OEL ⚬ DEUTERONOMY ⚬ KINGS
ANIAH ⚬ HEBREW⸱ HI
CHRONICLES ⚬ ECCLESIASTES
ATIANS ⚬ EXODUS ⚬ PHILEMON
LEVITICUS ⚬ HAGGAI ⚬ PSALMS
MIAH ⚬ EZEKIEL ⚬ ESTHER ⚬ JOB
PHILIPPIANS ⚬ JAMES ⚬ NAHUM
ADIAH ⚬ TIMOTHY ⚬ EPHESIANS
GALATIANS ⚬ ACTS ⚬ JEREMIAH
I ⚬ SONG OF SOLOMON ⚬ JUDE
ROMANS ⚬ REVELATION ⚬ LUKE
LACHI ⚬ HEBREWS ⚬ MATTHEW
DEUTERONOMY ⚬ KINGS ⚬ JOEL
EWS ⚬ MALACHI ⚬ ZEPHANIAH
ANS ⚬ NUMBERS ⚬ REVELATION
MATTHEW ⚬ TITUS ⚬ PROVERBS
ANS ⚬ JONAH ⚬ RUTH ⚬ EXODUS
ESSALONIANS ⚬ PSALMS ⚬ JOB
SAMUEL ⚬ COLOSSIANS ⚬ JOHN
MOTHY ⚬ EPHESIANS ⚬ NAHUM
CHARIAH ⚬ JUDGES ⚬ OBADIAH
UDE ⚬ THESSALONIANS ⚬ EZRA
NICLES ⚬ SONG OF SOLOMON
ON ⚬ AMOS ⚬ MATTHEW ⚬ LUKE
INTHIANS ⚬ JONAH ⚬ HEBREWS

THE
READER'S
DIGEST
BIBLE

THE READER'S DIGEST BIBLE

CONDENSED FROM
THE REVISED STANDARD VERSION
OLD AND NEW TESTAMENTS

General Editor
BRUCE M. METZGER
Ph.D., D.D., L.H.D., D.Theol.
Princeton Theological
Seminary

THE READER'S DIGEST ASSOCIATION
PLEASANTVILLE, NEW YORK
LONDON, MONTREAL, SYDNEY, CAPE TOWN, HONG KONG

Note:
The full-length text of
the Revised Standard Version is available
from the following:

Holman Bible Publishers
Thomas Nelson Publishers
Oxford University Press Inc.
World Bible Publishers Inc.
The Zondervan Corporation

First Edition

CONTENTS

PREFACE

The age-old effort to spread knowledge of the Bible and its message has today entered a new era. The twentieth century, in fact, has witnessed a near revolution in the field, and the Bible may now be read in a remarkable variety of versions and editions. There are any number of new translations made from the ancient Hebrew and Greek originals. There are paraphrases, adaptations, updatings, amplifications, abridgments, selections, modernizations. While in each case the manner of presentation differs, all these editions are designed for a single purpose: in one way or another to reduce the formidable length, complexity, or obscurity of the Scriptures and thus to bring them ever closer to the mind and heart of the general reader.

Prompted by this atmosphere of ferment and renewal, Reader's Digest some six years ago took up a task it had long contemplated, condensation of the Bible as a whole. For many years the Digest has been aware that in the experience and skills of its editors it possessed a literary method for producing a version of the Scriptures that could be of unique value: a text significantly shortened and clarified, yet which retains all sixty-six books, carefully preserves every incident, personality, and teaching of substance, and keeps as well the true essence and flavor of the language. Such an unprecedented version could be achieved only through the condensation methods developed by Reader's Digest during more than half a century of use on all types of writing, including some of the world's foremost literature.

As practiced by the Digest, condensation is basically different from other methods of reducing the length of a text, such as abridgment. Condensation concerns itself with every individual word of the text, every phrase, sentence, paragraph, and chapter, as well as the larger portions or blocks of text, in relation both to the immediate context and to the whole. At the same time infinite care is taken to leave the essential fabric intact. By contrast, abridgment merely eliminates whole books or sizable sections of books, or brings together selected passages.

Though it is the inspired word of God, the Bible is still a written document— actually a library of many books—employing the language of mortals. Like all things mortal, language, too, is subject to change. Forms of literary expression, habits of thought, structure of language, preferences in vocabulary have altered considerably over the centuries. The device of repetition—in word, thought, and incident—and the multiplying of words for rhetorical effect were practices favored in ancient times. Today they tend to confuse and exhaust the reader's attention. Also, of course, a certain percentage of the Old Testament text, particularly details concerning the ritual and history presented in some of the earlier books, holds a less immediate relevance for Christian belief and practice. The special technique of condensation employed by the Digest smooths away such features and frees for the modern reader a text that shines forth with simplicity and directness, without in the least reshaping its fundamental character.

The task of producing such a version of the Bible was one which, in all its subtle complexity, went far beyond anything that Digest editors had faced before. Consequently, the first approaches were made with unusual care. Exhaustive preliminary studies of the text were carried out, and special problems were isolated and analyzed. In repeated experiment, methods were carefully tested, book by book, and were modified where necessary. As the work of condensation progressed, the editors made constant reference to standard commentaries on the Bible, in order to be guided by the best approved opinion.

Serving in the capacity of General Editor was the Reverend Bruce M. Metzger, Ph.D., D.D., L.H.D., D.Theol., Professor of New Testament Language and Literature, Princeton Theological Seminary. Dr. Metzger was actively involved at every stage of the work, from the initial studies on each of the sixty-six books through all subsequent editorial reviews. The finished condensation has received his full approval. Nothing has been changed, he states, nothing added to or removed from the text that in any way diminishes its spirit, its teachings, or the familiar ring of its language. Further, he certifies that the work has been thoroughly objective, without bias toward or against any particular set of beliefs. Finally, he provided the Introductions to the Old and New Testaments and to each individual book.

In this condensed version the Biblical text has been reduced by an overall figure of some forty percent. The Old Testament, with its greater variety in form and language, understandably offered larger scope than the New Testament for reduction. It has been shortened by approximately one half, different books permitting different percentages of reduction. The New Testament, much sparer in form and language, was brought down by about one quarter. Apart from the preliminary studies, the actual work of condensation required a total time of three years and involved a team of seven editors.

The basic text of *The Reader's Digest Bible* is the Revised Standard Version, the New Testament of which was first published in 1946 and the Old Testament in 1952. This version was chosen for several reasons: it is in wide use, its scholarship is impeccable, it enjoys an established familiarity, and it is directly linked to the King James Version, a relationship that gives it a strong echo of that elevated and dignified tone cherished by so many generations. The King James Version itself, published in 1611, took notice of those English translations that had preceded it, including that of William Tyndale, the first English translation to be made directly from the original Hebrew and Greek. Later, the King James Version underwent extensive revision, emerging in 1901 as the American Standard Version, of which the present RSV is the authorized revision.

Not in any way intended to replace the full Biblical text, which will always remain available, *The Reader's Digest Bible* offers the general reader a more direct means of becoming intimately acquainted with the *whole* body of the Scriptures. It can be read more rapidly and with swifter comprehension, for inspiration, for instruction, even for pure heart-lifting enjoyment—the Bible is, after all, an unsurpassed collection of marvelous and stirring events linked to the divine will and purpose, compelling tales of men and women caught up in a courageous effort to live good and godly lives.

The Reader's Digest Bible is presented in the confident hope that readers, young and old, will find its quickened pace, its sharper focus, its smoothly flowing narratives an irresistible invitation to draw closer to the spiritual heart of the greatest book mankind possesses.

—The Editors

THE
OLD TESTAMENT

INTRODUCTION TO
THE
OLD TESTAMENT

The phrase "Old Testament" is the Christian name for a collection of sacred books that records the religious life and faith of ancient Israel—in short, the Jewish Bible. Composed at different times and places, by many different hands, over a period of some thousand years, these books set forth the mighty drama of divine revelation against a kaleidoscopic human background. From the very start of Christianity they have been an integral part of the Christian Scriptures, because in them is prefigured much of the religious teaching that reached the full flower of its development in the New Testament. "The New Testament was in the Old concealed," Saint Augustine explained, "the Old Testament is in the New revealed."

In the pages of the Old Testament may be found a wide variety of literary forms: prose, poetry, folktales, history, religious and secular laws, proverbs of the wise, oracles of the prophets, sacred hymns, a superb love song, laments, allegories, and much more. Originally written almost entirely in Hebrew, the Old Testament had a long history even after leaving the hands of the writers or editors who gave the separate books their present form. Until well into the Christian era it was the practice in writing the Hebrew text to represent only the consonants. As a result, depending on which vowels were supplied by the reader, some passages could yield more than one sense (in English, for example, the three consonants G-R-T might be read as GReaT, GReeT, GiRT, GRiT, GRaTe, eGReT, GRoaT). About A.D. 600 the manuscripts were supplied with strokes and dots, called vowel points, thus fixing the traditional Hebrew reading. This pointed text, known as the Masoretic text (from the Hebrew word for tradition), became the standard Hebrew Scriptures.

In the Hebrew Bible the separate books are grouped into three sections:

the Law (consisting of the first five books, known collectively as the Pentateuch), the Prophets, and the Writings. Of these three, the Law (Torah) is regarded by Jews as most important, but Christians view the Old Testament in a different light. All of its books are accepted as being equally inspired, and no gradation of rank or sacredness is imposed. Their sequence in the Christian Bible is also arranged differently, according to a more systematic plan.

In ancient times translations of the Jewish Scriptures were made for those who could not read the original Hebrew. The earliest of these was the Old Greek, called the Septuagint (after the seventy translators who supposedly worked on the Pentateuch). The Septuagint became the Old Testament of the early Christian Church, and later versions were made from it or patterned after it. Included in the Septuagint were certain books not found in the Masoretic text, and these books have since been regarded as canonical by the Roman Catholic Church. At the Reformation, however, Protestants refused to recognize the canonicity of these books, and to set them apart, translators grouped them in a section following the Old Testament, which they entitled the Apocrypha. Thus the Protestant canon of the Old Testament is exactly like the Masoretic, though with a difference in the order of the books.

The true sequence of the books of the Old Testament, as established by modern scholars on the basis of internal clues, differs greatly from their actual order as they stand in the Bible. This is so not only for the books as a whole, but also as regards their parts, for many of the books are of composite authorship. The process of compiling and editing occupied many centuries, and though in ancient times traditions of authorship became attached to some of the books, firm identification of the different authors is seldom possible. In most cases, material that existed much earlier was recast by one or more later writers and editors before reaching final form. These men—great creative artists who produced masterpieces of literature—were unconcerned about their own names being preserved. Above all, it was important to them that readers should be guided in understanding God's will and in gaining a fuller appreciation of his purpose.

Until recently the oldest known manuscripts containing major sections of the Hebrew Bible dated from only the ninth and tenth centuries of the Christian era, with the oldest dated manuscript of the entire Hebrew Bible coming from A.D. 1008. But discoveries made during the mid-twentieth century, in caves at Qumran near the Dead Sea, have brought to light much older manuscripts, most of them fragmentary, of all the books of the Old Testament except Esther. Several of these "Dead Sea Scrolls," as they are now called, go back to the second century B.C. or even earlier.

Frequently New Testament writers quote from the Old Testament, a practice that forms an obvious bond between the two parts of the Bible. Some of these quotations are direct, some are vague and allusive, while still others show considerable variation from the wording of the older Scriptures. For the variations there are several causes: first, the New Testament writers all apparently quoted from the Greek of the Septuagint; second, many of them must frequently have quoted from memory; third, they sometimes abridged or expanded the original, in order to gain force of expression or derive a new meaning.

The remarkable variety of the Old Testament is evident even to the casual reader. Yet running as a golden thread through all this wide-ranging diversity there is a unifying, never failing sense of the presence and activity of the living God, who reveals himself to his people and who desires their fellowship. And in both Testaments it is the selfsame God who is revealed, a circumstance that is memorably expressed in the opening words of the Letter to the Hebrews: "In many and various ways God spoke of old to our fathers by the prophets; but in these last days he has spoken to us by a Son."

GENESIS

Although Genesis is silent as to its author, Jewish and Christian thought had long accepted it as the work of Moses. However, nearly all modern scholars agree that, like the other books of the Pentateuch, it is a composite of several sources, embodying traditions that go back in some cases to Moses. The book falls into two parts. The first includes the stories of the creation, the Garden of Eden, Cain and Abel, Noah and the Flood, and the Tower of Babel. The second deals with the "fathers" of Israel. It begins with God's call to Abram (later renamed Abraham) to leave his own country for one that God would give him. He is promised an innumerable posterity, among whom chief attention is given to Joseph. The lengthy saga of Joseph explains how the Israelites came to be in Egypt, thus providing the background for the narrative of their deliverance, recounted in the next book, Exodus.

Theologically, Genesis is basic to both the Old and the New Testament. The covenant between God and his chosen people, expressed in the promises given to Abraham and renewed to Isaac and to Jacob, is fundamental to the Old Testament as a whole. New Testament writers, who frequently refer to Genesis, presuppose its accounts of creation and of the fall, and reiterate the covenant-keeping character of God.

IN THE BEGINNING God created the heavens and the earth. The earth was without form and void, and darkness was upon the face of the deep; and the Spirit of God was moving over the face of the waters.

God said, "Let there be light"; and there was light. And God saw that the light was good; and God separated the light from the darkness. God called the light Day, and the darkness he called Night. And there was evening and morning, one day.

God said, "Let there be a firmament in the midst of the waters." And God made the firmament and separated the waters which were under the firmament from the waters which were above it. And God called the firmament Heaven. And there was evening and morning, a second day.

God said, "Let the waters under the heavens be gathered together, and let the dry land appear." And it was so. God called the dry land Earth, and the waters he called Seas. God said, "Let the earth put forth vegetation, plants yielding seed, and trees bearing fruit in which is their seed, each according to its kind." It was so, and God saw that it was good. And there was evening and morning, a third day.

God said, "Let there be lights in the firmament of the heavens to separate day from night; let them be for signs and seasons and days and years, and let them give light upon the earth." God made the two great lights, the greater to rule the day, the lesser to rule the night; he made the stars also, and set them in the heavens. God saw that it was good. And there was evening and morning, a fourth day.

God said, "Let the waters bring forth swarms of living creatures, and let birds fly across the heavens." So God created the great sea monsters and every living creature with which the waters swarm, and every winged bird. And God saw that it was good, and blessed them, saying, "Be fruitful and multiply." And there was evening and morning, a fifth day.

God said, "Let the earth bring forth living creatures: cattle and creeping things and beasts of the earth." So God made the beasts of the earth, and the cattle, and everything that creeps upon the ground according to its kind. And God saw that it was good.

Then God said, "Let us make man in our image, after our likeness; and let them have dominion over all the earth." So God created man in his own image, in the image of God he created him; male and female he created them. And God blessed them, saying, "Be fruitful and multiply, and fill the earth and subdue it; and have dominion over the fish of the sea and the birds of the air and every living thing that moves upon the earth." And God said, "Behold, I have given you every plant yielding seed, and every tree with seed in its fruit; you shall have them for food. And to every beast and every bird, to everything that has the breath of life, I have given every green plant for food." And it was so. God saw that everything he had made was very good. And there was evening and morning, a sixth day.

Thus the heavens and the earth were finished, and on the seventh day God rested from all his work. God blessed and hallowed the seventh day, because on it he rested from all his work of creation.

WHEN THE LORD God made the earth and heavens, no plant was yet in the earth, no herb of the field had yet sprung up—for the LORD God had not caused it to rain upon the earth, and there was no man to till the ground; but a mist went up from the earth and watered the ground—then the LORD God formed man of dust from the ground, and breathed into his nostrils the breath of life; and man became a living being.

To the east, in Eden, the LORD God planted a garden. Out of the ground he made to grow every tree that is pleasant to the sight and good for food, the tree of life also, in the midst of the garden, and the tree of the knowledge of good and evil. A river flowed out of Eden to water the garden, and there it divided and became four rivers. The first is the Pishon, which flows around the land of Havilah, where there is gold; the second is the Gihon, which flows around the land of Cush; the third is the Tigris, which flows east of Assyria. The fourth river is the Euphrates.

The LORD God took the man and put him in the garden of Eden to till it and keep it. He commanded the man, saying, "You may freely eat of every tree of the garden; but of the tree of the knowledge of good and evil you shall not eat, for in the day that you eat of it you shall die."

Then the LORD God said, "It is not good that the man should be alone; I will make a helper fit for him." Out of the ground he formed every beast and bird, and brought them to the man; and whatever the man called every living creature, that was its name. The man gave names to all cattle, to the birds of the air, and to every beast of the field; but there was not found a helper fit for him. So the LORD God caused a deep sleep to fall upon the man, and while he slept took one of his ribs and closed up its place with flesh; and the rib which the LORD God had taken from the man he made into a woman and brought her to the man. "This at last is bone of my bones and flesh of my flesh," the man said. "She shall be called Woman, because she was taken out of Man." Therefore a man leaves his father and mother and cleaves to his wife, and they become one flesh. The man and his wife were both naked, and were not ashamed.

Now the serpent was more subtle than any other wild creature that the LORD God had made. He said to the woman, "Did God say, 'You shall not eat of any tree of the garden'?" The woman replied, "We may eat fruit, but God said, 'You shall not eat fruit from the tree in the midst of the garden, lest you die.'"

"You will not die," the serpent said. "God knows that when you eat of it your eyes will be opened, and you will be like God, knowing good and evil." So the woman, seeing that the tree was good for food and was to be desired to make one wise, ate of its fruit. She gave some to her husband, and he also ate. Then the eyes of both were opened, and they knew that they were naked, and they sewed fig leaves together and made aprons for themselves.

In the cool of the day they heard the LORD God walking in the garden, and hid themselves among the trees. But the LORD God called to the man, "Where are you?" The man said, "I heard thee in the garden, and was afraid, because I was naked; and I hid myself." God said, "Who told you that you were naked? Have you eaten of the tree of which I commanded you not to eat?" The man replied, "The woman whom thou gavest to be with me gave me the fruit, and I ate." Then the LORD God said to the woman, "What is this you have done?" The woman said, "The serpent beguiled me, and I ate."

"Because you have done this," the Lord God said to the serpent, "you are cursed above all animals. Upon your belly you shall go, and you shall eat dust all your life. I will put enmity between you and the woman, and between your seed and her seed; he shall bruise your head, and you shall bruise his heel." To the woman he said, "In pain you shall bring forth children, yet your desire shall be for your husband, and he shall rule over you." To Adam he said, "Because you have listened to the voice of your wife, and have eaten of the tree of which I commanded you not to eat, cursed is the ground because of you. In toil you shall eat of it all your life, and it shall bring forth thorns and thistles to you. In the sweat of your face you shall eat bread till you return to the ground, for out of it you were taken; you are dust, and to dust you shall return." The man called his wife's name Eve, because she was the mother of all living, and the Lord God made garments of skins for them and clothed them.

Then the Lord God said, "Man has become like one of us, knowing good and evil. Now he might eat also of the tree of life, and live for ever." So the Lord God drove man out of the garden of Eden, to till the ground from which he was taken. East of Eden he placed the cherubim, and a flaming sword which turned every way, to guard the way to the tree of life.

Adam knew Eve his wife, and she conceived and bore Cain, saying, "I have gotten a man with the help of the Lord." Again, she bore his brother Abel. Now Abel was a keeper of sheep, and Cain a tiller of the ground. In the course of time Cain brought to the Lord an offering of the fruit of the ground, and Abel brought the firstlings of his flock and of their fat portions. The Lord had regard for Abel and his offering, but not for Cain and his. So Cain was very angry. "Why are you angry?" the Lord said to him. "If you do well, will you not be accepted? If you do not do well, sin is couching at the door; its desire is for you, but you must master it."

Cain said to Abel, "Let us go out to the field," and when they were there, Cain rose up against his brother and killed him. "Where is Abel?" the Lord asked Cain. "I do not know," he replied. "Am I my brother's keeper?" The Lord said, "What have you done? The voice of your brother's blood is crying to me from the ground. Now you are cursed from the ground, which has opened its mouth to receive your brother's blood from your hand. When you till the ground, it shall no longer yield to you its strength; you shall be a wanderer on the earth."

"My punishment is greater than I can bear," said Cain. "I shall be hidden from thy face, a fugitive. Whoever finds me will slay me." But the Lord said, "Not so! If any one slays Cain, vengeance shall be taken on him sevenfold." He put a mark on Cain, lest any who came upon him should kill him. Then Cain went away from the presence of the Lord, and dwelt in the land of Nod, east of Eden.

Cain knew his wife, and she conceived and bore Enoch. And Cain built a city, and named the city after his son, Enoch. To Enoch was born Irad; and

Irad was the father of Mehujael, and Mehujael the father of Methushael, and Methushael the father of Lamech. Lamech took two wives, Adah and Zillah. Adah bore Jabal; he was the father of those who dwell in tents and have cattle. His brother Jubal was the father of those who play the lyre and pipe. Zillah bore Tubal-cain, the forger of all instruments of bronze and iron.

THIS IS THE book of the generations of Adam. When God created man, he made him in the likeness of God. Male and female he created them, and he blessed them and named them Man. When Adam had lived a hundred and thirty years, he became the father of a son in his own likeness, after his image, and named him Seth. The days of Adam after he became the father of Seth were eight hundred years; and he had other sons and daughters. Thus all the days that Adam lived were nine hundred and thirty years; and he died.

Seth became the father of Enosh, and also had other sons and daughters. All the days of Seth were nine hundred and twelve years; and he died. Enosh became the father of Kenan, and also had other sons and daughters. All the days of Enosh were nine hundred and five years; and he died. Kenan became the father of Mahalalel, and also had other sons and daughters. All the days of Kenan were nine hundred and ten years; and he died. Mahalalel became the father of Jared, and also had other sons and daughters. All the days of Mahalalel were eight hundred and ninety-five years; and he died. Jared became the father of Enoch, and also had other sons and daughters. All the days of Jared were nine hundred and sixty-two years; and he died.

Enoch became the father of Methuselah, and also had other sons and daughters. All the days of Enoch were three hundred and sixty-five years. Enoch walked with God; and then he was not, for God took him.

Methuselah became the father of Lamech, and also had other sons and daughters. All the days of Methuselah were nine hundred and sixty-nine years; and he died. Lamech became the father of a son, and called him Noah, saying, "Out of the ground which the LORD has cursed this one shall bring us relief from our toil." All the days of Lamech were seven hundred and seventy-seven years; and he died. After Noah was five hundred years old, he became the father of Shem, Ham, and Japheth.

WHEN MEN BEGAN to multiply on earth, and daughters were born to them, the sons of God saw that the daughters of men were fair, and took to wife such as they chose. The LORD said, "My spirit shall not abide in man for ever, for he is flesh; his days shall be a hundred and twenty years." The Nephilim were on the earth in those days, and also afterward, when the sons of God came in to the daughters of men, who bore children to them. These were the mighty men of old, men of renown.

Now the LORD saw that the wickedness of man was great, and his every imagination continually evil. It grieved him to his heart that he had made man on earth, so he said, "I will blot out man from the face of the earth, man and beast and creeping things and birds, for I am sorry I made them." But Noah found favor in the eyes of the LORD. A righteous man, blameless in his generation, Noah walked with God.

The earth was corrupt in God's sight, and filled with violence; for all flesh had corrupted their way upon the earth. God said to Noah, "I have determined to destroy all flesh, for the earth is filled with violence through them. You are to make an ark of gopher wood, and cover it with pitch. Make it four hundred and fifty feet long, seventy-five feet wide, and forty-five feet high. Make a roof for the ark, and set the door of the ark in its side; make it with lower, second, and third decks. For I will bring a flood upon the earth, and everything shall die. But I will establish my covenant with you, and you shall come into the ark, you, your sons, your wife, and your sons' wives. You shall bring two, male and female, of every living thing into the ark, to keep them alive with you: birds, animals, creeping things, according to their kinds. Also take with you every sort of food, and store it up for you and them." Noah did all that God commanded him.

In the six hundredth year of Noah's life, in the second month, on the seventeenth day of the month, all the fountains of the deep burst forth, and the windows of the heavens were opened. On the very same day Noah and his wife, his sons, Shem and Ham and Japheth, and their wives entered the ark. Every beast, all the cattle, every creeping thing, and bird of every sort went into the ark with Noah, two and two, male and female, as God had commanded, and the LORD shut them in.

The flood continued. Rain fell upon the earth for forty days and forty nights. The waters increased, and bore up the ark, and it rose high above the earth, floating on the face of the waters. The waters prevailed so mightily that all the high mountains were covered more than twenty feet deep. All flesh died; everything on dry land in whose nostrils was the breath of life died. Man and animals, creeping things and birds—all were blotted out from the earth. Only Noah and those with him in the ark were left. The waters prevailed upon the earth a hundred and fifty days, but God remembered Noah and all with him in the ark. He made a wind blow, and the waters subsided. The rain was restrained, the waters receded, and in the seventh month, on the seventeenth day of the month, the ark came to rest upon the mountains of Ararat. The waters continued to abate until, on the first day of the tenth month, the tops of the mountains were seen.

Noah opened the window of the ark and sent forth a raven; to and fro it went until the waters were dried up from the earth. Then Noah sent forth a dove, to see if the waters had subsided; but the dove, finding no place to set her foot, returned. So he put forth his hand and brought her into the ark. He waited seven days, and again sent the dove out. She came back in the evening, and in her mouth was a freshly plucked olive leaf, so Noah knew that the waters had subsided from the earth. He waited another seven days, then again sent forth the dove, and she did not return any more.

Removing the covering of the ark, Noah looked about. The ground was dry. God said to Noah, "Go forth from the ark with your wife, your sons and their wives. Bring forth with you every living thing, that they may be fruitful and multiply upon the earth." So they all went forth by families out of the ark, and Noah built an altar to the LORD, and offered burnt offerings. When the LORD smelled the pleasing odor, he said in his heart, "I will never again curse the ground because of man, for the imagination of man's heart is evil from his youth; neither will I ever again destroy every living creature. While the earth remains, seedtime and harvest, cold and heat, summer and winter, day and night, shall not cease."

God blessed Noah and his sons, saying, "Be fruitful and multiply, and fill the earth. The fear and dread of you shall be upon every beast of the earth, and every bird of the air, upon everything that creeps on the ground and all the fish of the sea; into your hand they are delivered. Every moving thing that lives shall be food for you; and as I gave you the green plants, I give you everything. Only you shall not eat flesh with its life, that is, its blood. For your lifeblood I will surely require a reckoning; of every beast I will require it and of man. Whoever sheds the blood of man, by man shall his blood be shed; for God made man in his own image."

Then God said to Noah and his sons, "I establish my covenant with you and your descendants, and every living creature for all future generations. Never again shall there be a flood to destroy the earth. This is the sign of the covenant: I set my bow in the cloud. When I bring clouds over the earth and the bow is in the clouds, I will look upon it and remember my covenant; and the waters shall never again become a flood to destroy all flesh."

Noah was the first tiller of the soil. He planted a vineyard, drank of the wine, became drunk, and lay uncovered in his tent. Ham, the father of Canaan, saw the nakedness of his father, and told his two brothers. Shem and Japheth laid a garment upon both their shoulders, walked backward, their faces turned away, and covered the nakedness of their father. When Noah awoke from his wine and knew what his youngest son had done to him, he said, "Cursed be Canaan; a slave shall he be to his brothers. Blessed by the LORD my God be Shem, and let Canaan be his slave. God enlarge Japheth, and let Canaan be his slave." After the flood Noah lived three hundred and fifty years, and all his days were nine hundred and fifty years. From the families of his sons the nations spread abroad on the earth after the flood.

Now the whole earth had one language and few words. As men migrated from the east, they settled on a plain in the land of Babylon. "Come," they said to one another, "let us make bricks, and burn them thoroughly." Then they had brick for stone, and bitumen for mortar. "Let us build a city," they said, "and a tower with its top in the heavens, and let us make a name for ourselves."

The LORD came down to see the city and the tower which the sons of men had built. "Behold," he said, "they are one people with one language, and this is only the beginning. Nothing they propose to do will now be impossible for them. Let us confuse their language, that they may not understand one another." So the LORD scattered them abroad over the face of the earth, and they stopped building the city; it was called Babel, because there the LORD confused their language and from there he scattered them over all the earth.

THESE ARE THE descendants of Shem, who became the father of Arpachshad two years after the flood: Arpachshad became the father of Shelah, Shelah the father of Eber, and Eber the father of Peleg. Peleg became the father of Reu, Reu the father of Serug, Serug the father of Nahor, and Nahor the father of Terah. Terah became the father of Abram, Nahor, and Haran. Haran became the father of Lot, and died before his father, Terah, in the land of his birth, Ur of the Chaldeans. Abram and Nahor took wives. Abram's wife was Sarai, and Nahor's wife was Milcah, the daughter of Haran. Abram's wife, Sarai, was barren; she had no child. Terah took his son Abram, his daughter-in-law Sarai, and his grandson Lot, the son of Haran, and they went forth together from Ur to go into the land of Canaan. But when they came to Haran, they settled there, and Terah died in Haran.

Now the LORD said to Abram, "Go from your country and your kindred to the land I will show you. I will make of you a great nation, and make your name great. I will bless you and those who bless you, and curse him who curses you. By you all the families of the earth shall be blessed." So Abram, who was seventy-five years old, departed from Haran with Sarai his wife, Lot his brother's son, and all their possessions, and the persons that they had gotten in Haran. When they came to Canaan, Abram passed through the land to the oak of Moreh near Shechem. There the LORD appeared to him and said, "To your descendants I will give this land." So Abram built an altar to the LORD at Shechem; then he moved on to the mountain east of Bethel, pitched his tent, and built another altar and called on the name of the LORD. Then he journeyed on, still going toward the Negeb.

There was a famine in the land, so Abram went down to Egypt to sojourn there. As they were about to enter Egypt, Abram said to Sarai, "When the Egyptians see that you are a woman beautiful to behold, they will say, 'This is his wife.' Then they will kill me, but let you live. Say you are my sister, that it may go well with me because of you, and my life may be spared."

In Egypt the princes of Pharaoh saw that Sarai was very beautiful, and they praised her to Pharaoh, who took her into his house. For her sake Pharaoh dealt well with Abram, giving him sheep, oxen, asses, servants, and camels. But because of Sarai the LORD afflicted Pharaoh and his house with great plagues. So Pharaoh called Abram. "What is this you have done to me?" he said. "Why did you say, 'She is my sister,' so that I took her for my wife? Now, take her, and be gone." And Pharaoh's men set Abram on the way, with his wife and all that he had.

Abram, very rich in cattle, silver, and gold, went up from Egypt, he and his

wife, and Lot with him, into the Negeb. They journeyed on as far as Bethel, to the place where Abram's tent had been, and where he had made an altar. Now Lot also had many flocks, herds, and tents. So great were the possessions of Abram and Lot that the land could not support both of them dwelling together, and there was strife between their herdsmen.

"Let there be no strife between you and me," Abram said to Lot, "for we are kinsmen. Is not the whole land before you? Separate yourself from me. If you take land to the left, then I will go right; if you go right, I will go to the left." Lot saw that the Jordan valley was well watered everywhere like the garden of the LORD, like the land of Egypt, so he chose for himself all the Jordan valley, and journeyed east. Thus they separated. Abram dwelt in the land of Canaan, while Lot dwelt among the cities of the valley and moved his tent as far as Sodom, where the men were wicked, great sinners against the LORD.

"Lift up your eyes," the LORD said to Abram after Lot had gone. "From where you are, look northward, southward, eastward, and westward. I will give all the land you see to you and your descendants for ever. I will make your descendants as the dust of the earth; if one can count the dust, your descendants also can be counted. Arise. Walk the length and the breadth of the land, for I will give it to you." So Abram moved his tent, and dwelt by the oaks of Mamre, at Hebron; and there he built an altar to the LORD.

NOW AMRAPHEL KING of Babylon, Arioch king of Ellasar, Chedorlaomer king of Elam, and Tidal king of Goiim made war with the Canaanite kings of Sodom, Gomorrah, Admah, Zeboiim, and Zoar. For twelve years the Canaanite kings had served Chedorlaomer, but in the thirteenth year they rebelled. When Chedorlaomer and the kings who were with him came and subdued all the country as far as the border of the wilderness, the Canaanite kings went out and joined battle, five kings against four, in the Valley of Siddim (that is, the Salt Sea). But the Valley of Siddim was full of bitumen pits, and as the forces of the kings of Sodom and Gomorrah fled, some fell into them; the rest fled to the mountain. So the enemy took all the goods of Sodom and Gomorrah, and they captured Lot, Abram's kinsman who dwelt in Sodom, took his goods, and departed.

Then one who had escaped came and told Abram, living by the oaks of Mamre, that his kinsman had been taken captive. Abram led forth his trained men, born in his house, three hundred and eighteen of them, and went in pursuit as far as Dan. He divided his forces against the enemy by night, routed them, and pursued them to Hobah, north of Damascus. He brought back all the goods, and Lot with his goods and people.

As Abram was returning, the king of Sodom came out to meet him at the King's Valley. And Melchizedek, king of Salem and priest of God Most High, brought out bread and wine, and blessed him, saying, "Blessed be Abram by God Most High, maker of heaven and earth; and blessed be God Most High, who has delivered your enemies into your hand!" And Abram gave him a tenth of everything.

The king of Sodom said to Abram, "Give me the persons, but take the goods for yourself." But Abram said, "I have sworn to the LORD God Most High, maker of heaven and earth, that I would not take a thread or a sandal-thong of yours, lest you should say, 'I have made Abram rich.' I will take nothing but what the young men have eaten."

After these things the word of the LORD came to Abram in a vision: "Fear not, Abram, I am your shield; your reward shall be very great." But Abram said, "O Lord GOD, what wilt thou give me? For I continue childless, and Eliezer of Damascus, a slave in my house, will be my heir." Then the word of the LORD came: "This man shall not be your heir; your own son shall be your heir." The LORD brought Abram outside and said, "Look toward heaven, and number the stars, if you are able to. So shall your descendants be." Abram believed, and the LORD reckoned it to him as righteousness, and said, "I am the LORD who brought you from Ur of the Chaldeans, to give you this land to possess. Your descendants will be sojourners in a land not theirs. They will be slaves there, oppressed for four hundred years; but I will bring judgment on the nation which they serve. Afterward they shall come out with great posses-sions, and come back here in the fourth generation. As for yourself, you shall go to your fathers in peace, and be buried in a good old age."

ABRAM HAD DWELT ten years in the land of Canaan, and Sarai, his wife, had borne him no children. "The LORD has prevented me from bearing children," she said to Abram. "Go in to my maid, Hagar; it may be that I shall obtain children by her." Abram hearkened to Sarai's voice, so Sarai took Hagar, her Egyptian maid, and gave her to Abram as a wife. He went in to Hagar, and she conceived; and then she looked with contempt on her mistress. "May the wrong done to me be on you!" Sarai said to Abram. "I gave my maid to your embrace, and when she conceived, she looked on me with contempt." Abram said, "Your maid is in your power. Do to her as you please." Then Sarai dealt harshly with Hagar, and Hagar fled. But the angel of the LORD found her by a spring of water in the wilderness, and he said, "Hagar, where have you come from and where are you going?" She replied, "I am fleeing from my mistress Sarai."

"Return and submit to your mistress," the angel said, "and I will so greatly multiply your descendants that they cannot be numbered. You are with child, and shall bear a son. Call his name Ishmael, because the LORD has given heed to your affliction. He shall be a wild ass of a man, his hand against every man and every man's hand against him; and he shall dwell over against all his kinsmen." Hagar said, "Have I really seen God and remained alive after see-ing him?" And Hagar bore Abram a son, and Abram called him Ishmael.

When Abram was ninety-nine, the LORD appeared to him and said, "I am God Almighty; walk before me, and be blameless. My covenant is with you.

No longer shall your name be Abram, but your name shall be Abraham, for I have made you the father of a multitude of nations. I will establish my covenant between me and you, an everlasting covenant, to be God to you and to your descendants, and I will give to you and your descendants all the land of Canaan for an everlasting possession. As a sign of the covenant between us, you and your descendants, every male among you, shall be circumcised in the flesh of your foreskins. He that is eight days old shall be circumcised; every male throughout your generations, both he that is born in your house and he that is bought with your money. Any uncircumcised male shall be cut off from his people; he has broken my covenant.

"As for your wife, you shall not call her Sarai, but Sarah shall be her name. I will bless her, and give you a son by her. She shall be a mother of nations; kings shall come from her."

Abraham fell on his face and laughed, and said to himself, "Shall a child be born to a man who is a hundred years old? Shall Sarah, who is ninety years old, bear a child?" To God he said, "O that Ishmael might live in thy sight!" God said, "I have heard you. I will bless Ishmael and make him fruitful; I will make him a great nation. But Sarah your wife shall bear you a son at this season next year, and you shall call his name Isaac. I will establish my covenant with him as an everlasting covenant for his descendants after him." When God had finished talking with him, Abraham took Ishmael his son and all the male slaves in his house, and he circumcised them that very day.

THE LORD APPEARED to Abraham by the oaks of Mamre, as he sat at the door of his tent in the heat of the day. Abraham lifted up his eyes, and there before him stood three men. He ran to meet them, and bowed, saying, "My lords, do not pass by your servant. Let a little water be brought. Wash your feet, and rest under the tree, while I fetch food. Refresh yourselves, and after that you may pass on." Abraham ran to the herd, took a tender calf, and gave it to the servant to prepare. Then he took curds, milk, and the prepared calf, set it before the men, and stood by them under the tree while they ate.

"Where is Sarah your wife?" they asked. And Abraham said, "She is in the tent." The LORD said, "I will surely return to you in the spring, and Sarah your wife shall have a son." Sarah was listening at the tent door, and she laughed to herself, saying, "After I have grown old, and my husband is old, shall I have pleasure?"

"Why did Sarah laugh?" the LORD said to Abraham. "Is anything too hard for the LORD?" But Sarah denied it, saying, "I did not laugh," for she was afraid. "No, but you did laugh," the LORD said.

The men set out toward Sodom, and Abraham went with them to set them on their way. "Shall I hide from Abraham what I am about to do," the LORD asked himself, "seeing that he shall become a great and mighty nation? No, for I have chosen him and his household after him to keep the way of the LORD by doing righteousness and justice." So the LORD said to Abraham,

"The outcry against Sodom and Gomorrah is great. I will go down to see whether their sin is as grave as the outcry which has come to me."

The men turned toward Sodom, but Abraham, still standing before the LORD, drew near, and said, "Wilt thou indeed destroy the righteous with the wicked? Suppose there are fifty righteous within the city; wilt thou not spare it for the fifty righteous? Far be it from thee to slay the righteous with the wicked! Shall not the Judge of all the earth do right?" The LORD said, "If I find at Sodom fifty righteous, I will spare the whole place for their sake."

"Behold," Abraham said, "I who am but dust and ashes have taken upon myself to speak to the Lord. Suppose only forty righteous are found. Wilt thou destroy the whole city?" The LORD replied, "For the sake of forty I will not do it." Abraham said, "Suppose thirty are found." The LORD answered, "I will not do it, if I find thirty." Abraham said, "Suppose twenty are found." The LORD replied, "For the sake of twenty I will not destroy it." Abraham said, "Let not the Lord be angry, and I will speak again but this once. Suppose ten are found." The LORD answered, "For the sake of ten I will not destroy it." Then the LORD went his way, and Abraham returned to his place.

When the two angels came to Sodom in the evening, Lot was sitting in the city gate. He rose, bowed, and said, "My lords, turn aside to your servant's house and spend the night. Then you may rise up early and go on your way."

"No," they said, "we will spend the night in the street." But Lot urged them strongly, so they entered his house, where he made a feast for them, and they ate. But before they lay down, the men of the city of Sodom, both young and old, surrounded the house and called to Lot, "Where are the men who came to you tonight? Bring them out, that we may know them."

Lot went out, shut the door after him, and said, "I beg you, my brothers, do not act so wickedly. I have two daughters who have not known man; let me bring them out to you. Do to them as you please; only do nothing to these men under the shelter of my roof."

"This fellow would play the judge!" the men of Sodom said. "We will deal worse with you than with them." They pressed hard against Lot, and drew near to break down the door. But the angels put forth their hands, brought Lot into the house, and shut the door. They struck with blindness the men outside, so that they wearied themselves groping for the door.

When morning dawned, the angels urged Lot to leave. "Take your wife, your two daughters, and any one else you have here, lest you be consumed in the punishment of the city, for the LORD has sent us to destroy it." But Lot lingered. The angels seized him and his wife and daughters by the hand, the LORD being merciful to him, and they brought them forth and set them outside the city. "Flee for your life," the angels said. "Do not look back or stop anywhere in the valley; flee to the hills, lest you be consumed."

"You have shown me great kindness in saving my life," said Lot, "but I cannot flee to the hills, lest disaster overtake me. Let me escape to yonder city—is it not a little one?—and my life will be saved!" The LORD said, "I grant you this favor also. I will not overthrow that city. Make haste, escape; for I can do nothing till you arrive there." The city was called Zoar, and the sun had risen when Lot came there.

Then the LORD rained on Sodom and Gomorrah brimstone and fire out of heaven; and he overthrew the valley, and all the inhabitants of the cities. But Lot's wife, behind him, looked back, and she became a pillar of salt. Early in the morning Abraham went to the place where he had stood before the LORD, and looked down toward Sodom and Gomorrah, and lo, the smoke of the land of the valley went up like the smoke of a furnace. So it was that, when God destroyed the cities of the valley, he remembered Abraham, and sent Lot out of the midst of the overthrow.

Lot was afraid to dwell in Zoar, so he went up to the hills and dwelt in a cave with his two daughters. "Our father is old," the first-born daughter said to the younger, "and there is not a man to come in to us after the manner of all the earth. Let us make our father drink wine, and we will lie with him, that we may preserve offspring through him." So they made their father drink wine that night, and the first-born went in, and lay with him; he did not know when she lay down or when she arose. The next night they made their father drink wine also, and the younger arose, and lay with him. Thus both the daughters of Lot were with child by their father. The first-born bore a son, and called him Moab; he is the father of the Moabites to this day. The younger also bore a son, and called him Ben-ammi; he is the father of the Ammonites to this day.

THE LORD VISITED Sarah and did as he had promised, and Sarah conceived and bore Abraham a son when he was a hundred years old. Abraham called his son Isaac, and he circumcised him when he was eight days old, as God had commanded. "God has made laughter for me," said Sarah. "Who would have said Sarah would suckle children? Yet I have borne Abraham a son in his old age."

The child grew, and Abraham made a great feast on the day Isaac was weaned. But Sarah saw Ishmael, the son of Hagar the Egyptian, playing with her son Isaac. "Cast out this slave woman with her son," Sarah said to Abraham, "for he shall not be heir with my son Isaac." This was very displeasing to Abraham, but God said to him, "Be not displeased. Do as Sarah tells you, for through Isaac shall your descendants be named. And I will make a nation of Hagar's son also, because he is your offspring." So Abraham took bread and a skin of water, and gave it to Hagar, putting it on her shoulder, and sent her away with the child, and they wandered in the wilderness of Beer-sheba.

When the water in the skin was gone, Hagar cast Ishmael under a bush, and sat down a good way off, saying, "Let me not look upon the death of my child." The lad lifted up his voice and wept. God heard, and the angel of God called to Hagar from heaven, "What troubles you, Hagar? Fear not; for God has heard the voice of the lad. Arise, lift him up, and hold him fast with your hand; for I will make him a great nation." God opened her eyes, and she saw a well of water. She filled the skin with water, and gave the lad a drink. And God was with Ishmael. He grew up, lived in the wilderness of Paran, and became an expert with the bow. His mother took a wife for him from the land of Egypt, and his sons dwelt opposite Egypt in the direction of Assyria.

AFTER THESE THINGS God tested Abraham, and said to him, "Take your son Isaac, whom you love, and go to the land of Moriah. Offer him there as a burnt offering upon one of the mountains of which I shall tell you." So Abraham rose early in the morning, cut wood for the burnt offering, saddled his ass, took two young men with him, and his son Isaac, and went toward the place of which God had told him. On the third day he saw the place afar off. "Stay here with the ass," he said to his young men. "The lad and I will go yonder and worship, and come again to you." He laid the wood on Isaac, and took in his hand the fire and the knife. "My father," Isaac said, "I behold the fire and the wood, but where is the lamb for a burnt offering?" Abraham said, "God will provide the lamb, my son."

When they came to the place of which God had told him, Abraham built an altar and laid the wood in order. He bound Isaac and laid him on the altar, upon the wood. Then he took the knife to slay his son. But the angel of the LORD called from heaven, "Abraham! Abraham! Do not lay your hand on the lad, for now I know that you fear God, seeing you have not withheld your son from me."

Abraham lifted up his eyes and looked, and there behind him was a ram, caught in a thicket by his horns. He took the ram, and offered it up as a burnt offering instead of his son. Then he called that place The LORD will provide; as it is said to this day, "On the mount of the LORD it shall be provided."

The angel of the LORD called to Abraham a second time, "Because you have done this, I will indeed bless you. I will multiply your descendants as the sand on the seashore. They shall possess the gate of their enemies, and all the nations of the earth shall be blessed by them, because you have obeyed my voice." So Abraham returned to his young men, and they went together to Beer-sheba, where Abraham dwelt.

SARAH LIVED A hundred and twenty-seven years; she died at Hebron, in the land of Canaan. Abraham mourned and wept for her, and buried her in the cave of the field of Machpelah, east of Mamre. And the field and the cave that is in it were sold to Abraham by the Hittites, the people of the land, as a burying place.

Now Abraham was old, and the LORD had blessed him in all things. To his oldest servant, who had charge of all that he had, Abraham said, "Swear by the LORD, the God of heaven and earth, that you will not take a wife for my son from the daughters of the Canaanites. Go to my country and to my kindred, and take a wife for Isaac."

"Perhaps the woman may not be willing to follow me to this land," the servant replied. "Must I then take your son back to the land from which you came?"

"Do not take my son back there," said Abraham. "The LORD, who took me from the land of my birth, spoke to me and swore, 'To your descendants I will give this land.' He will send his angel before you, and you shall take a wife for my son from there. If the woman is not willing to follow you, you will be free from this oath." So the servant swore to Abraham concerning this matter. Then he took ten of his master's camels, with all sorts of choice gifts, and departed.

The servant went to Mesopotamia, to Haran, the city of Abraham's brother, Nahor. Outside the city, he made the camels kneel down by the well at evening time when women go out to draw water. "O LORD, God of my master Abraham," he said, "grant me success today, and show steadfast love to my master. I am standing by the spring, and the daughters of the city are coming out to draw water. Let the maiden to whom I shall say, 'Pray let down your jar that I may drink,' and who shall say, 'Drink, and I will water your camels'—let her be the one whom thou hast appointed for thy servant Isaac."

Before he had done speaking, Rebekah, a virgin, very fair to look upon, and the granddaughter of Nahor, came out with her water jar upon her shoulder. She went down to the spring and filled her jar. As she came up, the servant ran to meet her, saying, "Pray give me a little water to drink from your jar." Rebekah said, "Drink, my lord," and she quickly let down her jar. Then she said, "I will draw for your camels also," and emptying her jar into the trough, she ran again to the well.

The man gazed at her in silence, and when the camels had done drinking, he took a gold ring and two bracelets for her arms and said, "Tell me whose daughter you are." Rebekah said, "I am the daughter of Bethuel who is the son of Nahor." Bowing his head, the servant said, "Blessed be the LORD, who has not forsaken his steadfast love toward my master, and has led me to the house of my master's kinsmen."

The maiden ran and told her mother's household about these things. When Rebekah's brother, Laban, saw the ring and the bracelets, and heard his sister's words, he went to the man standing by the camels at the spring. "Come in," he said. "Why do you stand outside? I have prepared the house and a place for the camels." So the man came into the house. Laban gave him straw and provender for the camels, and water to wash his feet. Food was set before him, but he said, "I will not eat until I have told my errand. I am Abraham's servant. The LORD has greatly blessed my master, and has given him flocks and herds, silver and gold, menservants and maidservants, camels and asses. Sarah my master's wife bore him a son when she was old; to this son he has given all he has. My master made me swear not to take a wife for his son from the daughters of the Canaanites, but from his kindred." Then the servant told everything that had happened at the well, and said to Rebekah's father and brother, "Now, tell me if you will deal loyally and truly with my master."

"This comes from the LORD," Laban and Bethuel answered. "Behold, Rebekah is before you. Take her and go, and let her be the wife of your master's son." When Abraham's servant heard their words, he bowed himself to the earth before the LORD. Then he brought forth jewelry of silver and gold, and raiment, and gave them to Rebekah; he also gave costly ornaments to her brother and mother. He ate and drank, and spent the night there.

When they arose in the morning, the servant said, "Send me back to my master." Rebekah's brother and mother said, "Let the maiden remain with us a few days. Then she may go." But he said, "Do not delay me, since the LORD has prospered my way." So they called Rebekah and said to her, "Will you go with this man?" She said, "I will go." Then they blessed her, and she and her maids arose, and rode upon the camels, following Abraham's servant.

Now Isaac was dwelling in the Negeb. One evening when he went out to meditate in the field, he lifted up his eyes and behold, there were camels coming. When Rebekah saw Isaac, she said to the servant, "Who is the man yonder, walking in the field to meet us?" The servant said, "It is my master's son." Rebekah alighted from the camel, took her veil, and covered herself. The servant told Isaac all that he had done; then Isaac brought Rebekah into the tent. She became his wife, and he loved her. So Isaac was comforted after his mother's death.

ABRAHAM BREATHED HIS last and died at the age of a hundred and seventy-five, and was gathered to his people. His sons, Isaac and Ishmael, buried him in the cave of Machpelah with Sarah his wife. After the death of Abraham God blessed Isaac.

Isaac was forty years old when he took to wife Rebekah, and he prayed to the LORD for his wife, because she was barren. The LORD granted his prayer, and Rebekah conceived. Within her, the children struggled together, and she said, "If it is thus, why do I live?" She inquired of the LORD, and the LORD said, "Two nations are in your womb. Two peoples, born of you, shall be divided. One shall be stronger than the other, and the elder shall serve the younger."

When Rebekah's days to be delivered were fulfilled, there were twins in her womb. The first came forth red, all his body hairy; so they called him Esau. Afterward his brother came forth, and his hand had taken hold of Esau's heel; so he was called Jacob (that is, he supplants). When the boys grew up, Esau was a skilful hunter, a man of the field, while Jacob was a quiet man, dwelling in tents. Isaac loved Esau, because he ate of his game; but Rebekah loved Jacob.

Once when Jacob was boiling pottage, Esau came in from the field. "Let me eat some of that," he said, "for I am famished!" But Jacob said, "First sell me your birthright." Esau said, "Here I am about to die. Of what use is a birthright to me?" Jacob said, "Swear to me first." So Esau swore, and sold his birthright to Jacob. Then Jacob gave bread and pottage of lentils to Esau, who ate and drank, and went his way. Thus Esau despised his birthright.

When Esau was forty years old, he took to wife Judith and Basemath, daughters of the Hittites, and Esau's wives made life bitter for Isaac and Rebekah.

ISAAC WAS OLD and his eyes were dim so that he could not see. "I am old," he said to Esau his older son. "I do not know the day of my death. Take your quiver and bow, and go out and hunt game for me. Prepare savory food, such as I love, and bring it to me to eat, that I may bless you before I die." Rebekah was listening, so when Esau went to hunt game, she told Jacob what she had heard. "Therefore, my son," she said, "obey my word. Go to the flock, and fetch me two good kids, that I may prepare savory food for your father. You shall bring it to him to eat, so that he may bless you before he dies." But Jacob said, "My brother Esau is a hairy man, and I am a smooth man. Perhaps my father will feel me. I shall seem to be mocking him, and bring a curse upon myself, not a blessing."

"Upon me be your curse, my son," Rebekah replied. "Go. Fetch the kids to me." So Jacob brought them to his mother, and she prepared savory food, such as his father loved. Then she took the best garments of Esau and put them on Jacob. She put the skins of the kids upon his hands and the smooth part of his neck. Then she gave him the food she had prepared, and Jacob went in to his father. "My father," he said.

"Here I am," said Isaac. "Who are you, my son?" Jacob said, "I am Esau your first-born. I have done as you told me. Sit up and eat of my game, that you may bless me." But Isaac said, "How did you find it so quickly, my son?"

"God granted me success," Jacob answered. "Come near," Isaac said, "that I may feel you, to know whether or not you are really my son Esau." So Jacob went near, and his father felt his hands, which were hairy like his brother Esau's hands. "Are you really Esau?" Isaac asked, and Jacob answered, "I am."

"The voice is Jacob's," Isaac said, "but these are the hands of Esau. Bring the game to me, that I may eat of it and bless you." So Jacob brought the food, and Isaac ate; Jacob brought him wine, and he drank. Then Isaac said, "Come, kiss me, my son." When Jacob came near and kissed him, Isaac smelled his garments, and said, "See, the smell of my son is as the smell of a field which the LORD has blessed!" And Isaac blessed Jacob, saying, "May God give you of the dew of heaven, of the fatness of the earth, and plenty of grain and wine. Let peoples serve you, and nations bow down to you. Cursed be those who curse you, and blessed be those who bless you!"

Jacob had scarcely left Isaac's presence when Esau came in from his hunting. Esau also prepared savory food, and brought it to his father, saying, "Arise and eat of your son's game, that you may bless me." But Isaac said,

"Who are you?" Esau answered, "I am your son, your first-born, Esau."

"Who was it then that hunted game and brought it to me?" Isaac asked, trembling. "I ate it all before you came, and I have blessed him—yes, and he shall be blessed." When Esau heard these words, he cried out bitterly, "Bless me, even me also, O my father!" But Isaac said, "Your brother came with guile, and he has taken away your blessing."

"Is he not rightly named Jacob?" Esau said. "For he has twice supplanted me. He has taken away my birthright, and now my blessing. Have you but one blessing, my father? Bless me also." And Esau lifted up his voice and wept. "Away from the fatness of the earth," Isaac answered, "shall your dwelling be, and away from the dew of heaven. By your sword you shall live, and you shall serve your brother; but when you break loose you shall break his yoke from your neck."

Now Esau hated Jacob because his father had blessed him. "The days of mourning for my father are approaching," Esau said to himself. "Then I will kill my brother Jacob." But his words were told to Rebekah, so she called Jacob. "Your brother Esau comforts himself by planning to kill you," she said. "Flee to Laban my brother in Haran. Stay with him until your brother's fury turns away, and he forgets what you have done to him."

Then Rebekah said to Isaac, "I am weary of my life because of the Hittite women. If Jacob marries one of them, what good will my life be to me?" So Isaac called Jacob, and charged him, "You shall not marry a Hittite. Go to Haran to the house of Bethuel your mother's father, and take as wife one of the daughters of Laban your mother's brother. God Almighty bless you and make you fruitful. May he give the blessing of Abraham to you and your descendants, that you may possess the land God gave to Abraham!"

Thus Isaac sent Jacob away; and Jacob went toward Haran. He came to a certain place, and stayed there that night, because the sun had set. Taking a stone, he put it under his head and lay down to sleep. Jacob dreamed that a ladder was set up on earth; its top reached to heaven, and the angels of God were ascending and descending on it! The LORD stood above it and said, "I am the LORD, the God of Abraham and Isaac. The land on which you lie I will give to you and your descendants, and you shall spread abroad to the west, east, north, and south; by you shall all the families of the earth be blessed. Behold, I am with you and will keep you wherever you go, and bring you back to this land." Jacob awoke and said, "Surely the LORD is in this place, and I did not know it." And he was afraid. "How awesome is this place!" he said. "This is none other than the house of God, and this is the gate of heaven."

Jacob took the stone he had put under his head, set it up for a pillar, and poured oil on the top of it. He called the place Bethel (that is, the house of God), vowing, "If God will be with me and keep me, and give me bread to eat and clothing to wear, so that I come again to my father's house in peace, then the LORD shall be my God. This stone, set up for a pillar, shall be God's house; and of all that thou givest me I will give the tenth to thee."

JACOB JOURNEYED ON TO THE land of the people of the east. There, in a field, he saw three flocks of sheep lying beside the well where they were watered. The stone on the well's mouth was large, and when all the flocks were gathered there, the shepherds would roll the stone from the mouth of the well, water the sheep, and put the stone back in place. "Where do you come from, my brothers?" Jacob asked the shepherds. When they said, "We are from Haran," Jacob asked, "Do you know Laban?" The shepherds said, "We know him. And see, Rachel his daughter is coming with the sheep which she keeps for her father!"

When Jacob saw Rachel the daughter of his mother's brother, he rolled the stone from the well's mouth, and watered the flock of Laban. Then Jacob kissed Rachel, and wept aloud. He told her that he was her father's kinsman, Rebekah's son, and Rachel ran and told her father. When Laban heard the tidings of his sister's son, he went to Jacob, embraced him, and brought him to his house, saying, "Surely you are my bone and my flesh."

Jacob stayed with Laban a month. Then Laban said, "Because you are my kinsman, should you therefore serve me for nothing? Tell me, what shall your wages be?" Now Laban had two daughters; the older was Leah, and the younger was Rachel. Leah's eyes were weak, but Rachel was beautiful, and Jacob loved her. "I will serve you seven years," he said, "for your younger daughter Rachel." Laban said, "It is better that I give her to you than to any other man. Stay with me." So Jacob served seven years for Rachel, and they seemed to him but a few days because of the love he had for her.

"My time is completed," he then said to Laban. "Give me my wife, that I may go in to her." So Laban made a feast. But in the evening he brought his daughter Leah, covered with her veil, to Jacob; and Jacob went in to her. Next morning, when Jacob saw that it was Leah, he said to Laban, "What is this you have done to me? Did I not serve with you for Rachel? Why then have you deceived me?"

"It is not so done in our country," said Laban, "to give the younger daughter before the first-born. Complete the marriage week of this one, and we will give you the other also in return for serving me another seven years." Jacob did so, completing Leah's week. Then Laban gave him Rachel to wife, so Jacob served Laban for another seven years. And he loved Rachel more than Leah.

When the LORD saw that Leah was hated, he opened her womb, but Rachel was barren. Leah conceived and bore four sons: first Reuben, then Simeon, then Levi, and then Judah; then she ceased bearing. But Rachel bore Jacob no children. She envied her sister, and said to Jacob, "Give me children, or I shall die!" This kindled Jacob's anger against Rachel. "Am I in the place of God," he said, "who has withheld from you the fruit of the womb?"

"Here is my maid Bilhah," said Rachel. "Go in to her, that I may have children through her." So Jacob went in to Bilhah, and she conceived and bore Jacob a son. "God has heard my voice," said Rachel, "and given me a son." She called his name Dan. Rachel's maid Bilhah conceived again and bore Jacob a second son; Rachel called him Naphtali.

When Leah saw that she had ceased bearing children, she gave her maid Zilpah to Jacob as a wife. Zilpah bore Jacob a son, and Leah named him Gad. Zilpah bore Jacob a second son, and Leah named him Asher. Then God hearkened to Leah, and she conceived again. She bore Jacob a fifth son, Issachar, and a sixth son, Zebulun. "Now my husband will honor me," Leah said, "because I have borne him six sons." Afterwards she bore a daughter, and called her name Dinah.

Then God remembered Rachel, and opened her womb. Rachel conceived and bore a son, and she called his name Joseph, saying, "May the LORD add to me another son!"

AFTER RACHEL HAD borne Joseph, Jacob said to Laban, "Give me my wives and children for whom I have served you, and let me go to my own home and country." But Laban said, "The LORD has blessed me because of you. Name your wages, and I will give it."

"You know how I have served you, and how your cattle have fared," said Jacob. "For you had little before I came, and it has increased abundantly. The LORD has blessed you wherever I turned. Now when shall I provide for my own household also?" But Jacob saw that Laban did not regard him with favor as before. Then the LORD said to Jacob, "Return to the land of your fathers and to your kindred, and I will be with you." So Jacob arose, set his sons and his wives on camels, and fled with all he had, to go to the land of Canaan to his father Isaac. Laban had gone to shear his sheep, and Jacob did not tell him that he intended to flee. Crossing the Euphrates, Jacob set his face toward the hill country of Gilead.

When Laban heard that Jacob had fled, he pursued him for seven days. But God came to Laban in a dream by night, and said, "Take heed that you say not a word to Jacob, either good or bad." Laban overtook Jacob in the hill country where Jacob had pitched his tent. "Why have you cheated me," he said, "and carried away my daughters like captives of the sword? Why did you not permit me to kiss them farewell?" Jacob answered, "Because I was afraid, for I thought you would take your daughters from me by force." Laban replied, "The daughters are my daughters, the children are my children, the flocks are my flocks, and all that you see is mine. But what can I do this day to these my daughters, or to their children? Come now, let us make a covenant, you and I. The LORD watch between you and me, when we are absent one from the other. If you ill-treat my daughters, or if you take wives besides my daughters, although no man is with us, remember, God is witness between you and me." Jacob offered a sacrifice on the mountain, and they ate bread and tarried there all night. Early in the morning Laban arose, kissed his grandchildren and his daughters, and blessed them. Then he departed and returned home.

Jacob went on his way and sent messengers before him to Esau his brother in the land of Seir, the country of Edom, instructing them to tell Esau that Jacob sought favor in his sight. The messengers returned, saying that Esau was coming with four hundred men. Jacob, greatly afraid, prayed to the LORD, saying, "Deliver me from the hand of my brother Esau, for I fear him, lest he come and slay us all, the mothers with the children. I am not worthy of thy steadfast love, but thou didst say, 'Return to your country and your kindred, and I will do you good.'"

That night Jacob took a present for Esau: droves of goats, ewes, rams, camels, cows, bulls, and asses. These he delivered into the hands of his servants, and said, "Pass on before me, and when Esau my brother meets you, you shall say, 'These are a present sent by your servant Jacob to my lord Esau.'" For Jacob thought, "I may appease Esau with the present, and afterwards, when I see his face, perhaps he will accept me." So the present passed on before him. The same night Jacob sent his two wives, his two maids, his eleven children, and everything he had across the ford of the river Jabbok. He was left alone in the camp. A man wrestled with him until the breaking of the day, but he did not prevail against Jacob. Then the man touched the hollow of Jacob's thigh, and it was put out of joint. "Let me go," he said to Jacob, "for the day is breaking." But Jacob said, "I will not let you go, unless you bless me."

"What is your name?" the man asked, and when Jacob told him, he said, "Your name shall no more be called Jacob, but Israel, for you have striven with God and with men, and have prevailed." Jacob asked him, "Tell me, I pray, your name." But the man said, "Why is it you ask my name?" And there he blessed Jacob. So Jacob called the name of the place Peniel, saying, "I have seen God face to face, and yet my life is preserved."

The sun rose upon Jacob as he passed on, limping because of his thigh. Then he lifted up his eyes and saw Esau coming with four hundred men. So he divided the children among Leah and Rachel and the two maids, putting Rachel and Joseph last of all. He himself went on before them, bowing himself to the ground as he came near to his brother. But Esau ran to meet him, and embraced him, and kissed him, and they wept.

"Who are these with you?" Esau asked, and Jacob said, "The children whom God has graciously given me." Then Esau asked, "And what did you mean by all this company I met?" Jacob answered, "To find favor in the sight of my lord." But Esau said, "I have enough, my brother; keep what you have for yourself." Jacob said, "No, I pray you accept my present, for truly to see your face is like seeing the face of God, with such favor have you received me. My gift is brought to you, because God has dealt graciously with me, and because I have enough." So Esau took it, and returned that day to Edom. But God said to Jacob, "Go to Bethel, and make there an altar to the God who appeared to you when you fled from your brother Esau." So Jacob and all the people with him went to Bethel, and there he built an altar.

They journeyed on, and when they were still some distance from Ephrath (that is, Bethlehem), Rachel travailed, and she had hard labor. "Fear not," the midwife said, "for now you will have another son." As her soul was departing (for she died), Rachel named the boy Ben-oni, but his father called him Benjamin. So Rachel died, and was buried, and Jacob set up a pillar upon her grave, the pillar of Rachel's tomb. And now the sons of Jacob were twelve.

Israel journeyed on, and came to his father Isaac at Mamre, where Abraham and Isaac had sojourned. Now the days of Isaac were a hundred and eighty years when he died and was gathered to his people. His sons Esau and Jacob buried him. Then Esau returned to the hill country of Edom, and Jacob dwelt in the land of his father's sojournings, in Canaan.

THIS IS THE history of the family of Jacob.

Joseph, being seventeen years old, was shepherding the flock with his brothers, and he brought an ill report of them to their father. Now Israel loved Joseph, the son of his old age, more than his other children, and he made him a long robe with sleeves. Because of this, Joseph's brothers hated him, and could not speak to him peaceably. When Joseph told his brothers of a dream he had, they only hated him the more. "I dreamed we were binding sheaves in the field," he said. "My sheaf arose and stood upright; and your sheaves gathered round it, and bowed down to my sheaf." His brothers said, "Are you indeed to have dominion over us?" Joseph dreamed another dream, and told it to his father and his brothers, saying, "The sun, the moon, and eleven stars were bowing down to me." His brothers were jealous, and his father rebuked him. "What is this dream? Shall we indeed come to bow before you?" But his father kept the saying in mind.

One day Israel sent Joseph to Shechem, where his brothers had gone to pasture their father's flock. "Go see if it is well with your brothers and the flock," he told Joseph, "and bring me word." When Joseph came to Shechem, a man found him wandering in the fields, and asked, "What are you seeking?" Joseph said, "I am seeking my brothers, who are pasturing the flock." The man said, "They have gone away. I heard them say, 'Let us go to Dothan.'" So Joseph went after his brothers and found them at Dothan.

They saw him afar off, and conspired against him. "Here comes this dreamer," they said to one another. "Let us kill him and throw him into one of the water pits, and say that a wild beast has devoured him. Then we shall see what will become of his dreams." But Reuben, hoping to rescue Joseph, said, "Do not take his life. Shed no blood. Cast him into this empty pit here in the wilderness, but lay no hand upon him." So when Joseph came to his brothers, they stripped him of his long robe, and they cast him into the empty pit.

As the brothers sat down to eat, they saw a caravan of Ishmaelites approaching, their camels bearing gum, balm, and myrrh. "Let us sell our brother to the Ishmaelites," Judah said, "and let not our hand be upon him."

His brothers heeded him, and when the caravan passed by, they drew Joseph up out of the pit, and sold him to the Ishmaelites for twenty shekels of silver. Then the brothers killed a goat, and dipped Joseph's robe in the blood, and brought the robe to their father, saying, "This we have found. Is it your son's robe?" Jacob recognized it, and said, "It is my son's. A wild beast has devoured him; Joseph is without doubt torn to pieces." Jacob rent his garments, and put sackcloth upon his loins, and mourned for his son many days. All Jacob's sons and daughters rose up to comfort him; but he refused to be comforted.

JOSEPH WAS TAKEN down to Egypt, where Potiphar, the captain of Pharaoh's guard, bought him from the Ishmaelites. The LORD was with Joseph, and he became a successful man in the house of his Egyptian master. Potiphar saw that the LORD caused all that Joseph did to prosper, so he made him his overseer, putting him in charge of all that he had.

Joseph was handsome, and after a time his master's wife cast her eyes upon him. "Lie with me," she said. But Joseph refused, saying, "My master has put everything that he has in my hand except yourself, because you are his wife. How then can I do this great wickedness, and sin against God?" Although she spoke to Joseph day after day, he would not lie with her. Then one day, when he came into the house to do his work, she caught him by his garment, saying, "Lie with me." But Joseph fled out of the house, leaving his garment in her hand. She called to the men of her household. "See how this Hebrew insults us," she said. "He came in to lie with me, and when I cried out, he left his garment and fled." When her husband came home, she told him the same story, and his anger was kindled. He took Joseph and put him into prison. But the LORD was with Joseph, showing him steadfast love, and giving him favor in the sight of the keeper of the prison, who committed to Joseph's care all the other prisoners. Whatever Joseph did, the LORD made it prosper.

Some time after this, Pharaoh was angry with his chief butler and chief baker, and he put them in the prison where Joseph was confined. They were placed in Joseph's care, and continued for some time in custody. One night the butler and the baker both dreamed—each his own dream with its own meaning. When Joseph came to them in the morning, he saw that they were troubled. "Why are your faces downcast today?" he asked. "We have had dreams," they said, "and there is no one to interpret them." Joseph said, "Do not interpretations belong to God? Tell them to me, I pray you."

"In my dream," said the butler, "there was a vine with three branches. It budded, blossomed, and the clusters ripened into grapes. Pharaoh's cup was in my hand. I took the grapes, pressed them into the cup, and placed it in Pharaoh's hand." Joseph said, "This is its interpretation: the three branches are three days. Within three days Pharaoh will restore you to your office, and you shall place Pharaoh's cup in his hand as formerly. Remember me then, I pray you. Mention me to Pharaoh. For I was stolen out of the land of the

Hebrews, and I have done nothing that they should put me into the dungeon." When the baker saw that the interpretation was favorable, he said to Joseph, "I also had a dream: there were three cake baskets on my head. In the uppermost basket was food baked for Pharaoh, but the birds were eating it." Joseph answered, "This is its interpretation: the three baskets are three days. Within three days Pharaoh will lift up your head—from you!—and hang you on a tree; and the birds will eat the flesh from you." On the third day, which was Pharaoh's birthday, he made a feast for all his servants. He restored the chief butler to his butlership; but he hanged the chief baker, as Joseph had interpreted. Yet the chief butler did not remember Joseph.

Two YEARS LATER, Pharaoh dreamed one night he was standing by the Nile, and seven cows, sleek and fat, came up out of the Nile to feed in the reed grass. Seven other cows, gaunt and thin, came up after them, and ate up the seven fat cows. Pharaoh awoke, but he fell asleep and dreamed a second time: seven ears of grain, plump and good, were growing on one stalk, and after them sprouted seven ears, thin and blighted. The thin ears swallowed up the plump ears. In the morning his spirit was troubled, so he sent for all of Egypt's wise men, and told them his dream. None could interpret it. Then the chief butler said, "I remember my faults today. When Pharaoh was angry with his servants, and put me and the chief baker in custody, we dreamed on the same night, each having a different dream. A young Hebrew was with us, and he interpreted our dreams, and as he interpreted, so it came to pass; I was restored to my office, and the baker was hanged."

Pharaoh sent for Joseph, and they brought him hastily out of the dungeon. When he had shaved himself and changed clothes, he came in before Pharaoh, who said, "I have heard that you can interpret dreams." Joseph answered, "It is not in me; God will give Pharaoh a favorable answer." So Pharaoh told Joseph his dream of the seven thin cows that ate the seven fat cows. "But when they had eaten them," Pharaoh said, "they were still as gaunt as at the beginning." He then told his dream of the seven good ears of grain and the seven blighted ears. "There is no one," Pharaoh said, "who can explain this to me."

"The dreams are one," Joseph said. "The seven good cows and seven good ears are seven years. The seven lean cows and seven blighted ears are also seven years. God has shown Pharaoh what he is about to do. There will come seven years of great plenty throughout Egypt, but after them will come seven years of famine, and the famine will consume the land. The doubling of Pharaoh's dream means that the thing is fixed by God, and will shortly come to pass. Therefore, let Pharaoh select a man discreet and wise, and set him over the land of Egypt. Let Pharaoh appoint overseers to lay up a fifth of the produce of the land of Egypt during the seven plenteous years that are coming. Let it be a reserve against the seven years of famine, so that the land may not perish."

This proposal seemed good to Pharaoh and to all his servants. "Can we find such a man as this," he asked, "in whom is the Spirit of God?" Then he said to Joseph, "Since God has shown you all this, there is none so discreet and wise as you. I shall set you over all the land of Egypt, and my people shall do as you command." He took his signet ring from his hand and put it on Joseph's hand. He arrayed Joseph in garments of fine linen, put a gold chain about his neck, and made him ride in his second chariot. Moreover, he gave to Joseph in marriage Asenath, the daughter of Potiphera, priest of On.

When Joseph entered the service of Pharaoh, he was thirty years old. During the seven plenteous years, he went through all of Egypt gathering and storing up grain in great abundance until, like the sand of the sea, it could not be measured. Before the years of famine came, Asenath bore Joseph two sons. The first-born he named Manasseh, and the second son he called Ephraim. After the seven years of plenty, the seven years of famine began to come. When all the land of Egypt was famished, the people cried to Pharaoh for bread, and Pharaoh said, "Go to Joseph." So Joseph opened all the storehouses, and sold to the Egyptians. Moreover, all the earth came to Egypt to buy grain, because the famine was severe everywhere.

WHEN JACOB LEARNED that there was grain in Egypt, he said to his sons, "Go down to Egypt and buy grain for us, that we may not die." So ten of Joseph's brothers, the sons of Israel, went down to buy grain in Egypt. But Jacob did not send Joseph's brother Benjamin, for he feared that harm might befall him.

Now Joseph was governor over the land. When his brothers came and bowed themselves before him, they did not know him, but Joseph knew them, and remembered the dreams he had dreamed of them. Yet he treated them like strangers and spoke roughly to them. "Where do you come from?" he said. They replied, "From the land of Canaan, to buy food." Joseph said, "You are spies. You have come to see the weakness of the land." But they said, "No, my lord, your servants come to buy food. We are all honest men, not spies. We are twelve brothers, the sons of one man in the land of Canaan. The youngest is this day with our father, and one is no more."

"Surely you are spies," said Joseph, "but by this shall your words be tested: if you are honest men, let one of your brothers remain here, confined in prison. Let the rest carry grain to your households. Then bring your youngest brother to me, so your words will be verified." And Joseph took Simeon from his other brothers and bound him before their eyes.

"Now comes a reckoning for Joseph's blood," the brothers said to one another, "for in truth we are guilty concerning him, in that we saw the distress of his soul when he besought us and we would not listen." They did not know that Joseph understood them, for there was an interpreter between them. And Joseph turned away from them and wept. Then he gave orders to fill their bags with grain, and to give them provisions for the journey. This was done, and the brothers departed. When they came to the land of Canaan, they told their father all that had befallen them. "You have bereaved me of my children," Jacob said. "Joseph is no more. Simeon is no more. Now you would take Benjamin. Why did you tell the man you had another brother?"

"The man, the lord of the land, took us to be spies and spoke roughly to us," they replied. "He questioned us carefully about ourselves and our kindred, and we answered. Could we know he would say, 'Bring your brother down'?"

"Benjamin shall not go with you," said Jacob, "for his brother is dead, and he only is left. If harm should befall him, you would bring down my gray hairs with sorrow to the grave."

But the famine continued. When they had eaten the grain brought from Egypt, Jacob said to his sons, "Go again. Buy us a little food." But Judah said to him, "The man who is lord of the land solemnly warned us, saying, 'Bring your youngest brother. Then I shall know you are not spies, and will deliver your other brother to you.' If you will not send Benjamin, we will not go. But if you send the lad with me, I will be surety for him. If I do not bring him back to you, then let me bear the blame for ever."

"If it must be so," said Jacob, "do this: carry a present down to the man, a little balm, a little honey, gum, myrrh, pistachio nuts, and almonds. Take also your brother Benjamin, and may God Almighty grant you mercy before the man, that he may send back your other brother, Simeon, and Benjamin. If I am bereaved of my children, I am bereaved."

So they took the present and Benjamin, and went down to Egypt. When Joseph saw Benjamin with them, he said to his steward, "Bring the men to my house, for they are to dine with me at noon." The steward did as he was bidden, but the brothers were afraid. "We are brought here," they said, "so that he may make slaves of us." But the steward said, "Do not be afraid." Then he brought Simeon to them, and gave them water to wash their feet, and provender for their asses.

When Joseph came home, they gave him the present they had brought, and bowed down to him. "Is your father well," Joseph inquired, "the old man of whom you spoke?" They said, "Our father is well." And they bowed their heads and made obeisance. Then Joseph saw his brother Benjamin, and his heart yearned for him. "Is this your youngest brother?" he asked. "God be gracious to you, my son!" And he made haste to enter his chamber, and wept there. Then he washed his face and came out. Controlling himself he said, "Let food be served." His brothers sat before him, the first-born according to his birthright and the youngest according to his youth. They looked at one another in amazement, and they drank and were merry with him.

Then Joseph commanded the steward of his house, "Fill the men's sacks with food, as much as they can carry, and put my cup, the silver cup, in the sack of the youngest." The steward did so, and as soon as the morning was light, the men were sent away with their asses. When they had gone but a short distance from the city, Joseph said to his steward, "Overtake the men, and say to them, 'Why have you returned evil for good? Why have you stolen the silver cup from which my lord drinks and by which he divines?' " When the steward overtook the brothers and spoke these words, they said, "Far be it from your servants to do such a thing! If it be found with one of us, let him die, and we also will be my lord's slaves." Then every man quickly lowered his sack to the ground, and opened it. The steward searched, beginning with the eldest and ending with the youngest, and the cup was found in Benjamin's sack. The brothers rent their clothes, and returned to Joseph's house, falling to the ground before him. "What deed is this you have done?" Joseph said. "Do you not know that such a man as I can indeed divine?" Judah said, "What shall we say? How can we clear ourselves? God has found out the guilt of your servants; behold, we are my lord's slaves, both we and he also in whose hand the cup has been found." But Joseph said, "Only that man shall be my slave. As for you, go in peace to your father."

Then Judah went up to Joseph and said, "O my lord, let your servant speak, and let not your anger burn against me. When our father said, 'Go again, buy us a little food,' we said, 'We cannot go unless our youngest brother is with us.' My father said, 'You know that my wife bore me two sons; one left me, and he has surely been torn to pieces. I have never seen him since. If you take this one also from me, and harm befalls him, you will bring down my gray hairs in sorrow to the grave.' Then I became surety for the lad to my father. Therefore, let me, I pray you, remain instead of the lad as a slave to my lord. How can I go back if the lad is not with me? I fear to see the evil that would come upon my father." Joseph could not control himself before all those who stood by him. He sent out all but his brothers, and he wept aloud as he made himself known. "I am your brother, Joseph, whom you sold into Egypt," he said. But they could not answer him, for they were dismayed.

"Now do not be distressed," Joseph said, "or angry with yourselves because you sold me. God sent me before you to preserve life in these years of famine, and to keep alive for you a remnant of survivors on earth. It was not you who sent me here, but God; and he has made me lord of Pharaoh's house and ruler over all the land. Go and bring my father to me. Do not tarry. You shall dwell near me in the land of Goshen, you and your children and your children's children, your flocks, and your herds. There I will provide for you, for there are yet five years of famine to come." Then he fell upon Benjamin's neck, and he kissed all his brothers and wept.

When Pharaoh heard that Joseph's brothers had come, he was pleased. "Say to your brothers," he told Joseph, "that the best of all the land of Egypt is theirs." So Joseph gave his brothers grain and provisions, and wagons for their wives and little ones and for his father on the journey. Then he sent them away, saying, "Do not quarrel on the way." When they came to the land of Canaan, they told their father that Joseph was still alive, and was ruler over all the land of Egypt. And Jacob's heart fainted, for he did not believe them. But when he saw the wagons which Joseph had sent to carry him, his spirit revived. "Joseph my son is alive," he said. "I will go and see him before I die."

So the sons of Israel carried their father, their little ones, and their wives in the wagons. They took their cattle and their goods, and came into Egypt. All the persons of the house of Jacob were seventy. Then Jacob sent Judah to Joseph, and Joseph made ready his chariot and went up and presented himself to his father in the land of Goshen. "Now let me die," said Jacob, "since I have seen your face and know that you are still alive." Joseph brought his father to Pharaoh, and Jacob blessed Pharaoh. And Joseph settled his father and his brothers, and gave them a possession in the land of Egypt, in the best of the land, as Pharaoh had commanded.

JACOB DWELT IN Egypt, in the land of Goshen, for seventeen years. When the days of his life were a hundred and forty-seven years, the time drew near that he must die. So Joseph, told that his father was ill, took his two sons, Manasseh and Ephraim, and went to him. Summoning his strength, Jacob sat up in bed. "God Almighty appeared to me," he said, "at Bethel in the land of Canaan. He blessed me and said he would give that land to my descendants for an everlasting possession. Now your two sons, Ephraim and Manasseh, shall be mine, as Reuben and Simeon are. The offspring born to you after them shall be yours, but shall be called by the name of their brothers in their inheritance."

Then Jacob called all his sons. "Gather yourselves together," he said, "that I may tell you what shall befall you in days to come. Assemble and hearken to Israel your father. Reuben, you are my first-born. Pre-eminent in pride and power, you are unstable as water. You shall not have pre-eminence. Simeon and Levi are brothers; weapons of violence are their swords. Cursed be their anger, for it is fierce; and their wrath, for it is cruel! I will divide them in Jacob and scatter them in Israel. Judah, your brothers shall praise you; your hand shall be on the neck of your enemies. Judah is a lion's whelp; from the prey, my son, you have gone up. He stooped down, he couched as a lion; who dares rouse him up? The scepter shall not depart from Judah, until he comes to whom it belongs; and to him shall be the obedience of the peoples.

"Zebulun shall dwell at the shore of the sea, a haven for ships, and his border shall be at Sidon. Issachar is a strong ass, crouching between the sheepfolds. He saw that a resting place was good, the land pleasant, so he bowed his shoulder and became a slave at forced labor. Dan shall judge his people as one of the tribes of Israel. He shall be a serpent in the path, that bites the horse's heels so that the rider falls backward. Raiders shall raid Gad, but he shall raid at their heels. Asher's food shall be rich, and he shall yield royal dainties. Naphtali is a hind let loose, that bears comely fawns.

"Joseph is a fruitful bough by a spring; his branches run over the wall. The archers fiercely attacked him, yet his bow remained unmoved. His arms were made agile by the Mighty One of Jacob (by the name of the Shepherd, the Rock of Israel), the God of your father who will help you, and bless you with

blessings of heaven above. Benjamin is a ravenous wolf, in the morning devouring the prey, and at even dividing the spoil."

All these are the twelve tribes of Israel, and thus their father Jacob blessed
them. Then he said to his sons, "I am to be gathered to my people. When I
came from Haran, Rachel to my sorrow died in the land of Canaan when
there was still some distance to go; and I buried her there on the way to
Ephrath. But bury me with my fathers in the cave that is in the field at
Machpelah, to the east of Mamre, in the land of Canaan. There they buried
Abraham and Sarah; there they buried Isaac and Rebekah; and there I buried
Leah." When he had finished, Jacob drew up his feet into the bed, and
breathed his last. Joseph fell on his father's face and wept over him, and
kissed him. Then he commanded the physicians to embalm his father. Forty
days were required for it, and the Egyptians wept for Jacob seventy days.

When the days of weeping were past, Joseph spoke to Pharaoh. "If now I
have found favor in your eyes," he said, "let me go up to the land of Canaan
and bury my father; then I will return." Pharaoh agreed. So with all the
servants of Pharaoh, all the elders of Egypt, and all his own household, Joseph went up to Canaan. There were chariots and horsemen; it was a very
great company. When the Canaanites saw this, they said, "This is a grievous
mourning to the Egyptians." Thus Jacob's sons did for him as he had commanded, and buried him in the cave of the field at Machpelah. Then Joseph
returned to Egypt with his brothers and all who had gone up with him.

Joseph's brothers, knowing that their father was dead, said, "It may be that
Joseph will hate us and pay us back for all the evil we did to him." They sent a
message to Joseph, praying for his forgiveness, and they came and fell down
before him, saying, "Behold, we are your servants." But Joseph said to them,
"Fear not, for am I in the place of God? You meant evil against me; but God
meant it for good, that many people should be kept alive, as they are today.
Do not fear; I will provide for you and your little ones." Thus he reassured
and comforted them.

So Joseph dwelt in Egypt. He saw Ephraim's children of the third generation, and children of the son of Manasseh were born upon his knees. And
Joseph said to his brothers, "I am about to die; but God will visit you, and
bring you up out of this land to the land which he swore to Abraham, to Isaac,
and to Jacob." Then Joseph took an oath of the sons of Israel, saying, "God
will visit you, and you shall carry up my bones from here." So Joseph died,
being a hundred and ten years old; and they embalmed him, and he was put in
a coffin in Egypt.

EXODUS

At the book's opening, several hundred years have passed since the close of Genesis, and the Israelites in Egypt are suffering as slaves under an oppressive new regime. First recounted is the story of Moses: his birth, his divine commission to free his fellow slaves, the ten plagues called down upon Egypt, the institution of Passover, and the miraculous escape of the Israelites through the Red Sea. The date of this "exodus" from Egypt has been calculated as between 1580 B.C. and 1215 B.C., with present opinion favoring the mid-thirteenth century B.C.

The narrative continues with the establishment, at Mount Sinai, of the covenant between God and his people. It is at the summit of this mountain, against the backdrop of a majestic theophany, that Moses receives the Ten Commandments from God.

Elsewhere in the Old Testament this deliverance of the Israelites from bondage is celebrated as the outstanding instance of God's love for his chosen people. It also plays a part in the New Testament, where the imagery of the Passover is applied to the sacrifice of Christ on Calvary. As with Genesis, several strands of literary tradition, some very ancient, some as late as the sixth century B.C., were combined in the makeup of the book.

———

JOSEPH DIED, AND all his brothers, and all that generation, but the descendants of Jacob were fruitful and increased greatly in Egypt for four hundred years; they multiplied and grew exceedingly strong, so that the land was filled with them. Now there arose a new king over Egypt, who did not know Joseph, and to his people he said, "The people of Israel are too many and too mighty for us. Come, let us deal shrewdly with them, lest, if war befall us, they join our enemies, fight against us, and escape from the land." So the Egyptians set taskmasters over the people of Israel to afflict them with heavy burdens, and make their lives bitter with hard service in mortar and brick, and work in the field, building for Pharaoh the store-cities of Pithom and Rameses. But the more the people of Israel were oppressed, the more they multiplied and spread abroad. And the Egyptians were in dread of them.

Then Pharaoh said to the Hebrew midwives, Shiphrah and Puah, "When you serve the Hebrew women, and see them upon the birthstool, if it is a son, you shall kill him; but if it is a daughter, she shall live." But the midwives feared God, and did not do as Pharaoh commanded. He then called them and said, "Why have you let the male children live?" The midwives said, "Because the Hebrew women are not like Egyptian women; they are vigorous and are delivered before the midwife comes to them." So God dealt well with the midwives, giving them families. And the people of Israel multiplied and grew so strong that Pharaoh then commanded all his people, "Every son born to the Hebrews shall be cast into the Nile, but let every daughter live."

Now Amram, a man from the house of Levi, had taken to wife Jochebed, a daughter of Levi, who conceived and bore a son. She saw that he was a goodly child, and hid him three months. Then, when she could hide him no longer, she took a basket made of bulrushes, daubed it with bitumen and pitch, put the child in it, and placed it among the reeds at the river's brink. The child's sister stood at a distance to see what would happen.

Soon the daughter of Pharaoh came down to bathe at the river. She saw the basket among the reeds, sent her maid to fetch it, opened it, and saw the child. The babe was crying, and she took pity on him. "This is one of the Hebrews' children," she said. Then his sister approached, saying, "Shall I go call a nurse from the Hebrew women to nurse the child for you?" Pharaoh's daughter said, "Go." So the girl called the child's mother. "Take this child away, and nurse him for me," Pharaoh's daughter told the mother, "and I will give you wages." The woman took the child, nursed him, and he grew; and then she brought him back. Thus the child became the son of Pharaoh's daughter; and she named him Moses.

ONE DAY, WHEN Moses was grown, he went out to his people, looked on their burdens, and saw an Egyptian beating a Hebrew. Moses looked around, and seeing no one near, he killed the Egyptian and hid him in the sand. Next day he went out again and saw two Hebrews struggling together. "Why do you strike your fellow?" Moses asked the man that did wrong. "Who made you a judge over us?" the man answered. "Do you mean to kill me as you killed the Egyptian?" Then Moses was afraid. "Surely the thing is known," he thought. And when Pharaoh heard of it, he sought to kill Moses.

But Moses fled from Pharaoh to the land of Midian. There he sat down by a well, and soon the seven daughters of Jethro, the priest of Midian, came and drew water for their father's flock. Shepherds came then, and drove the girls away; but Moses stood up and helped them, and watered their flock. When they returned to their father, he said, "How did you finish so soon today?" They replied, "An Egyptian delivered us from the shepherds, and even drew water for us and watered the flock." Jethro said, "Where is this man? Call him, that he may eat bread." And Moses stayed there, content to dwell with them. Jethro gave Moses his daughter Zipporah in marriage, and she bore him two sons. The first he named Gershom, that is, Sojourner, for he said, "I have been a sojourner in a foreign land," and the second Eliezer, "My God, my help."

IN THE COURSE of time the king of Egypt died, but the people of Israel still groaned under their bondage, and cried out for help. And God heard, and he remembered his covenant with Abraham, with Isaac, and with Jacob. Now Moses was keeping the flock of his father-in-law. He led it to the west side of the wilderness and came to Sinai, the mountain of God. There the angel of the LORD appeared to him in a flame of fire out of the midst of a bush. When Moses saw that the bush was burning yet was not consumed, he said, "I will turn aside and see this great sight." God called to him out of the bush, saying, "Moses, Moses!" Moses said, "Here am I." God said, "Do not come near; put off your shoes, for you are standing on holy ground. I am the God of your father, the God of Abraham, Isaac, and Jacob." And Moses hid his face, afraid to look at God.

Then the LORD said, "I have seen the affliction of my people in Egypt, and have heard their cry. I know their sufferings, and I have come down to deliver them out of that land to a good and broad land, flowing with milk and honey, to the place of the Canaanites. Come, I will send you to Pharaoh that you may bring forth my people, the sons of Israel, out of Egypt." But Moses said, "Who am I that I should go to Pharaoh?" Then God said, "I will be with you; and this shall be the sign for you, that I have sent you: when you have brought the people out of Egypt, you shall serve God upon this mountain."

Moses said, "If I say to the people of Israel, 'The God of your fathers has sent me,' and they ask, 'What is his name?' what shall I say to them?" God said, "I AM WHO I AM. Say this to the people of Israel, 'I AM has sent me to you.' This is my name for ever, and thus I am to be remembered throughout all generations. Say to the elders of Israel, 'The LORD, the God of your fathers, the God of Abraham, Isaac, and Jacob, has appeared to me, and promised to bring you up out of the affliction of Egypt, to the land of Canaan, a land flowing with milk and honey.' You and the elders shall go to Pharaoh and say, 'The LORD, the God of the Hebrews, has met with us; and now, we pray you, let us go a three days' journey into the wilderness, that we may sacrifice to the LORD our God.'"

"But the people will not believe me," Moses said. The LORD said to him, "Cast your rod on the ground." Moses did so, and the rod became a serpent; and Moses fled from it. But the LORD said, "Put out your hand, and take it by the tail." Moses did so, and the serpent became a rod in his hand. And God said, "If they will not believe that the LORD, the God of their fathers, has appeared to you, they may believe signs, and then they will heed your voice."

But Moses said, "Oh, my Lord, I am not eloquent. I am slow of speech and tongue." The LORD replied, "Who has made man's mouth? Who makes him dumb, or deaf, or seeing, or blind? Is it not I, the LORD? Now go. I will teach you what you shall speak." Moses said, "Oh, my Lord, send, I pray, some other person." Then the anger of the LORD was kindled against Moses and he said, "Aaron, your brother, can speak well; he is coming out to meet you, and when he sees you, he will be glad. You shall speak to him and put the words in his mouth. I will be with you and teach you. He shall speak for you to the people; he shall be a mouth for you, and you shall be to him as God. Take in your hand this rod, with which you shall do before Pharaoh all the miracles I have put in your power."

So Moses went to Jethro his father-in-law. "Let me go back to my kinsmen in Egypt," he said, "and see whether they are still alive." And Jethro said, "Go in peace." And the LORD said to Moses, "Go back to Egypt, for all the men who were seeking your life are dead." So Moses took his wife and his sons and set them on an ass, and went back to the land of Egypt; in his hand Moses took the rod of God.

THEN THE LORD said to Aaron, "Go into the wilderness to meet Moses." So Aaron went, and met him at the mountain of God, and kissed him; and Moses told Aaron all that the LORD had charged him to do. Then they gathered together all the elders of the people of Israel, and Aaron spoke the words which the LORD had spoken to Moses, and did the signs, and the people believed. When they heard that the LORD had visited the people of Israel and had seen their affliction, they bowed their heads and worshiped.

Afterward Moses and Aaron went to Pharaoh and said, "The LORD, the God of Israel, has met with us and says, 'Let my people go hold a feast to me in the wilderness.'" But Pharaoh said, "Who is the LORD, that I should heed his voice? I do not know the LORD, and I will not let Israel go." They said, "Let us go, we pray, a three days' journey into the wilderness, and sacrifice to the LORD our God, lest he fall upon us with pestilence or sword." Pharaoh said, "Moses and Aaron, why do you take the people away from their work? Get to your burdens." The same day Pharaoh commanded his taskmasters and their foremen, "You shall no longer give the people of Israel straw to make bricks. Let them gather straw for themselves. But do not lessen the daily number of bricks which they must make. For they are idle; therefore they cry, 'Let us go and offer sacrifice to our God.' Let heavier work be laid upon them."

The taskmasters and foremen told the people of Pharaoh's words, and the people were scattered throughout the land to gather straw. "Complete your work, your daily task," the taskmasters urged. And the foremen, whom Pharaoh's taskmasters had set over the people of Israel, were beaten, and were asked, "Why have you not done all your task of making bricks today, as hitherto?" The foremen, seeing they were in evil plight, went to Moses and

Aaron and said, "The LORD look upon you and judge. You have made us offensive to Pharaoh and his servants, and have put a sword in their hands to kill us."

"O LORD," Moses prayed, "why didst thou ever send me? For since I came to Pharaoh to speak in thy name, he has done evil to thy people, and thou hast not delivered them at all." The LORD replied, "Now you shall see what I will do to Pharaoh; for with a strong hand he will send them out; he will drive them out of his land. I am the LORD; tell Pharaoh all that I say to you. But I will harden Pharaoh's heart, and though I multiply my signs and wonders, Pharaoh will not listen to you; then I will lay my hand upon Egypt and bring forth my people, the sons of Israel, out of Egypt by great acts of judgment. For the Egyptians shall know that I am the LORD. When Pharaoh says to you, 'Prove yourselves by working a miracle,' then you shall say to Aaron, 'Cast your rod down before Pharaoh, that it may become a serpent.'"

So Moses and Aaron went to Pharaoh and did as the LORD commanded. But when Aaron cast down his rod before Pharaoh and it became a serpent, Pharaoh summoned the wise men and sorcerers of Egypt, and they did the same by their secret arts. Every man cast down his rod, and the rods became serpents. Then Aaron's rod swallowed up their rods. Still Pharaoh's heart was hardened, as the LORD had said, and he would not listen to them.

Then the LORD said to Moses, "Go to Pharaoh in the morning, as he is going out to the water; wait for him by the river's brink, and say to him, 'The LORD, the God of the Hebrews, sent me to you, saying, "Let my people go serve me in the wilderness." You have not yet obeyed. Now the LORD says, "By this you shall know that I am the LORD: the water in the Nile shall be turned to blood; the fish in the Nile shall die, and it shall become foul and loathsome."' Tell Aaron to stretch out his rod over the waters of Egypt, over their canals, ponds, and pools, that they may become blood; and there shall be blood throughout all the land of Egypt."

Moses and Aaron did as the LORD commanded; in the sight of Pharaoh and his servants, all the water in the Nile turned to blood. There was blood throughout Egypt. But the magicians of Egypt did the same by their secret arts; so Pharaoh's heart remained hardened, and he would not listen, as the LORD had said. Pharaoh turned and went into his house, and the Egyptians dug round about the Nile for water, for they could not drink from the Nile.

SEVEN DAYS PASSED. Then the LORD said to Moses, "Go tell Pharaoh the LORD says, 'If you refuse to let my people go serve me, I will plague your country with frogs. The Nile shall swarm with frogs which shall come up into your houses, and bedchambers, and beds, and into your ovens and kneading bowls; the frogs shall come up on you and all your people.' And tell Aaron to stretch out his rod, and cause frogs to come." So Aaron stretched out his hand over the waters of Egypt, and frogs came up and covered the land. But the magicians did the same by their secret arts.

Then Pharaoh called Moses and Aaron. "Entreat the LORD to take away the frogs," he said, "and I will let the people go to sacrifice." Moses said, "It shall be as you say, so that you may know there is no one like the LORD our God. The frogs shall depart." Moses and Aaron went out from Pharaoh; and Moses cried to the LORD concerning the frogs. The frogs died out of the houses and courtyards and fields; they were gathered together in heaps, and the land stank. But when Pharaoh saw there was a respite, he hardened his heart, as the LORD had said.

Then the LORD said to Moses, "Tell Aaron to strike with his rod the dust of the earth, that it may become gnats throughout all Egypt." Aaron struck the dust, and it became gnats on man and beast throughout the land. The magicians tried by their secret arts to bring forth gnats. When they could not, they said to Pharaoh, "This is the finger of God." But Pharaoh's heart was hardened, and he would not listen.

So the LORD said to Moses, "Rise up early in the morning, and tell Pharaoh the LORD says, 'If you will not let my people go, I will send swarms of flies on you and your people. But there shall be no swarms of flies in the land of Goshen, where my people dwell. So that you may know that I am the LORD, I will thus put a division between my people and your people. By tomorrow shall this sign be.'" And the LORD did so; all the land of Egypt was ruined by great swarms of flies.

Then Pharaoh called Moses and Aaron. "Go," he said. "Sacrifice to your God within the land." But Moses said, "It would not be right. For we shall sacrifice animals to our God—offerings abominable to the Egyptians. Will they not stone us? We must go three days' journey into the wilderness to sacrifice." Pharaoh said, "I will let you go sacrifice in the wilderness, only not very far away. Make entreaty for me." Moses said, "I will pray to the LORD that the swarms of flies may depart tomorrow; only let not Pharaoh deal falsely again." So Moses went out and prayed to the LORD, and the LORD removed the swarms of flies; not one remained. But Pharaoh hardened his heart this time also. He did not let the people go.

Then the LORD said to Moses, "Go tell Pharaoh that the LORD, the God of the Hebrews, says, 'Let my people go serve me. If you refuse, a very severe plague will fall upon your cattle which are in the field, the horses, asses, and camels, all your herds and flocks. But the LORD will make a distinction between the cattle of Israel and of Egypt; nothing that belongs to the people of Israel shall die.'" The LORD set a time, saying, "Tomorrow the LORD will do this." And on the morrow all the cattle of the Egyptians died, yet not one of the cattle of the Israelites died. But Pharaoh did not let the people go.

The LORD then said to Moses and Aaron, "Take handfuls of ashes from the kiln. Throw them toward heaven in the sight of Pharaoh, to become fine dust over all the land, and cause boils to break out on man and beast throughout Egypt." So they took ashes, stood before Pharaoh, and Moses threw them toward heaven. Boils broke out on man and beast; the magicians could not stand before Moses, for boils were upon them and all Egyptians. But the LORD hardened the heart of Pharaoh, and he did not listen.

Then the LORD said to Moses, "Rise up early, stand before Pharaoh, and tell him the God of the Hebrews says, 'Let my people go, or this time I will send all my plagues upon your heart, so that you may know there is none like me in all the earth. By now I could have struck you and your people with pestilence, and cut you off from the earth; but I have let you live, to show you my power, so my name may be declared throughout the earth. You are still exalting yourself against my people. Tomorrow I will cause very heavy hail to fall, such as never has been in Egypt. Get your cattle into safe shelter; for every man and beast in the field shall die.'" Then those among Pharaoh's servants who feared the word of the LORD made their slaves and cattle flee into the houses; but those who did not, left slaves and cattle in the field.

And the LORD said to Moses, "Stretch forth your hand toward heaven, that there may be hail." Moses stretched forth his rod, and the LORD sent thunder and hail upon the land, and fire flashing continually in the midst of the very heavy hail. The hail struck down every plant in the field. (The flax in the bud and the barley in the ear were ruined. But the wheat, which is late coming up, was not ruined.) The hail struck down every man and beast in the field throughout Egypt, and it shattered every tree. Only in the land of Goshen, where the people of Israel were, was there no hail.

Then Pharaoh sent for Moses and Aaron. "I have sinned this time," he said. "The LORD is right. Entreat the LORD, for there has been enough hail. I will let you go." Moses said, "I will stretch out my hands to the LORD; there will be no more hail, that you may know that the earth is the LORD's. But I know you do not yet fear the LORD God." So Moses went out of the city, and stretched out his hands to the LORD; the thunder and hail ceased. But when Pharaoh saw this, he sinned yet again, and did not let the people of Israel go.

MOSES AND AARON again went in to Pharaoh, and told him, "The LORD says, 'How long will you refuse to humble yourself before me? If you refuse to let my people go, behold, tomorrow I will bring locusts into your country, as neither your fathers nor your grandfathers have seen. The locusts shall cover the face of the land, fill your houses, and eat every plant that is left after the hail.'" Then Moses and Aaron turned and went out.

"How long shall this man be a snare to us?" Pharaoh's servants said to him. "Let the men go serve the LORD their God. Do you not yet understand that Egypt is ruined?" So Moses and Aaron were brought back. "Go, serve the LORD your God," Pharaoh said, "but who are to go?" Moses said, "Our young and old, our sons and daughters, and our flocks and herds, for we must hold a feast to the LORD." But Pharaoh said, "The LORD be with you, if ever I let you and your little ones go! No! You have some evil purpose in mind. Let the men among you go and serve the LORD, for that is what you desire." And they were driven out from Pharaoh's presence.

Then the LORD said to Moses, "Stretch out your hand, that the locusts may come." So Moses stretched forth his rod, and the LORD brought an east wind upon the land all that day and night; and the east wind brought locusts over all of Egypt. Such a dense swarm of locusts had never been before. They darkened the whole land, eating all plants and the fruit of all trees; not a green thing remained. In haste, Pharaoh called Moses and Aaron. "I have sinned against your God, and against you," he said. "Forgive my sin, I pray, and entreat the LORD your God to remove this death from me." So Moses entreated the LORD, and the LORD sent a very strong west wind, which lifted the locusts and drove them into the Red Sea; not a single locust was left. But Pharaoh did not let the children of Israel go.

The LORD then said to Moses, "Stretch out your hand toward heaven to bring darkness over Egypt, a darkness to be felt." So Moses stretched out his hand, and there was thick darkness in all the land. The Egyptians did not see one another nor rise from their places for three days; but the people of Israel had light where they dwelt. Then Pharaoh called Moses. "Go, serve the LORD," he said. "Your children may go with you; only let your flocks and herds remain behind." But Moses said, "We must take our cattle, for we do not know with what sacrifices and burnt offerings we must serve the LORD until we arrive there." Then the LORD hardened Pharaoh's heart, and Pharaoh said to Moses, "Get away from me. Never see my face again, or you shall die." Moses said, "As you say!"

But the LORD said to Moses, "Yet one plague more I will bring upon Pharaoh and Egypt. Afterwards he will let you go; he will drive you away. Speak now in the hearing of the people, that they ask, every man of his neighbor and every woman of her neighbor, jewelry of silver and of gold."

And Moses said to Pharaoh, "Thus says the LORD: 'About midnight I will go forth in Egypt, and all the first-born in the land shall die, from the first-born of Pharaoh upon his throne, to the first-born of the maidservant behind the mill, even to all the first-born of the cattle. There shall be a great cry throughout Egypt, such as has never been, nor shall be again. But against any of the people of Israel, either man or beast, not a dog shall growl; thus you will know that the LORD makes a distinction between the Egyptians and Israel.' And all your servants shall come and bow down to me, saying, 'Get out, you and all who follow you.' And after that I will go."

Moses then went out from Pharaoh in hot anger. And the LORD said to Moses, "Pharaoh will not listen to you, so that my wonders may be multiplied in the land of Egypt." Thus the LORD hardened Pharaoh's heart, and he did not let the people of Israel go.

THE LORD SAID to Moses and Aaron, "This month shall be for you the first month of the year. Tell all of Israel that on the tenth day of this month they shall take a lamb for each household, a lamb without blemish, a male a year old. Keep it until the fourteenth day of this month, when the whole congregation of Israel shall kill their lambs in the evening. Then they shall take some of the blood, and put it on the two doorposts and the lintel of the house in which they eat them. They shall eat the flesh that night, roasted; with unleavened bread and bitter herbs they shall eat it. Eat with your loins girded, your sandals on, your staff in hand; and eat in haste. It is the LORD's passover. For I will pass through the land of Egypt that night, and smite all the first-born, both man and beast; on the gods of Egypt I will execute judgments: I am the LORD. The blood shall be a sign for you; when I see blood upon your houses, I will pass over you, and no plague shall destroy you.

"This shall be a memorial day; keep it throughout your generations as a feast to the LORD. Seven days you shall eat unleavened bread; no leaven shall be found in your houses, for if any one eats what is leavened, that person shall be cut off from Israel. On the first day and on the seventh you shall hold a holy assembly; no work shall be done on those days. And you shall observe the feast of unleavened bread as an ordinance for ever."

Then Moses called all the elders of Israel. "Select and kill lambs for yourselves," he said, "according to your families. Dip a bunch of hyssop in the blood which is in the basin, and touch the lintel and doorposts; and none of you shall go out of his house until morning. For the LORD will pass through to slay the Egyptians; and when he sees the blood, he will pass over the door, and will not allow the destroyer to enter your houses to slay you. You shall observe this rite for ever. When you come to the land which the LORD will give you, as he has promised, you shall keep this service. And when your children say, 'What do you mean by this service?' you shall say, 'It is the sacrifice of the LORD's passover, for he passed over our houses and spared the people of Israel in Egypt, when he slew the Egyptians.'" And the people of Israel bowed their heads and worshiped. Then they did as the LORD had commanded.

At midnight the LORD smote all the first-born in the land of Egypt, from the first-born of Pharaoh to the first-born of the captive in the dungeon, even to the first-born of the cattle. Pharaoh rose up in the night, he, and all his servants; and there was a great cry in Egypt, for there was not a house where one was not dead. And he summoned Moses and Aaron by night and said, "Go forth, both you and the people of Israel. Go, serve the LORD, as you have said. Take your flocks and herds, and be gone; and bless me also!" So the people of Israel took their dough before it was leavened, their kneading bowls being bound up in their mantles on their shoulders. They had also done as Moses told them, and had asked of the Egyptians jewelry of silver and of gold, and clothing. And the LORD had given them favor in the sight of the Egyptians; moreover, Moses was very great in the sight of Pharaoh's servants. So the Egyptians let them have what they asked.

The people of Israel journeyed from Rameses to Succoth, about six hundred thousand men on foot, besides women and children. A mixed multitude also went with them, and many cattle, flocks, and herds. And they baked unleavened cakes of the dough which they had brought when they were thrust out of Egypt and could not tarry, neither had they prepared for themselves any provisions.

The people of Israel had dwelt in Egypt four hundred and thirty years. And at the end of that time, on that very day, all the hosts of the LORD went out from the land of Egypt. It was a night of watching by the LORD, to bring them out; so this same night is a night of watching kept to the LORD by all the people of Israel throughout their generations.

WHEN PHARAOH LET the people go, God did not lead them to Canaan by way of the land of the Philistines, although that was near; for God said, "If the people see war, they might repent and return to Egypt." So God led the people round by way of the wilderness toward the Red Sea. They went out of Egypt equipped for battle. And Moses took the bones of Joseph with him; for Joseph had solemnly sworn the people of Israel, saying, "God will visit you; carry my bones with you from here." They moved on from Succoth, and encamped at Etham, on the edge of the wilderness. The LORD led them by day in a pillar of cloud, and by night in a pillar of fire to give them light, that they might travel by day and by night, and he did not depart from before the people.

Then the LORD said to Moses, "Tell the people of Israel to turn back and encamp in front of Pihahiroth, by the sea. For Pharaoh will say, 'The people of Israel are entangled in the land; the wilderness has shut them in.' Then he will pursue them, and I will get glory over Pharaoh; the Egyptians shall know that I am the LORD." And the people did so.

Now when Pharaoh and his servants were told that the people of Israel had fled, their minds were changed toward them. "What is this we have done," they said, "to let Israel go from serving us?" So Pharaoh made ready his chariot and took his army with him, and six hundred picked chariots and all his horses and horsemen. He pursued the people of Israel, and overtook them encamped at the sea, by Pihahiroth. When the people of Israel saw that the Egyptians were marching after them, in great fear they cried out to the LORD; and they said to Moses, "Is it because there are no graves in Egypt that you have brought us out to die? What have you done to us? It would have been better for us to serve the Egyptians than to die in the wilderness."

"Fear not," said Moses, "stand firm, and see the salvation that the LORD will work for you today; for the Egyptians whom you see today, you shall never see again. The LORD will fight for you, and you have only to be still." Then the LORD said to Moses, "Tell the people of Israel to go forward. Lift up your rod over the sea and divide it, that the people may go through on dry ground. And I will harden the hearts of the Egyptians so that they shall go in after them. The Egyptians shall know that I am the LORD, when I have gotten glory over Pharaoh, his chariots, and his horsemen."

Then the angel of God who went before the host of Israel moved behind them; and the pillar of cloud moved from before them and stood behind them, coming between them and the host of Egypt. And there was darkness; and the night passed without one coming near the other. Moses stretched out his hand over the sea, and the LORD drove the sea back by a strong east wind all night, and made the sea dry land; the waters were divided. The people of Israel went into the midst of the sea on dry ground, the waters being a wall to them on their right hand and their left. The Egyptians pursued, and went in after them into the midst of the sea, all Pharaoh's horses, chariots, and horsemen. And at the morning watch the LORD in the pillar of fire and of cloud looked down upon the host of the Egyptians, and discomfited them, clogging their chariot wheels so that they drove heavily; and the Egyptians said, "Let us flee; for the LORD fights for Israel against us."

Then the LORD said to Moses, "Stretch out your hand over the sea, that the water may come back upon the Egyptians." Moses stretched forth his hand, and the sea returned to its wonted flow when the morning appeared; and the LORD routed the Egyptians. The waters covered their chariots and horsemen and all the host of Pharaoh; not so much as one of them remained. But the people of Israel walked on dry ground through the sea.

Thus the LORD saved Israel that day from the hand of the Egyptians; Israel saw them dead upon the seashore. And the people saw the great work which the LORD did, and they feared the LORD, and believed in him and in his servant Moses.

THEN MOSES AND the people of Israel sang this song:

I will sing to the LORD, for he has triumphed gloriously;
    the horse and his rider he has thrown into the sea.
The LORD is my strength and my song, and he has become
    my salvation; this is my God, and I will praise and exalt him.
The LORD is a man of war;
    the LORD is his name.

Pharaoh's chariots, his host, and his picked officers
    are sunk in the Red Sea.
The floods cover them; they went down into the depths like a stone.
Thy right hand, O LORD, glorious in power, shatters the enemy.
In thy majesty thou overthrowest thy adversaries;
    thou sendest forth thy fury; it consumes them like stubble.
At the blast of thy nostrils the waters piled up;
    the floods stood up in a heap;
    the deeps congealed in the heart of the sea.
The enemy said, "I will pursue, overtake, divide the spoil;
    my desire shall have its fill of them.
I will draw my sword, my hand shall destroy them."

Thou didst blow with thy wind, the sea covered them;
   they sank as lead in the mighty waters.
Who is like thee, O LORD, among the gods?
Majestic in holiness, terrible in glorious deeds, doing wonders?
Thou didst stretch out thy right hand, the earth swallowed them.
Thou hast led in thy steadfast love the people whom thou hast redeemed.
Thou wilt bring thy people in, and plant them on thy own mountain,
   the place, O LORD, which thou hast made for thy abode,
   the sanctuary which thy hands have established.
The LORD will reign for ever and ever.

Then Aaron's sister Miriam, the prophetess, took a timbrel in her hand; all the women went out after her with timbrels and dancing. And Miriam sang:

Sing to the LORD, for he has triumphed gloriously;
   the horse and his rider he has thrown into the sea.

THEN MOSES LED Israel onward from the Red Sea, three days into the wilderness of Shur, and they found no water. They came to Marah, but could not drink the water there because it was bitter, and the people murmured against Moses. "What shall we drink?" they said. Moses cried to the LORD; and the LORD showed him a tree; he threw it into the water, and the water became sweet. There the LORD made for them an ordinance to prove them, saying, "If you will hearken to the LORD your God, doing what is right in his eyes and keeping his statutes, I will put none of the diseases upon you which I put upon the Egyptians; for I am the LORD, your healer." Then they came to Elim, where there were springs and palm trees, and encamped by the water.

After Elim, on the fifteenth day of the second month after they had departed from Egypt, they came to the wilderness of Sin. And the whole congregation of Israel murmured against Moses and Aaron, saying, "Would that we had died by the hand of the LORD in Egypt, when we sat by the fleshpots and ate bread to the full. You have brought us out into this wilderness to kill us with hunger." Then the LORD said to Moses, "Behold, I will rain bread from heaven. The people shall gather a day's portion every day, that I may prove them, whether they will walk in my law or not. On the sixth day what they bring in will be twice as much as they gather daily."

And Moses said to Aaron, "Say to the people of Israel, 'Come near before the LORD, for he has heard your murmurings.'" The whole congregation looked, and the glory of the LORD appeared in the cloud. The LORD said to Moses, "I have heard the murmurings of the people; say to them, 'At twilight you shall eat flesh, and in the morning you shall be filled with bread; then you shall know that I am the LORD your God.'" So Moses and Aaron said to the people, "At evening you shall know that it was the LORD who brought you out of the land of Egypt, and in the morning you shall see his glory, because he has heard your murmurings against him. For what are we, that you murmur against us? Your murmurings are not against us but against the LORD."

In the evening, quails came up and covered the camp; in the morning, dew lay round about the camp. When the dew had gone, a flake-like thing, fine as hoarfrost, was left on the ground. "What is it?" the people asked. Moses said, "It is the bread which the LORD has given you to eat. The LORD has commanded: 'Gather of it, every man, as much as he can eat; a measure apiece according to the number of persons each has in his tent.'" And the people of Israel did so; some gathered more, some less. But when they measured it, he that gathered much had nothing over, and he that gathered little had no lack. And Moses said to them, "Let no man leave any till the morning." But they did not listen; some left part till the morning, and it bred worms and became foul; and Moses was angry with them.

Morning by morning they gathered the bread, but when the sun grew hot, it melted. On the sixth day they gathered twice as much. And Moses said to them, "The LORD has commanded: 'Tomorrow is a day of rest, a holy sabbath to the LORD; bake and boil what you will, and keep all the bread that is left over till the morning.'" So they laid it by till morning, and it did not become foul. Moses said, "Eat it today, for today is the seventh day, a sabbath to the LORD; today you will not find it in the field." Still some people went out to gather, and found none. The LORD said to Moses, "How long do you refuse to keep my laws? The LORD has given you the sabbath, therefore on the sixth day he gives you bread for two days. Let no man go out of his place on the seventh day." So the people rested on the seventh day.

Now the house of Israel called the bread manna; it was like coriander seed, white, and tasting like wafers made with honey. And Moses said, "The LORD has commanded: 'Let a measure of it be kept throughout your generations, that they may see the bread I fed you when I brought you out of Egypt.'" (And the people of Israel ate the manna forty years, till they came to a habitable land, to the border of the land of Canaan.)

The congregation of Israel then moved on from the wilderness of Sin by stages, according to the LORD's commandment. They camped at Rephidim, but there was no water to drink, and the people found fault with Moses. "Why do you find fault with me?" he said. "Why do you put the LORD to the proof?" But the people murmured against Moses. "Why did you bring us up out of Egypt," they said, "to kill us and our children and our cattle with thirst?" So Moses cried to the LORD, "What shall I do? These people are almost ready to stone me." The LORD replied, "Pass on before the people, taking with you some of the elders, and take your rod with which you struck the Nile. Go. I will stand before you there on the rock. Strike the rock, and water shall come out of it, that the people may drink." And Moses did so, in the sight of the elders of Israel. And he called the name of the place Massah (that is, Proof), and Meribah (that is, Contention), because the children of Israel put the LORD to the proof by saying, "Is the LORD among us or not?"

Then came Amalek and fought with Israel at Rephidim. To Joshua, Moses said, "Choose men and go out and fight with Amalek; tomorrow I will stand on the top of the hill with the rod of God in my hand." So Joshua fought with Amalek; and Moses, Aaron, and Hur went up the hill. Whenever Moses held up his hand, Israel prevailed; whenever he lowered his hand, Amalek prevailed. But Moses' arms grew weary, so they took a stone and put it under him, and he sat upon it, and Aaron and Hur held up his hands, one on each side, until the going down of the sun. And Joshua mowed down Amalek and his people with the sword. And the LORD said to Moses, "Write this as a memorial in a book and recite it in the ears of Joshua, that I will utterly blot out the remembrance of Amalek from under heaven." Then Moses built an altar and called the name of it, The LORD is my banner, saying, "A hand upon the banner of the LORD! The LORD will have war with Amalek from generation to generation."

JETHRO, THE PRIEST of Midian, Moses' father-in-law, heard of all that God had done, how the LORD had brought Israel out of Egypt. Now Zipporah, Moses' wife, and Gershom and Eliezer, her two sons, were with Jethro, and he came with them to where Moses was encamped in the wilderness. Moses went out to meet him, and did obeisance and kissed him; and they asked each other of their welfare, and went into the tent. Then Moses told his father-in-law all that the LORD had done to Pharaoh, all the hardship that had come upon them in the way, and how the LORD had delivered them. And Jethro said, "Blessed be the LORD, who has delivered you out of the hand of the Egyptians. Now I know that the LORD is greater than all gods." And Jethro offered a burnt offering and sacrifices to God; and Aaron came with all the elders of Israel to eat bread with Jethro before God.

On the morrow Moses sat to judge the people, from morning till evening. "What is this you are doing, and why do you sit alone, and all the people stand about you from morning till evening?" Jethro asked. "The people come to me to inquire of God, when they have a dispute. I make them know the statutes of God and his decisions," Moses replied. "The thing is too heavy for you," Jethro said. "I will give you counsel. You shall represent the people before God, and teach them the statutes and decisions. But choose able men from all the people, such as fear God, men who are trustworthy and hate a bribe; and place such men over the people as rulers of thousands, of hundreds, of fifties, and of tens. Every great matter they shall bring to you, but any small matter they shall decide themselves; they will bear the burden with you. Then all this people will go to their place in peace."

So Moses gave heed to the voice of his father-in-law and did all that he had said, choosing able men out of all Israel. Then Moses let Jethro depart, and he went his way to his own country.

On the day of the third new moon after the people of Israel had gone forth from Egypt, they came to the wilderness of Sinai, and encamped before the mountain. Moses went up, and the LORD called to him out of the mountain, saying, "These words you shall speak to the people of Israel: 'You have seen what I did to the Egyptians, how I bore you on eagles' wings and brought you to myself. Now, if you will obey my voice and keep my covenant, you shall be my own possession among all peoples; for all the earth is mine, and you shall be to me a kingdom of priests and a holy nation.'"

So Moses called the elders, and set before them the LORD's words. And the people answered, "All that the LORD has spoken we will do." Moses reported their words to the LORD, and the LORD said, "Lo, I am coming to you in a thick cloud, that the people may hear when I speak with you, and may believe you for ever. Go to the people, consecrate them, let them wash their garments and be ready; for on the third day the LORD will come down upon Mount Sinai in sight of the people. Set bounds for them, saying, 'Take heed that you do not go up into the mountain; whoever touches the mountain shall be put to death.' When the trumpet sounds a long blast, they shall come up to the mountain." So Moses went down from the mountain, and consecrated the people. On the morning of the third day there were thunders, lightnings, a thick cloud upon the mountain, and a very loud trumpet blast, so that all in the camp trembled. Moses brought the people out of the camp to meet God, and they took their stand at the foot of the mountain. Mount Sinai was wrapped in smoke, because the LORD descended upon it in fire; and the whole mountain quaked greatly. As the sound of the trumpet grew louder, Moses spoke, and God answered him in thunder. The LORD called Moses to the top of the mountain, and Moses went up.

And God spoke these words:

"I am the LORD your God, who brought you out of the land of Egypt, out of the house of bondage.

"You shall have no other gods before me.

"You shall not make for yourself a graven image, or any likeness of anything that is in heaven above, or that is in the earth beneath, or that is in the water under the earth; you shall not bow down to them or serve them; for I the LORD your God am a jealous God, visiting the iniquity of the fathers upon the children to the third and the fourth generation of those who hate me, but showing steadfast love to thousands of those who love me and keep my commandments.

"You shall not take the name of the LORD your God in vain; for the LORD will not hold him guiltless who takes his name in vain.

"Remember the sabbath day, to keep it holy. Six days you shall labor, and do all your work; but the seventh day is a sabbath to the LORD your God; in it you shall not do any work, you, or your son, or your daughter, your manservant, or your maidservant, or your cattle, or the sojourner who is within your gates; for in six days the LORD made heaven and earth, the sea, and all that is in them, and rested the seventh day; therefore the LORD blessed the sabbath day and hallowed it.

"Honor your father and your mother, that your days may be long in the land which the LORD your God gives you.

"You shall not kill.

"You shall not commit adultery.

"You shall not steal.

"You shall not bear false witness against your neighbor.

"You shall not covet your neighbor's house; you shall not covet your neighbor's wife, or his manservant, or his maidservant, or his ox, or his ass, or anything that is your neighbor's."

Now when the people perceived the thunderings, the lightnings, the sound of the trumpet, and the mountain smoking, they trembled with fear and stood afar off. "You speak to us, and we will hear," they said to Moses, "but let not God speak to us, lest we die." And Moses replied, "Do not fear; for God has come to prove you, that the fear of him may be before your eyes, that you may not sin."

WHILE THE PEOPLE stood afar off, Moses drew near to the thick darkness where God was, and the LORD said, "Thus you shall say to the people of Israel: 'You have seen for yourselves that I have talked with you from heaven. You shall not make for yourselves gods of silver or gold. Make for me an altar of earth and sacrifice on it your burnt offerings and peace offerings; in every place where I cause my name to be remembered I will come to you and bless you.'"

And the LORD said, "Now these are ordinances which you shall set before them: When you buy a Hebrew slave, he shall serve six years, and in the seventh he shall go out free. If he comes in single, he shall go out single; if he comes in married, then his wife shall go out with him.

"Whoever wilfully attacks a man so that he dies shall be put to death. Whoever strikes his father or his mother shall be put to death. Whoever curses his father or his mother shall be put to death. When a man strikes his slave, male or female, with a rod and the slave dies under his hand, he shall be punished. When a man strikes the eye of his slave and destroys it, he shall let the slave go free for the eye's sake. If he knocks out the tooth of his slave, he shall let the slave go free for the tooth's sake. When an ox gores a man or a woman to death, the ox shall be stoned; but the owner of the ox shall be clear. But if the ox has gored in the past, and its owner has not kept it in, and it kills a man or a woman, the ox shall be stoned, and its owner put to death.

"When one man's ox hurts another's, so that it dies, then they shall sell the live ox and divide the price of it; and the dead beast also they shall divide. If a man steals an ox or sheep, and kills or sells it, he shall pay five oxen for an ox, and four sheep for a sheep. He shall make restitution; if he has nothing, then he shall be sold for his theft. When a man lets his beast loose and it feeds in another man's field or vineyard, he shall make restitution from the best in his own field and vineyard. When fire breaks out and catches in thorns so that stacked or standing grain in the field is consumed, he that kindled the fire shall make full restitution. If a man borrows anything of his neighbor, and it is hurt or dies, he shall make full restitution. If you meet your enemy's ox or his ass going astray, you shall bring it back to him.

"You shall not permit a sorceress to live. Whoever lies with a beast shall be put to death. You shall not wrong a stranger or oppress him; you know the heart of a stranger, for you were strangers in Egypt. You shall not afflict any widow or orphan. If you do, I will surely hear their cry, and my wrath will burn; I will kill you, and your wives shall become widows and your children fatherless. If you lend money to any of my people who is poor, you shall not exact interest. If you take your neighbor's garment in pledge, you shall restore it to him before the sun goes down, for that is his only covering; in what else shall he sleep? And if he cries to me, I will hear, for I am compassionate. You shall not revile God, nor curse a ruler of your people. You shall not utter a false report. You shall not follow a multitude to do evil; nor shall you bear witness in a suit, turning aside after a multitude, so as to pervert justice; nor shall you be partial to a poor man in his suit. You shall take no bribe, for a bribe blinds officials, and subverts the cause of those in the right.

"For six years you shall sow your land and gather in its yield; but the seventh year you shall let it lie fallow, that the poor may eat; and what they leave the wild beasts may eat. You shall do likewise with your vineyard and olive orchard. Three times in the year you shall keep a feast to me. You shall keep the feast of unleavened bread, as I commanded you when you came out of Egypt. You shall keep the feast of harvest, of the first fruits of what you sow. You shall keep the feast of ingathering at the end of the year, when you gather in from the field the fruit of your labor. Three times in the year shall all your males appear before the Lord GOD.

"Behold, I send an angel before you, to guard you and bring you to the place I have prepared. Give heed to him, and do not rebel against him, for my name is in him. But if you hearken to his voice and do all that I say, then I will be an enemy to your enemies. I will bless your bread and your water; I will take sickness away from the midst of you. I will send my terror before you, and throw into confusion all the people against whom you shall come. And I will send hornets before you, which shall drive out the Canaanites. Little by little I will drive them out, until you possess the land from the Red Sea to the sea of the Philistines, and from the wilderness to the Euphrates. I will deliver the inhabitants of the land into your hand, and you shall drive them out before you. You shall make no covenant with them or with their gods, but you shall break the pillars of their gods in pieces. They shall not dwell in your land, lest they make you sin against me; for if you serve their gods, it will surely be a snare to you."

And God said to Moses, "Come up to the LORD with Aaron and his sons, Nadab and Abihu, and seventy elders of Israel, and worship. Moses alone shall come near to the LORD; but the others shall worship afar off, and the people shall not come up with him."

WHEN MOSES TOLD THE PEOPLE all the words of the LORD and all the ordinances, with one voice they said, "All the words which the LORD has spoken we will do." Then Moses wrote all the words of the LORD, and he built an altar at the foot of the mountain, and twelve pillars, according to the twelve tribes of Israel. He sent young men of Israel, who offered burnt offerings and sacrificed peace offerings of oxen to the LORD. Moses put half of the blood in basins, and half of the blood he threw against the altar. Then he took the book of the covenant, and read it in the hearing of the people; they said, "All that the LORD has spoken we will do, and we will be obedient."

Taking the blood, Moses threw it upon the people. "Behold the blood of the covenant," he said, "which the LORD has made with you in accordance with these words."

Then Moses and Aaron, Nadab and Abihu, and seventy of the elders of Israel went up, and saw the God of Israel. Under his feet was a pavement like sapphire stone, like the very heaven for clearness. He did not lay his hand on the chief men of the people of Israel; they beheld God, and ate and drank.

The LORD said to Moses, "Come up to me on the mountain, and wait there; I will give you tables of stone, with the law and the commandment, which I have written for their instruction." So Moses rose with his young servant Joshua to go up into the mountain of God. He said to the elders, "Tarry here, until we come to you again. Aaron and Hur are with you; let whoever has a cause go to them."

Then Moses went up on the mountain, and the cloud covered it. The glory of the LORD settled on Mount Sinai; the cloud covered it six days, and on the seventh day the LORD called to Moses out of the midst of the cloud. Now the glory of the LORD was like a devouring fire on the top of the mountain in the sight of the people of Israel. And Moses entered the cloud, up on the mountain. And Moses was on the mountain forty days and forty nights.

The LORD said to Moses, "Speak to the people of Israel, that they take for me an offering, from every man whose heart makes him willing. And this is the offering you shall receive from them: gold, silver, and bronze, blue and purple and scarlet stuff and fine twined linen, goats' hair, tanned rams' skins, goatskins, acacia wood, oil for lamps, spices for anointing oil and for fragrant incense, and onyx stones for setting. Let them make me a sanctuary, that I may dwell in their midst. According to all that I show you concerning the pattern of the tabernacle, and of all its furniture, so you shall make it.

"Make an ark of acacia wood, forty-five inches long, twenty-seven inches wide, and twenty-seven inches high. Overlay it with pure gold, within and without. Cast four rings of gold for it and put two on one side and two on the other. Make poles of acacia wood, and overlay them with gold, and put them into the rings, to carry the ark. Make a mercy seat of pure gold, with two cherubim of gold on the two ends, their faces one to another, and put the mercy seat on the top of the ark. And in the ark you shall put the tables of the law that I shall give you. There I will meet with you, and from above the mercy seat I will speak with you. Make the tabernacle (the tent of meeting to enclose the ark) with ten curtains of fine twined linen and blue and purple and scarlet stuff, with cherubim skilfully worked. Make curtains of goats' hair for a tent over the tabernacle, and a covering for the tent of tanned rams' skins and goatskins. Make upright frames for the tabernacle of acacia wood. Make a veil of blue and purple and scarlet stuff and fine twined linen, embroidered with cherubim; and hang it in the tabernacle upon four pillars of acacia wood overlaid with gold. Bring the ark within the veil; and the veil shall separate for you the holy place from the most holy.

"Make a table of acacia wood, and overlay it with pure gold; and you shall set the bread of the Presence on the table before me always. Make a lamp-stand of pure gold, with six branches, three on each side; and make seven lamps for it. Make an altar of acacia wood for burnt offerings, and overlay it with bronze. Make an altar to burn incense upon, of acacia wood overlaid with pure gold. And you shall also make a laver of bronze, with its base of bronze, for washing hands and feet.

"Make the court of the tabernacle, enclosed with hangings of fine twined linen. The length of the court shall be a hundred and fifty feet, the breadth seventy-five, and the height of the hangings seven and a half feet. Command the people that they bring pure beaten olive oil, that a lamp may be set up to burn continually. Aaron and his sons shall tend it from evening to morning before the LORD. It shall be a statute for ever to be observed by the people of Israel. And you shall make holy garments for Aaron your brother, for glory and for beauty. And you shall speak to all who have ability, whom I have endowed with an able mind, that they make Aaron's garments, to consecrate him for my priesthood, and also for his sons. Make a breastpiece of judgment, in skilled work, of gold, blue and purple and scarlet stuff and fine twined linen. Set in it twelve stones, for the twelve tribes of Israel, set in gold filigree. And you shall make a robe all of blue; on its skirts pomegranates, with bells of gold between them, a golden bell and a pomegranate, a golden bell and a pomegranate, round about on the skirts of the robe. And it shall be upon Aaron when he ministers, and its sound shall be heard when Aaron goes into the holy place before the LORD, and when he comes out.

"I will consecrate the tent of meeting and the altar. There I will meet with the people of Israel, and it shall be sanctified by my glory; Aaron also and his sons I will consecrate, to serve me as priests. I will dwell among the people of Israel, and they shall know that I am the LORD their God, who brought them forth out of the land of Egypt, that I might dwell among them; I am the LORD their God."

And the LORD said to Moses, "See, I have called by name Bezalel, of the tribe of Judah: and I have filled him with the Spirit of God, and with ability, intelligence, knowledge, and craftsmanship, to devise artistic designs, to work in gold, silver, and bronze, in cutting stones for setting, and in carving wood. I have appointed with him Oholiab, of the tribe of Dan; and I have given to all able men ability to make all that I command you. This they shall do."

When the LORD finished speaking with Moses upon Mount Sinai, he gave him the two tables of the law, tables of stone, written with the finger of God.

WHEN THE PEOPLE saw that Moses delayed to come down from the mountain, they gathered together and said to Aaron, "Make gods to go before us. As for this Moses, who brought us out of Egypt, we do not know what has become of him." And Aaron said, "Take off the golden earrings of your wives, sons, and daughters, and bring them to me." So all the people brought their golden earrings to Aaron. He received the gold, fashioned it with a graving tool, and made a molten calf; and the people worshiped it. Seeing this, Aaron built an altar before the golden calf, and made proclamation: "Tomorrow shall be a feast to the LORD." The people rose early on the morrow, offered burnt offerings and brought peace offerings; and they sat down to eat and drink, and rose up to play.

The LORD said to Moses, "Go down; for your people have corrupted themselves, turning quickly from the way which I commanded them. They have made for themselves a molten calf, have worshiped it and sacrificed to it. Behold, this is a stiff-necked people; now therefore let me alone, that my wrath may burn hot against them and that I may consume them; but of you I will make a great nation."

But Moses besought the LORD, saying, "O LORD, why does thy wrath burn hot against thy people, whom thou hast brought out of Egypt with a mighty hand? Why should the Egyptians say, 'With evil intent did he bring them forth, to slay them in the mountains, and to consume them from the face of the earth'? Turn from thy fierce wrath. Remember Abraham, Isaac, and Jacob, thy servants, to whom thou didst say, 'I will multiply your descendants as the stars of heaven, and all this land I will give to your descendants for ever.'" And the LORD repented of the evil which he thought to do to his people.

Then Moses went down from the mountain with the two tables of the law in his hands, tables that were the work of God; on both sides were they written, and the writing graven upon the tables was the writing of God. Joshua, hearing the people as they shouted, said to Moses, "There is a noise of war in the camp." But Moses said, "It is not shouting for victory, or the cry of defeat, but the sound of singing that I hear." As he came near the camp and saw the calf and the dancing, Moses' anger grew hot. He threw down the two tables and broke them at the foot of the mountain. He took the calf they had made, burnt it, ground it to powder, scattered it upon the water, and made the people of Israel drink it.

"What did this people do to you," Moses asked Aaron, "that you have brought a great sin upon them?" Aaron said, "Let not the anger of my lord burn hot; you know the people are set on evil. 'Make gods to go before us,' they said to me, 'for we do not know what has become of Moses.' I said, 'Let any who have gold take it off.' So they gave it to me, I threw it into the fire, and out came this calf."

And when Moses saw that the people were out of control (for Aaron had let them get out of control, to their shame among their enemies), Moses stood in the gate of the camp, saying, "Who is on the LORD's side? Come to me." All the sons of Levi gathered to him, and he said, "Thus says the LORD God of Israel, 'Let every man put on his sword, and go from gate to gate throughout the camp, and slay his brother, his companion, and his neighbor.'" The sons of Levi did according to the word of Moses, and three thousand of the people fell that day. "Today you have ordained yourselves for the service of the LORD," Moses said, "each one at the cost of son and brother, that the LORD may bestow a blessing upon you."

On the morrow Moses said to the people, "You have sinned a great sin. I will go up to the LORD; perhaps I can make atonement for your sin." So Moses returned to the LORD and said, "Alas, this people have made for themselves gods of gold. But now, if thou wilt, forgive their sin—and if not, blot me, I pray, out of thy book of life." The LORD said, "Whoever has sinned against me, him will I blot out of my book. But go now, lead the people to the place of which I have spoken. Nevertheless, I will visit their sin upon them." And the LORD sent a plague upon the people, because of the calf Aaron made.

NOW MOSES USED to take a tent and pitch it far off from the camp. When he entered the tent, the pillar of cloud would descend and stand at the door, and the LORD would speak with him. And when the people saw the cloud at the door, they would all rise up and worship, every man at his tent door. Thus the LORD used to speak to Moses face to face, as a man speaks to his friend.

Then Moses said to the LORD, "Thou sayest to me, 'Bring up this people.' But thou hast not let me know whom thou wilt send with me. I pray thee, show me now thy ways, that I may know thee. Consider too that this nation is thy people. If thy presence will not go with me, do not carry us up from here. For is it not in thy going with us that we are distinct, I and thy people, from all other people upon the face of the earth?" And the LORD said, "My presence will go with you, and I will give you rest. This I will do; for you have found favor in my sight, and I know you by name."

Moses said, "I pray thee, show me thy glory." And the LORD said, "I will make all my goodness pass before you, and will proclaim before you my name 'The LORD'; and I will be gracious to whom I will be gracious, show mercy on whom I will show mercy. But you cannot see my face; for man shall not see me and live. There is a place where you shall stand upon the rock. While my glory passes by I will put you in a cleft of the rock, and cover you with my hand until I have passed by. Then I will take away my hand, and you shall see my back; but my face shall not be seen."

The LORD said to Moses, "Cut two tables of stone like the first; I will write upon them the words that were on the first tables, which you broke. Be ready in the morning, and come up to Mount Sinai. Present yourself to me on the top of the mountain. No man shall come with you, and let no man be seen throughout the mountain; let no flocks or herds feed before that mountain." So Moses cut two tables of stone, and early in the morning he took them up on Mount Sinai. The LORD descended in the cloud and stood with him; then the LORD passed before him, and proclaimed his name: "The LORD, a God merciful and gracious, slow to anger, and abounding in faithfulness, keeping steadfast love for thousands, forgiving iniquity and transgression and sin, but who will by no means clear the guilty, visiting the iniquity of the fathers upon the children and the children's children, to the third and the fourth generation." Moses bowed his head toward the earth, and worshiped, saying, "If now I have found favor in thy sight, O Lord, I pray thee, go in the midst of us, although it is a stiff-necked people; pardon our iniquity and sin, and take us for thy inheritance."

The LORD said, "Behold, I make a covenant. Before all your people I will do marvels, such as have not been wrought in all the earth; and all the people among whom you are shall see the work of the LORD; for it is a terrible thing that I will do with you."

When Moses came down from Mount Sinai, with the two tables of the law in his hand, he did not know that the skin of his face shone because he had been talking with God. When Aaron and all the people of Israel saw this, they were afraid to come near him. But Moses called to them; and he talked with Aaron and the leaders of the congregation. Then all the people came near, and Moses gave them in commandment all that the LORD had spoken. When he finished, he put a veil on his face. Whenever Moses went in before the LORD, he took the veil off; when he came out and told the people what he was commanded, they saw that the skin of Moses' face shone; and Moses would put the veil on again, until he went in to speak with the LORD.

AFTER MOSES TOLD the congregation what the LORD had said concerning the sanctuary, all the men and women whose heart moved them to bring anything for the work brought it as their freewill offering to the LORD. Moses called Bezalel and Oholiab and every able man in whose mind the LORD had put ability, and they came to do the work. When the work was finished, the people of Israel brought to Moses the tabernacle, the tent, the veil, the ark of the tables of the law and the mercy seat, the table and the bread of the Presence, the lampstand, the golden altar, the oil and incense, the bronze altar and the laver, the hangings of the court, all the utensils for the service of the tabernacle, and the finely worked holy garments for Aaron and his sons to serve as priests. Moses saw all the work, and behold, the people of Israel had done it as the LORD had commanded. And Moses blessed them.

The LORD said to Moses, "On the first day of the first month you shall erect the tabernacle of the tent of meeting, and set its arrangements in order. Set up the court round about. Then take the anointing oil, anoint the tabernacle and all that is in it, and consecrate it and all its furniture; it shall become holy. Consecrate the altar; it shall be most holy. Then bring Aaron and his sons to the door of the tent of meeting, and wash them with water. Put upon Aaron the holy garments, anoint him, and consecrate him, that he may serve me. Put coats on his sons and anoint them: and their anointing shall admit them to a perpetual priesthood throughout their generations."

On the first day of the first month in the second year, the tabernacle was erected. Moses laid its bases, set up its frames, and raised up its pillars. He put the tables of the law into the ark, and set the mercy seat on the ark; he brought the ark into the tabernacle, and set up the veil. He put the table in the tent of meeting, and set the bread in order on it before the LORD. He set up the lampstand and put the golden altar before the veil, and burnt fragrant incense upon it. He set the altar of burnt offering at the door of the tabernacle, and offered upon it the burnt offering. He set the laver between the tent of meeting and the altar, and put water in it for washing; when Moses and Aaron and his sons went into the tent of meeting and approached the altar, they washed their hands and feet, as the LORD had commanded. And Moses erected the court round the tabernacle and altar. So he finished the work.

Then the cloud covered the tent of meeting; and Moses was not able to enter, because the cloud abode upon it, and the glory of the LORD filled the tabernacle. Throughout their journeys, whenever the cloud was taken up from over the tabernacle, the people of Israel would go onward; but they did not go onward till the day that it was taken up. For throughout all their journeys the cloud of the LORD was upon the tabernacle by day, and fire was in it by night, in the sight of all the house of Israel.

LEVITICUS

The word Leviticus means "pertaining to the Levites," and the book contains the system of laws, administered by the Levitical priesthood, under which the Israelites lived. Included are regulations concerning kinds of sacrifices, the consecration of priests to their office, the distinction between clean and unclean, the ceremony for the annual Day of Atonement, and various precepts concerning Israel's life as a holy people *("You shall be holy; for I the Lord your God am holy")*.

The language and theology of Leviticus are reflected in the words and ideas of certain New Testament writers, notably in the Letter to the Hebrews. There the priesthood of Jesus Christ is contrasted with the Levitical priesthood. It is also significant that of all the many precepts contained in this book, Jesus singles out the command *"You shall love your neighbor as yourself"* as second only to the primary command of love toward God. The oldest part is probably the Code of Holiness (pages 61–65), which was combined with other traditional material in the sixth century B.C.

THE LORD CALLED Moses, and spoke to him from the tent of meeting, saying, "Speak to the people of Israel, and say, When any man of you brings an offering to the LORD, bring cattle from the herd or from the flock. If it is a burnt offering from the herd, offer a male without blemish; offer it at the door of the tent of meeting, to be accepted before the LORD; lay your hand upon its head, and it shall be accepted to make atonement for you. Then kill the bull before the LORD; Aaron's sons the priests shall present the blood, and throw it round about against the altar at the door of the tent of meeting. Flay the burnt offering and cut it into pieces; the sons of Aaron shall put fire on the altar, lay wood upon the fire, and lay the pieces, the head, and the fat, in order upon the wood. The entrails and legs shall be washed with water, and the priest shall burn the whole on the altar, as a burnt offering, an offering by fire, a pleasing odor to the LORD.

"If the burnt offering is from the flock, sheep or goats, offer a male without blemish; kill it on the north side of the altar before the LORD, and the priests shall throw its blood against the altar round about. Cut it into pieces, and the priest shall lay them upon the wood that is on the fire. The entrails and legs shall be washed with water, and the priest shall offer the whole, and burn it on the altar; it is a burnt offering, a pleasing odor to the LORD.

"If your offering is a burnt offering of birds, then bring a turtledove or young pigeon. The priest shall bring the offering to the altar and wring off its head. Its blood shall be drained out on the side of the altar, and its crop, with the feathers, cast beside the altar in the place for ashes. Tear it by its wings, but do not divide it asunder. The priest shall burn it on the altar, an offering by fire, a pleasing odor to the LORD.

"When any one brings a cereal offering to the LORD, it shall be of fine flour; pour oil upon it, and put frankincense on it, and bring it to Aaron's sons the priests. Take from it a handful which the priest shall burn as its memorial portion upon the altar, an offering by fire, a pleasing odor to the LORD. What is left of the cereal offering shall be for Aaron and his sons, a most holy part of the offerings by fire to the LORD. No cereal offering shall be made with leaven; you shall burn no leaven or honey as an offering by fire to the LORD. Season all your cereal offerings with salt; do not let the salt of the covenant with your God be lacking from your cereal offering; with all your offerings you shall offer salt.

"If you offer a cereal offering of first fruits to the LORD, offer crushed new grain from fresh ears, parched with fire. Put oil upon it, lay frankincense on it, and the priest shall burn its memorial portion as an offering by fire to the LORD.

"If, as a sacrifice of peace offering, you offer an animal from the herd, male or female, offer it without blemish before the LORD. Lay your hand upon its head and kill it at the door of the tent of meeting; Aaron's sons the priests shall throw the blood against the altar round about. Offer the fat that is on the entrails, the two kidneys with the fat on them, and the appendage of the liver. Aaron's sons shall burn them on the altar upon the burnt offering, which is upon the wood on the fire; it is an offering by fire, a pleasing odor to the LORD.

"If your sacrifice of peace offering is an animal from the flock, male or female, offer it without blemish. If it is a lamb, offer it before the LORD, laying your hand upon its head and killing it before the tent of meeting; Aaron's sons shall throw its blood against the altar, and the priest shall burn its fat as food offered by fire to the LORD. All fat is the LORD's. It shall be a perpetual statute throughout your generations, that you eat neither fat nor blood."

The LORD said to Moses, "If any one of the common people sins unwittingly in doing any of the things which the LORD has commanded not to be done, he shall offer a female goat without blemish for the sin which he has committed. He shall lay his hand on the head of the sin offering, and kill it.

The priest shall burn it upon the altar, and make atonement for him, and he shall be forgiven.

"If any one commits a breach of faith against the LORD by deceiving his neighbor in a matter of deposit, or through robbery, or if he has oppressed his neighbor, or has found what was lost and lied about it, swearing falsely—in any of these sins of which men become guilty, he shall restore what he took by robbery, or got by oppression, or the deposit committed to him, or the lost thing he found, or anything about which he has sworn falsely; he shall restore it in full, add a fifth to it, and give it to him to whom it belongs, on the day of his guilt offering. He shall bring to the priest his guilt offering to the LORD, a ram without blemish out of the flock; the priest shall make atonement for him before the LORD, and he shall be forgiven."

The LORD said to Moses, "Command Aaron and his sons, saying, This is the law of the burnt offering: it shall be on the hearth upon the altar all night, and the fire of the altar shall be kept burning. In the morning the priest shall put on his linen garments, take up the ashes of the burnt offering, and put them beside the altar. Then he shall put off his garments, and put on other garments, and carry the ashes outside the camp to a clean place. The fire on the altar shall be kept burning continually; it shall not go out."

THE LORD SAID to Moses, "Take Aaron and his sons; take the garments, the anointing oil, the bull of the sin offering, two rams, and the basket of unleavened bread; and assemble the congregation at the door of the tent of meeting."

Moses did as the LORD commanded him, and said to the assembled congregation, "This the LORD has commanded be done." Then he washed Aaron and his sons with water. He put on Aaron the coat, the girdle, and the robe; he put the priestly apron upon him, girding him with its skilfully woven band. He placed the breastpiece on him, and he set the turban upon his head. On the turban he set the golden plate, the holy crown, as the LORD commanded. Then Moses took the anointing oil, and sprinkled it on the tabernacle and on all that was in it, and on the altar and all its utensils, to consecrate them. He poured some of the oil on Aaron's head, consecrating him, and he clothed Aaron's sons with coats, girded them, and bound caps on them, as the LORD commanded.

Then Moses brought the bull of the sin offering, and Aaron and his sons laid their hands upon its head. Moses killed it, and with his finger put some of the blood on the horns of the altar round about to purify it. He poured out the rest of the blood at the base of the altar to consecrate and make atonement for it. Then he took the fat on the entrails, the appendage of the liver, the two kidneys with their fat, and burned them on the altar. But the bull, its skin, its flesh, and its dung, Moses burned outside the camp, as the LORD commanded. Then Moses presented the ram of the burnt offering; Aaron and his sons laid their hands on its head, and Moses killed it, and threw the blood upon the altar. The ram was cut into pieces, and Moses burned it on the altar, a pleasing odor, an offering by fire to the LORD, as the LORD commanded.

Then Moses presented the other ram, the ram of ordination; Aaron and his sons laid their hands on its head. Moses killed it, and put some of its blood on the tip of Aaron's right ear, the thumb of his right hand, and the great toe of his right foot. He put blood on the tips of the right ears of Aaron's sons, on the thumbs of their right hands, and on the great toes of their right feet; then Moses threw the blood upon the altar. He took the fat tail, the fat on the entrails, the appendage of the liver, the two kidneys with their fat, and the right thigh; out of the basket of unleavened bread he took one unleavened cake, one cake of bread with oil, and one wafer, and placed them on the fat and on the right thigh; he put all these in the hands of Aaron and his sons, and waved them before the altar as a wave offering to the LORD. Then Moses took them from their hands, and burned them on the altar as an ordination offering to the LORD. Moses took the breast, and waved it before the altar; it was Moses' portion of the ram of ordination, as the LORD commanded.

Moses took anointing oil and some of the blood which was on the altar, and sprinkled it upon Aaron and his sons, consecrating them. "Boil the flesh of the ram at the door of the tent of meeting," Moses said to them, "and eat it there with the bread that is in the basket of ordination offerings. What remains you shall burn. Do not go out of the tent of meeting for seven days, for it will take seven days to ordain you. The LORD has commanded what has been done today, to make atonement for you. Remain at the door of the tent of meeting day and night for seven days, performing what the LORD has charged, lest you die; for so I am commanded." And Aaron and his sons did all the things the LORD commanded by Moses.

On the eighth day Moses called Aaron and his sons and the elders of Israel. "Take a bull calf for a sin offering," he said to Aaron, "and a ram for a burnt offering, both without blemish; offer them before the LORD. Say to the people of Israel, Take a male goat for a sin offering, a calf and a lamb, both without blemish, for a burnt offering, and an ox and a ram for peace offerings, to sacrifice before the LORD, and a cereal offering mixed with oil; for today the LORD will appear to you." They brought what Moses commanded before the tent of meeting, and the congregation drew near and stood before the LORD. "Draw near to the altar," Moses said to Aaron, "and offer your sin offering and burnt offering to make atonement for yourself; then bring the people's offering and make atonement for them, as the LORD has commanded."

So Aaron drew near to the altar. He presented his offering and the people's offering according to the ordinances. Then he lifted up his hands toward the people and blessed them; he came down from the altar and, with Moses, went into the tent of meeting. When they came out they blessed the people, and the glory of the LORD appeared to all. Fire came forth from before the LORD and consumed the offerings upon the altar; and the people, seeing it, shouted and fell on their faces.

Now Nadab and Abihu, sons of Aaron, each took a censer, put fire in it, laid incense on it, and offered unholy fire before the Lord, such as he had not commanded them. Fire came forth from the presence of the Lord, devouring them, and they died. "This," Moses said to Aaron, "is what the Lord has said: 'I will show myself holy among those who are near me, and before all the people I will be glorified.'" Aaron held his peace.

Then Moses called Mishael and Elzaphan, sons of Uzziel, Aaron's uncle. "Draw near," he said to them. "Carry your brethren from before the sanctuary out of the camp." So they carried them out in their coats, as Moses had said. Then Moses said to Aaron and his sons, Eleazar and Ithamar, "Do not let your hair hang loose, and do not rend your clothes in mourning, lest you die, and wrath come upon the congregation; but your brethren, the house of Israel, may bewail the burning which the Lord has kindled. And do not go out of the tent of meeting, lest you die; for the anointing oil of the Lord is upon you." They did according to the word of Moses.

The Lord said to Aaron, "Drink no wine nor strong drink, you nor your sons, when you go into the tent of meeting, lest you die; it shall be a statute throughout your generations. You are to distinguish between the holy and the common, between the unclean and the clean; and you are to teach the people of Israel the statutes which the Lord has spoken to them by Moses."

The Lord said to Moses and Aaron, "Say to the people of Israel, These are the living things which you may eat among all the beasts on earth. Whatever parts the hoof and is cloven-footed and chews the cud, you may eat. Nevertheless, among animals that chew the cud or part the hoof, you shall not eat these: the camel, the rock badger, and the hare. Because they chew the cud but do not part the hoof, they are unclean to you. The swine, because it parts the hoof and is cloven-footed but does not chew the cud, is unclean to you.

"These you may eat, of all that are in the waters: everything that has fins and scales, whether in the seas or in the rivers. But anything that has not fins and scales is an abomination to you. Of their flesh you shall not eat, and their carcasses you shall have in abomination.

"And these you shall have in abomination among the birds, they shall not be eaten: the eagle, the vulture, the osprey, the kite, the falcon, every raven according to its kind, the ostrich, the nighthawk, the sea gull, the hawk, the owl, the cormorant, the ibis, the water hen, the pelican, the carrion vulture, the stork, the heron, the hoopoe, and the bat.

"All winged insects that go upon all fours are an abomination to you. Yet among them you may eat those which have legs above their feet, with which to leap on the earth. Of them you may eat: the locust, the bald locust, the cricket, and the grasshopper according to its kind. But all other winged insects which have four feet are an abomination to you.

"And by these you shall become unclean; whoever touches their carcass shall be unclean until evening; whoever carries any part of their carcass shall wash his clothes and be unclean until evening. Every animal which parts the hoof but is not cloven-footed or does not chew the cud is unclean to you; every one who touches them shall be unclean. All that go on their paws, among animals that go on all fours, are unclean to you; whoever touches their carcass shall be unclean, and he who carries their carcass shall wash his clothes and be unclean until evening.

"These are unclean to you among the swarming things upon the earth: the weasel, the mouse, the great lizard, the gecko, the land crocodile, the lizard, the sand lizard, and the chameleon. Whoever touches them when they are dead shall be unclean until evening. Anything upon which any of them falls when they are dead shall be unclean, whether it is an article of wood, a garment, a skin or a sack, any vessel used for any purpose; it must be put into water, and it shall be unclean until evening; then it shall be clean. And if any part of their carcass falls into any earthen vessel, all that is in the vessel shall be unclean, and you shall break it. Any food in it, upon which water may come, shall be unclean; and all drink which may be drunk from every such vessel shall be unclean. Nevertheless, a spring or a cistern holding water shall be clean. And if any part of their carcass falls upon any seed that is to be sown, it is clean; but if water is put on the seed and any part of their carcass falls on it, it is unclean to you.

"If any animal of which you may eat dies, he who touches its carcass shall be unclean until evening; he who eats of its carcass shall wash his clothes and be unclean until evening; he also who carries the carcass shall wash his clothes and be unclean until evening.

"Whatever goes on its belly, whatever goes on all fours, whatever has many feet, all the swarming things that swarm upon the earth, you shall not eat; for they are an abomination. You shall not defile yourselves with them, lest you become unclean. For I am the LORD your God; consecrate yourselves therefore, and be holy, for I am holy. I brought you up out of Egypt, to be your God; you shall be holy, for I the LORD your God am holy."

This is the law pertaining to beast and bird and every living creature that moves through the waters and swarms upon the earth, to make a distinction between the unclean and the clean, between the living creature that may be eaten and the living creature that may not be eaten.

THE LORD SAID to Moses, "Say to the people of Israel, If a woman conceives, and bears a male child, then she shall be unclean seven days, as at the time of her menstruation. On the eighth day the flesh of the child's foreskin shall be circumcised. Then she shall continue for thirty-three days in the blood of her purifying; she shall not touch any hallowed thing, nor come into the sanctuary, until the days of her purifying are completed. But if she bears a female child, she shall be unclean two weeks, as in her menstruation, and she shall continue in the blood of her purifying for sixty-six days.

"When the days of her purifying are completed, whether for a son or a daughter, she shall bring to the priest at the door of the tent of meeting a year-old lamb for a burnt offering, and a young pigeon or turtledove for a sin offering; the priest shall offer it before the LORD, and make atonement for her; then she shall be clean from the flow of her blood. This is the law for her who bears a child, male or female. If she cannot afford a lamb, she shall take two turtledoves or two young pigeons, one for a burnt offering and the other for a sin offering; the priest shall make atonement for her, and she shall be clean."

THE LORD SAID to Moses, "This shall be the law of the leper for his day of cleansing. He shall be brought to the priest, and the priest shall go out of the camp and make an examination. If the leprous disease is healed, the priest shall command that two living clean birds, some cedarwood, scarlet thread, and hyssop be taken for him who is to be cleansed. One of the birds shall be killed in an earthen vessel over running water, and the priest shall dip the living bird, with the cedarwood, the scarlet thread, and the hyssop, in the blood of the bird that was killed; the priest shall sprinkle the blood seven times upon him who is to be cleansed of leprosy, then pronounce him clean, and let the living bird go into the open field. He who is to be cleansed shall wash his clothes, shave off all his hair, bathe himself in water, and he shall be clean; after that he shall come into the camp, but shall dwell outside his tent seven days. On the seventh day he shall shave off all his hair, his beard, and his eyebrows. Then he shall wash his clothes and bathe his body, and he shall be clean.

"On the eighth day the man who is to be cleansed shall take two male lambs and a year-old ewe lamb without blemish, a cereal offering, and a measure of oil. The priest shall offer these things to the LORD, to make atonement for him, and he shall be clean.

"But if he is poor and cannot afford so much, then he shall take one male lamb, a cereal offering, a measure of oil, and two turtledoves or two young pigeons, such as he can afford. On the eighth day he shall bring them to the priest, and the priest shall offer these and make atonement before the LORD for him who is being cleansed. This is the law for him in whom is a leprous disease, who cannot afford the offerings for his cleansing."

The LORD said to Moses and Aaron, "When you come into the land of Canaan, which I give you for a possession, and I put a leprous disease in a house there, the priest shall command that the house be emptied, lest all that is in it be declared unclean; then he shall examine the house. If the disease is in the walls with greenish or reddish spots, and if it appears to be deeper than the surface, the priest shall shut up the house seven days. On the seventh day he shall come again and look; if the disease has spread in the walls, the priest shall command that the diseased stones be taken and thrown into an unclean place outside the city; the inside of the house shall be scraped, and the plaster poured into an unclean place outside the city; then other stones shall be put in the place of those stones, and other plaster used to plaster the house.

"If the disease breaks out again, and spreads, it is a malignant leprosy in the house; it is unclean. He who owns the house shall break it down, and carry its stones, timber, and plaster out of the city to an unclean place. But if the priest makes an examination, and the disease has not spread after the house was plastered, then the priest shall make atonement for the house, and it shall be clean."

This is the law for any leprous disease: to show when it is unclean and when it is clean.

THE LORD SPOKE to Moses, after the death of Aaron's two sons, when they drew near before the LORD and died. The LORD said, "Tell Aaron your brother not to come at all times into the holy place within the veil, before the mercy seat which is upon the ark, lest he die; for I will appear in the cloud upon the mercy seat. But thus shall Aaron come into the holy place: with a young bull for a sin offering and a ram for a burnt offering. He shall bathe his body, put on the holy linen coat and breeches, be girded with the linen girdle, and wear the linen turban; these are the holy garments. He shall take from the congregation of the people of Israel two male goats for a sin offering, and one ram for a burnt offering.

"Aaron shall offer the bull as a sin offering, and make atonement for himself and for his house. Then he shall take the two goats, and set them before the LORD at the door of the tent of meeting; he shall cast lots upon the two goats, one lot for the LORD and the other for Azazel. Aaron shall offer the goat on which the lot fell for the LORD as a sin offering for the people. He shall kill it and sprinkle its blood upon and before the mercy seat; thus he shall make atonement for the holy place, because of the uncleannesses of the people of Israel, and because of all their sins; and so he shall do for the tent of meeting, which abides with them in the midst of their uncleannesses. There shall be no man in the tent of meeting when he enters the holy place, or until he comes out, after having made atonement for himself, for his house, and for all of Israel. Then he shall go out to the altar before the LORD and make atonement for it, sprinkling some blood of the bull and of the goat upon it with his finger seven times, to cleanse and hallow it from the uncleannesses of the people of Israel.

"When Aaron has made an end of atoning for the holy place and the tent of meeting and the altar, he shall present before the LORD the goat on which the lot fell for Azazel. He shall lay both his hands upon the head of the live goat, and confess over it all the iniquities of the people of Israel, all their transgressions, all their sins; he shall put these upon the head of the goat, and send it into the wilderness by the hand of a man who is in readiness. The goat shall bear the people's iniquities to a solitary land, and there it shall be let go. Then Aaron shall come into the tent of meeting, put off the linen garments, and leave them there; he shall bathe, put on his garments, come forth, offer his burnt offering and the burnt offering of the people, and make atonement for himself and for the people.

"And it shall be a statute for ever that on the tenth day of the seventh month, you shall fast, and do no work, either the native or the stranger who sojourns among you; for on this day shall atonement be made for you; from all your sins you shall be clean before the LORD. It is a sabbath of solemn rest to you. The priest, wearing the holy linen garments, shall make atonement for the sanctuary, for the tent of meeting, for the altar, for the priests, and for all the people of the assembly. This shall be an everlasting statute for you, that atonement may be made for the people of Israel once in the year because of all their sins." And Moses did as the LORD commanded him.

THE LORD SAID to Moses, "Say to the people of Israel, You shall be holy; for I the LORD your God am holy. Every one of you shall revere his mother and his father, and you shall keep my sabbaths. Do not turn to idols or make for yourselves molten gods: I am the LORD your God.

"You shall not steal, nor lie to one another. And you shall not swear by my name falsely, and so profane the name of your God. You shall not oppress your neighbor or rob him. The wages of a hired servant shall not remain with you all night until the morning. You shall not curse the deaf or put a stumbling block before the blind, but you shall fear your God: I am the LORD.

"You shall do no injustice in judgment; you shall not be partial to the poor or defer to the great, but in righteousness shall you judge your neighbor. You shall not hate your brother in your heart. You shall not take vengeance or bear any grudge against the sons of your own people, but you shall love your neighbor as yourself. And when a stranger sojourns with you in your land, you shall not do him wrong. He shall be to you as the native among you, and you shall love him as yourself; for you were strangers in the land of Egypt: I am the LORD your God.

"You shall do no wrong in judgment, in measures of length or weight or quantity. You shall have just balances, just weights. I am the LORD your God, who brought you out of the land of Egypt. You shall observe all my statutes and all my ordinances, and do them: I am the LORD."

THE LORD SAID to Moses, "Say to the people of Israel, My appointed feasts which you shall proclaim as holy convocations are these. Six days shall work be done; but on the seventh day, a sabbath of solemn rest, you shall do no work; it is a sabbath to the LORD in all your dwellings.

"These are the holy convocations, which you shall proclaim at the appointed time. On the fourteenth day of the first month, in the evening, is the LORD's passover. On the fifteenth day of the same month begins the feast of unleavened bread to the LORD; seven days you shall eat unleavened bread. On the first day you shall have a holy convocation; you shall do no laborious work. But you shall present an offering by fire to the LORD seven days; on the seventh day also there shall be a holy convocation; you shall do no laborious work."

The LORD said to Moses, "Say to the people of Israel, When you come into the land which I give you and reap its harvest, bring the sheaf of the first fruits of your harvest to the priest; on the morrow after the sabbath he shall wave it before the LORD, that you may find acceptance. On that day you shall offer a male lamb a year old without blemish as a burnt offering to the LORD. A cereal offering of fine flour mixed with oil shall be offered with it by fire to the LORD, a pleasing odor; the drink offering with it shall be of wine. You shall eat neither bread nor grain, parched or fresh, until you have brought the offering of your God: it is a statute for ever in all your dwellings.

"Count from the day you brought the sheaf of the wave offering seven full weeks, counting fifty days to the morrow after the seventh sabbath; then present a cereal offering of new grain to the LORD. Bring from your dwellings two loaves of bread to be waved, made of fine flour and baked with leaven, as first fruits to the LORD. Present also seven lambs, one young bull, and two rams as a burnt offering, a pleasing odor to the LORD. Offer one male goat for a sin offering, and two male lambs a year old as a sacrifice of peace offerings. The priest shall wave them before the LORD with the bread of the first fruits; they shall be holy to the LORD for the priest. You shall make proclamation on the same day, and hold a holy convocation, and do no laborious work: it is a statute for ever throughout your generations.

"When you reap the harvest, you shall not reap your field to its very border, nor shall you gather the gleanings after your harvest; leave them for the poor and for the stranger: I am the LORD your God."

The LORD said to Moses, "Say to the people of Israel, On the first day of the seventh month, observe a day of solemn rest, a memorial proclaimed with blast of trumpets, a holy convocation. You shall do no laborious work, and you shall present an offering by fire to the LORD.

"On the tenth day of this seventh month is the day of atonement, a time of holy convocation; you shall fast, present an offering by fire to the LORD, and do no work on this day; for it is a day of atonement, to make atonement for you before the LORD your God. Whoever does not fast on this day shall be cut off from his people; whoever does any work, that person I will destroy from among his people. It shall be to you a sabbath of solemn rest; on the ninth day of the month, beginning at evening, from evening to evening shall you keep your sabbath.

"On the fifteenth day of this seventh month, when you have gathered in the produce of the land, you shall keep the feast of booths to the LORD for seven days; on the first and eighth days shall be a solemn rest. Take on the first day the fruit of goodly trees, branches of palm trees, boughs of leafy trees, and willows of the brook; rejoice before the LORD your God seven days. It is a statute for ever; keep it as a feast to the LORD seven days in the seventh month. All Israel shall dwell in booths for seven days, that your generations may know that I made the people of Israel dwell in booths when I brought them out of Egypt: I am the LORD your God."

Thus Moses declared to the people of Israel the appointed feasts of the LORD.

NOW AN ISRAELITE woman's son, whose father was an Egyptian, quarreled in the camp with a man of Israel, and her son blasphemed the Name, and cursed. The people brought him to Moses, and put him in custody, till the will of the LORD should be declared to them.

The LORD said to Moses, "Bring out of the camp him who cursed; let all who heard him lay their hands upon his head, and let the congregation stone him. Say to the people of Israel, Whoever curses his God shall bear his sin. The sojourner as well as the native, when he blasphemes the name of the LORD, shall be put to death; all the congregation shall stone him.

"And he who kills a man shall be put to death. He who kills a beast shall make it good, life for life. When a man causes a disfigurement in his neighbor, as he has done it shall be done to him, fracture for fracture, eye for eye, tooth for tooth. You shall have one law for the sojourner and for the native; for I am the LORD your God." So Moses spoke to the people of Israel; and they brought him who had cursed out of the camp, and stoned him. Thus the people did as the LORD commanded Moses.

THE LORD SAID to Moses on Mount Sinai, "Say to the people of Israel, When you come into the land which I give you, the land shall keep a sabbath to the LORD. Six years you shall sow, prune, and gather, but the seventh year you shall not; it shall be a year of solemn rest for the land.

"You shall count seven times seven years, forty-nine years. Then you shall send abroad the loud trumpet on the day of atonement. And you shall hallow the fiftieth year, and proclaim liberty throughout the land; it shall be a jubilee for you, when each of you shall return to his property and to his family. For the land shall not be sold in perpetuity; the land is mine, and you are strangers and sojourners with me. In all the country you possess, you shall grant a redemption of the land.

"If your brother becomes poor, sells part of his property, and has not sufficient means to get it back, then what he sold shall remain in the hand of him who bought it until the year of jubilee; then it shall be released, and he shall return to his property. If your brother becomes poor, and cannot maintain himself, you shall maintain him; as a stranger and a sojourner he shall live with you. Take no interest from him or increase, but fear your God; that your brother may live beside you.

"And if your brother becomes poor beside you, and sells himself to you, you shall not make him serve as a slave: he shall be as a hired servant and a sojourner. He shall serve with you until the year of the jubilee; then he shall go out from you, he and his children with him, and go back to his own family, returning to the possession of his fathers. For to me the people of Israel are servants, my servants whom I brought forth out of the land of Egypt: I am the LORD your God.

"YOU SHALL MAKE for yourselves no idols, erect no graven image or pillar to bow down to; for I am the LORD your God. You shall keep my sabbaths and reverence my sanctuary: I am the LORD.

"If you walk in my statutes and observe my commandments, I will give you rains in their season, and the land shall yield its increase, the trees shall yield their fruit. Your threshing shall last to the time of vintage, and the vintage shall last to the time for sowing; you shall eat bread to the full, and dwell in your land securely. I will give peace, and none shall make you afraid; I will remove evil beasts, and the sword shall not go through your land. You shall chase your enemies, and they shall fall before you. I will make you fruitful, and will confirm my covenant with you. I will make my abode among you; my soul shall not abhor you. I will be your God, and you shall be my people. I am the LORD your God, who brought you out of Egypt, that you should not be slaves; I have broken the bars of your yoke and made you walk erect.

"But if you will not do all these commandments, if you spurn my statutes, if your soul abhors my ordinances, so that you break my covenant, I will appoint over you sudden terror, consumption, and fever that waste the eyes and cause life to pine away. You shall sow your seed in vain, for your enemies shall eat it; I will set my face against you, and you shall be smitten before your enemies; those who hate you shall rule you, and you shall flee when none pursues. If in spite of this you will not hearken to me, then I will chastise you again sevenfold; I will break the pride of your power, and make your heavens like iron and your earth like brass; your strength shall be spent in vain, for your land shall not yield its increase, and the trees shall not yield their fruit.

"Then if you will not hearken to me, I will bring more plagues upon you, sevenfold as many as your sins. I will let loose the wild beasts among you, to rob you of your children, destroy your cattle, and make you few in number. And if by this discipline you are not turned to me, but walk contrary to me, then I also will walk contrary to you; I myself will smite you. I will bring a sword upon you, that shall execute vengeance for the covenant; if you gather within your cities, I will send pestilence among you. When I break your staff of bread, ten women shall bake your bread in one oven, and you shall eat, but not be satisfied.

"If in spite of this you will not hearken to me, but walk contrary to me, then I, in fury, will chastise you myself sevenfold for your sins. You shall eat the flesh of your sons and daughters. I will destroy your high places, cut down your incense altars, and cast your dead bodies upon the dead bodies of your idols; my soul will abhor you. I will make your sanctuaries desolate, and I will not smell your pleasing odors. I will devastate the land, so that your enemies who settle in it shall be astonished at it. And I will scatter you among the nations; your land shall be a desolation, and your cities shall be a waste.

"Then, while you are in your enemies' land, the land shall enjoy its sabbaths. It shall have rest, the rest it had not when you dwelt upon it. As for those of you that are left, I will send faintness into your hearts in the lands of your enemies; at the sound of a driven leaf you shall flee as one flees from the sword, stumbling over one another and falling though none pursues. You shall have no power to stand before your enemies. You shall perish among nations, and the land of your enemies shall eat you up. Those of you that are left shall pine away in your enemies' lands because of your iniquity and the iniquities of your fathers.

"But if you confess your iniquity and the treachery of your fathers, committed against me; if your uncircumcised heart is humbled and you make amends; then I will remember my covenant with Jacob, with Isaac, and with Abraham, and I will remember the land. I will not spurn you, neither will I abhor you so as to destroy you utterly and break my covenant; for I am the LORD your God; I will remember the covenant with your forefathers, whom I brought forth out of the land of Egypt in the sight of the nations, that I might be your God: I am the LORD."

These are the statutes and ordinances and laws which the LORD commanded Moses for the people of Israel on Mount Sinai.

NUMBERS

Prior to their arrival at the border of the Promised Land, the Israelites wandered in the wilderness for nearly forty years, mostly in the vicinity of an oasis near Kadesh. The Book of Numbers relates the varied experiences of these years, including the often discontented murmuring of the people. The unknown compiler of these traditions emphasizes that God, though he disciplined the Israelites for their faithlessness, was at the same time marvelously guiding and sustaining them throughout their long and difficult journey. In addition, within the narrative there are miscellaneous laws and ceremonial ordinances, which supplement the Sinaitic code and anticipate the settlement in Canaan. The New Testament has several references to the events in this book, including the bronze serpent, the revolt of Korah and its consequences, the prophecies of Balaam, and the water that Moses brought gushing from the rock. The book derives its name from the account, at the beginning, of the census or numbering of the Israelite people.

———

THE LORD SPOKE to Moses in the wilderness of Sinai, in the tent of meeting, on the first day of the second month, in the second year after they had come out of Egypt, saying, "Take a census of the people of Israel, by families, by fathers' houses, every male, from twenty years old and upward; all in Israel who are able to go forth to war, you and Aaron shall number them, company by company. There shall be with you a man from each tribe, each being the head of the house of his fathers. And these are the men who shall attend you: from the tribe of Reuben, Elizur; from the tribe of Simeon, Shelumiel; from Judah, Nahshon; from Issachar, Nethanel; from Zebulun, Eliab; from the sons of Joseph, from Ephraim, Elishama, and from Manasseh, Gamaliel; from Benjamin, Abidan; from Dan, Ahiezer; from Asher, Pagiel; from Gad, Eliasaph; and from Naphtali, Ahira." These were the chosen leaders of their ancestral tribes, the heads of the clans of Israel.

So Moses and Aaron assembled the congregation, and with the help of the leaders of Israel, they numbered them. And their whole number was six hundred and three thousand five hundred and fifty. But the Levites were not numbered by their ancestral tribe. For the LORD said to Moses, "You shall not take a census of the tribe of Levi among the people of Israel; but appoint the Levites over the tabernacle of the testimony; they are to carry and tend the tabernacle and all its furnishings, and they shall encamp around it. When the tabernacle is to set out, the Levites shall take it down; and when the tabernacle is to be pitched, they shall set it up. If any one else comes near, he shall be put to death. The people of Israel shall pitch their tents by their companies, every man by his own camp and his own standard; but the Levites shall encamp around the tabernacle of the testimony, and keep charge of it, that there may be no wrath upon the congregation." And the people of Israel did all that the LORD commanded Moses.

The LORD said to Moses and Aaron, "The people of Israel shall encamp, each with the ensign of his fathers' house, facing the tent of meeting on every side. Those to encamp on the east side toward the sunrise shall be of the standard of the camp of Judah by their companies, the leader of the people of Judah being Nahshon, and his host as numbered being seventy-four thousand six hundred. Next to him shall encamp the tribe of Issachar, their leader being Nethanel, and their number being fifty-four thousand four hundred. Then the tribe of Zebulun, led by Eliab, and numbering fifty-seven thousand four hundred. The whole camp of Judah, by their companies, is a hundred and eighty-six thousand four hundred. They shall set out first on the march.

"On the south side shall be the camp of Reuben by their companies, the leader of the people of Reuben being Elizur, his host being forty-six thousand five hundred. Next to him shall encamp the tribe of Simeon, led by Shelumiel, his host numbering fifty-nine thousand three hundred. Then the tribe of Gad, led by Eliasaph, and numbering forty-five thousand six hundred and fifty. The whole camp of Reuben is a hundred and fifty-one thousand four hundred and fifty. They shall set out second.

"Then the tent of meeting shall set out, with the camp of the Levites in the midst of the other camps; as they encamp, so shall they set out, each in position.

"On the west side shall be the standard of the camp of Ephraim, the leader of the people of Ephraim being Elishama, his host being forty thousand five hundred. Next to him shall be the tribe of Manasseh, their leader being Gamaliel, and their number being thirty-two thousand two hundred. Then the tribe of Benjamin, led by Abidan, and numbering thirty-five thousand four hundred. The whole camp of Ephraim, numbering a hundred and eight thousand one hundred, shall set out third on the march.

"On the north side shall be the camp of Dan, the leader of the people of Dan being Ahiezer, his host being sixty-two thousand seven hundred. Next to him shall encamp the tribe of Asher, led by Pagiel, and numbering forty-one thousand five hundred. Then the tribe of Naphtali, their leader being Ahira, and their number being fifty-three thousand four hundred. The whole camp of Dan, numbering a hundred and fifty-seven thousand six hundred, shall set out last, standard by standard."

Thus the people of Israel, according to all that the LORD commanded Moses, encamped by their standards, and so they set out, every one according to his fathers' house.

THE LORD SAID to Moses, "Command the people of Israel to put out of the camp every leper, every one having a discharge, and every one unclean through contact with the dead; put out both male and female, that they may not defile their camp, in the midst of which I dwell." And the people drove them outside the camp, as the LORD said.

The LORD said to Moses, "Say to the people of Israel, When a man or woman sins, breaking faith with the LORD, that person shall confess the sin committed, and make full restitution, adding a fifth to it, and giving it to him to whom he did the wrong. But if there is no kinsman to whom restitution may be made, the restitution shall go to the LORD for the priest, in addition to the ram of atonement. Every offering, all the holy things that the people of Israel bring to the priest, shall be his."

The LORD said to Moses, "Say to the people of Israel, If any man's wife goes astray and acts unfaithfully, if a man lies with her carnally, hidden from the eyes of her husband, and there is no witness against her, since she was not taken in the act; and if the spirit of jealousy comes upon the husband whose wife has defiled herself; or if he is jealous of his wife, though she has not defiled herself; then the man shall bring his wife to the priest, with a cereal offering of jealousy. The priest shall set her before the LORD; then he shall take holy water in an earthen vessel, and put some of the dust from the floor of the tabernacle into the water. He shall unbind the woman's hair, and place in her hands the cereal offering of jealousy. In his hand the priest shall have the water of bitterness that brings the curse. Then the priest shall make her take the oath of the curse, saying to her, 'If no man has lain with you, be free from this water of bitterness that brings the curse. But if you have gone astray, though you are under your husband's authority, and if some man other than your husband has lain with you, then the LORD make you an execration among your people; may this water that brings the curse pass into your bowels and make your body swell and your thigh fall away.' And the woman shall say, 'Amen, Amen.'

"Then the priest shall write these curses in a book, and wash them off into the water of bitterness. He shall take the cereal offering of jealousy out of the woman's hand, wave it before the LORD, and burn a handful of it upon the altar as its memorial portion. Afterward he shall make the woman drink the water of bitterness that brings the curse; if she has acted unfaithfully against her husband, the water shall enter into her and cause bitter pain; her body shall swell, her thigh shall fall away, and she shall become an execration among her people. But if the woman has not defiled herself, then she shall be free and shall conceive children."

The LORD said to Moses, "Say to the people of Israel, When a man or woman makes the vow of a Nazirite, to separate himself to the LORD, he shall separate himself from wine and strong drink; he shall drink no vinegar made from wine, shall drink no juice of grapes, and shall eat no grapes, fresh or dried. All the days of his separation he shall eat nothing produced by the grapevine. All the days of his vow no razor shall come upon his head; until the time of his separation to the LORD is completed, he shall be holy, letting his hair grow long. While he separates himself he shall not go near a dead body. Neither for his father nor mother, nor for brother or sister, if they die, shall he make himself unclean; because his separation to God is upon his head. He is holy to the LORD. If any man dies suddenly beside him, defiling his consecrated head, then he shall shave his head on the day of his cleansing; on the seventh day he shall shave it. On the eighth day he shall bring two turtle-doves or two young pigeons to the tent of meeting, and the priest shall offer one for a sin offering and the other for a burnt offering, and make atonement for him. He shall consecrate his head that same day, and separate himself to the LORD for the days of his separation; but the former time shall be void, because his separation was defiled.

"This is the law for the Nazirite, when his time of separation has been completed: he shall be brought to the door of the tent of meeting, and he shall offer his gift to the LORD, one male lamb for a burnt offering, one ewe lamb as a sin offering, one ram as a peace offering, and a basket of unleavened bread, cakes, and wafers. The priest shall present the offerings before the LORD and shall offer also cereal and drink offerings. The Nazirite shall shave his conse-crated head at the door of the tent of meeting, and put the hair on the fire under the sacrifice of the peace offering. The priest shall put the shoulder of the ram, when it is boiled, one unleavened cake, and one unleavened wafer upon the hands of the Nazirite after he has shaven. Then the priest shall wave them for a wave offering before the LORD; they are a holy portion for the priest; and after that the Nazirite may drink wine. This is the law for the Nazirite in accordance with his vow."

The LORD said to Moses, "Say to Aaron and his sons, Thus you shall bless the people of Israel: you shall say to them, The LORD bless you and keep you; the LORD make his face to shine upon you, and be gracious to you; the LORD lift up his countenance upon you, and give you peace. So shall they put my name upon the people of Israel, and I will bless them."

ON THE DAY Moses finished setting up the tabernacle, after he had anointed and consecrated it with all its furnishings, the leaders of Israel, heads of their fathers' houses, brought their offerings before the LORD: six covered wagons and twelve oxen. They offered them before the tabernacle, and the LORD said to Moses, "Accept these to be used in doing the service of the tent of meeting, and give them to the Levites." So Moses took the wagons and the oxen, and gave them to the Levites.

Then the leaders offered offerings for the dedication of the altar. The LORD said to Moses, "They shall offer their offerings, one leader each day, for twelve days." At the end of the twelve days, this was the dedication offering for the altar from the leaders of Israel: twelve silver plates, twelve silver basins, twelve golden dishes, each silver plate weighing a hundred and thirty shekels and each basin seventy, the twelve golden dishes, full of incense, weighing ten shekels apiece according to the shekel of the sanctuary; all the cattle for the burnt offering: twelve bulls, twelve rams, twelve male lambs a year old, with their cereal offering; twelve male goats for a sin offering; and all the cattle for the sacrifice of peace offerings: twenty-four bulls, sixty rams, sixty male goats, and sixty male lambs a year old. And when Moses went into the tent of meeting to speak with the LORD, he heard the voice speaking to him from above the mercy seat upon the ark of the testimony.

Now the LORD said to Moses, "Take the Levites from among the people of Israel, and cleanse them. Sprinkle the water of expiation upon them, and let them shave all their body, wash their clothes, and cleanse themselves. Then let them take a young bull and its cereal offering, and you shall take another young bull for a sin offering. Present the Levites before the tent of meeting, and assemble the congregation. The people of Israel shall lay their hands upon the Levites, and Aaron shall offer the Levites before the LORD as a wave offering from the people of Israel, to do the service of the LORD. Then the Levites shall lay their hands upon the heads of the bulls; and you shall offer one for a sin offering and the other for a burnt offering, to make atonement for the Levites. And the Levites shall attend Aaron and his sons.

"Thus you shall separate the Levites to do service at the tent of meeting. They are wholly given to me from among the people of Israel, instead of all that open the womb. For the first-born of Israel, both man and beast, are mine; on the day I slew all the first-born in Egypt I consecrated them for myself, and I have taken the Levites instead of all the first-born of Israel. I have given the Levites to Aaron and his sons, to do service at the tent of meeting, and to make atonement, that there may be no plague among the people of Israel in case the people should come near the sanctuary."

Thus Moses, Aaron, and the congregation did all that the LORD commanded Moses concerning the Levites. And the Levites went in to do their service in the tent of meeting. The LORD said to Moses, "From twenty-five years old and upward the Levites shall perform work in the tent of meeting; and from the age of fifty years they shall withdraw and serve no more, but minister to their brethren in the tent of meeting, to keep the charge."

THE LORD SPOKE to Moses in the wilderness of Sinai, in the first month of the second year after they had come out of Egypt, saying, "Let the people of Israel keep the passover at its appointed time, on the fourteenth day of this month, in the evening, according to all its ordinances." So Moses told the people of Israel, and they kept the passover in the wilderness of Sinai, according to all that the LORD commanded. But certain men were unclean through touching a dead body, so they could not keep the passover. They came before Moses and Aaron on that day, and said, "We are unclean through touching the dead body of a man; why are we kept from offering the LORD's offering at its appointed time?" Moses answered, "Wait, that I may hear what the LORD will command concerning you."

The LORD said to Moses, "Say to the people, If any of you is unclean through touching a dead body, or is afar off on a journey, he shall still keep the passover to the LORD, not in the first month, but in the second month on the fourteenth day in the evening. But the man who is clean and is not on a journey, yet refrains from keeping the passover at its appointed time, shall be cut off from his people; he shall bear his sin. And if a stranger sojourns among you, and will keep the passover to the LORD, according to its ordinance, so shall he do; have one statute for both sojourner and native."

On the day the tabernacle was set up, the cloud covered the tent of the testimony; at evening it was over the tabernacle like the appearance of fire until morning. So it was continually; the cloud by day, and the appearance of fire by night. Whenever the cloud was taken up, the people of Israel set out; and in the place where the cloud settled down, the people of Israel encamped. Even if the cloud continued over the tabernacle many days, they remained in camp; and when the cloud was taken up, they set out.

The LORD said to Moses, "Make two silver trumpets of hammered work; use them for summoning the congregation, and for breaking camp. The sons of Aaron, the priests, shall blow the trumpets. When both trumpets are blown, the congregation shall assemble at the tent of meeting. But if only one is blown, the leaders, the heads of the tribes of Israel, shall gather. An alarm is to be sounded whenever the tribes are to set out. When the first alarm is blown, the camps on the east side shall set out, and when the second is blown, the camps on the south side shall set out. The trumpets shall be a perpetual statute throughout your generations. When you go to war, sound an alarm, that you may be remembered before the LORD your God, and be saved from your enemies. On the day of your gladness also, at your appointed feasts, and at the beginnings of your months, blow the trumpets over your burnt offerings and peace offerings; they shall serve you for remembrance before your God: I am the LORD your God."

IN THE SECOND year, on the twentieth day of the second month, the cloud was taken up from over the tabernacle, and the people of Israel set out by stages from the wilderness of Sinai. The ark of the covenant of the LORD went before them, to seek out a resting place. The cloud of the LORD was over them by day, whenever they set out from the camp. And whenever the ark set out, Moses said, "Arise, O LORD, and let thy enemies be scattered; let them that hate thee flee before thee." And when it rested, he said, "Return, O LORD, to the ten thousand thousands of Israel."

Now the people complained about their misfortunes; and when the LORD heard, his anger was kindled, and the fire of the LORD burned among them, and consumed outlying parts of the camp. Then the people cried to Moses, who prayed to the LORD, and the fire abated. So that place was called Taberah, that is, Burning, because the fire of the LORD burned there.

But the rabble that was among them had a strong craving; and the people of Israel also wept again, and said, "O that we had meat to eat! We remember the fish we ate in Egypt, the cucumbers, melons, leeks, onions, and garlic; but now there is nothing but this manna to look at." The manna was like coriander seed; it fell, with the dew, on the camp in the night. The people gathered it, ground it in mills or beat it in mortars, boiled it, and made cakes of it, which tasted like cakes baked with oil.

Moses heard the people weeping; the anger of the LORD blazed hotly, and Moses was displeased. He said to the LORD, "Why dost thou lay the burden of all this people upon me? Did I conceive them? Did I bring them forth, that thou shouldst tell me to carry them in my bosom, as a nurse carries the sucking child, to the land which thou didst swear to give their fathers? Where am I to get meat to give to all who weep before me? I am not able to carry all this people alone, the burden is too heavy. If thou wilt deal thus with me, kill me at once, that I may not see my wretchedness."

The LORD said to Moses, "Gather seventy of the elders of Israel; bring them to the tent of meeting, and I will come down and talk with you there. I will take some of the spirit which is upon you and put it upon them; and they shall bear the burden of the people with you. Say to the people, Consecrate yourselves for tomorrow, and you shall eat meat; for you have wept in the hearing of the LORD, saying, 'Who will give us meat to eat?' Therefore the LORD will give you meat, and you shall eat, not one or two days, or five or ten or twenty days, but a whole month, until it comes out at your nostrils and becomes loathsome to you, because you have rejected the LORD who is among you, saying, 'Why did we come forth out of Egypt?'" But Moses said, "The people number six hundred thousand on foot; and thou hast said, 'I will give them meat to eat for a whole month!' Shall flocks and herds be slaughtered to suffice them? Or shall all the fish of the sea be gathered to suffice them?" The LORD said, "Is the LORD's hand shortened? You shall see whether my word will come true or not."

So Moses told the people the words of the LORD, and he gathered seventy elders in the tent. Then the LORD came down in the cloud, and took some of the spirit that was upon Moses and put it upon the seventy; and when the spirit rested upon them, they prophesied. But they did not do so again.

Now two men, Eldad and Medad, had not gone to the tent, but had remained in the camp. And the spirit rested upon them, so they prophesied in the camp. A young man ran and told Moses, "Eldad and Medad are prophesying in the camp." And Joshua the son of Nun, the minister of Moses, one of his chosen men, said, "My lord Moses, forbid them." But Moses said, "Are you jealous for my sake? Would that all the LORD's people were prophets, that the LORD would put his spirit upon them!" And Moses and the elders of Israel returned to the camp.

Then there went forth a wind from the LORD, and it brought quails from the sea, and let them fall round about the camp. All that day, all night, and all the next day the people gathered the quails. Each gathered at least one hundred bushels, which they spread out to dry in the sun, all around the camp. While the meat was yet between their teeth, the anger of the LORD was kindled against the people, and the LORD smote them with a very great plague. That place was called Kibroth-hattaavah, that is, Graves of craving, because there they buried the people who had the craving. From Kibroth-hattaavah the people journeyed to Hazeroth, where they remained.

MIRIAM AND AARON spoke against Moses because he had married a Cushite woman. "Has the LORD indeed spoken only through Moses?" they said. "Has he not spoken through us also?" And the LORD heard, and his anger was kindled against them. Now Moses was very meek, more than all men on earth. And the LORD said to Moses, Aaron, and Miriam, "Come, you three, to the tent of meeting." They came, and the LORD came down in a pillar of cloud, stood at the door of the tent, and called Aaron and Miriam. When they came forward, he said, "Hear my words: If there is a prophet among you, I the LORD make myself known to him in a vision, I speak with him in a dream. Not so with my servant Moses. With him I speak mouth to mouth, clearly, and not in dark speech; and he beholds the form of the LORD. Why then were you not afraid to speak against Moses?" Then the LORD departed, and when the cloud removed from over the tent, behold, Miriam was leprous, as white as snow. Aaron, seeing this, said to Moses, "Oh, my lord, do not punish us because we have sinned. Let her not be as one dead, of whom the flesh is half consumed." Moses cried to the LORD, "Heal her, O God, I beseech thee." But the LORD said, "If her father had but spit in her face, should she not be shamed seven days? Let her be shut up outside the camp seven days; after that she may be brought in." So Miriam was shut up seven days; and the people did not march till she returned. Then they set out from Hazeroth, and encamped in the wilderness of Paran.

The LORD said to Moses, "Send men to spy out the land of Canaan, which I give to Israel; from each tribe of their fathers send one man, every one a leader." So Moses sent from the wilderness of Paran, according to the LORD's command, these men who were heads of the people of Israel: from the tribe of Reuben, Shammua; from the tribe of Simeon, Shaphat; from Judah, Caleb; from Issachar, Igal; from Ephraim, Joshua; from Benjamin, Palti; from Zebulun, Gaddiel; from Manasseh, Gaddi; from Dan, Ammiel; from Asher, Scthur; from Naphtali, Nahbi; and from Gad, Geuel. "Go up into the

Negeb yonder," Moses said to them. "Go up into the hill country, and see what the land is, whether it is good or bad, rich or poor, whether the people who dwell in it are strong or weak, few or many, and whether their cities are camps or strongholds. Be of good courage, and bring back some of the fruit of the land." It was the season of the first ripe grapes.

So the men of Israel spied out the land from the wilderness of Zin to Rehob; they went up into the Negeb, and came to Hebron, where they saw the descendants of Anak, men of great stature. In the Valley of Eshcol they cut down a branch with a single cluster of grapes, which they carried on a pole between two of them; they brought also some pomegranates and figs. At the end of forty days they returned, and came to Moses, Aaron, and all the congregation in the wilderness of Paran, at Kadesh. They showed them the fruit of the land, but gave an evil report. "The land to which you sent us flows with milk and honey," they told Moses, "and this is its fruit. Yet the people who dwell there are strong, and the cities are fortified and very large; and besides, we saw the descendants of Anak there." But Caleb quieted the people. "Let us go up at once, and occupy the land," he said, "for we are well able to overcome it." Then the men who had gone up with him said, "We are not able to, for the people are stronger than we. All that we saw there are men of great stature, such as the sons of Anak; we seemed to ourselves like grasshoppers, and so we seemed to them."

That night the people of Israel wept, and murmured against Moses and Aaron. "Would that we had died in Egypt or in this wilderness!" they said. "Why does the LORD bring us here to fall by the sword? Our wives and little ones will become a prey. Let us choose a captain, and go back to Egypt." Then Moses and Aaron fell on their faces before the assembly. Joshua and Caleb, who were among those who had spied out the land, rent their clothes, saying, "The land we passed through is exceedingly good. If the LORD delights in us, he will bring us into this land which flows with milk and honey. Only, do not rebel against the LORD; and do not fear the people of the land; their protection is removed, and the LORD is with us." But the congregation said to stone them. Then the glory of the LORD appeared to the people of Israel. And the LORD said to Moses, "How long will this people despise me and not believe in me, in spite of all the signs I have wrought among them in Egypt and in the wilderness? I will strike them with pestilence and disinherit them, and I will make of you a nation greater than they."

But Moses said to the LORD, "Then the Egyptians will hear of it, and they will tell the inhabitants of this land, who have heard that thou, O LORD, art in the midst of this people. If thou dost kill this people, then the nations will say, 'Because the LORD was not able to bring them into the land he swore to give to them, he has slain them in the wilderness.' Now, I pray thee, let the power of the LORD be great as thou hast promised, saying, 'The LORD is slow to anger, and abounding in steadfast love, forgiving iniquity and transgression, but he will by no means clear the guilty, visiting the iniquity of fathers upon children, to the third and fourth generation.' Pardon the iniquity of this people, I pray thee, according to the greatness of thy steadfast love, as thou hast forgiven them from Egypt until now."

Then the LORD said, "I have pardoned, according to your word; but truly, as I live, none of the men who have seen my glory and my signs, and yet have not hearkened to my voice, shall see the land I swore to give to their fathers; none of those who despised me shall see it. Now, since the Canaanites dwell in the valleys, turn tomorrow and set out for the wilderness by way of the Red Sea. Tell the people of Israel, Of all your number, numbered from twenty years old and upward, who have murmured against me, not one shall come into the land where I swore that I would make you dwell, except Caleb and Joshua, who have followed me fully. But your little ones, who you said would become a prey, I will bring in; they shall know the land which you have despised. As for you, your dead bodies shall fall in this wilderness. Your children shall be shepherds in the wilderness forty years, suffering for your faithlessness until the last of your dead bodies lies in the wilderness. You shall bear your iniquity a year for every day of the forty days you spied out the land. For forty years you shall know my displeasure.

"I, the LORD, have spoken; surely this will I do to this wicked congregation gathered together against me: in this wilderness they shall die."

And the men whom Moses sent to spy out the land, and who returned bringing an evil report, died by plague before the LORD. Only Joshua and Caleb remained alive.

Moses told the LORD's words to the people of Israel, and they mourned greatly. They rose early in the morning, and went up toward the hill country, saying, "We will go up to the place which the LORD has promised; for we have sinned." But Moses said, "Why now are you transgressing the command of the LORD, for that will not succeed? Do not go lest you be struck down before your enemies, for the LORD is not among you. The Canaanites are before you, and you shall fall by the sword, because you have turned back from following the LORD." But they presumed to go, although neither the ark of the covenant of the LORD, nor Moses, departed out of the camp. Then the Canaanites who dwelt in that hill country came down, and defeated them and pursued them, even to Hormah.

Now KORAH, a son of Levi, and Dathan, Abiram, and On, sons of Reuben, rose up before Moses, with two hundred and fifty leaders of the congregation. They assembled themselves together against Moses and Aaron, and said, "You have gone too far! For all the congregation are holy, every one of them, and the LORD is among them; why then do you exalt yourselves above the assembly of the LORD?" When Moses heard this, he said to Korah and his company, "The LORD will show who is his, and who is holy, and will cause him to come near to him. Do this: take censers, put fire in them, and put incense upon them before the LORD. The man whom the LORD chooses shall be the holy one. You have gone too far, you sons of Levi! Is it too small a thing for you that the God of Israel has separated you from the congregation, to bring you near to himself, to do service in the tabernacle of the LORD, and to minister to the congregation? Would you seek the priesthood also? It is against the LORD that you have gathered together; what is Aaron, that you murmur against him?"

Then Moses summoned Dathan and Abiram, but they said, "We will not come up. Is it a small thing that you, having brought us out of a land flowing with milk and honey, to kill us in the wilderness, must also make yourself a prince over us? Moreover you have not brought us into a land flowing with milk and honey, nor given us inheritance of fields and vineyards. We will not come up." Moses was very angry, and said to the LORD, "Do not respect their offering. I have not taken one ass from them, and I have not harmed them."

Moses then said to Korah, "Be present, you and all your company, before the LORD; and every one of you bring his censer, two hundred and fifty censers." So every man took his censer, put fire in it, and laid incense upon it, and they stood at the entrance of the tent of meeting with Moses and Aaron. Then Korah assembled all the congregation against them, and the glory of the LORD appeared. The LORD said to Moses and to Aaron, "Separate yourselves from this congregation, that I may consume them." But Moses and Aaron fell on their faces. "O God," they said, "if one man sins, wilt thou be angry with all the congregation?"

Then the LORD said to Moses, "Say to the congregation, Get away from the dwellings of Dathan and Abiram." So Moses rose and went to Dathan and Abiram. The elders of Israel followed him, and Moses said, "Depart from the tents of these wicked men; touch nothing of theirs, lest you be swept away with all their sins." Then Dathan and Abiram came out and stood at the door of their tents, with their wives, sons, and little ones. Moses said, "Hereby you shall know that the LORD has sent me to do these works, and that it has not been of my own accord. If these men die the common death of all men, then the LORD has not sent me. But if the ground opens its mouth, and swallows them up alive, with all that belongs to them, then you shall know that these men have despised the LORD." As he finished speaking, the ground under Dathan and Abiram split asunder; the earth swallowed them up, with their households and all their goods. It closed over them, and they perished. All Israel that were round about them fled at their cry.

Then fire came forth from the LORD, and consumed Korah and his company, the two hundred and fifty men offering the incense. The LORD said to Moses, "Tell Eleazar, the son of Aaron the priest, to take the censers out of the blaze, and scatter the fire far and wide. For the censers of these men who have sinned at the cost of their lives are holy; they were offered before the LORD. Let them be hammered into plates as a covering for the altar, to be a sign to the people of Israel." So Eleazar the priest took the bronze censers, and they were hammered out as a covering for the altar, to remind the people that no one who is not a priest, a descendant of Aaron, should burn incense before the LORD, lest he become as Korah and his company.

But on the morrow all the congregation of Israel murmured against Moses and Aaron, saying, "You have killed the people of the LORD." And behold, the cloud covered the tent of meeting, and the glory of the LORD appeared. The LORD said to Moses, "Get away from the midst of this congregation, that I may consume them." Moses and Aaron fell on their faces, and Moses said to Aaron, "Take your censer, put fire from the altar therein, and lay incense on it; carry it quickly to the congregation, and make atonement for them, for wrath has gone forth from the LORD; the plague has begun." So Aaron took the censer and ran into the midst of the assembly. He stood between the dead and the living; and the plague was stopped. But fourteen thousand seven hundred died by the plague, besides those who died in the affair of Korah. When the plague was stopped, Aaron returned to Moses.

The LORD said to Moses, "Speak to the people of Israel; get from their leaders twelve rods, one rod for the head of each fathers' house. Write each man's name upon his rod, and write Aaron's name upon the rod of Levi. Deposit the rods in the tent of meeting before the testimony, where I meet with you. The rod of the man whom I choose shall sprout; thus I will make to cease the murmurings of the people of Israel against you." Moses spoke to the people, and each leader gave him a rod. The rod of Aaron was among them, and Moses deposited the rods before the LORD in the tent.

On the morrow Moses went into the tent, and behold, the rod of Aaron for the house of Levi had sprouted, put forth buds, produced blossoms, and it bore ripe almonds. Moses brought out all the rods; the people of Israel looked, and each man took his rod. But the LORD said to Moses, "Put back the rod of Aaron before the testimony, to be kept as a sign for the rebels to make an end to their murmurings against me, lest they die." As the LORD commanded, so Moses did.

THE PEOPLE OF Israel, the whole congregation, came into the wilderness of Zin in the first month, and the people stayed in Kadesh; and Miriam died there, and was buried there.

Now there was no water for the congregation. They assembled themselves against Moses and Aaron, and contended with Moses, saying, "Would that we had died when our brethren died before the LORD! Why have you brought the assembly of the LORD into this wilderness, that we should die here, both we and our cattle? Why have you made us come up out of Egypt, to bring us to this evil place? It is no place for grain, or figs, or vines, or pomegranates; and there is no water to drink." Then Moses and Aaron went from the presence of the assembly to the tent of meeting, and fell on their faces. The glory of the LORD appeared to them, and the LORD said to Moses, "Take the rod, and assemble the congregation, you and Aaron your brother, and tell the rock before their eyes to yield its water; so you shall bring water out of the rock; so you shall give drink to the congregation and their cattle." Moses took the rod as the LORD commanded, and he gathered the assembly before the rock.

"Hear now, you rebels," Moses said, "shall we bring forth water for you out of this rock?" He lifted up his hand and struck the rock with his rod twice; water came forth abundantly, and the congregation drank, and their cattle. But the LORD said to Moses and Aaron, "Because you did not believe in me, to sanctify me in the eyes of the people, you shall not bring this assembly into the land which I have given them." These are the waters of Meribah, where the people of Israel contended with the LORD, and he showed himself holy among them.

Moses sent messengers from Kadesh to the king of Edom, saying, "You know all the adversity that has befallen us, your brother Israel: how our fathers went down to Egypt, and the Egyptians dealt harshly with us; and when we cried to the LORD, he heard our voice, and brought us forth out of Egypt; and here we are in Kadesh, a city on the edge of your territory. Now let us pass through your land. We will not pass through field or vineyard; we will go along the King's Highway, and will pay if we drink of your water; let us pass through on foot, nothing more." But the king said, "You shall not pass through," and Edom came out against them with a strong force of many men, and refused to give Israel passage.

So the people of Israel turned away, and journeyed from Kadesh to Mount Hor. The LORD said to Moses and Aaron, "Aaron shall be gathered to his people. He shall not enter the land I have given to Israel, because both of you rebelled at the waters of Meribah. Bring Aaron and Eleazar his son up to Mount Hor; strip Aaron of his garments, and put them upon Eleazar; and Aaron shall die there." Moses did as the LORD commanded; they went up Mount Hor in the sight of all the congregation, and Aaron died there. Then Moses and Eleazar came down, and all the house of Israel wept for Aaron thirty days.

From Mount Hor they set out by the way to the Red Sea, to go around the land of Edom. On the way, the people became impatient, and spoke against God and Moses. "Why have you brought us up out of Egypt to die in the wilderness? For there is no water, and we loathe this worthless food." Then the LORD sent fiery serpents among them, and the serpents bit the people, so that many Israelites died. The people came to Moses, and said, "We have sinned, for we have spoken against the LORD and against you; pray to the LORD, that he take away the serpents from us." So Moses prayed for the people. And the LORD said to Moses, "Make a fiery serpent, and set it on a pole; every one who is bitten, when he sees it, shall live." So Moses made a bronze serpent, and set it on a pole; and if a serpent bit any man, the man would look at the bronze serpent and live.

The people of Israel went on to the valley lying in the region of Moab by the top of Pisgah, which looks down upon the desert. Then Israel sent messengers to Sihon the king of the Amorites, who dwelt at Heshbon, saying, "Let us pass through your land." But Sihon would not allow Israel to pass. He gathered his men and went out and fought against them. And Israel slew him, and took possession of the land of the Amorites. Then they turned and went up by the way to Bashan; and Og the king of Bashan came out to battle against them at Edrei. But the LORD said to Moses, "Do not fear him, for I have given him into your hand; and you shall do to him as you did to Sihon." So they slew him, and all his people; and they possessed his land.

THEN THE PEOPLE of Israel encamped in the plains of Moab beyond the Jordan at Jericho. Balak the king of Moab saw all that Israel had done to the Amorites, and Moab was in great dread of the people of Israel, because they were many. The Moabites said to the elders of Midian, "This horde will now lick up all that is round about us, as the ox licks up the grass of the field." So Balak sent messengers to call Balaam the son of Beor at Pethor, which is near the river Euphrates, saying, "Behold, a people has come out of Egypt; they cover the face of the earth, and are dwelling opposite me. Come, curse this people, for they are too mighty for me; perhaps I shall be able to drive them from the land; for I know that he whom you bless is blessed, and he whom you curse is cursed."

So the elders of Moab and Midian departed with the fees for divination in their hand. When they gave Balak's message to Balaam, he said to them, "Lodge here this night. I will bring back word to you, as the LORD speaks to me." So they stayed, and God came to Balaam and said, "Who are these men?" Balaam said, "Balak the king of Moab has sent them to me, saying, 'A people has come out of Egypt, and covers the face of the earth; come, curse them for me; perhaps I shall be able to drive them out.'" God said to Balaam, "You shall not go; you shall not curse the people, for they are blessed." Balaam rose in the morning, and said to the elders, "Go to your own land; the LORD has refused to let me go with you." So they returned to Balak, and said, "Balaam refuses to come."

Once again Balak sent messengers to Balaam, saying, "Let nothing hinder you from coming, for I will surely do you great honor, and whatever you say to me I will do. Come, curse this people for me." But Balaam said to the servants of Balak, "Though Balak were to give me his house full of silver and gold, I could not go beyond the command of the LORD my God. Pray tarry here this night also, that I may know what more the LORD will say to me." And God came to Balaam at night and said, "If the men have come to call you, rise, go with them; but do only what I bid you."

So Balaam rose in the morning, saddled his ass, and went with the elders of Moab. But God's anger was kindled, and the angel of the LORD took his stand in the way as Balaam was riding. The ass saw the angel of the LORD standing in the road, with a drawn sword in his hand, and turned aside into the field; so Balaam struck the ass, to turn her into the road. Then the angel stood in a narrow path between the vineyards, with a wall on either side. When the ass saw the angel, she pushed against the wall, pressing Balaam's foot against it; so he struck her again. Then the angel went ahead, and stood in a place so narrow there was no way to turn. When the ass saw this, she lay down under Balaam. Balaam's anger was kindled, and he struck the ass with his staff. Then the LORD opened the mouth of the ass. "What have I done to you," she said to Balaam, "that you have struck me these three times?" And Balaam said, "You have made sport of me. If I had a sword in my hand, I would kill you." But the ass said, "Am I not your ass, upon which you have ridden all your life? Was I ever accustomed to do so to you?" And Balaam said, "No."

Then the LORD opened Balaam's eyes; he saw the angel standing with drawn sword, and he bowed his head, and fell on his face. "Why have you struck your ass these three times?" the angel said. "Behold, I have come to withstand you, because your way is perverse before me. If the ass had not turned aside, I would have slain you." Then Balaam said, "I have sinned, for I did not know that thou didst stand in the road against me. If it is evil in thy sight, I will go back." But the angel said, "Go with the men; but speak only the words which I bid you." So Balaam went on with the servants of Balak.

When Balak heard that Balaam had come, he went out to meet him, and said, "Why did you not come to me? Am I not able to honor you?" Balaam answered, "Lo, I have come to you! Have I now any power at all to speak anything? The word that God puts in my mouth, that must I speak."

On the morrow Balak took Balaam up into the high places, and from there he saw the people of Israel. "Build for me here seven altars," Balaam said to Balak, "and provide seven bulls and seven rams." Balak did so, and they offered on each altar a bull and a ram. "Stand beside your burnt offering," Balaam said, "and I will go yonder; perhaps the LORD will meet me, and whatever he shows me I will tell you." So Balaam went to a bare height, and God met him. The LORD put words in Balaam's mouth, and said, "Return to Balak, and speak thus."

Balaam returned, and found Balak and all the princes of Moab standing beside his burnt offering. Balaam took up his discourse, saying, "From Mesopotamia Balak has brought me: 'Come, curse Israel for me!' How can I curse whom God has not cursed? From the top of the mountains I see a people dwelling alone, and not reckoning itself among the nations! Who can count the dust of Israel? Let me die the death of the righteous, and let my end be like his!"

Then Balak said to Balaam, "What have you done to me? I took you to curse my enemies, and you have done nothing but bless them." Balaam answered, "Must I not speak what the LORD puts in my mouth?" Balak said, "Come with me to another place, from which you may see only the nearest of the people of Israel, not all of them; then curse them for me from there." He took Balaam to the top of Pisgah, and built seven altars, and offered a bull and a ram on each. "Stand here beside your burnt offering," Balaam said, "while I meet the LORD yonder." The LORD again put words in Balaam's mouth. He returned to Balak and the princes of Moab, and took up his discourse, saying, "Rise, Balak, and hear: God is not man, that he should lie, or a son of man, that he should repent. Has he spoken, and will he not fulfil it? He has blessed, and I cannot revoke it. He has not beheld misfortune in Israel. The LORD their God is with them, and the shout of a king is among them. God brings them out of Egypt; they have as it were the horns of the wild ox. There is no divination against Israel; now it shall be said of Israel, 'What has God wrought!' Behold, a people! As a lioness it rises up; it devours the prey, and drinks the blood of the slain."

Then Balak said to Balaam, "Neither curse them, nor bless them." But Balaam answered, "Did I not tell you, 'All that the LORD says, that I must do'?" And Balak said, "Come now, I will take you to another place; perhaps it will please God that you may curse them for me from there." So Balak took Balaam to the top of Peor, that overlooks the desert. Balak built seven altars there, and offered a bull and a ram on each. When Balaam saw that it pleased the LORD to bless Israel, he did not go, as at other times, to look for omens, but set his face toward the wilderness. He lifted up his eyes, and saw Israel encamping tribe by tribe. The Spirit of God came upon him, and he said, "The oracle of Balaam, the man whose eye is opened, the oracle of him who hears the words of God: how fair are your encampments, O Israel! Like valleys that stretch afar, like gardens beside a river. Water shall flow from his buckets, and his kingdom shall be exalted. God brings him out of Egypt; he shall eat up his adversaries, break their bones in pieces, and pierce them with his arrows. He lay down like a lion; who will rouse him up? Blessed be those who bless you, and cursed be those who curse you."

Balak's anger was kindled; he struck his hands together, and said to Balaam, "I called you to curse my enemies, and you have blessed them these three times. Now flee to your place; I said I would honor you, but the LORD has held you back from honor." Balaam replied, "Did I not tell your messengers I would not be able to do either good or bad of my own will? What the LORD speaks, that will I speak. Now I am going to my people; but come, I will let you know what this people will do to your people in the latter days." And he took up his discourse, saying, "The oracle of Balaam, the man whose eye is opened, the oracle of him who knows the knowledge of the Most High: I see him, but not now; I behold him, but not nigh: a star shall come forth out of Jacob, and a scepter shall rise out of Israel; it shall crush the forehead of Moab, and Edom also shall be dispossessed. By Israel shall dominion be exercised, and the survivors of cities be destroyed!" Then Balaam rose, and went back to his place; and Balak also went his way.

WHILE ISRAEL DWELT in Shittim, the people began to play the harlot with the daughters of Moab, who invited them to the sacrifices of their gods. They ate, and bowed down to Baal of Peor. And the LORD, his anger kindled against Israel, said to Moses, "Take all the chiefs of the people, and hang them in the sun before the LORD." So Moses said to the judges of Israel, "Every one of you slay his men who have yoked themselves to Baal of Peor."

And behold, one of the people of Israel brought a Midianite woman to his family, in the sight of Moses and the whole congregation at the tent of meeting. When Phinehas the son of Eleazar, son of Aaron the priest, saw it, he left the congregation, took a spear, went after them into the inner room, and pierced both of them through her body. Thus the plague which the LORD had sent was stayed from the people of Israel. Nevertheless twenty-four thousand died. The LORD said to Moses, "Phinehas, jealous with my jealousy, has turned back my wrath from the people of Israel. Therefore I give my covenant of peace to him and his descendants, the covenant of a perpetual priesthood, because he was jealous for his God, and made atonement for the people of Israel." The slain man was Zimri, a Simeonite, and the Midianite woman who was slain with him was Cozbi, daughter of a prince of Midian. And the LORD said to Moses, "Harass the Midianites, and smite them; for they have harassed you with their wiles in the matter of Peor, and of Cozbi, their sister, who was slain on the day of the plague."

After the plague the LORD said to Moses and to Eleazar the son of Aaron, "Take another census of the people of Israel, from twenty years old and upward, by their fathers' houses, all who are able to go forth to war." Moses and Eleazar did as the LORD commanded; and the people numbered six hundred and one thousand seven hundred and thirty. The LORD said to Moses, "To these the land shall be divided for inheritance; according to the names of the tribes of their fathers they shall inherit." But not a man of these, except Caleb and Joshua, was among those numbered by Moses and Aaron in the wilderness. For the LORD had said of them, "They shall die in the wilderness."

Then drew near the daughters of Zelophehad, of the tribe of Manasseh. Their names were: Mahlah, Noah, Hoglah, Milcah, and Tirzah. They stood before Moses and Eleazar, and all the congregation at the tent of meeting, saying, "Our father died in the wilderness; he was not among those who gathered together against the LORD in the company of Korah, but died for his own sin; and he had no sons. Why should the name of our father be taken away from his family, because he had no son? Give to us a possession among our father's brethren."

Moses brought their case before the LORD. And the LORD said, "The daughters of Zelophehad are right; you shall cause the inheritance of their father to pass to them. Say to the people of Israel, If a man dies, and has no son, then his inheritance shall pass to his daughter. If he has no daughter, give his inheritance to his brothers; if he has no brothers, give it to his father's brothers; and if his father has no brothers, then give his inheritance to the next kinsman of his family. This shall be to the people of Israel a statute and ordinance."

Then the LORD said to Moses, "Go up into the mountains of Abarim, and see the land which I have given to the people of Israel. When you have seen it, you also shall be gathered to your people, as Aaron was, because you rebelled against my word at the waters of Meribah." Moses said, "Let the LORD, the God of the spirits of all flesh, appoint a man over the congregation, who shall lead them out and bring them in; that the congregation of the LORD may not be as sheep with no shepherd." And the LORD said, "Take Joshua the son of Nun, a man in whom is the spirit, and lay your hand upon him; cause him to stand before Eleazar the priest, and commission him in the sight of all the congregation. Invest him with some of your authority, that the people of Israel may obey; at his word they shall go out and come in, all the people with him, the whole congregation." And Moses did as the LORD directed.

THE LORD SAID to Moses, "Avenge the people of Israel on the Midianites; afterward you shall be gathered to your people." So Moses said to the people, "Arm men for war, that they may execute the LORD's vengeance on Midian. Send a thousand from each of the tribes of Israel." So there were provided twelve thousand armed men, and Moses sent them to the war, together with Phinehas the son of Eleazar, with the vessels of the sanctuary and the trumpets for the alarm in his hand. They warred against Midian, as the LORD commanded, and slew every male. They slew the five kings of Midian; and they also slew Balaam the son of Beor with the sword. They took captive the women of Midian and their little ones; and they took as booty all their cattle, flocks, and goods. They burned their cities and all their encampments. Then they brought the captives and the booty to Moses and Eleazar the priest, and to the congregation of the people of Israel, at the camp on the plains of Moab by the Jordan at Jericho.

Moses, Eleazar, and the leaders of the congregation went to meet them outside the camp. And Moses was angry with the officers of the army who had come from service in the war. "Have you let all the women live?" he said. "These caused the people of Israel, by the counsel of Balaam, to act treacherously against the LORD at Peor, and so the plague came. Now therefore, kill every male among the little ones, and kill every woman who has known man by lying with him. But keep alive for yourselves all the young girls who have not known man. Encamp outside the camp seven days; whoever of you has killed any person, or touched any slain, purify yourselves and your captives on the third day and on the seventh day. You must wash your clothes on the seventh day, and afterward you shall be clean and shall come into the camp."

The LORD said to Moses, "Count the booty that was taken, both of man and of beast, and divide it into two parts, between the warriors who went out to battle and all the congregation. Levy for the LORD a tribute from the men of war; from their half take one out of five hundred, both of persons and of beasts, to give to Eleazar the priest as an offering to the LORD. From the people of Israel's half take one of every fifty, both of persons and of beasts, and give them to the Levites who have charge of the tabernacle of the LORD." Moses and Eleazar did as the LORD commanded Moses, and divided the booty remaining of the spoil that the men of war had taken, which was: six hundred and seventy-five thousand sheep, seventy-two thousand cattle, sixty-one thousand asses, and thirty-two thousand women who had not known man by lying with him.

Now THE SONS of Reuben and the sons of Gad had a multitude of cattle; and when they saw that the lands of Jazer and Gilead were a good place for cattle, they came to Moses and Eleazar, and to the leaders of the congregation, and said, "If we have found favor in your sight, let this land be given to us for a possession; do not take us across the Jordan." But Moses said to them, "Shall your brethren go to the war while you sit here? Will you discourage the people of Israel from going over into the land which the LORD has given them? Thus did your fathers in the wilderness of Paran, when I sent them from Kadesh to see the land. They discouraged the heart of the people. The LORD's anger was kindled that day, and he swore that none of the men who came up out of Egypt would see the land promised to Abraham, Isaac, and Jacob; none except Caleb and Joshua, who had wholly followed the LORD. And the LORD made Israel wander in the wilderness forty years. Now you have risen in your fathers' stead, a brood of sinful men, to increase still more the LORD's fierce anger! For if you turn away, he will again abandon Israel in the wilderness; and you will destroy this people."

But the sons of Gad and of Reuben said, "We will build sheepfolds here for our flocks, and cities for our little ones. Then we will take up arms and go with Israel. Our little ones, our wives, our flocks and cattle, shall remain in the fortified cities of Gilead, but we will not return to our homes until we have brought all the people of Israel to their place. For we will not inherit with them on the other side of the Jordan; our inheritance has come to us here on the east side." So Moses said to them, "If you will do this, if you will take up arms to go before the LORD for the war, then after that you shall return here, and this land shall be your possession before the LORD. But if you will not do so, you have sinned against the LORD, and your sin will find you out. Build cities now, and folds for your sheep, and do what you have promised." And they said to Moses, "Your servants will do as my lord commands." So Moses gave to the sons of Gad and of Reuben, and to the half-tribe of Manasseh, the kingdom of the Amorites and the kingdom of Bashan, the land and its cities throughout the country. And the sons of Gad and of Reuben, and of Machir the son of Manasseh, built fortified cities, and folds for sheep. They gave names to the cities which they built; they took villages, and dispossessed the people, and they settled there.

WHEN THE PEOPLE of Israel had gone forth out of the land of Egypt under the leadership of Moses and Aaron, Moses had written down their starting places, stage by stage, by command of the LORD. These are their stages according to their starting places. They set out from Rameses on the fifteenth day of the first month, the day after the passover. They went out triumphantly in the sight of the Egyptians, while the Egyptians were burying all their first-born, whom the LORD had struck down. They encamped at Succoth, then at Etham on the edge of the wilderness, then turned back to Pihahiroth, by the Red Sea. They passed through the midst of the sea, went a three days' journey in the wilderness of Shur, and encamped at Marah, then came to Elim, where there were twelve springs of water and seventy palm trees, and encamped there. They set out from Elim, encamped by the Red Sea, then in the wilderness of Sin, and then at Rephidim, where there was no water for the people to drink. They set out from Rephidim, encamped in the wilderness of Sinai, then at Kibroth-hattaavah, and then at Hazeroth. They set out from Hazeroth, and encamped at Rithmah, and at Ezion-geber, and in the wilderness of Zin (that is, Kadesh). Then they set out from Kadesh, and encamped at Mount Hor, on the edge of the land of Edom.

Aaron the priest went up Mount Hor at the command of the LORD, and died there, in the fortieth year after the people of Israel had come out of Egypt. Aaron was a hundred and twenty-three years old when he died.

The people of Israel set out from Mount Hor, and entered the territory of Moab. They encamped in the mountains of Abarim, before Mount Nebo, and then in the plains of Moab by the Jordan at Jericho. The LORD said to Moses, "Say to the people of Israel, When you pass over the Jordan into the land of Canaan, drive out all the inhabitants of the land, destroy their figured stones and molten images, and demolish all their high places; take possession of the land and settle in it, for I have given it to you. You shall inherit the land by lot according to the tribes of your fathers. But if you do not drive out the inhabitants of the land, those whom you let remain shall be as pricks in your eyes and thorns in your sides. And I will do to you as I thought to do to them."

The LORD said to Moses in the plains of Moab, "Command the people of Israel to give from their inheritance forty-two cities to the Levites, for them to dwell in, and pasture lands round about the cities for their livestock. In addition, give them six cities of refuge. Give three cities beyond the Jordan, and three in the land of Canaan. These six cities shall be for the people of Israel, for the stranger, and for the sojourner among them, that any one who kills without intent may flee there.

"But if any one strikes a person down with an instrument of iron, a stone in the hand, or a weapon of wood, so that the person dies, he is a murderer and shall be put to death. The avenger of blood shall himself put the murderer to death, when he meets him. And if any one stabs a person from hatred, or hurls at him, lying in wait, or in enmity strikes him down with his hand, so that he dies, then he who struck the blow shall be put to death; he is a murderer; the avenger of blood shall put him to death, when he meets him.

"But if any one kills without intent, the congregation shall judge, in accordance with these ordinances, and shall rescue him from the hand of the avenger of blood; and he shall live in his city of refuge until the death of the high priest. But if the manslayer shall at any time go beyond the bounds of his city of refuge, and the avenger of blood finds him, and slays him, the avenger shall not be guilty of blood. For the man must remain in his city of refuge until the death of the high priest, after which he may return to the land of his possession.

"These things shall be a statute to you throughout your generations. If any one kills a person, the murderer shall be put to death on the evidence of witnesses; but no person shall be put to death on the testimony of one witness. Accept no ransom for the life of a murderer; he shall be put to death. For blood pollutes the land, and no expiation can be made for blood that is shed, except by the blood of him who shed it. You shall not defile the land in which you live, for I the LORD dwell in the midst of the people."

THE HEADS OF the families of the tribe of Manasseh came and spoke before Moses and the leaders of the people of Israel. "The LORD commanded my lord to give land for inheritance by lot to the people," they said, "and to give the inheritance of Zelophehad, our brother, to his daughters. But if they marry sons of other tribes, then their inheritance will be taken from the inheritance of our fathers, and added to the inheritance of the other tribe. When the year of jubilee comes, their inheritance will be added to the inheritance of the tribe to which they belong, and taken from the inheritance of the tribe of our fathers."

And Moses commanded the people of Israel according to the word of the LORD, saying, "The tribe of Manasseh is right concerning the daughters of Zelophehad. Let them marry whom they think best; only, they shall marry within the family of the tribe of their father. The inheritance of the people of Israel shall not be transferred from one tribe to another. Every daughter who possesses an inheritance in any tribe shall be wife to one of the family of the tribe of her father, so that every one of the people may possess the inheritance of his fathers. Each of the tribes shall cleave to its own inheritance."

The daughters of Zelophehad did as the LORD commanded Moses; for Mahlah, Tirzah, Hoglah, Milcah, and Noah married sons of their father's brothers. They were married into the families of the sons of Manasseh, and their inheritance remained in the tribe of their father.

These are the ordinances which the LORD commanded by Moses to the people of Israel in the plains of Moab by the Jordan at Jericho.

DEUTERONOMY

The Israelites have now almost reached the land of Canaan, where they are to settle, and Moses speaks to them for the last time. He reviews the mighty acts of the Lord, solemnly warns of the temptations to be found in Canaan, and pleads for fidelity to God as the condition for life in the Promised Land.

Deuteronomy, which means "second law," amplifies the law proclaimed at Mount Sinai, and repeats some Israelite history from earlier books. Its compilation is generally assigned to the seventh century B.C., though it rests upon much older tradition, some of it from Moses' time. The distinctive oratorical style of the book, in which absolute monotheism is strongly emphasized, sets it apart from the other Pentateuchal writings. At the emergence of Christianity, Deuteronomy shared with the Psalms a preeminent position among Old Testament books. Jesus quoted from it in overcoming his threefold temptation in the desert, and in explaining the first and greatest commandment: *"The Lord our God is one Lord; and you shall love the Lord your God with all your heart, and with all your soul, and with all your might."*

THESE ARE THE words that Moses spoke to all Israel beyond the Jordan in the wilderness, in the land of Moab. In the fortieth year, on the first day of the eleventh month, Moses undertook to explain to the people all the law that the LORD had given him in commandment to them, saying, "The LORD our God said to us at Sinai, 'You have stayed long enough at this mountain; turn and take your journey to the hill country of the Amorites, and to all their neighbors in the lowland, and in the Negeb, and by the seacoast, the land of the Canaanites, and Lebanon, as far as the great river Euphrates. Go take possession of the land which the LORD swore to give to your fathers, Abraham, Isaac, and Jacob, and to their descendants.'

"At that time I said to you, 'The LORD your God has multiplied you, and behold, you are as the stars of heaven. May the LORD make you a thousand times as many as you are, and bless you, as he has promised! But how can I bear alone the burden of you and your strife? Choose wise, understanding, and experienced men, according to your tribes, and I will appoint them as your heads.' And you answered, 'That is good for us to do.' So I set wise and experienced men over you, throughout your tribes. I charged your judges, 'Hear cases between your brethren, and judge righteously. Do not be partial; hear the small and the great alike. Do not be afraid of the face of man, for the judgment is God's; the case that is too hard for you, bring to me, and I will hear it.' And I commanded you at that time all the things that you should do.

"We set out from Sinai, and after going through that great and terrible wilderness, as the LORD commanded us, we came to Kadesh. 'You have come to the hill country of the Amorites,' I said. 'Behold, the LORD your God has set the land before you; go up, take possession, as the LORD has told you; do not fear or be dismayed.' But you said, 'Let us send men before us to explore the land, and bring word of the way by which we must go up and the cities into which we shall come.' So I sent twelve men, one for each tribe, into the hill country to spy it out. They returned, bringing in their hands some of the fruit of the land, and said, 'It is a good land which the LORD our God gives us.'

"Yet you would not go up, but rebelled against the command of the LORD, and murmured in your tents. 'Because the LORD hated us,' you said, 'he has brought us forth out of Egypt, to give us into the hand of the Amorites, to destroy us. Our brethren have made our hearts melt, saying that the people are greater and taller than we, for the sons of the Anakim are there; and their cities are fortified up to heaven.' Then I said to you, 'Do not be in dread of them. The LORD your God who goes before you will himself fight you, just as he did in Egypt, and in the wilderness. You have seen how the LORD bore you, as a man bears his son, all the way to this place, going before you to show you the way, in fire by night, and in the cloud by day.' Yet in spite of this you did not believe.

"The LORD heard your words, and was angered, and he swore, 'Not one man of this evil generation shall see the good land I swore to give to your fathers, except Caleb and Joshua, who have wholly followed the LORD!' The LORD was angry with me also on your account, and said, 'You also shall not go in there; encourage Joshua, who stands before you, for he shall cause Israel to inherit it. Moreover your little ones, who you said would become a prey, shall go in and possess the land. But as for you, turn, and journey into the wilderness.'

"'We have sinned against the LORD,' you answered; 'we will go up and fight, as the LORD commanded us.' You girded on weapons, and thought it easy to go up into the hill country. The LORD told me to say to you, 'Do not go up or fight, lest you be defeated, for I am not in the midst of you.' But you would not hearken; you were presumptuous and went up into the hill country. The Amorites who lived there came out against you and chased you as bees do and beat you. Returning, you wept before the LORD; but the LORD did not give ear to you. So we remained at Kadesh many days.

"Then we turned and journeyed into the wilderness in the direction of the Red Sea, as the LORD told me; and for many days we went about Mount Seir. And the LORD said, 'You have been going about this mountain country long enough; turn northward. But do not contend with your brethren the sons of Esau, who live in Edom; for I will not give you any of their land, no, not so much as for the sole of the foot to tread on, because I have given Edom to Esau as a possession.' So we turned in the direction of the wilderness of Moab, away from our brethren the sons of Esau. And the LORD said, 'Do not harass Moab or contend with them in battle, for I will not give you any of their land. I have given it to the sons of Lot for a possession. Now rise up, and go over the brook Zered.' So we went over. Thirty-eight years had passed from the time we left Kadesh until we crossed the brook Zered, and the entire generation, the men of war, had perished from the camp, as the LORD had sworn.

"When all the men of war were dead, the LORD said to me, 'This day you are to pass over the boundary of Moab. When you approach the frontier of the sons of Ammon, do not contend with them, for I will not give you any of their land. I have given it also to the sons of Lot. Take your journey over the valley of the Arnon; behold, I have given into your hand Sihon, the Amorite king, and his land; contend with him in battle, and take possession of it. This day I will begin to put the fear of you upon the peoples that are under the whole heaven, who shall hear the report of you and shall tremble and be in anguish.'

"So I sent messengers to Sihon, with words of peace, saying, 'Let me pass through your land; I will go only by the road, and will not turn aside. Sell me food and water, and let me pass through on foot, and I will go over the Jordan into the land which the LORD our God gives to us.' But Sihon would not let us pass, for the LORD hardened his spirit, that he might give him into our hand. Sihon and all his people came out to battle against us, and the LORD gave him over to us, and we defeated him. We captured all his cities and utterly destroyed the men, women, and children; we left none remaining; only the cattle we took as spoil.

"Then we turned and went up to Bashan; and Og the king of Bashan and all his people came out to battle against us. But the LORD gave them into our hand also. There was not a city we did not take from them—sixty cities, the whole kingdom of Bashan, all fortified with high walls, gates, and bars—besides very many unwalled villages. We utterly destroyed them, as we did Sihon the king of the Amorites, until no survivor was left. But all the cattle and the spoil of the cities we took as booty. And behold, the iron bedstead of Og the king of Bashan was thirteen and a half feet long, and six feet wide.

"So we took the land of the two kings, from the valley of the Arnon to Mount Hermon, all Gilead and all Bashan. To the Reubenites and the Gadites I gave the territory which is on the edge of the valley of the Arnon, and half the hill country of Gilead; the rest of Gilead and all Bashan I gave to the half-tribe of Manasseh. 'The LORD has given you this land,' I said to them. 'Your wives, your little ones, and your cattle (I know you have many cattle) shall remain in the cities. But all your men of valor shall pass over armed before your brethren, the people of Israel, until the LORD gives rest to them, as to you, and they also occupy the land which the LORD gives them beyond the Jordan. Then you shall return to this possession which I have given you.'

"I besought the LORD at that time, saying, 'O Lord GOD, thou hast only begun to show thy servant thy greatness; for what god is there in heaven or on earth who can do such mighty acts as thine? Let me go over, I pray, and see the good land beyond the Jordan.' But the LORD was angry with me on your account, and would not hearken. 'Speak no more of this matter,' he said to me. 'Go up to the top of Pisgah, and lift up your eyes westward, northward, southward, and eastward, and behold the land; for you shall not go over this Jordan. Encourage and strengthen Joshua, for he shall lead this people and put them in possession of the land which you shall see.' So we remained in the valley opposite Beth-peor."

"AND NOW, O Israel," said Moses, "give heed to the statutes and ordinances I teach you. You shall not add to the word which I command you, nor take from it; that you may keep the commandments of the LORD. Your eyes have seen how the LORD destroyed all who followed the Baal of Peor; but you who held fast to the LORD your God are alive this day. Behold, I have taught you statutes and ordinances, as the LORD commanded me. Keep them and do them in the land which you are entering, for that will be your wisdom in the sight of the peoples, who, when they hear all these statutes, will say, 'Surely this great nation is a wise and understanding people.' For what great nation has a god so near to it as the LORD our God is to us, whenever we call upon him? And what great nation has statutes and ordinances so righteous as all this law which I set before you this day?

"Only take heed, lest you forget the things your eyes have seen. Make them known to your children and your children's children—how, at Sinai, the LORD said to me, 'Gather the people to me, that I may let them hear my words, so they may learn to fear me all the days that they live, and may teach their children so.' And you came near and stood at the foot of the mountain, which was wrapped in darkness, cloud, and gloom, and burned with fire to the heart of heaven. The LORD spoke to you out of the midst of the fire; you heard the words, but saw no form; there was only a voice. He declared his covenant, the ten commandments, for you to perform; and he wrote them upon two tables of stone.

"Therefore take heed. Since you saw no form on the day that the LORD spoke to you at Sinai, beware lest you act corruptly by making a graven image for yourselves, in the form of any figure, male or female, the likeness of any beast on earth, any bird that flies, anything that creeps on the ground, or any fish in the water under the earth. And beware lest you lift up your eyes to heaven, and seeing the sun, moon, and stars, be drawn away to worship them, things which the LORD has allotted to all peoples under the whole heaven. Take heed, lest you forget the covenant of the LORD. For the LORD your God is a devouring fire, a jealous God.

"When you beget children and children's children, and have grown old in the land, if you act corruptly by doing what is evil in the sight of the LORD, I call heaven and earth to witness against you this day, that you will soon utterly perish from the land which you are going over the Jordan to possess. The LORD will scatter you, and you will be left few in number among the nations where the LORD will drive you. There you will serve gods of wood and stone, the work of men's hands, that neither see, nor hear, nor eat, nor smell. But from there you will seek the LORD your God, and you will find him, if you search after him with all your heart and with all your soul. When you are in tribulation, and these things come upon you, you will return to the LORD and obey his voice, for the LORD your God is merciful; he will not fail you or destroy you or forget the covenant with your fathers.

"For ask now, since the day God created man upon the earth, whether such a great thing as this has ever happened. Did any people ever hear the voice of a god speaking out of the midst of the fire, as you have heard, and still live? Or has any god ever attempted to take a nation for himself from the midst of another nation, by trials, by signs, by wonders, and by war, by a mighty hand and an outstretched arm, and by great terrors, as the LORD your God did for you in Egypt? To you it was shown, that you might know that the LORD is God; there is no other besides him. Out of heaven he let you hear his voice, that he might discipline you; and on earth he let you see his great fire. He loved your fathers and chose their descendants, and brought you out of Egypt with his own presence, driving out before you nations mightier than yourselves, to give you their land for an inheritance. Know therefore this day, and lay it to your heart, that the LORD is God in heaven above and on the earth beneath; there is no other. Keep his commandments, that it may go well with you, and with your children, and that you may prolong your days in the land which the LORD your God gives you for ever."

Then Moses set apart three cities of refuge east of the Jordan, that the manslayer who kills his neighbor unintentionally might flee to one of them and save his life: Bezer on the tableland for the Reubenites, Ramoth in Gilead for the Gadites, and Golan in Bashan for the Manassites.

THIS IS THE law, these are the testimonies, statutes, and ordinances, which Moses spoke to the children of Israel east of the Jordan in the valley opposite Beth-peor, under the slopes of Pisgah. Summoning all Israel, he said, "Hear, O Israel, the statutes which I speak this day; learn them and be careful to do them. The LORD our God made a covenant with us at Sinai. Out of the midst of the fire he spoke, saying, 'I am the LORD your God, who brought you out of the land of Egypt, out of the house of bondage.

" 'You shall have no other gods before me.

" 'You shall not make for yourself a graven image, or any likeness of anything that is in heaven above, or that is on the earth beneath, or that is in the water under the earth; you shall not bow down to them or serve them; for I the LORD your God am a jealous God, visiting the iniquity of the fathers upon the children to the third and fourth generation of those who hate me, but showing steadfast love to thousands of those who love me and keep my commandments.

" 'You shall not take the name of the LORD your God in vain: for the LORD will not hold him guiltless who takes his name in vain.

" 'Observe the sabbath day, to keep it holy, as the LORD your God commanded you. Six days you shall labor, and do all your work; but the seventh day is a sabbath to the LORD your God; in it you shall not do any work, you, or your son, or your daughter, or your manservant, or your maidservant, or your ox, or your ass, or any of your cattle, or the sojourner who is within your gates, that your manservant and your maidservant may rest as well as you. You shall remember that you were a servant in the land of Egypt, and the LORD your God brought you out thence with a mighty hand and an outstretched arm; therefore the LORD your God commanded you to keep the sabbath day.

" 'Honor your father and your mother, as the LORD your God commanded you; that your days may be prolonged, and that it may go well with you, in the land which the LORD your God gives you.

" 'You shall not kill.

" 'Neither shall you commit adultery.

" 'Neither shall you steal.

" 'Neither shall you bear false witness against your neighbor.

" 'Neither shall you covet your neighbor's wife; and you shall not desire your neighbor's house, his field, or his manservant, or his maidservant, his ox, or his ass, or anything that is your neighbor's.'

"These words the LORD spoke to all your assembly at the mountain out of the midst of the fire, with a loud voice; and he added no more. When you heard the voice, you came to me, saying, 'Behold, the LORD our God has shown us his glory. But this great fire will consume us; if we hear the voice of the LORD any more, we shall die. For who of all flesh has heard the voice of the living God, as we have, and still lived? Go near, and hear all that the LORD will say; then speak it to us, and we will hear and do it.'

"And the LORD said to me, 'I have heard the words of this people; they have rightly spoken. Oh that they had such a mind always, to fear me and keep my commandments, that it might go well with them and with their children for ever! Let them return to their tents, but you, stand here by me, and I will tell you all the statutes and ordinances which you shall teach them, that they may do them in the land which I give them to possess.'

"Now these are the statutes and ordinances which the LORD commanded me to teach you. Hear therefore, and do them; that you may multiply greatly, as the LORD, the God of your fathers, has promised you, in a land flowing with milk and honey.

"Hear, O Israel: The LORD our God is one LORD; and you shall love the LORD your God with all your heart, and with all your soul, and with all your might. These words shall be upon your heart; teach them diligently to your children, and talk of them when you sit in your house, when you walk by the way, when you lie down, and when you rise. Bind them as a sign upon your hand, and they shall be as frontlets between your eyes. Write them on the doorposts of your house and on your gates.

"And when the LORD your God brings you into the land which he swore to your fathers, Abraham, Isaac, and Jacob, to give you, a land with great and goodly cities, which you did not build, houses full of all good things, which you did not fill, cisterns hewn out, which you did not hew, and vineyards and olive trees, which you did not plant, and when you eat and are full, then take heed, lest you forget the LORD. You shall fear the LORD your God, serve him, and swear by his name. You shall not go after other gods, lest the anger of the LORD be kindled against you, and he destroy you.

"You shall not put the LORD your God to the test, as you tested him at Massah. Diligently keep his commandments, and do what is right and good in his sight.

"When your son asks, 'What is the meaning of the ordinances which the LORD our God has commanded you?' you shall say, 'We were Pharaoh's slaves in Egypt; and the LORD brought us out with a mighty hand, that he might give us the land which he swore to give to our fathers. And the LORD commanded us to do all these statutes, to fear the LORD our God, for our good always, that he might preserve us alive, as at this day.'

"When the LORD your God brings you into the land you are to possess, and gives many nations over to you, nations greater and mightier than yourselves, then you must utterly destroy them; make no covenant with them, and show no mercy to them. Do not make marriages with them, giving your daughters to their sons or taking their daughters for your sons. For they would turn away your sons to serve other gods; then the anger of the LORD would be kindled against you, and he would destroy you. But thus shall you deal with them: break down their altars and pillars, and burn their graven images.

"For you are a people holy to the LORD your God, who has chosen you for his own possession, out of all the peoples on earth. It was not because you were more numerous than others that the LORD chose you, for you were the fewest of all peoples; but it is because the LORD loves you, and is keeping the oath which he swore to your fathers, that he has redeemed you from the house of bondage of Pharaoh king of Egypt. Know therefore that the LORD your God is God, the faithful God who keeps covenant and steadfast love with those who love him and keep his commandments, to a thousand generations, and requites to their face those who hate him, by destroying them.

"And because you hearken to these ordinances, and keep them, the LORD will love you, bless you, and multiply you; he will bless the fruit of your body and the fruit of your ground, your grain, your wine, and your oil, the increase of your cattle and your flocks. You shall be blessed above all peoples; there shall not be male or female barren among you, or among your cattle. The LORD will take away from you all sickness and evil diseases, and will inflict them upon all who hate you. You shall destroy all the peoples that the LORD will give over to you, your eye shall not pity them; neither shall you serve their gods, for that would be a snare to you.

"If you say in your heart, 'These nations are greater than I; how can I dispossess them?' you shall remember what the LORD did to Pharaoh and all Egypt, the great trials, the signs, and the wonders; so will the LORD do to the peoples you fear. Moreover the LORD will send hornets among them, until those who hide themselves from you are destroyed. Do not be in dread of them; for the LORD is in the midst of you, a great and terrible God. The LORD will clear away these nations little by little; you may not make an end of them at once, lest the wild beasts grow too numerous for you. But the LORD will throw them into great confusion. He will give their kings into your hand, and their name shall perish from under heaven; not a man shall be able to stand against you. You shall burn the graven images of their gods, but do not covet the silver or gold on them, or take it for yourselves, lest you be ensnared; for it is an abomination to the LORD. Do not bring an abominable thing into your house, and become accursed like it; you shall utterly detest and abhor it.

"Remember the way the LORD your God has led you these forty years in the wilderness, testing you to know what was in your heart. He humbled you and let you hunger and fed you with manna, that he might make you know that man does not live by bread alone, but by everything that proceeds out of the mouth of the LORD. Your clothing did not wear out upon you, and your foot did not swell, these forty years. Know then in your heart that, as a man disciplines his son, the LORD your God disciplines you. So keep the commandments of the LORD, by walking in his ways and by fearing him. For the LORD is bringing you into a good land, a land of brooks, fountains, and springs, a land of wheat and barley, of vines, fig trees, and pomegranates, of olive trees and honey, a land in which you will lack nothing, a land whose stones are iron, and out of whose hills you can dig copper. You shall eat and be full, and you shall bless the LORD your God for the good land he has given you.

"Take heed lest, when you have eaten and are full, and when your herds and flocks, your silver and gold, and all that you have is multiplied, you say in your heart, 'My power and the might of my hand have gotten me this wealth.' Remember it is the LORD who gives you power to get wealth; that he may confirm his covenant which he swore to your fathers.

"Know that the LORD your God is not giving you this good land because of your righteousness; for you are a stubborn people. Do not forget how you provoked the LORD in the wilderness; from the day you came out of Egypt, until you came to this place, you have been rebellious. Even at Sinai you provoked the LORD to such wrath that he was ready to destroy you. I went up the mountain, and at the end of forty days and forty nights the LORD gave me the two tables of the covenant, and said, 'Arise, go down quickly; for your people have acted corruptly, turning aside from the way I commanded them; they have made themselves a molten image. This people is a stubborn people. Let me alone, that I may destroy them and blot out their name from under heaven; and I will make of you a nation mightier and greater than they.'

"So I came down from the mountain, the two tables of the covenant in my hands. I looked, and behold, you had made yourselves a molten calf. So I cast the two tables out of my hands, and broke them before your eyes. Then I took the sinful thing, the calf which you had made, and burned it and crushed it, grinding it fine as dust; and I threw the dust into the brook that descended out of the mountain.

"I lay prostrate before the LORD for forty days and forty nights; I neither ate bread nor drank water, because of the sin which you had committed. For I was afraid of the anger the LORD bore against you, so that he was ready to destroy you. 'O Lord GOD,' I prayed, 'destroy not thy people and thy heritage, whom thou hast brought out of Egypt with a mighty hand. Remember thy servants, Abraham, Isaac, and Jacob; do not regard the stubbornness, wickedness, or sin of this people, lest the inhabitants of the land from which thou didst bring them say, "Because the LORD was not able to bring them into the land which he promised them, and because he hated them, he has brought them out to slay them in the wilderness." For they are thy people and thy heritage, whom thou hast redeemed through thy greatness.'

"The LORD hearkened to me, and said, 'Hew two tables of stone like the first, make an ark of wood, and come up to me on the mountain.' So I made an ark of acacia wood, hewed two tables of stone like the first, and took them up the mountain. And the LORD wrote on the tables, as at the first writing, the ten commandments which he had spoken to you on the mountain out of the midst of the fire; and he gave them to me. I came down from the mountain, and put the tables in the ark I had made; and there they are, as the LORD commanded."

"AND NOW, ISRAEL," Moses said, "what does the LORD your God require of you, but to fear the LORD, to walk in all his ways, to love him and serve him with all your heart and with all your soul, and to keep his commandments and statutes, which I command you this day for your good? To the LORD your God belong the heavens, the earth with all that is in it; yet the LORD set his heart in love upon your fathers and chose their descendants after them, you above all peoples. Therefore be no longer stubborn. For the LORD your God is God of gods and Lord of lords, the great, the mighty, and the terrible God, who is not partial and takes no bribe. He executes justice for the fatherless and the widow, and loves the sojourner, giving him food and clothing. Love the sojourner therefore; for you were sojourners in the land of Egypt. Fear the LORD; serve him, cleave to him, and swear by his name. He is your praise; he is your God, who has done for you great and terrible things. Your fathers went down to Egypt seventy persons; and now the LORD your God has made you as the stars of heaven for multitude.

"You shall therefore love the LORD your God, and keep his commandments always, that you may live long in the land which the LORD swore to give to your fathers and their descendants, a land flowing with milk and honey. For the land you are entering is not like Egypt, where you sowed your seed and watered it with your feet, like a garden of vegetables. The land you are to possess is a land of hills and valleys, which drinks rain from heaven, a land which the LORD your God cares for; his eyes are always upon it, from the beginning to the end of the year. If you will love the LORD your God, as I command you this day, and serve him with all your heart and with all your soul, he will give rain for your land in its season, that you may gather in your grain, your wine, and your oil. He will give grass for your cattle, and you shall eat and be full. Take heed, lest your heart be deceived, and you worship other gods, kindling the anger of the LORD against you, and he shut up the heavens, so that there be no rain, and the land yield no fruit, and you perish quickly off the good land which the LORD gives you.

"When you dwell in the land of your inheritance, and you say, 'I will set a king over me, like the nations round about me'; you may indeed set as king over you him whom the LORD your God will choose, one from among your brethren, not a foreigner. Only he must not multiply horses for himself, or cause the people to return to Egypt to multiply horses, since the LORD has said to you, 'You shall never return that way again.' And he shall not multiply wives for himself, lest his heart turn away; nor shall he greatly multiply for himself silver and gold. And when he sits on the throne, he shall write for himself in a book a copy of this law. It shall be with him, and he shall read in it all the days of his life, that he may learn to fear the LORD, by keeping and doing all the words of these statutes; that his heart may not be lifted up above his brethren, and he and his children may continue long in his kingdom.

"In the land the LORD gives you, the Levitical priests shall have no inheritance with Israel; the LORD is their inheritance, as he promised them; they shall eat the offerings by fire to the LORD. From a sacrifice of ox or sheep, you shall give them the shoulder, two cheeks, and the stomach. And you shall give them the first fruits of your grain, your wine, and your oil, and the first fleece of your sheep. For the LORD has chosen them out of all your tribes, to minister in the name of the LORD for ever.

"When you come into the land the LORD gives you, do not follow the abominable practices of those nations you dispossess. There shall not be found among you any one who burns his son or daughter as an offering, or practices divination, a soothsayer, augur, sorcerer, charmer, medium, wizard, or necromancer. For whoever does these things is an abomination to the LORD;

and because of these practices the LORD your God is driving those nations out before you. They give heed to soothsayers and diviners; but as for you, the LORD your God has not allowed you so to do. You shall be blameless before the LORD.

"The LORD your God will raise up a prophet like me from among you—him you shall heed. This you desired of the LORD at Sinai on the day of the assembly, when you said, 'Let me not hear again the voice of the LORD my God, or see this great fire any more, lest I die.' And the LORD said to me, 'They have rightly spoken. I will raise up a prophet like you from among their brethren; I will put my words in his mouth, and he shall speak to them all that I command. Whoever will not give heed to my words which he shall speak in my name, I myself will require it of him. But the prophet who presumes to speak a word in my name which I have not commanded, or who speaks in the name of other gods, that same prophet shall die.' You may say in your heart, 'How can we know the word which the LORD has not spoken?' When a prophet speaks in the name of the LORD, if the word does not come to pass, that is a word the LORD has not spoken; the prophet has spoken it presumptuously, you need not be afraid of him.

"When the LORD your God cuts off the nations whose land he gives you, and you dispossess them and dwell in their cities and houses, you shall set apart three cities of refuge, by dividing into three parts the area of the land which the LORD gives you, and preparing the roads, so that the manslayer who kills his neighbor unintentionally can flee to them. And if the LORD enlarges your border—provided you keep all this commandment, by loving the LORD your God and walking ever in his ways—then you shall add three other cities to these three, lest innocent blood be shed in the land of your inheritance, and the guilt of bloodshed be upon you. But if any man hates his neighbor, lies in wait for him, attacks, and wounds him mortally, and then flees into one of these cities, the elders of his city shall fetch him, and hand him over to the avenger of blood, so that he may die. Your eye shall not pity him, but you shall purge the guilt of innocent blood from Israel.

"In the land the LORD gives you, a single witness shall not prevail against a man for any crime or offense he has committed; only on the evidence of two or three witnesses shall a charge be sustained. If a malicious witness rises against any man to accuse him of wrongdoing, then both parties to the dispute shall appear before the LORD, before the priests and judges who are in office. The judges shall inquire diligently, and if the witness has accused his brother falsely, then you shall do to him as he had meant to do to his brother; so you shall purge the evil from your midst. And the rest shall hear, and fear, and never again commit such evil. Your eye shall not pity; it shall be life for life, eye for eye, tooth for tooth, hand for hand, foot for foot.

"You shall not see your brother's ox or sheep go astray, and withhold your help; take it back to your brother. If he is not near, or if you do not know him, bring it home to your house, to be with you until he seeks it; then restore it to him. And so you shall do with his ass, his garment, or any lost thing of your brother's which you find. And if you see your brother's ass or ox fallen down by the way, help him to lift it up again. You may not withhold your help.

"A woman shall not wear anything that pertains to a man, nor shall a man put on a woman's garment; whoever does these things is an abomination to the LORD.

"If you chance upon a bird's nest, in a tree or on the ground, with the mother sitting upon the young or upon the eggs, you shall let the mother go, but the young you may take to yourself.

"When you build a new house, make a parapet for your roof, that you may not bring the guilt of blood upon your house, if any one fall from it.

"Do not sow your vineyard with two kinds of seed. Do not plow with an ox and an ass together. Do not wear a mingled stuff, wool and linen together.

"If any man takes a wife, goes in to her, and then spurns her, and charges her with shameful conduct, saying, 'I took this woman, and when I came near her, I did not find in her the tokens of virginity,' then the father and mother of the young woman shall bring out the tokens of her virginity and spread the garment before the elders of the city. And the father shall say, 'These are the tokens of my daughter's virginity.' Then the elders shall take the man and whip him; they shall fine him a hundred shekels of silver, to be given to the father of the young woman, because this man has brought an evil name upon a virgin of Israel; and she shall be his wife; he may not put her away all his days. But if the tokens of virginity are not found in the young woman, then she shall be brought to the door of her father's house, and the men of her city shall stone her to death, because she has wrought folly in Israel by playing the harlot in her father's house; so you shall purge evil from your midst.

"If a man is found lying with another man's wife, both the man who lay with her and the woman shall die; so you shall purge evil from Israel.

"If a man meets a betrothed virgin in the city and lies with her, bring them both out to the gate of that city, and stone them to death, the young woman because she did not cry for help though she was in the city, and the man because he violated his neighbor's wife. But if a man meets a betrothed young woman in the open country, seizes her, and lies with her, then only the man shall die. To the young woman you shall do nothing, for in the open country, though the woman cried for help, there was no one to rescue her.

"If a man meets a virgin who is not betrothed, seizes her, lies with her, and they are found, then he shall give to her father fifty shekels of silver, and she shall be his wife, because he has violated her; he may not put her away all his days.

"A man shall not take his father's wife, nor uncover her who is his father's.

"If a man takes a wife, and then she finds no favor in his eyes because he has found some indecency in her, let him put a bill of divorce in her hand, and send her out of his house. If she becomes another man's wife, and he also dislikes her and writes her a bill of divorce, or if he dies, then her former husband, who sent her away, may not take her again to be his wife, after she has been defiled; that is an abomination before the LORD, and you shall not bring guilt upon the land which the LORD gives you for an inheritance.

"A newly married man shall not go out with the army or be charged with any business; he shall be free at home one year, to be happy with his wife.

"If a man steals one of his brethren, and treats him as a slave or sells him, then that thief shall die; so you shall purge evil from your midst.

"When you make your neighbor a loan, do not go into his house to fetch his pledge. Stand outside, and he shall bring the pledge out to you. If he is poor, and pledges his cloak, do not sleep in it; when the sun goes down, restore it to him that he may sleep in it and bless you; and this shall be righteousness to you before the LORD.

"You shall not oppress a poor and needy hired servant, whether he is one of your brethren or a sojourner in your land; give him his hire on the day he earns it, before the sun goes down (for he is poor, and sets his heart upon it); lest he cry against you to the LORD, and it be sin in you.

"The fathers shall not be put to death for the children, nor the children for the fathers; every man shall be put to death for his own sin.

"When you reap your harvest and forget a sheaf in the field, do not go back to get it; it shall be for the sojourner, the fatherless, and the widow; that the LORD your God may bless you in all the work of your hands. When you beat your olive trees, do not go over the boughs again; when you gather the grapes of your vineyard, do not glean it afterward; what is left shall be for the sojourner, the fatherless, and the widow. Remember that you were a slave in Egypt; therefore I command you to do this.

"If there is a dispute between men, and the guilty man is condemned to be beaten, the judge shall cause him to be beaten in his presence with a number of stripes in proportion to his offense. Not more than forty stripes may be given, lest your brother be degraded in your sight.

"You shall not muzzle an ox when it treads out the grain.

"If brothers dwell together, and one dies leaving no son, the widow shall not be married outside the family; her husband's brother shall take her as his wife, and perform the duty of a husband's brother to her. The first son she bears shall succeed to the name of the brother who is dead, that his name may not be blotted out of Israel. If the man does not wish to take his brother's wife, she shall go to the elders of the city, and say, 'My husband's brother refuses to perpetuate his brother's name in Israel.' Then the elders shall speak to him; and if he persists, saying, 'I do not wish to take her,' then his brother's wife, in the presence of the elders, shall pull his sandal off his foot, spit in his face, and say, 'So shall it be done to the man who does not build up his brother's house.'

"You shall not have in your bag or in your house two kinds of measures, a large and a small. A full and just weight you shall have, a full and just measure, that your days may be prolonged in the land which the LORD your God gives you. For all who act dishonestly are an abomination to the LORD your God.

"Remember how Amalek attacked you as you came out of Egypt, when you were faint and weary. He cut off at your rear all who lagged behind you, and he did not fear God. Therefore when the LORD has given you rest from your enemies, in the land of your inheritance, you shall blot out the remembrance of Amalek from under heaven; you shall not forget."

NOW MOSES AND the elders of Israel commanded the people, saying, "On the day you pass over the Jordan to the land which the LORD your God gives you, set up large stones on Mount Ebal. Plaster them, and write upon them all the words of this law very plainly. Then build an altar of unhewn stones to the LORD your God, and make offerings. Eat there, and rejoice before the LORD."

Moses charged the people, saying, "Behold, I set before you a blessing and a curse: the blessing, if you obey the commandments of the LORD, and the curse, if you do not obey, but turn aside to go after other gods. When you have passed over the Jordan, you shall set the blessing on Mount Gerizim and the curse on Mount Ebal. These shall stand upon Mount Gerizim to bless the people: Simeon, Levi, Judah, Issachar, Joseph, and Benjamin. And these shall stand upon Mount Ebal for the curse: Reuben, Gad, Asher, Zebulun, Dan, and Naphtali. And the Levites shall declare to all Israel with a loud voice:

"'Cursed be the man who makes a graven or molten image, an abomination to the LORD, made by the hands of a craftsman, and sets it up in secret.

"'Cursed be he who dishonors his father or his mother.

"'Cursed be he who removes his neighbor's landmark.

"'Cursed be he who misleads a blind man on the road.

"'Cursed be he who perverts the justice due to the sojourner, the fatherless, and the widow.

"'Cursed be he who lies with his father's wife, because he has uncovered her who is his father's.

"'Cursed be he who lies with any kind of beast.

"'Cursed be he who lies with his sister, whether the daughter of his father or of his mother.

"'Cursed be he who lies with his mother-in-law.

"'Cursed be he who slays his neighbor in secret.

"'Cursed be he who takes a bribe to slay an innocent person.

"'Cursed be he who does not confirm the words of this law by doing them.' And all the people shall say, 'Amen.'

"If you obey the voice of the LORD your God, being careful to do all his commandments, the LORD will set you high above all nations, and these blessings shall come upon you. Blessed shall you be in the city, and in the field. Blessed shall be the fruit of your body, and of your ground, the increase of your cattle, and the young of your flock. Blessed shall be your basket and your kneading-trough. Blessed shall you be when you come in, and when you go out. The LORD will cause your enemies to be defeated. He will establish you as a people holy to himself, if you walk in his ways. All the peoples of the earth shall see that you are called by the name of the LORD; and they shall be afraid of you. The LORD will make you abound in prosperity, and will open his good treasury, the heavens, to give rain to your land in its season and to bless the work of your hands. You shall lend to many nations, but you shall not borrow. And the LORD will make you the head, not the tail; you shall tend upward only, not downward; if you obey the commandments of the LORD your God, and do not turn aside to serve other gods.

"But if you will not obey the voice of the LORD your God, then all these curses shall come upon you. Cursed shall you be in the city, and in the field. Cursed shall be your basket and your kneading-trough. Cursed shall be the fruit of your body, and of your ground, the increase of your cattle, and the young of your flock. Cursed shall you be when you come in, and when you go out. The LORD will send upon you confusion and frustration in all that you undertake, until you perish, on account of your evil doings. The heavens over your head shall be brass, and the earth under you shall be iron. The LORD will make the rain of your land powder and dust; from heaven it shall come down upon you until you are destroyed.

"The LORD will cause you to be defeated before your enemies, and you shall be a horror to all the earth's kingdoms. Your dead body shall be food for birds and beasts; and there shall be no one to frighten them away. The LORD will smite you with the boils of Egypt, and with ulcers, scurvy, and itch, of which you cannot be healed. He will afflict you with madness, blindness, and confusion of mind; you shall grope at noonday, as the blind grope in darkness; you shall not prosper; you shall be oppressed and robbed continually, and no one shall help you. You shall betroth a wife, and another man shall lie with her; you shall build a house, and not dwell in it; you shall plant a vineyard, and not use its fruit. Your ox shall be slain before your eyes, and you shall not eat of it; your ass shall be violently taken away, and not be restored to you; your sheep shall be given to your enemies, and no one shall help you. Your sons and daughters shall be given to another people, while your eyes look on and fail with longing for them; and it shall not be in your power to prevent it. The sojourner among you shall mount above you higher and higher, and you shall come down lower and lower. He shall lend to you, and you shall not lend to him; he shall be the head and you shall be the tail. All these curses shall come upon you and destroy you, because you did not obey the voice of the LORD your God. They shall be upon you as a sign and a wonder, and upon your descendants for ever.

"Because you did not serve the LORD your God with joyfulness, by reason of the abundance of all things, therefore you shall serve your enemies in hunger, thirst, and nakedness. The LORD will bring a nation against you from afar, a nation of stern countenance, whose language you do not understand, who shall not regard the person of the old or show favor to the young, and shall eat the offspring of your cattle and the fruit of your ground. That nation

shall besiege your towns, until your high fortified walls come down. In your
distress you shall eat the offspring of your own body, the flesh of your sons
and daughters. Whereas you were a multitude as the stars of heaven, you
shall be left few in number. The LORD will scatter you among all peoples,
from one end of the earth to the other; and there you shall serve other gods.
Among these nations you shall find no ease, and have no assurance for your
life. The LORD will give you a trembling heart, failing eyes, and a languishing
soul; night and day you shall be in dread. In the morning you shall say,
'Would it were evening!' and at evening you shall say, 'Would it were morning!' because of the fear in your heart, and the sights your eyes shall see. And
the LORD will bring you back in ships to Egypt, a journey I promised you
should never make again; there you shall offer yourselves for sale to your
enemies as slaves, but no man will buy you."

THESE ARE THE words of the covenant which the LORD commanded Moses to
make with the people of Israel in the land of Moab, besides the covenant he
had made with them at Sinai. Summoning all Israel, Moses said, "You have
seen all that the LORD did before your eyes. The secret things belong to the
LORD our God; but the things that are revealed belong to us and our children
for ever, that we may do all the words of this law.

"And when all these things come upon you, the blessing and the curse, and
you call them to mind among the nations where the LORD has driven you, and
return to the LORD your God, you and your children, obeying his voice in all
that I command you this day, then the LORD will restore your fortunes, have
compassion upon you, and gather you again from where he has scattered you.
From the uttermost parts of heaven he will fetch you, and bring you into the
land which your fathers possessed. He will make you abundantly prosperous
in all the work of your hand, and in the fruit of your body, your cattle, and
your ground; for the LORD will again take delight in prospering you, if you
keep his commandments and turn to him with all your heart and with all your
soul.

"For this commandment is not too hard for you, neither is it far off. It is not
in heaven, that you should say, 'Who will go up to heaven, and bring it to us,
that we may hear it and do it?' Neither is it beyond the sea, that you should
say, 'Who will go over the sea, and bring it to us, that we may hear it and do
it?' But the word is very near you; it is in your mouth and in your heart, so
that you can do it.

"See, I have set before you life and good, death and evil. If you obey the
commandments of the LORD your God, by loving him and walking in his
ways, then you shall live and multiply, and the LORD your God will bless you.
But if your heart turns away, and you will not hear, but worship other gods,
you shall perish; you shall not live long in the land which you are going over
the Jordan to enter and possess. I call heaven and earth to witness this day,
that I have set before you life and death, blessing and curse; therefore choose

life, loving the LORD your God, obeying his voice, and cleaving to him, that you and your descendants may live long in the land which the LORD swore to your fathers, to Abraham, Isaac, and Jacob, to give them."

THEN MOSES SAID to all Israel, "I am a hundred and twenty years old this day; I am no longer able to go out and come in. The LORD has said to me, 'You shall not go over this Jordan.' The LORD your God himself will go over before you, destroying nations, so that you shall dispossess them; and Joshua will go over at your head. Be of good courage, for the LORD goes with you; he will not fail you or forsake you."

When Moses had finished writing the words of the law in a book, he said to the Levites, "Take this book of the law, and put it by the side of the ark of the covenant of the LORD your God, that it may be there for a witness against you. Every seven years, during the feast of booths, when all Israel appears before the LORD at the place which he will choose, you shall read this law. Assemble the people, men, women, little ones, and the sojourner within your towns, that they may hear and learn to fear the LORD, and do all the words of this law. For I know how rebellious and stubborn you are today, while I am yet with you; how much more after my death!"

And the LORD said to Moses, "Behold, the days approach when you must die; call Joshua, and present yourselves in the tent of meeting, that I may commission him." Moses and Joshua presented themselves, and the LORD appeared by the door of the tent of meeting in a pillar of cloud. The LORD commissioned Joshua, saying, "Be strong and of good courage; for you shall bring the children of Israel into the land which I swore to give them: I will be with you."

To Moses the LORD said, "You are about to sleep with your fathers; then this people will play the harlot after strange gods, and forsake me and break my covenant. My anger will be kindled against them, and many troubles will come upon them. 'Have not these evils come upon us,' they will say, 'because our God is not among us?' And I will surely hide my face in that day, because they have turned to other gods. Now therefore write this song, and teach it to the people; put it in their mouths, that it may be a witness for me against the people of Israel. For I know the purposes they are already forming, before I have brought them into the land flowing with milk and honey. When they have eaten and grown fat, they will despise me and break my covenant. And when many evils have come upon them, this song shall confront them as a witness, living unforgotten in the mouths of their descendants." So Moses wrote this song the same day, and taught it to the people of Israel, saying, "Give ear, O heavens, and let the earth hear my words. May my speech distil as the dew, and my teaching drop as gentle rain upon the tender grass. For I will proclaim the name of the LORD. He is the Rock, his work is perfect; for all his ways are justice. A God of faithfulness is he, without iniquity.

"They have dealt corruptly with him; no longer his children because of

their blemish, they are a perverse and crooked generation. Do you thus re-
quite the LORD, you senseless people? Is he not your father, who created you?
Remember the days of old; ask your elders, and they will tell you. When the
Most High gave the nations their inheritance, he separated the sons of men,
and fixed the bounds of the peoples according to the number of the sons of
God. But the LORD's portion is his people, Jacob his allotted heritage.

"He found him in a desert land, a howling waste of wilderness; he encircled him, cared for him as the apple of his eye. Like an eagle that flutters over
its young, spreading out its wings, catching them, bearing them on its pinions, the LORD alone did lead him; no foreign god was with him. He made him
ride on the high places of the earth, eat the produce of the field, and suck
honey out of the rock.

"But Israel waxed fat, grew thick, became sleek; then he forsook God who
made him, and scoffed at the Rock of his salvation.

"The LORD saw it, and said, 'I will hide my face from them, and see what
their end will be, for they are children in whom there is no faithfulness. They
have provoked me with their idols. I will provoke them with a foolish nation.
For a fire is kindled by my anger; it devours the earth, and sets on fire the
foundations of the mountains. I will heap evils upon them; they shall be
wasted with hunger, devoured with poisonous pestilence; I will send the
teeth of beasts, the venom of crawling things against them. In the open the
sword shall bereave, and in the chambers terror shall destroy young man and
virgin, the sucking child, and the man of gray hairs. I would have said, "I will
scatter them afar, and make remembrance of them cease among men," had I
not feared, lest their adversaries should judge amiss, saying, "Our hand is
triumphant, the LORD has not wrought all this."'

"For they are a nation void of counsel, with no understanding. If they were
wise, they would discern their latter end! How should one chase a thousand,
and two put ten thousand to flight, unless their Rock had sold them, and the
LORD had given them up? For the rock of our enemies is not as our Rock.
Their vine comes from the vine of Sodom, and the fields of Gomorrah; their
grapes are grapes of poison; their wine is the cruel venom of asps. But the day
of their calamity is at hand. For the LORD will vindicate his people and have
compassion, when he sees that their power is gone. Then he will say, 'Where
are the gods who ate the fat of your sacrifices, and drank the wine of your
drink offering? Let them rise up and be your protection! See now that I, even
I, am he, and there is no god beside me; I kill and I make alive; I wound and I
heal; none can deliver out of my hand. For I lift up my hand to heaven, and
swear, As I live for ever, I will take vengeance on my adversaries. I will make
my arrows drunk with the blood of the slain and the captives, and my sword
shall devour flesh.'

"Praise his people, O you nations; for he avenges the blood of his servants,
and makes expiation for the land of his people."

When Moses had finished reciting this song to the people of Israel, he said,

"Lay to heart all the words which I enjoin upon you this day, that you may command them to your children. For this law is no trifle for you; it is your life, and thereby you shall live long in the land you are going over the Jordan to possess."

THE LORD SAID to Moses that very day, "Ascend this mountain of the Abarim, Mount Nebo, in the land of Moab, opposite Jericho, and view the land of Canaan. Because you broke faith with me in the midst of the people of Israel at the waters of Meribah, and did not revere me as holy, you shall not go into the land I give to the people of Israel. You shall die on the mountain and be gathered to your people, as Aaron your brother died on Mount Hor."

This is the blessing with which Moses the man of God blessed the children of Israel before his death: "The LORD came from Sinai, and shone forth from Paran; he came from the ten thousands of holy ones. Yea, he loved his people; those consecrated to him were in his hand, following in his steps, receiving direction from him, when Moses commanded a law. Thus the LORD became king in Israel."

Of Reuben he said, "Let Reuben live, and not die, nor let his men be few." And this he said of Judah, "Hear, O LORD, the voice of Judah; bring him in to his people, and be a help against his adversaries." Of Levi he said, "Levi, who has observed thy word, and kept thy covenant, shall teach Israel thy law, and put incense and burnt offering upon thy altar. Bless, O LORD, his substance, and accept the work of his hands; crush those that hate him, that they rise not again." And of Benjamin he said, "The beloved of the LORD dwells in safety by him; the LORD encompasses him, and makes his dwelling between his shoulders."

Of Joseph he said, "Blessed by the LORD be his land, with the choicest gifts of heaven above, and of the deep that couches beneath, with the choicest fruits of the sun, the abundance of the everlasting hills, and the favor of him that dwelt in the bush. Let these come upon the head of Joseph, prince among his brothers. His firstling bull has majesty, and his horns are the horns of a wild ox; with them he shall push the peoples to the ends of the earth; such are the ten thousands of Ephraim, and the thousands of Manasseh."

Of Zebulun and Issachar he said, "Rejoice, Zebulun, in your going out; and Issachar, in your tents. They shall offer right sacrifices; for they suck the affluence of the seas and the hidden treasures of the sand." Of Gad he said, "Blessed be he who enlarges Gad! He chose the best of the land for himself, a commander's portion, and with Israel he executed the commands and just decrees of the LORD." Of Dan he said, "Dan is a lion's whelp, that leaps forth from Bashan." Of Naphtali he said, "O Naphtali, full of the blessing of the LORD, possess the lake and the south." And of Asher he said, "Blessed be Asher, favorite of his brothers; let him dip his foot in oil. Your bars shall be iron and bronze; and as your days, so shall your strength be.

"There is none like God, O Israel, who rides through the heavens to your help. The eternal God is your dwelling place, and underneath are the everlasting arms. He thrust out the enemy before you, and Israel dwelt in safety, in a land of grain and wine; yea, his heavens drop down dew. Happy are you, O Israel! Who is like you, a people saved by the LORD, the shield of your help, and sword of your triumph! Your enemies shall come fawning to you, and you shall tread upon their high places."

Then Moses went up from the plains of Moab to Mount Nebo, to the top of Pisgah, which is opposite Jericho. And the LORD showed him all the land, Gilead as far as Dan, all Naphtali, the land of Ephraim and Manasseh, all Judah as far as the Western Sea, the Negeb, and the valley of Jericho the city of palm trees, as far as Zoar. And the LORD said to him, "This is the land I swore to give to the descendants of Abraham, Isaac, and Jacob. I have let you see it, but you shall not go over there." So Moses the servant of the LORD died there, according to the word of the LORD, and the LORD buried him in the valley in the land of Moab; but no man knows the place of his burial to this day. Moses was a hundred and twenty years old when he died; his eye was not dim, nor his natural force abated. And the people of Israel wept for Moses in the plains of Moab thirty days; then the days of mourning ended.

And Joshua the son of Nun was full of the spirit of wisdom, for Moses had laid his hands upon him; so the people of Israel obeyed Joshua, as the LORD had commanded. There has not arisen a prophet since in Israel like Moses, whom the LORD knew face to face, none like him for all the signs and wonders which the LORD sent him to do in the land of Egypt, and for all the mighty power and all the great and terrible deeds which Moses wrought in the sight of all Israel.

JOSHUA

With the passing of Moses, Joshua assumes leadership of the Israelites. This book tells how, under Joshua, the land of Canaan is conquered and divided among the twelve tribes. It is thus a sequel to Deuteronomy, tracing the history of the Israelites up to the death of Joshua. Its better-known incidents are the hiding of Israelite spies in Jericho by Rahab the harlot, the miraculous crossing of the Jordan, the fall of Jericho, and the deception practiced by the Gibeonites in order to become allies of the Israelites. Just before his death, the aged Joshua gathers all Israel about him in a solemn assembly at Shechem, where the people take upon themselves a covenant with the Lord similar to the one their forebears accepted at Mount Sinai.

The general impression conveyed by the book as a whole is that of a complete conquest of Canaan by Israel within a period of a few years. The Book of Judges, however, suggests that in reality the conquest was somewhat slower, rather confused, and not complete. Although some of the book's sources may date from the ninth century B.C. or even earlier, it probably did not reach its present form until the sixth century B.C. or later. Its compilers were also the final editors of Judges, 1 and 2 Samuel, and 1 and 2 Kings.

AFTER THE DEATH of Moses the servant of the Lord, the Lord said to Joshua the son of Nun, Moses' minister, "Moses my servant is dead; now therefore arise, go over this Jordan, you and all this people, into the land which I am giving to them. Every place that the sole of your foot will tread upon I have given to you, as I promised to Moses. From the wilderness and this Lebanon as far as the river Euphrates, to the Great Sea toward the going down of the sun shall be your territory. No man shall be able to stand before you all the days of your life; as I was with Moses, so I will be with you; I will not fail you or forsake you. Be strong and of good courage; for you shall cause this people to inherit the land which I swore to give them. Only be strong, and be careful to keep all the law which Moses my servant commanded you; turn not from it to the right hand or to the left. This book of the law shall not depart out of your mouth, but you shall meditate on it day and night, that you may be careful to do according to all that is written in it; for then you shall make your way prosperous, and then you shall have good success. Have I not commanded you? Be not frightened, neither be dismayed; for the LORD your God is with you wherever you go."

Joshua then sent two men secretly from Israel's camp at Shittim as spies. "Go, view the land," he said, "especially Jericho." The two went, and coming to the house of a harlot whose name was Rahab, they lodged there. When the king of Jericho heard that certain men of Israel had come as spies, he sent to Rahab, saying, "Bring forth the men who entered your house; for they have come to search out the land." But the woman had hidden them. "True, men came to me," she said, "but I did not know where they came from, and when the gate was to be closed, at dark, they went out. Where they went I do not know; pursue them quickly, for you will overtake them." When the king's men left, Rahab went up to the roof where she had hidden the men with stalks of flax, and she said, "I know that the LORD has given you the land, and fear has fallen upon us, and all the inhabitants melt away before you. We have heard how the LORD dried up the water of the Red Sea when you came out of Egypt, and how you utterly destroyed the two kings beyond the Jordan, Sihon and Og. As soon as we heard it, our hearts melted, and there was no courage left in any man; for the LORD your God is he who is God in heaven above and on earth beneath. Now then, swear to me by the LORD that as I have dealt kindly with you, you also will deal kindly with my father's house, and spare my father and mother, my brothers and sisters, and all who belong to them." And the men said, "Our life for yours! If you do not tell this business of ours, we will deal kindly and faithfully with you when the LORD gives us the land."

She let them down by a rope through the window, for her house was built into the city wall. "Go into the hills," she said, "lest the pursuers meet you. Hide yourselves there three days; then you may go your way." The men said, "We will be guiltless with respect to the oath you have made us swear. Behold, when we come into the land, bind this scarlet cord in the window through which you let us down, and gather into your house all your father's household. If any one goes into the street, his blood shall be upon his head, and we shall be guiltless; but if a hand is laid upon any one who is with you in the house, his blood shall be on our head." She said, "According to your words, so be it," and she bound the scarlet cord in the window.

After three days in the hills, the men returned to Joshua, and told him all that had befallen them. "Truly the LORD has given the land into our hands," they said, "and moreover all the inhabitants are fainthearted because of us."

Early in the morning Joshua set out from Shittim, with the people of Israel; they came to the Jordan, and lodged there before they passed over. At the end of three days the officers went through the camp and commanded the people,

"When you see the ark of the covenant of the LORD your God being carried by the Levitical priests, set out and follow it, that you may know the way you shall go, for you have not passed this way before. Keep a space between you and the ark, a distance of about a thousand yards; do not come near it." And Joshua said to the people, "Sanctify yourselves; for tomorrow the LORD will do wonders among you."

The LORD said to Joshua, "Command the priests who bear the ark, 'When you come to the brink of the waters, stand still in the Jordan.'"

Joshua said to the people, "Come hither, and hear the words of the LORD your God. Hereby you shall know that the living God is among you, and that he will without fail drive out the inhabitants of the land. Behold, the ark of the covenant of the Lord of all the earth is to pass before you into the Jordan. When the soles of the feet of the priests who bear the ark shall rest in the Jordan, the waters shall be stopped from flowing."

The people set out from their tents to pass over the Jordan, and when the feet of the priests were dipped in the water (the Jordan overflows all its banks throughout the time of harvest), the waters coming down from above rose up in a heap far off, at the city of Adam, and those flowing down toward the Salt Sea were wholly cut off. The people passed over opposite Jericho on dry ground, while the priests stood in the midst of the Jordan.

When all the nation had finished passing over, the LORD said to Joshua, "Appoint twelve men from the people, from each tribe a man, and command them, 'Take twelve stones from the midst of the Jordan, and carry them with you.'" Joshua appointed the twelve men, and said to them, "Pass into the midst of the Jordan, and take up each of you a stone upon his shoulder, according to the number of the tribes of the people of Israel." And the men of Israel did as Joshua commanded. Then the LORD said to Joshua, "Command the priests who bear the ark to come up out of the Jordan." When the priests came up, the waters of the Jordan returned to their place and overflowed its banks, as before. On that day the LORD exalted Joshua in the sight of all Israel; and they stood in awe of him, as they had stood in awe of Moses, all the days of his life.

The people came up out of the Jordan on the tenth day of the first month, and encamped in Gilgal on the east border of Jericho. There Joshua set up the twelve stones from the Jordan, saying, "When your children ask their fathers in time to come, 'What do these stones mean?' you shall say, 'Israel passed over this Jordan on dry ground.' For the LORD your God dried up the waters of the Jordan for you, as he dried up the Red Sea for us, so that all the peoples of the earth may know that the hand of the LORD is mighty; that you may fear the LORD your God for ever." While the people of Israel were encamped in Gilgal they kept the passover on the fourteenth day of the month at evening in the plains of Jericho. On the morrow they ate of the produce of the land, unleavened cakes and parched grain. The manna ceased, and the people ate of the fruit of the land of Canaan.

WHEN JOSHUA WAS BY JERICHO, he lifted up his eyes, and behold, a man stood before him with drawn sword. "Are you for us, or for our adversaries?" Joshua asked. "As commander of the army of the LORD I have now come," he said. Joshua fell on his face to the earth, and worshiped.

Now Jericho was shut up from within and without because of the people of Israel; none went out, and none came in. And the LORD said to Joshua, "See, I have given into your hand Jericho, with its king and mighty men of valor. All your men of war shall march around the city once, for six days. Seven priests shall bear seven trumpets of rams' horns before the ark; and on the seventh day you shall march around the city seven times, the priests blowing the trumpets. When they make a long blast with the ram's horn, all the people shall shout with a great shout; and the wall of the city will fall down flat." So Joshua commanded the priests and the people, and they went forward, the trumpets blowing continually. "You shall not let your voice be heard," Joshua commanded, "until the day I bid you shout; then you shall shout." So he caused the ark of the LORD to compass the city, going about it once, and thus they did for six days.

On the seventh day they rose at dawn, and marched around the city in the same manner seven times. At the seventh time, when the priests had blown a long blast with the trumpets, Joshua said to the people, "Shout; for the LORD has given you the city. All within it shall be devoted to the LORD for destruction; only Rahab the harlot and her household shall live, because she hid the messengers that we sent. But you, keep yourselves from the things devoted to destruction, lest you take any and bring trouble upon the camp of Israel. All silver and gold, and vessels of bronze and iron, are sacred to the LORD; they shall go into the LORD's treasury." So the people raised a great shout, and the wall fell down flat, and they went up into the city, and took it.

Then Joshua said to the two men who had spied out the land, "Go into the harlot's house, and bring out the woman, and all who belong to her, as you swore." So they brought out Rahab and her kindred, and set them outside the camp of Israel. Then they utterly destroyed all in the city, both men and women, young and old, oxen, sheep, and asses, with the edge of the sword, and they burned the city, and all within it. Only the silver and gold, and the vessels of bronze and iron, they put into the treasury of the house of the LORD. Thus Joshua saved Rahab and her kindred, and she dwelt in Israel, because she hid the spies whom Joshua sent. And Joshua pronounced an oath: "Cursed before the LORD be the man that rises up and rebuilds this city, Jericho. At the cost of his first-born shall he lay its foundation, and at the cost of his youngest son shall he set up its gates."

So the LORD was with Joshua; and his fame was in all the land.

BUT THE PEOPLE of Israel broke faith; for Achan the son of Carmi, son of Zabdi, son of Zerah, of the tribe of Judah, took some of the devoted things; and the anger of the LORD burned against Israel.

Joshua sent men from Jericho to Ai, east of Bethel, to spy out the land. On their return they said, "Let about two or three thousand men go up and attack Ai; do not make the whole people toil up there, for they are but few." So about three thousand went up; but they fled before the men of Ai, who killed about thirty-six of them, and chased them as far as Shebarim, and slew them. The hearts of the people melted, and became as water. Joshua rent his clothes, and fell upon his face before the ark, he and the elders of Israel; and they put dust upon their heads. "Alas, O Lord GOD," Joshua said, "why hast thou brought this people over the Jordan at all, to give us into the hands of our enemies? Would that we had been content to dwell beyond the Jordan! O LORD, what can I say, when Israel has turned their backs before their enemies! The Canaanites and all the inhabitants of the land will hear of it, and will surround us, and cut off our name from the earth; and what wilt thou do for thy great name?"

The LORD said to Joshua, "Arise, why have you thus fallen upon your face? Israel has transgressed my covenant; they have taken some of the devoted things. I will be with you no more, unless you destroy the devoted things from among you. Up, sanctify the people, and say, 'Thus says the LORD, God of Israel, "There are devoted things in the midst of you; you cannot stand before your enemies, until you take them away." In the morning therefore you shall be brought near by your tribes and families and households; and the household which the LORD chooses shall come near, man by man. He who is found with the devoted things shall be burned, he and all that he has, because he has transgressed the covenant of the LORD, and done a shameful thing in Israel.'"

In the morning Joshua brought Israel near, tribe by tribe, and the tribe of Judah was chosen by the sacred lot; he brought near the families of Judah, and the family of the Zerahites was chosen; he brought near the Zerahites, and the household of Zabdi was chosen; he brought near his household, man by man, and Achan the son of Carmi was chosen. "My son," Joshua said to Achan, "give glory to the LORD God of Israel, and tell me now what you have done; do not hide it from me." Achan answered, "Of a truth I have sinned against the LORD. When I saw among the spoil a beautiful mantle from Babylon, and two hundred shekels of silver, and a bar of gold weighing fifty shekels, I coveted them, and took them. They are hidden in the earth inside my tent." Joshua sent messengers to the tent, and they found the devoted things and brought them. Then Joshua, and all Israel with him, took Achan, with the silver, the mantle, the bar of gold, his sons and daughters, his oxen, asses, and sheep, his tent, and all that he had, and they brought them to the Valley of Achor. And Joshua said, "Why did you bring trouble on us? The LORD brings trouble on you today." And all Israel stoned them and burned them. They raised over Achan a great heap of stones that remains to this day; then the LORD turned from his burning anger.

The LORD said to Joshua, "Do not fear or be dismayed; take all the fighting men with you, and go up to Ai; see, I have given into your hand the king, and his people, his city, and his land; you shall do to Ai as you did to Jericho; only its spoil and its cattle you shall take as booty for yourselves. Lay an ambush against the city, behind it." So Joshua chose thirty thousand men, and sent them forth by night. "Lie in ambush against the city, behind it," he commanded. "Hold yourselves in readiness; I, and all the people who are with me, will approach the city. When they come out against us, as before, we shall flee, and they will come after us. Then you shall rise up from the ambush, and seize the city; for the LORD your God will give it into your hand. When you have taken the city, set it on fire, doing as the LORD has bidden." So they went to the place of ambush, to the west of Ai.

Early in the morning Joshua mustered the people, and they encamped on the north side of the city, with a ravine between them and Ai. When the king of Ai saw this, he and his men hastened to meet Israel in battle. Joshua and his men made a pretense of being beaten, and fled, so all in the city were called together to pursue them. There was not a man left in Ai, and they left the city open. Then the LORD said to Joshua, "Stretch out your javelin toward Ai; for I will give it into your hand." Joshua stretched out his javelin, and the men in ambush rose quickly, taking the city and setting it on fire. The men of Ai looked back, and saw the smoke of the city rising to heaven; but they had no power to flee this way or that, for when Joshua and his men saw the smoke, they turned back against the men of Ai, and the others came forth from the city against them. So they were in the midst of Israel, some on this side, and some on that side; and Israel smote them until none survived or escaped. But the king of Ai they took alive, and brought to Joshua.

All Israel returned to Ai, and smote it with the edge of the sword. Those who fell that day, both men and women, were twelve thousand, all the people of Ai. For Joshua did not draw back his javelin until he had utterly destroyed all the inhabitants. The cattle and the spoil Israel took as their booty, according to the word of the LORD. So Joshua burned Ai, and made it for ever a heap of ruins, as it is to this day. He hanged the king of Ai on a tree until evening, when they took his body down, and cast it at the entrance of the city, and raised over it a great heap of stones, which stands there to this day.

Then, on Mount Ebal, Joshua built an altar to the LORD of unhewn stones, as Moses had commanded, and they made burnt offerings, and sacrificed peace offerings. In the presence of the people, Joshua wrote upon the stones a copy of the law of Moses. All Israel, with elders, officers, and judges, stood on opposite sides of the ark, facing the Levitical priests who carried it. Half of them stood in front of Mount Gerizim and half of them in front of Mount Ebal, as Moses had commanded. Afterward Joshua read all the words of the law, the blessing and the curse, before the assembly of Israel.

WHEN THE INHABITANTS of Gibeon heard what Joshua had done to Jericho and to Ai, they acted with cunning. They made ready dry and moldy provisions, and put worn-out sacks and mended wineskins upon their asses. Wearing patched sandals and worn-out clothes, they went to Joshua in the camp at Gilgal. "We are your servants," they said. "Come now, make a covenant with us." But the men of Israel said, "Perhaps you live among us; then how can we make a covenant with you? Who are you? And where do you come from?" They replied, "From a very far country your servants have come, because we have heard all that the LORD your God did in Egypt, and all that he did to the two kings, Sihon and Og. Here is our bread. It was still warm when we took it from our houses, but now, behold, it is dry and moldy. These wineskins were new when we filled them, and behold, they are burst. These garments and shoes of ours are worn out from the very long journey." So the men of Israel partook of their provisions, and did not ask direction from the LORD. Joshua made peace with them, and a covenant, and the leaders of the congregation swore to them.

Then, three days later, the people of Israel heard that the Gibeonites were their neighbors. They set out and reached their cities on the third day, but they did not kill them, because the leaders had sworn to them by the LORD. When the congregation of Israel murmured, the leaders said, "We have sworn to them by the LORD, and now we may not touch them, lest wrath be upon us."

Summoning the inhabitants of Gibeon, Joshua said, "Why did you deceive us? Now therefore you are cursed, and some of you shall always be slaves, hewers of wood and drawers of water for the house of my God." They answered, "Because we were told for a certainty that the LORD your God had commanded his servant Moses to give you all the land, and to destroy all the inhabitants, we feared greatly for our lives. Now, behold, we are in your hand: do to us as it seems good and right in your sight." So Joshua made them hewers of wood and drawers of water for the house of the LORD.

WHEN ADONIZEDEK KING of Jerusalem heard how Joshua had taken Ai, and how the inhabitants of Gibeon had made peace with Israel, he feared greatly, because Gibeon was a great city, greater than Ai, and all its men were mighty. So he sent to the Amorite kings of Hebron, Jarmuth, Lachish, and Eglon, saying, "Come up and help me, and let us smite Gibeon; for it has made peace with the people of Israel." Then these five kings gathered their forces, and went up to make war against Gibeon.

The Gibeonites sent to Joshua at the camp in Gilgal for help. So, with all the mighty men of valor, he went up. And the LORD said to Joshua, "Do not fear them, for I have given them into your hands; there shall not a man of them stand before you." Having marched all night from Gilgal, Joshua came upon them suddenly. And the LORD threw them into a panic before Israel, who slew them with a great slaughter at Gibeon, and chased them by the way of the ascent of Beth-horon. As they fled, the LORD threw great stones from heaven upon them, and they died; more died because of the hailstones than by the sword.

Then Joshua spoke to the LORD in the sight of Israel, "Sun, stand thou still at Gibeon, and thou Moon in the valley of Aijalon." And the sun stood still, and the moon stayed, until the nation took vengeance on their enemies. Is this not written in the Book of Jashar? The sun stayed in the midst of heaven, and did not hasten to go down for about a whole day. There has been no day like it before or since, when the LORD hearkened to the voice of a man; for the LORD fought for Israel.

The five kings fled, and hid themselves in the cave at Makkedah. "Roll great stones against the mouth of the cave," Joshua said, "and set men to guard it. Then pursue your enemies, and do not let them enter their cities; for the LORD your God has given them into your hand." When Joshua and the men of Israel had finished slaying all of them, except the remnant which had entered into the fortified cities, they returned to Makkedah; not a man moved his tongue against any of the people of Israel.

Then Joshua said, "Bring those five kings out to me from the cave," and he summoned all the men of Israel. To the chiefs of war he said, "Come near, put your feet upon the necks of these kings." They did so, and Joshua said, "Do not be afraid or dismayed; be strong and of good courage; for thus the LORD will do to all your enemies against whom you fight." Afterward Joshua put the kings to death, and hung them on five trees. At the going down of the sun, at Joshua's command, they took them down, threw them into the cave where they had hidden, and set great stones against the mouth of the cave, which remain to this very day. Then Joshua took Makkedah, and smote it and its king with the edge of the sword until none remained.

So Joshua defeated the southern hill country and utterly destroyed all that breathed, as the LORD God of Israel commanded. Then he returned, and all Israel with him, to the camp at Gilgal.

WHEN THE KING of Hazor heard of this, he sent to the kings in the northern hill country. They came out, with all their troops, a great host, in number like the sand upon the seashore, with very many horses and chariots, and joined their forces at the waters of Merom, to fight with Israel. The LORD said to Joshua, "Do not be afraid of them, for tomorrow at this time I will give over all of them, slain, to Israel; you shall hamstring their horses, and burn their chariots." So Joshua came suddenly with all his people of war by the waters of Merom, and fell upon them. The LORD gave them into the hand of Israel, who smote them until they left none remaining. Joshua did as the LORD bade; he hamstrung their horses, and burned their chariots. Then he took their cities, and smote them with the edge of the sword, utterly destroying them, as Moses had commanded. The people of Israel took the spoil of these cities and the cattle for their booty.

Joshua made war a long time; for there was not a city that made peace with the people of Israel, except Gibeon. It was the LORD's doing to harden their hearts that they should come against Israel in battle, in order that they should be utterly destroyed, and receive no mercy. At that time Joshua came and wiped out the Anakim, a people great and tall, from the hill country. Only in Gaza, in Gath, and in Ashdod did some remain. So Joshua took the whole land, according to all that the LORD had spoken to Moses; and Joshua gave it for an inheritance to Israel. And the land had rest from war.

JOSHUA SUMMONED THE Reubenites, the Gadites, and the half-tribe of Manasseh, and said to them, "You have kept all that Moses and I have commanded you; you have not forsaken your brethren these many days, but have been careful to keep the charge of the LORD your God. Now the LORD has given rest to your brethren, as he promised them; therefore turn and go to your home in the land which Moses gave you on the other side of the Jordan. Take good care to observe the commandment and the law which Moses commanded you, to love the LORD your God, to walk in all his ways, to keep his commandments, to cleave to him, and to serve him with all your heart and with all your soul." So the Reubenites, the Gadites, and the half-tribe of Manasseh returned home, parting from the people of Israel at Shiloh, in Canaan, to go to Gilead, their own land.

When they came to the region about the Jordan, they built an altar of great size at the frontier, on the side that belongs to Israel. The people of Israel heard of it, and gathered at Shiloh, to make war. They sent Phinehas the son of Eleazar the priest, and with him ten chiefs, to say, "What is this treachery which you have committed, by building yourselves an altar in rebellion against the LORD? Have we not had enough of the sin at Peor from which even yet we have not cleansed ourselves, and for which there came a plague? If you rebel against the LORD today, he will be angry with the whole congregation of Israel tomorrow. But now, if your land is unclean, pass over into the LORD's land where the LORD's tabernacle stands, and take for yourselves a possession among us; only do not rebel, or make us as rebels by building yourselves an altar other than the altar of the LORD our God. Did not Achan break faith in the matter of the devoted things, and bring wrath upon all the congregation of Israel? And he did not perish alone for his iniquity."

Then the Reubenites, the Gadites, and the half-tribe of Manasseh said, "The Mighty One, God, the LORD! He knows; and let Israel itself know! If it was in rebellion or in breach of faith toward the LORD, spare us not today for building an altar; or if we did so to make offerings, may the LORD himself take vengeance. Nay, but we did it from fear that in time to come your children might say to our children, 'What have you to do with the LORD, the God of Israel? For the LORD has made the Jordan a boundary between us and you; you have no portion in the LORD.' So your children might make our children cease to worship the LORD. Therefore we said, 'Let us now build an altar, not for offerings or sacrifice, but to be a witness between us and you, and between the generations after us, that we do perform the service of the LORD in his presence.' If it should be said to us or to our descendants, 'You have no portion in the LORD,' we should say, 'Behold the copy of the altar of the LORD, which our fathers made, to be a witness between us and you.' Far be it from us that we should turn away from following the LORD by building an altar other than the altar of the LORD our God that stands before his tabernacle!"

When Phinehas and the others heard these words, it pleased them well. "Today we know that the LORD is in the midst of us," Phinehas said, "because you have not committed this treachery against the LORD; now you have saved the people of Israel from the hand of the LORD." Then Phinehas and the chiefs returned, and their report pleased the people, who blessed God and spoke no more of making war.

A LONG TIME afterward, when the LORD had given rest to Israel, Joshua summoned all the people, their elders, judges, and officers, and he said, "I am now well advanced in years; and you have seen all that the LORD your God has done to these nations for your sake. Behold, I have allotted to you as an inheritance those nations that remain, along with all the nations that I have already cut off, from the Jordan to the Great Sea in the west. The LORD will push them back before you, and you shall possess their land, as the LORD promised you. Therefore keep the law of Moses, turning aside from it neither to the right hand nor to the left; cleave to the LORD your God as you have done to this day. No man has been able to withstand you. One man of you puts to flight a thousand, since it is the LORD who fights for you, as he promised. Therefore love the LORD your God. For if you turn back, and join the remnant of these nations, and make marriages with them, know assuredly that the LORD will not continue to drive them out; but they shall be a snare and a trap for you, a scourge on your sides, and thorns in your eyes, till you perish from off this good land which the LORD has given you. Now I am about to go the way of all the earth, and you know in your hearts and souls, all of you, that not one thing has failed of all the good things which the LORD your God promised you."

THEN JOSHUA GATHERED the tribes of Israel to Shechem, and they presented themselves before God. And Joshua said to the people, "Thus says the LORD, the God of Israel, 'Your fathers lived of old beyond the Euphrates, and they served other gods. Then I took Abraham from beyond the River and led him through all the land of Canaan, and made his offspring many. I gave him Isaac; and to Isaac I gave Jacob and Esau. I gave Esau the hill country of Seir to possess, but Jacob and his children went down to Egypt. I sent Moses and Aaron, and I plagued Egypt; and afterwards I brought you out. You lived in the wilderness a long time. Then I brought you to the land of the Amorites, who lived east of the Jordan; they fought with you, and I gave them into your hand, and you took possession of their land. Then Balak king of Moab arose and fought against Israel; and he invited Balaam the son of Beor to curse you, but I would not listen to Balaam; therefore he blessed you; so I delivered you out of his hand. You went over the Jordan, and the inhabitants of the land fought against you. I sent the hornet before you, which drove them out; it was not by your sword or by your bow. I gave you a land on which you had not labored, and cities which you had not built, and you dwell therein; you eat the fruit of vineyards and oliveyards which you did not plant.' Now therefore fear the LORD, and serve him in sincerity and in faithfulness. If you be unwilling to serve the LORD, choose this day whom you will serve, whether the gods your fathers served in the region beyond the River, or the gods of the peoples in whose land you dwell; but as for me and my house, we will serve the LORD."

The people answered, "Far be it from us that we should forsake the LORD, to serve other gods; for it is the LORD our God who brought us from the land of Egypt, out of the house of bondage, and who did those great signs in our sight, and preserved us in all the way that we went, and drove out before us all the peoples who lived in the land; therefore we also will serve the LORD, for he is our God." But Joshua said, "The LORD will not forgive your transgressions or your sins. If you forsake the LORD and serve foreign gods, he will turn and do you harm, and consume you, after having done you good."

The people said, "Nay; but we will serve the LORD." Then Joshua said, "You are witnesses against yourselves that you have chosen the LORD, to serve him." And they said, "We are witnesses." He said, "Then put away the foreign gods which are among you, and incline your heart to the LORD, the God of Israel." The people said, "The LORD our God we will serve, and his voice we will obey." So Joshua made a covenant with the people that day, and made statutes and ordinances for them at Shechem. He wrote these words in the book of the law of God; and he set up a great stone under the oak in the sanctuary of the LORD. "Behold," he said to the people, "this stone, which has heard all the words of the LORD, shall be a witness against you, lest you deal falsely with your God." Then he sent the people away, every man to his inheritance.

After these things Joshua the son of Nun, the servant of the LORD, died, being a hundred and ten years old. They buried him in his own inheritance at Timnath-serah in the hill country of Ephraim. Israel served the LORD all the days of Joshua, and all the days of the elders who outlived Joshua and had known all the work which the LORD did for Israel.

The bones of Joseph which the people of Israel brought up from Egypt were buried at Shechem. And Eleazar the son of Aaron died; and they buried him at Gibeah, the town of Phinehas his son, which had been given him in the hill country of Ephraim.

JUDGES

With the death of Joshua, the people of Israel are ruled for several centuries by a series of tribal patriots and religious reformers. They are known as judges (the traditional translation of the Hebrew word), but settling disputes is only a part of their task. Mainly, because the Israelites are so often under attack by their neighbors, the judges serve as war leaders. The book came into being when some unknown editor gathered colorful stories about these leaders and about the Israelites' early life in the Promised Land, and placed them within a religious framework. His primary concern is not with simple history but with driving home to the people a fundamental moral and theological lesson: The repeated sequence of sin, punishment, repentance, and deliverance demonstrates that obedience to the divine commands leads to national success, while disobedience leads to disaster. This same theme also appears in classical form in the Book of Deuteronomy.

AFTER THE DEATH of Joshua there arose another generation, who did not know the LORD or the work he had done for Israel. The people did what was evil in the sight of the LORD; they forsook the God of their fathers, who had brought them out of Egypt, and they bowed down to the gods of the peoples who were round about them. So the anger of the LORD was kindled against Israel, and he gave them over to plunderers, and sold them into the power of their enemies. Whenever they marched out, the hand of the LORD was against them for evil, as the LORD had warned; and they were in sore straits.

Then the LORD raised up judges, who saved Israel out of the power of those who plundered them. The LORD was with the judge, saving the Israelites from the hand of their enemies all the days of the judge; for the LORD was moved to pity by their groaning under those who afflicted and oppressed them. But whenever the judge died, they turned back and behaved worse than their fathers, serving other gods; they did not drop any of their practices or their stubborn ways. So the LORD said, "Because this people have transgressed my covenant which I commanded their fathers, I will not henceforth drive out before them any of the nations that Joshua left when he died. By them I will test Israel, whether they will take care to walk in the way of the LORD as their fathers did, or not." These are the nations which the LORD left, to test all in Israel who had no experience of any war in Canaan: the Philistines, the Canaanites, the Sidonians, and the Hivites who dwelt on Mount Lebanon. So the Israelites dwelt among the people of these nations. They took their daughters for wives, and their own daughters they gave to their sons; and they served their gods.

Therefore the anger of the LORD was kindled against Israel, and he sold them into the hand of Cushan-rishathaim king of Mesopotamia. The people of Israel served Cushan-rishathaim eight years. But when the people cried to the LORD, he raised up a deliverer for them, Othniel the son of Kenaz, Caleb's younger brother. The Spirit of the LORD came upon him, and he judged Israel; he went out to war, and the LORD gave Cushan-rishathaim into his hand. So the land had rest for forty years. Then Othniel died.

THE PEOPLE OF Israel again did what was evil in the sight of the LORD; and the LORD strengthened Eglon king of Moab against them. Eglon defeated Israel, and Israel served him eighteen years. But when the people of Israel cried to the LORD, the LORD raised up for them a deliverer, Ehud, a left-handed man, the son of Gera, the Benjaminite. Israel sent tribute by him to Eglon. Now Ehud had made for himself a sword with two edges, a foot and a half in length; and he girded it on his right thigh under his clothes. Then he presented the tribute to Eglon king of Moab. When he had finished presenting the tribute, he sent away the people that carried it, but he himself turned back and said, "I have a secret message for you, O king." Eglon commanded, "Silence," and all his attendants went out from his presence. Ehud came to him, as he was sitting alone in his cool roof chamber, and said, "I have a message from God for you." Now Eglon was a very fat man. He arose from his seat, and Ehud reached with his left hand, took the sword from his right thigh, and thrust it into Eglon's belly. The hilt went in after the blade, and the fat closed over the blade, for Ehud did not withdraw the sword. Then Ehud went out, closed the doors of the roof chamber, and locked them.

When he had gone, the servants came; and when they saw that the doors were locked, they thought, "He is only relieving himself in the closet." They waited till they were utterly at a loss; but when he still did not open the doors, they took the key and went in, and there lay their lord dead on the floor. While they delayed, Ehud escaped.

When he arrived in the hill country of Ephraim, he sounded the trumpet, and the people of Israel came down from the hills. "Follow after me," Ehud said, "for the LORD has given your enemies the Moabites into your hand." So they went down after him, and seized the fords of the Jordan against the Moabites, and allowed none to pass over. They killed at that time about ten thousand of the enemy, all strong, able-bodied men; not a man escaped. So Moab was subdued that day under the hand of Israel. And the land had rest for eighty years.

THE PEOPLE OF Israel again did what was evil in the sight of the LORD, after Ehud died. And the LORD sold them into the hand of Jabin king of Canaan, who reigned in Hazor; the commander of his army was Sisera. The people of Israel cried to the LORD for help; for Sisera had nine hundred chariots of iron, and oppressed the people of Israel cruelly for twenty years.

Now Deborah, a prophetess, the wife of Lappidoth, was judging Israel at that time. She used to sit under the palm of Deborah in the hill country of Ephraim; and the people of Israel came up to her for judgment. She summoned Barak the son of Abinoam from Kedesh in Naphtali, and said to him, "The LORD, the God of Israel, commands you, 'Go, gather your men at Mount Tabor, taking ten thousand from the tribes of Naphtali and Zebulun. I will draw out Sisera to meet you by the river Kishon with his chariots and his troops; and I will give him into your hand.'" Barak said to Deborah, "If you will go with me, I will go; but if you will not go with me, I will not go." She said, "I will surely go with you; nevertheless, the road on which you are going will not lead to your glory, for the LORD will sell Sisera into the hand of a woman." Then Deborah arose, and went with Barak to Kedesh. Barak summoned Zebulun and Naphtali, and ten thousand men went up at his heels to Mount Tabor.

When Sisera was told that Barak had gone up to Mount Tabor, he called out his nine hundred chariots of iron, and all his men, to the river Kishon. Deborah said to Barak, "Up! For this is the day in which the LORD has given Sisera into your hand. Does not the LORD go out before you?" So Barak and his men went down from Mount Tabor, and the LORD routed Sisera and all his chariots and all his army before them at the edge of the sword. Barak pursued the chariots and the army, and all the troops of Sisera fell by the edge of the sword; not a man was left.

But Sisera fled on foot to the tent of Jael, the wife of Heber the Kenite. Jael came out to meet Sisera, saying, "Turn aside, my lord, turn aside to me; have no fear." So he turned aside into the tent, and she covered him with a rug. "Pray, give me a little water to drink," he said, "for I am thirsty." So she opened a skin of milk and gave him a drink. "Stand at the door of the tent," he told her, "and if any man comes and asks you, 'Is any one here?' say, No." But later, as Sisera was lying fast asleep from weariness, Jael took a tent peg and a hammer in her hand, went softly to him, and drove the peg into his temple, till it went down into the ground. So he died. And behold, as Barak pursued Sisera, Jael went out to meet him, saying, "Come, I will show you the man you seek." He went in to her tent; and there lay Sisera dead, with the tent peg in his temple.

So on that day God subdued Jabin the king of Canaan. And the hand of the

people of Israel bore harder and harder on Jabin, until they destroyed him.
  Then sang Deborah and Barak the son of Abinoam on that day:

That the leaders took the lead in Israel,
   that the people offered themselves willingly,
   bless the LORD!
Hear, O kings; give ear, O princes;
   to the LORD I will sing,
   I will make melody to the LORD, the God of Israel.

LORD, when thou didst go forth from Seir,
   when thou didst march from the region of Edom,
the earth trembled,
   and the heavens dropped,
   yea, the clouds dropped water.
The mountains quaked before the LORD,
   yon Sinai before the LORD, the God of Israel.

In the days of Shamgar, son of Anath,
   in the days of Jael, caravans ceased
   and travelers kept to the byways.
The peasantry ceased in Israel, they ceased
   until you arose, Deborah,
   arose as a mother in Israel.
When new gods were chosen,
   then war was in the gates.
Was shield or spear to be seen
   among forty thousand in Israel?
My heart goes out to the commanders of Israel
   who offered themselves willingly among the people.
   Bless the LORD.
Tell of it, you who ride on tawny asses,
   you who sit on rich carpets,
   and you who walk by the way.
To the sound of musicians at the watering places,
   there they repeat the triumphs of the LORD,
   the triumphs of his peasantry in Israel.

Then down to the gates marched the people of the LORD.

Awake, awake, Deborah!
   Awake, awake, utter a song!
Arise, Barak, lead away your captives,
   O son of Abinoam.

Then down marched the remnant of the noble;
    the people of the LORD marched down for him against the mighty.

The kings came, they fought;
    then fought the kings of Canaan,
at Taanach, by the waters of Megiddo;
    they got no spoils of silver.
From heaven fought the stars,
    from their courses they fought against Sisera.
The torrent Kishon swept them away,
    the onrushing torrent, the torrent Kishon.
    March on, my soul, with might!

Most blessed of women be Jael,
    the wife of Heber the Kenite,
    of tent-dwelling women most blessed.
He asked water and she gave him milk,
    she brought him curds in a lordly bowl.
She put her hand to the tent peg
    and her right hand to the workmen's mallet;
she struck Sisera a blow,
    she crushed his head,
    she shattered and pierced his temple.
He sank, he fell,
    he lay still at her feet;
at her feet he sank, he fell;
    where he sank, there he fell dead.

Out of the window she peered,
    the mother of Sisera gazed through the lattice:
"Why is his chariot so long in coming?
    Why tarry the hoofbeats of his chariots?"
Her wisest ladies make answer,
    nay, she gives answer to herself,
"Are they not finding and dividing the spoil?—
    A maiden or two for every man;
spoil of dyed stuffs for Sisera,
    spoil of dyed stuffs embroidered,
    two pieces of dyed work embroidered for my neck as spoil?"

So perish all thine enemies, O LORD!
    But thy friends be like the sun as he rises in his might.

And the land had rest for forty years.

THE PEOPLE OF ISRAEL DID what was evil in the sight of the LORD; and the LORD gave them into the hand of Midian for seven years. Because of Midian the people of Israel made for themselves dens in the mountains, and caves and strongholds. For whenever the Israelites put in seed the Midianites and the Amalekites and the people of the East would come up and attack them; they would destroy the produce of the land, as far as the neighborhood of Gaza, and leave no sustenance in Israel, and no sheep or ox or ass. They would come up with their cattle and their tents, coming like locusts for number, so that they wasted the land as they came. Israel was brought very low because of Midian; and the people of Israel cried for help to the LORD.

Now Gideon, the son of Joash of the clan of Abiezer, was beating out wheat in the wine press, to hide it from the Midianites. The LORD appeared to him and said, "The LORD is with you, you mighty man of valor." Gideon said, "If the LORD is with us, why then has all this befallen us? Where are all his wonderful deeds which our fathers recounted to us? Now the LORD has cast us off, and given us into the hand of Midian." And the LORD said, "Go and deliver Israel from the hand of Midian; do not I send you?" Gideon said, "Pray, Lord, how can I deliver Israel? My clan is the weakest in Manasseh, and I am the least in my family." The LORD said to him, "But I will be with you, and you shall smite the Midianites as one man."

Then all the Midianites, the Amalekites, and the people of the East came together, and crossing the Jordan they encamped in the Valley of Jezreel. But the Spirit of the LORD took possession of Gideon; he sounded the trumpet, and the Abiezrites were called out to follow him. He sent messengers throughout all Manasseh, and to Asher, Zebulun, and Naphtali; and they too went up.

Then Gideon said to God, "Behold, I am laying a fleece of wool on the threshing floor; if there is dew on the fleece alone, and it is dry on all the ground, then I shall know that thou wilt deliver Israel by my hand, as thou hast said." And it was so. When he rose early next morning and squeezed the fleece, he wrung enough dew from it to fill a bowl with water. Then Gideon said to God, "Let not thy anger burn against me; let me make trial this once more with the fleece; pray, let it be dry only on the fleece, and on all the ground let there be dew." And God did so that night; for it was dry on the fleece only, and on all the ground there was dew.

Then Gideon and all the people who were with him rose early and encamped beside the spring of Harod, south of the camp of Midian. The LORD said to Gideon, "The people with you are too many for me to give the Midianites into their hand, lest Israel vaunt themselves against me, saying, 'My own hand has delivered me.' Therefore proclaim in the ears of the people, saying, 'Whoever is fearful and trembling, let him return home.'" And Gideon tested them; twenty-two thousand returned, and ten thousand remained. The LORD said, "The people are still too many; take them down to the water and I will test them for you there." So Gideon brought the people down to the water; and the LORD said, "Every one that laps the water with his tongue, as a dog laps, you shall set by himself; likewise every one that kneels down to drink." The number of those that lapped, putting their hands to their mouths, was three hundred men; the rest of the people knelt down to drink. The LORD said, "With the three hundred men that lapped I will deliver you; let all the others go every man to his home." So Gideon sent all these home, but retained the three hundred men; and the camp of Midian was below him in the valley.

That same night the LORD said to him, "Arise, attack the camp; for I have given it into your hand. But if you fear to attack, go down to the camp with Purah your servant; you shall hear what they say, and afterward your hands shall be strengthened." So Gideon went down with Purah his servant to the outposts of the camp. The Midianites, the Amalekites, and the people of the East lay along the valley like locusts for multitude; their camels were without number, as the sand upon the seashore. When Gideon came, behold, a man was telling a dream to his comrade: "I dreamed a cake of barley bread tumbled into the camp of Midian, and struck the tent, and turned it upside down, so that the tent lay flat." His comrade answered, "This is no other than the sword of Gideon the son of Joash, a man of Israel; into his hand God has given Midian and all the host."

When Gideon heard the telling of the dream and its interpretation, he worshiped. Then he returned to the camp of Israel and said, "Arise; for the LORD has given the host of Midian into your hand." He divided the three hundred men into three companies, and put trumpets into their hands and empty jars, with torches inside the jars. "Look at me," he said, "and when I come to the outskirts of the camp, do as I do. When I blow the trumpet, then blow the trumpets also on every side of the camp, and shout, 'For the LORD and for Gideon.'"

So Gideon and the hundred men who were with him came to the outskirts of the camp at the beginning of the middle watch. The three companies blew the trumpets and smashed the jars, holding in their left hands the torches, and in their right hands the trumpets to blow; and they cried, "A sword for the LORD and for Gideon!" They stood every man in his place round about the camp, and all the army cried out and fled.

Then Gideon sent messengers throughout the hill country of Ephraim, saying, "Come down against the Midianites, as far as the Jordan." So all the men of Ephraim were called out. As they pursued Midian, they took the two princes, Oreb and Zeeb, and killed them; and they brought their heads to Gideon beyond the Jordan. "What is this that you have done to us," the men of Ephraim said, "not to call us when you went to fight with Midian?" And they upbraided him violently. "What have I done now in comparison with you?" Gideon replied. "Is not the gleaning of the grapes of Ephraim better than the vintage of Abiezer? God has given into your hands the princes of Midian, Oreb and Zeeb; what have I been able to do in comparison with you?'' And their anger against him was abated. So Midian was subdued before the people of Israel, and the land had rest for forty years. And Gideon died in a good old age, and was buried in the tomb of Joash his father, at Ophrah of the Abiezrites.

THE PEOPLE OF Israel again did what was evil in the sight of the LORD, and served the Baals, the gods of Syria, of the Ammonites, and of the Philistines; they forsook the LORD, and did not serve him. The anger of the LORD was kindled against Israel, and he sold them into the hands of the Philistines and the Ammonites. For eighteen years they oppressed all the people of Israel that were beyond the Jordan in the land of the Amorites, which is in Gilead. And the Ammonites crossed the Jordan to fight also against Judah, Benjamin, and the house of Ephraim; so that Israel was sorely distressed.

The people cried to the LORD, saying, "We have sinned against thee, because we have forsaken our God and have served the Baals." The LORD said, "Did I not deliver you from the Egyptians? Yet you have forsaken me and served other gods; therefore I will deliver you no more. Cry to the gods whom you have chosen; let them deliver you in the time of your distress." The people said, "We have sinned; do to us whatever seems good to thee; only deliver us, we pray thee, this day." So they put away the foreign gods and served the LORD; and he became indignant over the misery of Israel.

Now Jephthah the Gileadite was a mighty warrior, but he was the son of a harlot. His father's wife also bore sons; and when the wife's sons grew up, they thrust Jephthah out, saying, "You shall not inherit in our father's house; for you are the son of another woman." Jephthah fled from his brothers, and dwelt in the land of Tob; and worthless fellows collected round Jephthah, and went raiding with him. When the Ammonites made war against Israel, the elders of Gilead went to bring Jephthah from the land of Tob. "Come and be our leader," they said, "that we may fight the Ammonites." But Jephthah said, "Did you not hate me, and drive me out of my father's house? Why have you come to me now when you are in trouble?" The elders said, "We have turned to you now, that you may go with us and fight the Ammonites, and be our head over all the inhabitants of Gilead." Jephthah said, "If you bring me home again to fight the Ammonites, and the LORD gives them over to me, I will be your head." The elders said, "The LORD will be witness between us; we will surely do as you say." So Jephthah went with the elders of Gilead, and the people made him leader over them; and Jephthah spoke all his words before the LORD at Mizpah.

Then Jephthah sent messengers to the king of the Ammonites and said, "What have you against me, that you come to fight against my land?" The king answered, "Because Israel on coming from Egypt took away my land; now therefore restore it peaceably." Jephthah sent messengers again, who said, "Thus says Jephthah: Israel did not take away the land of the Ammonites. When they came up from Egypt, Israel sent messengers to Sihon king of the Amorites, king of Heshbon, and said, 'Let us pass, we pray, through your land to our country.' But Sihon did not trust Israel to pass through his territory; so he gathered all his people together, and fought with Israel. And the LORD, the God of Israel, gave Sihon and his people into the hand of Israel; so Israel took possession of the land of the Amorites, from the Arnon to the Jabbok and from the wilderness to the Jordan. Then the LORD dispossessed the Amorites from before his people Israel; and are you now to take possession of them? Will you not possess what Chemosh your god gives you to possess? All that the LORD our God has dispossessed before us, we will possess. The LORD, the Judge, decide this day between the people of Israel and the people of Ammon." But the king of the Ammonites did not heed the message Jephthah sent him.

Then the Spirit of the LORD came upon Jephthah, and he passed through Gilead and Manasseh, to where the Ammonites were encamped. Jephthah made a vow to the LORD, "If thou wilt give the Ammonites into my hand, then whoever comes forth from the doors of my house to meet me, when I return victorious, shall be the LORD'S, and I will offer him up for a burnt offering." Jephthah crossed over to the Ammonites to fight against them; and the LORD gave them into his hand. He smote twenty cities, with a very great slaughter.

As Jephthah came to his home at Mizpah, behold, his daughter came out to meet him with timbrels and with dances; she was his only child. When he saw her, he rent his clothes, and said, "Alas, my daughter! you have brought me very low; for I have opened my mouth to the LORD, and I cannot take back my vow." She said, "My father, do to me according to what has gone forth from your mouth, now that the LORD has avenged you on your enemies. But let this one thing be done for me. Let me alone two months, that I may go and wander on the mountains, I and my companions, and bewail that I must die a virgin." He said, "Go." She departed, with her companions, and bewailed her virginity upon the mountains. At the end of two months, she returned to her father, who did with her according to his vow. She had never known a man. And it became a custom that the daughters of Israel went year by year to lament the daughter of Jephthah the Gileadite four days in the year.

After the Ammonites were subdued, the men of Ephraim said to Jephthah, "Why did you cross over to fight against the Ammonites, and not call us to go with you? We will burn your house over you." Jephthah replied, "I and my people had a great feud with the Ammonites; and when I called you, you did not deliver me from them. Therefore I took my life in my hand, and crossed over against the Ammonites, and the LORD gave them into my hand; why then have you come this day, to fight against me?" Then Jephthah gathered all the men of Gilead and fought with Ephraim; and the men of Gilead smote Ephraim. They took the fords of the Jordan, and held them against the Ephraimites. When any fugitive of Ephraim said, "Let me go over," the men of Gilead said to him, "Are you an Ephraimite?" When he said, "No," they said, "Then say Shibboleth," and he said, "Sibboleth," for he could not pronounce it right; then they seized him and slew him at the fords of the Jordan. There fell at that time forty-two thousand of the Ephraimites.

Jephthah judged Israel six years. Then Jephthah died, and was buried in his city in Gilead.

THE PEOPLE OF Israel again did what was evil in the sight of the LORD; and the LORD gave them into the hand of the Philistines for forty years.

Now there was a certain man of the tribe of the Danites, whose name was Manoah; his wife was barren and had no children. The angel of the LORD appeared to her and said, "Behold, you are barren, but you shall conceive and bear a son. Therefore beware, and drink no wine or strong drink, and eat nothing unclean. No razor shall come upon the boy's head, for he shall be a Nazirite, consecrated to God from birth; and he shall begin to deliver Israel from the hand of the Philistines." The woman told her husband of the man, and she said, "His countenance was like the countenance of the angel of God, very terrible; I did not ask him whence he was, and he did not tell me his name." Now they did not know that the man was the angel of the LORD.

Then Manoah entreated the LORD, "I pray thee, O LORD, let the man whom thou didst send come again to us, and teach us what we are to do with the boy that will be born." God listened, and the angel came again to the woman as she sat in the field; but Manoah was not with her. The woman ran in haste and told her husband, "Behold, the man has appeared to me again." Manoah went with his wife and said to the man, "When your words come true, what is to be the boy's manner of life, and what is he to do?" The angel said, "Of all that I said to the woman let her beware. She may not eat of anything that comes from the vine, neither let her drink wine or strong drink, or eat any unclean thing; all that I commanded her let her observe." Manoah said, "Pray, let us detain you, and prepare a kid for you." The angel replied, "If you detain me, I will not eat of your food; but if you make ready a burnt offering, then offer it to the LORD." Manoah asked, "What is your name, so that, when your words come true, we may honor you?" The angel said, "Why do you ask my name, seeing it is wonderful?" So Manoah took the kid with the cereal offering, and offered it upon the rock to the LORD, to him who works wonders. When the flame went up toward heaven from the altar, the angel ascended in the flame while Manoah and his wife looked on; and they fell on their faces, and they knew that the man was the angel of the LORD. "We shall surely die," Manoah said, "for we have seen God." But his wife said, "If the LORD had meant to kill us, he would not have accepted an offering at our hands, or announced to us such things as these." And the woman bore a son, and called his name Samson; the boy grew, and the LORD blessed him. And the Spirit of the LORD began to stir him.

Samson went down to Timnah, and there he saw one of the daughters of the Philistines. He asked his father and mother to get her as his wife. "Is there not a woman among your kin," they asked, "or among all our people, that you must take a wife from the uncircumcised Philistines?" But Samson said, "Get her for me; for she pleases me well." His father and mother did not know that this request was from the LORD; for he was seeking an occasion against the Philistines, who had dominion over Israel.

Then Samson went again to Timnah, and in the vineyards a young lion roared against him. The Spirit of the LORD came mightily upon him, and although he had nothing in his hand, he tore the lion asunder as one tears a kid. But he did not tell his father or his mother what he had done. Then he went down and talked with the woman, and she pleased him well. After a while, when he returned to marry her, he turned aside to see the carcass of the lion, and behold, there was a swarm of bees in the body, and honey. He scraped the honey into his hands, and went on, eating as he went. When he came to his father and mother, he gave some to them, and they ate. But he did not tell them that he had taken the honey from the carcass of the lion.

Samson made a marriage feast in Timnah, and when the people saw him, they brought thirty companions to be with him. "Let me now put a riddle to you," Samson said. "If you can tell me what it is, within the seven days of the feast, I will give you thirty linen garments and thirty festal garments; but if not, then you shall give the same to me." They said, "Put your riddle, that we may hear it." And he said, "Out of the eater came something to eat. Out of the strong came something sweet." And they could not in three days tell what the riddle was.

On the fourth day they said to Samson's wife, "Have you invited us here to impoverish us? Entice your husband to tell us what the riddle is, lest we burn you and your father's house." Samson's wife wept before him. "You hate me," she said, "you do not love me; you have put a riddle to my countrymen, and you have not told me what it is." He said, "I have not told my father nor my mother, and shall I tell you?" She wept before him the seven days that their feast lasted; and on the seventh day he told her, because she pressed him hard. Then she told the riddle to her countrymen. On the seventh day before the sun went down they said to Samson, "What is sweeter than honey? What is stronger than a lion?" Samson said, "If you had not plowed with my heifer, you would not have found out my riddle." The Spirit of the LORD came mightily upon him, and he went down to Ashkelon and killed thirty men of the town, and took their spoil and gave the festal garments to those who had told the riddle. In hot anger he went back to his father's house, and his wife was given to his companion, who had been his best man.

After a while, at the time of wheat harvest, Samson went to visit his wife. "I will go in to my wife in the chamber," he said. But her father would not allow him to go in. "I really thought that you utterly hated her," he said, "so I gave her to your companion. Is not her younger sister fairer than she? Pray take her instead." Samson said, "This time I shall be blameless in regard to the Philistines, when I do them mischief." He caught three hundred foxes, and took torches; and he tied the foxes tail to tail, putting a torch between each pair. After setting fire to the torches, he let the foxes go into the standing grain of the Philistines, and burned up the shocks and the standing grain, as well as the olive orchards. "Who has done this?" the Philistines asked. And they were told, "Samson, the son-in-law of the Timnite, because he has given Samson's wife to his companion." Then the Philistines came and burned both her and her father. "If this is what you do," Samson said to them, "I swear I will be avenged upon you, and after that I will quit." He smote them hip and thigh with great slaughter, and went down and stayed in the cleft of the rock of Etam.

The Philistines came up and encamped in Judah, and made a raid on Lehi. "Why have you come up against us?" the men of Judah asked. "We have come up to bind Samson," they replied, "to do to him as he did to us." Then three thousand men of Judah went down to Etam, and they asked Samson, "Do you not know that the Philistines are rulers over us? What is this that you have done?" Samson said, "As they did to me, so have I done to them." And they said, "We have come down to bind you, that we may give you into the hands of the Philistines." Samson said, "Swear to me that you will not fall upon me yourselves." They said, "No, we will only bind you and give you into their hands; we will not kill you." So they bound him with two new ropes, and brought him up from the rock.

At Lehi, the Philistines came shouting to meet him; and the Spirit of the LORD came mightily upon him. The ropes on his arms became as flax that has caught fire, and his bonds melted off his hands. He found a fresh jawbone of an ass, and seized it, and with it he slew a thousand men. And Samson said, "With the jawbone of an ass, heaps upon heaps, with the jawbone of an ass have I slain a thousand men." He was very thirsty, and called on the LORD, saying, "Thou hast granted this great deliverance by the hand of thy servant; and shall I now die of thirst, and fall into the hands of the uncircumcised?" God split open the hollow place that is at Lehi, and there came water from it; when he drank, his spirit returned, and he revived.

Samson went to Gaza where he saw a harlot, and he went in to her. When the Gazites were told, "Samson has come here," they surrounded the place and lay in wait for him at the gate of the city. All night they kept quiet, saying, "Let us wait till the light of the morning; then we will kill him." But at midnight Samson arose and took hold of the doors of the gate of the city and the two posts, and pulled them up, bar and all, and carried them on his shoulders to the top of the hill that is before Hebron.

After this he loved a woman in the valley of Sorek, whose name was Delilah. The lords of the Philistines came to her and said, "Entice him, and see wherein his great strength lies, and by what means we may overpower him; we will each give you eleven hundred pieces of silver." So Delilah said to Samson, "Please tell me wherein your great strength lies, and how you might be bound, that one could subdue you." Samson said, "Bind me with seven fresh bowstrings which have not been dried; then I shall be like any other man." The lords of the Philistines brought her seven such bowstrings, and she bound him. Now she had men lying in wait in an inner chamber. And she said to him, "The Philistines are upon you, Samson!" But he snapped the bowstrings, as a string of tow snaps when it touches the fire. So the secret of his strength was not known. "You have mocked me," Delilah said, "and told me lies; please tell me how you might be bound." Samson said, "Bind me with new ropes that have not been used; then I shall be like any other man." So Delilah took new ropes and bound him, and said, "The Philistines are upon you, Samson!" But he snapped the ropes off his arms like a thread. "Until now you have mocked me, and told me lies," she said. "Tell me how you might be bound." He said, "If you weave the seven locks of my head into the cloth on the loom and make it tight with the pin, then I shall become weak, and be like any other man." So while he slept, Delilah took the seven locks of his head and wove them into the cloth, and made them tight with the pin. Then she said to him, "The Philistines are upon you, Samson!" But he awoke from his sleep, and pulled away the pin, the loom, and the cloth.

"How can you say, 'I love you,' when your heart is not with me?" she asked. "You have mocked me these three times, and you have not told me wherein your great strength lies." When she pressed him hard with her words day after day, and urged him, his soul was vexed to death. He told her all his mind, and said, "A razor has never come upon my head; for I have been a Nazirite to God from my mother's womb. If I be shaved, then my strength will leave me." When Delilah saw that he had told her all his mind, she sent for the lords of the Philistines. They came, and brought the money in their hands. She made Samson sleep upon her knees; and she called a man to shave off the seven locks of his head, and his strength left him. "The Philistines are upon you, Samson!" she said. Waking from his sleep, he said, "I will go out as at other times, and shake myself free." He did not know that the LORD had left him. Then the Philistines seized him and gouged out his eyes, and they brought him down to Gaza. There they bound him with bronze fetters, and put him in prison, where he ground at the mill. But the hair of his head began to grow again.

Now the lords of the Philistines gathered to rejoice, and to offer a great sacrifice to Dagon their god; for they said, "Our god has given Samson our enemy into our hand." When the hearts of the people were merry, they said, "Call Samson, to make sport for us." So they called Samson out of the prison, and he said to the lad who led him by the hand, "Let me feel the pillars on which the temple rests, that I may lean against them." Now the temple was full of men and women; all the lords of the Philistines were there, and on the roof there were about three thousand men and women, looking on. Samson called to the LORD, "O Lord GOD, remember me, I pray, and strengthen me only this once, that I may be avenged upon the Philistines for one of my two eyes." He grasped the two middle pillars upon which the temple rested, and leaned his weight upon them, his right hand on the one and his left hand on the other. "Let me die with the Philistines," he said. Then he bowed with all his might; and the temple fell upon the lords and upon all the people that were in it. So those he slew at his death were more than those he had slain during his life. Then his family came down and took him and buried him in the tomb of Manoah his father. He had judged Israel twenty years.

Now there was a young man of Bethlehem in Judah, of the family of Judah, who was a Levite; and he departed from Bethlehem, to live where he could find a place. As he journeyed, he came to the hill country of Ephraim to the house of a man whose name was Micah. "From where do you come?" Micah asked him. "I am a Levite of Bethlehem in Judah, and I am going to sojourn where I may find a place," he replied. "Stay with me," Micah said, "and be to me a father and a priest. I will give you ten pieces of silver a year, a suit of apparel, and your living." The Levite was content to dwell with him, and became like one of his sons. "Now I know that the Lord will prosper me," Micah said, "because I have a Levite as priest." And Micah had a shrine with idols and a silver image.

In those days the tribe of the Danites was seeking for itself an inheritance to dwell in. Until then no inheritance among the tribes of Israel had fallen to them, for the Amorites did not allow them to come down to the plain, to the land Joshua had apportioned them. So the Danites sent five able men to spy out and explore the land. They came to the hill country of Ephraim, to the house of Micah, and lodged there. When they recognized the voice of the young Levite, they said to him, "What are you doing in this place?" He answered, "Micah has hired me, and I have become his priest." They said to him, "Inquire of God, we pray thee, that we may know whether our journey will succeed." The Levite said, "Go in peace. The journey on which you go is under the eye of the Lord."

The five men departed, and came to Laish, and saw that the people there dwelt in security, quiet and unsuspecting, lacking nothing that is in the earth, and possessing wealth; and they had no dealings with any one. Returning to their brethren, they said, "Arise, and let us go up against them; for we have seen the land, and behold, it is very fertile. Do not be slow to enter in and possess the land. You will come to an unsuspecting people. Yea, God has given into your hands a place where there is no lack of anything that is in the earth."

So six hundred armed men of the tribe of Dan set forth, and came to the hill country of Ephraim. "Do you know," the five spies said to their brethren, "that in one of these houses there are idols and a graven image of silver? Therefore consider what you will do." And the five men turned aside to Micah's house, and asked him of his welfare. Then they entered the house and took the idols and the silver image. The six hundred Danites stood by the entrance to the village with the Levite; and when the five men approached with the idols and the image, the Levite asked, "What are you doing?" They said, "Keep quiet, put your hand upon your mouth, and come with us, and be to us a father and a priest. Is it better for you to be priest to the house of one man, or to a tribe and family in Israel?" The priest's heart was glad. He took the idols and the graven image, and went with the Danites.

When they had gone a good way, the men in the houses near Micah's house were called out, and they overtook the Danites. They shouted to the Danites, who turned round and said to Micah, "What ails you that you come with such a company?" He said, "You take my gods, and the priest, and go away. What have I left? How then do you ask me, 'What ails you?'" The Danites said, "Do not let your voice be heard among us, lest angry fellows fall upon you, and you lose your life with the lives of your household." Then the Danites went their way; and Micah, seeing they were too strong for him, went back to his home.

The Danites came to Laish, to a people quiet and unsuspecting, and smote them with the edge of the sword, and burned the city. There was no deliverer because they had no dealings with any one. The Danites rebuilt the city, and dwelt in it, and named it Dan, after their ancestor, who was born to Jacob. The Danites set up the graven image for themselves; and Jonathan the son of Gershon, son of Moses, and his sons were priests to the tribe until the day of the captivity of the land.

IN THOSE DAYS, when there was no king in Israel, a certain Levite sojourning in the remote parts of the hill country of Ephraim took to himself a concubine from Bethlehem in Judah. She became angry with him, and went away to her father's house, and was there about four months. Then her husband went after her, to speak kindly to her and bring her back. He had with him his servant and a couple of asses. When he came to her father's house, the father came with joy to meet him, and made him stay; he remained with him three days. On the fourth day he arose early and prepared to go, but the father said, "Strengthen your heart with a morsel of bread, and after that you may go." So the two men sat and ate and drank together; and the girl's father said, "Be pleased to spend the night, and let your heart be merry." He urged him till he lodged there again. On the fifth day he arose early to depart, and the father said, "Strengthen your heart, and tarry until the day declines." So they ate. When the man and his concubine and his servant rose up to depart, the father said, "Behold, now the day has waned toward evening; pray tarry all night, and let your heart be merry; tomorrow you shall arise early and go home."

But the man would not spend the night; the three departed, and arrived opposite Jebus (that is, Jerusalem) when the day was far spent. "Come now," the servant said, "let us turn aside to this city of the Jebusites, and spend the night in it." His master said, "We will not turn aside into the city of foreigners, who do not belong to the people of Israel; but we will pass on to Gibeah or Ramah." They passed on, and the sun went down on them near Gibeah, which belongs to Benjamin, and they turned aside to spend the night there.

But no man would take them into his house, so they sat down in the open square of the city.

At evening an old man was coming from his work in the field; he was from the hill country of Ephraim, but was sojourning in Gibeah, where the men were Benjaminites. Seeing the wayfarer in the square, he asked, "Where are you going? and whence do you come?" The wayfarer replied, "We are passing from Bethlehem in Judah back to my home in the hill country of Ephraim; and nobody takes us into his house. We have straw and provender for our asses, and bread and wine for us; there is no lack of anything." The old man said, "Peace be to you; I will care for all your wants; only do not spend the night in the square." He brought them into his house, and gave the asses provender; and they washed their feet, and ate and drank.

As they were making their hearts merry, behold, the men of the city, base fellows, beset the house round about, beating on the door; and they said to the old man, the master of the house, "Bring out the man who came into your house, that we may know him." The master went out to them and said, "No, my brethren, do not act so wickedly; seeing that this man has come into my house, do not do this vile thing. Behold, here are my virgin daughter and his concubine; let me bring them out now. Ravish them and do with them what seems good to you; but against this man do not do so vile a thing." But the men would not listen to him. So the Levite seized his concubine, and put her out to them; and they knew her, and abused her all night. As the dawn began to break, they let her go, and she came and fell down at the door of the house.

In the morning, when her master opened the door to go on his way, behold, there was his concubine lying with her hands on the threshold. "Get up," he said to her, "let us be going." But there was no answer; she was dead. He put her body upon an ass, and went away to his home. When he entered his house, he took a knife, and laying hold of his concubine he divided her, limb by limb, into twelve pieces, and sent the pieces throughout all the territory of Israel. All who saw it said, "Such a thing has never happened or been seen from the day that the people of Israel came up out of the land of Egypt until this day; consider it, take counsel, and speak."

Then the people of Israel came out, from Dan to Beersheba, including the land of Gilead, and the congregation assembled at Mizpah, four hundred thousand men on foot that drew the sword. (Now the Benjaminites heard that the people of Israel had gone up to Mizpah.) "Tell us," the Israelites said, "how was this wickedness brought to pass?" The husband of the woman who was murdered told what the Benjaminites of Gibeah had done, and asked, "People of Israel, all of you, give your advice and counsel."

The people arose as one man, saying, "None of us will go to his tent or return to his house. We will go up to requite Gibeah of Benjamin for the wanton crime which they have committed in Israel." So the men of Israel gathered, and sent men through all the tribe of Benjamin, saying, "What wickedness is this that has taken place among you? Give up the base fellows in Gibeah, that we may put them to death, and put away evil from Israel." But the Benjaminites would not listen to the voice of their brethren, and twenty-six thousand seven hundred men came to Gibeah, to go out to battle against Israel. Among these were seven hundred picked men who were left-handed; every one could sling a stone at a hair, and not miss.

Then the men of Israel went out to battle, and the Benjaminites came out of Gibeah and they felled on that day twenty-two thousand Israelites. The people of Israel went up and wept before the LORD until the evening; and they inquired of the LORD, "Shall we again battle against our brethren the Benjaminites?" The LORD said, "Go up against them." The people took courage, and again formed the battle line in the same place where they had formed it on the first day.

Benjamin went against them out of Gibeah the second day, and felled eighteen thousand Israelites. Then all the people of Israel, the whole army, wept; they sat before the LORD, and fasted until evening, and offered burnt offerings and peace offerings. And they inquired of the LORD, "Shall we yet again go out to battle against our brethren the Benjaminites, or shall we cease?" The LORD said, "Go up; for tomorrow I will give them into your hand."

So Israel set men in ambush round about Gibeah, and went up against the Benjaminites on the third day. The men of Israel gave ground to Benjamin, because they trusted to the men in ambush; and the Benjaminites were drawn away from the city. Then the men in ambush rushed upon Gibeah, and smote all the city with the edge of the sword. Now the appointed signal between the men of Israel and the men in ambush was that when they made a great cloud of smoke rise up out of the city, the men of Israel should turn in battle. Benjamin had begun to smite Israel; but when the signal began to rise out of the city in a column of smoke, they looked behind them; and behold, the whole of the city went up in smoke to heaven. Then the men of Israel turned, and the men of Benjamin were dismayed, for they saw that disaster was close upon them. They turned their backs before the men of Israel in the direction of the wilderness; but the battle overtook them. Eighteen thousand men of Benjamin fell. The rest turned and fled toward the rock of Rimmon; five thousand were cut down in the highways, and two thousand more were pursued hard to Gidom, where they were slain. But six hundred men fled to the rock of Rimmon, and abode there. So all of Benjamin who fell that day were twenty-five thousand men that drew the sword, all of them men of valor.

In those days there was no king in Israel; every man did what was right in his own eyes.

RUTH

Renowned in world literature as a masterpiece of idyllic narrative, the Book of Ruth is from the hand of an unknown author. The incidents relate to the later days of the judges, before 1000 B.C., and this explains why in the English Bible the book follows immediately after the Book of Judges (in the Hebrew Bible it follows Proverbs). Linguistic features of the narrative, however, suggest a date of composition after the Babylonian Exile, that is, sometime in the sixth century B.C. Besides providing information about King David's ancestors, the story testifies that piety and trust in God will be rewarded, and that God's goodness is not constricted by nationalistic frontiers.

IN THE DAYS when the judges ruled there was a famine in the land of Judah, and a certain man of Bethlehem named Elimelech went to sojourn in the country of Moab with his wife, Naomi, and his two sons, Mahlon and Chilion. But Elimelech died, and Naomi was left with her two sons in Moab. The sons took Moabite wives, one named Orpah and the other Ruth. They had lived there about ten years when Mahlon and Chilion died, so that Naomi was bereft of both husband and sons.

Then she heard that the LORD had visited his people in Judah and had given them food, so she set out to return to Bethlehem. Her two daughters-in-law went with her, but Naomi said, "Turn back, my daughters, return to your mothers. May the LORD deal kindly with you, as you have dealt with the dead and with me. May he grant that you find a home, each of you in the house of her husband!" She kissed them, and they lifted up their voices and wept, saying, "Let us return with you to your people." But Naomi said, "Why will you go with me? Have I yet sons in my womb to become your husbands? Would you refrain from marrying? No, my daughters, for it is bitter to me for your sake that the hand of the LORD has gone forth against me."

Then the daughters-in-law wept again, and Orpah kissed Naomi and returned to her people. But Ruth clung to her mother-in-law. "Entreat me not to leave you," she said, "or to return from following you. Where you go I will go, and where you lodge I will lodge; your people shall be my people, and your God my God; where you die I will die, and there will I be buried. May the LORD punish me if even death parts me from you." When Naomi saw that Ruth was determined, she said no more.

Naomi and Ruth went on till they came to Bethlehem, and there the whole town was stirred because of them. "Is this Naomi?" the women asked. She answered, "Do not call me Naomi, call me Mara, for the Almighty has dealt very bitterly with me." Now it happened that the two had come to Bethlehem at the beginning of barley harvest. "Let me go to the field," Ruth said, "and glean among the ears of grain." Naomi answered, "Go, my daughter."

Gleaning after the reapers, Ruth came by chance to the part of the field belonging to Boaz, a man of wealth, who was of the family of Elimelech, Naomi's husband. When Boaz saw her, he said to the servant in charge of the reapers, "Who is that maiden working in the field?" The servant answered, "It is the Moabite maiden who came back with Naomi. She asked to glean after the reapers, and she has continued without resting even for a moment."

To Ruth, Boaz said, "Now, listen, my daughter, keep close to my maidens in this field. I have charged the young men not to molest you. When you are thirsty, go to the vessels and drink. And when you are hungry, eat some bread and dip it into the wine." Ruth fell on her face, bowing to the ground. "You are most gracious, my lord," she said. "Why should you take notice of me, when I am a foreigner?"

"All that you have done for your mother-in-law," Boaz said, "since the death of your husband has been fully told me, and how you left your father and mother and came to a people that you did not know. A full reward be given you by the God of Israel, under whose wings you have come to take refuge!" When Ruth rose to glean, he instructed his young men, "Let her glean even among the sheaves, and do not reproach her. Also pull out some grain from the bundles, and leave it for her."

Ruth worked in the field until evening; then she beat out the barley she had gleaned, and it was about a bushel. She took it up and went into the city and showed it to her mother-in-law. "In whose field did you glean today?" Naomi asked. "Blessed be the man who took notice of you." Ruth answered, "In the field of a man named Boaz."

"Blessed be he by the LORD," Naomi said, "whose kindness has not forsaken the living or the dead! The man is a relative, one of our nearest kin."

Until the end of the barley and wheat harvests, Ruth gleaned in the field. Then Naomi said, "My daughter, should I not seek a home for you? Is not Boaz our kinsman? See, he is winnowing barley tonight. Therefore anoint yourself, put on your best clothes, and go down to the threshing floor. Do not make yourself known to the man, but when he lies down to sleep, go and uncover his feet and lie down, and he will tell you what to do."

So Ruth went to the threshing floor, and when Boaz fell asleep at the end of the heap of grain, she came softly, and uncovered his feet and lay down. At midnight he awoke, and behold, a woman lay at his feet! "Who is that?" he said. "Ruth, your maidservant," she answered. "Spread your cloak over me, for you are next of kin."

"My daughter," Boaz said, "you have made this last kindness greater than the first, in that you have not gone after younger men. Do not fear. I will do for you what you ask, for all the city knows that you are a woman of worth. But though it is true that I am a near kinsman, there is a kinsman nearer than I. Remain this night, and in the morning, I will ask him if he will do his part for you. If he is not willing, then, as the LORD lives, I will do it myself."

She lay at his feet until morning, but they arose before dawn so that it should not be known that she had come to the threshing floor. "Bring your mantle," he said, "and hold it out." Pouring six measures of barley into the mantle, he said, "You must not go back empty-handed to your mother-in-law."

When Naomi heard all that Boaz had done for Ruth, she said, "Wait, my daughter. The man will not rest, but will settle the matter today."

And Boaz went up to the gate of the city, and when the next of kin came by, Boaz said, "Turn aside, friend, and sit down here." Then he took ten elders of the city, and asked them also to sit down. "Naomi, who has come back from the country of Moab," he said to the next of kin, "is selling the land which belonged to our kinsman Elimelech. If you will, buy it in the presence of the elders sitting here. But if you will not redeem it, tell me, so that I may redeem it myself, for I am next of kin after you." The man said, "I will redeem it." And Boaz said, "The day you buy the field, you are also buying Ruth, the widow of Mahlon, to restore the name of the dead to his inheritance." The next of kin answered, "Then I cannot redeem it, lest I impair my own inheritance." In former times in Israel, this was the custom: to confirm a transaction, a man drew off his sandal and gave it to the other. Saying, "Buy it for yourself," the next of kin drew off his sandal and gave it to Boaz.

"You are witnesses this day," Boaz said to the elders, "that I have bought the land that belonged to Elimelech. Also Ruth the Moabitess, the widow of Mahlon, I have bought to be my wife, to perpetuate the name of the dead."

"We are witnesses," the elders said. "May the LORD make the woman, who is coming into your house, be like Rachel and Leah, who together built up the house of Israel."

So Ruth became the wife of Boaz; and the LORD gave her conception, and she bore a son. To Naomi, the women of the neighborhood said, "Blessed be the LORD, who has not left you this day without next of kin! He shall be to you a restorer of life and a nourisher of your old age, for your daughter-in-law, who is more to you than seven sons, has borne him." Then Naomi laid the child in her bosom and became his nurse. And the women of the neighborhood gave him the name of Obed, saying, "A son has been born to Naomi." And Obed was the father of Jesse, who was the father of David.

1 SAMUEL

The two books of Samuel were originally a single book in Hebrew, which was first written down probably in the sixth century B.C., before the Babylonian Exile. Together they carry Israelite history from the era of the judges to the establishment of David's kingdom. Chief participants are the prophet Samuel, King Saul, and King David.

The first book is woven of two main literary strands, known as the Early Source and the Late Source. The Early Source, probably dating to the reign of Solomon, is of such exceptional historical and literary quality that its unknown author deserves to be called the father of history (a title usually given to the Greek writer Herodotus, who lived five hundred years later). A noble but tragic figure, King Saul wins remarkable victories but falls into conflict between his own self-will and obedience to the will of God. Eventually he is rejected, and shows symptoms of psychosis in his attitude toward David, whose popularity threatens to eclipse his own. Finally, defeated by his enemies, alienated from his associates as well as from his God, he dies in battle. The real hero is David, but he is a very human hero who is not above ignoble deeds. As so often in the Old Testament, the narrative insists that, despite sin and human failing, God's providence accomplishes its ends.

———

THERE WAS A certain man of Ramah, in the hill country of Ephraim, whose name was Elkanah. He had two wives, Hannah and Peninnah. Now Peninnah had children, but Hannah had none.

Elkanah and his family used to go every year to worship the LORD at Shiloh, where Eli and his two sons were priests. When Elkanah sacrificed, he would give many portions to Peninnah and her children to eat; but to Hannah, although he loved her, he could give only one portion, because the LORD had closed her womb. Peninnah used to provoke her sorely because of this, to irritate her, and so it went on year by year, as often as they went up to Shiloh.

Hannah would weep and would not eat, and Elkanah would say to her, "Hannah, why is your heart sad? Am I not more to you than ten sons?"

At last Hannah went to the temple, deeply distressed and weeping bitterly. "O LORD of hosts," she prayed, "if thou wilt indeed look on the affliction of thy maidservant, and remember me, and give me a son, I will give him to the LORD all the days of his life." Now Eli the priest was sitting beside the doorpost of the temple, and as Hannah was praying, he observed her. She was speaking in her heart; her lips moved but her voice was not heard, and Eli took her to be a drunken woman. "How long will you be drunken?" he said. "Put away your wine from you."

"No, my lord," Hannah answered, "I am a woman sorely troubled. I have drunk neither wine nor strong drink, but I have been pouring out my soul before the LORD, speaking out of my great anxiety and vexation."

"Go in peace," Eli said, "and the God of Israel grant your petition." So she went her way, and was no longer sad. In the morning they rose and went back to Ramah, and Elkanah knew Hannah, and the LORD remembered her. In due time she bore a son, and she called him Samuel.

After she had weaned her son, she brought him to the house of the LORD at Shiloh, along with a three-year-old bull, a measure of flour, and a skin of wine. They slew the bull for a sacrifice, and then they brought the child to Eli. "Oh, my lord!" said Hannah. "I am the woman who was standing here in your presence, praying to the LORD. For this child I prayed, and the LORD has granted my petition. Therefore I have given him to the LORD for as long as he lives." Then she went home to Ramah, leaving Samuel at the temple. And the boy ministered to the LORD in the presence of Eli.

Now the sons of Eli, Hophni and Phinehas, were worthless priests, with no regard for the LORD; they treated his offering with contempt. When any man offered sacrifice at Shiloh, the priest's servant would come while the meat was boiling and thrust a three-pronged fork into the pot; all that the fork brought up the priest took for himself. Moreover, before the fat was burned for the sacrifice, the servant would come and say, "Give raw meat for the priest to roast; if not, I will take it by force." Thus their sin was great in the sight of the LORD. When Eli heard all that his sons were doing, he said, "My sons, why do you do such things? If a man sins against a man, God will mediate for him; but if he sins against the LORD, who can intercede for him?" But they would not listen, for it was the will of the LORD to slay them.

Now Samuel was ministering to the LORD, a boy girded with a priestly apron. Each year his mother would make a little robe and take it to him when she went up with Elkanah for the yearly sacrifice, and the boy continued to grow in stature and in favor with the LORD and with men. But the word of the LORD came rarely in those days; there was no frequent vision.

At that time Eli, whose eyesight had grown dim, was lying down in his room; it was near dawn, and Samuel was sleeping within the temple, where the ark was. Then the LORD called, "Samuel! Samuel!"

"Here I am!" he said, and ran to Eli. "Here I am, for you called me." But Eli said, "I did not call; lie down again." So he went and lay down. The LORD called again, "Samuel!" And Samuel arose and went to Eli. "I did not call, my son," said Eli; "lie down again."

The LORD called Samuel the third time, and again he arose and went to Eli. Then Eli perceived that the LORD was calling the boy. "Lie down," he said, "and if he calls, you shall say, 'Speak, LORD, for thy servant hears.'" So Samuel lay down, and the LORD came forth, calling, "Samuel! Samuel!"

"Speak," said Samuel, "for thy servant hears."

"Behold," said the LORD, "I am about to do a thing at which the two ears of every one that hears it will tingle. I am about to punish Eli's house for ever, for he knew that his sons were blaspheming God, and he did not restrain them. Therefore I swear that the iniquity of Eli's house shall not be expiated by sacrifice or offering for ever." In the morning Samuel was afraid to tell the vision to Eli, but Eli called him. "My son," he said, "what was it he told you? Do not hide it from me." So Samuel told him everything. "It is the LORD," said Eli. "Let him do what seems good to him."

Samuel grew, and the LORD was with him, and he became acknowledged as a prophet. Year by year he went on a circuit to Bethel, Gilgal, and Mizpah, and he judged Israel in all those places. Then he would come back to Ramah, for his home was there.

NOW ISRAEL WENT out to battle against the Philistines, and in the first fighting Israel was defeated. "Why has the LORD put us to rout today?" the elders of Israel said. "Let us bring the ark of the covenant of the LORD here from Shiloh, that he may save us from our enemies."

So the people brought the ark from Shiloh, and the two sons of Eli were with it. When the ark came into the camp, all Israel gave a mighty shout, so that the earth resounded, and the Philistines heard it. "What does this great shouting in the camp of the Hebrews mean?" they asked; and learning that the ark of the LORD had come, they were afraid. "Woe to us!" they said. "This is the god who smote the Egyptians with plagues. Take courage and acquit yourselves like men, O Philistines, lest you become slaves to the Hebrews." So the Philistines fought, and again Israel was defeated and fled, every man to his home. There was a great slaughter, the ark of God was captured, and the two sons of Eli were slain.

A man of the tribe of Benjamin ran from the battle and came to Shiloh the same day, with his clothes rent and earth upon his head. Eli was sitting upon his seat by the road watching, for his heart trembled for the ark of God. "I am come from the battle," the man said to Eli. "Israel has fled before the Philistines, your two sons are dead, and the ark of God has been captured." Hearing this, Eli fell over backward from his seat; his neck was broken and he died, for he was an old man, and heavy. He had judged Israel forty years.

For seven months the ark of the LORD was in the country of the Philistines.

The hand of God was very heavy there, and there was a deathly panic, for he afflicted both young and old with plague. Those who did not die were stricken with tumors, and at last the people said, "Send away the ark of the God of Israel, and let it return to its own place." So the Philistines put the ark on a cart, and followed it as far as the border at Beth-shemesh. The people there were reaping their harvest, and when they saw the ark, they rejoiced, and they sent messengers to Kiriath-jearim, saying, "The Philistines have returned the ark of the LORD. Come and take it." So the men of Kiriath-jearim came and took the ark, and brought it to the house of Abinadab on the hill.

THERE WAS A wealthy man of Benjamin whose name was Kish. He had a son named Saul, and there was not a man of Israel handsomer than he, and he was head and shoulders taller than any of them.

Now the asses of Kish were lost, so he said to Saul, "Take one of the servants and go and look for the asses." They passed through the land of Benjamin, and the hill country of Ephraim, but they did not find them. When they came to the land of Zuph, Saul said to his servant, "Come, let us go back, lest my father become anxious about us." But the servant said, "Behold, there is in Ramah a man of God who is held in honor; all that he says comes true. Let us go there; perhaps he can help us in our journey."

"If we go," Saul said, "what have we to bring for a present?"

"I have the fourth part of a shekel of silver," the servant answered, "and I will give it to him."

As they went toward the city, they met young maidens coming out to draw water. "Is the prophet here?" they asked.

"He is," the maidens answered, "but make haste, for the people have a sacrifice today on the high place, and they will not eat till he comes, since he must bless it." As they were entering the city, they saw Samuel coming toward them on his way to the high place.

Now the day before, the LORD had revealed to Samuel: "Tomorrow I will send you a man of Benjamin. You shall anoint him to be prince over my people Israel, and he shall save them from the Philistines." When Samuel saw Saul, the LORD told him, "Here is the man who shall rule over my people."

Now Saul approached Samuel, saying, "Tell me where is the house of the prophet?"

"I am the prophet," Samuel answered; "go up before me to the high place, for today you shall eat with me, and in the morning I will tell you all that is on your mind. As for your lost asses, do not set your mind on them, for they have been found."

Samuel brought Saul into the hall, where he placed him at the head of those who had been invited. To the cook, he said, "Bring the portion I gave you to put aside," and the cook set the leg and the upper portion before Saul. "Eat," said Samuel, "because it was kept for you that you might eat with the guests." When they came down into the city, a bed was spread for Saul on the roof, and he lay down to sleep. At dawn Samuel called to him, "Up, that I may send you on your way." So Saul arose, and they went to the outskirts of the city. "Tell the servant to pass on before us," said Samuel, "that I may make known to you the word of God."

Then Samuel took a vial of oil and poured it on Saul's head, and kissed him. "Has not the LORD anointed you to be prince over his people Israel?" he said. "You shall reign over them and save them from their enemies. And this shall be the sign to you: When you depart today, you will meet two men by Rachel's tomb at Zelzah, and they will say to you, 'The asses you went to seek are found, and now your father is anxious about you.' After that you shall come to Gibeah, where there is a garrison of the Philistines; and there you will meet a band of prophets, prophesying. The spirit of the LORD will come mightily upon you, and you shall prophesy with them. Now when these signs meet you, do whatever your hand finds to do, for God is with you."

When Saul left Samuel, God gave him another heart; and all these signs came to pass that day. When he came to Gibeah, a band of prophets met him; and the Spirit of God came upon him, and he prophesied among them. When all who knew him before saw how he prophesied, they said to one another, "What has come over the son of Kish? Is Saul also among the prophets?" When he had finished prophesying, he came home.

Now Samuel called the people of Israel together at Mizpah. "You have asked for a king," he said. "Now therefore present yourselves before the LORD by your tribes and families." He brought all the tribes near, and the tribe of Benjamin was chosen by sacred lot. Family by family he brought the Benjaminites near, and the Matrites were chosen by lot; then, man by man, he brought the Matrites near, and Saul the son of Kish was chosen by lot; and when he stood among the people, he was head and shoulders taller than any. "Do you see him whom the LORD has chosen?" Samuel cried. "There is none like him." And the people shouted, "Long live the king!"

Samuel told the people the rights and duties of the kingship, and then sent them home. Saul went home to Gibeah, and with him went men of valor whose hearts God had touched. But some worthless fellows despised him and said, "How can this man save us?" But Saul held his peace.

Then Nahash the Ammonite besieged Jabesh-gilead. The men of Jabesh said, "Make a treaty with us, and we will serve you." Nahash replied, "On this condition I will make a treaty, that I gouge out all your right eyes." So the elders of Jabesh sent messengers throughout Israel for help. When they came to Gibeah and reported the matter, all the people wept aloud. Saul, who was coming from the field behind his oxen, asked, "What ails you, that you are weeping?" When they told him the tidings from Jabesh, the Spirit of God came upon him, and his anger was kindled. He killed two oxen, cut them in pieces, and sent them throughout Israel by messengers, saying, "Whoever does not come to Saul and Samuel, so shall it be done to his oxen!"

The dread of the LORD fell upon the people, and they came out as one man.

Saul mustered them at Bezek, across the Jordan valley from Jabesh-gilead, and they sent a message to the men of Jabesh: "Tomorrow, by the time the sun is hot, you shall have deliverance." The men of Jabesh were glad, and said to Nahash, "Tomorrow we will give ourselves up to you, and you may do to us whatever seems good to you."

That night Saul put the people in three companies. They crossed the Jordan valley and came into the camp of the Ammonites in the morning watch, and cut them down until the heat of the day; of those who survived no two were left together. "Who was it who said, 'Shall Saul reign over us?'" the people cried. "Bring them, that we may put them to death."

"No man shall be put to death this day," Saul answered, "for today the LORD has wrought deliverance in Israel." Afterward Saul fought valiantly against his enemies on every side, against Moab, the Ammonites, Edom, the kings of Zobah, and the Philistines. Wherever he turned he put them to the worse, and delivered Israel out of the hands of those who plundered her. But all his days he had hard fighting against the Philistines, and when he saw any strong man, he attached him to himself.

The sons of Saul were Jonathan, Ishbosheth, Abinadab, and Malchishua; the name of his first-born daughter was Merab, the name of the younger Michal. His wife was Ahinoam the daughter of Ahimaaz.

Now SAMUEL SAID to Saul, "The LORD sent me to anoint you king over Israel; now therefore hearken to his words. Thus says the LORD of hosts, 'I will punish what Amalek did to Israel when they came up out of Egypt. Now go and smite Amalek, and utterly destroy them; kill both man and woman, infant and suckling, ox and sheep, camel and ass.'" So Saul summoned the men, and they came to the city of Amalek and defeated the Amalekites. They destroyed all the people with the sword, except Agag the king, and they spared the best of the sheep and the oxen and all that was good.

Then the word of the LORD came in the night to Samuel: "I repent that I have made Saul king, for he has not performed my commandments." Samuel was angry, and he rose early and came to Saul. "Blessed be you to the LORD," Saul said; "I have performed his commandment."

"What then is this bleating of sheep and lowing of oxen in my ears?" said Samuel. "The people brought them from the Amalekites," Saul said, "for they spared the best of the sheep and oxen to sacrifice to the LORD; the rest we have utterly destroyed."

"Stop!" said Samuel. "Did not the LORD say to go and utterly destroy the Amalekites? Why then did you not obey? Why did you fear the people and allow them to take spoil, and do what was evil in the sight of the LORD?"

"I have obeyed the LORD," said Saul; "I have brought back Agag the king of Amalek, and I have utterly destroyed the Amalekites. But the people took the best of the spoil to sacrifice to the LORD in Gilgal."

"Has the LORD as great delight in sacrifice as in obedience?" said Samuel.

"Because you have rejected the word of the LORD, he has also rejected you from being king." As Samuel turned to go, Saul seized the skirt of his robe, and it tore. "The LORD has torn the kingdom from you this day," said Samuel, "and has given it to one better than you."

"I have sinned," Saul said, "yet honor me now before Israel, and return with me to Gilgal, that I may worship the LORD." So Samuel turned back with him, and Saul worshiped the LORD. "Now bring me the king of the Amalekites," said Samuel, and Agag came to him cheerfully, saying, "Surely the bitterness of death is past."

"As your sword has made women childless," Samuel answered, "so shall your mother be childless among women." And he hewed Agag in pieces before the LORD in Gilgal.

Then Samuel went home to Ramah, grieving over Saul, and Saul went to his house in Gibeah. Now the LORD said to Samuel, "How long will you grieve over Saul? Fill your horn with oil, and go to Jesse the Bethlehemite, for I have provided for myself a king among his sons."

"How can I go?" said Samuel. "If Saul hears it, he will kill me."

The LORD said, "Take a heifer with you, and say, 'I have come to sacrifice to the LORD,' and invite Jesse to the sacrifice; you shall anoint him whom I name to you." So Samuel came to Bethlehem, where he consecrated Jesse and seven of his sons, and invited them to the feast of the sacrifice. When they came, Jesse made his sons pass before Samuel. "The LORD has not chosen these," Samuel said to him. "Are all your sons here?"

"There remains the youngest," said Jesse. "He is keeping the sheep."

"Send and fetch him," said Samuel, "for we will not sit down till he comes." So Jesse sent and brought him in. Now David was ruddy, and had beautiful eyes, and was handsome. The LORD said to Samuel, "Arise, anoint him; for this is he." Samuel took the horn of oil and anointed him in the midst of his brothers; and from that day forward, the Spirit of the LORD came mightily upon David.

Now the Spirit of the LORD left Saul, and an evil spirit tormented him. His servants said to him, "Let our lord command his servants to seek out a man skilful in playing the lyre; and when the evil spirit is upon you, he will play, and you will be well." Saul agreed, and one of the young men said, "I have seen a son of Jesse the Bethlehemite, who is skilful in playing, prudent in speech, and a man of good presence." So Saul sent messengers to Jesse, saying, "Send me David your son." And David came to Saul, and entered his service. Saul loved him greatly, and when the evil spirit was upon him, David played the lyre; so Saul was refreshed, and the evil spirit left him.

Now the Philistines gathered their armies for battle in Judah, and Saul and the men of Israel drew up against them, with a valley between. Out from the Philistine camp, his shield-bearer going before him, came a champion named Goliath, of Gath, who was more than nine feet tall. He wore a bronze helmet and a heavy coat of mail. Upon his legs were bronze greaves, and a bronze javelin was slung between his shoulders; its shaft was like a weaver's beam, the head weighing fifteen pounds. "I defy the ranks of Israel," Goliath shouted. "Choose a man, and if he is able to fight with me and kill me, then we will be your servants; but if I prevail and kill him, then you shall serve us."

When Saul and all Israel heard this, they were dismayed. But David said to Saul, "Who is this uncircumcised Philistine, that he should defy the armies of the living God? Let no man's heart fail; your servant will go and fight him."

"You cannot go against this Philistine," said Saul; "you are but a youth, and he has long been a man of war."

"I used to keep sheep for my father," David answered, "and when a lion took a lamb from the flock, I went after him and smote him and delivered it; and if he attacked me, I caught him by his beard, and smote him and killed him. The LORD who delivered me from the lion will deliver me from this Philistine." So Saul said, "Go, and the LORD be with you!" He clothed David with his armor and put a helmet of bronze on his head. Girding the king's sword over the armor, David tried to go, but in vain, for he was not used to these things. "I cannot go with these," he said, and took them off.

Then David took his staff and his sling, and he chose five smooth stones from the brook. Putting them in his shepherd's bag, he drew near to the Philistine. When Goliath saw David, he disdained him. "Am I a dog," he said, "that you come to me with sticks?"

"I come to you in the name of the LORD of hosts," said David, "the God of the armies of Israel, whom you have defied." Then he put his hand in his bag and took out a stone, and slung it, and struck the Philistine on his forehead. The stone sank in and Goliath fell to the ground. David ran and stood over him, and took Goliath's sword out of its sheath and killed him, and cut off his head with it. When the Philistines saw that their champion was dead, they fled, and the men of Israel and Judah rose with a shout and pursued them as far as Gath and the gates of Ekron. When they came back, they plundered the Philistine camp.

As they were going home, the women came out of all the cities to greet King Saul with music and dancing and songs of joy. "Saul has slain his thousands," they sang to one another, "and David his ten thousands." Saul was very angry. "They have ascribed to David ten thousands," he said, "and to me only thousands; what more can he have but the kingdom?" And he eyed David from that day on, fearing him because the LORD was with him but had departed from Saul. So Saul removed David from his presence, and made him a troop commander of a thousand. David had success in all his undertakings, and when Saul saw this, he stood in awe of him.

Now Saul's daughter Michal loved David, and Saul thought, "Let me give her to him, that she may be a snare for him." So he commanded his servants to speak to David and say, "Behold, the king has delight in you; now then become the king's son-in-law." But David said, "Does it seem easy to you to become the king's son-in-law, seeing that I am a poor man and of no repute?"

This the servants of Saul reported, and Saul told them to reply, "The king desires no marriage present except a hundred foreskins of the Philistines, that he may be avenged of his enemies." For Saul thought to make David fall by the hand of the Philistines. But David was well pleased, and he went with his men and killed two hundred Philistines and brought their foreskins to the king. So Saul gave him his daughter Michal for a wife.

Now Saul saw that all Israel loved David, and he became his enemy continually. He spoke to Jonathan his son, and to his servants, that they should kill David. But the soul of Jonathan was knit to the soul of David, and Jonathan loved him as his own soul, for they had made a vow of friendship. "My father seeks to kill you," Jonathan said. "Hide yourself, and I will speak to him about you; if I learn anything I will tell you."

To Saul, Jonathan spoke well of David. "Let not the king sin against David," he said, "because he has not sinned against you, and he has been of good service to you; for he took his life in his hand and slew the Philistine. You saw it, and rejoiced; why then will you kill him without cause?" Saul hearkened to the voice of his son. "As the LORD lives," he swore, "he shall not be put to death." So Jonathan called David and brought him to Saul, and he was accepted in his presence as before.

Again the Philistines came out to battle, and David made a great slaughter among them, so that they fled before him. Then an evil spirit rushed upon Saul, and he raved within his house while David was playing the lyre, as he did day by day. Saul had his spear in his hand, and he cast it, seeking to pin David to the wall; but David eluded him, so that the spear struck into the wall. And David fled.

That night Saul sent messengers to David's house to watch him, that he might kill him in the morning. But Michal told David, "If you do not escape tonight, tomorrow you will be killed." She let him down from the window, then she laid an image on the bed and put a pillow of goats' hair at its head, and covered it with the bedclothes. When Saul's messengers came to take David, she said, "He is sick," and sent them away. But Saul said, "Bring him up to me in the bed, that I may kill him." When the messengers came in, behold, the image was in the bed, with the pillow of goats' hair at its head.

"Why have you deceived me thus," said Saul to Michal, "and let my enemy escape?" Michal answered, "He said to me, 'Let me go; why should I have to kill you?'"

DAVID FLED TO Nob, to Ahimelech the priest, the great-grandson of Eli, who met him with respect. "Why are you alone?" asked Ahimelech. "The king charged me with a secret matter," David replied. "I am to meet my men. What have you at hand? Give me five loaves of bread, or whatever is here."

"I have no common bread," said the priest, "but there is holy bread; if only the young men have kept themselves from women."

"Of a truth, women are kept from us even when it is a common expedition," David answered; "how much more today will their bodies be holy?" So the priest gave him the bread of the Presence, which is removed from before the LORD and replaced by hot bread. "Do you have a spear or a sword at hand?" asked David. "I did not bring my weapons with me because the king's business required haste."

"The sword of Goliath whom you killed is here wrapped in a cloth," the priest replied. "There is none like that," David said; "give it to me."

Now Doeg the Edomite, Saul's chief herdsman, was there that day, serving in the temple. So David departed and fled to the cave of Adullam. When his brothers and all his father's house heard it, they went down there to him. And every one in distress, every one in debt, and every one who was discontented gathered to him; and he became captain over them. And there were with him about four hundred men.

At Gibeah, Saul was sitting under the tamarisk tree on the height, with his spear in his hand and all his servants about him. Doeg the Edomite stood with them. "I saw the son of Jesse coming to Nob," he said to Saul, "and Ahimelech gave him provisions and the sword of Goliath the Philistine." Then the king sent to summon Ahimelech and all his father's house, the priests who were at Nob; and all of them came to the king. "Why have you conspired against me," Saul said to Ahimelech, "you and the son of Jesse, in that you have given him bread and a sword, and have inquired of God for him, so that he has risen against me?"

"Who among all your servants," Ahimelech answered, "is so faithful as David who is the king's son-in-law, and captain over your bodyguard, and honored in your house? No! Let not the king impute anything to me, for I have known nothing of all this."

"You shall surely die, Ahimelech," said the king, "you and all your father's house." Then he said to the guards, "Turn and kill them, for they also are with David, and they knew that he fled, and did not disclose it to me." But the guards would not fall upon the priests of the LORD, so the king said to Doeg, "You turn and fall upon the priests." So Doeg the Edomite fell upon them, and he killed on that day eighty-five persons who wore the priestly apron. And in Nob, the city of the priests, he put men and women, children and sucklings, oxen, asses, and sheep to the sword.

But one of Ahimelech's sons, named Abiathar, escaped and fled after David, and told him that Saul had killed the priests. "I knew on that day, when Doeg the Edomite was there," said David, "that he would surely tell Saul. I have occasioned the death of all your father's house. Stay with me, fear not; for he that seeks my life seeks your life; with me you shall be safe."

David and his men were in the wilderness of Maon, south of Ziph, and Saul and his men went there to seek him. David was told, and he took refuge in the mountain there. Saul sought him on one side of the mountain, while David and his men were on the other side, but as Saul was closing in, a messenger came to him, saying, "Make haste and come; for the Philistines have made a raid upon the land." So Saul returned from pursuing David and went against the Philistines; therefore that place was called the Rock of Escape.

Now Samuel died; and all Israel assembled and mourned for him, and they buried him in his house at Ramah.

THERE WAS IN Maon a very rich man named Nabal; he had three thousand sheep and a thousand goats. His wife, Abigail, was of good understanding and beautiful, but the man, a Calebite, was churlish and ill-behaved.

David, in the wilderness, heard that Nabal was shearing his sheep at Carmel, so he chose ten young men and said, "Go to Nabal, and greet him in my name thus: 'Peace be to you, and to your house. I hear that you have shearers; now your shepherds have been with us, and we did them no harm, and they missed nothing, for we guarded them all the time they were in the wilderness. Ask your young men, and they will tell you. Therefore let my young men find favor in your eyes, for we come on a feast day. Pray, give whatever you have at hand to them and to your son David.'" The young men came to Nabal and said all this in the name of David; and then they waited. "Who is David?" Nabal answered. "There are many servants nowadays who are breaking away from their masters. Shall I take my bread and wine and meat that I have killed for my shearers, and give it to men who come from I do not know where?" David's men came back and told him all this.

"This fellow has returned me evil for good," said David. "God punish me if by morning I leave alive so much as one male of all who belong to him." To his men, he said, "Every man gird on his sword!" Every man did so, and David also. He now had about six hundred men; four hundred went with him, while two hundred remained with the baggage.

But one of Nabal's young men told Abigail how her husband had received David's messengers. "Yet they were very good to us," he told her, "all the while we were with them. Consider what you should do; for evil is determined against our master, and he is so ill-natured one cannot speak to him."

Abigail made haste and took two hundred loaves, two skins of wine, five sheep ready dressed, five measures of parched grain, a hundred clusters of raisins, and two hundred cakes of figs. She laid them on asses and departed, but she did not tell Nabal. As she came near the mountain, behold, David and his men were coming down toward her. When she saw David, she alighted from the ass and fell before him to the ground.

"Upon me alone, my lord, be the guilt," she said; "pray hear the words of your handmaid. Let not my lord pay attention to this ill-natured fellow, Nabal, for folly is with him; but I your handmaid did not see the young men you sent. Now then, my lord, seeing that the LORD has restrained you from bloodguilt, and from taking vengeance with your own hand, let this present which your servant has brought be given to your young men. Pray forgive my trespass, for your life shall be in the care of the LORD your God, and the lives of your enemies he shall sling out as from the hollow of a sling. And when the

LORD has dealt well with you, my lord, then remember your handmaid."

"Blessed be the God of Israel," David replied, "who sent you this day to meet me! Blessed be your discretion, and blessed be you, who have kept me from bloodguilt and from avenging myself with my own hand!" And he received from her what she had brought him. "Go in peace to your house," he said. "I have hearkened to you and granted your petition."

When Abigail returned, Nabal was holding a feast in his house, like the feast of a king. His heart was merry, for he was very drunk, so she told him nothing at all until the morning light. In the morning, when the wine had gone out of him, she told him these things, and his heart died within him, and he became as a stone. About ten days later he died.

When David heard that Nabal was dead, he wooed Abigail, sending his servants to her at Carmel to say, "David has sent us to take you to him as his wife." Abigail bowed with her face to the ground. "Behold," she said, "your handmaid is a servant to wash the feet of the servants of my lord." Then she rose and mounted an ass, and with five maidens attending her, she followed the messengers of David, and became his wife. David also took Ahinoam of Jezreel; and both of them became his wives. But Saul had given Michal to Paltiel the son of Laish when David became a fugitive.

THE ZIPHITES CAME to Saul at Gibeah, saying, "Is not David hiding himself on the mountain in the wilderness of Ziph?" So Saul arose and returned to the wilderness with three thousand chosen men of Israel, and encamped on the mountain. Hearing that Saul was coming after him, David sent out spies and learned of a certainty that Saul had come. He came close to Saul's encampment and saw where he was lodged with Abner, the commander of his army. "Who will go down with me into the camp of Saul?" said David to his men. "I will go with you," said Abishai the son of Zeruiah, David's sister.

So David and Abishai went down to the encampment by night. Saul was sleeping with his spear stuck in the ground at his head; and Abner and the army lay around him. "God has given your enemy into your hand this day," said Abishai; "let me pin him to the earth with one stroke of the spear."

"Do not destroy him," David said. "As the LORD lives, the LORD will smite him; or his day shall come to die; or he shall perish in battle. The LORD forbid that I should raise my hand against the LORD's anointed; but let us take now his spear and the jar of water and go." So David took the spear and the jar of water, and they went away. No man saw it, or knew it, nor did any awake.

Then David went to the other side, and stood afar off on top of the mountain, and he called to Saul's army, "Will you not answer, Abner?"

"Who are you that calls to the king?" Abner answered.

"Are you not a man?" said David. "Why have you not kept watch over your king, the LORD's anointed? As the LORD lives, you deserve to die. Where is the king's spear, and the jar of water that was at his head?"

Saul recognized David's voice. "Is this your voice, David?" he said.

"It is my voice," replied David. "Why does my lord pursue his servant? What have I done? What guilt is on my hands? If it is the LORD who has stirred you up against me, may he accept an offering; but if it is men, may they be cursed before the LORD, for they have driven me out, and my lord has come to seek my life, like one who hunts a partridge in the mountains."

Then Saul said, "I have done wrong; return, my son David, for I will no more do you harm; I have played the fool, and have erred exceedingly."

"Here is the spear, O king!" David answered. "Let one of the young men come over and fetch it. As your life was precious this day in my sight, so may my life be precious in the sight of the LORD, and may he deliver me out of all tribulation."

"Blessed be you, my son David!" said Saul. "You will do many things and will succeed in them."

So David went his way, and Saul returned to Gibeah. But David said in his heart, "I shall perish one day by the hand of Saul; there is nothing better for me than to escape to the land of the Philistines; then Saul will despair of seeking me any longer." So he went over with his six hundred men to Achish, king of Gath; and they dwelt at Gath, and Saul sought him no more.

Now David and his men made raids upon the Amalekites and other inhabitants of the land from of old, as far as the land of Egypt. He smote the land and left neither man nor woman alive, but took away the livestock and the garments and came back to Achish. But when Achish asked, "Against whom have you made a raid today?" David would say, "Against the Negeb of Judah," and he spared neither man nor woman, lest they bring tidings to Gath. Such was David's custom while he dwelt with the Philistines, and Achish trusted him, thinking, "He has made himself utterly abhorred by Israel; therefore he shall be my servant always."

Then David said to Achish, "If I have found favor in your eyes, let me be given a country town to dwell in; for why should your servant dwell in the royal city with you?" So Achish gave him Ziklag, and to this day Ziklag has belonged to the kings of Judah.

IN THOSE DAYS the Philistines again gathered forces for war against Israel. "You and your men are to go out with me in the army," Achish said to David. "Very well," David replied, "you shall know what your servant can do."

When the Philistines assembled their forces at Shunem, David and his men were in the rear with Achish as the lords of the Philistines passed by with their men. "What are these Hebrews doing here?" they said. "Is not this David, the servant of Saul?" Achish replied. "Since he deserted to me I have found no fault in him." But the commanders were angry. "Send the man back," they said; "he shall not go down with us to battle, lest he become an adversary. For how could this fellow reconcile himself to his lord?"

So Achish called David. "As the LORD lives," he said, "you have been honest, and to me it seems right that you should march with me in the campaign. Nevertheless the lords do not approve of you. Go back now peaceably, that you may not displease them." So early in the morning David set out with his men to return to the land of the Philistines.

Now the Amalekites had made a raid upon Ziklag, and when David and his men came to the city on the third day, they found it burned, and their wives and sons and daughters taken captive. David wept, and he was greatly distressed; for the people were bitter in soul for their sons and daughters and spoke of stoning him. But David strengthened himself in the LORD his God, and inquired of the LORD, "Shall I pursue this band?" The LORD answered, "Pursue; for you shall surely overtake and surely rescue."

So David set out with his six hundred men. When they came to the brook Besor, two hundred men stayed behind, too exhausted to cross. But David and four hundred men went on with the pursuit. In the open country they found an Egyptian who had not eaten or drunk water for three days and nights. They gave him water and figs and raisins, and when he had eaten, his spirit revived. "Where are you from?" David asked him.

"I am an Egyptian," he replied, "servant to an Amalekite. My master left me behind because I fell sick three days ago. We had made a raid upon the Negeb, and we burned Ziklag."

"Will you take me to this band?" David said.

"Swear to me that you will not kill me," the man said, "or deliver me into the hands of my master, and I will." He took them to the band, and behold, the Amalekites were spread over the land, eating and drinking and dancing, because of all the spoil they had taken from the land of Judah. And David smote them, and not a man of them escaped, except some who mounted camels and fled. David recovered all that they had taken, including Ahinoam and Abigail, and he captured all their flocks and herds. The people drove those cattle before him, saying, "This is David's spoil."

When David came to the two hundred men who had been left at the brook Besor, he saluted them. Then the wicked fellows among the men who had gone with David said, "Because they did not go with us, we will not give them any of the spoil." But David said, "Not so, my brothers. The LORD has preserved us and given into our hand the band that came against us. As his share is who goes into battle, so shall his share be who stays by the baggage; they shall share alike." And from that day this was an ordinance for Israel.

When David came back to Ziklag, he sent part of the spoil to his friends, the elders of Judah, in all the places where he and his men had roamed.

Now SAUL GATHERED all Israel, and they encamped at Mount Gilboa. When he saw the army of the Philistines, he was afraid, and his heart trembled; but when he inquired of the LORD, the LORD did not answer him, either by dreams, or by the sacred lot, or by prophets. "Seek out a woman who is a medium," Saul said to his servants, "that I may go and inquire of her."

"Behold, there is a medium at Endor," they replied.

So Saul disguised himself and went with two men to the woman by night. "Tell me the future through a spirit," he said, "and bring up for me whomever I shall name to you."

"Whom shall I bring up?" the woman asked.

"Bring up Samuel for me," Saul said. But when the woman saw Samuel, she cried out with a loud voice.

"What do you see?" the king said to her.

"I see a spirit coming up out of the earth," she said, "like an old man wrapped in a robe." Saul knew that it was Samuel, and he bowed with his face to the ground and did obeisance.

"Why have you disturbed me by bringing me up?" Samuel said to Saul.

"I am in great distress," Saul answered, "for the Philistines are warring against me, and God has turned away from me and answers me no more, either by prophets or by dreams; therefore I have summoned you to tell me what to do."

"The LORD has done to you as he spoke through me," said Samuel, "for he has torn the kingdom out of your hand and given it to David because you did not obey him and carry out his fierce wrath against Amalek. Moreover the LORD will give Israel into the hand of the Philistines, and tomorrow you and your sons shall be with me." Then Saul fell full length upon the ground, filled with fear, and there was no strength in him. But his servants, together with the woman, urged him; and he rose and went away.

The next day the Philistines fought against Israel, and the men of Israel fled before them, and fell slain on Mount Gilboa. The Philistines overtook Saul and slew Jonathan and Abinadab and Malchishua, his sons. The battle pressed hard upon Saul, and the archers found him, and he was badly wounded. "Draw your sword," he said to his armor-bearer, "and thrust me through with it, lest these uncircumcised come and make sport of me." But his armor-bearer would not; for he feared greatly. Therefore Saul took his own sword, and fell upon it.

Thus Saul died, and his sons, and all his men, on the same day together. When the people heard that the men of Israel had fled and that Saul and three of his sons were dead, they fled from their cities; and the Philistines came and dwelt in them.

On the morrow, when the Philistines came to strip the slain, they found Saul on Mount Gilboa. They cut off his head, and stripped off his armor, and sent messengers throughout their land to carry the good news to their gods and to the people. They put his armor in the temple of Astarte, and they fastened his body to the wall of Beth-shan. But when the inhabitants of Jabesh-gilead heard what the Philistines had done to Saul, the valiant men arose and went all night, and took Saul's body from the wall. Then they came back to Jabesh and burned the body, and buried the bones under the tamarisk tree in Jabesh, and they fasted seven days.

2 SAMUEL

The central figure of 2 Samuel is David, the successor to Saul, Israel's first king. David's reign begins at Hebron, at first over the kingdom of Judah only. Later, after a successful war against the house of Saul, it is established at Jerusalem, this time over all Israel. David's reign of forty years is not without many difficulties, and a considerable part of the book describes the domestic and political troubles that plague him. The unknown author of 2 Samuel derived most of his material from the Early Source (see 1 Samuel Introduction), and consequently the narrative is unified and easily followed. Theologically, the most significant contribution from the Late Source is the prophecy of Nathan promising David an everlasting dynasty. This pronouncement becomes the basis for the development of royal messianism throughout the Bible.

AFTER THE DEATH of Saul, when David had returned from the slaughter of the Amalekites, he remained two days in Ziklag. On the third day a man came from Saul's camp, his clothes rent and earth upon his head. When he came to David, he fell to the ground and did obeisance. "Where do you come from?" asked David.

"I have escaped from the camp of Israel at Gilboa," the man replied. "The people have fled from the battle, many have fallen, and Saul and his son Jonathan are dead."

Then David took hold of his clothes and rent them, and so did all the men who were with him. They mourned and wept and fasted for Saul and Jonathan and for the people of the LORD fallen by the sword. And David lamented: "Thy glory, O Israel, is slain upon thy high places! How are the mighty fallen! Tell it not in Gath, publish it not in the streets of Ashkelon, lest the daughters of the Philistines rejoice. Ye mountains of Gilboa, let no dew or rain fall upon you, O treacherous fields; for there the shield of Saul was defiled. Saul and Jonathan, beloved and lovely! They were swifter than eagles; they were stronger than lions. How are the mighty fallen in the midst of the battle! Jonathan lies slain upon thy high places. I am distressed for you, my brother Jonathan; very pleasant have you been to me; your love to me was wonderful, passing the love of women. How are the mighty fallen, and the weapons of war perished!"

AFTER THIS, DAVID inquired of the LORD, "Shall I go up into the cities of Judah?" The LORD answered, "Go up to Hebron." So David went up, with his wives and all his men, every one with his household; and they dwelt in the towns of Hebron. Then the men of Judah came, and they anointed David king over the house of Judah.

When they told David, "It was the men of Jabesh-gilead who buried Saul," he sent messengers to them in Gilead, saying, "May you be blessed by the LORD for this loyalty to Saul your lord. I will do good to you because of this. Now therefore be strong; for Saul is dead, and the house of Judah has anointed me king over them." But Abner, Saul's cousin and commander of his army, had taken Saul's young son Ishbosheth, and brought him over to Mahanaim in Gilead; and he made him king over Gilead and Benjamin and all Israel north of Judah.

Now Abner and Ishbosheth's men marched from Mahanaim across the Jordan to Gibeon. So Joab, the son of David's sister Zeruiah, went out with David's men and met them at the pool of Gibeon. They sat down, Abner's company on one side of the pool and Joab's on the other. "Let the young men arise for single combat," said Abner to Joab. "Let them arise," Joab answered. So the young men arose, twelve on a side. Each caught his opponent by the hair and thrust his sword into his opponent, so that they all fell down together. The battle spread and became very fierce.

The three sons of David's sister Zeruiah were there that day, Joab, Abishai, and Asahel. Now Asahel was as swift of foot as a wild gazelle, and he pursued Abner, turning neither right nor left from following him. Abner looked back and said to Asahel, "Turn aside, and seize one of the young men." But Asahel would not, and Abner said again, "Turn aside; why should I smite you? How then could I lift up my face to your brother Joab?" When Asahel refused again, Abner smote him in the belly with his spear, so that it came out at his back; and Asahel fell there and died. And all who came to that place stood still in grief.

Joab and Abishai took up the pursuit of Abner. As the sun was going down they came to a hill in the wilderness of Gibeon. Here Abner and his people took their stand. "Shall the sword devour for ever?" Abner called to Joab. "Do you not know that the end will be bitter? How long before you bid your people turn from the pursuit of their brethren?"

"As God lives," Joab replied, "if you had not spoken, surely the men would have continued until morning." Then he blew the trumpet; and all his men stopped and pursued Abner no more. When Joab gathered his people together, there were missing nineteen besides Asahel; but they had slain three hundred and sixty of Abner's men. They took up Asahel and buried him in the tomb of his father at Bethlehem. Then they marched all night, and the day broke upon them at Hebron.

Now THERE WAS a long war between the house of Saul and the house of David. While David grew stronger and stronger, the house of Saul became weaker and weaker. And while there was war, Abner was making himself strong in the house of Saul.

Now Saul had a concubine, Rizpah, and Ishbosheth said to Abner, "Why have you gone in to my father's concubine?" Abner was very angry at this. "Am I a dog's head of Judah?" he said. "I show loyalty to the house of Saul, and have not given you over to David; and yet you charge me today with a fault concerning a woman. God punish me if I do not accomplish for David what the LORD has sworn to him, to set up his throne over Israel and Judah, from Dan to Beer-sheba." Then Abner sent word to David at Hebron, saying, "To whom does this land belong? Make your covenant with me, and my hand shall be with you to bring over all Israel to you."

"I will make a covenant with you," David replied. "But one thing I require: you shall not see my face unless you bring Michal, Saul's daughter, when you come." Then he sent messengers to Ishbosheth, saying, "Give me my wife Michal, whom I betrothed at the price of a hundred foreskins of the Philistines." So Ishbosheth took Michal from her husband Paltiel; and her husband went with her, weeping, until Abner commanded him to return.

And Abner conferred with the elders of Israel, saying, "For some time past you have been seeking David as king. Now then bring it about, for the LORD has promised David that he will save our people from the hand of all their enemies." Then Abner went to Hebron to tell David all that the elders of Israel thought good to do. David made a feast for him, and Abner said, "Now I will arise and go, and I will gather all Israel to my lord the king, that they may make a covenant with you." So Abner went away in peace.

Just then Joab arrived from a raid; and he was told that Abner had come to talk with the king and that the king had let him go. "Why have you sent Abner away in peace?" Joab said to the king. "You know that he came to deceive you and to know all that you are doing." When he came out from David's presence, Joab sent messengers after Abner, and they brought him back to Hebron. Joab and Abishai his brother took Abner into the inner part of the gate to speak with him privately, and because he had killed their brother Asahel in the battle at Gibeon, they smote him in the belly and he died.

When David heard of it, he said, "I and my kingdom are guiltless before the LORD for the blood of Abner. May it fall upon the head of Joab and upon all his father's house." Then to Joab and all the people who were with him he said, "Rend your clothes and mourn before Abner. Do you not know that a prince and a great man has fallen in Israel?" They buried Abner at Hebron, and David lamented at his grave, saying, "Should Abner die as a fool dies? Your hands were not bound, your feet were not fettered; as one falls before the wicked, you have fallen." The people wept, and all Israel understood that it had not been the king's will to slay Abner.

When Ishbosheth heard that Abner had died, his courage failed, and all Israel was dismayed. Two brothers named Baanah and Rechab, both captains of raiding bands, set out for Mahanaim, and in the heat of the day they came to the house of Ishbosheth. The doorkeeper had grown drowsy and slept, so Rechab and Baanah slipped into his chamber. As Ishbosheth lay on his bed they smote him and beheaded him. Then they took his head and traveled all night through the Arabah, and brought it to David at Hebron. "Here is the head of Ishbosheth, the son of Saul, your enemy," they said to the king. "The LORD has avenged my lord the king this day on Saul and his offspring."

"When wicked men have slain a righteous man in his own house," David answered, "shall I not now require his blood at your hand and destroy you from the earth?" And he commanded his young men, and they hanged Rechab and Baanah beside the pool at Hebron. But they took the head of Ishbosheth and buried it in the tomb of Abner.

Then all the tribes of Israel came to David at Hebron, and said, "Behold, we are your bone and flesh. When Saul was king over us, it was you that led us out and brought us in, and the LORD said to you, 'You shall be prince over my people Israel.'" So David made a covenant with the elders of Israel before the LORD, and they anointed him king. He was thirty years old, and he had reigned over Judah seven years and six months. He reigned over both Israel and Judah thirty-three years.

NOW THE KING and his men went to Jerusalem against the Jebusites, the inhabitants of the land, and they took the stronghold of Zion. David dwelt there in the fortress and called it the city of David. And he became greater and greater, for the LORD, the God of hosts, was with him. Hiram king of Tyre sent cedar trees to him and carpenters and masons who built him a house. And David perceived that the LORD had exalted his kingdom for the sake of his people Israel.

Sons had been born to David at Hebron: his first-born was Amnon, by Ahinoam of Jezreel, and his second Chileab, by Abigail; then Absalom, the son of Maacah, daughter of the king of Geshur; and Adonijah, and Shephatiah, and Ithream. Now David took more concubines and wives from Jerusalem, and more sons and daughters were born to him.

When the Philistines heard that David had been anointed king over Israel, they went up in search of him in the valley of Rephaim. David inquired of the LORD, "Shall I go up against the Philistines?" The LORD said, "Go up; for I will certainly give the Philistines into your hand." And David defeated them and carried away their idols. Then the Philistines came up again. When David inquired of the LORD, he said, "You shall not go up; go around to their rear, and come upon them opposite the balsam trees. When you hear the sound of marching in the balsam trees, then bestir yourself; for the LORD has gone out before you to smite the army of the Philistines." And David did as the LORD commanded him.

Now David gathered the chosen men of Israel and went with them to Kiriath-jearim to bring up from there the ark of the LORD of hosts. They brought the ark out of the house of Abinadab on the hill, and carried it, with shouting and the sound of the horn, on a cart to the city of David. David sacrificed an ox and a fatling, and he danced before the LORD with all his might, girded with a priestly apron.

As the ark of the LORD came into the city, Michal the daughter of Saul looked out of the window and saw King David leaping and dancing before the LORD; and she despised him in her heart. They set the ark in its place in the tent David had pitched for it, and he made burnt offerings before the LORD. Then he blessed the people in the name of the LORD of hosts, and distributed to each a portion of meat and a cake of raisins. When he returned to bless his own household, Michal came out to meet him. "How the king of Israel honored himself today," she said, "uncovering himself before his servants' maids, as vulgar fellows shamelessly do!"

"It was before the LORD," said David, "who chose me above your father and all his house as prince over Israel—and I will make merry before him. I will make myself yet more contemptible than this in your eyes. But by the maids of whom you have spoken I shall be held in honor." And Michal had no child to the day of her death.

Now when the king dwelt in his house and the LORD had given him rest from all his enemies round about, he said to Nathan the prophet, "See now, I dwell in a house of cedar, but the ark of God dwells in a tent."

That night the word of the LORD came to Nathan: "Go and tell my servant David, 'Thus says the LORD: Would you build me a house to dwell in? I have not dwelt in a house since the day I brought up the people of Israel from Egypt. Wherever I have moved with them, did I speak a word with any of the judges, saying, "Why have you not built me a house of cedar?"'

"Now therefore you shall say to my servant David, 'I took you from following the sheep to be prince over my people Israel, and I have been with you wherever you went; and I will make for you a great name, like the great ones of the earth. And I will appoint a place for my people Israel, that they may dwell there and be disturbed no more; and I will give you rest from all your enemies. Moreover the LORD declares to you that he will build you a house. When your days are fulfilled and you lie down with your fathers, I will raise up your son after you, who shall come forth from your body, and I will establish his kingdom. He shall build a house for my name. I will be his father, and he shall be my son. When he commits iniquity, I will chasten him with the rod of men; but I will not take my steadfast love from him, as I took it from Saul. And your kingdom shall be established for ever.'" In accordance with all these words, and in accordance with all this vision, Nathan spoke to David.

Then King David went in and sat before the LORD and said, "Who am I, O LORD, and what is my family, that thou hast brought me thus far? And yet this was a small thing in thy eyes, O LORD; thou hast also shown me future generations. Because of thy promise, and according to thy own heart, thou hast wrought all this greatness. Thou hast said, 'I will build you a house'; therefore I have found courage to pray this prayer to thee. Thy words are true, and thou hast promised this good thing to thy servant; and now may it please thee to bless the house of thy servant, that it may continue for ever before thee."

AFTER THIS, DAVID did as the LORD commanded him, and subdued the Philistines from Gibeon to Gezer. And he defeated Moab, making them lie down on the ground in three lines; two lines he measured to be put to death, and one full line to be spared. David also defeated Hadadezer, son of the king of Zobah, as he went to restore his power at the river Euphrates. And David took from him a thousand and seven hundred horsemen, and twenty thousand foot soldiers. When the Syrians of Damascus came to help Hadadezer, David slew twenty-two thousand of their men. When he returned, he slew eighteen thousand Edomites in the Valley of Salt and put garrisons throughout Edom. And his enemies became David's servants and brought tribute.

The LORD gave victory to David wherever he went. And David took all the articles of silver, gold, and bronze that had been given to him as tribute and dedicated them to the LORD. So David reigned over all Israel and administered justice and equity to his people.

IN THE SPRING of the year, the time when kings go forth to battle, David sent Joab and the army against the Ammonites, and they besieged Rabbah. But David remained at Jerusalem.

It happened late one afternoon, when David arose from his couch and was walking upon the roof of his house, that he saw a woman bathing; and the woman was very beautiful. David sent and inquired about her. One servant said, "Is not this Bathsheba, the wife of Uriah the Hittite, who is with the army in Ammon?" So David sent messengers, and they brought Bathsheba to him, and he lay with her; then she returned to her house. She conceived; and she sent and told David, "I am with child."

David sent word to Joab, "Send me Uriah the Hittite." When Uriah came, David asked how the people fared and how the war prospered. Then he said, "Go down to your house and rest." Uriah left, but he slept at the door of the king's house with the soldiers and did not go down to his house.

When they told David this, he said to Uriah, "Have you not come from a journey? Why did you not go down to your house?"

"The ark dwells in a tent," Uriah answered, "and my lord Joab and your soldiers are camping in the open field; shall I then go to my house to eat and to drink and to lie with my wife? As your soul lives, I will not do this thing."

"Then remain here today also," David said, "and tomorrow I will let you depart." Uriah remained in Jerusalem that day and the next. David invited him, and Uriah ate and drank in his presence, so that David made him drunk. But again in the evening Uriah went out to lie on his couch with the soldiers, and he did not go down to his house.

In the morning David wrote a letter to Joab, and sent it by the hand of Uriah. "Set Uriah in the forefront of the hardest fighting," he wrote, "and then draw back from him, that he may be struck down and die." So Joab assigned Uriah to a place in the siege lines where he knew the foe had valiant men. The men of the city came out and attacked; some of David's soldiers fell, and Uriah the Hittite was slain also. Then Joab sent David all the news about the fighting; and he instructed the messenger, "If the king's anger rises and he says to you, 'Why did you go so near the city wall to fight?' you shall say, 'Your servant Uriah the Hittite is dead also.'"

The messenger came to David and said, "We drove the enemy back to the gate of the city. Then the archers shot at us from the wall; some of the king's servants are dead; and your servant Uriah the Hittite is dead also."

"Thus shall you say to Joab," David replied. "'Do not let this matter trouble you, for the sword devours now one and now another; strengthen your attack upon the city, and overthrow it.'" When Bathsheba heard that Uriah her husband was dead, she made lamentation for him. But when the mourning was over, David brought her to his house, and she became his wife and bore him a son.

The thing David had done displeased the LORD, and he sent Nathan the prophet to him. "There were two men in a certain city," Nathan said to David, "one rich and the other poor. The rich man had many flocks and herds; but the poor man had nothing but one little ewe lamb. It grew up with his children; it used to eat of his morsel, and drink from his cup, and it was like a daughter to him. Now there came a traveler to the rich man, and he was unwilling to slaughter one of his own flock for the wayfarer, so he took the poor man's lamb and prepared it for the feast."

David's anger was greatly kindled. "As the LORD lives," he said to Nathan, "the man who has done this deserves to die because he had no pity."

"You are the man," said Nathan. "Thus says the LORD, 'I anointed you king over Israel, and I delivered you from Saul; and I gave you the house of Israel and of Judah; and if this were too little, I would add to you as much more. Why have you despised the word of the LORD, to do what is evil in his sight? You have smitten Uriah the Hittite with the sword of the Ammonites, and have taken his wife to be your wife. Now therefore the sword shall never depart from your house.' Thus says the LORD, 'Behold, I will raise up evil against you out of your own house; and I will take your wives and give them to another, and he shall lie with them in the sight of this sun. For you did it secretly, but I will do this thing before all Israel.'"

"I have sinned against the LORD," said David.

"And the LORD has put away your sin," replied Nathan; "you shall not die. Nevertheless, because by this deed you have utterly scorned the LORD, the child that is born to you shall die." The LORD struck the child that Uriah's wife bore to David, and it became sick. David besought God for the child, and he fasted and went in and lay all night upon the ground. The elders of his house tried to raise him up; but he would not rise, nor did he eat food with them. On the seventh day the child died. The servants of David feared to tell him, for they said, "How can we say to him the child is dead? He may do himself some harm."

But when David saw them whispering together, he asked, "Is the child dead?" And they replied, "He is dead." David arose from the earth, and washed, and changed his clothes; and he went into the house of the LORD and worshiped; then he went to his own house, and when they set food before him, he ate.

"You fasted and wept for the child while it was alive," his servants said, "but when it died, you arose and ate food."

David answered, "I fasted and wept, for I said, 'Who knows whether the LORD will be gracious to me, that the child may live?' But now he is dead. Why should I fast? Can I bring him back again? I shall go where he is, but he will not return to me." Then David comforted his wife, Bathsheba, and went in to her and lay with her; and she bore a son, and he called his name Solomon. And the LORD loved him.

NOW ABSALOM, DAVID'S son, had a beautiful sister whose name was Tamar, and Amnon, David's eldest son, loved her. Amnon was so tormented that he made himself ill because of Tamar; for she was a virgin, and it seemed impossible to him to do anything to her. But Amnon had a friend, Jonadab, who said to him, "O son of the king, why are you so haggard morning after morning? Will you not tell me?" Amnon answered him, "I love Tamar, my brother Absalom's sister."

"Lie down on your bed," Jonadab said, "and pretend to be ill. When your father comes to see you, say to him, 'Let my sister Tamar come and prepare food in my sight, that I may eat it from her hand.'" Amnon pretended to be ill, and when the king came to see him, he spoke as Jonadab had told him. So David sent Tamar, and she took dough and kneaded it and baked cakes in Amnon's sight; but he refused to eat. "Send out every one from me," he said, "then bring the food into the chamber, that I may eat from your hand." When every one left, Tamar brought the cakes into the chamber. As she came near him, Amnon took hold of her and said, "Come, lie with me, my sister."

"No, my brother, do not force me," she answered him. "Where could I carry my shame? As for you, you would be as a wanton fool in Israel. Now therefore, I pray you, speak to the king, for he will not withhold me from you." But he would not listen to her; and being stronger than she, he forced her, and lay with her.

Then Amnon's hatred for Tamar became greater than his love for her. "Arise, be gone," he said. "No, my brother," she answered, "for sending me away is a greater wrong than the other which you did to me." But he would not listen, and to his servant he said, "Put this woman out of my presence, and bolt the door after her." Tamar put ashes on her head, and rent her long robe; and she laid her hand on her head, and went away, crying aloud. She dwelt, a desolate woman, in her brother Absalom's house.

When King David heard of all these things, he was very angry. But Absalom spoke to Amnon neither good nor bad, for he hated Amnon because he had forced his sister Tamar.

Two years later Absalom had sheepshearers at his lands at Baalhazor, and he invited all the king's sons. He came to the king and said, "Behold, your servant has sheepshearers; pray let the king and his household visit me."

"No, my son," replied the king, "let us not all go, lest we be burdensome."

Absalom pressed him, but the king would not go. "If not you," said Absalom, "pray let my brother Amnon go with us." And Absalom urged the king until he let Amnon and all his other sons go to Baalhazor. Then Absalom commanded his servants, "Mark when Amnon's heart is merry with wine, and when I say to you, 'Strike Amnon,' then kill him." So the servants did to Amnon as Absalom had commanded. Then the king's sons arose, and each mounted his mule and fled. When they brought the tidings to the king, they lifted up their voices and wept; and the king also and all his servants wept very bitterly.

Absalom fled to his grandfather Talmai king of Geshur and was there three years. David mourned for his son Amnon day after day, but he became comforted about him, seeing he was dead, and his spirit longed to go forth to Absalom. Now Joab perceived that the king's heart went out to Absalom, and he sent to Tekoa for a wise woman. "Behave like a woman who has been mourning many days for the dead," he said to her, "and go to the king and speak thus to him." So Joab put the words in her mouth.

When the woman of Tekoa came to the king, she fell on her face and did obeisance, and said, "Help, O king."

"What is your trouble?" the king asked.

"Alas," she said, "I am a widow, and I had two sons, and they quarreled with one another in the field. One struck the other and killed him. Now the whole family has risen against me, and they say, 'Give up your son, that we may kill him for the life of his brother.' And so they would destroy the heir also, and leave to my husband neither name nor remnant upon the face of the earth."

"Go to your house," the king said. "I will give orders about you."

"Pray let the king invoke the LORD," said the woman, "that the avenger of blood slay no more, and my son be not destroyed."

"As the LORD lives," the king replied, "not one hair of your son shall fall to the ground."

"Pray let your handmaid speak a word further to my lord the king," the woman said. "In giving this decision the king convicts himself, inasmuch as he does not bring his banished son home again. We must all die, we are like water spilt on the ground; but God will not take the life of him who brings home his banished one. Now I have come to say this because my lord the king is like the angel of God to discern good and evil." The king answered, "Do not hide anything from me. Is the hand of Joab with you in all this?"

"As surely as you live, my lord the king, one cannot hide anything from you. In order to change the course of affairs, your servant Joab put these words into my mouth."

Sending for Joab, the king said, "Behold now, I grant this; go, bring back the young man Absalom." Joab fell on his face and did obeisance, and blessed the king. Then he arose and went to Geshur, and brought Absalom to Jerusalem. "Let him dwell apart in his own house," said the king; "he is not to come into my presence." And so it was.

After Absalom had dwelt two full years in Jerusalem without coming into the king's presence, he sent for Joab, to intercede for him with the king. But Joab would not come. Absalom sent a second time, but still Joab would not come. Then Absalom said to his servants, "See, Joab's barley field is next to mine; go and set it on fire." So they set the field on fire. Then Joab went to Absalom. "Why have your servants set my field on fire?" he said. "Behold," Absalom answered, "I wanted to send you to the king to ask, 'Why have I come from Geshur? It would be better for me to be there still.' Now therefore let me go into his presence; and if there is guilt in me, let him kill me." Joab told the king, and David summoned Absalom. Coming to the king, Absalom bowed himself on his face to the ground before him; and the king kissed him.

In all Israel there was no one so much to be praised for his beauty as Absalom; from the sole of his foot to the crown of his head there was no blemish in him. And when he cut his hair (for at the end of every year he cut it when it was heavy on him), it weighed five pounds by the king's weight.

Now Absalom got himself a chariot and horses, and fifty men to run before him. He would rise early and stand by the gate, and when any man had a suit he wanted to bring before the king for judgment, Absalom would say to him, "See, your claims are good and right; but there is no man deputed by the king to hear you. Oh that I were judge in the land! Then every man might come to me, and I would give him justice." And whenever a man did obeisance to him, he would take hold of him, and kiss him. Thus Absalom did to all who came to the king for judgment; so he stole the hearts of the men of Israel.

After four years Absalom said to the king, "While I dwelt at Geshur I vowed a vow, saying, 'If the LORD will indeed bring me back to Jerusalem, then I will offer worship to the LORD.' Pray let me go and pay my vow in Hebron." And the king answered, "Go in peace." Absalom took with him two hundred men from Jerusalem, invited guests, who went in their simplicity and knew nothing. But Absalom sent secret messengers throughout Israel, saying, "As soon as you hear the sound of the trumpet, then say, 'Absalom is king at Hebron!'" And while he was offering the sacrifices at Hebron, he sent for Ahithophel, David's counselor. And the conspiracy grew strong, and the people with Absalom kept increasing.

At last messengers came to David, saying, "The hearts of the men of Israel have gone after Absalom." And David said to all who were with him at Jerusalem, "Arise, and let us flee, lest Absalom overtake us quickly, and smite the city with the sword." So the king went forth with his household, leaving ten concubines to keep the house. At the last house of the city he halted while all his servants and all the Cherethites and Pelethites, and all the six hundred Gittites who had followed him from Gath, passed on before him. Then the king crossed the brook Kidron, and all the country wept aloud as he passed on toward the wilderness.

Abiathar and Zadok the priests came up, bearing the ark of God, and they set it down until the people had all passed out of the city. Then the king said to Zadok, "Carry the ark of God back into the city. If I find favor in the eyes of the LORD, he will bring me back and let me see it. Go back to the city in peace, you and Abiathar, with Ahimaaz your son, and Jonathan the son of Abiathar. I will wait by the Jordan, at the fords of the wilderness, until word comes from you." So Zadok and Abiathar carried the ark of God back to Jerusalem; and they remained there.

But David, barefoot and weeping, climbed the Mount of Olives, and all the people with him covered their heads and wept. And it was told David that his counselor Ahithophel was among the conspirators. "O LORD," David said, "I pray thee, turn the counsel of Ahithophel into foolishness." When David came to the summit, behold, Hushai the Archite, his other counselor, came to meet him with his coat torn and earth upon his head. David said to him, "If you go on with me, you will be a burden to me. But if you return to the city and say to Absalom, 'O king, as I have been your father's servant in time past, so now I will be your servant,' then you will defeat for me the counsel of Ahithophel. Are not Zadok and Abiathar the priests with you there? Whatever you hear from the king's house, tell it to them. By their two sons you shall send me everything you hear." So Hushai came into Jerusalem just as Absalom was entering the city.

When King David came to Bahurim, near the border, there came out a man of the family of Saul whose name was Shimei. As he came he cursed continually, threw stones at David, and at all the mighty men who were on his right hand and on his left. "Begone, begone, you worthless fellow!" Shimei shouted. "The LORD has avenged upon you all the blood of the house of Saul and given the kingdom to your son Absalom. See, your ruin is on you, for you are a man of blood."

"Why should this dead dog curse my lord the king?" said Abishai. "Let me go over and take off his head."

"Behold," said the king, "my own son seeks my life; how much more now may this Benjaminite! Let him alone, and let him curse; for the LORD has bidden him. It may be that the LORD will look upon my affliction and repay me with good for this cursing of me today." So David and his men went on the road, while Shimei went along on the hillside opposite and cursed as he went and threw stones and dust at him. The king and the people with him arrived weary at the Jordan; and there he refreshed himself.

Now Absalom and his people, the men of Israel, came to Jerusalem, and Ahithophel with him. And Hushai, David's counselor, came to Absalom. "Long live the king! Long live the king!" he cried.

"Is this your loyalty to my father?" Absalom asked.

"He whom the LORD and all Israel have chosen, his I will be," Hushai answered. "As I have served your father, so I will serve you." Then Absalom said to Ahithophel, "Give your counsel. What shall we do?"

"Go in to your father's concubines," said Ahithophel, "and all Israel will hear that you have made yourself odious to him, and our hands will be strengthened." So they pitched a tent for Absalom upon the roof, and he went in to his father's concubines in the sight of all Israel.

In those days the counsel of Ahithophel was as if one consulted the oracle of God; it was so esteemed by both David and Absalom. Now Ahithophel said to Absalom, "Let me set out with twelve thousand men tonight and come upon David while he is weary and discouraged, and throw him and all his people into a panic. I will strike down the king only, and I will bring the people back to you as a bride comes home to her husband." The advice pleased Absalom and the elders of Israel. But Absalom said, "Call Hushai the Archite also, and let us hear what he has to say." When Hushai came, Absalom said, "Thus has Ahithophel spoken; shall we do as he advises? If not, you speak."

"This time," said Hushai, "the counsel of Ahithophel is not good. Your father and his men are mighty men, and they are enraged, like a bear robbed of her cubs. Besides, your father is expert in war; he will not spend the night with the people. My counsel is that all Israel be gathered to you, from Dan to Beer-sheba, as the sand by the sea for multitude, and that you go to battle in person. So we shall come upon him as the dew falls on the ground; and of him and all his men not one will be left." And Absalom and the elders said, "The counsel of Hushai the Archite is better than the counsel of Ahithophel." When Ahithophel saw that his good counsel was not followed, he went off home to his own city. He set his house in order, and then he hanged himself, and he was buried in the tomb of his father.

But Hushai did not know that the LORD had ordained to defeat the counsel of Ahithophel. He said to Zadok and Abiathar, "Send quickly to your sons that they may tell David, 'Do not lodge tonight at the fords of the wilderness, but by all means pass over the water, lest you and all your people be swallowed up tonight.'" So David and all the people with him crossed the Jordan;

and they came to Mahanaim in Gilead. And Absalom also crossed the Jordan with the men of Israel, and encamped in the land of Gilead, having set Amasa his cousin over his army.

Then David mustered his men and sent forth the army, one third under the command of Joab, one third under Joab's brother Abishai, and one third under Ittai the Gittite, who with the men of Gath had been loyal to David. "I myself will also go out with you," the king said. "You shall not go out," the men told him. "If half of us die, they will not care about us. But you are worth ten thousand of us; therefore it is better that you send us help from the city."

"Whatever seems best to you I will do," the king replied. So he stood by the gate at Mahanaim, while the army marched out by its hundreds and its thousands. "Deal gently for my sake with the young man Absalom," the king ordered his three commanders. And all the people heard him.

So the army went out into the field against Absalom, and the battle was fought in the forest nearby. Absalom's men were defeated there by the servants of David, and the slaughter was great on that day. The battle spread over the face of all the country; the forest devoured more people than the sword.

Now Absalom was riding upon his mule, and the mule chanced to go under the thick branches of a great oak. Absalom's head caught fast in the branches, and he was left hanging between heaven and earth, while the mule under him went on. One of David's servants saw it, and told Joab. "What, you saw him!" cried Joab. "Why then did you not strike him there to the ground? I would have been glad to give you ten pieces of silver."

"Even for a thousand pieces of silver I would not put forth my hand against the king's son; for in our hearing the king commanded you to protect him."

"I will not waste time like this with you," said Joab. He took three darts and went and thrust them into Absalom's heart while he was still alive in the oak. Then ten of Joab's young men surrounded Absalom and struck him, and killed him. Joab blew the trumpet, and the troops came back from the pursuit. They took Absalom and threw him into a pit in the forest, and raised over him a great heap of stones; and his men fled every one to his own home.

At Mahanaim, David was sitting by the gate. The watchman went up to the roof of the gate, and he called out to tell the king that he saw a man running alone. "If he is alone," said the king, "there are tidings in his mouth." The runner came apace, and drew near. Now the watchman called again and said, "See, another man running alone!"

"He also brings tidings," said the king.

"I think the running of the foremost is like the running of Ahimaaz the son of Zadok," the watchman said. "He is a good messenger," said the king, "and comes with good tidings."

Then Ahimaaz came and cried out to the king, "All is well." And he bowed before the king with his face to the earth and said, "Blessed be the Lord, who has delivered up the men who raised their hand against my lord the king."

"Is it well with the young man Absalom?" the king asked.

"When Joab sent me, I saw a great tumult," Ahimaaz replied, "but I do not know what it was."

"Turn aside," the king said, "and stand here." So Ahimaaz turned aside, and stood still. Then the second messenger came. "Good tidings for my lord the king!" he cried. "For the LORD has delivered you this day from the power of all who rose up against you."

"Is it well with the young man Absalom?" asked the king.

"May the enemies of my lord the king, and all who rise up against you for evil, be like that young man," the messenger replied.

The king was deeply moved and went up to the chamber over the gate and wept; and as he went, he said, "O my son Absalom, my son, my son Absalom! Would I had died instead of you, O Absalom, my son, my son!"

SO THE KING came back to the Jordan; and the men of Judah came to meet him and to bring him across the river. And all the people of Judah, and also half the people of Israel, brought him on his way.

Now there happened to be there a worthless fellow, Sheba, the son of Bichri, a Benjaminite; and he blew the trumpet and then said, "We have no portion in David, nor inheritance in the son of Jesse; every man to his tents, O Israel!" So all the men of Israel withdrew from David and followed Sheba. But the men of Judah followed their king steadfastly from the Jordan to Jerusalem.

When David came to his house there, he took the ten concubines he had left to care for it and put them in a house under guard. He provided for them, but did not go in to them, so they were shut up until the day of their death, living as if in widowhood. Then David said to Abishai, "Sheba the son of Bichri will do us more harm than Absalom; take the army and pursue him." So Abishai went out from Jerusalem with Joab his brother and all the mighty men, and they pursued Sheba northward through all the tribes of Israel to Abel of Beth-maacah; and they besieged him there. They cast up a mound against the rampart, and were battering the wall when a wise woman called from the city for Joab. He came near her, and the woman said, "Listen to the words of your maidservant. I am one of those who are peaceable and faithful in Israel. You seek to destroy a city which is a mother in Israel; why will you swallow up the heritage of the LORD?"

"Far be it from me that I should swallow up or destroy!" Joab answered. "But a man called Sheba has lifted up his hand against King David; give him up, and I will withdraw from the city."

"Behold," said the woman, "his head shall be thrown to you over the wall." She went to all the people of the city in her wisdom, and they cut off Sheba's head and threw it out. So Joab blew the trumpet; they dispersed from the city and returned to Jerusalem to the king.

NOW THE KING SAID TO JOAB and the commanders of the army, "Go through all the tribes of Israel, from Dan to Beer-sheba, and number the people, that I may know their number." But Joab said, "May the LORD add to the people a hundred times as many as they are, but why does my lord the king delight in this thing?" But David's word prevailed, so Joab and his commanders went out to number the people of Israel. When they had gone through all the land, they came to Jerusalem after nine months and twenty days, and Joab gave the sum of the numbering to the king: in Israel there were eight hundred thousand men who drew the sword, and the men of Judah were five hundred thousand. But David's heart smote him after he had numbered the people, and he said to the LORD, "I have sinned greatly, O LORD; I pray thee, take away the iniquity of thy servant; for I have done very foolishly."

So the LORD sent a pestilence upon Israel, and there died seventy thousand of the people from Dan to Beer-sheba. The angel of the LORD was by the threshing floor of Araunah the Jebusite, and he was stretching forth his hand to destroy Jerusalem when David spoke to the LORD. "Lo, I have sinned," he said, "and I have done wickedly; but these sheep, what have they done? Let thy hand, I pray thee, be against me." The prophet Gad came that day to David and said, "Go up, rear an altar to the LORD on the threshing floor of Araunah the Jebusite." So David went up as the LORD commanded. When Araunah saw the king and his servants coming up, he did obeisance, asking, "Why has my lord the king come to his servant?"

"To buy the threshing floor of you," David replied, "in order to build an altar to the LORD, that the plague may be averted from the people."

"Let my lord the king take the oxen for the burnt offering," said Araunah, "and the threshing sledges and the yokes of the oxen for the wood. All this, O king, Araunah gives to the king."

"No," said the king; "but I will buy it of you for a price; I will not offer burnt offerings to the LORD which cost me nothing." So David bought the threshing floor and the oxen, and he built there an altar to the LORD, and offered burnt offerings and peace offerings. So the plague was averted.

THIS IS THE oracle of David, the son of Jesse, the oracle of the man who was raised on high, the anointed of the God of Jacob, the sweet psalmist of Israel: "The Spirit of the LORD speaks by me; his word is upon my tongue. The God of Israel has said to me: 'When one rules justly over men, ruling in the fear of God, he dawns on them like the morning light, like the sun shining forth upon a cloudless morning, like rain that makes grass to sprout.'

"Yea, does not my house stand so with God? For he has made with me an everlasting covenant, ordered in all things and secure. But godless men are all like thorns; for they cannot be taken with the hand, or a man touch them except with the shaft of a spear; and they must be destroyed with fire."

1 KINGS

In the two books of Kings, originally a single book in Hebrew, the history of Israel is continued. This book opens with the last days of King David, and continues with the reign of King Solomon and the building of the temple in Jerusalem. After Solomon's death, what had been a single nation splits into two separate kingdoms, Judah and Israel. Through the remainder of the book the successive rulers in each kingdom are treated alternately. While the author evidently had access to several purely historical sources, his main interest is religious. He ascribes a dominant role to the prophet Elijah, and he judges every king by his obedience to God's commandments and his rejection of idol worship. By that standard, all the kings of Israel fail, and only two kings of Judah are thoroughly good, Hezekiah and Josiah. The author's message, reflecting the theme of Deuteronomy, is that national success depends on obedience to the will of God, while abandonment of religious faith inevitably brings divine punishment. The bulk of 1 and 2 Kings seems to have been written about 600 B.C., with additions made some fifty years later.

Now KING DAVID was old and advanced in years, and although they covered him with clothes, he could not get warm. Therefore his servants said to him, "Let a young maiden be sought to wait upon my lord the king and be his nurse; let her lie in your bosom, that you may be warm." So they sought throughout all Israel and found Abishag the Shunammite, and brought her to the king. She was very beautiful, and she became the king's nurse and ministered to him; but the king knew her not.

Now Adonijah the son of David, born next after Absalom, exalted himself, saying, "I will be king." He was a very handsome man, and his father had never displeased him by asking, "Why have you done thus and so?" He prepared chariots and horsemen, with fifty men to run before him, and he conferred with Joab and with Abiathar the priest, and they followed him. But Zadok the priest, and Benaiah the commander of the king's bodyguard, and

Nathan the prophet, and David's mighty men were not with him. Adonijah sacrificed sheep and oxen at En-rogel, outside Jerusalem, and he invited all his brothers except Solomon, and all the royal officials of Judah.

Then Nathan said to Bathsheba the mother of Solomon, "Have you not heard that Adonijah has become king and David does not know it? Go in at once to King David and say, 'Did you not swear to your maidservant, saying, "Solomon your son shall reign after me"? Why then is Adonijah king?'"

Bathsheba went to the king in his chamber, where Abishag was ministering to him. "My lord," she said, "you swore to your maidservant, saying, 'Solomon your son shall reign after me.' But now, behold, Adonijah is king. My lord the king, the eyes of all Israel are upon you, to tell them who shall sit on the throne after you. Otherwise, when my lord sleeps with his fathers, I and my son Solomon will be in danger."

"As the LORD lives," the king said, "as I swore to you that Solomon should reign after me, even so will I do this day." Then he summoned Zadok, Nathan, and Benaiah. "Take with you my bodyguard," he said, "and cause Solomon my son to ride on my own mule, and bring him down to Gihon; and let Zadok and Nathan there anoint him king over Israel; then blow the trumpet and say, 'Long live King Solomon!' For I have appointed him to be king over Israel and Judah in my stead."

"Amen!" said Benaiah. "May the LORD make his throne greater than the throne of my lord King David."

ADONIJAH AND HIS guests, as they finished feasting, heard playing on pipes and rejoicing. "What does this uproar in the city mean?" said Joab. While he was still speaking, Jonathan the son of Abiathar came. "Our lord King David has made Solomon king," he said. "Zadok and Nathan have anointed him at Gihon, and they have gone up from there rejoicing, so that the city is in an uproar. This is the noise that you have heard."

Then all the guests of Adonijah trembled and rose, and each went his own way. Adonijah feared Solomon, and he went to the tent of the LORD and caught hold of the horns of the altar, saying, "Let King Solomon swear to me that he will not slay me with the sword." And it was told Solomon, and he said, "If he prove to be a worthy man, not one of his hairs shall fall to the earth; but if wickedness is found in him, he shall die." Then they brought Adonijah down from the altar, and he came and did obeisance to the king; and Solomon said to him, "Go to your house."

When David's time to die drew near, he charged Solomon, saying, "I am about to go the way of all the earth. Be strong, and show yourself a man, and walk in the ways of the LORD and keep his commandments, as it is written in the law of Moses, that you may prosper in all that you do and that the LORD may establish his word concerning me, saying, 'If your sons take heed to their way, to walk before me in faithfulness with all their heart, there shall not fail you a man on the throne of Israel.' Moreover, you know what Joab did to

me, how he murdered Abner, the commander of the army of Israel, avenging
in time of peace blood which had been shed in war, and putting innocent
blood upon me. Do not let his gray head go down to Sheol in peace." Then
David slept with his fathers, and was buried in the city of David; and Solomon sat upon his throne.

Now Adonijah came to Bathsheba the mother of Solomon. "You know that
the kingdom was mine," he said, "and that all Israel fully expected me to
reign; however, the kingdom has turned about and become my brother's, for
it was his from the LORD. And now I have one request to make of you; pray
ask King Solomon—he will not refuse you—to give me Abishag the
Shunammite as my wife."

"Very well," Bathsheba replied. "I will speak for you to the king." She
went to King Solomon, and the king rose and bowed to her; then he had a
seat brought, and she sat on his right. "I have one small request to make of
you," she said. "Let Abishag the Shunammite be given to Adonijah your
brother as his wife."

"And why do you ask this for Adonijah?" King Solomon answered. "Ask
for him the kingdom also; for he is my elder brother, and on his side are
Abiathar and Joab. God punish me if this word does not cost Adonijah his life
this day!" So King Solomon sent Benaiah, and Benaiah struck Adonijah
down, and he died. To Abiathar Solomon said, "Go to your estate. You deserve death, but I will not at this time put you to death, because you bore the
ark of the LORD before David my father, and because you shared in all his
affliction." Solomon expelled Abiathar as priest to the LORD, thus fulfilling
the word the LORD had spoken concerning the house of Eli.

When the news came to Joab, he fled to the tent of the LORD and caught
hold of the horns of the altar. When it was told King Solomon, he summoned
Benaiah, saying, "Go, strike Joab down." So Benaiah came to the tent of the
LORD. "The king commands, 'Come forth,'" he said. "No, I will die here,"
Joab replied. Benaiah brought word of this to the king. "Do as he has said,"
the king replied. "Strike him down there, and thus take away from my father's house the guilt for the blood which Joab shed without cause." So
Benaiah went back and struck Joab down and killed him; and he was buried
in his own house in the wilderness. Then the king put Benaiah over the army
in place of Joab, and Zadok the priest in the place of Abiathar; and so the
kingdom was firmly established in the hand of Solomon.

SOLOMON MADE A marriage alliance with Pharaoh king of Egypt; he brought
Pharaoh's daughter into the city of David until he had finished building his
own house and the house of the LORD. Now Solomon loved the LORD, walking
in the statutes of David his father; but because no temple had yet been built
for the LORD, he sacrificed at the high places. He went to Gibeon to sacrifice
(for that was the great high place), and there the LORD appeared to him in a
dream by night. "Ask what I should give you," the LORD said.

"O Lord my God," Solomon answered, "thou hast made thy servant king in place of David my father, although I do not know how to go out or come in. Give thy servant therefore an understanding mind to govern thy great people, that I may discern between good and evil."

It pleased the Lord that Solomon had asked this. "Because you have not asked for yourself long life or riches or the life of your enemies," he said, "behold, I now give you a wise and discerning mind, so that none like you has been before and none shall arise after you. I give you also what you have not asked, both riches and honor, so that no other king shall compare with you all your days. And if you will walk in my ways, keeping my commandments, as your father David walked, then I will lengthen your days."

Solomon awoke, and behold, it was a dream. He came to Jerusalem, and stood before the ark of the Lord, and offered up burnt offerings, and made a feast for all his servants.

Then two harlots came to the king. "Oh, my lord," one of them said, "this woman and I dwell in the same house, and I gave birth to a child there. On the third day after I was delivered, this woman also gave birth; and we two were alone in the house. This woman's son died in the night, because she lay on it; so she arose at midnight, and took my son from beside me while I slept, and laid it in her bosom, and laid her dead son in my bosom. When I rose in the morning to nurse my child, behold, it was dead; but when I looked at it closely, it was not the child that I had borne."

"The living child is mine," said the other woman.

"No, the dead child is yours," said the first.

Then the king said, "Bring me a sword." So a sword was brought, and the king said, "Divide the living child in two, and give half to one woman and half to the other."

Then the heart of the first woman yearned for her son. "Oh, my lord," she said, "give her the child, and by no means slay it."

"It shall be neither mine nor yours," said the other. "Divide it."

Then the king answered and said, "Give the living child to the first woman, and by no means slay it; she is its mother." All Israel heard of the judgment the king had rendered, and they stood in awe of him, because they perceived that the wisdom of God was in him.

King Solomon had twelve officers over the twelve districts of Israel; each man had to provide food for the king and his household for one month in the year. Solomon's provision for one day was three hundred and thirty bushels of fine flour, and six hundred and sixty bushels of meal, ten fat oxen, and twenty pasture-fed cattle, a hundred sheep, besides harts, gazelles, roebucks, and fatted fowl. King Solomon also had four thousand stalls of horses for his chariots. And those officers supplying provisions let nothing be lacking. Barley and straw for the horses they brought to the place where it was required.

Judah and Israel were as many as the sand by the sea; they ate and drank and were happy. They dwelt in safety, from Dan even to Beer-sheba, every man under his vine and under his fig tree; for Solomon ruled over all the kingdoms from the Euphrates to the border of Egypt; they brought tribute and served Solomon all the days of his life. Solomon's wisdom surpassed the wisdom of all the people of the east, so that his fame was in all the nations round about. He also uttered three thousand proverbs, and his songs were a thousand and five; and men came from all peoples to hear his wisdom.

HIRAM KING OF Tyre sent his servants to Solomon when he heard that he was anointed king in place of his father; for Hiram always loved David. Solomon sent word back, "You know that my father could not build a house for the name of the LORD his God because of the warfare with which his enemies surrounded him. But now the LORD has given me rest on every side; there is neither adversary nor misfortune. And so I purpose to build a house for his name, as the LORD foretold to David my father. Now therefore command that cedars of Lebanon be cut for me; and my servants will join your servants, and I will pay you for your servants such wages as you set; for you know that no one knows how to cut timber like the Sidonians."

When Hiram heard these words, he rejoiced greatly, and sent to Solomon, saying, "I am ready to do all you desire. My servants shall bring the cedar and cypress timber down to the sea; and I will make it into rafts to go by sea to the place you direct, and I will have them broken up there." Year by year Hiram supplied Solomon with all the timber that he desired, while Solomon gave Hiram wheat and beaten oil for his household.

Solomon also raised a levy of thirty thousand men out of all Israel and placed Adoniram in charge. He sent them to Lebanon as forced labor, ten thousand a month in relays. And he had seventy thousand burden-bearers and eighty thousand hewers of stone in the hill country, with three thousand three hundred officers over the work. They quarried out great, costly stones for the foundation of the house. And so, in the four hundred and eightieth year after the people of Israel came out of Egypt, in the fourth year of his reign, in the month of Ziv, which is the second month, Solomon began to build the house of the LORD.

The temple was ninety feet long, thirty feet wide, and forty-five feet high. Solomon lined the walls with boards of cedar and covered the floor with cypress. The inner sanctuary he prepared in the innermost part of the house, to set there the ark of the covenant. It was thirty feet long, thirty feet wide, and thirty feet high; and he overlaid it with pure gold. In it he placed two cherubim of olivewood, each fifteen feet high. The wings of the two cherubim were spread out so that a wing of each touched each wall, and their other wings touched in the middle. And he overlaid the cherubim with gold.

Solomon was seven years in building the house of the LORD, and in the eleventh year of his reign, in the month of Bul, which is the eighth month, it was finished in all its parts. Then he assembled in Jerusalem the elders of

Israel and the heads of the tribes, to bring the ark of the covenant up from the city of David, which is Zion, to the temple. The priests took up the ark and brought it to its place in the inner sanctuary, in the most holy place, underneath the wings of the cherubim. There was nothing in the ark except the two tablets of stone which Moses put there at Sinai, where the LORD made a covenant with the people of Israel when they came out of Egypt. And when the priests came out of the holy place, a cloud filled the house of the LORD, so that the priests could not minister; for the glory of the LORD filled his house.

Then Solomon knelt before the altar in the presence of all the assembly of Israel, and spread forth his hands toward heaven and said, "O LORD, God of Israel, the highest heaven cannot contain thee; how much less this house which I have built! Yet hearken thou to the supplication of thy servant and of thy people Israel when they pray toward this place; yea, hear thou in heaven; and when thou hearest, forgive. For thou didst separate thy people from among all the peoples of the earth to be thy heritage, as thou didst declare through Moses, thy servant, when thou didst bring our fathers out of Egypt, O Lord GOD." As Solomon finished, he arose and stood before the altar and blessed the assembly. Then he and all Israel with him offered sacrifice before the LORD of twenty-two thousand oxen and a hundred and twenty thousand sheep. So the king and all the people dedicated the house of the LORD. Solomon held the feast at that time, a great assembly before the LORD, seven days. On the eighth day he sent the people away; and they went to their homes joyful and glad of heart.

When Solomon had finished building the house of the LORD and his own house and all that he desired to build, the LORD appeared to him a second time, as he had at Gibeon. And the LORD said, "I have heard your prayer, and I have consecrated this house which you have built. As for you, if you will walk before me with integrity of heart and uprightness, keeping my statutes and my ordinances, then I will establish your royal throne over Israel for ever, as I promised David your father. But if you turn aside from following me, you or your children, and go and worship other gods, then I will cut off Israel from the land which I have given them. The house which I have consecrated for my name will become a heap of ruins, and Israel will become a proverb and a byword among all peoples."

NOW WHEN THE queen of Sheba heard of the fame of Solomon, she came to test him with hard questions. With a great retinue she came to Jerusalem, with camels bearing spices, gold, and precious stones, and when she met Solomon, she told him all that was on her mind. Solomon answered all her questions; there was nothing he could not explain to her. When the queen had seen all his wisdom, the palace he had built, and his manner of life, she said to him, "I did not believe the reports of your prosperity and your wisdom until my own eyes had seen it; and, behold, the half was not told me. Happy are your wives! Happy are these your servants, who continually stand before you and hear your wisdom! Blessed be the LORD your God, who has delighted in you!" Then she gave the king a very great quantity of gold and precious stones, and an abundance of spices. And the king gave to the queen of Sheba all that she desired before she went back to her own land.

Now the weight of gold that came to Solomon in one year was six hundred and sixty-six talents, besides that which came from the traders and all the kings of Arabia and the governors of the land. All the king's drinking vessels were of gold; silver was not considered as anything in the days of Solomon. For the king had a fleet of ships of Tarshish at sea with the fleet of Hiram, and every three years it came bringing gold, silver, ivory, apes, and peacocks.

Now Solomon loved many foreign women from the nations round about, concerning which the LORD had said, "You shall not enter into marriage with them, for surely they will turn away your heart after their gods." But Solomon clung to them in love. He had seven hundred wives, princesses, and three hundred concubines; and when he was old, his wives turned away his heart after other gods, and he was not wholly true to the LORD his God, as was David his father. For Solomon built a high place for Chemosh the abomination of Moab, and for Molech the abomination of the Ammonites, on the mountain east of Jerusalem. And so he did for all his foreign wives who sacrificed to their gods.

So Solomon did what was evil in the sight of the LORD, and the LORD was angry, and said to him, "Since you have not kept my covenant and my statutes, I will surely tear the kingdom from you and will give it to your servant." Then the LORD raised up an adversary against Solomon, Jeroboam the son of Nebat. When Solomon saw that the man Jeroboam was very able and industrious, he gave him charge over the forced labor of the house of Joseph.

About that time Jeroboam went out of Jerusalem, and the prophet Ahijah the Shilonite found him on the road. The two of them were alone in the open country, and Ahijah, who had clad himself in a new cloak, laid hold of it and tore it into twelve pieces. "Take for yourself ten pieces," he said to Jeroboam; "for thus says the LORD: 'Behold, I am about to tear the kingdom from the hand of Solomon, because he has forsaken me and worshiped foreign gods. Nevertheless, for the sake of David my servant I will not take the whole kingdom out of his hand during the days of his life, but I will take it out of his son's hand, and will give it to you, ten tribes. Yet to his son I will give one tribe, that David may always have a lamp before me in Jerusalem. You shall be king over Israel, and if you will keep my statutes and my commandments, as David my servant did, I will be with you, and will build you an enduring house.'" Solomon sought therefore to kill Jeroboam; but Jeroboam fled to Shishak king of Egypt.

Now the rest of the acts of Solomon, and all that he did, and his wisdom, are they not written in the book of the acts of Solomon? After he had reigned over all Israel for forty years, Solomon slept with his fathers, and was buried in the city of David; and Rehoboam his son reigned in his stead.

REHOBOAM WENT TO SHECHEM, for the northern tribes had come there to make him king; and when Jeroboam heard of it, he returned from Egypt. And they sent and called him; and Jeroboam and all the assembly of Israel came and said to Rehoboam, "Your father made our yoke heavy. Now therefore lighten his hard service, and we will serve you." And he said, "Depart for three days, then come again to me." When the people went away, Rehoboam conferred with the old men, the counselors of Solomon his father. "How do you advise me to answer this people?" he asked them. "If you will be a servant to this people," they answered, "and speak good words to them, they will be your servants for ever."

Then he asked counsel of the young men who had grown up with him. "Thus shall you speak," they replied. "'My little finger is thicker than my father's loins. And now, whereas my father laid upon you a heavy yoke, I will add to it. My father chastised you with whips, but I will chastise you with scorpions.'"

Jeroboam and all the people came to Rehoboam the third day, as he had said. And the king spoke to them harshly, according to the counsel of the young men. Now when Israel saw that the king did not hearken to them, the people answered him, "What portion have we in David? We have no inheritance in the son of Jesse. To your tents, O Israel! Look now to your own house, David." So Israel departed to their tents.

Then King Rehoboam sent Adoniram to them, who was taskmaster over the forced labor; but they stoned him to death, and the king made haste to mount his chariot to flee to Jerusalem. So Rehoboam reigned over the people who dwelt in the cities of Judah, and so Israel has been in rebellion against the house of David to this day.

Now they called Jeroboam to the assembly and made him king over all Israel. None followed the house of David, but the tribe of Judah only.

When Rehoboam returned to Jerusalem, he assembled all the house of Judah to fight to restore Israel to his rule. But the word of God came to Shemaiah the man of God: "Say to Rehoboam, king of Judah, and to the rest of the people, 'Thus says the LORD: You shall not go up or fight against your kinsmen. Return every man to his home, for this thing is from me.'" So they hearkened to the word of the LORD and went home again.

THEN JEROBOAM DWELT in Shechem, in the hill country of Ephraim; and he said in his heart, "If this people go up to offer sacrifices in the house of the LORD at Jerusalem, their hearts will turn again to Rehoboam, and they will kill me and return to the house of David." So Jeroboam took counsel, and made two calves of gold; he set one in Bethel and the other in Dan. He also built temples on high places, and appointed priests who were not Levites. And this thing became a sin.

"You have gone up to Jerusalem long enough," Jeroboam said to the people. "Behold your gods, O Israel, who brought you up out of the land of

Egypt." Then he ordained a feast for the people of Israel at Bethel, and he went up to the altar that he had made to burn incense. And behold, a man of God came out of Judah to Bethel, and the man cried against the altar and said, "O altar, altar, thus says the LORD: 'Behold, a son shall be born to the house of David, Josiah by name; and he shall sacrifice upon you the priests of the high places who burn incense upon you, and men's bones shall be burned upon you.' And this is the sign that the LORD has spoken: 'Behold, the altar shall be torn down, and the ashes that are upon it shall be poured out.'"

Jeroboam stretched out his hand against the man of God, saying, "Lay hold of him." But his hand dried up, so that he could not draw it back. The altar also was torn down, and the ashes poured out from it, according to the sign the man of God had given. Then the king said to the man, "Entreat now the favor of the LORD your God and pray for me, that my hand may be restored." So the man entreated the LORD; and the king's hand became as it was before. "Come home with me and refresh yourself," said the king, "and I will give you a reward."

"If you give me half your house," replied the man of God, "I will not go in with you, nor eat bread or drink water in this place; for so was it commanded me by the word of the LORD." So he departed.

Now Jeroboam did not turn from his evil way, but consecrated any from among the people who desired to be priests of the high places. And this thing became sin to the house of Jeroboam, so as to cut it off and destroy it from the face of the earth.

At that time Abijah the son of Jeroboam fell sick, and Jeroboam said to his wife, "Arise, and go to Shiloh to Ahijah the prophet, who said of me that I should be king over this people. Take with you ten loaves, some cakes, and a jar of honey; he will tell you what shall happen to the child." In Shiloh she came to the house of Ahijah. Now Ahijah could not see, for his eyes were dim from age, and the LORD said to him, "Behold, the wife of Jeroboam is coming to inquire concerning her son. Thus and thus shall you say to her."

When she came, she pretended to be another woman. But when Ahijah heard the sound of her feet at the door, he said, "Come in, wife of Jeroboam; why do you pretend to be another? I am charged with heavy tidings for you. Go, tell Jeroboam, 'Thus says the LORD, the God of Israel: "I exalted you from among the people and made you leader over Israel; yet you have done evil above all that were before you and have made for yourself molten images, provoking me to anger. Therefore I will bring evil upon your house and will utterly consume it, as a man burns up dung until it is all gone."' Arise therefore; go to your house. When your feet enter the city of Tirzah, the child shall die. Moreover, the LORD will smite the people of Israel and root them out of this good land which he gave to their fathers, and scatter them beyond the Euphrates, because of the sins of Jeroboam, and those which he made Israel to sin." Then Jeroboam's wife departed; and as she came to the threshold of her house, the child died, according to the word of the LORD.

Now the rest of the acts of Jeroboam, how he warred and how he reigned, are written in the Book of the Chronicles of the Kings of Israel. And the time that Jeroboam reigned was twenty-two years; and he slept with his fathers, and Nadab his son reigned in his stead.

Now Rehoboam the son of Solomon reigned seventeen years in Jerusalem. Judah provoked the Lord by their sins more than all that their fathers had done. For they also placed idols on the high places, and there were male cult prostitutes in the land. They did according to all the abominations of the nations which the Lord drove out before the people of Israel.

In the fifth year of King Rehoboam, Shishak king of Egypt came up against Jerusalem; he took away the treasures of the house of the Lord and of the king's house; he took away everything. And there was war between Rehoboam and Jeroboam continually.

Then Rehoboam slept with his fathers, and Abijam his son reigned in his stead. Abijam reigned for three years in Jerusalem, and he walked in all the sins which his father did before him. Nevertheless, for David's sake the Lord gave him a lamp in Jerusalem, setting up his son after him, because David did what was right in the eyes of the Lord all the days of his life, except in the matter of Uriah the Hittite.

Nadab the son of Jeroboam reigned over Israel two years, and walked in the sinful way of his father. Then Baasha, of the house of Issachar, conspired against him. Now Nadab and his army were laying siege to Gibbethon, which belonged to the Philistines; and Baasha killed him there and reigned at Tirzah in his stead. As soon as Baasha was king, he killed all the house of Jeroboam, leaving not one that breathed, until he had destroyed it according to the word of the Lord. Then Baasha slept with his fathers, and Elah his son reigned in his stead; but Zimri, commander of half his chariots, conspired against Elah. When Elah was at Tirzah, drinking himself drunk in the house of his chamberlain, Zimri came in and struck him down and killed him, and reigned in his stead for seven days.

Now the troops were again encamped against the Philistines at Gibbethon, and when they heard that Zimri had killed the king, they made Omri, the commander of the army, king over Israel that day in the camp. So Omri took the army and went up from Gibbethon and besieged Tirzah. When Zimri saw that the city was taken, he went into the king's house and burned it over him and died.

Omri reigned for twelve years over Israel, six years in Tirzah. Then he bought the hill of Samaria for two talents of silver; and he fortified it, and called the city which he built Samaria, after the name of Shemer, the owner of the hill. Omri did what was evil in the sight of the Lord, more than all who were before him. And he slept with his fathers, and was buried in Samaria; and Ahab his son reigned in his stead.

AHAB REIGNED OVER ISRAEL in Samaria twenty-two years. As if it were a light thing for him to walk in the sins of Jeroboam, he also took for wife Jezebel the daughter of the king of the Sidonians, and he went and served Baal, and he built a temple for Baal in Samaria. Ahab did more to provoke the LORD to anger than all the kings of Israel who were before him. In his days Hiel of Bethel built Jericho; he laid its foundation at the cost of Abiram his first-born, and set up its gates at the cost of his youngest son Segub, according to the word of the LORD, which he spoke by Joshua the son of Nun.

Now Elijah the prophet said to Ahab, "As the LORD the God of Israel lives, there shall be neither dew nor rain these years, except by my word." Then the word of the LORD came to Elijah: "Depart from here and hide yourself by the brook Cherith, east of the Jordan. You shall drink from the brook, and I have commanded the ravens to feed you there." So Elijah went and dwelt by the brook Cherith, and the ravens brought him bread and meat in the morning and in the evening. After a while the brook dried up, because there was no rain in the land; and again the word of the LORD came: "Arise, go to Zare-phath, which belongs to Sidon, and dwell there. Behold, I have commanded a widow there to feed you." So Elijah went, and at the gate of Zarephath a widow was gathering sticks.

"Bring me a little water in a vessel," he called to her, "and bring me also a morsel of bread."

"As the LORD lives," she said, "I have nothing baked, only a handful of meal in a jar, and a little oil in a cruse; and now I am gathering sticks, that I may go in and prepare it for myself and my son."

"Fear not," Elijah replied. "Go and do as you have said; but first make a little cake for me, and afterward make for yourself and your son. For thus says the LORD: 'The jar of meal shall not be spent, and the cruse of oil shall not fail, until the day the LORD sends rain upon the earth.'" The woman did as Elijah said; and she, and he, and her household ate for many days.

After this the son of the woman became ill, so that there was no breath left in him. "What have you against me, O man of God?" she cried to Elijah. "You have come to me to bring my sin to remembrance, and to cause the death of my son!"

"Give me your son," Elijah said; and he took up the child and laid him upon his own bed. Then he stretched himself upon the child three times. "O LORD my God," he cried, "let this child's soul come into him again." The LORD hearkened to the voice of Elijah; and the soul of the child came into him again. Then Elijah brought him to the widow. "See, your son lives," he said. "Now I know that you are a man of God," she said, "and that the word of the LORD in your mouth is truth."

In the third year of the drought the word of the LORD came to Elijah, say-ing, "Go, show yourself to Ahab; and I will send rain upon the earth." So Elijah went to show himself to Ahab. The famine was severe in Samaria, and Ahab called Obadiah, who was over his household. (Obadiah revered the

LORD greatly; and when Jezebel persecuted the prophets of the LORD, Obadiah took a hundred of them and hid them in a cave, and fed them with bread and water.) "Go through the land," said Ahab. "Go to all the springs of water and to all the valleys; perhaps we may find grass to keep the horses and mules alive." As Obadiah was on the way, behold, Elijah met him. Obadiah recognized him and fell on his face. "Is it you, my lord Elijah?" he said.

"It is I. Go, tell your lord, 'Behold, Elijah is here.'"

"Wherein have I sinned," Obadiah replied, "that you would give me into the hand of Ahab, to kill me? As the LORD lives, there is no nation whither Ahab has not sent to seek you; and now you say, 'Go, tell your lord that Elijah is here.' As soon as I have left you, the Spirit of the LORD will carry you whither I know not; and when Ahab cannot find you, he will kill me, although I have revered the LORD from my youth."

"As the LORD lives," Elijah replied, "I will surely show myself to him today." So Obadiah told Ahab; and Ahab went to meet Elijah. "Is it you, you troubler of Israel?" Ahab said when he saw Elijah.

"I have not troubled Israel," Elijah answered, "but you have, because you have forsaken the LORD and followed Baal. Now therefore send and gather all Israel to me at Mount Carmel, and the prophets of Baal, who eat at Jezebel's table." So Ahab gathered all the people and the prophets together at Mount Carmel. "How long will you go limping about with two different opinions?" Elijah cried to them. "If the LORD is God, follow him; but if Baal, then follow him." The people did not answer him a word.

Then Elijah said, "Only I am left a prophet of the LORD, but Baal's prophets are four hundred and fifty. Let two bulls be brought; and let them choose one and cut it in pieces and lay it on the wood, but put no fire to it; and I will prepare the other bull and lay it on the wood, and put no fire to it. And you call on your god and I will call on the LORD; the God who answers by fire, he is God."

"It is well spoken," the people answered.

The prophets of Baal took a bull and prepared it, and called on the name of Baal from morning until noon, saying, "O Baal, answer us!" But there was no voice, and no one answered.

"Cry aloud," Elijah mocked them, "for he is a god; either he is musing, or he is on a journey, or perhaps he is asleep and must be awakened." They raved on, and cut themselves after their custom until the blood gushed out, but there was no voice; no one heeded.

Then Elijah said to the people, "Come near to me." And taking twelve stones, according to the number of the tribes of Israel, he built an altar in the name of the LORD, and made a trench about it. He put the wood in place, and cut the bull in pieces and laid it on the wood. "Fill four jars with water," he said, "and pour it on the offering, and on the wood." He had them do it a second time, and a third time, so that the water ran round about the altar, and filled the trench also.

Then Elijah came near and said, "O LORD, God of Abraham, Isaac, and Israel, let it be known this day that thou art God in Israel, and I am thy servant, and that I have done all these things at thy word. Answer me, O LORD, that this people may know thou art God." Then the fire of the LORD fell, and consumed the burnt offering, and the wood, and the stones, and licked up the water in the trench. And when the people saw it, they fell on their faces. "The LORD, he is God," they cried. "The LORD, he is God."

"Seize the prophets of Baal," Elijah told them; "let not one escape." And the people seized the prophets and brought them down to the brook Kishon, and killed them there.

Then Elijah went up to the top of Carmel and bowed himself down upon the earth. "Go up now," he said to his servant, "look toward the sea." The servant went up and looked. "There is nothing," he said. "Go again seven times," said Elijah. At the seventh time the servant said, "Behold, a little cloud like a man's hand is rising out of the sea." "Go up," said Elijah, "and say to Ahab, 'Prepare your chariot and go down, lest the rain stop you.'" In a little while the heavens grew black with clouds and wind, and there was a great rain. Ahab rode to Jezreel; but the hand of the LORD was on Elijah, and he girded up his loins and ran before Ahab to the entrance of the city.

AHAB TOLD HIS wife Jezebel all that Elijah had done, and how he had slain all the prophets of Baal. Jezebel sent a messenger to Elijah, saying, "May the gods punish me if I do not make your life as the life of the prophets of Baal by this time tomorrow." Then Elijah was afraid, and he arose and went for his life, and came to Beer-sheba, in Judah, and left his servant there.

But he himself went a day's journey into the wilderness, and came and sat under a broom tree; and he asked that he might die, saying, "It is enough; now, O LORD, take away my life; for I am no better than those who came before me." He lay down and slept; and behold, an angel touched him, and said, "Arise and eat." At his head there was a cake baked on hot stones and a jar of water. He ate and drank, and lay down again. The angel came a second time, and touched him, and said, "Arise and eat, else the journey will be too great for you." So he arose, and ate and drank, and went in the strength of that food forty days and forty nights to Sinai, the mount of God. He came to a cave, and lodged there; and behold, the word of the LORD came to him, saying, "What are you doing here, Elijah?"

"I have been very jealous for the LORD, the God of hosts," Elijah answered; "for the people of Israel have forsaken thy covenant, thrown down thy altars, and slain thy prophets with the sword; and I, even I only, am left; and they seek my life, to take it away." The LORD said, "Go forth, and stand upon the mount before me."

And behold, the LORD passed by, and a great and strong wind rent the mountains, but the LORD was not in the wind; and after the wind an earthquake, but the LORD was not in the earthquake; and after the earthquake a fire, but the LORD was not in the fire; and after the fire a still small voice. When Elijah heard it, he wrapped his face in his mantle.

"Go," the LORD said to him, "return on your way to Damascus; when you arrive, you shall anoint Hazael king over Syria; and Jehu the son of Nimshi you shall anoint king over Israel; and Elisha the son of Shaphat you shall anoint to be prophet in your place. And him who escapes from the sword of Hazael shall Jehu slay; and him who escapes from the sword of Jehu shall Elisha slay. Yet I will leave seven thousand in Israel, all the knees that have not bowed to Baal, and every mouth that has not kissed him."

So Elijah departed, and found Elisha the son of Shaphat, who was plowing with twelve yoke of oxen; and he cast his mantle upon him. Elisha left the oxen and ran after Elijah. "Let me kiss my father and my mother," he said, "and then I will follow you." And Elijah replied, "Go back." So Elisha went back and took a yoke of oxen, and slew them, and boiled their flesh, and gave it to the people, and they ate. Then he arose and went after Elijah, and ministered to him.

NOW NABOTH THE Jezreelite had a vineyard in Jezreel, beside the country palace of Ahab king of Samaria. "Give me your vineyard," Ahab said to him, "that I may have it for a vegetable garden, because it is near my house; and I will give you a better vineyard for it; or, if it seems good to you, I will give you its value in money." Naboth replied, "The LORD forbid that I should give you the inheritance of my fathers."

So Ahab went into his house vexed and sullen, and he lay down on his bed, and turned away his face, and would eat no food. "Why is your spirit so vexed?" asked Jezebel. When Ahab told her, she said, "Do you govern Israel or not? Arise and eat, and let your heart be cheerful; I will give you Naboth's vineyard." She wrote letters in Ahab's name and sealed them with his seal, and she sent them to the elders of Jezreel. She wrote in the letters, "Proclaim a fast, and set Naboth on high among the people; then set two base fellows opposite him, and let them bring a charge against him, saying, 'You have cursed God and the king.' Then take him out and stone him to death." And the elders did as Jezebel had written. Then they sent to Jezebel, saying, "Naboth is dead." As soon as Jezebel heard this, she said to Ahab, "Arise, take possession of Naboth's vineyard, for he is dead." And Ahab did so.

Then the word of the LORD came to Elijah, saying, "Arise, go to meet Ahab king of Israel, who is in the vineyard of Naboth, where he has gone to take possession. And you shall say to him, 'Thus says the LORD: "Have you killed, and also taken possession? In the place where dogs licked up the blood of Naboth shall dogs lick your own blood."'"

So Elijah went down to meet the king. "Have you found me, O my enemy?" said Ahab. "I have found you," Elijah answered, "because you have sold yourself to do what is evil in the sight of the LORD. Behold, I will utterly sweep you away; I will destroy every son of the house of Ahab for the anger you have provoked in me. And the LORD also has said, 'The dogs shall eat Jezebel within the bounds of Jezreel.'" For there was none who sold himself to do what was evil in the sight of the LORD like Ahab, whom Jezebel incited.

NOW JEHOSHAPHAT THE great-grandson of Rehoboam began to reign over Judah in the fourth year of Ahab king of Israel. He did what was right in the sight of the LORD, although the people still sacrificed on the high places. He also made peace with the king of Israel and came to visit him. Then Ahab said to his servants, "Do you know that Ramoth-gilead belongs to us, yet we keep quiet and do not take it from the king of Syria?" And he said to Jehoshaphat, "Will you go with me to battle at Ramoth-gilead?"

"I am as you are," Jehoshaphat replied, "my people as your people, my horses as your horses. But inquire first for the word of the LORD." Gathering the prophets together, Ahab asked them, "Shall I go to battle against Ramoth-gilead, or shall I forbear?"

"Go up," they replied; "for the LORD will give it into the hand of the king." But Jehoshaphat said, "Is there not here another prophet of the LORD of whom we may inquire?"

"There is yet one man," said the king, "but I hate him, for he never prophesies good concerning me." Then he summoned an officer and said, "Bring quickly Micaiah the son of Imlah." Now Ahab and Jehoshaphat were sitting on their thrones, arrayed in their robes, outside the gate of Samaria; and all the prophets were prophesying before them, saying, "Go up to Ramoth-gilead and triumph; the LORD will give it into the hand of the king." The messenger who went to summon Micaiah said to him, "Behold, the words of the prophets with one accord are favorable to the king; let your word be like theirs, and speak favorably."

"As the LORD lives," Micaiah answered, "what the LORD says to me, that I will speak." When he came to King Ahab, the king said to him, "Micaiah, shall we go to Ramoth-gilead to battle, or shall we forbear?"

"Go up and triumph," Micaiah answered him. "The LORD will give it into the hand of the king."

"How many times shall I adjure you to speak nothing but the truth in the name of the LORD?" the king said.

Now Micaiah answered, "I saw Israel scattered upon the mountains, as sheep that have no shepherd; and the LORD said, 'These have no master; let each return to his home in peace.'"

"Did I not tell you," Ahab said to Jehoshaphat, "that he would not prophesy good concerning me, but evil?"

"Therefore hear the word of the LORD," Micaiah continued. "I saw the LORD sitting on his throne, and all the host of heaven standing on his right hand and on his left; and the LORD said, 'Who will entice Ahab, that he may go up and fall at Ramoth-gilead?' And a spirit came forward, saying, 'I will entice him. I will be a lying spirit in the mouth of all his prophets.' And the

LORD said, 'Go forth and entice him.' Now therefore, behold, the LORD has put a lying spirit in the mouth of all these your prophets; the LORD has spoken evil concerning you."

Then Zedekiah the son of Chenaanah came near and struck Micaiah on the cheek, and said, "How did the Spirit of the LORD go from me to speak to you?" Micaiah answered, "You shall see on that day when you go into an inner chamber to hide yourself." And the king cried, "Seize Micaiah. Take him back to the city, and put him in prison, and feed him on bread and water until I return in peace."

"If you ever return in peace," Micaiah answered, "the LORD has not spoken by me." And he added, "Hear, all you peoples!"

The kings of Israel and Judah went up to Ramoth-gilead, and Ahab said to Jehoshaphat, "I will disguise myself to go into battle, but you shall wear your royal robes." So the king of Israel disguised himself, and they went into battle. Now the king of Syria had commanded his captains, "Fight with neither small nor great, but only with the king of Israel." When the captains saw Jehoshaphat in his robes, they said, "It is surely the king of Israel," and they turned to fight against him. But Jehoshaphat cried out, and when the captains saw that he was not the king of Israel, they turned away. Then a certain man drew his bow at a venture, and, unknowing, struck King Ahab between the joints of his armor. "Turn about," Ahab said to his chariot driver, "and carry me out of the battle, for I am wounded."

The battle grew hot that day. The king was propped up in his chariot facing the Syrians; the blood of his wound flowed into the bottom of the chariot, until at evening he died. And about sunset a cry went through the army, "Every man to his city!" King Ahab was brought to Samaria and buried there. They washed out the chariot by the pool of Samaria, and the dogs licked up his blood, according to the word of the LORD.

Now the rest of the acts of Ahab, all that he did, and the ivory house and the cities which he built, are they not written in the Book of the Chronicles of the Kings of Israel? So Ahab slept with his fathers; and Ahaziah his son reigned in his stead.

2 KINGS

The first part of the book describes the miracles performed by the prophet Elisha, successor to Elijah, among them restoring life to a dead child and cleansing a Syrian commander of leprosy. Elisha also directs Jehu to grasp the throne of Israel from King Ahab and his Baal-worshipping queen, Jezebel. In Judah, where Baal-worship had been extended by Ahab's daughter, Athaliah, the rightful heir, King Joash, restores the worship of God in the temple.

The latter part of the book continues the story of the Hebrew monarchies. Assyria, growing in power, constantly threatens Israel, until at last King Shalmaneser conquers it in 721 B.C. Judah is also threatened in the time of King Hezekiah, but through the intervention of the prophet Isaiah, Jerusalem is wonderfully preserved. And though King Josiah reforms and purifies religious practice, the short-lived kings who come after him are unable to hold out against Egypt and Babylon. Finally, Judah is conquered in 586 B.C. and its people are exiled to Babylon.

Now Ahaziah fell through the lattice in his upper chamber in Samaria and lay injured; so he sent messengers, telling them, "Go, inquire of Baal-zebub, the god of Ekron, whether I shall recover." But the angel of the LORD said to Elijah the prophet, "Arise, go up to meet the messengers of the king of Samaria, and say to them, 'Is it because there is no God in Israel that you are going to inquire of Baal-zebub?' Now therefore thus says the LORD, 'You shall not come down from the bed to which you have gone, but you shall surely die.'" So Elijah went.

The messengers returned to the king, and they told him what had happened. "What kind of man was he who told you these things?" King Ahaziah asked. "He wore a garment of haircloth," they replied, "with a girdle of leather about his loins." And the king said, "It is Elijah the Tishbite."

Then the king sent a captain and fifty men to Elijah, who was sitting on top of a hill. "O man of God," said the captain, "the king says, 'Come down.'"

Elijah answered, "If I am a man of God, let fire come down from heaven and consume you." Then fire came down from heaven and consumed the captain and his fifty. The king sent another captain with his fifty, but again the fire of God came down and consumed them. Then the king sent a third captain with his fifty. But this captain fell on his knees before Elijah and entreated him, "I pray you, O man of God, let my life and the lives of these servants of yours be precious in your sight." Then the angel of the LORD said to Elijah, "Go down with him; do not be afraid of him." So Elijah arose and went down with the captain to King Ahaziah, and he said to the king, "Thus says the LORD, 'Because you have sent to inquire of Baal-zebub—is it because there is no God in Israel?—therefore you shall not come down from your bed, but you shall surely die.'" So Ahaziah died according to the word of the LORD, and Joram his brother became king of Israel in his stead, because Ahaziah had no son.

WHEN THE LORD was about to take Elijah up to heaven, he and Elisha were on their way from visiting the prophets in Gilgal. "Tarry here, I pray you," Elijah said to Elisha, "for the LORD has sent me as far as Bethel." Elisha answered, "As the LORD lives, and as you yourself live, I will not leave you." So they went down to Bethel, and there the prophets came out to Elisha. "Do you know," they said to him, "that today the LORD will take your master away from you?" And he answered, "Yes, I know it. Hold your peace."

Again Elijah said, "Elisha, tarry here, I pray you; for the LORD has sent me on to Jericho." But Elisha replied, "As the LORD lives, I will not leave you." So they came to Jericho, and the prophets there drew near to Elisha, and said, "Do you know that today the LORD will take your master away from you?" And he answered, "Yes, I know it. Hold your peace."

Then Elijah said to him, "Tarry here, I pray you; for the LORD has sent me to the Jordan." But Elisha said, "As the LORD lives, I will not leave you." So the two of them went on. Fifty of the prophets also went, and stood at some distance from them as they were standing by the river Jordan. Then Elijah took his mantle and rolled it up and struck the water, and the water was parted, so that the two of them could go over on dry ground. When they had crossed, Elijah said to Elisha, "Ask what I should do for you, before I am taken from you."

"I pray you," said Elisha, "let me inherit a double share of your spirit."

"You have asked a hard thing," said Elijah; "yet, if you see me as I am being taken from you, it shall be so. But if you do not see me, it shall not be so."

As they went on, behold, a chariot of fire and horses of fire separated the two of them, and Elijah went up by a whirlwind into heaven. Elisha saw it. "My father, my father!" he cried; "the chariots of Israel and its horsemen!" And he saw Elijah no more. Then Elisha rent his clothes, and he took up the mantle of Elijah that had fallen from him, and he went back to the river Jordan. He struck the water with the mantle, saying, "Where is the LORD, the

God of Elijah?'' And the water was parted, and Elisha returned to the other side. When the prophets of Jericho saw him on their side, they said, "The spirit of Elijah rests on Elisha." And they bowed to the ground before him.

Now the men of the city said to Elisha, "Behold, the situation of this city is pleasant, as my lord sees; but the water is bad, and the land is unfruitful." Elisha said, "Bring me a new bowl, and put salt in it." When they had brought it, he went to the spring and threw salt in it. "Thus says the LORD," he said, "I have made this water wholesome; henceforth neither death nor miscarriage shall come from it." So the spring has been wholesome to this day, according to the word which Elisha spoke.

NOW THE WIFE of one of the prophets cried to Elisha, "Your servant my husband is dead. You know that he feared the LORD, but the creditor has come to take my two children to be his slaves."

"What shall I do for you?" Elisha asked. "Tell me, what have you in the house?" She answered, "I have nothing in the house, except a jar of oil." Then Elisha said, "Go outside; borrow empty vessels of all your neighbors—and not too few. Then go in and shut the door upon yourself and your sons, and pour into all these vessels; and when one is full, set it aside." She went from him and shut the door upon herself and her sons; and as she poured they brought the vessels to her. When all of them were full, the oil stopped flowing, and the woman came and told the man of God. "Go," he said, "sell the oil and pay your debts, and you and your sons can live on the rest."

One day Elisha went to Shunem. A wealthy woman who lived there urged him to eat some food. Whenever he passed that way, he would turn in at her house. She said to her husband, "Behold now, I perceive that this is a holy man of God. Let us make a small chamber on the roof, and put there for him a bed, a table, a chair, and a lamp, so that when he comes to us, he can go in there." One day Elisha came and turned into the chamber and rested there. "Call this Shunammite woman," he said to his servant Gehazi. When she stood before him, he said to her, "See, you have taken all this trouble for us; what is to be done for you? Shall I speak a word on your behalf to the king or to the commander of the army?"

"I dwell among my own people," she answered. "I am content." Later Elisha said to Gehazi, "What then is to be done for her?" Gehazi answered, "Well, she has no son, and her husband is old."

"Call her," said Elisha. And when she stood in the doorway, he said, "At this season, when the year comes round again, you shall embrace a son."

"No, my lord, O man of God," she said, "do not lie to your maidservant." But the woman conceived, and she bore a son about that time the following spring, as Elisha had said. When the child had grown, he went out one day to his father among the reapers. "Oh, my head, my head!" the child cried to his father. "Carry him to his mother," the father said to a servant. And when the servant brought him to his mother, the child sat on her lap till noon, and then he died.

The woman went up and laid him on the bed of the man of God, and shut the door upon him. Then she called to her husband, "Send me a servant and one of the asses, that I may quickly go to the man of God and come back again." She saddled the ass, and did not slacken her pace until she came to the man of God at Mount Carmel.

When Elisha saw her coming, he said to Gehazi, "Yonder is the Shunammite; run at once to meet her, and say, 'Is it well with you? Is it well with the child?'" She answered, "It is well." But when she came to the mountain to the man of God, she caught hold of his feet. Gehazi came to thrust her away. But the man of God said, "Let her alone, for she is in bitter distress; and the LORD has hidden it from me." Then the woman said, "Did I ask my lord for a son? Did I not say, 'Do not deceive me'?"

Elisha told Gehazi, "Take my staff in your hand, and go with the woman and lay my staff upon the face of the child." But the mother said to Elisha, "As the LORD lives, I will not leave you." So he arose and followed her. Gehazi went on ahead and laid the staff upon the face of the child, but there was no sound or sign of life. He returned and told Elisha, "The child has not awaked."

When Elisha went into the chamber where the child was lying dead on his bed, he shut the door and prayed to the LORD. Then he lay upon the child, putting his mouth upon the child's mouth, his eyes upon his eyes, and his hands upon his hands; and as he stretched himself upon the child, its flesh became warm. Elisha got up and walked once to and fro in the house, and then he stretched himself again upon the child. The child sneezed seven times and opened his eyes. Elisha summoned Gehazi, saying, "Call this Shunammite." When she came to him, he said, "Take up your son." She fell at his feet, bowing to the ground; then she took up her son and went out.

When Elisha came again to Gilgal, there was famine in the land, and as the prophets were sitting before him, he said to his servant, "Set on the great pot, and boil pottage for the prophets." One of them went out into the field and gathered wild gourds and cut them up into the pot, not knowing what they were. Then they poured out pottage, but while they were eating, the prophets cried out, "O man of God, there is death in the pot!" And they could not eat it. "Then bring meal," Elisha said. He threw the meal into the pot, and said, "Pour out for the men, that they may eat." And now there was no harm in the pot.

A man came bringing bread of the first fruits, twenty loaves of barley, and fresh grain in his sack. "Give to the men, that they may eat," Elisha said. But the servant asked, "How am I to set this before a hundred men?" Elisha repeated, "Give it to them, for thus says the LORD, 'They shall eat and have some left.'" So the servant set it before them, and they ate, and had some left, according to the word of the LORD.

NAAMAN, COMMANDER OF THE SYRIAN army, was in high favor with his master the king, because through him the LORD had given victory to Syria. He was a mighty man of valor, but he was a leper. Now the Syrians on one of their raids had carried off a little maid from the land of Israel, and she waited on Naaman's wife. "Would that my lord were with the prophet Elisha who is in Samaria!" she said to her mistress. "He would cure him of his leprosy." So Naaman told his lord, "Thus and so spoke the maiden from Israel." And the king of Syria said, "Go now, and I will send a letter to the king of Israel." Naaman went, taking with him talents of silver and shekels of gold and festal garments, and the letter to the king of Israel, which read, "I have sent to you Naaman my servant, that you may cure him of his leprosy."

When the king of Israel read the letter, he rent his clothes. "Am I God, to kill and to make alive," he said, "that this man sends word to me to cure a man of his leprosy? Only consider, and see how he is seeking a quarrel with me!" But when Elisha heard of this, he sent to the king, saying, "Why have you rent your clothes? Let Naaman come now to me, that he may know that there is a prophet in Israel." So Naaman came with his horses and chariots to the door of Elisha's house, and Elisha sent a messenger to him, saying, "Go and wash in the Jordan seven times, and your flesh shall be restored."

Naaman turned and went away in a rage. "Behold," he said, "I thought he would surely come out and call on the name of his God, and wave his hand over the place, and cure the leper. Are not the rivers of Damascus better than all the waters of Israel? Could I not wash in them and be clean?"

His servants came near and said to him, "My father, if the prophet had commanded you to do some great thing, would you not have done it? How much rather, then, when he says to you, 'Wash, and be clean'?" So Naaman went down and dipped himself seven times in the Jordan, and his flesh was restored like the flesh of a little child.

Then he and all his company returned and stood before Elisha. "Behold," he said, "I know that there is no God in all the earth but in Israel; so accept now a present from your servant." And Elisha answered, "As the LORD lives, whom I serve, I will receive none." Then Naaman said, "If not, I pray you, let me have two mules' burden of earth; for henceforth I will not offer sacrifice to any god but the LORD. And when my master goes into the house of Rimmon to worship, leaning on my arm, and I bow myself there, may the LORD pardon your servant in this matter." Elisha answered, "Go in peace."

When Naaman had gone a short distance, Gehazi, Elisha's servant, said to himself, "See, my master has spared this Syrian in not accepting the gift that he brought. As the LORD lives, I will run after him and get something from him." When Naaman saw some one running after him, he alighted from the chariot. "Is all well?" he said. Gehazi answered, "All is well, but my master has sent me to say, 'There have just come to me from the hill country of Ephraim two young prophets; pray, give them a talent of silver and two festal garments.'" Naaman tied up the silver and garments in two bags, and laid them upon two of his servants; and they carried them before Gehazi. Near Elisha's house, Gehazi took them from their hands and sent the men away. Then he went in and stood before his master.

"Where have you been, Gehazi?" said Elisha. Gehazi said, "Your servant went nowhere." Elisha answered, "Did I not go with you in spirit when Naaman turned from his chariot to meet you? Was it a time to accept money and garments? Because of this, the leprosy of Naaman shall cleave to you and to your descendants for ever." So Gehazi went out from Elisha's presence a leper, as white as snow.

Now the prophets said to Elisha, "See, the place where we dwell under your charge is too small for us. Let us go to the Jordan and each of us get there a log, and let us make a place for us to dwell there." So Elisha went with them, and when they came to the Jordan, they cut down trees. But as one was felling a log, his axe head fell into the water; and he cried, "Alas, my master! It was borrowed." Then the man of God said, "Where did it fall?" When he showed him the place, Elisha cut off a stick, and threw it in there, and made the iron float. "Take it up," he said. So the young man reached out his hand and took it.

WHEN THE KING of Syria was warring against Israel, Elisha would send word to the king of Israel, "Beware that you do not pass such and such a place, for the Syrians are going down there." And the king of Israel more than once thus saved himself.

The king of Syria was greatly troubled because of this, and he said to his servants, "Show me who of us is for the king of Israel." One of them answered, "None, my lord; but Elisha the prophet tells the king of Israel the words you speak in your bedchamber." The king said, "Go and see where he is, that I may send and seize him."

It was told him that Elisha was in Dothan, to the north of Samaria; so he sent there horses and chariots and a great army; and they came by night, and surrounded the city. When Elisha's servant rose early in the morning and went out, behold, an army was round about the city. "Alas, my master!" he cried; "what shall we do?" Elisha answered, "Fear not, for those who are with us are more than those with them." Then he prayed, "O LORD, open his eyes that he may see." So the LORD opened the eyes of the servant, and he saw that the mountain was full of horses and chariots of fire round about Elisha.

When the Syrians came down against him, Elisha prayed again to the LORD, and said, "Strike this people, I pray thee, with blindness." So the LORD struck them with blindness, and Elisha said to them, "This is not the way; follow me, and I will bring you to the man whom you seek." He led them to Samaria, and as soon as they entered the city, the LORD opened their eyes; and lo, they were in the midst of Samaria. When the king of Israel saw them, he asked Elisha, "My father, shall I slay them?" Elisha answered, "You shall not slay them. Would you slay those whom you have taken captive with your sword? Set food before them, that they may eat and drink and go to their master." So the king prepared for them a great feast; and when they had eaten and drunk, he sent them back to their master. And for some time the Syrians came no more on raids into Israel.

AFTERWARD BEN-HADAD KING of Syria mustered his entire army and went up and besieged Samaria. There was a great famine there, until an ass's head was sold for eighty shekels of silver and a portion of dove's dung for five shekels. Now as the king of Israel was passing by upon the wall, a woman cried out to him, saying, "Help, my lord, O king!" The king said, "If the LORD will not help you, whence shall I help you? What is your trouble?" She answered, "This woman said to me, 'Give your son, that we may eat him today, and we will eat my son tomorrow.' So we boiled my son, and ate him. And on the next day I said to her, 'Give your son, that we may eat him'; but she has hidden her son."

When the king heard these words, he rent his clothes, and the people saw that he wore sackcloth beneath them. "May God punish me," he said, "if the head of Elisha remains on his shoulders today."

Elisha was sitting in his house with the elders when the king came down to him. "This trouble is from the LORD!" the king said. "Why should I wait for him any longer?" But Elisha answered, "Thus says the LORD, 'Tomorrow about this time a measure of fine meal shall be sold for a shekel, and two measures of barley for a shekel, at the gate of Samaria.'" Then a captain of the king said to Elisha, "If the LORD himself should make windows in heaven, could this thing be?" And Elisha said to him, "You shall see it with your own eyes, but you shall not eat of it."

Now there were four lepers at the entrance to the gate. "Why do we sit here till we die?" they said to one another. "If we enter the city, the famine is there and we shall die there; and if we sit here, we die also. So let us go over to the camp of the Syrians; if they spare our lives we shall eat, and if they kill us we shall but die." They arose at twilight; but when they came to the edge of the camp of the Syrians, behold, there was no one there. For the LORD had made the Syrians hear the sound of the chariots and horses of a great army, so that they said to one another, "Behold, the king of Israel has hired the king of Egypt to come against us." So they fled for their lives, and forsook their tents, their horses, and their asses, leaving the camp as it was.

When the lepers came to the camp, they went into a tent and ate and drank, and carried off silver and gold and clothing, and so with another tent. But then they said to one another, "We are not doing right. This is a day of good news. If we are silent until the morning light, punishment will overtake us. Now therefore let us go and tell the king's household." So they came back and told the city gatekeepers, and the gatekeepers called out. When it was told within the king's household, the king said to his servants, "The Syrians know that we are hungry. Therefore they have gone to hide themselves in the open country, thinking, 'When the people come out of the gate, we shall take them alive and get into the city.'" One of the servants said, "Let us send and see," so the king sent two mounted men after the Syrians. They went as far as the Jordan, and lo, all the way was littered with garments and equipment which the Syrians had thrown away in their haste.

Then the people went out and plundered the Syrian camp. So a measure of fine meal was sold for a shekel at the gate of Samaria, and two measures of barley for a shekel, according to the word of the LORD. But the captain whom the king had placed in charge of the gate was trod upon by the people, so that he died, as Elisha had foretold when he said to him, "You shall see it with your own eyes, but you shall not eat of it."

IN THE FIFTH year of Joram the son of Ahab, king of Israel, Jehoram the son of Jehoshaphat began to reign in Judah. Jehoram was thirty-two years old when he became king, and he reigned eight years in Jerusalem. He walked in the way of the kings of Israel, as the house of Ahab had done, for the daughter of Ahab was his wife. And he did what was evil in the sight of the LORD. Yet the LORD did not destroy Judah, for the sake of David his servant, since he promised to give a lamp to him and to his sons for ever.

In his days Edom revolted from the rule of Judah, and set up a king of their own. Then the city of Libnah revolted at the same time. When Jehoram slept with his fathers, he was buried in the city of David; and Ahaziah his son reigned in his stead.

It was in the twelfth year of Joram the son of Ahab, king of Israel, that Ahaziah began to reign in Jerusalem. His mother was Athaliah, daughter of Ahab, and he did what was evil in the sight of the LORD, as the house of Ahab had done. Ahaziah went with King Joram and all Israel to make war against the Syrians, who were threatening Ramoth-gilead. Joram was wounded, and he returned to be healed in Jezreel. Ahaziah went down to see him there.

Now Elisha called one of the young prophets. "Gird up your loins," he said to him, "and take this flask of oil and go to Ramoth-gilead. Look there for Jehu the son of Jehoshaphat and go in and lead him to an inner chamber. Then take the flask of oil and pour it on his head, and say, 'Thus says the LORD, I anoint you king over Israel.' Then open the door and flee. Do not tarry."

When the young prophet went to Ramoth-gilead, the commanders of the army were in council there. "I have an errand to you, O commander," the prophet said. "To which of us all?" said Jehu. "To you," the prophet replied.

Jehu arose and went into the house; and the young man poured the oil on his head, saying, "Thus says the LORD the God of Israel, I anoint you king over Israel. You shall strike down the house of Ahab, that I may avenge on Jezebel the blood of my prophets. The whole house of Ahab shall perish, and the dogs shall eat Jezebel in Jezreel and none shall bury her." Then he opened the door and fled.

When Jehu came out, the commanders asked him, "Why did this mad fellow come to you?" Jehu answered, "He spoke to me, saying, 'Thus says the LORD, I anoint you king over Israel.'" Then in haste every man of them took his cloak and put it under Jehu on the bare steps, and they blew the trumpet and proclaimed, "Jehu is king." Thus Jehu conspired against Joram. "If this is your mind," he said to the commanders, "let no one slip away to tell the news in Jezreel." Then he mounted his chariot and went to Jezreel, where Joram lay wounded and Ahaziah king of Judah had come to visit him.

Now the watchman standing on the tower in Jezreel spied the company of Jehu as he came. "I see a company," he cried. "Send a horseman to meet them," Joram commanded, "and let him say, 'Is it peace?'" But Jehu answered the horseman, "What have you to do with peace? Turn round and ride behind me."

The watchman on the tower reported, "The messenger reached them, but he is not coming back. And the driving is like the driving of Jehu, for he drives furiously."

"Make ready," Joram ordered, and they made ready his chariot. Then Joram and Ahaziah set out, each in his chariot, and they met Jehu at the vineyard of Naboth the Jezreelite. "Is it peace, Jehu?" Joram asked. "What peace can there be," answered Jehu, "so long as the harlotries and the sorceries of your mother Jezebel are so many?" Then Joram reined about and fled, saying, "Treachery, O Ahaziah!"

Jehu drew his bow with his full strength and shot Joram between the shoulders, so that the arrow pierced his heart, and he sank in his chariot. "Take him up," Jehu told his aide, "and cast him on the plot of ground belonging to Naboth, in accordance with the word of the LORD." When Ahaziah king of Judah saw this, he fled south. Jehu pursued him and shot him in his chariot at the ascent of Gur. Ahaziah fled to Megiddo and died there. Then his servants carried him in a chariot to Jerusalem and buried him with his fathers in the city of David.

When Jehu came to Jezreel, Jezebel heard of it. She painted her eyes and adorned her head. As Jehu entered the gate, she looked out of the window and said, "Is it peace, you murderer of your master?" Jehu lifted up his face. "Who is on my side? Who?" he called. Two or three eunuchs looked out at him. "Throw her down," he ordered. So they threw her down; and some of her blood spattered on the wall and on the horses, and they trampled on her.

Then Jehu went in and ate and drank. "Now bury this cursed woman," he ordered, "for she is a king's daughter." But when they went to bury her, they found no more of her than the skull and the feet and the palms of her hands. "This is the word of the LORD," Jehu said, "which he spoke by his servant Elijah the prophet: 'In the territory of Jezreel the dogs shall eat the flesh of Jezebel, and her corpse shall be as dung upon the face of the field, so that no one can say, This is Jezebel.'"

Thus Jehu wiped out Baal from Israel, but he did not turn aside from the sins of Jeroboam, which he made Israel to sin—the golden calves that were in

Bethel and in Dan. And in those days the LORD began to cut off parts of Israel. Hazael king of Syria defeated them throughout their territory from the Jordan eastward, all the land of Gilead and Bashan.

Jehu reigned over Israel for twenty-eight years. Then he slept with his fathers, and Jehoahaz his son reigned in his stead.

WHEN ATHALIAH THE mother of Ahaziah, king of Judah, saw that her son was dead, she arose and destroyed all his sons except Joash, whom Ahaziah's sister stole away. She was the wife of Jehoiada the priest, and Joash remained with her six years, hid in the house of the LORD, while Athaliah reigned over the land. But in the seventh year Jehoiada had the captains of the guards come to him in the house of the LORD. Then he brought out Joash and put the crown upon him; and they proclaimed him king, and anointed him, and clapped their hands, and said, "Long live the king!"

When Athaliah heard the noise, she went into the house of the LORD; and when she looked, there was the king standing by the pillar, according to the custom. Athaliah rent her clothes. "Treason! Treason!" she cried. Then Jehoiada commanded the captains, "Bring her out between the ranks, but let her not be slain in the house of the LORD." So they laid hands on her; and she went through the horses' entrance to the king's house, and there she was slain. So Joash took his seat on the throne of the kings, and all the people of the land rejoiced.

Joash was seven years old when he began to reign in the seventh year of Jehu king of Israel, and he reigned forty years in Jerusalem. He did what was right in the eyes of the LORD all his days, as Jehoiada the priest instructed him. Nevertheless the high places were not taken away; the people continued to sacrifice there.

At that time Hazael king of Syria went up and took Gath, and then he set his face to go up against Jerusalem. But Joash took all the votive gifts that his fathers, the kings of Judah, had dedicated and all the gold that was found in the temple and in the king's house, and sent these to Hazael. Then Hazael went away from Jerusalem.

Now the servants of Joash arose and made a conspiracy and struck him down, so that he died. They buried him with his fathers in the city of David, and Amaziah his son reigned in his stead.

IN THE TWENTY-THIRD year of Joash king of Judah, Jehoahaz the son of Jehu began to reign over Israel in Samaria, and he reigned seventeen years. In the thirty-seventh year of Joash king of Judah, Jehoash the grandson of Jehu began to reign over Israel in Samaria. He also did what was evil in the sight of the LORD; he did not depart from the sins of Jeroboam, which he made Israel to sin. So the anger of the LORD was kindled against Israel, and he gave them continually into the hand of Hazael king of Syria and of Ben-hadad his son. For there was not left to Israel an army of more than fifty horsemen and ten chariots and ten thousand footmen; the king of Syria had destroyed them and made them like the dust at threshing.

Now when Elisha had fallen sick with the illness of which he was to die, Jehoash went down to him and wept before him, crying, "My father, my father! The chariots of Israel and its horsemen!"

"Take a bow and arrows," Elisha said; so he took a bow and arrows. "Draw the bow"; and he drew it. Then Elisha laid his hands upon the king's hands. "Open the window eastward," he said; and he opened it. Then Elisha said, "Shoot"; and he shot.

"The LORD'S arrow of victory," Elisha cried. "The arrow of victory over Syria! For you shall fight the Syrians until you have made an end of them." Then he said, "Take the arrows and strike the ground with them"; so the king struck three times, and stopped. But the man of God was angry with him. "You should have struck five or six times," he said; "then you would have made an end of it, but now you will strike down Syria only three times." So Elisha died, and they buried him.

When Hazael king of Syria died, Jehoash took back from Ben-hadad his son the cities which had been taken in war. Three times Jehoash defeated him and recovered the cities of Israel.

So Jehoash slept with his fathers and was buried in Samaria with the kings of Israel; and Jeroboam II, his son, reigned in his stead.

In the second year of Jehoash, Amaziah the son of Joash began to reign in Jerusalem, and he did what was right in the eyes of the LORD, yet not like David. As soon as the royal power was firmly in his hand, Amaziah killed those who had slain his father, King Joash.

In Jerusalem they made a conspiracy against Amaziah, and he fled to Lachish. But they sent after him to Lachish and slew him there. They brought him upon horses, and he was buried in Jerusalem with his fathers in the city of David. And all the people of Judah took Uzziah his son, and made him king.

In the twenty-seventh year of Jeroboam II, king of Israel, Uzziah the son of Amaziah, king of Judah, began to reign. He was sixteen years old, and he reigned fifty-two years in Jerusalem. He did what was right in the eyes of the LORD, according to all that his father Amaziah had done. Nevertheless the high places were not taken away; the people still sacrificed and burned incense there. And the LORD smote the king, so that he was a leper to the day of his death, and he dwelt in a separate house. Jotham his son was over the household, governing the people of the land. And when Uzziah slept with his fathers, Jotham reigned in his stead.

IN THE FIFTEENTH year of Amaziah king of Judah, Jeroboam II began to reign in Samaria, and he reigned forty-one years. Although he did what was evil in the sight of the LORD, he restored the border of Israel from Damascus as far as the Sea of the Arabah, according to the word of the LORD, which he spoke by his servant Jonah the prophet. For the LORD saw that the affliction of Israel was very bitter, and that there was none to help them; so he saved them by the hand of Jeroboam II.

When Jeroboam II slept with his fathers, Zechariah his son reigned in his stead, and he reigned over Israel six months. Shallum the son of Jabesh conspired against him, and struck him down and killed him, and reigned in his stead. (This was the promise which the LORD gave to Jehu, "Your sons shall sit upon the throne of Israel to the fourth generation." And so it came to pass.) But Shallum reigned only one month in Samaria, for Menahem the son of Gadi came up from Tirzah and struck him down and slew him. At that time Menahem sacked the towns around Tirzah because they did not open to him, and he ripped up all the women there who were with child.

Menahem began to reign over Israel in the thirty-ninth year of Uzziah king of Judah, and he reigned ten years in Samaria. He did what was evil in the sight of the LORD. The king of Assyria came against the land, and Menahem gave him a thousand talents of silver, that he might help him to confirm his hold of the royal power, exacting the money from all the wealthy men of Israel. So the king of Assyria turned back, and did not stay there in the land.

Then Menahem slept with his fathers, and Pekahiah his son reigned in his stead. Pekahiah reigned two years in Samaria; but Pekah the son of Remaliah, Pekahiah's captain, conspired against him with fifty men of Gilead, and slew him in the citadel of the king's house, and reigned in his stead.

In the fifty-second year of Uzziah king of Judah, Pekah began to reign over Israel in Samaria. He reigned twenty years, and he did what was evil in the sight of the LORD. Now Tiglath-pileser king of Assyria came and captured Gilead and Galilee and Syria, and he carried the people captive to Assyria.

Now Hoshea the son of Elah made a conspiracy against Pekah, and struck him down and slew him, and reigned in his stead.

Hoshea began to reign over Israel in the twelfth year of Ahaz king of Judah. He did what was evil in the sight of the LORD, yet not as the kings who were before him. Against him came Shalmaneser king of Assyria. Hoshea became his vassal and paid him tribute. But Shalmaneser found treachery in Hoshea, for he had sent messengers to the king of Egypt and offered no tribute, as he had done year by year. Therefore Shalmaneser shut Hoshea up in prison. Then he invaded all the land and came to Samaria, and for three years he besieged it. In the ninth year of Hoshea he captured it, and he carried the Israelites away to Assyria and placed them on the river Habor and in the cities of the Medes.

This was so, because the people of Israel had sinned against the LORD their God, who had brought them up out of Egypt. They had feared other gods and burned incense on all the high places. They would not listen when the LORD warned them by every prophet and seer. They despised his statutes, and his covenant that he made with their fathers, and the warnings which he gave them. They went after false idols, and made for themselves molten images of two calves. They burned their sons and their daughters as offerings, and used divination and sorcery. They sold themselves to do evil, provoking the LORD to anger. Therefore he removed them out of his sight to Assyria. None was left but the tribe of Judah only.

The king of Assyria also brought people from Babylon and Syria, and they took possession of Samaria and dwelt in its cities. At the beginning of their dwelling there, they did not fear the LORD. Therefore the LORD sent lions among them. The king of Assyria was told, "The nations which you have placed in the cities of Samaria do not know the law of the god of the land; therefore he sent lions among them, and behold, the lions are killing them." Then the king of Assyria commanded, "Send there one of the priests whom you carried away, and let him go and dwell there and teach them the law of the god of the land." So one of the priests came back and dwelt in Bethel and taught them how they should fear the LORD.

But every nation still made gods of its own; so these nations feared the LORD, but also served their own graven images; their children likewise, and their children's children—as their fathers did, so they do to this day.

WHEN AHAZ KING of Judah slept with his fathers, Hezekiah his son reigned in his stead. He did what was right in the eyes of the LORD, according to all that David his father had done. He removed the high places, and he broke in pieces the bronze serpent of Moses, for until those days the people of Israel had burned incense to it. He trusted in the LORD the God of Israel; so that there was none like him among all the kings of Judah. And the LORD was with him; wherever he went forth, he prospered. In those days Hezekiah became sick and was at the point of death. And Isaiah the prophet, the son of Amoz, came to him and said, "Thus says the LORD, 'Set your house in order, for you shall die; you shall not recover.'" Then Hezekiah turned his face to the wall, and prayed to the LORD, saying, "Remember, O LORD, I beseech thee, how I have walked before thee in faithfulness and with a whole heart, and have done what is good in thy sight." And he wept bitterly.

Then the word of the LORD came to Isaiah the prophet: "Go and say to Hezekiah, 'Thus says the LORD: I have heard your prayer, I have seen your tears; behold, I will heal you; on the third day you shall go up to the house of the LORD. And I will add fifteen years to your life.'" When he had spoken thus to Hezekiah, Isaiah said, "Bring a cake of figs. And let them take and lay it on the boil, that he may recover."

"What shall be the sign that the LORD will heal me?" Hezekiah asked. Isaiah replied, "This is the sign to you from the LORD: shall the shadow on the dial of Ahaz go forward ten steps, or go back ten steps?" And Hezekiah answered, "It is an easy thing for the shadow to lengthen ten steps; rather let the shadow go back ten steps." Then Isaiah the prophet cried to the LORD; and he brought the shadow back ten steps, by which the sun had declined on the dial of Ahaz.

Now in the fourteenth year of King Hezekiah he rebelled against the king of Assyria and would not serve him. So Sennacherib king of Assyria came up against all the fortified cities of Judah and took them. Then he sent the Rabshakeh, his chief of staff, with a great army to Jerusalem. When they arrived, they came and stood by the water conduit from the upper pool and called for King Hezekiah. There came out to them Eliakim the son of Hilkiah, who was over the household.

The Rabshakeh said to him, "Say to Hezekiah, 'Thus says the great king Sennacherib: On what do you rest this confidence of yours, that you have rebelled against me? Do you think mere words are strategy and power? Behold, you are relying now on Egypt, that broken reed of a staff, which will pierce the hand of any man who leans on it. How then can you repulse the least of my captains? But if you say to me, "We rely on the LORD our God," is it without the LORD that I have come up against this place to destroy it? The LORD said to me, Go up against this land, and destroy it.'"

"Pray, speak to your servant in the Aramaic language," said Eliakim, "for I understand it. Do not speak in the language of Judah within hearing of the people on the wall." The Rabshakeh replied, "Has my master sent me to speak these words to your master and not to the men sitting on the wall, who are doomed with you to eat their own dung and to drink their own urine?"

Then the Rabshakeh stood and called out in a loud voice in the language of Judah: "Hear the word of the great king, the king of Assyria! Thus says the king: 'Do not let Hezekiah deceive you, for he will not be able to deliver you out of my hand. And do not listen when he misleads you by saying, "The LORD will surely deliver us." Has any of the gods of the nations ever delivered his land out of the hand of the king of Assyria? Where are the gods of Samaria? Have they delivered Samaria out of my hand, that the LORD should deliver Jerusalem?'"

But Eliakim was silent, for the king's command was, "Do not answer him." Then he came to Hezekiah and told him the words of the Rabshakeh. Hezekiah rent his clothes and covered himself with sackcloth and went into the house of the LORD. He sent Eliakim and the senior priests, covered with sackcloth, to the prophet Isaiah. "Thus says Hezekiah," they said to him, "'It may be that the LORD your God heard all the words of the Rabshakeh, whom the king of Assyria has sent to mock the living God, and will rebuke them; therefore lift up your prayer for the remnant of Israel that is left.'"

Isaiah replied, "Say to your master, 'Thus says the LORD concerning the king of Assyria: He shall not come into this city or shoot an arrow there, or come before it with a shield or cast up a siege mound against it. By the way he came, by the same he shall return, says the LORD, and I will cause him to fall by the sword in his own land. For I will defend this city to save it, for my own sake and for the sake of my servant David.'"

That night the angel of the LORD went forth and slew a hundred and eighty-five thousand in the camp of the Assyrians; and when men arose early

in the morning, behold, these were all dead bodies. Then Sennacherib king of
Assyria departed and went home to Nineveh. And as he was worshiping in
the house of his god, two of his sons slew him with the sword, and escaped
into Ararat. And Esarhaddon his son reigned in his stead.

THEN HEZEKIAH SLEPT with his fathers, and Manasseh his son reigned. For
fifty-five years Manasseh reigned in Jerusalem, and he did what was evil in the
sight of the LORD. He rebuilt the high places which his father had destroyed;
and he erected new altars for Baal in the house of the LORD, of which the LORD
had said to David and to Solomon his son, "In this house and in Jerusalem I
will put my name." Manasseh also practiced soothsaying and augury, and
dealt with mediums and with wizards, provoking the LORD to anger. Moreover he shed much innocent blood, till he had filled Jerusalem from one end
to another.

And the LORD said by his prophets, "Because Manasseh has committed
these abominations and has made Judah to sin with his idols, therefore thus
says the LORD: Behold, I am bringing upon Jerusalem such evil that the ears of
every one who hears of it will tingle. I will stretch over Jerusalem the measuring line of Samaria, and the plummet of the house of Ahab; and I will wipe
Jerusalem as one wipes a dish, wiping it and turning it upside down. And I
will cast off the remnant of my heritage, and they shall become a prey to all
their enemies, because they have done what is evil in my sight."

When Manasseh slept with his fathers, Amon his son reigned two years in
Jerusalem. But his servants conspired against him and killed him, and the
people of the land made Josiah his son king in his stead.

JOSIAH WAS EIGHT years old when he began to reign, and he reigned thirty-one
years in Jerusalem. He did what was right in the eyes of the LORD, and walked
in all the ways of David his father, and he did not turn aside to the right hand
or to the left.

In the eighteenth year King Josiah sent Shaphan the secretary to the temple. "Go up to Hilkiah the high priest," he said, "that he may reckon the
amount of money the people have brought into the house of the LORD, and let
it be given to the workmen who are repairing the house." To Shaphan,
Hilkiah said, "I have found a book of the law in the house of the LORD," and
he gave the book to Shaphan. After reading it, Shaphan returned to the king,
saying, "Your servants have delivered the money that was found in the temple into the hand of the workmen." Then he said, "Hilkiah the priest has
given me a book," and he read the book before the king.

When the king heard the words of the book of the law, he rent his clothes.
"Go," he commanded Hilkiah and Shaphan, "inquire of the LORD for me and
for all Judah concerning the words of this book. Great is the wrath of the
LORD against us, because our fathers have not obeyed its words."

They went to Huldah the prophetess, who dwelt in Jerusalem in the Second

Quarter, and she said to them, "Thus says the LORD: 'Tell the man who sent you, Behold, I will bring evil upon this place and upon its inhabitants. Because they have forsaken me and have burned incense to other gods, therefore my wrath will be kindled against them, and it will not be quenched.' But as to the king of Judah, thus shall you say to him: 'Because your heart was penitent, and you humbled yourself before me when you heard how I spoke against this place, and you have rent your clothes and wept before me, I also have heard you,' says the LORD. 'Therefore, behold, I will gather you to your fathers in peace, and your eyes shall not see all the evil which I will bring upon this place.'"

Then the king went up to the house of the LORD, and with him the priests and the prophets and all the people, both small and great; and he read in their hearing the book of the law which had been found in the house of the LORD. And the king stood by the pillar and made a covenant before the LORD, to walk after him and to keep his commandments and his statutes with all his heart and all his soul; and all the people joined in the covenant.

Commanding Hilkiah to bring out of the temple all the vessels made for Baal, King Josiah burned them outside Jerusalem and carried their ashes to Bethel. And he broke down the houses of the male cult prostitutes which were in the house of the LORD, and defiled the high places where the priests had burned incense, from Geba to Beer-sheba. And he removed the horses that the kings of Judah had dedicated to the sun, and burned the chariots of the sun with fire. And he defiled the high places east of Jerusalem, which Solomon had built for Ashtoreth the abomination of the Sidonians, and for Milcom the abomination of the Ammonites.

Moreover he pulled down and broke in pieces the altar at Bethel, the high place erected by Jeroboam the son of Nebat, crushing its stones to dust. As he turned he saw the tombs on the mountain, and he said, "What is yonder monument?"

"It is the tomb of the man of God who came from Judah and predicted these things you have done against the altar at Bethel," the men of the city told him. "Let him be," Josiah said; "let no man move his bones." And he removed all the high places in the cities of Samaria which kings of Israel had made. Then he returned to Jerusalem where he commanded the people, "Keep the passover to the LORD your God, as it is written in this book of the covenant." For no such passover had been kept since the days of the judges, nor during all the days of the kings of Israel or of Judah.

Josiah put away the mediums and the wizards and all the abominations that were seen in the land of Judah, that he might establish the words of the law. Before him there was no king like him, who turned to the LORD with all his heart and with all his soul and with all his might, according to the law of Moses; nor did any like him arise after him. Still the LORD did not turn from the fierceness of his great wrath against Judah, because of all the provocations of Manasseh.

NOW IN THE DAYS OF JOSIAH, Pharaoh Neco of Egypt went up to the river Euphrates to help the king of Assyria against Babylon. King Josiah went to meet him; and Pharaoh Neco slew him in battle at Megiddo. His servants carried him dead in a chariot to Jerusalem, and buried him there; and the people took Jehoahaz his son and made him king in his father's stead.

Jehoahaz reigned only three months in Jerusalem, for Pharaoh Neco took him away in bonds to Egypt and made his brother Jehoiakim king in his place. Jehoiakim reigned eleven years in Jerusalem, and he did what was evil in the sight of the LORD. He gave tribute to Pharaoh, but he exacted silver and gold from the people, from every one according to his assessment.

In the days of Jehoiakim, Nebuchadnezzar king of Babylon came up against the king of Egypt, and took all that belonged to Pharaoh from the Brook of Egypt to the river Euphrates. Jehoiakim became the servant of Nebuchadnezzar three years; then he turned and rebelled against him. And the LORD sent against him bands of the Babylonians, and the Syrians, and the Moabites, and the Ammonites—sent them against Judah to destroy it, according to the word of the LORD which he spoke by his prophets. Then Jehoiakim slept with his fathers, and Jehoiachin his son reigned in his stead.

Jehoiachin was eighteen years old when he became king, and he reigned three months in Jerusalem. He did what was evil in the sight of the LORD, and at that time Nebuchadnezzar sent his army and besieged Jerusalem, so that Jehoiachin gave himself up. Nebuchadnezzar carried him away to Babylon; the king's mother, the king's wives, his princes, and his officials he also took into captivity in Babylon. And he made Zedekiah, Jehoiachin's uncle, king in his stead.

Zedekiah was twenty-one years old when he became king, and he reigned eleven years in Jerusalem. He did what was evil in the sight of the LORD, and because of the anger of the LORD it came to the point in Jerusalem and Judah that he cast them out from his presence.

Zedekiah rebelled against the king of Babylon, and in the ninth year of his reign Nebuchadnezzar came with all his army and laid siege to Jerusalem. So the city was besieged till the eleventh year of King Zedekiah. The famine was so severe in the city that there was no food for the people. Then a breach was made in the walls, and the king with all his men of war fled by night by way of the king's garden, though the Babylonians were around the city. They fled in the direction of the Arabah, but the Babylonians pursued them and overtook the king in the plains of Jericho, and scattered his army. Capturing the king, they brought him up to Nebuchadnezzar at Riblah in Syria. When Nebuchadnezzar had passed sentence upon him, they slew Zedekiah's sons before his eyes. Then they put out his eyes and bound him in fetters and took him to Babylon.

In the fifth month of the eleventh year, on the seventh day of the month, Nebuzaradan, the captain of the bodyguard of King Nebuchadnezzar, came to Jerusalem with an army. And he burned the house of the LORD and the king's house and all the houses of Jerusalem; and the army broke down the walls around Jerusalem. The pillars of bronze and the bronze sea that Solomon had made for the temple, they broke in pieces and carried to Babylon, along with the dishes for incense and all the vessels used in the temple service. What was of gold they cut in pieces and took away as so much gold, and what was of silver, as so much silver.

The people were carried into exile, though Nebuzaradan left some of the poorest in the land to be vinedressers and plowmen. Seraiah the chief priest, the three keepers of the threshold, five men of the king's council, and sixty of the men of the land were brought to the king of Babylon at Riblah. And Nebuchadnezzar smote them and put them to death. So Judah was taken into exile out of its land.

In the thirty-seventh year of the exile of Jehoiachin king of Judah before his uncle Zedekiah, Evil-merodach king of Babylon, in the year that he began to reign, graciously freed Jehoiachin from prison. He spoke kindly to him and gave him a seat above the seats of the other kings who were with him in Babylon. So Jehoiachin put off his prison garments, and every day of his life he dined at the king's table. And an allowance was given him by the king, every day as long as he lived.

1 CHRONICLES

The two books of Chronicles, also originally a single book, cover the same period of history as 1 and 2 Kings. But some events and personages are left out (the prophets Elijah and Elisha, for example), while other materials and a more religious emphasis have been added. In 1 Chronicles the long rule of King David is described, with the author underlining his glory and omitting the less praiseworthy episodes in his life. Much attention is also given to David's preparations for the building of the temple in Jerusalem and his establishment of the proper rituals to be conducted there. Because of the Chronicler's concern with the role of Levites and singers, it is thought that he himself may have been a Levite and a singer. The date usually assigned to his work is the latter part of the fourth century B.C.

———

ADAM, SETH, METHUSELAH, Noah; the sons of Noah: Shem, Ham, and Japheth.

The sons of Shem: Elam, Asshur, and Arpachshad. Arpachshad was the father of Shelah, and Shelah of Eber. To Eber were born two sons, Peleg and Joktan. Among the descendants of Peleg was Terah; and Terah was the father of Abram, that is, Abraham.

Abraham was the father of Isaac. The sons of Isaac: Esau and Israel (Jacob).

These are the sons of Israel: Reuben, Simeon, Levi, Judah, Issachar, Zebulun, Dan, Joseph, Benjamin, Naphtali, Gad, and Asher.

Judah became strong among his brothers. He had five sons in all: three by Bathshua the Canaanitess, and his daughter-in-law Tamar also bore him Zerah and Perez.

The descendants of Perez were Hezron, Ram, and Amminadab, and Amminadab was the father of Nahshon, prince of the sons of Judah. Nahshon was the father of Salma, Salma of Boaz, Boaz of Obed, Obed of Jesse; and Jesse was the father of David.

NOW MEN CAME TO DAVID AT Ziklag while he could not move about freely because of Saul the son of Kish; and they were among the mighty men who helped him in war. They were bowmen, and could shoot arrows and sling stones with either the right or the left hand; they were Benjaminites, Saul's kinsmen.

From the Gadites there went over to David at the stronghold in the wilderness mighty and experienced warriors, expert with shield and spear, whose faces were like the faces of lions and who were swift as gazelles upon the mountains. David went out to meet them. "If you have come in friendship to help me," he said, "my heart will be knit to you; but if to betray me to my adversaries, then may the God of our fathers see and rebuke you."

Then the Spirit came upon Amasai, chief of the warriors, and he said, "We are yours, O David, and with you, O son of Jesse! Peace, peace to you, and peace to your helpers! For your God helps you." David received them and made them officers of his troops.

Some of the men of Manasseh deserted to David when he came with the Philistines to Gilboa for the battle against Saul. (Yet he did not help the Philistines, for they took counsel and sent him away, saying, "At peril to our heads he will desert to his master Saul.") From day to day mighty men of valor kept coming to David, until there was a great army, like an army of God.

NOW THE PHILISTINES fought against Israel, and the men of Israel fled before them, and fell slain on Mount Gilboa. The Philistines overtook Saul and slew Jonathan and Abinadab and Malchishua, his sons. The battle pressed hard upon Saul, and the archers found him and wounded him. "Draw your sword," he said to his armor-bearer, "and thrust me through with it, lest these uncircumcised come and make sport of me." But his armor-bearer would not; for he feared greatly. Therefore Saul took his own sword and fell upon it.

Thus Saul died, and his sons, and all his men. When the men of Israel down in the valley saw that their army had fled and that Saul and his sons were dead, they forsook their cities, and the Philistines came and dwelt in them.

On the morrow, when the Philistines came to strip the slain, they found Saul and his sons fallen on Mount Gilboa. They stripped Saul and took his head and his armor and sent messengers throughout their land to carry the good news to the people. They put his armor in the temple of their gods and fastened his head in the temple of Dagon. But when Jabesh-gilead heard what the Philistines had done, the valiant men arose and took the bodies of Saul and his sons from the battlefield and brought them to Jabesh. They buried their bones under the oak in Jabesh and fasted seven days.

So Saul died for his unfaithfulness, in that he did not keep the command of the LORD and also consulted a medium, seeking guidance. Therefore the LORD slew him and turned the kingdom over to David the son of Jesse.

ALL ISRAEL GATHERED TO DAVID AT Hebron, and said, "Behold, we are your bone and flesh. Even when Saul was king it was you that led us out and brought us in, and the LORD said to you, 'You shall be shepherd of my people Israel, and prince over my people Israel.'" So the elders of Israel came to Hebron with full intent to make David king. David made a covenant with them before the LORD, and they anointed him king over all Israel, according to the word of the LORD by Samuel. They were there with David for three days, eating and drinking, for their brethren had made preparation for them, bringing abundant provisions of meal, cakes of figs, clusters of raisins, and wine and oil, oxen and sheep; for there was joy in Israel.

After this, David went to Jerusalem, where the Jebusites were, the inhabitants of the land. "You will not come in here!" they told David. Nevertheless David took the stronghold of Zion. Then he said, "Whoever shall smite the Jebusites first shall be chief and commander." And Joab the son of Zeruiah, David's sister, went up first, so he became chief. David took the stronghold of Zion, and then dwelt there; and it was called the city of David. And David became greater and greater, for the LORD of hosts was with him.

Now these are the chiefs of David's mighty men, who gave him strong support to make him king. Jashobeam was chief of the three; he wielded his spear against three hundred whom he slew at one time. Next to him was Eleazar the son of Dodo. At Pas-dammim against the Philistines, David's men had fled, but Eleazar took his stand in the midst of a plot of barley and slew the Philistines; and the LORD saved them by a great victory.

Abishai the brother of Joab was the most renowned of the thirty mighty men and became their commander, but he did not attain to the three. And Benaiah was a valiant man, a doer of great deeds. He went down and slew a lion in a pit on a day when snow had fallen. He also slew an Egyptian, a man of great stature, who had in his hand a spear like a weaver's beam; but Benaiah snatched it out of his hand and slew him with his own spear. Benaiah was renowned among the thirty, and David set him over his bodyguard.

DAVID CONSULTED WITH the commanders, and with every leader; then he said to the assembly of Israel, "If it seems good to you, let us send abroad to our brethren in all the land of Israel, and to the priests and Levites, that we may bring again the ark of our God to us; for we neglected it in the days of Saul." And the thing was right in the eyes of all the people. So David assembled all Israel from the border of Egypt to Syria, and they went up to Kiriath-jearim to bring up from there the ark of the LORD. They carried the ark upon a new cart from the house of Abinadab upon the hill, and Uzzah his son was driving the cart. David and all Israel were making merry before God with all their might, with song and lyres and tambourines and trumpets. But it happened that the oxen stumbled, and Uzzah put out his hand to hold the ark. The anger of the LORD was kindled against him, and he smote him because he had touched the ark; and Uzzah died there before God. David was afraid, because the LORD had broken forth upon Uzzah, and he said, "How can I bring the ark of God home to me?" So he did not take the ark into the city of David, but took it aside to the house of Obed-edom the Gittite. And the ark of God remained there three months; and the LORD blessed the household of Obed-edom and all that he had.

WHEN THE PHILISTINES heard that David had been anointed king over all Israel, they went in search of him. David heard of it and went out against them. Now the Philistines made a raid in the valley of Rephaim, and David inquired of God, "Shall I go up against the Philistines?" and the LORD said, "Go up, and I will give them into your hand." David went up to Baal-perazim, and defeated them there; the Philistines left their gods behind, and David gave command, and they were burned.

The Philistines made another raid in the valley. When David again inquired of God, God said, "You shall not go up after them; go around and come upon them opposite the balsam trees. When you hear the sound of marching in the tops of the trees, then go out to battle; for God has gone out before you to smite the army of the Philistines." David did as God commanded, and they smote the Philistine army from Gibeon to Gezer. The fame of David went out into all lands, and the LORD brought the fear of him upon all nations.

HIRAM KING OF Tyre sent messengers to David, and cedar trees, also masons and carpenters. David built houses for himself in the city of David; and he prepared a place for the ark of God and pitched a tent for it. Then he said, "No one but the Levites may carry the ark of God, for the LORD chose them to carry it and to minister to him for ever."

Now David assembled all Israel at Jerusalem, to bring up the ark of the LORD to the place he had prepared for it; and he summoned the priests and the Levites. "Sanctify yourselves, you and your brethren," he said, "so that you may bring up the ark of the LORD to the place that I have prepared for it. Because you did not carry it the first time, the LORD broke forth upon us." The priests and the Levites sanctified themselves, and the Levites carried the ark of God upon their shoulders with the poles, as Moses had commanded according to the word of the LORD. David also commanded the Levites to appoint their brethren as the singers who should play on harps and lyres and cymbals, to raise sounds of joy.

David and the elders of Israel went to bring up the ark of the covenant from the house of Obed-edom with rejoicing, and they sacrificed seven bulls and seven rams. David was clothed with a robe of fine linen, and he wore a priestly apron. All Israel brought up the ark of the LORD with shouting, to the sound of the horn, trumpets, and cymbals, and made loud music on harps and lyres. They set the ark inside the tent which David had pitched for it; and David offered burnt offerings and peace offerings before God. When he had finished, he blessed the people and distributed to each a loaf of bread, a portion of meat, and a cake of raisins.

Moreover he appointed certain of the Levites as ministers before the ark of the LORD, to invoke, to thank, and to praise the LORD. Asaph was the chief; he was to sound the cymbals, and Benaiah and Jahaziel the priests were to blow trumpets continually before the ark of the covenant. On that day David first appointed that thanksgiving be sung to the LORD by Asaph and his brethren. Then all the people said "Amen!" and praised the LORD.

NOW WHEN DAVID dwelt in his house, he said to Nathan the prophet, "Behold, I dwell in a house of cedar, but the ark of the LORD is under a tent."

That same night the word of the LORD came to Nathan, "Go and tell my servant David, 'Thus says the LORD: You shall not build me a house. For I have not dwelt in a house since the day I led Israel from Egypt. In all places where I have moved with Israel, did I speak a word with any of the judges, saying, "Why have you not built me a house of cedar?"' Now therefore shall you say to my servant David, 'Thus says the LORD of hosts, I took you from following the sheep, that you should be prince over my people Israel, and I have been with you wherever you went; and I will make for you a name like the great ones of the earth. When your days are fulfilled, I will raise up one of your own sons, and he shall build a house for me. I will be his father, and he shall be my son; I will not take my steadfast love from him, as I took it from Saul, but his throne shall be established for ever.'" In accordance with all these words, Nathan spoke to David.

Then King David went in and sat before the LORD, and said, "Who am I, O LORD God, and what is my family, that thou hast brought me thus far? And what more can David say to thee? For thou knowest thy servant. For thy servant's sake, O LORD, and according to thy own heart, thou hast wrought all this greatness. Thou hast revealed to him that thou wilt build a house for him; therefore I have found courage to pray before thee. May it please thee to bless the house of thy servant, that it may continue for ever before thee."

AFTER THIS, DAVID defeated the Philistines and subdued them; and he defeated Moab, and the Moabites became his servants and brought tribute. David also defeated Hadadezer king of Zobah, toward Hamath in the north, and when the Syrians came to help Hadadezer, David slew twenty-two thousand of them, and put garrisons in Damascus; and the Syrians became his servants and brought tribute. From the cities of Hadadezer David took very much bronze; with it Solomon made the bronze sea and the pillars and the vessels of bronze for the temple.

Also Abishai the son of Zeruiah slew eighteen thousand Edomites in the Valley of Salt, and the Edomites became David's servants. And the LORD gave victory to David wherever he went. So David reigned over all Israel; and he administered justice and equity to all his people. Joab the brother of Abishai was over the army; and Zadok the son of Ahitub, and Ahimelech the son of Abiathar were priests; and Benaiah was over the Cherethites and the Pelethites of the bodyguard; and David's sons were the chief officials in the service of the king.

AFTER NAHASH THE king of the Ammonites died, David said, "I will deal loyally with Hanun the son of Nahash, for his father dealt loyally with me." So David sent messengers to console Hanun concerning his father.

But the princes of the Ammonites said to Hanun, "Do you think that David is honoring your father? Have not his servants come to spy out the land?" So Hanun took David's servants and shaved them and cut off their garments at their hips and sent them away. When David was told, he sent to meet the men, for they were greatly ashamed. "Remain at Jericho until your beards have grown," he told them, "and then return."

In the spring of the year, the time when kings go forth to battle, Joab led out the army. He ravaged the country of the Ammonites, and came and smote Rabbah, their chief city, and overthrew it. And David took Hanun's crown from his head, and it was placed on David's head. And he brought forth the spoil of the city, and the people who were in it, and set them to labor with saws and picks and axes. Thus David did to all the cities of the Ammonites. Then he returned to Jerusalem.

SATAN STOOD UP against Israel and incited David to number the people. "Go, number Israel from Beer-sheba to Dan," David said to Joab, "and bring me a report."

"May the LORD add to his people a hundred times as many as they are!" Joab replied. "Are they not all of them my lord's servants? Why then should my lord require this? Why should he bring guilt upon Israel?"

But the king's word prevailed, so Joab departed and went throughout all Israel, and came back to Jerusalem and gave the number of the people to David. In all Israel there were one million one hundred thousand men who drew the sword, and in Judah four hundred and seventy thousand. But Joab did not include Levi and Benjamin in the numbering, for the king's command was abhorrent to him.

God was displeased with this thing, and he smote Israel. David said to God, "I have sinned greatly in doing this, but now, I pray thee, take away the iniquity of thy servant."

And the LORD spoke to Gad, David's seer, saying, "Go and say to David, 'Thus says the LORD, Three things I offer you; choose one, that I may do it to you.'" So Gad came to David and said, "Thus says the LORD, 'Take which you will: either three years of famine; or three months of devastation by the sword of your enemies; or three days of pestilence upon the land, and the angel of the LORD destroying throughout all Israel.' Now decide what answer I shall return to him who sent me."

"Let me fall into the hand of the Lord," David replied, "for his mercy is very great; but let me not fall into the hand of man."

So the Lord sent a pestilence upon Israel, and there fell seventy thousand men. God sent the angel to Jerusalem to destroy it, and the angel of the Lord was standing by the threshing floor of Ornan the Jebusite. David lifted his eyes and saw the destroying angel standing between earth and heaven, and in his hand a drawn sword stretched out over Jerusalem. Then David and the elders, clothed in sackcloth, fell upon their faces, and David said to God, "It is I who have sinned by numbering the people; but these sheep, what have they done? Let thy hand, I pray thee, O Lord my God, be against me and my father's house; but let not the plague be upon thy people." The Lord repented of the evil; and he said to the destroying angel, "It is enough; now stay your hand."

Then the angel of the Lord commanded Gad the seer to say to David that David should go up and rear an altar to the Lord on the threshing floor of Ornan. So David went up at Gad's word, which he had spoken in the name of the Lord. Now Ornan was threshing wheat; he turned and saw the angel, and his four sons who were with him hid themselves. Then Ornan looked and saw David coming, and he went forth and did obeisance to David with his face to the ground.

"Give me the site of the threshing floor," said David, "that I may build on it an altar to the Lord, that the plague may be averted from the people."

"Take it," said Ornan, "and let my lord the king do what seems good to him; see, I give the oxen for burnt offerings, and the threshing sledges for the wood, and the wheat for a cereal offering. I give it all."

"No," answered King David, "but I will buy it for the full price; I will not take for the Lord what is yours, or offer burnt offerings which cost me nothing." So David paid Ornan six hundred shekels of gold for the site, and he built there an altar to the Lord and presented burnt offerings and called upon the Lord; and the Lord answered him with fire from heaven upon the altar. Then the Lord commanded the angel to put his sword back into its sheath.

When David saw that the Lord had answered him, he said, "Here shall be the house of the Lord God and here the altar of burnt offering for Israel." Then he called for Solomon his son. "My son," he said, "I had it in my heart to build a house to the name of the Lord my God. But the Lord said, 'You shall not build a house to my name, because you have waged great wars and shed much blood upon the earth. Behold, a son shall be born to you, a man of peace. His name shall be Solomon, and I will give him peace from all his enemies round about. He shall build a house for my name, and I will establish his royal throne in Israel for ever.' Now, my son, the Lord be with you, so that you may succeed in building the house of the Lord your God. Only, may the Lord grant you discretion and understanding, that when he gives you charge over Israel you may observe his statutes and ordinances. Be strong, and fear not; be not dismayed. Arise and be doing! The Lord be with you!"

Then David commanded the aliens who were in the land of Israel to prepare dressed stones for building the temple. He also provided great stores of iron, as well as bronze in quantities beyond weighing, and cedar timbers without number. For David said, "Solomon my son is young and inexperienced, and the house that is to be built for the LORD must be exceedingly magnificent, of fame and glory throughout all lands." David also commanded the leaders of Israel to help Solomon, saying, "Arise and build the sanctuary of the LORD God, so that the ark of the covenant and the holy vessels of God may be brought into a house built for the name of the LORD."

And he assembled all the leaders of Israel and the priests and the Levites, saying, "The LORD has given peace to his people, and he dwells in Jerusalem for ever, so the Levites no longer need to carry the tabernacle or any of the things for its service; but their duty shall be to assist the sons of Aaron for the service of the temple, having the care of the courts and the chambers, the cleansing of all that is holy, and any work for the service of the temple; to assist also with the showbread, the wafers of unleavened bread, the baked offering, and the offering mixed with oil. And they shall stand every morning and evening, thanking and praising the LORD, and whenever burnt offerings are offered on sabbaths, new moons, and feast days. Thus they shall keep charge of the sanctuary, and shall attend the sons of Aaron, their brethren, for the service of the temple."

Now King David assembled at Jerusalem all the officials of Israel and of the tribes, all the mighty men, and all the seasoned warriors. Then he rose to his feet. "Hear me, my brethren and my people," he said. "I had it in my heart to build a house for the ark of the covenant of the LORD, but God said to me, 'You may not build a house for my name, for you are a warrior and have shed blood. It is Solomon your son who shall build my house, and I will establish his kingdom for ever if he keeps my commandments and my ordinances.' Now therefore in the sight of all Israel and in the hearing of our God, observe all the commandments of the LORD, that you may possess this good land, and leave it for an inheritance to your children for ever. And you, Solomon my son, take heed now, for the LORD has chosen you to build a house for the sanctuary; be strong, and do it."

Then David gave Solomon the plan of the vestibule of the temple, and of its treasuries, its upper rooms, and its inner chambers, and of the room for the mercy seat; and the plan of all that he had in mind for the divisions of the priests and Levites in the service of the temple; also his plan for the golden chariot of the cherubim that spread their wings and covered the ark of the covenant. All this he made clear by an edict from the hand of the LORD, and all the work was to be done according to the plan.

And David said to the assembly, "Now I have provided for the house of my God, so far as I was able, the gold for the things of gold, the silver for the things of silver, the bronze, the iron, and the wood, besides great quantities of precious stones and marble. Who then will offer willingly, consecrating himself today to the Lord?'' Then all made their freewill offerings for the service of the temple, and the people rejoiced, for with a whole heart they had offered freely to the Lord.

David also rejoiced greatly, and he blessed the Lord in the presence of all the assembly, saying, "Blessed art thou, O Lord, the God of Israel our father, for ever and ever. Thine is the greatness, and the power, and the glory, and the victory, and the majesty; for thine is the kingdom, O Lord, and thou art exalted as head above all. And now we thank thee, our God, and praise thy glorious name.

"But who am I, and what is my people, that we should be able thus to offer willingly? For we are strangers before thee, and sojourners, as all our fathers were; our days on the earth are like a shadow, and there is no abiding. O Lord our God, all this abundance that we have provided for building thee a house for thy holy name comes from thy hand and is all thy own. I know that thou triest the heart and hast pleasure in uprightness; in the uprightness of my heart I have freely offered all these things, and now I have seen thy people here offering freely and joyously to thee. O Lord, the God of Abraham, Isaac, and Israel, our fathers, keep for ever such purposes and thoughts in the hearts of thy people, and direct their hearts toward thee."

Then David said to all the assembly, "Bless the Lord your God." And all the assembly blessed the Lord, the God of their fathers, and bowed their heads, and worshiped the Lord, and did obeisance to the king. And they performed sacrifices to the Lord, and on the next day offered burnt offerings to the Lord, a thousand bulls, a thousand rams, and a thousand lambs, with their drink offerings, and sacrifices in abundance for all Israel; and they ate and drank before the Lord on that day with great gladness.

When David was old, he made Solomon his son king over Israel. All the leaders and the mighty men, and also the other sons of King David, pledged their allegiance to King Solomon. He prospered, and all Israel obeyed him, and the Lord gave him great repute. David had reigned over Israel forty years, and he died in a good old age, full of riches and honor.

2 CHRONICLES

This book begins by describing the grandeur of the reign of David's son Solomon, emphasizing his zeal in constructing the temple and instituting its services. Most of the book deals with the period of the divided monarchy that followed Solomon's death. The unknown author, however, writes as little as possible about the northern kingdom, since to him the apostasy of the ten tribes from the worship of God means that they no longer represent the true Israel. Though the people of the southern kingdom of Judah sometimes go badly astray, suffering divine punishment for their sins, they still remain God's chosen people even as they are led into exile. The author accepts the view of Deuteronomy that national calamity is the result of national sin, and he emphasizes the blessings that come from respect for the law of God.

———

SOLOMON THE SON of David established himself in his kingdom, and the LORD was with him and made him exceedingly great.

Solomon spoke to all Israel, to the commanders, to the judges, and the heads of fathers' houses. He, and all the assembly with him, went to the high place at Gibeon, for there stood the tabernacle of God which Moses had made in the wilderness. They sought the LORD, and Solomon went up to the bronze altar and offered a thousand burnt offerings upon it.

In that night God appeared to him, and said, "Ask what I should give you."

"O LORD God, thou hast made me king over a people as many as the dust of the earth," Solomon said. "Give me wisdom and knowledge to rule them."

God answered, "Because you have not asked possessions, wealth, honor, or the life of those who hate you, wisdom and knowledge are granted to you. I will also give you riches and honor surpassing those of other kings."

WHEN SOLOMON DECIDED to build a temple for the name of the LORD and a royal palace for himself, he sent word to Hiram king of Tyre: "Behold, I am about to build a house for the name of the LORD my God, for the burning of sweet spices and burnt offerings before him. It will be great and wonderful, for our God is greater than all gods, and even heaven cannot contain him. Send me a man skilled to work in gold, silver, bronze, and iron, and in purple, crimson, and blue fabrics, trained also in engraving, to be with the craftsmen in Judah whom David my father provided. Send me also cedar and cypress from Lebanon. My servants will be with your servants to prepare timber in abundance, and I will give for your servants two hundred and twenty thousand bushels of crushed wheat, two hundred and twenty thousand bushels of barley, a hundred and eighty thousand gallons of wine, and a hundred and eighty thousand gallons of oil."

Hiram answered in a letter, "Because the LORD loves his people he has made you king over them. Now I have sent a man, endowed with understanding and trained to execute with your craftsmen any design that may be assigned him. Therefore the wheat and barley, oil and wine, of which my lord has spoken, let him send them to Lebanon; and we will cut whatever timber you need and bring it to you in rafts by sea to Joppa."

Solomon took a census of all the aliens who were in the land of Israel, and there were found a hundred and fifty-three thousand six hundred. Seventy thousand of them he assigned to bear burdens, eighty thousand to quarry in the hill country, and three thousand six hundred as overseers to make the people work. Then in the second month of the fourth year of his reign, Solomon began to build the house of the LORD in Jerusalem on Mount Moriah, where the angel had appeared to David his father on the threshing floor of Ornan the Jebusite. He adorned the house with settings of precious stones, lined it with gold, and carved cherubim on the walls.

In the inner sanctuary he placed two cherubim of wood and overlaid them with gold. The cherubim stood together facing the nave. Their wings extended thirty feet: one wing of each touched opposite walls of the house, and the other wings joined in the middle. Solomon made the veil of blue and purple and crimson fabrics and fine linen, and worked cherubim on it. In front of the temple he set two high pillars; one on the south he called Jachin, the other on the north Boaz. He made all the things that were in the temple: the golden altar, the tables for the bread of the Presence, the lamps to burn before the inner sanctuary, the tongs, snuffers, basins, and firepans, all of purest gold.

When the work for the house of the LORD was finished, Solomon assembled the elders of Israel and the heads of the tribes in Jerusalem to bring up the ark of the covenant out of the city of David, which is Zion. The king and all the congregation were before the ark, sacrificing so many sheep and oxen that they could not be counted. Then the Levites took up the ark and brought it to its place in the inner sanctuary, in the most holy place, underneath the wings of the cherubim. There was nothing in the ark except the two tablets which Moses put there at Sinai, where the LORD made a covenant with Israel after they came out of Egypt.

When the priests came out of the holy place, a song in praise to the LORD was raised by the Levitical singers, with lyres, harps, trumpets, and cymbals. The temple was filled with a cloud, so that the priests could not stand to minister, for the glory of the LORD filled his house.

Then Solomon stood before the altar in the presence of all the assembly of Israel, and spread forth his hands. "O LORD, God of Israel," he said, "behold, heaven and the highest heaven cannot contain thee—how much less this house which I have built! Yet hearken thou to the supplications of thy people Israel when they pray toward this place; yea, hear thou from heaven thy dwelling place; and when thou hearest, forgive." When Solomon had ended his prayer, fire came down from heaven and consumed the burnt offering and the sacrifices, and the glory of the LORD filled the temple. And the children of Israel bowed down with their faces to the earth and gave thanks to the LORD. Then Solomon held a feast for seven days, and on the eighth day he sent the people away to their homes, joyful and glad of heart.

The LORD appeared to Solomon in the night and said to him, "I have heard your prayer, and have chosen this place for myself as a house of sacrifice. When I shut up the heavens so that there is no rain, or command the locust to devour the land, if my people seek my face and turn from their wicked ways, I will forgive their sin and heal their land. My ears will be attentive to the prayer that is made in this place. As for you, if you walk before me as David your father walked, keeping my statutes and my ordinances, I will establish your royal throne, as I covenanted with David, saying, 'There shall not fail you a man to rule Israel.' But if you turn aside and serve other gods, then I will pluck you up from the land I have given you; and this house, which I have consecrated for my name, I will cast out of my sight, and will make it a proverb and a byword among all peoples."

AT THE END of twenty years, during which he had built the house of the LORD and his own palace, Solomon rebuilt the cities which Hiram had given to him, and settled the people of Israel in them. He built Tadmor in the wilderness and store-cities in Hamath. He also built fortified cities with walls and gates, and cities for his chariots and for his horsemen. He built whatever he desired in Jerusalem, in Lebanon, and in the whole of his dominion. Solomon made a forced levy of all the people in the land who were not of Israel, and so they are to this day. But of the people of Israel, Solomon made no slaves for his work; they were soldiers and officers, commanders of chariots, and horsemen.

When the queen of Sheba heard of the fame of Solomon, she came to Jerusalem to test him with hard questions, bringing a very great retinue and camels bearing spices and much gold and precious stones. She told Solomon all that was on her mind, and he answered all her questions; there was nothing he could not explain to her. When the queen had seen his wisdom, the house he had built, and his manner of living, she said to him, "I did not believe the reports of your affairs and your wisdom until my own eyes had seen it; and behold, half your greatness was not told me. Happy are your wives! Happy are these your servants, who continually stand before you and hear your wisdom! Blessed be the LORD your God, who has delighted in you and set you on his throne as king." Then she gave the king a very great quantity of gold, spices, and precious stones before she went back to her own land.

Now the weight of gold that came to Solomon in one year was fifty thousand pounds, besides that which the traders and merchants and all the kings of Arabia brought. The king made a great ivory throne overlaid with pure gold; the like of it was never made in any kingdom. It had six steps and a footstool of gold attached to the throne, and on each side of the seat were arm rests and two lions standing beside the arm rests. Lions also stood on the ends of each of the six steps. All the king's drinking vessels were of gold; silver was not considered as anything in his days. For his ships went to Tarshish with the servants of Hiram, and once every three years they used to come bringing gold, silver, ivory, apes, and peacocks.

Thus King Solomon excelled all the kings of the earth in riches and in wisdom. Every one of them sought his presence and brought him articles of silver and gold, myrrh, spices, horses, and mules, so much year by year. He had four thousand stalls for horses and chariots, and twelve thousand horsemen, whom he stationed in the chariot cities and in Jerusalem. And he ruled over all the kings from the Euphrates to the border of Egypt. After Solomon had reigned over all Israel forty years, he slept with his fathers and was buried in the city of David; and Rehoboam his son reigned in his stead.

REHOBOAM WENT TO Shechem, for the northern tribes had come there to make him king. When Jeroboam the son of Nebat heard of it (for he was in Egypt, whither he had fled from King Solomon), he returned to Israel; and they sent and called him to Shechem. Then he and all Israel came to Rehoboam. "Your father made our yoke heavy," they said. "Now therefore lighten his hard service and we will serve you."

"Come to me again in three days," King Rehoboam said. Then he conferred with the old men who had counseled Solomon his father. "How do you advise me to answer this people?" he asked them. "If you will be kind to this people," they answered, "and speak good words to them, they will be your servants for ever."

Now Rehoboam took counsel with the young men who had grown up with him. "What do you advise that I answer this people?" he said. "Thus shall you speak to them," they replied. " 'My little finger is thicker than my father's loins, and whereas my father chastised you with whips, I will chastise you with scorpions.' "

Jeroboam and the people of Israel came to Rehoboam the third day, as he had said. But the king forsook the counsel of the old men. He answered them harshly, saying, "My father made your yoke heavy, but I will add to it." When the people saw that the king did not hearken to them, they answered him,

"What portion have we in David? We have no inheritance in the son of Jesse. Each of you to your tents, O Israel! Look now to your own house, David." So all Israel departed to their tents.

Then King Rehoboam sent Adoram, the taskmaster over forced labor, to them. But the people of Israel stoned him to death, and King Rehoboam made haste to mount his chariot to flee to Jerusalem. Rehoboam reigned only over the people who dwelt in the cities of Judah, and Israel has been in rebellion against the house of David to this day.

In Jerusalem, Rehoboam assembled the house of Judah to fight against Israel and restore it to his rule. But the word of the LORD came to Shemaiah the man of God: "Say to Rehoboam, king of Judah, and to the rest of the people, 'Thus says the LORD, You shall not fight against your brethren. Return every man to his home, for this thing is from me.'" So they hearkened to the word of the LORD, and did not go against Jeroboam in Israel.

Rehoboam dwelt in Jerusalem, and he made fortresses in Bethlehem and other cities in Judah and Benjamin. The priests and the Levites of all Israel left their holdings and came to Jerusalem from wherever they lived, because Jeroboam had cast them out from serving as priests of the LORD. He had appointed his own priests for the high places and for the golden calves which he had made. So those from all the tribes of Israel who had set their hearts to seek the LORD strengthened the kingdom of Judah. For three years they made Rehoboam secure, because they walked in the way of David and Solomon.

Rehoboam took eighteen wives and sixty concubines, but he loved above all Maacah the granddaughter of Absalom, who bore him Abijam. He appointed Abijam chief prince among his brothers, for he intended to make him king. But when the rule of Rehoboam was established and strong, he forsook the law of the LORD. Because the people of Judah had been unfaithful to the LORD, Shishak king of Egypt came and took their fortified cities and came up against Jerusalem; he took away the treasures of the temple and the king's house; he took away everything. But when Rehoboam humbled himself, the wrath of the LORD turned from him, so as not to make a complete destruction; moreover, conditions were good in Judah.

King Rehoboam reigned seventeen years in Jerusalem, and there were continual wars between him and Jeroboam. Then Rehoboam slept with his fathers, and was buried in the city of David; and Abijam his son reigned in his stead.

In the eighteenth year of King Jeroboam, Abijam began to reign over Judah. Now there was war between the two kings. Abijam went out to battle in the hill country of Ephraim with an army of valiant men. Jeroboam drew up his line of battle against him with twice as many mighty warriors. Then Abijam stood up and called, "Hear me, O Jeroboam and all Israel! Ought you not to know that the LORD gave the kingship over Israel for ever to David and his sons by a covenant of salt? Yet Jeroboam, a servant of Solomon, rose up and rebelled against his lord; and certain worthless scoundrels gathered about him and defied Rehoboam the son of Solomon when he was young and irresolute. And now you think to withstand the sons of David, because you are a great multitude and have with you the golden calves of Jeroboam. Have you not driven out the priests of the LORD and made priests for yourselves like the peoples of other lands? But as for us, we keep the charge of the LORD. Behold, his priests are at our head with their trumpets to sound the call to battle against you. O sons of Israel, do not fight against the LORD, the God of your fathers, for you cannot succeed."

Now Jeroboam had sent an ambush around behind them, and when Judah looked, behold, his troops were before and behind them. They cried to the LORD, and the priests blew the trumpets. When they raised the battle shout, the men of Israel fled, and Abijam and his people slew them with a great slaughter. Thus Judah prevailed, because it relied upon the LORD.

Jeroboam did not recover his power in the days of Abijam; and the LORD smote him, and he died. But Abijam grew mighty; and he took fourteen wives, and had twenty-two sons and sixteen daughters. When he slept with his fathers, they buried him in the city of David.

NOW JEHOSHAPHAT THE grandson of Abijam reigned in Jerusalem and strengthened himself against Israel. The LORD was with him, because he walked in his commandments. Therefore the LORD established the kingdom in his hand, and all Judah brought him tribute. The fear of the LORD fell upon all the kingdoms round about Judah, so that they made no war against Jehoshaphat. Some of the Philistines brought him silver for tribute, and the Arabs brought him more than seven thousand rams and seven thousand he-goats.

Jehoshaphat made a marriage alliance with Ahab king of Israel, and after some years he went down to visit the king in Samaria. Ahab killed an abundance of sheep and oxen for him and asked him to go up with him against the Syrians at Ramoth-gilead. "I am as you are; my people are as your people," Jehoshaphat answered. "But inquire first for the word of the LORD." Ahab gathered the prophets together. "Shall we go to battle against Ramoth-gilead," he asked them, "or shall I forbear?"

"Go up," they said, "for God will give it into the hand of the king." But Jehoshaphat said, "Is there not here another prophet of the LORD of whom we may inquire?"

"There is yet one," King Ahab replied, "but I hate him, for he never prophesies good concerning me." Then he summoned an officer and said, "Bring quickly Micaiah the son of Imlah."

Now the kings were sitting on their thrones, arrayed in their robes, outside the gate of Samaria; and all the prophets were prophesying before them, saying, "Go up to Ramoth-gilead and triumph; the LORD will give it into the hand of the king." When Micaiah came before them, King Ahab said to him, "Micaiah, shall we go to Ramoth-gilead to battle, or shall I forbear?" Micaiah answered, "Go up; the Syrians will be given into your hand."

"How many times shall I adjure you that you speak to me nothing but the truth in the name of the LORD?" King Ahab said.

Then Micaiah replied, "I saw all Israel scattered upon the mountains, as sheep that have no shepherd; and the LORD said, 'These have no master; let each return to his home in peace.'"

"Did I not tell you," said Ahab to Jehoshaphat, "that he would not prophesy good concerning me, but evil?"

"Therefore hear the word of the LORD," Micaiah continued. "I saw the LORD sitting on his throne, and all the host of heaven standing on his right hand and on his left; and the LORD said, 'Who will entice Ahab that he may go up and fall at Ramoth-gilead?' And a spirit came forward, saying, 'I will entice him. I will be a lying spirit in the mouth of all his prophets.' And the LORD said, 'Go forth and entice him.' Now therefore behold, the LORD has put a lying spirit in the mouth of these your prophets."

Then Zedekiah the son of Chenaanah came near and struck Micaiah on the cheek. "How did the Spirit of the LORD go from me to speak to you?" he said. "Behold," Micaiah replied, "you shall see on that day when you go into an inner chamber to hide yourself."

"Seize Micaiah," the king cried, "and put him in prison, and feed him with scant fare of bread and water until I return in peace."

"If you return in peace," Micaiah answered, "the LORD has not spoken by me." And he added, "Hear, all you peoples!"

So the kings of Israel and Judah went up to Ramoth-gilead. Ahab said to Jehoshaphat, "I will disguise myself to go into battle, but you shall wear your royal robes." And thus they went into battle.

Now the king of Syria had commanded his captains, "Fight with neither small nor great, but only with King Ahab of Israel." So when the captains saw King Jehoshaphat, they said, "It is the king of Israel," and they turned to fight against him. But Jehoshaphat cried out, and the LORD helped him, drawing them away. But a certain man drew his bow at a venture, and, unknowing, struck King Ahab between the scales of his armor. "Turn about," Ahab said to his chariot driver, "and carry me out of the battle, for I am wounded." The battle grew hot that day. King Ahab propped himself up in his chariot facing the Syrians until evening; then at sunset he died.

Jehoshaphat returned in safety to his house in Jerusalem. But Jehu the son of Hanani went out to meet him, and said, "Should you help the wicked and love those who hate the LORD? Because of this, wrath has gone out against you from the LORD." So Jehoshaphat went out again among the people, from Beer-sheba to the hill country of Ephraim, and brought them back to the LORD, the God of their fathers. Moreover, in Jerusalem he appointed certain Levites and priests to give judgment for the LORD and to decide disputed cases; and he charged them to deal in faithfulness, and in fear of the LORD.

After this the Moabites and Ammonites, and with them some of the men of Mount Seir, came against Jehoshaphat for battle. Jehoshaphat feared, and he stood in the assembly of Judah in the house of the LORD and said, "O LORD, God of our fathers, we are powerless against this great multitude that is coming against us. We do not know what to do, but our eyes are upon thee."

Meanwhile all the men of Judah stood before the LORD, with their little ones and their wives. And the Spirit of the LORD came upon Jahaziel the son of Zechariah in the midst of the assembly. And he said, "Hearken, all Judah and King Jehoshaphat: Thus says the LORD, 'Be not dismayed at this great multitude; for the battle is not yours but God's. Behold, tomorrow they will come up by the ascent of Ziz, at the end of the valley. You will not need to fight; take your position, stand still, and see the victory of the LORD on your behalf.' Fear not; go out against them, and the LORD will be with you." Then Jehoshaphat bowed his head to the ground, and all Judah fell down before the LORD.

They rose early in the morning and went out into the wilderness of Tekoa; and Jehoshaphat appointed those who were to praise the LORD in holy array as they went before the army, saying, "Give thanks to the LORD, for his steadfast love endures for ever." When they began to sing, the LORD set an ambush against those who had come against Judah, so that they were routed. The men of Ammon and Moab rose against the inhabitants of Mount Seir, destroying them utterly; and then they all turned to attack one another.

When Jehoshaphat and his people came to the watchtower of the wilderness, they beheld only dead bodies lying on the ground; none had escaped. They were three days in taking the spoil, for they found cattle in great numbers, goods, and precious things. On the fourth day they returned to Jerusalem with joy. And the fear of God came on all the kingdoms when they heard that the LORD had fought against the enemies of Judah. So the realm of Jehoshaphat was quiet, for his God gave him rest round about. Jehoshaphat reigned twenty-five years in Jerusalem. Then he slept with his fathers, and was buried in the city of David; and Jehoram his son reigned in his stead.

When Jehoram was established, he slew all his brothers with the sword, and also some of the princes of Israel. And he walked in the way of the kings of Israel, for Athaliah the daughter of Ahab was his wife, and he did what was evil in the sight of the LORD. Yet the LORD would not destroy the house of David because of the covenant he had made with David.

But a letter came to Jehoram from Elijah the prophet, saying, "Thus says the LORD, 'Because you have walked in the way of the kings of Israel, and have led Judah into unfaithfulness, behold, the LORD will bring a great plague on your people, and you yourself will have a severe sickness, until your bowels come out because of it, day by day.'"

After this the LORD smote him in his bowels, and at the end of two years he died in great agony. His people made no fire in his honor, like the fires made for his fathers, and he departed with no one's regret. They buried him in the city of David, but not in the tombs of the kings, and they made Ahaziah his son king in his stead.

AHAZIAH REIGNED ONE YEAR IN Jerusalem. His mother was Athaliah, the daughter of Ahab and Jezebel. He did what was evil in the sight of the LORD, for his mother was his counselor. He even followed her advice and went with Joram the son of Ahab to make war against Syria at Ramoth-gilead. The Syrians wounded Joram, and he returned to be healed in Jezreel, and Ahaziah went down to see him there.

It was ordained by God that the downfall of Ahaziah should come about through this visit. At Jezreel he went out with Joram to meet Jehu the son of Nimshi, whom the LORD had anointed to destroy the house of Ahab. When Jehu was executing judgment upon the house of Ahab, he captured Ahaziah and put him to death.

Now when Athaliah saw that her son was dead, she arose and destroyed all his sons except Joash, whom Ahaziah's sister stole away. She was the wife of Jehoiada the priest, and Joash remained with them six years, hid in the house of God, while Athaliah reigned over the land. But in the seventh year Jehoiada the priest took courage and entered into a compact with the captains of the army; and they went about through Judah and gathered the Levites from all the cities, and the heads of fathers' houses; and they came to the house of God in Jerusalem.

"Behold, Joash the king's son!" Jehoiada said to them. "Let him reign, as the LORD spoke concerning the sons of David. The Levites shall surround him, each with his weapons in his hand; and whoever enters the house of the LORD shall be slain." Then he brought out Joash the king's son, and put the crown upon him. The Levites and all Judah proclaimed him king, and Jehoiada anointed him, and they cried, "Long live the king!"

When Athaliah heard the people praising the king, she went into the house of the LORD; and when she looked, there was Joash standing by the king's pillar with the captains and the trumpeters. All the people were rejoicing, and the singers with their musical instruments led in the celebration. "Treason! Treason!" Athaliah cried, and she rent her clothes.

Then Jehoiada brought out the captains of the army. "Bring Athaliah out between the ranks," he said to them. "Do not slay her in the house of the LORD." So they laid hands on her and took her into the entrance of the horse gate of the king's house, and they slew her there.

Then all the people went to the house of Baal and tore it down. Baal's altars and images they broke in pieces, and they slew his priest before the altar. Jehoiada posted watchmen for the house of the LORD under the direction of the priests and the Levites, as it is written in the law of Moses. Then he and all the people of the land brought the king down to the king's house and set him upon the royal throne. The people rejoiced, and the city was quiet.

JOASH WAS SEVEN years old when he began to reign, and he reigned forty years in Jerusalem. He did what was right in the eyes of the LORD all the days of Jehoiada the priest.

Now Joash decided to restore the house of the LORD; for the sons of Athaliah, that wicked woman, had broken into the temple, and used all the dedicated things for the Baals. He said to the priests and the Levites, "Go out to the cities of Judah and gather money to repair the house of your God, and see that you hasten the matter." Then they made a chest and set it outside the gate of the house of the LORD; and proclamation was made throughout Judah to bring in the tax for the LORD. And whenever the Levites saw that there was much money in the chest, the king's secretary and Jehoiada would give it to those who had charge of the repair. They hired masons and carpenters to restore the house of the LORD to its proper condition, and they made burnt offerings there continually all the days of Jehoiada.

When he was a hundred and thirty years old, Jehoiada died and they buried him among the kings, because he had done good in Israel. After this, King Joash and the princes of the people forsook the God of their fathers and served idols. The LORD sent prophets among them to bring them back to him, but they would not give heed.

Then the Spirit of God took possession of Zechariah the son of Jehoiada, and he stood up among the people. "Thus says God," he said. "'Why do you transgress the commandments of the LORD, so that you cannot prosper? Because you have forsaken the LORD, he has forsaken you.'" But by the command of King Joash the people stoned Zechariah in the court of the temple. "May the LORD see and avenge!" he said as he was dying.

At the end of the year the Syrian army came up against Joash. They destroyed all the princes of the people and sent their spoil to Damascus. Though the Syrians had come with few men, the LORD delivered Judah into their hand, because they had forsaken the God of their fathers.

When the Syrians had departed, leaving Joash severely wounded, his servants conspired against him and slew him on his bed because of the blood of Zechariah. They buried him in the city of David, but not in the tombs of the kings; and Amaziah his son reigned in his stead.

AMAZIAH WAS TWENTY-FIVE years old when he began to reign in Jerusalem, and he did what was right in the eyes of the LORD, yet not with a blameless heart. As soon as the royal power was firmly in his hand, he killed those who had slain his father. He turned away from the LORD, and they made a conspiracy against him in Jerusalem and slew him. Then the people of Judah took Uzziah his son, who was sixteen years old, and made him king instead.

Uzziah built Elath and restored it to Judah, and he did what was right in the eyes of the LORD; and as long as he sought the LORD, he prospered. He made war against the Philistines, and God helped him. The Ammonites paid him tribute, and his fame spread even to the border of Egypt. He built towers in the wilderness and hewed out many cisterns. He had large herds in the plain, and he had farmers and vinedressers in the fertile lands, for he loved the soil. In Jerusalem he made engines, invented by skilful men, to shoot arrows and great stones. And Uzziah's fame spread far, for he was marvelously helped, till he was strong.

But when he was strong he grew proud, to his destruction. He was false to the LORD and entered the temple to burn incense on the altar. Azariah the priest went in after him with eighty priests who were men of valor; and they said to King Uzziah, "It is not for you, Uzziah, to burn incense to the LORD, but for the priests the sons of Aaron. Go out of the sanctuary, for you have done wrong."

Because Uzziah became angry with the priests, the LORD smote him with leprosy on his forehead, and the priests thrust him quickly from the temple. And King Uzziah was a leper to the day of his death, and dwelt in a separate house, excluded from the house of the LORD. Jotham his son was over the king's household, governing the people of the land.

When Uzziah slept with his fathers, Jotham his son reigned in his stead. He prevailed against the Ammonites and became mighty, because he ordered his ways before the LORD his God.

After Jotham slept with his fathers, his son Ahaz reigned sixteen years in Jerusalem. He did not do what was right in the eyes of the LORD, but walked in the ways of the kings of Israel. He made molten images for the Baals; he sacrificed on the high places, and on the hills, and under every green tree; and he even burned his sons as an offering. Therefore the LORD gave him into the hands of the king of Syria and of Pekah king of Israel, who defeated him with great slaughter.

The men of Israel took captive two hundred thousand of their kinsfolk in Judah, women, sons, and daughters; they also took much spoil and brought it to Samaria. Oded a prophet of the LORD went out to meet the army and said to them, "Behold, because the LORD, the God of your fathers, was angry with Judah, he gave them into your hand; but you have slain them in a rage which has reached up to heaven. And now you intend to subjugate the people of Judah as your slaves. Have you not sins of your own against the LORD? Now hear me, and send back the kinsfolk whom you have taken, for your guilt is already great."

So the men of Israel rose and clothed with the spoil all that were naked among the captives, provided them with food and drink, and anointed them. Carrying the feeble among them on asses, they brought them to their kinsfolk at Jericho, the city of palm trees.

At that time King Ahaz sent to Tiglath-pileser king of Assyria for help, for the Edomites had again invaded Judah and carried away captives, and the Philistines had made raids and taken Beth-shemesh. Tiglath-pileser came against Ahaz instead of strengthening him. Ahaz gave tribute, but it did not help him.

In the time of his distress he became yet more faithless to the LORD—this same King Ahaz. For he said, "Because the gods of the kings of Syria helped them, I will sacrifice to them, that they may help me." But they were the ruin of Ahaz, and of all Judah, for he cut in pieces the vessels of the temple, and he shut up its doors; and he made himself heathen altars in every corner of Jerusalem, provoking the LORD to anger.

WHEN AHAZ SLEPT with his fathers, Hezekiah his son reigned in his stead. Hezekiah reigned twenty-nine years in Jerusalem, and he did what was right in the eyes of the LORD, according to all that David his father had done. In the first month of his reign he opened the doors of the temple and repaired them, and he assembled the priests and the Levites in the square on the east. "Hear me, Levites!" he said to them. "Now sanctify yourselves, and carry out the filth from the holy place. For our fathers have been unfaithful and have done what was evil in the sight of the LORD; therefore his wrath has come on Judah and Jerusalem. He has made them an object of horror, of astonishment, and of hissing, as you see with your own eyes. Our fathers have fallen by the sword, and our children and our wives are in captivity for this. Now it is in my heart to make a covenant with the LORD, that his fierce anger may turn away from us. My sons, do not now be negligent, for the LORD has chosen you to stand in his presence and to be his ministers."

Then the Levites arose and sanctified themselves and went in as the king had commanded to cleanse the house of the LORD. They began on the first day of the month, and on the sixteenth day they finished. Then they went in to Hezekiah and said, "We have cleansed all the house of the LORD, and we have made ready all the utensils which King Ahaz discarded."

Then Hezekiah rose early and gathered the officials of the city and went up to the temple. They brought seven bulls, seven rams, seven lambs, and seven he-goats, and Hezekiah commanded the priests to offer them for a sin offering for all Israel on the altar of the LORD. So they killed the bulls, and the priests received the blood and threw it against the altar; and so with the rams, and the lambs, and the he-goats.

Then the king stationed the Levites in the temple with cymbals, harps, and lyres, according to the commandment of David. When the burnt offering began, the song to the LORD began also, and continued until the offering was finished. Thus the service of the house of the LORD was restored. And Hezekiah and the people rejoiced because of what God had done for them; for the thing came about suddenly.

Now the king and all the assembly in Jerusalem decreed to make a proclamation that the people should come and keep the passover at Jerusalem. Couriers went throughout all Israel and Judah with letters from the king, saying, "O people of Israel, return to the LORD, the God of Abraham, Isaac, and Israel, that he may turn again to the remnant of you who have escaped from the hand of the kings of Assyria. Do not now be stiff-necked as your fathers were, but yield yourselves to the LORD, and come to his sanctuary, that his fierce anger may turn away from you. For if you return to the LORD, your brethren and your children will find compassion with their captors and return to this land. The LORD is merciful and will not turn away his face from you if you return to him."

Sojourners out of Israel and Judah came together in Jerusalem to keep the feast of unleavened bread, a very great assembly. There were many who had not sanctified themselves; therefore the Levites had to kill the passover lamb for every one who was not clean, to make it holy to the LORD. And Hezekiah prayed for them, saying, "The good LORD pardon every one who sets his heart to seek the LORD, even though not according to the sanctuary's rules of cleanness." The LORD heard Hezekiah and healed the people. There was great joy in Jerusalem, for there had been nothing like this since the time of Solomon.

Thus Hezekiah did what was good and right before the LORD. But after these acts of faithfulness, Sennacherib king of Assyria came and invaded Judah and encamped against the fortified cities, thinking to win them for himself. Hezekiah built up the wall of Jerusalem and raised towers upon it. He also made weapons in abundance and set combat commanders over the people. Then he gathered the people together in the square at the gate of the city. "Be strong and of good courage," he said to them. "Do not be dismayed before the king of Assyria and his horde, for with us there is one greater than he; with us is the LORD, to help us and to fight our battles." And the people took confidence from his words.

After this, Sennacherib, who was besieging Lachish, sent his servants to Jerusalem. "Thus says Sennacherib king of Assyria," they said. "'On what are you relying, that you stand siege in Jerusalem? Is not Hezekiah misleading you when he tells you, "The LORD will deliver us"? Do you not know what I and my fathers have done to the peoples of other lands? Were the gods of those nations able to deliver their lands out of my hand? How much less will your God be able to deliver you! Now therefore do not let Hezekiah deceive you in this fashion.'" His servants shouted with a loud voice in the language of Judah to the people upon the wall in order to frighten them.

Then Hezekiah and Isaiah the prophet, the son of Amoz, prayed to heaven, and the LORD sent an angel who cut off all the mighty warriors in the Assyrian camp. So Sennacherib returned with shame of face to his own land, and when he came into the house of his god, some of his own sons struck him down with the sword. Thus the LORD saved Hezekiah and Jerusalem from the hand of the Assyrians, and he gave them rest on every side.

Hezekiah had very great riches and honor, and flocks and herds in abundance. This same Hezekiah closed the upper outlet of the waters of Gihon and directed them down to the west side of the city of David. And he prospered in all his works. Then he slept with his fathers, and all Judah did him honor at his death; and Manasseh his son reigned in his stead.

MANASSEH REIGNED FIFTY-FIVE years in Jerusalem, and he did what was evil in the sight of the LORD. For he rebuilt the high places which his father had broken down, and erected an altar to Baal in the house of God. And he burned his sons as an offering and practiced soothsaying and sorcery. Manasseh seduced Judah, so that they did more evil than the nations whom the LORD drove out before the people of Israel.

The LORD spoke to Manasseh and to his people, but they gave no heed. Therefore the LORD brought upon him the army of the king of Assyria, who took Manasseh with hooks and bound him with fetters and brought him to Babylon. In his distress Manasseh entreated the favor of the LORD and humbled himself greatly before the God of his fathers. He prayed to him, and God heard his supplication and brought him again to Jerusalem into his kingdom. Then Manasseh knew that the LORD was God.

Afterwards he took away the foreign gods from the house of the LORD, and he threw them outside of the city. He also restored the altar of the LORD and offered upon it sacrifices of thanksgiving; and he commanded Judah to serve the LORD God of Israel.

When Manasseh slept with his fathers, Amon his son reigned for two years in Jerusalem. He did what was evil in the sight of the LORD, and his servants conspired against him and killed him, and the people of the land made Josiah his son king in his stead.

JOSIAH WAS EIGHT years old when he began to reign, and he reigned thirty-one years in Jerusalem. He did what was right in the eyes of the LORD and walked in the ways of David his father; he did not turn aside to the right or to the left. For in the twelfth year of his reign he began to purge Judah of the high places and the molten images. He also burned the bones of their priests and hewed down all the incense altars throughout the land.

Now in the eighteenth year of his reign he sent Shaphan the secretary to Hilkiah the high priest to see to the repair of the temple, which the kings of Judah had let go to ruin. While Shaphan was bringing out the money that had been collected, Hilkiah the priest found the book of the law of the LORD given through Moses. "I have found the book of the law in the house of the LORD," he told Shaphan, and he gave the book to him.

Shaphan reported to the king, "Hilkiah has given me a book." And Shaphan read it before the king.

When the king heard the words of the law he rent his clothes. "Go, inquire of the LORD for me concerning the words of the book that has been found," he commanded Hilkiah and Shaphan. "Great is the wrath of the LORD on us, because our fathers have not done according to its words."

So Hilkiah and Shaphan went to Huldah the prophetess, who dwelt in Jerusalem in the Second Quarter, and spoke to her. "Thus says the LORD, the God of Israel," she replied. "'Behold, I will bring evil upon this place and upon its inhabitants, all the curses that are written in the book which was read before the king. Because they have forsaken me and have burned incense to other gods, therefore my wrath will be poured out upon them. But to the king of Judah, thus shall you say to him: Because your heart was penitent and you humbled yourself and wept before God when you heard his words against this place, I also have heard you, says the LORD. Behold, I will gather you to your fathers in peace, and your eyes shall not see all the evil which I will bring upon this place and its inhabitants.'" And they brought back this word to the king.

Then the king sent and gathered together all the elders of Judah. He went up to the house of the LORD with them and all the people both great and small; and he read in their hearing the book which had been found in the house of the LORD. And the king stood in his place and made a covenant before the LORD, to walk after him and to keep his commandments with all his heart and soul. Then he made all who were present promise to adhere to it. And Josiah took away all the abominations from the territory of Israel, and all his days the people did not turn away from following the LORD.

IN THE EIGHTEENTH year of the reign of Josiah he said to the Levites, who were holy to the LORD, "Now serve the LORD your God and his people Israel. Kill the passover lamb, and sanctify yourselves, and prepare for your brethren, to do according to the word of the LORD by Moses."

Then Josiah contributed as passover offerings lambs and kids from his own flock to the number of thirty thousand. When the service had been prepared, the priests, the sons of Aaron, stood in their place, and the Levites in their divisions according to the directions of David king of Israel. The Levites killed the passover lambs, and the sons of Aaron sprinkled the blood which they received from them. And the priests distributed the burnt offerings to the lay people to sacrifice to the LORD, as it is written in the book of Moses. The singers were in their place, according to the command of David, and the gatekeepers were at each gate; they did not need to depart from their service, for their brethren the Levites prepared burnt offerings for them. So the people of Israel kept the passover that day, and the feast of unleavened bread seven days, according to the command of King Josiah. No passover like it had been kept since the days of Samuel the prophet.

After all this, Neco king of Egypt went up to fight at Carchemish on the Euphrates, and Josiah went out against him. But Neco sent envoys to him, saying, "What have we to do with each other, king of Judah? I am not coming against you this day, but against the house with which I am at war; and God has commanded me to make haste. Cease opposing God, who is with me, lest he destroy you."

Nevertheless Josiah did not listen to the words of Neco from the mouth of God, but joined battle with him in the plain of Megiddo. And the archers shot him, and he said to his servants, "Take me away, for I am badly wounded." So his servants carried King Josiah in his chariot to Jerusalem, and he died and was buried with his fathers. All Judah mourned for Josiah. Jeremiah the prophet also uttered a lament for him; and all the singing men and women have spoken of Josiah in their laments to this day.

THE PEOPLE TOOK JEHOAHAZ THE son of Josiah and made him king in his father's stead. But Jehoahaz reigned only three months in Jerusalem, for the king of Egypt deposed him and took him to Egypt and made Jehoiakim his brother king in his place.

Jehoiakim reigned eleven years in Jerusalem, and he did what was evil in the sight of the LORD. Nebuchadnezzar king of Babylon came up against him, and bound him in fetters to take him to Babylon; and Jehoiachin his son reigned in his stead.

Jehoiachin was eighteen years old when he began to reign, and he reigned three months and ten days in Jerusalem. In the spring of the year King Nebuchadnezzar sent and brought him to Babylon, and made his brother Zedekiah king over Judah.

Zedekiah reigned eleven years in Jerusalem. He did what was evil in the sight of the LORD, and did not humble himself before Jeremiah the prophet, who spoke from the mouth of the LORD. He also rebelled against King Nebuchadnezzar, and he hardened his heart against turning to the LORD. All the leading priests and the people likewise were exceedingly unfaithful, following all the abominations of the nations. The LORD sent persistently to them by his messengers, but they kept scoffing at his prophets. So the wrath of the LORD rose against his people, till there was no remedy.

Therefore he brought up against them Nebuchadnezzar king of Babylon. He slew their young men with the sword in their sanctuary, and had no compassion on young man or virgin, old man or aged. The LORD gave them all into his hand. And all the treasures of the house of God, and the treasures of the king, all these he brought to Babylon. And they burned the house of God, and broke down the wall of Jerusalem, and burned all its palaces with fire. Nebuchadnezzar took into exile in Babylon those who had escaped from the sword, and they became servants to him and to his sons until the establishment of the kingdom of Persia, to accomplish the word of the LORD by the mouth of Jeremiah. All the days that the land lay desolate it kept sabbath, to fulfil seventy years.

NOW IN THE first year of Cyrus king of Persia, that the word of the LORD by the mouth of Jeremiah might be accomplished, the LORD stirred up the spirit of Cyrus, so that he made a proclamation throughout all his kingdom: "Thus says Cyrus king of Persia, 'The LORD, the God of heaven, has given me all the kingdoms of the earth, and he has charged me to build him a house at Jerusalem, which is in Judah. Whoever is among you of all his people, may the LORD his God be with him. Let him go up.'"

EZRA

The books of Ezra and Nehemiah, which in Hebrew form a single book, are a continuation of the books of Chronicles, telling about the return of the Jews from exile in Babylon. In 586 B.C. the Babylonians conquered Judah, but they in turn were conquered by Cyrus, king of Persia. In 538, Cyrus issued an edict permitting the Jews to leave Babylon. Many do so, and under the leadership of Sheshbazzar they begin to rebuild the temple in Jerusalem. Because of local opposition, however, the temple has to be left unfinished. During the reign of Darius I (521–485 B.C.) a second returning group, led by Zerubbabel and Jeshua, and encouraged by the prophets Haggai and Zechariah, manages in the face of opposition to complete the temple by the spring of 515 B.C. Still later another large group of Jews returns, under the leadership of Ezra, a Jewish scribe. With him Ezra brings a codification of the Mosaic law, and he also introduces reforms, notably in the matter of mixed marriages. Because of intermarriage with Gentiles, he charges, the Jews are in danger of blending with the nations around them. He therefore requires the eviction of Gentile wives from Jewish families.

IN THE FIRST year of Cyrus king of Persia, that the word of the LORD by the mouth of Jeremiah might be accomplished, the LORD stirred up the spirit of the king, so that he made a proclamation throughout all his kingdom:

"Thus says Cyrus king of Persia: The LORD, the God of heaven, has given me all the kingdoms of the earth, and he has charged me to build him a house at Jerusalem, which is in Judah. Whoever is among you of all his people, let him go up and rebuild the house of the LORD, the God of Israel—he is the God who is in Jerusalem; and let each survivor be assisted by the men of his place with silver and gold, with goods and with beasts."

Then rose up the heads of the families of Judah, and the priests and the Levites, every one whose spirit God had stirred to go up to rebuild the temple in Jerusalem; and all who were about them aided them with vessels of silver,

with gold, with goods, with beasts, and with costly wares. Cyrus also brought
out the vessels of the temple, which Nebuchadnezzar had carried away from
Jerusalem, and the treasurer counted them out to Sheshbazzar the prince of
Judah. The vessels of gold and of silver were five thousand four hundred and
sixty-nine. All these did Sheshbazzar bring up to Jerusalem.

When the seventh month came, and the sons of Israel were back in the
towns, the people gathered as one man to Jerusalem, and they built the altar
of the God of Israel for burnt offerings, as it is written in the law of Moses.
For fear was upon them because of the peoples of the lands round about, and
they made burnt offerings to the LORD daily, morning and evening. And they
kept the feast of booths, as it is written. But the foundation of the temple was
not yet laid, so they gave money to the masons and the carpenters, and food,
drink, and oil to the Sidonians and the Tyrians to bring cedar trees from
Lebanon by sea to Joppa.

When the builders laid the foundation of the temple, the priests in their
vestments came forward with trumpets, and the Levites with cymbals, to
praise the LORD, according to the directions of David the king; and they sang
responsively, praising and giving thanks to the LORD: "For he is good, for his
steadfast love endures for ever toward Israel." And all the people shouted
with a great shout when they praised the LORD, because the foundation of his
house was laid. But many of the old men who had seen the first house wept
when they saw the foundation being laid, though many shouted aloud for joy;
so that the people could not distinguish the sound of the joyful shout from
that of the people's weeping, and the sound was heard afar.

Now when the Samaritans heard that the returned exiles were building a
temple to the LORD, they approached them and said, "Let us build with you;
for we worship your God as you do, and we have been sacrificing to him ever
since Esarhaddon king of Assyria brought us here." But all Israel said to
them, "You have nothing to do with us in building a house to our God; we
alone will build to the God of Israel, as King Cyrus has commanded us."

Then the Samaritans discouraged the people of Judah, and made them
afraid to build, and hired counselors against them at court to frustrate their
purpose, all the days of Cyrus. So the work on the house of God in Jerusalem
ceased until the second year of the reign of Darius king of Persia.

That year the prophets Haggai and Zechariah the son of Iddo prophesied
to the Jews in Jerusalem in the name of the God of Israel. Then Zerubbabel
the son of She-alti-el and Jeshua the son of Jozadak arose and began to rebuild
the temple, the prophets helping them.

At the same time Tattenai the governor of the province Beyond the River
came and spoke to them thus: "Who gave you a decree to build this house
and to finish this structure?" But the eye of their God was upon the Jews, and
Tattenai did not stop them till a report should reach Darius and answer be
returned. His report read as follows:

"To Darius the king, all peace. Be it known to the king that we went to the province of Judah, to the house of the great God. It is being built with huge stones, and timber is laid in the walls; this work goes on diligently and prospers. We spoke to the elders thus: 'Who gave you a decree to build this house and to finish this structure?' This was their reply: 'We are the servants of the God of heaven and earth, and we are rebuilding the house built many years ago by a great king of Israel. But because our fathers had angered the God of heaven, he gave them into the hand of Nebuchadnezzar king of Babylon, who destroyed this house and carried away the people to Babylonia. However, in the first year of Cyrus the king, Cyrus made a decree that this house of God should be rebuilt. And he delivered the gold and silver vessels, which Nebuchadnezzar had taken out of the temple in Jerusalem and brought to Babylon, to one Sheshbazzar, whom he had made governor, saying, "Take these vessels to Jerusalem, and let the temple be rebuilt on its site." Then this Sheshbazzar came and laid the foundations of the temple in Jerusalem; and it is not yet finished.' Therefore, if it seem good to the king, let search be made in the royal archives for such a decree issued by Cyrus. And let the king send us his pleasure in this matter."

Then Darius the king had search made, and a record was found: "In the first year of Cyrus the king, he issued a decree: Concerning the house of God at Jerusalem, let the house be rebuilt, and let the cost be paid from the royal treasury. Also let the gold and silver vessels of the temple, which Nebuchadnezzar brought to Babylon, be restored and brought back to Jerusalem."

"Now therefore," Darius decreed, "Tattenai, governor of the province Beyond the River, keep away; let the governor and the elders of the Jews rebuild this temple on its site. Moreover, the cost is to be paid in full and without delay from the royal revenue, the tribute of the province Beyond the River. And whatever is needed—young bulls, rams, or sheep for burnt offerings to the God of heaven, wheat, salt, wine, or oil, as the priests at Jerusalem require—let that be given to them day by day without fail, that they may offer pleasing sacrifices to the God of heaven, and pray for the life of the king and his sons. If any one alters this edict, a beam shall be pulled out of his house, and he shall be impaled upon it, and his house shall be made a dunghill. I Darius make a decree; let it be done with all diligence."

Then Tattenai did with all diligence what Darius had ordered; and the Jews built and prospered, through the prophesying of Haggai and Zechariah. They finished their building by command of the God of Israel and by decree of Cyrus and Darius; and the temple was finished on the third day of the month of Adar, in the sixth year of the reign of Darius.

The people of Israel, the priests and the Levites, and the rest of the returned exiles celebrated the dedication of this temple with joy. They offered sacrifices: one hundred bulls, two hundred rams, four hundred lambs, and as a sin offering twelve he-goats, according to the number of the tribes of Israel. And they set the priests and the Levites in their divisions for the service of God, as it is written in the book of Moses.

On the fourteenth day of the first month the returned exiles kept the passover. The priests and the Levites killed the passover lamb for all the exiles, for their fellow priests, and for themselves; it was eaten by them, and also by every one who had separated himself from the pollutions of the peoples of the land to worship the God of Israel. And they kept the feast of unleavened bread seven days with joy; for the LORD had made them joyful, and had turned to them the heart of the king of Persia.

NOW IN THE seventh year of the reign of Artaxerxes king of Persia, Ezra the son of Seraiah went up from Babylonia to Jerusalem. He was a scribe skilled in the law of Moses, and the king granted him all that he asked, for the hand of the LORD was upon him. Ezra had set his heart to study the law of the LORD, and to do it, and to teach his statutes and ordinances in Israel. King Artaxerxes gave him this letter: "Artaxerxes, king of kings, to Ezra the priest, the scribe of the law of the God of heaven. Now I make a decree that any of the people of Israel who freely offer to go to Jerusalem may go with you. For you are sent by the king and his seven counselors to make inquiries about Judah and Jerusalem according to the law of your God, which is in your hand, and also to convey the silver and gold which the king and his counselors have freely offered to the God of Israel, whose dwelling is in Jerusalem. With this money, then, you shall with all diligence buy bulls, rams, and lambs, and you shall offer them upon the altar of the temple. And whatever else is required for the house of your God, you may provide it out of the king's treasury.

"And I, Artaxerxes the king, make a decree to all the treasurers in the province Beyond the River: Whatever Ezra the priest, the scribe of the law, requires of you, be it done with all diligence, lest the wrath of the God of heaven be against the realm of the king and his sons.

"And you, Ezra, according to the wisdom of your God which is in your hand, appoint magistrates and judges who may judge all the people in the province Beyond the River such as know the laws of your God; and those who do not know them, you shall teach. Whoever will not obey the law of your God and the law of the king, let judgment be strictly executed upon him, for death or banishment or confiscation of goods or imprisonment."

BLESSED BE THE LORD, the God of our fathers, who put it into the heart of the king to beautify the temple in Jerusalem, and who extended to me his steadfast love before all the king's mighty officers. I took courage, for the hand of the LORD was upon me, and I gathered leading men from Israel to go up with me from Babylonia. I gathered them to the river that runs to Ahava, and there we encamped three days.

I proclaimed a fast, that we might humble ourselves before our God, to seek from him a straight way for ourselves, our children, and all our goods. For I was ashamed to ask the king for soldiers to protect us on our way, since we had told him, "The hand of our God is for good upon all that seek him, and the power of his wrath is against all that forsake him." So we fasted and besought our God for this, and he listened to our entreaty.

Then I set apart twelve of the leading priests, and I weighed out to them the silver and the gold and the vessels which the king had offered for the temple. "You are holy to the LORD," I said to them, "and the vessels are holy, and the silver and the gold are a freewill offering to the LORD. Guard them and keep them until you weigh them before the chief priest at Jerusalem, within the chambers of the temple." So the priests took the silver and the gold and the vessels, to bring them to Jerusalem.

Then we departed from the river on the twelfth day of the first month, to go to Jerusalem; the hand of our God was upon us, and he delivered us from the enemy and from ambushes by the way. We came to Jerusalem on the first day of the fifth month. On the fourth day, within the temple, the silver and the gold and the vessels were weighed into the hands of Meremoth the priest, and the weight of everything was recorded. At that time those who had come from captivity offered burnt offerings to the God of Israel. They also delivered the king's commissions to the governors of the province Beyond the River, and they aided the people and the house of God.

THE OFFICIALS APPROACHED me and said, "The people of Israel and the priests and the Levites have not separated themselves from the peoples of the lands round about, with their abominations. For they have taken their daughters to be wives for themselves and for their sons, so that the holy race has mixed itself with the peoples of the lands. And in this faithlessness the chief men have been foremost."

When I heard this, I rent my garments and pulled hair from my head and beard, and sat appalled until evening. At the evening sacrifice I rose from my fasting, and fell upon my knees and spread out my hands to the LORD my God, saying: "O my God, I am ashamed to lift my face to thee, for our iniquities have risen higher than our heads, and our guilt has mounted to the heavens. From the days of our fathers to this day we have been in great guilt; and for our iniquities we, our kings, and our priests have been given to the sword, to captivity, to plundering, and to utter shame, as at this day. But now for a brief moment favor has been shown by the LORD to leave us a remnant, and to give us a secure hold within his holy place, that he may brighten our eyes and grant us a little reviving in our bondage. We are bondmen; yet our God has not forsaken us in our bondage, but has extended to us his steadfast love before the kings of Persia, to set up the house of our God, to repair its ruins, and to give us protection in Judea.

"And now, O our God, what shall we say after this? For we have forsaken thy commandments, which thou didst command by the prophets, saying, 'The land you are entering to possess is a land unclean with the pollutions of its peoples, whose abominations have filled it from end to end. Therefore give not your daughters to their sons, neither take their daughters for your sons, and never seek their peace or prosperity, that you may be strong, and eat the good of the land, and leave it for an inheritance to your children for ever.' And after all that has come upon us for our evil deeds, and seeing that thou, our God, hast punished us less than our iniquities deserved, shall we break thy commandments again and intermarry with the peoples who practice these abominations? Wouldst thou not be angry with us till thou wouldst consume us, so that there should be no remnant, nor any to escape? O LORD, thou art just. Behold, we are before thee in our guilt, for none can stand before thee because of this.''

While Ezra prayed, weeping and casting himself down before the house of God, a very great assembly of men, women, and children gathered to him out of Israel, and the people wept bitterly. Shecaniah the son of Jehiel addressed Ezra: ''We have broken faith with our God and have married foreign women, but even now there is hope for Israel in spite of this. Therefore let us make a covenant with our God to put away all these wives and their children, according to the counsel of my lord; and let it be done according to the law. Arise, for it is your task, and we are with you; be strong and do it.''

Then Ezra arose and made all Israel take oath that they would do as had been said. Then he withdrew from before the temple and went to the chamber of Jehohanan the son of Eliashib, where he spent the night, neither eating bread nor drinking water; for he was mourning over the faithlessness of the exiles. And a proclamation was made throughout Judah that all the returned exiles should assemble at Jerusalem. Any one who did not come within three days should be banned from the congregation of the exiles, and all his property forfeited.

All the men of Judah came within the three days. On the twentieth day of the ninth month they sat in the open square before the temple, trembling because of this matter and because of heavy rain. Then Ezra the priest stood up. ''You have trespassed and married foreign women,'' he said to them, ''and so increased the guilt of Israel. Now then make confession to the LORD, and do his will; separate yourselves from the foreign wives.''

''It is so,'' the assembly answered; ''we must do as you have said. But the people are many, and it is a time of heavy rain; we cannot stand in the open. Nor is this a work for one day or for two; for we have greatly transgressed in this matter. Let our officials stand for the whole assembly; let all in our cities who have taken foreign wives come at appointed times, and with them their elders and judges, till the fierce wrath of our God over this matter be averted from us.''

This the returned exiles did. Ezra selected heads of fathers' houses, and on the first day of the tenth month they sat down to examine the matter. By the first day of the first month they had come to the end of all the men who had married foreign women. These pledged themselves to put away their wives, and they put them away with their children.

NEHEMIAH

The Book of Nehemiah embodies the first-person "memoirs" (a form unique in the Old Testament) of this Jewish leader of the postexilic period. Nehemiah, cupbearer to the Persian king Artaxerxes (465–424 B.C.), is allowed to visit Jerusalem in order to assist with the city's restoration. His narrative contains stirring accounts of conflicts with enemies who plot against the rebuilding of the city walls. Despite this opposition, the work of restoration is finally completed, and the people then enter into a covenant to observe God's law as given by Moses. Nehemiah also tells of Ezra reading the Mosaic law to a great assembly of the people, while the Levites interpret the law to them, after which Ezra leads the assembly in a confession of sins and in the worship of God. Both books, Ezra and Nehemiah, were written by the same man (who was probably also the author of the books of Chronicles), sometime between 350 and 300 B.C.

T HE WORDS OF Nehemiah the son of Hacaliah. Now it happened in the month of Chislev, in the nineteenth year of King Artaxerxes, as I was in Susa the winter capital, that Hanani, one of my brethren, came with certain men out of Judah; and I asked them concerning the Jews that survived, who had escaped exile, and concerning Jerusalem.

"The survivors are in great trouble and shame," they replied. "The wall of Jerusalem is broken down, and its gates are destroyed by fire."

When I heard these words, I sat down and wept, and mourned for days, fasting and praying before the God of heaven. "O LORD," I said, "the great and terrible God who keeps covenant and steadfast love with those who love him and keep his commandments; hear thy servant confessing the sins of the people of Israel. We have acted very corruptly against thee, and have not kept the ordinances thou didst command thy servant Moses, saying, 'If you are unfaithful, I will scatter you among the peoples; but if you keep my commandments and do them, though your exiles be under the farthest skies, I will bring them thence to the place I have chosen, to make my name dwell there.' They are thy servants and thy people, whom thou hast redeemed by thy great power and strong hand.''

Now I was cupbearer to the king. In the month of Nisan, I took up wine and gave it to him. I had not been sad before in his presence, and the king said to me, "Why is your face sad, seeing you are not sick? This is nothing else but sadness of the heart.''

Then I was very much afraid. "Let the king live for ever!" I said. "Why should not my face be sad, when the city, the place of my fathers' sepulchres, lies waste, and its gates have been destroyed by fire?''

"For what do you make request?" the king asked.

So I prayed to the God of heaven, "O LORD, let thy ear be attentive to the prayer of thy servant, and give him success today, and grant him mercy in the sight of this man." Then I said to the king, "If it pleases the king, and if your servant has found favor in your sight, send me to Jerusalem, that I may rebuild it.''

"How long will you be gone, and when will you return?" the king said to me (the queen sitting beside him).

So it pleased him to send me; and I set him a time. "If it pleases the king," I said, "let letters be given me to the governors of the province Beyond the River, that they may let me pass through to Judah; and a letter to Asaph, the keeper of the king's forest, that he may give me timber to make beams for the wall of the city, and for the house I shall occupy." The king granted what I asked, for the good hand of my God was upon me.

Then I came to the governors of the province Beyond the River and gave them the king's letters; but when Sanballat the governor of Samaria heard this, it displeased him greatly that some one had come to seek the welfare of the children of Israel.

I came to Jerusalem. After three days there, I arose in the night, I and a few men with me. Telling no one what my God had put into my heart to do for Jerusalem, I went out by night by the Valley Gate, and inspected the walls of Jerusalem which were broken down and its gates which had been destroyed. I went on to the Fountain Gate and to the King's Pool, and entered again by the Valley Gate. The officials did not know where I had gone or what I was doing; and I had not yet told the Jews, the priests, the nobles, and the rest that were to do the work.

"You see the trouble we are in," I then said to the Jews, "how Jerusalem lies in ruins with its gates burned. Come, let us rebuild the wall, that we may no longer suffer disgrace." And I told them how the hand of my God had been upon me for good, and also the words the king had spoken to me.

"Let us rise up and build," they said. So they strengthened their hands for the good work.

Then Eliashib the high priest rose up with his brethren the priests and they built the Sheep Gate; and next to him the men of Jericho built. Joiada the son of Paseah repaired the Old Gate; he laid its beams and set its doors, its bolts, and its bars. And Hanun and the inhabitants of Zanoah repaired the Valley Gate and fifteen hundred feet of the wall, as far as the Dung Gate. Others repaired opposite their houses.

So we built the wall; and all the wall was joined together to half its height. For the people had a mind to work.

When Sanballat and Tobiah the Ammonite and Geshem the Arab heard of it, they derided us. "What is this thing that you are doing?" they asked. "Are you rebelling against the king?"

"The God of heaven will make us prosper," I replied to them, "and we his servants will arise and build; but you have no portion or right or memorial in Jerusalem."

Sanballat ridiculed us in the presence of his brethren. "What are these feeble Jews doing?" he cried. "Will they restore things? Will they finish up in a day? Will they revive the stones out of the heaps of rubbish, and burned ones at that?"

Tobiah said, "Yes, what they are building—if a fox goes up on it, he will break down their stone wall!"

Hear, O our God, for we are despised; turn back their taunt upon their own heads, and give them up to be plundered in a land where they are captives. Do not cover their guilt.

Sanballat and Tobiah and the Arabs were very angry; they all plotted to fight against Jerusalem and to cause confusion in it. We prayed to our God, and set a guard against them day and night.

But the Jews said, "The strength of the burden-bearers is failing, and there is much rubbish; we are not able to work on the wall." Our enemies said, "They will not know or see till we come into the midst of them and kill them and stop the work." The Jews who lived near them came and said to us ten times, "From all the places where they live they will come up against us."

So in open places behind the wall I stationed the people according to their families, with their swords, their spears, and their bows. "Do not be afraid of them," I said to the nobles and the people. "Remember the Lord, who is great and terrible, and fight for your brethren, your sons, your daughters, your wives, and your homes."

Our enemies heard that their plan was known to us and that God had frustrated it. We all returned to the wall, each to his work. From that day on, half of my servants worked on construction, and half held the spears, shields, bows, and coats of mail; and the leaders stood behind all who were building on the wall. Those who carried burdens were laden in such a way that each held his weapon in one hand, and each of the builders had his sword girded at his side while he built. The trumpeter was beside me. "The work is great and widely spread," I said to the people, "and we are separated on the wall, far from one another. In the place where you hear the sound of the trumpet, rally to us there. Our God will fight for us."

So we labored at the work, and half held the spears from the break of dawn till the stars came out. I also had every man and his servant pass the night within Jerusalem, that they might be a guard for us by night and labor by day. So neither I nor my brethren nor the men of the guard took off our clothes; each kept his weapon in his hand.

NOW THERE AROSE a great outcry of the people against their Jewish brethren: "We are mortgaging our fields, our vineyards, and our houses to get grain because of the famine." Others said, "We have borrowed money upon our fields and our vineyards to pay the king's tax. Our flesh is as the flesh of our brethren, our children are as their children; yet we are forcing our sons and daughters to be slaves, and some of our daughters have already been enslaved, that we may buy grain in order to live; but it is not in our power to help it, for our brethren have our fields and our vineyards."

I was very angry when I heard their outcry. I took counsel with myself, and I brought charges against the nobles and officials. "You are exacting interest, each from his brother," I said to them; and I held a great assembly against them. "We, as far as we are able, have bought back our Jewish brethren who have been sold to the nations," I told them; "but you even sell your brethren that they may be sold back to us!" They were silent, finding not a word to say.

"What you are doing is not good," I said. "Ought you not to walk in the fear of our God to prevent the taunts of our enemies? Leave off this interest. Return to your brethren this very day their fields, their vineyards, their olive orchards, and their houses, and the hundredth of money, grain, wine, and oil which you have been exacting of them each month."

"We will restore these and require nothing from them," they replied. "We will do as you say."

Then I called the priests, who took an oath of them. I also shook out my lap and said, "So may God shake out every man from his house who does not perform this promise. May he be shaken out and emptied." All the assembly said "Amen" and praised the LORD. And the people did as they promised.

Moreover from the time I was appointed governor of Judah, from the twentieth year to the thirty-second year of Artaxerxes the king, twelve years, neither I nor my brethren took the food allowance of the governor. Former governors laid heavy burdens upon the people, and took from them food and wine, besides forty shekels of silver. Even their servants lorded it over the people. But I did not do so, because of the fear of God. I also held to the work on the wall, and acquired no land; and all my servants were gathered there for the work. Moreover there were at my table a hundred and fifty Jews who came to us from the nations about us. There was prepared for one day one ox and six choice sheep, and fowls likewise, and every ten days skins of wine in abundance; yet with all this I did not demand the food allowance of the governor, because the servitude was heavy upon this people. Remember for my good, O my God, all that I have done for this people.

Now WHEN IT WAS REPORTED to Sanballat and to Geshem the Arab that I had built the wall and that there was no breach left in it (although I had not yet set up the doors in the gates), they sent to me, saying, "Come and let us meet together." But they intended to do me harm, so I sent messengers to them, saying, "I am doing a great work, and why should the work stop while I leave it and come to you?" They sent to me four times in this way.

Then Sanballat for the fifth time sent his servant to me with an open letter in his hand. In it was written, "It is reported among the nations that you and the Jews intend to rebel; that is why you are building the wall; and you wish to become their king. You have set up prophets to proclaim you in Jerusalem, 'There is a king in Judah.' It will be reported to the king. So now come, and let us take counsel together."

"No such things as you say have been done," I replied to him, "for you are inventing them out of your own mind." They wanted to frighten us, thinking, "Their hands will drop from the work, and it will not be done." But now, O God, strengthen thou my hands.

Now when I went into the house of Shemaiah, who had pronounced a prophecy against me, he said, "Let us meet together in the house of God, within the temple, and close the doors; for they are coming to kill you; at night they are coming to kill you."

"Should such a man as I flee?" I answered. "And what man such as I could go into the temple and live? I will not go in." I understood that God had not sent him, but that Tobiah and Sanballat had hired him, so that I should be afraid and act in this way and sin, so they could give me an evil name. Remember Tobiah and Sanballat, O my God, according to these things that they did, and also the rest of the prophets who wanted to make me afraid.

So the wall was finished on the twenty-fifth day of the month Elul, in fifty-two days. When our enemies heard of it, they were afraid, for they perceived that this work had been accomplished with the help of our God.

Now when the wall had been built and I had set up the doors, and the gatekeepers had been appointed, I gave my brother Hanani charge over Jerusalem, for he was a more faithful and God-fearing man than many.

"Let not the gates of Jerusalem be opened until the sun is hot," I told him, "and while they are still standing guard in the evening, let them shut and bar the doors. Appoint guards from among the inhabitants of Jerusalem, each to a station opposite his own house." The city was wide and large, but the people within it were few and no new houses had been built. The people who came up out of captivity had returned each to his town.

Then God put it into my mind to assemble the nobles and the people to consult together. After this the leaders of the people came to live in Jerusalem; the rest of the people cast lots to bring one out of ten to live in the holy city, while nine tenths remained in the other towns. The people blessed all who willingly offered to live in Jerusalem.

Then they sought the Levites in all their places, to bring them to celebrate the dedication of the wall with thanksgivings and singing, with cymbals, harps, and lyres. The priests and the Levites purified themselves; then they purified the people and the gates and the wall. I brought up the princes of Judah upon the wall, and appointed two great companies which went in procession upon the wall. One went to the right. The other, which I followed with half of the people, went to the left, and we came to a halt at the Gate of the Guard. Then both companies went and stood in the house of God, and they offered great sacrifices that day and rejoiced with great joy; the women and children also rejoiced, and the joy of Jerusalem was heard afar off.

IN THE THIRTY-SECOND year of King Artaxerxes, I went back to Babylon. After some time I again asked leave of the king and returned to Jerusalem. I found that while I was not there, the portions of the Levites, who did the work, had not been given to them, so that they had fled each to his field. So I remonstrated with the officials: "Why is the house of God forsaken?" I gathered the Levites together to set them in their stations. Then all Judah brought the tithes of grain, wine, and oil, and I appointed faithful treasurers over the storehouses, whose duty was to distribute to their brethren.

I also discovered that Eliashib the priest, who was connected with Tobiah the Ammonite, had prepared for Tobiah a large chamber in the temple where they had previously put the frankincense, the vessels, and the tithes of grain, wine, and oil for the Levites and the priests. I was very angry, and I threw all the household furniture of Tobiah out. Then I gave orders, and they cleansed the chamber, and I brought back thither the vessels of the temple, with the frankincense.

Remember me, O my God, concerning this, and wipe not out my good deeds that I have done for the house of my God and for his service.

In those days I saw in Judah men treading wine presses on the sabbath, and bringing in heaps of grain and loading them on asses; also wine, grapes, and figs, which they brought into Jerusalem on the sabbath day. Men of Tyre also, who lived in the city, brought in fish and all kinds of wares and sold them on the sabbath. Then I remonstrated with the nobles of Judah: "What is this evil thing you are doing, profaning the sabbath day? Did not your fathers act in this way, and did not our God bring evil on us and on this city? Yet you bring more wrath upon Israel."

Before the sabbath, when it began to be dark, I gave orders that the gates should be shut and not opened until after the sabbath. Then the merchants lodged outside the gates once or twice; but I said to them, "Why do you lodge before the wall? If you do so again, I will lay hands on you." From that time on, they did not come on the sabbath. Remember this also in my favor, O my God, and spare me according to the greatness of thy steadfast love.

In those days also I saw Jews who had married foreign women, and half of their children could not speak the language of Judah. I contended with them and cursed them and beat some of them and pulled out their hair; and I made them take oath in the name of God, saying, "You shall not give your daughters to their sons, or take their daughters for your sons or for yourselves. Did not Solomon king of Israel sin on account of such women? Among the nations there was no king like him, and he was beloved by his God, who made him king over all Israel; nevertheless foreign women made even him to sin. Shall we then act treacherously against our God by marrying foreign women?"

And one of the grandsons of Eliashib the high priest was the son-in-law of Sanballat; therefore I chased him from me. Remember them, O my God, because they have defiled the covenant of the priesthood and the Levites.

Thus I cleansed them from everything foreign, and I established the duties of the priests and Levites. Remember me, O my God, for good.

Because of all this we now make a firm covenant and write it, and our princes, our Levites, and our priests set their seal to it. The rest of the people, all who have knowledge and understanding, join with their brethren and enter into a curse and an oath to walk in God's law given by Moses, and to observe all his commandments. We will not give our daughters to the peoples of the land or take their daughters for our sons; nor will we buy from the peoples on the sabbath; and we will forego the crops of the seventh year and the exaction of every debt.

We also lay upon ourselves the yearly obligation of the third part of a shekel for the service of the temple. We have likewise cast lots for the wood offering, to bring it into the temple to burn upon the altar of the LORD, as it is written in the law. We obligate ourselves to bring the first fruits of our ground and of every tree, year by year, to the house of the LORD; also the first-born of our sons and of our cattle, as it is written in the law, and to bring our contributions of fruit and wine and oil to the priests, and the tithes to the Levites, for it is the Levites who collect the tithes in all our rural towns. We will not neglect the house of our God.

WHEN THE SEVENTH month had come, all the people gathered as one man into the square before the Water Gate; and they told Ezra the scribe to bring the book of the law of Moses which the LORD had given to Israel. So Ezra brought the law before the assembly on the first day of the seventh month. He stood on a wooden pulpit which they had made for the purpose, and when he opened the book in the sight of all, the people stood. He read from it, facing the square from early morning until midday, in the presence of both men and women; and they were attentive to the law.

Ezra blessed the LORD, the great God; and all the people answered, "Amen, Amen," lifting up their hands; and they bowed their heads and worshiped the LORD with their faces to the ground. The Levites helped the people to understand the law, giving the sense so that they understood the reading.

"This day is holy to the LORD your God," said Ezra to the people; "do not mourn or weep." For all the people wept when they heard the words of the law. "Go your way, eat the fat and drink sweet wine and send portions to him for whom nothing is prepared; for this day is holy to our Lord; and do not be grieved, for the joy of the LORD is your strength."

So the people went their way to eat and drink and to send portions and to make great rejoicing, because they had understood the reading.

On the second day the heads of families, with the priests and the Levites, came to Ezra the scribe to study the words of the law. They found it written that the LORD had commanded by Moses that the people of Israel should dwell in booths during the feast of the seventh month, and that they should go out to the hills and bring branches of olive, myrtle, palm, and other leafy trees to make booths. So the people went out and brought them and made booths for themselves, each on his roof, and in the courts of the temple, and in the square at the Water Gate. All those who had returned from the captivity made booths and dwelt in them, and there was very great rejoicing. Day by day, from the first day to the last day, Ezra read from the book of the law of God. They kept the feast seven days; and on the eighth day there was a solemn assembly, according to the ordinance.

Now on the twenty-fourth day of the ninth month, the people of Israel were assembled with fasting and in sackcloth, and with earth upon their heads; they separated themselves from all foreigners, and stood and confessed their sins and the iniquities of their fathers. They stood and listened to the book of the law for a fourth of the day; for another fourth they made confession and worshiped the LORD.

Then Ezra said: "Thou art the LORD, thou alone; thou hast made the heavens with all their host, the earth and all that is on it, the seas and all that is in them; and thou preservest all of them; and the host of heaven worships thee. Thou art the God who didst choose Abram and bring him forth out of Ur of the Chaldeans and give him the name Abraham; and thou didst find his heart faithful before thee, and didst make with him the covenant to give to his descendants the land of Canaan; and thou hast fulfilled thy promise, for thou art righteous.

"And thou didst see the affliction of our fathers in Egypt and hear their cry at the Red Sea, and didst perform signs and wonders against Pharaoh and all his people. Thou didst divide the sea before them, so that they went through the midst of the sea on dry land; and thou didst cast their pursuers into the depths, as a stone into mighty waters. By a pillar of cloud thou didst lead them in the day, and by a pillar of fire in the night to light their way. Thou didst come down upon Mount Sinai, and speak with them and give them right ordinances and good statutes and commandments by Moses thy servant. Thou didst give them bread from heaven for their hunger and bring forth water from the rock for their thirst, and tell them to go in to possess the land which thou hadst sworn to give them.

"But they and our fathers acted presumptuously and did not obey thy commandments, and were not mindful of the wonders thou didst perform among them. But thou art a God gracious and merciful, slow to anger and abounding in steadfast love, and thou didst not forsake them. Even when they had made for themselves a molten calf and said, 'This is your God who brought you up out of Egypt,' and had committed great blasphemies, thou in thy great mercies didst not forsake them in the wilderness; the pillar of cloud which led them did not depart from them by day, nor the pillar of fire by night. Forty years didst thou sustain them in the wilderness, and they lacked nothing; their clothes did not wear out and their feet did not swell. Thou didst multiply their descendants as the stars of heaven, and bring them into the land thou hadst told their fathers to possess. So the descendants went in and captured fortified cities and a rich land, and took possession of houses full of all good things, cisterns hewn out, vineyards, olive orchards and fruit trees in abundance; so they ate, and were filled and became fat, and delighted themselves in thy great goodness.

"Nevertheless they were disobedient and cast thy law behind their back and killed thy prophets, and they committed great blasphemies. Therefore thou didst give them into the hand of the peoples of the lands. Yet thou didst not make an end of them; for thou art a gracious and merciful God.

"Now therefore, our God, the great and mighty and terrible God, who keepest covenant and steadfast love, let not all the hardship that has come upon us seem little to thee. Yet thou hast been just in all that has come upon us, for we have acted wickedly, and behold, we are slaves this day; in the land thou gavest our fathers, behold, we are slaves. Its rich yield goes to the kings whom thou hast set over us because of our sins; they have power also over our bodies and over our cattle at their pleasure, and we are in great distress."

ESTHER

During the reign of the Persian king Ahasuerus (that is, Xerxes I, 486–465
B.C.), the Jews are so hated by the grand vizier, Haman, that he schemes to
have them all put to death by the king's order. Esther hears of the plot
through Mordecai, her cousin, and is able, at some risk to herself, to turn the
tables on the plotter. Although there may be a historical basis for the story, in
its present form it seems to be a popular romance. The book does not mention God or religion, and the probable reason for its inclusion in the canon of
the Old Testament was that it describes the institution of Purim, an annual
feast still kept by Jews. Nothing is known of the book's author or date. There
are no quotations from it in the New Testament, nor have any fragments of it
been found among the Biblical manuscripts at Qumran.

IN THE DAYS of Ahasuerus, the Ahasuerus who reigned from India to Ethiopia
over one hundred and twenty-seven provinces, in those days when King
Ahasuerus sat on his royal throne in Susa the capital, in the third year of his
reign he gave a banquet for all his princes and servants, the army chiefs of
Persia and Media, and the nobles and governors of the provinces. For a hundred and eighty days he showed his riches and the splendor of his majesty.
When these days were completed, he gave for all the people in Susa a banquet
lasting seven days, in the garden court of the palace. There were white cotton
curtains and blue hangings caught up with cords of fine linen; also couches of
gold and silver on a mosaic pavement of marble, mother-of-pearl, and precious stones. The royal wine was lavished according to the bounty of the king,
and served in golden goblets. Queen Vashti also gave a banquet for the
women.

On the seventh day, when the king's heart was merry with wine, he commanded his chamberlains to bring Queen Vashti before him, in order to show
the peoples and the princes her beauty. But she refused to come. At this the
king was enraged. "According to the law," he asked his wise men, seven
princes versed in law and judgment, "what is to be done to Queen Vashti,

who has not performed my command?" Memucan, one of the princes, answered, "Not only to the king has Queen Vashti done wrong, but also to all the peoples who are in all the provinces of the king. For her deed will be made known to all women, causing them to look with contempt upon their husbands. They will say, 'King Ahasuerus commanded Queen Vashti to be brought before him, and she did not come.' If it please the king, let a royal order be written among the laws of the Persians and the Medes so that it may not be altered, that Vashti is to come no more before King Ahasuerus, and let the king give her royal position to another who is better than she. When the decree is proclaimed throughout the kingdom, all women will honor their husbands, high and low." This advice pleased the king, and he did as Memucan proposed.

Then the king's servants said, "Let officers be appointed in all the provinces to gather beautiful young virgins to the harem in Susa, under custody of Hegai the eunuch in charge of the women. Let the maiden who pleases the king be queen instead of Vashti." This also pleased the king, and he did so.

Now there was a Jew in Susa named Mordecai, the son of Jair, son of Shimei, son of Kish, a Benjaminite, who had been carried away from Jerusalem among the captives taken by King Nebuchadnezzar of Babylon. Mordecai had brought up Hadassah, that is Esther, the daughter of his uncle, for her father and mother had died. Esther was beautiful, so when the king's order was proclaimed, she was one of the maidens taken into the palace and put in Hegai's custody. But she did not make known her people, for Mordecai had charged her not to. She won Hegai's favor, and he provided her with seven chosen maids and advanced her to the best place in the harem. And every day Mordecai walked in front of the harem court to learn how Esther fared.

Each maiden was to go in turn to King Ahasuerus after twelve months of beautifying: six months with oil of myrrh and six months with spices and ointments. In the evening she went to the palace, and in the morning she came back to the second harem in custody of Shaashgaz the eunuch in charge of the concubines. She did not go in to the king again, unless he delighted in her and she was summoned by name.

Now Esther found favor in the eyes of all who saw her, and when she was taken to the king, in the seventh year of his reign, he loved her more than all others, so he set the royal crown on her head and made her queen. Then he gave a great banquet in her honor, granted a remission of taxes to the provinces, and gave gifts with royal liberality.

One day, as Mordecai was sitting at the king's gate, it came to his knowledge that Bigthana and Teresh, two of the king's eunuchs who guarded the threshold, sought to lay hands on King Ahasuerus. He told Queen Esther, and she told the king in the name of Mordecai. When the affair was investigated and found to be so, the men were hanged. It was recorded in the Book of the Chronicles in the king's presence.

AFTER THESE THINGS KING AHASUERUS promoted Haman the Agagite, son of Hammedatha, above all the princes. The servants at the king's gate bowed down to Haman, for the king had so commanded. But Mordecai did not bow down, and when Haman saw this, he was filled with fury. He had been told that the people of Mordecai were Jews, but he disdained to lay hands on Mordecai alone, and sought to destroy all Jews throughout the kingdom.

In the first month, in the twelfth year of King Ahasuerus, they cast Pur, that is the lot, before Haman, and the lot fell on the twelfth month, the month of Adar. Then Haman said to King Ahasuerus, "There is a certain people dispersed in your kingdom whose laws are different from those of every other people. They do not keep the king's laws, so it is not for the king's profit to tolerate them. Let it be decreed that they be destroyed, and I will pay ten thousand talents of silver into the king's treasuries." The king took off his signet ring and gave it to Haman, saying, "The money is given to you, the people also. Do with them as it seems good to you."

On the thirteenth day of the first month, secretaries were summoned. An edict, according to all that Haman commanded, was written to the governors and princes of the provinces, to slay all Jews in one day, the thirteenth day of the twelfth month, the month of Adar, and to plunder their goods. The edict was written in the name of King Ahasuerus and sealed with his ring, and a copy of it was to be issued as a decree in every province and in Susa the capital.

When Mordecai learned all that had been done, he rent his clothes and put on sackcloth and ashes, and went through the city, wailing loudly. He went only as far as the entrance of the king's gate, for no one might enter clothed with sackcloth. In every province, wherever the king's command came, there was mourning among the Jews.

Esther's maids came and told her, and the queen was deeply distressed. She ordered Hathach, one of the eunuchs who attended her, to go to Mordecai to learn why this was. Mordecai gave Hathach a copy of the decree, that he might show it to Esther and charge her to entreat the king for her people. Hathach did so, and Esther gave him a message for Mordecai, saying, "If any man or woman goes to the king inside the inner court without being called, there is but one law; all alike are to be put to death, unless the king holds out the golden scepter. I have not been called to the king these thirty days."

Mordecai answered, "Think not that in the king's palace you will escape any more than the other Jews. For if you keep silence at such a time as this, deliverance will rise for the Jews from another quarter, but you and your father's house will perish. And who knows whether you have not come to the kingdom for such a time as this?" Esther replied, "Go, gather all the Jews in Susa, and hold a fast on my behalf for three days. I will also fast. Then I will go to the king, though it is against the law; and if I perish, I perish." Mordecai then did as Esther had ordered.

On the third day Esther put on her royal robes and stood in the inner court, opposite the king's hall. The king was sitting on his throne, and when he saw Queen Esther, she found favor in his sight and he held out the golden scepter. Esther approached and touched the top of the scepter. "What is your request?" said the king. "It shall be given you, even to the half of my kingdom." Esther said, "If it please the king, let him come this day with Haman to a dinner that I have prepared." So the king and Haman came to the dinner, and as they were drinking wine, the king said to Esther, "What is your petition? It shall be granted you." Esther said, "If it please the king, let him come again with Haman tomorrow to the dinner which I will prepare, and tomorrow I will answer."

Haman went out glad of heart. But when he saw Mordecai in the king's gate, that he neither rose nor trembled before him, he was filled with wrath. He went home, and recounted to his friends and his wife the riches and promotions with which the king had honored him. "Even Queen Esther," he added, "let no one come with the king to the banquet she prepared but myself. Tomorrow also I am invited. Yet all this does me no good, so long as I see Mordecai the Jew sitting at the king's gate." Then his wife and his friends said, "Let a gallows be made, and in the morning tell the king to have Mordecai hanged upon it; then go merrily to the dinner." This counsel pleased Haman, and he had the gallows made. That night the king could not sleep, and he ordered that the book of memorable deeds, the chronicles, be read to him. It was found written how Mordecai had told about Bigthana and Teresh, who had sought to lay hands upon the king. "What honor or dignity has been bestowed on Mordecai for this?" the king asked, and his servants told him nothing had been done.

When Haman entered the court to speak to the king about having Mordecai hanged, the king said to him, "What shall be done to the man whom the king delights to honor?" Haman, thinking to himself, "Whom more than me would the king delight to honor?" said, "Let royal robes be brought, which the king has worn, and the horse which the king has ridden, and let one of the king's most noble princes array the man and conduct him on horseback through the open square of the city, proclaiming: 'Thus shall it be done to the man whom the king delights to honor.'" The king said, "Make haste, and do as you have said to Mordecai the Jew. Leave out nothing that you have mentioned." So Haman arrayed Mordecai and made him ride through the open square of the city, proclaiming, "Thus shall it be done to the man whom the king delights to honor." When Mordecai returned to the king's gate, Haman hurried to his house, mourning, and told his wife and his friends what had befallen him. They said, "If Mordecai, before whom you have begun to fall, is of the Jewish people, you will not prevail against him, but will surely fall before him." While they were talking, the king's eunuchs arrived and brought Haman in haste to the banquet that Esther had prepared.

The king and Haman feasted with Esther, and as they were drinking wine, the king said, "What is your petition, Queen Esther? It shall be fulfilled."

Esther answered, "O king, let my life be given me at my petition, and my people at my request. For we are sold, to be slain and to be annihilated."

"Who is he, and where is he, that would presume to do this?" asked the king. "A foe and enemy!" Esther said. "This wicked Haman!" Then Haman was in terror. The king rose in wrath and went into the garden; but Haman stayed to beg his life from Queen Esther, for he saw that the king determined evil against him. The king returned as Haman was falling on the couch where Esther was. "Will he even assault the queen in my own house?" said the king. Then Harbona, one of the king's attendants, said, "Haman has prepared a gallows for Mordecai, whose word saved the king. It is standing at his house." The king said, "Hang him on that." So they hanged Haman on the gallows he had prepared for Mordecai, and King Ahasuerus gave Esther the house of Haman.

That day Mordecai came before the king, for Esther had told what he was to her. The king took off his signet ring, which he had taken from Haman, and gave it to Mordecai, and Esther set Mordecai over the house of Haman. Then she fell at the king's feet and besought him with tears to avert the evil plot which Haman had devised against the Jews. The king held out the golden scepter to her, and she rose and stood before him. "If it please the king," she said, "let the edict which Haman wrote to destroy the Jews be revoked. For how can I endure to see the destruction of my people?"

"I have given Esther the house of Haman," King Ahasuerus said to Esther and to Mordecai, "and they have hanged him on the gallows, because he would lay hands on the Jews. You may write as you please with regard to the Jews, in the name of the king, and seal it with the king's ring, for an edict so written cannot be revoked."

The king's secretaries were summoned, and an edict was written according to all that Mordecai commanded, and sent by couriers riding on swift horses to the governors and princes of all the provinces, and also to the Jews. The writing was in the name of King Ahasuerus and sealed with his ring. It allowed the Jews to defend their lives, to annihilate any armed force that might attack them, with their children and women, and to plunder their goods, upon one day, the thirteenth day of the twelfth month, the month of Adar.

Mordecai went out from the king's presence in royal robes, with a golden crown, while the city of Susa rejoiced. Wherever the king's edict came, there was gladness among the Jews. And many declared themselves Jews, for fear of the Jews had fallen upon them.

On the thirteenth day of Adar, the very day when the enemies of the Jews had hoped to get mastery over them, the Jews gathered to lay hands on such as sought their hurt. No one could stand against them. The royal officials also helped the Jews, for fear of Mordecai, who grew more and more powerful. In Susa the capital itself the Jews slew five hundred men, also the ten sons of Haman; but they laid no hand on the plunder.

When this was reported to the king, he said to Queen Esther, "Now what is your petition? It shall be granted." Esther said, "If it please the king, let the Jews in Susa be allowed tomorrow also to do according to this day's edict. And let the bodies of Haman's sons be hanged on the gallows." So the king commanded this to be done.

The Jews in the provinces slew seventy-five thousand of their enemies, but laid no hands on the plunder. This was on the thirteenth day of Adar, and on the fourteenth they rested. But the Jews in Susa gathered on the thirteenth day and the fourteenth, and rested on the fifteenth, making that a holiday. Mordecai recorded these things, and sent letters to all the Jews, enjoining them that they should keep the fourteenth day of Adar and the fifteenth, year by year, as the days on which the Jews got relief from their enemies; that they should make them days of feasting and gladness, days for sending choice portions to one another and gifts to the poor. The Jews called these days Purim, after the term Pur, and they ordained that without fail the commemoration of these two days should never cease among their descendants. The command of Queen Esther fixed these practices of Purim, and it was recorded in writing.

The full account of the high honor of Mordecai, to which King Ahasuerus advanced him, is it not written in the Book of the Chronicles of the kings of Media and Persia? For Mordecai the Jew was next in rank to King Ahasuerus, and he was great among the Jews and popular with the multitude of his brethren, for he sought their welfare and spoke peace to all his people.

JOB

Why do good people, the righteous and the innocent, sometimes suffer great sorrow and affliction? In the Book of Job this age-old problem, perhaps the deepest mystery of human life, is brilliantly and movingly discussed.

Job, a good man who is greatly afflicted, rejects the traditional view that suffering is the result of sin, for he has no doubt about his innocence. But he is thoroughly perplexed why God should have sent such calamity upon him, since he does not doubt that God is just. After a searching dialogue between Job and his friends, God himself speaks out of a whirlwind, reminding Job that the universe and the creatures in it are really beyond the understanding of mortals. How then can they presume to argue with God about what he chooses to do? No explicit solution to the problem is offered, but Job is satisfied by an experience of immediate communion with God (*"now my eye sees thee"*), his humility and trust deepened by his sufferings. The book's historical background is uncertain, and the author is unknown. Modern opinion favors a date of composition in the fifth century B.C.

THERE WAS A man in the land of Uz, whose name was Job; and that man was blameless and upright, one who feared God, and turned away from evil. There were born to him seven sons and three daughters. He had seven thousand sheep, three thousand camels, five hundred yoke of oxen, five hundred she-asses, and very many servants; so that this man was the greatest of all the people of the east. His sons used to hold a feast, each in turn in his own house, and they would invite their sisters to eat and drink with them. When the days of the feast had run their course, Job would send and sanctify them, and he would rise early and offer burnt offerings according to the number of them all; for he said, "It may be that my sons have sinned, and cursed God in their hearts." Thus Job did continually.

Now there was a day when the sons of God came to present themselves before the LORD, and Satan also came among them. The LORD said to Satan,

"Whence have you come?" Satan answered, "From going to and fro on the earth, and from walking up and down on it." And the LORD said, "Have you considered my servant Job, that there is none like him on the earth, a blameless and upright man, who fears God and turns away from evil?" Satan answered, "Does Job fear God for nought? Hast thou not put a hedge about him on every side? Thou hast blessed the work of his hands, and his possessions have increased in the land. But put forth thy hand and touch all that he has, and he will curse thee to thy face." And the LORD said, "Behold, all that he has is in your power; only upon himself do not put your hand." So Satan went forth from the presence of the LORD.

Now there was a day when Job's sons and daughters were eating and drinking wine in their eldest brother's house. A messenger came to Job, and said, "The oxen were plowing and the asses feeding beside them; the Sabeans fell upon them and took them, and slew the servants; and I alone have escaped to tell you." While he was yet speaking, there came another, and said, "The fire of God fell from heaven and burned up the sheep and the servants; and I alone have escaped to tell you." Then came another, saying, "The Chaldeans made a raid upon the camels and took them, and slew the servants; and I alone have escaped to tell you." While he was yet speaking, there came one other, and said, "Your sons and daughters were feasting in their eldest brother's house; and behold, a great wind struck the four corners of the house, and it fell upon the young people, and they are dead; and I alone have escaped to tell you."

Then Job rent his robe, and shaved his head, and fell upon the ground and worshiped. "Naked I came from my mother's womb," he said, "and naked shall I return; the LORD gave, and the LORD has taken away; blessed be the name of the LORD." In all this Job did not sin or charge God with wrong.

Again there was a day when the sons of God came before the LORD, and Satan also came among them. The LORD said to Satan, "Whence have you come?" and Satan answered, "From going to and fro on the earth, and from walking up and down on it." And the LORD said, "Have you considered my servant Job, that there is none like him? He still holds fast his integrity, although you moved me against him, to destroy him without cause." Satan answered, "Skin for skin! All that a man has he will give for his life. But touch his bone and his flesh, and he will curse thee." And the LORD said to Satan, "Behold, he is in your power; only spare his life."

So Satan went forth, and afflicted Job with loathsome sores from the sole of his foot to the crown of his head. And Job took a potsherd with which to scrape himself, and sat among the ashes. "Do you still hold fast your integrity?" his wife said to him. "Curse God, and die." But Job said, "You speak as a foolish woman. Shall we receive good at the hand of God and not receive evil?" In all this Job did not sin with his lips.

Now when Job's three friends, Eliphaz the Temanite, Bildad the Shuhite, and Zophar the Naamathite, heard of all that had come upon him, they made an appointment together to go and comfort him. When they saw him from afar, they did not recognize him; and they wept, and rent their robes, and sprinkled dust upon their heads. They sat with him on the ground seven days and seven nights, and no one spoke a word to him, for they saw that his suffering was very great.

After this, Job opened his mouth and cursed the day of his birth, saying, "Let the day perish wherein I was born, and the night which said, 'A man-child is conceived.' Let that day be darkness! Yea, let that night be barren; let no joyful cry be heard in it. Let the stars of its dawn be dark; let it hope for light, but have none, nor see the eyelids of the morning; because it did not shut the doors of my mother's womb.

"Why did I not die at birth? Why did the knees receive me? Or why the breasts, that I should suck? For then I should have slept, and been at rest with kings and counselors of the earth. Or why was I not as a hidden untimely birth, as infants that never see the light? There the wicked cease from troubling, and the weary are at rest. The small and the great are there, and the slave is free from his master.

"Why is light given to him that is in misery, and life to the bitter in soul, who long for death and who rejoice exceedingly when they find the grave? Why is light given to a man whose way is hid, whom God has hedged in? For my groanings are poured out like water, and what I dread befalls me. I am not at ease, I have no rest; but trouble comes."

THEN ELIPHAZ THE Temanite answered:

"If one ventures a word with you, will you be offended? Yet who can keep from speaking? Behold, you have instructed many. Your words have upheld him who was stumbling, and you have made firm the feeble knees. But now it has come to you, and you are impatient; it touches you, and you are dismayed. Is not your fear of God your confidence, and the integrity of your ways your hope? Think now, who that was innocent ever perished? As I have seen, those who sow trouble reap the same. By the blast of God's anger they are consumed. The teeth of the young lions are broken. The strong lion perishes for lack of prey, and the whelps of the lioness are scattered.

"Now a word was brought to me stealthily. Amid thoughts from visions of the night, when deep sleep falls on men, dread came upon me, and trembling made all my bones shake. A spirit glided past my face; the hair of my flesh stood up. It stood still, but I could not discern its appearance. Then I heard a voice: 'Can mortal man be righteous before God? Can a man be pure before his Maker? Even in his servants he puts no trust, and his angels he charges with error; how much more those who dwell in houses of clay, whose foundation is in the dust, who are crushed before the moth. Between morning and evening they are destroyed; they perish for ever without any regarding it. If their tent-cord is plucked up within them, do they not die, and that without wisdom?'

"Call now; is there any one who will answer you? To which of the holy ones will you turn? Surely vexation kills the fool, and jealousy slays the simple. I have seen the fool taking root, but his sons are far from safety; they are crushed in the gate, and there is no one to deliver them. His harvest the hungry eat, and the thirsty pant after his wealth. For affliction does not come from the dust, nor does trouble sprout from the ground; but man is born to trouble as the sparks fly upward.

"As for me, I would seek God, and to him commit my cause. He sets on high those who are lowly, and those who mourn are lifted to safety. He takes the wise in their own craftiness, and the schemes of the wily are brought to a quick end. But he saves the needy from the hand of the mighty. So the poor have hope, and injustice shuts her mouth.

"Behold, happy is the man whom God reproves; despise not the chastening of the Almighty. For he wounds, but his hands heal. He will deliver you from six troubles; in seven shall no evil touch you. In famine he will redeem you from death, and in war from the sword. You shall be in league with the stones of the field, and the beasts of the earth shall be at peace with you. You shall know that your tent is safe; you shall inspect your fold and miss nothing. You shall know also that your descendants shall be many. And you shall come to your grave in ripe old age, as grain comes up to the threshing floor in its season. Lo, this we have searched out; it is true."

THEN JOB ANSWERED:

"Oh, that my vexation were weighed, and all my calamity laid in the balances! It would be heavier than the sand of the sea; therefore my words have been rash. For the arrows of the Almighty are in me; my spirit drinks their poison; the terrors of God are arrayed against me. Does the wild ass bray when he has grass? Can that which is tasteless be eaten without salt? Oh, that God would grant my desire; that it would please him to crush me, to let loose his hand and cut me off! This would be my consolation; I would even exult in pain unsparing; for I have not denied the words of the Holy One. What is my end, that I should be patient? Is my strength the strength of stones, or is my flesh bronze?

"He who withholds kindness from a friend forsakes the fear of the Almighty. My brethren are treacherous as a torrent-bed, as streams that pass away when it is hot, vanishing from their place. Caravans turn aside from their course, go up into the waste, and perish. They look for water, and are disappointed because they were confident. Such you have now become to me; you see my calamity, and are afraid. Have I said, 'Make me a gift,' or 'Offer a bribe for me,' or 'Ransom me from oppressors'? Teach me, and I will be silent; make me understand how I have erred. Be pleased to look at me; for I will not lie to your face. My vindication is at stake. Is there any wrong on my tongue?

"Has not man a hard service upon earth? Like a slave who longs for the shadow, or a hireling who looks for his wages, so I am allotted months of emptiness and nights of misery. When I lie down I say, 'When shall I arise?' But the night is long, and I am full of tossing till the dawn. My flesh is clothed with worms and dirt; my skin hardens, then breaks out afresh. My days are swifter than a weaver's shuttle, and come to their end without hope.

"Remember, O God, that my life is a breath; my eye will never again see good. While thy eyes are upon me, I shall be gone. As the cloud fades and vanishes, so he who goes down to Sheol does not come up; he returns no more to his house. Therefore I will not restrain my mouth; I will speak in the anguish of my spirit: Am I the sea, or a sea monster, that thou settest a guard over me? When I say, 'My bed will comfort me,' then thou dost terrify me with dreams. I loathe my life; I would not live for ever. What is man, that thou dost make so much of him, and set thy mind upon him, dost visit him every morning, and test him every moment? How long wilt thou not look away from me, nor let me alone till I swallow my spittle? If I sin, what do I do to thee, thou watcher of men? Why hast thou made me thy mark? Why dost thou not pardon my transgression and take away my iniquity? For now I shall lie in the earth; thou wilt seek me, but I shall not be."

THEN BILDAD THE Shuhite answered:

"How long will you say these things, and the words of your mouth be a great wind? Does God pervert justice? If your children have sinned against him, he has delivered them into the power of their transgression. If you will seek God, if you are pure and upright, surely then he will reward you with a rightful habitation. And though your beginning was small, your latter days will be very great.

"Inquire, I pray you, of bygone ages, and consider what the fathers have found. Will they not teach you out of their understanding? Can papyrus grow where there is no marsh? Can reeds flourish where there is no water? While yet in flower, they wither. Such are the paths of all who forget God. The hope of the godless man shall perish; his confidence breaks, and his trust is a spider's web. He thrives before the sun, his shoots spread over his garden, his roots twine about the stoneheap. But if he is destroyed from his place, it will deny him, saying, 'I have never seen you,' and out of the earth others will spring. Behold, God will not reject a blameless man, nor take the hand of evildoers. He will yet fill your mouth with laughter. Those who hate you will be clothed with shame, and the tent of the wicked will be no more."

THEN JOB ANSWERED:

"Truly I know that it is so. But how can a man be just before God? If one wished to contend with him, one could not answer him once in a thousand times. He is wise in heart and mighty in strength—who has hardened himself against him and succeeded?—he who overturns mountains in his anger; who shakes the earth out of its place; who commands the sun and it does not rise;

who seals up the stars; who alone stretched out the heavens and trampled the waves of the sea; who does marvelous things without number. Lo, he passes by me, and I see him not. Behold, he snatches away; who can hinder him? Who will say to him, 'What doest thou'? God will not turn back his anger. How then can I answer him? Though I am innocent, I cannot; I must appeal for mercy to my accuser. If I summoned him and he answered me, I would not believe he was listening to my voice. For he crushes me with a tempest, and multiplies my wounds without cause; he will not let me get my breath, but fills me with bitterness. Though I am innocent, my own mouth would condemn me; though I am blameless, he would prove me perverse. Therefore I say, he destroys both the blameless and the wicked. When disaster brings sudden death, he mocks at the calamity of the innocent. The earth is given into the hand of the wicked, and he covers the faces of its judges. If it is not he, who then is it?

"My days are swifter than a runner; they go by like an eagle swooping on the prey. If I say, 'I will forget my complaint and put off my sad countenance,' I become afraid of all my suffering, for I know thou wilt not hold me innocent. I shall be condemned; why then do I labor in vain? If I wash myself with snow, and cleanse my hands with lye, yet thou wilt plunge me into a pit, and my own clothes will abhor me.

"For he is not a man, as I am, that I might answer him, that we should come to trial together. There is no umpire between us, who might lay his hand upon us both. Let him take his rod away from me, and let not dread of him terrify me. Then I would speak without fear of him.

"I will give free utterance to my complaint. I will say to God, Let me know why thou dost contend against me. Hast thou eyes of flesh? Dost thou see as man sees? Are thy days as the days of man, that thou dost seek out my iniquity, although thou knowest I am not guilty, and there is none to deliver out of thy hand? Remember that thou hast made me of clay; wilt thou turn me to dust again? Didst thou not pour me out like milk and curdle me like cheese? Thou didst clothe me with skin and flesh, and knit me together with bones and sinews. Thou hast granted me life and steadfast love; and thy care has preserved my spirit. Yet these things thou didst hide in thy heart; I know that this was thy purpose. If I sin, thou dost not acquit me. If I am righteous, I am filled with disgrace. If I lift myself up, thou dost hunt me like a lion. Why didst thou bring me forth from the womb? Would that I had died before any eye had seen me. Are not the days of my life few? Let me alone, that I may find a little comfort before I go whence I shall not return, to the land of gloom and chaos, where light is as darkness."

THEN ZOPHAR THE Naamathite answered:

"Should a multitude of words go unanswered, and a man full of talk be vindicated? Should your babble silence men, and when you mock, shall no one shame you? For you say, 'My doctrine is pure, and I am clean in God's eyes.' But oh, that God would open his lips to you and tell you the secrets of wisdom! Know that God exacts of you less than your guilt deserves. Can you find out the deep things of God? Can you find out the limit of the Almighty? It is higher than heaven—what can you do? Deeper than Sheol—what can you know? Its measure is longer than the earth, and broader than the sea. If he passes through, and calls to judgment, who can hinder him? If you set your heart aright, you will stretch out your hands toward him. Surely then you will lift up your face without blemish; you will forget your misery, and your life will be brighter than the noonday. You will have confidence, because there is hope. You will lie down, and none will make you afraid.''

THEN JOB ANSWERED:

"No doubt you are the people, and wisdom will die with you. But I have understanding as well as you. Who does not know such things as these? I am a laughingstock to my friends; I, who called upon God and he answered me, am a laughingstock. In the thought of one who is at ease there is contempt for misfortune; it is ready for those whose feet slip. The tents of robbers are at peace, and those who provoke God are secure. But ask the beasts and the birds, or the plants and the fish, and they will tell you. Who among all these does not know that the hand of the LORD has done this? In his hand is the life of every living thing. Does not the ear try words as the palate tastes food? Is wisdom with the aged, and understanding in length of days? With God are wisdom and might. If he tears down, none can rebuild; if he shuts a man in, none can open. The deceived and the deceiver are his. He leads counselors away stripped, and judges he makes fools. He pours contempt on princes, and looses the belt of the strong. He makes nations great, and he destroys them. He takes away understanding from the chiefs of the people, and makes them wander in a pathless waste.

"Lo, my eye has seen all this, my ear has heard and understood it. What you know, I also know. But I would speak to the Almighty; I desire to argue my case with God. As for you, you whitewash with lies; worthless physicians are you all. Oh, that you would keep silent, and it would be your wisdom! Hear now my reasoning. Will you speak falsely for God? Will you show partiality toward him, will you plead the case for him? Will it be well with you when he searches you out? Or can you deceive him, as one deceives a man? He will surely rebuke you if in secret you show partiality. Will not his majesty terrify you? Your maxims are proverbs of ashes, your defenses are defenses of clay. Let me have silence, and I will speak; let come on me what may. I will take my life in my hand. Behold, he will slay me. I have no hope; yet I will defend my ways to his face. This will be my salvation, that a godless man shall not come before him. Listen carefully to my words. I have prepared my case; I know I shall be vindicated.

"Only grant two things, O God, then I will not hide myself from thy face: withdraw thy hand far from me, and let not dread of thee terrify me. Then call, and I will answer; or let me speak, and do thou reply. How many are my iniquities? Make me know my sin. Why dost thou hide thy face, and count me as thy enemy? Wilt thou frighten a driven leaf? For thou writest bitter things against me, and makest me inherit the iniquities of my youth. Thou puttest my feet in the stocks, and watchest all my paths; thou settest a bound to the soles of my feet.

"Man that is born of a woman is of few days, and full of trouble. He comes forth like a flower, and withers; he flees like a shadow. And dost thou open thy eyes upon such a one and bring him into judgment with thee? Who can bring a clean thing out of an unclean? There is not one. Since the number of his days is with thee, and thou hast appointed his bounds, look away from him, and desist, that he may enjoy, like a hireling, his day. For there is hope for a tree, if it be cut down, that it will sprout again. But man dies, and is laid low; man breathes his last, and where is he? As waters fail from a lake, and a river wastes away and dries up, so man lies down and rises not again; till the heavens are no more he will not awake, or be roused out of his sleep. Oh, that thou wouldst hide me in Sheol until thy wrath be past, and appoint me a set time, and remember me! If a man die, shall he live again? All the days of my service I would wait till my release should come. Thou wouldst call, and I would answer; thou wouldst long for the work of thy hands. For then thou wouldst number my steps, and not keep watch over my sin; my transgression would be sealed up in a bag, and thou wouldst cover over my iniquity. But the mountain falls and crumbles; the waters wear away the stones; the torrents wash away the soil of the earth; so thou destroyest the hope of man. Thou prevailest for ever against him, and he passes. His sons come to honor, and he does not know it; they are brought low, and he perceives it not. He feels only the pain of his own body, and he mourns only for himself."

THEN ELIPHAZ THE Temanite answered:

"Should a wise man fill himself with the east wind? Should he argue in words with which he can do no good? You are doing away with the fear of God, hindering meditation before him. For you choose the tongue of the crafty. Your own mouth condemns you, not I. Are you the first man that was born? Have you listened in the council of God? And do you limit wisdom to yourself? What do you understand that is not clear to us? Both the gray-haired and the aged are among us, older than your father. Are the consolations of God too small for you, or the word that deals gently with you? Why does your heart carry you away, why do your eyes flash, that you turn your spirit against God, and let such words out of your mouth? What is man born of a woman, that he can be righteous? Behold, God puts no trust in his holy ones, and the heavens are not clean in his sight; how much less one who is abominable and corrupt, who drinks iniquity like water!

"Hear me; what I have seen I will declare. The wicked man writhes in pain all his days. Terrifying sounds are in his ears; in prosperity the destroyer will come upon him. He wanders abroad for bread, saying, 'Where is it?' He knows a day of darkness is at hand. Because he has stretched forth his hand against God, running stubbornly against him; because he has lived in houses destined to become ruins, his wealth will not endure, nor will he strike root in the earth; the flame will dry up his shoots, and his blossom will be swept away by the wind. Let him not trust in emptiness, deceiving himself; for emptiness will be his recompense. It will be paid in full before his time, and his branch will not be green. He will shake off his unripe grape, like the vine. For the company of the godless is barren. They conceive mischief and bring forth evil, and their heart prepares deceit.''

THEN JOB ANSWERED:

"I have heard many such things; miserable comforters are you all. Shall windy words have an end? Or what provokes you that you answer? I also could speak as you do, if you were in my place; I could join words together against you, and shake my head at you. But I would strengthen you with my mouth, and the solace of my lips would assuage your pain.

"If I speak, my pain is not assuaged, and if I forbear, how much of it leaves me? Surely now God has worn me out; he has shriveled me up, which is a witness against me. He has torn me in his wrath, and hated me; my adversary sharpens his eyes against me. Men have gaped at me, and struck me on the cheek; they mass together against me. God gives me up to the ungodly. I was at ease, and he seized me by the neck and dashed me to pieces; he set me up as his target, his archers surround me. He slashes open my kidneys; he pours out my gall on the ground. I have sewed sackcloth on my skin, and laid my strength in the dust. My face is red with weeping, and on my eyelids is deep darkness; although there is no violence in my hands, and my prayer is pure.

"O earth, cover not my blood, and let my cry find no resting place. Even now, behold, my witness is in heaven, and he that vouches for me is on high. My friends scorn me; my eye pours out tears to God, that he would maintain the right of a man with God, like that of a man with his neighbor. For when a few years have come, I shall go the way whence I shall not return. My spirit is broken; the grave is ready for me. Surely there are mockers about me, and my eye dwells on their provocation.

"Lay down a pledge for me with thyself; who is there that will give surety for me? Since thou hast closed their minds to understanding, therefore thou wilt not let them triumph. He who informs against his friends, the eyes of his children will fail.

"I am made a byword, one before whom men spit. My eye has grown dim from grief, and all my members are like a shadow. Upright men are appalled at this. Yet the righteous holds to his way, and he that has clean hands grows stronger and stronger. Come on again, all of you, and I shall not find a wise man among you. My days are past, my plans are broken off. If I look for Sheol as my house and spread my couch in darkness, if I say to the pit, 'You are my father,' and to the worm, 'My mother,' or 'My sister,' where then is my hope? Who will see my hope? Will it go down to the bars of Sheol? Shall we descend together into the dust?''

THEN BILDAD THE Shuhite answered:

"How long will you hunt for words? Why are we counted as cattle, stupid in your sight? You who tear yourself in your anger, shall the earth be forsaken for you?

"Yea, the light of the wicked is put out; it is dark in his tent. His strong steps are shortened; he is cast into a net by his own feet. A trap seizes him by the heel, a rope is hid for him in the ground. He is torn from the tent in which he trusted, and brought to the king of terrors. Brimstone is scattered upon his habitation. His roots dry up and his branches wither. His memory perishes from the earth; he has no name in the street, and no survivor where he used to live. They of the west are appalled at his day, and horror seizes them of the east. Surely such is the place of him who knows not God."

THEN JOB ANSWERED:

"How long will you torment me? Are you not ashamed to wrong me? If it be true that I have erred, my error remains with myself. If you make my humiliation an argument against me, know then that God has put me in the wrong, and closed his net about me. Behold, I cry out, 'Violence!' but I am not answered. He has walled up my way, so I cannot pass; he has stripped from me my glory; he breaks me down on every side, and my hope has he pulled up like a tree. He counts me as his adversary. His troops have cast up siegeworks against me, and encamp about my tent. He has put my brethren far from me. My kinsfolk and close friends have failed me; the guests in my house have forgotten me; my maidservants count me a stranger. I am repulsive to my wife, loathsome to the sons of my own mother; even young children despise me. My bones cleave to my flesh, and I have escaped by the skin of my teeth. Have pity on me, have pity on me, O you my friends, for the hand of God has touched me! Why do you, like God, pursue me? Why are you not satisfied with my flesh?

"Oh, that my words were inscribed in a book! Oh, that with an iron pen they were graven in the rock for ever! For I know that my Redeemer lives, and at last he will stand upon the earth; and after my skin has been thus destroyed, then from my flesh I shall see God on my side. My heart faints within me! If you say, 'How we will pursue him!' and, 'The root of the matter is found in him'; be afraid, for wrath brings the punishment of the sword, that you may know there is a judgment."

THEN ZOPHAR THE Naamathite answered:

"My thoughts hasten within me. I hear censure which insults me, and out of my understanding a spirit answers me. Do you not know, since man was placed upon earth, that the exulting of the wicked is short? Though his head reach to the clouds, he will perish like his own dung. He will be chased away like a vision of the night. Though wickedness is sweet in his mouth, though he hides it under his tongue, yet his food is turned in his stomach; it is the gall of asps within him. He swallows down riches and vomits them up again; from the profit of his trading he will get no enjoyment. For he has crushed the poor, he has seized a house which he did not build. Because his greed knew no rest, he will not save anything in which he delights. All the force of misery will come upon him. A bronze arrow will strike him through; the glittering point comes out of his gall; terrors come upon him. The heavens will reveal his iniquity, and the earth will rise up against him. The possessions of his house will be dragged off in the day of God's wrath. This is the wicked man's portion from God.''

THEN JOB ANSWERED:

"Listen carefully to my words, and let this be your consolation to me. Bear with me, and after I have spoken, mock on. As for me, is my complaint against man? Why should I not be impatient? Look at me, and be appalled. When I think of it, shuddering seizes my flesh. Why do the wicked live, reach old age, and grow mighty in power? Their children are established in their presence, their houses are safe from fear, and no rod of God is upon them. Their bull breeds without fail; their cow does not cast her calf. Their children dance to the tambourine and the lyre, and rejoice to the sound of the pipe. They spend their days in prosperity, and in peace they go down to Sheol. They say to God, 'Depart from us! We do not desire the knowledge of thy ways. What is the Almighty, that we should serve him? What profit do we get if we pray to him?' Behold, is not their prosperity in their hand? The counsel of the wicked is far from me.

"How often is it that the lamp of the wicked is put out? That their calamity comes upon them? That God distributes pains in his anger? You say, 'God stores up their iniquity for their sons.' Let him recompense it to themselves, that they may know it; let their own eyes see their destruction, for what do they care for their houses after them? Will any teach God knowledge, seeing that he judges those that are on high? One dies in full prosperity, wholly at ease, his body fat and the marrow of his bones moist. Another dies in bitterness of soul, never having tasted of good. They lie down alike in the dust, and the worms cover them.

"Have you not asked those who travel the roads, and do you not accept their testimony that the wicked man is spared in the day of calamity, that he is rescued in the day of wrath? Who requites him for what he has done? When he is borne to the grave, watch is kept over his tomb. The clods of the valley are sweet to him; all men follow after him, and those who go before him are innumerable. How then will you comfort me with empty nothings? There is nothing left of your answers but falsehood.''

THEN ELIPHAZ THE Temanite answered:

"Can a man be profitable to God? Surely he who is wise is profitable to himself. Is it any pleasure to the Almighty if you are righteous? Is it for your fear of him that he reproves you? There is no end to your iniquities. You have exacted pledges of your brothers for nothing, stripped the naked of their clothing, withheld bread from the hungry, sent widows away empty. Therefore snares are round about you, and sudden terror overwhelms you; your light is darkened, so that you cannot see, and a flood of water covers you. Is not God high in the heavens? See the highest stars, how lofty they are! Therefore you say, 'What does God know? Can he judge through the deep darkness? Thick clouds enwrap him, so that he does not see, and he walks on the vault of heaven.' Will you keep to the old way which wicked men have trod? They were snatched away before their time; their foundation was washed away. The righteous see it and are glad, the innocent laugh them to scorn, saying, 'Surely our adversaries are cut off, and what they left the fire has consumed.'

"Agree with God, and be at peace; thereby good will come to you. Lay up his words in your heart. If you return to the Almighty and humble yourself, if you remove unrighteousness from your tents, if you lay gold in the torrent bed, and if the Almighty is your gold, then you will delight yourself in the Almighty and lift up your face to God. You will make your prayer, and he will hear you. For God abases the proud, but he saves the lowly. He delivers the innocent man; you will be delivered through the cleanness of your hands."

THEN JOB ANSWERED:

"Today also my complaint is bitter, his hand is heavy in spite of my groaning. Oh, that I knew where I might find him, that I might come even to his seat! I would lay my case before him and learn what he would answer me. He would give heed to me; an upright man could reason with him, and I should be acquitted for ever by my judge.

"Behold, I go forward, but he is not there, and backward, but I cannot perceive him; on the left hand I seek him, and on the right, but I cannot see him. But he knows the way that I take; when he has tried me, I shall come forth as gold. My foot has held fast to his steps, and I have treasured in my bosom the words of his mouth. But who can turn him? What he desires, that he does. For he will complete what he appoints for me, and many such things are in his mind. Therefore, when I consider, I am in dread of him. God has made my heart faint.

"Why are not times of judgment kept by the Almighty, and why do those who know him never see his days? Men remove landmarks, seize flocks and pasture them, drive away the ass of the fatherless, take the widow's ox for a pledge, and thrust the poor off the road. The poor hide themselves, seeking prey in the wilderness as food for their children; they lie all night naked in the cold; they are wet with the rain of the mountains, and cling to the rock for want of shelter. From out of the city the dying groan, and the soul of the wounded cries for help. Yet God pays no attention to their prayer.

"There are those who rebel against the light and do not stay in its paths. The murderer rises in the dark, that he may kill the poor and needy. The eye of the adulterer also waits for the twilight, and he disguises his face. In the dark they dig through houses, by day they shut themselves up, for deep darkness is morning to all of them. You say, 'Their portion is cursed in the land. Drought and heat snatch away the snow; so does Sheol those who have sinned.' Yet God prolongs the life of the mighty. He gives them security, and his eyes are upon their ways. If it is not so, who will prove there is nothing in what I say?"

Then Bildad the Shuhite answered:

"Dominion and fear are with God; he makes peace in his high heaven. Is there any number to his armies? Upon whom does his light not arise? How then can man be righteous before God? Behold, even the moon is not bright and the stars are not clean in his sight; how much less man, who is a worm!"

Then Job answered:

"How you have helped him who has no power! How you have counseled him who has no wisdom! With whose help have you uttered words, and whose spirit has come forth from you?

"The shades below tremble before God. He stretches out the north over the void, and hangs the earth upon nothing. He binds up the waters in his thick clouds, and covers the face of the moon. He has described a circle upon the waters at the boundary between light and darkness. By his power he stilled the sea; by his wind the heavens were made fair; his hand pierced the fleeing serpent. Lo, these are but the outskirts of his ways.

"As God lives, who has made my soul bitter, as long as my breath is in me, and the spirit of God is in my nostrils, my tongue will not utter deceit. Far be it from me to say that you are right. Till I die I will not put away my integrity from me; my heart does not reproach me for any of my days.

"Surely there is a mine for silver, and a place for gold which they refine. Iron is taken out of the earth, and copper is smelted from the ore. Men search out to the farthest bound the ore in gloom and deep darkness. They open shafts in a valley away from where men live; forgotten by travelers, they hang afar from men, they swing to and fro. As for the earth, out of it comes bread; but underneath it is turned up as by fire. Its stones are the place of sapphires, and it has dust of gold. Man puts his hand to the flinty rock, and overturns mountains by the roots. He cuts out channels in the rocks, and his eye sees every precious thing. He binds up the streams so that they do not trickle, and the thing that is hid he brings forth to light.

"But where shall wisdom be found? And where is the place of understanding? Man does not know the way to it, and it is not found in the land of the living. The deep says, 'It is not in me,' and the sea says, 'It is not with me.' It cannot be gotten for gold, and silver cannot be weighed as its price. It cannot be valued in precious onyx or sapphire, nor can it be exchanged for jewels. The price of wisdom is above pearls. Whence then comes wisdom? Where is the place of understanding? It is hid from the eyes of all living, and concealed from the birds of the air.

"But God understands the way to it, for he sees everything under the heavens. When he gave to the wind its weight, and measured out the waters; when he made a decree for the rain, and a way for the lightning and thunder; then he saw it and declared it; he established it, and searched it out. And he said to man, 'Behold, the fear of the Lord, that is wisdom; and to depart from evil is understanding.'"

And Job again took up his discourse, saying, "Oh, that I were as in the months of old when God watched over me, when his lamp shone upon my head, when my children were about me, when my steps were washed with milk, and the rock poured out for me streams of oil! At the gate of the city, or when I sat in the square, the young men withdrew, and the aged stood; the princes refrained from talking, the voice of the nobles was hushed. The blessing of him who was about to perish came upon me, and I caused the widow's heart to sing for joy. I put on righteousness, and it clothed me. I was eyes to the blind, and feet to the lame. I was a father to the poor, and I searched out the cause of him whom I did not know. I broke the fangs of the unrighteous, and made him drop his prey from his teeth. Then I thought, 'I shall die in my nest, and I shall multiply my days as the sand, my glory fresh with me, and my bow ever new in my hand.' Men listened to my counsel. After I spoke they did not speak again; my word dropped upon them. They waited for me, and opened their mouths as for the spring rain. I smiled on them when they had no confidence, and the light of my countenance they did not cast down. I chose their way, and dwelt like a king among his troops, like one who comforts mourners.

"But now they make sport of me, men who are younger than I, whose fathers I would have disdained to set with the dogs of my flock. I have become their song, a byword to them. They do not hesitate to spit at the sight of me. Because God has humbled me, the rabble rise against me. As through a wide breach they come. My honor is pursued as by the wind, and my prosperity has passed away like a cloud. And now my soul is poured out within me; the pain that gnaws me takes no rest; it binds me about like the collar of my tunic. God has cast me into the mire.

"I cry to thee and thou dost not heed me. Thou hast turned cruel to me; thou liftest me up on the wind, thou makest me ride on it. Yea, I know that thou wilt bring me to death, to the house appointed for all living.

"Yet does not one in a heap of ruins stretch out his hand for help? Did not I weep for him whose day was hard? Was not my soul grieved for the poor? But when I looked for good, evil came. My heart is in turmoil; I go about blackened, but not by the sun. I am a brother of jackals. My skin turns black and falls from me, and my bones burn with heat.

"I have made a covenant with my eyes; how then could I look upon a virgin? What would be my portion from God above? Does not he see my ways, and number all my steps? If I have walked with falsehood, if my step has turned aside from the way, and my heart has gone after my eyes; if any spot has cleaved to my hands, then let me sow, and another eat; and let what grows for me be rooted out. If my heart has been enticed to a woman, and I have lain in wait at my neighbor's door, then let my wife grind for another. For that would be a heinous crime to be punished by the judges, a fire which would burn all my increase to the root.

"If I have withheld anything that the poor desired, or caused the eyes of the widow to fail, or eaten my morsel alone, and the fatherless has not eaten of it; if I have seen any one perish for lack of clothing; if I have raised my hand against the fatherless because I saw help in the gate, then let my arm be broken from its socket. For I was in terror of God and could not have faced his majesty.

"If I have made gold my trust; if I have looked at the sun when it shone, or the moon moving in splendor, and my heart has been secretly enticed; this also would be an iniquity to be punished by the judges, for I should have been false to God above. If I have rejoiced at the ruin of him that hated me, or exulted when evil overtook him; if the men of my tent have not said, 'Who is there that has not been filled with his meat?'; if I have concealed my transgressions from men because I stood in fear of the multitude so that I kept silence, and did not go out of doors— Oh, that I had one to hear me! Let the Almighty answer me! Oh, that I had the indictment written by my adversary! Surely I would carry it on my shoulder, I would bind it on me as a crown; I would give him an account of all my steps; like a prince I would approach him. If my land has cried out against me, and its furrows have wept together; if I have eaten its yield without payment, let thorns grow instead of wheat, and foul weeds instead of barley."

The words of Job are ended.

SO THESE THREE men ceased to answer Job, because he was righteous in his own eyes. Then Elihu the son of Barachel the Buzite, of the family of Ram, became angry. He was angry at Job because he justified himself rather than God, and at Job's friends because they had found no answer, although they had declared Job to be wrong. Elihu had waited to speak because they were older than he.

NOW ELIHU ANSWERED:

"I am young in years, and you are aged; therefore I was afraid to declare my opinion. But it is the spirit in a man, the breath of the Almighty, that makes him understand. It is not the old that are wise. Therefore I say, 'Listen to me.'

While you searched out what to say, I waited. And, behold, there was none among you that confuted Job. Beware lest you say, 'We have found wisdom; God may vanquish him, not man.' Job has not directed his words against me, and I will not answer him with your speeches. But I am full of words. My heart is like wine that has no vent; like new wineskins, it is ready to burst. I must speak, that I may find relief. I will not show partiality to any person or use flattery toward any man. For I do not know how to flatter, else would my Maker soon put an end to me.

"Now hear my speech, O Job. My words declare the uprightness of my heart; for the spirit of God has made me, and his breath gives me life. Answer me, if you can; take your stand. Behold, I am toward God as you are; I too was formed from a piece of clay. No fear of me need terrify you; my pressure will not be heavy upon you.

"Surely, I have heard you say, 'I am pure, and there is no iniquity in me; yet God finds occasions against me, he counts me as his enemy; he puts my feet in the stocks, and watches all my paths.' In this you are not right. I answer that God is greater than man. Why do you contend against him, saying, 'He will answer none of my words'? For God speaks in one way, and in two, though man does not perceive it. In a dream, while they slumber, he opens the ears of men, and terrifies them with warnings, that he may turn man aside from his deed, and cut off his pride; and he keeps back his soul from the Pit.

"Man is also chastened with pain upon his bed, so that his life loathes bread. His flesh wastes away and his bones stick out. His soul draws near the Pit, and his life to those who bring death. If there be for him an angel, a mediator, to declare to man what is right for him; if he is gracious to him, and says, 'Deliver him from the Pit, I have found a ransom, let his flesh become fresh with youth'; then man prays to God, and he accepts him, he comes into his presence with joy, and he sings before men: 'I sinned, and perverted what was right, and it was not requited to me. He has redeemed my soul, and my life shall see the light.'

"Behold, God does all these things, twice, three times, with a man, to bring back his soul from the Pit, that he may see the light of life. Give heed, O Job. If you have anything to say, speak, for I desire to justify you. If not, be silent, and I will teach you wisdom."

Then Elihu said, "Hear my words, you wise men. Let us determine among ourselves what is good. For Job has said, 'I am innocent, and God has taken away my right; my wound is incurable, though I am without transgression.' What man is like Job, who drinks up scoffing like water and walks with evildoers? For he has said, 'It profits a man nothing that he should take delight in God.' Therefore, hear me, you men of understanding. Far be it from God that he should do wrong. For according to the work of a man he will requite him. Of a truth, the Almighty will not pervert justice. Who gave him charge over the whole world? If he should take back his spirit, and gather his breath to himself, all flesh would return to dust.

"If you have understanding, O Job, listen. Shall one who hates justice govern? Will you condemn him who is righteous and mighty, who says to a king, 'Worthless one,' and shows no partiality to princes, nor regards the rich more than the poor? They are all the work of his hands. In a moment they die; at midnight the people pass away, and the mighty are taken by no human hand. For his eyes are upon the ways of a man, and there is no darkness where evildoers may hide. For he has not appointed a time for any man to go before him in judgment. He shatters the mighty without investigation and sets others in their place. Knowing their works, he overturns them in the night, and they are crushed because they turned aside from his ways and caused the cry of the afflicted to come to him. When he is quiet, who can condemn? When he hides his face, who can behold him, whether it be a nation or a man? For has any one said to God, 'I have borne chastisement; I will not offend any more; teach me what I do not see; if I have done iniquity, I will do it no more'? Will he then make requital to suit you? You must choose, not I; declare what you know. The wise man who hears me will say: 'Job speaks without knowledge, his words are without insight.' Would that Job were tried to the end, because he answers like wicked men. For he adds rebellion to his sin; he claps his hands among us, and multiplies his words against God.

"Do you think this to be just? Do you say, 'It is my right before God,' that you ask, 'How am I better off than if I had sinned?' I will answer you and your friends with you. Look at the heavens and behold the clouds, which are higher than you. If you have sinned, what do you accomplish against him? If you are righteous, what do you give to him? Your wickedness concerns a man like yourself, and your righteousness a son of man.

"Because of the multitude of oppressions people cry for help; but none says, 'Where is God my Maker, who gives songs in the night, who teaches us more than the beasts of the earth, and makes us wiser than the birds of the air?' They cry out, but he does not answer, because of the pride of evil men. Surely God does not regard an empty cry. How much less when you say that you do not see him, that the case is before him, and you are waiting for him! And now, because his anger does not punish, Job opens his mouth in empty talk, he multiplies words without knowledge.

"Bear with me, for I have yet something to say on God's behalf. I will fetch my knowledge from afar, and ascribe righteousness to my Maker. For truly my words are not false; one who is perfect in knowledge is with you. Behold, God is mighty, and does not despise any; he does not keep the wicked alive, but gives the afflicted their right. He does not withdraw his eyes from the righteous, but with kings he sets them for ever. And if they are caught in the cords of affliction, he declares to them their transgressions, and commands that they return from iniquity. If they hearken, they complete their years in pleasantness. But if they do not, they die without knowledge.

"But you are full of the judgment on the wicked. Beware lest wrath entice you into scoffing; and let not the greatness of the ransom turn you aside. Will your cry avail to keep you from distress? Take heed, do not turn to iniquity, for this you have chosen rather than affliction. Behold, God is exalted in his power; who is a teacher like him? Who has prescribed for him his way, or who can say, 'Thou hast done wrong'? Remember to extol his work, of which men have sung.

"Behold, God is great, and we know him not; the number of his years is unsearchable. Can any one understand the spreading of the clouds, the thunderings of his pavilion? He scatters his lightning about him, and commands it to strike the mark. Its crashing declares concerning him, who is jealous with anger against iniquity. At this my heart trembles, and leaps out of its place. God thunders wondrously with his voice; he does great things which we cannot comprehend. To the snow he says, 'Fall on the earth'; and to the rain, 'Be strong.' He seals up the hand of every man, that all men may know his work; and then the beasts go into their lairs and remain there. From its chamber comes the whirlwind, and cold from the scattering winds. By the breath of God ice is given. He loads the thick clouds with moisture; they turn round and round by his guidance, to accomplish all that he commands them on the face of the habitable world. Whether for correction, or for his land, or for love, he causes it to happen.

"Hear this, O Job; stop and consider the wondrous works of God. Can you, like him, spread out the skies, hard as a molten mirror? Teach us what we shall say to him; we cannot draw up our case because of darkness. Shall it be told him that I would speak? Did a man ever wish that he would be swallowed up? The Almighty—we cannot find him; he is great in power and justice, and abundant righteousness he will not violate. Therefore men fear him; he does not regard any who are wise in their own conceit."

THEN THE LORD answered Job out of the whirlwind:

"Who is this that darkens counsel by words without knowledge? Gird up your loins like a man; I will question you, and you shall declare to me. Where were you when I laid the foundation of the earth? Tell me, if you have understanding. Who determined its measurements—surely you know! On what were its bases sunk, or who laid its cornerstone, when the morning stars sang together, and all the sons of God shouted for joy? Who shut in the sea with doors, when it burst forth from the womb; when I made clouds its garment and thick darkness its swaddling band, and prescribed bounds for it, and said, 'Thus far shall you come, and no farther; here shall your proud waves be stayed'?

"Have you commanded the morning since your days began, and caused the dawn to know its place, that it might take hold of the skirts of the earth, and the wicked be shaken out of it? Have you entered into the springs of the sea, or walked in the recesses of the deep? Have the gates of death been revealed to you? Have you comprehended the expanse of the earth? Declare, if you know all this. Where is the way to the dwelling of light, and where is the place of darkness, that you may discern the paths to its home? You know, for you were born then, and the number of your days is great!

"Have you entered the storehouses of the snow, or seen the hail, which I have reserved for the time of trouble, the day of war? What is the way to the place where the east wind is scattered? Who has cleft a channel for the torrents, and a way for the thunderbolt, to bring rain on the desert, and make the ground put forth grass? Has the rain a father, or who has begotten the drops of dew? From whose womb did the ice and the hoarfrost come forth?

"Can you bind the chains of the Pleiades, or loose the cords of Orion? Do you know the ordinances of the heavens? Can you establish their rule on the earth? Can you lift up your voice to the clouds, that a flood of waters may cover you? Can you send forth lightnings, that they may say to you, 'Here we are'? Who has put wisdom in the clouds? Who can number them? Or who can tilt the waterskins of the heavens, when the dust runs into a mass and the clods cleave fast together?

"Can you hunt the prey for the lion, or satisfy the appetite of the young lions, when they lie in wait in their covert? Who provides for the raven its prey, when its young ones cry to God, and wander about for lack of food? Do you know when the mountain goats bring forth? Do you observe the calving of the hinds? Their young become strong, grow up in the open, go forth, and do not return to them.

"Who has let the wild ass go free, the swift ass to whom I have given the steppe for his home? He scorns the tumult of the city; he hears not the shouts of the driver. He ranges the mountains as his pasture, and searches after every green thing. Is the wild ox willing to serve you? Will he spend the night at your crib? Can you bind him in the furrow with ropes, will he harrow the valleys after you? Will you depend on him because his strength is great, and will you leave to him your labor? Do you have faith that he will return, and bring your grain to your threshing floor?

"The wings of the ostrich wave proudly; but are they the pinions and plumage of love? For she leaves her eggs to be warmed on the ground, forgetting that a wild beast may trample them. She deals cruelly with her young, as if they were not hers; though her labor be in vain, yet she has no fear because God has given her no share in understanding. When she rouses herself to flee, she laughs at the horse and his rider.

"Do you give the horse his might? Do you clothe his neck with strength? Do you make him leap like the locust? His majestic snorting is terrible. He paws in the valley, and exults in his strength; he goes out to meet the weapons. He laughs at fear. Upon him rattle the quiver, the flashing spear, and the javelin. With rage he swallows the ground; he cannot stand still at the sound of the trumpet. He says 'Aha!' and smells the battle from afar, the thunder of the captains, and the shouting.

"Is it by your wisdom that the hawk soars, and spreads his wings toward the south? Is it at your command that the eagle mounts up and makes his nest on high? On the rock he dwells and makes his home in the fastness of the rocky crag. Thence he spies out the prey; his eyes behold it afar off. His young ones suck up blood; and where the slain are, there is he."

And the LORD said to Job, "Shall a faultfinder contend with the Almighty? He who argues with God, let him answer it."

THEN JOB ANSWERED the LORD:
"Behold, I am of small account; what shall I answer thee? I lay my hand on my mouth. I have spoken once, and I will not answer; twice, but I will proceed no further."

THEN THE LORD answered Job out of the whirlwind:
"Gird up your loins like a man; I will question you, and you declare to me. Will you even put me in the wrong? Will you condemn me that you may be justified? Have you an arm like God, and can you thunder with a voice like his? Deck yourself with majesty and dignity; clothe yourself with glory. Pour forth your anger; look on every one that is proud, and bring him low; tread down the wicked where they stand. Hide them all in the dust together; bind their faces in the world below. Then will I also acknowledge that your own right hand can give you victory.

"Behold Behemoth, which I made as I made you; he eats grass like an ox. Behold his strength in his loins and in the muscles of his belly. He makes his tail stiff like a cedar; his bones are tubes of bronze, his limbs like bars of iron. He is the first of the works of God; let him who made him bring near his sword! For the mountains yield food for him where all the wild beasts play. In the covert of the reeds he lies; for his shade the lotus trees cover him, and the willows of the brook surround him. Behold, if the river is turbulent he is not frightened; he is confident though Jordan rushes against his mouth. Can one take him with hooks, or pierce his nose with a snare?

"Can you draw out Leviathan with a fishhook, or put a rope in his nose? Will you play with him as with a bird, or put him on leash for your maidens? Can you fill his skin with harpoons, or penetrate his double coat of mail? Who can open the doors of his face? Round about his teeth is terror. His back is made of rows of shields, shut up closely as with a seal. Out of his mouth go flaming torches, and out of his nostrils comes forth smoke. He makes the deep boil like a pot; behind him he leaves a shining wake. Upon earth there is not his like, a creature without fear. He is king over all the sons of pride. Behold, the hope of a man is laid low even at the sight of him.

"Who then is he that can stand before me? Who has given to me, that I should repay him? Whatever is under the whole heaven is mine."

THEN JOB ANSWERED the LORD:
"I know that thou canst do all things, and that no purpose of thine can be thwarted. Thou hast said, 'Who is this that hides counsel without knowl-

edge?' Therefore I have uttered what I did not understand, things too wonderful for me, which I did not know. Thou hast said, 'Hear, and I will speak; I will question you, and you declare to me.' I had heard of thee by the hearing of the ear, but now my eye sees thee; therefore I despise myself, and repent in dust and ashes."

AFTER THE LORD had spoken to Job, he said to Eliphaz the Temanite: "My wrath is kindled against you and against your two friends; for you have not spoken of me what is right, as my servant Job has. Now take seven bulls and seven rams, and go to Job, and offer up for yourselves a burnt offering. Job shall pray for you, for I will accept his prayer not to deal with you according to your folly." So Eliphaz, Bildad, and Zophar did what the LORD told them. And the LORD restored the fortunes of Job, when he had prayed for his friends, giving him twice as much as he had before. Then all his brothers and sisters and all who had known him came and ate bread with him, and comforted him for the evil the LORD had brought upon him; and each of them gave him a piece of money and a ring of gold. And the LORD blessed the latter days of Job more than his beginning; he had fourteen thousand sheep, six thousand camels, a thousand yoke of oxen, and a thousand she-asses. He had also seven sons and three daughters. He named the first daughter Jemimah, the second Keziah, and the third Keren-happuch. In all the land there were no women so fair as Job's daughters, and he gave them inheritance among their brothers. After this, Job lived a hundred and forty years, and saw his sons, and his sons' sons, four generations. And Job died, an old man, and full of days.

PSALMS

Since a time well before Christ, the Book of Psalms has been the great hymnal of the Jews, and subsequently of Christendom. Its spiritual depth and beauty make it an unparalleled treasury of resources for public and private devotion. The original Hebrew title means "Praises," and praise is certainly one of the book's themes. But there is far more than this, for the poems vary widely in tone and subject. Some express contrition or call down curses. Others are meant to teach, and still others seem to have been adapted for use on special occasions, such as a coronation or a royal wedding. Some are regarded as messianic, being quoted in this light by New Testament writers.

Divided into five books, the individual Psalms are of differing date and authorship, with many attributed to King David. Most took their present form during the time of the second temple, somewhere between 537 B.C. and 100 B.C. Standard numbers for the Psalms in this selection may be found by a glance at the Index, under *Psalms*, where opening phrases are listed.

BOOK I

Blessed is the man
who walks not in the counsel of the wicked,
nor stands in the way of sinners,
    nor sits in the seat of scoffers;
but his delight is in the law of the LORD,
    and on his law he meditates day and night.
He is like a tree
    planted by streams of water,
that yields its fruit in its season,
    and its leaf does not wither.
In all that he does, he prospers.
The wicked are not so,

but are like chaff which the wind drives away.
Therefore the wicked will not stand in the judgment,
 nor sinners in the congregation of the righteous;
for the Lord knows the way of the righteous,
 but the way of the wicked will perish.

Why do the nations conspire,
 and the peoples plot in vain?
The kings of the earth set themselves,
 and the rulers take counsel together,
 against the Lord and his anointed, saying,
"Let us burst their bonds asunder,
 and cast their cords from us."
He who sits in the heavens laughs;
 the Lord has them in derision.
Then he will speak to them in his wrath,
 and terrify them in his fury, saying,
"I have set my king
 on Zion, my holy hill."
I will tell of the decree of the Lord:
He said to me, "You are my son,
 today I have begotten you.
Ask of me, and I will make the nations your heritage,
 and the ends of the earth your possession.
You shall break them with a rod of iron,
 and dash them in pieces like a potter's vessel."
Now therefore, O kings, be wise;
 be warned, O rulers of the earth.
Serve the Lord with fear,
 with trembling kiss his feet,
lest he be angry, and you perish in the way;
 for his wrath is quickly kindled.
Blessed are all who take refuge in him.

Give ear to my words, O Lord;
 give heed to my groaning.
Hearken to the sound of my cry,
 my King and my God,
 for to thee do I pray.
O Lord, in the morning thou dost hear my voice;
 in the morning I prepare a sacrifice for thee, and watch.
For thou art not a God who delights in wickedness;

evil may not sojourn with thee.
But I through the abundance of thy steadfast love
   will enter thy house.

Lead me, O LORD, in thy righteousness
   because of my enemies;
   make thy way straight before me.
For there is no truth in their mouth;
   their heart is destruction,
their throat is an open sepulchre,
   they flatter with their tongue.
Make them bear their guilt, O God;
   let them fall by their own counsels;
because of their many transgressions cast them out,
   for they have rebelled against thee.
But let all who take refuge in thee rejoice,
   let them ever sing for joy.
For thou dost bless the righteous, O LORD;
   thou dost cover him with favor as with a shield.

O LORD, rebuke me not in thy anger,
   nor chasten me in thy wrath.
Be gracious to me, O LORD, for I am languishing;
   O LORD, heal me, for my bones are troubled.
My soul also is sorely troubled.
   But thou, O LORD—how long?

Turn, O LORD, save my life;
   deliver me for the sake of thy steadfast love.
For in death there is no remembrance of thee;
   in Sheol who can give thee praise?
I am weary with my moaning;
   every night I flood my bed with tears;
   I drench my couch with my weeping.
My eye wastes away because of grief,
   it grows weak because of all my foes.

Depart from me, all you workers of evil;
   for the LORD has heard the sound of my weeping.
The LORD has heard my supplication;
   the LORD accepts my prayer.
All my enemies shall be ashamed and sorely troubled;
   they shall turn back, and be put to shame in a moment.

O Lord, our Lord,
   how majestic is thy name in all the earth!
Thou whose glory above the heavens is chanted
   by the mouth of babes and infants,
thou hast founded a bulwark because of thy foes,
   to still the enemy and the avenger.
When I look at thy heavens, the work of thy fingers,
   the moon and the stars which thou hast established;
what is man that thou art mindful of him,
   and the son of man that thou dost care for him?
Yet thou hast made him little less than God,
   and dost crown him with glory and honor.
Thou hast given him dominion over the works of thy hands;
   thou hast put all things under his feet,
all sheep and oxen,
   and also the beasts of the field,
the birds of the air, and the fish of the sea,
   whatever passes along the paths of the sea.
O Lord, our Lord,
   how majestic is thy name in all the earth!

How long, O Lord? Wilt thou forget me for ever?
   How long wilt thou hide thy face from me?
How long must I bear pain in my soul,
   and have sorrow in my heart all the day?
How long shall my enemy be exalted over me?
Consider and answer me, O Lord my God;
   lighten my eyes, lest I sleep the sleep of death;
lest my enemy say, "I have prevailed over him";
   lest my foes rejoice because I am shaken.
But I have trusted in thy steadfast love;
   my heart shall rejoice in thy salvation.
I will sing to the Lord,
   because he has dealt bountifully with me.

The fool says in his heart,
   "There is no God."
They are corrupt, they do abominable deeds,
   there is none that does good.
The Lord looks down from heaven upon the children of men,
   to see if there are any that act wisely,

that seek after God.
They have all gone astray, they are all alike corrupt;
 there is none that does good,
 no, not one.

Have they no knowledge, all the evildoers
 who eat up my people as they eat bread,
 and do not call upon the LORD?
There they shall be in great terror,
 for God is with the generation of the righteous.
You would confound the plans of the poor,
 but the LORD is his refuge.
O that deliverance for Israel would come out of Zion!
 When the LORD restores the fortunes of his people,
 Jacob shall rejoice, Israel shall be glad.

O LORD, who shall sojourn in thy tent?
 Who shall dwell on thy holy hill?
He who walks blamelessly, and does what is right,
 and speaks truth from his heart;
who does not slander with his tongue,
 and does no evil to his friend,
 nor takes up a reproach against his neighbor;
in whose eyes a reprobate is despised,
 but who honors those who fear the LORD;
who swears to his own hurt and does not change;
who does not put out his money at interest,
 and does not take a bribe against the innocent.
He who does these things shall never be moved.

Preserve me, O God, for in thee I take refuge.
 I say to the LORD, "Thou art my Lord;
 I have no good apart from thee."
As for the saints in the land, they are the noble,
 in whom is all my delight.
Those who choose another god multiply their sorrows;
 their libations of blood I will not pour out
 or take their names upon my lips.
The LORD is my chosen portion and my cup;
 thou holdest my lot.
The lines have fallen for me in pleasant places;
 yea, I have a goodly heritage.

I bless the LORD who gives me counsel;
   in the night also my heart instructs me.
I keep the LORD always before me;
   because he is at my right hand, I shall not be moved.
Therefore my heart is glad, and my soul rejoices;
   my body also dwells secure.
For thou dost not give me up to Sheol,
   or let thy godly one see the Pit.
Thou dost show me the path of life;
   in thy presence there is fulness of joy,
   in thy right hand are pleasures for evermore.

I love thee, O LORD, my strength.
   The LORD is my rock, and my fortress, and my deliverer,
   my God, my rock, in whom I take refuge,
   my shield, and the horn of my salvation, my stronghold.
In my distress I called upon the LORD;
   to my God I cried for help.
From his temple he heard my voice,
   and my cry to him reached his ears.
Then the earth reeled and rocked;
   the foundations of the mountains trembled
   and quaked, because he was angry.
Smoke went up from his nostrils,
   and devouring fire from his mouth;
   glowing coals flamed forth from him.
He bowed the heavens, and came down;
   thick darkness was under his feet.
He rode on a cherub, and flew;
   he came swiftly upon the wings of the wind.
He made darkness his covering around him,
   his canopy thick clouds dark with water.
Out of the brightness before him
   there broke through his clouds
   hailstones and coals of fire.
The LORD also thundered in the heavens,
   and the Most High uttered his voice.
And he sent out his arrows, and scattered them;
   he flashed forth lightnings, and routed them.
Then the channels of the sea were seen,
   and the foundations of the world were laid bare,
at thy rebuke, O LORD,
   at the blast of the breath of thy nostrils.

He reached from on high, he took me,
   he drew me out of many waters.
The LORD rewarded me according to my righteousness;
   according to the cleanness of my hands he recompensed me.
For I have kept the ways of the LORD,
   and have not wickedly departed from my God.

With the loyal thou dost show thyself loyal;
   with the blameless man thou dost show thyself blameless;
with the pure thou dost show thyself pure;
   and with the crooked thou dost show thyself perverse.
For thou dost deliver a humble people;
   but the haughty eyes thou dost bring down.
Yea, thou dost light my lamp;
   the LORD my God lightens my darkness.
Yea, by thee I can crush a troop;
   and by my God I can leap over a wall.
This God—his way is perfect;
   he is a shield for all those who take refuge in him.
He made my feet like hinds' feet,
   and set me secure on the heights.
He trains my hands for war,
   so that my arms can bend a bow of bronze.
I pursued my enemies and overtook them;
   and did not turn back till they were consumed.
I thrust them through, so that they were not able to rise;
   they fell under my feet.
For thou didst gird me with strength for the battle;
   thou didst make my assailants sink under me.
Thou didst make my enemies turn their backs to me,
   and those who hated me I destroyed.
They cried for help, but there was none to save,
   they cried to the LORD, but he did not answer them.
I beat them fine as dust before the wind;
   I cast them out like the mire of the streets.
Thou didst deliver me from strife with the peoples;
   thou didst make me the head of the nations;
   people whom I had not known served me.

For this I will extol thee, O LORD, among the nations,
   and sing praises to thy name.
Great triumphs he gives to his king,
   and shows steadfast love to his anointed,
   to David and his descendants for ever.

The heavens are telling the glory of God;
    and the firmament proclaims his handiwork.
Day to day pours forth speech,
    and night to night declares knowledge.
There is no speech, nor are there words;
    their voice is not heard;
yet their voice goes out through all the earth,
    and their words to the end of the world.
In them he has set a tent for the sun,
which comes forth like a bridegroom leaving his chamber,
    and like a strong man runs its course with joy.
Its rising is from the end of the heavens,
    and its circuit to the end of them;
    and there is nothing hid from its heat.

The law of the LORD is perfect,
    reviving the soul;
the testimony of the LORD is sure,
    making wise the simple;
the precepts of the LORD are right,
    rejoicing the heart;
the commandment of the LORD is pure,
    enlightening the eyes;
the fear of the LORD is clean,
    enduring for ever;
the ordinances of the LORD are true,
    and righteous altogether.
More to be desired are they than gold,
    even much fine gold;
sweeter also than honey
    and drippings of the honeycomb.
Moreover by them is thy servant warned;
    in keeping them there is great reward.
But who can discern his errors?
    Clear thou me from hidden faults.
Keep back thy servant also from presumptuous sins;
    let them not have dominion over me!
Then I shall be blameless,
    and innocent of great transgression.

Let the words of my mouth and the meditation of my heart
    be acceptable in thy sight,
    O LORD, my rock and my redeemer.

My God, my God, why hast thou forsaken me?
Why art thou so far from helping me,
    from the words of my groaning?
O my God, I cry by day, but thou dost not answer;
    and by night, but find no rest.
Yet thou art holy,
    enthroned on the praises of Israel.
In thee our fathers trusted;
    they trusted, and thou didst deliver them.
To thee they cried, and were saved;
    in thee they trusted, and were not disappointed.

But I am a worm, and no man;
    scorned by men, and despised by the people.
All who see me mock at me,
    they make mouths at me, they wag their heads;
"He committed his cause to the LORD; let him deliver him,
    let him rescue him, for he delights in him!"
Yet thou art he who took me from the womb;
    thou didst keep me safe upon my mother's breasts.
Upon thee was I cast from my birth,
    and since my mother bore me thou hast been my God.
Be not far from me,
    for trouble is near
    and there is none to help.
Many bulls encompass me,
    strong bulls of Bashan surround me;
they open wide their mouths at me,
    like a ravening and roaring lion.
I am poured out like water,
    and all my bones are out of joint;
my heart is like wax,
    it is melted within my breast;
my strength is dried up like a potsherd,
    and my tongue cleaves to my jaws;
    thou dost lay me in the dust of death.
Yea, dogs are round about me;
    a company of evildoers encircle me;
    they have pierced my hands and feet—
I can count all my bones—
    they stare and gloat over me;
they divide my garments among them,
    and for my raiment they cast lots.

But thou, O LORD, be not far off!
　O thou my help, hasten to my aid!
Deliver my soul from the sword,
　my life from the power of the dog!
Save me from the mouth of the lion,
　my afflicted soul from the horns of the wild oxen!

I will tell of thy name to my brethren;
　in the midst of the congregation I will praise thee:
You who fear the LORD, praise him!
　all you sons of Jacob, glorify him,
　and stand in awe of him, all you sons of Israel!
For he has not despised or abhorred
　the affliction of the afflicted;
and he has not hid his face from him,
　but has heard, when he cried to him.
From thee comes my praise in the great congregation;
　my vows I will pay before those who fear him.
The afflicted shall eat and be satisfied;
　those who seek him shall praise the LORD!
　May your hearts live for ever!
All the ends of the earth shall remember
　and turn to the LORD;
and all the families of the nations
　shall worship before him.
For dominion belongs to the LORD,
　and he rules over the nations.
Yea, to him shall all the proud of the earth bow down;
　before him shall bow all who go down to the dust,
　and he who cannot keep himself alive.
Posterity shall serve him;
　men shall tell of the Lord to the coming generation,
and proclaim his deliverance to a people yet unborn,
　that he has wrought it.

The LORD is my shepherd, I shall not want;
　he makes me lie down in green pastures.
He leads me beside still waters;
　he restores my soul.
He leads me in paths of righteousness
　for his name's sake.
Even though I walk through the valley of the shadow of death,
　I fear no evil;

for thou art with me;
   thy rod and thy staff,
   they comfort me.
Thou preparest a table before me
   in the presence of my enemies;
thou anointest my head with oil,
   my cup overflows.
Surely goodness and mercy shall follow me
   all the days of my life;
and I shall dwell in the house of the LORD
   for ever.

The earth is the LORD's and the fulness thereof,
   the world and those who dwell therein;
for he has founded it upon the seas,
   and established it upon the rivers.
Who shall ascend the hill of the LORD?
   And who shall stand in his holy place?
He who has clean hands and a pure heart,
   who does not lift up his soul to what is false,
   and does not swear deceitfully.
He will receive blessing from the LORD,
   and vindication from the God of his salvation.
Such is the generation of those who seek him,
   who seek the face of the God of Jacob.

Lift up your heads, O gates!
   and be lifted up, O ancient doors!
   that the King of glory may come in.
Who is the King of glory?
   The LORD, strong and mighty,
   the LORD, mighty in battle!
Lift up your heads, O gates!
   and be lifted up, O ancient doors!
   that the King of glory may come in.
Who is this King of glory?
   The LORD of hosts,
   he is the King of glory!

The LORD is my light and my salvation;
   whom shall I fear?
The LORD is the stronghold of my life;

of whom shall I be afraid?
When evildoers assail me,
   uttering slanders against me,
my adversaries and foes,
   they shall stumble and fall.
Though a host encamp against me,
   my heart shall not fear;
though war arise against me,
   yet I will be confident.
One thing have I asked of the LORD,
   that will I seek after;
that I may dwell in the house of the LORD
   all the days of my life,
to behold the beauty of the LORD,
   and to inquire in his temple.
For he will hide me in his shelter
   in the day of trouble;
he will conceal me under the cover of his tent,
   he will set me high upon a rock.
And now my head shall be lifted up
   above my enemies round about me;
and I will offer in his tent
   sacrifices with shouts of joy;
I will sing and make melody to the LORD.

Hear, O LORD, when I cry aloud,
   be gracious to me and answer me!
Thou hast said, "Seek ye my face."
   My heart says to thee,
"Thy face, LORD, do I seek."
   Hide not thy face from me.
Turn not thy servant away in anger,
   thou who hast been my help.
Cast me not off, forsake me not,
   O God of my salvation!
For my father and my mother have forsaken me,
   but the LORD will take me up.

Teach me thy way, O LORD;
   and lead me on a level path
   because of my enemies.
Give me not up to the will of my adversaries;
   for false witnesses have risen against me,
   and they breathe out violence.

I believe that I shall see the goodness of the LORD
    in the land of the living!
Wait for the LORD;
    be strong, and let your heart take courage;
    yea, wait for the LORD!

Ascribe to the LORD, O heavenly beings,
    ascribe to the LORD glory and strength.
Ascribe to the LORD the glory of his name;
    worship the LORD in holy array.
The voice of the LORD is upon the waters;
    the God of glory thunders,
    the LORD, upon many waters.
The voice of the LORD is powerful,
    the voice of the LORD is full of majesty.
The voice of the LORD breaks the cedars,
    the LORD breaks the cedars of Lebanon.
He makes Lebanon to skip like a calf,
    and Mount Hermon like a young wild ox.
The voice of the LORD flashes forth flames of fire.
The voice of the LORD shakes the wilderness,
    the LORD shakes the wilderness of Kadesh.
The voice of the LORD makes the oaks to whirl,
    and strips the forests bare;
    and in his temple all cry, "Glory!"
The LORD sits enthroned over the flood;
    the LORD sits enthroned as king for ever.
May the LORD give strength to his people!
    May the LORD bless his people with peace!

I will extol thee, O LORD, for thou hast drawn me up,
    and hast not let my foes rejoice over me.
O LORD my God, I cried to thee for help,
    and thou hast healed me.
O LORD, thou hast brought up my soul from Sheol,
    restored me to life from among those gone down to the Pit.
Sing praises to the LORD, O you his saints,
    and give thanks to his holy name.
For his anger is but for a moment,
    and his favor is for a lifetime.
Weeping may tarry for the night,
    but joy comes with the morning.

As for me, I said in my prosperity,
  "I shall never be moved."
By thy favor, O Lord,
  thou hadst established me as a strong mountain;
thou didst hide thy face,
  I was dismayed.
To thee, O Lord, I cried;
  and to the Lord I made supplication:
"What profit is there in my death,
  if I go down to the Pit?
Will the dust praise thee?
  Will it tell of thy faithfulness?
Hear, O Lord, and be gracious to me!
  O Lord, be thou my helper!"
Thou hast turned for me my mourning into dancing;
  thou hast loosed my sackcloth
  and girded me with gladness,
that my soul may praise thee and not be silent.
  O Lord my God, I will give thanks to thee for ever.

Blessed is he whose transgression is forgiven,
  whose sin is covered.
Blessed is the man to whom the Lord imputes no iniquity,
  and in whose spirit there is no deceit.
When I declared not my sin, my body wasted away
  through my groaning all day long.
For day and night thy hand was heavy upon me;
  my strength was dried up as by the heat of summer.
I acknowledged my sin to thee,
  and I did not hide my iniquity;
I said, "I will confess my transgressions to the Lord";
  then thou didst forgive the guilt of my sin.

Therefore let every one who is godly offer prayer to thee;
at a time of distress, in the rush of great waters,
  they shall not reach him.
Thou art a hiding place for me,
  thou preservest me from trouble;
  thou dost encompass me with deliverance.

I will instruct you and teach you the way you should go;
  I will counsel you with my eye upon you.
Be not like a horse or a mule, without understanding,

which must be curbed with bit and bridle,
else it will not keep with you.
Many are the pangs of the wicked;
but steadfast love surrounds him who trusts in the LORD.
Be glad in the LORD, and rejoice, O righteous,
and shout for joy, all you upright in heart!

Rejoice in the LORD, O you righteous!
Praise befits the upright.
Praise the LORD with the lyre,
make melody to him with the harp of ten strings!
Sing to him a new song,
play skilfully on the strings, with loud shouts.
For the word of the LORD is upright;
and all his work is done in faithfulness.
He loves righteousness and justice;
the earth is full of the steadfast love of the LORD.
By the word of the LORD the heavens were made,
and all their host by the breath of his mouth.
He gathered the waters of the sea as in a bottle;
he put the deeps in storehouses.
Let all the earth fear the LORD,
let all the inhabitants of the world stand in awe of him!
For he spoke, and it came to be;
he commanded, and it stood forth.
The LORD brings the counsel of the nations to nought;
he frustrates the plans of the peoples.
The counsel of the LORD stands for ever,
the thoughts of his heart to all generations.
Blessed is the nation whose God is the LORD,
the people whom he has chosen as his heritage!
The LORD looks down from heaven,
he sees all the sons of men;
from where he sits enthroned he looks forth
on all the inhabitants of the earth,
he who fashions the hearts of them all,
and observes all their deeds.
A king is not saved by his great army;
a warrior is not delivered by his great strength.
The war horse is a vain hope for victory,
and by its great might it cannot save.
Behold, the eye of the LORD is on those who fear him,
on those who hope in his steadfast love,

that he may deliver their soul from death,
    and keep them alive in famine.
Our soul waits for the LORD;
    he is our help and shield.
Yea, our heart is glad in him,
    because we trust in his holy name.
Let thy steadfast love, O LORD, be upon us,
    even as we hope in thee.

Fret not yourself because of the wicked,
    be not envious of wrongdoers!
For they will soon fade like the grass,
    and wither like the green herb.
Trust in the LORD, and do good;
    so you will dwell in the land, and enjoy security.
Take delight in the LORD,
    and he will give you the desires of your heart.
Commit your way to the LORD;
    trust in him, and he will act.
He will bring forth your vindication as the light,
    and your right as the noonday.
Be still before the LORD, and wait patiently for him;
    fret not yourself over him who prospers in his way,
    over the man who carries out evil devices!
Refrain from anger, and forsake wrath!
    Fret not yourself; it tends only to evil.
For the wicked shall be cut off;
    but those who wait for the LORD shall possess the land.
Yet a little while, and the wicked will be no more;
    though you look well at his place, he will not be there.
But the meek shall possess the land,
    and delight themselves in abundant prosperity.
The wicked plots against the righteous,
    and gnashes his teeth at him;
but the LORD laughs at the wicked,
    for he sees that his day is coming.
The wicked draw the sword and bend their bows,
    to bring down the poor and needy,
    to slay those who walk uprightly;
their sword shall enter their own heart,
    and their bows shall be broken.
Better is a little that the righteous has
    than the abundance of many wicked.

For the arms of the wicked shall be broken;
  but the LORD upholds the righteous.
The LORD knows the days of the blameless,
  and their heritage will abide for ever;
they are not put to shame in evil times,
  in the days of famine they have abundance.
But the wicked perish;
  the enemies of the LORD are like the glory of the pastures,
  they vanish—like smoke they vanish away.
The wicked borrows, and cannot pay back,
  but the righteous is generous and gives;
for those blessed by the LORD shall possess the land,
  but those cursed by him shall be cut off.
The steps of a man are from the LORD,
  and he establishes him in whose way he delights;
though he fall, he shall not be cast headlong,
  for the LORD is the stay of his hand.
I have been young, and now am old;
  yet I have not seen the righteous forsaken
  or his children begging bread.
He is ever giving liberally and lending,
  and his children become a blessing.
Depart from evil, and do good;
  so shall you abide for ever.
For the LORD loves justice;
  he will not forsake his saints.
The righteous shall be preserved for ever,
  but the children of the wicked shall be cut off.
The righteous shall possess the land,
  and dwell upon it for ever.
The mouth of the righteous utters wisdom,
  and his tongue speaks justice.
The law of his God is in his heart;
  his steps do not slip.
The wicked watches the righteous,
  and seeks to slay him.
The LORD will not abandon him to his power,
  or let him be condemned when he is brought to trial.
Wait for the LORD, and keep to his way,
  and he will exalt you to possess the land;
  you will look on the destruction of the wicked.
I have seen a wicked man overbearing,
  and towering like a cedar of Lebanon.
Again I passed by, and, lo, he was no more;

though I sought him, he could not be found.
Mark the blameless man, and behold the upright,
  for there is posterity for the man of peace.
But transgressors shall be altogether destroyed;
  the posterity of the wicked shall be cut off.
The salvation of the righteous is from the LORD;
  he is their refuge in the time of trouble.
The LORD helps them and delivers them;
  he delivers them from the wicked, and saves them,
  because they take refuge in him.

I said, "I will guard my ways,
  that I may not sin with my tongue;
I will bridle my mouth,
  so long as the wicked are in my presence."
I was dumb and silent,
  I held my peace to no avail;
my distress grew worse,
  my heart became hot within me.
As I mused, the fire burned;
  then I spoke with my tongue:
"LORD, let me know my end,
  and what is the measure of my days;
  let me know how fleeting my life is!
Behold, thou hast made my days a few handbreadths,
  and my lifetime is as nothing in thy sight.
Surely every man stands as a mere breath!
  Surely man goes about as a shadow!
Surely for nought are they in turmoil;
  man heaps up, and knows not who will gather!
And now, Lord, for what do I wait?
  My hope is in thee.
Deliver me from all my transgressions.
  Make me not the scorn of the fool!
I am dumb, I do not open my mouth;
  for it is thou who hast done it.
Remove thy stroke from me;
  I am spent by the blows of thy hand.
When thou dost chasten man
  with rebukes for sin,
thou dost consume like a moth what is dear to him;
  surely every man is a mere breath!
Hear my prayer, O LORD,

and give ear to my cry;
    hold not thy peace at my tears!
For I am thy passing guest,
    a sojourner, like all my fathers.
Look away from me, that I may know gladness,
    before I depart and be no more!''

I waited patiently for the LORD;
    he inclined to me and heard my cry.
He drew me up from the desolate pit,
    out of the miry bog,
and set my feet upon a rock,
    making my steps secure.
He put a new song in my mouth,
    a song of praise to our God.
Many will see and fear,
    and put their trust in the LORD.
Blessed is the man who makes the LORD his trust,
who does not turn to the proud,
    to those who go astray after false gods!
Thou hast multiplied, O LORD my God,
    thy wondrous deeds and thy thoughts toward us;
    none can compare with thee!
Sacrifice and offering thou dost not desire;
    but thou hast given me an open ear.
Burnt offering and sin offering
    thou hast not required.
Then I said, "I delight to do thy will, O my God;
    thy law is within my heart."
I have told the glad news of deliverance
    in the great congregation;
lo, I have not restrained my lips,
    as thou knowest, O LORD.
I have not hid thy saving help within my heart,
    I have spoken of thy faithfulness and thy salvation.

Do not thou, O LORD, withhold
    thy mercy from me,
let thy steadfast love and thy faithfulness
    ever preserve me!
For evils have encompassed me
    without number;
my iniquities have overtaken me,

till I cannot see.
Be pleased, O LORD, to deliver me!
    O LORD, make haste to help me!
Let them be put to shame and confusion altogether
    who seek to snatch away my life!
Let them be appalled because of their shame
    who say to me, "Aha, Aha!"
But may all who seek thee
    rejoice and be glad in thee;
may those who love thy salvation
    say continually, "Great is the LORD!"
As for me, I am poor and needy;
    but the Lord takes thought for me.
Thou art my help and my deliverer;
    do not tarry, O my God!

Blessed is he who considers the poor!
    The LORD delivers him in the day of trouble;
the LORD protects him and keeps him alive;
    he is called blessed in the land;
    thou dost not give him up to the will of his enemies.
The LORD sustains him on his sickbed;
    in his illness thou healest all his infirmities.

As for me, I said, "O LORD, be gracious to me;
    heal me, for I have sinned against thee!"
My enemies say of me in malice:
    "When will he die, and his name perish?"
And when one comes to see me, he utters empty words,
    while his heart gathers mischief;
    when he goes out, he tells it abroad.
All who hate me whisper together about me;
    they imagine the worst for me.
They say, "A deadly thing has fastened upon him;
    he will not rise again from where he lies."
Even my bosom friend in whom I trusted,
    who ate of my bread, has lifted his heel against me.
But do thou, O LORD, be gracious to me,
    and raise me up, that I may requite them!
By this I know that thou art pleased with me,
    in that my enemy has not triumphed over me.
But thou hast upheld me because of my integrity,
    and set me in thy presence for ever.

Blessed be the LORD, the God of Israel,
from everlasting to everlasting!
Amen and Amen.

BOOK II

As a hart longs
for flowing streams,
so longs my soul
for thee, O God.
My soul thirsts for God,
for the living God.
When shall I come and behold
the face of God?
My tears have been my food
day and night,
while men say to me continually,
"Where is your God?"
These things I remember,
as I pour out my soul:
how I went with the throng,
and led them in procession to the house of God,
with glad shouts and songs of thanksgiving,
a multitude keeping festival.
Why are you cast down, O my soul,
and why are you disquieted within me?
Hope in God; for I shall again praise him,
my help and my God.

My soul is cast down within me,
therefore I remember thee
from the land of Jordan and of Hermon,
from Mount Mizar.
Deep calls to deep
at the thunder of thy cataracts;
all thy waves and thy billows
have gone over me.
By day the LORD commands his steadfast love;
and at night his song is with me,
a prayer to the God of my life.
I say to God, my rock:
"Why hast thou forgotten me?

Why go I mourning
    because of the oppression of the enemy?"
As with a deadly wound in my body,
    my adversaries taunt me,
while they say to me continually,
    "Where is your God?"
Why are you cast down, O my soul,
    and why are you disquieted within me?
Hope in God; for I shall again praise him,
    my help and my God.

Vindicate me, O God, and defend my cause
    against an ungodly people;
from deceitful and unjust men
    deliver me!
For thou art the God in whom I take refuge;
    why hast thou cast me off?
Why go I mourning
    because of the oppression of the enemy?

Oh send out thy light and thy truth;
    let them lead me,
let them bring me to thy holy hill
    and to thy dwelling!
Then I will go to the altar of God,
    to God my exceeding joy;
and I will praise thee with the lyre,
    O God, my God.
Why are you cast down, O my soul,
    and why are you disquieted within me?
Hope in God; for I shall again praise him,
    my help and my God.

My heart overflows with a goodly theme;
    I address my verses to the king;
    my tongue is like the pen of a ready scribe.

You are the fairest of the sons of men;
    grace is poured upon your lips;
    therefore God has blessed you for ever.
Gird your sword upon your thigh, O mighty one,
    in your glory and majesty!

In your majesty ride forth victoriously
>   for the cause of truth and to defend the right;
>   let your right hand teach you dread deeds!
Your arrows are sharp
>   in the heart of the king's enemies;
>   the peoples fall under you.

Your divine throne endures for ever and ever.
>   Your royal scepter is a scepter of equity;
>   you love righteousness and hate wickedness.
Therefore God, your God, has anointed you
>   with the oil of gladness above your fellows;
>   your robes are all fragrant with
>   myrrh and aloes and cassia.
From ivory palaces stringed instruments make you glad;
>   daughters of kings are among your ladies of honor;
>   at your right hand stands the queen in gold of Ophir.

Hear, O daughter, consider, and incline your ear;
>   forget your people and your father's house;
>   and the king will desire your beauty.
Since he is your lord, bow to him;
>   the people of Tyre will sue your favor with gifts,
>   the richest of the people with all kinds of wealth.

The princess is decked in her
>   chamber with gold-woven robes,
>   in many-colored robes she is led to the king,
>   with her virgin companions, her escort, in her train.
With joy and gladness they are led along
>   as they enter the palace of the king.

Instead of your fathers shall be your sons;
>   you will make them princes in all the earth.
I will cause your name to be celebrated in all generations;
>   therefore the peoples will praise you for ever and ever.

God is our refuge and strength,
>   a very present help in trouble.
Therefore we will not fear, though the earth should change,
>   though the mountains shake in the heart of the sea;
though its waters roar and foam,
>   though the mountains tremble with its tumult.

There is a river whose streams make glad the city of God,
    the holy habitation of the Most High.
God is in the midst of her, she shall not be moved;
    God will help her right early.
The nations rage, the kingdoms totter;
    he utters his voice, the earth melts.
The LORD of hosts is with us;
    the God of Jacob is our refuge.

Come, behold the works of the LORD,
    how he has wrought desolations in the earth.
He makes wars cease to the end of the earth;
    he breaks the bow, and shatters the spear,
    he burns the chariots with fire!
"Be still, and know that I am God.
    I am exalted among the nations,
    I am exalted in the earth!"
The LORD of hosts is with us;
    the God of Jacob is our refuge.

Hear this, all peoples!
    Give ear, all inhabitants of the world,
both low and high,
    rich and poor together!
My mouth shall speak wisdom;
    the meditation of my heart shall be understanding.
I will incline my ear to a proverb;
    I will solve my riddle to the music of the lyre.

Why should I fear in times of trouble,
    when the iniquity of my persecutors surrounds me,
men who trust in their wealth
    and boast of the abundance of their riches?
Truly no man can ransom himself,
    or give to God the price of his life,
for the ransom of his life is costly,
    and can never suffice,
that he should continue to live on for ever,
    and never see the Pit.
Yea, he shall see that even the wise die,
    the fool and the stupid alike must perish
    and leave their wealth to others.
Their graves are their homes for ever,

their dwelling places to all generations,
    though they named lands their own.
Man cannot abide in his pomp,
    he is like the beasts that perish.

This is the fate of those who have foolish confidence,
    the end of those who are pleased with their portion.
Like sheep they are appointed for Sheol;
    Death shall be their shepherd;
straight to the grave they descend,
    and their form shall waste away;
    Sheol shall be their home.
But God will ransom my soul from the power of Sheol,
    for he will receive me.
Be not afraid when one becomes rich,
    when the glory of his house increases.
For when he dies he will carry nothing away;
    his glory will not go down after him.
Though, while he lives, he counts himself happy,
    and though a man gets praise when he does well,
he will go to the generation of his fathers,
    who will never more see the light.
Man cannot abide in his pomp,
    he is like the beasts that perish.

Have mercy on me, O God, according to thy steadfast love;
    according to thy abundant mercy blot out my transgressions.
Wash me thoroughly from my iniquity,
    and cleanse me from my sin!
For I know my transgressions,
    and my sin is ever before me.
Against thee, thee only, have I sinned,
    and done that which is evil in thy sight,
so that thou art justified in thy sentence
    and blameless in thy judgment.
Behold, I was brought forth in iniquity,
    and in sin did my mother conceive me.

Behold, thou desirest truth in the inward being;
    therefore teach me wisdom in my secret heart.
Purge me with hyssop, and I shall be clean;
    wash me, and I shall be whiter than snow.
Fill me with joy and gladness;

let the bones which thou hast broken rejoice.
Hide thy face from my sins,
   and blot out all my iniquities.
Create in me a clean heart, O God,
   and put a new and right spirit within me.
Cast me not away from thy presence,
   and take not thy holy Spirit from me.
Restore to me the joy of thy salvation,
   and uphold me with a willing spirit.

Then I will teach transgressors thy ways,
   and sinners will return to thee.
Deliver me from bloodguiltiness, O God,
    thou God of my salvation,
   and my tongue will sing aloud of thy deliverance.
O Lord, open thou my lips,
   and my mouth shall show forth thy praise.
For thou hast no delight in sacrifice;
    were I to give a burnt offering,
    thou wouldst not be pleased.
The sacrifice acceptable to God is a broken spirit;
    a broken and contrite heart, O God, thou wilt not despise.

Do good to Zion in thy good pleasure;
    rebuild the walls of Jerusalem,
then wilt thou delight in right sacrifices,
    in burnt offerings and whole burnt offerings;
    then bulls will be offered on thy altar.

Give ear to my prayer, O God;
   and hide not thyself from my supplication!
Attend to me, and answer me;
   I am overcome by my trouble.
I am distraught by the noise of the enemy,
   because of the oppression of the wicked.
Fear and trembling come upon me,
   and horror overwhelms me.
And I say, "O that I had wings like a dove!
   I would fly away and be at rest;
yea, I would wander afar,
   I would lodge in the wilderness,
I would haste to find me a shelter
   from the raging wind and tempest."

It is not an enemy who taunts me—
    then I could bear it;
it is not an adversary who deals insolently with me—
    then I could hide from him.
But it is you, my equal,
    my companion, my familiar friend.
We used to hold sweet converse together;
    within God's house we walked in fellowship.
Let death come upon them;
    let them go down to Sheol alive;
    let them go away in terror into their graves.
My companion stretched out his hand against his friends,
    he violated his covenant.
His speech was smoother than butter,
    yet war was in his heart;
his words were softer than oil,
    yet they were drawn swords.

Cast your burden on the LORD,
    and he will sustain you;
he will never permit
    the righteous to be moved.

But thou, O God, wilt cast them down
    into the lowest pit;
men of blood and treachery
    shall not live out half their days.
But I will trust in thee.

Hear my cry, O God,
    listen to my prayer;
from the end of the earth I call to thee,
    when my heart is faint.

Lead thou me
    to the rock that is higher than I;
for thou art my refuge,
    a strong tower against the enemy.

Let me dwell in thy tent for ever!
    Oh to be safe under the shelter of thy wings!
For thou, O God, hast heard my vows,
    thou hast given me the heritage of those who fear thy name.

Prolong the life of the king;
  may his years endure to all generations!
May he be enthroned for ever before God;
  bid steadfast love and faithfulness watch over him!

So will I ever sing praises to thy name,
  as I pay my vows day after day.

For God alone my soul waits in silence;
  from him comes my salvation.
He only is my rock and my salvation,
  my fortress; I shall not be greatly moved.
How long will you set upon a man
    to shatter him, all of you,
    like a leaning wall, a tottering fence?
They only plan to thrust him down from his eminence.
  They take pleasure in falsehood.
They bless with their mouths,
  but inwardly they curse.
For God alone my soul waits in silence,
  for my hope is from him.
He only is my rock and my salvation,
  my fortress; I shall not be shaken.
On God rests my deliverance and my honor;
  my mighty rock, my refuge is God.

Trust in him at all times, O people;
    pour out your heart before him;
    God is a refuge for us.
Men of low estate are but a breath,
  men of high estate are a delusion;
in the balances they go up;
  they are together lighter than a breath.
Put no confidence in extortion,
  set no vain hopes on robbery;
  if riches increase, set not your heart on them.

Once God has spoken;
  twice have I heard this:
that power belongs to God;
  and that to thee, O Lord, belongs steadfast love.
For thou dost requite a man
  according to his work.

O God, thou art my God, I seek thee,
   my soul thirsts for thee;
my flesh faints for thee,
   as in a dry and weary land where no water is.
So I have looked upon thee in the sanctuary,
   beholding thy power and glory.
Because thy steadfast love is better than life,
   my lips will praise thee.
So I will bless thee as long as I live;
   I will lift up my hands and call on thy name.
My soul is feasted as with marrow and fat,
   and my mouth praises thee with joyful lips,
when I think of thee upon my bed,
   and meditate on thee in the watches of the night;
for thou hast been my help,
   and in the shadow of thy wings I sing for joy.
My soul clings to thee;
   thy right hand upholds me.

But those who seek to destroy my life
   shall go down into the depths of the earth;
they shall be given over to the power of the sword,
   they shall be prey for jackals.
But the king shall rejoice in God;
   all who swear by him shall glory;
   for the mouths of liars will be stopped.

Praise is due to thee,
   O God, in Zion;
and to thee shall vows be performed,
   O thou who hearest prayer!
To thee shall all flesh come
   on account of sins.
When our transgressions prevail over us,
   thou dost forgive them.
Blessed is he whom thou dost choose and bring near,
   to dwell in thy courts!
We shall be satisfied with the goodness of thy house,
   thy holy temple!
By dread deeds thou dost answer us with deliverance,
   O God of our salvation,
who art the hope of all the ends of the earth,

and of the farthest seas;
who by thy strength hast established the mountains,
 being girded with might;
who dost still the roaring of the seas,
 the roaring of their waves,
 the tumult of the peoples;
so that those who dwell at earth's farthest bounds
 are afraid at thy signs;
thou makest the outgoings of the morning and the evening
 to shout for joy.

Thou visitest the earth and waterest it,
 thou greatly enrichest it;
the river of God is full of water;
 thou providest their grain,
 for so thou hast prepared it.
Thou waterest its furrows abundantly,
 settling its ridges,
softening it with showers,
 and blessing its growth.
Thou crownest the year with thy bounty;
 the tracks of thy chariot drip with fatness.
The pastures of the wilderness drip,
 the hills gird themselves with joy,
the meadows clothe themselves with flocks,
 the valleys deck themselves with grain,
 they shout and sing together for joy.

May God be gracious to us and bless us
 and make his face to shine upon us,
that thy way may be known upon earth,
 thy saving power among all nations.
Let the peoples praise thee, O God;
 let all the peoples praise thee!
Let the nations be glad and sing for joy,
 for thou dost judge the peoples with equity
 and guide the nations upon earth.
Let the peoples praise thee, O God;
 let all the peoples praise thee!
The earth has yielded its increase;
 God, our God, has blessed us.
God has blessed us;
 let all the ends of the earth fear him!

Save me, O God!
    For the waters have come up to my neck.
I sink in deep mire,
    where there is no foothold;
I have come into deep waters,
    and the flood sweeps over me.
I am weary with my crying;
    my throat is parched.
My eyes grow dim
    with waiting for my God.
More in number than the hairs of my head
    are those who hate me without cause;
mighty are those who would destroy me,
    those who attack me with lies.
What I did not steal
    must I now restore?
O God, thou knowest my folly;
    the wrongs I have done are not hidden from thee.

Let not those who hope in thee be put to shame through me,
    O Lord GOD of hosts.
For it is for thy sake that I have borne reproach,
    that shame has covered my face.
For zeal for thy house has consumed me,
    and the insults of those who insult thee have fallen on me.

But as for me, my prayer is to thee, O LORD.
    At an acceptable time, O God,
    in the abundance of thy steadfast love answer me.
With thy faithful help rescue me
    from sinking in the mire;
let me be delivered from my enemies
    and from the deep waters.
Thou knowest my reproach,
    and my shame and my dishonor;
    my foes are all known to thee.
They gave me poison for food,
    and for my thirst they gave me vinegar to drink.
Let their own table before them become a snare;
    let their sacrificial feasts be a trap.
Let their eyes be darkened, so that they cannot see;
    and make their loins tremble continually.
May their camp be a desolation,

let no one dwell in their tents.
For they persecute him whom thou hast smitten,
   and him whom thou hast wounded, they afflict still more.
Let them be blotted out of the book of the living;
   let them not be enrolled among the righteous.

But I am afflicted and in pain;
   let thy salvation, O God, set me on high!

I will praise the name of God with a song;
   I will magnify him with thanksgiving.
Let the oppressed see it and be glad.
For the LORD hears the needy,
   and does not despise his own that are in bonds.
Let heaven and earth praise him,
   the seas and everything that moves therein.
For God will save Zion
   and rebuild the cities of Judah;
and his servants shall dwell there and possess it;
   the children of his servants shall inherit it,
   and those who love his name shall dwell in it.

Give the king thy justice, O God,
   and thy righteousness to the royal son!
May he judge thy people with righteousness,
   and thy poor with justice!
Let the mountains bear prosperity for the people,
   and the hills, in righteousness!
May he defend the cause of the poor of the people,
   give deliverance to the needy,
   and crush the oppressor!
May he live while the sun endures,
   and as long as the moon, throughout all generations!
May he be like rain that falls on the mown grass,
   like showers that water the earth!
In his days may righteousness flourish,
   and peace abound, till the moon be no more!
May he have dominion from sea to sea,
   and from the river Euphrates to the ends of the earth!
May his foes bow down before him,
   and his enemies lick the dust!
May the kings of Tarshish and of the isles
   render him tribute,

may the kings of Sheba and Seba bring gifts!
May all kings fall down before him,
   all nations serve him!
For he delivers the needy when he calls,
   the poor and him who has no helper.
He has pity on the weak and the needy,
   and saves the lives of the needy.
From oppression and violence he redeems their life;
   and precious is their blood in his sight.

Long may he live,
   may gold of Sheba be given to him!
May prayer be made for him continually,
   and blessings invoked for him all the day!
May there be abundance of grain in the land;
   on the tops of the mountains may it wave;
   may its fruit be like Lebanon;
and may men blossom forth from the cities
   like the grass of the field!
May his name endure for ever,
   his fame continue as long as the sun!
May men bless themselves by him,
   all nations call him blessed!

Blessed be the LORD, the God of Israel,
   who alone does wondrous things.
Blessed be his glorious name for ever;
   may his glory fill the whole earth!
   Amen and Amen!

BOOK III

Truly God is good to the upright,
   to those who are pure in heart.
But as for me, my feet had almost stumbled,
   my steps had well nigh slipped.
For I was envious of the arrogant,
   when I saw the prosperity of the wicked.
For they have no pangs;
   their bodies are sound and sleek.
They are not in trouble as other men are;
   they are not stricken like other men.

Therefore pride is their necklace;
   violence covers them as a garment.
Their eyes swell out with fatness,
   their hearts overflow with follies.
They scoff and speak with malice;
   loftily they threaten oppression.
They set their mouths against the heavens,
   and their tongue struts through the earth.
Therefore the people turn and praise them;
   and find no fault in them.
And they say, "How can God know?
   Is there knowledge in the Most High?"
Behold, these are the wicked;
   always at ease, they increase in riches.
All in vain have I kept my heart clean
   and washed my hands in innocence.
For all the day long I have been stricken,
   and chastened every morning.

If I had said, "I will speak thus,"
   I would have been untrue to the generation of thy children.
But when I thought how to understand this,
   it seemed to me a wearisome task,
until I went into the sanctuary of God;
   then I perceived their end.
Truly thou dost set them in slippery places;
   thou dost make them fall to ruin.
How they are destroyed in a moment,
   swept away utterly by terrors!
They are like a dream when one awakes,
   on awaking you despise their phantoms.
When my soul was embittered,
   when I was pricked in heart,
I was stupid and ignorant,
   I was like a beast toward thee.
Nevertheless, I am continually with thee;
   thou dost hold my right hand.
Thou dost guide me with thy counsel,
   and afterward thou wilt receive me to glory.
Whom have I in heaven but thee?
   And there is nothing upon earth that I desire besides thee.
My flesh and my heart may fail,
   but God is the strength of my heart for ever.
For, lo, those who are far from thee shall perish;

thou dost put an end to those who are false to thee.
But for me it is good to be near God;
    I have made the Lord GOD my refuge,
    that I may tell of all thy works.

Give ear, O my people, to my teaching;
    incline your ears to the words of my mouth!
I will open my mouth in a parable;
    I will utter dark sayings from of old,
things that we have heard and known,
    that our fathers have told us.
We will not hide them from their children,
    but tell to the coming generation
the glorious deeds of the LORD, and his might,
    and the wonders which he has wrought.
He established a testimony in Jacob,
    and appointed a law in Israel,
which he commanded our fathers
    to teach to their children;
that the next generation might know them,
    the children yet unborn,
and arise and tell them to their children,
    so that they should set their hope in God,
and not forget the works of God,
    but keep his commandments;
and that they should not be like their fathers,
    a stubborn and rebellious generation,
a generation whose heart was not steadfast,
    whose spirit was not faithful to God.

In the sight of their fathers he wrought marvels
    in the land of Egypt, in the fields of Zoan.
He divided the sea and let them pass through it,
    and made the waters stand like a heap.
In the daytime he led them with a cloud,
    and all the night with a fiery light.
He cleft rocks in the wilderness,
    and gave them drink abundantly as from the deep.
Yet they sinned still more against him,
    rebelling against the Most High in the desert.
They tested God in their heart
    by demanding the food they craved.
They spoke against God, saying,

"Can God spread a table in the wilderness?
He smote the rock so that water gushed out
 and streams overflowed.
Can he also give bread,
 or provide meat for his people?"

Therefore, when the LORD heard, he was full of wrath;
 his anger mounted against Israel;
because they had no faith in God,
 and did not trust his saving power.
Yet he commanded the skies above,
 and opened the doors of heaven;
and he rained down upon them manna to eat,
 and gave them the grain of heaven.
He rained flesh upon them like dust,
 winged birds like the sand of the seas;
he let them fall in the midst of their camp,
 all around their habitations.
And they ate and were well filled,
 for he gave them what they craved.
But before they had sated their craving,
 while the food was still in their mouths,
the anger of God rose against them
  and he slew the strongest of them,
  and laid low the picked men of Israel.

In spite of all this they still sinned;
 despite his wonders they did not believe.
Their heart was not steadfast toward him;
 they were not true to his covenant.
Yet he, being compassionate,
 forgave their iniquity,
 and did not destroy them;
he restrained his anger often,
 and did not stir up all his wrath.
He remembered that they were but flesh,
 a wind that passes and comes not again.
He led them in safety, so that they were not afraid.
And he brought them to his holy land,
 to the mountain which his right hand had won.
He drove out nations before them;
 he apportioned them for a possession
 and settled the tribes of Israel in their tents.
Yet they tested and rebelled against the Most High God,

and did not observe his testimonies,
    but turned away and acted treacherously like their fathers;
        they twisted like a deceitful bow.
For they provoked him to anger with their high places;
        they moved him to jealousy with their graven images.
When God heard, he was full of wrath,
        and he utterly rejected Israel.
He forsook his dwelling at Shiloh,
        the tent where he dwelt among men,
and delivered his power to captivity,
        his glory to the hand of the foe.
He gave his people over to the sword,
        and vented his wrath on his heritage.
Fire devoured their young men,
        and their maidens had no marriage song.
Their priests fell by the sword,
        and their widows made no lamentation.

Then the Lord awoke as from sleep,
        like a strong man shouting because of wine.
And he put his adversaries to rout;
        he put them to everlasting shame.
He rejected the tent of Joseph,
        he did not choose the tribe of Ephraim;
but he chose the tribe of Judah,
        Mount Zion, which he loves.
He built his sanctuary like the high heavens,
        like the earth, which he has founded for ever.
He chose David his servant,
        and took him from the sheepfolds;
from tending the ewes that had young he brought him
        to be the shepherd of Jacob his people.
With upright heart he tended them,
        and guided them with skilful hand.

God has taken his place in the divine council;
        in the midst of the gods he holds judgment:
"How long will you judge unjustly
        and show partiality to the wicked?
Give justice to the weak and the fatherless;
        maintain the right of the afflicted and the destitute.
Rescue the weak and the needy;
        deliver them from the hand of the wicked."

They have neither knowledge nor understanding,
    they walk about in darkness;
    all the foundations of the earth are shaken.
I say, "You are gods,
    sons of the Most High, all of you;
nevertheless, you shall die like men,
    and fall like any prince."

Arise, O God, judge the earth;
    for to thee belong all the nations!

How lovely is thy dwelling place,
    O LORD of hosts!
My soul longs, yea, faints
    for the courts of the LORD;
my heart and flesh sing for joy
    to the living God.
Even the sparrow finds a home,
    and the swallow a nest for herself,
    where she may lay her young,
at thy altars, O LORD of hosts,
    my King and my God.
Blessed are those who dwell in thy house,
    ever singing thy praise!
Blessed are the men whose strength is in thee,
    in whose heart are the highways to Zion.
As they go through the valley of Baca
    they make it a place of springs;
    the early rain also covers it with pools.
They go from strength to strength;
    the God of gods will be seen in Zion.

O LORD God of hosts, hear my prayer;
    give ear, O God of Jacob!
Behold our shield, O God;
    look upon the face of thine anointed!

For a day in thy courts is better
    than a thousand elsewhere.
I would rather be a doorkeeper in the house of my God
    than dwell in the tents of wickedness.
For the LORD God is a sun and shield;
    he bestows favor and honor.

No good thing does the LORD withhold
   from those who walk uprightly.
O LORD of hosts,
   blessed is the man who trusts in thee!

On the holy mount stands the city he founded;
   the LORD loves the gates of Zion
   more than all the dwelling places of Jacob.
Glorious things are spoken of you,
   O city of God.

Among those who know me I mention Rahab and Babylon;
   behold, Philistia and Tyre, with Ethiopia—
   "This one was born there," they say.
And of Zion it shall be said,
   "This one and that one were born in her";
   for the Most High himself will establish her.
The LORD records as he registers the peoples,
"This one was born there."
Singers and dancers alike say,
   "All my springs are in you."

O LORD, my God, I call for help by day;
   I cry out in the night before thee.
Let my prayer come before thee,
   incline thy ear to my cry!
For my soul is full of troubles,
   and my life draws near to Sheol.
I am reckoned among those who go down to the Pit;
   I am a man who has no strength,
like one forsaken among the dead,
   like the slain that lie in the grave,
like those whom thou dost remember no more,
   for they are cut off from thy hand.
Thou hast put me in the depths of the Pit,
   in the regions dark and deep.
Thy wrath lies heavy upon me,
   and thou dost overwhelm me with all thy waves.
Thou hast caused my companions to shun me;
   thou hast made me a thing of horror to them.
I am shut in, so that I cannot escape;
   my eye grows dim through sorrow.

Every day I call upon thee, O Lord;
    I spread out my hands to thee.
Dost thou work wonders for the dead?
    Do the shades rise up to praise thee?
Is thy steadfast love declared in the grave,
    or thy faithfulness in Abaddon?
Are thy wonders known in the darkness,
    or thy saving help in the land of forgetfulness?

But I, O Lord, cry to thee;
    in the morning my prayer comes before thee.
O Lord, why dost thou cast me off?
    Why dost thou hide thy face from me?
Afflicted and close to death from my youth up,
    I suffer thy terrors; I am helpless.
Thy wrath has swept over me;
    thy dread assaults destroy me.
They surround me like a flood all day long;
    they close in upon me together.
Thou hast caused lover and friend to shun me;
    my companions are in darkness.

I will sing of thy steadfast love, O Lord, for ever;
    I will proclaim thy faithfulness to all generations.
For thy steadfast love was established for ever,
    thy faithfulness is firm as the heavens.
Thou hast said, "I have made a covenant with my chosen one,
    I have sworn to David my servant:
'I will establish your descendants for ever,
    and build your throne for all generations.'"
Let the heavens praise thy wonders, O Lord,
    thy faithfulness in the assembly of the holy ones!
O Lord God of hosts,
    who is mighty as thou art?
The heavens are thine, the earth also is thine;
    the world and all that is in it, thou hast founded them.
Righteousness and justice are the foundation of thy throne;
    steadfast love and faithfulness go before thee.

Blessed are the people who know the festal shout,
    who walk, O Lord, in the light of thy countenance,
who exult in thy name all the day,
    and extol thy righteousness.

For thou art the glory of their strength;
    by thy favor our horn is exalted.
For our shield belongs to the LORD,
    our king to the Holy One of Israel.

Of old thou didst speak in a vision
    to thy faithful one, and say:
"I have set the crown upon one who is mighty,
    I have exalted one chosen from the people.
I have found David, my servant;
    with my holy oil I have anointed him;
so that my hand shall ever abide with him,
    my arm also shall strengthen him.
The enemy shall not outwit him,
    the wicked shall not humble him.
I will crush his foes before him
    and strike down those who hate him.
And I will make him the first-born,
    the highest of the kings of the earth.
My steadfast love I will keep for him for ever,
    and my covenant will stand firm for him.
I will establish his line for ever
    and his throne as the days of the heavens.
If his children forsake my law
    and do not walk according to my ordinances,
if they violate my statutes
    and do not keep my commandments,
then I will punish their transgression with the rod
    and their iniquity with scourges;
but I will not remove from him my steadfast love,
    or be false to my faithfulness."

But now thou hast cast off and rejected,
    thou art full of wrath against thy anointed.
Thou hast renounced the covenant with thy servant;
    thou hast defiled his crown in the dust.
Thou hast breached all his walls;
    thou hast laid his strongholds in ruins.
All that pass by despoil him;
    he has become the scorn of his neighbors.
Thou hast exalted the right hand of his foes;
    thou hast made all his enemies rejoice.
Yea, thou hast turned back the edge of his sword,
    and thou hast not made him stand in battle.

Thou hast removed the scepter from his hand,
    and cast his throne to the ground.
Thou hast cut short the days of his youth;
    thou hast covered him with shame.

How long, O LORD? Wilt thou hide thyself for ever?
    How long will thy wrath burn like fire?
Remember, O Lord, what the measure of life is,
    for what vanity thou hast created all the sons of men!
What man can live and never see death?
    Who can deliver his soul from the power of Sheol?
Lord, where is thy steadfast love of old,
    which by thy faithfulness thou didst swear to David?
Remember, O Lord, how thy servant is scorned;
    how I bear in my bosom the insults of the peoples,
with which thy enemies taunt, O LORD,
    with which they mock the footsteps of thy anointed.

    Blessed be the LORD for ever!
    Amen and Amen.

BOOK IV

Lord, thou hast been our dwelling place
    in all generations.
Before the mountains were brought forth,
    or ever thou hadst formed the earth and the world,
    from everlasting to everlasting thou art God.
Thou turnest man back to the dust,
    and sayest, "Turn back, O children of men! "
For a thousand years in thy sight
    are but as yesterday when it is past,
    or as a watch in the night.
Thou dost sweep men away; they are like a dream,
    like grass which is renewed in the morning:
in the morning it flourishes and is renewed;
    in the evening it fades and withers.

For we are consumed by thy anger;
    by thy wrath we are overwhelmed.
Thou hast set our iniquities before thee,
    our secret sins in the light of thy countenance.

For all our days pass away under thy wrath,
 our years come to an end like a sigh.
The years of our life are threescore and ten,
 or even by reason of strength fourscore;
yet their span is but toil and trouble;
 they are soon gone, and we fly away.
Who considers the power of thy anger,
 and thy wrath according to the fear of thee?
So teach us to number our days
 that we may get a heart of wisdom.

Return, O LORD! How long?
 Have pity on thy servants!
Satisfy us in the morning with thy steadfast love,
 that we may rejoice and be glad all our days.
Make us glad as many days as thou hast afflicted us,
 and as many years as we have seen evil.
Let thy work be manifest to thy servants,
 and thy glorious power to their children.
Let the favor of the LORD our God be upon us,
 and establish thou the work of our hands upon us,
yea, the work of our hands establish thou it.

He who dwells in the shelter of the Most High,
 who abides in the shadow of the Almighty,
will say to the LORD, "My refuge and my fortress;
 my God, in whom I trust."
For he will deliver you from the snare of the fowler
 and from the deadly pestilence;
he will cover you with his pinions,
 and under his wings you will find refuge;
 his faithfulness is a shield and buckler.
You will not fear the terror of the night,
 nor the arrow that flies by day,
nor the pestilence that stalks in darkness,
 nor the destruction that wastes at noonday.
A thousand may fall at your side,
 ten thousand at your right hand;
 but it will not come near you.
You will only look with your eyes
 and see the recompense of the wicked.
Because you have made the LORD your refuge,
 the Most High your habitation,

no evil shall befall you,
  no scourge come near your tent.
For he will give his angels charge of you
  to guard you in all your ways.
On their hands they will bear you up,
  lest you dash your foot against a stone.
You will tread on the lion and the adder,
  the young lion and the serpent you will trample under foot.

Because he cleaves to me in love, I will deliver him;
  I will protect him, because he knows my name.
When he calls to me, I will answer him;
  I will be with him in trouble,
  I will rescue him and honor him.
With long life I will satisfy him,
  and show him my salvation.

It is good to give thanks to the LORD,
  to sing praises to thy name, O Most High;
to declare thy steadfast love in the morning,
  and thy faithfulness by night,
to the music of the lute and the harp,
  to the melody of the lyre.
For thou, O LORD, hast made me glad by thy work;
  at the works of thy hands I sing for joy.

How great are thy works, O LORD!
  Thy thoughts are very deep!
The dull man cannot know,
  the stupid cannot understand this:
that, though the wicked sprout like grass
  and all evildoers flourish,
they are doomed to destruction for ever,
  but thou, O LORD, art on high for ever.
For, lo, thy enemies, O LORD, shall perish;
  all evildoers shall be scattered.

But thou hast exalted my horn like that of the wild ox;
  thou hast poured over me fresh oil.
My eyes have seen the downfall of my enemies,
  my ears have heard the doom of my evil assailants.
The righteous flourish like the palm tree,

and grow like a cedar in Lebanon.
They are planted in the house of the LORD,
   they flourish in the courts of our God.
They still bring forth fruit in old age,
   they are ever full of sap and green,
to show that the LORD is upright;
   he is my rock, and there is no unrighteousness in him.

O come, let us sing to the LORD;
   let us make a joyful noise to the rock of our salvation!
Let us come into his presence with thanksgiving;
   let us make a joyful noise to him with songs of praise!
For the LORD is a great God,
   and a great King above all gods.
In his hand are the depths of the earth;
   the heights of the mountains are his also.
The sea is his, for he made it;
   for his hands formed the dry land.
O come, let us worship and bow down,
   let us kneel before the LORD, our Maker!
For he is our God,
   and we are the people of his pasture,
   and the sheep of his hand.

O that today you would hearken to his voice!
   Harden not your hearts, as at Meribah,
   as on the day at Massah in the wilderness,
when your fathers tested me,
   and put me to the proof, though they had seen my work.
For forty years I loathed that generation
   and said, "They are a people who err in heart,
   and they do not regard my ways."
Therefore I swore in my anger
   that they should not enter my rest.

O sing to the LORD a new song;
   sing to the LORD, all the earth!
Sing to the LORD, bless his name;
   tell of his salvation from day to day.
Declare his glory among the nations,
   his marvelous works among all the peoples!
For great is the LORD, and greatly to be praised;

he is to be feared above all gods.
For all the gods of the peoples are idols;
   but the LORD made the heavens.
Honor and majesty are before him;
   strength and beauty are in his sanctuary.
Ascribe to the LORD, O families of the peoples,
   ascribe to the LORD glory and strength!
Ascribe to the LORD the glory due his name;
   bring an offering, and come into his courts!
Worship the LORD in holy array;
   tremble before him, all the earth!
Say among the nations, "The LORD reigns!
   Yea, the world is established, it shall never be moved;
   he will judge the peoples with equity."
Let the heavens be glad, and let the earth rejoice;
   let the sea roar, and all that fills it;
   let the field exult, and everything in it!
Then shall all the trees of the wood sing for joy
   before the LORD, for he comes,
   for he comes to judge the earth.
He will judge the world with righteousness,
   and the peoples with his truth.

The LORD reigns; let the earth rejoice;
   let the many coastlands be glad!
Clouds and thick darkness are round about him;
   righteousness and justice are the foundation of his throne.
Fire goes before him,
   and burns up his adversaries round about.
His lightnings lighten the world;
   the earth sees and trembles.
The mountains melt like wax before the LORD,
   before the Lord of all the earth.
The heavens proclaim his righteousness;
   and all the peoples behold his glory.
All worshipers of images are put to shame,
   who make their boast in worthless idols;
   all gods bow down before him.
Zion hears and is glad,
   and the daughters of Judah rejoice,
   because of thy judgments, O God.
For thou, O LORD, art most high over all the earth;
   thou art exalted far above all gods.

The LORD loves those who hate evil;
    he preserves the lives of his saints;
    he delivers them from the hand of the wicked.
Light dawns for the righteous,
    and joy for the upright in heart.
Rejoice in the LORD, O you righteous,
    and give thanks to his holy name!

O sing to the LORD a new song,
    for he has done marvelous things!
His right hand and his holy arm have gotten him victory.
The LORD has made known his victory,
    he has revealed his vindication in the sight of the nations.
He has remembered his steadfast love and faithfulness
    to the house of Israel.
All the ends of the earth have seen
    the victory of our God.

Make a joyful noise to the LORD, all the earth;
    break forth into joyous song and sing praises!
Sing praises to the LORD with the lyre,
    with the lyre and the sound of melody!
With trumpets and the sound of the horn
    make a joyful noise before the King, the LORD!
Let the sea roar, and all that fills it;
    the world and those who dwell in it!
Let the floods clap their hands;
    let the hills sing for joy together
before the LORD, for he comes
    to judge the earth.
He will judge the world with righteousness,
    and the peoples with equity.

Make a joyful noise to the LORD, all the lands!
    Serve the LORD with gladness!
    Come into his presence with singing!
Know that the LORD is God!
    It is he that made us, and we are his;
    we are his people, and the sheep of his pasture.
Enter his gates with thanksgiving,
    and his courts with praise!
    Give thanks to him, bless his name!

For the LORD is good;
   his steadfast love endures for ever,
   and his faithfulness to all generations.

Hear my prayer, O LORD;
   let my cry come to thee!
Do not hide thy face from me
   in the day of my distress!
Incline thy ear to me;
   answer me speedily in the day when I call!

For I eat ashes like bread,
   and mingle tears with my drink,
because of thy indignation and anger;
   for thou hast taken me up and thrown me away.
My days are like an evening shadow;
   I wither away like grass.

But thou, O LORD, art enthroned for ever;
   thy name endures to all generations.
Thou wilt arise and have pity on Zion;
   it is the time to favor her;
   the appointed time has come.

Let this be recorded for a generation to come,
   so that a people yet unborn may praise the LORD:
that he looked down from his holy height,
   from heaven the LORD looked at the earth,
to hear the groans of the prisoners,
   to set free those who were doomed to die;
that men may declare in Zion the name of the LORD,
   and in Jerusalem his praise,
when peoples gather together,
   and kingdoms, to worship the LORD.

He has broken my strength in mid-course;
   he has shortened my days.
"O my God," I say, "take me not hence
   in the midst of my days,
thou whose years endure
   throughout all generations!"
Of old thou didst lay the foundation of the earth,
   and the heavens are the work of thy hands.

They will perish, but thou dost endure;
 they will all wear out like a garment.
Thou changest them like raiment, and they pass away;
 but thou art the same, and thy years have no end.
The children of thy servants shall dwell secure;
 their posterity shall be established before thee.

Bless the Lord, O my soul;
 and all that is within me, bless his holy name!
Bless the Lord, O my soul,
 and forget not all his benefits,
who forgives all your iniquity,
 who heals all your diseases,
who redeems your life from the Pit,
 who crowns you with steadfast love and mercy,
who satisfies you with good as long as you live,
 so that your youth is renewed like the eagle's.

The Lord works vindication and
 justice for all who are oppressed.
He made known his ways to Moses,
 his acts to the people of Israel.
The Lord is merciful and gracious,
 slow to anger and abounding in steadfast love.
He will not always chide,
 nor will he keep his anger for ever.
He does not deal with us according to our sins,
 nor requite us according to our iniquities.
For as the heavens are high above the earth,
 so great is his steadfast love toward those who fear him;
as far as the east is from the west,
 so far does he remove our transgressions from us.
As a father pities his children,
 so the Lord pities those who fear him.
For he knows our frame;
 he remembers that we are dust.

As for man, his days are like grass;
 he flourishes like a flower of the field;
for the wind passes over it, and it is gone,
 and its place knows it no more.
But the steadfast love of the Lord
 is from everlasting to everlasting

upon those who fear him,
   and his righteousness to children's children,
to those who keep his covenant
   and remember to do his commandments.

The LORD has established his throne in the heavens,
   and his kingdom rules over all.
Bless the LORD, O you his angels,
   you mighty ones who do his word,
   hearkening to the voice of his word!
Bless the LORD, all his hosts,
   his ministers that do his will!
Bless the LORD, all his works,
   in all places of his dominion.
Bless the LORD, O my soul!

Bless the LORD, O my soul!
   O LORD my God, thou art very great!
Thou art clothed with honor and majesty,
   who coverest thyself with light as with a garment,
who hast stretched out the heavens like a tent,
   who hast laid the beams of thy chambers on the waters,
who makest the clouds thy chariot,
   who ridest on the wings of the wind,
who makest the winds thy messengers,
   fire and flame thy ministers.

Thou didst set the earth on its foundations,
   so that it should never be shaken.
Thou didst cover it with the deep as with a garment;
   the waters stood above the mountains.
At thy rebuke they fled;
   at the sound of thy thunder they took to flight.
The mountains rose, the valleys sank down
   to the place which thou didst appoint for them.
Thou didst set a bound which they should not pass,
   so that they might not again cover the earth.
Thou makest springs gush forth in the valleys;
   they flow between the hills.
Thou dost cause the grass to grow for the cattle,
   and plants for man to cultivate,
that he may bring forth food from the earth,
   and wine to gladden the heart of man,

oil to make his face shine,
   and bread to strengthen man's heart.
The trees of the LORD are watered abundantly,
   the cedars of Lebanon which he planted.
In them the birds build their nests;
   the stork has her home in the fir trees.
The high mountains are for the wild goats;
   the rocks are a refuge for the badgers.
Thou hast made the moon to mark the seasons;
   the sun knows its time for setting.
Thou makest darkness, and it is night,
   when all the beasts of the forest creep forth.
The young lions roar for their prey,
   seeking their food from God.
When the sun rises, they get them away
   and lie down in their dens.
Man goes forth to his work
   and to his labor until the evening.
O LORD, how manifold are thy works!
   In wisdom hast thou made them all;
   the earth is full of thy creatures.
Yonder is the sea, great and wide,
   which teems with things innumerable,
   living things both small and great.
There go the ships,
   and Leviathan which thou didst form to sport in it.

May the glory of the LORD endure for ever,
   may the LORD rejoice in his works,
who looks on the earth and it trembles,
   who touches the mountains and they smoke!
I will sing to the LORD as long as I live;
   I will sing praise to my God while I have being.
May my meditation be pleasing to him,
   for I rejoice in the LORD.
Let sinners be consumed from the earth,
   and let the wicked be no more!
Bless the LORD, O my soul!
Praise the LORD!

Blessed be the LORD, the God of Israel,
   from everlasting to everlasting!
And let all the people say, "Amen!"

BOOK V

Ogive thanks to the LORD, for he is good;
    for his steadfast love endures for ever!
Let the redeemed of the LORD say so,
    whom he has redeemed from trouble
and gathered in from the lands,
    from the east and from the west,
    from the north and from the south.

Some wandered in desert wastes,
    finding no way to a city to dwell in;
hungry and thirsty,
    their soul fainted within them.
Then they cried to the LORD in their trouble,
    and he delivered them from their distress;
he led them by a straight way,
    till they reached a city to dwell in.
Let them thank the LORD for his steadfast love,
    for his wonderful works to the sons of men!
For he satisfies him who is thirsty,
    and the hungry he fills with good things.

Some sat in darkness and in gloom,
    prisoners in affliction and in irons,
for they had rebelled against the words of God,
    and spurned the counsel of the Most High.
Their hearts were bowed down with hard labor;
    they fell down, with none to help.
Then they cried to the LORD in their trouble,
    and he delivered them from their distress;
he brought them out of darkness and gloom,
    and broke their bonds asunder.
Let them thank the LORD for his steadfast love,
    for his wonderful works to the sons of men!
For he shatters the doors of bronze,
    and cuts in two the bars of iron.

Some were sick through their sinful ways,
    and because of their iniquities suffered affliction;
they loathed any kind of food,
    and they drew near to the gates of death.

Then they cried to the LORD in their trouble,
    and he delivered them from their distress;
he sent forth his word, and healed them,
    and delivered them from destruction.
Let them thank the LORD for his steadfast love,
    for his wonderful works to the sons of men!
And let them offer sacrifices of thanksgiving,
    and tell of his deeds in songs of joy!

Some went down to the sea in ships,
    doing business on the great waters;
they saw the deeds of the LORD,
    his wondrous works in the deep.
For he commanded, and raised the stormy wind,
    which lifted up the waves of the sea.
They mounted up to heaven, they went down to the depths;
    their courage melted away in their evil plight;
they reeled and staggered like drunken men,
    and were at their wits' end.
Then they cried to the LORD in their trouble,
    and he delivered them from their distress;
he made the storm be still,
    and the waves of the sea were hushed.
Then they were glad because they had quiet,
    and he brought them to their desired haven.
Let them thank the LORD for his steadfast love,
    for his wonderful works to the sons of men!
Let them extol him in the congregation of the people,
    and praise him in the assembly of the elders.

He turns rivers into a desert,
    springs of water into thirsty ground,
a fruitful land into a salty waste,
    because of the wickedness of its inhabitants.
He turns a desert into pools of water,
    a parched land into springs of water.
And there he lets the hungry dwell,
    and they establish a city to live in;
they sow fields and plant vineyards,
    and get a fruitful yield.
By his blessing they multiply greatly;
    and he does not let their cattle decrease.
When they are diminished and brought low
    through oppression, trouble, and sorrow,

he pours contempt upon princes
    and makes them wander in trackless wastes;
but he raises up the needy out of affliction,
    and makes their families like flocks.
The upright see it and are glad;
    and all wickedness stops its mouth.
Whoever is wise, let him give heed to these things;
    let men consider the steadfast love of the LORD.

My heart is steadfast, O God,
    my heart is steadfast!
I will sing and make melody!
    Awake, my soul!
Awake, O harp and lyre!
    I will awake the dawn!
I will give thanks to thee, O LORD, among the peoples,
    I will sing praises to thee among the nations.
For thy steadfast love is great above the heavens,
    thy faithfulness reaches to the clouds.

Be exalted, thyself, O God, above the heavens!
    Let thy glory be over all the earth!
That thy beloved may be delivered,
    give help by thy right hand, and answer me!

God has promised in his sanctuary:
    "With exultation I will divide up Shechem,
    and portion out the Vale of Succoth.
Gilead is mine; Manasseh is mine;
    Ephraim is my helmet;
    Judah my scepter.
Moab is my washbasin;
    upon Edom I cast my shoe;
    over Philistia I shout in triumph."

Who will bring me to the fortified city?
    Who will lead me to Edom?
Hast thou not rejected us, O God?
    Thou dost not go forth, O God, with our armies.
O grant us help against the foe,
    for vain is the help of man!
With God we shall do valiantly;
    it is he who will tread down our foes.

The LORD says to my lord:
   "Sit at my right hand,
till I make your enemies your footstool."
The LORD sends forth from Zion
   your mighty scepter.
   Rule in the midst of your foes!
Your people will offer themselves freely
   on the day you lead your host
   upon the holy mountains.
From the womb of the morning
   like dew your youth will come to you.
The LORD has sworn
   and will not change his mind,
"You are a priest for ever
   after the order of Melchizedek."
The Lord is at your right hand;
   he will shatter kings on the day of his wrath.
He will execute judgment among the nations,
   filling them with corpses;
he will shatter chiefs
   over the wide earth.
He will drink from the brook by the way;
   therefore he will lift up his head.

Praise the LORD.
I will give thanks to the LORD with my whole heart,
   in the company of the upright, in the congregation.
Great are the works of the LORD,
   studied by all who have pleasure in them.
Full of honor and majesty is his work,
   and his righteousness endures for ever.
He has caused his wonderful works to be remembered;
   the LORD is gracious and merciful.
He provides food for those who fear him;
   he is ever mindful of his covenant.
He has shown his people the power of his works,
   in giving them the heritage of the nations.
The works of his hands are faithful and just;
   all his precepts are trustworthy,
they are established for ever and ever,
   to be performed with faithfulness and uprightness.
He sent redemption to his people;

he has commanded his covenant for ever.
　Holy and terrible is his name!
The fear of the LORD is the beginning of wisdom;
　a good understanding have all those who practice it.
　His praise endures for ever!

When Israel went forth from Egypt,
　the house of Jacob from a people of strange language,
Judah became his sanctuary,
　Israel his dominion.
The sea looked and fled,
　Jordan turned back.
The mountains skipped like rams,
　the hills like lambs.
What ails you, O sea, that you flee?
　O Jordan, that you turn back?
O mountains, that you skip like rams?
　O hills, like lambs?
Tremble, O earth, at the presence of the Lord,
　at the presence of the God of Jacob,
who turns the rock into a pool of water,
　the flint into a spring of water.

I love the LORD, because he has heard
　my voice and my supplications.
Because he inclined his ear to me,
　therefore I will call on him as long as I live.
The snares of death encompassed me;
　the pangs of Sheol laid hold on me;
　I suffered distress and anguish.
Then I called on the name of the LORD:
　"O LORD, I beseech thee, save my life!"
Gracious is the LORD, and righteous;
　our God is merciful.
The LORD preserves the simple;
　when I was brought low, he saved me.
Return, O my soul, to your rest;
　for the LORD has dealt bountifully with you.
For thou hast delivered my soul from death,
　my eyes from tears,
　my feet from stumbling;
I walk before the LORD

in the land of the living.
I kept my faith, even when I said,
    "I am greatly afflicted";
I said in my consternation,
    "Men are all a vain hope."

What shall I render to the LORD
    for all his bounty to me?
I will lift up the cup of salvation
    and call on the name of the LORD,
I will pay my vows to the LORD
    in the presence of all his people.
Precious in the sight of the LORD
    is the death of his saints.
O LORD, I am thy servant;
    I am thy servant, the son of thy handmaid.
    Thou hast loosed my bonds.
I will offer to thee the sacrifice of thanksgiving
    and call on the name of the LORD.
I will pay my vows to the LORD
    in the presence of all his people,
in the courts of the house of the LORD,
    in your midst, O Jerusalem.
Praise the LORD!

Praise the LORD, all nations!
    Extol him, all peoples!
For great is his steadfast love toward us;
    and the faithfulness of the LORD endures for ever.
Praise the LORD!

O give thanks to the LORD, for he is good;
    his steadfast love endures for ever!

Out of my distress I called on the LORD;
    the LORD answered me and set me free.
With the LORD on my side I do not fear.
    What can man do to me?
The LORD is on my side to help me;
    I shall look in triumph on those who hate me.
It is better to take refuge in the LORD
    than to put confidence in man.

It is better to take refuge in the LORD
 than to put confidence in princes.
All nations surrounded me on every side;
 they blazed like a fire of thorns;
 in the name of the LORD I cut them off!
I was pushed hard, so that I was falling,
 but the LORD helped me.
The LORD is my strength and my song;
 he has become my salvation.
Hark, glad songs of victory
 in the tents of the righteous.

I thank thee that thou hast answered me
 and hast become my salvation.
The stone which the builders rejected
 has become the head of the corner.
This is the LORD's doing;
 it is marvelous in our eyes.
This is the day which the LORD has made;
 let us rejoice and be glad in it.
Save us, we beseech thee, O LORD!
 O LORD, we beseech thee, give us success!

Blessed be he who enters in the name of the LORD!
O give thanks to the LORD, for he is good;
 for his steadfast love endures for ever!

Blessed are those whose way is blameless,
 who walk in the law of the LORD!
Blessed are those who keep his testimonies,
 who seek him with their whole heart,
who also do no wrong,
 but walk in his ways!
Thou hast commanded thy precepts
 to be kept diligently.
O that my ways may be steadfast
 in keeping thy statutes!
Then I shall not be put to shame,
 having my eyes fixed on all thy commandments.
I will praise thee with an upright heart,
 when I learn thy righteous ordinances.
I will observe thy statutes;
 O forsake me not utterly!

Thy word is a lamp to my feet
and a light to my path.
I have sworn an oath and confirmed it,
to observe thy righteous ordinances.
I am sorely afflicted;
give me life, O LORD, according to thy word!
Accept my offerings of praise, O LORD,
and teach me thy ordinances.
I hold my life in my hand continually,
but I do not forget thy law.
The wicked have laid a snare for me,
but I do not stray from thy precepts.
Thy testimonies are my heritage for ever;
yea, they are the joy of my heart.
I incline my heart to perform thy statutes
for ever, to the end.

Thy testimonies are wonderful;
therefore my soul keeps them.
The unfolding of thy words gives light;
it imparts understanding to the simple.
With open mouth I pant,
because I long for thy commandments.
Turn to me and be gracious to me,
as is thy wont toward those who love thy name.
Keep steady my steps according to thy promise,
and let no iniquity get dominion over me.
Redeem me from man's oppression,
that I may keep thy precepts.
Make thy face shine upon thy servant,
and teach me thy statutes.
My eyes shed streams of tears,
because men do not keep thy law.

Princes persecute me without cause,
but my heart stands in awe of thy words.
I rejoice at thy word
like one who finds great spoil.
I hate and abhor falsehood,
but I love thy law.
Seven times a day I praise thee
for thy righteous ordinances.
Great peace have those who love thy law;
nothing can make them stumble.

I hope for thy salvation, O Lord,
   and I do thy commandments.
My soul keeps thy testimonies;
   I love them exceedingly.
I keep thy precepts and testimonies,
   for all my ways are before thee.

Let my cry come before thee, O Lord;
   give me understanding according to thy word!
Let my supplication come before thee;
   deliver me according to thy word.
My lips will pour forth praise
   that thou dost teach me thy statutes.
My tongue will sing of thy word,
   for all thy commandments are right.
Let thy hand be ready to help me,
   for I have chosen thy precepts.
I long for thy salvation, O Lord,
   and thy law is my delight.
Let me live, that I may praise thee,
   and let thy ordinances help me.
I have gone astray like a lost sheep;
   seek thy servant,
      for I do not forget thy commandments.

I lift up my eyes to the hills.
   From whence does my help come?
My help comes from the Lord,
   who made heaven and earth.
He will not let your foot be moved,
   he who keeps you will not slumber.
Behold, he who keeps Israel
   will neither slumber nor sleep.
The Lord is your keeper;
   the Lord is your shade
   on your right hand.
The sun shall not smite you by day,
   nor the moon by night.
The Lord will keep you from all evil;
   he will keep your life.
The Lord will keep
   your going out and your coming in
   from this time forth and for evermore.

I was glad when they said to me,
   "Let us go to the house of the LORD!"
Our feet have been standing
   within your gates, O Jerusalem!
Jerusalem, built as a city
   which is bound firmly together,
to which the tribes go up,
   the tribes of the LORD,
as was decreed for Israel,
   to give thanks to the name of the LORD.
There thrones for judgment were set,
   the thrones of the house of David.

Pray for the peace of Jerusalem!
   "May they prosper who love you!
Peace be within your walls,
   and security within your towers!"
For my brethren and companions' sake
   I will say, "Peace be within you!"
For the sake of the house of the LORD our God,
   I will seek your good.

To thee I lift up my eyes,
   O thou who art enthroned in the heavens!
Behold, as the eyes of servants
   look to the hand of their master,
as the eyes of a maid
   to the hand of her mistress,
so our eyes look to the LORD our God,
   till he have mercy upon us.
Have mercy upon us, O LORD, have mercy upon us,
   for we have had more than enough of contempt.
Too long our soul has been sated
   with the scorn of those who are at ease,
   the contempt of the proud.

Unless the LORD builds the house,
   those who build it labor in vain.
Unless the LORD watches over the city,
   the watchman stays awake in vain.
It is in vain that you rise up early

and go late to rest,
eating the bread of anxious toil;
   for he gives to his beloved sleep.
Lo, sons are a heritage from the LORD,
   the fruit of the womb a reward.
Like arrows in the hand of a warrior
   are the sons of one's youth.
Happy is the man who has
   his quiver full of them!
He shall not be put to shame
   when he speaks with his enemies in the gate.

Blessed is every one who fears the LORD,
   who walks in his ways!
You shall eat the fruit of the labor of your hands;
   you shall be happy, and it shall be well with you.
Your wife will be like a fruitful vine
   within your house;
your children will be like olive shoots
   around your table.
Lo, thus shall the man be blessed
   who fears the LORD.
The LORD bless you from Zion!
   May you see the prosperity of Jerusalem
   all the days of your life!
May you see your children's children!
   Peace be upon Israel!

Out of the depths I cry to thee, O LORD!
   Lord, hear my voice!
Let thy ears be attentive
   to the voice of my supplications!
If thou, O LORD, shouldst mark iniquities,
   Lord, who could stand?
But there is forgiveness with thee,
   that thou mayest be feared.

I wait for the LORD, my soul waits,
   and in his word I hope;
my soul waits for the Lord
   more than watchmen for the morning.
O Israel, hope in the LORD!

For with the LORD there is steadfast love,
and with him is plenteous redemption.
And he will redeem Israel from all his iniquities.

O LORD, my heart is not lifted up,
my eyes are not raised too high;
I do not occupy myself with things
too great and too marvelous for me.
But I have calmed and quieted my soul,
like a child quieted at its mother's breast;
like a child that is quieted is my soul.
O Israel, hope in the LORD
from this time forth and for evermore.

Behold, how good and pleasant it is
when brothers dwell in unity!
It is like the precious oil upon the head,
running down upon the beard,
upon the beard of Aaron,
running down on the collar of his robes!
It is like the dew of Hermon,
which falls on the mountains of Zion!
For there the LORD has commanded the blessing,
life for evermore.

By the waters of Babylon,
there we sat down and wept,
when we remembered Zion.
On the willows there
we hung up our lyres.
For there our captors required of us songs,
and our tormentors, mirth, saying,
"Sing us one of the songs of Zion!"
How shall we sing the LORD's song in a foreign land?

If I forget you, O Jerusalem,
let my right hand wither!
Let my tongue cleave to the roof of my mouth,
if I do not remember you,
if I do not set Jerusalem
above my highest joy!

Remember, O L<small>ORD</small>, against the Edomites
    the day of Jerusalem,
how they said, "Raze it, raze it!
    Down to its foundations!"
O daughter of Babylon, you devastator!
    Happy shall he be who requites you
    with what you have done to us!
Happy shall he be who takes your little ones
    and dashes them against the rock!

O L<small>ORD</small>, thou hast searched me and known me!
Thou knowest when I sit down and when I rise up;
    thou discernest my thoughts from afar.
Thou searchest out my path and my lying down,
    and art acquainted with all my ways.
Even before a word is on my tongue,
    lo, O L<small>ORD</small>, thou knowest it altogether.
Thou dost beset me behind and before;
    and layest thy hand upon me.
Such knowledge is too wonderful for me;
    it is high, I cannot attain it.
Wither shall I go from thy Spirit?
    Or whither shall I flee from thy presence?
If I ascend to heaven, thou art there!
    If I make my bed in Sheol, thou art there!
If I take the wings of the morning
    and dwell in the uttermost parts of the sea,
even there thy hand shall lead me,
    and thy right hand shall hold me.
If I say, "Let only darkness cover me,
    and the light about me be night,"
even the darkness is not dark to thee,
    the night is bright as the day;
    for darkness is as light with thee.

For thou didst form my inward parts,
    thou didst knit me together in my mother's womb.
I praise thee, for thou art fearful and wonderful.
    Wonderful are thy works!
Thou knowest me right well;
    my frame was not hidden from thee,
when I was being made in secret,
    intricately wrought in the depths of the earth.

Thy eyes beheld my unformed substance;
    in thy book were written, every one of them,
the days that were formed for me,
    when as yet there was none of them.
How precious to me are thy thoughts, O God!
    How vast is the sum of them!
If I would count them, they are more than the sand.
    When I awake, I am still with thee.

O that thou wouldst slay the wicked, O God,
    and that men of blood would depart from me,
men who maliciously defy thee,
    who lift themselves up against thee for evil!
Do I not hate them that hate thee, O LORD?
    And do I not loathe them that rise up against thee?
I hate them with perfect hatred;
    I count them my enemies.
Search me, O God, and know my heart!
    Try me and know my thoughts!
And see if there be any wicked way in me,
    and lead me in the way everlasting!

Blessed be the LORD, my rock,
who trains my hands for war,
    and my fingers for battle;
my rock and my fortress,
    my stronghold and my deliverer,
my shield and he in whom I take refuge,
    who subdues the peoples under him.

I will sing a new song to thee, O God;
    upon a ten-stringed harp I will play to thee,
who givest victory to kings,
    who rescuest David thy servant.

May our sons in their youth
    be like plants full grown,
our daughters like corner pillars
    cut for the structure of a palace;
may our garners be full,
    providing all manner of store;
may our sheep bring forth thousands
    and ten thousands in our fields;

may our cattle be heavy with young,
    suffering no mischance or failure in bearing;
may there be no cry of distress in our streets!
Happy the people to whom such blessings fall!
    Happy the people whose God is the LORD!

I will extol thee, my God and King,
    and bless thy name for ever and ever.
Every day I will bless thee,
    and praise thy name for ever and ever.
Great is the LORD, and greatly to be praised,
    and his greatness is unsearchable.
One generation shall laud thy works to another,
    and shall declare thy mighty acts.
On the glorious splendor of thy majesty,
    and on thy wondrous works, I will meditate.
Men shall proclaim the might of thy terrible acts,
    and I will declare thy greatness.
They shall pour forth the fame of thy abundant goodness,
    and shall sing aloud of thy righteousness.

The LORD is gracious and merciful,
    slow to anger and abounding in steadfast love.
The LORD is good to all,
    and his compassion is over all that he has made.

All thy works shall give thanks to thee, O LORD,
    and all thy saints shall bless thee!
They shall speak of the glory of thy kingdom,
    and tell of thy power,
to make known to the sons of men thy mighty deeds,
    and the glorious splendor of thy kingdom.
Thy kingdom is an everlasting kingdom,
    and thy dominion endures throughout all generations.

The LORD is faithful in all his words,
    and gracious in all his deeds.
The LORD upholds all who are falling,
    and raises up all who are bowed down.
The eyes of all look to thee,
    and thou givest them their food in due season.
Thou openest thy hand,
    thou satisfiest the desire of every living thing.

The LORD is just in all his ways,
    and kind in all his doings.
The LORD is near to all who call upon him,
    to all who call upon him in truth.
He fulfils the desire of all who fear him,
    he also hears their cry, and saves them.
The LORD preserves all who love him;
    but all the wicked he will destroy.
My mouth will speak the praise of the LORD,
    and let all flesh bless his holy name for ever and ever.

Praise the LORD!
Praise the LORD from the heavens,
    praise him in the heights!
Praise him, all his angels,
    praise him, all his host!
Praise him, sun and moon,
    praise him, all you shining stars!
Praise him, you highest heavens,
    and you waters above the heavens!
Let them praise the name of the LORD!
    For he commanded and they were created.
And he established them for ever and ever;
    he fixed their bounds which cannot be passed.
Praise the LORD from the earth,
    you sea monsters and all deeps,
fire and hail, snow and frost,
    stormy wind fulfilling his command!
Mountains and all hills,
    fruit trees and all cedars!
Beasts and all cattle,
    creeping things and flying birds!
Kings of the earth and all peoples,
    princes and all rulers of the earth!
Young men and maidens together,
    old men and children!
Let them praise the name of the LORD,
    for his name alone is exalted;
    his glory is above earth and heaven.
He has raised up a horn for his people,
    praise for all his saints,
    for the people of Israel who are near to him.
Praise the LORD!

Praise the LORD!
Praise God in his sanctuary;
　　praise him in his mighty firmament!
Praise him for his mighty deeds;
　　praise him according to his exceeding greatness!
Praise him with trumpet sound;
　　praise him with lute and harp!
Praise him with timbrel and dance;
　　praise him with strings and pipe!
Praise him with sounding cymbals;
　　praise him with loud clashing cymbals!
Let everything that breathes praise the LORD!
Praise the LORD!

PROVERBS

This book is a compendium of religious and moral instruction as given to Jewish youth by professional sages in the postexilic period. The overall concept is "wisdom," but this does not mean merely knowing many things or being very clever. It means knowing the right thing to do *and doing it.* Wisdom is a practical thing of daily life; it is not nationalistic, but is individual and universal. As it stands, the book represents a gathering of several different collections of proverbs, stemming from various localities during the ninth to the third century B.C. Some sections offer extended admonition and warning, others provide pithy two-line maxims, all appealing to the lessons of experience. The frequent use of the book by New Testament writers (nearly a dozen quotations and more than twenty allusions) indicates the respect of early Christians for these wise thoughts of Israel's ancient sages.

———

THE PROVERBS OF Solomon, son of David, king of Israel:

That men may know wisdom, understand words of insight, receive instruction in wise dealing, righteousness, justice, and equity; that prudence may be given to the simple, knowledge and discretion to the youth—the man of understanding acquire skill, to understand a proverb and a figure, the words of the wise and their riddles.

The fear of the LORD is the beginning of knowledge; fools despise wisdom and instruction.

Hear, my son, your father's instruction, and reject not your mother's teaching; for they are a fair garland for your head. My son, if sinners entice you, if they say, "Come, let us lie in wait for blood, let us ambush the innocent; we shall fill our houses with spoil"—my son, hold back your foot from their paths. For in vain is a net spread in the sight of any bird; but these men set an ambush for their own lives. Such are the ways of all who get gain by violence; it takes away the life of its possessors.

Wisdom cries aloud in the street: "How long, O simple ones, will you love being simple? How long will fools hate knowledge? Give heed to my reproof. Because I have called and you refused to listen, I will laugh when panic strikes you like a storm. Then you will seek me, but you will not find me. Because you hated knowledge and did not choose the fear of the LORD, therefore you shall eat the fruit of your way and be sated with your own devices. For the complacence of fools destroys them; but he who listens to me will be at ease, without dread of evil."

My son, if you treasure up my commandments, if you cry out for insight and seek it like hidden treasure, you will understand the fear of the LORD and find the knowledge of God; for the LORD stores up sound wisdom for the upright, guarding the paths of justice and preserving the way of his saints. Then knowledge will be pleasant to your soul; discretion will watch over you, delivering you from the ways of darkness, from men of perverted speech, whose paths are crooked, and who are devious in their ways. You will be saved from the adventuress with her smooth words, who forsakes the companion of her youth and forgets the covenant of her God. You will walk in the way of good men, for the upright will inhabit the land.

My son, let not loyalty and faithfulness forsake you; write them on the tablet of your heart. So you will find favor and good repute in the sight of God and man. Trust in the LORD with all your heart, and do not rely on your own insight. In all your ways acknowledge him, and he will make straight your paths. Be not wise in your own eyes, and turn away from evil. It will be healing to your flesh and refreshment to your bones.

Do not despise the LORD's discipline or be weary of his reproof, for the LORD reproves him whom he loves, as a father the son in whom he delights.

Happy is the man who finds wisdom, for her profit is better than gold. Long life is in her right hand; in her left are riches and honor. Her ways are ways of pleasantness, and all her paths are peace. She is a tree of life to those who lay hold of her; those who hold her fast are called happy.

Do not withhold good from those to whom it is due, when it is in your power to do it. Do not say to your neighbor, "Go, and come again, tomorrow I will give it"—when you have it with you. Do not plan evil against your neighbor who dwells trustingly beside you. Do not envy a man of violence and do not choose any of his ways; for the perverse man is an abomination to the LORD, but the upright are in his confidence.

When I was a son with my father, tender, the only one in the sight of my mother, he taught me, "The beginning of wisdom is this: Get wisdom, and whatever you get, get insight. Prize her highly, and she will exalt you." I have taught you the way of wisdom, my son; guard her, for she is your life. Do not enter the path of the wicked; turn away from it and pass on. For the way of the wicked is like deep darkness; they do not know over what they stumble. But the path of the righteous is like the light of dawn, which shines brighter and brighter until full day.

The lips of a loose woman drip honey, and her speech is smoother than oil; but in the end she is bitter as wormwood, sharp as a two-edged sword. She does not take heed to the path of life; her feet go down to death. O sons, keep your way far from her; do not go near her door, lest you give your honor to others and your years to the merciless; and at the end of your life you groan, when your flesh and body are consumed, and you say, "How I hated discipline, and my heart despised reproof! I was at the point of utter ruin in the assembled congregation."

Drink water from your own cistern, flowing water from your own well. Let your fountain be blessed, and rejoice in the wife of your youth, a lovely hind, a graceful doe. Let her affection fill you with delight, be infatuated at all times with her love. Why should you embrace the bosom of an adventuress, my son? For a man's ways are before the eyes of the LORD, and he watches all his paths.

Go to the ant, O sluggard; consider her ways, and be wise. Without having any chief, officer or ruler, she prepares her food in summer, and gathers her sustenance in harvest. How long will you lie there, O sluggard? When will you arise from your sleep? A little sleep, a little slumber, a little folding of the hands to rest, and poverty will come upon you like a robber, and want like an armed man.

There are six things which the LORD hates, seven which are an abomination to him: haughty eyes, a lying tongue, and hands that shed innocent blood, a heart that devises wicked plans, feet that make haste to run to evil, a false witness who breathes out lies, and a man who sows discord among brothers.

Through the window of my house I have seen among the simple a young man passing along the street in the twilight, at the time of night and darkness. And lo, a woman meets him, dressed as a harlot, wily of heart. She is loud and wayward; her feet do not stay at home. Now in the street, now in the market, and at every corner she lies in wait. She seizes him and kisses him, and with impudent face she says: "I had to offer sacrifices, and today I have paid my vows; so now I have come to seek you. I have decked my couch with colored linen; I have perfumed my bed with myrrh. Come, let us delight ourselves with love till morning. For my husband has gone on a journey; only at full moon will he return."

With her smooth talk she persuades him. All at once he follows her, as an ox goes to the slaughter. He does not know that it will cost him his life. For many a victim has she laid low; yea, all her slain are a mighty host. Her house is the way to Sheol, going down to the chambers of death.

Does not wisdom call, does not understanding raise her voice? On the heights beside the way, beside the gates in front of the town, she cries aloud: "To you, O men, I call. O foolish ones, pay attention. Hear, for I will speak noble things; my mouth will utter truth. Take my instruction instead of silver, and knowledge rather than gold. I, wisdom, dwell in prudence, and I find knowledge and discretion. I have counsel, I have insight, I have strength. By me kings reign, and rulers decree what is just. I love those who love me, and those who seek me diligently find me. I walk in the way of righteousness, in the paths of justice, endowing with wealth those who love me, and filling their treasuries.

"The LORD created me at the beginning of his work, the first of his acts of old. Ages ago I was set up, before the beginning of the earth. When there were no depths, I was brought forth, before the mountains had been shaped. Before the LORD made the first dust of the world, when he established the heavens, I was there. When he made firm the skies above, when he assigned to the sea its limit, when he marked out the foundations of the earth, then I was beside him. Like a little child, I was daily his delight, rejoicing in his inhabited world, rejoicing in the sons of men.

"He who finds me finds life and obtains favor from the LORD; but he who misses me injures himself. All who hate me love death."

Wisdom has built her house, she has set up her seven pillars. She has slaughtered her beasts, she has mixed her wine, she has also set her table. She has sent out her maids to call from the highest places in the town, "Whoever is simple, let him turn in here!" To him who is without sense she says, "Come, eat of my bread and drink of the wine I have mixed. Leave simpleness, and live, and walk in the way of insight."

A foolish woman is noisy; she is wanton and knows no shame. She sits at the door of her house, calling to those who pass by, "Whoever is simple, let him turn in here!" And to those without sense she says, "Stolen water is sweet, and bread eaten in secret is pleasant." But they do not know that the dead are there, that her guests are in the depths of Sheol.

THE PROVERBS OF Solomon.

A wise son makes a glad father,
   but a foolish son is a sorrow to his mother.
The LORD does not let the righteous go hungry,
   but he thwarts the craving of the wicked.
A slack hand causes poverty,
   but the hand of the diligent makes rich.
The memory of the righteous is a blessing,
   but the name of the wicked will rot.

He who walks in integrity walks securely,
    but he who perverts his ways will stumble.
He who winks the eye causes trouble,
    but he who boldly reproves makes peace.
The mouth of the righteous is a fountain of life,
    but the mouth of the wicked conceals violence.
Hatred stirs up strife,
    but love covers all offenses.
The lips of the righteous feed many,
    but fools die for lack of sense.
The blessing of the LORD makes rich,
    and he adds no sorrow with it.
When the tempest passes, the wicked is no more,
    but the righteous is established for ever.
Like vinegar to the teeth, and smoke to the eyes,
    so is the sluggard to those who send him.
The fear of the LORD prolongs life,
    but the years of the wicked will be short.
A false balance is an abomination to the LORD,
    but a just weight is his delight.
When pride comes, then comes disgrace;
    but with the humble is wisdom.
Riches do not profit in the day of wrath,
    but righteousness delivers from death.
Where there is no guidance, a people falls;
    but in an abundance of counselors there is safety.
Like a gold ring in a swine's snout
    is a beautiful woman without discretion.
One man gives freely, yet grows all the richer;
    another withholds, and only suffers want.
He who trusts in his riches will wither,
    but the righteous will flourish like a green leaf.
If the righteous is requited on earth,
    how much more the wicked and the sinner!
A good wife is the crown of her husband,
    but she who brings shame is like rottenness in his bones.
Better is a man of humble standing who has bread
    than one who plays the great man but lacks it.
A righteous man has regard for the life of his beast,
    but the mercy of the wicked is cruel.
The strong tower of the wicked comes to ruin,
    but the root of the righteous stands firm.
The way of a fool is right in his own eyes,
    but a wise man listens to advice.

The vexation of a fool is known at once,
   but the prudent man ignores an insult.
Truthful lips endure for ever,
   but a lying tongue is but for a moment.
Anxiety in a man's heart weighs him down,
   but a good word makes him glad.
A wise son heeds his father's instruction,
   but a scoffer does not listen to rebuke.
The soul of the sluggard craves, and gets nothing,
   while the soul of the diligent is richly supplied.
Hope deferred makes the heart sick,
   but a desire fulfilled is a tree of life.
The ground of the poor yields much food,
   but it is swept away through injustice.
He who spares the rod hates his son,
   but he who loves him is diligent to discipline him.
Wisdom builds her house,
   but folly with her own hands tears it down.
The heart knows its own bitterness,
   and no stranger shares its joy.
The house of the wicked will be destroyed,
   but the tent of the upright will flourish.
There is a way which seems right to a man,
   but its end is the way to death.
Even in laughter the heart is sad,
   and the end of joy is grief.
A perverse man will be filled with the fruit of his ways,
   and a good man with the fruit of his deeds.
The simple believes everything,
   but the prudent looks where he is going.
The evil bow down before the good,
   the wicked at the gates of the righteous.
In all toil there is profit,
   but mere talk tends only to want.
The fear of the LORD is a fountain of life,
   that one may avoid the snares of death.
A tranquil mind gives life to the flesh,
   but passion makes the bones rot.
He who oppresses a poor man insults his Maker,
   but he who is kind to the needy honors him.
A soft answer turns away wrath,
   but a harsh word stirs up anger.
The sacrifice of the wicked is an abomination to the LORD,
   but the prayer of the upright is his delight.

All the days of the afflicted are evil,
  but a cheerful heart has a continual feast.
Better is a little with the fear of the LORD
  than great treasure and trouble with it.
To make an apt answer is a joy to a man,
  and a word in season, how good it is!
The LORD tears down the house of the proud,
  but maintains the widow's boundaries.
The LORD is far from the wicked,
  but he hears the prayer of the righteous.
The light of the eyes rejoices the heart,
  and good news refreshes the bones.
The plans of the mind belong to man,
  but the answer of the tongue is from the LORD.
The LORD has made everything for its purpose,
  even the wicked for the day of trouble.
When a man's ways please the LORD,
  even his enemies will be at peace with him.
A just balance and scales are the LORD's;
  all the weights are his work.
It is an abomination to kings to do evil,
  for the throne is established by righteousness.
Pride goes before destruction,
  and a haughty spirit before a fall.
It is better to be of a lowly spirit with the poor
  than to divide the spoil with the proud.
Better is a dry morsel with quiet
  than a house full of feasting with strife.
The crucible is for silver, and the furnace is for gold,
  and the LORD tries hearts.
Fine speech is not becoming to a fool;
  still less is false speech to a prince.
He who forgives an offense seeks love,
  but he who dwells on a matter alienates a friend.
A rebuke goes deeper into a man of understanding
  than a hundred blows into a fool.
Let a man meet a she-bear robbed of her cubs,
  rather than a fool in his folly.
If a man returns evil for good,
  evil will not depart from his house.
The beginning of strife is like letting out water;
  so quit before the quarrel breaks out.
A friend loves at all times,
  and a brother is born for adversity.

A cheerful heart is a good medicine,
  but a downcast spirit dries up the bones.
Even a fool who keeps silent is considered wise;
  when he closes his lips, he is deemed intelligent.
A fool takes no pleasure in understanding,
  but only in expressing his opinion.
The words of a whisperer are like delicious morsels;
  they go down into the inner parts of the body.
He who is slack in his work
  is a brother to him who destroys.
If one gives answer before he hears,
  it is his folly and shame.
A man's spirit will endure sickness;
  but a broken spirit who can bear?
He who states his case first seems right,
  until the other comes and examines him.
When a man's folly brings his way to ruin,
  his heart rages against the LORD.
Wealth brings many new friends,
  but a poor man is deserted by all.
It is not fitting for a fool to live in luxury,
  much less for a slave to rule over princes.
A king's wrath is like the growling of a lion,
  but his favor is like dew upon the grass.
A foolish son is ruin to his father,
  and a wife's quarreling is a continual dripping of rain.
House and wealth are inherited from fathers,
  but a prudent wife is from the LORD.
Many are the plans in the mind of a man,
  but it is the purpose of the LORD that will be established.
The sluggard buries his hand in the dish,
  and will not even bring it back to his mouth.
Who can say, "I have made my heart clean;
  I am pure from my sin"?
Even a child makes himself known by his acts,
  whether what he does is pure and right.
The hearing ear and the seeing eye,
  the LORD has made them both.
If one curses his father or his mother,
  his lamp will be put out in utter darkness.
Do not say, "I will repay evil";
  wait for the LORD, and he will help you.
A man's steps are ordered by the LORD;
  how then can man understand his way?

It is a snare for a man to say rashly, "It is holy,"
  and to reflect only after making his vows.
Blows that wound cleanse away evil;
  strokes make clean the innermost parts.
The king's heart is a stream of water in the hand of the LORD;
  he turns it wherever he will.
To do righteousness and justice
  is more acceptable to the LORD than sacrifice.
The getting of treasures by a lying tongue
  is a fleeting vapor and a snare of death.
He who closes his ear to the cry of the poor
  will himself cry out and not be heard.
A gift in secret conceals anger;
  and a bribe in the bosom, strong wrath.
A man who wanders from the way of understanding
  will rest in the assembly of the dead.
It is better to live in a desert land
  than with a fretful woman.
"Scoffer" is the name of the proud, haughty man
  who acts with arrogant pride.
All day long the wicked covets,
  but the righteous gives and does not hold back.
No wisdom, no understanding, no counsel
  can avail against the LORD.
The horse is made ready for the day of battle,
  but the victory belongs to the LORD.
A good name is to be chosen rather than great riches,
  and favor is better than silver or gold.
The rich and the poor meet together;
  the LORD is the maker of them all.
A prudent man sees danger and hides himself;
  but the simple go on, and suffer for it.
The reward for humility and fear of the LORD
  is riches and honor and life.
Train up a child in the way he should go,
  and when he is old he will not depart from it.
The rich rules over the poor,
  and the borrower is the slave of the lender.
He who loves purity of heart
  will have the king as his friend.
The sluggard says, "There is a lion outside!
  I shall be slain in the streets!"
He who oppresses the poor to increase his own wealth
  will only come to want.

HAVE I NOT WRITTEN SAYINGS OF admonition and knowledge, to show you what is right and true, that you may give a wise answer to those who ask you?

Do not rob the poor, because he is poor, or crush the afflicted at the gate; for the LORD will plead their cause and despoil of life those who despoil them.

Make no friendship with a wrathful man, lest you learn his ways and entangle yourself in a snare.

Do you see a man skilful in his work? He will stand before kings.

When you sit down to eat with a ruler, observe carefully what is before you; and put a knife to your throat if you are a man given to appetite. Do not desire a king's delicacies, for they are deceptive food.

Do not toil to acquire wealth; be wise enough to desist. When your eyes light upon it, it is gone; for suddenly it takes wing, flying like an eagle toward heaven.

Do not eat the bread of a man who is stingy; do not desire his delicacies; for he is like one who is inwardly reckoning. "Eat and drink!" he says to you; but his heart is not with you.

Do not remove an ancient landmark or enter the fields of the fatherless; for their Redeemer is strong; he will plead their cause against you.

My son, if your heart is wise, my heart too will be glad. My soul will rejoice when your lips speak what is right. Let not your heart envy sinners, nor desire to be with them, but continue in the fear of the LORD all the day. Surely there is a future, and your hope will not be cut off.

Who has sorrow? Who has strife? Who has wounds without cause? Those who tarry over wine, who try mixed wine. Do not look at wine when it sparkles in the cup. Though it goes down smoothly, at the last it stings like an adder. Your eyes will see strange sights, and your mind utter perverse things. You will be like one sleeping in a stormy sea, lying on top of the mast. "They struck me," you will say, "but I was not hurt; they beat me, but I did not feel it. When shall I awake? I will seek another drink."

By wisdom a house is built; by knowledge the rooms are filled with all precious and pleasant riches.

A wise man is mightier than a strong man, and a man of knowledge than he who has strength; for by wise guidance you can wage war, and in abundance of counselors there is victory.

If you faint in the day of adversity, your strength is small. Rescue those who are being taken away to death. If you say, "Behold, we did not know this," does not he who weighs the heart perceive it, and will he not requite you according to your work?

Do not rejoice when your enemy falls, and let not your heart be glad when he stumbles; lest the LORD see it, and be displeased, and turn away his anger from him.

Fear the LORD and the king, and do not disobey either of them; for disaster from them will rise suddenly, and who knows the ruin that will come?

THESE ALSO ARE PROVERBS OF Solomon which the men of Hezekiah king of Judah copied.

It is the glory of God to conceal things, but the glory of kings is to search things out. As the heavens for height, and the earth for depth, so the mind of kings is unsearchable. Take away the dross from the silver, and the smith brings forth a vessel; take away the wicked from the presence of the king, and his throne will be established in righteousness.

Do not put yourself forward in the king's presence or stand in the place of the great; for it is better to be told, "Come up here," than to be put lower in the presence of the prince.

What your eyes have seen, do not hastily bring into court; for what will you do in the end, when your neighbor puts you to shame? Argue your case with your neighbor himself, and do not disclose his secret; lest he bring shame upon you, and your ill repute have no end.

A word fitly spoken
    is like apples of gold in a setting of silver.
Like clouds without rain
    is a man who boasts of a gift he does not give.
With patience a ruler may be persuaded,
    and a soft tongue will break a bone.
A faithless man in time of trouble
    is like a bad tooth or a foot that slips.
He who sings songs to a heavy heart
    is like vinegar on a wound.
If your enemy is hungry, give him bread to eat;
    and if he is thirsty, give him water to drink;
for you will heap coals of fire on his head,
    and the LORD will reward you.
The north wind brings forth rain,
    and a backbiting tongue, angry looks.
Like cold water to a thirsty soul,
    so is good news from a far country.
Like a muddied spring or a polluted fountain
    is a righteous man who falters before the wicked.
Like snow in summer or rain in harvest,
    so honor is not fitting for a fool.
Like a sparrow in its flitting, like a swallow in its flying,
    a curse that is causeless does not alight.
A whip for the horse, a bridle for the ass,
    and a rod for the back of fools.
Answer not a fool according to his folly,
    lest you be like him yourself.

Answer a fool according to his folly,
  lest he be wise in his own eyes.
Like a dog that returns to his vomit
  is a fool that repeats his folly.
Do you see a man who is wise in his own eyes?
  There is more hope for a fool than for him.
As a door turns on its hinges,
  so does a sluggard on his bed.
The sluggard is wiser in his own eyes
  than seven men who can answer discreetly.
He who meddles in a quarrel not his own
  is like one who takes a passing dog by the ears.
Like a madman who throws firebrands and arrows
  is the man who deceives his neighbor and says, "I am only joking!"
For lack of wood the fire goes out;
  and where there is no whisperer, quarreling ceases.

He who hates, dissembles with his lips; when he speaks graciously, believe
him not, for there are seven abominations in his heart. Though his hatred be
covered with guile, his wickedness will be exposed. He who digs a pit will fall
into it, and a stone will come back upon him who starts it rolling.

Do not boast about tomorrow,
  for you do not know what a day may bring forth.
Let another praise you, and not your own mouth;
  a stranger, and not your own lips.
A stone is heavy, and sand is weighty,
  but a fool's provocation is heavier than both.
Wrath is cruel, anger is overwhelming;
  but who can stand before jealousy?
Better is open rebuke
  than hidden love.
Sincere are the wounds of a friend;
  perverse are the kisses of an enemy.
He who blesses his neighbor with a loud voice
  will be counted as cursing.
Iron sharpens iron,
  and one man sharpens another.
As in water face answers to face,
  so the mind of man reflects the man.
The wicked flee when no one pursues,
  but the righteous are bold as a lion.
A chieftain who oppresses the poor
  is a beating rain that leaves no food.

He who augments his wealth by interest and increase
   gathers it for him who is kind to the poor.
When the righteous triumph, there is great glory;
   but when the wicked rise, men hide themselves.
He who conceals his transgressions will not prosper,
   but he who confesses them will obtain mercy.
Like a roaring lion or a charging bear
   is a wicked ruler over a people.
If a man is burdened with the blood of another,
   let him be a fugitive until death.
A miserly man hastens after wealth,
   and does not know that want will come upon him.
He who is often reproved, yet stiffens his neck,
   will suddenly be broken beyond healing.
If a ruler listens to falsehood,
   all his officials will be wicked.
If a king judges the poor with equity,
   his throne will be established for ever.
When the wicked are in authority, transgression increases;
   but the righteous will look upon their downfall.
Do you see a man who is hasty in his words?
   There is more hope for a fool than for him.
Many seek the favor of a ruler,
   but from the LORD a man gets justice.

THE WORDS OF Agur son of Jakeh of Massa.

Surely I am too stupid to be a man. I have not the understanding of a man. I
have not learned wisdom, nor have I knowledge of the Holy One. Who has
ascended to heaven and come down? Who has gathered the wind in his fists?
Who has wrapped up the waters in a garment? Who has established all the
ends of the earth? What is his name, and what is his son's name? Surely you
know!

Every word of God proves true. Do not add to his words, lest he rebuke
you, and you be found a liar.

Two things I ask of thee; deny them not to me before I die: Remove far
from me falsehood and lying; give me neither poverty nor riches; feed me
with the food that is needful for me, lest I be full and deny thee, or lest I be
poor and steal, and profane the name of my God.

The leech has two daughters; "Give, give," they cry. Three things are never
satisfied; four never say, "Enough": Sheol, the barren womb, the earth ever
thirsty for water, and the fire which never says, "Enough."

Three things are too wonderful for me; four I do not understand: the way of an eagle in the sky, the way of a serpent on a rock, the way of a ship on the high seas, and the way of a man with a maiden.

Under three things the earth trembles; under four it cannot bear up: a slave when he becomes king, a fool when he is filled with food, an unloved woman when she gets a husband, and a maid when she succeeds her mistress.

THE WORDS OF Lemuel, king of Massa, which his mother taught him:

What, my son? What, son of my womb? Give not your strength to women, my son, your ways to those who destroy. It is not for kings, O Lemuel, it is not for kings to drink wine, lest they forget what has been decreed, and pervert the rights of all. Give strong drink to him who is perishing, to those in bitter distress. Let them drink and remember their misery no more. Open your mouth for the dumb, my son, for the rights of the desolate. Open your mouth, maintain the rights of the poor.

A good wife who can find? She is far more precious than jewels. The heart of her husband trusts in her, and he will have no lack of gain. She does him good, and not harm, all the days of her life. She is like the ships of the merchant, she brings her food from afar. She rises while it is yet night and works with willing hands. She considers a field and buys it; with the fruit of her hands she plants a vineyard. She opens her hand to the poor, and reaches out her hands to the needy. She is not afraid of snow; all her household are clothed in wool. Her husband is known in the gates; he sits among the elders of the land. She makes fine linen and purple; her lamp does not go out at night. Strength and dignity are her clothing, and she laughs at the time to come. She opens her mouth with wisdom, and the teaching of kindness is on her tongue. Her children call her blessed; her husband also, and he praises her: "Many women have done excellently, but you surpass them all." Charm is deceitful, and beauty is vain, but a woman who fears the LORD is to be praised.

ECCLESIASTES

The author of this book has reflected deeply on the frustrations of human existence, and has become disappointed with the so-called good things of life. Yet, in spite of his pessimism, he advises his readers to work hard, to overdo nothing, and to enjoy the gifts of God as much and as long as they can. Although the first section is written in the person of Solomon, the son of David, the subject matter and language make it clear that the book is the work of an unknown writer who lived centuries later, perhaps 350 B.C. Ecclesiastes was thus one of the latest books to be admitted into the canon of Hebrew Scripture. Its title is an interpretation of the Hebrew word *Qoheleth*, meaning a teacher or preacher in an assembly. The New Testament contains no quotation of this book, and no certain allusion. Fragments of it have been found among the Dead Sea Scrolls at Qumran.

———

THE WORDS OF the Preacher, the son of David, king in Jerusalem.

VANITY OF VANITIES, says the Preacher, vanity of vanities! All is vanity. What does man gain by all the toil at which he toils under the sun? A generation goes, and a generation comes, but the earth remains for ever. The sun rises and the sun goes down, and hastens to the place where it rises. The wind blows to the south, and goes round to the north; round and round goes the wind, and on its circuits the wind returns. All streams run to the sea, but the sea is not full; to the place where the streams flow, there they flow again.

All things are full of weariness; a man cannot utter it; the eye is not satisfied with seeing, nor the ear filled with hearing. What has been is what will be, and what has been done is what will be done; and there is nothing new under the sun. Is there a thing of which it is said, "See, this is new"? It has been already, in the ages before us. There is no remembrance of former things, nor will there be any remembrance of things yet to happen among those who come after.

I the Preacher have been king over Israel in Jerusalem. And I applied my mind to search out by wisdom all that is done under heaven. It is an unhappy business that God has given to the sons of men to be busy with. I have seen everything that is done under the sun; and behold, all is vanity and a striving after wind. What is crooked cannot be made straight, and what is lacking cannot be numbered.

I said to myself, "I have acquired great wisdom, surpassing all who were over Jerusalem before me." I perceived that this also is but a striving after wind. For in much wisdom is much vexation, and he who increases knowledge increases sorrow.

I said to myself, "Come now, I will make a test of pleasure." But this also was vanity. I said of laughter, "It is mad," and of pleasure, "What use is it?" I searched with my mind how to cheer my body with wine and how to lay hold on folly, till I might see what was good for the sons of men to do under heaven during the few days of their life. I made great works; I built houses and planted vineyards for myself; I made gardens and parks, and pools from which to water the forest of growing trees. I had also great herds and flocks, more than any who had been before me in Jerusalem. I gathered silver and gold and the treasure of kings and provinces. I got singers, both men and women, and many concubines, man's delight. Whatever my eyes desired I did not keep from them. I kept my heart from no pleasure, and this was my reward for all my toil. Then I considered all that my hands had done, and behold, all was vanity and a striving after wind.

So I turned to consider wisdom and madness and folly. I saw that wisdom excels folly as light excels darkness. The wise man has his eyes in his head, but the fool walks in darkness; and yet I perceived that one fate comes to all of them. I said to myself, "Why then have I been so very wise?" So I hated all my toil in which I had toiled under the sun, seeing that I must leave it to the man who will come after me; and who knows whether he will be a wise man or a fool? This is vanity and a great evil.

FOR EVERYTHING THERE is a season, and a time for every matter under heaven: a time to be born, and a time to die; a time to plant, and a time to pluck up what is planted; a time to kill, and a time to heal; a time to break down, and a time to build up; a time to weep, and a time to laugh; a time to mourn, and a time to dance; a time to cast away stones, and a time to gather stones together; a time to embrace, and a time to refrain from embracing; a time to seek, and a time to lose; a time to keep, and a time to cast away; a time to rend, and a time to sew; a time to keep silence, and a time to speak; a time to love, and a time to hate; a time for war, and a time for peace. What gain has the worker from all his toil?

I have seen the business that God has given to the sons of men to be busy with. He has made everything beautiful in its time; also he has put eternity into man's mind, yet so that he cannot find out what God has done from the beginning to the end. I know that there is nothing better for men than to be happy and enjoy themselves as long as they live. It is God's gift to man that every one should eat and drink and take pleasure in his toil. I know that whatever God does endures for ever; nothing can be added to it, nor anything taken from it. God has made it so, in order that men should fear before him. That which is, already has been; that which is to be, already has been; and God seeks what has been driven away.

I saw under the sun that in the place of justice there was wickedness, and in the place of righteousness there was wickedness. I said in my heart, God will judge the righteous and the wicked, for he has appointed a time for every matter, and for every work. I said in my heart that God is testing the sons of men to show them that they are but beasts. For their fate and the fate of beasts is the same. All have the same breath; all go to one place; all are from the dust, and all turn to dust again. Who knows whether the spirit of man goes upward and the spirit of the beast goes down to the earth? And who can bring man to see what will be after him?

Again I saw all the oppressions that are practiced under the sun. And behold, the tears of the oppressed, and they had no one to comfort them! Power was on the side of their oppressors. I thought the dead more fortunate than the living; but better than both is he who has not yet been, and has not seen the evil deeds that are done under the sun.

Then I saw that toil and skill in work come from a man's envy of his neighbor. I saw a person who has no one, either son or brother, yet there is no end to all his toil, and his eyes are never satisfied with riches. He never asks, "For whom am I toiling and depriving myself of pleasure?" This is vanity and an unhappy business.

He who loves money will not be satisfied with money; nor he who loves wealth, with gain. Sweet is the sleep of a laborer, whether he eats little or much; but the surfeit of the rich will not let him sleep.

There is a grievous evil under the sun: riches kept by their owner to his hurt are lost in a bad venture. He is father of a son, but he has nothing in his hand. As he came from his mother's womb he shall go again, naked as he came, and shall take nothing for his toil. What gain has he that he toiled for the wind, and spent all his days in darkness and grief, in much vexation and sickness and resentment? A man to whom God has given the power to accept his lot and find enjoyment in his toil—this is the gift of God. For he will not reflect much on the days of his life; God keeps him occupied with joy in his heart. But a man to whom God gives wealth, possessions, and honor, so that he lacks nothing that he desires, yet does not give him the power to enjoy them; this is a sore affliction. If a man begets a hundred children, and lives many years, but does not enjoy life's good things, I say that an untimely birth is better off than he. For it comes into vanity and goes into darkness; moreover it has not seen the sun or known anything, yet it finds rest rather than he.

All the toil of a man is for his mouth, yet his appetite is not satisfied. Better is the sight of the eyes than the wandering of desire; this also is a striving after the wind. Whatever has come to be has already been named, and it is known what man is, and that he is not able to dispute with one stronger than he. The more words, the more vanity, and what is man the better?

A GOOD NAME is better than precious ointment; and the day of death better than the day of birth. It is better to go to the house of mourning than to go to the house of feasting; for this is the end of all men, and the living will lay it to heart. Sorrow is better than laughter, for by sadness of countenance the heart is made glad. The heart of the wise is in the house of mourning; but the heart of fools is in the house of mirth. It is better for a man to hear the rebuke of the wise than to hear the song of fools. For as the crackling of thorns under a pot, so is the laughter of fools; this also is vanity.

Surely oppression makes the wise man foolish, and a bribe corrupts the mind. Better is the end of a thing than its beginning; and the patient in spirit is better than the proud in spirit. Be not quick to anger, for anger lodges in the bosom of fools. Say not, "Why were the former days better than these?" For it is not from wisdom that you ask this. Wisdom is good with an inheritance, an advantage to those who see the sun. For the protection of wisdom is like the protection of money; and the advantage of knowledge is that wisdom preserves the life of him who has it. In the day of prosperity be joyful, and in the day of adversity consider; God has made the one as well as the other, so that man may not find out anything that will be after him.

In my vain life I have seen everything; there is a righteous man who perishes in his righteousness, and there is a wicked man who prolongs his life in his evil-doing. Be not righteous overmuch, and do not make yourself over-wise; why should you destroy yourself? It is good that you should take hold of this, and from that withhold not your hand; for he who fears God shall come forth from them all. Wisdom gives strength to the wise man more than ten rulers that are in a city. Surely there is not a righteous man on earth who does good and never sins.

All this I have tested by wisdom; I said, "I will be wise"; but it was far from me. That which is, is far off, and deep, very deep; who can find it out? I turned my mind to know and to search out wisdom and the sum of things, and to know the wickedness of folly and the foolishness which is madness. Behold, this is what I found, says the Preacher, adding one thing to another to find the sum, which my mind has sought repeatedly, but I have not found. One man among a thousand I found, but a woman among all these I have not found. Behold, this alone I found, that God made man upright, but they have sought out many devices.

KEEP THE KING'S command, and go from his presence when the matter is unpleasant, for he does whatever he pleases. He who obeys a command will meet no harm, and the mind of a wise man will know the time and way. For every matter has its time and way, although man's trouble lies heavy upon him, for he does not know what is to be. No man has power to retain the spirit, or authority over the day of death; there is no discharge from war, nor will wickedness deliver those who are given to it. All this I observed while applying my mind to all that is done under the sun, while man lords it over man to his hurt. Then I saw all the work of God, that man cannot find out the work that is done under the sun. Even though a wise man claims to know, he cannot find it out.

All this I laid to heart, examining it, how the righteous and the wise and their deeds are in the hand of God; whether it is love or hate man does not know. Everything before them is vanity, since one fate comes to all, to the righteous and the wicked, to the clean and the unclean, to him who sacrifices and him who does not sacrifice.

The hearts of men are full of evil and madness while they live, and after that they go to the dead. But he who is joined with the living has hope, for a living dog is better than a dead lion. The living know that they will die, but the dead know nothing.

Go, eat your bread with enjoyment, and drink your wine with a merry heart, for God has already approved what you do. Enjoy life with the wife whom you love all the days of your vain life which he has given you under the sun. Whatever your hand finds to do, do it with your might, for there is no work or thought or knowledge or wisdom in death, to which you are going.

Again I saw that the race is not to the swift, nor the battle to the strong, nor bread to the wise, nor riches to the intelligent, nor favor to the men of skill; but time and chance happen to them all. For man does not know his time. Like fish which are taken in an evil net, so the sons of men are snared at an evil time, when it suddenly falls upon them.

I have also seen this example of wisdom under the sun, and it seemed great to me. There was a little city with few men in it, and a great king besieged it. But there was found in it a poor wise man, and he by his wisdom delivered the city. Yet no one remembered that poor man. But I say that wisdom is better than might, though the poor man's wisdom is despised, and his words are not heeded. The words of the wise heard in quiet are better than the shouting of a ruler among fools. Wisdom is better than weapons of war, but one sinner destroys much good.

There is an evil under the sun, as it were an error proceeding from the ruler: folly is set in many high places, and the rich sit in a low place. I have seen slaves on horses, and princes walking on foot like slaves.

Cast your bread upon the waters, for you will find it after many days. Give a portion to seven, or even to eight, for you know not what evil may happen on earth. If the clouds are full of rain, they empty themselves on the earth, and where a tree falls, there it will lie. As you do not know how the spirit comes to the bones in the womb of a woman with child, so you do not know the work of God who makes everything. In the morning sow your seed, and at evening withhold not your hand; for you do not know which will prosper, this or that, or whether both alike will be good.

Light is sweet, and it is pleasant for the eyes to behold the sun. If a man lives many years, let him rejoice in them all; but let him remember that the days of darkness will be many. All that comes is vanity.

Rejoice, O young man, in your youth, and let your heart cheer you; walk in the ways of your heart and the sight of your eyes. But know that for all these things God will bring you into judgment.

Remember also your Creator before the evil days come, and the years draw nigh, when you will say, "I have no pleasure in them"; before the sun and the light and the moon and the stars are darkened and the clouds return after the rain; in the day when the keepers of the house tremble, and the strong men are bent, and the grinders cease because they are few, and those that look through the windows are dimmed, and the doors on the street are shut; when the sound of the grinding is low, and one rises up at the voice of a bird, and all the daughters of song are brought low. They are afraid also of what is high, and terrors are in the way; the almond tree blossoms, the grasshopper drags itself along and desire fails; because man goes to his eternal home, and the mourners go about the streets; before the silver cord is snapped, or the golden bowl is broken, or the pitcher is broken at the fountain, or the wheel broken at the cistern, and the dust returns to the earth as it was, and the spirit returns to God who gave it. Vanity of vanities, says the Preacher; all is vanity.

BESIDES BEING WISE, the Preacher also taught the people knowledge, weighing and studying and arranging proverbs with great care. The Preacher sought to find pleasing words, and uprightly he wrote words of truth. The sayings of the wise are like goads, and like nails firmly fixed are the collected sayings which are given by one Shepherd. My son, beware of anything beyond these. Of making many books there is no end, and much study is a weariness of the flesh.

The end of the matter; all has been heard. Fear God, and keep his commandments; for this is the whole duty of man. For God will bring every deed into judgment, with every secret thing, whether good or evil.

SONG OF SOLOMON

Different from all other books of the Bible, the Song of Solomon is more like love poetry. It contains no outright mention of religion, and the word God does not occur even once. Its inclusion in the Jewish and Christian canon is due to its acceptance as an allegory of God's love for Israel, or of Christ's love for the church. The book is not a single poem, but a collection of several rather disconnected poems, which are spoken by characters as in a play. In places the sense is difficult to follow, but the theme is clear: mainly it is a dialogue between a rustic Jewish maiden (the Shulammite) and her lover, with several other people present as onlookers. Also known as the Song of Songs or Canticles, the book had long been ascribed to Solomon. Modern scholars see it as a product of the third or fourth century B.C.

THE SONG OF SONGS, which is Solomon's.

> O that you would kiss me with the kisses of your mouth!
> For your love is better than wine,
> your anointing oils are fragrant,
> your name is oil poured out;
> therefore the maidens love you.
> Draw me after you, let us make haste.
> The king has brought me into his chambers.
> We will exult and rejoice in you;
> we will extol your love more than wine;
> rightly do they love you.

> I AM VERY dark, but comely,
> O daughters of Jerusalem,
> like the tents of Kedar,

like the curtains of Solomon.
Do not gaze at me because I am swarthy,
    because the sun has scorched me.
My mother's sons were angry with me,
    they made me keeper of the vineyards;
    but my own vineyard I have not kept!
Tell me, you whom my soul loves,
    where you pasture your flock,
    where you make it lie down at noon;
for why should I be like one who wanders
    beside the flocks of your companions?

If you do not know,
    O fairest among women,
follow in the tracks of the flock,
    and pasture your kids
    beside the shepherds' tents.

I COMPARE YOU, my love,
    to a mare of Pharaoh's chariots.
Your cheeks are comely with ornaments,
    your neck with strings of jewels.
We will make you ornaments of gold,
    studded with silver.

While the king was on his couch,
    my nard gave forth its fragrance.
My beloved is to me a bag of myrrh,
    that lies between my breasts.
My beloved is to me a cluster of henna blossoms
    in the vineyards of Engedi.

Behold, you are beautiful, my love;
    behold, you are beautiful;
    your eyes are doves.
Behold, you are beautiful, my beloved,
    truly lovely.
Our couch is green;
    the beams of our house are cedar,
    our rafters are pine.

I am a rose of Sharon,
    a lily of the valleys.

As a lily among brambles,
  so is my love among maidens.

As an apple tree among the trees of the wood,
  so is my beloved among young men.
With great delight I sat in his shadow,
  and his fruit was sweet to my taste.
He brought me to the banqueting house,
  and his banner over me was love.
Sustain me with raisins,
    refresh me with apples;
  for I am sick with love.
O that his left hand were under my head,
  and that his right hand embraced me!
I adjure you, O daughters of Jerusalem,
that you stir not up nor awaken love
    until it please.

THE VOICE OF my beloved!
  Behold, he comes,
leaping upon the mountains,
  bounding over the hills.
My beloved is like a gazelle,
  or a young stag.
Behold, there he stands
  behind our wall,
gazing in at the windows,
  looking through the lattice.
My beloved speaks and says to me:
"Arise, my love, my fair one,
  and come away;
for lo, the winter is past,
  the rain is over and gone.
The flowers appear on the earth,
  the time of singing has come,
and the voice of the turtledove
  is heard in our land.
The fig tree puts forth its figs,
  and the vines are in blossom;
  they give forth fragrance.
Arise, my love, my fair one,
  and come away.
O my dove, in the clefts of the rock,

in the covert of the cliff,
let me see your face,
   let me hear your voice,
for your voice is sweet,
   and your face is comely.
Catch us the foxes,
   the little foxes,
that spoil the vineyards,
   for our vineyards are in blossom.''

My beloved is mine and I am his,
   he pastures his flock among the lilies.
Until the day breathes
   and the shadows flee,
turn, my beloved, be like a gazelle,
   or a young stag upon rugged mountains.

UPON MY BED by night
   I sought him whom my soul loves;
I sought him, but found him not;
   I called him, but he gave no answer.
"I will rise now and go about the city,
   in the streets and in the squares;
I will seek him whom my soul loves."
   I sought him, but found him not.
The watchmen found me,
   as they went about in the city.
"Have you seen him whom my soul loves?"
Scarcely had I passed them,
   when I found him whom my soul loves.
I held him, and would not let him go
   until I had brought him into my mother's house,
   and into the chamber of her that conceived me.
I adjure you, O daughters of Jerusalem,
that you stir not up nor awaken love
   until it please.

WHAT IS THAT coming up from the wilderness,
   like a column of smoke,
perfumed with myrrh and frankincense,
   with all the fragrant powders of the merchant?
Behold, it is the litter of Solomon!

About it are sixty mighty men
  of the mighty men of Israel,
all girt with swords
  and expert in war,
each with his sword at his thigh,
  against alarms by night.
King Solomon made himself a palanquin
  from the wood of Lebanon.
He made its posts of silver,
  its back of gold, its seat of purple;
it was lovingly wrought within
  by the daughters of Jerusalem.
Go forth and behold King Solomon,
  on the day of the gladness of his heart.

BEHOLD, YOU ARE beautiful, my love,
  behold, you are beautiful!
Your eyes are doves behind your veil.
Your hair is like a flock of goats,
  moving down the slopes of Gilead.
Your teeth are like a flock of shorn ewes
  that have come up from the washing.
Your lips are like a scarlet thread,
  and your mouth is lovely.
Your cheeks are like halves of a pomegranate
  behind your veil.
Your neck is like the tower of David,
  built for an arsenal,
whereon hang a thousand bucklers,
  all of them shields of warriors.
Your two breasts are like two fawns,
  twins of a gazelle,
    that feed among the lilies.
Until the day breathes
  and the shadows flee,
I will hie me to the mountain of myrrh
  and the hill of frankincense.
You are all fair, my love;
  there is no flaw in you.
Come with me from Lebanon, my bride;
  come with me from Lebanon.
Depart from the peak of Amana,
  from the peak of Senir and Hermon.

You have ravished my heart, my sister, my bride,
    you have ravished my heart with a glance of your eyes,
    with one jewel of your necklace.
How sweet is your love, my sister, my bride!
    how much better is your love than wine,
    and the fragrance of your oils than any spice!
Your lips distil nectar, my bride;
    honey and milk are under your tongue;
the scent of your garments is like the scent of Lebanon.
A garden locked is my sister, my bride,
    a garden locked, a fountain sealed.
Your shoots are an orchard of pomegranates
    with all choicest fruits,
    with all trees of frankincense,
myrrh and aloes,
    with all chief spices—
a garden fountain, a well of living water,
    and flowing streams from Lebanon.

Awake, O north wind,
    and come, O south wind!
Blow upon my garden,
    let its fragrance be wafted abroad.
Let my beloved come to his garden,
    and eat its choicest fruits.

I come to my garden, my sister, my bride,
    I gather my myrrh with my spice,
    I eat my honeycomb with my honey,
    I drink my wine with my milk.

I SLEPT, BUT my heart was awake.
Hark! my beloved is knocking.
"Open to me, my sister, my love,
    my dove, my perfect one;
for my head is wet with dew,
    my locks with the drops of the night."
I had put off my garment,
    how could I put it on?
I had bathed my feet,
    how could I soil them?
My beloved put his hand to the latch,
    and my heart was thrilled within me.

I arose to open to my beloved,
    and my hands dripped with myrrh,
my fingers with liquid myrrh,
    upon the handles of the bolt.
I opened to my beloved,
    but my beloved had turned and gone.
My soul failed me when he spoke.
I sought him, but found him not;
    I called him, but he gave no answer.
The watchmen found me,
    as they went about in the city;
they beat me, they wounded me,
    they took away my mantle,
    those watchmen of the walls.
I adjure you, O daughters of Jerusalem,
    if you find my beloved,
that you tell him
    I am sick with love.

What is your beloved more than another beloved,
    O fairest among women?
What is your beloved more than another beloved,
    that you thus adjure us?

My beloved is all radiant and ruddy,
    distinguished among ten thousand.
His head is the finest gold;
    his locks are wavy,
    black as a raven.
His eyes are like doves
    beside springs of water.
His cheeks are like beds of spices,
    yielding fragrance.
His lips are lilies,
    distilling liquid myrrh.
His arms are rounded gold,
    set with jewels.
His body is ivory work,
    encrusted with sapphires.
His legs are alabaster columns,
    set upon bases of gold.
His appearance is like Lebanon,
    choice as the cedars.
His speech is most sweet,

and he is altogether desirable.
This is my beloved,
     O daughters of Jerusalem.

Whither has your beloved gone,
     O fairest among women?
Whither has your beloved turned,
     that we may seek him with you?

My beloved has gone down to his garden,
     to the beds of spices,
to pasture his flock in the gardens,
     and to gather lilies.
I am my beloved's and my beloved is mine;
     he pastures his flock among the lilies.

YOU ARE BEAUTIFUL as Tirzah, my love,
     comely as Jerusalem,
     terrible as an army with banners.
Turn away your eyes from me,
     for they disturb me.
There are sixty queens and eighty concubines,
     and maidens without number.
My dove, my perfect one, is only one,
     the darling of her mother,
     flawless to her that bore her.
The maidens saw her and called her happy;
     the queens and concubines also, and they praised her.
"Who is this that looks forth like the dawn,
     fair as the moon, bright as the sun,
     terrible as an army with banners?"

I WENT DOWN to the nut orchard,
     to look at the blossoms of the valley,
to see whether the vines had budded,
     whether the pomegranates were in bloom.
Before I was aware, my fancy set me
     in a chariot beside my prince.

RETURN, RETURN, O Shulammite,
     return, return, that we may look upon you.

Why should you look upon the Shulammite,
   as upon a dance before two armies?

How graceful are your feet in sandals,
   O queenly maiden!
Your rounded thighs are like jewels,
   the work of a master hand.
Your navel is a rounded bowl
   that never lacks mixed wine.
Your belly is a heap of wheat,
   encircled with lilies.
Your two breasts are like two fawns,
   twins of a gazelle.
Your neck is like an ivory tower.
Your eyes are pools in Heshbon,
   by the gate of Bath-rabbim.
Your head crowns you like Carmel,
   and your flowing locks are like purple;
   a king is held captive in the tresses.

How fair and pleasant you are,
   O loved one, delectable maiden!
You are stately as a palm tree,
   and your breasts are like its clusters.
I say I will climb the palm tree
   and lay hold of its branches.
Oh, may your breasts be like clusters of the vine,
   and the scent of your breath like apples,
and your kisses like the best wine
   that goes down smoothly,
   gliding over lips and teeth.

I AM MY beloved's,
   and his desire is for me.
Come, my beloved,
   let us go forth into the fields,
   and lodge in the villages;
let us go out early to the vineyards,
   and see whether the vines have budded,
whether the grape blossoms have opened
   and the pomegranates are in bloom.
There I will give you my love.
The mandrakes give forth fragrance,

and over our doors are all choice fruits,
new as well as old,
    which I have laid up for you, O my beloved.

WHO IS THAT coming up from the wilderness,
    leaning upon her beloved?

Under the apple tree I awakened you.
There your mother was in travail with you,
    there she who bore you was in travail.

Set me as a seal upon your heart,
    as a seal upon your arm;
for love is strong as death,
    jealousy is cruel as the grave.
Its flashes are flashes of fire,
    a most vehement flame.
Many waters cannot quench love,
    neither can floods drown it.
If a man offered for love
    all the wealth of his house,
    it would be utterly scorned.

MAKE HASTE, MY beloved,
    and be like a gazelle
or a young stag
    upon the mountains of spices.

ISAIAH

Isaiah received his call to prophesy in the form of a vision in the temple at Jerusalem about 740 B.C. Thus he lived during the critical period in which Israel was annexed by the Assyrians, and Judah became a tributary, threatened with the same fate. The first part of the book warns the sinners of Israel and Judah that God will punish their faithlessness through the Assyrians, but it also forecasts the wonderful reign of the Prince of Peace. The next section tells of Sennacherib's attack in 701 and how God kept Jerusalem safe—the greatest event of Isaiah's time. The latter part of the book, which appears to be of a later date, emphasizes God's majesty and mercy. In it the writer declares that God has forgiven the sins of Israel so that the people's sufferings will be at an end.

The prominent part played by Isaiah in his country's affairs made him a national figure, but he was also a poet of genius. His brilliant style and fresh imagery make his work preeminent in the literature of the Bible. From New Testament times onward, his prophecies of the coming Messiah have frequently been referred by Christian writers to the historic Christ.

THE VISION OF Isaiah the son of Amoz, which he saw concerning Judah and Jerusalem in the days of Uzziah, Jotham, Ahaz, and Hezekiah, kings of Judah.

Hear, O heavens, and give ear, O earth; for the LORD has spoken: "Sons have I reared, but they have rebelled against me. The ox knows its owner, and the ass its master's crib; but Israel does not know, my people do not understand."

Ah, sinful nation, a people laden with iniquity, offspring of evildoers, sons who deal corruptly! They have forsaken the LORD, despised the Holy One of Israel; they are utterly estranged. Why will you still be smitten, that you continue to rebel? The whole head is sick, and the whole heart faint. From the sole of the foot to the head, there is no soundness in it, but bruises and sores and bleeding wounds. Your country lies desolate, your cities are burned; in your very presence aliens devour your land; it is desolate, as overthrown by aliens. And the daughter of Zion is left like a booth in a vineyard, like a besieged city. If the LORD of hosts had not left us a few survivors, we should have been like Sodom and Gomorrah.

Hear the word of the LORD, you rulers of Sodom! Give ear to the teaching of our God, you people of Gomorrah!

"What to me is the multitude of your sacrifices? I have had enough of burnt offerings. I do not delight in the blood of bulls. When you appear before me, who requires of you this trampling of my courts? Bring no more vain offerings; incense is an abomination to me. New moon and sabbath and solemn assembly I cannot endure. When you spread forth your hands, I will hide my eyes from you; though you make many prayers, I will not listen; your hands are full of blood.

"Wash yourselves; make yourselves clean; cease to do evil, learn to do good; seek justice, correct oppression; defend the fatherless, plead for the widow.

"Come now, let us reason together, says the LORD: though your sins are like scarlet, they shall be as white as snow; though they are red like crimson, they shall become like wool. If you are willing and obedient, you shall eat the good of the land; but if you refuse and rebel, you shall be devoured by the sword; for the mouth of the LORD has spoken."

How the faithful city has become a harlot, she that was full of justice! Righteousness lodged in her, but now murderers. Your silver has become dross, your wine mixed with water. Your princes are rebels and companions of thieves. Every one loves a bribe and runs after gifts. They do not defend the fatherless, and the widow's cause does not come to them. Therefore the LORD, the Mighty One of Israel, says: "Ah, I will vent my wrath on my enemies. I will turn my hand against you and smelt away your dross as with lye. And I will restore your judges as at the beginning. Afterward you shall be called the faithful city."

Zion shall be redeemed by justice, and those in her who repent, by righteousness. But rebels and sinners shall be destroyed together, and those who forsake the LORD shall be consumed. You shall be ashamed of the oaks in which you delighted, and blush for the gardens you have chosen. For you shall be like an oak whose leaf withers, and like a garden without water. The strong shall become straw, and his work a spark, and both of them shall burn together, with none to quench them.

THE WORD WHICH Isaiah the son of Amoz saw concerning Judah and Jerusalem.

It shall come to pass in the latter days that the mountain of the house of the LORD shall be established as the highest of the mountains, and all the nations shall flow to it. Many peoples shall come, and say: "Come, let us go up to the mountain of the LORD, that he may teach us his ways and that we may walk in his paths." For out of Zion shall go forth the law, and the word of the LORD from Jerusalem. He shall judge between the nations, and shall decide for many peoples; they shall beat their swords into plowshares, and their spears into pruning hooks; nation shall not lift up sword against nation, neither shall they learn war any more.

O HOUSE OF Jacob, come, let us walk in the light of the LORD.

FOR THOU HAST rejected thy people, the house of Jacob, because they are full of diviners and soothsayers like the Philistines; and they strike hands with foreigners. Their land is filled with silver and gold, with horses and chariots; and they bow down to idols their own fingers have made. So men are brought low—forgive them not!

Enter into the rock, and hide from the terror of the LORD. For the LORD of hosts has a day against all that is proud and lifted up; against all the cedars of Lebanon and all the lofty hills; against every high tower and fortified wall; against all the beautiful ships of Tarshish. And the haughtiness of man shall be humbled and the LORD alone exalted in that day. In that day men will cast forth their idols to the moles and the bats, to enter the caverns of the rocks from before the terror of the LORD and the glory of his majesty, when he rises to terrify the earth.

Turn away from man in whose nostrils is breath, for of what account is he?

For behold, the LORD enters into judgment with the elders and princes of his people: "It is you who have devoured the vineyard, the spoil of the poor is in your houses. What do you mean by crushing my people, by grinding the face of the poor?"

And the LORD said: Because the daughters of Zion are haughty and walk with outstretched necks, glancing wantonly with their eyes, mincing along as they go, tinkling with their feet; the Lord will smite with a scab the heads of the daughters of Zion.

In that day the Lord will take away the finery of the anklets, the headbands, and the crescents; the pendants, the bracelets, and the scarfs; the head-dresses, the armlets, the sashes, the perfume boxes, and the amulets; the signet rings and nose rings; the festal robes, the mantles, the cloaks, and the handbags; the garments of gauze, the linen garments, the turbans, and the veils. Instead of perfume there will be rottenness; instead of a girdle, a rope; instead of well-set hair, baldness; and instead of a rich robe, a girding of sackcloth; instead of beauty, shame.

Your men shall fall by the sword and your mighty men in battle. Her gates shall lament and mourn; ravaged, she shall sit upon the ground. Seven women shall take hold of one man in that day, saying, "We will eat our own bread and wear our own clothes, only let us be called by your name; take away our reproach."

In that day the branch of the LORD shall be beautiful and glorious, and the fruit of the land shall be the pride and glory of the survivors of Israel.

LET ME SING FOR MY BELOVED a love song concerning his vineyard: My beloved
had a vineyard on a very fertile hill. He digged it and cleared it of stones, and
planted it with choice vines; he built a watchtower in the midst of it, and
hewed out a wine vat in it; and he looked for it to yield grapes, but it yielded
wild grapes.

Now, O men of Judah, judge, I pray you, between me and my vineyard.
What more was there to do for my vineyard that I have not done in it? When I
looked for it to yield grapes, why did it yield wild grapes? Now I will tell you
what I will do to my vineyard. I will remove its hedge, and it shall be devoured
and trampled down. I will make it a waste; it shall not be pruned or hoed, and
briers shall grow up; I will also command the clouds that they rain no rain
upon it.

For the vineyard of the LORD of hosts is the house of Israel, and the men of
Judah are his pleasant planting; and he looked for justice, but behold, bloodshed; for righteousness, but behold, a cry!

WOE TO THOSE who join house to house, who add field to field until there is no
more room and you dwell alone in the land. The LORD of hosts has sworn in
my hearing: "Surely many houses shall be desolate, large and beautiful
houses, without inhabitant. For a field shall yield but a tenth of the seed put
in."

Woe to those who rise early in the morning, that they may run after strong
drink, who tarry late into the evening till wine inflames them! They have harp
and flute and wine at their feasts; but they do not regard the deeds of the
LORD, or see the work of his hands.

Therefore my people go into exile for want of knowledge; their honored
men are dying of hunger, their multitude of thirst. Therefore the grave has
enlarged its appetite beyond measure, and the nobility of Jerusalem and her
multitude go down. Men are brought low, and the eyes of the haughty are
humbled. But the LORD of hosts is exalted in justice, and holy in righteousness. Then shall lambs graze as in their pasture, fatlings and kids shall feed
among the ruins.

Woe to those who draw iniquity with cords of falsehood, who draw sin as
with cart ropes; who say: "Let him make haste, that we may see his work; let
the purpose of the Holy One draw near, that we may know it!" Woe to those
who call evil good and good evil! Woe to those who are wise in their own
eyes! Woe to those who are heroes at drinking wine, but acquit the guilty for a
bribe and deprive the innocent of his right!

Therefore, as the tongue of fire devours the stubble, and dry grass sinks in
the flame, so their root will be as rottenness, and their blossom go up like
dust; for they have despised the word of the Holy One of Israel. Therefore the
anger of the LORD was kindled against his people, and he stretched out his
hand and smote them, and the mountains quaked; and their corpses were as
refuse in the streets. For all this his anger is not turned away and his hand is

stretched out still. He will raise a signal for a nation afar off, and whistle for it from the ends of the earth; and lo, speedily it comes! None stumbles, not a waistcloth is loose; their arrows are sharp, all their bows are bent. Like young lions they roar; they seize their prey, and none can rescue. They will growl over it on that day, like the roaring of the sea. And if one look to the land, behold, darkness and distress.

In the year that King Uzziah died I saw the Lord sitting upon a throne, high and lifted up; and his train filled the temple. Above him stood the seraphim; each had six wings: with two he covered his face, and with two he covered his feet, and with two he flew. And one called to another and said: "Holy, holy, holy is the Lord of hosts; the whole earth is full of his glory." And the foundations shook at the voice of him who called, and the house was filled with smoke. And I said: "Woe is me! For I am lost; for I am a man of unclean lips, and I dwell in the midst of a people of unclean lips; for my eyes have seen the King, the Lord of hosts!"

Then flew one of the seraphim to me, having in his hand a burning coal which he had taken with tongs from the altar. And he touched my mouth, and said: "Behold, this has touched your lips; your guilt is taken away, and your sin forgiven." And I heard the voice of the Lord saying, "Whom shall I send, and who will go for us?" Then I said, "Here am I! Send me."

And he said, "Go, and say to this people: 'Hear and hear, but do not understand; see and see, but do not perceive.' Make the heart of this people fat, and their ears heavy, and shut their eyes; lest they see with their eyes, and hear with their ears, and understand with their hearts, and turn and be healed."

Then I said, "How long, O Lord?"

And he said: "Until cities lie waste without inhabitant, and houses without men, and the forsaken places are many in the midst of the land. And though a tenth remain in it, it will be burned again, like a terebinth or an oak, whose stump remains standing when it is felled." The holy seed is its stump.

In the days of Ahaz the king of Judah, Rezin the king of Syria and Pekah the son of Remaliah, king of Israel, came up to Jerusalem to wage war against it, but they could not conquer it. When the house of David was told, "Syria is in league with Ephraim," his heart and the heart of his people shook as the trees of the forest shake before the wind.

And the Lord said to Isaiah, "Go forth to meet Ahaz, you and Shear-jashub your son, on the highway to the Fuller's Field. Say to him, 'Do not let your heart be faint because of these two smoldering stumps of firebrands, Rezin and the son of Remaliah. Because Syria, with Ephraim, has devised evil against you, saying, "Let us go up against Judah and conquer it for ourselves, and set up the son of Tabe-el as king," thus says the Lord God: It shall not come to pass. For the head of Syria is Damascus, and the head of Damascus is Rezin. And the head of Ephraim is Samaria, and the head of Samaria is Pekah the son of Remaliah. If you will not believe, you shall not be established.'"

Again the LORD spoke to Ahaz, "Ask a sign of the LORD your God; let it be deep as Sheol or high as heaven." But Ahaz said, "I will not ask, and I will not put the LORD to the test."

And Isaiah said, "O house of David! Is it too little for you to weary men, that you weary my God also? Therefore the LORD himself will give you a sign. Behold, a young woman shall conceive and bear a son, and shall call his name Immanuel. He shall eat curds and honey when he knows how to refuse the evil and choose the good. For before the child knows evil from good, the land whose kings you dread will be deserted. The LORD will bring upon you and your father's house such days as have not come since Ephraim departed from Judah."

Then the LORD said to me, "Take a large tablet and write upon it, 'Belonging to Maher-shalal-hashbaz.'" ("The spoil speeds, the prey hastes.") I got reliable witnesses to attest for me. And I went to the prophetess, and she conceived and bore a son. Then the LORD said, "Call his name Maher-shalal-hashbaz; for before he knows how to cry 'Father' or 'Mother,' the wealth of Damascus and the spoil of Samaria will be carried away. Because this people have refused the waters of Shiloah that flow gently, and melt in fear before Rezin and the son of Remaliah; therefore, behold, the Lord is bringing up against them the waters of the mighty River, the king of Assyria and all his glory. It will rise over all its banks and sweep on into Judah, reaching even to the neck; and its outspread wings will fill the breadth of your land, O Immanuel."

Give ear, all you far countries; gird yourselves and be dismayed. Take counsel together, but it will come to nought; for God is with us.

For the LORD spoke thus to me with his strong hand upon me, and warned me: "Do not call conspiracy all that this people call conspiracy, nor fear what they fear. But the LORD of hosts, him you shall regard as holy; let him be your fear. And he will become a stone of offense, and a rock of stumbling to both houses of Israel, a trap to the inhabitants of Jerusalem. And many shall stumble thereon; they shall fall and be broken; they shall be snared and taken."

BIND UP THE testimony, seal the teaching among my disciples. I will wait for the LORD, who is hiding his face from the house of Jacob, and I will hope in him. Behold, I and the children whom the LORD has given me are signs and portents from the LORD of hosts, who dwells on Mount Zion. And when they say to you, "Consult the mediums and the wizards who chirp and mutter," should not a people consult their God? Should they consult the dead on behalf of the living? To the teaching and to the testimony! Surely for this which they speak there is no dawn. They will pass through the land, greatly distressed and hungry; and they will curse their king and their God, and turn their faces upward; and they will look to the earth, but behold, distress and the gloom of anguish; and they will be thrust into thick darkness.

But there will be no gloom for her that was in anguish. In the latter time he will make glorious the land beyond the Jordan, Galilee of the nations.

The people who walked in darkness have seen a great light; those who dwelt in a land of deep darkness, on them has light shined. Thou hast multiplied the nation, thou hast increased its joy; they rejoice before thee as with joy at the harvest. For the yoke of his burden and the rod of his oppressor thou hast broken. Every boot of the tramping warrior in battle tumult and every garment rolled in blood will be burned as fuel for the fire.

For to us a child is born, to us a son is given; and the government will be upon his shoulder, and his name will be called "Wonderful Counselor, Mighty God, Everlasting Father, Prince of Peace." Of the increase of his government and of peace there will be no end, upon the throne of David, and over his kingdom, to establish it, and to uphold it with justice and with righteousness from this time forth and for evermore. The zeal of the LORD of hosts will do this.

THE LORD HAS sent a word against Jacob, and it will light upon Israel; and all the people will know, Ephraim and the inhabitants of Samaria, who say in pride and in arrogance of heart: "The bricks have fallen, but we will build with dressed stones; the sycamores have been cut down, but we will put cedars in their place."

So the LORD stirs up their enemies. The Syrians on the east and the Philistines on the west devour Israel with open mouth. For all this his anger is not turned away and his hand is stretched out still.

The people did not turn to him who smote them. So the LORD cut off from Israel head and tail, palm branch and reed in one day—the elder is the head, and the prophet who teaches lies is the tail; for those who lead this people lead them astray. Therefore the Lord does not rejoice over their young men, and has no compassion on their fatherless and widows; for every one is godless and every mouth speaks folly. For all this his anger is not turned away and his hand is stretched out still.

Through the wrath of the LORD of hosts the land is burned, and the people are like fuel for the fire; no man spares his brother. Each devours his neighbor's flesh, Manasseh Ephraim, and Ephraim Manasseh, and together they are against Judah. For all this his anger is not turned away and his hand is stretched out still.

THERE SHALL COME forth a shoot from the stump of Jesse, and a branch shall grow out of his roots. And the Spirit of the LORD shall rest upon him, the spirit of wisdom and understanding, the spirit of counsel and might, the spirit of knowledge and the fear of the LORD. And his delight shall be in the fear of the LORD.

He shall not judge by what his eyes see, or decide by what his ears hear; but with righteousness he shall judge the poor and the meek of the earth; with the breath of his lips he shall slay the wicked. Righteousness shall be the girdle of his waist and faithfulness the girdle of his loins.

The wolf shall dwell with the lamb, and the leopard shall lie down with the kid, and the calf and the lion and the fatling together; and a little child shall lead them. The sucking child shall play over the hole of the asp, and the weaned child shall put his hand on the adder's den. They shall not hurt or destroy in all my holy mountain; for the earth shall be full of the knowledge of the LORD as the waters cover the sea.

In that day the root of Jesse shall stand as an ensign to the peoples; him shall the nations seek, and his dwellings shall be glorious. In that day the Lord will extend his hand yet a second time to assemble the outcasts of Israel, and gather the dispersed of Judah from the four corners of the earth. Ephraim shall not be jealous of Judah, and Judah shall not harass Ephraim. But together they shall swoop down upon the Philistines, and put forth their hand against Edom and Moab. The LORD will utterly destroy the tongue of the sea of Egypt. And there will be a highway from Assyria for the remnant which is left of his people, as there was for Israel when they came up from the land of Egypt.

You will say in that day: "I will give thanks to thee, O LORD, for though thou wast angry with me, thy anger turned away, and thou didst comfort me. Behold, God is my salvation; I will trust, and will not be afraid; for the LORD GOD is my strength and my song." With joy you will draw water from the wells of salvation. And you will say: "Give thanks to the LORD; make known his deeds among the nations, proclaim that his name is exalted. Shout, and sing for joy, O inhabitant of Zion, for great in your midst is the Holy One of Israel."

THE ORACLE CONCERNING Babylon which Isaiah the son of Amoz saw.

On a bare hill raise a signal, cry aloud to them; wave the hand for them to enter the gates of the nobles. I myself have commanded my consecrated ones, my mighty men, to execute my anger. Hark, a tumult on the mountains, an uproar of nations gathering together! The LORD of hosts is mustering a host for battle. They come from the end of the heavens, the LORD and the weapons of his indignation, to destroy the whole earth.

Wail, for the day of the LORD is near; as destruction from the Almighty it will come! Therefore every man's heart will melt; pangs and agony will seize them; they will be in anguish like a woman in travail. They will look aghast at one another; their faces will be aflame.

Behold, the day of the LORD comes, cruel, with fierce anger. The stars and the moon will not shed their light; and the sun will be dark at its rising. I will punish the world for its evil; I will put an end to the pride of the arrogant and lay low the ruthless. I will make men more rare than fine gold. Therefore I will make the heavens tremble, and the earth will be shaken out of its place at the wrath of the LORD of hosts in the day of his anger. And like sheep with none to gather them, every man will flee to his own land. Whoever is caught will fall by the sword. Their infants will be dashed in pieces, their houses plundered, their wives ravished.

The LORD will have compassion on Jacob and will again choose Israel, and will set them in their own land, and aliens will join them and will cleave to the house of Jacob. The house of Israel will take captive those who were their captors, and rule over those who oppressed them. When the LORD has given you rest from your pain and turmoil and the hard service which you were made to serve, you will take up this taunt against the king of Babylon:

"How the oppressor has ceased! The LORD has broken the scepter of rulers that smote the peoples with unceasing blows. The whole earth is at rest; they break forth into singing. The cedars of Lebanon rejoice at you, saying, 'Since you were laid low, no hewer comes up against us.' Sheol beneath is stirred up to meet you; it rouses the shades to greet you. All who were kings of the nations will say: 'You too have become as weak as we!' Your pomp is brought down; maggots are the bed beneath you, and worms are your covering.

"How you are fallen from heaven, O Day Star, son of Dawn! How you are cut to the ground, you who laid the nations low! You said in your heart, 'I will set my throne above the clouds, I will make myself like the Most High.' But you are brought down to the Pit. Those who see you will stare at you and ponder over you: 'Is this the man who shook kingdoms, who made the world like a desert and did not let his prisoners go home?' All the kings of the nations lie in glory, each in his own tomb; but you are cast out like a loathed untimely birth. You will not be joined with them in burial, because you have destroyed your land, you have slain your people.

"May the descendants of evildoers nevermore be named! Prepare slaughter for his sons because of the guilt of their fathers, lest they rise and possess the earth."

THE LORD OF hosts has sworn: "As I have planned, so shall it be, that I will break the Assyrian in my land and upon my mountains trample him under foot; and his yoke shall depart from them, and his burden from their shoulder." This is the purpose that the LORD of hosts has purposed, and who will annul it? His hand is stretched out over all the nations, and who will turn it back?

IN THE YEAR that King Ahaz died came this oracle: "Rejoice not, O Philistia, all of you, that the rod which smote you is broken, for from the serpent's root will come forth an adder, and its fruit will be a flying serpent. The poor will feed and the needy lie down in safety, but I will kill your root with famine. Wail, O city; melt in fear, all of you! For smoke comes out of the north, and there is no straggler in his ranks."

What will one answer the messengers of the nation? "The LORD has founded Zion, and in her the afflicted of his people find refuge."

AN ORACLE CONCERNING DAMASCUS.

Behold, Damascus will cease to be a city and become a heap of ruins. Her cities, deserted for ever, will be for flocks, which will lie down, and none will make them afraid. The fortress will disappear from Ephraim, and the kingdom from Damascus; and the remnant of Syria will be like the glory of the children of Israel.

And in that day the glory of Jacob will be brought low, and the fat of his flesh will grow lean. And it shall be as when the reaper gathers grain in the Valley of Rephaim. Gleanings will be left in it, as when an olive tree is beaten—two or three berries in the highest bough, four or five on a fruit tree, says the LORD God of Israel.

For you have forgotten the God of your salvation, and have not remembered the Rock of your refuge; therefore, though you plant pleasant plants and set out slips of an alien god, though you make them blossom on the day you plant them, yet the harvest will flee away in a day of grief and incurable pain.

Ah, the thunder of many peoples, they thunder like the thundering of the sea! The nations roar like the roaring of mighty waters; but he will rebuke them, and they will flee, chased like whirling dust before the storm. At evening time, behold, terror! Before morning, they are no more! This is the portion of those who plunder us.

AH, LAND OF whirring wings which is beyond the rivers of Ethiopia; which sends ambassadors by the Nile, in vessels of papyrus upon the waters! Go, you swift messengers, to a nation tall and smooth, to a people feared near and far, a nation mighty and conquering, whose land the rivers divide.

All you inhabitants of the world, when a signal is raised on the mountains, look! When a trumpet is blown, hear!

For thus the LORD said to me: "I will quietly look from my dwelling like clear heat in sunshine, like a cloud of dew in the heat of harvest."

For before the harvest, when the blossom is over, and the flower becomes a ripening grape, he will cut off the shoots with pruning hooks, and the spreading branches he will hew away. They shall all of them be left to the birds of prey of the mountains and to the beasts of the earth.

At that time gifts will be brought to the LORD of hosts from a people tall and smooth, whose land the rivers divide.

AN ORACLE CONCERNING Egypt.

Behold, the LORD is riding on a swift cloud and comes to Egypt; the idols of Egypt will tremble and the heart of the Egyptians melt within them. I will stir up Egyptians against Egyptians, and they will fight, every man against his brother; and the spirit within them will be emptied out, and I will confound their plans. They will consult the idols and the mediums and the wizards; and I will give over the Egyptians into the hand of a hard master, says the LORD of hosts. And the waters of the Nile will be dried up; its canals will become foul, reeds and rushes will rot away, and all that is sown on the brink of the Nile will dry up and be no more. The fishermen will lament, all who cast hook in the Nile and spread nets upon it. The workers in combed flax will be in despair, and the weavers of white cotton. Those who are the pillars of the land will be crushed.

The princes of Zoan and Memphis have become fools; the wise counselors of Pharaoh give stupid counsel. How can you say to Pharaoh, "I am a son of the wise, a son of ancient kings"? Where then are your wise men? Let them tell you what the LORD of hosts has purposed against Egypt. Those who are the cornerstones of her tribes have led Egypt astray. The LORD has mingled within her a spirit of confusion; and they have made her stagger as a drunken man in all her doings. And there will be nothing for Egypt which head or tail, palm branch or reed, may do.

In that day the Egyptians will tremble with fear before the hand which the LORD of hosts shakes over them. And Judah will become a terror to them because of the purpose which the LORD has purposed against them.

In that day there will be five cities in the land of Egypt which speak the language of Canaan and swear allegiance to the LORD of hosts. There will be an altar to the LORD in the midst of Egypt, and a pillar to the LORD at its border. It will be a sign and a witness; when they cry to the LORD because of oppressors he will send them a savior, and will defend and deliver them. The LORD will make himself known to the Egyptians; and they will know him and worship with sacrifice; they will make vows to the LORD and perform them. And the LORD will smite Egypt, smiting and healing, and they will return to the LORD, and he will heed their supplications and heal them.

In that day there will be a highway from Egypt to Assyria, and the Assyrian will come into Egypt, and the Egyptian into Assyria, and the Egyptians will worship with the Assyrians. Israel will be the third with Egypt and Assyria, a blessing in the midst of the earth, whom the LORD of hosts has blessed, saying, "Blessed be Egypt my people, and Assyria the work of my hands, and Israel my heritage."

THE ORACLE CONCERNING Tyre and Sidon.

Wail, O ships of Tarshish, for Tyre is laid waste, without house or haven! From the land of Cyprus it is revealed. Be still, O merchants of Sidon; your messengers passed over the sea; your revenue was the harvest of the Nile; you were the merchant of the nations. Be ashamed, O Sidon, for the sea has spoken, saying: "I have neither travailed nor given birth."

When the report comes to Egypt, they will be in anguish over Tyre. Pass over to Tarshish, wail, O inhabitants of the coast! Is this your exultant city whose origin is from days of old, whose feet carried her to settle afar? Who has purposed this against Tyre, the bestower of crowns, whose traders were the honored of the earth?

The LORD of hosts has purposed it, to defile the pride of all glory, to dishonor all the honored of the earth. Overflow your land like the Nile, O daughter of Tarshish; there is no restraint any more. He has stretched out his hand over the sea, he has shaken the kingdoms; the LORD has given command concerning Canaan to destroy its strongholds.

Behold the land of the Chaldeans! This is the people; it was not Assyria. They destined Tyre for wild beasts. They erected their siege towers, they razed her palaces, they made her a ruin.

In that day Tyre will be forgotten for seventy years, like the days of one king. At the end of seventy years, it will happen to Tyre as in the song of the harlot: "Take a harp, go about the city, O forgotten harlot! Make sweet melody, sing many songs, that you may be remembered."

At the end of seventy years, the LORD will visit Tyre, and she will return to her hire, and will play the harlot with all the kingdoms of the world. Her merchandise and her hire will be dedicated to the LORD; it will supply abundant food and fine clothing for those who dwell before the LORD.

ON THIS MOUNTAIN the LORD of hosts will make a feast for all peoples. He will destroy the veil that is spread over all nations. He will swallow up death for ever, and the Lord GOD will wipe away tears from all faces, and the reproach of his people he will take away from all the earth; for the LORD has spoken.

This song will be sung in the land of Judah: "We have a strong city; he sets up salvation as walls and bulwarks. Open the gates, that the nation which keeps faith may enter in. Thou dost keep him in perfect peace, whose mind is stayed on thee, because he trusts in thee. Trust in the LORD for ever, for the LORD GOD is an everlasting rock. He has brought low the lofty city; he casts it to the dust, and the foot tramples it, the feet of the poor."

Thou dost make smooth the way of the righteous. In the path of thy judgments, O LORD, we wait for thee; thy memorial name is the desire of our soul. My soul yearns for thee. For when thy judgments are in the earth, the inhabitants learn righteousness. If favor is shown to the wicked, he does not learn; he deals perversely. O LORD, thy hand is lifted up, but they see it not. Let them be ashamed. Let the fire for thy adversaries consume them.

O LORD, thou wilt ordain peace for us, thou hast wrought for us all our works. O LORD our God, other lords besides thee have ruled over us, but thy name alone we acknowledge. They are dead, they will not live; they are shades, they will not arise; to that end thou hast wiped out all remembrance of them. But thou, O LORD, thou hast increased the nation; thou art glorified.

O LORD, in distress they sought thee when thy chastening was upon them. Like a woman with child, who writhes and cries out when she is near her time, so were we because of thee, O LORD; we were with child, we writhed, we have as it were brought forth wind. We have wrought no deliverance in the earth.

Thy dead shall live, their bodies shall rise. O dwellers in the dust, awake and sing for joy! For thy dew is a dew of light, and on the land of the shades thou wilt let it fall.

Come, my people, enter your chambers, and shut your doors behind you; hide yourselves for a little while. For behold, the LORD is coming forth out of his place to punish the inhabitants of the earth for their iniquity, and the earth will disclose the blood shed upon her, and will no more cover her slain.

In that day the LORD with his hard and great and strong sword will punish Leviathan the fleeing serpent; he will slay the dragon that is in the sea.

In that day: "A pleasant vineyard, sing of it! I the LORD am its keeper; every moment I water it. Lest any one harm it, I guard it night and day; I have no wrath. Would that I had thorns and briers to battle! I would set out against them, I would burn them up together. Or let them lay hold of my protection, let them make peace with me."

In days to come Jacob shall take root, Israel shall blossom and put forth shoots, and fill the whole world with fruit.

Have they been slain as their slayers were slain? He removed them with his fierce blast. Therefore by this the guilt of Jacob will be expiated, when no incense altars will remain standing.

In that day, O people of Israel, a great trumpet will be blown, and those who were lost in Assyria and those who were driven out to the land of Egypt will come and worship the LORD on the holy mountain at Jerusalem.

WOE TO THE proud crown of the drunkards of Ephraim, and to the fading flower on the head of the rich valley! Behold, the Lord has one who is mighty and strong, like a storm of hail. The proud crown of the drunkards of Ephraim will be trodden under foot; and the fading flower of its glorious beauty will be like a first-ripe fig before the summer: when a man sees it, he eats it up as soon as it is in his hand.

In that day the LORD of hosts will be a crown of glory to the remnant of his people, a spirit of justice to him who sits in judgment, and strength to those who turn back the battle at the gate.

These also stagger with strong drink, the priest and the prophet; they are confused with wine, they err in vision, they stumble in giving judgment. "Whom will he teach," they say, "to whom explain the message? Those weaned from the milk? For it is precept upon precept, precept upon precept, line upon line, line upon line, here a little, there a little."

Nay. By men of strange lips and alien tongue the LORD will speak to this people, to whom he has said, "This is rest; give rest to the weary; and this is repose"; yet they would not hear. Therefore the word of the LORD will be to them precept upon precept, precept upon precept, line upon line, line upon line, here a little, there a little; that they may fall backward, and be broken, and snared, and taken.

Hear the word of the LORD, you scoffers who rule this people in Jerusalem! Because you have said, "We have made a covenant with death and an agreement with Sheol; when the overwhelming scourge passes through, it will not come to us, for we have made lies our refuge, and in falsehood we have taken shelter"; therefore thus says the Lord GOD, "Behold, I am laying in Zion for a foundation a stone, a tested stone, a precious cornerstone, of a sure foundation: 'He who believes will not be in haste.' And I will make justice the line, and righteousness the plummet; and hail will sweep away the refuge of lies, and waters will overwhelm the shelter."

Then your covenant with death will be annulled, and when the overwhelming scourge passes through, you will be beaten down by it. As often as it passes through, it will take you, morning by morning, by day and by night; and it will be sheer terror to understand the message. For the bed is too short to stretch oneself on it, and the covering too narrow to wrap oneself in it. Now therefore do not scoff, lest your bonds be made strong; for I have heard a decree of destruction from the Lord GOD of hosts upon the whole land.

Give ear, and hear my voice. Does he who plows for sowing plow continually? Does he continually harrow his ground? When he has leveled its surface, does he not scatter dill, sow cummin, and put in wheat in rows? For he is instructed aright; his God teaches him.

Dill is not threshed with a sledge, nor is a cart wheel rolled over cummin; but dill is beaten out with a stick, and cummin with a rod. Does one crush bread grain? No, he does not thresh it for ever. This also comes from the LORD of hosts; he is excellent in wisdom.

AND THE LORD said: "Because this people draw near with their mouth and honor me with their lips, while their hearts are far from me, and their fear of me is a commandment of men learned by rote; therefore, behold, I will again do marvelous things with this people, and the wisdom of their wise men shall perish." Woe to those who hide deep from the LORD their counsel, whose deeds are in the dark, and who say, "Who sees us? Who knows us?" You turn things upside down! Shall the potter be regarded as the clay; that the thing made should say of its maker, "He did not make me"; or the thing formed say of him who formed it, "He has no understanding"?

"Woe to the rebellious children," says the LORD, "who carry out a plan, but not mine; who make a league, but not of my spirit; who set out, without asking my counsel, to take refuge in the protection of Pharaoh! Shelter in the shadow of Egypt shall turn to humiliation. For every one comes to shame through a people that cannot profit them. And Egypt's help is worthless and empty."

Now go, write it before them on a tablet, inscribe it in a book, that it may be for the time to come as a witness for ever. For they are a rebellious people, lying sons, who say to the prophets, "Prophesy not what is right; speak to us smooth things, prophesy illusions; turn aside from the path, let us hear no more of the Holy One of Israel."

Therefore thus says the Holy One of Israel, "Because you despise this word, and trust in oppression and perverseness, this iniquity shall be to you like a break in a high wall, about to collapse, whose crash comes suddenly, its breaking like that of a potter's vessel smashed so ruthlessly that not a fragment is found with which to dip up water from the cistern."

For thus said the Lord God, "In returning and rest you shall be saved; in quietness and in trust shall be your strength." And you would not. You said, "No! We will speed away upon horses." Therefore your pursuers shall be swift. A thousand shall flee at the threat of one, at the threat of five you shall flee, till you are left like a flagstaff on the top of a mountain.

THEREFORE THE LORD waits to be gracious to you; he exalts himself to show mercy to you. For he is a God of justice; blessed are those who wait for him. O people in Jerusalem, you shall weep no more. Surely at the sound of your cry he will answer you. Though he give you the bread of adversity and the water of affliction, yet your Teacher will not hide himself any more, but your eyes shall see him. Your ears shall hear a word behind you, saying, "This is the way, walk in it," when you turn to the right or turn to the left. Then you will scatter your graven images as unclean things and say to them, "Begone!" And he will give rain for the seed you sow, and grain will be plenteous. Your cattle will graze in large pastures. And upon every high hill there will be brooks running with water. Moreover the light of the moon will be as the light of the sun, and the light of the sun sevenfold, in the day when the LORD binds up the hurt of his people.

Behold, the name of the LORD comes from far, burning with his anger; his breath is like an overflowing stream that reaches up to the neck.

You shall have a song as in the night when a holy feast is kept; and gladness of heart, as when one sets out to the sound of the flute to go to the mountain of the LORD. And the LORD will cause his majestic voice to be heard and the descending blow of his arm to be seen, in furious anger and a flame of devouring fire. The Assyrians will be terror-stricken at the voice of the LORD, when he smites with his rod. For a burning place has long been prepared; yea, for the king it is made ready, its pyre with fire and wood in abundance; the breath of the LORD, like a stream of brimstone, kindles it.

Woe to those who trust in chariots because they are many and in horsemen because they are strong, but do not consult the LORD! He does not call back his words, but will arise against evildoers and the helpers of those who work iniquity. The Egyptians are men, and not God; their horses are flesh, and not spirit. When the LORD stretches out his hand, the helper will stumble, and he who is helped will fall, and they will all perish together.

For thus the LORD said to me: As a lion growls over his prey, and when a band of shepherds is called forth against him is not daunted by their shouting, so the LORD of hosts will come down to fight upon Mount Zion. Like birds hovering, the LORD of hosts will protect Jerusalem. And the Assyrian shall fall by a sword, not of man, and his officers desert the standard in panic.

DRAW NEAR, O PEOPLES, TO HEAR! Let the earth listen, and all that fills it. For the
LORD is enraged against all the nations and has given them over for slaughter.
Their slain shall be cast out, and the stench of their corpses shall rise. All the
host of heaven shall rot away and fall like leaves falling from the fig tree, and
the skies roll up like a scroll. For my sword has drunk its fill in the heavens;
and behold, it descends for judgment upon Edom, the people I have doomed.
Their land shall be soaked with blood.

For the LORD has a day of vengeance. The streams of Edom shall be turned
into pitch, and her soil into brimstone; its smoke shall go up for ever. From
generation to generation it shall lie waste; none shall pass through it. But the
hawk and the porcupine shall possess it. They shall name it No Kingdom
There, and all its princes shall be nothing. Thorns shall grow over its fortresses. It shall be the haunt of jackals, an abode for ostriches. The satyr shall
cry to his fellow; yea, there shall the night hag alight and find a resting place.
For the mouth of the LORD has commanded and his hand has portioned it out
to them; from generation to generation they shall dwell in it.

THE WILDERNESS AND the dry land shall be glad, the desert shall rejoice and
blossom; like the crocus it shall blossom abundantly, and rejoice with joy and
singing. They shall see the glory of the LORD, the majesty of our God.
Strengthen the weak hands, and make firm the feeble knees. Say to those who
are of a fearful heart, "Be strong, fear not! Behold, your God will come with
vengeance, with the recompense of God. He will come and save you."

Then the eyes of the blind shall be opened, and the ears of the deaf un-
stopped; then shall the lame man leap like a hart, and the tongue of the dumb
sing for joy. For waters shall break forth in the wilderness, and streams in the
desert; the burning sand shall become a pool, and the thirsty ground springs
of water. And a highway shall be there, and it shall be called the Holy Way;
the unclean shall not pass over it, and fools shall not err therein. No lion nor
any ravenous beast shall come up on it, but the redeemed shall walk there.
And the ransomed of the LORD shall return to Zion with singing; everlasting
joy shall be upon their heads, and sorrow and sighing shall flee away.

IN THE FOURTEENTH year of King Hezekiah, Hezekiah became sick and was at
the point of death. And Isaiah the prophet, the son of Amoz, came to him and
said, "Thus says the LORD: 'Set your house in order; for you shall die, you
shall not recover.'" Then Hezekiah turned his face to the wall, and prayed to
the LORD, saying, "Remember now, O LORD, I beseech thee, how I have
walked before thee in faithfulness and with a whole heart, and have done
what is good in thy sight." And he wept bitterly.

Then the word of the LORD came to Isaiah: "Go and say to Hezekiah, 'Thus
says the LORD: I have heard your prayer, I have seen your tears; behold, I will
add fifteen years to your life.'" And Isaiah said, "Bring a cake of figs, and
apply it to the boil, that he may recover. And this is the sign to you from the

LORD: Behold, I will make the shadow cast by the declining sun on the dial of Ahaz turn back ten steps." So the sun turned back on the dial ten steps.

A writing of Hezekiah king of Judah, after he had recovered:

I said, In the noontide of my days I must depart; I am consigned to the grave. I said, I shall not see the LORD in the land of the living; I shall look upon man no more. Like a weaver I have rolled up my life; he cuts me off from the loom; from day to night thou dost bring me to an end; I cry for help until morning. O Lord, I am oppressed; be thou my security! But what can I say? For he himself has done it. All my sleep has fled because of the bitterness of my soul.

O Lord, in these things is the life of my spirit. Oh, restore me to health! Lo, it was for my welfare that I had great bitterness; but thou hast held back my life from the Pit, thou hast cast my sins behind thy back. For the dead cannot thank thee; those who go down to the Pit cannot hope for thy faithfulness. The living, the living, he thanks thee, as I do this day; the father makes known to the children thy faithfulness. And we will sing to stringed instruments all the days of our life, at the house of the LORD.

SENNACHERIB KING OF Assyria came up against all the fortified cities of Judah and took them. Then he sent the Rabshakeh, his chief of staff, with a great army to Jerusalem. And he stood by the water conduit. There came out to him Eliakim the son of Hilkiah, who was over the household.

The Rabshakeh said to him, "Say to Hezekiah, 'Thus says the great King Sennacherib: On what do you rest this confidence of yours, that you have rebelled against me? Do you think mere words are strategy and power? Behold, you are relying on Egypt, that broken reed of a staff, which will pierce the hand of any man who leans on it. How then can you repulse the least of my captains? But if you say to me, "We rely on the LORD our God," is it without the LORD that I have come up against this land to destroy it? The LORD said to me, Go up against this land, and destroy it.'"

"Pray, speak to your servant in Aramaic," said Eliakim, "for I understand it. Do not speak in the language of Judah within hearing of the people on the wall." The Rabshakeh replied, "Has my master sent me to speak these words to your master and not to the men sitting on the wall, who are doomed with you to eat their own dung and drink their own urine?"

Then the Rabshakeh stood and called out in a loud voice in the language of Judah: "Hear the word of the great king, the king of Assyria! Thus says the king: 'Do not let Hezekiah deceive you, for he will not be able to deliver you. And do not listen when he misleads you by saying, "The LORD will surely deliver us." Has any of the gods of the nations delivered his land out of the hand of the king of Assyria? Where are the gods of Samaria? Have they delivered Samaria out of my hand, that the LORD should deliver Jerusalem?'"

But Eliakim was silent, for the king's command was, "Do not answer him." Then he came to Hezekiah and told him the words of the Rabshakeh.

Hezekiah rent his clothes and covered himself with sackcloth and went into the house of the LORD. He sent Eliakim and the senior priests, clothed with sackcloth, to the prophet Isaiah. "Thus says Hezekiah," they said to him. " 'It may be that the LORD your God heard the words of the Rabshakeh, whom the king of Assyria has sent to mock the living God, and will rebuke them; therefore lift up your prayer for the remnant that is left.' "

Isaiah replied, "Say to your master, 'Thus says the LORD concerning the king of Assyria: He shall not come into this city, or shoot an arrow there, or come before it with a shield or cast up a siege mound against it. By the way that he came, he shall return, says the LORD, and I will make him fall by the sword in his own land. For I will defend this city to save it, for my own sake and for the sake of my servant David.' "

And the angel of the LORD went forth and slew a hundred and eighty-five thousand in the camp of the Assyrians; and when men arose early in the morning, behold, these were all dead bodies. Then Sennacherib king of Assyria departed and went home to Nineveh. And as he was worshiping in the house of his god, two of his sons slew him with the sword and escaped into Ararat. And Esarhaddon his son reigned in his stead.

COMFORT, COMFORT MY people, says your God. Speak tenderly to Jerusalem, and cry to her that her warfare is ended, that her iniquity is pardoned, that she has received from the LORD's hand double for all her sins.

A voice cries: "In the wilderness prepare the way of the LORD, make straight in the desert a highway for our God. Every valley shall be lifted up, and every hill made low; and the glory of the LORD shall be revealed, and all flesh shall see it together, for the mouth of the LORD has spoken."

A voice says, "Cry!" And I said, "What shall I cry?" All flesh is grass, and all its beauty is like the flower of the field. The grass withers, the flower fades, when the breath of the LORD blows upon it; surely the people is grass. The grass withers, the flower fades; but the word of our God will stand for ever.

Get you up to a high mountain, O Zion, herald of good tidings, lift up your voice, fear not; say to the cities of Judah, "Behold your God!" Behold, the Lord GOD comes with might, and his arm rules for him; behold, his recompense is with him. He will feed his flock like a shepherd; he will carry the lambs in his bosom and gently lead those that are with young.

Who has measured the waters in the hollow of his hand, marked off the heavens with a span, and weighed the mountains in scales? Who has directed the Spirit of the LORD, or as his counselor has instructed him? Who taught him knowledge and showed him the way of understanding? Behold, the nations are like a drop from a bucket, and accounted as dust on the scales. Lebanon would not suffice for fuel, nor are its beasts enough for a burnt offering. All the nations are as nothing before him.

To whom then will you liken God, what likeness compare with him? The idol! a workman casts it, a goldsmith overlays it with gold; he who is impoverished chooses wood that will not rot and seeks out a craftsman to set up an image.

Have you not known? Have you not heard? Has it not been told you from the beginning? Have you not understood from the foundations of the earth? It is he who sits above the circle of the earth, and its inhabitants are like grasshoppers; he who stretches out the heavens like a curtain.

To whom then will you compare me, that I should be like him? says the Holy One. Lift up your eyes on high and see: who created these? He who brings out their host by number, calling them all by name; and because he is strong in power, not one is missing.

Why do you say, O Jacob, O Israel, "My way is hid from the Lord, and my right is disregarded by my God"?

Have you not known? Have you not heard? The Lord is the everlasting God, the Creator of the ends of the earth. He does not faint or grow weary, his understanding is unsearchable. He gives power to the faint, and to him who has no might he increases strength. Even youths shall faint and be weary, and young men shall fall exhausted; but they who wait for the Lord shall renew their strength, they shall mount up with wings like eagles, they shall run and not be weary, they shall walk and not faint.

BEHOLD MY SERVANT, whom I uphold, my chosen, in whom my soul delights; I have put my Spirit upon him, he will bring forth justice to the nations. He will not cry or lift up his voice, or make it heard in the street; a bruised reed he will not break, and a dimly burning wick he will not quench. He will not fail or be discouraged till he has established justice in the earth; and the coastlands wait for his law.

Thus says the Lord, who created the heavens, who spread forth the earth, who gives breath and spirit to those who walk in it: "I am the Lord, I have called you in righteousness, I have taken you by the hand; I have given you as a covenant to the people, a light to the nations, to open eyes that are blind, to bring out from prison those who sit in darkness. I am the Lord, that is my name; my glory I give to no other, nor my praise to graven images. Behold, the former things have come to pass, and new things I now declare; before they spring forth I tell you of them."

Sing to the Lord a new song, his praise from the end of the earth! Let the sea roar and all that fills it, the coastlands and their inhabitants. Let the desert and its cities lift up their voice. Let them shout from the top of the mountains. Let them give glory to the Lord. The Lord goes forth like a man of war; he shows himself mighty against his foes.

For a long time I have held my peace, I have kept still and restrained myself. Now I will cry out like a woman in travail. I will lay waste mountains; I will turn the rivers into islands and dry up the pools. And I will lead the blind in paths they have not known. I will turn the darkness before them into light, the rough places into level ground. These are the things I will do. And they shall be turned back and utterly put to shame, who trust in graven images, who say to molten images, "You are our gods."

Hear, you deaf; look, you blind, that you may see! Who is blind but my servant, or deaf as my messenger? Who is blind as my dedicated one, blind as the servant of the LORD? He sees many things, but does not observe them; his ears are open, but he does not hear. The LORD was pleased, for his righteousness' sake, to magnify his teaching and make it glorious. But this is a people robbed and plundered, trapped in holes, hidden in prisons; they have become a prey with none to rescue. Who among you will listen for the time to come? Who gave up Jacob to the spoiler and Israel to the robbers? Was it not the LORD, whose law they would not obey? So he poured upon Jacob the heat of his anger; it set him on fire round about, but he did not understand.

BUT NOW THUS says the LORD, he who created you, O Jacob, O Israel: "Fear not, for I have redeemed you; I have called you by name, you are mine. When you pass through the waters, I will be with you; when you walk through fire, the flame shall not consume you. For I am the LORD your God, the Holy One of Israel, your Savior.

"I give Egypt and Ethiopia as your ransom. Because you are precious in my eyes, and honored, and I love you, I give peoples in exchange for your life. Fear not, for I am with you; I will gather your offspring from east and west; I will say to the north and the south, Give up; bring my sons from afar and my daughters from the end of the earth, every one who is called by my name, whom I created for my glory."

Bring forth the people who are blind, yet have eyes, who are deaf, yet have ears! Let the nations assemble. Who among them can show us the former things? Let them bring their witnesses to justify them, and let them hear and say, It is true.

"You are my witnesses," says the LORD, "and my servant whom I have chosen, that you may know and believe me and understand that I am He. Before me no god was formed, nor shall there be any after me. I, I am the LORD. Besides me there is no savior. I declared and saved when there was no strange god among you. I am God, and also henceforth I am He; there is none who can deliver from my hand; I work and who can hinder it?"

Thus says the LORD, your Redeemer: "For your sake I will send to Babylon and break down all the bars, and the shouting of the Chaldeans will be turned to lamentations. I am the LORD, the Creator of Israel, your King." Thus says the LORD, who makes a way in the sea, who brings forth army and warrior: "Remember not the things of old. Behold, I am doing a new thing; now it springs forth, do you not perceive it? I will make a way in the wilderness. The wild beasts will honor me, for I make rivers in the desert to give drink to my people, the people I formed for myself, that they might declare my praise.

"Yet you did not call upon me, O Jacob; you have been weary of me, O Israel! You have not brought me your sheep for burnt offerings. You have not bought me sweet cane with money or honored me with your sacrifices. But you have burdened me with your sins.

"I, I am He who blots out your transgressions for my own sake; I will not remember your sins. Let us argue together; set forth your case. Your first father sinned, and your mediators transgressed against me. Therefore I profaned the princes of the sanctuary, I delivered Jacob to utter destruction.

"But now hear, O Jacob my servant, Israel whom I have chosen! Thus says the LORD who made you: Fear not, for I will pour water on the thirsty land; I will pour my Spirit upon your descendants, and they shall spring up like willows by flowing streams. This one will say, 'I am the LORD's,' another will call himself Jacob, and another will write on his hand, 'The LORD's,' and surname himself Israel."

Thus says the LORD of hosts: "I am the first and I am the last; besides me there is no God. Who is like me? Let him declare it before me. Who has announced from of old the things to come? Let them tell us what is yet to be. Fear not; have I not told you from of old? And you are my witnesses! Is there a God besides me? There is no Rock; I know not any."

All who make idols are nothing, and the things they delight in do not profit; their witnesses neither see nor know, that they may be put to shame. Who fashions a god or casts an image that is profitable for nothing? The craftsmen are but men; let them stand forth, they shall be put to shame together. The ironsmith fashions it over the coals; he shapes it with hammers and forges it with his strong arm; he becomes hungry and his strength fails. The carpenter marks it out with a pencil and fashions it with planes; he shapes it into the figure of a man, with the beauty of a man, to dwell in a house. He chooses an oak and lets it grow strong in the forest; he plants a cedar and the rain nourishes it. Then it becomes fuel for a man; he takes a part of it and kindles a fire and bakes bread. Over half of it he roasts meat; also he warms himself. And the rest of it he makes into a god, his idol, and worships it; he prays, "Deliver me, for thou art my god!" They know not, nor do they discern; for he has shut their eyes and their minds. No one considers, nor is there discernment to say, "Half of it I burned in the fire, I baked bread, I roasted flesh and have eaten; and shall I make the residue an abomination? Shall I fall down before a block of wood?" A deluded mind has led him astray. He cannot deliver himself or say, "Is there not a lie in my right hand?"

Remember these things, O Jacob, and Israel, for you are my servant; I have swept away your transgressions like a cloud; return to me, for I have redeemed you. Sing, O heavens, shout, O earth; break forth into singing, O forest, and every tree in it! For the LORD has redeemed Jacob, and will be glorified in Israel.

THUS SAYS THE LORD, your Redeemer: "I am the LORD, who stretched out the heavens alone—Who was with me?—who frustrates the omens of liars; who turns wise men back and makes their knowledge foolish; who confirms the word of his servant and performs the counsel of his messengers; who says of Jerusalem, 'She shall be inhabited,' and of the cities of Judah, 'I will raise up their ruins'; who says of Cyrus, 'He is my shepherd, he shall fulfil my purpose'; and of the temple, 'Your foundation shall be laid.'"

Thus says the LORD to his anointed, to Cyrus, whose right hand I have grasped, to subdue nations and ungird the loins of kings:

"I will go before you and level the mountains, I will break in pieces the doors of bronze, I will give you the treasures in secret places, that you may know that it is I, the LORD, the God of Israel, who call you by your name. For the sake of my servant Jacob, and Israel my chosen, I call you by your name, I surname you, though you do not know me.

"I am the LORD, and there is no other, besides me there is no God; I gird you, though you do not know me, that men may know, from the rising of the sun and from the west, that there is none besides me. I form light and create darkness, I make weal and create woe.

"Woe to him who strives with his Maker, an earthen vessel with the potter! Does the clay say to him who fashions it, 'What are you making?' or 'Your work has no handles'? Woe to him who says to a father, 'What are you begetting?' or to a woman, 'With what are you in travail?'"

Therefore thus says the LORD: "Will you question me, or command me, concerning the work of my hands? I made the earth and created man upon it; I have aroused Cyrus in righteousness, and he shall build my city and set my exiles free, not for price or reward," says the LORD of hosts.

Thus says the LORD: "The wealth of Egypt and the merchandise of Ethiopia, and the Sabeans, men of stature, shall come over to you and be yours; they shall come over in chains and make supplication to you, saying: 'God is with you only, and there is no other, no god besides him.'"

Israel is saved by the LORD with everlasting salvation. For thus says the LORD, who formed the earth (he established it; he did not create it a chaos, he formed it to be inhabited!): "I am the LORD, and there is no other. I did not speak in secret, in a land of darkness; I did not say to the offspring of Jacob, 'Seek me in chaos.' I the LORD speak the truth, I declare what is right. There is no other god besides me, a righteous God and a Savior. Turn to me and be saved, all the ends of the earth! By myself I have sworn, from my mouth has gone forth in righteousness a word that shall not return: 'To me every knee shall bow, every tongue shall swear.' In the LORD all the offspring of Israel shall triumph and glory."

LISTEN TO ME, O coastlands, and peoples from afar. The LORD called me from the womb, from the body of my mother he named my name. He made my mouth like a sharp sword, in the shadow of his hand he hid me; he made me a polished arrow, in his quiver he hid me away. And he said to me, "You are my servant, Israel, in whom I will be glorified."

But I said, "I have labored in vain, I have spent my strength for nothing and vanity; yet surely my right is with the LORD, and my recompense with my God."

And now the LORD says, who formed me from the womb to be his servant, to bring Jacob back to him, and that Israel might be gathered to him, for I am honored in the eyes of the LORD, and my God has become my strength—he says: "It is too light a thing that you should be my servant to restore the preserved of Israel; I will give you as a light to the nations, that my salvation may reach to the end of the earth."

But Zion said, "The LORD has forsaken me, my Lord has forgotten me."

"Can a woman forget her sucking child, that she should have no compassion on the son of her womb? Even these may forget, yet I will not forget you."

Thus says the LORD: "Where is your mother's bill of divorce, with which I put her away? Or which of my creditors is it to whom I have sold you? Behold, for your iniquities you were sold, and for your transgressions your mother was put away. Why, when I called, was there no one to answer? Is my hand shortened, that it cannot redeem? Or have I no power to deliver?"

THE LORD GOD has given me the tongue of those who are taught, that I may know how to sustain with a word him that is weary. Morning by morning he wakens my ear to hear as those who are taught. The Lord GOD has opened my ear, and I was not rebellious, I turned not backward. I gave my back to the smiters, and my cheeks to those who pulled out the beard; I hid not my face from shame and spitting. For the Lord GOD helps me; therefore I have not been confounded; I have set my face like a flint and I know I shall not be put to shame; he who vindicates me is near.

Who will contend with me? Let us stand up together. Who is my adversary? Behold, the Lord GOD helps me; who will declare me guilty? Behold, all of them will wear out like a garment; the moth will eat them up. Who among you fears the LORD and obeys the voice of his servant, who walks in darkness and has no light, yet trusts in the name of the LORD and relies upon his God? Behold, all you who kindle a fire, who set brands alight! Walk by the light of your fire, and by the brands which you have kindled! This shall you have from my hand: you shall lie down in torment.

"HEARKEN TO ME, you who pursue deliverance, you who seek the LORD; look to the rock from which you were hewn. Look to Abraham your father and to Sarah who bore you; when he was but one I called him, and I blessed him and made him many. For the LORD will comfort Zion; he will make her wilderness like Eden; and gladness will be found in her, thanksgiving, and the voice of song.

"Listen to me, my nation; for a law will go forth from me for a light to the peoples. My deliverance draws near speedily, my salvation has gone forth; the coastlands wait for me, for my arm they hope. Lift up your eyes to the heavens, and look at the earth beneath; for the heavens will vanish like smoke, and the earth will wear out like a garment, but my salvation will be for ever.

"Hearken, you who know righteousness, you in whose heart is my law; fear not the reproach of men, be not dismayed at their revilings, for the moth will eat them up like wool; but my deliverance will be for all generations."

Awake, awake, O arm of the LORD, as in days of old. Was it not thou that didst cut the sea monster Rahab in pieces, thou that didst dry up the sea for the redeemed to pass over? And the ransomed of the LORD shall return to Zion with singing; everlasting joy shall be upon their heads, and sorrow and sighing shall flee away.

"I, I am he that comforts you; who are you that you are afraid of man who dies, and have forgotten the LORD, your Maker; you who fear continually all the day because of the fury of the oppressor, when he sets himself to destroy? And where is the fury of the oppressor? He who is bowed down shall speedily be released; he shall not die and go down to the Pit, neither shall his bread fail. For I am the LORD your God, who stirs up the sea so that its waves roar—the LORD of hosts is his name. And I have hid you in the shadow of my hand, saying to Zion, 'You are my people.'"

Rouse yourself, rouse yourself, O Jerusalem, you who have drunk at the hand of the LORD the cup of his wrath, who have drunk to the dregs the bowl of staggering. There is none to guide her among all the sons she has borne, none to take her by the hand. These things have befallen you—devastation, famine, and sword; who will comfort you? Your sons have fainted, they lie at the head of every street like an antelope in a net, full of the wrath of your God.

Therefore hear this, you who are drunk, but not with wine: Thus says your God who pleads the cause of his people: "Behold, I have taken from your hand the bowl of my wrath. I will put it into the hand of your tormentors, who have said to you, 'Bow down, that we may pass over'; and you have made your back like the street for them to pass over."

Awake, awake, put on your strength, O Zion; put on your beautiful garments, O Jerusalem, the holy city; for there shall no more come into you the uncircumcised and the unclean. Shake yourself from the dust, arise, loose the bonds from your neck, O captive daughter of Zion.

For thus says the LORD: "You were sold for nothing, and you shall be redeemed without money. My people went down at first into Egypt to sojourn there; and the Assyrian oppressed them for nothing. Now therefore what have I here, seeing that my people are taken away for nothing? Their rulers wail, and my name is despised. Therefore my people shall know my name; in that day they shall know that it is I who speak; here am I."

How beautiful upon the mountains are the feet of him who brings good tidings, who publishes peace, who brings good tidings of good, who publishes salvation, who says to Zion, "Your God reigns." Hark, your watchmen lift up their voice, together they sing for joy; for eye to eye they see the return of the LORD to Zion. Break forth together into singing, you waste places of

Jerusalem; for the LORD has comforted his people, he has redeemed Jerusalem. The LORD has bared his holy arm, and all the ends of the earth shall see the salvation of our God.

Depart, depart, go out thence, purify yourselves, you who bear the vessels of the LORD. And you shall not go in flight, for the LORD will go before you, and the God of Israel will be your rear guard.

BEHOLD, MY SERVANT shall prosper, he shall be exalted and lifted up. As many were astonished at him—his appearance was so marred, beyond human semblance, and his form beyond that of the sons of men—so shall he startle many nations; kings shall shut their mouths because of him; for that which has not been told them they shall see, and that which they have not heard they shall understand.

Who has believed what we have heard? And to whom has the arm of the LORD been revealed? For he grew up before him like a root out of dry ground; he had no form or comeliness that we should look at him, and no beauty that we should desire him. He was despised and rejected by men; a man of sorrows, and acquainted with grief; and as one from whom men hide their faces he was despised, and we esteemed him not.

Surely he has borne our griefs and carried our sorrows; yet we esteemed him stricken, smitten by God. But he was wounded for our transgressions; upon him was the chastisement that made us whole, and with his stripes we are healed. All we like sheep have gone astray; we have turned every one to his own way; and the LORD has laid on him the iniquity of us all.

He was oppressed, and he was afflicted, yet he opened not his mouth; like a lamb that is led to the slaughter, like a sheep that before its shearers is dumb, so he opened not his mouth. By oppression and judgment he was taken away; and as for his generation, who considered that he was cut off out of the land of the living, stricken for the transgression of my people? And they made his grave with the wicked and with a rich man in his death, although he had done no violence, and there was no deceit in his mouth.

Yet it was the will of the LORD to bruise him; he has put him to grief; when he makes himself an offering for sin, he shall see his offspring, he shall prolong his days; the will of the LORD shall prosper in his hand; he shall see the fruit of the travail of his soul and be satisfied; by his knowledge shall the righteous one, my servant, make many to be accounted righteous; and he shall bear their iniquities. Therefore I will divide him a portion with the great, and he shall divide the spoil with the strong; because he poured out his soul to death, and was numbered with the transgressors; yet he bore the sin of many, and made intercession for the transgressors.

"SING, O BARREN one, who did not bear! For the children of the desolate one will be more than the children of her that is married, says the LORD. Enlarge the place of your tent, for you will spread abroad to right and left, and your descendants will possess the nations. You will forget the shame of your youth and the reproach of your widowhood. For your Maker is your husband, the LORD of hosts is his name; and the Holy One of Israel is your Redeemer, the God of the whole earth he is called. He has called you like a wife forsaken and grieved in spirit. For a brief moment I forsook you, in overflowing wrath, but with everlasting love I will have compassion on you, says the LORD, your Redeemer. This is like the days of Noah to me: as I swore that the waters of Noah should no more go over the earth, so I have sworn that I will not be angry with you. The mountains may be removed, but my steadfast love, my covenant of peace, shall not be removed.

"O afflicted one, storm-tossed, behold, I will set your stones in antimony, and lay your foundations with sapphires. I will make your pinnacles of agate, your gates of carbuncles, and all your wall of precious stones. All your sons shall be taught by the LORD, and great shall be their prosperity. In righteousness you shall be established; oppression and terror shall not come near you. If any one stirs up strife, it is not from me; whoever stirs up strife with you shall fall because of you. Behold, I have created the smith who produces a weapon; I have also created the ravager. No weapon that is fashioned against you shall prosper; you shall confute every tongue that rises against you in judgment. This is the heritage of the servants of the LORD, says the LORD."

"HO, EVERY ONE who thirsts, come to the waters; and he who has no money, come, buy and eat! Buy wine and milk without money and without price. Why do you spend your money for that which is not bread, and your labor for that which does not satisfy? Hearken diligently to me, and eat what is good, and delight yourselves in fatness. Come to me; hear, that your soul may live, and I will make with you an everlasting covenant, my steadfast, sure love for David. Behold, I made him a witness to the peoples, a leader for the peoples. You shall call nations that you know not, and nations that knew you not shall run to you because of the LORD your God, for he has glorified you.

"Seek the LORD while he may be found, call upon him while he is near; let the wicked forsake his way and the unrighteous man his thoughts; let him return to the LORD, that he may have mercy on him, and to our God, for he will abundantly pardon. My thoughts are not your thoughts, neither are your ways my ways, says the LORD. As the heavens are higher than the earth, so are my ways higher than your ways, and my thoughts than your thoughts. As rain and snow come down from heaven, and return not thither but water the earth, making it bring forth and sprout, giving seed to the sower and bread to the eater, so shall my word that goes forth from my mouth not return to me empty; but it shall accomplish that which I purpose.

"You shall go out in joy and peace; the mountains before you shall break forth into singing, and all the trees shall clap their hands. Instead of the thorn shall come up the cypress, instead of the brier, the myrtle; and it shall be to the LORD for an everlasting sign which shall not be cut off."

THUS SAYS THE LORD: "KEEP justice, and do righteousness, for soon my salvation will come, and my deliverance be revealed. Blessed is the man who does this, who keeps the sabbath, not profaning it, and keeps his hand from doing any evil."

Let not the foreigner who has joined himself to the LORD say, "The LORD will surely separate me from his people"; and let not the eunuch say, "Behold, I am a dry tree." For thus says the LORD: "To the eunuchs who keep my sabbaths, and hold fast my covenant, I will give within my walls a monument and a name better than sons and daughters; an everlasting name which shall not be cut off.

"The foreigners who join themselves to the LORD, to minister to him, and to be his servants, every one who keeps the sabbath, and does not profane it, and holds fast my covenant—these I will bring to my holy mountain, and make them joyful in my house of prayer; their burnt offerings and their sacrifices will be accepted on my altar; for my house shall be called a house of prayer for all peoples."

All you beasts of the field, come to devour. His watchmen are blind, without knowledge; they are all dumb dogs, they cannot bark; dreaming, lying down, loving to slumber. The dogs have a mighty appetite; they never have enough. The shepherds also have no understanding; they have all turned to their own way, each to his own gain. "Come," they say, "let us fill ourselves with strong drink; tomorrow will be like this day, great beyond measure."

"CRY ALOUD, SPARE not, lift up your voice like a trumpet; declare to my people their transgression. Yet they seek me daily, as if they were a nation that did righteousness, and they ask of me righteous judgments. 'Why have we fasted, and thou seest it not? Why have we humbled ourselves, and thou takest no knowledge of it?' Behold, in the day of your fast you seek your own pleasures and oppress all your workers. You fast only to quarrel and to fight and to hit with wicked fist. Fasting like yours this day will not make your voice to be heard on high. Is such the fast that I choose, a day for a man to humble himself? Is it to bow down his head, and spread sackcloth and ashes under him? Will you call this a fast, and a day acceptable to the LORD?

"Is not this the fast that I choose: to loose the bonds of wickedness, to let the oppressed go free, and to break every yoke? Is it not to share your bread with the hungry, and bring the homeless poor into your house; when you see the naked, to cover him? Then shall your light break forth like the dawn, and your righteousness go before you. Then you shall call, and the LORD will answer, Here I am.

"If you take away from the midst of you the yoke, the pointing of the finger, and speaking wickedness, if you pour yourself out for the hungry and the afflicted, then the LORD will guide you continually and satisfy your desire with good things; you shall be like a spring whose waters fail not. And your ancient ruins shall be rebuilt; you shall raise up the foundations of many generations; you shall be called the repairer of the breach, the restorer of streets to dwell in.

"If you turn back your foot from doing your pleasure on my holy day and call the sabbath a delight; if you honor it, not going your own ways, then I will make you ride upon the heights of the earth; I will feed you with the heritage of Jacob your father, for the mouth of the LORD has spoken."

BEHOLD, THE LORD's hand is not shortened, that it cannot save; but your sins have made a separation between you and your God. For your hands are defiled with blood, and your tongue mutters wickedness. No one goes to law honestly; they speak lies, they conceive mischief and bring forth iniquity. They hatch adders' eggs, they weave the spider's web; he who eats their eggs dies, and their webs will not serve as clothing. Deeds of violence are in their hands, and their feet run to evil; their thoughts are thoughts of iniquity. Desolation and destruction are in their highways; they have made their roads crooked, no one who goes in them knows peace.

Therefore justice and righteousness are far from us; we look for light, but we walk in gloom and grope for the wall like the blind. We all growl like bears, we moan and moan like doves; we look for justice, but there is none; for salvation, but it is far from us.

For our sins are multiplied before thee and testify against us. We know our iniquities: transgressing, and turning away from following our God, speaking oppression and revolt, conceiving and uttering from the heart lying words. Justice is turned back, and righteousness stands afar off; for truth has fallen in the public squares, and uprightness cannot enter. Truth is lacking, and he who departs from evil makes himself a prey.

The LORD saw it, and it displeased him that there was no justice. He wondered that there was no man to intervene; then his own arm brought him victory. He put on righteousness as a breastplate, and a helmet of salvation upon his head; he put on garments of vengeance for clothing, and wrapped himself in fury as a mantle. According to their deeds will he repay. So they shall fear the name of the LORD from the west, and his glory from the rising of the sun; for he will come like a rushing stream which the wind of the LORD drives.

"He will come to Zion as Redeemer, to those in Jacob who turn from transgression, says the LORD.

"This is my covenant, says the LORD: my Spirit which is upon you, and my words which I have put in your mouth, shall not depart out of your mouth, or out of the mouth of your children, or out of the mouth of your children's children, from this time forth and for evermore."

ARISE, SHINE; FOR your light has come, and the glory of the LORD has risen upon you. For behold, darkness shall cover the earth, and thick darkness the peoples; but the LORD will arise upon you, and his glory will be seen upon you. And nations shall come to your light, and kings to the brightness of your rising.

Lift up your eyes and see; they all gather together, your sons from far, your daughters carried in the arms. Then you shall see and be radiant, your heart shall thrill and rejoice; because the abundance of the sea and the wealth of the nations shall come to you. A multitude of camels shall come, the young camels of Midian and Sheba. They shall bring gold and frankincense, and proclaim the praise of the LORD. All the flocks of Kedar shall come up with acceptance on my altar; and I will glorify my glorious house.

Who are these that fly like a cloud, like doves to their windows? The ships of Tarshish first, to bring your sons from far, their silver and gold with them, for the name of the LORD your God, because he has glorified you.

Foreigners shall build up your walls, and their kings shall minister to you; for in my wrath I smote you, but in my favor I have had mercy on you. Your gates shall be open day and night, that men may bring you the wealth of the nations, with their kings led in procession. For the nation and kingdom that will not serve you shall perish. The glory of Lebanon shall come to you, the cypress, the plane, and the pine, to beautify the place of my sanctuary; and I will make the place of my feet glorious. The sons of those who oppressed you shall bow down at your feet; they shall call you the City of the LORD.

Whereas you have been forsaken and hated, I will make you majestic for ever, a joy from age to age. You shall suck the milk of nations; and you shall know that I, the LORD, am your Savior and your Redeemer, the Mighty One of Jacob. Instead of bronze I will bring gold, and instead of iron I will bring silver; instead of wood, bronze, instead of stones, iron. I will make your overseers peace and righteousness. Violence shall no more be heard in your land; you shall call your walls Salvation and your gates Praise.

The sun shall be no more your light by day, nor the moon by night; but the LORD will be your everlasting light, and your days of mourning shall be ended. Your people shall all be righteous; they shall possess the land for ever, the shoot of my planting, that I might be glorified. The least one shall become a clan, the smallest a mighty nation; I am the LORD; in its time I will hasten it.

THE SPIRIT OF the Lord GOD is upon me, because the LORD has anointed me to bring good tidings to the afflicted; he has sent me to bind up the broken-hearted, to proclaim liberty to the captives, and the opening of the prison to those who are bound; to proclaim the year of the LORD's favor and the day of vengeance of our God; to grant to those who mourn in Zion a garland instead of ashes, the mantle of praise instead of a faint spirit, that they may be called oaks of righteousness, the planting of the LORD, that he may be glorified. They shall build up the ancient ruins and repair the devastations.

Aliens shall stand and feed your flocks, foreigners shall be your plowmen; but you shall be called the priests of the LORD, the ministers of our God; you shall eat the wealth of the nations and in their riches you shall glory. Instead of dishonor you shall rejoice in your lot; yours shall be everlasting joy.

I the LORD love justice, I hate robbery and wrong; I will faithfully give them their recompense, and I will make an everlasting covenant with them. Their descendants shall be known among the nations; all who see them shall acknowledge that they are a people whom the LORD has blessed.

My soul shall exult in my God, for he has clothed me with the garments of salvation, he has covered me with the robe of righteousness, as a bridegroom decks himself with a garland, and a bride with her jewels. As the earth brings forth its shoots, so the Lord GOD will cause righteousness and praise to spring forth before all the nations.

WHO IS THIS that comes from Edom, in crimsoned garments from Bozrah, he that is glorious in his apparel, marching in the greatness of his strength?

"It is I, announcing vindication, mighty to save."

Why is thy apparel red, thy garments like his that treads in the wine press?

"I have trodden the wine press alone; from the peoples no one was with me; I trod them in my anger and trampled them in my wrath; their lifeblood is sprinkled upon my garments and I have stained all my raiment. For the day of vengeance was in my heart and my year of redemption has come. I looked, but there was no one to help; I was appalled, but there was no one to uphold me, so my own arm brought me victory. I trod down the peoples in my anger, I made them drunk in my wrath, and I poured out their lifeblood on the earth."

I WILL RECOUNT the steadfast love of the LORD, the praises of the LORD, according to the great goodness to the house of Israel which he has granted them. For he said, Surely they are my people, sons who will not deal falsely; and he became their Savior. In their affliction he was afflicted, and the angel of his presence saved them; in his love and pity he redeemed them; he lifted them up and carried them all the days of old.

But they rebelled and grieved his holy Spirit; therefore he himself fought against them. Then he remembered the days of Moses his servant. Where is he who brought up out of the sea the shepherds of his flock? Where is he who put in the midst of them his holy Spirit, who caused his glorious arm to go at the right hand of Moses, who divided the waters before them? So thou didst lead thy people, to make for thyself a glorious name.

Look down and see, from thy holy habitation. Where are thy zeal and thy compassion? For thou art our Father, though Abraham does not know us; thou, O LORD, art our Father, our Redeemer from of old. O LORD, why dost thou make us err from thy ways and harden our heart, so that we fear thee not? Return for the sake of thy servants. Thy holy people possessed thy sanctuary a little while; our adversaries have trodden it down. We have become like those over whom thou hast never ruled, like those who are not called by thy name.

Yet, O LORD, thou art our Father; we are the clay, and thou art our potter; we are all the work of thy hand. O LORD, remember not iniquity for ever. Consider, we are all thy people. Thy holy cities have become a wilderness. Our holy and beautiful house, where our fathers praised thee, has been burned by fire; all our pleasant places are ruins. Wilt thou keep silent, O LORD, and afflict us sorely?

I WAS READY to be sought by those who did not ask for me; I was ready to be found by those who did not seek me. I said, "Here am I, here am I," to a nation that did not call on my name.

I spread out my hands all day to a rebellious people, who provoke me continually, sacrificing in gardens and burning incense; who sit in tombs; who eat swine's flesh and broth of abominable things; who say, "Keep to yourself, I am set apart from you." These are a smoke in my nostrils, a fire that burns all the day.

Behold, it is written before me: "I will not keep silent, but I will repay their iniquities and their fathers' iniquities together, says the LORD; because they burned incense upon the mountains and reviled me upon the hills, I will measure into their bosom payment for their former doings."

Thus says the LORD: "As the wine is found in the cluster, and they say, 'Do not destroy it, for there is a blessing in it,' so I will do for my servants' sake, and not destroy them all. I will bring forth descendants from Jacob, and from Judah inheritors of my mountains, and my servants shall dwell there.

"For behold, I create new heavens and a new earth; and the former things shall not come into mind. Be glad, for I create Jerusalem a rejoicing, and her people a joy. I will rejoice in Jerusalem; no more shall be heard in it the sound of weeping; no more shall there be in it an infant that lives but a few days, or an old man who does not fill out his days.

"They shall build houses and inhabit them; they shall plant vineyards and eat their fruit. They shall not build and another inhabit, or plant and another eat. They shall not labor in vain, or bear children for calamity; for they shall be the offspring of the blessed of the LORD. Before they call I will answer, while they are yet speaking I will hear. The wolf and the lamb shall feed together, the lion shall eat straw like the ox; and dust shall be the serpent's food. They shall not hurt or destroy in all my holy mountain, says the LORD."

THUS SAYS THE LORD: "Heaven is my throne and the earth is my footstool; what is the house which you would build for me, and what is the place of my rest? All these things my hand has made, so all these things are mine. But this is the man to whom I will look, he that is humble and contrite in spirit, and trembles at my word.

"He who slaughters an ox is like him who kills a man; he who sacrifices a lamb, like him who breaks a dog's neck; he who presents a cereal offering, like him who offers swine's blood; he who makes an offering of frankincense, like him who blesses an idol. These have chosen their own ways; their soul delights in abominations. I also will choose affliction for them, because when I spoke they did not listen, but did what was evil in my eyes."

Hear the word of the LORD, you who tremble at his word: "Your brethren who hate you and cast you out for my name's sake have said, 'Let the LORD be glorified, that we may see your joy'; but it is they who shall be put to shame.

"Hark, an uproar from the city! A voice from the temple! The voice of the LORD, rendering recompense to his enemies!

"Before she was in labor she gave birth; before her pain came upon her she was delivered of a son. Who has heard such a thing? Shall a land be born in one day? For as soon as Zion was in labor she brought forth her sons. Shall I bring to the birth and not cause to bring forth? says the LORD; shall I, who cause to bring forth, shut the womb?

"Rejoice with Jerusalem, all you who love her; rejoice, that you may drink deeply from the abundance of her glory. Behold, I will extend prosperity to her like an overflowing stream; and you shall suck and be carried upon her hip, and dandled upon her knees. As one whom his mother comforts, so I will comfort you; your heart shall rejoice; your bones shall flourish; and it shall be known that the hand of the LORD is with his servants, and his indignation is against his enemies.

"Behold, the LORD will come in fire, and his chariots like the stormwind, to render his anger in fury. By fire will the LORD execute judgment, and by his sword, upon all flesh; and those slain by the LORD shall be many.

"Those who sanctify and purify themselves to go into the gardens, following one in the midst, eating swine's flesh and the abomination and mice, shall come to an end together, says the LORD.

"I am coming to gather all nations and tongues; they shall come and shall see my glory, and I will set a sign among them. And from them I will send survivors to the nations, to Tarshish, and to the coastlands afar off that have not seen my glory; and they shall declare my glory among the nations. And they shall bring all your brethren from all the nations as an offering to the LORD, upon horses, and in chariots, and in litters, and upon mules, and upon dromedaries, to my holy mountain Jerusalem, says the LORD, just as the Israelites bring their cereal offering in a clean vessel to the house of the LORD. And some of them also I will take for priests and for Levites, says the LORD.

"For as the new heavens and the new earth which I will make shall remain before me, so shall your descendants and your name remain. From new moon to new moon, and from sabbath to sabbath, all flesh shall come to worship before me, says the LORD.

"And they shall go forth and look on the dead bodies of the men that have rebelled against me; for their worm shall not die, their fire shall not be quenched, and they shall be an abhorrence to all flesh."

JEREMIAH

The life of Jeremiah is much better known than that of any other Old
Testament prophet. He was called by God in 627 B.C., while still a young
man. With great eloquence, backed by threats of judgment and doom, he
summoned his people to moral reform, proclaiming the goodness and power
of the Lord. He warned the people of Judah to forsake idols, return to righteousness, and cultivate purity of heart, lest God's justice bring them catas-
trophe. Eventually he aroused the hostility of the Jewish establishment, and
he was imprisoned. When Jerusalem fell, in 586 B.C., he was not among
those taken into exile in Babylon, but later a band of conspirators took him
with them to Egypt, where his story ends.

The influence of Jeremiah increased after his death, when his secretary,
Baruch, gathered his prophecies together, though not in strict chronological
order. Despite the thundering associated with his name, he was a man of
great sensitivity, even tenderness. One of the high points of his teaching is the
promise that God will make a new covenant with his people, writing his law
on their hearts. Then, he predicts, both Jews and Gentiles will enjoy a new
day under the rule of a messianic king.

THE WORDS OF Jeremiah, the son of Hilkiah, of the priests who were in
Anathoth in the land of Benjamin, to whom the word of the LORD came in the
days of Josiah, king of Judah, in the thirteenth year of his reign. It came also in
the days of Jehoiakim the son of Josiah, and until the end of the eleventh year
of Zedekiah the son of Josiah, until the captivity of Jerusalem in the fifth
month.

Now the word of the LORD came to me, saying, "Before I formed you in the
womb I knew you, and before you were born I consecrated you; I appointed
you a prophet to the nations."

Then I said, "Ah, Lord GOD! Behold, I do not know how to speak, for I am only a youth." But the LORD said to me, "Do not say, 'I am only a youth'; for to all to whom I send you you shall go, and whatever I command you you shall speak. Be not afraid of them, for I am with you to deliver you." Then the LORD put forth his hand and touched my mouth, and said, "Behold, I have put my words in your mouth. See, I have set you this day over nations and over kingdoms, to pluck up and to break down, to destroy and to overthrow, to build and to plant."

The word of the LORD came to me, saying, "Jeremiah, what do you see?" I said, "I see a rod of almond." The LORD said, "You have seen well, for I am watching over my word to perform it."

The word of the LORD came to me a second time, saying, "What do you see?" And I said, "I see a boiling pot, facing away from the north." The LORD said, "Out of the north evil shall break forth upon all the inhabitants of the land. For lo, I am calling all the tribes of the kingdoms of the north, says the LORD; and they shall come and every one shall set his throne at the entrance of the gates of Jerusalem, against all its walls round about, and against all the cities of Judah. And I will utter my judgments against them, for all their wickedness in forsaking me; they have burned incense to other gods, and worshiped the works of their own hands.

"But you, gird up your loins; arise, and say to them everything that I command you. Do not be dismayed by them, lest I dismay you before them. And I, behold, I make you this day a fortified city, an iron pillar, and bronze walls, against the whole land, against the kings of Judah, its princes, its priests, and the people of the land. They will fight against you; but they shall not prevail against you, for I am with you, says the LORD, to deliver you."

THE WORD OF the LORD came to me, saying, "Go and proclaim in the hearing of Jerusalem, Thus says the LORD, I remember the devotion of your youth, your love as a bride, how you followed me in the wilderness, in a land not sown. Israel was holy to the LORD, the first fruits of his harvest. What wrong did your fathers find in me that they went far from me, and went after worthlessness? I brought you into a plentiful land to enjoy its fruits and good things; but you made my heritage an abomination. The priests did not say, 'Where is the LORD?' Those who handle the law did not know me; the rulers transgressed against me; the prophets prophesied by Baal.

"Therefore I still contend with you, says the LORD, and with your children's children I will contend. Has a nation changed its gods, even though they are no gods? My people have changed their glory for that which does not profit. Be appalled, O heavens, for my people have committed two evils: they have forsaken me, the fountain of living waters, and hewed out cisterns for themselves, broken cisterns, that can hold no water.

"How can you say, 'I am not defiled, I have not gone after the Baals'? Look at your way in the valley; know what you have done. As a thief is shamed when caught, so the house of Israel shall be shamed: they, their kings, their princes, their priests, and their prophets, who say to a tree, 'You are my father,' and to a stone, 'You gave me birth.' For they have turned their back to me, and not their face. But in the time of their trouble they say, 'Arise and save us!' Where then are your gods that you made for yourself? Let them arise, if they can save you; for as many as your cities are your gods, O Judah."

"IF A MAN divorces his wife and she goes from him and becomes another man's wife, will he return to her? Would not that land be greatly polluted? You have played the harlot with many lovers; and would you return to me? says the LORD. Lift up your eyes to the bare heights, and see! Where have you not been lain with? You have polluted the land with your vile harlotry. Therefore the showers have been withheld, and the spring rain has not come; yet you refuse to be ashamed.

"Have you not just now called to me, 'My father, thou art the friend of my youth—will he be angry for ever?' Behold, you have spoken, but you have done all the evil that you could."

The LORD said to me in the days of King Josiah: "Have you seen what she did, that faithless one, Israel, how on every high hill and under every green tree she played the harlot? I thought, 'After she has done all this she will return to me'; but she did not. Her false sister Judah saw it; she saw that for all the adulteries I had sent Israel away with a decree of divorce. Yet Judah did not fear, but she too went and played the harlot, polluting the land, committing adultery with stone and tree. Yet for all this, Judah did not return to me with her whole heart, but in pretense.

"Faithless Israel has shown herself less guilty than false Judah. Go, proclaim these words toward the north: 'Return, faithless Israel, for I am merciful, says the LORD; I will not be angry for ever. Only acknowledge your guilt, that you rebelled against the LORD your God and have not obeyed my voice. Return, O faithless children, says the LORD; for I am your master; I will take you, one from a city and two from a family, and I will bring you to Zion. I will give you shepherds after my own heart, who will feed you with knowledge and understanding. And when you have multiplied and increased in the land, Jerusalem shall be called the throne of the LORD, and all nations shall gather to it, to the presence of the LORD, and they shall no more stubbornly follow their own evil heart. The house of Judah shall join the house of Israel, and together they shall come from the north to the land that I gave your fathers.

"'I thought how I would set you among my sons, and give you a pleasant land, a heritage most beauteous of all nations. And I thought you would call me, My Father, and would not turn from following me. Surely, as a faithless wife leaves her husband, so have you been faithless to me, O house of Israel, says the LORD.'"

A voice on the bare heights is heard, the weeping and pleading of Israel's sons, because they have perverted their way. They have forgotten the LORD their God.

"Return, O faithless sons, I will heal your faithlessness."

"Behold, we come to thee; for thou art the LORD our God. Truly the hills are a delusion, the orgies on the mountains. Truly in the LORD our God is the salvation of Israel. But from our youth Baal has devoured all for which our fathers labored. Let us lie down in our shame, and let our dishonor cover us; for we have sinned against the LORD our God, we and our fathers, from our youth even to this day."

"If you return, O Israel, says the LORD, to me you should return. If you remove your abominations and do not waver, if you swear, 'As the LORD lives,' in truth, in justice, and in uprightness, then nations shall bless themselves in him, and in him shall they glory."

For thus says the LORD to the men of Judah: "Break up your fallow ground, and sow not among thorns. Circumcise yourselves to the LORD, remove the foreskin of your hearts; lest my wrath go forth like fire, and burn with none to quench it, because of the evil of your doings."

PROCLAIM IN JERUSALEM: "Blow the trumpet through the land; cry aloud, 'Assemble, and let us go into the fortified cities!' Flee for safety, for I bring evil from the north. A lion has gone up from his thicket, a destroyer of nations has set out from his place to make your land a waste; your cities will be ruins without inhabitant. Gird you with sackcloth, lament and wail; for the fierce anger of the LORD has not turned back from us."

"In that day, says the LORD, courage shall fail both king and princes; the priests and the prophets shall be astounded." Then I said, "Ah, Lord GOD, surely thou hast utterly deceived this people, saying, 'It shall be well with you'; whereas the sword has reached their very life."

At that time it will be said to Jerusalem, "A hot wind from the desert toward the daughter of my people—not to winnow or cleanse, a wind too full for this—comes for me. Now it is I who speak in judgment upon them."

Behold, he comes up like clouds, his chariots like the whirlwind; his horses swifter than eagles—woe to us! O Jerusalem, wash your heart from wickedness, that you may be saved. How long shall your evil thoughts lodge within you? For a voice proclaims from Mount Ephraim: "Besiegers come from a distant land; they shout against Judah. Like keepers of a field are they against her round about, because she has rebelled against me, says the LORD. Your ways and your doings have brought this upon you. This is your doom; it has reached your very heart."

My anguish, my anguish! I writhe in pain! Oh, the walls of my heart! My heart is beating wildly; I cannot keep silent; for I hear the alarm of war. Disaster follows disaster, the whole land is laid waste. How long must I hear the sound of the trumpet?

"My people are foolish, they know me not; they have no understanding. They are skilled in doing evil, but how to do good they know not."

I looked on the earth, and lo, it was void; and to the heavens, and they had no light. I looked on the mountains, and they were quaking. I looked, and there was no man, and all the birds of the air had fled. I looked, and the fruitful land was a desert, and its cities were laid in ruins before the LORD, before his fierce anger.

For thus says the LORD, "The whole land shall be a desolation; yet I will not make a full end. The earth shall mourn, and the heavens be black; for I have spoken; I have not relented nor will I turn back."

At the noise of horseman and archer every city takes to flight; they enter thickets; they climb among rocks. And you, O desolate one, what do you mean that you dress in scarlet, deck yourself with ornaments of gold, enlarge your eyes with paint? In vain you beautify yourself. Your lovers despise you; they seek your life. I heard a cry as of one bringing forth her first child, the daughter of Zion gasping for breath, stretching out her hands, "Woe is me! I am fainting before murderers."

THE WORD THAT came to Jeremiah from the LORD: "Stand in the gate of the LORD's house, and proclaim there, Hear the word of the LORD, all you men of Judah who enter these gates to worship. Amend your ways, and I will let you dwell in this place. Do not trust in these deceptive words: 'This is the temple of the LORD, the temple of the LORD, the temple of the LORD.' For if you truly amend your doings, if you truly execute justice one with another, if you do not oppress the alien, the fatherless, or the widow, or shed innocent blood in this place, and if you do not go after other gods to your own hurt, then I will let you dwell in this land that I gave to your fathers for ever.

"Behold, you trust in deceptive words to no avail. Will you steal, murder, commit adultery, swear falsely, burn incense to Baal, and then stand before me in this house, which is called by my name, and say, 'We are delivered!'—only to go on doing all these abominations?

"Has this house become a den of robbers in your eyes? Behold, I myself have seen it, says the LORD. Go now to my place that was in Shiloh, where I made my name dwell at first, and see what I did to it for the wickedness of my people Israel. And now, because you have done all these things, says the LORD, and when I called you, you did not answer, therefore I will do to this house as I did to Shiloh. And I will cast you out of my sight, as I cast out your kinsmen of Ephraim.

"As for you, do you pray for this people, and do not intercede for them with me, for I do not hear you. Do you not see what they are doing in the streets of Jerusalem? The children gather wood, the fathers kindle fire, and the women knead dough to make cakes for the queen of heaven; and they pour out drink offerings to other gods, to provoke me to anger. Is it I whom they provoke? says the LORD. Is it not themselves, to their own confusion? Therefore my wrath will be poured out on this place, upon man and beast, upon the trees of the field and the fruit of the ground; it will burn and not be quenched."

Thus says the LORD of hosts, the God of Israel: "Add your burnt offerings to your sacrifices, and eat the flesh. For in the day that I brought them out of Egypt, I did not speak to your fathers concerning burnt offerings. But this command I gave them, 'Obey my voice, and I will be your God, and you shall be my people; and walk in all the way that I command you, that it may be well with you.' They did not obey, but walked in their own counsels, and went backward and not forward. From the day your fathers came out of Egypt to this day, I have persistently sent the prophets to this people; yet they did not incline their ear, but stiffened their neck. They did worse than their fathers.

"So you shall speak all these words to them, but they will not listen. You shall say to them, 'This is the nation that did not obey the voice of their God, and did not accept discipline; truth has perished; it is cut off from their lips. Raise a lamentation on the heights, for the LORD has rejected and forsaken the generation of his wrath.'"

MY GRIEF IS beyond healing, my heart is sick within me. Hark, the cry of the daughter of my people from the length and breadth of the land: "Is the LORD not in Zion? Is her King not in her? The harvest is past, the summer is ended, and we are not saved." For the wound of the daughter of my people is my heart wounded, I mourn, and dismay has taken hold on me.

Is there no balm in Gilead? Is there no physician there? Why then has the health of the daughter of my people not been restored? O that my head were waters, and my eyes a fountain of tears, that I might weep day and night for the slain of the daughter of my people!

O THAT I had in the desert a wayfarers' lodging place, that I might go away from my people! For they are treacherous men. They bend their tongue like a bow; falsehood has grown strong in the land; they proceed from evil to evil, says the LORD. Let every one beware of his neighbor, and put no trust in any brother; for every brother is a supplanter, and every neighbor a slanderer, and no one speaks the truth; they commit iniquity and are too weary to repent. Heaping deceit upon deceit, they refuse to know me.

Therefore thus says the LORD of hosts: "Behold, I will refine and test them, for what else can I do? Their tongue is a deadly arrow; with his mouth each speaks peaceably to his neighbor, but in his heart he plans an ambush for him. Shall I not punish them for these things?

"Take up weeping and wailing for the mountains, and a lamentation for the pastures because they are laid waste; the lowing of cattle is not heard; the birds and the beasts have fled. I will make Jerusalem a lair of jackals, and the cities of Judah a desolation."

Who is the man so wise that he can understand this? To whom has the mouth of the LORD spoken, that he may declare it? Why is the land ruined, so that no one passes through? And the LORD says: "Because they have forsaken my law and have not obeyed my voice, but have gone after the Baals. Therefore I will feed this people with wormwood. I will scatter them among nations whom neither they nor their fathers have known; and I will send the sword after them, until I have consumed them.

"Hear, O women, the word of the LORD; teach to your daughters a lament, and each to her neighbor a dirge. For death has come up into our windows, it has entered our palaces, cutting off the children from the streets and the young men from the squares."

Thus says the LORD: "Let not the wise man glory in his wisdom, let not the mighty man glory in his might, let not the rich man glory in his riches; but let him who glories glory in this, that he understands and knows me, that I am the LORD who practice steadfast love, justice, and righteousness in the earth; for in these things I delight."

THE WORD THAT came to Jeremiah from the LORD: "Hear the words of this covenant, and speak to the men of Judah and the inhabitants of Jerusalem. You shall say to them, Thus says the LORD, the God of Israel: Cursed be the man who does not heed the words of this covenant which I commanded your fathers when I brought them out of the land of Egypt, saying, Listen to my voice, and do all that I command you. So shall you be my people, and I will be your God, that I may perform the oath which I swore to your fathers, to give them a land flowing with milk and honey, as at this day." Then I answered, "So be it, LORD."

And the LORD said to me, "I solemnly warned your fathers, warning them persistently even to this day, saying, Obey my voice. Yet they did not, but every one walked in the stubbornness of his evil heart. Therefore I brought upon them all the words of this covenant, which I commanded them to do, but they did not."

Again the LORD said to me, "There is revolt among the men of Judah. They have turned back to the iniquities of their forefathers, who refused to hear my words; they have gone after other gods; the houses of Israel and Judah have broken my covenant which I made with their fathers. Therefore, thus says the LORD, Behold, I am bringing evil upon them which they cannot escape; though they cry to me, I will not listen to them. Then they will go and cry to the gods to whom they burn incense, but they cannot save them in time of trouble. For as many as the streets of Jerusalem, O Judah, are the altars you have set up to Baal.

"Therefore do not pray for this people, or lift up a cry on their behalf, for I will not listen when they call. What right has my beloved in my house, when she has done vile deeds? Can vows and sacrificial flesh avert your doom? The LORD once called you, 'A green olive tree, fair with goodly fruit'; but with the roar of a great tempest he will set fire to it, and its branches will be consumed. The LORD of hosts, who planted you, has pronounced evil against you, because of the evil which you have done, provoking me to anger by burning incense to Baal."

THE LORD MADE KNOWN TO ME the evil deeds of my neighbors of Anathoth. But I was like a gentle lamb led to the slaughter. I did not know it was against me they devised schemes, saying, "Let us cut him off from the land of the living, that his name be remembered no more." O LORD of hosts, who judgest righteously, let me see thy vengeance upon them, for to thee have I committed my cause.

Concerning the men of Anathoth, who say, "Do not prophesy in the name of the LORD or you will die by our hand," thus says the LORD: "Behold, I will bring evil upon the men of Anathoth."

Righteous art thou, O LORD, when I complain to thee; yet I would plead my case before thee. Why does the way of the wicked prosper? Why do all who are treacherous thrive? Thou plantest them, and they bring forth fruit; thou art near in their mouth and far from their heart. But thou knowest me, and triest my mind toward thee. Pull them out like sheep for the slaughter.

"If you have raced with men on foot and they have wearied you, how will you compete with horses? And if in a safe land you fall down, how will you do in the jungle of the Jordan? For even your brothers and the house of your father have dealt treacherously with you; even they are in full cry after you; believe them not, though they speak fair words to you."

"I HAVE FORSAKEN my house, I have given the beloved of my soul into the hands of her enemies. My heritage has become to me like a lion in the forest, she has lifted up her voice against me; therefore I hate her. Is my heritage to me like a speckled bird of prey, with other birds of prey against her round about? Go, assemble all the wild beasts; bring them to devour.

"Many shepherds have destroyed my vineyard, they have made my pleasant portion a wilderness. Desolate, it mourns to me, but no man lays it to heart. Upon the heights in the desert destroyers have come; the sword of the LORD devours from one end of the land to the other; no flesh has peace. They have sown wheat and reaped thorns, they have tired themselves out but profit nothing. They shall be ashamed of their harvests because of the fierce anger of the LORD."

Thus says the LORD concerning all my evil neighbors who touch the heritage given my people Israel: "Behold, I will pluck them up from their land, and Judah from among them. After I have plucked them up, I will again have compassion on them, and bring them again each to his heritage. This shall come to pass, if they will diligently learn the ways of my people: to swear by my name, 'As the LORD lives,' even as they taught my people to swear by Baal. But if any nation will not listen, then I will utterly pluck it up and destroy it, says the LORD."

THE LORD SAID to me, "Go and buy a linen waistcloth, and put it on your loins, and do not dip it in water." So I bought a waistcloth and put it on my loins. The word of the LORD came to me a second time, "Take the waistcloth which is upon your loins, go to the Euphrates, and hide it there in a cleft of the rock." So I went, and hid it by the Euphrates, as the LORD commanded. After many days the LORD said to me, "Arise, take the waistcloth I commanded you to hide." Then I went to the Euphrates, and dug, and I took the waistcloth from where I had hidden it. And behold, it was spoiled, good for nothing.

Then the word of the LORD came to me: "Even so will I spoil the pride of Judah and the great pride of Jerusalem. This stubborn people who follow their own heart and have gone after other gods shall be like this waistcloth, which is good for nothing. For as the waistcloth clings to the loins of a man, so I made the houses of Israel and Judah cling to me, says the LORD, that they might be for me a people, a name, a praise, and a glory, but they would not listen.

"You shall speak to them this word: 'Thus says the LORD, the God of Israel: Every jar shall be filled with wine.' They will say, 'Do we not indeed know that?' Then you shall say, 'Thus says the LORD: Behold, I will fill with drunkenness all the inhabitants of this land: the kings who sit on David's throne, the priests, the prophets, and all the inhabitants of Jerusalem. And I will dash them one against another, fathers and sons together, says the LORD.'

"Can the Ethiopian change his skin or the leopard his spots? Then also you can do good who are accustomed to do evil. I will scatter you like chaff driven by the wind from the desert. This is the portion I have measured out to you, says the LORD, because you have trusted in lies. I have seen your abominations on the hills in the field. Woe to you, O Jerusalem! How long will it be before you are made clean?"

THE WORD OF the LORD which came to Jeremiah concerning the drought:

"Judah mourns and her gates languish; her people lament on the ground, and the cry of Jerusalem goes up. Her nobles send their servants for water; they come to the cisterns, find no water, return with their vessels empty; confounded, they cover their heads. Because of the ground which is dismayed since there is no rain, the farmers are ashamed and cover their heads. The hind in the field forsakes her newborn calf because there is no grass. The wild asses stand on the bare heights, they pant for air like jackals.

"Though our iniquities testify against us, act, O LORD, for thy name's sake; for our backslidings are many. O thou hope of Israel, why shouldst thou be like a stranger in the land, like a man confused, like a mighty man who cannot save? Yet thou, O LORD, art in the midst of us, and we are called by thy name; leave us not."

Thus says the LORD concerning this people: "They have loved to wander, they have not restrained their feet; therefore the LORD does not accept them, now he will remember their iniquity."

The LORD said to me: "Do not pray for the welfare of this people. Though they fast, I will not hear their cry; but I will consume them by the sword, by famine, and by pestilence." Then I said: "Ah, Lord GOD, behold, the prophets say to them, 'You shall not see the sword or famine, but I will give you assured peace in this place.'" And the LORD said: "Those prophets are prophesying lies in my name: I did not send them or speak to them. They are prophesying the deceit of their own minds. Therefore thus says the LORD: By sword and famine those prophets shall be consumed. The people to whom they prophesy shall be cast out in the streets of Jerusalem, victims of famine and sword, with none to bury them, their wives, sons, and daughters. For I will pour out their wickedness upon them."

"WHO WILL HAVE pity on you, O Jerusalem? Who will turn aside to ask about your welfare? You have rejected me, says the LORD; so I have stretched out my hand against you—I am weary of relenting. I have winnowed my people with a winnowing fork, I have destroyed them; they did not turn from their ways. I have made their widows more in number than the sand of the seas; I have brought against the mothers of young men a destroyer at noonday; I have made terror fall upon them suddenly. She who bore seven has swooned away, her sun went down while it was yet day. And the rest of them I will give to the sword before their enemies, says the LORD."

WOE IS ME, my mother, that you bore me, a man of strife and contention to the whole land! I have not lent, nor have I borrowed, yet all of them curse me. So let it be, O LORD, if I have not entreated thee for their good, if I have not pleaded with thee on behalf of the enemy in the time of distress! Can one break iron, iron from the north, and bronze?

O LORD, thou knowest; remember me and visit me, and take vengeance for me on my persecutors. Know that for thy sake I bear reproach. Thy words were found, and I ate them, and thy words became to me the delight of my heart; for I am called by thy name, O LORD, God of hosts. I did not sit in the company of merrymakers; I sat alone, because thy hand was upon me, for thou hadst filled me with indignation. Why is my pain unceasing, my wound incurable, refusing to be healed? Wilt thou be to me like a deceitful brook, like waters that fail?

Therefore thus says the LORD: "If you return, I will restore you. If you utter what is precious, and not what is worthless, you shall be as my mouth. They shall turn to you, but you shall not turn to them. And I will make you to this people a fortified wall of bronze; they will fight against you, but they shall not prevail, for I am with you, says the LORD. I will deliver you out of the hand of the wicked."

THE WORD OF the LORD came to me: "You shall not take a wife, nor shall you have sons or daughters in this place. For thus says the LORD concerning the sons and daughters born in this place, and the mothers who bore them and the fathers who begot them: They shall die of deadly diseases. They shall perish by sword and famine, and their bodies be food for the beasts.

"Do not enter the house of mourning to bemoan them; for I have taken away my peace from this people, my steadfast love and mercy. Both great and small shall die and not be buried, and no one shall lament for them. No one shall break bread for the mourner, to comfort him; nor shall any give him the cup of consolation. You shall not go into the house of feasting to sit with them. For behold, I will make to cease from this place in your days the voice of mirth and the voice of gladness, the voice of the bridegroom and the voice of the bride.

"And when you tell this people these words, and they say to you, 'Why has the LORD pronounced all this great evil against us? What is the sin that we have committed against the LORD our God?' then you shall say to them: 'Because your fathers have forsaken me and gone after other gods, says the LORD, and have not kept my law; and because you have done worse than your fathers, every one of you following his stubborn evil will, refusing to listen to me; therefore I will hurl you into a land which neither you nor your fathers have known, and there you shall serve other gods day and night, for I will show you no favor.'

"Behold, I am sending for many fishers, says the LORD, and they shall catch them; and afterwards I will send for many hunters, and they shall hunt them from every mountain, and out of the clefts of the rocks. For my eyes are upon all their ways; their iniquity is not hid from me. And I will doubly recompense their sin, because they have polluted my land with the carcasses of their detestable idols.

"The sin of Judah is written with a pen of iron; with a point of diamond it is engraved on the tablet of their heart, and on the horns of their altars, while their children remember their altars beside every green tree. Your wealth and all your treasures I will give for spoil as the price of your sin. You shall loosen your hand from your heritage which I gave to you, and I will make you serve your enemies in a land which you do not know, for in my anger a fire is kindled which shall burn for ever."

THUS SAYS THE LORD: "Cursed is the man who trusts in man and whose heart turns away from the LORD. He is like a shrub in the desert; he shall dwell in parched places, in an uninhabited salt land.

"Blessed is the man who trusts in the LORD. He is like a tree planted by water, that sends out its roots by the stream, and does not fear when heat comes, for its leaves remain green, and is not anxious in the year of drought, for it does not cease to bear fruit."

The heart is deceitful above all things; who can understand it? "I the LORD search the mind and try the heart, to give to every man according to the fruit of his doings."

Like the partridge that gathers a brood which she did not hatch, so is he who gets riches but not by right; in the midst of his days they will leave him, and at his end he will be a fool.

A glorious throne set on high from the beginning is the place of our sanctuary. O LORD, the hope of Israel, all who turn away from thee shall be written in the earth, for they have forsaken the LORD, the fountain of living water.

HEAL ME, O LORD, and I shall be healed; save me, and I shall be saved; for thou art my praise. Behold, they say to me, "Where is the word of the LORD? Let it come!"

I have not pressed thee to send evil, thou knowest; that which came out of my lips was before thy face. Be not a terror to me; thou art my refuge in the day of evil. Let those be put to shame who persecute me, but let me not be put to shame; let them be dismayed; bring upon them the day of evil!

THE LORD SAID to me: "Go and stand in the Benjamin Gate, by which the kings of Judah enter and go out, and say: 'Hear the word of the LORD, you kings of Judah, and all Judah, and all who enter by these gates: Take heed for the sake of your lives, and do not bear a burden on the sabbath day or do any work, but keep the sabbath holy, as I commanded your fathers. Yet they did not incline their ear, but stiffened their neck, that they might not receive instruction. If you listen to me, says the LORD, and keep the sabbath holy, then there shall enter by the gates of this city kings who sit on the throne of David, riding in chariots and on horses, they and their princes, the men of Judah and the inhabitants of Jerusalem; and this city shall be inhabited for ever. And people shall come from the cities of Judah round about, bringing thank offerings to the house of the LORD. But if you do not listen to me, to keep the sabbath day holy, then I will kindle a fire in these gates, and it shall devour the palaces of Jerusalem and shall not be quenched.'"

THE WORD THAT came to Jeremiah from the LORD: "Arise, and go down to the potter's house, and there I will let you hear my words." So I went to the potter's house, and there he was working at his wheel. And the vessel he was making of clay was spoiled in his hand, and he reworked it into another vessel, as it seemed good to him to do.

Then the word of the LORD came to me: "O house of Israel, can I not do with you as this potter has done? Like the clay in the potter's hand, so are you in my hand. If at any time I declare concerning a nation that I will pluck up and destroy it, and if that nation then turns from its evil, I will repent of the evil I intended to do to it. And if I declare concerning a nation that I will build and plant it, and it does evil in my sight, then I will repent of the good I had intended to do to it. Now therefore say to the men of Judah: 'Thus says the LORD, Behold, I am devising a plan against you. Return, every one from his evil way.'

"But they say, 'That is in vain! We will follow our own plans, and will every one act according to the stubbornness of his heart.'"

Thus said the LORD, "Go, buy a potter's earthen flask, and take some of the elders of the people and senior priests, and go out to Topheth in the valley of the son of Hinnom at the entry of the Potsherd Gate, and proclaim there these words that I tell you: 'Hear the word of the LORD, O kings of Judah and inhabitants of Jerusalem. Behold, I am bringing such evil upon this place that the ears of every one who hears of it will tingle. Because the people have profaned this place by burning incense in it to other gods, and have filled it with the blood of innocents, and built the high places to burn their sons as offerings to Baal, which I did not command or decree, nor did it come into my mind; therefore days are coming, says the LORD, when this place shall no more be called Topheth, or the valley of the son of Hinnom, but the valley of Slaughter. In this place I will make void the plans of Judah and Jerusalem, and will cause their people to fall by the sword before their enemies, and I will give their dead bodies for food to the birds of the air and to the beasts of the earth. I will make this city a horror, a thing to be hissed at. I will make them eat the flesh of their sons and their daughters, and every one shall eat the flesh of his neighbor in the siege, and in the distress with which those who seek their life afflict them.'

"Then you shall break the earthen flask in the sight of the men who go with you, and say to them, 'Thus says the LORD of hosts: So will I break this city, as one breaks a potter's vessel, so it can never be mended. Men shall bury in Topheth because there will be no place else to bury. Thus will I do to this place, making this city like Topheth. The houses of Jerusalem and the houses of the kings of Judah—all the houses upon whose roofs incense has been burned and drink offerings poured out to other gods—shall be defiled like the place of Topheth.'"

Then Jeremiah came from Topheth, where the LORD had sent him to prophesy, and he stood in the court of the LORD's house, and said to all the people: "Thus says the LORD of hosts, Behold, I am bringing upon this city all the evil I have pronounced against it, because they have refused to hear my words."

NOW PASHHUR THE priest, who was chief officer in the house of the LORD, heard Jeremiah prophesying these things. Then Pashhur beat Jeremiah, and put him in the stocks that were in the upper Benjamin Gate of the house of the LORD.

On the morrow, when Pashhur released him from the stocks, Jeremiah said, "The LORD does not call your name Pashhur, but Terror on every side. For thus says the LORD: I will make you a terror to yourself and to all your friends. They shall fall by the sword of their enemies while you look on. And I will give all Judah into the hand of the king of Babylon; he shall carry them captive to Babylon and slay them with the sword. Moreover, I will give all the treasures of the city and of the kings of Judah into the hand of their enemies. And you, Pashhur, shall go into captivity; to Babylon you shall go; there you shall die and be buried, you and all your friends, to whom you have prophesied falsely."

O LORD, THOU HAST DECEIVED me, and I was deceived; thou art stronger than I, and thou hast prevailed. Every one mocks me. For whenever I speak, I shout, "Violence and destruction!" The word of the LORD has become for me a reproach and derision all day long. If I say, "I will not speak any more in his name," there is in my heart as it were a burning fire shut up in my bones, and I am weary with holding it in, and I cannot. Terror is on every side! "Denounce him! Let us denounce him!" say all my familiar friends, watching for my fall. "Perhaps he will be deceived, and then we can overcome him and take our revenge."

But the LORD is with me as a dread warrior. Therefore my persecutors will stumble. They will be greatly shamed, for they will not succeed. O LORD of hosts, who triest the righteous, who seest the heart and the mind, to thee have I committed my cause.

Sing to the LORD; praise the LORD! For he has delivered the life of the needy from the hand of evildoers.

THIS IS THE word which came to Jeremiah from the LORD, when Zedekiah king of Judah sent to him Zephaniah the priest and another, saying, "Inquire of the LORD for us, for Nebuchadrezzar king of Babylon is making war against us; perhaps the LORD will deal with us according to all his wonderful deeds, and will make him withdraw from us."

Jeremiah said: "Say to Zedekiah, 'Thus says the LORD: Behold, I will turn back the weapons of war with which you are fighting against the king of Babylon and the Chaldeans besieging your walls; and I will bring them together into this city. I myself will fight against you with outstretched hand and strong arm in great wrath, and I will smite the inhabitants of this city, both man and beast; they shall die of a great pestilence. Afterward I will give Zedekiah, and his servants, and the people in this city who survive the pestilence and sword, into the hand of Nebuchadrezzar king of Babylon. He shall not pity or spare them.'

"And to this people you shall say: 'Thus says the LORD: Behold, I set before you the way of life and the way of death. He who stays in this city shall die; but he who goes out and surrenders to the Chaldeans shall have his life as a prize of war. For I have set my face against this city for evil and not for good, says the LORD; it shall be given into the hand of the king of Babylon, and he shall burn it with fire.'"

THUS SAYS THE LORD: "Go down to the house of the king, and say, Hear the word of the LORD, O King of Judah, who sit on the throne of David, you, and your servants, and your people: Do justice and righteousness, and deliver from the hand of the oppressor him who has been robbed. And do no wrong or violence to the alien, the fatherless, and the widow, nor shed innocent blood in this place. For if you will indeed obey this word, then there shall enter these gates kings who sit on the throne of David. But if you will not heed these words, I swear by myself, says the Lord, that this house shall become a desolation. For you are as Gilead to me, as the summit of Lebanon, yet surely I will make you a desert. I will prepare destroyers against you and they shall cut down your choicest cedars and cast them into the fire. Many nations will pass by, and every man will say to his neighbor, 'Why has the Lord dealt thus with this great city?' And they will answer, 'Because they forsook the covenant of the Lord their God, and worshiped other gods.'"

Weep not for him who is dead; but weep bitterly for him who goes away, for he shall return no more to see his native land. Thus says the Lord concerning Jehoahaz the son of Josiah, king of Judah, who reigned instead of his father, and went away from this place: "He shall return here no more, but in the place where they have carried him captive, there shall he die."

"Woe to him who builds his house by unrighteousness, who makes his neighbor serve him and does not give him his wages; who says, 'I will build myself a great house with spacious upper rooms,' and cuts out windows for it, paneling it with cedar, and painting it with vermilion. Do you think you are a king because you compete in cedar? Did not your father eat and drink and do justice and righteousness? He judged the cause of the poor and needy; then it was well with him. Is not this to know me? says the Lord. But you have eyes and heart only for your dishonest gain, and for practicing oppression and violence."

Therefore thus says the Lord concerning Jehoiakim the son of Josiah, king of Judah: "They shall not lament for him, saying, 'Ah my brother!' or 'Ah his majesty!' With the burial of an ass he shall be buried, dragged, and cast forth beyond the gates of Jerusalem."

"Go up to Lebanon, and cry out, for all your lovers are destroyed. I spoke to you in your prosperity, but you said, 'I will not listen.' This has been your way from your youth. The wind shall shepherd all your shepherds, and your lovers shall go into captivity; then you will be confounded because of your wickedness. How you will groan when pangs come upon you, pain as of a woman in travail!"

"As I live, says the Lord, though Jehoiachin the son of Jehoiakim, king of Judah, were the signet ring on my right hand, yet I would tear you off and give you into the hand of those of whom you are afraid, even Nebuchadrezzar king of Babylon and the Chaldeans. I will hurl you and the mother who bore you into another country, where you were not born, and there you shall die."

Is this man Jehoiachin a despised, broken pot, a vessel no one cares for? Why are he and his children hurled into a land which they do not know? O land, land, land, hear the word of the Lord: Write this man down as childless, a man who shall not succeed in his days; for none of his offspring shall succeed in sitting on the throne of David, and ruling again in Judah.

"WOE TO THE SHEPHERDS WHO destroy and scatter the sheep of my pasture!" says the LORD. "You have driven my flock away, and you have not attended to them. Behold, I will attend to you for your evil doings. Then I will gather the remnant of my flock out of all the countries and bring them back to their fold, and they shall be fruitful and multiply. I will set shepherds over them who will care for them, and they shall fear no more, nor be dismayed, neither shall any be missing.

"Behold, the days are coming, says the LORD, when I will raise up for David a righteous Branch, and he shall reign as king and deal wisely, and shall execute justice and righteousness in the land. In his days Judah will be saved, and Israel will dwell securely. And this is the name by which he will be called: 'The LORD is our righteousness.' Men shall no longer say, 'As the LORD lives who brought up the people of Israel out of Egypt,' but 'As the LORD lives who brought the descendants of the house of Israel out of the north country and all the countries where he had driven them.' Then they shall dwell in their own land."

THUS SAYS THE LORD of hosts: "Do not listen to the words of the prophets who fill you with vain hopes; they speak visions of their own minds, not from the LORD. They say continually to those who despise the word of the LORD, 'It shall be well with you'; and to every one who stubbornly follows his own heart, they say, 'No evil shall come upon you.'"

For who among them has stood in the council of the LORD or given heed to his word? "I did not send the prophets, yet they ran; I did not speak to them, yet they prophesied. But if they had stood in my council, they would have proclaimed my words to my people, and they would have turned them from their evil way.

"Am I a God at hand, says the LORD, and not a God afar off? Can a man hide himself so I cannot see him? Do I not fill heaven and earth? I have heard what the prophets say who prophesy lies in my name: 'I have dreamed, I have dreamed!' How long shall prophets prophesy the deceit of their own heart, who think to make my people forget my name by their dreams which they tell one another, even as their fathers forgot my name for Baal? Let the prophet who has a dream tell the dream, but let him who has my word speak my word faithfully. What has straw in common with wheat? says the LORD. Is not my word like fire, and like a hammer which breaks the rock in pieces? Therefore, behold, I am against the prophets who steal my words from one another. I am against the prophets who use their tongues and say, 'Says the LORD.' I am against those who lead my people astray by their lies and recklessness when I did not send them or charge them. They do not profit this people at all, says the LORD.

"When one of this people, or a prophet, or a priest asks you, 'What is the burden of the LORD?' you shall say to them, 'You are the burden, and I will cast you off, says the LORD.'"

AFTER NEBUCHADREZZAR KING OF BABYLON had taken into exile from Jerusalem Jehoiachin the son of Jehoiakim, king of Judah, together with the princes, the craftsmen, and the smiths, and had brought them to Babylon, the LORD showed me this vision: Behold, two baskets of figs placed before the temple of the LORD. One basket had very good figs, like first-ripe figs, but the other basket had very bad figs. And the LORD said to me, "What do you see, Jeremiah?" I said, "Figs, the good figs very good, and the bad figs so bad that they cannot be eaten."

The LORD said, "Like these good figs, so I will regard as good the exiles from Judah, whom I have sent to the land of the Chaldeans. I will set my eyes upon them for good, and bring them back to this land; I will plant them, and not uproot them. I will give them a heart to know that I am the LORD; and they shall be my people and I will be their God, for they shall return to me with their whole heart.

"But like the bad figs which are so bad they cannot be eaten, so will I treat Zedekiah the king of Judah, his princes, the remnant of Jerusalem in this land, and those who dwell in Egypt. I will make them a horror to all the kingdoms of the earth, a reproach, a byword, and a curse in all the places where I shall drive them. And they shall be utterly destroyed from the land which I gave to them and their fathers."

THE WORD THAT came to Jeremiah concerning all the people of Judah, in the fourth year of Jehoiakim the son of Josiah, king of Judah (that was the first year of Nebuchadrezzar king of Babylon), which Jeremiah the prophet spoke: "For twenty-three years, from the thirteenth year of Josiah to this day, the word of the LORD has come to me, and I have spoken to you. But you have not inclined your ears to hear, although the LORD persistently sent you all his servants the prophets, saying, 'Turn now, every one of you, from his wrong doings, and dwell upon the land which the LORD has given you; do not go after other gods, or provoke me to anger with the work of your hands. Then I will do you no harm.' Yet you have not listened to me, says the LORD, that you might provoke me to anger.

"Therefore thus says the LORD of hosts: Behold, I will send for all the tribes of the north, and for Nebuchadrezzar the king of Babylon, my servant, and I will bring them against this land and all these nations round about. I will banish from these nations the voice of mirth and gladness, the voice of the bridegroom and the bride, the grinding of the millstones and the light of the lamp. And they shall serve the king of Babylon seventy years. Then, after seventy years, I will punish the king of Babylon and the Chaldeans for their iniquity, says the LORD. I will bring upon that land all the words I have uttered against it, everything written in this book, which Jeremiah prophesied against all the nations. For many nations and great kings shall make slaves even of them; for I will recompense them according to their deeds."

Thus the LORD, the God of Israel, said to me: "Take from my hand this cup of the wine of wrath, and make all the nations to whom I send you drink it. They shall drink and stagger and be crazed because of the sword which I am sending among them."

So I took the cup from the LORD's hand, and made all the nations to whom the LORD sent me drink it: Judah, its kings and princes; Pharaoh of Egypt, all his people, and all the foreign folk among them; all the kings of the north, far and near; all the kingdoms on the face of the earth. And after them the king of Babylon shall drink.

"Then you shall say, 'Thus says the God of Israel: Drink, fall, rise no more, because of the sword I am sending among you.'

"And if they refuse to accept the cup from your hand, then you shall say, 'Thus says the LORD of hosts: You must drink! For behold, I begin to work evil at the city which is called by my name, and shall you go unpunished? You shall not go unpunished, for I am summoning a sword against all the inhabitants of the earth.'"

IN THE BEGINNING of the reign of Jehoiakim this word came from the LORD: "Stand in the court of the LORD's house, and speak there all the words that I command you; do not hold back a word. It may be they will listen, and that I may repent of the evil I intend to do them. You shall say, 'Thus says the LORD: If you will not walk in my law and heed the words of my servants the prophets whom I send you urgently, then I will make this house like Shiloh, and this city a curse for all the nations of the earth.'"

The priests and the prophets and all the people heard Jeremiah speaking these words in the house of the LORD. And when he had finished, they laid hold of him, saying, "You shall die! Why have you prophesied in the name of the LORD, saying, 'This house shall be like Shiloh, and this city without inhabitant'?" And all the people gathered about Jeremiah. When the princes of Judah heard these things, they came up from the king's house and took their seat in the entry of the New Gate of the house of the LORD. The priests and prophets said to the princes and to all the people, "This man deserves the sentence of death, because he has prophesied against this city, as you have heard with your own ears."

Then Jeremiah spoke to all the princes and all the people, saying, "The LORD sent me to prophesy against this house and this city. Now therefore amend your ways, and obey the voice of the LORD your God, and the LORD will repent of the evil he has pronounced against you. But as for me, behold, I am in your hands. Do with me as seems right to you. Only know for certain that if you put me to death, you will bring innocent blood upon yourselves and upon this city, for in truth the LORD sent me to you to speak all these words in your ears."

Then the princes and all the people said to the priests, "This man does not deserve death, for he has spoken to us in the name of the LORD our God." And certain of the elders arose and spoke to the assembled people, saying,

"Micah prophesied in the days of King Hezekiah to the people of Judah: 'Thus says the LORD, Zion shall be plowed as a field; Jerusalem shall become a heap of ruins, and the mountain of the house a wooded height.' Did Hezekiah put him to death? Did he not fear the LORD, and did not the LORD repent of the evil he had pronounced against them? But we are about to bring great evil upon ourselves."

The hand of Ahikam the son of Shaphan was with Jeremiah, so that he was not given over to the people to be put to death.

IN THE BEGINNING of the reign of Zedekiah the son of Josiah, king of Judah, the LORD said to me: "Make yourself thongs and yoke-bars, and put them on your neck. Send word to the kings of Edom, Moab, and Ammon, and the kings of Tyre and Sidon by the hand of the envoys who have come to Jerusalem to Zedekiah. Give them this charge: 'Thus says the LORD of hosts, the God of Israel, to your masters: It is I who by my great power have made the earth, with the men and animals that are on it, and I give it to whomever it seems right to me. Now I have given all these lands into the hand of Nebuchadrezzar, the king of Babylon, my servant, and I have given him also the beasts of the field to serve him. All the nations shall serve him and his son and his grandson, until the time of his own land comes.'"

To Zedekiah king of Judah I spoke thus: "Bring your necks under the yoke of the king of Babylon, serve him, and live. Why will you die, as the LORD has spoken concerning any nation which will not serve the king of Babylon? Do not listen to prophets who say, 'You shall not serve Nebuchadrezzar,' for I have not sent them, says the LORD. They prophesy falsely in my name, says the LORD, with the result that I will drive you out and you will perish, you and those prophets."

Then I spoke to the priests and to all this people: "Do not listen to prophets who say, 'Behold, the vessels of the LORD's house will now shortly be brought back from Babylon,' for it is a lie. Do not listen to them; serve the king of Babylon and live. If they are prophets and the word of the LORD is with them, then let them intercede with him, that the vessels which are still in the house of the LORD, in the house of the king of Judah, and in Jerusalem may not go to Babylon. For thus says the LORD concerning the pillars, the sea, the stands, and the rest of the vessels which Nebuchadrezzar did not take when he took into exile Jehoiachin king of Judah: They shall be carried to Babylon and remain there until the day when I give attention to them. Then I will restore them to this place."

In that same year, at the beginning of the reign of Zedekiah, Hananiah the prophet from Gibeon spoke to me in the house of the LORD, saying, "Thus says the LORD of hosts: I have broken the yoke of the king of Babylon. Within two years I will bring back to this place all the vessels of the LORD's house which Nebuchadrezzar carried to Babylon. I will also bring back Jehoiachin the son of Jehoiakim, and all the exiles from Judah, says the LORD."

Then Jeremiah spoke to Hananiah in the presence of all the people: "Amen! May the LORD make your words come true and bring back from Babylon all the vessels and all the exiles. Yet hear now this word. The prophets who preceded you and me from ancient times prophesied war, famine, and pestilence against many countries. As for the prophet who prophesies peace, when the word of that prophet comes to pass, then it will be known that the LORD has truly sent the prophet."

Then Hananiah took the yoke-bars from the neck of Jeremiah and broke them. And he spoke, saying, "Thus says the LORD: Even so will I break the yoke of Nebuchadrezzar king of Babylon from the neck of all the nations within two years." But Jeremiah the prophet went his way.

Sometime after this, the word of the LORD came to Jeremiah: "Go, tell Hananiah, 'Thus says the LORD: You have broken wooden bars, but I will make in their place bars of iron. For I have put upon the neck of all these nations an iron yoke of servitude to the king of Babylon, for I have given to him even the beasts of the field.'" Jeremiah said, "Listen, Hananiah, the LORD has not sent you, and you have made this people trust in a lie. Therefore thus says the LORD: 'Behold, I will remove you from the face of the earth. This very year you shall die, because you have uttered rebellion against the LORD.'"

In that same year, in the seventh month, the prophet Hananiah died.

THE WORD THAT came to Jeremiah from the LORD: "Write in a book all the words I have spoken to you. For behold, days are coming when I will restore the fortunes of my people and bring them back to the land I gave to their fathers."

These are the words the LORD spoke concerning Israel and Judah: "We have heard a cry of panic, and no peace. Ask now, can a man bear a child? Why then do I see every man with his hands on his loins like a woman in labor? Why has every face turned pale? Alas! that day is so great there is none like it; it is a time of distress for Jacob; yet he shall be saved out of it. And it shall come to pass in that day that I will break the yoke from off their neck, and I will burst their bonds, and strangers shall no more make servants of them. But they shall serve the LORD their God and David their king, whom I will raise up for them.

"Then fear not, O Jacob my servant, says the LORD, for lo, I will save you from afar, and your offspring from captivity. Jacob shall return, and none shall make him afraid. For I am with you to save you, says the LORD; I will make a full end of all the nations among whom I scattered you, but of you I will not make a full end. I will chasten you in just measure.

"Your wound is grievous. There is none to uphold your cause, no healing for you. All your lovers have forgotten you; for I have dealt you the blow of an enemy, because your guilt is great. Why do you cry out over your hurt? Your pain is incurable. Because your sins are flagrant, I have done this to you.

"Yet all who devour you shall be devoured, and your foes, every one of them, shall go into captivity; all who prey on you I will make a prey. For I will restore health to you, and your wounds I will heal, says the LORD. Behold, I will restore the fortunes of the tents of Jacob; the city shall be rebuilt upon its mound, and the palace shall stand where it used to be. Out of them shall come songs of thanksgiving, and the voices of those who make merry. I will multiply them, and make them honored. Their children shall be as they were of old, their congregation established before me. Their prince, their ruler, shall come forth from their midst; I will make him draw near, and he shall approach me, for who would dare of himself to approach me? says the LORD. You shall be my people, and I will be your God."

Behold the storm of the LORD! A whirling tempest will burst upon the head of the wicked. The fierce anger of the LORD will not turn back until he has accomplished the intents of his mind. In the latter days you will understand this.

"At that time, says the LORD, I will be the God of all the families of Israel, and they shall be my people."

Thus says the LORD: "The people who survived the sword found grace in the wilderness; when Israel sought for rest, the LORD appeared to him from afar. I have loved you with an everlasting love; therefore I have continued my faithfulness to you. Again I will build you, O virgin Israel! Again you shall adorn yourself with timbrels and go forth in the dance of the merrymakers. Again you shall plant vineyards upon the mountains of Samaria and enjoy the fruit. For there shall be a day when watchmen will call in the hill country of Ephraim: 'Arise, and let us go up to Zion, to the LORD our God.'"

For thus says the LORD: "Sing aloud with gladness for Jacob, give praise, and say, 'The LORD has saved his people, the remnant of Israel.' Behold, I will gather them from the farthest parts of the earth, among them the blind and the lame, the woman with child and her who is in travail; a great company, they shall return. With consolations I will lead them back, I will make them walk by brooks of water, in a path in which they shall not stumble; for I am a father to Israel, and Ephraim is my first-born.

"Hear the word of the LORD, O nations, and declare in the coastlands afar off: 'He who scattered Israel will gather him, and will keep him as a shepherd keeps his flock.' For the LORD has ransomed Jacob from hands too strong for him. They shall come and sing aloud on the height of Zion, they shall be radiant over the goodness of the LORD, over the grain, the wine, and the oil, and over the young of the flock and the herd; their life shall be like a watered garden. Then shall the maidens rejoice in the dance, and young men and old shall be merry. I will give them gladness for sorrow. I will feast the soul of the priests with abundance, and my people shall be satisfied with my goodness."

Thus says the LORD: "A voice is heard in Ramah, lamentation and bitter weeping. Rachel is weeping for her children; she refuses to be comforted, because they are not.

"Keep your eyes from tears. There is hope for your future, and your children shall come back to their own country, says the LORD. I have heard Ephraim bemoaning, 'Thou hast chastened me like an untrained calf; bring me back, that I may be restored. For after I had turned away, I repented; and after I was instructed, I smote upon my thigh; I was confounded, because I bore the disgrace of my youth.' Is Ephraim my dear son? Is he my darling child? For as often as I speak against him, I do remember him still. Therefore my heart yearns for him; I will surely have mercy on him, says the LORD.

"Set up waymarks for yourself, make yourself guideposts; consider well the highway, the road by which you went. Return, O virgin Israel, return to these your cities. How long will you waver, O faithless daughter? For the LORD has created a new thing on the earth: a woman protects a man.

"Once more they shall use these words in the land of Judah and in its cities, when I restore their fortunes: 'The LORD bless you, O habitation of righteousness, O holy hill!' And Judah and all its cities shall dwell there together, and the farmers and those who wander with their flocks. For I will satisfy the weary soul, and every languishing soul I will replenish."

Thereupon I awoke and looked, and my sleep was pleasant to me.

"Behold, the days are coming, says the LORD, when I will sow the house of Israel and the house of Judah with the seed of man and the seed of beast. And it shall come to pass that as I have watched over them to pluck up and break down, to destroy, and bring evil, so I will watch over them to build and to plant. In those days they shall no longer say: 'The fathers have eaten sour grapes, and the children's teeth are set on edge.' But every one shall die for his own sin; each man who eats sour grapes, his teeth shall be set on edge.

"Behold, the days are coming when I will make a new covenant with Israel and Judah, not like the covenant which I made with their fathers when I took them by the hand to bring them out of Egypt, my covenant which they broke, though I was their husband, says the LORD. But this is the covenant which I will make with Israel: I will put my law within them, and I will write it upon their hearts; and I will be their God, and they shall be my people. And no longer shall each man teach his neighbor and each his brother, saying, 'Know the LORD,' for they shall all know me, from the least of them to the greatest; for I will forgive their iniquity, and I will remember their sin no more."

Thus says the LORD, who gives the sun for light by day and the fixed order of the moon and the stars for light by night, who stirs up the sea so that its waves roar—the LORD of hosts is his name: "If this fixed order departs from before me, then shall the descendants of Israel cease from being a nation for ever. If the heavens above can be measured, and the foundations of the earth below explored, then I will cast off all the descendants of Israel."

IN THE TENTH year of Zedekiah king of Judah, which was the eighteenth year of Nebuchadrezzar, when the army of the king of Babylon was besieging Jerusalem, Jeremiah the prophet was shut up in the court of the guard in the palace of the king. For Zedekiah had imprisoned him, saying, "Why do you prophesy, 'Thus says the LORD: I am giving this city into the hand of the king of Babylon; and Zedekiah shall surely not escape the Chaldeans, but shall speak with the king of Babylon face to face, and eye to eye; and he shall take Zedekiah to Babylon'?"

Jeremiah said, "The word of the LORD came to me: Behold, Hanamel the son of your uncle will come to you and say, 'Buy my field which is at Anathoth, for the right of purchase is yours.' Then my cousin came to me in the court of the guard and said, 'Buy my field which is at Anathoth in the land of Benjamin, for the right of possession is yours; buy it for yourself,' And I knew that this was the word of the LORD.

"I bought the field from Hanamel my cousin, and weighed out the money to him, seventeen shekels of silver. I signed the deed, sealed it, got witnesses, and weighed the money on scales. Then I took the sealed deed of purchase, containing the terms and conditions, and the open copy; and I gave the deed of purchase to Baruch the son of Neriah, in the presence of Hanamel my cousin and the witnesses who signed the deed, and in the presence of all the Jews who were sitting in the court of the guard. I charged Baruch, saying: 'Take these deeds, both this sealed deed of purchase and this open deed, and put them in an earthenware vessel, that they may last for a long time. For thus says the LORD: Houses and fields and vineyards shall again be bought in this land.'

"After I had given the deed to Baruch, I prayed to the LORD: 'Ah, Lord GOD! It is thou who hast made the heavens and the earth by thy outstretched arm! Nothing is too hard for thee, who showest steadfast love to thousands, but dost requite the guilt of fathers to their children after them, O great and mighty God whose name is the LORD of hosts. Thou didst bring thy people Israel out of Egypt with signs and wonders, and thou gavest them this land, a land flowing with milk and honey; and they took possession of it. But they did nothing of all thou didst command them to do. Therefore thou hast made all this evil come upon them. Behold, the siege mounds have come up to the city to take it. What thou didst speak has come to pass, and thou seest it. Yet thou, O Lord GOD, hast said to me, "Buy the field for money and get witnesses"—though the city is given into the hands of the Chaldeans.'"

The word of the LORD came to Jeremiah: "I am the LORD, the God of all flesh; is anything too hard for me? Behold, I am giving this city into the hand of Nebuchadrezzar king of Babylon. The Chaldeans shall set this city on fire, and burn the houses on whose roofs incense has been offered to Baal and drink offerings poured out to other gods. This city has aroused my anger from the day it was built. I will remove it from my sight because of all the evil the sons of Israel and of Judah did to provoke me. They have turned to me their back and not their face; they have not listened to instruction. They set up their abominations in the house which is called by my name, to defile it. They built the high places of Baal to offer up their sons and daughters to Molech.

"Now thus says the LORD: Behold, I will gather them from all the countries to which I drove them in my great indignation; I will bring them back to this place, and I will make them dwell in safety. They shall be my people, and I will be their God. I will give them one heart and one way, that they may fear me for ever, for their own good and the good of their children after them. I will make with them an everlasting covenant, that I will not turn away from doing good to them; and I will put the fear of me in their hearts, that they may not turn from me. I will rejoice in doing them good, and I will plant them in this land in faithfulness, with all my heart and all my soul.

"For thus says the LORD: Just as I have brought all this great evil upon this people, so I will bring upon them all the good that I promise them. Fields shall be bought in this land of which you are saying, It is a desolation, without man or beast; it is given into the hands of the Chaldeans. Deeds shall be signed and sealed and witnessed, in the land of Benjamin, in the places about Jerusalem, and in the cities of Judah, in the cities of the hill country, in the Shephelah, and the Negeb; for I will restore their fortunes."

THE WORD WHICH came to Jeremiah from the LORD in the days of Jehoiakim the son of Josiah, king of Judah: "Go to the house of the Rechabites, and bring them to the house of the LORD, into one of the chambers; then offer them wine to drink." So I took Jaazaniah, and his brothers, and all his sons, and the whole house of the Rechabites. I brought them to the house of the LORD and into a chamber near the chamber of the princes.

Then I set before the Rechabites pitchers full of wine, and cups; and I said to them, "Drink." But they answered, "We will drink no wine, for our father, Jonadab the son of Rechab, commanded us, 'You shall not drink wine, neither you nor your sons for ever; you shall not build a house; you shall not sow seed; you shall not plant a vineyard; but you shall live in tents, that you may live many days in the land where you sojourn.' We have obeyed the voice of Jonadab our father in all that he commanded us. We have no vineyard or field or seed; and we have lived in tents. But when Nebuchadrezzar king of Babylon came up against the land, we said, 'Come, let us go to Jerusalem for fear of the army of the Chaldeans.' So we are living in Jerusalem."

Then the word of the LORD came to Jeremiah: "Go and say to the inhabitants of Jerusalem, Will you not receive instruction? says the LORD. The command which Jonadab the son of Rechab gave to his sons, to drink no wine, has been kept; and they drink none to this day. I have spoken to you persistently, but you have not obeyed me. Therefore, behold, I am bringing on Judah and all the inhabitants of Jerusalem all the evil I have pronounced against them; because I have called to them and they have not answered."

But Jeremiah said to the Rechabites, "Because you have obeyed the command of your father, and kept all his precepts, therefore thus says the LORD of hosts, the God of Israel: Jonadab the son of Rechab shall never lack a man to stand before me."

IN THE FOURTH YEAR OF JEHOIAKIM, king of Judah, this word came to Jeremiah from the LORD: "Take a scroll and write on it all the words I have spoken to you against Israel and Judah from the days of Josiah until today. It may be that the house of Judah will hear the evil I intend to do them, so that every one may turn from his evil way and I may forgive."

Then Jeremiah called Baruch the son of Neriah, and Baruch wrote upon a scroll at the dictation of Jeremiah all the words the LORD had spoken to him. And Jeremiah ordered Baruch, saying, "I am debarred from going to the house of the LORD; so you are to go, and on a fast day in the hearing of all the people you shall read the words of the LORD from this scroll. You shall read them also in the hearing of all the men of Judah who come out of their cities. It may be that their supplication will come before the LORD, and that every one will turn from his evil way, for great is the wrath that the LORD has pronounced against them." And Baruch did as Jeremiah ordered him.

The next year, in the ninth month, all the people in Jerusalem and all the people who came to Jerusalem from the cities of Judah proclaimed a fast before the LORD. Then, in the hearing of the people, Baruch read the words of Jeremiah from the scroll in the house of the LORD, in the chamber of Gemariah the son of Shaphan the secretary, which was in the upper court, at the entry of the New Gate of the LORD's house.

When Micaiah the son of Gemariah heard all the words from the scroll, he went down to the king's house, into the secretary's chamber, where all the princes were sitting. And Micaiah told them all he had heard Baruch read. Then the princes sent Jehudi the son of Nethaniah to say to Baruch, "Take in your hand that scroll, and come." So Baruch took it and came. "Sit down and read it," they said. So he read them all the words of the LORD from the scroll, and they turned one to another in fear, and said, "We must report this to the king." Then they asked Baruch, "Tell us, how did you write these words? Was it at his dictation?" Baruch answered them, "He dictated the words to me, while I wrote them with ink on the scroll." Then they said to Baruch, "Go and hide, you and Jeremiah, and let no one know where you are."

So the princes went into the court to King Jehoiakim, having put the scroll in the chamber of Elishama the secretary, and reported all the words to him. Then the king sent Jehudi to get the scroll, and Jehudi read it to the king and all the princes. It was the ninth month, and the king was sitting in the winter house and there was a fire burning in the brazier before him. As Jehudi read three or four columns, the king would cut them off with a penknife and throw them into the brazier, until the entire scroll was consumed in the fire. Yet neither the king, nor any of his servants who heard all these words, was afraid. Even when some urged the king not to burn the scroll, he would not listen. And the king commanded Jerahmeel his son and two others of his court to seize Baruch and Jeremiah the prophet; but the LORD hid them.

Now, after the king had burned the scroll, the word of the LORD came to Jeremiah: "Take another scroll and write on it all the words that were in the first scroll. And concerning Jehoiakim king of Judah you shall say, 'Thus says the LORD, You have burned this scroll, saying, "Why have you written in it that the king of Babylon will certainly destroy this land, and will cut off from it man and beast?" Therefore thus says the LORD concerning Jehoiakim, He shall have none to sit upon the throne of David, and his dead body shall be cast out to the heat by day and the frost by night. And I will punish him and his offspring and his servants; I will bring upon them, upon Jerusalem, and upon Judah, all the evil that I have pronounced against them, but they would not hear.'"

Then Jeremiah took another scroll and gave it to Baruch, who wrote on it at his dictation all the words of the scroll which Jehoiakim had burned; and many similar words were added to them.

ZEDEKIAH THE SON of Josiah, whom Nebuchadrezzar king of Babylon made king in the land of Judah, reigned instead of Jehoiachin the son of Jehoiakim. But neither he nor the people listened to the words of the LORD which he spoke through Jeremiah the prophet.

King Zedekiah sent Jehucal the son of Shelemiah, and Zephaniah the priest, to Jeremiah, saying, "Pray for us to the LORD our God." Now Jeremiah was still going in and out among the people, for he had not yet been put in prison. At that time the army of Pharaoh had come out of Egypt; and when the Chaldeans besieging Jerusalem heard news of them, they withdrew from the city.

Then the word of the LORD came to Jeremiah: "Say to the king, 'Behold, Pharaoh's army which came to help you is about to return to Egypt. And the Chaldeans shall come back and take this city. Do not deceive yourselves, saying, "The Chaldeans will surely stay away from us," for they will not. For even if you should defeat their whole army, and there remained of them only wounded men, every man in his tent, they would rise up and burn this city.'"

Now when the Chaldean army had withdrawn at the approach of Pharaoh's army, Jeremiah set out from Jerusalem to go to the land of Benjamin to receive his portion there. When he was at the Benjamin Gate, a sentry there named Irijah the son of Shelemiah seized him, saying, "You are deserting to the Chaldeans." And Jeremiah said, "It is false; I am not deserting to the Chaldeans." But the sentry would not listen, and brought him to the princes. And the princes were enraged at Jeremiah, and they beat him and imprisoned him in the house of Jonathan the secretary, for it had been made a prison.

When Jeremiah had remained in the dungeon cells many days, King Zedekiah sent for him, and questioned him secretly: "Is there any word from the LORD?" Jeremiah said, "There is. You shall be delivered into the hand of the king of Babylon."

Jeremiah then said to King Zedekiah, "What wrong have I done to you or this people, that you have put me in prison? Where are your prophets who said to you, 'The king of Babylon will not come against this land'? Now hear,

I pray you, O my lord the king: do not send me back to the house of Jonathan the secretary, lest I die there." So King Zedekiah gave orders, and they committed Jeremiah to the court of the guard; and a loaf of bread was given him daily from the bakers' street, until all the bread of the city was gone. So Jeremiah remained in the court of the guard.

Now JEHUCAL THE son of Shelemiah, and three others, heard the words that Jeremiah was saying to all the people, "Thus says the LORD, He who stays in this city shall die by the sword, by famine, and by pestilence; but he who goes out to the Chaldeans shall live. This city shall surely be taken." Then the princes went to the king and said, "Let this man be put to death, for he is weakening the hands of the soldiers who are left in this city, and of all the people. He is not seeking their welfare, but their harm." King Zedekiah said, "Behold, he is in your hands; for the king can do nothing against you." So they took Jeremiah and cast him into the cistern in the court of the guard, letting him down by ropes. There was no water in the cistern, but only mire, and Jeremiah sank in the mire.

When Ebed-melech the Ethiopian, a eunuch in the king's house, heard that they had put Jeremiah into the cistern, he went to the king and said, "My lord, these men have done evil in that they cast Jeremiah the prophet into the cistern; he will die there." Then the king commanded Ebed-melech, "Take three men with you from here, and lift Jeremiah out of the cistern before he dies." So Ebed-melech took the men and went to the house of the king, to a wardrobe of the storehouse, and took from there old rags and worn-out clothes, which he let down to Jeremiah in the cistern by ropes. Ebed-melech said to Jeremiah, "Put the rags and clothes between your armpits and the ropes." Jeremiah did so, and they drew him up out of the cistern. And Jeremiah remained in the court of the guard.

King Zedekiah sent for Jeremiah the prophet and received him at the third entrance of the temple of the LORD. The king said, "I will ask you a question; hide nothing from me." Jeremiah said, "If I tell you, will you not be sure to put me to death? And if I give you counsel, you will not listen to me." Then Zedekiah swore secretly, "As the LORD lives, I will not put you to death or deliver you into the hand of these men who seek your life."

Then Jeremiah said, "Thus says the LORD, If you will surrender to the king of Babylon, this city shall not be burned with fire, and you and your house shall live. But if you do not, the Chaldeans shall take the city and burn it, and you shall not escape from their hand." But Zedekiah said, "I am afraid of the Jews who have deserted to the Chaldeans, lest I be handed over to them and they abuse me." Jeremiah said, "You shall not be given to them. Obey now the voice of the LORD, and it shall be well with you. But if you refuse, this is the vision which the LORD has shown to me: Behold, all the women left in the house of the king of Judah were being led out to the princes of the king of Babylon and were saying, 'Your trusted friends have deceived you; now that your feet are sunk in the mire, they turn away from you.' Your wives and sons shall be led out to the Chaldeans, and you yourself shall be seized by the king of Babylon."

Then Zedekiah said, "Let no one know of these words and you shall not die. If the princes hear that I have spoken with you and come to you and say, 'Tell us what you said to the king and he to you; hide nothing and we will not put you to death,' then you shall say to them, 'I made a humble plea to the king that he would not send me back to the dungeon to die there.'" All the princes did ask, and Jeremiah answered as the king had instructed. So they left him, for the conversation had not been overheard. And Jeremiah remained in the court of the guard until the day that Jerusalem was taken.

In the eleventh year of Zedekiah, in the fourth month, on the ninth day of the month, a breach was made in the city. When Jerusalem was taken, all the princes and officers of the king of Babylon came and sat in the middle gate. When Zedekiah and his soldiers saw them, they fled at night by way of the king's garden through the gate between the two walls; and they went toward the Arabah. But the army of the Chaldeans pursued them, and overtook Zedekiah in the plains of Jericho; and they brought him up to Nebuchadrezzar king of Babylon, at Riblah; and he passed sentence upon him. The king of Babylon slew the sons of Zedekiah at Riblah before his eyes, and he also slew all the nobles of Judah. He put out the eyes of Zedekiah, and bound him in fetters to take him to Babylon.

The Chaldeans burned the king's house and the house of the people, and broke down the walls of Jerusalem. Then the captain of the guard carried into exile the rest of the people who were left in the city, and those who had deserted to him. But he left in Judah some of the poor people who owned nothing, and gave them vineyards and fields at the same time.

Nebuchadrezzar gave command concerning Jeremiah through the captain of the guard, saying, "Look after him well and do him no harm, but deal with him as he tells you." So the chief officers of the king of Babylon took Jeremiah from the court of the guard. They entrusted him to the governor whom Nebuchadrezzar had appointed in Judah, Gedaliah the son of Ahikam, son of Shaphan, that he should take him home. So he dwelt among the people.

Now the word of the LORD had come to Jeremiah while he was shut up in the court of the guard: "Go, and say to Ebed-melech the Ethiopian, 'Thus says the LORD of hosts: Behold, I will fulfil my words against this city for evil and not for good. But I will deliver you on that day, and you shall not be given into the hand of the men of whom you are afraid. For I will surely save you; you shall not fall by the sword, but shall have your life as a prize of war, because you have put your trust in me, says the LORD.'"

WHEN ALL THE captains of the forces in the open country and their men heard that the king of Babylon had appointed Gedaliah governor of Judah, they went to him at Mizpah. Among these were Ishmael the son of Nethaniah of the royal family, and Johanan the son of Kareah. Gedaliah swore to them and their men, saying, "Do not be afraid to serve the king of Babylon, and it shall be well with you. I will dwell at Mizpah, to stand for you before the Chaldeans who will come to us; but as for you, gather wine and summer fruits and oil, and store them in your vessels, and dwell in your cities that you have taken." Likewise, when all the Jews who were in Moab or among the Ammonites or in other lands heard that the king of Babylon had left a remnant in Judah, they also returned to Gedaliah at Mizpah; and they gathered wine and summer fruits in great abundance.

Now Johanan and other leaders came and said to Gedaliah, "Do you know that the king of the Ammonites has sent Ishmael the son of Nethaniah to take your life?" Gedaliah would not believe them. Then Johanan spoke to him secretly, "Let me go and slay Ishmael, and no one will know it. Why should he take your life, so that all the Jews who are gathered about you would be scattered, and the remnant of Judah would perish?" But Gedaliah said, "You shall not do this thing, for you are speaking falsely of Ishmael."

In the seventh month, Ishmael came with ten men to Gedaliah. As they ate bread together there at Mizpah, Ishmael and the men with him rose up and struck down Gedaliah with the sword. Then Ishmael took away captive the king's daughters and all those whom Nebuchadrezzar had committed to Gedaliah, and set out to cross over to the Ammonites.

When Johanan and the captains with him heard of the evil Ishmael had done, they took their men and went to fight against him. They came upon him at the great pool in Gibeon. And all the people Ishmael had carried away captive saw Johanan, and rejoiced and went to him. But Ishmael escaped with eight men to the Ammonites. Then Johanan took all the rest of the people back from Gibeon. And they stayed at Geruth Chimham near Bethlehem, intending to go to Egypt because of the Chaldeans; for they were afraid of them, because Ishmael had slain Gedaliah, whom the king of Babylon had made governor.

THEN JOHANAN AND Azariah the son of Hoshaiah, and all the commanders of the forces, and all the people from the least to the greatest, came to Jeremiah the prophet. "Pray to the LORD for us," they said, "for all this remnant (for we are left but a few of many), that the LORD may show us the way we should go, and the thing that we should do." Jeremiah said to them, "I will pray to the LORD according to your request, and whatever he answers I will tell you." They said, "May the LORD be a true and faithful witness against us if we do not act according to all the word the LORD sends to us. Whether it is good or evil, we will obey the voice of the LORD our God, that it may be well with us."

At the end of ten days the word of the LORD came to Jeremiah. Then he summoned Johanan and all the people, and said, "Thus says the LORD, to whom you sent me to present your supplication: If you will remain in this land, then I will build you up and not pull you down; I will plant you, and not pluck you up; for I repent of the evil which I did to you. Do not fear the king of Babylon, for I am with you. I will grant you mercy, that he may have mercy on you and let you remain in your own land.

"But if you disobey, saying, 'No, we will go to Egypt, where we shall not see war or be hungry for bread,' then hear the word of the LORD, O remnant of Judah: If you set your faces to enter Egypt, then the sword which you fear shall overtake you there, and the famine shall follow hard after you. All who go to Egypt to live shall die; they shall have no survivor from the evil I will bring upon them.

"For thus says the LORD to you, O remnant of Judah: 'Do not go to Egypt.' Know that I have warned you this day that you go astray at the cost of your lives. For you sent me to the LORD, saying, 'Whatever the LORD says, we will do it.' And I have this day declared it to you. Now therefore know for a certainty that you shall die by the sword, by famine, and by pestilence in the place you desire to go to live."

When Jeremiah finished speaking, Azariah and Johanan and all the insolent men said to him, "You are telling a lie. The LORD did not send you to say, 'Do not go to Egypt to live'; but Baruch the son of Neriah has set you against us, to deliver us to the Chaldeans, that they may kill us or take us into exile in Babylon."

So Johanan and all the commanders of the forces took all the remnant who had returned to Judah from the nations to which they had been driven—the men, the women, the children, the princesses—and every person whom Nebuchadrezzar's captain of the guard had left with Gedaliah, also Jeremiah the prophet and Baruch the son of Neriah. And they came into Egypt, for they did not obey the voice of the LORD. And they arrived at Tahpanhes.

There the word of the LORD came to Jeremiah: "Take in your hands large stones, and hide them in the mortar in the pavement at the entrance to Pharaoh's palace in Tahpanhes, in the sight of the men of Judah, and say to them, 'Thus says the LORD of hosts, the God of Israel: Behold, I will send Nebuchadrezzar the king of Babylon, my servant, and he will set his throne above these stones and spread his royal canopy over them. He shall come and smite Egypt, giving to the pestilence those who are doomed to the pestilence, to captivity those who are doomed to captivity, and to the sword those who are doomed to the sword. He shall kindle a fire in the temples of the gods of Egypt; he shall clean the land of Egypt, as a shepherd cleans his cloak of vermin; and he shall go away from there in peace. He shall break the obelisks of Heliopolis; and the temples of the gods of Egypt he shall burn.'"

THE WORD THAT came to Jeremiah concerning all the Jews that dwelt in the land of Egypt, at Migdol, at Tahpanhes, at Memphis, and in the land of Pathros, "Thus says the LORD of hosts, the God of Israel: You have seen all the evil that I brought upon Jerusalem and the cities of Judah. Behold, this day they are a desolation, because they went to burn incense and serve gods that they knew not, neither they, nor you, nor your fathers. Yet I persistently sent to you all my servants the prophets, saying, 'Oh, do not do this abominable thing that I hate!' But they did not listen. Therefore my wrath was kindled and the cities of Judah became a waste, as at this day.

"And now thus says the LORD God of hosts: Why do you commit this great evil against yourselves, to cut off man and woman, infant and child, from the midst of Judah, leaving you no remnant? Why do you provoke me to anger, burning incense to other gods in Egypt, that you may become a curse among all the nations of the earth? Have you forgotten the wickedness of your fathers, of the kings of Judah and their wives, your own wickedness, and the wickedness of your wives, which they committed in the streets of Jerusalem? They have not humbled themselves even to this day, nor walked in my law which I set before you and your fathers.

"Therefore, behold, I will set my face against you for evil, to cut off all Judah. The remnant who have come to Egypt to live shall not return to Judah, except some fugitives."

Then all the men who knew that their wives had offered incense to other gods, and all the women who stood by, a great assembly, answered Jeremiah: "As for the word which you have spoken to us in the name of the LORD, we will not listen. We will burn incense to the queen of heaven and pour out libations to her, as we did, both we and our fathers, our kings and our princes, in the streets of Jerusalem; for then we had plenty of food, and prospered. But since we left off, we have lacked everything and have been consumed by sword and famine." And the women said, "Was it without our husbands' approval that we made cakes for the queen of heaven bearing her image and poured out libations to her?"

Then Jeremiah said to all the men and women who had given him this answer: "As for the incense that you burned in Judah, did not the LORD remember it? The LORD could no longer bear the abominations which you committed. It is because you sinned against the LORD and did not walk in his law that evil has befallen you, as at this day. Hear now the word of the LORD, all you of Judah who dwell in Egypt: You have declared, 'We will surely perform our vows to the queen of heaven and pour out libations to her.' Confirm your vows and perform your vows! Therefore, behold, I have sworn by my great name, says the LORD, that my name shall no more be invoked by the mouth of any man of Judah in all Egypt, saying, 'As the Lord GOD lives.'

"Behold, I am watching over them for evil and not for good; all the men of Judah in Egypt shall be consumed until there is an end of them. Those who do escape shall return to Judah, few in number; and all the remnant shall know whose word will stand, mine or theirs. This shall be the sign to you, says the LORD, that I will punish you in this place, in order that you may know that my words will surely stand against you for evil: Behold, I will give Pharaoh Hophra king of Egypt into the hand of his enemies, as I gave Zedekiah king of Judah into the hand of Nebuchadrezzar king of Babylon, who sought his life."

THE WORD THAT JEREMIAH THE PROPHET spoke to Baruch the son of Neriah, when he wrote these words in a book at the dictation of Jeremiah, in the fourth year of Jehoiakim the son of Josiah, king of Judah: "Thus says the LORD, the God of Israel, to you, O Baruch: You said, 'Woe is me! for the LORD has added sorrow to my pain; I am weary with my groaning, and I find no rest.' Thus says the LORD: Behold, what I have built I am breaking down, and what I have planted I am plucking up—that is, the whole land. And do you seek great things for yourself? Seek them not; for behold, I am bringing evil upon all flesh, says the LORD; but I will give you your life as a prize of war in all places to which you may go."

THE WORD OF the LORD which came to Jeremiah the prophet concerning the nations.

About Egypt. Concerning the army of Pharaoh Neco, king of Egypt, which was by the river Euphrates at Carchemish and which Nebuchadrezzar king of Babylon defeated in the fourth year of Jehoiakim, king of Judah:

"Prepare buckler and shield, and advance for battle! Harness the horses; mount, O horsemen! Take your stations, polish your spears, put on your coats of mail!

"Why have I seen it? They have turned backward. Their warriors have fled; they look not back—terror on every side! says the LORD. In the north by the river Euphrates they have stumbled and fallen.

"Who is this, rising like the Nile, like rivers whose waters surge? Egypt rises like the Nile. He said, I will cover the earth, destroy its cities. Advance, O horses! Let the warriors go forth!

"That day is the day of the Lord GOD, to avenge himself on his foes. The sword shall devour, and drink its fill of their blood. For the Lord GOD holds a sacrifice by the river Euphrates. Go up to Gilead, and take balm, O daughter of Egypt! In vain you have used many medicines; there is no healing for you. The nations have heard of your shame, and the earth is full of your cry; for warrior has stumbled against warrior; they have both fallen together."

THE WORD WHICH the LORD spoke to Jeremiah about the coming of Nebuchadrezzar king of Babylon to smite the land of Egypt:

"Declare in Egypt, in Migdol, Memphis, and Tahpanhes; say, 'Be prepared, for the sword shall devour round about you.' Why has Apis fled, why did your bull not stand? Because the LORD thrust him down. Your multitude stumbled and fell, and said one to another, 'Arise! Let us go back to our own land, because of the sword of the oppressor.' Call the name of Pharaoh, king of Egypt, 'Noisy one who lets the hour go by.'

"As I live, says the King, whose name is the LORD of hosts, like Tabor among the mountains shall one come! Prepare your baggage for exile, O inhabitants of Egypt! For Memphis shall become a waste, a ruin. A beautiful heifer is Egypt, but a gadfly has come upon her. Even her hired soldiers, in her midst like fatted calves, have turned and fled; they did not stand; the day of their calamity has come.

"She makes a sound like a serpent gliding away, for her enemies march against her with axes. They shall cut down her forest, says the LORD, impenetrable though it is; for they are more numerous than locusts. The daughter of Egypt shall be put to shame.

"Behold, I am bringing punishment upon Egypt and her gods and her kings, upon Pharaoh and those who trust in him. I will deliver them into the hand of Nebuchadrezzar king of Babylon. Afterward Egypt shall be inhabited as in the days of old, says the LORD.

"But fear not, O Israel my servant, for I am with you. I will make a full end of all the nations to which I have driven you. But of you I will not make a full end. I will chasten you in just measure."

THE WORD OF the LORD that came to Jeremiah concerning the Philistines, before Pharaoh smote Gaza.

"Thus says the LORD: Behold, waters are rising out of the north, and they shall overflow the land and all who dwell in it, and every inhabitant shall wail. At the noise of the stamping of stallions and the rumbling of chariot wheels, the fathers look not back to their children, so feeble are their hands. For the LORD is destroying the Philistines. Baldness has come upon Gaza, Ashkelon has perished.

"Ah, sword of the LORD! How long till you are quiet? Put yourself into your scabbard, rest and be still!

"How can it be quiet, when the LORD has given it a charge? Against Ashkelon and against the seashore he has appointed it."

CONCERNING MOAB. THUS says the LORD of hosts, the God of Israel: "Woe to Nebo, for it is laid waste! Kiriathaim is put to shame, it is taken; the fortress is broken down; the renown of Moab is no more. Hark! a cry from Horonaim. Moab is destroyed.

"Flee! Save yourselves! Be like a wild ass in the desert! Because you trusted in strongholds and treasures, you shall be taken; Chemosh shall go into exile with his priests. No city shall escape, and the valley shall perish, as the LORD has spoken.

"Cursed is he who does the work of the LORD with slackness; and cursed is he who keeps back his sword from bloodshed. Moab has been at ease from his youth and has settled on his lees; he has not been emptied from vessel to vessel, nor has he gone into exile; so his taste remains in him. Therefore the days are coming, says the LORD, when I shall send to him tilters who will tilt him, and empty his vessels, and break his jars in pieces. Then Moab shall be ashamed of Chemosh.

"Make Moab drunk, because he magnified himself against the LORD; so he shall wallow in his vomit, and he too shall be held in derision. Was not

Israel a derision to you? Was he found among thieves, that whenever you spoke of him you wagged your head? Dwell in the rock, O inhabitants of Moab, like the dove that nests in the sides of a gorge.

"We have heard of the pride of Moab—he is very proud—and of the haughtiness of his heart. I know his insolence, says the LORD; his boasts are false. Therefore I wail for all Moab. Upon your summer fruits and your vintage the destroyer has fallen. Gladness and joy have been taken away from the fruitful land; I have made the wine cease from the wine presses; no one treads them with shouts of joy; the shouting is not the shout of joy. On housetops, in the squares, there is nothing but lamentation; for I have broken Moab like a vessel for which no one cares.

"Woe to you, O Moab! The people of Chemosh is undone; your sons have been taken captive, and your daughters. Yet I will restore the fortunes of Moab in the latter days, says the LORD." Thus far is the judgment on Moab.

CONCERNING THE AMMONITES. Thus says the LORD: "Behold, the days are coming when I will cause the battle cry to be heard against Rabbah of the Ammonites; it shall become a desolate mound; then Israel shall dispossess those who dispossessed him. Wail, O Heshbon! Cry, O daughters of Rabbah! Gird yourselves with sackcloth, and run to and fro among the hedges! For Milcom shall go into exile, with his priests and his princes. You shall be driven out, every man straight before him, with none to gather the fugitives. But afterward I will restore the fortunes of the Ammonites, says the LORD."

CONCERNING EDOM. THUS says the LORD of hosts: "Is wisdom no more in Teman? Has counsel perished from the prudent? Dwell in the depths, O inhabitants of Dedan! For I will bring the calamity of Esau upon him when I punish him. If thieves came by night, would they not destroy only enough for themselves? But I have stripped Esau bare, I have uncovered his hiding places. His brothers are destroyed, and his neighbors; and he is no more.

"Leave your fatherless children, I will keep them alive; and let your widows trust in me."

For thus says the LORD: "If those who did not deserve to drink the cup must drink it, will you go unpunished? You shall not; you must drink. For I have sworn by myself, says the LORD, that Bozrah shall become a taunt, a waste, and a curse. Every one who passes by Edom will be horrified, and no man shall sojourn in her.

"Behold, one shall mount up and fly swiftly like an eagle, and spread his wings against Bozrah, and the heart of the warriors of Edom shall be in that day like the heart of a woman in her pangs."

CONCERNING DAMASCUS. "DAMASCUS has become feeble, she turned to flee, and panic seized her. How the famous city is forsaken, the joyful city! All her soldiers shall be destroyed in that day, says the LORD of hosts."

Concerning Kedar and the kingdoms of Hazor which Nebuchadrezzar king of Babylon smote. Thus says the Lord: "Rise up, advance against Kedar! Destroy the people of the east! Their tents, their camels, and their flocks shall be taken, and all their goods, and men shall cry to them: 'Terror on every side!' Flee, wander far away, O inhabitants of Hazor! says the Lord. For Nebuchadrezzar king of Babylon has made a plan against you.

"Rise up, advance against a nation at ease, that dwells securely, that has no gates or bars, that dwells alone. Their camels shall become booty, their cattle a spoil. I will scatter to every wind those who cut short their hair, and I will bring calamity on them from every side, says the Lord. Hazor shall become a haunt of jackals."

Concerning Elam. Thus says the Lord of hosts: "Behold, I will break the bow of Elam, the mainstay of their might; and I will bring upon Elam the four winds from the four quarters of heaven; and I will scatter them to all those winds, and there shall be no nation to which those driven out of Elam shall not come. But in the latter days I will restore the fortunes of Elam."

The word which the Lord spoke concerning Babylon, by Jeremiah the prophet:
"Declare among the nations, set up a banner and proclaim: 'Babylon is taken! Her idols are put to shame.' For out of the north a nation has come up against her which shall make her land a desolation. In those days, says the Lord, the people of Israel and the people of Judah shall come together, weeping as they come; and they shall seek the Lord their God. They shall ask the way to Zion, with faces turned toward it, saying, 'Come, let us join ourselves to the Lord in an everlasting covenant.' Because of the sword of the oppressor, every one shall turn to his own people, and every one shall flee to his own land.

"Israel is a hunted sheep driven away by lions. First the king of Assyria devoured him, and now the king of Babylon has gnawed his bones. Therefore thus says the Lord: Behold, I am bringing punishment on Babylon, as I punished Assyria. I will restore Israel to his pasture, and he shall feed on Carmel, and be satisfied on the hills of Ephraim. In those days, says the Lord, iniquity shall be sought in Israel and Judah, and none shall be found; for I will pardon those whom I leave as a remnant.

"Hark! they escape from Babylon, to declare in Zion the vengeance of the Lord our God, vengeance for his temple.

"Thus says the Lord of hosts: The people of Israel are oppressed, and the people of Judah with them; all who took them captive have held them fast, they refuse to let them go. Their Redeemer is strong; the Lord of hosts is his name. He will surely plead their cause, that he may give rest to the earth, but unrest to the inhabitants of Babylon.

"A sword upon the Chaldeans, says the Lord, upon the inhabitants of

Babylon, upon her princes and her wise men! A sword upon the diviners, that they may become fools! A sword upon her warriors, that they may be destroyed! A sword upon her horses and upon her chariots, and upon all the foreign troops in her midst, that they may become women! A sword upon all her treasures, that they may be plundered!

"Behold, like a lion coming up against a strong sheepfold, I will suddenly make them run away from her; and I will appoint over her whomever I choose. For who is like me? Who will summon me? What shepherd can stand before me? Therefore hear the plan which the LORD has made against Babylon. Babylon was a golden cup in the LORD's hand; the nations drank of her wine, therefore the nations went mad. Suddenly she has fallen and been broken; wail for her! We would have healed Babylon, but she was not healed. Forsake her, and let us go each to his own country; for her judgment has reached up to heaven. The LORD has brought forth our vindication; come, let us declare in Zion the work of the LORD our God.

"The LORD has stirred up the spirit of the kings of the Medes, because his purpose is to destroy Babylon, for that is the vengeance of the LORD for his temple. O you who dwell by many waters, rich in treasures, your end has come, the thread of your life is cut. The LORD of hosts has sworn by himself: Surely I will fill you with men, as many as locusts, and they shall raise the shout of victory over you.

"You are my hammer and weapon of war: with you I break nations in pieces; with you I break the horse and his rider, the chariot and the charioteer; with you I break in pieces man and woman, the young man and the maiden; with you I break in pieces the shepherd and his flock, the farmer and his team; with you I break in pieces governors and commanders.

"But now I will requite Babylon and all the inhabitants of Chaldea before your very eyes for all the evil they have done in Zion. Behold, I am against you, O destroying mountain, which destroys the whole earth; I will stretch out my hand and roll you down from the crags, and make you a burnt mountain. No stone shall be taken from you for a corner and no stone for a foundation, but you shall be a perpetual waste, says the LORD."

Let Jerusalem say, "Nebuchadrezzar the king of Babylon has crushed me; he has made me an empty vessel, he has swallowed me like a monster; he has filled his belly with my delicacies, he has rinsed me out. The violence done to me and to my kinsmen be upon Babylon."

Therefore thus says the LORD: "Behold, I will plead your cause and take vengeance for you. They shall roar together like lions; they shall growl like lions' whelps. While they are inflamed I will prepare them a feast and make them drunk, till they swoon away and sleep a perpetual sleep.

"How Babylon is taken, the praise of the whole earth seized! I will punish Baal in Babylon, and take out of his mouth what he has swallowed. The nations shall flow to him no longer.

"Go out of the midst of her, my people! Let every man save his life from the fierce anger of the LORD! Babylon must fall for the slain of Israel, as for Babylon have fallen the slain of all the earth. You that have escaped from the sword, go, stand not still! Remember the LORD, let Jerusalem come into your mind: 'Dishonor has covered our face, for aliens have come into the holy places of the LORD's house.' Therefore, behold, the days are coming, says the LORD, when I will execute judgment upon her images. Though Babylon should mount up to heaven and fortify her strong height, yet destroyers would come from me upon her, says the LORD.

"Hark! a cry from Babylon! For the LORD is laying Babylon waste and will still her mighty voice; a destroyer has come upon her, upon Babylon. The LORD is a God of recompense, he will surely requite."

THE WORD WHICH Jeremiah the prophet commanded Seraiah the son of Neriah, when he went with Zedekiah king of Judah to Babylon, in the fourth year of his reign. Seraiah was the quartermaster. Jeremiah wrote in a book all the evil that should come upon Babylon, all these words that are written concerning Babylon. And Jeremiah said to Seraiah: "When you come to Babylon, see that you read all these words, and say, 'O LORD, thou hast said concerning this place that thou wilt cut it off, so that nothing shall dwell in it, neither man nor beast, and it shall be desolate for ever.' When you finish reading this book, bind a stone to it, and cast it into the midst of the Euphrates, and say, 'Thus shall Babylon sink, to rise no more, because of the evil that I am bringing upon her.'"

Thus far are the words of Jeremiah.

LAMENTATIONS

The Book of Lamentations is a collection of five laments, communal and personal, over the sack of Jerusalem in 586 B.C., and for other sufferings inflicted on the Jews by their Babylonian conquerors. The common theme is the agony of the people, their apparent desertion by God, and the hope that God will yet restore a humbled and repentant Israel to its former glory. The name of the author is uncertain. Tradition assigns the book to Jeremiah, but in many ways it is quite unlike his acknowledged work. The writing of Lamentations can probably be dated in about the year 538 B.C., when the Jews were allowed to return from their exile in Babylon to a Jerusalem in ruins.

─────────

How lonely sits the city that was full of people! How like a widow is she that was great among the nations! A princess among cities has become a vassal. She weeps in the night, tears on her cheeks; among all her lovers she has none to comfort her; her friends have become her enemies.

Judah has gone into exile; she finds no resting place; her pursuers have overtaken her in her distress.

The roads to Zion mourn, for none come to appointed feasts; all her gates are desolate; her priests groan; her maidens have been dragged away; her foes prosper. The LORD has made her suffer for the multitude of her transgressions. From the daughter of Zion has departed all majesty. Her princes have become like stags that find no pasture; they have fled without strength before the pursuer.

Jerusalem remembers in the days of her bitterness the precious things that were hers of old. When her people fell and there was none to help her, the foe gloated, mocking at her downfall. Jerusalem sinned grievously, therefore she became filthy; all who honored her despise her, for they have seen her nakedness; yea, she herself turns her face away. She took no thought of her doom, therefore her fall is terrible. "O LORD, behold my affliction, for the enemy has triumphed!"

The enemy has stretched out his hands over all her precious things; she has seen the nations invade her sanctuary, those whom thou didst forbid to enter thy congregation. All her people groan as they search for bread; they trade their treasures for food. "Look, O LORD, behold, I am despised."

"Is it nothing to you, all you who pass by? Look, see if there is any sorrow like the sorrow the LORD inflicted upon me on the day of his anger. From on high he sent fire into my bones; he spread a net for my feet. My transgressions were bound into a yoke, and by his hand they were set upon my neck; he caused my strength to fail.

"The Lord flouted my mighty men in the midst of me; he summoned an assembly against me to crush my young men; the Lord has trodden as in a wine press the virgin daughter of Judah. For these things I weep."

Zion stretches out her hands, but there is none to comfort her; the LORD has commanded against Jacob that his neighbors should be his foes.

"The LORD is in the right, for I have rebelled against his word; but behold my suffering, all you peoples; my maidens and young men have gone into captivity. I called to my lovers but they deceived me; my priests and elders perished in the city while seeking food.

"Behold, O LORD, my soul is in tumult, my heart is wrung within me, because I have been rebellious. In the street the sword bereaves; in the house it is like death.

"All my enemies have heard of my trouble; they are glad that thou hast done it. Bring thou the day thou hast announced, and let them be as I am. Let all their evil-doing come before thee; and deal with them as thou hast dealt with me because of all my transgressions; for my groans are many and my heart is faint."

How THE LORD in his anger has set the daughter of Zion under a cloud! He has cast down from heaven the splendor of Israel. He has destroyed without mercy the habitations of Jacob, and brought to dishonor the kingdom and its rulers. He has bent his bow like an enemy, and has slain the pride of Zion; he has poured out his fury like fire. The Lord has destroyed Israel, all its palaces and strongholds, and has multiplied in Judah lamentation and mourning.

The Lord has laid in ruins the place of his worship; he has ended in Zion sabbath and feast. The Lord has scorned his altar, disowned his sanctuary, and delivered them into the enemy's hand.

He determined to lay in ruins the wall of Jerusalem; he restrained not his hand, causing rampart and wall to languish together. Her gates have sunk into the ground; her princes are exiled; the law is no more, and her prophets obtain no vision from the LORD. The elders sit silent in sackcloth; the maidens bow their heads to the ground.

My eyes are spent with weeping, because of the destruction of my people, because infants and babes faint in the streets. "Where is bread?" they cry, as their life is poured out on their mothers' bosom. What can I say, O daughter of Zion, to comfort you? Vast as the sea is your ruin; who can restore you?

Your prophets have seen for you false and deceptive visions; they have not exposed your iniquity to restore your fortunes.

All who pass by wag their heads at Jerusalem. "Is this the city once called the perfection of beauty, the joy of all the earth?" Your enemies rail against you; they cry: "We have destroyed her! This is the day we longed for; now we see it!" The LORD has done what he purposed long ago.

Cry aloud to the Lord, O daughter of Zion! Let tears stream down without respite! Arise, cry out in the night! Pour out your heart like water before the Lord! Lift your hands to him for the lives of your children, who hunger.

O LORD, with whom hast thou dealt thus? Should women eat the children of their tender care? Should priest and prophet be slain in thy sanctuary? In the dust lie the young and the old; in the day of thy anger thou hast slain them without mercy. Thou didst invite as to an appointed feast my terrors on every side; none escaped or survived that day; those I pampered and reared my enemy destroyed.

I AM THE man afflicted by the rod of his wrath; he turns his hand against me the whole day long. He has made my flesh waste away and broken my bones; he has made me dwell in darkness like the dead of long ago. He has walled me about so I cannot escape; though I cry for help, he shuts out my prayer; he has blocked my ways with hewn stones, he has made my paths crooked.

He is to me like a bear lying in wait; he led me off my way and tore me to pieces. His bow drove into my heart the arrows of his quiver; I have become the laughingstock of all peoples, the burden of their songs. He has made my teeth grind on gravel, and made me cower in ashes; my soul is bereft of peace, I have forgotten what happiness is; so I say, "Gone is my glory, my expectation from the LORD."

Remember my affliction and my bitterness, the wormwood and the gall! My soul is bowed down within me. But this I call to mind, and therefore I have hope: the steadfast love of the LORD never ceases, his mercies never come to an end; they are new every morning; great is thy faithfulness. "The LORD is my portion," says my soul, "therefore I will hope in him."

The LORD is good to those who wait for him, to the soul that seeks him. It is good to wait quietly for his salvation. It is good for a man to bear the yoke in his youth. Then let him sit alone in silence; let him put his mouth in the dust—there may yet be hope.

For the Lord will not cast off for ever, but, though he cause grief, he will have compassion according to the abundance of his steadfast love; for he does not willingly afflict or grieve the sons of men. To crush under foot the prisoners of the earth, to turn aside the right of a man in the presence of the Most High, to subvert a man in his cause, the Lord does not approve.

Whose command has come to pass, unless the Lord has ordained it? Is it not from the mouth of the Most High that good and evil come? Why should a living man complain about the punishment of his sins?

Let us examine our ways, and return to the LORD! Lift hearts and hands to God in heaven: "We have rebelled, and thou hast not forgiven. Thou hast wrapped thyself with anger and pursued us; thou hast wrapped thyself with a cloud no prayer can pass through. Thou hast made us as refuse among the peoples. Panic has come upon us; my eyes will flow with tears unceasing because of the destruction of my people, until the LORD from heaven looks down and sees.

"I have been hunted like a bird by those who were my enemies without cause; they flung me into the pit and cast stones on me; water closed over my head; I said, 'I am lost.' I called on thy name, O LORD, from the depths; thou didst hear my plea and didst come near, saying, 'Do not fear!'

"Thou hast redeemed my life, O LORD. Thou hast seen the wrong done me; judge thou my cause. Thou hast heard their taunts; their lips and thoughts are against me all day. I am the burden of their songs.

"Thou wilt requite them, O LORD, according to the work of their hands. Thou wilt give them dullness of heart; thy curse will be on them. Thou wilt pursue them in anger and destroy them."

HOW THE GOLD has grown dim, how the pure gold is changed! The holy stones lie scattered at the head of every street. The precious sons of Zion, worth their weight in fine gold, how they are reckoned as earthen pots, the work of a potter's hands!

Even the jackals give the breast to their young, but the daughter of my people has become cruel. The tongue of the nursling cleaves to the roof of its mouth for thirst; the children beg for food. Those who feasted on dainties perish in the streets; those brought up in purple lie on ash heaps. For the chastisement of the daughter of my people has been greater than the punishment of Sodom, which was overthrown in a moment. Her princes were whiter than milk, their bodies more ruddy than coral. Now blacker than soot, they are not recognized in the streets; their skin has shriveled dry as wood. Happier were the victims of the sword than the victims of hunger, stricken by want. The hands of compassionate women have boiled their own children for food.

The LORD gave full vent to his wrath. He poured out hot anger, and kindled a fire in Zion which consumed its foundations. The kings of the earth did not believe, nor any inhabitants of the world, that foe or enemy could enter Jerusalem's gates. It happened because of the sins of her prophets and priests, who shed in her midst the blood of the righteous. They wandered, blind, through the streets, so defiled with blood that none could touch their garments. "Away! Unclean!" men cried. "Touch not!" So they became fugitives, wanderers; men said among the nations, "They shall stay with us no longer." The LORD himself has scattered them; no honor was shown to the priests, no favor to the elders.

Our eyes failed, ever watching for help; we watched for a nation which could not save. Men dogged our steps, we could not walk in our streets; our days were numbered, for our end had come. Our pursuers were swifter than vultures; they chased us on the mountains, they lay in wait for us in the wilderness. He who was the breath of our nostrils, the LORD's anointed, was taken in their traps; he of whom we said, "Under his shadow we shall live among the nations."

Rejoice, O daughter of Edom, dweller in the land of Uz; but to you also the cup shall pass; you shall be drunk and strip yourself naked. The punishment of your iniquity, O daughter of Zion, is accomplished; he will keep you in exile no longer. But you, O daughter of Edom, he will punish; your sins he will bare.

REMEMBER, O LORD, what has befallen us; behold our disgrace! Our inheritance has been turned over to strangers; we have become orphans. We must pay for the water we drink, the wood we get. With a yoke on our necks we are driven hard. We have held out our hands to Egypt, and to Assyria, to get enough bread.

Our fathers sinned, and are no more; we bear their iniquities. Slaves rule over us; there is none to deliver us. We get our bread at peril of our lives because of the sword in the wilderness. Our skin is hot as an oven with the burning heat of famine.

Women are ravished, princes hung up by their hands; no respect is shown to the elders. Young men are compelled to grind at the mill; boys stagger under loads of wood. The old men have quit the city gate, the young men their music. Our dancing has been turned to mourning.

The crown has fallen from our head; woe to us, we have sinned! Our heart has become sick, our eyes have grown dim, Mount Zion lies desolate.

But thou, O LORD, dost reign for ever; thy throne endures to all generations. Why dost thou so long forsake us? Restore us to thyself, O LORD! Renew our days as of old! Or hast thou in thine anger rejected us utterly?

EZEKIEL

Eleven years before the fall of Jerusalem (586 B.C.), Ezekiel was deported, with other Jewish captives, to a settlement in Babylon. Here he received visions and was called to preach to his fellow exiles, a task he pursued faithfully for at least twenty-five years. He was a man of stern and inflexible energy of will and character, and his work consisted not only in sermons but also in prophetic behavior, such as sleeping on one side, not mourning over the sudden death of his wife, and eating a book. His prophecy falls into three main divisions: a warning to his people to repent or perish; judgments of doom directed against seven surrounding nations; and, after the fall of Jerusalem, prophecies of restoration and return, as in the vision of the valley of dry bones. Unlike other prophets of Israel, Ezekiel was also a priest, which accounts for his special interest in how the temple in Jerusalem should be restored after the Exile ended. His book explicitly revokes the principle that the sins of the fathers are visited on the children, and stresses the idea of personal responsibility before God.

I N THE THIRTIETH year, in the fourth month, on the fifth day of the month, as I was among the exiles by the river Chebar, the heavens were opened, and I saw visions of God. On the fifth day of the month (it was the fifth year of the exile of King Jehoiachin), the word of the LORD came to Ezekiel the priest, the son of Buzi, in the land of the Chaldeans by the river Chebar; and the hand of the LORD was upon him there.

As I looked, behold, a stormy wind came out of the north, and a great cloud, with brightness round about it, and fire flashing forth continually, and in the midst of the fire, as it were gleaming bronze. From the midst of it came the likeness of four living creatures. They had the form of men, but each had four faces and four wings. Their legs were straight, and the soles of their feet were like the sole of a calf's foot; they sparkled like burnished bronze. Under their wings on their four sides they had human hands. As for the likeness of their faces, each had the face of a man in front, the face of a lion on the right side, the face of an ox on the left side, and the face of an eagle at the back. Such were their faces. And each creature had two wings spread out above, each of which touched the wing of another, while two covered their bodies. And each went straight forward; wherever the spirit would go, they went, without turning. In the midst of the living creatures there was something that looked like burning coals of fire, like torches moving to and fro among the living creatures; the fire was bright, and out of it went forth lightning. And the living creatures darted to and fro, like a flash of lightning.

Now as I looked, I saw a wheel upon the earth beside the living creatures, one for each of the four of them. As for the wheels, their appearance was like the gleaming of a chrysolite; and the four had the same likeness, their construction being as it were a wheel within a wheel. When they went, they went in any of their four directions without turning. The wheels had rims and spokes; and their rims were full of eyes round about. When the living creatures went, the wheels went beside them; and when the living creatures rose from the earth, the wheels rose. Wherever the spirit would go, they went, and the wheels rose along with them; for the spirit of the living creatures was in the wheels. When those went, these went; and when those stood, these stood; and when those rose from the earth, the wheels rose along with them; for the spirit of the living creatures was in the wheels.

Over the heads of the living creatures there was the likeness of a firmament, shining like crystal, spread out above their heads. Under the firmament their wings were stretched out straight, one toward another; and each creature had two wings covering its body. When they went, I heard the sound of their wings like the sound of many waters, like the thunder of the Almighty, a sound of tumult like the sound of a host; when they stood still, they let down their wings. And there came a voice from above the firmament over their heads.

And above the firmament over their heads there was the likeness of a throne, in appearance like sapphire; seated above it was a likeness as it were of a human form. Upward from what had the appearance of his loins I saw gleaming bronze, like the appearance of fire enclosed round about; and downward I saw as it were the appearance of fire. There was brightness round about him. Like the bow that is in the cloud on the day of rain, so was the brightness round about.

Such was the appearance of the likeness of the glory of the LORD. When I saw it, I fell upon my face, and I heard a voice: "Son of man, stand upon your feet, and I will speak with you." When he spoke, the Spirit entered into me and set me upon my feet. "Son of man," he said, "I send you to the people of Israel, to a nation of rebels; they and their fathers have transgressed against me to this very day. The people also are impudent and stubborn. You shall say to them, 'Thus says the Lord GOD.' And whether they hear or refuse to hear, they will know there has been a prophet among them. Be not afraid of them, though briers and thorns are with you and you sit upon scorpions; be not afraid of their words, nor dismayed at their looks. Speak my words to them, whether they hear or refuse to hear; for they are a rebellious house.

"But you, son of man, hear what I say to you; be not rebellious. Open your mouth, and eat what I give you." And behold, a hand was stretched out to me, and a scroll was in it. He spread it before me, and written on the front and on the back were words of lamentation and woe. "Son of man," he said, "eat what is offered to you; eat this scroll, and go, speak to the house of Israel." So I opened my mouth, and he gave me the scroll to eat. It was in my mouth as sweet as honey. "Son of man, go," he said. "Speak with my words to the house of Israel. For you are not sent to a people of foreign speech and a hard language, whose words you cannot understand. Surely, if I sent you to such, they would listen to you. But the house of Israel will not listen, for they are not willing to listen to me; they are of a hard forehead and a stubborn heart. But I have made your face hard against their faces, and your forehead hard against their foreheads. Harder than flint have I made your forehead; fear them not. All my words that I shall speak to you receive in your heart. Get you to the exiles, your people, and say to them, 'Thus says the Lord GOD,' whether they hear or refuse to hear."

Then the Spirit lifted me up, and as the glory of the LORD arose from its place, I heard behind me the sound of a great earthquake; it was the sound of the wings of the living creatures as they touched one another, and the sound of the wheels beside them. The Spirit lifted me up and took me away, and I went in the heat of my spirit, the hand of the LORD being strong upon me; and I came to the exiles at Tel-abib, who dwelt by the river Chebar. I sat there overwhelmed among them seven days.

At the end of seven days the word of the LORD came to me: "Son of man, I have made you a watchman for the house of Israel; whenever you hear a word from my mouth, you shall give them warning from me. If I say to the wicked, 'You shall surely die,' and you give him no warning to turn from his wicked way in order to save his life, that man shall die in his iniquity; but his blood I will require at your hand. But if you warn him, and he does not turn from his wickedness, he shall die in his iniquity; but you will have saved your life. Again, if a righteous man turns from his righteousness and commits iniquity, and you do not warn him, he shall die for his sin, and his righteous deeds shall not be remembered; but his blood I will require at your hand. Nevertheless if you warn the righteous man not to sin, and he does not sin, he shall surely live, because he took warning; and you will have saved your life."

The hand of the LORD was there upon me. "Arise," he said, "go forth into the plain, and there I will speak with you." So I went into the plain; and lo, the glory of the LORD stood there, like the glory which I had seen by the river Chebar; and I fell on my face. But the Spirit entered into me, and set me upon my feet. "Go," he said, "shut yourself within your house. And behold, O son of man, cords will be placed upon you, and you shall be bound with them, so that you cannot go out among the people; and I will make your tongue cleave to the roof of your mouth, so that you shall be dumb and unable to reprove them; for they are a rebellious house. But when I speak with you, I will open your mouth, and you shall say to them, 'Thus says the Lord GOD'; he that will hear, let him hear, and he that will refuse to hear, let him refuse.

"And you, O son of man, take a brick and lay it before you, and portray upon it a city, even Jerusalem. Build a siege wall against it, and cast up a mound; set camps also against it, and plant battering rams round about. Take an iron plate, and place it as a wall between you and the city; set your face toward it, and press the siege against it. This is a sign for the house of Israel. Then lie on your left side, and I will lay the punishment of the house of Israel upon you; for three hundred and ninety days, the number of the years of their punishment, you shall bear the punishment of the house of Israel. When you have completed these, you shall lie on your right side and bear the punishment of the house of Judah; forty days I assign you, a day for each year. And you shall set your face toward the siege of Jerusalem and prophesy against the city. And behold, I will put cords upon you, so that you cannot turn from one side to the other, till you have completed the days of your siege.

"Take wheat and barley, beans and lentils, millet and spelt, and make bread of them. During the days that you lie on your side you shall eat it by weight, eight ounces a day. Water you shall drink by measure, a quart a day; once a day you shall eat and drink. And you shall bake your bread in the people's sight on human dung. Thus shall the people of Israel eat their bread unclean, among the nations whither I will drive them."

"Ah Lord GOD!" I said. "I have never defiled myself; from my youth up till now I have never eaten what died of itself or was torn by beasts, nor has foul flesh come into my mouth." Then he said, "See, I will let you have cow's dung instead of human dung, on which to prepare your bread. But I will break the staff of bread in Jerusalem; they shall eat bread by weight and with fearfulness, and drink water by measure and in dismay. I will do this that they may lack bread and water, and waste away under their punishment.

"And you, O son of man, take a sharp sword; use it as a barber's razor over your head and beard; then take balances for weighing, and divide the hair. A third you shall burn in the fire in the midst of the city when the days of the siege are completed; a third you shall take and strike with the sword round about the city; and a third you shall scatter to the wind, and I will unsheathe the sword after them. You shall take from these a small number, and bind them in the skirts of your robe. Of these again you shall take some, and burn them in the fire; from there a fire will come forth into all the house of Israel.

"This is Jerusalem; I have set her in the center of the nations, with countries round about her, and she has wickedly rebelled against my ordinances more than the other nations.

"Therefore thus says the Lord GOD: Because you are more turbulent than the nations round about you, and have not walked in my statutes, therefore I, even I, am against you; and I will execute judgments in the midst of you in the sight of the nations. Because of all your abominations I will do with you what I have never yet done, and the like of which I will never do again. Fathers shall eat their sons in the midst of you, and sons shall eat their fathers; any of you who survive I will scatter to all the winds. Wherefore, as I live, says the Lord GOD, surely, because you have defiled my sanctuary with your detestable things, therefore I will cut you down; my eye will not spare. A third of you shall die of pestilence and be consumed with famine in the midst of you; a third shall fall by the sword; and a third I will scatter to all the winds and will unsheathe the sword after them. Thus shall my anger spend itself; and they shall know that I the LORD have spoken in my jealousy.

"Yet I will leave some of you alive. Those of you who escape will remember me among the nations where they are carried captive, and they will be loathsome in their own sight for evils they have committed. They shall know that I am the LORD; I have not said in vain that I would do this evil to them."

IN THE SIXTH year, in the sixth month, on the fifth day of the month, as I sat in my house, with the elders of Judah sitting before me, the hand of the Lord GOD fell upon me. And lo, I beheld a form that had the appearance of a man; below what appeared to be his loins it was fire, and above, it was like the appearance of brightness, like gleaming bronze. He put forth the form of a hand, and took me by a lock of my head. The Spirit lifted me up between earth and heaven, and brought me in visions of God to Jerusalem, to the entrance of the gateway of the inner court that faces north, where was the seat of the image of jealousy, which provokes to jealousy. And behold, the glory of the God of Israel was there, like the vision that I saw in the plain. "Son of man," he said, "lift up your eyes now in the direction of the north." So I lifted up my eyes, and behold, north of the altar gate, in the entrance, was this image of jealousy. "Son of man," he said, "do you see the great abominations that the house of Israel are committing here, to drive me from my sanctuary? You will see still greater abominations."

He brought me to the door of the court; and behold, there was a hole in the wall. "Son of man," he said, "dig in the wall"; and when I dug, lo, there was a door. "Go in," he said, "and see the vile abominations they are committing here." So I went in, and there, portrayed upon the wall round about, were all kinds of creeping things, and loathsome beasts, and all the idols of the house of Israel. Before them stood seventy elders, each with his censer in his hand, and the smoke of the cloud of incense went up. "Son of man," he said, "have you seen what the elders of the house of Israel are doing in the dark, every man in his room of pictures? For they say, 'The LORD does not see us, the LORD has forsaken the land.' You will see still greater abominations which they commit."

Then he brought me to the entrance of the north gate of the house of the LORD; and behold, there sat women weeping for an alien god. "Have you seen this, O son of man?" he said. "You will see still greater abominations." He brought me into the inner court of the house of the LORD; and behold, at the door, between the porch and the altar, were about twenty-five men, with their backs to the temple of the LORD and their faces toward the east, worshiping the sun. "Have you seen this, O son of man?" he said. "Is it too slight a thing for the house of Judah to commit these abominations, that they should fill the land with violence, and provoke me further to anger? Therefore I will deal in wrath; my eye will not spare, nor will I have pity; and though they cry in my ears, I will not hear them."

Then he cried with a loud voice, saying, "Draw near, you executioners of the city, each with his destroying weapon." And lo, six men came from the direction of the upper gate, which faces north, every man with his weapon in his hand, and with them was a man clothed in linen, a writing case at his side. They went in and stood beside the bronze altar.

Now the glory of the God of Israel had gone up from the cherubim on which it rested to the threshold of the house; and he called to the man clothed in linen, and said, "Go through Jerusalem, and put a mark upon the foreheads of the men who sigh and groan over all the abominations that are committed in it." To the others he said, "Pass through the city after him, and smite; your eye shall not spare, and you shall show no pity; slay old men outright, young men and maidens, little children and women, but touch no one upon whom is the mark. Begin at my sanctuary." So they began with the elders who were before the house. Then he said to them, "Defile the house, and fill the courts with the slain. Go forth." So they went forth, and smote in the city. While they were smiting, and I was left alone, I fell on my face and cried, "Ah Lord GOD! wilt thou destroy all that remains of Israel in the outpouring of thy wrath upon Jerusalem?" He said, "The guilt of the house of Israel and Judah is exceedingly great; the land is full of blood, and the city full of injustice; for they say, 'The LORD has forsaken the land, and the LORD does not see.' As for me, my eye will not spare, nor will I have pity, but I will requite their deeds upon their heads."

And lo, the man clothed in linen, with the writing case at his side, brought back word, saying, "I have done as thou didst command me."

THE WORD OF the LORD came to me: "Son of man, how does the wood of the vine surpass any which is among the trees of the forest? Is wood taken from it to make anything? Do men take a peg from it to hang any vessel on? Lo, it is given to the fire for fuel; when the fire has consumed both ends of it, and the middle is charred, is it useful for anything? When it was whole, it was used for nothing; how much less, when the fire has charred it, can it ever be used for anything! Therefore thus says the Lord GOD: Like the wood of the vine which I have given to the fire for fuel, so will I give up the inhabitants of Jerusalem. I will set my face against them, and you will know that I am the LORD. I will make the land desolate, because they have acted faithlessly."

Again the word of the LORD came to me: "Son of man, make known to Jerusalem her abominations. Say to her, Thus says the Lord GOD: Your origin is of the land of the Canaanites; your father was an Amorite, and your mother a Hittite. As for your birth, on the day you were born your navel string was not cut, nor were you washed with water, nor rubbed with salt, nor swathed with bands. No eye pitied you, to do any of these things for you. You were cast out on the open field, for you were abhorred. When I passed by, and saw you weltering in your blood, I said to you, 'Live, and grow up like a plant of the field.' And you grew up and arrived at full maidenhood; your breasts were formed, and your hair had grown; yet you were naked and bare.

"When I passed by you again, behold, you were at the age for love; and I spread my skirt over you, and covered your nakedness: yea, I plighted my troth to you and entered into a covenant with you, and you became mine. I bathed you with water and anointed you with oil. I shod you with leather, swathed you in fine linen, and covered you with silk. I decked you with gold and silver, putting bracelets on your arms, a chain on your neck, earrings in your ears, and a beautiful crown upon your head. You ate fine flour and honey and oil. You came to regal estate, and your renown went forth among the nations because of your beauty, for it was perfect through the splendor which I had bestowed upon you.

"But you trusted in your beauty, and played the harlot because of your renown. You took some of your garments, and made for yourself gaily decked shrines, and on them played the harlot; the like has never been, nor ever shall be. You also took your jewels of my gold and my silver and made images of men, setting before them my oil, my incense, and my bread, made with fine flour and oil and honey. And you took the sons and daughters you had borne to me, and these you sacrificed to them. Were your harlotries so small a matter that you delivered my children up as an offering by fire to them? In all your abominations you did not remember the days of your youth, when you were naked and bare, weltering in your blood.

"After all your wickedness (woe, woe to you! says the Lord GOD), you built yourself a vaulted chamber, and a lofty place at the head of every street, offering yourself to any passer-by. You played the harlot with the Egyptians, your lustful neighbors, to provoke me to anger. Therefore I stretched out my hand against you, and delivered you to your enemies, the daughters of the Philistines, who were ashamed of your lewd behavior. You played the harlot also with the Assyrians, because you were insatiable; yea, you multiplied your harlotry with the trading land of Chaldea, and even with this you were not satisfied.

"Wherefore, O Jerusalem, thus says the Lord GOD: Because your shame was laid bare, and because of all your idols, and the blood of your children that you gave to them, therefore, behold, I will gather all your lovers against you from every side, and will uncover your nakedness to them, that they may see it. I will judge you as women who break wedlock and shed blood are

judged, and bring upon you the blood of wrath and jealousy. I will give you
into the hand of your lovers, and they shall break down your lofty places; they
shall strip you bare. They shall bring up a host against you, and stone you, and
cut you to pieces with their swords. They shall execute judgments upon you
in the sight of many women; I will make you stop playing the harlot. So will I
satisfy my fury on you, and my jealousy shall depart from you; I will no more
be angry. But because you have not remembered the days of your youth, and
have enraged me, therefore I will requite your deeds upon your head, says the
Lord God.

"Behold, every one who uses proverbs will use this proverb about you,
'Like mother, like daughter,' for you are the true daughter of your mother,
who loathed her husband and children; and you are the true sister of your
sisters, who loathed their husbands and children. Your elder sister is Samaria, to the north of you; and your younger sister, to the south, is Sodom.
Yet you were not content to do according to their abominations; within a very
little time you were more corrupt than they. As I live, says the Lord God,
Sodom and her daughters have not done as you and your daughters have
done. Behold, this was the guilt of Sodom: she and her daughters had pride,
surfeit of food, and prosperous ease, but did not aid the poor and needy. They
were haughty, and did abominable things; therefore I removed them. Samaria also has not committed half your sins. You have made your sisters
appear righteous by all the abominations you have committed. So be
ashamed, and bear your disgrace. I will restore the fortunes of Sodom and of
Samaria, and I will restore your fortunes in the midst of them, that you may
be ashamed of all that you have done, becoming a consolation to them. Was
not your sister Sodom a byword in your mouth in the day of your pride,
before your wickedness was uncovered? Now you have become like her an
object of reproach for those round about who despise you. You bear the
penalty of your lewdness, says the LORD.

"Yet I will remember my covenant with you in the days of your youth, and I
will establish with you an everlasting covenant. Then you will remember your
ways, and be ashamed when I take your sisters and give them to you as daughters. I will establish my covenant with you, and you shall know that I am the
LORD, that you may be confounded, and never open your mouth again because of your shame, when I forgive you all that you have done, says the Lord
God."

THE WORD OF the LORD came to me: "Son of man, propound a riddle, and
speak an allegory to the house of Israel; say, Thus says the Lord God: A great
eagle with great wings and long pinions, rich in plumage of many colors,
came to Lebanon and broke off the topmost young twig of the cedar. Carrying it to a land of trade, he set it in a city of merchants. Then he took of the
seed of the land and planted it in fertile soil beside abundant waters. It
sprouted and became a low spreading vine, and its branches turned toward

him. But there was another great eagle with great wings and much plumage; and behold, this vine now shot forth its branches toward him, that he might water it. From its bed he transplanted it, that it might bear fruit and become a noble vine. Behold, when it is transplanted, will it thrive? Will it not utterly wither when the east wind strikes it—wither away on the bed where it grew?"

Then the word of the LORD came to me: "Say now to the rebellious house, Do you not know what these things mean? Tell them, Behold, the king of Babylon came to Jerusalem, and took her king and princes and brought them to Babylon. He took one of the seed royal and made a covenant with him, putting him under oath. But the prince rebelled against the king of Babylon by sending ambassadors to Egypt, that they might give him horses and a large army. Will he succeed? Can he break the covenant and yet escape? As I live, says the Lord GOD, surely in the place where the king dwells who made him king, whose oath he despised, and whose covenant with him he broke, in Babylon he shall die. Pharaoh with his mighty army will not help him in war, when mounds are cast up and siege walls built. Because he despised the oath, because he gave his hand and yet did all these things, he shall not escape. My covenant which he broke I will requite upon his head. I will enter into judgment with him for the treason he has committed. The pick of his troops shall fall by the sword, and the survivors shall be scattered to every wind; you shall know that I, the LORD, have spoken."

Thus says the Lord GOD. "I myself will take a sprig from the lofty top of the cedar, and on the mountain height of Israel will I plant it, that it may bring forth boughs and bear fruit, and become a noble cedar. Under it will dwell all kinds of beasts; in the shade of its branches birds of every sort will nest. And all the trees of the field shall know that I the LORD bring low the high tree, and make high the low tree, dry up the green tree, and make the dry tree flourish. I the LORD have spoken, and I will do it."

THE WORD OF the LORD came to me again: "What do you mean by repeating this proverb concerning the land of Israel, 'The fathers have eaten sour grapes, and the children's teeth are set on edge'? As I live, says the Lord GOD, this proverb shall no more be used by you in Israel. Behold, all souls are mine; the soul of the father as well as the soul of the son: the soul that sins shall die.

"If a man does what is lawful and right—if he does not lift up his eyes to idols, does not defile his neighbor's wife, does not oppress any one, but restores to the debtor his pledge, commits no robbery, gives his bread to the hungry and covers the naked, does not lend at interest, withholds his hand from iniquity, executes true justice between man and man, walks in my statutes, and is careful to observe my ordinances—he is righteous, he shall surely live, says the Lord GOD.

"If he begets a son who is a robber, a shedder of blood, who does none of these duties, but commits abomination; shall this son then live? He shall not.

He has done abominable things; his blood shall be upon himself. But if this son begets a son who sees all the sins which his father has done, and fears, and does not do likewise, but observes my ordinances, and walks in my statutes, the son shall not die for his father's iniquity; he shall live.

"Yet you say, 'Why should not the son suffer for the iniquity of the father?' When the son has done what is lawful and right, he shall surely live. The soul that sins shall die. The son shall not suffer for the iniquity of the father, nor the father for the iniquity of the son; the righteousness of the righteous shall be upon himself, and the wickedness of the wicked shall be upon himself. But if a wicked man turns away from all his sins, he shall not die. None of his transgressions shall be remembered against him; for the righteousness he has done he shall live. Have I any pleasure in the death of the wicked, says the Lord GOD, and not prefer that he should turn from his way and live? But when a righteous man turns away from his righteousness and does the same abominable things that the wicked man does, shall he live? None of his righteous deeds shall be remembered; for the treachery of which he is guilty and the sin he has committed, he shall die.

"Yet you say, 'The way of the Lord is not just.' Hear now, O house of Israel: Is my way not just? Is it not your ways that are not just? When a righteous man turns away from his righteousness and commits iniquity, he shall die. Again, when a wicked man turns away from the wickedness he has committed and does what is right, he shall save his life. Yet the house of Israel says, 'The way of the Lord is not just.' O house of Israel, are my ways not just? Is it not your ways that are not just?

"Therefore I will judge you, O house of Israel, every one according to his ways. Repent, lest iniquity be your ruin. Cast away all the transgressions which you have committed against me, and get yourselves a new heart and a new spirit! Why will you die, O Israel? For I have no pleasure in the death of any one, says the Lord GOD; so turn, and live."

IN THE SEVENTH year, in the fifth month, on the tenth day of the month, certain of the elders of Israel came to inquire of the LORD, and sat before me. And the word of the LORD came to me: "Son of man, speak to the elders, and say, Thus says the Lord GOD: Is it to inquire of me that you come? As I live, says the Lord GOD, I will not be inquired of by you. Will you judge them, son of man, will you judge them? Then let them know the abominations of their fathers. Say to them, On the day when I chose Israel, I swore to the seed of the house of Jacob, making myself known to them in the land of Egypt, saying, I am the LORD your God. I swore that I would bring them into a land flowing with milk and honey, the most glorious of all lands. I said to them, Cast away the detestable things your eyes feast on, every one of you, and do not defile yourselves with the idols of Egypt; I am the LORD your God. But they would not listen.

"Then I thought I would spend my anger against them in the midst of the land of Egypt. But I acted for the sake of my name, that it should not be profaned in the sight of the nations among whom they dwelt. I led them into the wilderness, and gave them my statutes and ordinances, by whose observance man shall live. Moreover I gave them my sabbaths, as a sign between me and them, that they might know that I the LORD sanctify them. But the house of Israel rebelled against me; they rejected my ordinances, and profaned my sabbaths; their heart went after idols.

"Wherefore, son of man, say to the house of Israel, After the manner of your fathers, you defile yourselves with all your idols to this day. Shall I be inquired of by you, O Israel? As I live, says the Lord GOD, I will not. With a mighty hand and an outstretched arm, and with wrath poured out, I will be king over you. I will gather you out of the countries where you are scattered, and bring you into the wilderness of the peoples. There I will enter into judgment with you face to face. I will purge the rebels from among you; they shall not enter the land of Israel. Then you will know that I am the LORD. Go serve your idols, now and hereafter, if you will not listen to me; but my holy name you shall no more profane.

"For on my holy mountain, the mountain height of Israel, says the Lord GOD, all the house of Israel, all of them, shall serve me; there I will accept you, and there I will require the choicest of your gifts, with all your sacred offerings. I will manifest my holiness among you in the sight of the nations. And you shall know that I am the LORD, when I bring you into the land which I swore to give to your fathers. There you shall remember all the doings with which you have polluted yourselves, and you shall loathe yourselves. You shall know that I am the LORD, when I deal with you for my name's sake, not according to your evil ways, O house of Israel, says the Lord GOD."

THE WORD OF the LORD came to me: "Son of man, preach against the south, and say, Thus says the Lord GOD: Behold, I will kindle a fire in you, and it shall devour every green tree and every dry tree; the blazing flame shall not be quenched. All faces from south to north shall be scorched by it, and all flesh shall see that I the LORD have kindled it." Then I said, "Ah Lord GOD! they are saying of me, 'Is he not a maker of allegories?'"

The word of the LORD came to me: "Son of man, set your face toward Jerusalem and preach against the sanctuaries; say to the land of Israel, Thus says the LORD: Behold, I am against you, and will draw forth my sword out of its sheath, and cut off both righteous and wicked. All flesh shall know that I the LORD have drawn my sword; it shall not be sheathed again. Sigh therefore, son of man; sigh with breaking heart and bitter grief before their eyes. And when they say, 'Why do you sigh?' you shall say, 'Because of the tidings. When it comes, every heart will melt and all hands will be feeble, every spirit will faint and all knees will be weak as water. Behold, it comes and it will be fulfilled.' A sword is sharpened and polished, sharpened for slaughter, polished to flash like lightning! You have despised the rod, my son, so the sword is sharpened to be given into the hand of the slayer. Cry and wail, son of man, for it is against my people. I will satisfy my fury; I the LORD have spoken.''

The word of the LORD came to me again: "Son of man, mark two ways for the sword of the king of Babylon to come. Mark a way for the sword to come to Rabbah of the Ammonites, and to Judah, to Jerusalem the fortified. For the king of Babylon stands at the head of the two ways, to use divination; he shakes arrows, he consults idols, he looks at the liver. Into his right hand comes the lot for Jerusalem, where he is to set battering rams against the gates, cast up mounds, and build siege towers. To them it will seem like a false divination; but he brings their guilt to remembrance, that they may be captured. For thus says the Lord GOD: Because you have made your guilt to be remembered, so that in all your doings your sins appear, you shall be taken in them. And you, O unhallowed wicked one, prince of Israel, whose day has come, thus says the Lord GOD: Take off the crown; things shall not remain as they are; exalt that which is low, and abase that which is high. A ruin, ruin, ruin I will make it; there shall not be even a trace of it until he comes whose right it is; and to him I will give it.''

THE WORD OF the LORD came to me: "Son of man, there were two women, the daughters of one mother; they played the harlot in Egypt in their youth; there their virgin breasts were handled. Oholah was the elder and Oholibah her sister. They became mine, and they bore sons and daughters. As for their names, Oholah is Samaria, and Oholibah is Jerusalem.

"Oholah played the harlot while she was mine; she doted on her lovers the Assyrians, warriors clothed in purple, governors and commanders, the choicest men of Assyria; and she defiled herself with all the idols of every one on whom she doted. Therefore I delivered her into the hands of her lovers the Assyrians. These uncovered her nakedness; they seized her sons and daughters; and her they slew with the sword; she became a byword among women when judgment had been executed upon her.

"Oholibah saw this, yet she was more corrupt than her sister. She also doted upon the Assyrians, but she carried her harlotry further than Oholah. She saw men portrayed upon the wall, girded with belts on their loins, with flowing turbans on their heads, images of Babylonians whose native land was Chaldea. She doted upon them, and sent messengers to them. The Babylonians came and defiled her with their lust; and after she was polluted by them, she turned from them in disgust. When she carried on her harlotry so openly, I turned in disgust from her, as I had turned from her sister. Yet she increased her harlotry, remembering her paramours in Egypt.

"Therefore, O Oholibah, I will bring your lovers against you from every side: the Babylonians and all the Assyrians. With chariots they shall come, and I will direct my indignation against you, that they may deal with you in fury. Thus I will put an end to your lewdness. For thus says the Lord GOD: Behold, I will deliver you into the hands of those whom you hate, and they shall deal with you in hatred. They shall take away the fruit of your labor and leave you naked. You have gone the way of your sister; therefore I will give her cup into your hand, a cup of horror and desolation. You shall drain it, and pluck out your hair and tear your breasts; for I have spoken. Because you have forgotten me and cast me behind your back, therefore bear the consequences."

The LORD said to me: "Son of man, will you judge Oholah and Oholibah? Then declare to them their abominable deeds. For blood is upon their hands; with their idols they have committed adultery; they have even offered up to them for food the sons they had borne to me. Moreover they have defiled my sanctuary. For when they had slaughtered their children in sacrifice to their idols, on the same day they came into my sanctuary to profane it. This is what they did in my house. A messenger was sent to summon men from far, and lo, the men came. For them you bathed yourself, painted your eyes, and decked yourself with ornaments; you sat upon a stately couch, with a table spread before it on which you had placed my incense and my oil. The sound of a carefree multitude was heard, and men of the common sort, drunkards, were brought from the wilderness.

"Then I said, Do not men now commit adultery when they practice harlotry with them? For as men go in to a harlot, thus they went in to Oholah and Oholibah. But righteous men shall pass judgment on them with the sentence of adulteresses; because they are adulteresses, and blood is upon their hands. Bring up a host against them, and make them an object of terror. The host shall stone them and dispatch them with swords; they shall slay their sons and daughters, and burn up their houses. Thus will I put an end to lewdness in the land, that all women may take warning. You shall bear the penalty for your sinful idolatry; and you shall know that I am the Lord GOD."

IN THE NINTH year, in the tenth month, on the tenth day of the month, the word of the LORD came to me: "Son of man, write down the name of this day. The king of Babylon has laid siege to Jerusalem this very day. Utter an allegory to the rebellious house and say, Thus says the Lord GOD: Set on the pot, pour in water; put in it the pieces of flesh, the good pieces, thigh and shoulder; fill it with choice bones, take the choicest of the flock. Pile the logs under it; boil its pieces, boil also its bones in it.

"Therefore thus says the Lord GOD: Woe to the bloody city, to the pot whose rust is in it, and whose rust has not gone out of it! Take out piece after piece, without making any choice. For the blood she has shed is still in the midst of her; she did not pour it on the ground to cover it with dust. To take vengeance, I have set on the bare rock the blood she has shed, that it may not be covered. Woe to the bloody city! I also will make the pile great: heap on the logs, kindle the fire, boil well the flesh, empty out the broth, let the bones be burned up. Then set the empty pot upon the coals, that it may become hot and its copper burn, that its filthiness may be melted in it, its rust consumed.

In vain I have wearied myself; its thick rust does not go out of it by fire. This rust is your filthy lewdness. Because I would have cleansed you and you were not cleansed, you shall not be cleansed any more till I have satisfied my fury upon you. I the LORD have spoken; I will do it; I will not spare; according to your ways and your doings I will judge you."

Also the word of the LORD came to me: "Son of man, behold, I am about to take the delight of your eyes away from you at a stroke; yet you shall not mourn, nor shall your tears run down. Sigh, but not aloud; make no mourning for the dead. Bind on your turban, and put your shoes on your feet; do not cover your lips, nor eat the bread of mourners."

So I spoke to the people in the morning, and at evening my wife died. On the next morning I did as I was commanded.

The people said to me, "Will you not tell us what these things mean for us, that you are acting thus?" I said, "The word of the LORD came to me: 'Say to the house of Israel, Thus says the Lord GOD: Behold, I will profane my sanctuary, the pride of your power, the delight of your eyes, and the desire of your soul; and your sons and daughters whom you left behind shall fall by the sword. And you shall do as I have done; you shall not cover your lips, nor eat the bread of mourners. Your turbans shall be on your heads and your shoes on your feet; you shall not mourn or weep, but you shall pine away in your iniquities and groan to one another. Thus shall Ezekiel be to you a sign; according to all that he has done, you shall do. When this comes, then you will know that I am the Lord GOD.'

"And you, son of man, on the day when I take from them their joy and glory, the delight of their eyes and their heart's desire, and also their sons and daughters, on that day a fugitive will come to you to report the news. The hand of the LORD will be upon you the evening before he comes, but in the morning your mouth will be opened to the fugitive, and you shall speak and be no longer dumb. So you will be a sign to them; and they will know that I am the LORD."

THE WORD OF the LORD came to me: "Son of man, prophesy against the Ammonites, and say, Thus says the Lord GOD: Because you said, 'Aha!' over my sanctuary when it was profaned, and over the land of Israel when it was made desolate; therefore I am handing you over to the people of the East for a possession, and they shall set their encampments among you; they shall eat your fruit and drink your milk. Because you have clapped your hands and stamped your feet and rejoiced with all the malice within you against the land of Israel, therefore, behold, I will cut you off from the peoples and make you perish out of the countries; I will destroy you. Then you will know that I am the LORD.

"Thus says the Lord GOD: Because Moab said, 'Behold, the house of Judah is like all the other nations,' therefore I will lay open the flank of Moab and give it along with the Ammonites to the people of the East as a possession, that it may be remembered no more among the nations. Then they will know that I am the LORD.

"Thus says the Lord GOD: Because Edom acted revengefully against the house of Judah, therefore I will stretch out my hand against Edom, and make it desolate. They shall know my vengeance.

"Thus says the Lord GOD: Because the Philistines took vengeance with malice of heart to destroy in never-ending enmity; therefore I will stretch out my hand against the Philistines, and execute great vengeance upon them with wrathful chastisements. Then they will know that I am the LORD."

Moreover the word of the LORD came to me: "Son of man, raise a lamentation over the king of Tyre, and say, Thus says the Lord GOD: You were the signet of perfection, full of wisdom and perfect in beauty. You were in Eden, the garden of God; every precious stone was your covering, and wrought in gold were your settings. On the day you were created they were prepared. With an anointed guardian cherub I placed you; you were on the holy mountain of God; in the midst of the stones of fire you walked.

"You were blameless in your ways from the day you were created, till iniquity was found in you. In the abundance of your trade you were filled with violence, and you sinned; so I cast you as a profane thing from the mountain of God, and the guardian cherub drove you out from the midst of the stones of fire. Your heart was proud because of your beauty; you corrupted your wisdom for the sake of your splendor. I cast you to the ground; I exposed you before kings, to feast their eyes on you. I brought forth fire from the midst of you; it consumed you, and I turned you to ashes upon the earth. All who know you are appalled at you; you have come to a dreadful end and shall be no more for ever."

The word of the LORD came to me: "Son of man, set your face toward Sidon; prophesy against her, and say, Thus says the Lord GOD: Behold, I am against you, O Sidon; I will manifest my glory in the midst of you. And they shall know that I am the LORD when I execute judgments and manifest my holiness in her; for I will send pestilence into her, and blood into her streets; and the slain shall fall in the midst of her, by the sword that is against her on every side.

"And for the house of Israel there shall be no more a brier to prick or a thorn to hurt them among all their neighbors who have treated them with contempt. When I gather them from the peoples among whom they are scattered, and manifest my holiness in them in the sight of the nations, then they shall dwell in their own land which I gave to my servant Jacob. They shall dwell securely in it, and build houses and plant vineyards. Then they will know that I am the LORD their God."

IN THE TENTH year, in the tenth month, on the twelfth day of the month, the word of the LORD came to me: "Son of man, set your face against Pharaoh and all Egypt; speak, and say, Thus says the Lord GOD: Behold, I am against you, Pharaoh king of Egypt, the great dragon that lies in the midst of his streams, that says, 'My Nile is my own; I made it.' I will put hooks in your jaws, and make the fish of your streams stick to your scales; and I will draw you up out of your streams, with the fish sticking to you. I will cast you forth into the wilderness, you and the fish; you shall fall upon the open field and not be buried. To the beasts and the birds I have given you as food. Then all the inhabitants of Egypt shall know that I am the LORD.

"Because you have been a staff of reed to the house of Israel—when they grasped you with the hand, you broke, and tore their shoulders; when they leaned upon you, you broke, and made their loins to shake—therefore, says the Lord GOD, I will bring a sword upon you and cut off from you man and beast. Because you said, 'The Nile is mine, and I made it,' therefore I am against you and your streams, and I will make the land of Egypt an utter waste and desolation. No foot of man or beast shall pass through it; it shall be uninhabited forty years, and I will scatter the Egyptians among the nations. At the end of forty years I will bring them back to the land of their origin; and there they shall be the most lowly of kingdoms. I will make them so small that they will never again rule over the nations. And Egypt shall never again be the reliance of the house of Israel, recalling their iniquity when they turn to them for aid.

"Nebuchadrezzar king of Babylon made his army labor hard against Tyre; every head was made bald and every shoulder rubbed bare; yet neither he nor his army got anything from Tyre to pay for the labor they had performed against it. Therefore thus says the Lord GOD: Behold, I will give the land of Egypt to Nebuchadrezzar as recompense, because he worked for me. He shall carry off its wealth and plunder it; and it shall be the wages for his army.

"On that day, son of man, I will cause a horn to spring forth to the house of Israel, and I will open your lips among them. Then they will know that I am the LORD."

IN THE ELEVENTH year, in the third month, on the first day of the month, the word of the LORD came to me: "Son of man, say to Pharaoh king of Egypt and to his multitude: Whom are you like in your greatness? Behold, I will liken you to a cedar in Lebanon, with fair branches and forest shade, and of great height, its top among the clouds. The waters nourished it, the deep made it grow tall, making its rivers flow round the place of its planting. So it towered high above all the trees of the forest. The birds made their nests in its boughs; under its branches the beasts brought forth their young; and under its shadow dwelt all great nations. No tree in the garden of God was like it in beauty, and all the trees of Eden envied it.

"Therefore thus says the Lord GOD: Because it towered high, and its heart was proud of its height, I will give it into the hand of a mighty one of the nations; he shall deal with it as it deserves. I have cast it out. Foreigners, the most terrible of the nations, will cut it down. On the mountains and in the valleys its branches will fall, and its boughs will lie broken in the water-courses of the land. All the peoples of the earth will go from its shadow and leave it. Upon its ruin will dwell the birds and the beasts. All this is in order that no trees by the waters may set their tops among the clouds; for they are all given over to death, to the nether world among mortal men, with those who go down to the Pit.

"Thus says the Lord GOD: When it goes down to Sheol, I will make the deep mourn for it and restrain its rivers; I will clothe Lebanon in gloom, and the trees of the field shall faint because of it. I will make the nations quake at the sound of its fall, and all the trees of Eden will be comforted in the nether world.

"Whom are you thus like in glory and in greatness among the trees of Eden? You shall be brought down with them; you shall lie among the uncircumcised, with those who are slain by the sword. This is Pharaoh, and all his multitude, says the Lord GOD."

IN THE TWELFTH year, in the first month, on the fifteenth day of the month, the word of the LORD came to me: "Son of man, wail over the multitude of Egypt, and send them with the daughters of majestic nations to those who have gone down to the Pit. Say to them, 'Whom do you surpass in beauty? Go down, and be laid with the uncircumcised.' They shall fall amid those who are slain by the sword, and the mighty chiefs shall speak of them out of the midst of Sheol: 'They have come down, they lie still, the uncircumcised, slain by the sword.'

"Assyria is there, and all her company, their graves round about her set in the uttermost parts of the Pit; all of them slain, fallen by the sword, who spread terror in the land of the living. Elam is there, and her multitude, and Meshech and Tubal; all of them slain by the sword; for they spread terror in the land of the living. They do not lie with the fallen mighty men of old who went down to Sheol with their weapons of war, whose swords were laid under their heads, and whose shields are upon their bones. So you, Pharaoh, with all your multitude, shall be broken and lie among the uncircumcised, with those slain by the sword."

IN THE TWELFTH year of our exile, in the tenth month, on the fifth day of the month, a man who had escaped from Jerusalem came to me and said, "The city has fallen." Now the hand of the LORD had been upon me the evening before the fugitive came, but he had opened my mouth by the time the man came to me, so I was no longer dumb.

The word of the LORD came to me: "Son of man, the inhabitants of these waste places in the land of Israel keep saying, 'Abraham was only one man, yet he got possession of the land; but we are many; the land is surely given us to possess.' Therefore say to them, Thus says the Lord GOD: You eat flesh with the blood, and lift up your eyes to your idols; you resort to the sword, and each of you defiles his neighbor's wife; shall you then possess the land? As I live, surely those who are in the waste places shall fall by the sword; him that is in the open field I will give to the beasts to be devoured; and those who are in strongholds and in caves shall die by pestilence. I will make the land a desolation, and her proud might shall come to an end. Then they will know that I am the LORD.

"As for you, son of man, your people who talk together about you by the walls and at the doors of the houses, say to one another, 'Come, and hear what the word is that comes forth from the LORD.' And they come to you and sit before you. They hear what you say but they will not do it; for with their lips they show much love, but their heart is set on their gain. And lo, you are to them like one who sings love songs with a beautiful voice, for they hear what you say, but they will not do it. But when this comes—and come it will!—then they will know that a prophet has been among them."

THE WORD OF the LORD came to me: "Son of man, prophesy against the shepherds of Israel, and say, Thus says the Lord GOD: Ho, shepherds of Israel who have been feeding yourselves! Should not shepherds feed the sheep? You eat the fat, you clothe yourselves with the wool, you slaughter the fatlings; but you do not feed the sheep. The weak you have not strengthened, the sick you have not healed, the crippled you have not bound up, the strayed you have not brought back, and with force and harshness you have ruled them. So because there was no shepherd, they became food for all the wild beasts. My sheep wandered over all the mountains, and were scattered over the face of the earth, with none to seek for them.

"Therefore, you shepherds, hear the word of the LORD: Because my sheep have become food for wild beasts, and because my shepherds have fed themselves, and have not fed my sheep, I am against the shepherds. I will require my sheep at their hand; I will rescue my sheep from their mouths, that they may not be food for them.

"For thus says the Lord GOD: Behold, I, I myself will search for my sheep, as a shepherd seeks out his flock. I will rescue them from all places where they have been scattered on a day of clouds and thick darkness. I will gather them from the countries and bring them into their own land; and I will feed them with good pasture upon the mountain heights of Israel. I myself will be the shepherd of my sheep. I will seek the lost and bring back the strayed; I will bind up the crippled; I will strengthen the weak, and the fat and the strong I will watch over; I will feed them in justice.

"As for you, my flock, thus says the Lord GOD: Behold, I judge between sheep and sheep, rams and he-goats. Is it not enough for you to feed on the good pasture, that you must tread down the rest of it; and to drink of clear water, that you must foul the rest with your feet? Must my sheep eat what you have trodden and drink what you have fouled with your feet? Therefore behold, I, I myself will judge between the fat sheep and the lean sheep. Because you push with side and shoulder, and thrust at all the weak with your horns, till you have scattered them abroad, I will save my flock. They shall no longer be a prey; and I will judge between sheep and sheep. I will set up over them one shepherd, my servant David, and he shall feed them. I the LORD will be their God, and my servant David shall be prince among them; I, the LORD, have spoken.

"I will make with them a covenant of peace and banish wild beasts from the land, so that they may dwell securely in the wilderness and sleep in the woods. I will make them and the places round about my hill a blessing; and I will send down the showers in their season; they shall be showers of blessing. The trees of the field shall yield their fruit, and the earth shall yield its increase, and they shall be secure in their land. I will provide for them prosperous plantations, so that they shall no more be consumed with hunger, and no longer suffer the reproach of the nations. They shall know that I, the LORD their God, am with them, and that they, the house of Israel, are my people. You are my sheep, the sheep of my pasture, and I am your God, says the Lord GOD."

The word of the LORD came to me: "Son of man, when the house of Israel dwelt in their own land, they defiled it. So I poured out my wrath upon them; in accordance with their conduct and their deeds I judged them. But when they came to the nations to which I scattered them, they profaned my holy name, in that men said of them, 'These are the people of the LORD, and yet they had to go out of his land.'

"Therefore say to the house of Israel, Thus says the Lord GOD: It is not for your sake, O Israel, that I am about to act, but for the sake of my holy name, which you have profaned among the nations to which you came. Through you I will vindicate the holiness of my great name, and the nations will know that I am the LORD. For I will gather you from them and bring you into your own land. I will sprinkle clean water upon you; from all your idols I will cleanse you. A new heart I will give you, and a new spirit I will put within you; I will take out of your flesh the heart of stone and give you a heart of flesh. And I will put my spirit within you, and cause you to walk in my statutes. You shall dwell in the land which I gave to your fathers; and you shall be my people, and I will be your God. I will make the fruit of the tree and the increase of the field abundant, that you may never again suffer the disgrace of famine. Then you will remember your evil ways and loathe yourselves for your abominable deeds. It is not for your sake that I will act, says the Lord GOD; let that be known to you. Be ashamed and confounded for your ways, O house of Israel.

"Thus says the Lord GOD: On the day that I cleanse you from all your iniquities, I will cause the waste places to be rebuilt, and all who pass by will say, 'This land that was desolate has become like the garden of Eden; and the ruined cities are now inhabited and fortified.' Then the nations that are left round about you shall know that I the LORD have rebuilt the ruined places and replanted that which was desolate; I, the LORD, have spoken, and I will do it."

THE HAND OF THE LORD WAS UPON me, and he brought me out by the Spirit of the LORD, and set me down in the midst of the valley; it was full of bones. He led me round among them; and behold, there were very many upon the valley; and lo, they were very dry. "Son of man," he said, "can these bones live?" I answered, "O Lord GOD, thou knowest." Again he said, "Prophesy to these bones, and say, O dry bones, hear the word of the LORD. Thus says the Lord GOD to these bones: Behold, I will cause breath to enter you, and you shall live. I will lay sinews upon you, and cause flesh to come upon you, and cover you with skin; and you shall know that I am the LORD."

So I prophesied as I was commanded; and as I prophesied, there was a rattling; and the bones came together, bone to its bone. As I looked, there were sinews on them, and flesh had come upon them, and skin had covered them; but there was no breath in them. Then he said, "Prophesy to the breath, son of man, and say, Thus says the Lord GOD: Come from the four winds, O breath, and breathe upon these slain, that they may live." So I prophesied as he commanded, and the breath came into them. They lived, and stood upon their feet, an exceedingly great host.

Then he said, "Son of man, these bones are the whole house of Israel. They say, 'Our bones are dried up, and our hope is lost; we are clean cut off.' Therefore say to them, Thus says the Lord GOD: Behold, I will open your graves, and raise you from them, O my people; and I will bring you home into the land of Israel. I will put my Spirit within you, and you shall live, and I will place you in your own land; then you shall know that I, the LORD, have spoken, and I have done it."

The word of the LORD came to me: "Son of man, take a stick and write on it, 'For Judah, and the children of Israel associated with him'; then take another stick and write upon it, 'For Joseph (the stick of Ephraim) and all the house of Israel associated with him'; and join them together into one stick. When your people say to you, 'Will you not show us what you mean by these?' say to them, Thus says the Lord GOD: Behold, I am about to take the stick of Joseph and join with it the stick of Judah, and make them one. I will gather the people of Israel and bring them to their own land; I will make them one nation upon the mountains of Israel; one king shall be king over them all, and they shall be no longer divided into two kingdoms. They shall not defile themselves any more with their detestable things. I will save them from all the backslidings in which they have sinned, and will cleanse them; they shall be my people, and I will be their God.

"My servant David shall be king over them; and they shall all have one shepherd. They shall follow my ordinances and be careful to observe my statutes. They shall dwell where your fathers dwelt, in the land that I gave to my servant Jacob; they and their children and their children's children shall dwell there for ever; and David my servant shall be their prince for ever. I will make a covenant of peace with them, an everlasting covenant; and I will bless them and multiply them, and will set my sanctuary in the midst of them for evermore. My dwelling place shall be with them; I will be their God, and they shall be my people. Then the nations will know that I the LORD sanctify Israel, when my sanctuary is in the midst of them for evermore."

THE WORD OF the LORD came to me: "Son of man, set your face toward Gog, of the land of Magog, the chief prince of Meshech and Tubal; prophesy against him, and say, Thus says the Lord GOD: Behold, I am against you, O Gog, and I will put hooks into your jaws, and bring you forth with all your army, clothed in full armor, a great company, all wielding swords; Persia, Cush, and Put are with them; Gomer and all his hordes; Beth-togarmah from the uttermost parts of the north—many peoples are with you. Be ready, you and all the hosts assembled about you. In the latter years you will go against the land where people were gathered from many nations upon the mountains of Israel and now dwell securely. You will advance like a storm, you and all your hordes. On that day thoughts will come into your mind, and you will devise an evil scheme, and say, 'I will go up against the land of unwalled villages; I will fall upon the quiet people who dwell securely, without bars or gates.' Therefore, son of man, prophesy, and say to Gog, Thus says the Lord GOD: On that day, when my people Israel are dwelling securely, you will come from the uttermost parts of the north, you and a mighty army. I will bring you against my land, that the nations may know me, when through you, O Gog, I vindicate my holiness before their eyes.

"Thus says the Lord GOD: Are you he of whom I spoke in former days by my servants the prophets of Israel, who in those days prophesied that I would bring you against them? On that day, when Gog shall come against Israel, my wrath will be roused. There shall be a great shaking in the land of Israel; the fish of the sea, the birds of the air, the beasts of the field, all creeping things that creep on the ground, and all the men that are upon the face of the earth, shall quake at my presence; mountains shall be thrown down, cliffs shall fall, and every wall shall tumble to the ground. I will summon every kind of terror against Gog; every man's sword will be against his brother. With pestilence and bloodshed I will enter into judgment with him, and I will rain upon him and the many peoples with him, torrential rains and hailstones, fire and brimstone. So I will show my greatness and my holiness and make myself known in the eyes of many nations. Then they will know that I am the LORD."

IN THE TWENTY-FIFTH year of our exile, at the beginning of the year, on the tenth day of the month, in the fourteenth year after the city was conquered, on that very day, the hand of the LORD was upon me. In visions of God he brought me into the land of Israel, and set me down upon a very high mountain. A structure like a city was opposite me, and when he brought me there, behold, there was a man, whose appearance was like bronze, standing in the gateway. He had a line of flax and a measuring reed in his hand. And the man said to me, "Son of man, look with your eyes, and hear with your ears; set your mind upon all that I show you, for you were brought here that I might show it to you; declare all you see to the house of Israel."

And behold, there was a wall around the outside of the temple area. The man measured its thickness, ten and a half feet; and its height, ten and a half feet. Then he went into the gateway facing east. Going up its steps, he measured the threshold of the gate, ten and a half feet deep; and the three side rooms on either side of the gate, each ten and a half feet long and ten and a half feet broad. He measured the vestibule of the gateway, thirty-five feet in length and fourteen feet in breadth; all around the vestibule was the outer court. The gateway had windows round about, narrowing inwards into their jambs in the side rooms, and likewise the vestibule had windows round about, and on the jambs were carved palm trees.

He brought me into the outer court; and behold, there were thirty chambers fronting on a pavement round about the court; this was the lower pavement. He went before me to the gate of the outer court which faced north, and measured its length and breadth. Its side rooms and jambs, its windows, vestibule, and palm trees were of the same size as those of the gate facing east. He led me to the south gate, and measured its jambs and vestibule; they had the same size as the others. Then he brought me to the inner court, and measured the south gate; it was the same size as the others, but its vestibule faced the outer court. He measured the gates to the inner court on the east and north sides; they were the same size as the one on the south.

There was a chamber with its door in the vestibule of the gate, where the burnt offering was to be washed. Four tables were inside the vestibule, and four outside, on which the sacrifices were to be slaughtered. There were also four tables of hewn stone on which to lay the instruments with which the burnt offerings were to be slaughtered. Hooks, a handbreadth long, were fastened round about within.

There were two chambers in the inner court, one at the side of the north gate facing south, the other at the side of the south gate facing north. "This chamber which faces south," the man said, "is for the priests who have charge of the temple, and the chamber which faces north is for the priests who have charge of the altar; these are the sons of Zadok, who alone among the sons of Levi may come near to the LORD to minister to him." He brought me to the vestibule of the temple; ten steps led up to it, and then he brought me to the nave. He went alone into the inner room, beyond the nave. "This," he said, "is the most holy place."

When the man had finished measuring the interior of the temple area, he led me out to the gate facing east. And behold, the glory of the God of Israel came from the east; the sound of his coming was like the sound of many waters; and the earth shone with his glory. The vision I saw was like the vision I had seen by the river Chebar; and I fell upon my face. As the glory of the LORD entered the temple, the Spirit lifted me up, and brought me into the inner court; and behold, the glory of the LORD filled the temple.

While the man was standing beside me, I heard one speaking to me out of the temple. "Son of man," he said, "this is the place of my throne and the place of the soles of my feet, where I will dwell in the midst of the people of Israel for ever. The house of Israel shall no more defile my holy name, neither they, nor their kings. Describe to them the temple and its plan, that they may be ashamed of their iniquities. And if they are ashamed of all that they have done, portray the temple, its arrangement, its exits and entrances, and its whole form. Make known to them all its ordinances and laws, that they may observe and perform them. This is the law of the temple: the whole territory upon the top of the mountain shall be most holy."

Then the man brought me back to the outer gate of the sanctuary, which faces east; and it was shut. "This gate," he said, "shall not be opened; for the LORD, the God of Israel, has entered by it. Only the prince may sit in it to eat bread before the LORD."

He brought me by way of the north gate to the front of the temple; and behold, the glory of the LORD filled the temple of the LORD; and I fell upon my face. "Son of man," the LORD said, "mark well those who may be admitted to the temple and those who are to be excluded from the sanctuary. No foreigner, uncircumcised in heart and flesh, of all the foreigners who are among the people of Israel, shall enter my sanctuary. The Levites who went far from me, going after idols when Israel went astray, shall bear their punishment. They shall be ministers, having oversight at the gates of the temple, and serving in it; they shall slay the sacrifice for the people and attend on the people, to serve them; but they shall not come near me to serve me as priest, nor come near any of my sacred things.

"The Levitical priests, the sons of Zadok, who kept the charge of my sanctuary when the people of Israel went astray, shall come near me to minister to me; they shall enter my sanctuary, approach my table, and keep my charge. They shall teach my people the difference between the holy and the common, and show them how to distinguish between the unclean and the clean. In a controversy they shall act as judges, and judge it according to my judgments. They shall keep my laws in all my appointed feasts, and they shall keep my sabbaths holy, says the Lord GOD."

Then the man brought me back to the door of the temple; and behold, water was issuing from below the threshold of the temple toward the east (for the temple faced east); the water was flowing down from below the south end of the threshold of the temple, south of the altar. He brought me out by way of the north gate, and led me round on the outside to the outer gate, which faces east; and the water was coming out on the south side. Going on eastward with a line in his hand, the man measured fifteen hundred feet, and then led me through the water; it was ankle-deep. Again he measured fifteen hundred feet, and led me through the water; it was knee-deep. Again he measured fifteen hundred feet, and led me through the water; it was up to the loins. Again he measured fifteen hundred feet, and the water was deep enough to swim in, a river that could not be passed through. "Son of man," he said, "have you seen this?"

Then he led me back along the bank of the river, and I saw very many trees on both sides. "This water flows toward the eastern region," he said, "and goes down into the Arabah. When it enters the stagnant waters of the sea, the water will become fresh. Wherever the river goes every living creature which swarms will live. Fishermen will stand beside the sea, and it will be a place for the spreading of nets; its fish will be of very many kinds, like the fish of the Great Sea. But its swamps and marshes will not become fresh; they are to be left for salt. On the banks, on both sides of the river, there will grow all kinds of trees for food. Their leaves will not wither nor their fruit fail; they will bear fresh fruit every month, because the water for them flows from the sanctuary. Their fruit will be for food, and their leaves for healing."

THUS SAYS THE Lord GOD: "You shall divide the land for inheritance among you according to the tribes of Israel. You shall allot it as an inheritance for yourselves and for the aliens who reside among you and have begotten children among you. They shall be to you as native-born sons of Israel. In whatever tribe the alien resides, there you shall assign him his inheritance, says the Lord GOD.

"Adjoining the territory of Judah, from the east side to the west, shall be the portion which you shall set apart for the LORD, with the sanctuary in the midst of it. A special portion from the holy portion of the land shall belong to the consecrated priests, the sons of Zadok. Alongside the territory of the priests, the Levites shall have an allotment. They shall not sell or exchange any of it; they shall not alienate this choice portion of the land, for it is holy to the LORD.

"The remainder shall be for dwellings and for open country. In the midst of it shall be the city, one and a half miles square. The exits of the city shall be twelve, three on each of the four sides, the gates being named after the tribes of Israel. And the name of the city henceforth shall be, The LORD is there."

DANIEL

Two themes recur in the stories about Daniel and his friends during their exile in Babylon. First is the religious challenge arising from their hostile, foreign environment. Will they remain loyal to the Levitical laws on kosher diet? Will they pray to the king? Will they worship idols? Because they are faithful in these matters, defying their captors, they are sentenced to death, by fire or by being eaten alive. The second theme is Daniel's wisdom. As a sage and an interpreter of dreams, he proves far superior to all the wise men of Babylon, especially in the incident of "the handwriting on the wall." The book ends with a series of dream visions granted to Daniel, visions full of a dense symbolism (only the first is retained herein). Most scholars hold that the book was compiled during the persecutions (168–165 B.C.) of the Jewish people by Antiochus Epiphanes. It encourages the reader to be faithful to God and his law, and to trust that he is Lord of the secrets of world history.

―――――

IN THE THIRD year of the reign of Jehoiakim, king of Judah, Nebuchadnezzar, king of Babylon, besieged Jerusalem. And the Lord gave Jehoiakim into his hand, with some of the vessels of the house of God; and he brought the vessels to Babylon, where he placed them in the treasury of his god.

The king also brought some of the youths of Israel, of the royal family and the nobility, those without blemish, endowed with knowledge, and competent to serve in the king's palace. They were assigned a daily portion of rich food and wine, and they were to be educated for three years in the literature and language of Babylon.

Among these youths were Daniel, Hananiah, Mishael, and Azariah of the tribe of Judah. To them the chief eunuch gave new names: Daniel he called Belteshazzar, Hananiah he called Shadrach, Mishael he called Meshach, and Azariah he called Abednego. To all four God had given skill in letters and wisdom, and Daniel had understanding in all visions and dreams.

Now Daniel resolved that he would not defile himself with the king's rich food, so he asked the chief eunuch to allow him only vegetables and water. But the chief eunuch said, "I fear lest the king should see that you were in poorer condition than the other youths. You would endanger my head."

Then Daniel said to the steward whom the chief eunuch had appointed over them, "Test us for ten days on vegetables and water. Then let our appearance be observed, and according to what you see deal with us." So he tested them, and at the end of ten days it was seen that they were better in appearance and fatter in flesh than all the other youths. So the steward took away their rich food and gave them vegetables.

At the end of the appointed time the chief eunuch brought all the youths in before Nebuchadnezzar. The king spoke with them, and none was found like Daniel, Shadrach, Meshach, and Abednego; therefore they entered the king's service.

IN THE SECOND year of his reign, Nebuchadnezzar had dreams; his spirit was troubled, and his sleep left him. Then he commanded that the magicians and sorcerers be summoned. They came in and stood before the king, and he said to them, "I had a dream, and my spirit is troubled to understand it."

"O king, live for ever!" they said. "Tell your servants the dream, and we will show the interpretation."

"The word from me is sure," the king answered. "If you do not make known to me both the dream and its interpretation, you shall be torn limb from limb, and your houses shall be laid in ruins. But if you show the dream and its interpretation, you shall receive rewards and great honor."

"Let the king tell his servants the dream," they answered a second time, "and we will show its interpretation."

"I know that you are trying to gain time," the king said, "because you see that the word from me is sure. You have agreed to speak lying words before me till the times change. Therefore tell me what the dream was, and I shall know that you can show me its interpretation."

"There is not a man on earth who can meet the king's demand," they answered, "for no great king ever asked such a thing. None can show it to the king except the gods, whose dwelling is not with flesh."

At this the king was furious, and he commanded that all the wise men of Babylon be destroyed. So the decree went forth, and they sought Daniel and his companions, to slay them. But Daniel spoke to Arioch, the captain of the king's guard, asking, "Why is the decree of the king so severe?" Arioch explained, and Daniel went to his house and made the matter known to Shadrach, Meshach, and Abednego. He told them to seek mercy of the God of heaven concerning this mystery, so that they might not perish with the rest of the wise men. Then, in a vision of the night, the mystery was revealed to Daniel, and he blessed the God of heaven in these words:

"Blessed be the name of God for ever and ever, to whom belong wisdom and might. He changes times and seasons; he removes kings and sets up kings; he gives wisdom to the wise and knowledge to those who have under-standing; he reveals deep and mysterious things; he knows what is in the darkness, and the light dwells with him. To thee, O God of my fathers, I give thanks and praise."

After this, Daniel went again to Arioch. "Do not destroy the wise men of Babylon," he said; "bring me in before the king, and I will show the interpre-tation." Arioch brought him before the king and said, "I have found a man who can make known the interpretation."

"Are you able to make known to me both the dream and its interpreta-tion?" the king asked Daniel.

"No wise men can show the mystery which the king has asked," Daniel answered, "but there is a God in heaven who reveals mysteries, and he has made known to King Nebuchadnezzar what will be in the latter days. This was the dream: You saw as you lay in bed, O king, a great image, mighty and of exceeding brightness. Its appearance was frightening. The head was of fine gold, its breast and arms of silver, its belly and thighs of bronze, its legs of iron, its feet partly of iron and partly of clay. As you looked, a stone was cut out from a mountain by no human hand, and it smote the image on its feet and broke them in pieces. Then the iron, the clay, the bronze, the silver, and the gold, all together were broken in pieces, and became like the chaff of the summer threshing floors. And the wind carried them away, so that not a trace of them could be found. But the stone that struck the image became a great mountain and filled the whole earth.

"That was the dream; now we will tell its interpretation. You, O king, to whom the God of heaven has given the kingdom, the power, the might, and the glory, you are the head of gold. After you shall arise another kingdom inferior to you, and yet a third kingdom, of bronze, which shall rule over all the earth. And there shall be a fourth kingdom, strong as iron, and it shall break and crush all these. And as you saw the feet and toes partly of clay and partly of iron, it shall be a divided kingdom. As the toes were partly iron and partly clay, so the kingdom shall be partly strong and partly brittle. As you saw the iron mixed with clay, so they will mix with one another in marriage, but they will not hold together, just as iron does not mix with clay.

"And in the days of those kings the God of heaven will set up a kingdom which shall never be destroyed, nor shall its sovereignty be left to another people. It shall break in pieces all these kingdoms and bring them to an end, and it shall stand for ever. A great God has made known to the king what shall be hereafter. The dream is certain, and its interpretation sure."

Then King Nebuchadnezzar fell upon his face, and did homage to Daniel. "Truly, your God is God of gods and Lord of kings," he said, "and a revealer of mysteries." He gave Daniel high honors and many great gifts, and made him ruler over the whole province of Babylon, and chief prefect over all the wise men. At Daniel's request he also appointed Shadrach, Meshach, and Abednego to administer the affairs of the province of Babylon.

KING NEBUCHADNEZZAR MADE AN IMAGE of gold, ninety feet high and nine feet broad. He set it up on the plain of Dura, in Babylon. Then he assembled the satraps, governors, counselors, justices, and all the officials of the provinces for the dedication. They stood before the image, and the herald proclaimed, "You are commanded, that when you hear the sound of the horn, lyre, harp, bagpipe, and every kind of music, you are to fall down and worship the golden image. Whoever does not worship shall immediately be cast into a burning fiery furnace." As soon as the people heard the sound of the music, all fell down and worshiped the golden image.

At that time certain men came to King Nebuchadnezzar and maliciously accused the Jews. "O king, live for ever!" they said. "You, O king, have made a decree, that every man shall fall down and worship the golden image; and whoever does not worship shall be cast into a burning fiery furnace. There are certain Jews whom you have appointed over the affairs of the province of Babylon: Shadrach, Meshach, and Abednego. These men, O king, pay no heed to you; they do not serve your gods or worship the golden image."

In a furious rage, Nebuchadnezzar commanded that Shadrach, Meshach, and Abednego be brought before him. "Is it true that you do not serve my gods or worship the golden image?" he asked. "Now if you are ready, when you hear the sound of the music, fall down and worship. If you do not, you shall immediately be cast into a burning fiery furnace; and who is the god that will deliver you out of my hands?"

"O Nebuchadnezzar," the three said, "we have no need to answer you in this matter. If it be so, our God whom we serve is able to deliver us from the burning fiery furnace. But if he does not, be it known to you, O king, that we will not serve your gods or worship the golden image."

His face full of fury, Nebuchadnezzar ordered the furnace heated seven times more than its usual heat. And he ordered Shadrach, Meshach, and Abednego to be bound and cast into it. Because the furnace was very hot, the flame of the fire slew those men who took up the three to cast them in.

Then King Nebuchadnezzar was astonished, and he rose up in haste. "Did we not cast three men bound into the fire?" he said to his counselors. "I see four men loose, walking in the midst of the fire, and they are not hurt; and the appearance of the fourth is like a son of the gods." He came near to the door of the furnace. "Shadrach, Meshach, and Abednego," he called, "servants of the Most High God, come forth!"

The three came out, and everyone saw that the fire had not had any power over their bodies; the hair of their heads was not singed, their clothes were not harmed, and no smell of fire had come upon them.

"Blessed be the God of Shadrach, Meshach, and Abednego," the king said, "who has sent his angel and delivered his servants, who trusted in him, and set at nought the king's command, and yielded up their bodies rather than serve and worship any god except their own God. Therefore I make a decree: Any people, nation, or language that speaks anything against the God of these men shall be torn limb from limb, and their houses laid in ruins; for there is no other god who is able to deliver in this way." Then the king promoted Shadrach, Meshach, and Abednego in the province of Babylon.

A PROCLAMATION OF King Nebuchadnezzar to all peoples and nations that dwell in the earth: Peace be multiplied to you! It has seemed good to me to show the signs and wonders that the Most High God has wrought toward me. How great are his signs, how mighty his wonders! His kingdom is an everlasting kingdom, and his dominion is from generation to generation.

I, Nebuchadnezzar, was at ease and prospering in my palace. As I lay in bed I had a dream which alarmed me. Therefore I called all the wise men of Babylon that they might interpret the dream, but they could not. At last Daniel came before me, and I told him the dream, saying, "I saw a great tree in the midst of the earth; its top reached to heaven, and it was visible to the end of the whole earth. Its leaves were fair and its fruit abundant, and in it was food for all. The beasts of the field found shade under it, and the birds of the air dwelt in its branches, and all flesh was fed from it. And behold, a watcher, a holy one, came down from heaven. He cried aloud and said thus, 'Hew down the tree and cut off its branches, strip off its leaves and scatter its fruit. But leave the stump of its roots in the earth, bound with a band of iron and bronze, amid the tender grass of the field. Let him be wet with the dew of heaven; let his lot be with the beasts in the grass of the earth; let his mind be changed from a man's, and let a beast's mind be given to him; and let seven years pass over him. The sentence is by the decree of the watchers, the decision by the word of the holy ones, so that the living may know that the Most High rules the kingdom of men, gives it to whom he will, and sets over it the lowliest of men.'"

Daniel was dismayed for a moment, and his thoughts alarmed him. "My lord," he said, "may the dream be for those who hate you and its interpretation for your enemies! The great tree you saw, O king, is you. Your greatness reaches to heaven, and your dominion to the ends of the earth. And this is the interpretation: It is a decree of the Most High that you shall be driven from among men, and your dwelling shall be with the beasts of the field. You shall be made to eat grass like an ox, and you shall be wet with the dew of heaven. Seven years shall pass over you, till you know that the Most High rules the kingdom of men, and gives it to whom he will. And as it was commanded to leave the stump of the tree, your kingdom shall be sure for you from the time that you know that Heaven rules. Therefore, O king, break off your iniquities by showing mercy to the oppressed, that there may perhaps be a lengthening of your tranquillity."

All this came upon me. At the end of twelve months I was walking on the roof of the royal palace. "Is not this great Babylon," I said, "which I have built by my mighty power?" While the words were still in my mouth, there fell a voice from heaven, "O King Nebuchadnezzar, to you it is spoken: The kingdom has departed from you." Immediately the word was fulfilled. I was driven from among men, and ate grass like an ox, and my body was wet with the dew of heaven till my hair grew as long as eagles' feathers, and my nails were like birds' claws.

At the end of the days I lifted my eyes to heaven, and my reason returned to me, and I blessed the Most High, and praised and honored him who lives for ever; for his dominion is an everlasting dominion, and his kingdom endures from generation to generation. He does according to his will in the host of heaven and among the inhabitants of the earth; and none can stay his hand or say to him, "What doest thou?"

At the same time my majesty and splendor returned to me. My counselors and my lords sought me, and I was established in my kingdom, and still more greatness was added to me. Now I, Nebuchadnezzar, praise and extol and honor the King of heaven; for all his works are right and his ways are just. Those who walk in pride he is able to abase.

KING BELSHAZZAR OF Babylon made a great feast for a thousand of his lords, and he commanded that the vessels of gold and of silver which had been taken out of the temple in Jerusalem be brought. Then the king and his lords, his wives, and his concubines drank from them, while they praised their gods of gold and silver, bronze, iron, wood, and stone.

Immediately the fingers of a man's hand appeared and wrote on the wall of the palace, opposite the lampstand; and the king saw the hand as it wrote. His color changed, his limbs gave way, and his knees knocked together. He cried aloud to bring in the wise men, and he said, "Whoever reads this writing, and shows me its interpretation, shall be clothed with purple, and have a chain of gold about his neck, and shall be the third ruler in the kingdom." But all the wise men could not read the writing or make known the interpretation. Then King Belshazzar was greatly alarmed, and his lords were perplexed.

The queen came into the banqueting hall, and she said, "O king, live for ever! Let not your thoughts alarm you or your color change. There is in your kingdom a man in whom is the spirit of the holy gods. In the days of your father, understanding and wisdom were found in him. Now let this Daniel be called, and he will show the interpretation." When Daniel was brought in, the king said, "I have heard that the spirit of the holy gods is in you. Now the wise men could not show the interpretation of this matter. If you can do so, you shall be clothed with purple and a chain of gold, and shall be the third ruler in the kingdom."

"Let your gifts be for yourself," Daniel answered, "and give your rewards to another; nevertheless I will read the writing and make known the interpretation. O king, the Most High God gave Nebuchadnezzar your father kingship and majesty; and all peoples trembled before him. But when his spirit was hardened so that he dealt proudly, he was deposed, and his glory was taken from him, until he knew that the Most High God rules the kingdom of men. You, his son, though you knew all this, have not humbled your heart. The vessels of the Lord's house have been brought in, and you and your company have drunk wine from them. You have praised gods which do not see or hear or know, but the God in whose hand is your breath you have not honored. From his presence the hand was sent, and this is the writing: MENE, MENE, TEKEL, and PARSIN. This is the interpretation of the matter: MENE, God has numbered the days of your kingdom and brought it to an end; TEKEL, you have been weighed in the balances and found wanting; PERES, your kingdom is divided and given to the Medes and Persians."

Then Belshazzar clothed Daniel with purple, a chain of gold was put about his neck, and proclamation was made that he should be the third ruler in the kingdom. That very night Belshazzar was slain, and Darius the Mede received the kingdom.

IT PLEASED DARIUS to set over the kingdom a hundred and twenty satraps, and over them three presidents, of whom Daniel was one. Because an excellent spirit was in him, Daniel became distinguished above all, and the king planned to set him over the whole kingdom. When the presidents and the satraps heard this, they sought a ground for complaint against Daniel, but they could find no fault in him. Then they said, "We shall not find any complaint against this Daniel unless we find it in connection with the law of his God."

The presidents and satraps came by agreement to the king and said, "O King Darius, live for ever! We are all agreed that the king should establish an ordinance that whoever makes petition to any god or man for thirty days, except to you, O king, shall be cast into the den of lions. Now, O king, establish the interdict according to the law of the Medes and the Persians, which cannot be revoked." King Darius signed the document.

When Daniel heard of this, he went to his house, where he had windows in his upper chamber open toward Jerusalem; and three times a day he got down upon his knees and prayed, as he had done previously. Then these men found Daniel making supplication before his God, and they went to the king and said, "O king! Daniel pays no heed to your interdict, but makes his petition three times a day."

At these words the king was much distressed for Daniel, and he set his mind to rescue him. But those men came back and said, "Know, O king, that it is a law of the Medes and Persians that no interdict which the king establishes can be changed."

Then the king commanded Daniel to be brought and cast into the den of lions. "May your God, whom you serve continually, deliver you!" he said. A stone was laid upon the mouth of the den, and sealed with the king's own signet, and with the signet of his lords. In his palace, the king spent the night fasting; no diversions were brought to him, and sleep fled from him.

At break of day the king arose and went in haste to the den of lions. "O

Daniel," he cried in a tone of anguish, "has your God been able to deliver you?"

"O king, live for ever!" Daniel answered. "My God sent his angel and shut the lions' mouths, and they have not hurt me, because I was found blameless before him; and before you also, O king, I have done no wrong." The king was exceedingly glad, and he commanded that Daniel be taken up out of the den. No kind of hurt was found upon him, because he had trusted in his God. And the king commanded that those men who had accused Daniel be brought and cast among the lions—they, their children, and their wives; and before they reached the bottom of the den the lions overpowered them and broke all their bones in pieces.

Then King Darius wrote to all the peoples and nations that dwell in the earth: "Peace be multiplied to you. I make a decree, that in all my royal dominion men tremble before the God of Daniel, for he is the living God, enduring for ever. His kingdom shall never be destroyed and his dominion shall be to the end. He delivers and rescues, he works signs and wonders in heaven and on earth, he who has saved Daniel from the power of the lions."

So Daniel prospered during the reign of Darius and the reign of Cyrus the Persian.

IN THE FIRST year of Belshazzar king of Babylon, Daniel had a dream as he lay in bed. Then he wrote down the dream, and told the sum of the matter:

"Behold, the four winds of heaven were stirring up the great sea. And four great beasts came up out of the sea. The first was like a lion and had eagles' wings. Then its wings were plucked off, and it was made to stand upon two feet like a man; and the mind of a man was given to it. The second was like a bear. It was raised up on one side; it had three ribs between its teeth; and it was told, 'Arise, devour much flesh.' Another was like a leopard, with four wings on its back; and it had four heads, and dominion was given to it. The fourth beast was terrible and dreadful and exceedingly strong, and it had great iron teeth; it devoured and broke in pieces, and stamped the residue with its feet; and it had ten horns. I considered the horns, and behold, there came up among them another horn, a little one, before which three of the first horns were plucked up by the roots. In this horn were eyes like a man's, and a mouth speaking great things.

"As I looked, thrones were placed, and one that was ancient of days took his seat; his raiment was white as snow, and the hair of his head like pure wool; his throne was fiery flames, its wheels were burning fire. A stream of fire came forth from before him; a thousand thousands served him, and ten thousand times ten thousand stood before him. The court sat in judgment, and the books were opened. I looked then because of the sound of the great words which the horn was speaking. And as I looked, the beast was slain, and its body given over to be burned. As for the rest of the beasts, their dominion was taken away, but their lives were prolonged for a season and a time.

"I saw in the night visions, and behold, with the clouds of heaven there came one like a son of man, and he came to the Ancient of Days and was presented before him. And to him was given dominion and glory and kingdom, that all peoples, nations, and languages should serve him; his dominion is an everlasting dominion, which shall not pass away, and his kingdom one that shall not be destroyed.

"As for me, Daniel, my spirit was anxious and the visions alarmed me. I approached one of those who stood there and asked him the truth concerning all this. So he made known to me the interpretation: 'These four great beasts are four kings who shall arise out of the earth. But the saints of the Most High shall receive the kingdom, and possess the kingdom for ever, for ever and ever.' Then I desired to know the truth concerning the fourth beast, which was exceedingly terrible, and concerning the ten horns, and the other horn which came up. As I looked, this horn made war with the saints, and prevailed over them, until the Ancient of Days came, and judgment was given for the saints of the Most High, and the time came when the saints received the kingdom.

"Thus he said: 'As for the fourth beast, there shall be a fourth kingdom on earth, different from all, and it shall devour the whole earth. As for the ten horns, out of this kingdom ten kings shall arise, and another shall arise after them; he shall be different from the former ones, and shall put down three kings. He shall speak words against the Most High, and shall wear out the saints of the Most High, and shall think to change the times and the law; and they shall be given into his hand for a time, two times, and half a time. But the court shall sit in judgment, and his dominion shall be taken away, to be consumed to the end. And the kingdom and the dominion and the greatness of the kingdoms under the whole heaven shall be given to the people of the saints of the Most High; their kingdom shall be an everlasting kingdom, and all dominions shall serve and obey them.'"

HOSEA

Telling the story of his own tragic home life, Hosea interprets his experiences with his unfaithful wife, Gomer, as a parable of God's enduring love for the wayward nation of Israel. Concerned about idolatry among the people and their ruthless oppression of the poor, he develops the theme of Israel's apostasy and unfaithfulness, for which divine judgment rests upon the nation. The book closes with the promise that eventually Israel will be restored. A younger contemporary of Amos (eighth century B.C.), Hosea is the first Biblical writer to describe the relation between God and his people in terms of marriage. This symbolism is carried on in the New Testament with the imagery of the church as the bride of Christ.

———————

THE WORD OF the LORD that came to Hosea the son of Beeri, in the days of Uzziah, Jotham, Ahaz, and Hezekiah, kings of Judah, and in the days of Jeroboam the son of Joash, king of Israel.

When he first spoke through Hosea, the LORD said to him, "Go, take to yourself a wife of harlotry, for the land commits great harlotry by forsaking the LORD. Love a woman who is an adulteress; even as the LORD loves the people of Israel, though they turn to other gods."

So Hosea took Gomer the daughter of Diblaim to be his wife, and she conceived and bore him a son. "Name him Jezreel," the LORD said, "for in a little while I will punish the house of Jehu for the blood which was shed at Jezreel, and I will put an end to the kingdom of Israel. On that day I will break the bow of Israel in the valley of Jezreel." Gomer conceived again and bore a daughter. "Name her Not pitied," the LORD said, "for I will no more have pity on the house of Israel." When she had weaned Not pitied, Gomer conceived and bore another son. "Name him Not my people," the LORD said, "for you are not my people, and I am not your God."

Yet in the place where it was said to the people of Israel, "You are not my people," it shall be said to them, "Sons of the living God." And the people of Judah and Israel shall be gathered together. They shall appoint for themselves one head, and they shall go up from the land, for great shall be the day of Jezreel. Then you shall say to your brother, "My people," and to your sister, "She has obtained pity."

Plead with your mother, plead—for she is not my wife, and I am not her husband—that she put away her harlotry, lest I strip her naked as in the day she was born and make her like a parched land, and slay her with thirst. Upon her children also I will have no pity, because they are children of harlotry. Their mother has acted shamefully. "I will go after my lovers," she has said, "who give me my bread and my water, my wool and my flax, my oil and my drink." Therefore I will hedge up her way with thorns, so that she cannot find her paths. She shall pursue her lovers, but not overtake them. Then she shall say, "I will return to my husband, for it was better with me then than now."

She did not know that it was I who gave her the grain, the wine, and the oil, and who lavished upon her the silver and gold which she used for Baal. Therefore I will take back my grain in its time, and my wine in its season; I will take away my wool and my flax, which were to cover her nakedness. I will uncover her lewdness in the sight of her lovers, and I will put an end to all her mirth, her feasts, her new moons, and her sabbaths. I will lay waste her vines and her fig trees, of which she said, "These my lovers have given me." And I will punish her for the days when she decked herself with jewelry and burned incense to the Baals, and forgot me, says the LORD.

Then, behold, I will allure her, and bring her into the wilderness, and speak tenderly to her. There I will give her her vineyards, and make the valley of trouble a door of hope. And there she shall answer as in the days of her youth, when she came out of the land of Egypt.

In that day, says the LORD, you will call me, "My husband," and no longer will you call me, "My Baal." For I will remove the names of the Baals from your mouth, and they shall be mentioned no more. I will make for you a covenant with the beasts of the field, the birds of the air, and the creeping things of the ground; I will abolish war from the land, and make you lie down in safety. I will betroth you to me for ever in righteousness and in justice, in steadfast love, and in mercy. I will betroth you to me in faithfulness; and you shall know the LORD. In that day I will answer the heavens and they shall answer the earth; and the earth shall answer the cry of Jezreel with grain, and wine, and oil. I will have pity on Not pitied, and I will say to Not my people, "You are my people"; and he shall say, "Thou art my God."

HEAR THE WORD of the LORD, O people of Israel; for the LORD has a controversy with the inhabitants of the land. There is no faithfulness or kindness, and no knowledge of God in the land; there is swearing, lying, killing, stealing, and committing adultery; they break all bounds and murder follows murder. Therefore the land mourns, and all who dwell in it languish. Like a stubborn heifer, Israel is stubborn. Can the LORD now feed them like a lamb in a broad pasture? Joined to idols, a band of drunkards, they love shame more than their glory. A wind shall wrap them in its wings, and they shall be ashamed because of their altars.

Hear this, O priests! Give heed, O Israel! Hearken, O house of the king! For I will chastise all of you. You have played the harlot; Israel is defiled. Their deeds do not permit them to return to their God. With their flocks and herds they shall seek the LORD, but they will not find him; he has withdrawn from them. They have dealt faithlessly with the LORD; for they have borne alien children. Now the new moon shall devour them with their fields.

Blow the horn in Gibeah; sound the alarm at Beth-aven; tremble, O Benjamin! Yet you shall become a desolation in the day of punishment. Among the tribes of Israel I declare what is sure. The princes of Judah have abused their power; Israel was determined to go after vanity. Therefore I am like a moth to Israel, and like dry rot to the house of Judah.

When Israel saw his sickness, and Judah his wound, Israel went to Assyria, and sent to the great king. But he is not able to cure them or heal their wound. For I will be like a lion to Israel, and like a young lion to the house of Judah. I will rend and go away. I will carry off, and none shall rescue. Then I will return again to my place, until they acknowledge their guilt and seek me in their distress, saying, "Let us return to the LORD; for he has torn, that he may heal us; he has stricken, and he will bind us up. After two days he will revive us; on the third day he will raise us up, that we may live before him. Let us press on to know the LORD; he will come to us as the spring rains that water the earth."

What shall I do with you, O Israel? What shall I do with you, O Judah? Your love is like a morning cloud, like the dew that goes early away. Therefore I have slain you by the words of my mouth. For I desire steadfast love, not sacrifice, the knowledge of God, rather than burnt offerings.

When I would restore the fortunes of my people, when I would heal Israel, their corruption is revealed. They deal falsely but do not consider that I remember all their evil works. Now their deeds encompass them; they are before my face. By their wickedness they make the king glad, and the princes by their treachery. On the day of their king, the princes become sick with the heat of wine; and the king joins hands with mockers. Their hearts burn with intrigue. Hot as an oven, they devour their rulers. All their kings have fallen; and none of them calls upon me.

Israel mixes himself with the peoples; aliens devour his strength. Gray hairs are sprinkled upon him, and he knows it not. The pride of Israel witnesses against him; yet they do not return to the LORD, for all this.

Israel is like a dove, silly and without sense, calling upon Egypt, going to Assyria for help. As they go, I will spread my net over them and bring them down. I will chastise them for their wicked deeds. Woe to them, for they have strayed from me! Destruction to them, for they have rebelled against me! I would redeem them, but they speak lies against me. They do not cry to me from the heart but wail upon their beds. For grain and wine they gash themselves. Although I trained and strengthened their arms, they devise evil against me. They return to Baal.

Israel has multiplied altars, but they have become altars for sinning. Were I to write for them my laws by ten thousands, they would be regarded as a strange thing. They love sacrifice; they sacrifice flesh and eat it; but the LORD has no delight in them. Now he will remember their iniquity, and punish their sins. They shall return to Egypt.

REJOICE NOT, O Israel! You have loved a harlot's hire, forsaking your God. Threshing floor and winevat shall not feed them. They shall not remain in the land of the LORD. Behold, they are going to Assyria! Egypt shall gather them; Memphis shall bury them. The days of punishment have come; Israel shall know it. The prophet is a fool, made mad by your great iniquity. A snare is on all his paths, and hatred in the house of his God. They have deeply corrupted themselves; now the LORD will punish their sins.

LIKE GRAPES IN the wilderness, I found Israel. Like the first fruit on the fig tree, I saw your fathers. But they came to Baal-peor, and consecrated themselves to Baal, and became detestable like the thing they loved. Israel's glory shall fly away like a bird—no birth, no pregnancy, no conception! Even if they bring up children, I will bereave them till none is left. Woe to them when I depart from them! Give them, O LORD—what wilt thou give? Give them a miscarrying womb and dry breasts

Every evil of theirs is in Gilgal; there I began to hate them. Because of the wickedness of their deeds I will drive them out of my house. I will love them no more. Israel is stricken, their root is dried up, they shall bear no fruit. Even though they bring forth, I will slay their beloved children.

My God will cast them off, because they have not hearkened to him; they shall be wanderers among the nations.

ISRAEL IS A luxuriant vine that yields its fruit. The more his fruit increased, the more altars he built; as his country improved, he improved his pillars. Their heart is false; now they must bear their guilt. The LORD will break down their altars and destroy their pillars. Then they will say: "We have no king, for if we fear not the LORD, what could a king do for us?" They utter mere words; with empty oaths they make covenants; so judgment springs up like poisonous weeds in the furrows of the field.

The inhabitants of Samaria shall mourn for the calf of Beth-aven. Its idolatrous priests shall wail over its departed glory. Yea, the thing itself shall be carried to Assyria as tribute to the great king, and Israel shall be ashamed of his idol. Samaria's king shall perish, like a chip of wood on the face of the waters; the sin of Israel shall be destroyed. Thorn and thistle shall grow up on the altars; and the people shall say to the mountains, "Cover us," and to the hills, "Fall upon us."

FROM THE DAYS OF GIBEAH YOU have sinned, O Israel. You were a trained heifer that loved to thresh, and I spared your fair neck; but I will put you to the yoke. Sow for yourselves righteousness, reap the fruit of steadfast love; break up your fallow ground, for it is the time to seek the LORD, that he may come and rain salvation upon you.

But you have plowed iniquity, you have reaped injustice, you have eaten the fruit of lies. Because you have trusted in your chariots and in the multitude of your warriors, the tumult of war shall arise among you. As Beth-arbel was destroyed on the day of battle, and mothers were dashed in pieces with their children, thus it shall be done to you, O house of Israel.

When Israel was a child, I loved him, and out of Egypt I called my son. The more I called, the more they went from me. They kept sacrificing to the Baals, and burning incense to idols. Yet it was I who taught Israel to walk. I took them up in my arms; but they did not know that I healed them. I led them with cords of compassion, with bands of love.

How can I give you up, O Israel? How can I hand you over? My heart recoils within me; my compassion grows warm and tender. I will not execute my fierce anger. I will not again destroy Israel, for I am God and not man, the Holy One in your midst, and I will not come to destroy. My sons shall come trembling like birds from Egypt, and like doves from the land of Assyria; and I will return them to their homes, says the LORD.

WHEN ISRAEL SPOKE, men trembled; he was exalted. But he incurred guilt through Baal and died. And now they sin more and more, and make for themselves molten images, idols skilfully made of silver. "Sacrifice to these," they say. Therefore they shall be like the morning mist or like smoke from a window.

I AM THE LORD your God from the land of Egypt; you know no God but me, and besides me there is no savior. It was I who cared for you in the wilderness, in the land of drought. But when you had fed to the full, and your heart was lifted up, you forgot me. So I will lurk and fall upon you like a leopard, tearing open your breast as a wild beast would.

If I destroy you, O Israel, who can help you? Where now is your king, to save you? Where are all your princes, to defend you—those of whom you said, "Give me a king and princes"? I have given them to you in my anger, and I have taken them away in my wrath.

The iniquity of Israel is kept in store. The pangs of childbirth come for him, but he is an unwise son; for he does not present himself at the mouth of the womb. Shall I ransom him from the power of Sheol? Shall I redeem him from Death? O Death, where are your plagues? O Sheol, where is your destruction? Compassion is hid from my eyes. Though Israel may flourish as the reed plant, the wind of the LORD shall come, rising from the wilderness; and it shall strip his treasury of every precious thing. Samaria shall bear her guilt.

RETURN, O ISRAEL, TO THE LORD your God. Return and say to the LORD, "Take away all iniquity; accept that which is good and we will render the fruit of our lips. Assyria shall not save us. We will not ride upon horses. We will say no more, 'Our God,' to the work of our hands. In thee the orphan finds mercy."

I WILL HEAL their faithlessness; I will love them freely, for my anger has turned from them. They shall return and dwell beneath my shadow; they shall flourish as a garden. I will be as the dew to Israel; he shall strike root as the poplar. His beauty shall be like the olive, his fragrance like Lebanon. What more has Israel to do with idols? It is I who answer and look after you. I am like an evergreen cypress; from me comes your fruit.

WHOEVER IS WISE, let him understand these things; whoever is discerning, let him know them; for the ways of the LORD are right, and the upright walk in them, but transgressors stumble.

JOEL

When a vast plague of locusts descends on Israel, first swarming into the countryside and then descending on the capital, the prophet Joel sees it as a portent of the Day of Judgment. His urgent call to repentance, expressed in apocalyptic language, is followed by a vision of the future, in which the Lord will compensate his people for their sufferings, as well as punish their enemies. Of Joel personally nothing is known. Most scholars assign his book to a time after the Exile, about 400 to 350 B.C. The passage predicting the outpouring of God's spirit on all flesh is cited in the Book of Acts as foreshadowing the gift of the Holy Spirit at Pentecost.

THE WORD OF the LORD that came to Joel, the son of Pethuel:

Hear this, you aged men, give ear, all inhabitants of the land! Has such a thing happened in your days, or in the days of your fathers? Tell your children of it, and let your children tell their children, and their children another generation.

What the cutting locust left, the swarming locust has eaten. What the swarming locust left, the hopping locust has eaten, and what the hopping locust left, the destroying locust has eaten. Awake, you drunkards, and weep; wail, all you drinkers of wine; the sweet wine is cut off from your mouth. An army has come up against my land, powerful and without number; its teeth are lions' teeth, and it has the fangs of a lioness. It has laid waste my vines, and splintered my fig trees. It has stripped off their bark; their branches are made white. The fields are laid waste; the ground mourns because the grain is destroyed.

Be confounded, O tillers of the soil, for the wheat and the barley have perished. Wail, O vinedressers. The vine withers. Pomegranate, palm, and apple, all languish. Gladness fails from the sons of men.

Gird on sackcloth and lament, O priests. Wail, O ministers of the altar. Pass the night in sackcloth, O ministers of my God! Cereal offering and drink offering are withheld from the house of your God. Sanctify a fast; call a solemn assembly. Gather all the inhabitants of the land, and cry to the LORD your God. For the day of the LORD is near; as destruction from the Almighty it comes. Is not the food cut off before our eyes, joy and gladness from the house of our God?

The seed shrivels under the clods; the storehouses are desolate. How the beasts groan! The herds of cattle are perplexed because there is no pasture for them; the flocks of sheep are dismayed. Even the wild beasts, O LORD, cry unto thee because the water brooks are dried up, and fire has devoured the pastures of the wilderness.

Blow the trumpet in Zion; sound the alarm on my holy mountain! Let all the inhabitants of the land tremble, for the day of the LORD is near, a day of darkness and gloom! Like blackness there is spread upon the mountains a great and powerful host; their like has never been from of old, nor ever will be again.

Crackling fire devours before them, and after them a desolate wilderness. Their appearance is like the appearance of horses, and like war horses they run. As with the rumbling of chariots, they leap on the tops of the mountains. Before them peoples are in anguish; all faces grow pale. Like warriors they charge; like soldiers they scale the wall. They march each on his way; they do not swerve from their paths. They burst through weapons and are not halted. They leap upon the city; they climb into the houses; they enter through the windows like a thief.

The earth quakes before them; the heavens tremble. The sun and the moon are darkened, and the stars withdraw their shining. The LORD thunders at the head of his army; mighty are those who obey his command. The day of the LORD is terrible—who can endure it?

"YET EVEN NOW," says the LORD, "return to me with all your heart, with fasting, with weeping, and with mourning." Return to the LORD your God, for he is gracious and merciful, slow to anger, abounding in steadfast love. Who knows whether he will not turn and repent?

Blow the trumpet in Zion; sanctify a fast; assemble the elders; gather all the people, even nursing infants. Let the bridegroom leave his room, and the bride her chamber. Between the vestibule and the altar let the priests, the ministers of the LORD, weep and say, "Spare thy people, O LORD, and make not thy heritage a reproach, a byword among the nations. Why should they say, 'Where is their God?'"

Then the LORD had pity on his people. He said to them, "Behold, I am sending you grain, wine, and oil. You will be satisfied; and I will no more make you a reproach among the nations. I will remove the destroyer far from you, and drive him into a desolate land, his front into the eastern sea, his rear into the western sea. Fear not, O land; be glad and rejoice, for the LORD has done great things! Fear not, you beasts of the field, for the pastures of the wilderness are green; the tree bears its fruit; the fig tree and vine give their full yield. Be glad, O sons of Zion; the LORD has poured down for you abundant rain, both autumn and spring rains, as before.

"The threshing floors shall be full of grain; the vats shall overflow with wine and oil. I will restore to you the years which the swarming locust has eaten, the hopper, the destroyer, and the cutter, the great army which I sent among you. You shall praise the name of the LORD, who has dealt wondrously with you. You shall know that I am in the midst of Israel, that I am the LORD your God; and there is none else. My people shall never again be put to shame.

"It shall come to pass afterward that I will pour out my spirit on all flesh; your sons and your daughters shall prophesy; your old men shall dream dreams, and your young men shall see visions. And I will give portents in the heavens and on the earth; the sun shall be turned to darkness, and the moon to blood, before the great and terrible day of the LORD comes. And it shall come to pass that all who call upon the name of the LORD shall be delivered.

"Behold, at that time, when I restore the fortunes of Judah and Jerusalem, I will bring all the nations down to the valley of Jehoshaphat, and I will enter into judgment with them there, because they have scattered my people Israel among the nations, and have divided up my land; they have cast lots for my people, and have given a boy for a harlot, and have sold a girl for wine."

PROCLAIM THIS AMONG the nations: Prepare war, stir up the mighty men. Let all the men of war draw near. Beat your plowshares into swords, and your pruning hooks into spears; let the weak say, "I am a warrior." Hasten and come to the valley of Jehoshaphat; there I will sit to judge all the nations round about, for their wickedness is great.

Multitudes, multitudes, in the valley of decision! The day of the LORD is near. The sun and the moon are darkened, and the stars withdraw their shining. The LORD roars from Zion, and utters his voice from Jerusalem; the heavens and the earth shake. But the LORD is a refuge and a stronghold to the people of Israel.

"YOU SHALL KNOW that I am the LORD your God, who dwell in Zion, my holy mountain. Jerusalem shall be holy, and strangers shall never again pass through it. And in that day the mountains shall drip sweet wine, and the hills shall flow with milk; all the streambeds of Judah shall flow with water; and a fountain shall come forth from the house of the LORD.

"Egypt shall become a desolation and Edom a wilderness for the violence done to the people of Judah, because they have shed innocent blood in their land. But Judah shall be inhabited for ever, and Jerusalem to all generations. I will avenge their blood, and I will not clear the guilty, for the LORD dwells in Zion."

AMOS

From a small Judean village, where he lived a shepherd's life, Amos was called to preach in the northern kingdom of Israel under Jeroboam II (786–746 B.C.). Israel was then at the peak of her political might and national prosperity, but was ridden with social injustices. Outraged at the hypocritical worship, oppression of the poor, and immorality, Amos denounced Israel uncompromisingly, and his forceful preaching soon brought him into conflict with the authorities of the day. He was expelled from the royal sanctuary at Bethel and commanded not to prophesy there again. It is thought that he returned to Judah, where he wrote down the essence of his public preaching, to become the first of a notable succession of writing prophets. His powerful book, which insists that social justice is inseparable from true piety, ends on a happier note, promising a glorious age to come.

THE WORDS OF Amos, who was among the shepherds of Tekoa, which he saw concerning Israel in the days of Uzziah king of Judah and in the days of Jeroboam the son of Joash, king of Israel, two years before the earthquake. And he said: "The LORD roars from Zion, and utters his voice from Jerusalem; the pastures of the shepherds mourn, and the top of Carmel withers."

Thus says the LORD: "For three transgressions of Damascus, and for four, I will not revoke the punishment. Because they have threshed Gilead with sledges of iron, I will break the bar of Damascus, and the people of Syria shall go into exile. For three transgressions of Gaza, and for four, I will not revoke the punishment. Because they carried into exile a whole people to deliver them up to Edom, I will send a fire upon the wall of Gaza, and it shall devour her strongholds. The remnant of the Philistines shall perish. For three transgressions of Tyre, and for four, I will not revoke the punishment. Because they delivered up a whole people to Edom, and did not remember the covenant of brotherhood, I will send a fire upon the wall of Tyre, and it shall devour her strongholds."

Thus says the LORD: "For three transgressions of Edom, and for four, I will not revoke the punishment. Because he pursued his brother with the sword, cast off all pity, and kept his wrath for ever, I will send a fire upon Teman, and it shall devour the strongholds of Bozrah. For three transgressions of the Ammonites, and for four, I will not revoke the punishment. Because they have ripped up women with child in Gilead, that they might enlarge their border, I will kindle a fire in the wall of Rabbah, and it shall devour her strongholds. Her king shall go into exile, he and his princes together. For three transgressions of Moab, and for four, I will not revoke the punishment. Because he burned to lime the bones of the king of Edom, I will send a fire upon Moab, and it shall devour the strongholds of Kerioth. Moab shall die amid shouting and the sound of the trumpet. For three transgressions of Judah, and for four, I will not revoke the punishment. Because they have rejected the law of the LORD, and have not kept his statutes, I will send a fire upon Judah, and it shall devour the strongholds of Jerusalem."

Thus says the LORD: "For three transgressions of Israel, and for four, I will not revoke the punishment. Because they sell the righteous for silver, and the needy for a pair of shoes—they that trample the head of the poor into the dust, and turn aside the way of the afflicted; a man and his father go in to the same maiden, so that my holy name is profaned; they lay themselves down beside every altar upon garments taken in pledge; and in the house of their God they drink the wine of those who have been fined.

"Yet I destroyed the Amorite before them, who was as strong as the oaks; I destroyed his fruit above, and his roots beneath. I brought you up out of Egypt, and led you forty years in the wilderness, to possess the land of the Amorite. I raised up some of your sons for prophets, and some for Nazirites. Is it not indeed so, O people of Israel?" says the LORD. "But you made the Nazirites drink wine, and commanded the prophets, saying, 'You shall not prophesy.'

"Behold, I will press you down in your place, as a cart full of sheaves presses down. Flight shall perish from the swift, and the strong shall not retain his strength; he who handles the bow shall not stand, nor shall he who rides the horse save his life; and he who is stout of heart shall flee away naked in that day," says the LORD.

HEAR THIS WORD that the LORD has spoken against you, O Israel, against the whole family brought up out of Egypt: "You only have I known of all the families of the earth; therefore I will punish you for all your iniquities.

"Do two walk together, unless they have made an appointment? Does a lion roar in the forest, when he has no prey? Does a bird fall in a snare on the earth, when there is no trap for it? Does evil befall a city, unless the LORD has done it? Surely the Lord GOD does nothing without revealing his secret to his servants the prophets. The lion has roared; who will not fear? The Lord GOD has spoken; who can but prophesy?"

Proclaim to the strongholds in Assyria and in the land of Egypt, and say, "Assemble yourselves upon the mountains of Samaria, and see the great tumults within her, the oppressions in her midst."

"They do not know how to do right," says the LORD, "those who store up violence and robbery in their strongholds." Therefore thus says the Lord GOD: "An adversary shall surround the land, and bring down your defenses; your strongholds shall be plundered. As the shepherd rescues from the mouth of the lion two legs, or a piece of an ear, so shall the people of Israel who dwell in Samaria be rescued. Hear, and testify against the house of Jacob, that on the day I punish Israel for his transgressions, I will punish the altars of Bethel, and the horns of the altar shall be cut off and fall to the ground. I will smite the winter house with the summer house; the houses of ivory shall perish."

Hear this word which I take up over you in lamentation, O Israel: "Fallen, no more to rise, is the virgin Israel; forsaken on her land, with none to raise her up."

Thus says the LORD to the house of Israel: "Seek me and live; but do not seek Bethel, and do not enter into Gilgal or cross over to Beer-sheba; for Gilgal shall surely go into exile, and Bethel shall come to nought."

Seek the LORD and live, lest he break out like fire to devour the house of Joseph, O you who turn justice to wormwood, and cast down righteousness to the earth! You hate him who reproves in the gate, and abhor him who speaks the truth. Therefore, because you trample upon the poor, though you have built houses of hewn stone, you shall not dwell in them; though you have planted pleasant vineyards, you shall not drink their wine. For I know how great are your sins. Seek good, not evil, that you may live; and so the LORD, the God of hosts, will be with you. Hate evil, love good, and establish justice in the gate; it may be that the LORD will be gracious to the remnant of Joseph.

Therefore thus says the LORD, the God of hosts: "In all the squares there shall be wailing; and in all the streets they shall say, 'Alas! alas!' They shall call the farmers to mourning, and in all vineyards there shall be wailing, for I will pass through the midst of you."

Woe to you who desire the day of the LORD! It is darkness, not light; as if a man fled from a lion, and a bear met him; or went into the house and leaned with his hand against the wall, and a serpent bit him. Is not the day of the LORD gloom with no brightness in it?

"I hate, I despise your feasts," says the LORD, "and I take no delight in your solemn assemblies. Even though you offer me your burnt offerings, I will not accept them, and the peace offerings of your fatted beasts I will not look upon. Take away from me the noise of your songs; to the melody of your harps I will not listen. But let justice roll down like waters, and righteousness like an ever-flowing stream. Did you bring to me sacrifices and offerings the forty years in the wilderness, O Israel? You shall take up your images, which you made for yourselves; I will take you into exile beyond Damascus.

"Woe to those who are at ease in Zion, who feel secure on the mountain of Samaria, the notable men to whom the people of Israel come! Pass over to Calneh, and see; go to Hamath the great; then go down to Gath of the Philistines. Are you better than these kingdoms? Is your territory greater than their territory, O you who put far away the evil day, and bring near the seat of violence?

"Woe to those who lie upon beds of ivory, and eat lambs from the flock; who sing idle songs to the sound of the harp, and like David invent for themselves instruments of music; who drink wine in bowls, and anoint themselves with the finest oils, but are not grieved over the ruin of Joseph! They shall be the first to go into exile, and their revelry shall pass away." The Lord GOD has sworn by himself: "I abhor the pride of Jacob, and hate his strongholds; I will deliver up the city and all that is in it."

For behold, the LORD commands, and the great house shall be smitten into fragments, the little house into bits. Do horses run upon rocks? Does one plow the sea with oxen? But you have turned justice into poison and the fruit of righteousness into wormwood—you who say, "Have we not by our own strength taken Karnaim for ourselves?"

"Behold, I will raise up against you a nation, O Israel," says the LORD, "and they shall oppress you from the entrance of Hamath to the Brook of the Arabah."

THUS THE LORD GOD showed me: behold, he was forming locusts. When they had finished eating the grass of the land, I said, "O Lord GOD, forgive, I beseech thee! How can Jacob stand? He is so small!" The LORD repented concerning this, and said, "It shall not be."

Thus the Lord GOD showed me: behold, he was calling for a judgment by fire, and it devoured the great deep and was eating up the land. "O Lord GOD," I said, "cease, I beseech thee! How can Jacob stand? He is so small!" The LORD repented concerning this, and said, "This also shall not be."

He showed me: behold, the Lord was standing beside a wall, with a plumb line in his hand. "Amos," the LORD said, "what do you see?" I said, "A plumb line." Then he said, "Behold, I am setting a plumb line in the midst of my people Israel; I will never again pass by them; the high places of Isaac shall be made desolate, the sanctuaries of Israel shall be laid waste, and I will rise against the house of Jeroboam with the sword."

Then Amaziah the priest of Bethel sent to Jeroboam king of Israel, saying, "Amos has conspired against you. He has said, 'Jeroboam shall die by the sword, and Israel must go into exile.' The land is not able to bear all his words." And Amaziah said to Amos, "O seer, go; flee to the land of Judah. Eat bread there, prophesy there. But never again prophesy at Bethel, for it is the king's sanctuary, a temple of the kingdom."

"I am no prophet," Amos answered, "nor a prophet's son; I am a herdsman, and a dresser of sycamore trees. The LORD took me from following the flock, and said, 'Go, prophesy to my people Israel.' You say, 'Do not prophesy against Israel, or preach against the house of Isaac.' Therefore thus says the LORD: 'Your wife shall be a harlot in the city, your sons and daughters shall fall by the sword, and your land shall be parceled out by line; you yourself shall die in an unclean land, and Israel shall surely go into exile.'"

Thus the Lord GOD showed me: behold, a basket of ripe summer fruit. "Amos," he said, "what do you see?" I said, "A basket of ripe summer fruit." Then the LORD said, "The end has come upon my people Israel; I will never again pass by them. The songs of the temple shall become wailings in that day; the dead bodies shall be many; in every place they shall be cast out in silence."

Hear this, you who trample upon the needy, saying, "When will the sabbath be over, that we may offer wheat for sale, and deal deceitfully with false balances, that we may buy the poor for silver and the needy for a pair of sandals?" The LORD has sworn: "Surely I will never forget any of their deeds. Shall not the land tremble on this account, and every one mourn who dwells in it? On that day I will make the sun go down at noon, and darken the earth in broad daylight. I will turn your feasts into mourning; I will bring sackcloth upon all loins, and baldness on every head; I will make it like the mourning for an only son.

"Behold, the days are coming," says the Lord GOD, "when I will send a famine on the land; not a famine of bread, nor a thirst for water, but of hearing the words of the LORD. They shall wander from sea to sea, and from north to east; they shall run to and fro, to seek the word of the LORD, but they shall not find it. In that day fair virgins and young men shall faint for thirst. Those who swear by the idols of Samaria shall fall, and never rise again."

I SAW THE LORD standing beside the altar, and he said: "Smite the capitals until the thresholds shake, and shatter them on the heads of all the people; what are left of them I will slay with the sword; not one shall escape. Though they dig into Sheol, from there shall my hand take them; though they climb up to heaven, from there I will bring them down. Though they hide on the top of Carmel, I will search them out; though they hide at the bottom of the sea, there I will command the serpent to bite them. And though they go into captivity, there I will command the sword to slay them; I will set my eyes upon them for evil and not for good."

The Lord, GOD of hosts, he who touches the earth and it melts, and all who dwell in it mourn; who builds his upper chambers in the heavens, and founds his vault upon the earth; who calls for the waters of the sea, and pours them out upon the surface of the earth—the LORD is his name.

"Are you not like the Ethiopians to me, O people of Israel?" says the LORD. "Did I not bring up Israel from Egypt, the Philistines from Caphtor and the Syrians from Kir? Behold, the eyes of the Lord GOD are upon the sinful kingdom, and I will destroy it; except that I will not utterly destroy the house of Jacob. For lo, I will shake the house of Israel among all the nations as one shakes with a sieve, but no pebble shall fall upon the earth. All the sinners of my people shall die by the sword, who say, 'Evil shall not overtake us.'

"In that day I will raise up the booth of David that is fallen and repair its breaches, and raise up its ruins, and rebuild it as in the days of old; that they may possess the remnant of Edom and all the nations who are called by my name," says the LORD who does this.

"Behold, the days are coming," says the LORD, "when the plowman shall overtake the reaper and the treader of grapes him who sows the seed; the mountains shall drip sweet wine, and all the hills shall flow with it. I will restore the fortunes of my people Israel, and they shall rebuild the ruined cities and inhabit them; they shall plant vineyards and drink their wine, and they shall make gardens and eat their fruit. I will plant them upon their land, and they shall never again be plucked up out of the land which I have given them," says the LORD your God.

OBADIAH

This is the shortest book of the Old Testament. The prophet, about whose life nothing is known, warns the land of Edom that, for its refusal to fight against the foreigners who conquered Jerusalem, divine judgment will fall on it. He also assures the exiled Israelites that they will be restored to the Promised Land, and then will rule over Edom as well. The disaster to Jerusalem described by Obadiah is probably the sack of the city by the Babylonians in 586 B.C. Since Edom fell to the Nabataeans in 312 B.C., Obadiah's prophecy may be placed between those two dates.

———

THE VISION OF Obadiah.

Thus says the Lord GOD concerning Edom: We have heard tidings from the LORD, and a messenger has been sent among the nations: "Rise up! let us rise against her for battle!" Behold, I will make you small among the nations; you shall be utterly despised. The pride of your heart has deceived you, you who live in the clefts of the rock, whose dwelling is high, who say in your heart, "Who will bring me down to the ground?" Though you soar like the eagle, though your nest is among the stars, I will bring you down, says the LORD.

If thieves came to you by night, would they not steal only enough for themselves? If grape gatherers came to you, would they not leave gleanings? But how Esau will be pillaged, his treasures sought out! Your allies will drive you to the border; your trusted friends will set a trap under you—there will be no understanding of it. Will I not on that day, says the LORD, destroy the wise men of Edom? Your mighty men shall be dismayed, so that every man from Mount Esau will be cut off by slaughter. For the violence done to your brother Jacob, you shall be cut off for ever. On the day that you stood aloof, on the day that strangers carried off his wealth, and foreigners entered his gates and cast lots for Jerusalem, you were like one of them. But you should not have gloated over the day of your brother in the day of his misfortune. You should not have stood at the parting of the ways to cut off his fugitives. You should not have delivered up his survivors in the day of distress.

For the day of the LORD is near upon all the nations. As you have done, it shall be done to you; your deeds shall return on your own head. All the nations round about shall drink of my wrath, and they shall stagger. It shall be as though they had not been. But on Mount Zion there shall be those that escape, and it shall be holy. The house of Jacob shall possess their own possessions. The house of Jacob shall be a fire, and the house of Joseph a flame; they shall burn and consume the house of Esau. There shall be no survivor, for the LORD has spoken. The exiles of the Negeb shall possess Mount Esau, and those of the Shephelah the land of the Philistines; they shall possess Ephraim and Samaria, and Benjamin shall possess Gilead. The exiles in Halah shall possess Phoenicia as far as Zarephath; and the exiles of Jerusalem who are in Sepharad shall possess the cities of the Negeb. Saviors shall go up to Mount Zion to rule Mount Esau; and the kingdom shall be the LORD's.

JONAH

Unlike the other prophetic books of the Old Testament, Jonah is almost entirely the story of the man himself as he answers God's call and preaches against the wickedness of Nineveh. When the Ninevites respond to his message and repent, however, he sulks with displeasure! The book teaches that God's loving care and tender mercy extend even to the inhabitants of a foreign city hated by Israel, and that the Lord is the universal God of Jew and Gentile alike. Clearly it implies that Israel's mission is to proclaim this truth to other nations. The book was probably written after the Babylonian Exile (sixth century B.C.), but Jonah himself lived and prophesied about two hundred years earlier. In the Gospels, Jesus refers more than once to the "sign of Jonah," which in Matthew is interpreted as a prophecy of his resurrection.

———————

THE WORD OF the LORD came to Jonah the son of Amittai, saying, "Arise, go to Nineveh, that great city, and cry against it; for their wickedness has come up before me." But Jonah rose to flee from the presence of the LORD. He went to Joppa, where he found a ship going to Tarshish. Paying the fare, he went on board.

But the LORD hurled a great wind upon the sea, and there was a mighty tempest that threatened to break up the ship. The mariners were afraid, and each cried to his god; to lighten the ship they threw the cargo overboard. Now Jonah had lain down below deck, and was fast asleep. Finding him, the captain cried, "What do you mean, you sleeper! Arise, call upon your god! Perhaps he will save us."

Then the mariners said to one another, "Let us cast lots, that we may know on whose account this evil has come upon us." So they cast lots, and the lot fell on Jonah.

"Tell us," they asked him, "what is your occupation? Whence do you come? Of what people are you?"

"I am a Hebrew," Jonah answered, "and I fear the LORD, the God of heaven, who made the sea and the dry land." And he told them that he was fleeing from the presence of the LORD.

The men were exceedingly afraid. "What have you done!" they asked. "What shall we do to you, that the sea may quiet down?"

"Take me up and throw me into the sea," he replied. "I know it is because of me that this great tempest has come upon you."

Nevertheless the men rowed hard to bring the ship back to land, but they could not, for the sea grew more and more tempestuous. "We beseech thee, O LORD," they cried, "let us not perish for taking this man's life, and lay not on us innocent blood; for thou, O LORD, hast done as it pleased thee." Then they threw Jonah into the sea, and the sea ceased from its raging. The men, fearing the LORD exceedingly, offered a sacrifice to him and made vows.

The LORD appointed a great fish to swallow up Jonah, and for three days and three nights he was in the belly of the fish. Then he prayed to the LORD his God from the belly of the fish, saying, "I called to the LORD, out of my distress; I cried, and thou didst hear my voice. For thou didst cast me into the heart of the seas; all thy waves and thy billows passed over me. The deep was round about me; weeds were wrapped about my head. I went down to the land whose bars closed upon me for ever; yet thou didst bring up my life from the Pit, O LORD my God. When my soul fainted within me, I remembered the LORD; and my prayer came to thee. With the voice of thanksgiving I will sacrifice to thee; what I have vowed I will pay. Deliverance belongs to the LORD!"

The LORD spoke to the fish, and it vomited out Jonah upon the dry land.

THE WORD OF the LORD came to Jonah the second time, saying, "Arise, go to Nineveh, that great city, and proclaim to it the message that I tell you." Jonah went to Nineveh, and entering the city, he cried, "In forty days Nineveh shall be overthrown!" The people of Nineveh believed God; they proclaimed a fast, and put on sackcloth, from the greatest of them to the least.

When tidings reached the king, he arose from his throne, removed his robe, covered himself with sackcloth, and sat in ashes. Then he published a proclamation throughout Nineveh: "Let neither man nor beast feed or drink water, but let man and beast be covered with sackcloth, and let them cry mightily to God; yea, let every one turn from his evil way and from the violence which is in his hands. Who knows, God may yet repent and turn from his fierce anger, so that we perish not."

When God saw how they turned from their wicked ways, he repented of the evil which he had said he would do to them; and he did not do it. This displeased Jonah exceedingly, and he prayed, "LORD, is not this what I said when I was yet in my country? That is why I made haste to flee to Tarshish; for I knew that thou art a gracious God and merciful, slow to anger, and abounding in steadfast love, and repentest of evil. Therefore now, O LORD, take my life from me, I beseech thee, for it is better for me to die than to live."

The LORD said, "Do you do well to be angry?"

Jonah went out to the east of the city, made a booth for himself, and sat under it till he should see what would become of Nineveh. God caused a plant to come up over the booth, for a shade, and Jonah was exceedingly glad. But at dawn the next day God caused a worm to attack the plant, so that it withered. When the sun rose, God sent a sultry east wind, and the sun beat upon Jonah so that he was faint; and he asked that he might die. "It is better for me to die than to live," he said.

"Do you do well to be angry for the plant?" God asked.

"Yes," Jonah answered, "angry enough to die."

"You pity the plant," the LORD said, "for which you did not labor, nor did you make it grow, which came into being in a night, and perished in a night. And should not I pity Nineveh, that great city, in which there are more than a hundred and twenty thousand persons who do not know their right hand from their left, and also much cattle?"

MICAH

A Judean prophet, Micah was a contemporary of Isaiah (eighth century B.C.). His book comprises numerous short oracles, uttered at different times, and later brought together, but without much effort to smooth the transitions. While Micah denounces Samaria and Jerusalem for religious hypocrisy and oppression of the poor, he also prophesies a glorious future for Israel, and the restoration of the Davidic kingdom. Noteworthy in the latter passage is Micah's prediction of the coming of a messianic ruler who is to be born at Bethlehem (quoted by Matthew in connection with the birth of Jesus). The remainder of the book contains miscellaneous oracles, including a summation of true religion as justice, kindness, and humble communion with God.

THE WORD OF the LORD that came to Micah of Moresheth in the days of Jotham, Ahaz, and Hezekiah, kings of Judah, which he saw concerning Samaria and Jerusalem.

HEAR, YOU PEOPLES, all of you; hearken, O earth, and all that is in it; and let the Lord GOD be a witness against you. For behold, the LORD is coming down from his holy temple, and will tread upon the high places of the earth. And the mountains will melt under him and the valleys will be cleft, like wax before the fire, like waters poured down a steep place. All this is for the transgression of Jacob and for the sins of the house of Israel.

What is the transgression of Jacob? Is it not Samaria? And what is the sin of the house of Judah? Is it not Jerusalem? Therefore I will make Samaria a heap in the open country, a place for planting vineyards; I will pour down her stones into the valley, and uncover her foundations.

FOR THIS I will wail and go naked. I will make lamentation like the jackals. For her wound is incurable, and it has come to Judah; it has reached to the gate of my people, to Jerusalem.

Hear, you heads of Jacob and rulers of the house of Israel! Is it not for you to know justice?—you who hate the good and love the evil, who tear the skin from off my people, break their bones in pieces, and chop them up like meat in a kettle.

They will cry to the Lord, but he will not answer them; he will hide his face from them, because they have made their deeds evil.

Thus says the Lord concerning the prophets who lead my people astray, who cry "Peace" when they have something to eat, but declare war against him who puts nothing into their mouths: Therefore it shall be night to you, without vision. The sun shall go down upon the prophets; the seers shall be disgraced, for there is no answer from God. As for me, I am filled with power, with the Spirit of the Lord, to declare to Jacob his transgression and to Israel his sin.

Hear this, you heads of the house of Jacob and rulers of the house of Israel, who pervert all equity, who build Zion with blood and Jerusalem with wrong. Its heads give judgment for a bribe, its priests teach for hire, its prophets divine for money. Yet they lean upon the Lord and say, "Is not the Lord in the midst of us? No evil shall come upon us." Therefore because of you Zion shall be plowed as a field; Jerusalem shall become a heap of ruins, and the mountain of the house a wooded height.

It shall come to pass in the latter days that the mountain of the house of the Lord shall be established as the highest of the mountains, and peoples shall flow to it. Many nations shall come, and say: "Come, let us go up to the mountain of the Lord, that he may teach us his ways and we may walk in his paths." For out of Zion shall go forth the law, and the word of the Lord from Jerusalem. He shall judge between many peoples, and shall decide for strong nations afar off; they shall beat their swords into plowshares, and their spears into pruning hooks; nation shall not lift up sword against nation, neither shall they learn war any more; but they shall sit every man under his fig tree, and none shall make them afraid. For all the peoples walk each in the name of its god, but we will walk in the name of the Lord our God for ever and ever.

In that day, says the Lord, I will assemble the lame and gather those who have been driven away. Those whom I have afflicted I will make the remnant; and those who were cast off, a strong nation; the Lord will reign over them in Mount Zion from this time forth and for evermore. And you, O tower of the flock, hill of the daughter of Zion, to you the former dominion shall come, the kingdom of the daughter of Jerusalem.

Now why do you cry aloud? Is there no king among you? Has your counselor perished, that pangs have seized you like a woman in labor? Writhe and groan, O daughter of Zion, for you shall go forth from the city and dwell in the open country. There the Lord will rescue you from the hand of your enemies.

Now many nations are assembled against you, saying, "Let Zion be profaned." But they do not know the thoughts of the LORD, they do not understand his plan, that he has gathered them as sheaves to the threshing floor. Arise and thresh, O daughter of Zion, for I will make your horn iron and your hoofs bronze. You shall beat in pieces many peoples, and shall devote their wealth to the Lord of the whole earth.

Now you are walled about; with a rod they strike upon the cheek the ruler of Israel. But you, O Bethlehem Ephrathah, who are little among the clans of Judah, from you shall come forth for me one who is to be ruler in Israel, whose origin is from ancient days. Therefore he shall give them up until the time when she who is in labor has brought forth a child. Then the rest of his brethren shall return, and he shall stand and feed his flock in the strength of the LORD, in the majesty of the name of the LORD his God. The people of Israel shall dwell secure, for now he shall be great to the ends of the earth. And this shall be peace.

HEAR WHAT THE LORD says: Arise, plead your case before the mountains. Hear, you enduring foundations of the earth, for the LORD has a controversy with his people, and he will contend with Israel.

"O MY PEOPLE, what have I done to you? In what have I wearied you? Answer me! For I brought you up from the land of Egypt, and redeemed you from the house of bondage. O my people, remember what Balak king of Moab devised, and what Balaam the son of Beor answered him, that you may know the saving acts of the LORD."

WITH WHAT SHALL I come before the LORD, and bow myself before God on high? Shall I come before him with burnt offerings, with calves a year old? Will the LORD be pleased with thousands of rams, with ten thousands of rivers of oil? Shall I give my first-born for my transgression, the fruit of my body for the sin of my soul?

He has showed you, O man, what is good; and what does the LORD require of you but to do justice, and to love kindness, and to walk humbly with your God?

THE VOICE OF the LORD cries to the city—and it is sound wisdom to fear his name: "Hear, O tribe and assembly of the city! Can I forget the treasures of wickedness in the house of the wicked? Shall I acquit the man with deceitful scales? Your rich men are full of violence; your inhabitants speak lies. Therefore I have begun to smite you, making you desolate because of your sins. You shall eat, but not be satisfied; you shall put away, but what you save I will give to the sword. For you have kept the statutes of Omri, and all the works of the house of Ahab; that I may make you a desolation, and your inhabitants a hissing."

Woe is me! For I have become as when the summer fruit has been gathered: there is no first-ripe fig which my soul desires. The godly man has perished from the earth, and there is none upright among men. Each hunts his brother with a net. Put no trust in a neighbor; guard the doors of your mouth from her who lies in your bosom; for the son treats the father with contempt, the daughter rises up against her mother; a man's enemies are the men of his own house. But as for me, I will look to the Lord, I will wait for the God of my salvation; my God will hear me.

Rejoice not over me, O my enemy; when I fall, I shall rise; when I sit in darkness, the Lord will be a light to me. I will bear the indignation of the Lord because I have sinned against him, until he pleads my cause. He will bring me forth to the light; I shall behold his deliverance. Then my enemy will see, and shame will cover her who said to me, "Where is the Lord your God?" Now she will be trodden down like the mire of the streets.

A day for the building of your walls! In that day the boundary shall be far extended. In that day they will come to you, from Assyria to Egypt, and from Egypt to the Euphrates, from sea to sea and from mountain to mountain. But the earth will be desolate because of its inhabitants, for the fruit of their doings.

Shepherd thy people with thy staff, the flock of thy inheritance, who dwell alone in a forest in the midst of a garden land; let them feed in Bashan and Gilead as in the days of old.

"As in the days when you came out of Egypt," says the Lord, "I will show them marvelous things." The nations shall see and be ashamed of all their might. They shall lick the dust like a serpent, like the crawling things of the earth. They shall come trembling out of their strongholds. They shall turn in dread to the Lord our God, and they shall fear because of thee.

Who is a God like thee, pardoning iniquity and passing over transgression for the remnant of his inheritance? He does not retain his anger for ever because he delights in steadfast love. He will again have compassion upon us, and cast all our sins into the depths of the sea. Thou wilt show faithfulness to Jacob and steadfast love to Abraham, as thou hast sworn to our fathers from the days of old.

NAHUM

In a rapid, excited style that reveals his strong feelings and his great sense of God's power, Nahum predicts the coming destruction of Nineveh, capital of the Assyrian Empire. For centuries Assyria had been like a lion preying on and dominating other nations of the Near East. Now, declares the prophet, the wrath of the Lord, which none can resist, will be poured out upon it. Nahum was a native of a small village in Galilee. He prophesied some years before the fall of Nineveh in 612 B.C.

AN ORACLE CONCERNING Nineveh. The book of the vision of Nahum of Elkosh.

The LORD is a jealous God and avenging; the LORD takes vengeance on his adversaries and keeps wrath for his enemies. The LORD is slow to anger and of great might; the LORD will by no means clear the guilty. His way is in whirlwind and storm; the clouds are the dust of his feet. The earth is laid waste before him, the world and all that dwell therein. Who can endure the heat of his anger? His wrath is poured out like fire, and the rocks are broken asunder by him. The LORD is good, a stronghold in the day of trouble. But with an overflowing flood he will make an end of his adversaries. "Though they be strong and many," says the LORD, "they will pass away. Though I have afflicted you, O Judah, I will afflict you no more. I will break his yoke from off you and will burst your bonds asunder."

The LORD has given commandment about you, O Nineveh. "No more shall your name be perpetuated; from the house of your gods I will cut off the graven image. I will make your grave, for you are vile." The shatterer has come against you, O Nineveh. Man the ramparts; watch the road; gird your loins; collect your strength. The shield of his mighty men is red, his soldiers are clothed in scarlet. The chariots flash like flame, the chargers prance. The river gates are opened, the palace is in dismay; its mistress is stripped, she is carried off, her maidens moaning like doves, and beating their breasts. Nineveh is like a pool whose waters flow away. "Halt! Halt!" they cry; but none turns back. Plunder the silver, plunder the gold! There is no end of treasure.

Desolation and ruin! Hearts faint and knees tremble. Where is the lions' den, where the lion brought his prey, where his cubs were, with none to disturb? The lion filled his caves with prey and his dens with torn flesh. Behold, I am against you, says the LORD, and the sword shall devour your young lions. I will cut off your prey from the earth, and the voice of your messengers shall no more be heard.

Woe to the bloody city, all full of lies and booty. The crack of whip, and rumble of wheel, galloping horse and bounding chariot! Horsemen charging, flashing sword and glittering spear, heaps of corpses, dead bodies without end! And all for the countless harlotries of the harlot, who betrays nations and peoples with her charms. I will throw filth at you and treat you with contempt. All who look on you will shrink from you and say, Wasted is Nineveh; whence shall I seek comforters for her?

Are you better than Thebes that sat by the Nile, her rampart a sea, and water her wall? Yet she was carried into captivity; her little ones were dashed in pieces, and her great men were bound in chains. You also will be drunken; you will seek refuge from the enemy. Your princes are like grasshoppers, your scribes like clouds of locusts settling on the fences in a day of cold—when the sun rises, they fly away; no one knows where they are. Your shepherds are asleep, your nobles slumber. There is no assuaging your hurt, your wound is grievous. All who hear the news of you clap their hands over you. For upon whom has not come your unceasing evil?

HABAKKUK

This book frankly confronts the age-old problem of God's justice: Why is God *"silent when the wicked swallows up the man more righteous"*? To this perennial cry the prophet receives an answer eternally valid: God is still sovereign, and in his own way and at the proper time will deal with the wicked. The Lord assures Habakkuk that *"the righteous shall live by his faith."* Because of its use by Paul, that sentence became important in Christian thought as the starting point of the theological concept of faith. Habakkuk wrote probably near the end of the sixth century B.C., when the Chaldeans (that is, the Babylonians) had conquered Assyria and were threatening Judah.

THE ORACLE OF God which Habakkuk the prophet saw.

O LORD, how long shall I cry for help, and thou wilt not hear? Or cry to thee "Violence!" and thou wilt not save? Why dost thou make me see wrongs and look upon trouble? Destruction and violence are before me; strife and contention arise. The law is slacked, for the wicked surround the righteous, so justice goes forth perverted.

Look among the nations, and see; wonder and be astounded. For I am doing a work in your days that you would not believe if told. I am rousing the Chaldeans, that bitter and impatient nation, who march through the breadth of the earth, to seize habitations not their own. Dread and terrible are they; their justice and judgment are of their own making. Their horses are swifter than leopards, more fierce than the evening wolves. Their horsemen come from afar, and fly like an eagle swift to devour. Terror of them goes before them, and they gather captives like sand. At kings they scoff, and of rulers they make sport. They take every fortress, then sweep by like the wind and go on, guilty men, whose own might is their god!

O LORD, thou hast ordained them as a judgment, and established them for chastisement. Thou who art of purer eyes than to behold evil and canst not look on wrong, why dost thou look on faithless men, and art silent when the wicked swallows up the man more righteous than he? Thou makest men like the fish of the sea. The wicked foe brings all of them up with a hook, and drags them out with his net. Then, rejoicing, he sacrifices to his net, for by it he lives in luxury, and his food is rich. Is he then to keep on emptying his net, and mercilessly slaying nations for ever?

I will take my stand to watch, and station myself on the tower, and look forth to see what he will say to me, and what I will answer concerning my complaint. And the LORD answered me: "Write the vision; make it plain upon tablets, so he may run who reads it. For still the vision awaits its time; it hastens to the end—it will not lie. If it seem slow, wait for it; it will surely come, it will not delay. Behold, he whose soul is not upright in him shall fail, but the righteous shall live by his faith. Moreover, the arrogant man shall not abide. His greed is as wide as the grave; like death he has never enough. He gathers for himself all nations, and collects as his own all peoples."

SHALL NOT ALL these take up their taunt against him, in scoffing derision, and say, "Woe to him who heaps up what is not his own and loads himself with pledges!" Will not your debtors suddenly arise and make you tremble? Then you will be booty for them. Because you have plundered many nations, all the remnant of the peoples shall plunder you.

Woe to him who gets evil gain for his house, to set his nest on high, safe from the reach of harm! You have shamed your house by cutting off many peoples; you have forfeited your life.

Woe to him who builds a town with blood, and founds a city on iniquity! Is it not from the LORD that nations weary themselves for nought?

Woe to him who makes his neighbors drink of the cup of his wrath, and makes them drunk, to gaze on their shame! You will be sated with contempt instead of glory. Drink, yourself, and stagger! The cup in the LORD's right hand will come around to you, and shame will come upon your glory!

What profit is an idol when its maker has shaped it, a metal image, a teacher of lies? Woe to him who says to a wooden thing, Awake; to a dumb stone, Arise! Can this give revelation? Behold, it is overlaid with gold and silver, and there is no breath at all in it. But the LORD is in his holy temple; let all the earth keep silence before him.

A PRAYER OF Habakkuk the prophet.

O LORD, I have heard the report of thee, and thy work do I fear. In the midst of the years renew it; in the midst of the years make it known; in wrath remember mercy.

God came from Teman, and the Holy One from Mount Paran. His glory covered the heavens, and the earth was full of his praise. His brightness was like the light, rays flashed from his hand. Before him went pestilence, and plague followed close behind. He stood and measured the earth; he looked and shook the nations; then the eternal mountains were scattered, the everlasting hills sank low.

I saw the tents of Cushan in affliction; the curtains of the land of Midian did tremble. Was thy wrath against the rivers, O LORD, or thy indignation against the sea, when thou didst ride upon thy horses, upon thy chariot of victory? Thou didst strip the sheath from thy bow, and put the arrows to the string. Thou didst cleave the earth with rivers. The mountains saw thee, and writhed; the raging waters swept on; the deep gave forth its voice. The sun and moon stood still in their habitation at the light of thine arrows as they sped. Thou didst bestride the earth in fury, trampling the nations in anger. Thou wentest forth for the salvation of thy people, and thou didst crush the head of the wicked, laying him bare from thigh to neck.

I hear, and my body trembles, my lips quiver at the sound; rottenness enters into my bones, my steps totter beneath me. I will quietly wait for the day of trouble to come upon people who invade us.

Though the fig tree do not blossom, nor fruit be on the vines, the produce of the olive fail and the fields yield no food, the flock be cut off from the fold and there be no herd in the stalls, yet I will rejoice in the LORD, I will joy in the God of my salvation. GOD, the Lord, is my strength; he makes my feet like hinds' feet, he makes me tread upon my high places.

ZEPHANIAH

A man of deep moral sensitivity, Zephaniah prophesied early in the reign of Josiah, king of Judah (640–609 B.C.). With vivid power he announces the coming day of the Lord, which is to be a day of catastrophic judgment upon all nations. Judah itself is condemned for its religious and moral corruption, springing from pride and rebelliousness. Hope is held out for the survival of a faithful remnant, but only those who repent and turn to the Lord, the prophet warns, will be spared from divine wrath. Profoundly Zephaniah lays bare the true essence of sin: it is an offense against the majesty of the living God.

THE WORD OF the LORD which came to Zephaniah the son of Cushi, son of Gedaliah, son of Amariah, son of Hezekiah, in the days of Josiah the son of Amon, king of Judah.

"I will utterly sweep away everything from the face of the earth," says the LORD, "man and beast, the birds of the air, and the fish of the sea. I will overthrow the wicked. I will stretch out my hand against Judah and Jerusalem, and cut off from this place the remnant of Baal and the idolatrous priests; those who bow down on the roofs to the stars, those who bow down to the LORD and yet swear by a foreign god, and those who have turned back from following the LORD."

Be silent before the Lord GOD! For his day is at hand. He has prepared a sacrifice and consecrated his guests. "On that day," says the LORD, "I will punish the officials and the king's sons, those who walk in foreign ways, and those who fill their master's house with violence and fraud. A cry will be heard from the Fish Gate in Jerusalem, a wail from the Second Quarter, a loud crash from the hills. Wail, O inhabitants of the city! For the traders are no more; all who weigh silver are cut off. I will search Jerusalem with lamps, and punish the men who are thickening upon their lees, who say in their hearts, 'The LORD will not do good, nor will he do ill.'"

The great day of the LORD is near, near and hastening fast; the sound of the day of the LORD is bitter, the mighty man cries aloud there. A day of wrath is that day, a day of distress and anguish, a day of ruin and devastation, a day of darkness and gloom, a day of clouds and thick darkness, a day of trumpet blast and battle cry against the fortified cities and against the lofty battlements. I will bring distress on men, so that they shall walk like the blind, because they have sinned against the LORD; their blood shall be poured out like dust, and their flesh like dung. Neither their silver nor their gold shall be able to deliver them on the day of the wrath of the LORD. In the fire of his jealous wrath, all the earth shall be consumed; for a full, yea, sudden end he will make of all the inhabitants of the earth.

Come together, O shameless nation, before the fierce anger of the LORD comes upon you. Seek the LORD, all you humble of the land, who do his commands; seek righteousness and humility; perhaps you may be hidden on the day of the wrath of the LORD.

Woe to you inhabitants of the seacoast, you nation of the Philistines! The word of the LORD is against you, and you will be destroyed till no inhabitant is left. The seacoast shall become meadows, where the remnant of the house of Judah shall pasture its flocks. In the houses of the Philistines they shall lie down at evening, for the LORD their God will be mindful of them.

"I have heard the taunts of Moab," says the LORD of hosts, the God of Israel, "and the revilings of the Ammonites against my people. Therefore, as I live, Moab shall become like Sodom, and the Ammonites like Gomorrah, a land possessed by nettles and salt pits, and a waste for ever. The survivors of my nation shall plunder and possess them." This shall be their lot, because they scoffed and boasted against the people of the LORD.

You also, O Ethiopians, shall be slain by the sword of the LORD. And he will destroy Assyria, and make Nineveh a dry waste like the desert. Herds shall lie down in the midst of her, and the vulture and the hedgehog shall lodge in her capitals. This is the exultant city that dwelt secure and said to herself, "I am and there is none else." What a desolation she has become, a lair for wild beasts! Every one who passes by her hisses and shakes his fist.

Woe to the rebellious Jerusalem! She does not trust in the LORD, or draw near to her God. Her officials are roaring lions, her judges evening wolves that leave nothing till the morning. Her prophets are wanton, faithless men; her priests profane what is sacred; they do violence to the law. Every morning the LORD shows forth his justice, but the unjust knows no shame.

"I have cut off nations," says the LORD, "so that none walks in their streets. I said, 'Surely she will fear me, she will accept correction.' But all the more they were corrupt. Therefore wait for me, for the day when I arise as a witness. For my decision is to gather nations, to pour out upon them all the heat of my anger.

"At that time I will change the speech of the peoples to a pure speech, that all may call on the name of the LORD and serve him with one accord. On that day you shall not be put to shame because you have rebelled against me, for I will remove from your midst your proudly exultant ones and leave a people humble and lowly. Those who are left in Israel shall seek refuge in the name of the LORD. They shall do no wrong, nor shall there be found in their mouth a deceitful tongue. They shall pasture and lie down, and none shall make them afraid."

Sing aloud, O daughter of Zion; shout, O Israel! Rejoice and exult with all your heart. The LORD has taken away the judgments against you and cast out your enemies. The LORD, your God, is in your midst, a warrior who gives victory; he will rejoice over you with gladness and renew you in his love. "I will remove disaster from you," says the LORD, "so that you will not bear reproach for it. I will deal with your oppressors, and I will save the lame and gather the outcast, and change their shame into praise. At that time I will bring you home; yea, I will make you renowned and praised among all the peoples of the earth."

HAGGAI

The purpose of Haggai's vigorous preaching was to awaken popular enthusiasm for the completion of the second temple, the first having been destroyed about seventy years before by Nebuchadnezzar. Since the return of the Jews to Jerusalem from the Babylonian Exile, about 538 B.C., nearly two decades had passed, but as yet only the temple's foundations had been laid down. Haggai urges the leaders of the Judean community to take personal charge, in order to hasten its completion. He also calls for the priests to purify the cultic worship, and he links earlier Israelite traditions with the promise of a coming messianic age. The book, which was probably put together by another hand, offers a summary of his teaching.

———

IN THE SECOND year of Darius the king, in the sixth month, on the first day of the month, the word of the LORD came by Haggai the prophet to Zerubbabel son of Shealtiel, governor of Judah, and to Joshua son of Jehozadak, the high priest, "Thus says the LORD of hosts: This people say the time has not yet come to rebuild the house of the LORD. Is it a time for you to dwell in your paneled houses, while this house lies in ruins? Now therefore consider how you have fared. You have sown much, and harvested little; you eat, but you never have enough; you clothe yourselves, but no one is warm; and he who earns wages puts them into a bag with holes. You looked for much, and it came to little; and when you brought it home, I blew it away. Why? Because my house lies in ruins, while you busy yourselves with your own. Therefore the heavens above you have withheld the dew, and the earth has withheld its produce. I have called for a drought upon the land, upon what the ground brings forth, upon men and cattle, and upon all their labors."

Then Zerubbabel, Joshua, and all the remnant of the people feared before the LORD. Haggai spoke to them with the LORD's message, "Go up to the hills and bring wood and build the house, that I may take pleasure in it and appear in my glory. I am with you." The LORD stirred up the spirit of the people, and they came and worked on the house of the LORD their God.

On the twenty-first day of the seventh month, the word of the LORD came by Haggai, "Say to Zerubbabel, Joshua, and all the people, 'Who among you saw this house in its former glory? How do you see it now? Is it not as nothing? Yet take courage; work, for my Spirit abides among you. In a little while I will shake all nations, so that their treasures shall come in; the silver and gold is mine, and I will fill this house with greater splendor than the former. In this place I will give prosperity.'"

On the twenty-fourth day of the ninth month, the word of the LORD came by Haggai, "Thus says the LORD: Ask the priests to decide this question, 'If one carries holy flesh in the skirt of his garment, and the skirt touches bread, or wine, or any kind of food, does the food become holy?'" The priests answered, "No." Then said Haggai, "If one who is unclean by contact with a dead body touches food, does it become unclean?" The priests answered, "It does." Haggai said, "So is it with this nation before me, says the LORD. What the people offer is unclean. Consider now what will come to pass. Before a stone was placed upon a stone in the temple of the LORD, how did you fare? When one came to a heap of twenty measures, there were but ten; when one came to the winevat to draw fifty measures, there were but twenty. I smote you and the products of your toil with blight and mildew, yet you did not return to me, says the LORD. But since the day that the foundation of the LORD's temple was laid, consider: From this day on I will bless you."

Then the word of the LORD came a second time to Haggai on the same day, "Say to Zerubbabel, governor of Judah, I am about to shake the heavens and the earth, and to overthrow the throne of kingdoms; I am about to destroy the strength of the nations, and overthrow the chariots and their riders; the horses and their riders shall go down, every one by the sword of his fellow. On that day I will take you, O Zerubbabel my servant, and make you like a signet ring; for I have chosen you, says the LORD of hosts."

ZECHARIAH

In the first section of this book, Zechariah encourages the returned exiles, especially their leaders Joshua and Zerubbabel, to proceed with the rebuilding of the temple at Jerusalem. His prophecies, which may be dated about 519 B.C., are notably different from those of his contemporaries, among whom was the prophet Haggai. They consist of symbolic visions, and dialogues between God, seer, and an interpreting angel. There follows a sermon on the observance of the commandments and the rewards for so doing. In the second section the tone is different, and the circumstances reflect an age subsequent to Zechariah. This later writer, who remains unknown, foresees battles and distress for Israel, followed by eventual redemption. The description of the triumphant coming of the humble king was taken by New Testament writers as prefiguring Christ's entry into Jerusalem on Palm Sunday.

IN THE EIGHTH month, in the second year of Darius, the word of the LORD came to Zechariah the son of Berechiah, son of Iddo, the prophet, saying, "The LORD was very angry with your fathers. Therefore say to the people, Thus says the LORD of hosts: Return to me, and I will return to you. Be not like your fathers, to whom the former prophets cried out, 'Return from your evil ways and from your evil deeds.' They did not heed me, says the LORD. Your fathers, where are they? And the prophets, do they live for ever? But my words and my statutes, which I commanded my servants the prophets, did they not overtake your fathers? So they repented and said, As the LORD of hosts purposed to deal with us for our ways and deeds, so has he dealt with us."

On the twenty-fourth day of the eleventh month, in the second year of Darius, the word of the LORD came to Zechariah; and Zechariah said, "I saw in the night a man riding upon a red horse among the myrtle trees in the glen; and behind him were other men on red, sorrel, and white horses. 'Who are these?' I asked. 'These are they whom the LORD has sent to patrol the earth,' the man among the myrtle trees answered. And the horsemen said, 'We have patrolled the earth, and behold, it remains at rest.' Then the angel of the LORD said, 'O LORD of hosts, how long wilt thou have no mercy on Jerusalem and Judah, against which thou hast had indignation these seventy years?' And the LORD answered with gracious and comforting words. So the angel who talked with me said, 'Cry out, Thus says the LORD of hosts: I am exceedingly jealous for Jerusalem and for Zion. And I am very angry with the nations that are at ease; for while I was angry but a little, they furthered the disaster. Therefore I have returned to Jerusalem with compassion; and my house shall be built in it. My cities shall again overflow with prosperity, and I will again comfort Zion.'"

I lifted my eyes, and behold, I saw four horns! "What are these?" I asked the angel. "These are the horns which have scattered Judah, Israel, and Jerusalem," he answered. Then the LORD showed me four smiths. "What are these men coming to do?" I asked the angel. "They have come to terrify the nations," he answered, "and cast down the horns that were lifted up against Judah to scatter it."

I lifted my eyes again, and behold, I saw a man with a measuring line in his hand! "Where are you going?" I asked him. "To measure Jerusalem," he replied, "to see what is its breadth and length." And behold, the angel who talked with me came forward, and another angel came to meet him, saying, "Run, say to that young man, 'Jerusalem shall be inhabited as villages without walls, because of the multitude of men and cattle in it. For I will be to her a wall of fire, says the LORD, and I will be the glory within her.'"

Flee from the land of the north, says the LORD; for I have spread you abroad as the four winds of the heavens. Escape to Zion, you who dwell with the daughter of Babylon. For thus said the LORD of hosts, after he sent me to the nations who plundered you, for he who touches you touches the apple of his eye: "Behold, I will shake my hand over them, and they shall become plunder for those who served them. Sing and rejoice, O daughter of Zion; for lo, I come and I will dwell in the midst of you. Many nations shall join themselves to the LORD in that day, and shall be my people. The LORD will inherit Judah as his portion in the holy land, and will again choose Jerusalem."

Then the angel who talked with me showed me Joshua the high priest standing before the angel of the LORD, and Satan standing at his right hand to accuse Joshua. And the LORD said to Satan, "The LORD who has chosen Jerusalem rebukes you, O Satan! Is not this a brand plucked from the fire?" Joshua was clothed with filthy garments, and the angel said to those who were standing before him, "Remove the filthy garments from him." To Joshua he said, "Behold, I have taken your iniquity away from you, and I will clothe you with rich apparel, and put a clean turban on your head."

Then the angel of the LORD enjoined Joshua, "Thus says the LORD of hosts: If you will walk in my ways and keep my charge, you shall rule my house, and I will give you the right of access among the angels standing here. Hear now, O Joshua the high priest, you and your friends who sit before you, all men of good omen: behold, I will bring my servant the Branch, and I will remove the guilt of this land in a single day. In that day every one of you will invite his neighbor under his vine and under his fig tree."

The angel who talked with me came again, and waked me, like a man that is wakened out of his sleep. "What do you see?" he asked. "A lampstand of gold," I said, "with a bowl on the top of it, and seven lamps on it, with seven lips on each of the lamps. There are two olive trees by it, one on the right of the bowl and the other on its left." And I asked the angel, "What are these, my lord?" The angel answered, "These seven are the eyes of the LORD, which range through the whole earth, and the olive trees are the two anointed ones who stand by him."

Then the angel said, "This is the word of the LORD to Zerubbabel: Not by might, nor by power, but by my Spirit, says the LORD. What are you, O great mountain? Before Zerubbabel you shall become a plain." Moreover the word of the LORD came to me, saying, "The hands of Zerubbabel have laid the foundation of my house; his hands shall also complete it. Whoever has despised the day of small things shall rejoice when he sees the plumb line in the hand of Zerubbabel."

Again I lifted my eyes, and behold, I saw a flying scroll! "What do you see?" the angel asked. "A flying scroll," I answered. "Its length is thirty feet, and its breadth fifteen." He said, "This is the curse that goes out over the face of the whole land; for every one who steals, and every one who swears falsely shall be cut off henceforth according to it. I will send it forth, says the LORD of hosts, and it shall enter the house of the thief, and the house of him who swears falsely by my name, and it shall abide there and consume it, both timber and stones."

Then the angel came forward and said to me, "Lift your eyes, and see the large basket that goes forth." So I lifted my eyes, and behold, the leaden cover of the basket was raised, and there was a woman sitting inside! "This is Wickedness," the angel said. And he pushed her back into the basket, and thrust down the leaden cover. Then I saw two women coming forward! They had wings like a stork's, and they lifted up the basket between earth and heaven. "Where are they taking it?" I asked the angel. "To the land of Shinar," he answered, "to build a house for it. When the house is prepared, they will set the basket down there on its own base."

Again I lifted my eyes, and behold, I saw four chariots come out from between two mountains of bronze. The first chariot had red horses, the second black, the third white, and the fourth dappled gray. "What are these, my lord?" I asked the angel. "They are going forth to the four winds of heaven," he answered, "after presenting themselves before the LORD of all the earth." The steeds were impatient to get off, so the angel said to them, "Go, patrol the earth." Then he cried to me, "Behold, those who go toward the north country have set my Spirit at rest."

Now the word of the LORD came to me: "Go to the exiles Heldai, Tobijah, and Jedaiah, who have arrived from Babylon, and to the house of Josiah the son of Zephaniah. Take from them silver and gold, and make a crown. Set it upon the head of Joshua the high priest, and say to him, 'Thus says the LORD of hosts: "Behold, the man whose name is the Branch, for he shall build the temple of the LORD. He shall bear royal honor, and shall sit and rule upon his throne. And there shall be a priest by his throne, and peaceful understanding shall be between them both."' And the crown shall be in the temple of the LORD as a reminder to Heldai, Tobijah, Jedaiah, and Josiah the son of Zephaniah. Those who are far off shall come and help to build the temple, and then you shall know that the LORD of hosts has sent me to you. This shall come to pass, if you will diligently obey the voice of the LORD your God."

The word of the LORD came to me again, saying, "Thus says the LORD of hosts: I will return to Zion, and will dwell in the midst of Jerusalem, and it shall be called the faithful city. Old men and old women shall again sit in the streets, each with staff in hand, and the city shall be full of boys and girls playing. If this seems marvelous to you in these days, should it also be marvelous in my sight? I will bring my people from the east country and from the west country to dwell in the midst of Jerusalem; and I will be their God, in faithfulness and in righteousness."

Therefore says the LORD of hosts: "Let your hands be strong, that the temple might be built. For before the days that its foundation was laid there was no wage for man or beast, neither was there any safety from the foe; for I set every man against his fellow. But I will not deal with the remnant of this people as in the former days. There shall be a sowing of peace; the ground shall give its increase, and the heavens shall give their dew. As you have been a byword of cursing among the nations, O house of Judah and house of Israel, so you shall be a blessing. Fear not, but let your hands be strong. Speak the truth to one another, render judgments that are true and make for peace. Do not devise evil in your hearts against one another, and love no false oath, for all these things I hate. Many peoples and strong nations shall come to Jerusalem to entreat the favor of the LORD. In those days ten men of every tongue shall take hold of the robe of a Jew, saying, 'Let us go with you, for we have heard that God is with you.'"

THE WORD OF the LORD is against the land of Hadrach and will rest upon Damascus. For to the LORD belong the cities of Aram, even as all the tribes of Israel; Hamath also, which borders thereon, and Tyre and Sidon. And the king shall perish from Gaza; Ashkelon shall be uninhabited; and I will make an end of the pride of Philistia. I will take away its blood from its mouth, and its abominations from between its teeth; it shall be like a clan in Judah. Then I will encamp at my house as a guard, so that none shall march to and fro; no oppressor shall again overrun them, for now I see with my own eyes.

Rejoice greatly, O daughter of Zion! Shout aloud, O daughter of Jerusalem! Lo, your king comes to you; triumphant and victorious is he, humble and riding on an ass, on a colt the foal of an ass. I will cut off the war horse from Jerusalem, and he shall command peace to the nations; his dominion shall be from sea to sea, and from the River to the ends of the earth.

As for you, because of the blood of my covenant with you, I will set your captives free from the waterless pit. Return to your stronghold, O prisoners of hope; today I declare that I will restore to you double.

On that day the LORD their God will save them, for they are the flock of his people; like the jewels of a crown they shall shine on his land. Yea, how good and how fair it shall be! Grain shall make the young men flourish, and new wine the maidens.

THE LORD MY God said to me: "Become shepherd of the flock doomed to slaughter. Those who buy them slay them and go unpunished; and those who sell them say, 'Blessed be the LORD, I have become rich.' Their own shepherds have no pity on them. For I will no longer have pity on the inhabitants of this land. I will cause men to fall each into the hand of his shepherd, and each into the hand of his king; and they shall crush the earth; I will deliver none from their hand." So I became the shepherd of the flock doomed to be slain for those who trafficked in the sheep. I took two staffs; one I named Grace, the other I named Union. But I became impatient with the sheep, and they also detested me. "I will not be your shepherd," I said. "What is to die, let it die; and let those that are left devour the flesh of one another." And I took my staff Grace, and I broke it, annulling the covenant which I had made with the peoples. And the traffickers in the sheep, who were watching me, knew that it was the word of the LORD. "If it seems right to you," I said to them, "give me my wages; but if not, keep them." And they weighed out as my wages thirty shekels of silver. Then the LORD said to me, "Cast it into the treasury"—the lordly price at which I was paid off by them. So I took the thirty shekels of silver and cast them into the treasury in the house of the LORD. Then I broke my second staff, Union, annulling the brotherhood between Judah and Israel.

Then the LORD said to me, "Take the implements of a worthless shepherd. For lo, I am raising up in the land a shepherd who does not care for the perishing, or seek the wandering, or heal the maimed, or nourish the hungry, but devours the flesh of the fat ones, tearing off even their hoofs. Woe to my worthless shepherd, who deserts the flock! May the sword smite his arm and his right eye! Let his arm be wholly withered, his right eye utterly blinded!"

THE WORD OF the LORD concerning Israel: Thus says the LORD, who stretched out the heavens and founded the earth and formed the spirit of man within him: "Lo, I am about to make Jerusalem a cup to send the peoples reeling. On that day I will make Jerusalem a heavy stone; all who lift it shall grievously hurt themselves. And all the nations of the earth will come together against it. I will strike every horse of the nations with panic, and its rider with madness. But upon the house of Judah I will open my eyes. Then the clans of Judah shall say to themselves, 'The inhabitants of Jerusalem have strength through the LORD of hosts, their God.' I will make Judah like a flaming torch among sheaves; they shall devour to the right and to the left all the peoples round about, while Jerusalem shall still be inhabited in its place. I will give victory to the tents of Judah first, that the glory of Jerusalem may not be exalted over that of Judah. But I will put a shield about the inhabitants of Jerusalem, so that the feeblest among them shall be like David, and the house of David shall be like God, like the angel of the LORD at their head.

"I will pour out on the house of David and the inhabitants of Jerusalem a spirit of compassion, so that when they look on him whom they have pierced, they shall mourn for him, as one mourns for an only child, and weep bitterly over him, as one weeps over a first-born. On that day the mourning in Jerusalem will be as great as the mourning in the plain of Megiddo. The land shall mourn, each family by itself; the family of the house of David by itself, and their wives by themselves; and all the other families, each by itself, and their wives by themselves.

"On that day there shall be a fountain opened for the house of David and the inhabitants of Jerusalem to cleanse them from sin. I will cut off the names of the idols from the land, and I will remove the prophets and the unclean spirit. If any one again appears as a prophet, his father and mother will say to him, 'You shall not live, for you speak lies in the name of the LORD'; and they shall pierce him through when he prophesies. Every prophet will be ashamed of his vision when he prophesies; he will not put on a hairy mantle in order to deceive, but he will say, 'I am no prophet, I am a tiller of the soil; for the land has been my possession since my youth.'"

"AWAKE, O SWORD, against my shepherd, against the man who stands next to me," says the LORD of hosts. "Strike the shepherd, that the sheep may be scattered; I will turn my hand against the little ones. In the whole land, two thirds shall be cut off and perish, and one third shall be left alive. I will put this third into the fire, and refine them as one refines silver, and test them as gold is tested. They will call on my name, and I will answer them. I will say, 'They are my people'; and they will say, 'The LORD is my God.'"

BEHOLD, A DAY of the LORD is coming when the spoil taken from you will be divided in the midst of you. For I will gather all the nations against Jerusalem to battle, and the city shall be plundered and the women ravished. Half of the people shall go into exile, but the rest shall not be cut off from the city. Then the LORD will go forth and fight against those nations as on a day of battle. His feet shall stand on the Mount of Olives which lies before Jerusalem on the east; and the mount shall be split in two from east to west by a very wide valley, so that one half shall withdraw northward, and the other half southward. And the valley of my mountains shall be stopped up, and you shall flee as you fled from the earthquake in the days of Uzziah king of Judah. Then the LORD your God will come, and all the holy ones with him. On that day there shall be neither cold nor frost. There shall be continuous day (it is known to the LORD), not day and not night. Living waters shall flow out from Jerusalem, half of them to the eastern sea and half of them to the western sea; it shall continue in summer as in winter. And the LORD will become king over all the earth; the LORD will be one and his name one. The whole land shall be turned into a plain from Geba to Rimmon south of Jerusalem. But Jerusalem shall remain aloft upon its site, and it shall dwell in security, for there shall be no more curse on it.

And this shall be the plague with which the LORD will smite all the peoples that wage war against Jerusalem: their flesh shall rot while they are still on their feet, their eyes shall rot in their sockets, their tongues in their mouths. Then every one that survives of all the nations that have come against Jerusalem shall go up year after year to worship the King, the LORD of hosts, and to keep the feast of booths. If any of the families of the earth do not go up to worship the LORD, there will be no rain upon them. And if the family of Egypt do not present themselves, the LORD will afflict them with the plague. This shall be the punishment to all the nations that do not go up to keep the feast of booths.

On that day there shall be inscribed on the bells of the horses, "Holy to the LORD." And the pots in the house of the LORD shall be as the bowls before the altar; every pot in Jerusalem and Judah shall be sacred to the LORD of hosts, so that all who come may boil the flesh of the sacrifice in them. And there shall no longer be a trader in the house of the LORD of hosts.

MALACHI

The Hebrew name Malachi means "my messenger," and the word may not be the actual name of the prophet. Whoever the writer was, he addresses his fellow Jews in the fifth century B.C., some decades after their return from the Babylonian Exile and after the rebuilding of the temple. For their slackness and faithlessness, he rebukes not only the people but also the priests. Like Zechariah, he speaks of the day of the Lord, when the Lord will come in blessing and in judgment. A new feature regarding that day is the promise of a messenger to be sent as a herald. In the New Testament this prophecy is taken by the Gospels as fulfilled in John the Baptist.

THE ORACLE OF the word of the LORD to Israel by Malachi.

"I have loved you," says the LORD. But you say, "How hast thou loved us?" "Is not Esau Jacob's brother?" says the LORD. "Yet I have loved Jacob and hated Esau; I have laid waste his hill country and left his heritage to jackals of the desert." If Edom says, "We are shattered but we will rebuild the ruins," the LORD of hosts says, "They may build, but I will tear down, till they are called the wicked country, the people with whom the LORD is angry for ever." Your own eyes shall see this, and you shall say, "Great is the LORD, beyond the border of Israel!"

Have we not all one father? Has not one God created us? Why then are we faithless to one another, profaning the covenant of our fathers? Judah has been faithless, and abomination has been committed in Jerusalem; for Judah has profaned the sanctuary of the LORD and has married the daughters of a foreign god. May the LORD cut off from the tents of Jacob any man who does this, even though he brings an offering to the LORD of hosts!

And this again you do. You cover the LORD's altar with tears, with weeping and groaning because he no longer regards your offering with favor. You ask, "Why does he not?" Because the LORD was witness to the covenant between you and the wife of your youth, to whom you have been faithless. Has not the one God made and sustained for us the spirit of life? And what does he desire? Godly offspring. So take heed to yourselves, and let none be faithless to the wife of his youth. "For I hate divorce," says the LORD the God of Israel, "and covering one's garment with violence."

"BEHOLD, I SEND my messenger to prepare the way before me, and the Lord whom you seek will suddenly come to his temple; the messenger of the covenant, behold, he is coming," says the LORD of hosts.

"But who can endure the day of his coming, and who can stand when he appears? For he is like a refiner's fire and like fullers' soap; he will sit and purify the sons of Levi and refine them like gold and silver, till they present right offerings to the LORD.

"Then I will draw near to you for judgment. I will be a swift witness against the sorcerers, against the adulterers, against those who oppress the hireling in his wages, the widow and the orphan, and those who thrust aside the sojourner, and do not fear me," says the LORD of hosts.

"For I the LORD do not change; therefore you, O sons of Jacob, are not consumed. From the days of your fathers you have turned aside from my statutes and have not kept them. Return to me, and I will return to you," says the LORD of hosts. "But you say, 'How shall we return?' Will man rob God? Yet you are robbing me. But you say, 'How are we robbing thee?' In your tithes and offerings. Bring the full tithes into the storehouse, that there may be food in my house. Thereby put me to the test," says the LORD of hosts, "and I will pour down for you an overflowing blessing. I will rebuke the locust, so that it will not destroy the fruits of your soil; and your vine in the field shall not fail to bear," says the LORD of hosts. "Then all nations will call you blessed, for you will be a land of delight."

Then those who feared the LORD spoke with one another; the LORD heeded and heard them, and a book of remembrance was written before him of those who feared the LORD and thought on his name. "They shall be mine," says the LORD of hosts, "my special possession on the day when I act, and I will spare them as a man spares his son. Then once more you shall distinguish between the righteous and the wicked, between one who serves God and one who does not serve him.

"For behold, the day comes, burning like an oven, when all the arrogant and all evildoers will be stubble; the day that comes shall burn them up," says the LORD of hosts, "so that it will leave them neither root nor branch. But for you who fear my name the sun of righteousness shall rise with healing in its wings. You shall go forth leaping like calves from the stall. And you shall tread down the wicked, for they will be ashes under the soles of your feet on the day when I act," says the LORD of hosts. "Remember the law of my servant Moses, the ordinances that I commanded him at Sinai for all Israel.

"Behold, I will send you Elijah the prophet before the great and terrible day of the LORD comes. And he will turn the hearts of fathers to their children and the hearts of children to their fathers, lest I smite the land with a curse."

THE
NEW TESTAMENT

INTRODUCTION TO
THE
NEW TESTAMENT

The New Testament is the distinctively Christian portion of the Bible. It consists of twenty-seven documents, varying greatly in length, each of which is traditionally known as a "book."

The first four books, the Gospels, record the fundamental facts about Jesus Christ, his birth, ministry, teaching, death, and resurrection. Three of the Gospels—Matthew, Mark, and Luke—are known collectively as the Synoptics, because they follow much the same plan and tell much the same story (in the present version some of this repetition from Gospel to Gospel has been eliminated). John's Gospel is rather different. It contains no parables in the Synoptic sense, and it provides a number of incidents, and sayings of Jesus, not given by the other three evangelists. Also, John frequently weaves Jesus' words so closely with his own deeply meditated interpretations of them that it is often hard to find the break between the two.

Composition of the Gospels is assigned by most scholars to a thirty-year period, about A.D. 65 to A.D. 95. It is thought that Mark wrote first, and John last. The books of Matthew and Luke, both of which made use of Mark's work as well as other sources, appeared in between.

The fifth book of the New Testament, the Acts of the Apostles, records the growth and spread of Christianity during the generation after Christ's resurrection. Written by Luke as a continuation of his Gospel, the narrative of Acts focuses first on the work of the chief apostle, Peter, and then on the far-flung missionary labors of Paul.

The next twenty-one books are all letters, or epistles, by which early church authorities sought to provide guidance in the Christian way of life. Thirteen of these letters are attributed to the apostle Paul, and were written mostly to local churches he had personally founded. Paul's letters, containing some of the best-known passages in world literature, were in circulation even before the written Gospels, starting about A.D. 51 with his first letter to the Thessalonians. This was only some twenty years after Christ's death and resurrection.

The final book of the New Testament, Revelation, belongs to a class of literature called apocalyptic. By means of an elaborate symbolism it announces the disclosure, or revelation, of God's will for the future, the consummation of the divine purpose.

All the books of the New Testament were originally written in koine, the everyday Greek of the time, which was spoken by most peoples of the Roman Empire. The various books show different levels of competence in koine, the most highly literary being the Letter to the Hebrews and 1 Peter. Least polished are the Gospel of Mark and Revelation. As scholars have shown, certain turns of expression in the Greek of the Gospels reflect traces of an underlying Aramaic idiom, which was the mother tongue of Jesus and his disciples.

The original manuscripts of the books of the New Testament have not survived. Almost all of the thousands of copies made during the first three or four centuries, painstakingly handwritten by scribes, have also disappeared. The reasons for the unfortunate loss are obvious: the writing material then commonly used, papyrus, soon wore out, and during persecutions the Christian Scriptures were often hunted out and destroyed.

The oldest existing portion of the New Testament is a tiny scrap of papyrus, dating from about A.D. 125, which contains a few verses from the Gospel of John. The oldest considerable manuscripts of the New Testament, containing most of John's Gospel and some of the letters of Paul, are two papyrus books dating from about A.D. 200. The earliest existing copy of the entire New Testament is the famous volume known as Codex Sinaiticus, dating from about A.D. 350, now preserved in the British Library, London. Aside from these treasured volumes, more than five thousand other Greek manuscripts of the New Testament, whole or in part, are known to exist today.

At first the books of the New Testament were probably written on scrolls, making it impracticable to include many of them in a single scroll. When Christians, in the second century, began using the codex, or page form of manuscript, it became possible to collect in one volume all the New Testament books. With this physical assembling, questions about what to include in the volume became urgent, and churchmen had to decide on a canon for the New Testament.

Derived from Greek, the word canon denotes a measuring rod, thus indicating a rule or norm. Applied to the Scriptures, the word came to mean a list of those books that were considered authoritative, marking them off in a special way from the rest of early Christian literature. The test for canonicity most frequently applied seems to have been twofold: apostolic authorship, or at least apostolic content, as well as agreement with what was called the rule of faith, that is, a general harmony with the rest of Scripture.

Exactly when it was in the first centuries that the present books were admitted into the New Testament canon, and in what manner, is hard to say, since explicit information has been lost to history. Apparently the process went rapidly in some parts of the early church, more slowly in others. During the second century most churches came to accept a canon that included the four Gospels, Acts, and most of the epistles. At length, official pronouncements were made, first by bishops of provincial churches, then by synods and church councils. Prior to these statements, however, there existed the intuitive insight of individual Christians regarding the inherent significance of these books. Saint Athanasius, in A.D. 367, was the first of whom there is record to name the present twenty-seven books as exclusively canonical.

THE GOSPEL ACCORDING TO
MATTHEW

In his account of the ministry of Jesus Christ, Matthew repeatedly shows how the words and deeds of Jesus fulfill Old Testament predictions, and frequently he touches on the relation of Jesus' teachings to Jewish law. These and other features indicate that the writer's main purpose is to proclaim Jesus' mission as part of a divine plan, and to demonstrate to Jewish readers that Jesus is the royal Messiah. Also characteristic of this Gospel is the fullness with which it records Jesus' message.

While Matthew's account is based largely on that of Mark, it also provides much additional information, for instance, on the birth of Jesus, on certain sayings of Jesus about the church, and on Jesus' final commission to teach and baptize all nations. Though the framework of the narrative is biographical, Matthew tends to group his materials by subject, rather than presenting them in strict chronological order. The method can best be appreciated in the five distinctive and lengthy discourses given by Jesus, each of which is actually a collection of Jesus' teachings on a specific theme. Among the five is the well-known Sermon on the Mount.

Now THE BIRTH of Jesus Christ took place in this way. When his mother Mary had been betrothed to Joseph, before they came together she was found to be with child of the Holy Spirit; and her husband Joseph, being a just man and unwilling to put her to shame, resolved to divorce her quietly. But an angel of the Lord appeared to him in a dream, saying, "Do not fear to take Mary your wife, for that which is conceived in her is of the Holy Spirit; she will bear a son, and you shall call him Jesus, for he will save his people from their sins."

All this took place to fulfil what the Lord had spoken by the prophet, "Behold, a virgin shall conceive and bear a son, and his name shall be called Emmanuel" (which means, God with us). When Joseph woke, he did as the angel commanded; he took his wife, but knew her not until she had borne a son; and he called him Jesus.

Now when Jesus was born in Bethlehem of Judea in the days of Herod the king, wise men from the East came to Jerusalem, saying, "Where is he who has been born king of the Jews? For we have seen his star in the East, and have come to worship him." At this, Herod was troubled, and assembling the chief priests and scribes, he inquired where the Christ was to be born. They told him, "In Bethlehem of Judea; for so it is written by the prophet: 'And you, O Bethlehem, in the land of Judah, are by no means least among the rulers of Judah; for from you shall come a ruler who will govern my people Israel.'"

Secretly Herod summoned the wise men and ascertained from them what time the star appeared. "Go, and when you have found the child," he said, "bring me word, that I too may come and worship him." They went their way, and lo, the star which they had seen in the East went before them, till it came to rest over the place where the child was. Going into the house, they saw the child with Mary his mother, and they fell down and worshiped him, and they offered him gifts, gold and frankincense and myrrh. Then, being warned in a dream not to return to Herod, they departed to their own country by another way.

Now an angel appeared to Joseph in a dream and said, "Rise, take the child and his mother, and flee to Egypt, and remain there till I tell you; for Herod is about to search for the child, to destroy him." And he took them by night and departed. This was to fulfil what the Lord had spoken by the prophet, "Out of Egypt have I called my son."

When Herod saw that he had been tricked, he was in a furious rage, and he sent and killed all the male children in Bethlehem and in all that region who were two years old or under, according to the time which he had ascertained. Then was fulfilled what was spoken by the prophet Jeremiah, "A voice was heard in Ramah, wailing and loud lamentation, Rachel weeping for her children; she refused to be consoled, because they were no more."

After Herod died, an angel appeared in a dream to Joseph in Egypt, saying, "Rise, take the child and his mother, and go to the land of Israel, for those who sought the child's life are dead." And they went to the land of Israel, but when Joseph heard that Archelaus reigned over Judea in place of his father Herod, he was afraid, and being warned in a dream he withdrew to the district of Galilee. And they dwelt in a city called Nazareth, that what was spoken by the prophets might be fulfilled, "He shall be called a Nazarene."

IN THOSE DAYS came John the Baptist, preaching in the wilderness of Judea, "Repent, for the kingdom of heaven is at hand." For this is he who was spoken of by the prophet Isaiah when he said, "The voice of one crying in the wilderness: Prepare the way of the Lord, make his paths straight." Now John wore a garment of camel's hair, and a leather girdle, and his food was locusts and wild honey. The people of Jerusalem and all Judea and the region about the Jordan went out to him, and they were baptized by him in the river Jordan, confessing their sins.

But when he saw many of the Pharisees and Sadducees coming for baptism, he said, "You brood of vipers! Who warned you to flee from the wrath to come? Bear fruit that befits repentance, and do not presume to say to yourselves, 'We have Abraham as our father'; for I tell you, God is able from these stones to raise up children to Abraham. Even now the axe is laid to the root of the trees; every tree therefore that does not bear good fruit is cut down and thrown into the fire.

"I baptize you with water for repentance, but he who is coming after me is mightier than I, whose sandals I am not worthy to carry; he will baptize you with the Holy Spirit and with fire. His winnowing fork is in his hand, and he will clear his threshing floor and gather his wheat into the granary, but the chaff he will burn with unquenchable fire."

Then Jesus came from Galilee to John, to be baptized by him. John would have prevented him, saying, "I need to be baptized by you, and do you come to me?"

"Let it be so now," Jesus answered, "for thus it is fitting for us to fulfil all righteousness." When Jesus was baptized, the heavens were opened and he saw the Spirit of God descending like a dove, and alighting on him; and a voice from heaven said, "This is my beloved Son, with whom I am well pleased."

Then Jesus was led by the Spirit into the wilderness to be tempted by the devil. He fasted forty days and forty nights, and the tempter came and said, "If you are the Son of God, command these stones to become loaves of bread." But he answered, "It is written, 'Man shall not live by bread alone, but by every word that proceeds from the mouth of God.'"

The devil took him to the holy city, and set him on the pinnacle of the temple, and said, "If you are the Son of God, throw yourself down; for it is written, 'He will give his angels charge of you,' and 'On their hands they will bear you up, lest you strike your foot against a stone.'" Jesus said, "Again it is written, 'You shall not tempt the Lord your God.'"

Then the devil took him to a very high mountain, and showed him all the kingdoms of the world, and he said, "All these I will give you, if you will fall down and worship me." Then Jesus said, "Begone, Satan! for it is written, 'You shall worship the Lord your God and him only shall you serve.'" The devil left him, and behold, angels came and ministered to him.

Now when Jesus heard that John had been arrested, he withdrew into Galilee and dwelt in Capernaum by the sea. From that time he began to preach, saying, "Repent, for the kingdom of heaven is at hand."

As he walked by the Sea of Galilee, he saw two brothers who were fishermen casting a net; Simon who is called Peter, and Andrew. "Follow me," he said, "and I will make you fishers of men." Immediately they followed him.

Then he saw two other brothers, James and John, in the boat with Zebedee their father, mending their nets, and he called them. Immediately they left the boat and followed him.

JESUS WENT ABOUT all Galilee, teaching in synagogues, preaching the gospel of the kingdom, and healing every disease and infirmity among the people. As his fame spread throughout all Syria, they brought him all the sick and the demoniacs, and he healed them.

Seeing the great crowds that followed him, he went up on the mountain and sat down. When his disciples came, he taught them, saying:

"Blessed are the poor in spirit, for theirs is the kingdom of heaven.

"Blessed are those who mourn, for they shall be comforted.

"Blessed are the meek, for they shall inherit the earth.

"Blessed are those who hunger and thirst for righteousness, for they shall be satisfied.

"Blessed are the merciful, for they shall obtain mercy.

"Blessed are the pure in heart, for they shall see God.

"Blessed are the peacemakers, for they shall be called sons of God.

"Blessed are those who are persecuted for righteousness' sake, for theirs is the kingdom of heaven.

"Blessed are you when men revile you and persecute you and utter all kinds of evil against you falsely on my account. Rejoice and be glad, for your reward is great in heaven, for so men persecuted the prophets who were before you.

"You are the salt of the earth; but if salt has lost its taste, how shall its saltness be restored? It is no longer good for anything except to be thrown out and trodden under foot by men.

"You are the light of the world. A city set on a hill cannot be hid. Nor do men light a lamp and put it under a bushel, but on a stand, and it gives light to all in the house. Let your light so shine before men, that they may see your good works and give glory to your Father who is in heaven.

"Think not that I have come to abolish the law and the prophets; I have come not to abolish them but to fulfil them. For truly, I say to you, till heaven and earth pass away, not an iota, not a dot, will pass from the law until all is accomplished. Whoever then relaxes one of the least of these commandments and teaches men so, shall be called least in the kingdom of heaven; but he who does them and teaches them shall be called great in the kingdom of heaven. For I tell you, unless your righteousness exceeds that of the scribes and Pharisees, you will never enter the kingdom of heaven.

"You have heard that it was said to the men of old, 'You shall not kill; and whoever kills shall be liable to judgment.' But I say to you that every one who is angry with his brother shall be liable to judgment; whoever insults his brother shall be liable to the council, and whoever says, 'You fool!' shall be liable to the hell of fire. So if you are offering your gift at the altar, and remember that your brother has something against you, leave your gift and go; first be reconciled to your brother, and then come and offer your gift. Make friends quickly with your accuser, while you are going with him to court, lest your accuser hand you over to the judge, and the judge to the guard, and you be put in prison; truly, I say to you, you will never get out till you have paid the last penny.

"You have heard that it was said, 'You shall not commit adultery.' But I say to you that every one who looks at a woman lustfully has already committed adultery with her in his heart. If your right eye causes you to sin, pluck it out; and if your right hand causes you to sin, cut it off; it is better that you lose one of your members than that your whole body be thrown into hell.

"It was also said, 'Whoever divorces his wife, let him give her a certificate of divorce.' But I say to you that every one who divorces his wife, except on the ground of unchastity, makes her an adulteress; and whoever marries a divorced woman commits adultery.

"Again you have heard that it was said to the men of old, 'You shall not swear falsely, but shall perform to the Lord what you have sworn.' But I say to you, Do not swear at all, either by heaven, for it is the throne of God, or by the earth, for it is his footstool, or by Jerusalem, for it is the city of the great King. And do not swear by your head, for you cannot make one hair white or black. Let what you say be simply 'Yes' or 'No'; anything more than this comes from evil.

"You have heard that it was said, 'An eye for an eye and a tooth for a tooth.' But I say to you, Do not resist one who is evil. But if any one strikes you on the right cheek, turn to him the other also; and if any one would sue you and take your coat, let him have your cloak as well; and if any one forces you to go one mile, go with him two miles. Give to him who begs from you, and do not refuse him who would borrow from you.

"You have heard that it was said, 'You shall love your neighbor and hate your enemy.' But I say to you, Love your enemies and pray for those who persecute you, so that you may be sons of your Father who is in heaven; for he makes his sun rise on the evil and on the good, and sends rain on the just and on the unjust. For if you love those who love you, what reward have you? Do not even the tax collectors do the same? And if you salute only your brethren, what more are you doing than others? Do not even the Gentiles do the same? You, therefore, must be perfect, as your heavenly Father is perfect.

"Beware of practicing your piety before men in order to be seen by them; for then you will have no reward from your Father who is in heaven.

"Thus, when you give alms, sound no trumpet before you, as the hypocrites do in the synagogues and in the streets, that they may be praised. Truly, I say to you, they have received their reward. But when you give alms, do not let your left hand know what your right hand is doing, so that your alms may be in secret; and your Father who sees in secret will reward you.

"And when you pray, you must not be like the hypocrites; for they love to stand and pray in the synagogues and at the street corners, that they may be seen by men. Truly, I say to you, they have received their reward. But when you pray, go into your room and shut the door and pray to your Father who is in secret; and your Father who sees in secret will reward you.

"And in praying do not heap up empty phrases as the Gentiles do; for they think that they will be heard for their many words. Do not be like them, for your Father knows what you need before you ask him. Pray then like this:

"Our Father who art in heaven, hallowed be thy name. Thy kingdom come, thy will be done, on earth as it is in heaven. Give us this day our daily bread; and forgive us our debts, as we also have forgiven our debtors; and lead us not into temptation, but deliver us from evil.

"For if you forgive men their trespasses, your heavenly Father also will forgive you; but if you do not forgive men their trespasses, neither will your Father forgive your trespasses.

"And when you fast, do not look dismal, like the hypocrites, for they disfigure their faces that their fasting may be seen by men. Truly, I say to you, they have received their reward. But when you fast, anoint your head and wash your face, that your fasting may not be seen by men but by your Father who is in secret; and your Father who sees in secret will reward you.

"Do not lay up for yourselves treasures on earth, where moth and rust consume and where thieves break in and steal, but lay up for yourselves treasures in heaven, where neither moth nor rust consumes and where thieves do not break in and steal. For where your treasure is, there will your heart be also.

"The eye is the lamp of the body. So, if your eye is sound, your whole body will be full of light; but if your eye is not sound, your whole body will be full of darkness. If then the light in you is darkness, how great is the darkness!

"No one can serve two masters; for either he will hate the one and love the other, or he will be devoted to the one and despise the other. You cannot serve God and mammon.

"Therefore I tell you, do not be anxious about your life, what you shall eat or what you shall drink, nor about your body, what you shall put on. Is not life more than food, and the body more than clothing? Look at the birds of the air: they neither sow nor reap nor gather into barns, and yet your heavenly Father feeds them. Are you not of more value than they? And which of you by being anxious can add one cubit to his span of life? And why are you anxious about clothing? Consider the lilies of the field, how they grow; they neither toil nor spin; yet I tell you, even Solomon in all his glory was not arrayed like one of these. But if God so clothes the grass of the field, which today is alive and tomorrow is thrown into the oven, will he not much more clothe you, O men of little faith? Therefore do not be anxious, saying, 'What shall we eat?' or 'What shall we drink?' or 'What shall we wear?' For the Gentiles seek all these things; and your heavenly Father knows that you need them all. But seek first his kingdom and his righteousness, and all these things shall be yours as well.

"Therefore do not be anxious about tomorrow, for tomorrow will be anxious for itself. Let the day's own trouble be sufficient for the day.

"Judge not, that you be not judged. For with the judgment you pronounce you will be judged, and the measure you give will be the measure you get. Why do you see the speck that is in your brother's eye, but do not notice the log that is in your own eye? Or how can you say to your brother, 'Let me take the speck out of your eye,' when there is the log in your own eye? You hypocrite, first take the log out of your own eye, and then you will see clearly to take the speck out of your brother's eye.

"Do not give dogs what is holy; and do not throw your pearls before swine, lest they trample them under foot and turn to attack you.

"Ask, and it will be given you; seek, and you will find; knock, and it will be opened to you. For every one who asks receives, and he who seeks finds, and to him who knocks it will be opened. Or what man of you, if his son asks him for bread, will give him a stone? Or if he asks for a fish, will give him a serpent? If you then, who are evil, know how to give good gifts to your children, how much more will your Father who is in heaven give good things to those who ask him! So whatever you wish that men would do to you, do so to them; for this is the law and the prophets.

"Enter by the narrow gate; for the gate is wide and the way is easy, that leads to destruction, and those who enter by it are many. For the gate is narrow and the way is hard, that leads to life, and those who find it are few.

"Beware of false prophets, who come to you in sheep's clothing but inwardly are ravenous wolves. You will know them by their fruits. Are grapes gathered from thorns, or figs from thistles? So, every sound tree bears good fruit, but the bad tree bears evil fruit. A sound tree cannot bear evil fruit, nor can a bad tree bear good fruit. Every tree that does not bear good fruit is cut down and thrown into the fire. Thus you will know them by their fruits.

"Not every one who says to me, 'Lord, Lord,' shall enter the kingdom of heaven, but he who does the will of my Father who is in heaven. On that day many will say to me, 'Lord, Lord, did we not prophesy in your name, and cast out demons in your name, and do many mighty works in your name?' And then will I declare to them, 'I never knew you; depart from me, you evildoers.'

"Every one then who hears these words of mine and does them will be like a wise man who built his house upon the rock; and the rain fell, and the floods came, and the winds blew and beat upon that house, but it did not fall, because it had been founded on the rock. And every one who hears these words of mine and does not do them will be like a foolish man who built his house upon the sand; and the rain fell, and the floods came, and the winds blew and beat against that house, and it fell; and great was the fall of it."

When Jesus finished, the crowds were astonished at his teaching, for he taught them as one who had authority, and not as their scribes.

Afterward, when he came down from the mountain, great crowds followed him, and as he entered Capernaum, a centurion came forward, beseeching, "Lord, my servant is lying paralyzed at home, in terrible distress." Jesus said, "I will come and heal him." But the centurion answered, "Lord, I am not worthy to have you come under my roof; but only say the word, and my servant will be healed. For I am a man under authority, with soldiers under me; and I say to one, 'Go,' and he goes, and to another, 'Come,' and he comes, and to my slave, 'Do this,' and he does it."

At this, Jesus marveled, and he said to those who followed, "Truly, I say to you, not even in Israel have I found such faith. I tell you, many will come from east and west and sit at table with Abraham, Isaac, and Jacob in the kingdom of heaven, while the sons of the kingdom will be thrown into the outer darkness; there men will weep and gnash their teeth." Then to the centurion he said, "Go; be it done for you as you have believed." And the servant was healed at that very moment.

Now when Jesus saw great crowds around him, he gave orders to go over to the other side of the Sea of Galilee, and he got into the boat with his disciples. And behold, there arose a great storm, so that the boat was being swamped by the waves; but he was asleep. They woke him, saying, "Save, Lord; we are perishing." And he said, "Why are you afraid, O men of little faith?" Then he rose and rebuked the winds and the sea; and there was a great calm. "What sort of man is this," they marveled, "that even winds and sea obey him?"

When they came to the other side, to the country of the Gadarenes, two fierce demoniacs came out of the tombs, and they cried, "What have you to do with us, O Son of God? Have you come here to torment us before the time?" Now a herd of swine was feeding there, and the demons begged, "If you cast us out, send us into the swine." He said to them, "Go," and they went into the swine; and the whole herd rushed down the steep bank and perished in the waters. The herdsmen fled to the city and told what had happened, and all the city came out, and when they saw Jesus, they begged him to leave their neighborhood.

Getting into a boat, he crossed over again, and as he passed on from there, he saw a man called Matthew sitting at the tax office; and he said, "Follow me." And he rose and followed him. And as Jesus sat at table in Matthew's house, many tax collectors and sinners came and sat down. Then the Pharisees said to his disciples, "Why does your teacher eat with tax collectors and sinners?" When Jesus heard it, he said, "Those who are well have no need of a physician, but those who are sick. Go and learn what this means, 'I desire mercy, and not sacrifice.' For I came not to call the righteous, but sinners."

Then the disciples of John came and asked, "Why do we and the Pharisees fast, but your disciples do not fast?"

"Can the wedding guests mourn," Jesus said, "as long as the bridegroom is with them? The days will come when the bridegroom is taken away from them, and then they will fast."

Afterward, a dumb demoniac was brought to Jesus. And when the demon had been cast out, the dumb man spoke; and the crowds marveled, saying, "Never was anything like this seen in Israel." But the Pharisees said, "He casts out demons by the prince of demons."

WHEN JESUS SAW the crowds that followed him, he had compassion for them, because they were harassed and helpless, like sheep without a shepherd. "The harvest is plentiful," he said to his disciples, "but the laborers are few; pray therefore the Lord of the harvest to send out laborers into his harvest." Then he gave his twelve disciples authority to cast out unclean spirits, and to heal every disease and infirmity. The names of the twelve are these: first, Simon called Peter, and Andrew his brother; James and John the sons of Zebedee; Philip and Bartholomew; Thomas and Matthew the tax collector; James the son of Alphaeus, and Thaddaeus; Simon the Cananaean, and Judas Iscariot, who betrayed him.

These twelve Jesus sent out, charging them, "Go nowhere among the Gentiles, and enter no town of the Samaritans, but go rather to the lost sheep of the house of Israel. And preach as you go, saying, 'The kingdom of heaven is at hand.' Heal the sick, raise the dead, cleanse lepers, cast out demons. You received without paying, give without pay. Take no gold, nor silver, nor copper in your belts, no bag for your journey, nor two tunics, nor sandals, nor a staff; for the laborer deserves his food. And whatever town or village you enter, find out who is worthy in it, and stay with him until you depart. As you enter the house, salute it. And if the house is worthy, let your peace come upon it; but if it is not worthy, let your peace return to you. And if any one will not receive you or listen to your words, shake off the dust from your feet as you leave. Truly, I say to you, it shall be more tolerable on the day of judgment for the land of Sodom and Gomorrah than for that town.

"Behold, I send you out as sheep in the midst of wolves; so be wise as serpents and innocent as doves. Beware of men; for they will deliver you up to councils, and flog you in their synagogues, and you will be dragged before governors and kings for my sake, to bear testimony before them and the Gentiles. When they deliver you up, do not be anxious how you are to speak or what you are to say; for what you are to say will be given to you in that hour; for it is not you who speak, but the Spirit of your Father speaking through you. Brother will deliver up brother to death, and the father his child, and children will rise against parents and have them put to death; and you will be hated by all for my name's sake. But he who endures to the end will be saved. When they persecute you in one town, flee to the next; for truly, I say to you, you will not have gone through all the towns of Israel, before the Son of man comes.

"A disciple is not above his teacher, nor a servant above his master; it is enough for the disciple to be like his teacher, and the servant like his master. If they have called the master of the house Beelzebul, how much more will they malign those of his household.

"So have no fear of them; for nothing is covered that will not be revealed, or hidden that will not be known. What I tell you in the dark, utter in the light; and what you hear whispered, proclaim upon the housetops. And do not fear those who kill the body but cannot kill the soul; rather fear him who can destroy both soul and body in hell. Are not two sparrows sold for a penny? And not one of them will fall to the ground without your Father's will. But even the hairs of your head are all numbered. Fear not, therefore; you are of more value than many sparrows. So every one who acknowledges me before men, I also will acknowledge before my Father who is in heaven; but whoever denies me before men, I also will deny before my Father who is in heaven.

"Do not think that I have come to bring peace on earth; I have not come to bring peace, but a sword. For I have come to set a man against his father, and a daughter against her mother, and a daughter-in-law against her mother-in-law; and a man's foes will be those of his own household. He who loves father or mother more than me is not worthy of me; and he who loves son or daughter more than me is not worthy of me; and he who does not take his cross and follow me is not worthy of me. He who finds his life will lose it, and he who loses his life for my sake will find it.

"He who receives you receives me, and he who receives me receives him who sent me. He who receives a prophet because he is a prophet shall receive a prophet's reward, and he who receives a righteous man because he is a righteous man shall receive a righteous man's reward. And whoever gives to one of these little ones even a cup of cold water because he is a disciple, truly, I say to you, he shall not lose his reward."

When John the Baptist heard in prison about the deeds of the Christ, he sent his disciples to ask, "Are you he who is to come, or shall we look for another?" Jesus answered, "Go and tell John what you hear and see: the blind receive their sight and the lame walk, lepers are cleansed and the deaf hear, the dead are raised up, and the poor have good news preached to them. And blessed is he who takes no offense at me."

Then he spoke to the crowds concerning John: "What did you go out into the wilderness to behold? A reed shaken by the wind? Why then did you go out? To see a man clothed in soft raiment? Behold, those who wear soft raiment are in kings' houses. Why then did you go out? To see a prophet? Yes, I tell you, and more than a prophet. This is he of whom it is written, 'Behold, I send my messenger before thy face, who shall prepare thy way before thee.' Truly, I say to you, among those born of women there has risen no one greater than John the Baptist; yet he who is least in the kingdom of heaven is greater than he. From the days of John the Baptist until now the kingdom of heaven has suffered violence, and men of violence take it by force. For all the prophets and the law prophesied until John; and if you are willing to accept it, he is Elijah who is to come. He who has ears to hear, let him hear. But to what shall I compare this generation? It is like children sitting in the market places and calling to their playmates, 'We piped to you, and you did not dance; we wailed, and you did not mourn.' For John came neither eating nor drinking, and they say, 'He has a demon'; the Son of man came eating and drinking, and they say, 'Behold, a glutton and a drunkard, a friend of tax collectors and sinners!' Yet wisdom is justified by her deeds."

Then he began to upbraid the cities where most of his mighty works had been done, because they did not repent. "Woe to you, Chorazin! woe to you, Bethsaida! for if the mighty works done in you had been done in Tyre and Sidon, they would have repented long ago in sackcloth and ashes. But I tell you, it shall be more tolerable on the day of judgment for Tyre and Sidon than for you. And you, Capernaum, will you be exalted to heaven? You shall be brought down to Hades. For if the mighty works done in you had been done in Sodom, it would have remained until this day. But I tell you that it shall be more tolerable on the day of judgment for the land of Sodom than for you."

At that time Jesus declared, "I thank thee, Father, Lord of heaven and earth, that thou hast hidden these things from the wise and understanding, and revealed them to babes; yea, Father, for such was thy gracious will. All things have been delivered to me by my Father; and no one knows the Son except the Father, and no one knows the Father except the Son and any one to whom the Son chooses to reveal him. Come to me, all who labor and are heavy laden, and I will give you rest. Take my yoke upon you, and learn from me; for I am gentle and lowly in heart, and you will find rest for your souls. For my yoke is easy, and my burden is light."

From there he went on, and he entered a synagogue, and behold, there was a man with a withered hand. The Pharisees asked him, "Is it lawful to heal on the sabbath?" so that they might accuse him.

"What man of you," he said, "if he has one sheep and it falls into a pit on the sabbath, will not lay hold of it and lift it out? Of how much more value is a man than a sheep! So it is lawful to do good on the sabbath." Then he said to the man, "Stretch out your hand." The man stretched it out, and it was restored, whole like the other. But the Pharisees went out and took counsel against him, how to destroy him. Jesus, aware of this, withdrew from there. And many followed him, and he healed them all, and ordered them not to make him known.

Then a blind and dumb demoniac was brought to him, and he healed him, so that he spoke and saw. All the people were amazed, and said, "Can this be the Son of David?" But when the Pharisees heard it they said, "It is only by Beelzebul, the prince of demons, that this man casts out demons."

Knowing their thoughts, Jesus said to them, "Every kingdom divided against itself is laid waste, and no city or house divided against itself will stand; and if Satan casts out Satan, he is divided against himself; how then will his kingdom stand? And if I cast out demons by Beelzebul, by whom do your sons cast them out? Therefore they shall be your judges. But if it is by the

Spirit of God that I cast out demons, then the kingdom of God has come upon you. Or how can one enter a strong man's house and plunder his goods, unless he first binds the strong man? Then indeed he may plunder his house. He who is not with me is against me, and he who does not gather with me scatters. Therefore I tell you, every sin and blasphemy will be forgiven men, but the blasphemy against the Spirit will not be forgiven. And whoever says a word against the Son of man will be forgiven; but whoever speaks against the Holy Spirit will not be forgiven, either in this age or in the age to come.

"Either make the tree good, and its fruit good; or make the tree bad, and its fruit bad; for the tree is known by its fruit. You brood of vipers! how can you speak good, when you are evil? For out of the abundance of the heart the mouth speaks. I tell you, on the day of judgment men will render account for every careless word they utter; for by your words you will be justified, and by your words you will be condemned."

Some of the scribes and Pharisees said, "Teacher, we wish to see a sign from you." But he answered, "An evil and adulterous generation seeks for a sign; but no sign shall be given to it except the sign of the prophet Jonah. For as Jonah was three days and three nights in the belly of the whale, so will the Son of man be three days and three nights in the heart of the earth. The men of Nineveh will arise at the judgment with this generation and condemn it; for they repented at the preaching of Jonah, and behold, something greater than Jonah is here. The queen of the South will arise at the judgment with this generation and condemn it; for she came from the ends of the earth to hear the wisdom of Solomon, and behold, something greater than Solomon is here."

While he was still speaking, his mother and his brothers stood outside, asking to speak to him. But he replied to the man who told him, "Who is my mother, and who are my brothers?" Stretching out his hand toward his disciples, he said, "Here are my mother and my brothers! For whoever does the will of my Father in heaven is my brother, and sister, and mother."

That same day Jesus went out and sat beside the sea, and great crowds gathered, so that he sat in a boat while the crowd stood on the beach. And he told them many things in parables, saying, "The kingdom of heaven may be compared to a man who sowed good seed in his field; but while men were sleeping, his enemy came and sowed weeds among the wheat, and went away. So when the plants came up and bore grain, then the weeds appeared also. And the servants of the householder came and said to him, 'Sir, did you not sow good seed in your field? How then has it weeds?' He said to them, 'An enemy has done this.' The servants said to him, 'Then do you want us to go and gather them?' But he said, 'No; lest in gathering the weeds you root up the wheat along with them. Let both grow together until the harvest; and at harvest time I will tell the reapers, Gather the weeds first and bind them in bundles to be burned, but gather the wheat into my barn.'"

Another parable he put before them, saying, "The kingdom of heaven is like a grain of mustard seed which a man took and sowed in his field; it is the smallest of all seeds, but when it has grown it is the greatest of shrubs and becomes a tree, so that the birds of the air come and make nests in its branches." And he told them another parable. "The kingdom of heaven is like leaven which a woman took and hid in three measures of flour, till it was all leavened." All this Jesus said to the crowds in parables; indeed he said nothing to them without a parable. This was to fulfil what was spoken by the prophet, "I will open my mouth in parables, I will utter what has been hidden since the foundation of the world."

When he left the crowds and went into the house, his disciples came to him, saying, "Explain to us the parable of the weeds of the field." He answered, "He who sows the good seed is the Son of man; the field is the world, and the good seed means the sons of the kingdom; the weeds are the sons of the evil one, and the enemy who sowed them is the devil; the harvest is the close of the age, and the reapers are angels. Just as the weeds are gathered and burned with fire, so will it be at the close of the age. The Son of man will send his angels, and they will gather out of his kingdom all causes of sin and all evildoers, and throw them into the furnace of fire; there men will weep and gnash their teeth. Then the righteous will shine like the sun in the kingdom of their Father. He who has ears, let him hear."

When Jesus had finished these parables, he went away. And coming to his own country he taught in the synagogue, so that they were astonished, and said, "Where did this man get this wisdom and these mighty works? Is not this the carpenter's son? Is not his mother called Mary? And are not his brothers James and Joseph and Simon and Judas? And are not all his sisters with us? Where then did this man get all this?" And they took offense at him. But Jesus said, "A prophet is not without honor except in his own country and in his own house." And he did not do many mighty works there, because of their unbelief.

At that time Herod the tetrarch heard about the fame of Jesus; and he said to his servants, "This is John the Baptist, he has been raised from the dead; that is why these powers are at work in him." For Herod had seized John and put him in prison for the sake of Herodias, his brother Philip's wife; because John said to him, "It is not lawful for you to have her." Herod wanted to put him to death, but he feared the people, because they held John to be a prophet.

When Herod's birthday came, the daughter of Herodias danced before the company, and pleased Herod, so that he promised with an oath to give her whatever she might ask. Prompted by her mother, she said, "Give me the head of John the Baptist on a platter." The king was sorry, but because of his oaths and his guests he commanded it to be done. John was beheaded in the prison, and his head was brought on a platter and given to the girl, and she brought it to her mother. Then John's disciples took the body and buried it; and they went and told Jesus.

Now when Jesus heard this, he withdrew from there in a boat to a lonely place. The crowds followed by land, and as he went ashore he saw a great throng, and he had compassion on them, and healed their sick. When it was evening, the disciples said, "The day is now over; send the crowds into the villages to buy food for themselves."

"They need not go away," Jesus said. "You give them something to eat." They said, "We have only five loaves and two fish."

Then Jesus ordered the crowds to sit down on the grass; and taking the five loaves and the two fish he looked up to heaven, and blessed, and broke and gave the loaves to the disciples, and the disciples gave them to the crowds. They all ate and were satisfied, and they took up twelve baskets full of the broken pieces left over. Those who ate were about five thousand men, besides women and children.

Then he made the disciples get into the boat and go before him to the other side, while he dismissed the crowds. After that he went up on the mountain by himself to pray. The boat by this time was many furlongs distant from the land, beaten by the waves; for the wind was against them. And in the fourth watch of the night he came to them, walking on the sea. But when the disciples saw him walking on the sea, they were terrified, saying, "It is a ghost!" And they cried out for fear. But immediately he spoke to them, saying, "Take heart, it is I; have no fear."

"Lord," said Peter, "if it is you, bid me come to you on the water." He said, "Come." So Peter got out of the boat and walked on the water and came to Jesus. But when he saw the wind, he was afraid, and beginning to sink he cried out, "Lord, save me." Jesus immediately reached out his hand and caught him, saying, "O man of little faith, why did you doubt?" When they got into the boat, the wind ceased, and those in the boat worshiped him, saying, "Truly you are the Son of God." And when they had crossed over, they came to land at Gennesaret. Then Pharisees and scribes came to Jesus from Jerusalem and said, "Why do your disciples transgress the tradition of the elders? For they do not wash their hands when they eat."

"And why," he answered, "do you transgress the commandment of God for the sake of your tradition? For God commanded, 'Honor your father and your mother,' and, 'He who speaks evil of father or mother, let him surely die.' But you say, 'If any one tells his father or his mother, What you would have gained from me is given to God, he need not honor his father.' So, for the sake of your tradition, you have made void the word of God. You hypocrites! Well did Isaiah prophesy of you when he said, 'This people honors me with their lips, but their heart is far from me; in vain do they worship me, teaching as doctrines the precepts of men.'"

Then he called the people to him and said, "Hear and understand: not what goes into the mouth defiles a man, but what comes out of the mouth, this defiles a man." And the disciples said, "Do you know that the Pharisees were offended when they heard this saying?"

"Every plant," he answered, "which my heavenly Father has not planted will be rooted up. Let them alone; they are blind guides. And if a blind man leads a blind man, both will fall into a pit." But Peter said, "Explain the parable to us."

"Are you also still without understanding?" he said. "Do you not see that whatever goes into the mouth passes into the stomach, and so passes on? But what comes out of the mouth proceeds from the heart, and this defiles a man. For out of the heart come evil thoughts, murder, adultery, fornication, theft, false witness, slander. These are what defile a man; but to eat with unwashed hands does not defile a man."

Now Jesus withdrew to the district of Tyre and Sidon, and there a Canaanite woman came to him and cried, "Have mercy on me, O Lord, Son of David; my daughter is severely possessed by a demon." But he did not answer her a word. And his disciples begged him, "Send her away, for she is crying after us." He answered, "I was sent only to the lost sheep of the house of Israel." But the woman knelt before him, saying, "Lord, help me."

"It is not fair," he answered, "to take the children's bread and throw it to the dogs." Then she said, "Yes, Lord, yet even the dogs eat the crumbs that fall from their masters' table."

"O woman," Jesus answered, "great is your faith! Be it done for you as you desire." And her daughter was healed instantly.

Passing along the Sea of Galilee, Jesus went up on the mountain, and great crowds came to him, bringing the sick, and he healed them. And the throng wondered, when they saw the dumb speaking, the maimed whole, the lame walking, and the blind seeing; and they glorified the God of Israel.

Then he called his disciples and said, "I have compassion on the crowd, because they have been with me now three days, and have nothing to eat; and I am unwilling to send them away hungry, lest they faint on the way." The disciples said, "Where are we to get bread enough in the desert to feed so great a crowd?" Jesus said, "How many loaves have you?" They said, "Seven, and a few small fish." Commanding the crowd to sit on the ground, he took the seven loaves and the fish, and having given thanks he broke them and gave them to the disciples, and the disciples gave them to the crowds. And they all ate and were satisfied; and they took up seven baskets full of the broken pieces left over. Those who ate were four thousand men, besides women and children. After sending away the crowds, he got into the boat and went to the region of Magadan.

Now the Pharisees and Sadducees came, and to test him they asked for a sign from heaven. He answered, "When it is evening, you say, 'It will be fair weather; for the sky is red.' And in the morning, 'It will be stormy today, for the sky is red and threatening.' You know how to interpret the appearance of the sky, but you cannot interpret the signs of the times. An evil and adulterous generation seeks for a sign, but no sign shall be given to it except the sign of Jonah." So he left them and departed.

When the disciples reached the other side, they had forgotten to bring any bread. Jesus said, "Take heed and beware of the leaven of the Pharisees and Sadducees." And they discussed it among themselves, saying, "We brought no bread." But Jesus, aware of this, said, "O men of little faith, why do you discuss among yourselves the fact that you have no bread? Do you not yet perceive? Do you not remember the five loaves of the five thousand, and how many baskets you gathered? Or the seven loaves of the four thousand, and how many baskets you gathered? How is it that you fail to perceive that I did not speak about bread? Beware of the leaven of the Pharisees and Sadducees." Then they understood.

When Jesus came into the district of Caesarea Philippi, he asked his disciples, "Who do men say that the Son of man is?" They said, "Some say John the Baptist, others say Elijah, and others Jeremiah or one of the prophets." He said to them, "But who do you say that I am?" Simon Peter replied, "You are the Christ, the Son of the living God."

"Blessed are you, Simon Bar-Jona!" Jesus answered, "for flesh and blood has not revealed this to you, but my Father who is in heaven. And I tell you, you are Peter, and on this rock I will build my church, and the powers of death shall not prevail against it. I will give you the keys of the kingdom of heaven, and whatever you bind on earth shall be bound in heaven, and whatever you loose on earth shall be loosed in heaven." Then he strictly charged the disciples to tell no one that he was the Christ.

From that time Jesus began to show his disciples that he must go to Jerusalem and suffer many things from the elders and chief priests and scribes, and be killed, and on the third day be raised. And Peter began to rebuke him, saying, "God forbid, Lord! This shall never happen to you." But he turned and said to Peter, "Get behind me, Satan! You are a hindrance to me; for you are not on the side of God, but of men." Then he told his disciples, "If any man would come after me, let him deny himself and take up his cross and follow me. For whoever would save his life will lose it, and whoever loses his life for my sake will find it. For what will it profit a man, if he gains the whole world and forfeits his life? Or what shall a man give in return for his life? For the Son of man is to come with his angels in the glory of his Father, and then he will repay every man for what he has done. Truly, I say to you, there are some standing here who will not taste death before they see the Son of man coming in his kingdom."

After six days Jesus took Peter and James and John and led them up a high mountain apart. And he was transfigured before them, and his face shone like the sun, and his garments became white as light. And behold, there appeared to them Moses and Elijah, talking with him. And Peter said to Jesus, "Lord, it is well that we are here; if you wish, I will make three booths here, one for you and one for Moses and one for Elijah." He was still speaking, when lo, a bright cloud overshadowed them, and a voice from the cloud said, "This is my beloved Son, with whom I am well pleased; listen to him." When the disciples heard this, they fell on their faces, and were filled with awe. But Jesus came and touched them, saying, "Rise, and have no fear." When they lifted up their eyes, they saw no one but Jesus only.

As they were coming down the mountain, Jesus commanded them, "Tell no one the vision, until the Son of man is raised from the dead." And they asked, "Then why do the scribes say that first Elijah must come?" He replied, "Elijah does come, and he is to restore all things; but I tell you that Elijah has already come, and they did not know him, but did to him whatever they pleased. So also the Son of man will suffer at their hands." Then the disciples understood that he was speaking of John the Baptist.

When they came to the crowd, a man knelt before him and said, "Lord, have mercy on my son, for he is an epileptic and he suffers terribly; for often he falls into the fire, and often into the water. And I brought him to your disciples, and they could not heal him."

"O faithless and perverse generation," Jesus answered, "how long am I to be with you? How long am I to bear with you? Bring him here to me." And Jesus rebuked the demon and it came out, and the boy was cured instantly. Then the disciples asked Jesus privately, "Why could we not cast it out?" And he said, "Because of your little faith. For truly, I say to you, if you have faith as a grain of mustard seed, you will say to this mountain, 'Move from here to there,' and it will move; and nothing will be impossible to you."

As they were gathering in Galilee, Jesus said to the disciples, "The Son of man is to be delivered into the hands of men, and they will kill him, and he will be raised on the third day." And they were greatly distressed. When they came to Capernaum, the collectors of the half-shekel tax said to Peter, "Does not your teacher pay the tax?" He said, "Yes." And when he came home, Jesus spoke to him first, saying, "What do you think, Simon? From whom do kings of the earth take toll or tribute? From their sons or from others?" When Peter said, "From others," Jesus said, "Then the sons are free. However, not to give offense to them, go to the sea and cast a hook, and take the first fish that comes up, and when you open its mouth you will find a shekel; take that and give it to them for me and for yourself."

AT THAT TIME the disciples came to Jesus, saying, "Who is the greatest in the kingdom of heaven?" Calling a child, he put him in the midst of them, and said, "Truly, I say to you, unless you turn and become like children, you will never enter the kingdom of heaven. Whoever humbles himself like this child, he is the greatest in the kingdom of heaven. Whoever receives one such child in my name receives me; but whoever causes one of these little ones who believe in me to sin, it would be better for him to have a great millstone fastened round his neck and to be drowned in the depth of the sea. Woe to the world for temptations to sin! For it is necessary that temptations come, but woe to the man by whom the temptation comes!

"See that you do not despise one of these little ones; for I tell you that in heaven their angels always behold the face of my Father who is in heaven. What do you think? If a man has a hundred sheep, and one of them has gone astray, does he not leave the ninety-nine on the mountains and go in search of the one that went astray? And if he finds it, truly, I say to you, he rejoices over it more than over the ninety-nine that never went astray. So it is not the will of my Father that one of these little ones should perish.

"If your brother sins against you, go and tell him his fault, between you and him alone. If he listens to you, you have gained your brother. But if he does not listen, take one or two others along with you, that every word may be confirmed by the evidence of two or three witnesses. If he refuses to listen to them, tell it to the church; and if he refuses to listen even to the church, let him be to you as a Gentile and a tax collector. Truly, I say to you, whatever you bind on earth shall be bound in heaven, and whatever you loose on earth shall be loosed in heaven. Again I say to you, if two of you agree on earth about anything they ask, it will be done for them by my Father in heaven. For where two or three are gathered in my name, there am I in the midst of them."

Then Peter said, "Lord, how often shall my brother sin against me, and I forgive him? As many as seven times?"

"I do not say to you seven times," Jesus answered, "but seventy times seven. Therefore the kingdom of heaven may be compared to a king who wished to settle accounts with his servants. One was brought who owed him ten thousand talents; and as he could not pay, his lord ordered him to be sold for payment, with his wife and children and all that he had. The servant fell on his knees, imploring, 'Lord, have patience with me, and I will pay you everything.' Out of pity the king released him and forgave him the debt. That same servant, as he went out, came upon one of his fellow servants who owed him a hundred denarii; and seizing him by the throat he said, 'Pay what you owe.' The man fell down and besought him, 'Have patience with me, and I will pay you.' But he refused and put him in prison till he should pay the debt. When his fellow servants saw this, they were greatly distressed, and they went and reported to their lord all that had taken place. Then the king summoned him and said, 'You wicked servant! I forgave you all that debt because you besought me; and should not you have had mercy on your fellow servant, as I had mercy on you?' And in anger the king delivered him to the jailers, till he should pay all his debt. So also my heavenly Father will do to every one of you, if you do not forgive your brother from your heart."

When Jesus had finished these sayings, he left Galilee for Judea. And Pharisees came to test him by asking, "Is it lawful to divorce one's wife for any cause?" He answered, "Have you not read that he who made them from the beginning made them male and female, and said, 'For this reason a man shall leave his father and mother and be joined to his wife, and the two shall become one flesh'? So they are no longer two but one flesh. What therefore God has joined together, let not man put asunder."

"Why then," they said, "did Moses command one to give a certificate of divorce, and to put her away?"

"For your hardness of heart," he answered, "Moses allowed you to divorce your wives, but from the beginning it was not so. And I say to you: whoever divorces his wife, except for unchastity, and marries another, commits adultery."

The disciples said, "If such is the case of a man with his wife, it is not expedient to marry."

"Not all men," Jesus said, "can receive this saying, but only those to whom it is given. For there are eunuchs who have been so from birth, and there are eunuchs who have been made eunuchs by men, and there are eunuchs who have made themselves eunuchs for the sake of the kingdom of heaven. He who is able to receive this, let him receive it."

Then children were brought to him that he might lay his hands on them and pray. When the disciples rebuked the people, Jesus said, "Let the children come to me, and do not hinder them; for to such belongs the kingdom of heaven." And he laid his hands on them and went away.

And behold, one came up to him, saying, "Teacher, what good deed must I do, to have eternal life?" And he said to him, "Why do you ask me about what is good? One there is who is good. If you would enter life, keep the commandments." He said, "Which?" And Jesus said, "You shall not kill, You shall not commit adultery, You shall not steal, You shall not bear false witness, Honor your father and mother, and, You shall love your neighbor as yourself." The young man said, "All these I have observed; what do I still lack?" Jesus said, "If you would be perfect, go, sell what you possess and give to the poor, and you will have treasure in heaven; and come, follow me." When the young man heard this he went away sorrowful; for he had great possessions.

And to his disciples Jesus said, "Truly, I say to you, it will be hard for a rich man to enter the kingdom of heaven. Again I tell you, it is easier for a camel to go through the eye of a needle than for a rich man to enter the kingdom of God." The disciples were greatly astonished, and said, "Who then can be saved?" But Jesus looked at them and said, "With men this is impossible, but with God all things are possible." Then Peter said, "Lo, we have left everything and followed you. What then shall we have?" Jesus said, "Truly, I say to you, in the new world, when the Son of man shall sit on his glorious throne, you who have followed me will also sit on twelve thrones, judging the twelve tribes of Israel. And every one who has left houses or brothers or sisters or father or mother or children or lands, for my name's sake, will receive a hundredfold, and inherit eternal life. But many that are first will be last, and the last first.

"For the kingdom of heaven is like a householder who went out early in the morning to hire laborers for his vineyard. After agreeing with the laborers for a denarius a day, he sent them into his vineyard. And going out about the third hour he saw others standing idle in the market place, and he said, 'You go into the vineyard too, and whatever is right I will give you.' So they went. About the sixth hour and the ninth hour he did the same. And about the eleventh hour he went out and found others standing, and he said, 'Why do you stand here idle all day?' They said, 'Because no one has hired us.' He said, 'You go into the vineyard too.'

"Now when evening came, the owner of the vineyard said to his steward, 'Call the laborers and pay them their wages, beginning with the last, up to the first.' When those hired about the eleventh hour came, each of them received a denarius. When the first came, they thought they would receive more; but each of them also received a denarius. And they grumbled at the householder, saying, 'These last worked only one hour, and you have made them equal to us who have borne the burden of the day and the scorching heat.' But he replied, 'I am doing you no wrong; did you not agree with me for a denarius? Take what belongs to you, and go; I choose to give to this last as I give to you. Am I not allowed to do what I choose with what belongs to me? Or do you begrudge my generosity?' So the last will be first, and the first last."

AS THEY WERE going up to Jerusalem, Jesus took the twelve disciples aside and said, "Behold, we are going up to Jerusalem; and the Son of man will be delivered to the chief priests and scribes, and they will condemn him to death, and deliver him to the Gentiles to be mocked and scourged and crucified, and he will be raised on the third day."

And when they drew near to Jerusalem and came to the Mount of Olives, Jesus sent two disciples, saying, "Go into the village opposite you, and immediately you will find an ass tied, and a colt with her; untie them and bring them to me. If any one says anything to you, you shall say, 'The Lord has need of them,' and he will send them immediately." This took place to fulfil what was spoken by the prophet, "Behold, your king is coming to you, humble, and mounted on an ass, and on a colt, the foal of an ass."

The disciples brought the ass and the colt, and put their garments on them, and Jesus sat thereon. The crowd spread garments on the road, and cut branches from trees and spread them also, and they shouted, "Hosanna to the Son of David! Blessed is he who comes in the name of the Lord! Hosanna in the highest!" And all Jerusalem was stirred.

Entering the temple, Jesus drove out all who sold and bought there, and he overturned the tables of the money-changers and the seats of those who sold pigeons. He said, "It is written, 'My house shall be called a house of prayer'; but you make it a den of robbers."

And the blind and the lame came to him in the temple, and he healed them. But when the chief priests and the scribes saw the wonderful things that he did, and the children crying out, "Hosanna to the Son of David!" they were indignant. "Do you hear what these are saying?" they asked. Jesus said, "Yes; have you never read, 'Out of the mouth of babes and sucklings thou hast brought perfect praise'?'' And leaving them, he went out of the city and lodged at Bethany.

The next day in the city the chief priests and the elders came to him as he was teaching in the temple, and said, "By what authority are you doing these things, and who gave you this authority?"

"I also will ask you a question," Jesus said, "and if you tell me the answer, then I also will tell you by what authority I do these things. The baptism of John, whence was it? From heaven or from men?"

They argued with one another, "If we say, 'From heaven,' he will say to us, 'Why then did you not believe him?' But if we say, 'From men,' we are afraid of the multitude; for all hold that John was a prophet." So they answered Jesus, "We do not know."

"Neither will I tell you," he said, "by what authority I do these things. Now what do you think? A man had two sons; and he went to the first and said, 'Son, go and work in the vineyard today.' And he answered, 'I will not'; but afterward he repented and went. And the man went to the second and said the same; and he answered, 'I go, sir,' but did not go. Which of the two did the will of his father?" They said, "The first."

"Truly," said Jesus, "the tax collectors and the harlots go into the kingdom of God before you. For John came to you in the way of righteousness, and you did not believe him, but the tax collectors and the harlots believed him; and even when you saw it, you did not afterward repent and believe him."

Again Jesus spoke in parables, saying, "The kingdom of heaven may be compared to a king who gave a marriage feast for his son, and he sent his servants to call those who were invited to the marriage feast; but they would not come. Again he sent other servants, saying, 'Tell those who are invited, Behold, I have made ready my dinner, my oxen and my fat calves are killed, and everything is ready; come to the marriage feast.' But they made light of it and went off, one to his farm, another to his business, while the rest seized his servants, treated them shamefully, and killed them. The king was angry, and he sent his troops and destroyed those murderers and burned their city. Then he said to his servants, 'The wedding is ready, but those invited were not worthy. Go therefore to the thoroughfares, and invite to the marriage feast as many as you find.' And those servants went out into the streets and gathered all whom they found, both bad and good; so the wedding hall was filled with guests. But when the king came in to look at the guests, he saw there a man who had no wedding garment; and he said, 'Friend, how did you get in here without a wedding garment?' And he was speechless. Then the king said to the attendants, 'Bind him hand and foot, and cast him into the outer darkness; there men will weep and gnash their teeth.' For many are called, but few are chosen."

Now the Pharisees took counsel how to entangle Jesus in his talk, and they sent their disciples to him, along with the Herodians. "Teacher, we know that you are true," they said, "and teach the way of God truthfully, and care for no man; for you do not regard the position of men. Tell us, then, what you think. Is it lawful to pay taxes to Caesar, or not?"

"Why put me to the test, you hypocrites?" he said. "Show me the money for the tax." They brought him a coin, and he asked, "Whose likeness and inscription is this?" They said, "Caesar's." Then he said, "Render therefore to Caesar the things that are Caesar's, and to God the things that are God's." Marveling, they left him and went away.

The same day Sadducees, who say that there is no resurrection, came to him, saying, "Teacher, Moses said, 'If a man dies, having no children, his brother must marry the widow, and raise up children for his brother.' Now there were seven brothers among us; the first married, and died, and having no children, left his wife to his brother. So too the second and third, down to the seventh. After them all, the woman died. In the resurrection, therefore, to which of the seven will she be wife? For they all had her."

"You are wrong," Jesus answered, "because you know neither the scriptures nor the power of God. For in the resurrection they neither marry nor are given in marriage, but are like angels in heaven. And as for the resurrection of the dead, have you not read what was said to you by God, 'I am the God of Abraham, and the God of Isaac, and the God of Jacob'? He is not God of the dead, but of the living." And the crowd was astonished at his teaching.

When the Pharisees heard that he had silenced the Sadducees, they came together, and one of them asked him a question, to test him. "Teacher, which is the great commandment in the law?" He said, "You shall love the Lord your God with all your heart, and with all your soul, and with all your mind. This is the great and first commandment. And a second is like it, You shall love your neighbor as yourself. On these two commandments depend all the law and the prophets."

Then Jesus asked the Pharisees a question. "What do you think of the Christ? Whose son is he?" They said, "The son of David." He said, "How is it then that David, inspired by the Spirit, calls him Lord, saying, 'The Lord said to my Lord, Sit at my right hand, till I put thy enemies under thy feet'? If David thus calls him Lord, how is he his son?" No one was able to answer, nor from that day did any one dare to ask him any more questions.

Then said Jesus to the crowds and to his disciples, "The scribes and the Pharisees sit on Moses' seat; so practice and observe whatever they tell you, but not what they do; for they preach, but do not practice. They bind heavy burdens, hard to bear, and lay them on men's shoulders; but they themselves will not move them with their finger. They do all their deeds to be seen by men; for they make their phylacteries broad and their fringes long, and they love the place of honor at feasts and the best seats in the synagogues, and salutations in the market places, and being called rabbi by men. But you are not to be called rabbi, for you have one teacher, and you are all brethren. And call no man your father on earth, for you have one Father, who is in heaven. Neither be called masters, for you have one master, the Christ. He who is greatest among you shall be your servant; whoever exalts himself will be humbled, and whoever humbles himself will be exalted.

"But woe to you, scribes and Pharisees, hypocrites! because you shut the kingdom of heaven against men; for you neither enter yourselves, nor allow those who would enter to go in. Woe to you, scribes and Pharisees, hypocrites! for you traverse sea and land to make a single proselyte, and when he becomes a proselyte, you make him twice as much a child of hell as yourselves.

"Woe to you, blind guides, who say, 'If any one swears by the temple, it is nothing; but if any one swears by the gold of the temple, he is bound by his oath.' You blind fools! For which is greater, the gold or the temple that has made the gold sacred? And you say, 'If any one swears by the altar, it is nothing; but if any one swears by the gift that is on the altar, he is bound by his oath.' You blind men! For which is greater, the gift or the altar that makes the gift sacred? So he who swears by the altar, swears by it and by everything on it; and he who swears by the temple, swears by it and by him who dwells in it; and he who swears by heaven, swears by the throne of God and by him who sits upon it.

"Woe to you, scribes and Pharisees, hypocrites! for you tithe mint and dill and cummin, and have neglected the weightier matters of the law, justice and mercy and faith; these you ought to have done, without neglecting the others. You blind guides, straining out a gnat and swallowing a camel!

"Woe to you, scribes and Pharisees, hypocrites! for you cleanse the outside of the cup and of the plate, but inside they are full of extortion and rapacity. You blind Pharisee! first cleanse the inside of the cup and of the plate, that the outside also may be clean.

"Woe to you, scribes and Pharisees, hypocrites! for you are like whitewashed tombs, which outwardly appear beautiful, but within they are full of dead men's bones and all uncleanness. So you also outwardly appear righteous to men, but within you are full of hypocrisy and iniquity.

"Woe to you, scribes and Pharisees, hypocrites! for you build the tombs of the prophets and adorn the monuments of the righteous, saying, 'If we had lived in the days of our fathers, we would not have taken part with them in shedding the blood of the prophets.' Thus you witness against yourselves, that you are sons of those who murdered the prophets. Fill up, then, the measure of your fathers. You serpents, you brood of vipers, how are you to escape being sentenced to hell? Therefore I send you prophets and wise men and scribes, some of whom you will kill and crucify, and some you will scourge in your synagogues and persecute from town to town, that upon you may come all the righteous blood shed on earth, from the blood of innocent Abel to the blood of Zechariah the son of Barachiah, whom you murdered between the sanctuary and the altar. Truly, I say to you, all this will come upon this generation.

"O Jerusalem, Jerusalem, killing the prophets and stoning those who are sent to you! How often would I have gathered your children together as a hen gathers her brood under her wings, and you would not! Behold, your house is forsaken and desolate. For I tell you, you will not see me again, until you say, 'Blessed is he who comes in the name of the Lord.' "

As Jesus was leaving the temple, his disciples pointed out to him the buildings of the temple. But he answered, "You see all these, do you not? Truly, I say to you, there will not be left here one stone upon another, that will not be thrown down." And as he sat on the Mount of Olives, the disciples came to him privately, saying, "Tell us, when will this be, and what will be the sign of your coming and of the close of the age?"

"Take heed," Jesus answered, "that no one leads you astray. For many will come in my name, saying, 'I am the Christ,' and they will lead many astray. And you will hear of wars and rumors of wars; see that you are not alarmed; for this must take place, but the end is not yet. For nation will rise against nation, and kingdom against kingdom, and there will be famines and earthquakes in various places: all this is but the beginning of the birth-pangs. Then they will deliver you up to tribulation, and put you to death; and you will be hated by all nations for my name's sake. And then many will fall away, and betray one another, and hate one another. And many false prophets will arise and lead many astray. And because wickedness is multiplied, most men's love will grow cold. But he who endures to the end will be saved. And this gospel of the kingdom will be preached throughout the whole world, as a testimony to all nations; and then the end will come.

"So when you see the desolating sacrilege spoken of by the prophet Daniel, standing in the holy place (let the reader understand), then let those who are in Judea flee to the mountains; let him who is on the housetop not go down to take what is in his house; and let him who is in the field not turn back to take his mantle. And alas for those who are with child and for those who give suck in those days! Pray that your flight may not be in winter or on a sabbath. For then there will be great tribulation, such as has not been from the beginning of the world until now, no, and never will be. And if those days had not been shortened, no human being would be saved; but for the sake of the elect those days will be shortened. Then if any one says to you, 'Lo, here is the Christ!' or 'There he is!' do not believe it. For false Christs and false prophets will arise and show great signs and wonders, so as to lead astray, if possible, even the elect. Lo, I have told you beforehand. So, if they say to you, 'Lo, he is in the wilderness,' do not go out; if they say, 'Lo, he is in the inner rooms,' do not believe it. For as the lightning comes from the east and shines as far as the west, so will be the coming of the Son of man. Wherever the body is, there the eagles will be gathered together.

"Immediately after the tribulation of those days the sun will be darkened, and the moon will not give its light, and the stars will fall from heaven, and the powers of the heavens will be shaken; then will appear the sign of the Son of man in heaven, and then all the tribes of the earth will mourn, and they will see the Son of man coming on the clouds of heaven with power and great glory; and he will send out his angels with a loud trumpet call, and they will gather his elect from the four winds, from one end of heaven to the other.

"From the fig tree learn its lesson: as soon as its branch becomes tender and puts forth its leaves, you know that summer is near. So also, when you see all these things, you know that he is near, at the very gates. Truly, I say to you, this generation will not pass away till all these things take place. Heaven and earth will pass away, but my words will not pass away.

"But of that day and hour no one knows, not even the angels of heaven, nor the Son, but the Father only. As were the days of Noah, so will be the coming of the Son of man. For as in those days before the flood they were eating and drinking, marrying and giving in marriage, until the day when Noah entered the ark, and they did not know until the flood came and swept them all away, so will be the coming of the Son of man. Then two men will be in the field; one is taken and one is left. Two women will be grinding at the mill; one is taken and one is left. Watch therefore, for you do not know on what day your Lord is coming. But know this, that if the householder had known in what part of the night the thief was coming, he would have watched and would not have let his house be broken into. Therefore you also must be ready; for the Son of man is coming at an hour you do not expect.

"Who then is the faithful and wise servant, whom his master has set over his household, to give them their food at the proper time? Blessed is that servant whom his master when he comes will find so doing. Truly, I say to you, he will set him over all his possessions. But if that wicked servant says to himself, 'My master is delayed,' and begins to beat his fellow servants, and eats and drinks with the drunken, the master of that servant will come on a day when he does not expect him and at an hour he does not know, and will punish him, and put him with the hypocrites; there men will weep and gnash their teeth.

"Then the kingdom of heaven shall be compared to ten maidens who took their lamps and went to meet the bridegroom. Five of them were foolish, and five were wise. For when the foolish took their lamps, they took no oil with them; but the wise took flasks of oil with their lamps. As the bridegroom was delayed, they all slumbered and slept. But at midnight there was a cry, 'Behold, the bridegroom! Come out to meet him.' Then all those maidens rose and trimmed their lamps. And the foolish said to the wise, 'Give us some of your oil, for our lamps are going out.' But the wise replied, 'Perhaps there will not be enough for us and for you; go rather to the dealers and buy for yourselves.' And while they went to buy, the bridegroom came, and those who were ready went in with him to the marriage feast; and the door was shut. Afterward the other maidens came also, saying, 'Lord, lord, open to us.' But he replied, 'Truly, I say to you, I do not know you.' Watch therefore, for you know neither the day nor the hour.

"For it will be as when a man going on a journey called his servants and entrusted to them his property; to one he gave five talents, to another two, to another one, to each according to his ability. Then he went away. He who had received the five talents went at once and traded with them; and he made five talents more. So also, he who had the two talents made two talents more. But he who had received the one talent went and dug in the ground and hid his master's money. Now after a long time the master of those servants came and settled accounts with them. And he who had received the five talents came forward, bringing five talents more, saying, 'Master, you delivered to me five talents; here I have made five talents more.' His master said, 'Well done, good and faithful servant; you have been faithful over a little, I will set you over much; enter into the joy of your master.' And he also who had the two talents came forward, saying, 'Master, you delivered to me two talents; here I have made two talents more.' His master said, 'Well done, good and faithful servant; you have been faithful over a little, I will set you over much; enter into the joy of your master.'

"Then he who had received the one talent came forward. 'Master, I knew you to be a hard man,' he said, 'reaping where you did not sow, and gathering where you did not winnow; so I was afraid, and I went and hid your talent in the ground. Here you have what is yours.' But his master answered him, 'You wicked and slothful servant! You knew that I reap where I have not sowed, and gather where I have not winnowed? Then you ought to have invested my money with the bankers, and at my coming I should have received what was my own with interest. So take the talent from him, and give it to him who has the ten talents. For to every one who has will more be given, and he will have abundance; but from him who has not, even what he has will be taken away. And cast the worthless servant into the outer darkness; there men will weep and gnash their teeth.'

"When the Son of man comes in his glory, and all the angels with him, then he will sit on his glorious throne. Before him will be gathered all the nations, and he will separate them one from another as a shepherd separates the sheep from the goats, and he will place the sheep at his right hand, but the goats at the left. Then the King will say to those at his right hand, 'Come, O blessed of my Father, inherit the kingdom prepared for you from the foundation of the world; for I was hungry and you gave me food, I was thirsty and you gave me drink, I was a stranger and you welcomed me, I was naked and you clothed me, I was sick and you visited me, I was in prison and you came to me.'

"Then the righteous will answer, 'Lord, when did we see thee hungry and feed thee, or thirsty and give thee drink? And when did we see thee a stranger and welcome thee, or naked and clothe thee? And when did we see thee sick or in prison and visit thee?' And the King will answer, 'Truly, I say to you, as you did it to one of the least of these my brethren, you did it to me.'

"Then he will say to those at his left hand, 'Depart from me, you cursed, into the eternal fire prepared for the devil and his angels; for I was hungry and you gave me no food, I was thirsty and you gave me no drink, I was a stranger and you did not welcome me, naked and you did not clothe me, sick and in prison and you did not visit me.'

"Then they also will answer, 'Lord, when did we see thee hungry or thirsty or a stranger or naked or sick or in prison, and did not minister to thee?' Then he will answer them, 'Truly, I say to you, as you did it not to one of the least of these, you did it not to me.' And they will go away into eternal punishment, but the righteous into eternal life."

WHEN JESUS HAD finished all these sayings, he said to his disciples, "You know that after two days the Passover is coming, and the Son of man will be delivered up to be crucified."

Then the chief priests and the elders gathered in the palace of the high priest Caiaphas, and took counsel together in order to arrest Jesus by stealth and kill him. But they said, "Not during the feast, lest there be a tumult among the people."

Now when Jesus was at Bethany in the house of Simon the leper, a woman came up to him with an alabaster flask of very expensive ointment, and she poured it on his head as he sat at table. But the disciples were indignant at this, saying, "Why this waste? The ointment might have been sold for a large sum, and given to the poor." Jesus said, "Why do you trouble the woman? She has done a beautiful thing to me. For you always have the poor with you, but you will not always have me. In pouring this ointment on my body she has done it to prepare me for burial. Truly, I say to you, wherever this gospel is preached in the whole world, what she has done will be told in memory of her."

Then one of the twelve, who was called Judas Iscariot, went to the chief priests and said, "What will you give me if I deliver him to you?" And they paid him thirty pieces of silver. And from that moment he sought an opportunity to betray him.

Now on the first day of Unleavened Bread the disciples asked Jesus, "Where will you have us prepare for you to eat the passover?" He said, "Go into the city to a certain one, and say to him, 'The Teacher says, My time is at hand; I will keep the passover at your house with my disciples.'" And the disciples did as Jesus had directed them.

When it was evening he sat at table with the twelve disciples. As they were eating, he said, "Truly, I say to you, one of you will betray me." They were very sorrowful, and said to him one after another, "Is it I, Lord?" He answered, "He who has dipped his hand in the dish with me, will betray me. The Son of man goes as it is written of him, but woe to that man by whom the Son of man is betrayed! It would have been better for that man if he had not been born." Judas, who betrayed him, said, "Is it I, Master?" He said to him, "You have said so."

As they were eating, Jesus took bread, and blessed, and broke it, and gave it to the disciples and said, "Take, eat; this is my body." And he took a cup, and when he had given thanks he gave it to them, saying, "Drink of it, all of you; for this is my blood of the covenant, which is poured out for many for the forgiveness of sins. I tell you I shall not drink again of this fruit of the vine until that day when I drink it new with you in my Father's kingdom."

When they had sung a hymn, they went out to the Mount of Olives. Then Jesus said, "You will all fall away because of me this night; for it is written, 'I will strike the shepherd, and the sheep of the flock will be scattered.' But after I am raised up, I will go before you to Galilee."

"Though they all fall away because of you," Peter declared, "I will never fall away."

"Truly, I say to you," Jesus answered, "this very night, before the cock crows, you will deny me three times."

"Even if I must die with you," Peter said, "I will not deny you." And so said all the disciples.

Then Jesus went with them to a place called Gethsemane. "Sit here," he said, "while I go yonder and pray." Taking with him Peter and the two sons of Zebedee, he began to be troubled. "My soul is very sorrowful," he said, "even to death; remain here, and watch with me." And going a little farther he fell on his face and prayed, "My Father, if it be possible, let this cup pass from me; nevertheless, not as I will, but as thou wilt." Coming to the disciples, he found them sleeping, and he said to Peter, "So, could you not watch with me one hour? Watch and pray that you may not enter into temptation; the spirit indeed is willing, but the flesh is weak."

For the second time he went away and prayed, "My Father, if this cannot pass unless I drink it, thy will be done." And again he came and found them sleeping, for their eyes were heavy. Leaving them, he went away and prayed for the third time, saying the same words. Then he came to the disciples and said, "Are you still sleeping and taking your rest? Behold, the hour is at hand, and the Son of man is betrayed into the hands of sinners. Rise, let us be going; see, my betrayer is at hand."

While he was still speaking, Judas came, and with him a great crowd with swords and clubs, from the chief priests and the elders. The betrayer had given them a sign, saying, "The one I shall kiss is the man; seize him." And he came up to Jesus and said, "Hail, Master!" And he kissed him. "Friend, why are you here?" Jesus said.

Then they seized Jesus, and one of those who were with Jesus drew his sword, and struck the slave of the high priest, and cut off his ear. "Put your sword back into its place," said Jesus, "for all who take the sword will perish by the sword. Do you think that I cannot appeal to my Father, and he will at once send me more than twelve legions of angels? But how then should the scriptures be fulfilled, that it must be so?" To the crowds he said, "Have you come out as against a robber, with swords and clubs to capture me? Day after day I sat in the temple teaching, and you did not seize me. But all this has taken place, that the scriptures of the prophets might be fulfilled." Then all the disciples forsook him and fled.

They led Jesus to Caiaphas the high priest, where the scribes and the elders had gathered. Peter followed, as far as the courtyard of the high priest, and there he sat with the guards.

Now the chief priests and the whole council sought false testimony against Jesus that they might put him to death, but they found none, though there were many false witnesses. At last two came forward and said, "This fellow said, 'I am able to destroy the temple of God, and to build it in three days.'"

"Have you no answer to make?" asked the high priest. "What is it that these men testify against you?" But Jesus was silent. And the high priest said to him, "I adjure you by the living God, tell us if you are the Christ, the Son of God."

"You have said so," Jesus replied. "But I tell you, hereafter you will see the Son of man seated at the right hand of Power, and coming on the clouds of heaven."

Then the high priest tore his robes, and said, "He has uttered blasphemy. Why do we still need witnesses? You have now heard his blasphemy. What is your judgment?" They answered, "He deserves death." Then they spat in his face, and some slapped him, saying, "Prophesy to us, you Christ! Who is it that struck you?"

Peter was sitting in the courtyard, and a maid said to him, "You also were with Jesus the Galilean." But he denied it before them all, saying, "I do not know what you mean." He went out to the porch, and another maid said to the bystanders, "This man was with Jesus of Nazareth." Again he denied it with an oath, "I do not know the man." After a little while the bystanders said, "Certainly you are also one of them, for your accent betrays you." Then Peter invoked a curse on himself and swore, "I do not know the man." Immediately the cock crowed, and Peter remembered the saying of Jesus, and he went out and wept bitterly.

When morning came, all the chief priests and the elders took counsel against Jesus to put him to death; and they bound him and delivered him to Pilate the governor.

Judas, seeing that Jesus was condemned, repented and brought back the thirty pieces of silver to the chief priests and the elders, saying, "I have sinned in betraying innocent blood." They said, "What is that to us? See to it yourself." Throwing down the pieces of silver in the temple, he departed; and he went and hanged himself. The chief priests, taking the pieces of silver, said, "It is not lawful to put them into the treasury, since they are blood money." So they bought with them the potter's field, to bury strangers in, and it has been called the Field of Blood to this day.

Now Jesus stood before Pilate, who asked, "Are you the King of the Jews?" Jesus answered, "You have said so." But when he was accused by the chief priests and elders, he made no answer. Then Pilate said, "Do you not hear how many things they testify against you?" But he gave no answer, so that Pilate wondered greatly.

Now at the feast Pilate was accustomed to release for the crowd any one prisoner whom they wanted. And they had then a notorious prisoner, called Barabbas. To the crowd Pilate said, "Whom do you want me to release for you, Barabbas or Jesus who is called Christ?" For he knew that it was out of envy that they had delivered him up. Besides, while he was sitting on the judgment seat, his wife sent word to him, "Have nothing to do with that righteous man, for I have suffered much over him today in a dream."

Now the chief priests and the elders persuaded the people to ask for Barabbas and destroy Jesus. The governor again asked, "Which do you want me to release?" They said, "Barabbas," and Pilate asked, "Then what shall I do with Jesus?" They all said, "Let him be crucified." Pilate said, "Why, what evil has he done?" But they shouted all the more, "Let him be crucified."

When Pilate saw that a riot was beginning, he took water and washed his hands before the crowd, saying, "I am innocent of this man's blood." And all the people answered, "His blood be on us and on our children!" Then he released Barabbas, and having scourged Jesus, delivered him to be crucified.

The soldiers took Jesus into the praetorium, before the whole battalion. They stripped him and put on him a scarlet robe and a crown of thorns, and a reed in his right hand. Kneeling, they mocked him, saying, "Hail, King of the Jews!" And they spat upon him, and took the reed and struck him on the head. Then they took off the robe, put his own clothes on him, and led him away to crucify him.

As they went, they came upon a man of Cyrene, Simon by name; this man they compelled to carry his cross. At Golgotha (which means the place of a skull), they offered Jesus wine to drink, mingled with gall; but when he tasted it, he would not drink it. And when they had crucified him, they divided his garments among them by casting lots; then they sat down and kept watch over him there. And over his head they put the charge against him, which read, "This is Jesus the King of the Jews."

Two robbers were crucified with him, one on the right and one on the left. And those who passed by derided him, wagging their heads and saying, "You who would destroy the temple and build it in three days, save yourself! If you are the Son of God, come down from the cross." So also the chief priests, with the scribes and elders, mocked him, saying, "He saved others; he cannot save himself. He is the King of Israel; let him come down now from the cross, and we will believe in him. He trusts in God; let God deliver him now, if he desires him; for he said, 'I am the Son of God.'" And the robbers who were crucified with him also reviled him in the same way.

Now from the sixth hour there was darkness over all the land until the ninth hour. And about the ninth hour Jesus cried with a loud voice, "Eli, Eli, lama sabachthani?" that is, "My God, my God, why hast thou forsaken me?" Some of the bystanders said, "This man is calling Elijah." And one of them at once ran and took a sponge, filled it with vinegar, put it on a reed, and gave it to him to drink. But the others said, "Wait, let us see whether Elijah will come to save him." And Jesus cried again with a loud voice and yielded up his spirit.

And behold, the curtain of the temple was torn in two, from top to bottom; and the earth shook, and the rocks were split; the tombs also were opened, and many bodies of the saints who had fallen asleep were raised, and coming out of the tombs after his resurrection they went into the holy city and appeared to many. When the centurion and those with him, keeping watch, saw the earthquake and what took place, they were filled with awe, and said, "Truly this was the Son of God!"

There were also many women there, looking on from afar, who had followed Jesus from Galilee, ministering to him; among whom were Mary Magdalene, and Mary the mother of James and Joseph, and the mother of the sons of Zebedee.

When it was evening, there came a rich man from Arimathea, named Joseph, who also was a disciple of Jesus. He asked Pilate for the body of Jesus, and Pilate ordered it to be given. Joseph took the body, wrapped it in a clean linen shroud, and laid it in his own new tomb, which he had hewn in the rock; and he rolled a great stone to the door of the tomb, and departed. Mary Magdalene and the other Mary were there, sitting opposite the sepulchre.

Next day, that is, after the day of Preparation, the chief priests and the Pharisees gathered before Pilate and said, "Sir, we remember how that impostor said, while he was still alive, 'After three days I will rise again.' Therefore order the sepulchre to be made secure until the third day, lest his disciples steal him away, and tell the people, 'He has risen from the dead,' and the last fraud will be worse than the first." Pilate said, "You have a guard; go, make it as secure as you can." So they made the sepulchre secure by sealing the stone and setting a guard.

Now after the sabbath, toward the dawn of the first day of the week, Mary Magdalene and the other Mary went to see the sepulchre. And behold, there was a great earthquake; for an angel of the Lord descended from heaven and came and rolled back the stone, and sat upon it. His appearance was like lightning, and his raiment white as snow. And for fear of him the guards trembled and became like dead men.

To the women the angel said, "Do not be afraid; for I know that you seek Jesus who was crucified. He is not here; for he has risen, as he said. Come, see the place where he lay. Then go quickly and tell his disciples that he has risen from the dead, and behold, he is going before you to Galilee; there you will see him. Lo, I have told you." The women departed quickly from the tomb with fear and great joy, and ran to tell his disciples. And behold, Jesus met them and said, "Hail!" And they came up and took hold of his feet and worshiped him. Then Jesus said, "Do not be afraid; go and tell my brethren to go to Galilee, and there they will see me."

   While they were going, some of the guard went into the city and told the chief priests all that had taken place. And when they had assembled with the elders and taken counsel, they gave a sum of money to the soldiers and said, "Tell people, 'His disciples came by night and stole him away while we were asleep.' And if this comes to the governor's ears, we will satisfy him and keep you out of trouble." So they took the money and did as they were directed; and this story has been spread among the Jews to this day.

   Now the eleven disciples went to Galilee, to the mountain to which Jesus had directed them. And when they saw him they worshiped him; but some doubted. And Jesus came and said to them, "All authority in heaven and on earth has been given to me. Go therefore and make disciples of all nations, baptizing them in the name of the Father and of the Son and of the Holy Spirit, teaching them to observe all that I have commanded you; and lo, I am with you always, to the close of the age."

THE GOSPEL ACCORDING TO

MARK

Widely regarded as the earliest of the four Gospels, Mark's account was written within perhaps thirty years of Christ's death and resurrection. Though it is anonymous (the title was added later), ancient tradition ascribes the book to a certain John Mark, a disciple of both Peter and Paul, who is said to have composed it at Rome as a summary of Peter's preaching. The text, in any case, shows considerable knowledge of Palestine and of the Aramaic language spoken there, while its occasional Latinisms suggest Rome's influence.

Originally written in koine, the everyday Greek of the time, Mark's is the least polished of the Gospels, though the author reveals a flair for graphic description. The narrative opens not with the birth of Jesus in Bethlehem but with the preaching of John the Baptist, who is presented as the fulfillment of prophecy. Following Jesus' baptism and temptation, his messianic ministry begins at once, leading swiftly to the climax—the week of Jesus' passion at Jerusalem, culminating in the crucifixion. The brief mention of the young man who runs away after the arrest of Jesus may be the "artist's signature," in which Mark refers to himself.

THE BEGINNING OF the gospel of Jesus Christ, the Son of God.

As it is written in Isaiah the prophet, "Behold, I send my messenger before thy face, who shall prepare thy way; the voice of one crying in the wilderness: Prepare the way of the Lord, make his paths straight."

John the baptizer appeared in the wilderness, preaching a baptism of repentance for the forgiveness of sins. There went out to him the people of Judea and Jerusalem, and they were baptized by him in the river Jordan, confessing their sins. Now John was clothed with camel's hair, and had a leather belt around his waist, and ate locusts and wild honey. "After me," he preached, "comes he who is mightier than I, the thong of whose sandals I am not worthy to untie. I have baptized you with water; he will baptize you with the Holy Spirit.''

In those days Jesus came from Nazareth of Galilee and was baptized by John. When he came up out of the water, he saw the heavens opened and the Spirit descending upon him like a dove. And a voice came from heaven, "Thou art my beloved Son; with thee I am well pleased." Then the Spirit drove him into the wilderness, and he was there for forty days, tempted by Satan. He was with the wild beasts, and the angels ministered to him.

After John was arrested, Jesus came into Galilee, preaching, "The time is fulfilled, and the kingdom of God is at hand; repent, and believe in the gospel.'' Passing along by the Sea of Galilee, he saw Simon and his brother Andrew, who were fishermen, casting a net in the sea. "Follow me," he said, "and I will make you fishers of men." Immediately they left their nets and followed him. Going on a little farther, he saw James and John the sons of Zebedee, in their boat mending the nets. He called them, and they left their father in the boat with the hired servants, and followed him.

They went into Capernaum, and on the sabbath Jesus entered the synagogue and taught. The people were astonished at his teaching, for he taught as one who had authority, not as the scribes. Suddenly a man with an unclean spirit cried out, "What have you to do with us, Jesus of Nazareth? Have you come to destroy us? I know who you are, the Holy One of God." Jesus rebuked him, saying, "Be silent, and come out of him!" The unclean spirit, convulsing the man and crying loudly, came out. All were amazed, so that they questioned, "What is this? A new teaching! With authority he commands even the unclean spirits, and they obey him." From that moment his fame began spreading.

Jesus left the synagogue, and entered the house of Simon and Andrew, with James and John, where Simon's mother-in-law lay sick with a fever. When they told him of her, he came and took her by the hand and lifted her up. The fever left her, and she served them. That evening they brought to him all who were sick or possessed with demons, and the whole city was gathered about the door. He healed many, and cast out many demons; but he would not permit the demons to speak, because they knew him.

Early in the morning he rose and went to a lonely place, and prayed. Pursuing him, Simon and the others found him and said, "Every one is searching for you."

"Let us go on to the next towns," Jesus said, "that I may preach there also, for that is why I came out." So, preaching in synagogues and casting out demons, he went throughout all Galilee.

Once a leper came beseeching him, and kneeling said, "If you will, you can make me clean." Moved with pity, Jesus stretched out his hand and touched him. "I will," he said. "Be clean." Immediately the leprosy left the man, and he was made clean. "Say nothing to any one," Jesus charged him, "but go, show yourself to the priest, and offer for your cleansing what Moses commanded, for a proof to the people." But the man talked freely and spread the news, so that Jesus could no longer openly enter a town. He stayed in the country, where people came to him from every quarter.

When he returned to Capernaum, it was reported he was at home, and many gathered together, so that there was no room, not even about the door. And they brought a paralytic on a pallet, carried by four men, and when they could not get near him, they made an opening in the roof and let down the pallet with the paralytic. Jesus, seeing their faith, said to the paralytic, "My son, your sins are forgiven." Now some scribes were sitting there, questioning in their hearts, "Why does this man speak thus? It is blasphemy! Who can forgive sins but God alone?"

"Why do you question thus in your hearts?" Jesus said. "Which is easier, to say, 'Your sins are forgiven,' or to say, 'Rise, take up your pallet and walk'? But that you may know that the Son of man has authority on earth to forgive sins"—he said to the paralytic—"I say to you, rise, take up your pallet and go home." The man rose, immediately took up the pallet and departed. They were all amazed and glorified God, saying, "We never saw anything like this!"

Jesus went out again beside the sea, and a crowd gathered, and he taught them. Later, as he walked along, he saw Levi the son of Alphaeus sitting at the tax office, and he said to him, "Follow me." And Levi rose and followed him. And as Jesus sat at table in Levi's house, many tax collectors and sinners were there. The scribes of the Pharisees, when they saw this, said to his disciples, "Why does he eat with tax collectors and sinners?" Jesus heard it and said, "Those who are well have no need of a physician, but those who are sick; I came not to call the righteous, but sinners."

Now John's disciples and the Pharisees were fasting, and people came and said to Jesus, "Why do these fast, but your disciples do not?"

"Can the wedding guests fast while the bridegroom is with them?" Jesus said. "As long as they have the bridegroom with them, they cannot fast. The days will come, when the bridegroom is taken away, and then they will fast. No one sews a piece of unshrunk cloth on an old garment; if he does, the patch tears away from it and a worse tear is made. And no one puts new wine into old wineskins; if he does, the wine will burst the skins. New wine is for fresh skins."

One sabbath Jesus was going through the grainfields, and his disciples plucked heads of grain. "Look," said the Pharisees, "why are they doing what is not lawful on the sabbath?"

"Have you never read what David did," Jesus said, "when he was in need and was hungry, he and those who were with him: how he entered the house of God and ate the bread of the Presence, which it is not lawful for any but the priests to eat, and also gave it to those who were with him? The sabbath was made for man, not man for the sabbath; so the Son of man is lord even of the sabbath."

Again Jesus entered the synagogue, and a man was there who had a withered hand. While the Pharisees watched to see whether he would heal on the sabbath, so that they might accuse him, Jesus said to the man, "Come here." Then he said to the Pharisees, "Is it lawful on the sabbath to do good or to do harm, to save life or to kill?" They were silent, and he looked around at them with anger, grieved at their hardness of heart. "Stretch out your hand," he said to the man. He stretched it out, and it was restored. Then the Pharisees left, and they immediately held counsel with the Herodians, how to destroy him.

Jesus withdrew with his disciples to the sea, and a great multitude came to him. He told his disciples to have a boat ready because of the crowd, for he had healed many, so that all who had diseases pressed upon him. And whenever the unclean spirits beheld him, they fell down and cried, "You are the Son of God." Strictly he ordered them not to make him known. Afterward he went up on the mountain, and called those whom he desired. Then he appointed twelve, to be with him, and to be sent out to preach and have authority to cast out demons. They were: Simon whom he surnamed Peter, James and John the sons of Zebedee whom he surnamed Boanerges (sons of thunder), Andrew, Philip, Bartholomew, Matthew, Thomas, James the son of Alphaeus, Thaddaeus, Simon the Cananaean, and Judas Iscariot, who betrayed him.

Then he went home, and the crowd came together again, so that they could not even eat. When his family heard of this, they went out to seize him, for people were saying, "He is beside himself." And the scribes who came down from Jerusalem said, "He is possessed by Beelzebul, and by the prince of demons he casts out the demons."

"How can Satan cast out Satan?" Jesus asked. "If a kingdom is divided against itself, that kingdom cannot stand. And if a house is divided against itself, that house will not stand. And if Satan has risen up against himself and is divided, he cannot stand, but is coming to an end. Truly, I say to you, all sins will be forgiven the sons of men, and whatever blasphemies they utter, but whoever blasphemes against the Holy Spirit never has forgiveness, but is guilty of an eternal sin"—for the scribes had said, "He has an unclean spirit." The crowd sitting about him said, "Your mother and your brothers are outside, asking for you." He replied, "Who are my mother and my brothers?" Looking around on those who sat about him, he said, "Here are my mother and my brothers! Whoever does the will of God is my brother, and sister, and mother."

Again he taught beside the sea, and a large crowd gathered, so that he got into a boat, and the crowd was on the land. "Listen!" he said. "A sower went out to sow. And some seed fell along the path, and the birds came and devoured it. Other seed fell on rocky ground, where it had not much soil, and immediately it sprang up, and when the sun rose it was scorched, and since it had no root it withered away. Other seed fell among thorns and the thorns choked it, and it yielded no grain. And other seeds fell into good soil and brought forth grain, yielding thirtyfold and sixtyfold and a hundredfold." And he said, "He who has ears to hear, let him hear."

When he was alone, those about him with the twelve asked him concerning the parables. "To you has been given the secret of the kingdom of God," he said, "but for those outside everything is in parables; so that they may indeed see but not perceive, and may indeed hear but not understand; lest they should turn again, and be forgiven. Do you not understand this parable? How then will you understand all the parables?

"The sower sows the word. These are the ones along the path; when they hear, Satan immediately comes and takes away the word sown in them. These in like manner are the ones sown upon rocky ground, who immediately receive the word with joy; they have no root, but endure for a while; when tribulation or persecution arises on account of the word, they fall away. Others are the ones sown among thorns; they are those who hear the word, but the cares of the world, and the delight in riches and other things, choke the word, and it proves unfruitful. But those that were sown upon the good soil are the ones who hear the word and accept it and bear fruit, thirtyfold and sixtyfold and a hundredfold."

And he said, "Take heed what you hear; the measure you give will be the measure you get, and still more will be given you. For to him who has will more be given; and from him who has not, even what he has will be taken away."

And he said, "The kingdom of God is as if a man should scatter seed upon the ground, and should sleep and rise night and day, and the seed should sprout and grow, he knows not how. The earth produces of itself, first the blade, then the ear, then the full grain in the ear. But when the grain is ripe, at once he puts in the sickle, because the harvest has come."

And he said, "With what can we compare the kingdom of God? It is like a grain of mustard seed, which, when sown upon the ground, is the smallest of all the seeds on earth; yet it grows up and becomes the greatest of all shrubs, and puts forth large branches, so that the birds of the air can make nests in its shade." With many such parables he spoke the word; he did not speak without a parable, but privately to his own disciples he explained everything.

When evening had come, Jesus said, "Let us go across to the other side." They took him in the boat, and a great storm of wind arose, and the waves beat into the boat, so that it was filling. Jesus was in the stern, asleep on the cushion. They woke him and said, "Teacher, do you not care if we perish?" Then he rebuked the wind, and said to the sea, "Peace! Be still!" And the wind ceased, and there was a great calm. "Why are you afraid?" he said. "Have you no faith?"

"Who then is this," they said in awe, "that even wind and sea obey him?"

They came to the other side, to the country of the Gerasenes. When he left the boat, he was met by a man with an unclean spirit, who lived among the tombs. No one could bind him any more, for chains and fetters he wrenched apart, and night and day among the tombs he was crying out, and bruising himself with stones. Seeing Jesus, he ran and worshiped him, crying, "What have you to do with me, Jesus, Son of the Most High God? I adjure you by God, do not torment me." For Jesus had said to him, "Come out of the man, you unclean spirit!"

"What is your name?" Jesus asked.

"My name is Legion," he replied, "for we are many."

Now a great herd of swine was feeding on the hillside, and the demons begged Jesus, "Send us to the swine, let us enter them." So he gave them leave, and the unclean spirits entered the swine, and the herd, numbering about two thousand, rushed down the steep bank into the sea and were drowned. The herdsmen fled, and told it everywhere, and people came to see what had happened. They saw Jesus, and saw the demoniac sitting there, clothed and in his right mind. At this they were afraid, and begged Jesus to depart from their neighborhood. As he was getting into the boat, the man who had been possessed begged that he might be with him. "Go home to your friends," Jesus said, "and tell them how the Lord has had mercy on you." The man went away and proclaimed in the Decapolis region how much Jesus had done for him; and all marveled.

When Jesus had crossed again to the other side, a great crowd gathered about him. Then there came a ruler of the synagogue, Jairus, who fell at his feet. "My little daughter is at the point of death," he said. "Come and lay your hands on her, that she may live." Jesus went with him, and a great crowd followed. Now in the crowd there was a woman who had had a flow of blood for twelve years, who had suffered much under many physicians, had spent all that she had, and was no better but rather grew worse. She came up behind Jesus and touched his garment. "If I touch even his garments," she said, "I shall be made well." Immediately the hemorrhage ceased, and she felt that she was healed. Perceiving that power had gone forth from him, Jesus turned about. "Who touched my garments?" he asked. His disciples said, "You see the crowd pressing around, yet you say, 'Who touched me?'" Then the woman, in fear and trembling, fell down before him and told him the truth. "Daughter," he said, "your faith has made you well. Go in peace."

While he was speaking, there came from the ruler's house some who said to Jairus, "Your daughter is dead. Why trouble the Teacher further?" But Jesus said, "Do not fear, only believe." He allowed no one to follow him except Peter, James, and John, and at the ruler's house he saw a tumult, with people weeping and wailing loudly. "Why do you weep?" Jesus asked. "The child is not dead but sleeping." They laughed at him, but he put them all outside, took the child's parents and his disciples, and went in where the child was (she was twelve years old). Taking her by the hand, he said, "Talitha cumi"; which means, "Little girl, I say to you, arise." Immediately the girl got up and walked, and all were overcome with amazement. And

Jesus strictly charged them that no one should know this, and told them to give her something to eat.

With his disciples, he went away from there and came to his own country; and on the sabbath he taught in the synagogue. Many who heard him were astonished. "Where did this man get all this?" they said, taking offense at him. "What is the wisdom given to him? What mighty works are wrought by his hands! Is not this the carpenter, the son of Mary and brother of James and Joses and Judas and Simon, and are not his sisters here with us?" Jesus marveled because of their unbelief. "A prophet is not without honor," he said, "except in his own country, and among his own kin, and in his own house." He could do no mighty work there, except that he laid his hands upon a few sick people and healed them.

After that, he went about among the villages teaching. The twelve he sent out two by two, and gave them authority over the unclean spirits. He charged them to take nothing except a staff; no bread, no bag, no money in their belts, to wear sandals and not put on two tunics. "Where you enter a house," he said, "stay there until you leave the place. If any place will not receive you and they refuse to hear you, when you leave shake the dust from your feet for a testimony against them." Thus they went out and preached that men should repent. They cast out many demons, and anointed with oil many that were sick and healed them.

King Herod heard of all this, for Jesus' name had become known, and he said, "John the baptizer, whom I beheaded, has been raised." For Herod had put John in prison for the sake of Herodias, his brother's wife. Herod had married her, and John had said, "It is not lawful for you to have your brother's wife." Herodias wanted to kill him, but she could not, for Herod feared John, knowing he was a righteous and holy man. But an opportunity came when Herod on his birthday gave a banquet. Herodias' daughter danced, and she pleased Herod and his guests. "Ask me for whatever you wish," the king vowed, "and I will grant it, even half my kingdom." The girl went out and said to her mother, "What shall I ask?"

"The head of John the baptizer," Herodias said. The girl returned and said to the king, "I want you to give me at once the head of John the Baptist on a platter." The king was exceedingly sorry, but because of his oaths and his guests he did not want to break his word. He sent a soldier of the guard, who beheaded John in the prison. The soldier brought the head on a platter, gave it to the girl, and the girl gave it to her mother. When John's disciples heard of this, they took his body and laid it in a tomb.

The apostles returned to Jesus, and told him all that they had done. Now many were coming and going, and they had no leisure even to eat, so Jesus said, "Come away by yourselves to a lonely place and rest a while." They left in a boat, but many saw them and knew where they were going, and they ran there from all the towns and got there first. As Jesus went ashore he saw a great throng, and he had compassion on them because they were like sheep without a shepherd; and he taught them. When it grew late, his disciples said, "This is a lonely place, and the hour is late. Send them into the villages to buy something to eat."

"You give them something to eat," he answered.

"Shall we buy two hundred denarii worth of bread?" they asked.

"How many loaves have you?" he said. When they had found out, they said, "Five, and two fish." He commanded them all to sit down by companies upon the green grass, so they sat down by hundreds and by fifties. Taking the five loaves and the two fish, he looked up to heaven, and blessed, and broke the loaves, and gave them to the disciples to set before the people; and he divided the two fish among them all. And they all ate and were satisfied, and they took up twelve baskets full of broken pieces of bread and fish. Those who ate the loaves were five thousand men.

Immediately Jesus made his disciples get into the boat and go before him to the other side, to Bethsaida, while he dismissed the crowd. Then he went up on the mountain to pray. When evening came, the boat was out on the sea, and he saw that they were making headway painfully, for the wind was against them. About the fourth watch of the night he came to them, walking on the sea. He meant to pass by them, but when they saw him walking on the sea they thought it was a ghost, and they cried out; for all saw him, and were terrified. "Take heart," he said, "it is I; have no fear." He got into the boat with them and the wind ceased. They were utterly astounded, for they did not understand about the loaves, but their hearts were hardened.

They came to land at Gennesaret, and moored to the shore. When they got out of the boat, immediately the people recognized Jesus, and they ran about the whole neighborhood and brought sick people on pallets to any place where they heard he was. Wherever he went, they laid the sick in the market places, and besought him that they might touch even the fringe of his garment; and as many as touched it were made well.

Now when the Pharisees, with some scribes from Jerusalem, met Jesus, they saw that some of his disciples ate with hands defiled, that is, unwashed. (The Pharisees, and all the Jews, do not eat unless they wash their hands and purify themselves, and they have many other traditions, including the washing of cups and pots and vessels of bronze.) "Why do your disciples not live according to the tradition of the elders," they asked, "but eat with hands defiled?"

"Well did Isaiah prophesy of you hypocrites," Jesus said, "as it is written, 'This people honors me with their lips, but their heart is far from me; in vain do they worship me, teaching as doctrines the precepts of men.' You have a fine way of rejecting the commandment of God, in order to keep your tradition! Moses said, 'Honor your father and your mother'; and, 'He who speaks evil of father or mother, let him surely die'; but you say, 'If a man tells his father or his mother, What you would have gained from me is Corban' (given to God), then you no longer permit him to do anything for his father or mother, thus making void the word of God through your tradition. And many such things you do."

And he called the people to him and said, "Hear me, all of you, and understand: There is nothing outside a man which by going into him can defile him. The things which come out of a man are what defile him." Then he left the people, and when he had entered the house his disciples asked him about the saying. "Are you also without understanding?" he said. "Do you not see that whatever goes into a man from outside cannot defile him, since it enters not his heart but his stomach, and so passes on? (Thus he declared all foods clean.) What comes out of a man's heart is what defiles him. For out of the heart of man come evil thoughts, fornication, theft, murder, adultery, coveting, wickedness, deceit, licentiousness, envy, slander, pride, foolishness. All these evil things come from within, and they defile a man."

From there Jesus arose and went to the region of Tyre and Sidon, where he entered a house, and would not have any one know it. But he could not be hid. A woman, whose little daughter was possessed by an unclean spirit, came and fell down at his feet. She was a Greek, a Syrophoenician by birth, and she begged him to cast the demon out of her daughter. "Let the children first be fed," he said, "for it is not right to take the children's bread and throw it to the dogs."

"Yes, Lord," she answered, "yet even the dogs under the table eat the children's crumbs."

"For this saying," he replied, "you may go your way; the demon has left your daughter." The woman went home, and found the child lying in bed, and the demon gone.

Returning from the region of Tyre and Sidon, Jesus went through the region of the Decapolis. And they brought to him a man who was deaf and had an impediment in his speech. Taking the man aside privately, Jesus put his fingers into the man's ears, and he spat and touched his tongue. Looking up to heaven, he sighed and said, "Ephphatha," that is, "Be opened." The man's ears were opened, his tongue was released, and he spoke plainly. Jesus charged the man's friends to tell no one, but they were astonished beyond measure, and they zealously proclaimed it. "He has done all things well," they said; "he even makes the deaf hear and the dumb speak."

In those days, when another great crowd had gathered, and they had nothing to eat, Jesus said to his disciples, "I have compassion on the crowd, because they have been with me now three days, and have nothing to eat. If I send them away hungry, they will faint, for some of them have come a long way."

"How can one feed these men," his disciples said, "with bread here in the desert?"

"How many loaves have you?" he asked.

"Seven," they said. He commanded the crowd to sit on the ground, and he took the seven loaves, and having given thanks he broke them and gave them to his disciples to set before the people. They also had a few small fish. Having blessed them, he commanded that these should be set before the crowd. About four thousand people ate and were satisfied; and they took up the broken pieces left over, seven baskets full. Then Jesus sent them away; and immediately he got into the boat with his disciples, and went to the district of Dalmanutha.

The Pharisees came and argued with Jesus, seeking from him a sign from heaven, to test him. Sighing deeply in his spirit, he said, "Why does this generation seek a sign? Truly, I say to you, no sign shall be given to this generation." He left them, and getting into the boat again, he departed to the other side. Now they had forgotten to bring bread, so that they had only one loaf in the boat. He cautioned them, "Take heed, beware of the leaven of the Pharisees and the leaven of Herod." But they continued to say, "We have no bread."

"Why do you discuss the fact that you have no bread?" Jesus said. "Do you not yet perceive or understand? Are your hearts hardened? Having eyes, do you not see, and having ears, do you not hear? And do you not remember? When I broke the five loaves for the five thousand, how many baskets full of broken pieces did you take up?" They said, "Twelve." "And the seven for the four thousand, how many baskets full of broken pieces did you take up?" They said, "Seven." And he said, "Do you not yet understand?"

When they came to Bethsaida, some people brought to him a blind man. He took the man by the hand, and led him out of the village. When he had spit on his eyes and laid his hands upon him, he asked, "Do you see anything?" The man looked up. "I see men," he said, "but they look like trees, walking." Again he laid his hands upon his eyes; and the man looked intently and saw everything clearly. Jesus sent him away to his home, saying, "Do not even enter the village."

Going with his disciples to the villages of Caesarea Philippi, on the way Jesus asked his disciples, "Who do men say that I am?" They told him, "John the Baptist; and others say, Elijah; and others one of the prophets."

"But who do you say that I am?" he asked.

"You are the Christ," Peter answered. Then Jesus charged them to tell no one about him.

And he began to teach them that the Son of man must suffer many things, and be rejected by the elders and the chief priests and the scribes, and be killed, and after three days rise again. And he said this plainly. Then Peter took him, and began to rebuke him. But Jesus, turning and seeing his disciples, rebuked Peter. "Get behind me, Satan!" he said. "For you are not on the side of God, but of men."

He called to him the multitude with his disciples, and said, "If any man would come after me, let him deny himself and take up his cross and follow me. For whoever would save his life will lose it; and whoever loses his life for my sake and the gospel's will save it. What does it profit a man, to gain the whole world and forfeit his life? What can a man give in return for his life? Whoever is ashamed of me and of my words in this adulterous and sinful generation, of him will the Son of man also be ashamed, when he comes in the glory of his Father with the holy angels. Truly, I say to you, there are some standing here who will not taste death before they see that the kingdom of God has come with power."

After six days Jesus took Peter, James, and John, and led them up a high mountain apart by themselves; and he was transfigured before them. His garments became glistening, intensely white, as no fuller on earth could bleach them. And there appeared Elijah with Moses, talking to Jesus. "Master," said Peter, "it is well that we are here. Let us make three booths, one for you and one for Moses and one for Elijah" (he did not know what else to say, for they were exceedingly afraid). Then a cloud overshadowed them, and a voice came out of the cloud, "This is my beloved Son; listen to him." Suddenly looking around, they no longer saw any one with them but Jesus only. As they were coming down the mountain, he charged them to tell no one what they had seen, until the Son of man should have risen from the dead. So they kept the matter to themselves, questioning what the rising from the dead meant.

"Why do the scribes say that first Elijah must come?" they asked.

"Elijah does come first to restore all things," Jesus said. "And how is it written of the Son of man, that he should suffer many things and be treated with contempt? But I tell you that Elijah has come, and they did to him whatever they pleased, as it is written of him."

When they came to the other disciples, they saw a great crowd about them, and scribes arguing with them. "What are you discussing?" Jesus asked. One of the crowd answered, "Teacher, I brought my son to you, for he has a dumb spirit. Wherever it seizes him, it dashes him down, and he foams and grinds his teeth and becomes rigid. I asked your disciples to cast it out, and they were not able." Jesus answered, "O faithless generation, how long am I to be with you? How long am I to bear with you? Bring him to me." They brought the boy, and when the spirit saw Jesus it convulsed the boy. He fell on the ground and rolled about, foaming at the mouth. "How long has he had this?" Jesus asked.

"From childhood," said the father, "and it has often cast him into the fire and into the water. If you can do anything, have pity on us and help us."

"If you can!" said Jesus. "All things are possible to him who believes."

Immediately the father cried, "I believe; help my unbelief!" Then Jesus rebuked the unclean spirit, saying, "You dumb and deaf spirit, I command you, come out of him, and never enter him again." Crying out and convulsing the boy terribly, the spirit came out, and the boy was like a corpse. But Jesus took him by the hand and lifted him up, and he arose. Later his disciples asked him privately, "Why could we not cast it out?" And he said, "This kind cannot be driven out by anything but prayer."

From there they passed through Galilee, and he would not have any one know it. For he was teaching his disciples, saying, "The Son of man will be delivered into the hands of men, and they will kill him; and when he is killed, after three days he will rise." But they did not understand the saying, and they were afraid to ask him.

They came to Capernaum, and when he was in the house he asked, "What were you discussing on the way?" They were silent, for they had discussed which of them was the greatest. "If any one would be first," Jesus said, "he must be last of all and servant of all." Then he took a child, and put him in the midst of them, and taking him in his arms, he said, "Whoever receives one such child in my name receives me; and whoever receives me, receives not me but him who sent me."

"Teacher," said John, "we saw a man casting out demons in your name, and we forbade him, because he was not following us."

"Do not forbid him," Jesus said, "for no one who does a mighty work in my name will be able soon after to speak evil of me. For he that is not against us is for us. Truly, I say to you, whoever gives you a cup of water because you bear the name of Christ, will by no means lose his reward. Whoever causes one of these little ones who believe in me to sin, it would be better for him if a great millstone were hung round his neck and he were thrown into the sea. If your hand causes you to sin, cut it off; it is better for you to enter life maimed than with two hands to go to hell. If your eye causes you to sin, pluck it out; it is better for you to enter the kingdom of God with one eye than with two eyes to be thrown into hell, where their worm does not die, and the fire is not quenched."

Leaving Capernaum, Jesus went to the region of Judea, where crowds gathered to him. As his custom was, he taught them, and soon Pharisees came to test him. "Is it lawful for a man to divorce his wife?" they asked. "What did Moses command you?" he answered. "Moses allowed a man to write a certificate of divorce," they said, "and to put her away."

"For your hardness of heart he wrote you this commandment," Jesus said. "But from the beginning of creation, 'God made them male and female.' 'For this reason a man shall leave his father and mother and be joined to his wife, and the two shall become one flesh.' So they are no longer two but one flesh. What therefore God has joined together, let not man put asunder." In the house the disciples asked about this matter, and he said, "Whoever divorces his wife and marries another, commits adultery against her; and if she divorces her husband and marries another, she commits adultery."

They were bringing children to him, that he might touch them, and the disciples rebuked them. When Jesus saw it he was indignant. "Let the children come to me," he said, "do not hinder them; for to such belongs the kingdom of God. Truly, I say to you, whoever does not receive the kingdom of God like a child shall not enter it."

As he was setting out on his journey to Jerusalem, a man ran up and knelt before him. "Good Teacher," he asked, "what must I do to inherit eternal life?"

"Why do you call me good?" Jesus said. "No one is good but God alone. You know the commandments: 'Do not kill, Do not commit adultery, Do not steal, Do not bear false witness, Do not defraud, Honor your father and mother.'"

"Teacher," said the man, "all these I have observed from my youth."

Jesus looking upon him loved him. "You lack one thing," he said. "Go, sell what you have, and give to the poor, and you will have treasure in heaven; and come, follow me." At that the man's countenance fell, and he went away sorrowful, for he had great possessions. Jesus looked around and said to his disciples, "How hard it will be for those who have riches to enter the kingdom of God!" The disciples were amazed, but Jesus said again, "Children, how hard it is to enter the kingdom of God! It is easier for a camel to go through the eye of a needle than for a rich man to enter the kingdom of God."

"Then who can be saved?" they asked, exceedingly astonished.

"With men it is impossible," Jesus said, "but not with God; for all things are possible with God."

"Lo," said Peter, "we have left everything and followed you."

"Truly," Jesus said, "there is no one who has left house or brothers or sisters or mother or father or children or lands, for my sake and for the gospel, who will not receive a hundredfold now in this time, houses and brothers and sisters and mothers and children and lands, with persecutions, and in the age to come eternal life. But many that are first will be last, and the last first."

As they were on the road, Jesus began to tell his disciples what was to happen to him. "Behold, we are going up to Jerusalem, and the Son of man will be delivered to the chief priests and the scribes, and they will condemn him to death, and deliver him to the Gentiles. They will mock him, and spit upon him, and scourge him, and kill him; and after three days he will rise."

James and John came forward and said, "Teacher, we want you to do for us whatever we ask of you. Grant us to sit, one at your right hand and one at your left, in your glory."

"You do not know what you are asking," Jesus said. "Are you able to drink the cup that I drink, or to be baptized with the baptism with which I am baptized?"

"We are able," they said.

"The cup that I drink you will drink," Jesus said, "and with the baptism with which I am baptized, you will be baptized. But to sit at my right hand or at my left is not mine to grant; it is for those for whom it has been prepared."

When the ten heard of this request, they were indignant at James and John. Jesus called them to him and said, "You know that those who are supposed to rule over the Gentiles lord it over them, and their great men exercise authority over them. But it shall not be so among you; whoever would be great among you must be your servant, and whoever would be first among you must be slave of all. For the Son of man also came not to be served but to serve, and to give his life as a ransom for many."

They came to Jericho, and as they were leaving, followed by a great multitude, a blind beggar named Bartimaeus was sitting by the roadside. When he heard it was Jesus, he cried out, "Jesus, Son of David, have mercy on me!" Many rebuked him, but he cried out all the more, "Son of David, have mercy on me!" Jesus stopped and said, "Call him." They said to the blind man, "Take heart; rise, he is calling you." Throwing off his mantle, Bartimaeus sprang up and came to Jesus. "Master," he said, "let me receive my sight." Jesus said, "Go your way; your faith has made you well." Immediately he received his sight and followed him on the way.

When they drew near to Jerusalem, Jesus called two of his disciples. "Go into the village opposite you," he said, "and as you enter it you will find a colt tied, on which no one has ever sat; untie it and bring it. If any one says to you, 'Why are you doing this?' say, 'The Lord has need of it and will send it back here immediately.'" They went and found a colt tied at a door, and they untied it. Those who stood there said, "What are you doing?" They told them what Jesus had said, and they let them go.

Bringing the colt to Jesus, they threw their garments on it, and he sat upon it. Many people spread garments on the road, others spread leafy branches, cut from the fields. Those who went before and those who followed cried, "Hosanna! Blessed is he who comes in the name of the Lord! Blessed is the kingdom of our father David that is coming! Hosanna in the highest!" When Jesus entered Jerusalem he went into the temple, where he looked round at everything. Then, as it was late, he went out to Bethany with the twelve.

On the following day, when they came from Bethany, Jesus was hungry. Seeing a fig tree in leaf, he looked to see if he could find anything on it. There was nothing but leaves, for it was not the season for figs. "May no one ever eat fruit from you again," he said. And his disciples heard it.

In Jerusalem he entered the temple and began to drive out those who sold and bought there. He overturned the tables of the money-changers and the seats of those who sold pigeons, and he would not allow any one to carry anything through the temple. "Is it not written," he said, "'My house shall be called a house of prayer for all the nations'? But you have made it a den of robbers." The chief priests and the scribes heard of this, and they sought to destroy Jesus, for they feared him because the multitude was astonished at his teaching. That evening he and his disciples again went out of the city.

In the morning, as they returned, they saw the fig tree withered away to its roots. "Master, look!" said Peter. "The fig tree you cursed has withered."

"Have faith in God," Jesus answered. "Truly, I say to you, whoever says to this mountain, 'Be taken up and cast into the sea,' and does not doubt in his heart, but believes that what he says will come to pass, it will be done for him. Therefore I tell you, whatever you ask in prayer, believe that you have received it, and it will be yours. And whenever you stand praying, forgive, if you have anything against any one; so that your Father also who is in heaven may forgive you your trespasses.''

They came again to Jerusalem, and as Jesus was walking in the temple, the chief priests, the scribes, and the elders came to him and said, "By what authority are you doing these things?''

"I will ask you a question,'' Jesus said. "Answer me, and I will tell you by what authority I do these things. Was the baptism of John from heaven or from men? Answer me.''

They argued with one another, "If we say, 'From heaven,' he will say, 'Why then did you not believe him?' But shall we say, 'From men'?''—they were afraid of the people, for all held that John was a real prophet. So they answered Jesus, "We do not know.''

"Neither will I tell you,'' said Jesus, "by what authority I do these things.''

Jesus then began to speak to them in a parable. "A man planted a vineyard, dug a pit for the wine press, then let it out to tenants and went into another country. Later he sent a servant to get from the tenants some of the fruit of the vineyard. They beat him, and sent him away empty-handed. He sent another servant, and they treated him shamefully. He sent another, and him they killed; and so with others, some they beat and some they killed. He had still one other, a beloved son; finally he sent him to them, saying, 'They will respect my son.' But those tenants said, 'This is the heir; come, let us kill him, and the inheritance will be ours.' So they killed him, and cast him out of the vineyard. Now what will the owner of the vineyard do? He will come and destroy the tenants, and give the vineyard to others.''

At this the chief priests and the elders wanted to arrest Jesus, for they perceived that he had told the parable against them. But they feared the multitude, so they left him and went away.

Some of the Pharisees and Herodians came to entrap him in his talk. "Teacher,'' they said, "we know that you are true, and do not regard the position of men, but truly teach the way of God. Is it lawful to pay taxes to Caesar, or not?'' Knowing their hypocrisy, Jesus said, "Why put me to the test? Bring me a coin, and let me look at it.'' They showed him one, and he said, "Whose likeness and inscription is this?'' They said, "Caesar's.'' Jesus said, "Render to Caesar the things that are Caesar's, and to God the things that are God's.'' And they were amazed at him.

Some of the Sadducees, who say that there is no resurrection, also came to him. "Teacher,'' they said, "Moses wrote for us that if a man's brother dies and leaves a wife, but leaves no child, the man must take the wife, and raise up children for his brother. There were seven brothers; the first took a wife, and when he died left no children; and the second took her, and died, leaving no children; and the third likewise; and the seven left no children. Last of all the woman also died. In the resurrection whose wife will she be?''

"Is not this why you are wrong,'' Jesus said, "that you know neither the scriptures nor the power of God? For when they rise from the dead, they neither marry nor are given in marriage, but are like angels in heaven. And as for the dead being raised, have you not read in the book of Moses, in the passage about the bush, how God said, 'I am the God of Abraham, and the God of Isaac, and the God of Jacob'? He is not God of the dead, but of the living; you are quite wrong."

One of the scribes, seeing that Jesus answered well, asked, "Which commandment is the first of all?" Jesus answered, "The first is, 'Hear, O Israel: The Lord our God, the Lord is one; and you shall love the Lord your God with all your heart, and with all your soul, and with all your mind, and with all your strength.' The second is this, 'You shall love your neighbor as yourself.' There is no other commandment greater than these."

"You are right, Teacher," the scribe said, "you have truly said that he is one, and there is no other but he; and to love him, and to love one's neighbor, is much more than all burnt offerings and sacrifices." When Jesus saw that the scribe answered wisely, he said, "You are not far from the kingdom of God." After that no one dared to ask Jesus any question.

Again he said, "Beware of the scribes, who like to go about in long robes, and to have salutations in the market places and the best seats in the synagogues and the places of honor at feasts, who devour widows' houses and for a pretense make long prayers. They will receive the greater condemnation." Sitting opposite the treasury, he watched the multitude putting in money. Many rich people put in large sums, and a poor widow came, and put in a penny. Jesus said to his disciples, "Truly, I say to you, this poor widow has put in more than all those others. For they all contributed out of their abundance; but she out of her poverty has put in everything she had, her whole living."

As he came out of the temple, one of his disciples said, "Look, Teacher, what wonderful stones and what wonderful buildings!"

"Do you see these great buildings?" Jesus answered. "There will not be left here one stone upon another, that will not be thrown down."

"When will this be," they asked, "and what will be the sign when these things are all to be accomplished?"

"Take heed that no one leads you astray," Jesus said. "Many will come in my name, saying, 'I am he!' and they will lead many astray. When you hear of wars and rumors of wars, do not be alarmed; this must take place, but the end is not yet. Nation will rise against nation, and kingdom against kingdom; there will be earthquakes in various places, there will be famines; this is but the beginning of the birth-pangs.

"But take heed to yourselves; for they will deliver you up to councils; and you will be beaten in synagogues; and you will stand before governors and kings for my sake, to bear testimony. And the gospel must first be preached to all nations. When they bring you to trial, do not be anxious what you are to say; but say whatever is given you, for it is not you who speak, but the Holy Spirit. Brother will deliver up brother to death, the father his child, children will rise against parents and have them put to death; and you will be hated by all for my name's sake. But he who endures to the end will be saved.

"But when you see the desolating sacrilege set up where it ought not to be, then let those who are in Judea flee to the mountains; let him who is on the housetop not go down to take anything away; let him who is in the field not turn back to take his mantle. Alas for those who are with child and for those who give suck in those days! Pray that it may not happen in winter. For in those days there will be such tribulation as has not been from the beginning of creation until now, and never will be. And if the Lord had not shortened the days, no human being would be saved; but for the sake of the elect, whom he chose, he shortened the days. Then if any one says to you, 'Look, here is the Christ!' or 'Look, there he is!' do not believe it. False Christs and false prophets will arise and show signs and wonders, to lead astray, if possible, the elect. But take heed; I have told you all things beforehand.

"But after that tribulation the sun will be darkened, the moon will not give its light, the stars will be falling from heaven, and the powers in the heavens will be shaken. Then they will see the Son of man coming in clouds with great power and glory, and he will send out the angels, and gather his elect from the ends of the earth to the ends of heaven.

"From the fig tree learn its lesson: as soon as its branch becomes tender and puts forth its leaves, you know that summer is near. So also, when you see these things taking place, you know that he is near, at the very gates. Truly, I say to you, this generation will not pass away before all these things take place. Heaven and earth will pass away, but my words will not pass away. But of that day or that hour no one knows, not even the angels in heaven, nor the Son, but only the Father. Take heed, watch; for you do not know when the time will come. And what I say to you I say to all: Watch."

It was now two days before the Passover and the feast of Unleavened Bread. The chief priests and the scribes were again seeking how to arrest Jesus by stealth, and kill him; for they said, "Not during the feast, lest there be a tumult of the people."

While he was at Bethany, as he sat at table a woman came with an alabaster flask of pure nard, very costly, and she poured it over his head. Some said indignantly, "Why was the ointment wasted? It might have been sold for more than three hundred denarii, and given to the poor."

"Let her alone," Jesus said. "She has done a beautiful thing to me. You always have the poor with you, and whenever you will, you can do good to them; but you will not always have me. She has anointed my body beforehand for burying. And truly, I say to you, wherever the gospel is preached, what she has done will be told in memory of her."

Then Judas Iscariot, one of the twelve, went to the chief priests in order to betray him. When the chief priests heard this they were glad, and promised to give Judas money. And he sought an opportunity to betray him.

On the first day of Unleavened Bread, when they sacrificed the passover lamb, the disciples asked, "Where will you have us prepare for the passover?" Jesus called two of them and said, "Go into the city, and a man carrying a jar of water will meet you; follow him. Wherever he enters, say to the householder, 'The Teacher says, Where is my guest room, where I am to eat the passover with my disciples?' He will show you a large upper room furnished and ready; there prepare for us." The disciples went to Jerusalem and found all as Jesus had told them.

That evening he came to the upper room with the twelve. As they were at table, he said, "Truly, I say to you, one of you will betray me; one who is eating with me." They began to be sorrowful, and to say one after another, "Is it I?" He said, "It is one of the twelve, one who is dipping bread into the dish with me. For the Son of man goes as it is written of him, but woe to that man by whom the Son of man is betrayed! It would have been better for that man if he had not been born."

As they were eating, he took bread, and blessed, and broke it, and gave it to them. "Take," he said; "this is my body." And he took a cup, and when he had given thanks he gave it to them, and they all drank of it. "This is my blood of the covenant," he said, "which is poured out for many. Truly, I say to you, I shall not drink again of the fruit of the vine until that day when I drink it new in the kingdom of God."

When they had sung a hymn, they went out to the Mount of Olives, and Jesus said, "You will all fall away; for it is written, 'I will strike the shepherd, and the sheep will be scattered.' But after I am raised up, I will go before you to Galilee."

"Even though they all fall away," Peter said, "I will not."

"Truly, I say to you," Jesus answered, "this very night, before the cock crows twice, you will deny me three times."

"If I must die with you," said Peter vehemently, "I will not deny you." And all said the same.

They went to a place called Gethsemane, and Jesus said, "Sit here, while I pray." Then he took with him Peter, James, and John, and he began to be greatly distressed and troubled. "My soul is very sorrowful," he said, "even to death; remain here, and watch." Going a little farther, he fell on the ground and prayed that, if it were possible, the hour might pass from him. "Abba, Father, all things are possible to thee," he said. "Remove this cup from me; yet not what I will, but what thou wilt." He came and found the three sleeping, and he said to Peter, "Simon, are you asleep? Could you not watch one hour? Watch and pray that you may not enter into temptation; the spirit indeed is willing, but the flesh is weak."

Again he went away and prayed, saying the same words. Again he came and found them sleeping, and they did not know what to answer him. Then he came the third time, and said, "Are you still sleeping and taking your rest? It is enough; the hour has come; the Son of man is betrayed into the hands of sinners. Rise, let us be going; see, my betrayer is at hand."

While he was still speaking, Judas came, and with him a crowd with swords and clubs, from the chief priests and the scribes and the elders. Now the betrayer had given them a sign, saying, "The one I shall kiss is the man; seize him and lead him away under guard." He went up to Jesus at once, said, "Master!" and kissed him. As they seized Jesus, one of those who stood by drew his sword, and struck the slave of the high priest and cut off his ear.

"Have you come out as against a robber, with swords and clubs to capture me?" Jesus asked. "Day after day I was with you in the temple teaching, and you did not seize me. But let the scriptures be fulfilled." Then all the disciples forsook him and fled. And a young man followed him, with nothing but a linen cloth about his body; they seized him, but he left the linen cloth and ran away naked.

They led Jesus to the high priest; and all the chief priests, the elders, and scribes were assembled. Peter had followed at a distance, right into the courtyard of the high priest, and he was sitting with the guards, warming himself at the fire. Now the chief priests and the council sought testimony against Jesus to put him to death; but they found none. Many bore false witness, but their witness did not agree. Others charged, "We heard him say, 'I will destroy this temple that is made with hands, and in three days I will build another, not made with hands.'" Yet not even so did their testimony agree.

"Have you no answer to make?" the high priest asked Jesus. "What is it that these men testify against you?" But Jesus was silent. Again the high priest asked, "Are you the Christ, the Son of the Blessed?"

"I am," Jesus said, "and you will see the Son of man seated at the right hand of Power, and coming with the clouds of heaven."

At this the high priest tore his garments. "Why do we still need witnesses?" he said. "You have heard his blasphemy. What is your decision?" They all condemned him as deserving death. Some began to spit on him, and they covered his face and struck him, saying, "Prophesy!" The guards received him with blows.

Below in the courtyard one of the maids of the high priest saw Peter warming himself. "You also were with the Nazarene, Jesus," she said. But he denied it, saying, "I neither know nor understand what you mean," and he went out into the gateway. The maid saw him and said to the bystanders, "This man is one of them." Again Peter denied it. After a while the bystanders said, "Certainly you are one of them; for you are a Galilean." But he invoked a curse on himself and swore, "I do not know this man of whom you speak." Immediately the cock crowed a second time, and Peter remembered how Jesus had said, "Before the cock crows twice, you will deny me three times." And he broke down and wept.

As soon as it was morning the chief priests, with the whole council, held a consultation; then they bound Jesus and delivered him to Pilate.

"Are you the King of the Jews?" Pilate asked.

"You have said so," Jesus answered.

The chief priests accused him of many things, and Pilate asked, "Have you no answer to make? See how many charges they bring against you." But Jesus made no further answer, so that Pilate wondered.

Now at the feast Pilate used to release one prisoner for whom the people asked. Among the rebels in prison was a man called Barabbas, who had committed murder. The crowd asked Pilate to do as he usually did. "Do you want me to release for you the King of the Jews?" he asked. (He perceived it was out of envy that the chief priests had delivered Jesus up.) But the chief priests stirred up the crowd to have Barabbas released instead. "What shall I do with the man whom you call the King of the Jews?" Pilate asked.

"Crucify him," they cried out.

"Why, what evil has he done?" asked Pilate. But they shouted all the more, "Crucify him." So Pilate, wishing to satisfy the crowd, released Barabbas. Then, having scourged Jesus, he delivered him to be crucified.

The soldiers led Jesus to the praetorium, where they clothed him in a purple cloak, and put on him a crown of thorns. "Hail, King of the Jews!" they saluted. They struck his head with a reed, and spat upon him, and knelt down in homage. When they had mocked him, they stripped him of the purple cloak, and put his own clothes on him. And they led him out to crucify him.

A passer-by, Simon of Cyrene, who was coming in from the country, was compelled to carry his cross. At the place called Golgotha (the place of a skull) they offered him wine mingled with myrrh, but he did not take it. And at the third hour they crucified him, and divided his garments, casting lots for them. The inscription of the charge against him read, "The King of the Jews."

They also crucified two robbers, one on his right and one on his left. Those who passed by derided him, wagging their heads, saying, "Aha! You who would destroy the temple and build it in three days, save yourself, and come down from the cross!" The chief priests also mocked him. "He saved others," they said; "he cannot save himself. Let the Christ, the King of Israel, come down now from the cross, that we may see and believe." Those who were crucified with him also reviled him. Many women were looking on from afar, among whom were Mary Magdalene, and Mary the mother of James and Joses, and Salome, who, when he was in Galilee, ministered to him; also many other women who came up with him to Jerusalem.

When the sixth hour had come, there was darkness over the whole land until the ninth hour. Then Jesus cried with a loud voice, "Eloi, Eloi, lama sabachthani?" ("My God, my God, why hast thou forsaken me?") Some of the bystanders said, "He is calling Elijah." One ran and, filling a sponge full of vinegar, put it on a reed and gave it to him to drink, saying, "Wait, let us see whether Elijah will come to take him down."

And Jesus uttered a loud cry, and breathed his last. And the curtain of the temple was torn in two, from top to bottom. When the centurion saw that Jesus thus breathed his last, he said, "Truly this man was the Son of God!"

When evening had come, since it was the day of Preparation, the day before the sabbath, Joseph of Arimathea, a respected member of the council, who was also looking for the kingdom of God, went to Pilate and asked for the body of Jesus. Pilate summoned the centurion and asked whether Jesus was already dead. When he learned he was, he granted the body to Joseph. And Joseph bought a linen shroud, and taking Jesus down, wrapped him in the shroud and laid him in a tomb hewn out of the rock. Then he rolled a large stone against the door of the tomb.

Mary Magdalene and Mary the mother of Joses saw where he was laid, and when the sabbath was past, with Salome they bought spices to anoint him. Very early on the first day of the week they went to the tomb when the sun had risen. They were saying, "Who will roll away the stone for us?" and looking up, they saw that the stone was rolled back. Entering the tomb, they saw a young man sitting on the right side, dressed in a white robe, and they were amazed.

"Do not be amazed," he said. "You seek Jesus of Nazareth, who was crucified. He has risen, he is not here; see the place where they laid him. But go, tell his disciples and Peter that he is going before you to Galilee; there you will see him, as he told you."

The women fled from the tomb, for trembling and astonishment had come upon them; and they said nothing to any one, for they were afraid.

Now when Jesus rose early on the first day of the week, he appeared first to Mary Magdalene, from whom he had cast out seven demons. She went and told the others, as they mourned and wept. But when they heard that he was alive, they would not believe it. After this he appeared in another form to two of them, as they were walking into the country. They went back and told the rest, but they did not believe them.

Afterward Jesus appeared to the eleven as they sat at table, and he upbraided them for their unbelief and hardness of heart, because they had not believed those who saw him after he had risen. And he said to them, "Go into all the world and preach the gospel to the whole creation. He who believes and is baptized will be saved; but he who does not believe will be condemned. And these signs will accompany those who believe: in my name they will cast out demons; they will speak in new tongues; they will pick up serpents, and if they drink any deadly thing, it will not hurt them; they will lay their hands on the sick, and they will recover."

So then the Lord Jesus, after he had spoken to them, was taken up into heaven, and sat down at the right hand of God. And they went forth and preached everywhere, while the Lord worked with them and confirmed the message by the signs that attended it. Amen.

THE GOSPEL ACCORDING TO

LUKE

Not an eyewitness to the life of Jesus, Luke was a physician and a companion of the apostle Paul. His Gospel, taken as a whole, is an eloquent literary composition, showing thoughtful use of material gathered from different sources. Its middle section contains the only record of several of the most beloved of Jesus' parables, including the Good Samaritan and the Prodigal Son. The book is dedicated to a certain Theophilus, probably a Greek or Roman of high rank.

Throughout the narrative Luke emphasizes Jesus' compassion for the needy, the sick, the brokenhearted, and the outcast, and he also stresses Jesus' severity toward the proud and those who put their trust in riches. More so than the other evangelists, Luke insists on the fact that the teachings of Jesus are universal, addressed to all people. He has a remarkable number of references to women, including Elizabeth, the prophetess Anna, and the widow of Nain, and it is Mary, not Joseph (as in Matthew), who plays the principal role in the stories about Jesus' birth. In the ministry of Jesus, Luke assigns a prominent place to both prayer and the action of the Holy Spirit.

———

INASMUCH AS MANY have undertaken to compile a narrative of the things which have been accomplished among us, just as they were delivered to us by those who from the beginning were eyewitnesses and ministers of the word, it seemed good to me also, having followed all things closely for some time past, to write an orderly account for you, most excellent Theophilus, that you may know the truth concerning the things of which you have been informed.

In the days of Herod, king of Judea, there was a priest named Zechariah, and he had a wife named Elizabeth. They were both righteous before God, walking in all the commandments, but they had no child, because Elizabeth was barren, and both were advanced in years.

When Zechariah's division was on duty, it fell to him by lot to enter the temple and burn incense, while the people were praying outside. And there appeared to him an angel standing on the right side of the altar. Fear fell upon Zechariah, but the angel said, "Do not be afraid, for your prayer is heard, and your wife Elizabeth will bear you a son, and you shall call his name John. And many will rejoice at his birth, for he will be great before the Lord, and he will be filled with the Holy Spirit, even from his mother's womb. He will turn many of the sons of Israel to the Lord their God, and he will go before him in the spirit and power of Elijah to make ready for the Lord a people prepared."

"How shall I know this?" said Zechariah. "For I am an old man, and my wife is advanced in years."

"I am Gabriel," the angel answered, "who stand in the presence of God; I was sent to bring you this good news. Behold, you will be silent and unable to speak until the day that these things come to pass, because you did not believe my words."

The people were waiting for Zechariah, and they wondered at his delay. When he came out, he could not speak, and they perceived that he had seen a vision; he made signs to them and remained dumb. When his time of service was ended, he went home. Afterward his wife conceived, and for five months she hid herself, saying, "Thus the Lord has taken away my reproach among men."

In the sixth month the angel Gabriel was sent from God to a city of Galilee named Nazareth, to a virgin betrothed to a man whose name was Joseph, of the house of David; and the virgin's name was Mary. "Hail, O favored one," the angel said, "the Lord is with you!" But Mary was greatly troubled at the saying, and considered what sort of greeting this might be. "Do not be afraid," the angel said, "for you have found favor with God. And behold, you will conceive and bear a son, and you shall call his name Jesus. He will be great, and will be called the Son of the Most High; and the Lord God will give to him the throne of his father David, and he will reign over the house of Jacob for ever; and of his kingdom there will be no end."

"How shall this be," Mary said, "since I have no husband?"

"The Holy Spirit will come upon you," the angel answered, "and the power of the Most High will overshadow you; therefore the child to be born will be called holy, the Son of God. Behold, your kinswoman Elizabeth in her old age has also conceived a son; and this is the sixth month with her who was called barren. For with God nothing will be impossible."

"Behold, I am the handmaid of the Lord," said Mary; "let it be to me according to your word." And the angel departed from her.

In those days Mary arose and went into the hill country, to the house of Zechariah. When Elizabeth heard the greeting of Mary, the babe leaped in her womb, and she was filled with the Holy Spirit. "Blessed are you among women," she exclaimed, "and blessed is the fruit of your womb! And why is this granted me, that the mother of my Lord should come to me? For behold, at your greeting the babe in my womb leaped for joy. And blessed is she who believed that there would be a fulfilment of what was spoken to her from the Lord."

"My soul magnifies the Lord," Mary said, "and my spirit rejoices in God my Savior, for he has regarded the low estate of his handmaiden. Henceforth all generations will call me blessed; for he who is mighty has done great things for me, and holy is his name. His mercy is on those who fear him from generation to generation. He has shown strength with his arm, he has scattered the proud in the imagination of their hearts, he has put down the mighty from their thrones, and exalted those of low degree; he has filled the hungry with good things, and the rich he has sent empty away. He has helped his servant Israel, in remembrance of his mercy, as he spoke to our fathers, to Abraham and to his posterity for ever." And Mary remained with Elizabeth about three months, then returned to her home.

Now when the time came, Elizabeth gave birth to a son. On the eighth day they came to circumcise the child; and they would have named him Zechariah after his father, but his mother said, "He shall be called John." They said, "None of your kindred is called by this name," and they made signs to his father, inquiring what he would have him called. He asked for a writing tablet, and wrote, "His name is John," and they all marveled. Immediately Zechariah's tongue was loosed, and he spoke, blessing God. Fear came on all their neighbors, and these things were talked about through the hill country of Judea; and all who heard them said, "What then will this child be?"

Then Zechariah was filled with the Holy Spirit, and he prophesied: "Blessed be the Lord God of Israel, for he has visited and redeemed his people, and has raised up a horn of salvation for us in the house of his servant David, as he spoke by the mouth of his holy prophets from of old. And you, child, will be called the prophet of the Most High; for you will go before the Lord to prepare his ways, to give knowledge of salvation to his people in the forgiveness of their sins, through the tender mercy of our God, when the day shall dawn upon us from on high to give light to those who sit in darkness and in the shadow of death, to guide our feet into the way of peace." And the child grew and became strong in spirit, and he was in the wilderness till the day of his manifestation to Israel.

In those days a decree went out from Caesar Augustus that all the world should be enrolled. This was the first enrollment, when Quirinius was governor of Syria, and all went to be enrolled, each to his own city. Joseph also went up from Nazareth to the city of David, which is called Bethlehem, because he was of the house and lineage of David, to be enrolled with Mary, his betrothed, who was with child. While they were there she gave birth to her first-born son and wrapped him in swaddling cloths, and laid him in a manger, because there was no place for them in the inn.

In that region there were shepherds keeping watch over their flock by night, and an angel appeared, and the glory of the Lord shone around them, and they were filled with fear. "Be not afraid," the angel said, "for behold, I bring you good news of a great joy which will come to all the people; for to you is born this day in the city of David a Savior, who is Christ the Lord. And this will be a sign; you will find a babe wrapped in swaddling cloths and lying in a manger." Suddenly there was with the angel a multitude of the heavenly host praising God and saying, "Glory to God in the highest, and on earth peace among men with whom he is pleased!"

When the angels went away into heaven, the shepherds said, "Let us go over to Bethlehem and see this thing that has happened, which the Lord has made known to us." They went with haste, and found Mary and Joseph, and the babe lying in a manger. And they made known the saying which had been told them concerning this child, and all who heard it wondered. But Mary kept all these things, pondering them in her heart. When, at the end of eight days, the child was circumcised, he was called Jesus, the name given by the angel before he was conceived in the womb.

At the time for purification according to the law of Moses, they brought the child up to Jerusalem to present him to the Lord, and to offer a sacrifice according to the law, "a pair of turtledoves, or two young pigeons." Now there was a man in Jerusalem, Simeon, who was righteous and devout. It had been revealed to him by the Holy Spirit that he should not die before he had seen the Lord's Christ. Now, inspired by the Spirit, he came into the temple; and when the parents brought in the child Jesus, he took him in his arms and blessed God and said, "Lord, now lettest thou thy servant depart in peace, according to thy word; for mine eyes have seen thy salvation which thou hast prepared in the presence of all peoples, a light for revelation to the Gentiles, and for glory to thy people Israel."

The child's father and mother marveled at what was said about him; and Simeon blessed them and said to Mary, "Behold, this child is set for the fall and rising of many in Israel, and for a sign that is spoken against (and a sword will pierce through your own soul also), that thoughts out of many hearts may be revealed."

There was also a prophetess, Anna, who was of a great age, having lived with her husband seven years from her virginity, and as a widow till she was eighty-four. She did not depart from the temple, worshiping with fasting and prayer night and day. Coming up at that very hour, she gave thanks to God, and spoke of the child to all who were looking for the redemption of Jerusalem. And when Joseph and Mary had performed everything according to the law, they returned to Nazareth. And the child grew and became strong, filled with wisdom; and the favor of God was upon him.

Now his parents went to Jerusalem every year for the Passover, and when Jesus was twelve years old, they went up according to custom. As they were returning, Jesus stayed behind in Jerusalem, and his parents, supposing him to be in the company, went a day's journey. When they sought him among their kinsfolk and acquaintances and did not find him, they returned to Jeru-

salem. After three days they found him in the temple, sitting among the teachers, listening and asking questions; and all who heard him were amazed at his
understanding and his answers. When they saw him they were astonished;
and his mother said, "Son, why have you treated us so? Behold, your father
and I have been looking for you anxiously."

"How is it that you sought me?" Jesus answered. "Did you not know that I
must be in my Father's house?" They did not understand this saying, but he
went down with them to Nazareth, and was obedient to them; and his mother
kept all these things in her heart.

IN THE FIFTEENTH year of the reign of Tiberius Caesar, Pontius Pilate being
governor of Judea, and Herod being tetrarch of Galilee, in the high-priest-
hood of Annas and Caiaphas, the word of God came to John the son of
Zechariah in the wilderness. And he went into all the region about the Jordan, preaching a baptism of repentance for the forgiveness of sins. As it is
written in the book of Isaiah the prophet, "The voice of one crying in the
wilderness: Prepare the way of the Lord, make his paths straight. Every valley
shall be filled, and every mountain and hill shall be brought low, and the
crooked shall be made straight, and the rough ways shall be made smooth;
and all flesh shall see the salvation of God."

To the multitudes that came to be baptized by him John said, "You brood
of vipers! Who warned you to flee from the wrath to come? Bear fruits that
befit repentance, and do not begin to say to yourselves, 'We have Abraham as
our father'; for I tell you, God is able from these stones to raise up children to
Abraham."

The multitudes asked him, "What then shall we do?" And he answered,
"He who has two coats, let him share with him who has none; and he who has
food, let him do likewise." Tax collectors also came to be baptized, and said,
"Teacher, what shall we do?" And he said, "Collect no more than is appointed you." Soldiers also asked, "And we, what shall we do?" And he said,
"Rob no one by violence or by false accusation, and be content with your
wages."

Now all the people questioned in their hearts concerning John, whether he
were the Christ. "I baptize you with water," he answered, "but he who is
mightier than I is coming, the thong of whose sandals I am not worthy to
untie; he will baptize you with the Holy Spirit and with fire. His winnowing
fork is in his hand, to clear his threshing floor, and to gather the wheat into
his granary, but the chaff he will burn with unquenchable fire."

So John preached good news to the people. But Herod the tetrarch, who
had been reproved by John for Herodias, his brother's wife, and for other evil
things, shut up John in prison.

Now when all the people were baptized, and when Jesus also had been
baptized and was praying, the heaven was opened, and the Holy Spirit descended upon him as a dove, and a voice came from heaven, "Thou art my

beloved Son; with thee I am well pleased." When he began his ministry, Jesus was about thirty years of age.

Full of the Holy Spirit, Jesus returned from the Jordan, and was led by the Spirit for forty days in the wilderness, tempted by the devil. He ate nothing, and when those days were ended he was hungry. The devil said to him, "If you are the Son of God, command this stone to become bread."

"It is written," Jesus answered, "'Man shall not live by bread alone.'"

The devil took him up and showed him all the kingdoms of the world in a moment of time, and said, "To you I will give all this, for it has been delivered to me, and I give it to whom I will. If you will worship me, it shall all be yours."

"It is written," Jesus answered, "'You shall worship the Lord your God, and him only shall you serve.'"

Then the devil took him to Jerusalem and set him on the pinnacle of the temple, and said, "If you are the Son of God, throw yourself down from here; for it is written, 'He will give his angels charge of you, to guard you,' and 'On their hands they will bear you up, lest you strike your foot against a stone.'"

"It is said," Jesus answered, "'You shall not tempt the Lord your God.'"

When the devil had ended every temptation, he departed until an opportune time. And Jesus returned in the power of the Spirit into Galilee, and a report concerning him went out through all the surrounding country. And he taught in their synagogues, being glorified by all.

At Nazareth, where he had been brought up, he went to the synagogue on the sabbath. He stood up to read, and there was given to him the book of the prophet Isaiah. Opening the book, he read: "The Spirit of the Lord is upon me, because he has anointed me to preach good news to the poor. He has sent me to proclaim release to the captives and recovering of sight to the blind, to set at liberty those who are oppressed, to proclaim the acceptable year of the Lord."

Closing the book, he gave it back to the attendant and sat down; and the eyes of all in the synagogue were fixed on him. "Today," he said, "this scripture has been fulfilled in your hearing." All spoke well of him, and wondered at the gracious words which proceeded out of his mouth; and they said, "Is not this Joseph's son?"

"Doubtless," Jesus said, "you will quote to me this proverb, 'Physician, heal yourself; what we have heard you did at Capernaum, do here also in your own country.' Truly, I say to you, no prophet is acceptable in his own country. But in truth, I tell you, there were many widows in Israel in the days of Elijah, when there came a great famine over the land; and Elijah was sent to none of them but only to Zarephath in Sidon, to a woman who was a widow. And there were many lepers in Israel in the time of the prophet Elisha; and none of them was cleansed but only Naaman the Syrian."

At this, all in the synagogue were filled with wrath. They rose up and put Jesus out of the city, and led him to the brow of a hill, that they might throw him down headlong. But he passed through the midst of them, and he went away to Capernaum, where he stayed at Simon Peter's house.

Now when the sun was setting, the sick were brought to him, and he laid his hands on every one of them and healed them. Demons also came out of many, crying, "You are the Son of God!" But he would not allow them to speak, because they knew that he was the Christ. When it was day he departed into a lonely place, and the people came to him and would have kept him from leaving, but he said, "I must preach the good news of the kingdom of God to the other cities also; for I was sent for this purpose." And he went preaching in the synagogues of Judea.

While he was standing by the lake of Gennesaret, the people pressed upon him to hear the word of God. Getting into Simon's boat, he asked him to put out a little from the land; then he sat down and taught the people from the boat. When he had ceased speaking, he said to Simon, "Put out into the deep and let down your nets for a catch."

"Master," Simon answered, "we toiled all night and took nothing! But at your word I will let down the nets." When they had done this, they enclosed a great shoal of fish; and as their nets were breaking, they beckoned to their partners in another boat to come and help them. They came and filled both boats, so that they began to sink. When Simon Peter saw it, he fell down at Jesus' knees. "Depart from me," he said, "for I am a sinful man, O Lord." He and all that were with him were astonished at the catch of fish, and so also were James and John, sons of Zebedee, who were his partners. "Do not be afraid," Jesus said; "henceforth you will be catching men." And when they had landed, they left everything and followed him.

After this, Jesus went on and saw a tax collector, named Levi, sitting at the tax office. "Follow me," he said. And Levi left everything and followed him. Later Levi made Jesus a great feast in his house, with a large company of tax collectors and others at table. And the Pharisees murmured against his disciples, saying, "Why do you eat and drink with tax collectors and sinners?"

"Those who are well have no need of a physician," Jesus answered, "but those who are sick; I have not come to call the righteous, but sinners to repentance."

"The disciples of John fast often and offer prayers," the Pharisees said, "and so do our disciples, but yours eat and drink."

"Can you make wedding guests fast while the bridegroom is with them?" Jesus asked. "The days will come, when the bridegroom is taken away from them, and then they will fast." Then he told them a parable: "No one tears a piece from a new garment and puts it upon an old garment; if he does, he will tear the new, and the piece from the new will not match the old. And no one puts new wine into old wineskins; if he does, the new wine will burst the skins and it will be spilled, and the skins will be destroyed. But new wine must be put into fresh wineskins. And no one after drinking old wine desires new; for he says, 'The old is good.'"

In these days he went out to the mountain, and all night he continued in prayer. When it was day, he called his disciples, and chose from them twelve, whom he named apostles: Simon, whom he named Peter, Andrew his brother, James and John, Philip, Bartholomew, Matthew, Thomas, James the son of Alphaeus, Simon who was called the Zealot, Judas the son of James, and Judas Iscariot, who became a traitor. Then he came down with them and stood on a level place, with a great crowd of his disciples and a great multitude of people who came to hear him and to be healed. All sought to touch him, for power came forth from him and healed them all.

Lifting up his eyes on his disciples, he said: "Blessed are you poor, for yours is the kingdom of God. Blessed are you that hunger now, for you shall be satisfied. Blessed are you that weep now, for you shall laugh. Blessed are you when men hate you, and when they exclude you and revile you on account of the Son of man! Rejoice in that day, and leap for joy, for behold, your reward is great in heaven; for so their fathers did to the prophets. But woe to you that are rich, for you have received your consolation. Woe to you that are full now, for you shall hunger. Woe to you that laugh now, for you shall mourn and weep. Woe to you, when all men speak well of you, for so their fathers did to the false prophets.

"But I say to you that hear, Love your enemies, do good to those who hate you, bless those who curse you, pray for those who abuse you. To him who strikes you on the cheek, offer the other also; and from him who takes away your coat do not withhold even your shirt. Give to every one who begs from you; and of him who takes away your goods do not ask them again. And as you wish that men would do to you, do so to them.

"If you love those who love you, what credit is that to you? For even sinners love those who love them. And if you do good to those who do good to you, what credit is that to you? For even sinners do the same. And if you lend to those from whom you hope to receive, what credit is that to you? Even sinners lend to sinners, to receive as much again. But love your enemies, and do good, and lend, expecting nothing in return; and your reward will be great, and you will be sons of the Most High; for he is kind to the ungrateful and the selfish. Be merciful, even as your Father is merciful. Judge not, and you will not be judged; condemn not, and you will not be condemned; forgive, and you will be forgiven; give, and it will be given to you; good measure, pressed down, shaken together, running over, will be put into your lap. For the measure you give will be the measure you get back.

"No good tree bears bad fruit, nor again does a bad tree bear good fruit; for each tree is known by its own fruit. For figs are not gathered from thorns, nor are grapes picked from a bramble bush. The good man out of the good treasure of his heart produces good, and the evil man out of his evil treasure produces evil; for out of the abundance of the heart his mouth speaks. Why do you call me 'Lord, Lord,' and not do what I tell you? Every one who hears my words and does them is like a man building a house, who dug deep, and laid the foundation upon rock; and when a flood arose, the stream broke against that house, and could not shake it. But he who hears my words and does not do them is like a man who built a house on the ground without a foundation; against which the stream broke, and immediately it fell, and the ruin of that house was great."

After this, Jesus entered Capernaum. Now a centurion had a slave who was dear to him and who was at the point of death. When he heard of Jesus, he sent elders of the Jews asking him to come and heal his slave. "He is worthy to have you do this for him," the elders said, "for he loves our nation, and he built us our synagogue." Jesus went with them, followed by a multitude, and when he was not far from the house, the centurion sent friends to say, "Lord, do not trouble yourself, for I am not worthy to have you come under my roof; therefore I did not presume to come to you. But say the word, and let my servant be healed. For I am a man set under authority, with soldiers under me; and I say to one, 'Go,' and he goes; and to another, 'Come,' and he comes; and to my slave, 'Do this,' and he does it." At this, Jesus marveled, and he said to the multitude, "I tell you, not even in Israel have I found such faith." When those who had been sent returned to the house, they found the slave well.

Soon afterward Jesus went with his disciples to a city called Nain. As he drew near, a man who had died was being carried out, the only son of his mother, and she was a widow; and a large crowd was with her. The Lord had compassion on her and said, "Do not weep." He touched the bier, and the bearers stood still, and he said, "Young man, I say to you, arise." The dead man sat up and began to speak, and Jesus gave him to his mother. Fear seized them all, and they glorified God, saying, "A great prophet has arisen among us!" and "God has visited his people!" The report of this spread through all the surrounding country.

The disciples of John the Baptist told him of all these things, and he sent two of them to the Lord to ask, "Are you he who is to come, or shall we look for another?" In that hour Jesus cured many of diseases and plagues and evil spirits, and on many that were blind he bestowed sight. "Go and tell John," he answered, "what you have seen and heard: the blind receive their sight, the lame walk, lepers are cleansed, and the deaf hear, the dead are raised up, the poor have good news preached to them. And blessed is he who takes no offense at me."

When the messengers had gone, Jesus began to speak to the crowds concerning John: "What did you go out into the wilderness to behold? A reed shaken by the wind? What then did you go out to see? A man clothed in soft clothing? Behold, those who are gorgeously appareled and live in luxury are in kings' courts. What then did you go out to see? A prophet? Yes, I tell you, and more than a prophet. This is he of whom it is written, 'Behold, I send my messenger before thy face, who shall prepare thy way before thee.' I tell you, among those born of women none is greater than John; yet he who is least in the kingdom of God is greater than he. To what then shall I compare the men of this generation? They are like children sitting in the market place and calling to one another, 'We piped to you, and you did not dance; we wailed, and you did not weep.' For John the Baptist has come eating no bread and drinking no wine; and you say, 'He has a demon.' The Son of man has come eating and drinking; and you say, 'Behold, a glutton and a drunkard, a friend of tax collectors and sinners!' Yet wisdom is justified by all her children."

One of the Pharisees, named Simon, asked Jesus to eat with him, and he took his place at table. A woman of the city, a sinner, when she learned where Jesus was, brought an alabaster flask of ointment, and coming up behind him, she began to weep and to wet his feet with her tears, and she wiped them with her hair, and kissed his feet, and anointed them. Now when the Pharisee saw this, he said to himself, "If this man were a prophet, he would have known what sort of woman this is who is touching him."

"Simon, " said Jesus, "I have something to say to you. A certain creditor had two debtors; one owed five hundred denarii, and the other fifty. When they could not pay, he forgave them both. Now which of them will love him more?"

"The one, I suppose," Simon answered, "to whom he forgave more."

"Do you see this woman?" Jesus said, turning toward her. "I entered your house, you gave me no water for my feet, but she has wet my feet with her tears and wiped them with her hair. You gave me no kiss, but from the time I came in she has not ceased to kiss my feet. You did not anoint my head with oil, but she has anointed my feet with ointment. Therefore I tell you, her sins, which are many, are forgiven, for she loved much; but he who is forgiven little, loves little." Then he said to the woman, "Your sins are forgiven." Those at table with him began to say among themselves, "Who is this, who even forgives sins?" To the woman Jesus said, "Your faith has saved you; go in peace."

Soon afterward he went on through cities and villages, bringing the good news of the kingdom of God. The twelve were with him, and also some women who had been healed of evil spirits and infirmities: Mary, called Magdalene, from whom seven demons had gone out, and Joanna, the wife of Chuza, Herod's steward, and Susanna, and many others, who provided for them out of their means. And when a great crowd came to him, he said, "A sower went out to sow his seed; and as he sowed, some fell along the path, and was trodden under foot, and the birds of the air devoured it. And some fell on the rock; and as it grew up, it withered away, because it had no moisture. And some fell among thorns; and the thorns grew with it and choked it. And some fell into good soil and grew, and yielded a hundredfold. He who has ears to hear, let him hear."

When his disciples asked him what this meant, he said, "To you it has been given to know the secrets of the kingdom of God; but for others they are in parables, so that seeing they may not see, and hearing they may not understand. Now the parable is this: The seed is the word of God. The ones along the path are those who have heard; then the devil comes and takes away the word from their hearts. The ones on the rock are those who, when they hear the word, receive it with joy; but these have no root, they believe for a while and in time of temptation fall away. As for what fell among the thorns, they are those who hear, but as they go on their way they are choked by the cares and riches and pleasures of life, and their fruit does not mature. What fell in the good soil are those who, hearing the word, hold it fast in an honest and good heart, and bring forth fruit with patience.

"No one after lighting a lamp covers it with a vessel, or puts it under a bed, but on a stand, that those who enter may see the light. For nothing is hid that shall not be made manifest, nor anything secret that shall not be known and come to light. Take heed then how you hear; for to him who has will more be given, and from him who has not, even what he thinks that he has will be taken away."

Then his mother and his brothers came to him, but they could not reach him for the crowd. He was told, "Your mother and your brothers are outside, desiring to see you." But he said, "My mother and my brothers are those who hear the word of God and do it."

One day he got into a boat with his disciples, saying, "Let us go across to the other side of the lake." As they sailed he fell asleep, and a storm of wind came down, and the boat was filling with water. "Master, Master," they said, waking him, "we are perishing!" He awoke and rebuked the wind and the raging waves, and they ceased, and there was a calm. "Where is your faith?" he asked. And they were afraid, and they marveled, saying, "Who then is this, that he commands even wind and water, and they obey him?"

Afterward Jesus called the twelve together and gave them power over all demons and to cure diseases, and he sent them out to preach the kingdom of God. "Take nothing for your journey," he said, "no staff, nor bag, nor bread, nor money; and do not have two tunics. Whatever house you enter, stay there, and from there depart. Wherever they do not receive you, when you leave that town shake off the dust from your feet as a testimony against them." So they departed and went through the villages, preaching the gospel and healing everywhere.

Now Herod the tetrarch heard of all that was done by Jesus, and he was perplexed, because it was said by some that John had been raised from the dead, by some that Elijah had appeared, and by others that one of the old prophets had risen. Herod said, "John I beheaded; but who is this about whom I hear such things?" And he sought to see Jesus.

On their return the apostles told Jesus what they had done. Then he withdrew with them to a city called Bethsaida, and the crowds followed, and he welcomed them and spoke of the kingdom of God, and cured those who had need of healing.

Now the day began to wear away, and the twelve came and said, "Send the crowd into the villages to lodge and get provisions, for we are here in a lonely place."

"You give them something to eat," Jesus said.

"We have no more than five loaves and two fish," they said, "unless we are to go and buy food for all these people." (There were about five thousand men.)

"Make them sit down," he said, "in companies, about fifty each." They did so; then taking the five loaves and the two fish, Jesus looked up to heaven, and blessed and broke them, and gave them to the disciples to set before the crowd. All ate and were satisfied, and they took up what was left over, twelve baskets of broken pieces.

Now it happened that as Jesus was praying, the disciples were with him; and he asked them, "Who do the people say that I am?"

"John the Baptist," they answered, "but others say, Elijah; and others, that one of the old prophets has risen."

"But who do you say that I am?" he asked.

"The Christ of God," Peter answered.

Then he commanded them strictly to tell this to no one. "The Son of man must suffer many things," he said, "and be rejected by the elders and chief priests and scribes, and be killed, and on the third day be raised." And he said to all, "If any man would come after me, let him deny himself and take up his cross daily and follow me. For whoever would save his life will lose it; and whoever loses his life for my sake, he will save it. For what does it profit a man if he gains the whole world and loses or forfeits himself? For whoever is ashamed of me and of my words, of him will the Son of man be ashamed when he comes in his glory. But I tell you truly, there are some standing here who will not taste death before they see the kingdom of God."

About eight days after this he took with him Peter and John and James, and went up on the mountain to pray. As he was praying, the appearance of his countenance was altered, and his raiment became dazzling white. And behold, two men talked with him, Moses and Elijah, who appeared in glory and spoke of his departure, which he was to accomplish at Jerusalem. Peter and the others were heavy with sleep, and when they wakened they saw his glory and the two men who stood with him. As the men were parting from him, Peter said, "Master, it is well that we are here; let us make three booths, one for you and one for Moses and one for Elijah." Then a cloud came and overshadowed them; and they were afraid as they entered the cloud. And a voice came out of the cloud: "This is my Son, my Chosen; listen to him!" When the voice had spoken, Jesus was found alone, and the disciples kept silence and told no one in those days anything of what they had seen.

When they had come down from the mountain, Jesus said to his disciples, "Let these words sink into your ears: the Son of man is to be delivered into the hands of men." But they did not understand this saying, and it was concealed from them, that they should not perceive it; and they were afraid to ask him about it. Then an argument arose among them as to which was the greatest. When Jesus perceived the thought of their hearts, he took a child and put him by his side, and said, "Whoever receives this child in my name receives me, and whoever receives me receives him who sent me; for he who is least among you all is the one who is great."

When the days drew near for him to be received up, he set his face to go to Jerusalem. And he sent messengers ahead, who entered a village of the Samaritans to make ready for him; but the people would not receive him because his face was set toward Jerusalem. Then his disciples James and John said, "Lord, do you want us to bid fire come down from heaven and consume them?" But he rebuked them; and they went on to another village. As they were walking, a man said to him, "I will follow you wherever you go." And Jesus said to him, "Foxes have holes, and birds of the air have nests; but the Son of man has nowhere to lay his head." To another he said, "Follow me." The man said, "Lord, let me first go and bury my father." But Jesus said, "Leave the dead to bury their own dead; but as for you, go and proclaim the kingdom of God." Another said, "I will follow you, Lord; but let me first say farewell to those at my home." And Jesus said, "No one who puts his hand to the plow and looks back is fit for the kingdom of God."

After this the Lord appointed seventy others, and sent them on ahead of him, two by two, into every town and place where he himself was about to come. "The harvest is plentiful," he said to them, "but the laborers are few; pray therefore the Lord of the harvest to send out laborers into his harvest. Go your way; behold, I send you out as lambs in the midst of wolves. Carry no purse, no bag, no sandals; and salute no one on the road. Whatever house you enter, first say, 'Peace be to this house!' And if a son of peace is there, your peace shall rest upon him; but if not, it shall return to you. Remain in the same house, eating and drinking what they provide, for the laborer deserves his wages; do not go from house to house. Whenever you enter a town and they receive you, eat what is set before you; heal the sick in it and say to them, 'The kingdom of God has come near to you.' But whenever they do not receive you, go into the streets and say, 'Even the dust of your town that clings to our feet, we wipe off against you; nevertheless, know that the kingdom of God has come near.' I tell you, it shall be more tolerable on that day for Sodom than for that town.

"Woe to you, Chorazin! woe to you, Bethsaida! for if the mighty works done in you had been done in Tyre and Sidon, they would have repented long ago, sitting in sackcloth and ashes. But in the judgment it shall be more tolerable for Tyre and Sidon than for you. And you, Capernaum, will you be exalted to heaven? You shall be brought down to Hades." To the seventy he said, "He who hears you hears me, and he who rejects you rejects me, and he who rejects me rejects him who sent me."

Afterward the seventy returned with joy, saying, "Lord, even the demons are subject to us in your name!" And he said to them, "I saw Satan fall like lightning from heaven. Behold, I have given you authority to tread upon serpents and scorpions, and over all the power of the enemy; and nothing shall hurt you. Nevertheless, do not rejoice in this, that the spirits are subject to you; but rejoice that your names are written in heaven."

In that same hour he rejoiced in the Holy Spirit and said, "I thank thee, Father, Lord of heaven and earth, that thou hast hidden these things from the wise and understanding and revealed them to babes; yea, Father, for such was thy gracious will. All things have been delivered to me by my Father; and no one knows who the Son is except the Father, or who the Father is except the Son and any one to whom the Son chooses to reveal him." Turning to the disciples, he said, "Blessed are the eyes which see what you see! For I tell you that many prophets and kings desired to see what you see, and did not see it, and to hear what you hear, and did not hear it."

Another time a lawyer stood up to put him to the test. "Teacher," he said, "what shall I do to inherit eternal life?"

"What is written in the law?" Jesus asked. "How do you read?"

"You shall love the Lord your God," the lawyer answered, "with all your heart, and with all your soul, and with all your strength, and with all your mind; and your neighbor as yourself."

"You have answered right," Jesus said; "do this, and you will live." But the lawyer, desiring to justify himself, said, "And who is my neighbor?"

"A man was going down from Jerusalem to Jericho," Jesus replied, "and he fell among robbers, who stripped him and beat him and left him half dead. Now a priest was going down that road; and when he saw him he passed by on the other side. So likewise a Levite, when he saw him, passed by. But a Samaritan came to where he was, and when he saw him he had compassion, and bound up his wounds, pouring on oil and wine. Then he brought him to an inn, and he gave two denarii to the innkeeper, saying, 'Take care of him; and whatever more you spend, I will repay you when I come back.' Which of these three, do you think, proved neighbor to the man who fell among the robbers?"

"The one who showed mercy on him," the lawyer said.

"Go and do likewise," said Jesus.

As they went on their way, he entered a village, and a woman named Martha received him into her house. She had a sister called Mary, who sat at the Lord's feet and listened to his teaching. But Martha was distracted with much serving, and she said, "Lord, do you not care that my sister has left me to serve alone? Tell her to help me." But the Lord answered, "Martha, Martha, you are anxious and troubled about many things; one thing is needful. Mary has chosen the good portion, which shall not be taken away from her."

He was praying in a certain place, and when he ceased, one of his disciples said, "Lord, teach us to pray, as John taught his disciples." And he said to them, "When you pray, say:

"Father, hallowed be thy name. Thy kingdom come. Give us each day our daily bread; and forgive us our sins, for we ourselves forgive every one who is indebted to us; and lead us not into temptation."

And he said to them, "Which of you who has a friend will go to him at midnight and say to him, 'Friend, lend me three loaves; for a friend of mine has arrived on a journey, and I have nothing to set before him'; and he will answer from within, 'Do not bother me; the door is now shut, and my children are with me in bed; I cannot get up and give you anything'? I tell you, though he will not get up and give him anything because he is his friend, yet because of his importunity he will rise and give him whatever he needs. And I tell you, ask, and it will be given you; seek, and you will find; knock, and it will be opened to you. For every one who asks receives, and he who seeks finds, and to him who knocks it will be opened. What father among you, if his son asks for an egg, will give him a scorpion? If you then, who are evil, know how to give good gifts to your children, how much more will the heavenly Father give the Holy Spirit to those who ask him!"

Once he was casting out a demon that was dumb, and when the dumb man spoke, the people marveled. But some said, "He casts out demons by Beelzebul, the prince of demons." Others, to test him, sought a sign from heaven. Knowing their thoughts, Jesus said, "Every kingdom divided against itself is laid waste, and a divided household falls. And if Satan also is divided against himself, how will his kingdom stand? You say that I cast out demons by Beelzebul. If I do, by whom do your sons cast them out? They shall be your judges. But if it is by the finger of God that I cast out demons, then the kingdom of God has come upon you. He who is not with me is against me, and he who does not gather with me scatters.

"When the unclean spirit has gone out of a man, that spirit passes through waterless places seeking rest; and finding none he says, 'I will return to my house.' When he comes he finds it swept and put in order. Then he brings seven other spirits more evil than himself, and they dwell there; and the last state of that man becomes worse than the first." As he said this, a woman in the crowd raised her voice and said, "Blessed is the womb that bore you, and the breasts that you sucked!" But he said, "Blessed rather are those who hear the word of God and keep it!"

When the crowds were increasing, he began to say, "This generation is an evil generation; it seeks a sign, but no sign shall be given to it except the sign of Jonah. For as Jonah became a sign to the men of Nineveh, so will the Son of man be to this generation. The queen of the South will arise at the judgment with the men of this generation and condemn them; for she came from the ends of the earth to hear the wisdom of Solomon, and behold, something greater than Solomon is here. The men of Nineveh will arise at the judgment with this generation and condemn it; for they repented at the preaching of Jonah, and behold, something greater than Jonah is here. No one after lighting a lamp puts it under a bushel, but on a stand, that those who enter may see. Your eye is the lamp of your body; when your eye is sound, your whole body is full of light; but when it is not sound, your body is full of darkness."

A Pharisee asked him to dine, so he went in and sat at table. The Pharisee was astonished to see that he did not wash before dinner, and the Lord said, "You Pharisees cleanse the outside of the cup, but inside you are full of extortion and wickedness. You fools! Did not he who made the outside make the inside also? But give for alms those things which are within; and behold, everything is clean for you. But woe to you Pharisees! for you tithe mint and rue and every herb, and neglect justice and the love of God; these you ought to have done, without neglecting the others. You love the best seat in the synagogues and salutations in the market places. Woe to you! for you are like graves which are not seen, and men walk over them without knowing it." As he went away from there, the scribes and the Pharisees began to press him hard, to provoke him to speak of many things, lying in wait for him, to catch at something he might say.

In the meantime, when so many thousands of the multitude had gathered together that they trod upon one another, he said to his disciples, "Beware of the leaven of the Pharisees, which is hypocrisy. Nothing is covered up that will not be revealed, or hidden that will not be known. Whatever you have whispered in private rooms shall be proclaimed upon the housetops. I tell you, my friends, do not fear those who kill the body, and after that have no more that they can do. But fear him who, after he has killed, has power to cast into hell; yes, I tell you, fear him! Are not five sparrows sold for two pennies? And not one of them is forgotten before God. Why, even the hairs of your head are all numbered. Fear not; you are of more value than many sparrows.

"I tell you, every one who acknowledges me before men, the Son of man will acknowledge before the angels of God; but he who denies me before men will be denied before the angels of God. Every one who speaks a word against the Son of man will be forgiven; but he who blasphemes against the Holy Spirit will not be forgiven. And when they bring you before synagogues and the authorities, do not be anxious how you are to answer, for the Holy Spirit will teach you in that very hour what you ought to say."

One of the multitude said, "Teacher, bid my brother divide the inheritance with me." But he replied, "Who made me a judge over you?" And he said to them, "Take heed, and beware of all covetousness; for a man's life does not consist in the abundance of his possessions." Then he told them a parable: "The land of a rich man brought forth plentifully; and he thought, 'What shall I do, for I have nowhere to store my crops? I will pull down my barns, and build larger ones, and I will say to my soul, you have ample goods laid up for many years; take your ease, eat, drink, be merry.' But God said to him, 'Fool! This night your soul is required of you; and the things you have prepared, whose will they be?' So is he who lays up treasure for himself, and is not rich toward God."

Then to his disciples he said, "Do not be anxious about your life, what you shall eat, nor about your body, what you shall put on. For life is more than food, and the body more than clothing. Consider the ravens; they neither sow nor reap, they have neither storehouse nor barn, and yet God feeds them. Of how much more value are you than the birds! And which of you by being anxious can add a cubit to his span of life? If then you are not able to do as small a thing as that, why are you anxious about the rest?

"Consider the lilies, how they grow; they neither toil nor spin; yet I tell you, even Solomon in all his glory was not arrayed like one of these. But if God so clothes the grass which is alive in the field today and tomorrow is thrown into the oven, how much more will he clothe you, O men of little faith! And do not seek what you are to eat and what you are to drink, nor be of anxious mind. For all the nations of the world seek these things; and your Father knows that you need them. Instead, seek his kingdom, and these things shall be yours as well.

"Fear not, little flock, for it is your Father's good pleasure to give you the kingdom. Sell your possessions, and give alms; provide yourselves with purses that do not grow old, with a treasure in the heavens that does not fail, where no thief approaches and no moth destroys. For where your treasure is, there will your heart be also. Let your lamps be burning, and be like men who are waiting for their master to come home from the feast, so that they may open to him at once. Blessed are those servants whom the master finds awake when he comes. You also must be ready; for the Son of man is coming at an unexpected hour."

"Lord," Peter asked, "are you telling this for us or for all?"

"Who then is the faithful and wise steward," said the Lord, "whom his master will set over his household, to give them food at the proper time? Blessed is that servant whom his master when he comes will find so doing. Truly, I say to you, he will set him over all his possessions. But if that servant says to himself, 'My master is delayed in coming,' and begins to beat the servants, and to eat and get drunk, the master will come when he does not expect him, and will punish him, and put him with the unfaithful. Every one to whom much is given, of him will much be required; and of him to whom men commit much they will demand the more.

"I came to cast fire upon the earth; and would that it were already kindled! I have a baptism to be baptized with; and how I am constrained until it is accomplished! Do you think that I have come to give peace on earth? No, I tell you, but rather division; for henceforth in one house there will be five divided, three against two and two against three."

He also said to the multitudes, "When you see a cloud rising in the west, you say at once, 'A shower is coming'; and so it happens. And when you see the south wind blowing, you say, 'There will be scorching heat'; and it happens. You hypocrites! You know how to interpret the appearance of earth and sky; but why do you not know how to interpret the present time?"

There were some present who told him of the Galileans whose blood Pilate had mingled with their sacrifices. "Do you think," he answered, "that these

Galileans were worse sinners than all the other Galileans, because they suffered thus? I tell you, No; but unless you repent you will all likewise perish." And he told this parable: "A man had a fig tree planted in his vineyard; and he came seeking fruit on it and found none. And he said to the vinedresser, 'Lo, these three years I have come seeking fruit on this fig tree, and I find none. Cut it down; why should it use up the ground?' And the vinedresser answered, 'Let it alone, sir, this year also, till I dig about it and put on manure. And if it bears fruit next year, well and good; but if not, you can cut it down.'"

Now he was teaching in one of the synagogues on the sabbath. And there was a woman who had had a spirit of infirmity for eighteen years; she was bent over and could not fully straighten herself. When Jesus saw her, he laid his hands upon her and said, "Woman, you are freed from your infirmity." Immediately she was made straight, and she praised God. But the ruler of the synagogue, indignant because Jesus had healed on the sabbath, said to the people, "There are six days on which work ought to be done; come on those days and be healed, and not on the sabbath day."

"You hypocrites!" the Lord answered. "Does not each of you on the sabbath untie his ox or his ass from the manger, and lead it away to water it? And ought not this woman be loosed from this bond on the sabbath day?" At this, all his adversaries were put to shame, and all the people rejoiced.

As he went through towns and villages, teaching, and journeying toward Jerusalem, some one asked, "Lord, will those who are saved be few?"

"Strive to enter by the narrow door," he replied, "for many will seek to enter and will not be able. When once the householder has shut the door, you will stand outside and knock, saying, 'Lord, open to us.' He will answer you, 'I do not know where you come from.' Then you will say, 'We ate and drank in your presence, and you taught in our streets.' But he will say, 'I tell you, I do not know where you come from; depart from me, all you workers of iniquity!' There you will weep and gnash your teeth, when you see Abraham and Isaac and Jacob and all the prophets in the kingdom of God and you yourselves thrust out. And men will come from east and west, and from north and south, and sit at table in the kingdom of God. And behold, some are last who will be first, and some are first who will be last."

At that very hour some Pharisees came, and said to him, "Get away from here, for Herod wants to kill you."

"Go and tell that fox," he said, "'Behold, I cast out demons and perform cures today and tomorrow, and the third day I finish my course. Nevertheless, I must go on my way, for it cannot be that a prophet should perish away from Jerusalem.' O Jerusalem, Jerusalem, killing the prophets and stoning those who are sent to you! How often would I have gathered your children together as a hen gathers her brood under her wings, and you would not! Behold, your house is forsaken. And I tell you, you will not see me until you say, 'Blessed is he who comes in the name of the Lord!'"

One sabbath when he went to dine at the house of a Pharisee, they were watching him, and there was a man there who had dropsy. "Is it lawful," Jesus asked, "to heal on the sabbath, or not?" But they were silent. Then he took the man and healed him, and he said, "Which of you, having a son or an ox that has fallen into a well, will not immediately pull him out on a sabbath day?" And they could not reply to this.

Now when he marked how those invited chose the places of honor, he told a parable: "When you are invited to a feast, do not sit down in a place of honor, lest a more eminent man than you be invited, and he who invited you will come and say, 'Give place to this man,' and then you will begin with shame to take the lowest place. But when you are invited, sit in the lowest place, so that your host may say, 'Friend, go up higher'; then you will be honored in the presence of all who sit at table. For every one who exalts himself will be humbled, and he who humbles himself will be exalted." He said also to the Pharisee who had invited him, "When you give a banquet, do not invite your friends or brothers or kinsmen or rich neighbors, lest they invite you in return, and you be repaid. But invite the poor, the maimed, the lame, the blind, and you will be blessed, because they cannot repay you. You will be repaid at the resurrection of the just."

When one of those at table heard this, he said, "Blessed is he who shall eat bread in the kingdom of God!"

"A man once gave a great banquet," Jesus said to him, "and invited many. He sent his servant to say to those invited, 'Come; for all is now ready.' But they all began to make excuses. The first said, 'I have bought a field, and I must go and see it; I pray you, have me excused.' Another said, 'I have bought five yoke of oxen, and I go to examine them; I pray you, have me excused.' Another said, 'I have married a wife, and therefore I cannot come.' When the servant reported this, the householder in anger said, 'Go out quickly to the streets and lanes of the city, and bring in the poor and maimed and blind and lame.' And the servant said, 'Sir, what you commanded has been done, and still there is room.' And the master said, 'Go out to the highways and hedges, and compel people to come in, that my house may be filled. For I tell you, none of those who were invited shall taste my banquet.'"

Now great multitudes accompanied Jesus; and he turned and said, 'If any one comes to me and does not hate his own father and mother and wife and children and brothers and sisters, yes, and even his own life, he cannot be my disciple. Whoever does not bear his own cross and come after me, cannot be my disciple. For which of you, desiring to build a tower, does not first sit down and count the cost? Otherwise, when he has laid a foundation, and is not able to finish, all who see it begin to mock him, saying, 'This man began to build, and was not able to finish.' So therefore, whoever of you does not renounce all that he has cannot be my disciple."

Now the tax collectors and sinners were all drawing near to hear him. And the Pharisees and the scribes murmured, "This man receives sinners and eats with them.'' So he told them this parable: "What man of you, having a hundred sheep, if he has lost one of them, does not leave the ninety-nine in the wilderness, and go after the one which is lost, until he finds it? And when he has found it, he lays it on his shoulders, rejoicing, and he calls together his friends, saying, 'Rejoice with me, for I have found my sheep which was lost.' Just so, I tell you, there will be more joy in heaven over one sinner who repents than over ninety-nine righteous persons who need no repentance.''

And he said, "There was a man who had two sons; and the younger said, 'Father, give me the share of property that falls to me.' And he divided his living between them. Not many days later, the younger son gathered all he had and took his journey into a far country, and there he squandered his property in loose living. And when he had spent everything, a great famine arose, and he began to be in want. So he joined himself to one of the citizens of that country, who sent him into his fields to feed swine. And he would gladly have fed on the pods that the swine ate; and no one gave him anything. But when he came to himself he said, 'How many of my father's hired servants have bread enough and to spare, but I perish here with hunger! I will arise and go to my father, and I will say to him, "Father, I have sinned against heaven and before you; I am no longer worthy to be called your son; treat me as one of your hired servants."' And he arose and came to his father. But while he was yet at a distance, his father saw him and had compassion, and ran and embraced him and kissed him. And the son said to him, 'Father, I have sinned against heaven and before you; I am no longer worthy to be called your son.' But the father said to his servants, 'Bring quickly the best robe, and put it on him; and put a ring on his hand, and shoes on his feet; and bring the fatted calf and kill it, and let us eat and make merry; for this my son was dead, and is alive again; he was lost, and is found.' And they began to make merry.

"Now his elder son was in the field; and as he came near to the house, he heard music and dancing. And he called a servant and asked what this meant. And he said, 'Your brother has come, and your father has killed the fatted calf, because he has received him safe and sound.' But he was angry and refused to go in. His father came out and entreated him, but he answered, 'Lo, these many years I have served you, and I never disobeyed your command; yet you never gave me a kid, that I might make merry with my friends. But when this son of yours came, who has devoured your living with harlots, you killed for him the fatted calf!' And he said to him, 'Son, you are always with me, and all that is mine is yours. It was fitting to make merry, for this your brother was dead, and is alive; he was lost, and is found.'''

Jesus also said to the disciples, "There was a rich man who had a steward, and charges were brought to him that this man was wasting his goods. And he called him and said, 'Turn in the account of your stewardship, for you can no longer be steward.' And the steward said to himself, 'What shall I do? I am not strong enough to dig, and I am ashamed to beg. I have decided what to do, so that people may receive me into their houses.' Summoning his master's debtors one by one, he said to the first, 'How much do you owe my master?' He said, 'A hundred measures of oil.' And he said, 'Take your bill, and sit down quickly and write fifty.' Then he said to another, 'And how much do you owe?' He said, 'A hundred measures of wheat.' He said, 'Take your bill, and write eighty.' The master commended the dishonest steward for his shrewdness; for the sons of this world are more shrewd in dealing with their own generation than the sons of light. And I tell you, make friends for yourselves by means of unrighteous mammon, so that when it fails they may receive you into the eternal habitations.

"He who is faithful in very little is faithful in much; he who is dishonest in very little is dishonest in much. If then you have not been faithful in the unrighteous mammon, who will entrust to you the true riches? And if you have not been faithful in that which is another's, who will give you that which is your own? No servant can serve two masters; for either he will hate the one and love the other, or he will be devoted to the one and despise the other. You cannot serve God and mammon."

And he said, "There was a rich man who feasted sumptuously every day. And at his gate lay a poor man named Lazarus, full of sores, who desired to be fed with what fell from the rich man's table; moreover, the dogs came and licked his sores. The poor man died and was carried by the angels to Abraham's bosom. The rich man also died and was buried; and in Hades, being in torment, he lifted up his eyes, and saw Abraham far off and Lazarus in his bosom. And he called out, 'Father Abraham, have mercy upon me, and send Lazarus to dip the end of his finger in water and cool my tongue; for I am in anguish in this flame.' But Abraham said, 'Son, remember that you in your lifetime received your good things, and Lazarus in like manner evil things; but now he is comforted here, and you are in anguish. And besides all this, between us and you a great chasm has been fixed, in order that those who would pass from here to you may not be able, and none may cross from there to us.' And the rich man said, 'Then I beg you, father, to send him to my father's house, for I have five brothers, so that he may warn them, lest they also come into this place of torment.' But Abraham said, 'They have Moses and the prophets; let them hear them.' And he said, 'No, father Abraham; but if some one goes to them from the dead, they will repent.' Abraham said to him, 'If they do not hear Moses and the prophets, neither will they be convinced if some one should rise from the dead.'"

And Jesus said to his disciples, "Temptations to sin are sure to come; but woe to him by whom they come! It would be better for him if a millstone were hung round his neck and he were cast into the sea, than that he should cause one of these little ones to sin. Take heed to yourselves; if your brother sins, rebuke him, and if he repents, forgive him; and if he sins against you seven times in the day, and turns to you seven times, and says, 'I repent,' you must forgive him."

On the way to Jerusalem he entered a village, where he was met by ten lepers who stood at a distance and lifted up their voices and said, "Jesus, Master, have mercy on us."

"Go and show yourselves to the priests," he said.

As they went they were cleansed, and one of them, a Samaritan, turned back, praising God with a loud voice; and he fell on his face at Jesus' feet, giving him thanks. "Were not ten cleansed?" Jesus asked. "Where are the nine? Was no one found to return and give praise to God except this foreigner? Rise and go your way; your faith has made you well."

Being asked by the Pharisees when the kingdom of God was coming, Jesus answered them, "The kingdom of God is not coming with signs to be observed; nor will they say, 'Lo, here it is!' or 'There!' for behold, the kingdom of God is in the midst of you."

And to the disciples he said, "The days are coming when you will desire to see one of the days of the Son of man, and you will not see it. And they will say to you, 'Lo, there!' or 'Lo, here!' Do not go, do not follow them. For as the lightning flashes and lights up the sky from one side to the other, so will the Son of man be in his day. But first he must suffer many things and be rejected by this generation. As it was in the days of Noah, so will it be in the days of the Son of man. They ate, they drank, they married, they were given in marriage, until the day when Noah entered the ark, and the flood came and destroyed them all. Likewise as it was in the days of Lot—they ate, they drank, they bought, they sold, they planted, they built, but on the day when Lot went out from Sodom fire and sulphur rained from heaven and destroyed them all—so will it be on the day when the Son of man is revealed. On that day, let him who is on the housetop, with his goods in the house, not come down to take them away; and likewise let him who is in the field not turn back. Remember Lot's wife. Whoever seeks to gain his life will lose it, but whoever loses his life will preserve it. I tell you, in that night there will be two in one bed; one will be taken and the other left. There will be two women grinding together; one will be taken and the other left." The disciples said to him, "Where, Lord?" And he said, "Where the body is, there the eagles will be gathered together."

And he told them a parable, to the effect that they ought always to pray and not lose heart. "In a certain city," he said, "there was a judge who neither feared God nor regarded man; and there was a widow in that city who kept coming to him and saying, 'Vindicate me against my adversary.' For a while he refused; but afterward he said to himself, 'Because this widow bothers me, I will vindicate her, or she will wear me out by her continual coming.' Hear what the unrighteous judge says. And will not God vindicate his elect, who cry to him day and night? I tell you, he will vindicate them speedily. Nevertheless, when the Son of man comes, will he find faith on earth?"

He also told this parable to some who trusted in themselves that they were righteous and despised others: "Two men went up into the temple to pray, one a Pharisee and the other a tax collector. The Pharisee prayed thus, 'God, I thank thee that I am not like other men, extortioners, unjust, adulterers, or even like this tax collector. I fast twice a week, I give tithes of all that I get.' But the tax collector, standing far off, would not even lift up his eyes to heaven, but beat his breast, saying, 'God, be merciful to me a sinner!' I tell you, this man went down to his house justified rather than the other; for every one who exalts himself will be humbled, but he who humbles himself will be exalted."

Now they were bringing even infants to him that he might touch them; and when the disciples saw it, they rebuked them. But Jesus called them to him, saying, "Let the children come to me, for to such belongs the kingdom of God. Truly, I say to you, whoever does not receive the kingdom of God like a child shall not enter it."

And a ruler asked him, "Good Teacher, what shall I do to inherit eternal life?"

"Why do you call me good?" Jesus said. "No one is good but God alone. You know the commandments: 'Do not commit adultery, Do not kill, Do not steal, Do not bear false witness, Honor your father and mother.'"

"All these I have observed from my youth," said the ruler.

"One thing you still lack," Jesus replied. "Sell all that you have and distribute to the poor, and you will have treasure in heaven; and come, follow me." But when the ruler heard this he became sad, for he was very rich. Jesus looking at him said, "How hard it is for those who have riches to enter the kingdom of God! For it is easier for a camel to go through the eye of a needle than for a rich man to enter the kingdom of God."

"Then who can be saved?" asked those who heard this saying.

"What is impossible with men," Jesus said, "is possible with God."

"Lo, we have left our homes," said Peter, "and followed you."

"Truly, I say to you," Jesus replied, "there is no man who has left house or wife or brothers or parents or children, for the sake of the kingdom of God, who will not receive manifold more in this time, and in the age to come eternal life."

Now taking the twelve, Jesus said to them, "Behold, we are going up to Jerusalem, and everything that is written of the Son of man by the prophets will be accomplished. For he will be delivered to the Gentiles, and will be mocked and shamefully treated and spit upon; they will scourge him and kill him, and on the third day he will rise." But this saying was hid from them, and they did not grasp what was said.

When he was passing through Jericho, a man named Zacchaeus, a chief tax collector, sought to see who Jesus was, but could not, on account of the crowd and because he was small of stature. So he ran ahead and climbed a sycamore tree. When Jesus came to the place, he looked up and said, "Zacchaeus, make haste and come down; for I must stay at your house today." He came down, and received him joyfully; and all murmured, "He has gone in to be the guest of a man who is a sinner." Then Zacchaeus stood and said,

"Behold, Lord, the half of my goods I give to the poor, and if I have defrauded any one of anything, I restore it fourfold."

"Today salvation has come to this house," Jesus said, "since he also is a son of Abraham. For the Son of man came to seek and to save the lost."

Jesus then proceeded to tell a parable, because he was near Jerusalem, and because the people supposed that the kingdom of God was to appear immediately: "A nobleman went into a far country to receive a kingdom and then return. Calling ten of his servants, he gave them ten pounds, and said, 'Trade with these till I come.' But his citizens hated him and sent an embassy after him, saying, 'We do not want this man to reign over us.' When he returned, having received the kingdom, he called his servants, that he might know what they had gained. The first said, 'Lord, your pound has made ten pounds more.' And he said, 'Well done, good servant! Because you have been faithful in a very little, you shall have authority over ten cities.' And the second said, 'Lord, your pound has made five pounds.' And he said, 'And you are to be over five cities.' Then another came, saying, 'Lord, here is your pound, which I kept laid away in a napkin; for I was afraid of you, because you are a severe man; you take up what you did not lay down, and reap what you did not sow.' The nobleman said, 'I will condemn you out of your own mouth, you wicked servant! You knew that I was a severe man. Why then did you not put my money into the bank, and I should have collected it with interest?' And he said to those who stood by, 'Take the pound from him, and give it to him who has the ten pounds. I tell you, that to every one who has will more be given; but from him who has not, even what he has will be taken away. But as for these enemies of mine, who did not want me to reign over them, bring them here and slay them before me.'"

After this, Jesus went on ahead, going up to Jerusalem. Near Bethany, at the mount that is called Olivet, he told two of the disciples, "Go into the village opposite, where on entering you will find a colt tied, on which no one has ever yet sat; untie it and bring it here. If any one asks you, 'Why are you untying it?' you shall say this, 'The Lord has need of it.'" Those who were sent found it as he had told them, and as they were untying the colt, its owners said, "Why are you untying the colt?" They said, "The Lord has need of it." And they brought it to Jesus, and throwing their garments on the colt they set Jesus upon it. As he rode along, they spread garments on the road and the whole multitude of the disciples began to rejoice and praise God with a loud voice for all the mighty works that they had seen. "Blessed is the King," they said, "who comes in the name of the Lord! Peace in heaven and glory in the highest!" Some of the Pharisees in the multitude said, "Teacher, rebuke your disciples." But he answered, "I tell you, if these were silent, the very stones would cry out."

When he drew near and saw the city he wept over it. "Would that even today you knew the things that make for peace!" he said. "But now they are hid from your eyes. For the days shall come upon you, when your enemies will cast up a bank about you and surround you, and hem you in on every side, and dash you to the ground, you and your children within you, and they will not leave one stone upon another, because you did not know the time of your visitation." In the city he entered the temple and began to drive out those who sold, saying to them, "It is written, 'My house shall be a house of prayer'; but you have made it a den of robbers."

While he was teaching daily in the temple, the chief priests and the scribes and the principal men of the people sought to destroy him. But they did not find anything they could do, for all the people hung upon his words. Then one day the chief priests and the scribes with the elders came up. "Tell us by what authority you do these things," they said, "or who it is that gave you this authority."

"I also will ask you a question," he answered. "Now tell me, was the baptism of John from heaven or from men?" They discussed it with one another, saying, "If we say, 'From heaven,' he will say, 'Why did you not believe him?' But if we say, 'From men,' all the people will stone us; for they are convinced that John was a prophet." So they answered that they did not know whence it was. And Jesus said to them, "Neither will I tell you by what authority I do these things."

And he told the people this parable: "A man planted a vineyard, and let it out to tenants, and went into another country. When the time came he sent a servant to the tenants, that they should give him some of the fruit, but the tenants beat him and sent him away empty-handed. He sent another servant, and him also they treated shamefully and sent away empty-handed. He sent yet a third, and this one they wounded and cast out. Then the owner of the vineyard said, 'I will send my beloved son; it may be they will respect him.' But when the tenants saw the son, they said to themselves, 'This is the heir; let us kill him, that the inheritance may be ours.' And they cast him out of the vineyard and killed him. What then will the owner of the vineyard do? He will come and destroy those tenants, and give the vineyard to others."

When the people heard this, they said, "God forbid!" But he looked at them and said, "What then is this that is written: 'The very stone which the builders rejected has become the head of the corner'? Every one who falls on that stone will be broken to pieces; but when it falls on any one it will crush him."

At that very hour the scribes and the chief priests tried to lay hands on him, for they perceived that he had told this parable against them; but they feared the people. So they watched him, and sent spies, who pretended to be sincere, that they might take hold of what he said, so as to deliver him up to the governor. They asked, "Teacher, we know that you speak and teach rightly, and show no partiality, but truly teach the way of God. Is it lawful for us to give tribute to Caesar, or not?" But he perceived their craftiness, and said, "Show me a coin. Whose likeness and inscription has it?" They said, "Caesar's." He said to them, "Then render to Caesar the things that are Caesar's, and to God the things that are God's." Marveling at his answer, they were silent.

There came to him some Sadducees, those who say that there is no resurrection. "Teacher," they said, "Moses wrote for us that if a man's brother dies, having a wife but no children, the man must take the wife and raise up children for his brother. Now there were seven brothers; the first took a wife, and died without children; and the second and the third took her, and likewise all seven left no children and died. Afterward the woman also died. In the resurrection, therefore, whose wife will the woman be? For the seven had her as wife."

"The sons of this age," Jesus answered, "marry and are given in marriage; but those who are accounted worthy to attain to that age and to the resurrection from the dead neither marry nor are given in marriage, for they are equal to angels and are sons of God, being sons of the resurrection. But that the dead are raised, even Moses showed, in the passage about the bush, where he calls the Lord the God of Abraham and the God of Isaac and the God of Jacob. Now he is not God of the dead, but of the living; for all live to him."

And in the hearing of all the people he said to his disciples, "Beware of the scribes, who like to go about in long robes, and love salutations in the market places and the best seats in the synagogues and the places of honor at feasts, who devour widows' houses and for a pretense make long prayers. They will receive the greater condemnation."

While some were speaking of the temple, how it was adorned with noble stones and offerings, Jesus said, "As for these things, the days will come when there shall not be left here one stone upon another." And they asked him, "Teacher, when will this be, and what will be the sign when this is about to take place?"

"Take heed that you are not led astray," he said, "for many will come in my name, saying, 'I am he!' and, 'The time is at hand!' Do not go after them. And when you hear of wars and tumults, do not be terrified; for this must first take place, but the end will not be at once. Nation will rise against nation, and kingdom against kingdom; there will be great earthquakes, and in various places famines and pestilences; and there will be terrors and great signs from heaven. But before all this they will persecute you, delivering you up to the synagogues and prisons, and you will be brought before kings and governors for my name's sake. This will be a time for you to bear testimony. Settle it therefore in your minds, not to meditate beforehand how to answer; for I will give you a mouth and wisdom, which none of your adversaries will be able to withstand. You will be delivered up even by parents and brothers and kinsmen and friends, and some of you they will put to death; you will be hated by all for my name's sake. But not a hair of your head will perish. By your endurance you will gain your lives.

"But when you see Jerusalem surrounded by armies, then know that its desolation has come near. Then let those who are in Judea flee to the mountains, and let those who are inside the city depart, and let not those who are out in the country enter it; for these are days of vengeance, to fulfil all that is written. Alas for those who are with child and for those who give suck in those days! For great distress shall be upon the earth and wrath upon this people; they will fall by the edge of the sword, and be led captive among all nations; and Jerusalem will be trodden down by the Gentiles, until the times of the Gentiles are fulfilled. And there will be signs in sun and moon and stars, and upon the earth distress of nations in perplexity at the roaring of the sea and the waves, men fainting with fear and with foreboding of what is coming on the world; for the powers of the heavens will be shaken. And then they will see the Son of man coming in a cloud with power and great glory. Now when these things begin to take place, look up, because your redemption is drawing near.

"Look at the fig tree, and all the trees; as soon as they come out in leaf, you know that summer is near. So also, when you see these things taking place, you know that the kingdom of God is near. Truly, I say to you, this generation will not pass away till all has taken place. Heaven and earth will pass away, but my words will not pass away. But take heed to yourselves lest your hearts be weighed down with dissipation and drunkenness and cares of this life, and that day come upon you suddenly like a snare; for it will come upon all who dwell upon the face of the whole earth. But watch at all times, praying that you may have strength to escape all these things, and to stand before the Son of man."

Now the feast of Unleavened Bread drew near, which is called the Passover. And the chief priests and the scribes were seeking how to put him to death; for they feared the people. Then Satan entered into Judas called Iscariot, one of the twelve. He conferred with the chief priests and officers how he might betray Jesus, and they were glad, and engaged to give him money. So he sought an opportunity to betray him in the absence of the multitude.

The day of Unleavened Bread came, on which the passover lamb had to be sacrificed, and Jesus told Peter and John, "Go and prepare the passover for us, that we may eat it."

"Where will you have us prepare it?" they asked.

"When you have entered the city," he said, "a man carrying a jar of water will meet you; follow him into the house which he enters, and tell the householder, 'The Teacher says to you, Where is the guest room, where I am to eat the passover with my disciples?' And he will show you a large upper room furnished; there make ready." They went and found it as he had told them; and they prepared the passover.

Now when the hour came, he sat at table with the apostles. "I have earnestly desired," he said, "to eat this passover with you before I suffer; for I tell you I shall not eat it until it is fulfilled in the kingdom of God." Then he took a cup, and when he had given thanks he said, "Take this, and divide it among yourselves; for I tell you that from now on I shall not drink of the fruit of the vine until the kingdom of God comes." And he took bread, and when he had given thanks he broke it and gave it to them. "This is my body," he said, "which is given for you. Do this in remembrance of me." Likewise he took the cup after supper, saying, "This cup which is poured out for you is the new covenant in my blood. But behold, the hand of him who betrays me is with me on the table. For the Son of man goes as it has been determined; but woe to that man by whom he is betrayed!" And they began to question one another, which of them it was that would do this.

A dispute also arose among them, which of them was to be regarded as the greatest. And he said to them, "The kings of the Gentiles exercise lordship over them. But not so with you: rather let the greatest among you become as the youngest, and the leader as one who serves. Which is the greater, one who sits at table, or one who serves? Is it not the one who sits at table? But I am among you as one who serves. You have continued with me in my trials; and I assign to you, as my Father assigned to me, a kingdom, that you may eat and drink at my table in my kingdom, and sit on thrones judging the twelve tribes of Israel.

"Simon, Simon, behold, Satan demanded to have you, that he might sift you like wheat, but I have prayed for you that your faith may not fail; and when you have turned again, strengthen your brethren."

"Lord," said Peter, "I am ready to go with you to prison and to death."

"I tell you, Peter," Jesus said, "the cock will not crow this day, until you three times deny that you know me."

And he said to them, "When I sent you out with no purse or bag or sandals, did you lack anything?" They said, "Nothing." He said to them, "But now, let him who has a purse take it, and likewise a bag. And let him who has no sword sell his mantle and buy one. For I tell you that this scripture must be fulfilled in me, 'And he was reckoned with transgressors'; for what is written about me has its fulfilment." And they said, "Look, Lord, here are two swords." And he said to them, "It is enough."

After this, taking his disciples he went, as was his custom, to the Mount of Olives. Withdrawing about a stone's throw, he knelt down and prayed, "Father, if thou art willing, remove this cup from me; nevertheless not my will, but thine, be done."

Then there appeared to him an angel from heaven, strengthening him. And being in an agony he prayed more earnestly; and his sweat became like great drops of blood falling down upon the ground. When he rose, he came to the disciples and found them sleeping for sorrow, and he said, "Why do you sleep? Rise and pray that you may not enter into temptation."

While he was still speaking, there came a crowd, with Judas leading them. He drew near to Jesus to kiss him, but Jesus said, "Judas, would you betray the Son of man with a kiss?" When those about him saw what would follow, one of them drew a sword and struck the slave of the high priest and cut off his right ear. But Jesus said, "No more of this!" He touched the slave's ear and healed him. To the chief priests and officers he said, "Have you come out as against a robber, with swords and clubs? When I was with you day after day in the temple, you did not lay hands on me. But this is your hour, and the power of darkness."

Then they seized him and led him away to the high priest's house. At a distance, Peter followed, and in the courtyard he sat down among the guards and servants at the fire. Then a maid, gazing at him, said, "This man also was with him."

"Woman, I do not know him," Peter said. A little later some one else saw him and said, "You also are one of them."

"Man, I am not," said Peter. After an interval of about an hour still another insisted, "Certainly this man also was with him; for he is a Galilean."

"Man," said Peter, "I do not know what you are saying." And immediately, while he was still speaking, the cock crowed. And the Lord turned and looked at Peter, and Peter remembered how he had said to him, "Before the cock crows today, you will deny me three times." And he went out and wept bitterly.

Now the men who were holding Jesus mocked him and beat him; they also blindfolded him and asked, "Prophesy! Who is it that struck you?" And they spoke many other words against him, reviling him.

When day came, the elders, the chief priests, and the scribes assembled in council. "If you are the Christ," they said to Jesus, "tell us."

"If I tell you," he replied, "you will not believe. But from now on the Son of man shall be seated at the right hand of the power of God."

"Are you the Son of God, then?" they all asked.

"You say that I am," he answered.

"What further testimony do we need?" they said. "We have heard it ourselves from his own lips."

Then the whole company of them arose, and brought him before Pilate, and they began to accuse him. "We found this man perverting our nation," they said, "and forbidding us to give tribute to Caesar, and saying that he himself is Christ a king."

"Are you the King of the Jews?" Pilate asked.

"You have said so," Jesus answered.

"I find no crime in this man," Pilate said to the chief priests and the multitudes. But they were urgent, saying, "He stirs up the people, teaching throughout all Judea, from Galilee even to this place."

When Pilate heard this, he asked whether Jesus was a Galilean, and when he learned that he was, he sent him to Herod, who was then in Jerusalem. Herod was glad to see Jesus, for he had long desired to meet him, and he was hoping to see some sign done by him. So he questioned him at length, but Jesus made no answer. The chief priests and the scribes stood by, vehemently accusing him. And Herod with his soldiers treated him with contempt and mocked him; then, arraying him in gorgeous apparel, he sent him back to Pilate.

Calling together the chief priests and the rulers and the people, Pilate said, "You brought me this man as one who was perverting the people; and after examining him before you, behold, I did not find this man guilty of any of your charges against him; neither did Herod, for he sent him back to us. Behold, nothing deserving death has been done by him; I will therefore chastise him and release him." Now he was obliged to release one man to them at the festival.

But they all cried out together, "Away with this man, and release to us Barabbas" (a man who had been arrested for insurrection and murder). Pilate addressed them once more, desiring to release Jesus; but they shouted, "Crucify, crucify him!"

"Why, what evil has he done?" Pilate asked. "I have found in him no crime deserving death; I will therefore chastise him and release him."

But they were urgent, demanding with loud cries that he should be crucified. And their voices prevailed. So Pilate gave sentence that their demand should be granted. He released Barabbas, whom they asked for, but Jesus he delivered up to their will.

As they led him away, they seized one Simon of Cyrene, who was coming in from the country, and laid the cross on him, to carry it behind Jesus. A great multitude followed, with many women who bewailed and lamented him. But Jesus, turning to them, said, "Daughters of Jerusalem, do not weep for me, but weep for yourselves and for your children. For behold, the days are coming when they will say, 'Blessed are the barren, and the wombs that never bore, and the breasts that never gave suck!' Then they will say to the mountains, 'Fall on us'; and to the hills, 'Cover us.' For if they do this when the wood is green, what will happen when it is dry?"

Two others, who were criminals, were led away to be put to death with him. When they came to the place called The Skull, there they crucified him, and the criminals, one on the right and one on the left. "Father, forgive them," Jesus said, "for they know not what they do." And they cast lots to divide his garments.

The people stood by, watching, but the rulers scoffed, "He saved others; let him save himself, if he is the Christ of God, his Chosen One!" The soldiers also mocked him, offering him vinegar, and saying, "If you are the King of the Jews, save yourself!" There was also an inscription over him, "This is the King of the Jews."

One of the criminals railed at him, saying, "Are you not the Christ? Save yourself and us!" But the other rebuked him, "Do you not fear God, since you are under the same sentence of condemnation? And we indeed justly; for we are receiving the due reward of our deeds; but this man has done nothing wrong." And he said, "Jesus, remember me when you come into your kingdom."

Jesus replied, "Truly, I say to you, today you will be with me in Paradise."

It was now about the sixth hour, and the sun's light failed, and there was darkness over the whole land until the ninth hour; and the curtain of the temple was torn in two. Then Jesus cried with a loud voice, "Father, into thy hands I commit my spirit!" And he breathed his last. Now when the centurion saw what had taken place, he praised God, and said, "Certainly this man was innocent!" And the multitudes, when they saw what had taken place, returned home beating their breasts. And all his acquaintances and the women who had followed him from Galilee stood at a distance and saw these things.

Now it was the day of Preparation, and the sabbath was beginning. A man named Joseph, of Arimathea, a member of the council, a righteous man who had not consented to their deed, went to Pilate and asked for the body of Jesus. Then he took it down and wrapped it in a linen shroud, and laid it in a rock-hewn tomb, where no one had yet been laid. The women followed, and saw the tomb, and how his body was laid; then they returned home, and prepared spices and ointments.

On the sabbath the women rested according to the commandment. But on the first day of the week, at early dawn, they went to the tomb, taking the spices. They found the stone rolled away from the tomb, but when they went in they did not find the body. While they were perplexed about this, behold, two men stood by them in dazzling apparel, and the women, frightened, bowed their faces to the ground.

"Why do you seek the living among the dead?" the men asked. "He is not here, but has risen. Remember how he told you, while he was still in Galilee, that the Son of man must be delivered into the hands of sinful men, and be crucified, and on the third day rise." The women remembered, and returning from the tomb they told all this to the eleven and the rest. Now it was Mary Magdalene and Joanna and Mary the mother of James and the other women with them who told this to the apostles; but these words seemed an idle tale, and they did not believe them. But Peter ran to the tomb and, stooping and looking in, he saw the linen cloths by themselves; and he went home wondering at what had happened.

That very day two of the disciples were going to a village named Emmaus, and while they walked, Jesus himself drew near and went with them. But their eyes were kept from recognizing him. "What is this conversation," Jesus asked, "which you are holding with each other?" They stood still, looking sad. Then one, Cleopas, answered, "Are you the only visitor to Jerusalem who does not know the things that have happened there?"

"What things?" Jesus asked.

"Concerning Jesus of Nazareth," they answered, "who was a prophet mighty in deed and word, and how our chief priests delivered him up to be crucified. Moreover, some of our women were at the tomb early in the morning and did not find his body. They came back saying they had seen angels, who said that he was alive. Some of us went to the tomb, and found it just as the women had said."

"O foolish men," said Jesus, "and slow of heart to believe all that the prophets have spoken! Was it not necessary that the Christ should suffer these things and enter into his glory?" And beginning with Moses and all the prophets, he interpreted in the scriptures the things concerning himself.

As they drew near to Emmaus, Jesus appeared to be going further, but they said, "Stay with us, for the day is now far spent." So he stayed, and when he was at table he took the bread and blessed, and broke it, and gave it to them. And their eyes were opened and they recognized him; and he vanished out of their sight. "Did not our hearts burn within us," they said, "while he talked to us on the road?" That same hour they returned to Jerusalem, and they found the eleven and the others gathered together, who said, "The Lord has risen indeed, and has appeared to Simon!" Then the two told what had happened on the road, and how he was known to them in the breaking of the bread.

As they were saying this, Jesus himself stood among them and said, "Peace to you!" Startled and frightened, they supposed that they saw a spirit. "Why are you troubled," Jesus asked, "and why do questionings rise in your hearts? See my hands and my feet, that it is I myself; handle me, and see; for a spirit has not flesh and bones as you see that I have." Still they disbelieved for joy, and wondered. "Have you anything here to eat?" he asked. They gave him a piece of broiled fish, and he ate before them.

Then he said to them, "These are my words which I spoke to you, while I was still with you, that everything written about me in the law of Moses and the prophets and the psalms must be fulfilled." He opened their minds to understand the scriptures, and he said, "Thus it is written, that the Christ should suffer and on the third day rise from the dead, and that repentance and forgiveness of sins should be preached in his name to all nations, beginning from Jerusalem. You are witnesses of these things. And behold, I send the promise of my Father upon you; but stay in the city, until you are clothed with power from on high."

Then he led them out as far as Bethany, and lifting up his hands he blessed them. While he blessed them, he parted from them, and was carried up into heaven. And they returned to Jerusalem with great joy, and were continually in the temple blessing God.

THE GOSPEL ACCORDING TO

JOHN

A strong and early tradition assigns the authorship of the fourth Gospel, produced near the close of the first century, to the aged apostle John. Whether the book was written directly by John, or indirectly (his teachings may have been edited by another), the church has accepted it as an authoritative supplement to the story of Jesus' ministry given by the other evangelists. Often called a "spiritual" Gospel, John's narrative attempts to go behind and beyond the physical events of Jesus' ministry in an effort to explain his divine origin. This purpose may be readily seen in the magnificent prologue, where John briefly treats the significance of the Incarnation.

In his narrative John recounts just seven of Jesus' miracles, which he calls "signs," each of them intended to convey a definite meaning. He also provides a number of long and pithy discourses of Jesus, dealing with such topics as the need to be born again, and the spiritual life of the believer. In these discourses Jesus' teachings are often set forth in symbols, all drawn from common experience (bread, water, light, darkness, shepherd, door), which help to make the meaning vivid and memorable.

———

IN THE BEGINNING was the Word, and the Word was with God, and the Word was God. He was in the beginning with God; all things were made through him, and without him was not anything made that was made. In him was life, and the life was the light of men. The light shines in the darkness, and the darkness has not overcome it.

There was a man sent from God, whose name was John. He came for testimony, to bear witness to the light, that all might believe through him. He was not the light, but came to bear witness to the light.

The true light that enlightens every man was coming into the world. He was in the world, and the world was made through him, yet the world knew him not. He came to his own home, and his own people received him not. But to all who received him, who believed in his name, he gave power to become children of God; who were born, not of blood nor of the will of the flesh nor of the will of man, but of God.

And the Word became flesh and dwelt among us, full of grace and truth; we have beheld his glory, glory as of the only Son from the Father. And from his fulness have we all received, grace upon grace. For the law was given through Moses; grace and truth came through Jesus Christ. No one has ever seen God; the only Son, who is in the bosom of the Father, he has made him known.

THIS IS THE testimony of John, when the Pharisees in Jerusalem sent priests and Levites to Bethany beyond the Jordan, where John was baptizing, to ask him, "Who are you?"

"I am not the Christ," he confessed.

"What then?" they asked. "Are you Elijah or the prophet?"

"I am not," he answered.

"Then who are you?" they said. "Let us have an answer for those who sent us. What do you say about yourself?"

"I am the voice," he said, "of one crying in the wilderness, 'Make straight the way of the Lord,' as the prophet Isaiah said."

"Then why are you baptizing," they asked, "if you are neither the Christ, nor Elijah, nor the prophet?"

"I baptize with water," John answered, "but among you stands one whom you do not know, even he who comes after me, the thong of whose sandal I am not worthy to untie."

The next day John saw Jesus coming toward him. "Behold, the Lamb of God," he said, "who takes away the sin of the world! This is he of whom I said, 'After me comes a man who ranks before me, for he was before me.' I myself did not know him; but for this I came baptizing with water, that he might be revealed to Israel. I saw the Spirit descend as a dove from heaven, and it remained on him. Now he who sent me to baptize with water said, 'He on whom you see the Spirit descend and remain, this is he who baptizes with the Holy Spirit.' And I have seen and have borne witness that this is the Son of God."

The next day again John was with two of his disciples, and he looked at Jesus as he walked, and said, "Behold, the Lamb of God!" The disciples heard him, and they followed Jesus. Jesus turned and saw them. "What do you seek?" he asked. "Rabbi, where are you staying?" they said. "Come and see," he said. They came and they stayed with him that day, for it was about the tenth hour. One of the two was Andrew, Simon Peter's brother. He went to his brother and said, "We have found the Messiah," and he brought him to Jesus, who looked at him, and said, "So you are Simon the son of John? You shall be called Cephas" (which means Peter).

The next day Jesus decided to go to Galilee. He found Philip, and said,

"Follow me." Now Philip was from Bethsaida, the city of Andrew and Peter. Philip found Nathanael, and said, "We have found him of whom Moses in the law and also the prophets wrote, Jesus of Nazareth, the son of Joseph."

"Can anything good come out of Nazareth?" Nathanael asked. Philip said, "Come and see."

Jesus saw Nathanael coming. "Behold," he said, "an Israelite indeed, in whom is no guile!"

"How do you know me?" Nathanael asked.

"Before Philip called you," Jesus answered, "when you were under the fig tree, I saw you."

"Rabbi, you are the Son of God!" Nathanael answered. "You are the King of Israel!"

"Because," said Jesus, "I said to you, I saw you under the fig tree, do you believe? You shall see greater things than these. Truly, I say to you, you will see heaven opened, and the angels of God ascending and descending upon the Son of man."

On the third day there was a marriage at Cana in Galilee, and the mother of Jesus was there; Jesus also was invited, with his disciples. When the wine gave out, the mother of Jesus said, "They have no wine."

"O woman," he said, "what have you to do with me? My hour has not yet come."

His mother said to the servants, "Do whatever he tells you." Now six stone jars were standing there, for the Jewish rites of purification, each holding twenty or thirty gallons. "Fill the jars with water," Jesus said. They filled them to the brim, and he said, "Draw some out, and take it to the steward." When the steward tasted the water now become wine, and did not know where it came from (though the servants knew), the steward called the bridegroom. "Every man serves the good wine first," he said, "and when men have drunk freely, then the poor wine; but you have kept the good wine until now." This first of his signs Jesus did at Cana, and manifested his glory; and his disciples believed in him.

The Passover of the Jews was at hand, and Jesus went up to Jerusalem. In the temple he found those who were selling oxen and sheep and pigeons, and the money-changers at their business. Making a whip of cords, he drove them all, with the sheep and oxen, out of the temple, and he poured out the coins of the money-changers and overturned their tables. He told those who sold pigeons, "Take these things away; you shall not make my Father's house a house of trade." His disciples remembered that it was written, "Zeal for thy house will consume me." The Jews then said, "What sign have you to show us for doing this?"

"Destroy this temple," he said, "and in three days I will raise it up."

"It has taken forty-six years to build this temple," the Jews said, "and will you raise it up in three days?" But he spoke of the temple of his body. When therefore he was raised from the dead, his disciples remembered he had said this; and they believed the scripture and the word which Jesus had spoken.

While he was in Jerusalem, many believed in his name when they saw the signs which he did; but Jesus did not trust himself to them, because he himself knew what was in man. Now there was a Pharisee named Nicodemus, who came to Jesus by night. "Rabbi," he said, "we know that you are a teacher from God; for no one can do these signs, unless God is with him."

"Truly, truly, I say to you," Jesus answered, "unless one is born anew, he cannot see the kingdom of God."

"How can a man be born when he is old?" Nicodemus asked. "Can he enter a second time into his mother's womb and be born?"

"Truly, truly, I say to you," said Jesus, "unless one is born of water and the Spirit, he cannot enter the kingdom of God. That which is born of the flesh is flesh, and that which is born of the Spirit is spirit. Do not marvel that I said to you, 'You must be born anew.' The wind blows where it wills, and you hear the sound of it, but you do not know whence it comes or whither it goes; so it is with every one who is born of the Spirit."

"How can this be?" Nicodemus asked.

"Are you a teacher of Israel," Jesus replied, "and yet you do not understand this? Truly, I say to you, we speak of what we know, and bear witness to what we have seen; but you do not receive our testimony. If I have told you earthly things and you do not believe, how can you believe if I tell you heavenly things? No one has ascended into heaven but he who descended from heaven, the Son of man. And as Moses lifted up the serpent in the wilderness, so must the Son of man be lifted up, that whoever believes in him may have eternal life."

For God so loved the world that he gave his only Son, that whoever believes in him should not perish but have eternal life. God sent the Son into the world, not to condemn, but that the world might be saved through him. He who believes in him is not condemned; he who does not believe is condemned already. The light has come into the world, and men loved darkness rather than light, for every one who does evil hates the light, lest his deeds should be exposed. But he who does what is true comes to the light, that it may be clearly seen that his deeds have been wrought in God.

After this, Jesus and his disciples went into the land of Judea; there he remained with them and baptized (though Jesus himself did not baptize, but only his disciples). John also was baptizing at Aenon near Salim, because there was much water there; for John had not yet been put in prison.

Now a discussion arose between John's disciples and a Jew over purifying. They came to John, and said, "Rabbi, he who was with you beyond the Jordan, to whom you bore witness, here he is, baptizing, and all are going to him."

"No one can receive anything," John answered, "except what is given him from heaven. You yourselves bear me witness, that I said, I am not the Christ, but I have been sent before him. He who has the bride is the bridegroom; the friend of the bridegroom, who stands and hears him, rejoices greatly at the bridegroom's voice; therefore this joy of mine is now full. He must increase, but I must decrease."

He who is of the earth belongs to the earth, and of the earth he speaks; he who comes from heaven is above all. He bears witness to what he has seen and heard, yet no one receives his testimony; he who receives his testimony sets his seal to this, that God is true. He whom God has sent utters the words of God, for it is not by measure that he gives the Spirit; the Father loves the Son, and has given all things into his hand. He who believes in the Son has eternal life; he who does not obey the Son shall not see life, but the wrath of God rests upon him.

Now when Jesus knew that the Pharisees had heard that he was making more disciples than John, he left Judea for Galilee. Passing through Samaria, he came to a town called Sychar, near the field that Jacob gave to his son Joseph. Jacob's well was there, and Jesus, wearied with his journey, sat down beside it while his disciples went into the town to buy food. It was about noon.

There came a woman from the town to draw water, and Jesus asked her for a drink. "How is it," the woman asked, "that you, a Jew, ask a drink of me, a woman of Samaria?" (Jews have no dealings with Samaritans.)

"If you knew the gift of God," Jesus answered, "and who it is that asks for a drink, you would ask him, and he would give you living water."

"Sir, you have nothing to draw with," said the woman, "and the well is deep; where do you get that living water? Are you greater than our father Jacob, who gave us the well?"

"Every one who drinks of this water will thirst again," replied Jesus, "but whoever drinks of the water that I shall give him will never thirst. It will become in him a spring of water welling up to eternal life."

"Sir, give me this water," said the woman, "that I may not thirst, nor come here to draw."

"Go, call your husband," said Jesus, "and come here."

"I have no husband," answered the woman.

"You are right, for you have had five husbands," Jesus said, "and he whom you now have is not your husband."

"Sir, I perceive that you are a prophet," said the woman. "Our fathers worshiped on this mountain, but you say that in Jerusalem is the place where men ought to worship."

"Woman, believe me," said Jesus, "the hour is coming when neither on this mountain nor in Jerusalem will you worship the Father. You worship what you do not know; we worship what we know, for salvation is from the Jews. But the hour is coming, and now is, when the true worshipers will worship the Father in spirit and truth, for such the Father seeks to worship him. God is spirit, and those who worship him must worship in spirit and truth."

"I know that the Messiah is coming," said the woman. "When he comes, he will show us all things."

Then Jesus said, "I who speak to you am he."

Just then his disciples came. They marveled that he was talking with a woman, but they said nothing. The woman, forgetting her water jar, hurried into the town, and said to the people, "Come, see a man who told me all that I ever did. Can this be the Christ?" Many believed the woman's testimony and went out to meet him.

Meanwhile the disciples besought him, saying, "Rabbi, eat." But he said, "I have food to eat of which you do not know." So the disciples said to one another, "Has any one brought him food?"

"My food is to do the will of him who sent me," said Jesus, "and to accomplish his work. Do you not say, 'There are yet four months, then comes the harvest'? Lift up your eyes, and see how the fields are already white for harvest. He who reaps receives wages, and gathers fruit for eternal life, so that sower and reaper may rejoice together. For here the saying holds true, 'One sows and another reaps.' I sent you to reap that for which you did not labor; others have labored, and you have entered into their labor."

When the people from the town came to him, they asked him to stay with them; and he stayed there two days. And many more believed because of his word. They said to the woman, "It is no longer because of your words that we believe, for we have heard for ourselves, and we know that this is indeed the Savior of the world."

After the two days he departed to Galilee, and he came again to Cana. Now at Capernaum there was an official whose son was at the point of death. When he heard that Jesus was nearby, he went and begged him to come down and heal his son. "Unless you see signs and wonders," Jesus said, "you will not believe."

"Sir," the official said, "come down before my child dies."

"Go," said Jesus, "your son will live."

The man believed, and as he was going down, his servants met him and told him that his son was living. He asked the hour when he began to mend. "Yesterday at the seventh hour," they said. The father knew that was the hour when Jesus had said, "Your son will live." This was now the second sign that Jesus did when he had come from Judea to Galilee.

After this there was a feast of the Jews, and Jesus went up to Jerusalem. Now there is in Jerusalem a pool (in Hebrew called Bethzatha), which has five porticoes. In these lay a multitude of invalids, blind, lame, paralyzed. One man there had been ill for thirty-eight years, and when Jesus saw him and knew he had been there a long time, he said, "Do you want to be healed?"

"Sir," he answered, "I have no man to put me into the pool when the water is troubled; while I am going another steps down before me."

"Rise," said Jesus, "take up your pallet, and walk." At once the man was healed, and he took up his pallet and walked.

Now that day was the sabbath. So the Jews said to the man, "It is the sabbath, it is not lawful for you to carry your pallet." But he answered, "The man who healed me told me to do so." They asked, "Who is the man?" Now he did not know who it was, for Jesus had withdrawn. Afterward Jesus found him in the temple, and said, "See, you are well! Sin no more, that nothing worse befall you." The man went and told the Jews that it was Jesus; and this was why the Jews persecuted him, because he did this on the sabbath. But Jesus answered them, "My Father is working still, and I am working." Then the Jews sought all the more to kill him, because he not only broke the sabbath but also called God his own Father, making himself equal with God.

Jesus said to the Jews, "The Son can do nothing of his own accord, but only what he sees the Father doing; for whatever he does, the Son does likewise. For the Father loves the Son, and shows him all that he is doing; and greater works than these will he show, that you may marvel. As the Father raises the dead, so also the Son gives life to whom he will. The Father judges no one, but has given all judgment to the Son, that all may honor the Son, even as they honor the Father. He who does not honor the Son does not honor the Father who sent him. He who hears my word and believes him who sent me, has eternal life; he does not come into judgment, but has passed from death to life. Truly, truly, I say to you, the hour is coming, and now is, when the dead will hear the voice of the Son of God, and those who hear will live. Do not marvel at this; for the hour is coming when all who are in the tombs will hear his voice and come forth, those who have done good, to the resurrection of life, and those who have done evil, to the resurrection of judgment.

"I can do nothing on my own authority; as I hear, I judge; and my judgment is just, because I seek not my own will but the will of him who sent me. If I bear witness to myself, my testimony is not true; there is another who bears witness to me, and I know that the testimony which he bears to me is true. You sent to John, and he has borne witness to the truth. Not that the testimony which I receive is from man; but I say this that you may be saved. He was a shining lamp, and you were willing to rejoice in his light. But my testimony is greater than that of John; for the works which the Father has granted me to accomplish, these very works I am doing, bear witness that the Father has sent me. And the Father has himself borne witness to me. His voice you have never heard, his form you have never seen; and you do not have his word abiding in you, for you do not believe him whom he has sent.

"You search the scriptures, because you think that in them you have eternal life; and it is they that bear witness to me; yet you refuse to come to me. I do not receive glory from men. But I know that you have not the love of God within you. I have come in my Father's name, and you do not receive me; if another comes in his own name, him you will receive. How can you believe, who receive glory from one another and do not seek the glory that comes from the only God? Do not think that I shall accuse you to the Father; it is Moses who accuses you, on whom you set your hope. If you believed Moses, you would believe me, for he wrote of me. But if you do not believe his writings, how will you believe my words?"

After this, Jesus went to the other side of the Sea of Galilee, and a multitude followed him. He went up on the mountain with his disciples, and saw the multitude. "How are we to buy bread," he said to Philip, "that these people may eat?" This he said to test him, for he himself knew what he would do.

"Two hundred denarii," said Philip, "would not buy enough bread for each of them to get a little." Andrew, Simon Peter's brother, said, "There is a lad here who has five barley loaves and two fish; but what are they among so many?"

"Make the people sit down," said Jesus.

Now there was much grass in the place; so the men sat down, in number about five thousand. Jesus then took the loaves, and when he had given thanks, he distributed them; so also the fish, as much as they wanted. When they had eaten their fill, he told his disciples, "Gather up the fragments left over, that nothing may be lost," and they filled twelve baskets with fragments from the five loaves. When the people saw this, they said, "This is indeed the prophet who is to come into the world!" Perceiving that they were about to take him by force to make him king, Jesus withdrew to the mountain by himself.

When evening came, his disciples got into a boat and started across to Capernaum. It was now dark, and the sea rose because a strong wind was blowing. When they had rowed three or four miles, they saw Jesus walking on the sea and drawing near to the boat.

They were frightened, but he said, "It is I; do not be afraid." Then they were glad to take him into the boat, and immediately the boat was at the land to which they were going.

Next day the people on the other side of the sea saw that there had been only one boat there, and that Jesus had not entered it, but that his disciples had gone away alone. However, other boats came near the place, so the people got into the boats and went to Capernaum, seeking Jesus.

When they found him on the other side, they said, "Rabbi, when did you come here?"

"Truly, truly," Jesus answered, "you seek me, not because you saw signs, but because you ate your fill of the loaves. Do not labor for the food which perishes, but for the food which endures to eternal life, which the Son of man will give to you; for on him has God the Father set his seal."

"What must we do," they said, "to be doing the works of God?"

"This is the work of God," Jesus answered, "that you believe in him whom he has sent."

"Then what sign do you do," they said, "that we may see, and believe you? What work do you perform? Our fathers ate the manna in the wilderness; as it is written, 'He gave them bread from heaven to eat.'"

"It was not Moses who gave you the bread from heaven," Jesus said. "My Father gives you the true bread from heaven. For the bread of God is that which comes down from heaven, and gives life to the world."

"Lord," they said, "give us this bread always."

"I am the bread of life," said Jesus. "He who comes to me shall not hunger, and he who believes in me shall never thirst. But I said that you have seen me and yet do not believe. All that the Father gives me will come to me; and him who comes to me I will not cast out. For I have come down from heaven, not to do my own will, but the will of him who sent me, that I should lose nothing he has given me. For this is the will of my Father, that every one who sees the Son and believes in him should have eternal life; and I will raise him up at the last day."

The Jews then murmured at him because he said, "I am the bread which came down from heaven." They asked, "Is not this Jesus, the son of Joseph, whose father and mother we know? How does he now say, 'I have come down from heaven'?"

"Do not murmur among yourselves," Jesus answered. "No one can come to me unless the Father draws him. It is written in the prophets, 'And they shall all be taught by God.' Every one who has learned from the Father comes to me. Not that any one has seen the Father except him who is from God. Your fathers ate the manna in the wilderness, and they died. I am the bread of life which comes down from heaven that a man may eat of it and not die. I am the living bread which came down from heaven; if any one eats of this bread, he will live for ever; and the bread which I shall give for the life of the world is my flesh."

The Jews disputed among themselves, saying, "How can this man give us his flesh to eat?"

"Truly," Jesus said, "unless you eat the flesh of the Son of man and drink his blood, you have no life in you; he who eats my flesh and drinks my blood has eternal life, and I will raise him up at the last day. For my flesh is food indeed, and my blood is drink indeed. He who eats my flesh and drinks my blood abides in me, and I in him. As the living Father sent me, and I live because of the Father, so he who eats me will live because of me."

Many of his disciples, when they heard this, said, "This is a hard saying; who can listen to it?" But Jesus, knowing that his disciples murmured, said, "Do you take offense at this? Then what if you were to see the Son of man ascending where he was before? It is the spirit that gives life, the flesh is of no avail; the words that I have spoken to you are spirit and life. But there are some of you that do not believe." For Jesus knew from the first who those were that did not believe, and who it was that would betray him. "This is why I told you," he said, "that no one can come to me unless it is granted him by the Father."

After this many of his disciples drew back and no longer went about with him. "Do you also wish to go away?" Jesus said to the twelve.

"Lord," Simon Peter answered, "to whom shall we go? You have the words of eternal life; and we have believed, and have come to know, that you are the Holy One of God."

"Did I not choose you, the twelve," Jesus answered, "and one of you is a devil?" He spoke of Judas the son of Simon Iscariot, for he, one of the twelve, was to betray him.

After this, Jesus went about in Galilee, but not in Judea, because the Jews sought to kill him. Now the Jews' feast of Tabernacles was at hand, so his brothers said to him, "Leave here and go to Judea, that your disciples may see the works you are doing. For no man works in secret if he seeks to be known openly. If you do these things, show yourself to the world." For even his brothers did not believe in him. "My time has not yet come," Jesus said, "but your time is always here. The world cannot hate you, but it hates me because I testify of it that its works are evil. Go to the feast yourselves; I am not going up to this feast, for my time has not yet fully come." But after his brothers had gone up, then he also went, not publicly but in private.

The Jews were looking for him at the feast, and there was much muttering about him among the people. While some said, "He is a good man," others said, "No, he is leading the people astray." Yet for fear of the Jews no one spoke openly of him. About the middle of the feast Jesus went into the temple and taught. The Jews marveled, saying, "How is it that this man has learning, when he has never studied?"

"My teaching is not mine," Jesus answered them, "but his who sent me; if any man's will is to do his will, he shall know whether the teaching is from God or whether I am speaking on my own authority. He who speaks on his own authority seeks his own glory; but he who seeks the glory of him who sent him is true, and in him there is no falsehood. Did not Moses give you the law? Yet none of you keeps the law. Why do you seek to kill me?"

"You have a demon!" the people answered. "Who is seeking to kill you?"

"I did one deed," Jesus answered, "and you all marvel at it. Moses gave you circumcision (not that it is from Moses, but from the fathers), and you circumcise a man upon the sabbath. If on the sabbath a man receives circumcision, so that the law of Moses may not be broken, are you angry with me because on the sabbath I made a man's whole body well? Do not judge by appearances, but judge with right judgment."

Some of the people of Jerusalem said, "Is not this the man whom they seek to kill? And here he is, speaking openly, and they say nothing to him! Can it be that the authorities really know that this is the Christ? Yet we know where this man comes from; and when the Christ appears, no one will know where he comes from." So Jesus proclaimed, as he taught in the temple, "You know me, and you know where I come from? But I have not come of my own accord; he who sent me is true, and him you do not know. I know him, for I come from him, and he sent me." So they sought to arrest him; but no one laid hands on him, because his hour had not yet come. Yet many of the people believed in him. "When the Christ appears," they said, "will he do more signs than this man has done?"

The Pharisees heard the crowd thus muttering about him, and the chief priests and Pharisees sent officers to arrest him. Jesus then said, "I shall be with you a little longer, and then I go to him who sent me; you will seek me and you will not find me; where I am you cannot come."

"Where does this man intend to go," the Jews said, "that we shall not find him? Does he intend to go to the Dispersion among the Greeks and teach the Greeks? What does he mean?"

On the last day of the feast, the great day, Jesus stood up, and proclaimed, "If any one thirst, let him come to me and drink. He who believes in me, as the scripture has said, 'Out of his heart shall flow rivers of living water.'" Now this he said about the Spirit, which those who believed in him were to receive; for as yet the Spirit had not been given, because Jesus was not yet glorified. When they heard these words, some people said, "This is really the prophet," or, "This is the Christ." But some said, "Is the Christ to come from Galilee? Has not the scripture said that the Christ is descended from David, and comes from Bethlehem, the village where David was?" So there was a division among the people over him. Some wanted to arrest him, but no one laid hands on him.

The officers then went back to the chief priests and Pharisees, who asked, "Why did you not bring him?"

"No man ever spoke like this man!" they answered.

"Are you led astray," the Pharisees said, "you also? Have any of the authorities believed in him? But this crowd, who do not know the law, are accursed." Nicodemus, who had gone to him before, and who was one of them, said, "Does our law judge a man without first giving him a hearing and learning what he does?"

"Are you from Galilee too?" they replied. "Search and you will see that no prophet is to rise from Galilee."

Early in the morning Jesus came again to the temple, and he sat down and taught, and the scribes and the Pharisees brought a woman caught in adultery. "Teacher, this woman has been caught in the act of adultery," they said. "Now in the law Moses commanded us to stone such. What do you say about her?" This they said to test him, that they might have some charge to bring against him. Jesus bent down and wrote with his finger on the ground. When they continued to ask him, he stood up, and said, "Let him who is without sin among you be the first to throw a stone at her." And once more he bent down and wrote with his finger on the ground. Then they went away, one by one, beginning with the eldest, and Jesus was left alone with the woman standing before him.

Jesus looked up, and said, "Woman, where are they? Has no one condemned you?"

"No one, Lord," she said.

"Neither do I condemn you," Jesus said. "Go, and do not sin again."

Jesus again spoke to the people, saying, "I am the light of the world; he who follows me will not walk in darkness, but will have the light of life."

"You are bearing witness to yourself," the Pharisees said. "Your testimony is not true."

"Even if I do bear witness to myself," Jesus answered, "my testimony is true, for I know whence I have come and whither I am going, but you do not know whence I come or whither I am going. You judge according to the flesh, I judge no one. Yet even if I do judge, my judgment is true, for it is not I alone that judge, but I and he who sent me. In your law it is written that the testimony of two men is true; I bear witness to myself, and the Father who sent me bears witness to me."

"Where is your Father?" they asked.

"You know neither me nor my Father," Jesus answered. "If you knew me, you would know my Father also." These words he spoke in the temple; but no one arrested him, because his hour had not yet come.

Again he said to the Jews, "I go away, and you will seek me and die in your sin; where I am going, you cannot come."

"Will he kill himself," they asked, "since he says, 'Where I am going, you cannot come'?"

"You are from below," he said, "I am from above; you are of this world, I am not of this world. I told you that you would die in your sins, for you will die in your sins unless you believe that I am he."

"Who are you?" they asked.

"Even what I have told you from the beginning," he replied. "I have much to say about you and much to judge; but he who sent me is true, and I declare to the world what I have heard from him." They did not understand that he spoke to them of the Father, so Jesus said, "When you have lifted up the Son of man, then you will know that I am he, and that I do nothing on my own authority but speak as the Father taught me." As he spoke thus, many of the Jews believed in him, and Jesus said to them, "If you continue in my word, you are truly my disciples, and you will know the truth, and the truth will make you free."

"We are descendants of Abraham," they said, "and have never been in bondage to any one. How is it that you say, 'You will be made free'?"

"Truly," said Jesus, "every one who commits sin is a slave to sin. The slave does not continue in the house for ever; the son continues for ever. So if the Son makes you free, you will be free indeed. I know that you are descendants of Abraham; yet you seek to kill me, because my word finds no place in you. I speak of what I have seen with my Father, and you do what you have heard from your father."

"Abraham is our father," they said.

"If you were Abraham's children," Jesus said, "you would do what Abraham did, but now you seek to kill me, a man who has told you the truth which

I heard from God; this is not what Abraham did. You do what your father did."

"We were not born of fornication," they said. "We have one Father, even God."

"If God were your Father," Jesus said, "you would love me, for I came forth from God; I came not of my own accord, but he sent me. Why do you not understand what I say? It is because you cannot bear to hear my word. You are of your father the devil, and your will is to do your father's desires. He was a murderer from the beginning, and has nothing to do with the truth, because there is no truth in him. When he lies, he speaks according to his own nature, for he is a liar and the father of lies. But, because I tell the truth, you do not believe me. Which of you convicts me of sin? If I tell the truth, why do you not believe me? He who is of God hears the words of God; the reason why you do not hear them is that you are not of God."

"Are we not right," the Jews asked, "in saying that you are a Samaritan and have a demon?"

"I have not a demon," Jesus answered, "but I honor my Father, and you dishonor me. Yet I do not seek my own glory; there is One who seeks it and he will be the judge. Truly, truly, I say to you, if any one keeps my word, he will never see death."

"Now we know that you have a demon," they said. "Abraham died, as did the prophets; and you say, 'If any one keeps my word, he will never taste death.' Are you greater than our father Abraham, who died? And the prophets died! Who do you claim to be?"

"If I glorify myself," Jesus answered, "my glory is nothing; it is my Father who glorifies me, of whom you say that he is your God. But you have not known him; I know him. If I said, I do not know him, I should be a liar like you; but I do know him and I keep his word. Your father Abraham rejoiced that he was to see my day; he saw it and was glad."

"You are not yet fifty years old," they said, "and have you seen Abraham?"

"Truly, truly, I say to you," Jesus replied, "before Abraham was, I am." Then they took up stones to throw at him; but Jesus hid himself, and went out of the temple.

As he passed by, he saw a man blind from birth, and his disciples asked, "Rabbi, who sinned, this man or his parents, that he was born blind?"

"It was not that this man sinned," Jesus said, "or his parents, but that the works of God might be made manifest in him. We must work the works of him who sent me, while it is day; night comes, when no one can work. As long as I am in the world, I am the light of the world." Then he spat on the ground and made clay and anointed the man's eyes, saying, "Go, wash in the pool of Siloam." So he went and washed and came back seeing. Those who knew the man said to him, "How were your eyes opened?" He told them, and they brought him to the Pharisees; now it was a sabbath day when Jesus opened the man's eyes. The Pharisees asked him how he had received his sight, and he said, "He put clay on my eyes, and I washed, and I see." Some of the Pharisees said, "This man is not from God, for he does not keep the sabbath." But others said, "How can a man who is a sinner do such signs?" There was a division among them, so they asked the blind man, "What do you say about him, since he has opened your eyes?" He said, "He is a prophet."

The Jews did not believe that the man had been blind until they called his parents, and asked, "Is this your son, who you say was born blind? How then does he now see?"

"We know that this is our son," they answered, "and that he was born blind; but how he now sees we do not know, nor do we know who opened his eyes. Ask him; he is of age, he will speak for himself." They said this out of fear, for the Jews had agreed that if any one should confess Jesus to be Christ, he was to be put out of the synagogue.

A second time they called the man who had been blind. "Give God the praise," they said; "we know that this man is a sinner."

"Whether he is a sinner," said the man, "I do not know; one thing I know, that though I was blind, now I see."

"What did he do to you?" they asked. "How did he open your eyes?"

"I have told you already," he said, "and you would not listen. Why do you want to hear it again? Do you too want to become his disciples?"

"You are his disciple," they said, reviling him, "but we are disciples of Moses. We know that God has spoken to Moses, but as for this man, we do not know where he comes from."

"Why, this is a marvel!" he replied. "You do not know where he comes from, yet he opened my eyes. We know God does not listen to sinners, but if any one is a worshiper of God and does his will, God listens to him. Never since the world began has it been heard that any one opened the eyes of a man born blind. If this man were not from God, he could do nothing."

"You were born in utter sin," they answered, "and would you teach us?" And they cast him out.

Jesus heard that they had cast the man out, and having found him he said, "Do you believe in the Son of man?"

"Who is he, sir," he asked, "that I may believe in him?"

"You have seen him," Jesus said, "and it is he who speaks to you."

"Lord," he said, "I believe"; and he worshiped him.

"For judgment I came into this world," Jesus said, "that those who do not see may see, and that those who see may become blind." Some of the Pharisees nearby heard this, and they said, "Are we also blind?"

"If you were blind," Jesus said, "you would have no guilt; but now that you say, 'We see,' your guilt remains. Truly, truly, I say to you, he who does not enter the sheepfold by the door but climbs in by another way, that man is a thief and a robber; but he who enters by the door is the shepherd. The sheep hear his voice, and he calls his own sheep by name and leads them out. A stranger they will not follow, for they do not know the voice of strangers."

They did not understand what he was saying, so he again said to them, "I am the door of the sheepfold; if any one enters by me, he will be saved, and will go in and out and find pasture. The thief comes only to steal and destroy; I came that they may have life, and have it abundantly. I am the good shepherd. The good shepherd lays down his life for the sheep. He who is a hireling, whose own the sheep are not, sees the wolf coming and leaves the sheep, and the wolf snatches them and scatters them. I am the good shepherd; I know my own and my own know me, as the Father knows me and I know the Father; and I lay down my life for the sheep. And I have other sheep that are not of this fold; I must bring them also, and they will heed my voice. So there shall be one flock, one shepherd. For this reason the Father loves me, because I lay down my life, that I may take it again. No one takes it from me, but I lay it down of my own accord. I have power to lay it down, and I have power to take it again; this charge I have received from my Father."

Because of these words, there was again a division among the Jews. Many of them said, "He has a demon, and he is mad; why listen to him?" Others said, "These are not the sayings of one who has a demon. Can a demon open the eyes of the blind?"

It was the feast of the Dedication at Jerusalem; it was winter, and Jesus was walking in the temple, in the portico of Solomon. So the Jews gathered round him, and said, "How long will you keep us in suspense? If you are the Christ, tell us plainly."

"I told you," Jesus answered, "and you do not believe. The works that I do in my Father's name, they bear witness to me; but you do not believe, because you do not belong to my sheep. My sheep hear my voice, and I know them, and they follow me; and I give them eternal life, and they shall never perish, and no one shall snatch them out of my hand. My Father, who has given them to me, is greater than all, and no one is able to snatch them out of the Father's hand. I and the Father are one."

The Jews took up stones again to stone him. "I have shown you many good works from the Father," Jesus said. "For which of these do you stone me?"

"It is not for a good work that we stone you," they answered, "but for blasphemy; because you, being a man, make yourself God."

Jesus answered, "Is it not written in your law, 'I said, you are gods'? If he called them gods to whom the word of God came (and scripture cannot be broken), do you say of him whom the Father consecrated and sent into the world, 'You are blaspheming,' because I said, 'I am the Son of God'? If I am not doing the works of my Father, then do not believe me; but if I do them, even though you do not believe me, believe the works, that you may know and understand that the Father is in me and I am in the Father." Again they tried to arrest him, but he escaped from their hands.

Now a certain man was ill, Lazarus of Bethany, the brother of Mary and her sister Martha. The sisters sent to Jesus, saying, "Lord, he whom you love is ill." But when Jesus heard it he said, "This illness is not unto death; it is for the glory of God, so that the Son of God may be glorified by means of it." He stayed two days longer where he was, then he said to the disciples, "Let us go into Judea again."

"Rabbi," the disciples said, "the Jews were but now seeking to stone you, and are you going there again?"

"Are there not twelve hours in the day?" Jesus answered. "If any one walks in the day, he does not stumble, because he sees the light of this world. But if any one walks in the night, he stumbles, because the light is not in him." Then he said, "Our friend Lazarus has fallen asleep, but I go to awake him out of sleep." He spoke of death, but the disciples thought that he meant taking rest in sleep. Then Jesus told them plainly, "Lazarus is dead; and for your sake I am glad that I was not there, so that you may believe. But let us go to him." Thomas, called the Twin, said, "Let us also go, that we may die with him."

When Jesus came to Bethany he found that Lazarus had already been in the tomb four days. Bethany was near Jerusalem, about two miles off, and many of the Jews had come to console Martha and Mary. When Martha heard that Jesus was coming, she went and met him. "Lord, if you had been here," she said, "my brother would not have died. Even now I know that whatever you ask from God, God will give you."

"Your brother will rise again," said Jesus.

"I know that he will rise again in the resurrection at the last day," Martha replied.

"I am the resurrection and the life," Jesus said. "He who believes in me, though he die, yet shall he live, and whoever lives and believes in me shall never die. Do you believe this?"

"Yes, Lord," she said, "I believe that you are the Christ, the Son of God, he who is coming into the world." Martha then went and called her sister, saying quietly, "The Teacher is here and is calling for you." Mary rose quickly, and when the Jews in the house saw her go out, they followed, supposing that she was going to the tomb. She came to Jesus and fell at his feet, saying, "Lord, if you had been here, my brother would not have died." When Jesus saw her weeping, and also the Jews, he was deeply moved in spirit and troubled. "Where have you laid him?" he asked. They said, "Lord, come and see." Then Jesus wept, so the Jews said, "See how he loved him!" But some said, "Could not he who opened the eyes of the blind man have kept this man from dying?"

Jesus, deeply moved again, came to the tomb; it was a cave, and a stone lay upon it. "Take away the stone," he said.

"Lord," said Martha, "by this time there will be an odor, for he has been dead four days."

"Did I not tell you," said Jesus, "that if you would believe you would see the glory of God?" They took away the stone, and Jesus lifted up his eyes and said, "Father, I thank thee that thou hast heard me. I knew that thou hearest me always, but I have said this on account of the people standing by, that they may believe that thou didst send me." Then he cried with a loud voice, "Lazarus, come out." The dead man came out, his hands and feet bound and his face wrapped with a cloth. Jesus said, "Unbind him, and let him go."

Many of the Jews who had come with Mary believed in him, but some went to the Pharisees and told what Jesus had done. So the chief priests and the Pharisees gathered the council, and said, "What are we to do? For this man performs many signs. If we let him go on thus, every one will believe in him, and the Romans will come and destroy both our holy place and our nation." But one of them, Caiaphas, who was high priest that year, said, "You know nothing at all; you do not understand that it is expedient for you that one man should die for the people, and that the whole nation should not perish." Thus he prophesied that Jesus should die for the nation, and not for the nation only, but to gather into one the children of God who are scattered abroad. So from that day on they took counsel how to put him to death. Jesus therefore no longer went about openly, but went to the country near the wilderness, to a town called Ephraim; and there he stayed with the disciples.

Now the Passover was at hand, and many went up to Jerusalem to purify themselves. They were looking for Jesus and saying to one another, "What do you think? That he will not come to the feast?" Now the chief priests and the Pharisees had given orders that if any one knew where he was, he should let them know, so that they might arrest him.

Six days before the Passover, Jesus came to Bethany, where they made him a supper. Martha served, and Lazarus was one of those at table with him. Mary took a pound of costly ointment of pure nard and anointed the feet of Jesus and wiped his feet with her hair; and the house was filled with the fragrance. But Judas Iscariot said, "Why was this ointment not sold for three hundred denarii and given to the poor?" Not that he cared for the poor, but he was a thief, and as he had the money box he used to take what was put into it. "Let her alone," Jesus said, "let her keep it for the day of my burial. The poor you always have with you, but you do not always have me."

When the Jews learned that he was there, they came, not only on account of Jesus but also to see Lazarus. So the chief priests planned to put Lazarus also to death, because on account of him many of the Jews were believing in Jesus. The next day a great crowd who had come to the feast heard that Jesus was coming to Jerusalem. They took palm branches and went to meet him, crying, "Hosanna! Blessed is he who comes in the name of the Lord, even the King of Israel!" The Pharisees then said, "You see that you can do nothing; look, the whole world has gone after him." And Jesus found a young ass and sat upon it; as it is written, "Fear not, daughter of Zion; behold, your king is coming, sitting on an ass's colt!" His disciples did not understand this at first; but when Jesus was glorified, then they remembered that this had been written of him and had been done to him.

Now among those at the feast were some Greeks. These said to Philip, "Sir, we wish to see Jesus." Philip and Andrew went and told Jesus, and Jesus said,

"The hour has come for the Son of man to be glorified. Truly, truly, I say to you, unless a grain of wheat falls into the earth and dies, it remains alone; but if it dies, it bears much fruit. He who loves his life loses it, and he who hates his life in this world will keep it for eternal life. If any one serves me, he must follow me; and where I am, there shall my servant be also; if any one serves me, the Father will honor him. Now is my soul troubled. And what shall I say? 'Father, save me from this hour'? No, for this purpose I have come to this hour. Father, glorify thy name."

Then a voice came from heaven, "I have glorified it, and I will glorify it again." The crowd heard it and said that it had thundered. Others said, "An angel has spoken to him."

"This voice has come for your sake," Jesus said, "not for mine. Now is the judgment of this world, now shall the ruler of this world be cast out; and I, when I am lifted up from the earth, will draw all men to myself." He said this to show by what death he was to die, but the crowd answered, "We have heard from the law that the Christ remains for ever. How can you say that the Son of man must be lifted up? Who is this Son of man?"

"The light is with you for a little longer," Jesus said. "Walk while you have the light, lest the darkness overtake you; he who walks in the darkness does not know where he goes. While you have the light, believe in the light, that you may become sons of light." Then he departed and hid himself from them. Though he had done many signs, yet they did not believe in him; it was so that the word spoken by the prophet Isaiah might be fulfilled: "Lord, who has believed our report, and to whom has the arm of the Lord been revealed?" Therefore they could not believe. For Isaiah again said, "He has blinded their eyes and hardened their heart, lest they should see with their eyes and perceive with their heart, and turn for me to heal them." Isaiah said this because he saw his glory and spoke of him.

Nevertheless, many even of the authorities did believe in him, but they did not confess it, lest they should be put out of the synagogue: for they loved the praise of men more than the praise of God.

Then Jesus cried out, "He who believes in me, believes not in me but in him who sent me. And he who sees me sees him who sent me. I have come as light into the world, that whoever believes in me may not remain in darkness. If any one hears my sayings and does not keep them, I do not judge him; for I did not come to judge the world but to save the world. He who rejects me has a judge; the word that I have spoken will be his judge on the last day. For I have not spoken on my own authority; the Father has given me commandment what to speak, and I know that his commandment is eternal life. What I say, I say as the Father has bidden me."

Before the feast of the Passover, when Jesus knew that his hour had come to depart to the Father, having loved his own, he loved them to the end. During supper, when the devil had already put it into the heart of Judas Iscariot to betray him, Jesus rose, laid aside his garments, and girded himself with a towel. He poured water into a basin, and began to wash the disciples' feet, and to wipe them with the towel. He came to Peter, who said, "Lord, do you wash my feet?"

"What I am doing," Jesus answered, "you do not know now, but afterward you will understand."

"You shall never wash my feet," Peter said.

"If I do not wash you," said Jesus, "you have no part in me."

"Lord," said Peter, "not my feet only but also my hands and my head!"

"He who has bathed," Jesus said, "does not need to wash, except for his feet, but he is clean all over; and you are clean, but not every one of you." He knew who was to betray him; that was why he said, "You are not all clean."

When he had washed their feet and resumed his place, he said, "Do you know what I have done to you? You call me Teacher and Lord; and you are right, for so I am. If I then, your Lord and Teacher, have washed your feet, you also ought to wash one another's feet, for I have given you an example. A servant is not greater than his master; nor is he who is sent greater than he who sent him. If you know these things, blessed are you if you do them. I am not speaking of you all; I know whom I have chosen; it is that the scripture may be fulfilled, 'He who ate my bread has lifted his heel against me.' I tell you this now, before it takes place, that when it does take place you may believe that I am he. Truly, truly, I say to you, he who receives any one whom I send receives me; and he who receives me receives him who sent me." Then he was troubled in spirit, and testified, "Truly, truly, I say to you, one of you will betray me."

The disciples looked at one another, uncertain of whom he spoke. One of his disciples, whom Jesus loved, was lying close to his breast, so Peter beckoned to him, and said, "Tell us who it is of whom he speaks." The disciple asked, "Lord, who is it?"

"It is he," answered Jesus, "to whom I shall give this morsel when I have dipped it," and he gave it to Judas Iscariot. Then Satan entered into Judas, and Jesus said to him, "What you are going to do, do quickly." No one at the table knew why he said this to him. Some thought that, because Judas had the money box, Jesus was telling him to buy what was needed for the feast, or that he should give something to the poor. After receiving the morsel, Judas immediately went out; and it was night.

"Now is the Son of man glorified," Jesus said, "and in him God is glorified; if God is glorified in him, God will also glorify him in himself, and at once. Little children, yet a little while I am with you. You will seek me; and as I said to the Jews, 'Where I am going you cannot come.' A new commandment I give to you, that you love one another, even as I have loved you. By this all men will know that you are my disciples, if you have love for one another."

"Lord, where are you going?" Peter asked.

"Where I am going," Jesus answered, "you cannot follow me now; but you shall follow afterward."

"Lord, why cannot I follow you now?" said Peter. "I will lay down my life for you."

"Will you lay down your life for me?" Jesus replied. "Truly, truly, I say to you, the cock will not crow, till you have denied me three times.

"Let not your hearts be troubled; believe in God, believe also in me. In my Father's house are many rooms; if it were not so, would I have told you that I go to prepare a place for you? And when I go and prepare a place for you, I will come again and will take you to myself, that where I am you may be also. And you know the way where I am going."

"Lord," said Thomas, "we do not know where you are going; how can we know the way?"

"I am the way, and the truth, and the life," Jesus said; "no one comes to the Father, but by me. If you had known me, you would have known my Father also; henceforth you know him and have seen him."

"Lord," said Philip, "show us the Father, and we shall be satisfied."

"Have I been with you so long, and yet you do not know me, Philip?" Jesus said. "He who has seen me has seen the Father. The words that I say to you I do not speak on my own authority; but the Father who dwells in me does his works. Believe me that I am in the Father and the Father in me; or else believe me for the sake of the works themselves. He who believes in me will also do the works that I do; and greater works than these will he do, because I go to the Father. Whatever you ask in my name, I will do it, that the Father may be glorified in the Son. If you love me, you will keep my commandments. And I will pray the Father, and he will give you another Counselor, to be with you for ever, even the Spirit of truth, whom the world cannot receive, because it neither sees him nor knows him; you know him, for he dwells with you, and will be in you. I will not leave you desolate; I will come to you. Yet a little while, and the world will see me no more, but you will see me; because I live, you will live also. In that day you will know that I am in my Father, and you in me, and I in you. He who keeps my commandments loves me; and he who loves me will be loved by my Father, and I will love him and manifest myself to him."

"Lord," said Judas (not Iscariot), "how is it that you will manifest yourself to us, and not to the world?"

"If a man loves me," answered Jesus, "he will keep my word, and my Father will love him, and we will make our home with him. These things I have spoken to you, while I am still with you. But the Counselor, the Holy Spirit, whom the Father will send in my name, he will teach you all things, and bring to your remembrance all that I have said to you. Peace I leave with you; my peace I give to you; not as the world gives do I give to you. Let not your hearts be troubled, neither let them be afraid. You heard me say to you, 'I go away, and I will come to you.' If you loved me, you would have rejoiced, because I go to the Father; for the Father is greater than I. I have told you before it takes place, so that when it does take place, you may believe. I will no longer talk much with you, for the ruler of this world is coming. He has no power over me; but I do as the Father has commanded me, so that the world may know that I love the Father.

"I am the true vine, and my Father is the vinedresser. Every branch of mine that bears no fruit, he takes away, and every branch that does bear fruit he prunes, that it may bear more fruit. As the branch cannot bear fruit by itself, unless it abides in the vine, neither can you, unless you abide in me. I am the vine, you are the branches. Apart from me you can do nothing. If you abide in me, and my words abide in you, ask whatever you will, and it shall be done for you. By this my Father is glorified, that you bear much fruit, and so prove to be my disciples. As the Father has loved me, so have I loved you. If you keep my commandments, you will abide in my love, just as I have kept my Father's commandments and abide in his love. These things I have spoken to you, that my joy may be in you, and that your joy may be full.

"This is my commandment, that you love one another as I have loved you. Greater love has no man than this, that he lay down his life for his friends. You are my friends if you do what I command. No longer do I call you servants, for the servant does not know what his master is doing; but all that I have heard from my Father I have made known to you. You did not choose me, but I chose you and appointed you, that you should go and bear fruit and that your fruit should abide; so that whatever you ask the Father in my name, he may give it to you. This I command you, to love one another.

"If the world hates you, know that it has hated me before it hated you. If you were of the world, the world would love its own; because you are not of the world, because I chose you out of the world, therefore the world hates you. Remember that I said to you, 'A servant is not greater than his master.' If they persecuted me, they will persecute you. But this they will do on my account, because they do not know him who sent me. He who hates me hates my Father also. If I had not done among them the works which no one else did, they would not have sin; but now they have seen and hated both me and my Father. It is to fulfil the word that is written in their law, 'They hated me without a cause.' But when the Counselor comes, the Spirit of truth, who proceeds from the Father, he will bear witness to me. And you also are witnesses, because you have been with me from the beginning.

"I have said all this to keep you from falling away. They will put you out of the synagogues; indeed, the hour is coming when whoever kills you will think he is offering service to God. And they will do this because they have not known the Father, nor me. But I have said these things to you, that when their hour comes you may remember that I told you of them. I did not say these things to you from the beginning, because I was with you. But now I am going to him who sent me, and because I have said these things, sorrow has filled your hearts. Nevertheless, it is to your advantage that I go away, for if I do not go, the Counselor will not come to you; but if I go, I will send him. When he comes, he will convince the world concerning sin and righteousness and judgment: concerning sin, because they do not believe in me; concerning righteousness, because I go to the Father, and you will see me no more; concerning judgment, because the ruler of this world is judged.

"I have yet many things to say to you, but you cannot bear them now. When the Spirit of truth comes, he will guide you into all the truth; for he will not speak on his own authority, but whatever he hears he will speak, and he will declare to you the things to come. He will glorify me, for he will take what is mine and declare it to you. All that the Father has is mine; therefore I said that he will take what is mine and declare it to you. A little while, and you will see me no more; again a little while, and you will see me."

Some of his disciples said to one another, "What is this that he says? We do not know what he means."

Jesus knew that they did not understand, so he said, "Truly, truly, I say to you, you will weep and lament, but the world will rejoice; you will be sorrowful, but your sorrow will turn into joy. When a woman is in travail she has sorrow, because her hour has come; but when she is delivered of the child, she no longer remembers the anguish, for joy that a child is born into the world. So you have sorrow now, but I will see you again and your hearts will rejoice, and no one will take your joy from you. In that day you will ask nothing of me, but if you ask anything of the Father, he will give it to you in my name; ask, and you will receive, that your joy may be full. I have said this to you in figures; the hour is coming when I shall no longer speak in figures but tell you plainly of the Father. The Father himself loves you, because you loved me and believed that I came from him. I came from the Father and have come into the world; again, I am leaving the world and going to the Father."

"Ah, now you are speaking plainly," the disciples said, "not in any figure! Now we know that you know all things, and need none to question you; by this we believe that you came from God."

"Do you now believe?" Jesus said. "The hour is coming, indeed it has come, when you will be scattered, every man to his home, and will leave me alone; yet I am not alone, for the Father is with me. I have said this to you, that in me you may have peace. In the world you have tribulation; but be of good cheer, I have overcome the world."

Jesus then lifted up his eyes to heaven, and said, "Father, the hour has come; glorify thy Son that the Son may glorify thee, since thou hast given him power over all flesh, to give eternal life to all whom thou hast given him. And this is eternal life, that they know thee the only true God, and Jesus Christ whom thou hast sent. I glorified thee on earth, having accomplished the work which thou gavest me to do; and now, Father, glorify thou me in thy own presence with the glory which I had with thee before the world was made.

"I have manifested thy name to the men whom thou gavest me out of the world, and they have kept thy word. Now they know that everything is from thee; for I have given them the words which thou gavest me, and they know in truth that I came from thee, that thou didst send me. I am praying for them, not for the world, but for those whom thou hast given me. All mine are thine, and thine are mine, and I am glorified in them. Holy Father, keep them in thy name that they may be one, even as we are one. While I was with them, I guarded them in thy name, and none of them is lost but the son of perdition, that the scripture might be fulfilled. But now I am coming to thee; and these things I speak in the world, that they may have my joy fulfilled in themselves. The world has hated them because they are not of the world. I do not pray that thou shouldst take them out of the world, but that thou shouldst keep them from the evil one. Sanctify them in the truth; thy word is truth. As thou didst send me into the world, so I have sent them into the world. And for their sake I consecrate myself, that they also may be consecrated in truth.

"I do not pray for these only, but also for those who believe in me through their word, that they may all be one. The glory which thou hast given me I have given to them, that they may be one even as we are one, I in them and thou in me, that they may become perfectly one, so that the world may know that thou hast sent me and hast loved them even as thou hast loved me. Father, I desire that they also may be with me where I am, to behold my glory which thou hast given me before the foundation of the world. O righteous Father, the world has not known thee, but I have known thee; and these know that thou hast sent me. I made known to them thy name, and I will make it known, that the love with which thou hast loved me may be in them, and I in them."

When Jesus had spoken these words, he went with his disciples across the Kidron valley to a garden, which they entered. Judas Iscariot also knew the place (for Jesus often met there with his disciples), so he procured a band of soldiers from the chief priests and the Pharisees, and went there with lanterns and weapons. Jesus, knowing all that was to befall him, came forward and said, "Whom do you seek?"

"Jesus of Nazareth," they answered.

"I am he," Jesus said.

At this they drew back and fell to the ground. Again he asked, "Whom do you seek?"

"Jesus of Nazareth," they said again.

"I told you that I am he," said Jesus. "If you seek me, let these men go." This was to fulfil the word which he had spoken, "Of those whom thou gavest me I lost not one."

Then Peter, having a sword, drew it and struck the high priest's slave (whose name was Malchus) and cut off his right ear. "Put your sword into its sheath," Jesus said. "Shall I not drink the cup which the Father has given me?" Then the soldiers seized Jesus and bound him, and they led him to Annas, the father-in-law of Caiaphas.

Peter and another disciple followed Jesus. As this other disciple was known to the high priest, he entered the court along with Jesus, while Peter stood outside. So the other disciple spoke to the maid who kept the door, and brought Peter in. The maid said to Peter, "Are not you also one of this man's disciples?" He said, "I am not." Now the soldiers had made a charcoal fire, and Peter stood with them, warming himself.

The high priest then questioned Jesus about his disciples and his teaching. "I have spoken openly to the world," Jesus answered. "I have always taught in synagogues and in the temple, where all Jews come together; I have said nothing secretly. Why do you ask me? Ask those who have heard me." At this, one of the officers struck Jesus with his hand, saying, "Is that how you answer the high priest?"

"If I have spoken wrongly," said Jesus, "bear witness to the wrong; but if I have spoken rightly, why do you strike me?" Annas then sent him bound to Caiaphas the high priest.

Now Peter was standing and warming himself. Some said to him, "Are not you also one of his disciples?" He denied it, and said, "I am not." One of the servants of the high priest, a kinsman of the man whose ear Peter had cut off, asked, "Did I not see you in the garden with him?" Peter again denied it; and at once a cock crowed.

Early in the morning they led Jesus from the house of Caiaphas to the praetorium. The Jews themselves did not enter the praetorium, that they might not be defiled, but might eat the passover, so Pilate went out to them. "What accusation do you bring against this man?" he asked.

"If this man were not an evildoer," they answered, "we would not have handed him over."

"Take him yourselves," said Pilate, "and judge him by your own law."

"It is not lawful for us to put any man to death," they said. This was to fulfil the word which Jesus had spoken to show by what death he was to die. Pilate entered the praetorium, called Jesus, and said, "Are you the King of the Jews?"

"Do you say this of your own accord," asked Jesus, "or did others say it to you about me?"

"Am I a Jew?" Pilate answered. "Your own nation and the chief priests have handed you over to me; what have you done?"

"My kingship is not of this world," Jesus answered. "If my kingship were of this world, my servants would fight, that I might not be handed over to the Jews; but my kingship is not from the world."

"So you are a king?" Pilate asked.

"You say that I am a king," Jesus replied. "For this I was born, and for this I have come into the world, to bear witness to the truth. Every one who is of the truth hears my voice."

"What is truth?" Pilate asked. Then he went out to the Jews again, and told them, "I find no crime in him. But you have a custom that I should release one man for you at the Passover; will you have me release for you the King of the Jews?" They cried out, "Not this man, but Barabbas!" Now Barabbas was a robber.

Then Pilate took Jesus and scourged him. And the soldiers plaited a crown of thorns, and put it on his head, and arrayed him in a purple robe. "Hail, King of the Jews!" they said, and struck him with their hands. Pilate went out again, and said to the crowd, "See, I am bringing him out to you, that you may know that I find no crime in him." Wearing the crown of thorns and the purple robe, Jesus came out.

"Behold the man!" Pilate said.

When the chief priests and the officers saw him, they cried out, "Crucify him, crucify him!"

"Take him yourselves," said Pilate, "and crucify him, for I find no crime in him."

"We have a law," the Jews answered, "and by that law he ought to die, because he has made himself the Son of God." When Pilate heard this, he was the more afraid; he entered the praetorium, and said to Jesus, "Where are you from?" But Jesus gave no answer. Pilate therefore said, "You will not speak to me? Do you not know that I have power to release you, and power to crucify you?"

"You would have no power over me," Jesus answered, "unless it had been given you from above; therefore he who delivered me to you has the greater sin."

Upon this, Pilate sought to release him, but the Jews cried out, "If you release this man, you are not Caesar's friend; every one who makes himself a king sets himself against Caesar." Then Pilate brought Jesus out and sat on the judgment seat at a place called The Pavement. Now it was the day of Preparation of the Passover, about the sixth hour. Pilate said to the Jews, "Behold your King!"

"Away with him," they cried out, "away with him, crucify him!"

"Shall I crucify your King?" Pilate asked.

"We have no king but Caesar," the chief priests answered. Then Pilate handed him over to be crucified.

They took Jesus, and he went out, bearing his own cross, to the place of the skull, called in Hebrew, Golgotha. There they crucified him, and with him two others, one on either side. Pilate also put a title on the cross in Hebrew, Latin, and Greek; it read, "Jesus of Nazareth, the King of the Jews." Many of the Jews read this title, for Golgotha was near the city, and the chief priests said to Pilate, "Do not write, 'The King of the Jews,' but, 'This man said, I am King of the Jews.'"

"What I have written," Pilate answered, "I have written."

The soldiers then took his garments and made four parts, one for each soldier. But the tunic was without seam, woven from top to bottom; so they said, "Let us not tear it, but cast lots for it." This was to fulfil the scripture, "They parted my garments among them, and for my clothing they cast lots."

Standing by the cross were his mother, and his mother's sister, Mary the wife of Clopas, and Mary Magdalene. When Jesus saw his mother, and the disciple whom he loved standing near, he said to his mother, "Woman, behold, your son!" Then he said to the disciple, "Behold, your mother!" From that hour the disciple took her to his own home.

After this, Jesus, knowing that all was now finished, said (to fulfil the scripture), "I thirst." A bowl full of vinegar stood there; so they put a sponge full of the vinegar on a reed and held it to his mouth. When Jesus had received the vinegar, he said, "It is finished"; and he bowed his head and gave up his spirit.

Since it was the day of Preparation, in order to prevent the bodies from remaining on the cross on the sabbath, the Jews asked Pilate that their legs might be broken, and that they might be taken away. So the soldiers broke the legs of the two who had been crucified with him. When they came to Jesus and saw that he was already dead, they did not break his legs, but a soldier pierced his side with a spear, and at once there came out blood and water. He who saw it has borne witness—his testimony is true, and he knows that he tells the truth—that you also may believe. For these things took place that the scriptures might be fulfilled, "Not a bone of him shall be broken," and, "They shall look on him whom they have pierced."

After this, Joseph of Arimathea, who was a secret disciple of Jesus, asked Pilate for the body, and Pilate gave him leave. Nicodemus, who had come to Jesus by night, brought a mixture of myrrh and aloes, about a hundred pounds' weight; then they bound the body of Jesus in linen cloths with the spices, as is the burial custom of the Jews. Now there was a garden nearby, and in it a new tomb where no one had ever been laid. There they laid Jesus.

Now on the first day of the week Mary Magdalene came to the tomb while it was still dark, and saw that the stone had been taken away. She ran to Peter and the other disciple, the one whom Jesus loved, and said, "They have taken the Lord out of the tomb, and we do not know where they have laid him." Peter then ran with the other disciple to the tomb, but the other disciple reached the tomb first. Stooping to look in, he saw the linen cloths lying there, but he did not go in. Then Peter came and went into the tomb, and he saw the linen cloths lying, and the napkin, which had been on Jesus' head, rolled up in a place by itself. Then the other disciple went in, and he saw and believed; for as yet they did not know the scripture, that he must rise from the dead. Then the two went home.

But Mary Magdalene stood weeping outside the tomb. She stooped to look in, and saw two angels in white sitting where the body of Jesus had lain, one at the head and one at the feet. "Woman," they said, "why are you weeping?"

"Because they have taken away my Lord," she said, "and I do not know where they have laid him." Then she turned and saw Jesus standing, but she did not know that it was he.

"Woman, why are you weeping?" Jesus said. "Whom do you seek?"

Supposing him to be the gardener, she said, "Sir, if you have carried him away, tell me where you have laid him, and I will take him away."

"Mary," said Jesus. She turned and said in Hebrew, "Rabboni!" (which means Teacher).

"Do not hold me," Jesus said, "for I have not yet ascended to the Father; but go to my brethren and say to them, I am ascending to my Father and your Father, to my God and your God." She went and said to the disciples, "I have seen the Lord," and she told them that Jesus had said these things to her.

That evening, the doors being shut where the disciples were, for fear of the Jews, Jesus came and stood among them. "Peace be with you," he said, and he showed them his hands and his side. Then the disciples were glad, and Jesus said, "As the Father has sent me, even so I send you." He breathed on them, and said, "Receive the Holy Spirit. If you forgive the sins of any, they are forgiven; if you retain the sins of any, they are retained."

Now Thomas, one of the twelve, called the Twin, was not there when Jesus came. So the other disciples told him, "We have seen the Lord." But he said, "Unless I see in his hands the print of the nails, and place my finger in the mark of the nails, and place my hand in his side, I will not believe." Eight days later the disciples were again in the house, and Thomas was with them. The doors were shut, but Jesus came and stood among them, and said, "Peace be with you." Then he said to Thomas, "Put your finger here, and see my hands; and put out your hand, and place it in my side; do not be faithless, but believing." Thomas answered, "My Lord and my God!"

"Have you believed because you have seen me?" Jesus said. "Blessed are those who have not seen and yet believe."

Now Jesus did many other signs in the presence of the disciples, which are not written in this book; but these are written that you may believe that Jesus is the Christ, the Son of God, and that believing, you may have life in his name.

AFTER THIS, JESUS revealed himself again to the disciples by the Sea of Galilee, in this way. Some of them were together, and Peter said, "I am going fishing." They all went out in the boat, but that night they caught nothing. As day was breaking, Jesus stood on the beach; yet the disciples did not know him. "Children," he said, "have you any fish?"

"No," they answered.

"Cast the net on the right side of the boat," he said, "and you will find some." They cast it, and now they were not able to haul it in, for the quantity of fish. That disciple whom Jesus loved said to Peter, "It is the Lord!" When Peter heard this, he sprang into the sea, but the others came in the boat, dragging the net full of fish.

On land, they saw a charcoal fire, with fish lying on it. "Bring some of the fish you caught," Jesus said. Peter hauled the net ashore, full of large fish, a hundred and fifty-three of them, and although there were so many, the net was not torn.

"Come and have breakfast," Jesus said. Now none of the disciples dared ask, "Who are you?" They knew it was the Lord. Jesus gave them some bread, and so with the fish. This was now the third time that Jesus was revealed to the disciples after he was raised from the dead.

When they had finished breakfast, Jesus said to Peter, "Simon, son of John, do you love me more than these?"

"Yes, Lord," said Peter, "you know that I love you."

"Feed my lambs," Jesus said. A second time he said to him, "Simon, son of John, do you love me?"

"Yes, Lord," said Peter, "you know that I love you."

"Tend my sheep," Jesus said. Then he said to him the third time, "Simon, son of John, do you love me?"

Peter was grieved because he asked this the third time, and he said, "Lord, you know everything; you know that I love you."

"Feed my sheep," Jesus said. "Truly, truly, I say to you, when you were young, you girded yourself and walked where you would; but when you are old, you will stretch out your hands, and another will gird you and carry you where you do not wish to go." (This he said to show by what death he was to glorify God.) Then he said, "Follow me." Peter turned and saw following them the disciple whom Jesus loved, who had lain close to his breast at the supper. "Lord," he asked, "what about this man?"

"If it is my will," Jesus answered, "that he remain until I come, what is that to you? Follow me!" The saying spread among the brethren that this disciple was not to die; yet Jesus did not say that he was not to die, but, "If it is my will that he remain until I come, what is that to you?" This is the disciple who is bearing witness to these things, and who has written these things; and we know that his testimony is true.

But there are also many other things which Jesus did; were every one of them to be written, I suppose that the world itself could not contain the books that would be written.

THE ACTS
OF THE APOSTLES

In its opening paragraph this book describes itself as a continuation of the Gospel according to Luke. It is the earliest account of the formation and spread of the Christian church after the resurrection of Jesus Christ. It tells of the first apostolic sermon, the first apostolic miracle, the first steps toward organization, the first persecution, the first Christian martyr, the first Gentile convert, the first European church. The book forms a natural transition between the four Gospel accounts and the twenty-one letters written by Paul and others.

Initially, the apostles Peter and John play the leading roles; then the narrative concentrates on the work of Paul, apostle to the Gentiles. In this section the author sometimes writes "we" instead of "they," suggesting that he has made verbatim use of a "travel diary." Nothing is said at the close of the book about Paul's fate in Rome. This is seen by some as indicating the date of composition, that is, about A.D. 68. Others prefer a date between 75 and 85.

A special feature is the emphasis on the work of the Holy Spirit in guiding the disciples and their converts. Luke also tries to reassure his readers that Christians are not a subversive political threat to the Roman Empire. The Christian faith, he explains, is the fulfillment of the Jewish religion, and membership is open to all who repent and believe the gospel.

IN THE FIRST book, O Theophilus, I have dealt with all that Jesus began to do and teach, until the day when he was taken up, after he had given commandment through the Holy Spirit to the apostles whom he had chosen. He presented himself alive after his passion by many proofs, appearing and speaking to them during forty days. And while staying with them he charged them not to depart from Jerusalem, but to wait for the promise of the Father. "John baptized with water," he said, "but before many days you shall be baptized with the Holy Spirit."

When the disciples had come together at Mount Olivet, they asked him, "Lord, will you at this time restore the kingdom to Israel?"

"It is not for you to know times or seasons," he said, "which the Father has fixed by his own authority. But you shall receive power when the Holy Spirit has come upon you; and you shall be my witnesses in Jerusalem and in all Judea and Samaria and to the end of the earth."

When he had said this he was lifted up, and a cloud took him out of their sight. And behold, two men stood by them in white robes and said, "Men of Galilee, why do you stand looking into heaven? This Jesus, who was taken up into heaven, will come in the same way as you saw him go." They returned to Jerusalem and went to the upper room, where they were staying. With one accord they devoted themselves to prayer, together with the women, and Mary the mother of Jesus, and his brothers.

In those days Peter stood up among the brethren (in all about a hundred and twenty). "The scripture had to be fulfilled," he said, "which the Holy Spirit spoke by the mouth of David, concerning Judas, who was one of our number and shared in this ministry. (This man bought a field with the reward of his wickedness; and falling headlong he burst open in the middle and all his bowels gushed out; that field is called Akeldama, Field of Blood.) Now it is written in the book of Psalms, 'His office let another take.' So one of the men who accompanied us during all the time that the Lord Jesus went in and out among us must become with us a witness to his resurrection." They put forward two men, and they prayed, "Lord, who knowest the hearts of all men, show which of these two thou hast chosen." Then they cast lots, and the lot fell on Matthias, and he was enrolled with the eleven apostles.

When the day of Pentecost had come, they were all together in one place. Suddenly there was a sound from heaven like the rush of a mighty wind, filling the house. And there appeared tongues as of fire, distributed and resting on each one of them. All were filled with the Holy Spirit, and they left the house and began to speak in other tongues, as the Spirit gave them utterance.

Now there were dwelling in Jerusalem devout Jews from every nation under heaven. And the multitude was amazed because each one heard them speaking in his own language. "Are not all these Galileans?" they said. "How is it that each of us hears in his own tongue?"

"They are filled with new wine," others mocked.

But Peter addressed the crowd in a loud voice. "Men of Judea and all who dwell in Jerusalem," he said, "give ear to my words. These men are not drunk, as you suppose, since it is still early morning. But this is what was spoken by the prophet Joel: 'And in the last days it shall be, God declares, that I will pour out my Spirit upon all flesh, and your sons and your daughters shall prophesy, and your young men shall see visions, and your old men shall dream dreams. And I will show wonders in the heaven above and signs on the earth beneath; the sun shall be turned into darkness and the moon into blood, before the day of the Lord comes. And whoever calls on the name of the Lord shall be saved.' Men of Israel, hear these words: Jesus of Nazareth, a man attested to you by God with mighty works and signs, delivered up according to the definite plan and foreknowledge of God, you crucified and killed by the hands of lawless men. But God raised him up, having loosed the pangs of death, because it was not possible for him to be held by it. For David says concerning him, 'Thou wilt not abandon my soul to Hades, nor let thy Holy One see corruption.' Now David both died and was buried, and his tomb is with us to this day. Being therefore a prophet, he foresaw and spoke of the resurrection of the Christ, that he was not abandoned to Hades, nor did his flesh see corruption. This Jesus God raised up, and of that we all are witnesses. Being therefore exalted at the right hand of God, and having received from the Father the promise of the Holy Spirit, he has poured out this which you see and hear."

When the people heard this they were cut to the heart. "Brethren," they said, "what shall we do?"

"Repent," said Peter, "and be baptized in the name of Jesus Christ for the forgiveness of your sins; and you shall receive the gift of the Holy Spirit. For the promise is to you and to your children and to all that are far off, every one whom the Lord our God calls to him. Save yourselves from this crooked generation." Those who received his word were baptized, and there were added that day about three thousand souls.

All who believed were together and had all things in common. They sold their possessions and goods and distributed them to all, as any had need. Attending the temple together and breaking bread in their homes, they partook of food with glad and generous hearts, praising God and having favor with all the people. And day by day the Lord added to their number.

Now as Peter and John were going up to the temple at the hour of afternoon prayer, a man lame from birth asked for alms. Peter directed his gaze at him and said, "I have no silver and gold, but I give you what I have; in the name of Jesus Christ of Nazareth, walk." And he took him by the right hand and raised him up, and immediately his feet and ankles were made strong. Leaping up, he entered the temple with them, walking and leaping and praising God. The people recognized him as the one who always sat for alms at the temple, a man more than forty years old, and they were filled with amazement at what had happened.

While he clung to Peter and John, all the people ran to them in the portico called Solomon's. "Men of Israel, why do you stare at us," said Peter, "as though by our own power or piety we had made him walk? The God of Abraham, Isaac, and Jacob glorified his servant Jesus, whom you delivered up and denied in the presence of Pilate. You denied the Holy and Righteous One, and killed the Author of life, whom God raised from the dead. To this we are witnesses. And the faith which is through Jesus has given this man perfect health in the presence of you all. I know that you acted in ignorance, brethren, as did also your rulers. But what God foretold by the prophets, that his

Christ should suffer, he thus fulfilled. Repent therefore, and turn again, that your sins may be blotted out, and that God may send the Christ appointed for you, Jesus, whom heaven must receive until the time for establishing all that God spoke by the mouth of his holy prophets from of old. You are the sons of the prophets and of the covenant which God gave to your fathers, saying to Abraham, 'In your posterity shall all the families of the earth be blessed.' God, having raised up his servant, sent him to you first, to bless you in turning every one of you from your wickedness."

As Peter and John were speaking, the priests and the captain of the temple and the Sadducees came up, annoyed because they were proclaiming in Jesus the resurrection from the dead. They arrested them and put them in custody until the morrow, for it was already evening. But many of those who heard the word believed; and the number of the men came to about five thousand.

The next day the rulers, elders, and scribes were gathered together, with Annas the high priest and Caiaphas and all who were of the high-priestly family, and with Peter and John set in their midst. "By what power or by what name did you do this?" they inquired.

"Rulers of the people and elders," said Peter, "if we are being examined today concerning a good deed done to a cripple, by what means this man has been healed, be it known that by the name of Jesus Christ of Nazareth, whom you crucified, whom God raised from the dead, by him this man is standing before you well. This is the stone which was rejected by you builders, but which has become the head of the corner. And there is salvation in no one else, for there is no other name under heaven given among men by which we must be saved."

When the rulers saw the boldness of Peter and John, and knowing that they were uneducated, common men, they wondered; and they recognized that they had been with Jesus. But seeing the man that had been healed standing beside them, they had nothing to say in opposition. Then they commanded Peter and John to go aside out of the council, and they conferred with one another. "What shall we do with these men?" they said. "For that a notable sign has been performed through them we cannot deny. In order that it may spread no further among the people, let us warn them to speak no more to any one in this name." Calling the two back, they charged them not to speak or teach at all in the name of Jesus. But Peter and John answered, "Whether it is right in the sight of God to listen to you rather than to God, you must judge. We cannot but speak of what we have seen and heard." When the rulers had further threatened them, they let them go, finding no way to punish them, because of the people; for all men praised God for what had happened.

Afterward Peter and John reported to their friends what the chief priests and the elders had said, and they all lifted their voices together to God. "Sovereign Lord," they prayed, "who didst make the heaven and the earth and the sea and everything in them, grant to thy servants to speak thy word with all boldness, while thou stretchest out thy hand to heal, and signs and wonders are performed through the name of thy holy servant Jesus." Then the place in which they were gathered together was shaken; and they were all filled with the Holy Spirit and spoke the word of God with boldness.

Now in the company of those who believed, no one said that any of the things which he possessed was his own. Those who had lands or houses sold them, and laid the proceeds at the apostles' feet. But a man named Ananias sold a piece of property, and with his wife's knowledge secretly kept back some of the proceeds. At this Peter said, "Ananias, why has Satan filled your heart to lie to the Holy Spirit? While the land remained unsold, was it not your own? And after it was sold, was it not at your disposal? You have not lied to men but to God." When Ananias heard these words, he fell down and died, and the young men wrapped him up and carried him out and buried him. About three hours later his wife, Sapphira, came in, not knowing what had happened. "Tell me," said Peter, "whether you sold the land for so much." She said, "Yes, for so much." Then Peter said to her, "How is it that you have agreed together to tempt the Spirit of the Lord? Hark, the feet of those that have buried your husband are at the door, and they will carry you out." Immediately she fell down and died. The young men carried her out and buried her beside her husband, and great fear came upon all who heard of these things.

Many signs and wonders were done by the hands of the apostles, and people even carried out the sick into the streets, and laid them on pallets, that as Peter came by at least his shadow might fall on them. From the towns around Jerusalem the sick were brought, and those afflicted with unclean spirits, and they were all healed. But at this the high priest and those with him, that is, the party of the Sadducees, were filled with jealousy. So they arrested the apostles and put them in the common prison. That night an angel of the Lord opened the prison doors and brought them out, saying, "Go and stand in the temple and speak to the people all the words of this Life." And at daybreak they entered the temple and taught.

Now the high priest called together the council and all the senate of Israel, and sent to the prison for the apostles. When the officers returned they reported, "We found the prison securely locked and the sentries standing at the doors, but when we opened it we found no one inside." At first the chief priests were much perplexed; then some one came and told them that the apostles were teaching in the temple. So the officers went and brought them, but without violence, for they were afraid of being stoned by the people.

Setting the apostles before the council, the high priest questioned them. "We strictly charged you, " he said, "not to teach in this name, yet here you have filled Jerusalem with your teaching and you intend to bring this man's blood upon us."

"We must obey God rather than men," they answered. "The God of our fathers raised Jesus whom you killed by hanging him on a tree. God exalted him at his right hand as Leader and Savior, to give repentance to Israel and forgiveness of sins. And we are witnesses to these things, and so is the Holy Spirit whom God has given to those who obey him."

At this the council was enraged and wanted to kill them. But a Pharisee named Gamaliel, a teacher held in honor by all the people, stood up and ordered the apostles to be put outside. "Men of Israel," he said to the council, "take care what you do. For before these days Theudas arose, giving himself out to be somebody, and about four hundred men joined him; but he was slain and his movement came to nothing. After him Judas the Galilean drew some of the people after him, but he also perished. So in the present case I tell you, let these men alone. If this undertaking is of men, it will fail; but if it is of God, you will not be able to overthrow them. You might even be found opposing God!" They called in the apostles, beat them, charged them not to speak in the name of Jesus, then let them go. And every day in the temple and at home the apostles did not cease preaching Jesus as the Christ.

Now in these days when the disciples were increasing in number, the Hellenists murmured against the Hebrews because their widows were neglected in the daily distribution. So the twelve summoned the disciples and said, "It is not right that we should give up preaching the word of God to serve tables. Therefore, brethren, pick out from among you seven men of good repute, full of the Spirit and of wisdom, whom we may appoint to this duty. We will devote ourselves to prayer and to the ministry of the word." This pleased the whole multitude, so they chose the seven and set them before the apostles, who prayed and laid hands upon them.

One of the seven was a man named Stephen. Full of grace and power, he did great wonders and signs among the people, and also disputed with those who belonged to the synagogue of the Freedmen, and others. But none could withstand the wisdom and the Spirit with which he spoke, so they secretly instigated men who said, "We have heard him speak blasphemous words against Moses and God." They also stirred up the people and the elders and the scribes. Finally they seized Stephen, brought him before the council, and set up false witnesses who said, "This man never ceases to speak words against this holy place and the law. We have heard him say that this Jesus of Nazareth will destroy this place, and will change the customs which Moses delivered to us."

"Is this so?" asked the high priest.

"Brethren, hear me," said Stephen. "The God of glory appeared to our father Abraham, and gave him the covenant of circumcision. And Abraham became the father of Isaac, and Isaac of Jacob, and Jacob of the twelve patriarchs. And the patriarchs, jealous of Joseph, sold him into Egypt; but God was with him, and rescued him out of all his afflictions. Then in Egypt God raised up Moses, and he led the people out, having performed wonders and signs in Egypt and at the Red Sea and in the wilderness. But our fathers refused to obey him. They thrust him aside, and they made a calf and offered a sacrifice to the idol and rejoiced in the works of their hands. Our fathers had the tent of witness in the wilderness, and so it was until Solomon built the temple, yet the Most High does not dwell in houses made with hands. As the prophet says, 'Heaven is my throne, and earth my footstool.'

"You stiff-necked people, uncircumcised in heart and ears! You always resist the Holy Spirit. As your fathers did, so do you. Which of the prophets did not your fathers persecute? They killed those who announced beforehand the coming of the Righteous One, whom you have now betrayed and murdered, you who received the law as delivered by angels and did not keep it."

When they heard these things they were enraged, and they ground their teeth against Stephen. But he, full of the Holy Spirit, gazed into heaven and saw the glory of God, and Jesus standing at his right hand. And Stephen's face was like the face of an angel. "Behold, I see the heavens opened," he said, "and the Son of man standing at the right hand of God." Then they cried out with a loud voice and stopped their ears and rushed together upon him. They cast him out of the city and stoned him, and as they were stoning him he prayed, "Lord Jesus, receive my spirit." Then he knelt down and cried with a loud voice, "Lord, do not hold this sin against them." And he fell asleep, and he was buried by devout men who made great lamentation over him.

Those who threw the stones had laid their garments at the feet of a man named Saul, who was consenting to Stephen's death. Now on that day a great persecution arose against the church in Jerusalem, and all except the apostles were scattered throughout the region of Judea and Samaria. Saul himself began ravaging the church, and entering house after house, he dragged off men and women and committed them to prison.

Those who were scattered went about preaching the word. Philip proclaimed the Christ in the city of Samaria, and the multitudes with one accord gave heed to what he said when they saw the signs he did; unclean spirits came out of many who were possessed, and many who were paralyzed or lame were healed. Also in Samaria there was a man named Simon, a magician, who amazed every one. All gave heed to him, from the least to the greatest, saying, "This man is that power of God which is called Great." But when Philip preached the good news about the kingdom of God and Jesus Christ, even Simon himself believed, and after being baptized he continued with Philip. But Simon's heart was not right before God.

When the apostles at Jerusalem heard that many Samaritans had received the word of God and been baptized, but that the Holy Spirit had not yet fallen on any of them, they sent Peter and John. The two laid their hands on them and they received the Holy Spirit. When Simon saw this, he offered them money. "Give me this power, " he said, "that any one on whom I lay my hands may receive the Holy Spirit."

"Your silver perish with you," said Peter, "because you thought you could obtain the gift of God with money! Repent and pray to the Lord that, if possible, this may be forgiven you. For I see that you are in the gall of bitterness and the bond of iniquity."

"Pray for me to the Lord," Simon answered, "that nothing of what you have said may come upon me." Peter and John then returned to Jerusalem, preaching the gospel to many villages of the Samaritans.

Now an angel of the Lord said to Philip, "Rise and go toward the south to the road that goes down from Jerusalem to Gaza." Philip went, and behold, he saw an Ethiopian, a eunuch, a minister of the Candace, queen of Ethiopia. He had come to Jerusalem to worship and was returning; seated in his chariot, he was reading aloud the prophet Isaiah. To Philip the Spirit said, "Go up and join this chariot." Philip ran up, heard him reading Isaiah, and asked, "Do you understand what you are reading?"

"How can I, unless some one guides me?" the eunuch replied, inviting Philip to sit with him. Now the passage he was reading was this: "As a sheep led to the slaughter or a lamb before its shearer is dumb, so he opens not his mouth. In his humiliation justice was denied him. Who can describe his generation? For his life is taken up from the earth."

"About whom," the eunuch asked, "does the prophet say this, about himself or about some one else?"

Then Philip, beginning with this scripture, told the good news of Jesus. As they went along the road they came to some water, and the eunuch said, "See, here is water! What is to prevent my being baptized?" He commanded the chariot to stop, and they both went down into the water, and the eunuch was baptized. And the Spirit of the Lord caught up Philip, and the eunuch saw him no more, and he went on his way rejoicing. But Philip was found at Azotus, and he preached the gospel to all the towns till he came to Caesarea.

About this time Saul, still breathing threats against the disciples, went to the high priest and asked for letters to the synagogues at Damascus, so that if he found any there belonging to the Way he might bring them bound to Jerusalem. Now as he approached Damascus on his journey, a light from heaven suddenly flashed about him. He fell to the ground and he heard a voice saying, "Saul, Saul, why do you persecute me?"

"Who are you, Lord?" Saul asked.

"I am Jesus, whom you are persecuting," said the voice. "But rise and enter the city, and you will be told what you are to do."

The men who were traveling with Saul stood speechless, hearing the voice but seeing no one. Saul arose, but he was without sight, so they led him by the hand into Damascus, and for three days he neither ate nor drank.

At Damascus there was a disciple named Ananias. To him the Lord said in a vision, "Rise and go to the street called Straight, and inquire in the house of Judas for a man of Tarsus named Saul; for behold, he is praying, and he has seen a man named Ananias come in and lay his hands on him so that he might regain his sight."

"Lord," Ananias answered, "I have heard from many about this man, how much evil he has done to thy saints at Jerusalem. He has authority from the chief priests to bind all who call upon thy name."

But the Lord said, "Go, for he is a chosen instrument of mine to carry my name before the Gentiles and kings and the sons of Israel; for I will show him how much he must suffer for the sake of my name."

Ananias departed, entered the house, and laid his hands on Saul. "Brother," he said, "the Lord Jesus, who appeared to you on the road by which you came, has sent me that you may regain your sight and be filled with the Holy Spirit." Immediately something like scales fell from Saul's eyes and he regained his sight. Then he rose and was baptized, and took food and was strengthened. Several days later, in the synagogues of Damascus, he proclaimed Jesus, saying, "He is the Son of God."

All who heard Saul were amazed. "Is not this the man who made havoc in Jerusalem of those who called on this name?" they said. "Has he not come here to bring them bound before the chief priests?" But Saul increased all the more in strength, and confounded the Jews who lived in Damascus by proving that Jesus was the Christ. At last the Jews plotted to kill him, and they were watching the gates night and day. The plot became known to Saul, so his disciples took him by night and let him down over the wall in a basket.

Going to Jerusalem, Saul attempted to join the disciples. But they were all afraid of him, for they did not believe that he had changed. Then Barnabas (a Levite and a native of Cyprus, whose name means Son of encouragement) brought him to the apostles, and told how, on the road to Damascus, Saul had seen and heard the Lord, and how he had afterward preached boldly in the name of Jesus. So Saul was accepted, and for a time he went in and out among them at Jerusalem. But when he spoke and disputed against the Hellenists, they were displeased and began seeking to kill him. When the brethren heard this, they brought Saul to Caesarea, then to Tarsus.

In those days, as Peter traveled here and there among the brethren, he visited the saints that lived at Lydda. A man was there named Aeneas, who had been bedridden for eight years and was paralyzed. Peter spoke to him, saying, "Aeneas, Jesus Christ heals you; rise and make your bed." Immediately he rose, and all the residents of Lydda saw him, and they turned to the Lord. After this, at Joppa, which was near Lydda, a disciple named Tabitha, full of good works and charity, fell sick and died. Hearing that Peter was at Lydda, the disciples sent men to entreat him to come without delay. Peter went with them, and at Joppa they took him to an upper room where all the widows were gathered, weeping and showing tunics and other garments which Tabitha had made. Putting them all outside, Peter knelt down and prayed. Then, turning to the body, he said, "Tabitha, rise." She opened her eyes, and when she saw Peter she sat up. He gave her his hand and lifted her from the bed. Then, calling the saints and widows, he presented her alive. This became known throughout all Joppa, and many believed in the Lord.

At Caesarea there was a man named Cornelius, a centurion of the Italian Cohort, a devout man who feared God with all his household, who gave alms liberally and prayed constantly. One day he saw clearly in a vision an angel of

God, and he stared at the angel in terror. "Cornelius," said the angel, "your prayers and your alms have ascended as a memorial before God. Now send men to Joppa, and bring one Simon who is called Peter; he is lodging with Simon, a tanner, whose house is by the seaside." Then Cornelius called two of his servants and a devout soldier and sent them off.

The next day, as the three men were nearing Joppa, Peter went up on the housetop to pray. He became hungry and asked for something to eat, but while food was being prepared, he fell into a trance. He saw the heaven opened, and something descending, like a great sheet, let down by its four corners upon the earth. In it were all kinds of animals and reptiles and birds of the air. And there came a voice: "Rise, Peter, kill and eat."

"No, Lord," said Peter, "for I have never eaten anything that is common or unclean." The voice came again: "What God has cleansed, you must not call common." This happened three times; then the thing was taken up at once to heaven.

While Peter was inwardly perplexed as to what the vision might mean, the men sent by Cornelius stood before the gate and called out to ask whether Peter was lodging there. To Peter the Spirit said, "Behold, three men are looking for you. Rise and go down, and accompany them without hesitation; for I have sent them." Peter went down and said, "I am the one you are looking for; what is the reason for your coming?"

"Cornelius, a centurion," they said, "an upright and God-fearing man, well spoken of by the whole Jewish nation, was directed by a holy angel to send for you, to hear what you have to say." Peter called them in to be his guests that night, and the next day he went off with them, accompanied by some of the brethren.

At Caesarea, Cornelius was expecting them, and he had called together his kinsmen and close friends. When Peter entered, Cornelius met him and, falling down at his feet, worshiped him. "Stand up," said Peter, lifting him, "I too am a man." Inside he found many persons gathered. "You yourselves know," Peter said to them, "how unlawful it is for a Jew to associate with or to visit any one of another nation. But God has shown me that I should not call any man common or unclean. So when I was sent for, I came without objection. I ask then why you sent for me."

Then Cornelius told Peter about his vision. "Now therefore," he said, "we are all here present in the sight of God, to hear all that you have been commanded by the Lord."

"Truly," answered Peter, "I perceive that God shows no partiality, but in every nation any one who fears him and does what is right is acceptable to him. You know the word which he sent to Israel, preaching good news of peace by Jesus Christ, the word which was proclaimed throughout all Judea: how God anointed Jesus of Nazareth with the Holy Spirit and with power, how he went about doing good and healing all that were oppressed by the devil, how they put him to death by hanging him on a tree, and how God raised him on the third day and made him manifest, not to all the people but to us who were chosen by God as witnesses, who ate and drank with him after he rose from the dead. And Jesus commanded us to preach to the people, and to testify that he is the one ordained by God to be judge of the living and the dead. To him all the prophets bear witness that every one who believes in him receives forgiveness of sins through his name."

While Peter was talking, the Holy Spirit fell on those listening, and they began speaking in tongues and extolling God. The brethren who came with Peter were amazed, because the gift of the Holy Spirit had been poured out even on the Gentiles. Then Peter declared, "Can any one forbid water for baptizing these people who have received the Holy Spirit just as we have?" And he commanded them to be baptized in the name of Jesus Christ.

Now the apostles and the brethren who were in Judea heard how the Gentiles at Caesarea had received the word of God. So when Peter went up to Jerusalem, the circumcision party criticized him. "Why did you go to uncircumcised men and eat with them?" they asked. Peter explained all that had happened at Joppa and at Caesarea. "The Holy Spirit fell on them," he said, "just as on us at the beginning. And I remembered the word of the Lord, how he said, 'John baptized with water, but you shall be baptized with the Holy Spirit.' If then God gave the same gift to them as he gave to us, who was I that I could withstand God?" When they heard this they glorified God, saying, "Then to the Gentiles also God has granted repentance unto life."

Those who scattered because of the persecution that arose over Stephen traveled as far as Phoenicia and Cyprus and Antioch, speaking the word to none except Jews. But in Antioch there were some who spoke to the Greeks also, preaching the Lord Jesus, and a great number believed. When news of this came to the church in Jerusalem, they sent Barnabas, a man full of the Holy Spirit, to Antioch. And he saw the grace of God and was glad, and he exhorted them all to remain faithful. Then he went to Tarsus to look for Saul, so that he might help in the work. When he had found him, he brought him to Antioch, and for a whole year they met with the church, teaching a large company of people. It was in Antioch that the disciples were for the first time called Christians.

In these days a prophet named Agabus came from Jerusalem to Antioch, and he foretold that there would be a great famine over all the world. This did take place in the days of Claudius, and the disciples at Antioch determined, every one according to his ability, to send relief to the brethren in Judea. They sent it by the hand of Barnabas and Saul, and when they had fulfilled their mission they returned, bringing with them John, whose other name was Mark.

About that time Herod the king laid violent hands upon some in the church. He killed James, the son of Zebedee, with the sword, and he arrested Peter, whom he put in prison. The night before Herod was to bring him out for trial, Peter was sleeping between two soldiers, bound with two chains, and there were sentries at the door. And behold, an angel of the Lord appeared, and a light shone in the cell. Striking Peter on the side, the angel said, "Get up quickly," and the chains fell off Peter's hands. "Put on your sandals," said the angel, "wrap your mantle around you and follow me." Peter thought he was seeing a vision, but he followed the angel. When they had passed the first and the second guard, they came to an iron gate. It opened to them of its own accord. They went out and passed on through one street; then the angel left him, and Peter came to himself. "Now I am sure," he said, "that the Lord has sent his angel and rescued me from the hand of Herod."

He went to the house of Mary, the mother of Mark, where many were gathered together and were praying for him. When he knocked at the door of the gateway, a maid named Rhoda came to answer. Recognizing Peter's voice, in her joy she did not open the gate but ran in and said that it was Peter.

"You are mad," they said. But she insisted that it was so. "It is his angel!" they said.

Peter continued knocking, and when they opened they saw him and were amazed. Motioning to them with his hand to be silent, he described how the Lord had brought him out of prison. "Tell this to all the brethren," he said. Then he departed and went to another place.

Next day there was no small stir among the guards over what had become of Peter. When Herod sought for him and could not find him, he examined the sentries and ordered that they be put to death. Then Herod went down from Judea to Caesarea, where an angel of the Lord smote him; and he was eaten by worms and died.

IN THE CHURCH at Antioch, among the prophets and teachers were Barnabas and Saul. Concerning these two the Holy Spirit said, "Set them apart for me, for the work to which I have called them." After fasting and praying, and the laying on of hands, they were sent off, with Mark to assist them.

The three sailed to Cyprus, and when they reached Salamis they proclaimed the word of God in the synagogues of the Jews. Going through the whole island as far as Paphos, they came upon a certain magician, a Jewish false prophet, named Elymas. He served the proconsul, Sergius Paulus, a man of intelligence, who summoned Barnabas and Saul and sought to hear the word of God. But Elymas withstood them, seeking to turn away the proconsul from the faith. Saul (who is also called Paul) was filled with the Holy Spirit, and he looked intently at Elymas. "You son of the devil," he said, "you enemy of all righteousness, full of all deceit and villainy, will you not stop making crooked the straight paths of the Lord? Behold, the hand of the Lord is upon you, and you shall be blind and unable to see the sun for a time." Immediately mist and darkness fell upon Elymas, and he went about seeking people to lead him by the hand. Then the proconsul, when he saw what had occurred, believed the teaching of the Lord.

Setting sail from Paphos, Paul and his company came to Perga in

Pamphylia, where Mark left them to return to Jerusalem. They passed on to Antioch of Pisidia, and on the sabbath day they went into the synagogue and sat down. After the reading of the law and the prophets, the rulers of the synagogue said to them, "Brethren, if you have any word of exhortation for the people, say it." Paul stood up, and motioning with his hand, he spoke, reminding the people how God had given them their land as an inheritance, and then had raised up for them judges, and Samuel the prophet, and when the people asked for a king had given them Saul for forty years, and then had raised up David.

"Of this man's posterity," said Paul, "God has brought to Israel a Savior, Jesus, as he promised. Brethren, sons of the family of Abraham, and those among you that fear God, to us has been sent the message of this salvation. Those who live in Jerusalem and their rulers, because they did not recognize Jesus or understand the utterances of the prophets, fulfilled these by condemning him. Though they could charge him with nothing deserving death, yet they asked Pilate to have him killed. And when they had fulfilled all that was written of him, they took him down from the tree, and laid him in a tomb. But God raised him from the dead; and for many days he appeared to those who came up with him from Galilee to Jerusalem, who are now his witnesses to the people. And we bring you the good news that what God promised to the fathers, this he has fulfilled to us their children by raising Jesus. As it is written in the second psalm, 'Thou art my Son, today I have begotten thee.' And as for the fact that he raised him from the dead, he spoke in this way in another psalm, 'Thou wilt not let thy Holy One see corruption.' Let it be known to you therefore, brethren, that through this man forgiveness of sins is proclaimed to you. By him every one that believes is freed from everything from which you could not be freed by the law of Moses. Beware, therefore, lest there come upon you what is said in the prophets: 'Behold, you scoffers, and wonder, and perish; for I do a deed in your days, a deed you will never believe, if one declares it to you.'"

As they left the synagogue, the people begged that more about these things might be told them the next sabbath, and many followed Paul and Barnabas, who spoke to them and urged them to continue in the grace of God. The next sabbath almost the whole city gathered together to hear the word of God. But when certain Jews saw the multitudes, they were filled with jealousy, and contradicted what was spoken by Paul, and reviled him. Then Paul said boldly, "It was necessary that the word of God should be spoken first to you. Since you thrust it from you, and judge yourselves unworthy of eternal life, behold, we turn to the Gentiles. For so the Lord has commanded us, saying, 'I have set you to be a light for the Gentiles, that you may bring salvation to the uttermost parts of the earth.'"

But the Jews incited the devout women of high standing and the leading men of the city, and they stirred up persecution against Paul and Barnabas, and drove them out of their district. Filled with joy and with the Holy Spirit, they shook off the dust from their feet against them, and went to Iconium. Here they entered the Jewish synagogue, and so spoke that a great company believed. Speaking boldly for the Lord, who granted signs and wonders to be done by their hands, they remained for a long time in Iconium. But the unbelieving Jews stirred up the Gentiles and poisoned their minds against the brethren, and the people of the city were divided, some siding with the Jews, some with the apostles. When an attempt was made by both Gentiles and Jews to molest the two and to stone them, they learned of it and fled to Lystra and Derbe, cities of Lycaonia.

Now at Lystra there was a man who was a cripple from birth. As he listened to Paul speaking, Paul looked intently at him and saw that he had faith to be made well. "Stand upright on your feet," said Paul in a loud voice. And the man sprang up and walked. When the crowds saw what Paul had done, they lifted up their voices, saying, "The gods have come down to us in the likeness of men!" Barnabas they called Zeus, and Paul, because he was the chief speaker, they called Hermes. The priest of Zeus brought oxen and garlands and wanted to offer sacrifice to them with the people.

At this Barnabas and Paul tore their garments and rushed out among the multitude. "Men, why are you doing this?" they cried. "We also are men, of like nature with you, and bring you good news, that you should turn from these vain things to a living God who made the heaven and the earth and the sea and all that is in them. In past generations he allowed all the nations to walk in their own ways; yet he did not leave himself without witness, for he did good and gave you from heaven rains and fruitful seasons, satisfying your hearts with food and gladness." With these words they scarcely restrained the people from offering sacrifice to them.

Later, Jews came to Lystra from Antioch and Iconium, and they managed to persuade the people against the apostles. They stoned Paul and dragged him out of the city, supposing that he was dead. But when the disciples gathered about him, he rose up and entered the city. The next day he went on with Barnabas to Derbe, where they preached the gospel and made many disciples. Then they returned to Lystra and to Iconium and to Antioch, strengthening the souls of the disciples and saying that through many tribulations we must enter the kingdom of God. And in every church, after prayer and fasting, they appointed elders.

They passed through Pamphylia, and when they had spoken the word in Perga, they went down to Attalia, from where they sailed back to Antioch. Here they gathered the church together and declared all that God had done with them, and how he had opened a door of faith to the Gentiles.

Afterward some of the brethren came to Antioch from Judea and were teaching, "Unless you are circumcised according to the custom of Moses, you cannot be saved." Paul and Barnabas had no small dissension and debate with them about this question, and the two, with some of the others, were appointed to go up to Jerusalem to confer with the apostles and elders. At

Jerusalem they were welcomed by the church and declared all that God had done with them. But some believers who belonged to the party of the Pharisees rose up and said, "It is necessary to circumcise the Gentiles, and to charge them to keep the law of Moses." To consider this matter, the apostles and elders gathered together, and after much debate, Peter arose.

"Brethren," he said, "you know that in the early days God made choice among you, that by my mouth the Gentiles should hear the word of the gospel and believe. And God who knows the heart bore witness to them, giving them the Holy Spirit just as he did to us; he made no distinction between us and them, but cleansed their hearts by faith. Now therefore why do you make trial of God by putting a yoke upon the neck of the disciples which neither our fathers nor we have been able to bear? But we believe that we shall be saved through the grace of the Lord Jesus, just as they will."

The assembly then listened to Barnabas and Paul as they related what signs and wonders God had done through them among the Gentiles. After they finished speaking, James, the brother of the Lord, arose. "Brethren, listen to me," he said. "Peter has related how God first visited the Gentiles, to take out of them a people for his name. And with this the words of the prophets agree, as it is written, 'After this I will return, and I will rebuild the dwelling of David, which has fallen; I will rebuild its ruins, and I will set it up, that the rest of men may seek the Lord, and all the Gentiles who are called by my name, says the Lord, who has made these things known from of old.' Therefore my judgment is that we should not trouble those of the Gentiles who turn to God, but should write to them to abstain from the pollutions of idols and from unchastity and from what is strangled and from blood. For from early generations Moses has had in every city those who preach him, for he is read every sabbath in the synagogues."

Then the apostles and the elders, with the whole church, chose men to send to Antioch with Paul and Barnabas. They sent Judas, called Barsabbas, and Silas, leading men among the brethren, with the following letter:

> The brethren, both the apostles and the elders, to the brethren who are of the Gentiles in Antioch and Syria and Cilicia, greeting. Since we have heard that some persons from us have troubled you with words, unsettling your minds, although we gave them no instructions, it has seemed good to us, having come to one accord, to choose men and send them to you with our beloved Barnabas and Paul, men who have risked their lives for the sake of our Lord Jesus Christ. We have therefore sent Judas and Silas, who themselves will tell you the same things by word of mouth. For it has seemed good to the Holy Spirit and to us to lay upon you no greater burden than these necessary things: that you abstain from what has been sacrificed to idols and from blood and from what is strangled and from unchastity. If you keep yourselves from these, you will do well. Farewell.

At Antioch, having gathered the congregation together, they read the letter, and the brethren rejoiced. Judas and Silas, after some time, were sent off in peace, but Paul and Barnabas remained in Antioch, teaching and preaching the word of the Lord.

After some days Paul said to Barnabas, "Come, let us return and visit the brethren in every city where we proclaimed the word of the Lord, and see how they are." Barnabas wanted to take Mark with them, but Paul thought best not to take one who had withdrawn in Pamphylia, and had not gone with them to the work. There arose a sharp contention, so that they separated from each other. Then Barnabas took Mark with him and sailed away to Cyprus. Paul chose Silas and departed for Syria and Cilicia.

At Lystra there was a disciple named Timothy, the son of a Jewish woman, who was a believer, and a Greek father. He was well spoken of by the brethren. Paul wanted Timothy to accompany him, so he had him circumcised, because of the Jews that were in those places, for they all knew that his father was a Greek. As they went through the cities, they delivered the decisions which had been reached at Jerusalem. So the churches were strengthened in the faith, and they increased in numbers daily.

When they had come opposite Mysia, they attempted to go into Bithynia, but the Spirit of Jesus did not allow them, so they went down to Troas. Here a vision appeared to Paul in the night: a man of Macedonia was beseeching him, "Come over to Macedonia and help us." Immediately we set sail for Macedonia, concluding that God had called to preach the gospel there.

We made a direct voyage to Samothrace, then to Neapolis, and from there to Philippi, the leading city of Macedonia and a Roman colony. We remained some days, and on the sabbath we went outside the gate to the riverside, where there was a place of prayer, and spoke to the women who had come there. One who heard was Lydia, a seller of purple goods, who was a worshiper of God. The Lord opened her heart to what was said by Paul, and when she was baptized, with her household, she said, "If you have judged me to be faithful to the Lord, come to my house and stay." And she prevailed upon us.

Another day, as we were going to the place of prayer, we were met by a slave girl who had a spirit of divination and brought her owners much gain by soothsaying. She followed us, crying, "These men are servants of the Most High God, who proclaim to you the way of salvation." She did this for many days, and at last Paul was annoyed. "In the name of Jesus Christ," he said to the spirit, "come out of her." And it came out that very hour.

But when the girl's owners saw that their hope of gain was gone, they seized Paul and Silas and dragged them into the market place before the magistrates. "These men are Jews," they said, "and they are disturbing our city. They advocate customs which it is not lawful for us Romans to accept or practice." The crowd joined in attacking them, and the magistrates tore the garments off them and gave orders to beat them with rods. And when they had inflicted many blows upon them, they threw them into prison, and their feet were fastened in the stocks.

About midnight Paul and Silas were praying and singing hymns, and the prisoners were listening to them. Suddenly there was a great earthquake, so that the foundations of the prison were shaken. Immediately all the doors were opened and every one's fetters were unfastened. When the jailer woke and saw that the prison doors were open, he supposed that the prisoners had escaped. He drew his sword and was about to kill himself when Paul cried loudly, "Do not harm yourself, for we are all here." The jailer called for lights and rushed in, and trembling with fear he fell down before Paul and Silas. Then he brought them out and took them to his house and washed their wounds. "Men," he said, "what must I do to be saved?"

"Believe in the Lord Jesus," they said, "and you will be saved, you and your household." And they spoke the word of the Lord to him and to all that were in his house. He was baptized at once, with all his family; then he set food before them, and rejoiced that he had believed in God.

When it was day, the magistrates sent the police, saying, "Let those men go." The jailer told Paul, but Paul said, "They have beaten us publicly, uncondemned, men who are Roman citizens, and have thrown us into prison. Do they now cast us out secretly? No! Let them come themselves and take us out." The police reported these words to the magistrates, who were afraid when they heard that Paul and Silas were Roman citizens. They came and apologized to them, took them out, and asked them to leave the city. When the two had exhorted the brethren, they departed.

Next they came to Thessalonica, where there was a synagogue of the Jews. As was his custom, Paul went in, and for three weeks he argued with them from the scriptures, explaining and proving that it was necessary for the Christ to suffer and to rise from the dead. "This Jesus," he said, "whom I proclaim to you, is the Christ." Some were persuaded and joined Paul and Silas, as did a great many of the devout Greeks and the leading women. But others of the Jews were jealous, and taking some wicked fellows of the rabble, they gathered a crowd, set the city in an uproar, and attacked the house of Jason, where Paul and Silas were staying. When they could not find them they dragged Jason and some of the brethren before the city authorities. "These men who have turned the world upside down," they cried, "have come here also, and Jason has received them; and they are all acting against the decrees of Caesar, saying that there is another king, Jesus." But when the authorities had taken security from Jason and the rest, they let them go.

The brethren immediately sent Paul and Silas away by night to Beroea, where they went into the Jewish synagogue. Now these Jews received the word with all eagerness, examining the scriptures to see if these things were so, and many believed. But when the Jews of Thessalonica learned of this, they came there too, stirring up and inciting the crowds. Then the brethren sent Paul off to Athens, with Silas and Timothy to follow as soon as possible.

At Athens, Paul saw that the city was full of idols, and his spirit was provoked. He argued in the synagogue with the Jews and the devout persons, and in the market place every day with those who chanced to be there. Some also of the Epicurean and Stoic philosophers met him. "He seems to be a preacher of foreign divinities," they said, because he preached Jesus and the resurrection. They brought him to the Areopagus, saying, "May we know what this new teaching is which you present? For you bring some strange things to our ears." Now all the Athenians and the foreigners who lived there spent their time in nothing except telling or hearing something new.

Paul stood in the middle of the Areopagus and spoke. "Men of Athens," he said, "I perceive that in every way you are very religious. For as I passed along and observed the objects of your worship, I found an altar with this inscription, 'To an unknown god.' What therefore you worship as unknown, this I proclaim to you. The God who made the world and everything in it, being Lord of heaven and earth, does not live in shrines made by man, nor is he served by human hands, as though he needed anything, since he himself gives to all men life and breath and everything. And he made from one every nation of men to live on all the face of the earth, having determined allotted periods and the boundaries of their habitation, that they should seek God, in the hope that they might feel after him and find him. Yet he is not far from each one of us, for 'In him we live and move and have our being'; as even some of your poets have said, 'For we are indeed his offspring.' Being then God's offspring, we ought not to think that the Deity is like gold, or silver, or stone, a representation by the art and imagination of man. The times of ignorance God overlooked, but now he commands all men everywhere to repent, because he has fixed a day on which he will judge the world in righteousness by a man whom he has appointed, and of this he has given assurance to all men by raising him from the dead."

When the listeners heard Paul speak of the resurrection of the dead, some mocked; others said, "We will hear you again about this." But some joined Paul and believed, among them Dionysius the Areopagite and a woman named Damaris.

After this Paul went to Corinth. Here he found a Jew named Aquila, lately come from Italy with his wife, Priscilla, after all Jews had been commanded to leave Rome. Because he was of the same trade he stayed with them, and they worked, for they were tentmakers. When Silas and Timothy arrived, Paul was occupied with testifying to the Jews that the Christ was Jesus. But when they opposed him, he shook out his garments and said, "Your blood be upon your heads! I am innocent. From now on I will go to the Gentiles."

Next door to the synagogue was the house of a man named Titius Justus, a worshiper of God. Here Paul preached, and Crispus, the ruler of the synagogue, believed in the Lord, together with all his household; and many Corinthians believed and were baptized. Then one night in a vision the Lord said to Paul, "Do not be afraid, but speak and do not be silent; for I am with you, and no man shall attack you to harm you; for I have many people in this city." For a year and six months Paul stayed in Corinth, teaching the word of God.

After this Paul took leave of the brethren, and with Priscilla and Aquila he sailed for Syria. At Cenchreae he cut his hair, for he had taken a vow of thanksgiving. At Ephesus he went into the synagogue and argued with the Jews. When they asked him to stay longer, he declined. "I will return to you if God wills," he said, and he set sail from Ephesus, leaving Priscilla and Aquila behind. At Caesarea he greeted the church, and then went down to Antioch, where he spent some time. Then he departed and went from place to place through Galatia and Phrygia, strengthening all the disciples.

Now a Jew named Apollos, an eloquent man, well versed in the scriptures, came to Ephesus. He knew the way of the Lord, and being fervent in spirit, he spoke and taught accurately the things concerning Jesus, though he knew only the baptism of John. But when Priscilla and Aquila heard him speaking in the synagogue, they expounded to him the way of God more accurately. When he wished to go to Corinth, the brethren wrote to the disciples to receive him, and he greatly helped those who through grace had believed. In public he powerfully confuted the Jews, showing by the scriptures that the Christ was Jesus.

While Apollos was at Corinth, Paul came back to Ephesus, where he found some disciples of Apollos, about twelve in all. "Did you receive the Holy Spirit when you believed?" he asked.

"No," they said, "we have never even heard that there is a Holy Spirit."

"Into what then," he said, "were you baptized?"

"Into John's baptism," they answered.

"John baptized with the baptism of repentance," Paul said, "telling the people to believe in the one who was to come after him, that is, Jesus."

On hearing this, they were baptized in the name of the Lord Jesus. And when Paul had laid his hands upon them, the Holy Spirit came on them; and they spoke with tongues and prophesied. Paul continued at Ephesus for two years, speaking in the hall of Tyrannus, so that all the residents of Asia heard the word of the Lord, both Jews and Greeks.

God did extraordinary miracles by the hands of Paul. When handkerchiefs or aprons were carried from his body to the sick, diseases and evil spirits left them. Seeing these things, some Jewish exorcists undertook to pronounce the name of the Lord Jesus over those who had evil spirits, saying, "I adjure you by the Jesus whom Paul preaches." Once the evil spirit answered them, "Jesus I know, and Paul I know; but who are you?" And the man who had the evil spirit leaped and overpowered them, so that they fled naked and wounded. This became known to the Jews and Greeks of Ephesus, and fear fell upon them all. Many who were believers came, confessing and divulging their practices; some who practiced magic arts brought their books together and burned them. So the word of the Lord grew and prevailed mightily.

About this time there arose no little stir concerning the Way. A silversmith named Demetrius, who made silver shrines of Artemis which brought no little business to the craftsmen, called together the workmen of like occupation. "Men, you know that from this business we have our wealth," he said.

"And you see and hear that not only at Ephesus but almost throughout all Asia this Paul has persuaded and turned away a considerable company of people, saying that gods made with hands are not gods. There is danger not only that this trade of ours may come into disrepute but also that the temple of the great goddess Artemis may count for nothing. She may even be deposed from her magnificence, she whom all Asia and the world worship."

At this the workmen were enraged. "Great is Artemis of the Ephesians!" they cried. The city was filled with confusion, and they rushed together into the theater, dragging with them Gaius and Aristarchus, Paul's companions. Paul wished to go in but the disciples would not let him. Now some cried one thing, some another, for the assembly was in confusion, and most did not know why they had come together. Some of the Jews put forward Alexander to make a defense, but when the people recognized that he was a Jew, for about two hours they cried out, "Great is Artemis of the Ephesians!"

Then the town clerk quieted the crowd. "Men of Ephesus," he said, "what man is there who does not know that the city of the Ephesians is temple keeper of the great Artemis, and of the sacred stone that fell from the sky? Since these things cannot be contradicted, you ought to be quiet and do nothing rash. You have brought these men here who are neither sacrilegious nor blasphemers of our goddess. If there is a complaint against any one, the courts are open. If you seek anything further, it shall be settled in the regular assembly. But we are in danger of being charged with rioting today, there being no cause that we can give to justify this commotion." He then dismissed the assembly.

After the uproar ceased, Paul sent for the disciples, and having exhorted them he departed for Macedonia and Achaia, intending to go to Jerusalem. "After I have been there," he said, "I must also see Rome." When he had gone through these parts and had given them much encouragement, he came to Troas, where he stayed for seven days.

At Troas, on the first day of the week, we gathered to break bread in an upper chamber where there were many lights. Paul talked, and he prolonged his speech until midnight. Sitting in the window was a young man named Eutychus, and he sank into a deep sleep as Paul talked. Being overcome, he fell out the window from the third story and was taken up dead. But Paul went down and embraced him. "Do not be alarmed," he said, "for his life is in him." They took the lad away alive, and were comforted.

Paul was hastening to be at Jerusalem, if possible, on the day of Pentecost, so he had decided to sail past Ephesus. But when he reached Miletus he sent to Ephesus for the elders of the church. When they came, he spoke to them. "You yourselves know," he said, "how I lived among you all the time from the first day that I set foot in Asia, serving the Lord with all humility and with tears and with trials which befell me through the plots of the Jews. I did not shrink from declaring to you anything that was profitable, and teaching you in public and from house to house, testifying both to Jews and to Greeks of repentance to God and of faith in our Lord Jesus Christ. Now I am going to Jerusalem, bound in the Spirit, not knowing what shall befall me there, except that the Holy Spirit testifies to me that imprisonment and afflictions await me. But I do not account my life of any value nor as precious to myself, if only I may accomplish my course and the ministry which I received from the Lord Jesus, to testify to the gospel of the grace of God. You will see my face no more. Therefore I testify that I am innocent of the blood of all of you, for I did not shrink from declaring to you the whole counsel of God. Take heed to yourselves and to all the flock, in which the Holy Spirit has made you overseers, to care for the church of God which he obtained with the blood of his own Son. I know that after my departure fierce wolves will come in among you, and from among your own selves will arise men speaking perverse things, to draw away the disciples after them. Therefore be alert. Now I commend you to God and to the word of his grace, which is able to give you the inheritance among all those who are sanctified. I coveted no one's silver or gold or apparel. You yourselves know that these hands ministered to my necessities, and to those who were with me. In all things I have shown you that by so toiling one must help the weak, remembering the words of the Lord Jesus, how he said, 'It is more blessed to give than to receive.'"

When he had spoken, he knelt down and prayed, and they wept and embraced him and kissed him, sorrowing because he said they should see his face no more.

When we left Miletus, we sailed by a straight course to Cos, the next day to Rhodes, then to Patara, where we found a cargo ship crossing to Phoenicia. We passed Cyprus on the left and sailed to Tyre, where the ship unloaded. Having sought out the disciples, we stayed at Tyre for seven days, and when we departed, all the disciples, with wives and children, accompanied us outside the city. Kneeling down, we prayed and bade one another farewell.

Sailing down the coast to Ptolemais, we greeted the brethren there and stayed one day. Next we came to Caesarea, where we stayed at the house of Philip the evangelist; he had four unmarried daughters who prophesied. While we were there, the prophet Agabus came to us from Judea. He took Paul's belt and bound his own feet and hands and said, "Thus says the Holy Spirit, 'So shall the Jews at Jerusalem bind the man who owns this belt and deliver him into the hands of the Gentiles.'" At this we and the people there begged Paul not to go up to Jerusalem.

"What are you doing," Paul answered, "weeping and breaking my heart? I am ready not only to be imprisoned but even to die at Jerusalem for the name of the Lord Jesus."

"The will of the Lord be done," we said.

After this we went up to Jerusalem, where the brethren received us gladly. To James and the elders Paul related one by one the things that God had done among the Gentiles through his ministry, and when they heard this, they glorified God. But then they cautioned him. "You see, brother," they said, "there are many thousands among the Jews of those who have believed, all zealous for the law. They have been told that you teach all the believing Jews who live among the Gentiles to forsake Moses, telling them not to circumcise their children or observe the customs. What then is to be done? They will certainly hear that you have come. Do therefore what we tell you. We have four men who are under a vow. Purify yourself along with them and pay their expenses. Thus all will know that you yourself live in observance of the law." The next day Paul purified himself with the four, and he gave notice at the temple that when the seven days of purification had been fulfilled, the offering would be presented for each of them.

When the seven days were almost completed, some Jews from Asia who had seen Paul in the temple stirred up the crowd and laid hands on him. "Men of Israel, help!" they cried. "This is the man who is teaching men everywhere against the people and the law and this place. He also brought Greeks into the temple, and he has defiled this holy place." (They had seen Trophimus the Ephesian with him in the city, and they supposed that Paul had brought him into the temple.) Then all the people ran together. They seized Paul, dragged him out of the temple, and tried to kill him.

Word of this came to the Roman tribune, and he at once took soldiers and ran down, and when the crowd saw the soldiers they stopped beating Paul. Then the tribune arrested Paul, ordered him to be bound with two chains, and inquired of the crowd who Paul was and what he had done. Some shouted one thing, some another; and since he could not learn the facts because of the uproar, the tribune ordered Paul to be brought into the barracks. The mob followed, crying, "Away with him!" and because of the violence of the crowd, Paul was actually carried up the steps by the soldiers.

As he was about to enter the barracks, Paul spoke to the tribune. "I am a Jew from Tarsus in Cilicia," he said, "a citizen of no mean city. I beg you, let me speak to the people." The tribune gave him leave, and when Paul, standing on the steps, motioned with his hand to the people, there was a great hush. "Brethren," he said in Hebrew, "hear the defense which I now make before you." When they heard that he addressed them in the Hebrew language, they were even more quiet.

"I am a Jew," Paul went on, "born at Tarsus but brought up in this city at the feet of Gamaliel, educated according to the strict law of our fathers, being zealous for God as you all are this day. At first I persecuted this Way to the death, as the high priest and the elders bear me witness. I even journeyed to Damascus to punish those also who were there. But near Damascus a great light from heaven suddenly blinded me, and I heard a voice saying, 'Saul, Saul, why do you persecute me? I am Jesus of Nazareth whom you are persecuting.' I asked what I should do, and the Lord said, 'Go into Damascus, and there you will be told.' I was led by the hand into Damascus, where a devout man came to me and said, 'Brother Saul, receive your sight.' I received my sight, and he said, 'The God of our fathers appointed you to know his will, to see the Just One and to hear a voice from his mouth; for you will be a witness for him to all men of what you have seen and heard. Rise and be baptized, and wash away your sins, calling on his name.' When I had returned to Jerusalem and was praying in the temple, I fell into a trance and saw the Lord saying to me, 'Make haste and get quickly out of Jerusalem, because they will not accept your testimony about me. Depart; for I will send you to the Gentiles.'"

Up to this the crowd had listened; now they lifted up their voices and cried, "Away with such a fellow from the earth! For he ought not to live." As they cried out and waved their garments and threw dust into the air, the tribune commanded Paul to be brought in and examined by scourging, to find out why they shouted against him. As they tied him with thongs, Paul said to the centurion standing by, "Is it lawful for you to scourge a man who is a Roman citizen, and uncondemned?" The centurion went to the tribune and said, "What are you about to do? This man is a Roman citizen." The tribune came and asked Paul, "Are you a Roman citizen?" And he said, "Yes, I was born a citizen." Instantly those who were about to scourge him withdrew.

The tribune, desiring to know the real reason why the Jews accused Paul, the next day commanded the chief priests and all the council to meet, and he set Paul before them. Looking intently at the council, Paul said, "Brethren, I have lived before God in all good conscience up to this day." At this the high priest Ananias commanded those nearby to strike him on the mouth.

"God shall strike you," Paul said, "you whitewashed wall! Are you sitting to judge me according to the law, and yet contrary to the law you order me to be struck?"

"Would you revile God's high priest?" asked those who stood by.

"I did not know, brethren," Paul answered, "that he was the high priest; for it is written, 'You shall not speak evil of a ruler of your people.'"

When Paul perceived that one part of the council were Sadducees and the other Pharisees, he cried, "Brethren, I am a Pharisee, a son of Pharisees; with respect to the resurrection of the dead I am on trial." With this a dissension arose between the two parties, for the Sadducees say that there is no resurrection, nor angel, nor spirit; but the Pharisees acknowledge them all. A great clamor arose, and some of the Pharisees stood up and contended, "We find nothing wrong in this man. What if it was a spirit or an angel that spoke to him?" When the dissension became violent, the tribune sent the soldiers to get Paul and bring him into the barracks. That night the Lord stood by Paul and said, "Take courage, for as you have testified about me at Jerusalem, so you must bear witness also at Rome."

When it was day, more than forty of the Jews made a plot to kill Paul, and they bound themselves by an oath neither to eat nor drink till they had done it. To the chief priests and elders they said, "We have bound ourselves by an oath to kill Paul. Give notice now to the tribune to bring him down to you, as though you were going to determine his case more exactly. We are ready to kill him before he comes near."

But the son of Paul's sister heard of the conspiracy, so he entered the barracks and told Paul. Calling one of the centurions, Paul said, "Take this young man to the tribune; for he has something to tell him." The centurion did so, and when the young man had told the tribune of the conspiracy, the tribune dismissed him, saying, "Tell no one that you have informed me of this." Then he called two centurions. "Tonight," he said, "get ready two hundred soldiers with seventy horsemen and two hundred spearmen to go as far as Caesarea. Provide a mount for Paul, and bring him safely to Felix the governor." Then he wrote the following letter:

Claudius Lysias to his Excellency the governor Felix, greeting. This man was seized by the Jews, and was about to be killed by them, when I came upon them with the soldiers and rescued him, having learned that he was a Roman citizen. And desiring to know the charge on which they accused him, I brought him down to their council. I found that he was accused about questions of their law, but charged with nothing deserving death or imprisonment. And when it was disclosed to me that there would be a plot against the man, I sent him to you at once, ordering his accusers also to state before you what they have against him.

The soldiers, according to their instructions, took Paul away at night and by the next day had delivered him to the governor at Caesarea. On reading the tribune's letter, Felix said, "I will hear you when your accusers arrive." After five days the high priest Ananias came down with some elders and a spokesman, one Tertullus. They laid their case before the governor, and when Paul was called, Tertullus spoke. "Through you, most excellent Felix, we enjoy much peace," he said, "and we accept this with all gratitude. But, to detain you no further, I beg you in your kindness to hear us briefly. We have found this man a pestilent fellow, an agitator among all the Jews throughout the world, and a ringleader of the sect of the Nazarenes. He even tried to profane the temple, but we seized him. By examining him yourself you will be able to learn about everything of which we accuse him."

Then the governor motioned Paul to speak, and he replied:

"Realizing that for many years you have been judge over this nation, I cheerfully make my defense. As you may ascertain, it is not more than twelve days since I went up to worship at Jerusalem; and they did not find me disputing with any one or stirring up a crowd. But this I admit, that according to the Way, which they call a sect, I worship the God of our fathers, believing everything laid down by the law or written in the prophets, having a hope in God which these themselves accept, that there will be a resurrection of both the just and the unjust. So I always take pains to have a clear conscience toward God and toward men. Now after some years I came to bring to my nation alms and offerings. As I was doing this, some Jews from Asia found me purified in the temple, without any crowd or tumult. They ought to be here before you and to make an accusation, if they have anything against me. Or else let these men themselves say what wrongdoing they found when I stood before the council—except this one thing which I cried out, 'With respect to the resurrection of the dead I am on trial before you this day.'"

Now Felix, having a rather accurate knowledge of the Way, put the matter off. "When Lysias the tribune comes down," he said, "I will decide the case." Then he gave orders that Paul should be kept in custody but should have some liberty, and that his friends could attend to his needs.

Some days later Felix and his wife, Drusilla, who was a Jewess, visited Paul and heard him speak upon faith in Christ Jesus. As Paul argued about justice and self-control and future judgment, Felix was alarmed. "Go away for the present," he said; "when I have an opportunity I will summon you." At the same time Felix hoped that money would be given him by Paul, so he often sent for him and conversed with him. But when two years had elapsed, Felix was succeeded by Porcius Festus. Desiring to do the Jews a favor, Felix left Paul in prison.

When Festus came into the province, he visited Jerusalem where the chief priests informed him against Paul. They asked, as a favor, to have Paul sent to Jerusalem, planning an ambush to kill him on the way. Festus replied that Paul was being kept at Caesarea. "So let the men of authority among you go down with me," he said, "and if there is anything wrong about the man, let them accuse him."

At Caesarea, Festus took his seat on the tribunal and ordered Paul to be brought. The Jews who had come from Jerusalem stood about him, bringing many serious charges which they could not prove. Festus, wishing to do the Jews a favor, said to Paul, "Do you wish to go up to Jerusalem, and there be tried on these charges before me?"

"I am standing before Caesar's tribunal," Paul answered, "where I ought to be tried. To the Jews I have done no wrong, as you know very well. If then I am a wrongdoer, and have committed anything for which I deserve to die, I do not seek to escape death. But if there is nothing in their charges against me, no one can give me up to them. I appeal to Caesar."

Festus, when he had conferred with his council, answered, "You have appealed to Caesar; to Caesar you shall go."

When some days had passed, Agrippa the king arrived at Caesarea to welcome Festus. He stayed many days, and Festus laid Paul's case before him, explaining that he was to be sent to Caesar. "I should like to hear the man myself," said Agrippa.

So the next day Agrippa entered the audience hall with the military tribunes and the prominent men of the city. Paul was brought in, and Festus said, "King Agrippa, you see this man about whom the whole Jewish people petitioned me, shouting that he ought not to live. But I found that he had done nothing deserving death; and as he himself appealed to the emperor, I decided to send him. But I have nothing definite to write about him. Therefore I have brought him before you, King Agrippa, that, after we have examined him, I may have something to write."

Agrippa said to Paul, "You have permission to speak for yourself." Then Paul, stretching out his hand, made his defense:

"I think myself fortunate that it is before you, King Agrippa, I am to make my defense. You are familiar with all customs and controversies of the Jews; therefore I beg you to listen to me patiently. My manner of life from my youth is known by all the Jews. They know that according to the strictest party of our religion I have lived as a Pharisee. And now I stand here on trial for hope in the promise made by God to our fathers. And for this hope I am accused by Jews, O king! Why is it thought incredible by any of you that God raises the dead? I myself was convinced that I ought to do many things in opposing the name of Jesus of Nazareth. I shut up many of the saints in prison, and when they were put to death I cast my vote against them. I punished them, tried to make them blaspheme, and in raging fury I persecuted them even to foreign cities. Then one day near Damascus I suddenly saw a light from heaven, brighter than the sun, and I heard a voice saying in Hebrew, 'Saul, Saul, why do you persecute me? It hurts you to kick against the goads. I am Jesus, whom you are persecuting. I will appoint you to serve and bear witness to the things in which you have seen me and to those in which I will appear to you, delivering you from the people and from the Gentiles—to whom I send you to open their eyes, that they may turn from darkness to light and from the power of Satan to God, that they may receive forgiveness of sins and a place among those who are sanctified by faith in me.'

"O King Agrippa, I was not disobedient to the heavenly vision, but declared to those at Damascus, at Jerusalem and throughout Judea, and also to the Gentiles, that they should repent and turn to God and perform deeds worthy of their repentance. For this reason the Jews seized me in the temple and tried to kill me. To this day I have had the help that comes from God, and so I stand here testifying both to small and great, saying nothing but what the prophets and Moses said would come to pass: that the Christ must suffer, and that, by being the first to rise from the dead, he would proclaim light both to the Jews and to the Gentiles."

"Paul, you are mad," said Festus in a loud voice; "your great learning is turning you mad."

"I am not mad, most excellent Festus," Paul replied, "but I am speaking the sober truth. For the king knows about these things, and to him I speak freely. I am persuaded that none of these things has escaped his notice, for this was not done in a corner. King Agrippa, do you believe the prophets? I know that you believe."

"In a short time," Agrippa said, "you think to make me a Christian!"

"Whether short or long," said Paul, "I would to God that not only you but also all who hear me this day might become such as I am—except for these chains."

Then the king and the governor rose, and those who were sitting with them; and when they had withdrawn, they said to one another, "This man is doing nothing to deserve death or imprisonment. He could have been set free if he had not appealed to Caesar."

When it was time for us to sail for Italy, they delivered Paul and some other prisoners to a centurion named Julius, who treated Paul kindly. Embarking in a ship bound for ports along the coast of Asia, we sailed east of Cyprus, and came to Myra in Lycia. There the centurion found a grain ship of Alexandria sailing for Italy, and put us on board (there were in all two hundred and seventy-six persons in the ship). We sailed slowly for a number of days, and arrived with difficulty off Cnidus, then sailed south to Crete. Coasting along with difficulty, we came to a harbor called Fair Havens. Because the season was late, the voyage was becoming dangerous, and since Fair Havens was not suitable to winter in, we sailed for Phoenix, a safer harbor of Crete. We were sailing close inshore when a tempestuous wind struck down from the land. The ship was caught and was driven seaward, violently storm-tossed. Next day the storm continued and they began to throw the cargo overboard. The third day they cast out the ship's tackle. When neither sun nor stars appeared for many days, and no small tempest lay on us, all hope of being saved was at last abandoned.

After they had been long without food, Paul came forward. "Men, I bid you take heart," he said, "for there will be no loss of life among you, but only of the ship. This very night there stood by me an angel of the God whom I worship, and he said, 'Do not be afraid, Paul; you must stand before Caesar; and lo, God has granted you all those who sail with you.' So take heart, men, for I have faith in God that it will be exactly as I have been told. But we shall have to run on some island."

When the fourteenth night had come, as we were drifting across the open sea, the sailors suspected that they were nearing land. They sounded and found twenty fathoms, and a little farther on they sounded again and found fifteen fathoms. Fearing that we might run on the rocks, they let out four sea anchors from the stern, and prayed for day to come. At dawn Paul urged all to take some food. "Today is the fourteenth day," he said, "that you have continued in suspense and without food. Therefore I urge you to eat; it will give you strength, since not a hair is to perish from the head of any of you." Then he took bread, and giving thanks to God in the presence of all, he broke it and began to eat. They were all encouraged and when they had eaten enough, they lightened the ship, throwing the grain into the sea.

When it was light, they saw land but did not recognize it. Then they noticed a bay with a beach, and here they planned if possible to bring the ship ashore. Casting off the anchors and hoisting the foresail to the wind, they made for the beach. But the vessel struck a shoal and ran aground. The bow stuck and remained immovable, while the stern was being broken up by the surf. Lest any of the prisoners should swim away and escape, the soldiers decided to kill them, but the centurion, wishing to save Paul, forbade it. He ordered those who could swim to throw themselves overboard and make for the land, and the rest to use planks or pieces of the ship. And so it was that all escaped.

On land we learned that the island was called Malta. The natives showed us unusual kindness, and because it had begun to rain and was cold, they kindled a fire. Paul had gathered a bundle of sticks, and as he put them on the fire a viper came out because of the heat and fastened on his hand. When the natives saw this they said, "No doubt this man is a murderer. Though he has escaped from the sea, justice has not allowed him to live." When Paul shook off the creature, they waited, expecting him to swell up or suddenly fall down dead. After a long time, when they saw no misfortune came to him, they changed their minds and said that he was a god.

The chief man of the island, Publius, received us and entertained us hospitably for three days. Now it happened that the father of Publius lay sick with fever and dysentery, so Paul visited him and prayed, and putting his hands on him healed him. After this, during the three months that we stayed on the island, the rest of the people who had diseases also came and were cured. They presented many gifts to us, and when we sailed, in another ship of Alexandria, they put on board whatever was needed.

At Syracuse we stayed three days, and at Rhegium one day. At Puteoli we found brethren and stayed with them for seven days. And so we came to Rome, and the brethren there, when they heard, came out of the city to meet us. In Rome, Paul was allowed to stay by himself, in his own hired dwelling, with the soldier that guarded him.

Soon Paul called together the local leaders of the Jews, and when they had gathered, he said, "Brethren, though I had done nothing against the people or the customs of our fathers, yet I was delivered prisoner from Jerusalem into the hands of the Romans. For this reason I have asked to see you and speak with you, since it is because of the hope of Israel that I am bound with this chain." The Jews answered that they had received no letters from Judea about Paul, nor had any of the brethren coming to Rome reported any evil against him. "But we desire to hear what your views are," they said, "for with regard to this sect we know that everywhere it is spoken against."

They appointed a day and they came to his lodging in great numbers. Paul expounded the matter to them from morning till evening, testifying to the kingdom of God and trying to convince them about Jesus both from the law of Moses and from the prophets. Some were convinced, while others disbelieved, and they disagreed among themselves. At this Paul made a statement: "The Holy Spirit was right in saying to your fathers through Isaiah the prophet: 'Go to this people, and say, You shall indeed hear but never understand, and you shall indeed see but never perceive. For this people's heart has grown dull.' Let it be known to you then that this salvation of God has been sent to the Gentiles; they will listen."

Paul lived in Rome two whole years at his own expense, and welcomed all who came to him, preaching the kingdom of God and teaching about the Lord Jesus Christ quite openly and unhindered.

ROMANS

After years of spreading the gospel and founding churches through Asia Minor, Macedonia, and Greece, the apostle Paul at last decided to visit Rome, where there already existed a thriving Christian community. It was to introduce himself to the Roman Christians, apparently, that he wrote this letter from Corinth, about A.D. 58. Fully and systematically he sets forth his message, producing what amounts to a theological treatise rather than an ordinary letter. Since the Roman Christians were already converted, however, Paul does not attempt to lay bare the Christian way of life in its entirety. Instead, he concentrates on certain fundamental truths he feels require mentioning. After the usual salutation and thanksgiving, he discusses the need of the world for redemption. Next he takes up God's saving act in the earthly ministry of Jesus Christ, describing both its nature and the new life that it has made available. After a section on the role of the Jewish nation in God's plan, Paul closes with an exhortation to maintain Christian behavior and unity.

Paul, a servant of Jesus Christ, called to be an apostle, set apart for the gospel of God which he promised beforehand through his prophets in the holy scriptures, the gospel concerning his Son, who was descended from David according to the flesh and designated Son of God in power according to the Spirit of holiness by his resurrection from the dead, Jesus Christ our Lord.

To all God's beloved in Rome, who are called to be saints: grace to you and peace from God our Father and the Lord Jesus Christ.

First, I thank my God through Jesus Christ for all of you, because your faith is proclaimed in all the world. For God is my witness that without ceasing I mention you always in my prayers, asking that somehow by God's will I may succeed in coming to you. For I long to see you, that I may impart to you some spiritual gift to strengthen you, that is, that we may be mutually encouraged by each other's faith, both yours and mine.

For I am not ashamed of the gospel: it is the power of God for salvation to every one who has faith. In it the righteousness of God is revealed through faith for faith; as it is written, "He who through faith is righteous shall live."

The wrath of God is revealed against all ungodliness of men who by their wickedness suppress the truth. For what can be known about God is plain to them, because God has shown it to them. Ever since the creation of the world his invisible nature, namely, his eternal power and deity, has been clearly perceived in the things that have been made. So they are without excuse; for although they knew God they did not honor him as God, or give thanks to him, but they became futile in their thinking and their senseless minds were darkened. Claiming to be wise, they became fools, and exchanged the glory of the immortal God for images resembling mortal man or birds or animals or reptiles.

Therefore God gave them up in the lusts of their hearts to impurity, to the dishonoring of their bodies among themselves, because they exchanged the truth about God for a lie and worshiped and served the creature rather than the Creator, who is blessed for ever! Amen.

For this reason God gave them up to dishonorable passions. Their women exchanged natural relations for unnatural, and the men gave up natural relations with women and were consumed with passion for one another, men committing shameless acts with men and receiving in their own persons the due penalty for their error. Since they did not see fit to acknowledge God, God gave them up to a base mind and to improper conduct. They were filled with all manner of wickedness, evil, covetousness, malice. Full of envy, murder, strife, deceit, malignity, they are gossips, slanderers, haters of God, insolent, haughty, boastful, inventors of evil, disobedient to parents, foolish, faithless, heartless, ruthless. Though they know God's decree that those who do such things deserve to die, they not only do them but approve those who practice them.

Therefore you have no excuse, O man, whoever you are, when you judge another; for in passing judgment upon him you condemn yourself, because you, the judge, are doing the very same things. Do you suppose, O man, you will escape the judgment of God? Or do you presume upon the riches of his forbearance and patience? Do you not know that God's kindness is meant to lead you to repentance? But by your impenitent heart you are storing up wrath for yourself on the day when God's judgment will be revealed. For he will render to every man according to his works: to those who by patience in well-doing seek for glory and honor and immortality, he will give eternal life; but for those who do not obey the truth there will be wrath and fury. For God shows no partiality.

All who have sinned without the law will perish without the law, and all who have sinned under the law will be judged by the law. For it is not the hearers of the law who are righteous before God, but the doers of the law. When Gentiles who have not the law do by nature what the law requires, they are a law to themselves. They show that the law is written on their hearts.

Their conscience also bears witness and their conflicting thoughts accuse or perhaps excuse them on that day when God judges the secrets of men by Christ Jesus.

But if you call yourself a Jew and rely upon the law, and if you are sure that you are a light to those who are in darkness, a corrector of the foolish, a teacher of children, having in the law the embodiment of knowledge and truth—you then who teach others, will you not teach yourself? While you preach against stealing, do you steal? You who say that one must not commit adultery, do you commit adultery? You who abhor idols, do you rob temples? You who boast in the law, do you dishonor God by breaking the law?

Circumcision indeed is of value if you obey the law; but if you break the law, your circumcision becomes uncircumcision. For he is not a real Jew who is one outwardly, nor is true circumcision something external and physical. He is a Jew who is one inwardly, and real circumcision is a matter of the heart, spiritual and not literal. Then what is the value of circumcision? Much in every way. To begin with, the Jews are entrusted with the oracles of God. What if some were unfaithful? Does their faithlessness nullify the faithfulness of God? By no means! Let God be true though every man be false.

What then? Are we Jews any better off? No, not at all; for all men are under the power of sin, as it is written: "None is righteous, no, not one; no one understands, no one seeks for God. All have turned aside, together they have gone wrong; no one does good, not even one."

Now we know that whatever the law says it speaks to those who are under the law, so that every mouth may be stopped, and the whole world may be held accountable to God. For no human being will be justified in his sight by works of the law, since through the law comes knowledge of sin.

But now the righteousness of God has been manifested apart from law, although the law and the prophets bear witness to it, through faith in Jesus Christ for all who believe. For there is no distinction; since all have sinned and fall short of the glory of God, they are justified by his grace as a gift, through the redemption which is in Christ Jesus. This was to show God's righteousness, because in his divine forbearance he had passed over former sins; it was to prove at the present time that he himself is righteous and that he justifies him who has faith in Jesus.

Then what becomes of our boasting? It is excluded. On what principle? On the principle of works? No, but on the principle of faith. For we hold that a man is justified by faith apart from works of law. Or is God the God of Jews only? Is he not the God of Gentiles also? Yes, of Gentiles also, since God is one; and he will justify the circumcised on the ground of their faith and the uncircumcised through their faith. Do we then overthrow the law by this faith? By no means! On the contrary, we uphold the law.

What then shall we say about Abraham, our forefather according to the flesh? For if Abraham was justified by works, he has something to boast about, but not before God. For what does the scripture say? "Abraham believed God, and it was reckoned to him as righteousness." Now to one who works, his wages are not reckoned as a gift but as his due. And to one who does not work but trusts him who justifies the ungodly, his faith is reckoned as righteousness. We say that faith was reckoned to Abraham as righteousness. How was it reckoned to him? Was it before or after he had been circumcised? It was not after, but before. He received circumcision as a sign or seal of the righteousness which he had by faith while he was still uncircumcised. The purpose was to make him the father of all who believe without being circumcised and who thus have righteousness reckoned to them, and likewise the father of the circumcised who also follow the example of the faith Abraham had before he was circumcised.

The promise to Abraham and his descendants, that they should inherit the world, did not come through the law but through the righteousness of faith. If it is the adherents of the law who are to be the heirs, faith is null and the promise is void. For the law brings wrath, but where there is no law there is no transgression. That is why it depends on faith, in order that the promise may rest on grace and be guaranteed to all his descendants—not only to the adherents of the law but also to those who share the faith of Abraham, for he is the father of us all, as it is written, "I have made you the father of many nations"—in the presence of the God in whom he believed, who gives life to the dead and calls into existence the things that do not exist. In hope he believed against hope, that he should become the father of many nations; as he had been told, "So shall your descendants be."

He did not weaken in faith when he considered his own body, which was as good as dead because he was about a hundred years old, or when he considered the barrenness of Sarah's womb. No distrust made him waver concerning the promise of God, but he grew strong in his faith as he gave glory to God, fully convinced that God was able to do what he had promised. That is why his faith was "reckoned to him as righteousness." But the words, "it was reckoned to him," were written not for his sake alone, but for ours also. It will be reckoned to us who believe in him that raised from the dead Jesus our Lord, who was put to death for our trespasses and raised for our justification.

Therefore, since we are justified by faith, we have peace with God through our Lord Jesus Christ. Through him we have obtained access to this grace in which we stand, and we rejoice in our hope of sharing the glory of God. More than that, we rejoice in our sufferings, knowing that suffering produces endurance, and endurance produces character, and character produces hope, and hope does not disappoint us, because God's love has been poured into our hearts through the Holy Spirit.

God shows his love for us in that while we were yet sinners Christ died for us. Since we are now justified by his blood, much more shall we be saved by him from the wrath of God. For if while we were enemies we were reconciled to God by the death of his Son, much more, now that we are reconciled, shall we be saved by his life.

Therefore as sin came into the world through one man and death through sin, and so death spread to all men because all men sinned—sin indeed was in the world before the law was given, but sin is not counted where there is no law. Yet death reigned from Adam to Moses, even over those whose sins were not like the transgression of Adam, who was a type of the one who was to come.

But the free gift is not like the trespass. For if many died through one man's trespass, much more have the grace of God and the free gift in the grace of that one man Jesus Christ abounded for many. And the free gift is not like the effect of that one man's sin. For the judgment following one trespass brought condemnation, but the free gift following many trespasses brings justification. If, because of one man's trespass, death reigned through that one man, much more will those who receive the abundance of grace and the free gift of righteousness reign in life through the one man Jesus Christ.

Then as one man's trespass led to condemnation for all men, so one man's act of righteousness leads to acquittal and life for all men. For as by one man's disobedience many were made sinners, so by one man's obedience many will be made righteous. Law came in, to increase the trespass; but where sin increased, grace abounded all the more, so that, as sin reigned in death, grace also might reign through righteousness to eternal life through Jesus Christ our Lord.

What shall we say then? Are we to continue in sin, that grace may abound? By no means! How can we who died to sin still live in it? Do you not know that all of us who have been baptized into Christ Jesus were baptized into his death? We were buried therefore with him by baptism into death, so that as Christ was raised from the dead by the glory of the Father, we too might walk in newness of life.

For if we have been united with him in a death like his, we shall certainly be united with him in a resurrection like his. We know that our old self was crucified with him so that the sinful body might be destroyed, and we might no longer be enslaved to sin. For he who has died is freed from sin. But if we have died with Christ, we believe that we shall also live with him. For we know that Christ being raised from the dead will never die again; death no longer has dominion over him. The death he died he died to sin, once for all, but the life he lives he lives to God. So you also must consider yourselves dead to sin and alive to God in Christ Jesus. Let not sin therefore reign in your mortal bodies, to make you obey their passions. For sin will have no dominion over you, since you are not under law but under grace.

Do you not know that if you yield yourselves as slaves, you are slaves of the one whom you obey, either of sin, which leads to death, or of obedience, which leads to righteousness? But thanks be to God, that you who were once slaves of sin have become obedient from the heart to the standard of teaching to which you were committed, and, having been set free from sin, have become slaves of righteousness. I am speaking in human terms, because of your natural limitations. For just as you once yielded your members to impurity and to greater and greater iniquity, so now yield your members to righteousness for sanctification.

When you were slaves of sin, you were free in regard to righteousness. But then what return did you get from the things of which you are now ashamed? The end of those things is death. But now that you have been set free from sin and have become slaves of God, the return you get is sanctification and its end, eternal life. For the wages of sin is death, but the free gift of God is eternal life in Christ Jesus our Lord.

Do you not know, brethren—for I am speaking to those who know the law—that the law is binding on a person only during his life? Thus a married woman is bound by law to her husband as long as he lives; but if her husband dies she is discharged from the law concerning the husband. Accordingly, she will be called an adulteress if she lives with another man while her husband is alive. But if her husband dies she is free from that law, and if she marries another man she is not an adulteress.

Likewise, my brethren, you have died to the law through the body of Christ, so that you may belong to another, to him who has been raised from the dead in order that we may bear fruit for God. While we were living in the flesh, our sinful passions, aroused by the law, were at work in our members to bear fruit for death. But now we are discharged from the law, dead to that which held us captive, so that we serve not under the old written code but in the new life of the Spirit.

What then shall we say? That the law is sin? By no means! Yet, if it had not been for the law, I should not have known sin. I should not have known what it is to covet if the law had not said, "You shall not covet." But sin, finding opportunity in the commandment, wrought in me all kinds of covetousness. Apart from the law sin lies dead. I was once alive apart from the law, but when the commandment came, sin revived and I died; the very commandment which promised life proved to be death to me. For sin, finding opportunity in the commandment, deceived me and by it killed me. So the law is holy, and the commandment is holy and just and good.

Did that which is good, then, bring death to me? By no means! It was sin, working death in me through what is good, in order that sin might be shown to be sin, and through the commandment might become sinful beyond measure. We know that the law is spiritual; but I am carnal, sold under sin. I do not understand my own actions. For I do not do what I want, but I do the very thing I hate. Now if I do what I do not want, I agree that the law is good. So then it is no longer I that do it, but sin which dwells within me. For I know that nothing good dwells within me, that is, in my flesh. I can will what is right, but I cannot do it. For I do not do the good I want, but the evil I do not want is what I do. Now if I do what I do not want, it is no longer I that do it, but sin which dwells within me.

So I find it to be a law that when I want to do right, evil lies close at hand.

For I delight in the law of God, in my inmost self, but I see in my members another law at war with the law of my mind and making me captive to the law of sin which dwells in my members. Wretched man that I am! Who will deliver me from this body of death? Thanks be to God through Jesus Christ our Lord! So then, I of myself serve the law of God with my mind, but with my flesh I serve the law of sin.

There is therefore now no condemnation for those who are in Christ Jesus. For the law of the Spirit of life in Christ Jesus has set me free from the law of sin and death. For God has done what the law, weakened by the flesh, could not do: sending his own Son in the likeness of sinful flesh and for sin, he condemned sin in the flesh, in order that the just requirement of the law might be fulfilled in us. Those who live according to the flesh set their minds on the things of the flesh, but those who live according to the Spirit set their minds on the things of the Spirit. The mind that is set on the flesh is hostile to God; it does not submit to God's law, indeed it cannot.

Any one who does not have the Spirit of Christ does not belong to him. But if Christ is in you, although your bodies are dead because of sin, your spirits are alive because of righteousness. If the Spirit of him who raised Jesus from the dead dwells in you, he who raised Christ Jesus from the dead will give life to your mortal bodies also, through his Spirit which dwells in you.

All who are led by the Spirit of God are sons of God. For you did not receive the spirit of slavery, but you have received the spirit of sonship. When we cry, "Abba! Father!" it is the Spirit himself bearing witness with our spirit that we are children of God, and if children, then heirs, heirs of God and fellow heirs with Christ, provided we suffer with him in order that we may also be glorified with him.

I consider that the sufferings of this present time are not worth comparing with the glory that is to be revealed to us. For the creation waits with eager longing for the revealing of the sons of God; because the creation itself will be set free from its bondage to decay and obtain the glorious liberty of the children of God. We know that the whole creation has been groaning in travail together until now; and not only the creation, but we ourselves, who have the first fruits of the Spirit, groan inwardly as we wait for adoption as sons, the redemption of our bodies. For in this hope we were saved. Now hope that is seen is not hope. Who hopes for what he sees? But if we hope for what we do not see, we wait for it with patience.

Likewise the Spirit helps us in our weakness; for we do not know how to pray as we ought, but the Spirit himself intercedes for us with sighs too deep for words. And he who searches the hearts of men knows what is the mind of the Spirit, because the Spirit intercedes for the saints according to the will of God.

We know that in everything God works for good with those who love him. Those whom he foreknew he also predestined to be conformed to the image of his Son. And those whom he predestined he also called; and those whom he called he also justified; and those whom he justified he also glorified.

What then shall we say to this? If God is for us, who is against us? He who did not spare his own Son but gave him up for us all, will he not also give us all things with him? It is God who justifies; who is to condemn? Is it Christ Jesus, who was raised from the dead and who is at the right hand of God, who indeed intercedes for us? Who shall separate us from the love of Christ? Shall tribulation, or distress, or persecution, or famine, or nakedness, or peril, or sword? No, in all these things we are more than conquerors through him who loved us. For I am sure that neither death, nor life, nor angels, nor principalities, nor things present, nor things to come, nor powers, nor height, nor depth, nor anything else in all creation, will be able to separate us from the love of God in Christ Jesus our Lord.

I am speaking the truth in Christ, I am not lying; my conscience bears me witness in the Holy Spirit that I have unceasing anguish in my heart. For I could wish that I myself were accursed and cut off from Christ for the sake of my kinsmen by race. They are Israelites, and to them belong the sonship, the glory, the covenants, the giving of the law, the worship, and the promises; to them belong the patriarchs, and of their race, according to the flesh, is the Christ. God, who is over all, be blessed for ever. Amen.

But it is not as though the word of God had failed. For not all who are descended from Israel belong to Israel, and not all are children of Abraham because they are his descendants; but "Through Isaac shall your descendants be named." This means that it is not the children of the flesh who are the children of God, but the children of the promise are reckoned as descendants. What shall we say then? Is there injustice on God's part? By no means! For he says to Moses, "I will have mercy on whom I have mercy, and I will have compassion on whom I have compassion." So it depends not upon man's will or exertion, but upon God's mercy. He has mercy upon whomever he wills, and he hardens the heart of whomever he wills.

You will say to me then, "Why does he still find fault? For who can resist his will?" But who are you, a man, to answer back to God? Will what is molded say to its molder, "Why have you made me thus?" Has the potter no right over the clay, to make out of the same lump one vessel for beauty and another for menial use? As indeed he says in Hosea, "Those who were not my people I will call 'my people,' and her who was not beloved I will call 'my beloved.'"

And Isaiah cries out concerning Israel: "Though the number of the sons of Israel be as the sand of the sea, only a remnant of them will be saved; for the Lord will execute his sentence upon the earth with rigor and dispatch."

What shall we say then? That Gentiles who did not pursue righteousness have attained it, that is, righteousness through faith; but that Israel who pursued the righteousness which is based on law did not succeed in fulfilling that law. Why? Because they did not pursue it through faith, but as if it were based on works. They have stumbled over the stumbling stone, as it is written, "Behold, I am laying in Zion a stone that will make men stumble, a rock that will make them fall; and he who believes in him will not be put to shame."

Brethren, my heart's desire and prayer to God for them is that they may be saved. I bear them witness that they have a zeal for God, but it is not enlightened. Being ignorant of the righteousness that comes from God, and seeking to establish their own, they did not submit to God's righteousness.

Moses writes that the man who practices the righteousness which is based on the law shall live by it. But the righteousness based on faith says, Do not say in your heart, "Who will ascend into heaven?" (that is, to bring Christ down) or "Who will descend into the abyss?" (that is, to bring Christ up from the dead). But what does it say? The word is near you, on your lips and in your heart (that is, the word of faith which we preach). If you confess with your lips that Jesus is Lord and believe in your heart that God raised him from the dead, you will be saved. For man believes with his heart and so is justified, and he confesses with his lips and so is saved. The same Lord is Lord of all, and the scripture says, "every one who calls upon the name of the Lord will be saved."

But how are men to call upon him in whom they have not believed? And how are they to believe in him of whom they have never heard? And how are they to hear without a preacher? And how can men preach unless they are sent? So faith comes from what is heard, and what is heard comes by the preaching of Christ.

But I ask, have they not heard? Indeed they have; for "Their voice has gone out to all the earth, and their words to the ends of the world." Again I ask, did Israel not understand? First Moses says, "I will make you jealous of those who are not a nation; with a foolish nation I will make you angry." Then Isaiah is so bold as to say, "I have been found by those who did not seek me; I have shown myself to those who did not ask for me." But of Israel he says, "All day long I have held out my hands to a disobedient people."

I ask, then, has God rejected his people? By no means! I myself am an Israelite, a member of the tribe of Benjamin. Do you not know what the scripture says of Elijah, how he pleads with God against Israel? "Lord, they have killed thy prophets, they have demolished thy altars, and I alone am left, and they seek my life." But what is God's reply to him? "I have kept for myself seven thousand men who have not bowed the knee to Baal." So too at the present time there is a remnant, chosen by grace. But if it is by grace, it is no longer on the basis of works; otherwise grace would no longer be grace.

What then? Israel failed to obtain what it sought. The elect obtained it, but the rest were hardened. So I ask, have they stumbled so as to fall? By no means! But through their trespass salvation has come to the Gentiles, so as to make Israel jealous. Now if their trespass means riches for the world, and if their failure means riches for the Gentiles, how much more will their full inclusion mean!

Now I am speaking to you Gentiles. Inasmuch then as I am an apostle to the Gentiles, I magnify my ministry in order to make my fellow Jews jealous, and thus save some of them. For if their rejection means the reconciliation of the world, what will their acceptance mean but life from the dead? If the dough offered as first fruits is holy, so is the whole lump; and if the root is holy, so are the branches.

But if some of the branches were broken off, and you, a wild olive shoot, were grafted in their place to share the richness of the olive tree, do not boast over the branches. Remember, it is not you that support the root, but the root that supports you. They were broken off because of their unbelief, but you stand fast only through faith. So do not become proud, but stand in awe. For if God did not spare the natural branches, neither will he spare you. Note then the kindness and the severity of God: severity toward those who have fallen, but kindness to you. And even the others, if they do not persist in their unbelief, will be grafted in again.

Lest you be wise in your own conceits, I want you to understand this mystery, brethren: a hardening has come upon part of Israel, until the full number of the Gentiles come in, and so all Israel will be saved. As regards the gospel, they are enemies of God, for your sake; but as regards election, they are beloved for the sake of their forefathers. For the gifts and the call of God are irrevocable. Just as you were once disobedient to God but now have received mercy because of their disobedience, so they have now been disobedient in order that by the mercy shown to you they also may receive mercy. For God has consigned all men to disobedience, that he may have mercy upon all.

O the depth of the riches and wisdom and knowledge of God! How unsearchable are his judgments and how inscrutable his ways! For from him and through him and to him are all things. To him be glory for ever. Amen.

I appeal to you therefore, brethren, to present your bodies as a living sacrifice, holy and acceptable to God, which is your spiritual worship. Do not be conformed to this world but be transformed by the renewal of your mind, that you may prove what is the will of God, what is good and acceptable and perfect.

For by the grace given to me I bid every one among you not to think of himself more highly than he ought to think, but to think with sober judgment, each according to the measure of faith which God has assigned him. For as in one body we have many members, and all the members do not have the same function, so we, though many, are one body in Christ, and individually members one of another. Having gifts that differ according to the grace given to us, let us use them: if prophecy, in proportion to our faith; if service, in our serving; he who teaches, in his teaching; he who exhorts, in his exhortation; he who contributes, in liberality; he who gives aid, with zeal; he who does acts of mercy, with cheerfulness.

Let love be genuine; hate what is evil, hold fast to what is good; love one another with brotherly affection; outdo one another in showing honor. Never flag in zeal, be aglow with the Spirit, serve the Lord. Rejoice in your hope, be patient in tribulation, be constant in prayer. Contribute to the needs of the saints, practice hospitality.

Bless those who persecute you; bless and do not curse them. Rejoice with those who rejoice, weep with those who weep. Live in harmony with one another; do not be haughty, but associate with the lowly; never be conceited. Repay no one evil for evil, but take thought for what is noble in the sight of all. If possible, so far as it depends upon you, live peaceably with all. Beloved, never avenge yourselves, but leave it to the wrath of God; for it is written, "Vengeance is mine, I will repay, says the Lord." No, "if your enemy is hungry, feed him; if he is thirsty, give him drink; for by so doing you will heap burning coals upon his head." Do not be overcome by evil, but overcome evil with good.

Let every person be subject to the governing authorities. For there is no authority except from God, and those that exist have been instituted by God. Therefore he who resists the authorities resists what God has appointed, and those who resist will incur judgment. For rulers are not a terror to good conduct, but to bad. Would you have no fear of him who is in authority? Then do what is good, and you will receive his approval, for he is God's servant for your good. But if you do wrong, be afraid, for he does not bear the sword in vain. Therefore one must be subject, not only to avoid God's wrath but also for the sake of conscience. For the same reason you also pay taxes, for the authorities are ministers of God, attending to this very thing. Pay all of them their dues, taxes to whom taxes are due, revenue to whom revenue is due, respect to whom respect is due, honor to whom honor is due.

Owe no one anything, except to love one another; for he who loves his neighbor has fulfilled the law. The commandments, "You shall not commit adultery, You shall not kill, You shall not steal, You shall not covet," and any other commandment, are summed up in this sentence, "You shall love your neighbor as yourself." Love does no wrong to a neighbor; therefore love is the fulfilling of the law.

The night is far gone, the day is at hand. Let us then cast off the works of darkness and put on the armor of light; let us conduct ourselves becomingly as in the day, not in reveling and drunkenness, not in debauchery and licentiousness, not in quarreling and jealousy. But put on the Lord Jesus Christ, and make no provision for the flesh, to gratify its desires.

Let us no more pass judgment on one another, but rather decide never to put a stumbling block or hindrance in the way of a brother. I know and am persuaded in the Lord Jesus that nothing is unclean in itself; but it is unclean for any one who thinks it unclean. If your brother is being injured by what you eat, you are no longer walking in love. Do not let what you eat cause the ruin of one for whom Christ died. So do not let your good be spoken of as evil. For the kingdom of God is not food and drink but righteousness and peace and joy in the Holy Spirit. Do not, for the sake of food, destroy the work of

God. Everything is indeed clean, but it is wrong for any one to make others fall by what he eats; it is right not to eat meat or drink wine or do anything that makes your brother stumble. The faith that you have, keep between yourself and God.

We who are strong ought to bear with the failings of the weak, and not to please ourselves; let each of us please his neighbor for his good, to edify him. Welcome one another, therefore, as Christ has welcomed you, for the glory of God. For I tell you that Christ became a servant to the circumcised to show God's truthfulness, in order to confirm the promises given to the patriarchs, and in order that the Gentiles might glorify God for his mercy. May the God of hope fill you with all joy and peace in believing, so that by the power of the Holy Spirit you may abound in hope.

I myself am satisfied about you, my brethren, that you yourselves are full of goodness, filled with all knowledge, and able to instruct one another. But on some points I have written to you very boldly by way of reminder, because of the grace given me by God to be a minister of Christ Jesus to the Gentiles. In Christ Jesus, then, I have reason to be proud of my work for God. For I will not venture to speak of anything except what Christ has wrought through me to win obedience from the Gentiles, so that from Jerusalem as far round as Illyricum I have fully preached the gospel, thus making it my ambition to preach not where Christ has already been named, lest I build on another man's foundation, but as it is written, "They shall see who have never been told of him, and they shall understand who have never heard of him."

This is the reason why I have so often been hindered from coming to you. But now, since I no longer have any room for work in these regions, and since I have longed for many years to come to you, I hope to see you in passing as I go to Spain. At present, however, I am going to Jerusalem with aid for the saints. Macedonia and Achaia have been pleased to make some contribution for the poor among the saints at Jerusalem; they were pleased to do it, for if the Gentiles have come to share in their spiritual blessings, they ought to be of service to them in material blessings. When I have completed this, I shall go on by way of you to Spain; and I know that when I come to you I shall come in the fulness of the blessing of Christ.

I commend to you our sister Phoebe, a deaconess of the church at Cenchreae, that you may help her in whatever she may require from you, for she has been a helper of many and of myself as well. Greet Prisca and Aquila, who risked their necks for my life, to whom not only I but also all the churches of the Gentiles give thanks; greet also the church in their house.

Now to him who is able to strengthen you according to my gospel and the preaching of Jesus Christ, according to the revelation of the mystery which was kept secret for long ages but is now disclosed and through the prophetic writings is made known to all nations, according to the command of the eternal God, to bring about the obedience of faith—to the only wise God be glory for evermore through Jesus Christ! Amen.

1 CORINTHIANS

Corinth was one of the most important cities of Greece. Not long after Paul had planted the Christian faith there and left the city, news reached him in Ephesus of problems beginning to trouble the young church. Factions had split the community, and there was a growing tendency to be overly impressed by a certain kind of human "wisdom." Also, some of the faithful were taking undue pride in their ability to speak with tongues. Paul deals forthrightly with these and other problems, and in his effort to guide this local church he has bequeathed to the universal church some of the most exalted passages in his correspondence. Especially notable are the hymn on Christian love and the teaching on the meaning of Christ's resurrection.

———

Paul, CALLED BY the will of God to be an apostle of Christ Jesus, and our brother Sosthenes, to the church of God which is at Corinth, to those sanctified in Christ Jesus, called to be saints together with all those who in every place call on the name of our Lord Jesus Christ, both their Lord and ours: Grace to you and peace from God our Father and the Lord Jesus Christ.

I give thanks to God always for you because of the grace of God which was given you in Christ Jesus, that in every way you were enriched in him, so that you are not lacking in any spiritual gift, as you wait for the revealing of our Lord Jesus Christ, who will sustain you to the end. God is faithful, by whom you were called into the fellowship of his Son.

I appeal to you, brethren, that there be no dissensions among you. For it has been reported to me by Chloe's people that there is quarreling. Each one of you says, "I belong to Paul," or "I belong to Apollos," or "I belong to Cephas," or "I belong to Christ." Is Christ divided? Was Paul crucified for you? Or were you baptized in the name of Paul? I am thankful that I baptized none of you except Crispus and Gaius; lest any one should say that you were baptized in my name. (I did baptize also the household of Stephanas. Beyond that, I do not know whether I baptized any one else.) For Christ did not send me to baptize but to preach the gospel, and not with eloquent wisdom, lest the cross of Christ be emptied of its power. For the word of the cross is folly to those who are perishing, but to us who are being saved it is the power of God. For it is written, "I will destroy the wisdom of the wise, and the cleverness of the clever I will thwart."

Has not God made foolish the wisdom of the world? For since, in the wisdom of God, the world did not know God through wisdom, it pleased God through the folly of what we preach to save those who believe. Jews demand signs and Greeks seek wisdom, but we preach Christ crucified, a stumbling block to Jews and folly to Gentiles, but to those who are called, both Jews and Greeks, Christ the power of God and the wisdom of God. For the foolishness of God is wiser than men, and the weakness of God is stronger than men.

Consider your call, brethren; not many of you were wise according to worldly standards, not many were powerful, not many were of noble birth; but God chose what is foolish in the world to shame the wise, what is weak in the world to shame the strong, what is low and despised, even things that are not, to bring to nothing things that are, so that no human being might boast in the presence of God. He is the source of your life in Christ Jesus, whom God made our wisdom, our righteousness and sanctification and redemption; therefore, as it is written, "Let him who boasts, boast of the Lord."

When I came to you, brethren, I did not proclaim the testimony of God in lofty words or wisdom. For I decided to know nothing among you except Jesus Christ and him crucified. I was with you in weakness and in much fear and trembling; and my speech and my message were not in plausible words of wisdom, but in demonstration of the Spirit and of power, that your faith might not rest in the wisdom of men but in the power of God.

Yet among the mature we do impart wisdom, although it is not a wisdom of this age or of the rulers of this age, who are doomed to pass away. But we impart a secret and hidden wisdom of God, decreed before the ages for our glorification. None of the rulers of this age understood this; for if they had, they would not have crucified the Lord of glory. But, as it is written, "What no eye has seen, nor ear heard, nor the heart of man conceived, what God has prepared for those who love him," God has revealed to us through the Spirit.

For the Spirit searches everything, even the depths of God. For what person knows a man's thoughts except the spirit of the man which is in him? So also no one comprehends the thoughts of God except the Spirit of God. Now we have received the Spirit which is from God, that we might understand the gifts bestowed on us by God. And we impart this in words not taught by human wisdom but taught by the Spirit, interpreting spiritual truths to those who possess the Spirit.

The unspiritual man does not receive the gifts of the Spirit of God, for they are folly to him, and he is not able to understand them because they are spiritually discerned. The spiritual man judges all things, but is himself to be judged by no one. "For who has known the mind of the Lord so as to instruct him?" But we have the mind of Christ.

But I, brethren, could not address you as spiritual men, but as men of the flesh, as babes in Christ. I fed you with milk, not solid food; for you were not ready for it; and even yet you are not ready, for you are still of the flesh. While there is jealousy and strife among you, are you not of the flesh, and behaving like ordinary men?

What then is Apollos? What is Paul? Servants through whom you believed, as the Lord assigned to each. I planted, Apollos watered, but God gave the growth. So neither he who plants nor he who waters is anything, but only God who gives the growth. He who plants and he who waters are equal, and each shall receive his wages according to his labor. For we are God's fellow workers; you are God's field, God's building.

Let no one deceive himself. If any one among you thinks he is wise in this age, let him become a fool, that he may become wise. For the wisdom of this world is folly with God. So let no one boast of men. For all things are yours, whether Paul or Apollos or Cephas or the world or life or death or the present or the future, all are yours; and you are Christ's; and Christ is God's.

This is how one should regard us, as servants of Christ and stewards of the mysteries of God. Moreover it is required of stewards that they be found trustworthy. But with me it is a very small thing that I should be judged by you or by any human court. I do not even judge myself. I am not aware of anything against myself, but I am not thereby acquitted. It is the Lord who judges me. Therefore do not pronounce judgment before the time, before the Lord comes, who will bring to light the things now hidden in darkness and will disclose the purposes of the heart. Then every man will receive his commendation from God.

I have applied all this to myself and Apollos for your benefit, brethren, that you may learn by us not to go beyond what is written, that none of you may be puffed up in favor of one against another. For who sees anything different in you? What have you that you did not receive? If then you received it, why do you boast as if it were not a gift?

I think that God has exhibited us apostles as last of all, like men sentenced to death; because we have become a spectacle to the world. We are fools for Christ's sake, but you are wise in Christ. We are weak, but you are strong. You are held in honor, but we in disrepute. To the present hour we hunger and thirst, we are ill-clad and buffeted and homeless, and we labor, working with our own hands. When reviled, we bless; when persecuted, we endure; when slandered, we try to conciliate; we have become, and are now, as the refuse of the world, the offscouring of all things.

I do not write this to make you ashamed, but to admonish you as my beloved children. For though you have countless guides in Christ, you do not have many fathers. I became your father in Christ Jesus through the gospel. I urge you, then, be imitators of me. I will come to you soon, if the Lord wills, and I will find out not the talk of these arrogant people but their power. For the kingdom of God does not consist in talk but in power. What do you wish? Shall I come to you with a rod, or with love in a spirit of gentleness?

IT IS ACTUALLY reported that there is immorality among you, and of a kind that is not found even among pagans; for a man is living with his father's wife. Let him who has done this be removed from among you. For though absent in body I am present in spirit, and I have already pronounced judgment in the name of the Lord Jesus on the man who has done such a thing. When you are assembled, you are to deliver this man to Satan for the destruction of the flesh, that his spirit may be saved.

I wrote to you in my letter not to associate with immoral men; not meaning the immoral of this world, since then you would need to go out of the world. Rather I wrote to you not to associate with any one who bears the name of brother if he is guilty of immorality, not even to eat with such a one. "Drive out the wicked person from among you." Do not be deceived; neither the immoral, nor idolaters, nor adulterers, nor sexual perverts, nor thieves, nor the greedy, nor drunkards, nor revilers, nor robbers will inherit the kingdom of God. And such were some of you. But you were washed, you were sanctified, you were justified in the name of the Lord Jesus Christ and in the Spirit of our God.

"All things are lawful for me," you say, but not all things are helpful. "All things are lawful for me," but I will not be enslaved by anything. "Food is meant for the stomach and the stomach for food"—and God will destroy both one and the other. The body is not meant for immorality, but for the Lord, and the Lord for the body. And God raised the Lord and will also raise us up by his power. Do you not know that your bodies are members of Christ? Shall I therefore take the members of Christ and make them members of a prostitute? Never! Shun immorality. Every other sin which a man commits is outside the body; but the immoral man sins against his own body. Do you not know that your body is a temple of the Holy Spirit within you, which you have from God? You are not your own; you were bought with a price. So glorify God in your body.

Now concerning the matters about which you wrote. It is well for a man not to touch a woman. But because of the temptation to immorality, each man should have his own wife and each woman her own husband. The husband should give to his wife her conjugal rights, and likewise the wife to her husband. For the wife does not rule over her own body, but the husband does; likewise the husband does not rule over his own body, but the wife does. Do not refuse one another except perhaps by agreement for a season, that you may devote yourselves to prayer; but then come together again, lest Satan tempt you through lack of self-control. I say this by way of concession, not of command. I wish that all were as I myself am. But each has his own special gift from God, one of one kind and one of another.

To the unmarried and the widows I say that it is well for them to remain single as I do. But if they cannot exercise self-control, they should marry. For it is better to marry than to be aflame with passion.

To the married I give charge, not I but the Lord, that the wife should not separate from her husband (but if she does, let her remain single or else be reconciled to her husband)—and that the husband should not divorce his wife.

To the rest I say, not the Lord, that if any brother has a wife who is an unbeliever, and she consents to live with him, he should not divorce her. If any woman has a husband who is an unbeliever, and he consents to live with her, she should not divorce him. For the unbelieving husband is consecrated through his wife, and the unbelieving wife is consecrated through her husband. Otherwise, your children would be unclean, but as it is they are holy. But if the unbelieving partner desires to separate, let it be so; in such a case the brother or sister is not bound. For God has called us to peace. Wife, how do you know whether you will save your husband? Husband, how do you know whether you will save your wife?

Only, let every one lead the life which the Lord has assigned to him, and in which God has called him. This is my rule in all the churches. In whatever state each was called, there let him remain with God.

Now concerning the unmarried, I have no command of the Lord, but I give my opinion as one who by the Lord's mercy is trustworthy. I think that in view of the present distress it is well for a person to remain as he is. Are you bound to a wife? Do not seek to be free. Are you free from a wife? Do not seek marriage. But if you marry, you do not sin, and if a girl marries, she does not sin. Yet those who marry will have worldly troubles, and I would spare you that. I mean, brethren, the appointed time has grown very short; from now on, let those who have wives live as though they had none, and those who mourn as though they were not mourning, and those who rejoice as though they were not rejoicing, and those who buy as though they had no goods, and those who deal with the world as though they had no dealings with it. For the form of this world is passing away.

I want you to be free from anxieties. The unmarried man is anxious about the affairs of the Lord, how to please the Lord; but the married man is anxious about worldly affairs, how to please his wife, and his interests are divided. And the unmarried woman or girl is anxious about the affairs of the Lord, how to be holy in body and spirit; but the married woman is anxious about worldly affairs, how to please her husband. I say this for your own benefit, not to lay any restraint upon you, but to promote good order and to secure your undivided devotion to the Lord.

If any one thinks that he is not behaving properly toward his betrothed, if his passions are strong, and it has to be, let him do as he wishes: let them marry—it is no sin. But whoever is firmly established in his heart, being under no necessity but having his desire under control, and has determined this in his heart, to keep her as his betrothed, he will do well. So that he who marries his betrothed does well; and he who refrains from marriage will do better.

A wife is bound to her husband as long as he lives. If the husband dies, she is free to be married to whom she wishes, only in the Lord. But in my judgment she is happier if she remains as she is. And I think that I have the Spirit of God.

AM I NOT free? Am I not an apostle? Have I not seen Jesus our Lord? Are not you my workmanship in the Lord? If to others I am not an apostle, at least I am to you; for you are the seal of my apostleship in the Lord. This is my defense to those who would examine me. Do we not have the right to our food and drink? Do we not have the right to be accompanied by a wife, as the other apostles and the brothers of the Lord and Cephas? Or is it only Barnabas and I who have no right to refrain from working for a living? Who serves as a soldier at his own expense? Who plants a vineyard without eating any of its fruit?

Do I say this on human authority? Does not the law say the same? For it is written in the law of Moses, "You shall not muzzle an ox when it is treading out the grain." Is it for oxen that God is concerned? Does he not speak entirely for our sake? If we have sown spiritual good among you, is it too much if we reap your material benefits? Do you not know that those who are employed in the temple service get their food from the temple? In the same way, the Lord commanded that those who proclaim the gospel should get their living by the gospel.

But I have made no use of any of these rights, nor am I writing this to secure any such provision. For I would rather die than have any one deprive me of my ground for boasting. For if I preach the gospel, that gives me no ground for boasting; necessity is laid upon me. Woe to me if I do not preach the gospel! If I do this of my own will, I have a reward; but if not of my own will, I am entrusted with a commission. What then is my reward? Just this: that in my preaching I may make the gospel free of charge, not making full use of my right in the gospel.

For though I am free from all men, I have made myself a slave to all, that I might win the more. To the Jews I became as a Jew, in order to win Jews; to those under the law I became as one under the law—though not being myself under the law—that I might win those under the law. To those outside the law I became as one outside the law—not being without law toward God but under the law of Christ—that I might win those outside the law. To the weak I became weak, that I might win the weak. I have become all things to all men, that I might by all means save some. I do it all for the sake of the gospel, that I may share in its blessings.

Do you not know that in a race all the runners compete, but only one receives the prize? So run that you may obtain it. Every athlete exercises self-control in all things. They do it to receive a perishable wreath, but we an imperishable. Well, I do not run aimlessly, I do not box as one beating the air; but I pommel my body and subdue it, lest after preaching to others I myself should be disqualified.

I want you to know, brethren, that our fathers were all under the cloud, and all passed through the sea, and all were baptized into Moses in the cloud and in the sea, and all ate the same supernatural food and all drank the same supernatural drink. For they drank from the supernatural Rock which followed them, and the Rock was Christ. Nevertheless, with most of them God was not pleased; for they were overthrown in the wilderness. Now these things are warnings for us. We must not indulge in immorality, must not put the Lord to the test, nor grumble. No temptation has overtaken you that is not common to man. God is faithful, and he will not let you be tempted beyond your strength, but with the temptation will also provide the way of escape.

Therefore, my beloved, shun the worship of idols. I speak as to sensible men; judge for yourselves what I say. The cup of blessing which we bless, is it not a participation in the blood of Christ? The bread which we break, is it not a participation in the body of Christ? Because there is one bread, we who are many are one body, for we all partake of the one bread. What pagans sacrifice they offer to demons and not to God. You cannot drink the cup of the Lord and the cup of demons. You cannot partake of the table of the Lord and the table of demons.

I commend you because you remember me in everything and maintain the traditions even as I have delivered them to you. But I want you to understand that the head of every man is Christ, the head of a woman is her husband, and the head of Christ is God. Any man who prays or prophesies with his head covered dishonors his head, but any woman who prays or prophesies with her head unveiled dishonors her head—it is the same as if her head were shaven. For if a woman will not veil herself, then she should cut off her hair; but if it is disgraceful for a woman to be shorn or shaven, let her wear a veil. For a man ought not to cover his head, since he is the image and glory of God; but woman is the glory of man. (For man was not made from woman, but woman from man. Neither was man created for woman, but woman for man.) That is why a woman ought to have a veil on her head, because of the angels. (Nevertheless, in the Lord woman is not independent of man nor man of woman; for as woman was made from man, so man is now born of woman. And all things are from God.)

In the following I do not commend you, because when you assemble as a church, I hear that there are divisions among you; and I partly believe it. When you meet together, it is not the Lord's supper that you eat. For in eating, each one goes ahead with his own meal, and one is hungry and another is drunk. What! Do you not have houses to eat and drink in? Or do you despise the church of God and humiliate those who have nothing? Shall I commend you in this? No, I will not.

For I received from the Lord what I also delivered to you, that the Lord Jesus on the night when he was betrayed took bread, and when he had given thanks, he broke it, and said, "This is my body which is for you. Do this in remembrance of me." In the same way also the cup, after supper, saying, "This cup is the new covenant in my blood. Do this, as often as you drink it, in remembrance of me." For as often as you eat this bread and drink the cup, you proclaim the Lord's death until he comes.

Whoever, therefore, eats the bread or drinks the cup of the Lord in an unworthy manner will be guilty of profaning the body and blood of the Lord. Let a man examine himself, and so eat of the bread and drink of the cup. For any one who eats and drinks without discerning the body eats and drinks judgment upon himself. That is why many of you are weak and ill, and some have died. But if we judged ourselves truly, we should not be judged. But when we are judged by the Lord, we are chastened so that we may not be condemned along with the world. My brethren, when you come together to eat, wait for one another—if any one is hungry, let him eat at home—lest you come together to be condemned.

Now concerning spiritual gifts, brethren, I do not want you to be uninformed. You know that when you were heathen, you were led astray to dumb idols, however you may have been moved. Therefore I want you to understand that no one speaking by the Spirit of God ever says "Jesus be cursed!" and no one can say "Jesus is Lord" except by the Holy Spirit.

Now there are varieties of gifts, but the same Spirit; and there are varieties of service, but the same Lord; and there are varieties of working, but it is the same God who inspires them all in every one. To each is given the manifestation of the Spirit for the common good. To one is given through the Spirit the utterance of wisdom, and to another the utterance of knowledge according to the same Spirit, to another faith by the same Spirit, to another gifts of healing by the one Spirit, to another the working of miracles, to another prophecy, to another the ability to distinguish between spirits, to another various kinds of tongues, to another the interpretation of tongues. All these are inspired by one and the same Spirit, who apportions to each one individually as he wills. For just as the body is one and has many members, and all the members of the body, though many, are one body, so it is with Christ. For by one Spirit we were all baptized into one body—Jews or Greeks, slaves or free—and all were made to drink of one Spirit.

The body does not consist of one member but of many. If all were a single organ, where would the body be? As it is, there are many parts, yet one body. The eye cannot say to the hand, "I have no need of you," nor again the head to the feet, "I have no need of you." On the contrary, the parts of the body which seem to be weaker are indispensable, and those parts of the body which we think less honorable we invest with the greater honor, and our unpresentable parts are treated with greater modesty, which our more presentable parts do not require. But God has so composed the body, giving the greater honor to the inferior part, that there may be no discord in the body, but that the members may have the same care for one another. If one member suffers, all suffer together; if one member is honored, all rejoice together.

Now you are the body of Christ and individually members of it. And God has appointed in the church first apostles, second prophets, third teachers, then workers of miracles, then healers, helpers, administrators, speakers in various kinds of tongues. Are all apostles? Are all prophets? Are all teachers? Do all work miracles? Do all possess gifts of healing? Do all speak with tongues? Do all interpret? But earnestly desire the higher gifts.

And I will show you a still more excellent way.

If I speak in the tongues of men and of angels, but have not love, I am a noisy gong or a clanging cymbal. And if I have prophetic powers, and understand all mysteries and all knowledge, and if I have all faith, so as to remove mountains, but have not love, I am nothing. If I give away all I have, and if I deliver my body to be burned, but have not love, I gain nothing.

Love is patient and kind; love is not jealous or boastful; it is not arrogant or rude. Love does not insist on its own way; it is not irritable or resentful; it does not rejoice at wrong, but rejoices in the right. Love bears all things, believes all things, hopes all things, endures all things.

Love never ends; as for prophecies, they will pass away; as for tongues, they will cease; as for knowledge, it will pass away. For our knowledge is imperfect and our prophecy is imperfect; but when the perfect comes, the imperfect will pass away. When I was a child, I spoke like a child, I thought like a child, I reasoned like a child; when I became a man, I gave up childish ways. For now we see in a mirror dimly, but then face to face. Now I know in part; then I shall understand fully, even as I have been fully understood. So faith, hope, love abide, these three; but the greatest of these is love.

Make love your aim, and earnestly desire the spiritual gifts, especially that you may prophesy. For one who speaks in a tongue speaks not to men but to God; for no one understands him, but he utters mysteries in the Spirit. On the other hand, he who prophesies speaks to men for their upbuilding and encouragement and consolation. He who speaks in a tongue edifies himself, but he who prophesies edifies the church. Now I want you all to speak in tongues, but even more to prophesy. He who prophesies is greater than he who speaks in tongues, unless some one interprets, so that the church may be edified. I thank God that I speak in tongues more than you all; nevertheless, in church I would rather speak five words with my mind, in order to instruct others, than ten thousand words in a tongue.

Brethren, do not be children in your thinking; be babes in evil, but in thinking be mature. Tongues are a sign not for believers but for unbelievers, while prophecy is not for unbelievers but for believers. If, therefore, the whole church assembles and all speak in tongues, and outsiders or unbelievers enter, will they not say that you are mad? But if all prophesy, and an unbeliever or outsider enters, he is convicted by all, he is called to account by all, the secrets of his heart are disclosed; and so, falling on his face, he will worship God and declare that God is really among you.

When you come together, each one has a hymn, a lesson, a revelation, a tongue, or an interpretation. If any speak in a tongue, let there be only two or at most three, and each in turn; and let one interpret. But if there is no one to interpret, let each of them keep silence in church and speak to himself and to God. Let two or three prophets speak, and let the others weigh what is said. If a revelation is made to another sitting by, let the first be silent. For you can all prophesy one by one, so that all may learn and all be encouraged; and the spirits of prophets are subject to prophets. For God is not a God of confusion but of peace.

As in all the churches of the saints, the women should keep silence. For they are not permitted to speak, but should be subordinate, as even the law says. If there is anything they desire to know, let them ask their husbands at home. For it is shameful for a woman to speak in church.

Now I would remind you, brethren, in what terms I preached to you the gospel, by which you are saved if you hold it fast. I delivered to you as of first importance that Christ died for our sins in accordance with the scriptures, that he was buried, that he was raised on the third day in accordance with the scriptures, and that he appeared to Cephas, then to the twelve. Then he appeared to more than five hundred brethren at one time, most of whom are still alive, though some have fallen asleep. Then he appeared to James, then to all the apostles. Last of all, as to one untimely born, he appeared also to me. For I am the least of the apostles, unfit to be called an apostle, because I persecuted the church of God. But by the grace of God I am what I am, and his grace toward me was not in vain. On the contrary, I worked harder than any of them, though it was not I, but the grace of God which is with me.

Now if Christ is preached as raised from the dead, how can some of you say that there is no resurrection of the dead? But if there is no resurrection of the dead, then Christ has not been raised; if Christ has not been raised, then our preaching is in vain and your faith is in vain. We are even found to be misrepresenting God, because we testified of God that he raised Christ, whom he did not raise if it is true that the dead are not raised. Then those also who have fallen asleep in Christ have perished. If for this life only we have hoped in Christ, we are of all men most to be pitied.

But in fact Christ has been raised from the dead, the first fruits of those who have fallen asleep. For as by a man came death, by a man has come also the resurrection of the dead. For as in Adam all die, so also in Christ shall all be made alive. But each in his own order: Christ the first fruits, then at his coming those who belong to Christ. Then comes the end, when he delivers the kingdom to God the Father after destroying every rule and every authority and power. For he must reign until he has put all his enemies under his feet. The last enemy to be destroyed is death. "For God has put all things in subjection under his feet." But when it says, "All things are put in subjection under him," it is plain that he is excepted who put all things under him. When all things are subjected to him, then the Son himself will also be subjected to him who put all things under him, that God may be everything to every one.

Otherwise, what do people mean by being baptized on behalf of the dead? If the dead are not raised at all, why are people baptized on their behalf? If the dead are not raised, "Let us eat and drink, for tomorrow we die." Do not be deceived: "Bad company ruins good morals." Come to your right mind, and sin no more. For some have no knowledge of God. I say this to your shame.

But some one will ask, "How are the dead raised? With what kind of body do they come?" You foolish man! What you sow does not come to life unless it dies. And what you sow is not the body which is to be, but a bare kernel, perhaps of wheat or of some other grain. But God gives it a body as he has chosen, and to each kind of seed its own body. For not all flesh is alike, but there is one kind for men, another for animals, another for birds, and another for fish. There are celestial bodies and there are terrestrial bodies; but the glory of the celestial is one, and the glory of the terrestrial is another. There is one glory of the sun, and another glory of the moon, and another glory of the stars; for star differs from star in glory.

So is it with the resurrection of the dead. What is sown is perishable, what is raised is imperishable. It is sown in dishonor, it is raised in glory. It is sown in weakness, it is raised in power. It is sown a physical body, it is raised a spiritual body. If there is a physical body, there is also a spiritual body. Thus it is written, "The first man Adam became a living being"; the last Adam became a life-giving spirit. But it is not the spiritual which is first but the physical, and then the spiritual. The first man was from the earth, a man of dust; the second man is from heaven. As was the man of dust, so are those who are of the dust; and as is the man of heaven, so are those who are of heaven. Just as we have borne the image of the man of dust, we shall also bear the image of the man of heaven. I tell you this, brethren: flesh and blood cannot inherit the kingdom of God, nor does the perishable inherit the imperishable.

Lo! I tell you a mystery. We shall not all sleep, but we shall all be changed, in a moment, in the twinkling of an eye, at the last trumpet. For the trumpet will sound, and the dead will be raised imperishable, and we shall be changed. For this perishable nature must put on the imperishable, and this mortal nature must put on immortality. When the perishable puts on the imperishable, and the mortal puts on immortality, then shall come to pass the saying that is written: "Death is swallowed up in victory." "O death, where is thy victory? O death, where is thy sting?" The sting of death is sin, and the power of sin is the law. But thanks be to God, who gives us the victory through our Lord Jesus Christ.

Therefore, my beloved brethren, be steadfast, immovable, always abounding in the work of the Lord, knowing that in the Lord your labor is not in vain.

NOW CONCERNING THE CONTRIBUTION for the saints: as I directed the churches of Galatia, so you also are to do. On the first day of every week, each of you is to put something aside and store it up, as he may prosper, so that contributions need not be made when I come. And when I arrive, I will send those whom you accredit by letter to carry your gift to Jerusalem. If it seems advisable that I should go also, they will accompany me.

I will visit you after passing through Macedonia, and perhaps I will stay with you or even spend the winter. But I will stay in Ephesus until Pentecost, for a wide door for effective work has opened to me, and there are many adversaries.

When Timothy comes, see that you put him at ease among you, for he is doing the work of the Lord, as I am. Speed him on his way in peace, that he may return to me. As for our brother Apollos, I strongly urged him to visit you with the other brethren, but it was not at all his will to come. He will come when he has opportunity.

The churches of Asia send greetings. Aquila and Prisca, together with the church in their house, send you hearty greetings in the Lord. All the brethren send greetings. Greet one another with a holy kiss.

I, Paul, write this greeting with my own hand. If any one has no love for the Lord, let him be accursed. Our Lord, come! The grace of the Lord Jesus be with you. My love be with you all in Christ Jesus. Amen.

2 CORINTHIANS

This letter was written about a year after 1 Corinthians. Its principal topic is Paul's personal relationship to the church at Corinth, which had taken a turn for the worse. Grieved by the wavering attitude of some of the Corinthians toward his authority and motives, Paul wrote them a severe letter (not known to us), *"out of much affliction and anguish of heart and with many tears."* Anxious to hear how they had reacted to this reprimand, he was overjoyed at the news brought by Titus of their change of heart. In relief and gratitude, Paul wrote the present letter to explain his actions and give news of his work. Because so much of 2 Corinthians is a response to the words and feelings of others, unrecorded here, it is sometimes hard to follow. Its pages preserve a good deal, however, that illuminates Paul's own life and ministry.

PAUL, AN APOSTLE of Christ Jesus by the will of God, and Timothy our brother. To the church of God which is at Corinth, with all the saints who are in the whole of Achaia: Grace to you and peace from God our Father and the Lord Jesus Christ.

Blessed be the God and Father of our Lord Jesus Christ, the Father of mercies, who comforts us in all our affliction, so that we may be able to comfort others. For as we share abundantly in Christ's sufferings, so through Christ we share abundantly in comfort too. If we are afflicted, it is for your comfort and salvation; and if we are comforted, it is for your comfort, when you patiently endure the same sufferings that we suffer.

For we do not want you to be ignorant, brethren, of the affliction we experienced in Asia; we were so utterly, unbearably crushed that we despaired of life itself. Why, we felt that we had received the sentence of death; but that was to make us rely not on ourselves but on God, who raises the dead; he delivered us from so deadly a peril, and he will deliver us; on him we have set our hope that he will deliver us again.

For our boast is this, the testimony of our conscience that we have behaved in the world, and still more toward you, with holiness and godly sincerity, not by earthly wisdom but by the grace of God. I hope you will understand that you can be proud of us as we can be of you, on the day of the Lord Jesus.

Because I was sure of this, I wanted to come to you first, so that you might have a double pleasure; I wanted to visit you on my way to Macedonia, and to come back to you from Macedonia and have you send me on my way to Judea. But I call God to witness, it was to spare you that I refrained from coming to Corinth. I made up my mind not to make you another painful visit. For if I cause you pain, who is there to make me glad but the one whom I have pained? And I wrote as I did, so that when I came I might not suffer pain from those who should have made me rejoice. I wrote you out of much affliction and anguish of heart and with many tears, not to cause you pain but to let you know the abundant love that I have for you.

But if any one has caused pain, he has caused it not to me, but in some measure—not to put it too severely—to you all. For such a one this punishment by the majority is enough; so you should rather turn to forgive and comfort him, or he may be overwhelmed by excessive sorrow. So I beg you to reaffirm your love for him. Any one whom you forgive, I also forgive. What I have forgiven, if I have forgiven anything, has been for your sake in the presence of Christ, to keep Satan from gaining the advantage over us; for we are not ignorant of his designs.

When I came to Troas to preach the gospel of Christ, a door was opened for me in the Lord; but my mind could not rest because I did not find my brother Titus there. So I took leave of them and went on to Macedonia. But thanks be to God, who in Christ always leads us in triumph, and through us spreads the fragrance of the knowledge of him everywhere. For we are the aroma of Christ to God among those who are being saved and among those who are perishing, to one a fragrance from death to death, to the other a fragrance from life to life.

Are we beginning to commend ourselves again? Or do we need letters of recommendation to you, or from you? You yourselves are our letter of recommendation, written on your hearts, to be read by all men; you are a letter from Christ delivered by us, written not with ink but with the Spirit of the living God, not on tablets of stone but on tablets of human hearts. Not that we claim anything as coming from us; our competence is from God, who has made us ministers of a new covenant, not in a written code but in the Spirit; for the written code kills, but the Spirit gives life.

Now if the dispensation of death, carved in letters on stone, came with such splendor that the Israelites could not look at Moses' face because of its brightness, will not the dispensation of the Spirit be attended with greater splendor? Since we have such a hope, we are very bold, not like Moses, who put a veil over his face. But their minds were hardened; for to this day, when they read the old covenant, that same veil remains unlifted, because only through Christ is it taken away. Yes, to this day, whenever Moses is read, a veil lies over their minds; but when a man turns to the Lord the veil is removed. And we all, with unveiled face, beholding the glory of the Lord, are being changed into his likeness from one degree of glory to another.

Therefore, having this ministry by the mercy of God, we do not lose heart. We have renounced disgraceful, underhanded ways; we refuse to practice cunning or to tamper with God's word, but by the open statement of the truth we would commend ourselves to every man's conscience in the sight of God. What we preach is not ourselves, but Jesus Christ as Lord, with ourselves as your servants for Jesus' sake. For it is the God who said, "Let light shine out of darkness," who has shone in our hearts to give the light of the knowledge of the glory of God in the face of Christ.

But we have this treasure in earthen vessels, to show that the transcendent power belongs to God and not to us. We are afflicted in every way, but not crushed; perplexed, but not driven to despair; persecuted, but not forsaken; struck down, but not destroyed; always carrying in the body the death of Jesus, so that the life of Jesus may also be manifested in our bodies. For while we live we are always being given up to death for Jesus' sake. Death is at work in us, but life in you. So we speak, knowing that he who raised the Lord Jesus will raise us also with Jesus and bring us with you into his presence. This slight momentary affliction is preparing for us an eternal weight of glory beyond all comparison, because we look not to the things that are seen but to the things that are unseen; for the things that are seen are transient, but the things that are unseen are eternal. For we know that if the earthly tent we live in is destroyed, we have a building from God, a house not made with hands, eternal in the heavens.

So we are always of good courage; we know that while we are at home in the body we are away from the Lord, for we walk by faith, not by sight. We would rather be away from the body and at home with the Lord. So we make it our aim to please him. For we must all appear before the judgment seat of Christ, so that each may receive good or evil, according to what he has done in the body.

Therefore, knowing the fear of the Lord, we persuade men; but what we are is known to God, and I hope it is known also to your conscience. We are not commending ourselves to you again but giving you cause to be proud of us, so that you may be able to answer those who pride themselves on a man's position and not on his heart. For if we are beside ourselves, it is for God; if we are in our right mind, it is for you. The love of Christ controls us, because we are convinced that one has died for all; therefore all have died. And he died for all, that those who live might live no longer for themselves but for him who for their sake died and was raised.

Therefore, if any one is in Christ, he is a new creation; the old has passed away, behold, the new has come. All this is from God, who through Christ reconciled us to himself and gave us the ministry of reconciliation; that is, in Christ God was reconciling the world to himself, not counting their trespasses against them, and entrusting to us the message of reconciliation. So we are ambassadors for Christ, God making his appeal through us. We beseech you on behalf of Christ, be reconciled to God.

Working together with him, then, we entreat you not to accept the grace of God in vain. For he says, "At the acceptable time I have listened to you, and helped you on the day of salvation." Behold, now is the acceptable time; now is the day of salvation. We put no obstacle in any one's way, so that no fault may be found with our ministry, but as servants of God we commend ourselves in every way: through great endurance, in afflictions, hardships, calamities, beatings, imprisonments, tumults, labors, watching, hunger; by purity, knowledge, forbearance, kindness, the Holy Spirit, genuine love, truthful speech, and the power of God; with the weapons of righteousness for the right hand and for the left; in honor and dishonor, in ill repute and good repute. We are treated as impostors, and yet are true; as unknown, and yet well known; as dying, and behold, we live; as punished, and yet not killed; as sorrowful, yet always rejoicing; as poor, yet making many rich; as having nothing, and yet possessing everything.

Do not be mismated with unbelievers. For what partnership have righteousness and iniquity? Or what fellowship has light with darkness? What accord has Christ with Belial? Or what has a believer in common with an unbeliever? What agreement has the temple of God with idols? For we are the temple of the living God.

Open your hearts to us; we have wronged no one, we have corrupted no one, we have taken advantage of no one. If I made you sorry with my letter, I do not regret it (though I did regret it), for I see that that letter grieved you. I rejoice, not because you were grieved, but because you were grieved into repenting; for you felt a godly grief, so that you suffered no loss through us. For godly grief produces a repentance that leads to salvation and brings no regret, but worldly grief produces death. See what earnestness this godly grief has produced in you, what eagerness to clear yourselves, what indignation, what alarm, what longing, what zeal, what punishment! At every point you have proved yourselves guiltless in the matter.

We want you to know, brethren, about the grace of God which has been shown in the churches of Macedonia, for in a severe test of affliction, their abundance of joy and their extreme poverty have overflowed in a wealth of liberality on their part. For they gave according to their means, as I can testify, and beyond their means, of their own free will, begging us earnestly for the favor of taking part in the relief of the saints. Accordingly, we have urged Titus that he should also complete among you this gracious work. Now as you excel in everything, see that you excel in this also. I say this not as a command, but to prove by the earnestness of others that your love also is genuine.

But thanks be to God, who puts the same earnest care for you into the heart of Titus. With him we are sending the brother who is famous among all the churches for his preaching of the gospel; he has been appointed by the churches to travel with us in this gracious work which we are carrying on, for the glory of the Lord and to show our good will.

We intend that no one should blame us about this liberal gift which we are administering, for we aim at what is honorable not only in the Lord's sight but also in the sight of men. I am sending the brethren so that you may be ready, as I said you would be; lest if some Macedonians come with me and find that you are not ready, we be humiliated—to say nothing of you—for being so confident. So I thought it necessary to urge the brethren to go on before me, and arrange in advance for this gift you have promised.

The point is this: he who sows sparingly will also reap sparingly, and he who sows bountifully will also reap bountifully. Each one must do as he has made up his mind, not reluctantly or under compulsion, for God loves a cheerful giver. And God is able to provide you with every blessing in abundance. The rendering of this service not only supplies the wants of the saints but also overflows in many thanksgivings to God. Under the test of this service, you will glorify God by your obedience in acknowledging the gospel of Christ, and by the generosity of your contribution for them and for all others.

I entreat you, by the meekness and gentleness of Christ—I who am humble when face to face with you, but bold to you when I am away!—that when I am present I may not have to show boldness with such confidence as I count on showing against some who suspect us of acting in worldly fashion. For though we live in the world we are not carrying on a worldly war, for the weapons of our warfare are not worldly but have divine power to destroy strongholds. We destroy arguments and every proud obstacle to the knowledge of God, and take every thought captive to obey Christ, being ready to punish every disobedience, when your obedience is complete.

Look at what is before your eyes. If any one is confident that he is Christ's, let him remind himself that as he is Christ's, so are we. For even if I boast a little too much of our authority, which the Lord gave for building you up and not for destroying you, I shall not be put to shame. I would not seem to be frightening you with letters. For they say, "His letters are weighty and strong, but his bodily presence is weak, and his speech of no account." Let such people understand that what we say by letter when absent, we do when present.

But we will not boast beyond limit, but will keep to the limits God has apportioned us, to reach even to you. We were the first to come all the way to you with the gospel of Christ. We do not boast beyond limit, in other men's labors; but our hope is that as your faith increases, our field among you may be greatly enlarged, so that we may preach the gospel in lands beyond you, without boasting of work already done in another's field. "Let him who boasts, boast of the Lord." For it is not the man who commends himself that is accepted, but the man whom the Lord commends.

I wish you would bear with me in a little foolishness. Do bear with me! I feel a divine jealousy for you, for I betrothed you to Christ to present you as a pure bride to her one husband. But I am afraid that as the serpent deceived Eve by his cunning, your thoughts will be led astray from a sincere and pure devotion to Christ. For if some one comes and preaches another Jesus than the one we preached, or if you receive a different spirit from the one you received, or if you accept a different gospel from the one you accepted, you submit to it readily enough. I think that I am not in the least inferior to these superlative apostles. Even if I am unskilled in speaking, I am not in knowledge; in every way we have made this plain to you in all things.

Let no one think me foolish; but even if you do, accept me as a fool, so that I too may boast a little. (What I am saying I say not with the Lord's authority but as a fool, in this boastful confidence; since many boast of worldly things, I too will boast.) For you gladly bear with fools, being wise yourselves!

Whatever any one dares to boast of—I am speaking as a fool—I also dare to boast of that. Are they Hebrews? So am I. Are they Israelites? So am I. Are they descendants of Abraham? So am I. Are they servants of Christ? I am a better one—I am talking like a madman—with far greater labors, far more imprisonments, with countless beatings, and often near death. Five times I have received at the hands of the Jews the forty lashes less one. Three times I have been beaten with rods; once I was stoned. Three times I have been shipwrecked; a night and a day I have been adrift at sea; on frequent journeys, in danger from rivers, danger from robbers, danger from my own people, danger from Gentiles, danger in the city, danger in the wilderness, danger at sea, danger from false brethren; in toil and hardship, through many a sleepless night, in hunger and thirst, often without food, in cold and exposure. And, apart from other things, there is the daily pressure upon me of my anxiety for all the churches. Who is weak, and I am not weak? Who is made to fall, and I am not indignant?

If I must boast, I will boast of the things that show my weakness. The God and Father of the Lord Jesus, he who is blessed for ever, knows that I do not lie. At Damascus, the governor under King Aretas guarded the city in order to seize me, but I was let down in a basket through a window in the wall and escaped his hands.

I must boast; there is nothing to be gained by it, but I will go on to visions and revelations of the Lord. I know a man in Christ who fourteen years ago was caught up to the third heaven—whether in the body or out of the body I do not know, God knows. And I know that this man was caught up into Paradise—whether in the body or out of the body I do not know, God knows—and he heard things that cannot be told, which man may not utter. On behalf of this man I will boast, but on my own behalf I will not boast, except of my weaknesses. And to keep me from being too elated by the abundance of revelations, a thorn was given me in the flesh, a messenger of Satan, to harass me. Three times I besought the Lord about this, that it should leave me; but he said to me, "My grace is sufficient for you, for my power is made perfect in weakness." For the sake of Christ, then, I am content with weaknesses, insults, hardships, persecutions, and calamities; for when I am weak, then I am strong.

Here for the third time I am ready to come to you. And I will not be a burden, for I seek not what is yours but you; for children ought not to lay up for their parents, but parents for their children. I will most gladly spend and be spent for your souls. If I love you the more, am I to be loved the less?

Have you been thinking all along that we have been defending ourselves before you? It is in the sight of God that we have been speaking in Christ, and all for your upbuilding, beloved. For I fear that perhaps I may come and find you not what I wish, and that you may find me not what you wish; that perhaps there may be quarreling, jealousy, anger, selfishness, slander, gossip, conceit, and disorder. I fear that when I come again my God may humble me before you, and I may have to mourn over many of those who sinned before and have not repented of the impurity, immorality, and licentiousness which they have practiced.

Any charge must be sustained by the evidence of two or three witnesses. I warned those who sinned before and all the others, and I warn them now while absent, that if I come again I will not spare them—since you desire proof that Christ is speaking in me. He is not weak in dealing with you, but is powerful in you. For he was crucified in weakness, but lives by the power of God. For we are weak in him, but in dealing with you we shall live with him by the power of God.

Examine yourselves, to see whether you are holding to your faith. Test yourselves. Do you not realize that Jesus Christ is in you?—unless indeed you fail to meet the test! I hope you will find out that we have not failed. For we cannot do anything against the truth, but only for the truth. We are glad when we are weak and you are strong. What we pray for is your improvement. I write this in order that when I come I may not have to be severe in my use of the authority which the Lord has given me.

Finally, brethren, farewell. Mend your ways, heed my appeal, agree with one another, live in peace, and the God of love and peace will be with you. Greet one another with a holy kiss. All the saints greet you.

The grace of the Lord Jesus Christ and the love of God and the fellowship of the Holy Spirit be with you all.

GALATIANS

Paul's reason for writing to the churches of Galatia, founded by him, is quite clear: he has just received news about other Christian preachers from Jerusalem who are telling Galatia's converts that they must obey the Mosaic law of circumcision, eat only kosher food, and honor all other Jewish religious observances. This was contrary to the gospel, and Paul writes at once to remind his readers that salvation is God's free gift to all who have faith in Christ, not something earned by the keeping of certain rules. Those who are "in Christ," he insists, are free from the law, and are to be guided by the Spirit. Then, lest anyone should use the doctrine as a reason for indifference to the moral code, he concludes with some practical applications of his teaching.

Paul an apostle—not from men nor through man, but through Jesus Christ and God the Father, who raised him from the dead—and all the brethren who are with me, to the churches of Galatia: Grace to you and peace from God the Father and our Lord Jesus Christ, who gave himself for our sins to deliver us from the present evil age.

I am astonished that you are so quickly turning to a different gospel—not that there is another gospel, but there are some who want to pervert the gospel of Christ. But even if an angel from heaven should preach to you a gospel contrary to that which we preached to you, let him be accursed.

I would have you know, brethren, that the gospel which was preached by me is not man's gospel. For I did not receive it from man, but it came through a revelation of Jesus Christ. You have heard of my former life in Judaism, how I persecuted the church of God, so extremely zealous was I for the traditions of my fathers. But when he who had set me apart before I was born was pleased to reveal his Son to me, in order that I might preach him among the Gentiles, I did not go up to Jerusalem to those who were apostles before me, but I went away into Arabia; and again I returned to Damascus. Then after three years I went up to Jerusalem to visit Cephas, and remained with him fifteen days. But I saw none of the other apostles except James the Lord's brother. (In what I am writing to you, before God, I do not lie!) Then I went into the regions of Syria and Cilicia. And I was still not known by sight to the churches of Christ in Judea; they only heard it said, "He who once persecuted us is now preaching the faith he once tried to destroy." And they glorified God because of me.

After fourteen years I went up again to Jerusalem with Barnabas and Titus. I laid before those who were of repute the gospel which I preach, lest somehow I should be running in vain. But even Titus was not compelled to be circumcised, though he was a Greek. False brethren tried to bring us into bondage, but we did not yield submission, even for a moment, that the truth of the gospel might be preserved for you. Those who were reputed to be something (what they were makes no difference to me; God shows no partiality) added nothing to me. On the contrary, when they saw that I had been entrusted with the gospel to the uncircumcised, just as Peter had been entrusted with the gospel to the circumcised, James and Cephas and John gave to me and Barnabas the right hand of fellowship.

But when Cephas came to Antioch I opposed him to his face, because he stood condemned. For before certain men came from James, he ate with the Gentiles; when they came he separated himself, fearing the circumcision party. And with him the rest of the Jews acted insincerely, so that even Barnabas was carried away by their insincerity. But when I saw this, I said to Cephas before them all, "If you, though a Jew, live like a Gentile, how can you compel the Gentiles to live like Jews?" We ourselves, who are Jews by birth, know that a man is not justified by works of the law but through faith in Jesus Christ, because by works of the law shall no one be justified. But if, in our endeavor to be justified in Christ, we ourselves were found to be sinners, is Christ then an agent of sin? Certainly not! But if I build up again those things which I tore down, then I prove myself a transgressor. For I through the law died to the law, that I might live to God. I have been crucified with Christ; it is no longer I who live, but Christ who lives in me; and the life I now live in the flesh I live by faith in the Son of God, who loved me and gave himself for me. I do not nullify the grace of God; for if justification were through the law, then Christ died to no purpose.

O foolish Galatians! Who has bewitched you, before whose eyes Jesus Christ was publicly portrayed as crucified? Did you receive the Spirit by works of the law, or by hearing with faith? Having begun with the Spirit, are you now ending with the flesh? Does he who supplies the Spirit to you and works miracles among you do so by works of the law, or by hearing with faith? Thus Abraham "believed God, and it was reckoned to him as righteousness." So you see that it is men of faith who are the sons of Abraham. And the scripture, foreseeing that God would justify the Gentiles by faith, preached the gospel beforehand to Abraham, saying, "In you shall all the nations be blessed." So then, those who are men of faith are blessed with Abraham who had faith.

To give a human example, brethren: no one annuls even a man's will, or adds to it, once it has been ratified. Now the promises were made to Abraham and to his offspring. It does not say, "And to offsprings," referring to many; but, referring to one, "And to your offspring," which is Christ. This is what I mean: the law, which came afterward, does not annul a covenant previously ratified by God. For if the inheritance is by the law, it is no longer by promise; but God gave it to Abraham by a promise. Why then the law? It was added because of transgressions, till the offspring should come to whom the promise had been made.

Before faith came we were confined under the law, so that the law was our custodian until Christ came. Now we are no longer under a custodian; for in Christ Jesus you are all sons of God, through faith. For as many of you as were baptized into Christ have put on Christ. There is neither Jew nor Greek, slave nor free, male nor female; for you are all one in Christ Jesus. And if you are Christ's, then you are Abraham's offspring, heirs according to promise.

The heir, as long as he is a child, is no better than a slave, but is under guardians and trustees. So with us; when we were children, we were slaves to the elemental spirits of the universe. But when the time had fully come, God sent forth his Son, born of woman, born under the law, to redeem those who were under the law, so that we might receive adoption as sons. And because you are sons, God has sent the Spirit of his Son into our hearts, crying, "Abba! Father!" So through God you are no longer a slave but a son, and if a son then an heir. Now that you have come to know God, or rather to be known by God, how can you turn back again to the weak and beggarly elemental spirits? You observe days, and months, and seasons, and years! I am afraid I have labored over you in vain.

Brethren, I beseech you, become as I am, for I also have become as you are. You received me as an angel of God, as Christ Jesus. What has become of the satisfaction you felt? For I bear you witness that, if possible, you would have plucked out your eyes and given them to me. Have I then become your enemy by telling you the truth? My little children, with whom I am again in travail until Christ be formed in you! I could wish to be present with you now and to change my tone, for I am perplexed about you.

Tell me, you who desire to be under law, do you not hear the law? For it is written that Abraham had two sons, one by a slave and one by a free woman. But the son of the slave was born according to the flesh, the son of the free woman through promise. Now this is an allegory: these women are two covenants. One is from Mount Sinai, bearing children for slavery; she is Hagar and corresponds to the present Jerusalem, for she is in slavery with her children. But the Jerusalem above is free, and she is our mother. For it is written, "Rejoice, O barren one who does not bear; break forth and shout, you who are not in travail; for the children of the desolate one are many more than the children of her that is married." Now we, brethren, like Isaac, are children of promise. But as at that time he who was born according to the flesh persecuted him who was born according to the Spirit, so it is now. But what does the scripture say? "Cast out the slave and her son; for the son of the slave shall not inherit with the son of the free woman." So, brethren, we are not children of the slave but of the free woman. Christ has set us free; stand fast therefore, and do not submit again to a yoke of slavery.

Now I, Paul, say to you that if you receive circumcision, Christ will be of no advantage to you. I testify again to every man who receives circumcision that he is bound to keep the whole law. You are severed from Christ, you who would be justified by the law; you have fallen away from grace. For in Christ Jesus neither circumcision nor uncircumcision is of any avail, but faith working through love. You were running well; who hindered you from obeying the truth? I have confidence in the Lord that you will take no other view than mine; and he who is troubling you will bear his judgment, whoever he is. But if I, brethren, still preach circumcision, why am I still persecuted? In that case the stumbling block of the cross has been removed. I wish those who unsettle you would mutilate themselves!

Brethren, do not use your freedom as an opportunity for the flesh, but through love be servants of one another. For the whole law is fulfilled in one word, "You shall love your neighbor as yourself." But if you bite and devour one another, take heed that you are not consumed by one another. Walk by the Spirit, and do not gratify the desires of the flesh. For the desires of the flesh are against the Spirit, and the desires of the Spirit are against the flesh. Now the works of the flesh are plain: fornication, impurity, licentiousness, idolatry, sorcery, enmity, strife, jealousy, anger, selfishness, dissension, party spirit, envy, drunkenness, carousing, and the like. I warn you, as I warned you before, that those who do such things shall not inherit the kingdom of God. But the fruit of the Spirit is love, joy, peace, patience, kindness, goodness, faithfulness, gentleness, self-control. And those who belong to Christ Jesus have crucified the flesh with its passions and desires.

Brethren, if a man is overtaken in any trespass, you who are spiritual should restore him in a spirit of gentleness. Look to yourself, lest you too be tempted. Bear one another's burdens, and so fulfil the law of Christ. For if any one thinks he is something, when he is nothing, he deceives himself. But let each one test his own work, and then his reason to boast will be in himself alone and not in his neighbor. For each man will have to bear his own load.

Do not be deceived; God is not mocked, for whatever a man sows, that he will also reap. For he who sows to his own flesh will from the flesh reap corruption; but he who sows to the Spirit will from the Spirit reap eternal life. And let us not grow weary in well-doing, for in due season we shall reap, if we do not lose heart. As we have opportunity, let us do good to all men, and especially to those who are of the household of faith.

The grace of our Lord Jesus Christ be with your spirit, brethren. Amen.

EPHESIANS

More like a sermon or meditation than Paul's other letters, Ephesians does not deal with the needs of one particular church, and it contains no personal messages. It may in fact have been an encyclical or "circular letter." Opening with an exposition of God's eternal purpose to redeem Jews and Gentiles alike, the whole letter is pervaded with the doctrine of the mystical body of Christ, the apostle's analogy of the perfect union of Christian believers. This provides, too, the best example for the ideal harmony of husbands and wives. Unlike the Old Testament, the New Testament has no book that is purely poetry. But Ephesians comes near to it.

———

PAUL, AN APOSTLE of Christ Jesus by the will of God, to the saints who are also faithful in Christ Jesus: Grace to you and peace from God our Father and the Lord Jesus Christ.

Blessed be the God and Father of our Lord Jesus Christ, who has blessed us in Christ with every spiritual blessing in the heavenly places, even as he chose us in him before the foundation of the world, that we should be holy and blameless before him. He destined us in love to be his sons through Jesus Christ, according to the purpose of his will. In him we have redemption through his blood, the forgiveness of our trespasses, according to the riches of his grace. For he has made known to us the mystery of his will, according to his purpose which he set forth in Christ as a plan for the fulness of time, to unite in him all things in heaven and on earth.

In him we who first hoped in Christ have been appointed to live for the praise of his glory. In him you also, who have heard the gospel and have believed, were sealed with the Holy Spirit, which is the guarantee of our inheritance. For this reason, because I have heard of your faith in the Lord Jesus and your love toward all the saints, I do not cease to give thanks for you, remembering you in my prayers, that God may give you a spirit of wisdom, so that you may know what is the hope to which he has called you, and what is the immeasurable greatness of his power in us who believe, according to the working of his great might which he accomplished in Christ when he raised him from the dead. He made him sit at his right hand, far above all rule and authority and power and dominion, and above every name that is named, not only in this age but also in that which is to come. He has put all things under his feet and has made him the head over all things for the church, which is his body, the fulness of him who fills all in all.

And you he made alive, when you were dead through sins. We all once lived in the passions of our flesh, following the desires of body and mind, and so we were by nature children of wrath, like the rest of mankind. But God, even when we were dead through our trespasses, made us alive together with Christ, and raised us up with him. For by grace you have been saved through faith; and this is not your own doing, it is the gift of God—not because of works, lest any man should boast. For we are his workmanship, created in Christ Jesus for good works, which God prepared beforehand, that we should walk in them.

Remember that at one time you Gentiles were separated from Christ, alienated from Israel and the covenants of promise, having no hope and without God in the world. But now you who once were far off have been brought near in the blood of Christ. For he has broken down the dividing wall of hostility, by abolishing in his flesh the law of commandments and ordinances, that he might create in himself one new man in place of the two, and might reconcile us both to God in one body through the cross. He came and preached peace to those both far off and near; for through him we both have access in one Spirit to the Father. So you are no longer strangers, but are members of the household of God, built upon the foundation of the apostles and prophets, Christ Jesus himself being the cornerstone.

For this reason I, Paul, am a prisoner for Christ Jesus on behalf of you Gentiles—assuming that you have heard how the mystery was made known to me by revelation. When you read this you can perceive my insight into the mystery of Christ, which was not made known to other generations as it has now been revealed to his holy apostles and prophets by the Spirit; that is, how the Gentiles are fellow heirs of the promise in Christ Jesus through the gospel. To me, though I am the very least of all the saints, this grace was given, to preach to the Gentiles the unsearchable riches of Christ, and to make all men see what is the plan of the mystery; that through the church the manifold wisdom of God might now be made known to the principalities and powers in the heavenly places. So I ask you not to lose heart over what I am suffering for you, which is your glory.

I bow my knees before the Father, that he may grant you to be strengthened through his Spirit in the inner man, and that Christ may dwell in your hearts through faith; that you, being rooted and grounded in love, may comprehend with all the saints what is the breadth and length and height and depth, and know the love of Christ which surpasses knowledge, that you may be filled with all the fulness of God.

Now to him who by the power at work within us is able to do far more abundantly than all that we ask or think, to him be glory in the church and in Christ Jesus to all generations. Amen.

I therefore, a prisoner for the Lord, beg you to lead a life worthy of the calling to which you have been called, with all lowliness and meekness, with patience, forbearing one another in love, eager to maintain the unity of the Spirit in the bond of peace. There is one body and one Spirit, just as you were called to the one hope that belongs to your call, one Lord, one faith, one baptism, one God and Father of us all, who is above all and through all and in all. But grace was given to each of us according to the measure of Christ's gift. His gifts were that some should be apostles, some prophets, some evangelists, some pastors and teachers, to equip the saints for the work of ministry, for building up the body of Christ, until we all attain to the unity of the faith and of the knowledge of the Son of God, to mature manhood, to the stature of the fulness of Christ; so that we may no longer be children, tossed to and fro with every wind of doctrine, by the cunning of men. Rather, speaking the truth in love, we are to grow up in every way into him who is the head, into Christ, from whom the whole body, joined together, when each part is working properly, upbuilds itself in love.

Now this I testify in the Lord, that you must no longer live as the Gentiles do, darkened in their understanding, alienated from the life of God because of ignorance, callous, given up to licentiousness. You did not so learn Christ! Put off your old nature and be renewed in the spirit of your minds; put on the new nature, created after the likeness of God in true righteousness and holiness. Let every one speak the truth with his neighbor, for we are members one of another. Be angry but do not sin; do not let the sun go down on your anger, and give no opportunity to the devil. Let the thief no longer steal, but rather let him do honest work with his hands, to be able to give to those in need. Let no evil talk come out of your mouths, but only such as is edifying, as fits the occasion. And do not grieve the Holy Spirit of God, in whom you were sealed for the day of redemption. Let all bitterness and clamor and slander be put away, with all malice, and be kind to one another, tenderhearted, forgiving, as God in Christ forgave you.

Therefore be imitators of God, as beloved children. And walk in love, as Christ loved us and gave himself up for us, a sacrifice to God.

But fornication and all impurity or covetousness must not even be named among you. No impure man, or one who is covetous (that is, an idolater), has any inheritance in the kingdom of Christ and of God. Once you were darkness, but now you are light in the Lord; walk as children of light (for the fruit of light is found in all that is good and right and true), and try to learn what is pleasing to the Lord. Take no part in the unfruitful works of darkness, but instead expose them.

Look carefully then how you walk, not as unwise men but as wise, making the most of the time, because the days are evil. Do not get drunk with wine, for that is debauchery; but be filled with the Spirit, addressing one another in psalms, singing to the Lord with all your heart, always giving thanks in the name of our Lord Jesus Christ to God the Father.

Be subject to one another out of reverence for Christ. Wives, be subject to your husbands, as to the Lord. For the husband is the head of the wife as Christ is the head of the church, his body, and is its Savior. Husbands, love your wives, as Christ loved the church and gave himself up for her, that he might sanctify her, having cleansed her by water with the word, that he might present the church in splendor, holy and without blemish. Even so husbands should love their wives as their own bodies. He who loves his wife loves himself. For no man ever hates his own flesh, but nourishes and cherishes it, as Christ does the church. "A man shall leave his father and mother and be joined to his wife, and the two shall become one flesh." This mystery is a profound one, and I am saying that it refers to Christ and the church.

Children, obey your parents in the Lord, for this is right. "Honor your father and mother" (this is the first commandment with a promise), "that it may be well with you and that you may live long on the earth." Fathers, do not provoke your children to anger, but bring them up in the discipline and instruction of the Lord.

Slaves, be obedient to your earthly masters, with fear and trembling, in singleness of heart, not as men-pleasers, but as servants of Christ, doing the will of God from the heart, rendering service with a good will. Know that whatever good any one does, he will receive the same again from the Lord, whether he is a slave or free. Masters, do the same to them, and forbear threatening, knowing that he who is both their Master and yours is in heaven, and that there is no partiality with him.

Finally, be strong in the Lord and in the strength of his might. Put on the whole armor of God, that you may be able to stand against the wiles of the devil. For we are not contending against flesh and blood, but against the spiritual hosts of wickedness in the heavenly places. Stand therefore, having girded your loins with truth, and having put on the breastplate of righteousness, and having shod your feet with the equipment of the gospel of peace; taking the shield of faith, with which you can quench all the flaming darts of the evil one. And take the helmet of salvation, and the sword of the Spirit, which is the word of God. Pray at all times in the Spirit. To that end keep alert with all perseverance, making supplication for all the saints, and also for me, that utterance may be given me to proclaim boldly the mystery of the gospel, for which I am an ambassador in chains.

Peace be to the brethren, and love with faith, from God the Father and the Lord Jesus Christ. Grace be with all who love our Lord Jesus Christ with love undying.

PHILIPPIANS

One of Paul's most cordial and affectionate letters, Philippians was addressed to a Christian community in Macedonia, at Philippi, the first of the churches he founded in Europe. Writing from prison, probably in Rome, the apostle thanks the Philippians for having sent him, through Epaphroditus, some things he needed. When, after some time, Epaphroditus wanted to return home, Paul sent him back with this letter to express his warm regard for his friends there and to give them news and encouragement. The entire letter shows Paul's radiant joy and serene happiness in Christ, even while in prison and in danger of death.

PAUL AND TIMOTHY, servants of Christ Jesus, to all the saints in Christ Jesus who are at Philippi, with the bishops and deacons: Grace to you and peace from God our Father and the Lord Jesus Christ.

I thank my God, always in every prayer, for your partnership in the gospel from the first day until now. I am sure that he who began a good work in you will bring it to completion at the day of Jesus Christ. You are all partakers with me of grace, both in my imprisonment and in the defense and confirmation of the gospel. For God is my witness, how I yearn for you all with the affection of Christ Jesus. It is my prayer that your love may abound, with knowledge and all discernment, so that you may be pure and blameless for the day of Christ, filled with the fruits of righteousness which come through Jesus Christ, to the glory and praise of God.

I want you to know, brethren, that what has happened to me has really served to advance the gospel, so that it has become known throughout the whole praetorian guard and to all the rest that my imprisonment is for Christ; and most of the brethren have been made confident in the Lord because of my imprisonment, and are much more bold to speak the word of God without fear.

I rejoice, for I know that through your prayers and the help of the Spirit of Jesus Christ this will turn out for my deliverance, as it is my eager expectation and hope that with full courage now as always Christ will be honored in my body, whether by life or by death. For to me to live is Christ, and to die is gain. If it is to be life in the flesh, that means fruitful labor for me. Yet I am hard pressed between the two. My desire is to depart and be with Christ. But to remain in the flesh is more necessary on your account. Convinced of this, I know that I shall remain and continue with you all, for your progress and joy in the faith.

Only let your manner of life be worthy of the gospel of Christ, so that whether I come and see you or am absent, I may hear of you that you stand firm in one spirit, striving side by side for the faith of the gospel, and not frightened in anything by your opponents.

So if there is any encouragement in Christ, any incentive of love, any participation in the Spirit, complete my joy by being in full accord and of one mind. Do nothing from selfishness or conceit, but in humility count others better than yourselves. Let each of you look not only to his own interests, but also to the interests of others. Have this mind among yourselves, which is yours in Christ Jesus, who, though he was in the form of God, did not count equality with God a thing to be grasped, but emptied himself, taking the form of a servant, being born in the likeness of men. And being found in human form he humbled himself and became obedient unto death, even death on a cross. Therefore God has highly exalted him and bestowed on him the name which is above every name, that at the name of Jesus every knee should bow, in heaven and on earth and under the earth, and every tongue confess that Jesus Christ is Lord, to the glory of God the Father.

Therefore, my beloved, as you have always obeyed, not only in my presence but much more in my absence, work out your own salvation with fear and trembling; for God is at work in you.

Do all things without grumbling or questioning, that you may be children of God without blemish in the midst of a crooked and perverse generation, among whom you shine as lights in the world, holding fast the word of life, so that in the day of Christ I may be proud that I did not run in vain or labor in vain. Even if I am to be poured as a libation upon the sacrificial offering of your faith, I am glad and rejoice with you all. Likewise you also should be glad and rejoice with me.

I hope in the Lord Jesus to send Timothy to you soon, so that I may be cheered by news of you. I have no one like him, who will be genuinely anxious for your welfare. Timothy's worth you know, how as a son with a father he has served with me in the gospel. I hope therefore to send him just as soon as I see how it will go with me; and I trust in the Lord that shortly I myself shall come also.

I have thought it necessary to send you Epaphroditus, your messenger and minister to my need. He has been longing for you all, and has been distressed because you heard that he was ill. Indeed he was ill, near to death, but God had mercy on him. So receive him in the Lord with all joy; and honor such men, for he nearly died for the work of Christ, risking his life to complete your service to me.

Finally, my brethren, look out for the dogs, look out for the evil-workers, look out for those who mutilate the flesh. For we are the true circumcision, who worship God in spirit, and glory in Christ Jesus, and put no confidence in the flesh. If any man thinks he has reason for confidence in the flesh, I have more: circumcised on the eighth day, of the people of Israel, of the tribe of Benjamin, a Hebrew born of Hebrews; as to the law a Pharisee, as to zeal a persecutor of the church, as to righteousness under the law blameless. But whatever gain I had, I counted as loss for the sake of Christ. Indeed I count everything as loss because of the surpassing worth of knowing Christ Jesus my Lord. For his sake I have suffered the loss of all things, and count them as refuse, in order that I may gain Christ and be found in him, not having a righteousness of my own, based on law, but that which is through faith in Christ, the righteousness from God that depends on faith; that I may know him and the power of his resurrection, and may share his sufferings, becoming like him in his death, that if possible I may attain the resurrection from the dead.

Not that I have already obtained this or am already perfect; but I press on to make it my own, because Christ Jesus has made me his own. Forgetting what lies behind and straining forward to what lies ahead, I press on toward the goal for the prize of the upward call of God in Christ Jesus. Let those of us who are mature be thus minded; and if in anything you are otherwise minded, God will reveal that also to you. Only let us hold true to what we have attained.

Brethren, join in imitating me, and mark those who so live as you have an example in us. For many, of whom I have often told you and now tell you even with tears, live as enemies of the cross of Christ. Their end is destruction, their god is the belly, and they glory in their shame, with minds set on earthly things. But our commonwealth is in heaven, and from it we await a Savior, the Lord Jesus Christ, who will change our lowly body to be like his glorious body, by the power which enables him even to subject all things to himself.

Therefore, my brethren, whom I love and long for, my joy and crown, stand firm thus in the Lord, my beloved.

I entreat Euodia and Syntyche to agree in the Lord. And I ask you also, true yokefellow, help these women, for they have labored side by side with me in the gospel together with Clement and the rest of my fellow workers, whose names are in the book of life.

Rejoice in the Lord always; again I will say, Rejoice. Let all men know your forbearance. The Lord is at hand. Have no anxiety about anything, but in everything by prayer and supplication with thanksgiving let your requests be made known to God. And the peace of God, which passes all understanding, will keep your hearts and your minds in Christ Jesus.

Finally, brethren, whatever is true, whatever is honorable, whatever is just, whatever is pure, whatever is lovely, whatever is gracious, if there is any excellence, if there is anything worthy of praise, think about these things.

I rejoice in the Lord greatly that you have revived your concern for me; you were indeed concerned for me, but you had no opportunity. Not that I complain of want; for I have learned, in whatever state I am, to be content. I know how to be abased, and I know how to abound; in any and all circumstances I have learned the secret of facing plenty and hunger, abundance and want. I can do all things in him who strengthens me. Yet it was kind of you to share my trouble. Not that I seek the gift; but I seek the fruit which increases to your credit. And my God will supply every need of yours according to his riches in glory in Christ Jesus. To our God and Father be glory for ever and ever. Amen.

Greet every saint in Christ Jesus. The brethren who are with me greet you. All the saints greet you, especially those of Caesar's household.

The grace of the Lord Jesus Christ be with your spirit.

COLOSSIANS

The Christian church at Colossae, a city not far from Ephesus in Asia Minor, had been founded by Epaphras, whom Paul had sent to preach there. The apostle wrote this letter, probably from a prison in Rome, in order to correct some serious errors that were being taught at Colossae, and to instruct the recipients in the Christian life. The letter resembles Ephesians in tone, especially in the emphasis on the doctrine of the mystical body of Christ. At the same time Paul does not forget to give instructions for the Christian's daily life in the world.

Paul, an apostle of Christ Jesus by the will of God, and Timothy our brother, to the saints and faithful brethren in Christ at Colossae: Grace to you and peace from God our Father.

We always thank God, the Father of our Lord Jesus Christ, when we pray for you, because we have heard of your faith in Christ Jesus and of the love which you have for all the saints, because of the hope laid up for you in heaven. Of this you have heard before in the gospel which has come to you, as indeed in the whole world it is bearing fruit and growing—so among yourselves, from the day you heard and understood the grace of God in truth, as you learned it from Epaphras our beloved fellow servant. He is a faithful minister of Christ on our behalf and has made known to us your love in the Spirit.

And so, from the day we heard of it, we have not ceased to pray for you, asking that you may be filled with the knowledge of his will in all spiritual wisdom and understanding, to lead a life worthy of the Lord, fully pleasing to him, bearing fruit in every good work. May you be strengthened with all power, for all endurance with joy, giving thanks to the Father, who has qualified us to share in the inheritance of the saints in light. He has delivered us from the dominion of darkness and transferred us to the kingdom of his beloved Son, in whom we have redemption, the forgiveness of sins.

He is the image of the invisible God, the first-born of all creation; for in him all things were created, in heaven and on earth, visible and invisible, whether thrones or dominions or principalities or authorities—all things were created through him and for him. He is before all things, and in him all things hold together. He is the head of the body, the church; he is the beginning, the first-born from the dead, that in everything he might be preeminent. For in him all the fulness of God was pleased to dwell, and through him to reconcile to himself all things, whether on earth or in heaven, making peace by the blood of his cross.

And you, who once were estranged and hostile in mind, doing evil deeds, he has now reconciled in his body of flesh by his death, in order to present you holy and irreproachable before him, provided that you continue in the faith, stable and steadfast, not shifting from the hope of the gospel, which has been preached to every creature under heaven, and of which I, Paul, became a minister.

Now I rejoice in my sufferings for your sake, and in my flesh I complete what is lacking in Christ's afflictions for the sake of his body, that is, the church, of which I became a minister according to the divine office given to me for you, to make the word of God fully known, the mystery hidden for ages and generations but now made manifest to his saints. To them God chose to make known how great among the Gentiles are the riches of the glory of this mystery, which is Christ in you, the hope of glory. Him we proclaim, warning and teaching every man in all wisdom, that we may present every man mature in Christ. For this I toil, striving with all the energy which he mightily inspires within me.

For I want you to know how greatly I strive for you, and for those at Laodicea, and for all who have not seen my face, that their hearts may be encouraged as they are knit together in love, to have all the riches of assured understanding and the knowledge of God's mystery, of Christ, in whom are hid all the treasures of wisdom and knowledge. I say this in order that no one may delude you with beguiling speech. Though I am absent in body, yet I am with you in spirit, rejoicing to see your good order and the firmness of your faith in Christ. Live in him, rooted and built up in him and established in the faith, just as you were taught, abounding in thanksgiving.

See to it that no one makes a prey of you by philosophy and empty deceit, according to human tradition, according to the elemental spirits of the universe, and not according to Christ. For in him the whole fulness of deity dwells bodily, and you have come to fulness of life in him, who is the head of all rule and authority. You were buried with him in baptism, in which you were also raised with him through faith in the working of God. And you, who were dead in trespasses, God made alive together with him, having forgiven us all our trespasses, having canceled the bond which stood against us with its legal demands; this he set aside, nailing it to the cross. He disarmed the principalities and powers and made a public example of them, triumphing over them in him.

Therefore let no one pass judgment on you in questions of food and drink or a festival or a sabbath. These are only a shadow of what is to come; but the substance belongs to Christ. Let no one disqualify you, insisting on self-abasement and worship of angels, taking his stand on visions, puffed up without reason by his sensuous mind, and not holding fast to the Head, from whom the whole body, nourished and knit together through its joints and ligaments, grows with a growth that is from God.

If then you have been raised with Christ, seek the things that are above, where Christ is, seated at the right hand of God. For you have died, and your life is hid with Christ in God. When Christ, who is our life, appears, then you also will appear with him in glory.

Put to death therefore what is earthly in you: fornication, impurity, passion, evil desire, and covetousness, which is idolatry. On account of these the wrath of God is coming. Put away anger, wrath, malice, slander, and foul talk. Do not lie to one another, seeing that you have put on the new nature, which is being renewed in knowledge after the image of its creator. Here there cannot be Greek and Jew, circumcised and uncircumcised, barbarian, Scythian, slave, free man, but Christ is all, and in all.

Put on then, as God's chosen ones, holy and beloved, compassion, kindness, lowliness, meekness, and patience, forbearing one another and, if one has a complaint against another, forgiving each other; as the Lord has forgiven you, so you also must forgive. And above all these put on love, which binds everything together in perfect harmony. And let the peace of Christ rule in your hearts, to which indeed you were called in the one body. Let the word of Christ dwell in you richly, teach and admonish one another in all wisdom, and sing psalms and hymns with thankfulness in your hearts to God. And whatever you do, in word or deed, do everything in the name of the Lord Jesus.

Wives, be subject to your husbands, as is fitting in the Lord. Husbands, love your wives, and do not be harsh with them. Children, obey your parents in everything, for this pleases the Lord. Fathers, do not provoke your children, lest they become discouraged. Slaves, obey in everything your earthly masters. Whatever your task, work heartily, as serving the Lord and not men, knowing that from the Lord you will receive the inheritance as your reward. For the wrongdoer will be paid back for the wrong he has done, and there is no partiality. Masters, treat your slaves justly and fairly, knowing that you also have a Master in heaven.

Continue steadfastly in prayer with thanksgiving; and pray for us also, that God may open to us a door for the word, to declare the mystery of Christ, on account of which I am in prison, that I may make it clear, as I ought to speak.

Conduct yourselves wisely toward outsiders, making the most of the time. Let your speech always be gracious, seasoned with salt, so that you may know how you ought to answer every one.

Tychicus will tell you all about my affairs; he is a beloved brother and faithful minister and fellow servant in the Lord. I have sent him to you for this very purpose, and that he may encourage your hearts, and with him Onesimus, the faithful and beloved brother, who is one of yourselves.

Aristarchus my fellow prisoner greets you, and Mark the cousin of Barnabas, and Jesus who is called Justus. These are the only men of the circumcision among my fellow workers for the kingdom of God, and they have been a comfort to me. Epaphras, who is one of yourselves, a servant of Christ Jesus, greets you, always remembering you earnestly in his prayers, that you may stand mature and fully assured in all the will of God. He has worked hard for you and for those in Laodicea and in Hierapolis. Luke the beloved physician and Demas greet you. Give my greetings to the brethren at Laodicea, and to Nympha and the church in her house. And when this letter has been read among you, have it read also in the church of the Laodiceans; and see that you read also the letter from Laodicea.

I, Paul, write this greeting with my own hand. Remember my fetters. Grace be with you.

1 THESSALONIANS

During his second missionary journey, about A.D. 51, Paul visited Thessalonica, the capital of Macedonia. Here he preached for several weeks, then was forced by enemies to leave the city. Arriving in Corinth, he remained anxious about the immature congregation he had left behind, now deprived of its leadership and persecuted by the opposition. Soon afterward he wrote this letter of encouragement and instruction, warning his readers against unchastity, dishonest conduct, and idleness. He also deals with questions that had begun to perplex the Thessalonians concerning the Second Coming of Christ. Christians who die before that hoped-for event, Paul says, will not be deprived of the blessings of the kingdom, but will rise first and then, together with the living, be united with Christ. He declines to make pronouncements on the time of these events, but bids his readers watch and be sober.

PAUL, SILVANUS, AND Timothy, to the church of the Thessalonians in God the Father and the Lord Jesus Christ: Grace to you and peace.

We give thanks to God always for you all, constantly mentioning you in our prayers. For we know, brethren beloved by God, that he has chosen you; for our gospel came to you in power and in the Holy Spirit and with full conviction, so that you became an example to all the believers in Macedonia and in Achaia. They themselves report how you turned to God from idols, to serve a living and true God, and to wait for his Son from heaven, whom he raised from the dead, Jesus who delivers us from the wrath to come.

You know, brethren, that our visit to you was not in vain. We had courage in our God to declare to you the gospel in the face of great opposition. But just as we have been entrusted with the gospel, so we speak, not to please men, but to please God, who tests our hearts. We never used words of flattery, or a cloak for greed, nor did we seek glory from men, though we might have made demands as apostles of Christ. We worked night and day, that we might not burden any of you, while we preached to you the gospel of God. Like a father with his children, we exhorted each one of you and encouraged you to lead a life worthy of God, who calls you into his own kingdom and glory.

But since we were bereft of you, brethren, for a short time, in person not in heart, we endeavored the more eagerly to see you face to face, but Satan hindered us. For what is our hope or joy or crown of boasting before our Lord Jesus at his coming? Is it not you? For you are our glory and joy. When we could bear it no longer, we sent Timothy to establish you in your faith and to exhort you, that no one be moved by these afflictions. You know that this is to be our lot, for when we were with you, we told you that we were to suffer affliction, just as it has come to pass. So I sent that I might know your faith, for fear that somehow the tempter had tempted you and that our labor would be in vain.

Now that Timothy has brought us the good news and reported that you always remember us kindly and long to see us, as we long to see you, we have been comforted; for now we live, if you stand fast in the Lord. What thanksgiving can we render to God for you, praying earnestly night and day that we may see you face to face and supply what is lacking in your faith?

Brethren, we exhort you in the Lord Jesus, that as you learned from us how you ought to live and to please God, you do so more and more. For this is the will of God, your sanctification: that you abstain from unchastity; that each one of you know how to take a wife for himself in holiness and honor, not in the passion of lust like heathen who do not know God; that no man transgress, and wrong his brother in this matter, because the Lord is an avenger in all these things, as we solemnly forewarned you. For God has not called us for uncleanness, but in holiness. Therefore whoever disregards this, disregards not man but God, who gives his Holy Spirit to you.

Concerning love of the brethren you have no need to have any one write to you, for you yourselves have been taught by God to love one another. But we exhort you to do so more and more, to aspire to live quietly, to mind your own affairs, and to work with your hands, as we charged you; so that you may command the respect of outsiders, and be dependent on nobody.

But we would not have you ignorant, brethren, concerning those who are asleep, that you may not grieve as others do who have no hope. For since we believe that Jesus died and rose again, even so, through Jesus, God will bring with him those who have fallen asleep. For this we declare to you by the word of the Lord, that we who are alive, who are left until the coming of the Lord, shall not precede those who have fallen asleep. For the Lord himself will descend from heaven with a cry of command, with the archangel's call, and with the sound of the trumpet of God. And the dead in Christ will rise first; then we who are alive, who are left, shall be caught up together with them in the clouds to meet the Lord in the air; and so we shall always be with the Lord. Therefore comfort one another with these words.

As to times and seasons, you know well that the day of the Lord will come like a thief in the night. When people say, "There is peace and security," then sudden destruction will come upon them as travail comes upon a woman with child. But you are not in darkness, brethren, for that day to surprise you like a thief. For you are all sons of light and sons of the day. So let us not sleep, as others do, but keep awake and be sober. For those who sleep sleep at night, and those who get drunk are drunk at night. Since we belong to the day, let us be sober, and put on the breastplate of faith and love, and for a helmet the hope of salvation. For God has not destined us for wrath, but to obtain salvation through our Lord Jesus Christ, who died for us so that whether we wake or sleep we might live with him.

We beseech you, brethren, to respect those who labor among you and are over you in the Lord. Admonish the idlers, encourage the faint-hearted, help the weak, be patient with them all. See that none of you repays evil for evil, but always seek to do good to one another and to all. Rejoice always, pray constantly, give thanks in all circumstances; for this is the will of God in Christ Jesus for you. Do not quench the Spirit, do not despise prophesying, but test everything; hold fast what is good, abstain from every form of evil.

May the God of peace himself sanctify you wholly; and may your spirit and soul and body be kept sound and blameless at the coming of our Lord Jesus Christ. He who calls you is faithful, and he will do it.

Brethren, pray for us. Greet all the brethren with a holy kiss. I adjure you by the Lord that this letter be read to all the brethren. The grace of our Lord Jesus Christ be with you.

2 THESSALONIANS

Not long after Paul sent his first letter to the Christians of Thessalonica he wrote again, probably because he had heard further disturbing news about them. They were suffering persecution in some way, it seems, and certain persons were still causing trouble by their mistaken ideas on the Second Coming of Christ. Reminding them of the apostolic tradition concerning the day of the Lord, Paul declares that the Second Coming might not be quite so near as some of them thought. Certain definite signs, he says, will precede that day, and he rebukes those who in their excitement over the Second Coming neglect their ordinary duties and live in idleness. The letter closes with a concluding note in Paul's own handwriting as a guarantee of genuineness.

———

Paul, Silvanus, and Timothy, to the church of the Thessalonians in God our Father and the Lord Jesus Christ: Grace to you and peace from God the Father and the Lord Jesus Christ.

We are bound to give thanks to God always for you, brethren, because your faith is growing abundantly, and the love of one for another is increasing. We ourselves boast of you in the churches of God for your steadfastness in the afflictions which you are enduring.

This is evidence of the righteous judgment of God, that you may be made worthy—since indeed God deems it just to repay with affliction those who afflict you, and to grant rest to you when the Lord Jesus is revealed from heaven with his mighty angels in flaming fire, inflicting vengeance upon those who do not know God and upon those who do not obey the gospel. They shall suffer eternal destruction and exclusion from the presence of the Lord, when he comes on that day to be glorified and marveled at in all who have believed.

Now concerning the coming of our Lord Jesus Christ and our assembling to meet him, we beg you, brethren, not to be quickly shaken in mind or excited, by spirit, by word, or by letter purporting to be from us, to the effect that the day of the Lord has come. For that day will not come, unless the rebellion comes first, and the man of lawlessness is revealed, the son of perdition, who exalts himself, proclaiming himself God. Do you not remember that when I was still with you I told you this? The mystery of lawlessness is already at work; only he who now restrains it will do so until he is out of the way. And then the lawless one will be revealed, and the Lord Jesus will slay him with the breath of his mouth and destroy him by his coming. The coming of the lawless one by the activity of Satan will be with all power and with wicked deception for those who are to perish, because they refused to love the truth. Therefore God sends upon them a strong delusion, so that all may be condemned who had pleasure in unrighteousness.

Now we command you, brethren, in the name of our Lord Jesus Christ, that you keep away from any brother who is living in idleness. For you know how you ought to imitate us; we were not idle when we were with you, we did not eat any one's bread without paying, but with toil and labor we worked night and day, that we might not burden any of you. It was not because we have not that right, but to give you in our conduct an example to imitate. If any one will not work, let him not eat. For we hear that some of you are living in idleness, mere busybodies. Now such persons we command in the Lord Jesus Christ to do their work in quietness and to earn their own living. Brethren, do not be weary in well-doing.

If any one refuses to obey what we say in this letter, note that man, and have nothing to do with him, that he may be ashamed. Do not look on him as an enemy, but warn him as a brother.

Now may the Lord of peace himself give you peace at all times in all ways. I, Paul, write this greeting with my own hand. This is the mark in every letter of mine; it is the way I write. The grace of our Lord Jesus Christ be with you all.

1 TIMOTHY

The two letters to Timothy, along with the one to Titus, are called the Pastoral Letters because they are concerned with the work of the two men as pastors of churches. Judging by differences in style and vocabulary from Paul's other letters, many modern scholars think that the Pastorals were not written by Paul. A loyal disciple, it is thought, expanded several previously unpublished messages of the apostle, perhaps a generation after Paul's death. In any case, the letters are especially valuable for the light they shed on early church organization and the discipline of the time. In this first letter the author offers Timothy suggestions for the regulation of public worship, defines the position of men and women in the community, lays down the qualifications of bishops and deacons, warns against false teachers, and concludes with various moral exhortations.

———

PAUL, AN APOSTLE of Christ Jesus by command of God our Savior and of Christ Jesus our hope, to Timothy, my true child in the faith: Grace, mercy, and peace from God the Father and Christ Jesus our Lord.

As I urged you when I was going to Macedonia, remain at Ephesus that you may charge certain persons not to teach any different doctrine, nor to occupy themselves with myths which promote speculations rather than the divine training that is in faith. The aim of our charge is love that issues from a pure heart, a good conscience and sincere faith. Certain persons by swerving from these have wandered into vain discussion, desiring to be teachers of the law, without understanding what they are saying.

Now we know that the law is good, if any one uses it lawfully. The law is not laid down for the just but for the disobedient, for the ungodly, for murderers, immoral persons, sodomites, kidnapers, liars, and whatever else is contrary to sound doctrine, in accordance with the glorious gospel.

I thank Christ Jesus our Lord because he judged me faithful by appointing me to his service, though I formerly persecuted him; but I had acted ignorantly, and the grace of our Lord overflowed for me. The saying is sure, that Christ Jesus came into the world to save sinners. And I am the foremost of sinners; but I received mercy, that in me Jesus Christ might display his perfect patience for an example to those who were to believe in him for eternal life.

This charge I commit to you, Timothy, my son, in accordance with the prophetic utterances which pointed to you, so that inspired by them you may wage the good warfare, holding faith and a good conscience. By rejecting conscience, certain persons have made shipwreck of their faith, among them Hymenaeus and Alexander, whom I have delivered to Satan, that they may learn not to blaspheme.

First of all I urge that prayers and thanksgivings be made for all men, for kings and all who are in high positions. This is good in the sight of God our Savior, who desires all men to be saved and to come to the knowledge of the truth. For there is one God, and there is one mediator between God and men, the man Christ Jesus, who gave himself as a ransom for all, the testimony to which was borne at the proper time.

I desire that in every place the men should pray, lifting holy hands without quarreling; also that women should adorn themselves modestly and sensibly, not with braided hair or gold or pearls or costly attire but by good deeds, as befits women who profess religion. Let a woman learn in silence with all submissiveness. I permit no woman to teach or to have authority over men; she is to keep silent. For Adam was formed first, then Eve; and Adam was not deceived, but the woman was deceived and became a transgressor. Yet woman will be saved through bearing children, if she continues in faith and love and holiness, with modesty.

If any one aspires to the office of bishop, he desires a noble task. A bishop must be above reproach, the husband of one wife, temperate, dignified, hospitable, an apt teacher, no drunkard, not violent, not quarrelsome, and no lover of money. He must manage his own household well, keeping his children submissive and respectful; for if a man does not know how to manage his own household, how can he care for God's church?

Deacons likewise must be serious, not double-tongued, not addicted to much wine, not greedy. Let them be tested first; then if they prove themselves blameless let them serve as deacons. The women likewise must be serious, no slanderers, but temperate, faithful in all things. Let deacons be the husband of one wife, and let them manage their children and their households well.

Now the Spirit expressly says that in later times some will depart from the faith by giving heed to deceitful spirits, through the pretensions of liars who forbid marriage and enjoin abstinence from foods which God created to be received with thanksgiving. Everything created by God is good, and nothing is to be rejected if it is received with thanksgiving; for then it is consecrated by the word of God and prayer.

Have nothing to do with godless and silly myths. Train yourself in godliness; for while bodily training is of some value, godliness is of value in every way, as it holds promise for the present life and also for the life to come. To this end we strive, because we have our hope set on the living God, who is the Savior of all men, especially of those who believe.

Command and teach these things. Let no one despise your youth, but set an example in speech and conduct. Attend to the public reading of scripture, to preaching, to teaching. Do not neglect the gift you have, which was given you by prophetic utterance when the council of elders laid their hands upon you. Practice these duties, devote yourself to them, for by so doing you will save both yourself and your hearers. Do not rebuke an older man but exhort him as you would a father; treat younger men like brothers, older women like mothers, younger women like sisters, in all purity.

If a widow has children or grandchildren, let them first learn their religious duty to their own family and make some return to their parents. She who is a widow, and is left all alone, has set her hope on God and continues in supplications and prayers night and day; whereas she who is self-indulgent is dead even while she lives. If any one does not provide for his relatives, and especially for his own family, he has disowned the faith and is worse than an unbeliever.

Let a widow be enrolled if she is not less than sixty years of age, having been the wife of one husband; and she must be well attested for her good deeds, as one who has brought up children, shown hospitality, washed the feet of the saints, relieved the afflicted, and devoted herself to doing good in every way. But refuse to enrol younger widows; for when they grow wanton against Christ they desire to marry, and so they incur condemnation for having violated their first pledge. Besides that, they learn to be idlers, gadding about from house to house, gossips and busybodies. So I would have younger widows marry, bear children, rule their households, and give the enemy no occasion to revile us.

Let the elders who rule well be considered worthy of double honor, especially those who labor in preaching and teaching; for the scripture says, "You shall not muzzle an ox when it is treading out the grain," and, "The laborer deserves his wages." Never admit any charge against an elder except on the evidence of two or three witnesses. As for those who persist in sin, rebuke them in the presence of all, so that the rest may stand in fear.

No longer drink only water, but use a little wine for the sake of your stomach and your frequent ailments.

The sins of some men are conspicuous, pointing to judgment, but the sins of others appear later. So also good deeds are conspicuous; and even when they are not, they cannot remain hidden. Let all who are under the yoke of slavery regard their masters as worthy of all honor, so that the name of God and the teaching may not be defamed. Those who have believing masters must not be disrespectful on the ground that they are brethren; rather they must serve all the better, since those who benefit by their service are believers and beloved.

Teach and urge these duties. If any one does not agree with the sound words of our Lord Jesus Christ, he is puffed up with conceit; he has a morbid craving for controversy and for disputes about words, which produce envy, dissension, slander, base suspicions, and wrangling among men who are depraved in mind and bereft of the truth, imagining that godliness is a means of gain. There is great gain in godliness with contentment; for we brought nothing into the world, and we cannot take anything out of the world; but if we have food and clothing, with these we shall be content. Those who desire to be rich fall into many senseless desires that plunge men into ruin. For the love of money is the root of all evils; it is through this craving that some have wandered from the faith and pierced their hearts with many pangs.

As for you, man of God, shun all this. Fight the good fight of the faith; take hold of the eternal life to which you were called. In the presence of God who gives life to all things, and of Christ Jesus who in his testimony before Pontius Pilate made the good confession, I charge you to keep the commandment unstained and free from reproach until the appearing of our Lord Jesus Christ. This will be made manifest at the proper time by the blessed and only Sovereign, the King of kings and Lord of lords, who alone has immortality and dwells in unapproachable light, whom no man has ever seen or can see. To him be honor and eternal dominion. Amen.

As for the rich, charge them not to be haughty, nor to set their hopes on uncertain riches but on God, who richly furnishes us with everything. They are to be rich in good deeds, thus laying up for themselves a good foundation for the future, so that they may take hold of the life which is life indeed.

O Timothy, guard what has been entrusted to you. Avoid the godless chatter and contradictions of what is falsely called knowledge, for by professing it some have missed the mark as regards the faith. Grace be with you.

2 TIMOTHY

In 2 Timothy, a much more personal letter than 1 Timothy, the author urges endurance as an essential quality for a preacher of the gospel. The emphasis is on courage and fidelity in standing fast against false teaching, and in becoming a vessel fit for the Master's use. The author warns Timothy of sufferings that are bound to come, and he closes with a moving reference to his own impending martyrdom. For modern opinion concerning date and authorship, see the Introduction to 1 Timothy.

PAUL, AN APOSTLE of Christ Jesus by the will of God according to the promise of the life which is in Christ Jesus, to Timothy, my beloved child: Grace, mercy, and peace from God the Father and Christ Jesus our Lord.

I thank God, whom I serve with a clear conscience, when I remember you in my prayers. As I remember your tears, I long to see you, that I may be filled with joy. I am reminded of your sincere faith, a faith that dwelt first in your grandmother Lois and your mother Eunice and now dwells in you. Rekindle the gift of God that is within you through the laying on of my hands; God did not give us a spirit of timidity but a spirit of power and love and self-control.

Do not be ashamed then of testifying to our Lord, nor of me his prisoner. Share in suffering for the gospel in the power of God, who called us with a holy calling in virtue of his own purpose and the grace which he gave us in Christ Jesus ages ago, and now through the appearing of our Savior Christ Jesus, who abolished death and brought life and immortality. For this gospel I was appointed a preacher and apostle and teacher, and therefore I suffer as I do. But I am not ashamed, for I know whom I have believed. Follow the pattern of the sound words which you have heard from me, in the faith and love which are in Christ Jesus; guard the truth that has been entrusted to you by the Holy Spirit who dwells within us.

My son, be strong in the grace that is in Christ Jesus, and what you have heard from me, entrust to faithful men who will be able to teach others also. Share in suffering as a good soldier of Christ Jesus. No soldier on service gets entangled in civilian pursuits, since his aim is to satisfy the one who enlisted him. An athlete is not crowned unless he competes according to the rules.

Remember Jesus Christ, risen from the dead, descended from David, as preached in my gospel, the gospel for which I am suffering and wearing fetters like a criminal. But the word of God is not fettered. Therefore I endure everything for the sake of the elect, that they also may obtain salvation in Christ Jesus with its eternal glory. The saying is sure: If we have died with him, we shall also live with him; if we endure, we shall also reign with him; if we deny him, he also will deny us; if we are faithless, he remains faithful—for he cannot deny himself.

Remind them of this, and charge them before the Lord to avoid disputing about words, which does no good, but only ruins the hearers. Do your best to present yourself to God as one approved, a workman who has no need to be ashamed, rightly handling the word of truth. Avoid godless chatter, for it will lead people into more and more ungodliness, and their talk will eat its way like gangrene. Among them are Hymenaeus and Philetus, who have swerved from the truth by holding that the resurrection is past already. They are upsetting the faith of some. But God's firm foundation stands, bearing this seal: "The Lord knows those who are his," and, "Let every one who names the name of the Lord depart from iniquity."

In a great house there are not only vessels of gold and silver but also of wood and earthenware, and some for noble use, some for ignoble. If any one purifies himself from what is ignoble, then he will be a vessel for noble use, consecrated and useful to the master of the house, ready for any good work. So shun youthful passions and aim at righteousness, faith, love, and peace, along with those who call upon the Lord from a pure heart. Have nothing to do with stupid, senseless controversies; you know that they breed quarrels. And the Lord's servant must not be quarrelsome but kindly to every one, an apt teacher, forbearing, correcting his opponents with gentleness.

But understand this, that in the last days there will come times of stress. For men will be lovers of self, lovers of money, proud, arrogant, abusive, disobedient to their parents, ungrateful, unholy, inhuman, implacable, slanderers, profligates, fierce, haters of good, treacherous, reckless, swollen with conceit, lovers of pleasure rather than lovers of God, holding the form of religion but denying the power of it. Avoid such people. As Jannes and Jambres opposed Moses, so these men also oppose the truth, men of corrupt mind and counterfeit faith; but they will not get very far, for their folly will be plain to all, as was that of those two men.

Now you have observed my teaching, my conduct, my aim in life, my faith, my patience, my love, my steadfastness, my persecutions, my sufferings, what befell me at Antioch, at Iconium, and at Lystra, what persecutions I endured; yet from them all the Lord rescued me. Indeed all who desire to live a godly life in Christ Jesus will be persecuted, while evil men and impostors will go on from bad to worse, deceivers and deceived. But as for you, continue in what you have learned and have firmly believed, knowing from whom you learned it and how from childhood you have been acquainted with the sacred writings which are able to instruct you for salvation through faith in Christ Jesus. All scripture is inspired by God and profitable for teaching, for reproof, for correction, and for training in righteousness, that the man of God may be complete, equipped for every good work.

I charge you in the presence of God and of Christ Jesus who is to judge the living and the dead, preach the word, be urgent in season and out of season, convince, rebuke, and exhort, be unfailing in patience and in teaching. For the time is coming when people will not endure sound teaching, but having itching ears they will accumulate for themselves teachers to suit their own likings, and will turn away from listening to the truth and wander into myths.

I am already on the point of being sacrificed; the time of my departure has come. I have fought the good fight, I have finished the race, I have kept the faith. Henceforth there is laid up for me the crown of righteousness, which the Lord, the righteous judge, will award to me on that Day, and not only to me but also to all who have loved his appearing.

Do your best to come to me soon. For Demas, in love with this present world, has deserted me and gone to Thessalonica; Crescens has gone to Galatia, Titus to Dalmatia. Luke alone is with me. Get Mark and bring him with you; for he is very useful in serving me. Bring the cloak that I left with Carpus at Troas, also the books, and above all the parchments. Alexander the coppersmith did me great harm; the Lord will requite him for his deeds. At my first defense no one took my part; all deserted me. May it not be charged against them! But the Lord stood by me and gave me strength to proclaim the message fully, that all the Gentiles might hear it. So I was rescued from the lion's mouth. The Lord will rescue me from every evil and save me for his heavenly kingdom. To him be the glory for ever and ever. Amen.

Do your best to come before winter. Eubulus sends greetings to you, as do Pudens and Linus and Claudia and all the brethren. The Lord be with your spirit. Grace be with you.

TITUS

Titus, a Greek, was probably one of the first Gentile Christians. For a time he served as a missionary companion of the apostle Paul. This brief letter to him, classed with 1 and 2 Timothy as Paul's Pastoral Letters, deals with those qualities that are required of leaders in the church. It treats the duties of various classes in society, sums up the Christian virtues, and closes with a warning against becoming entangled in theoretical arguments that only distract the attention and divert energy from the Christian cause. For modern opinion concerning date and authorship, see the Introduction to 1 Timothy.

PAUL, A SERVANT of God and an apostle of Jesus Christ, to further the faith of God's elect and their knowledge of the truth which accords with godliness, in hope of eternal life which God, who never lies, promised ages ago and at the proper time manifested in his word through the preaching with which I have been entrusted by command of God our Savior; to Titus, my true child in a common faith: Grace and peace from God the Father and Christ Jesus our Savior.

This is why I left you in Crete, that you might amend what was defective, and appoint elders in every town, if any man is blameless, the husband of one wife, and his children are believers and not profligate or insubordinate. A bishop must not be arrogant or quick-tempered or a drunkard or violent or greedy, but hospitable, a lover of goodness, master of himself, and holy. He must hold firm to the sure word as taught, that he may be able to give instruction in sound doctrine and confute those who contradict it.

For there are many insubordinate men, deceivers, especially the circumcision party; they must be silenced, since they are upsetting whole families by teaching for base gain what they have no right to teach. One of themselves, a prophet, said, "Cretans are always liars, evil beasts, lazy gluttons." This testimony is true. Therefore rebuke them sharply, that they may be sound in the faith, instead of giving heed to Jewish myths or to men who reject the truth. To the pure all things are pure, but to the corrupt and unbelieving nothing is pure; their very minds and consciences are corrupted. They profess to know God, but they deny him by their deeds; they are detestable, disobedient, unfit for any good deed.

As for you, teach what befits sound doctrine. Bid the older men be temperate, serious, sound in faith, in love, and in steadfastness. Bid the older women be reverent in behavior, not slanderers or slaves to drink; they are to train the young women to love their husbands and children, to be sensible, chaste, domestic, kind, and submissive to their husbands. Urge the younger men to control themselves. Show yourself a model of good deeds, and in your teaching show integrity, gravity, and speech that cannot be censured, so that an opponent may have nothing evil to say of us. Bid slaves be submissive to their masters, not to pilfer, but to show entire fidelity.

For the grace of God has appeared for the salvation of all, training us to renounce irreligion and worldly passions, and to live sober, godly lives, awaiting our blessed hope, the appearing of the glory of our God and Savior Jesus Christ, who gave himself for us to redeem us from all iniquity and to purify for himself a people of his own who are zealous for good deeds.

Declare these things; exhort and reprove with all authority. Let no one disregard you.

Remind our people to be submissive to rulers and authorities, to be ready for any honest work, to speak evil of no one, to avoid quarreling, to be gentle, and to show perfect courtesy toward all. For we ourselves were once foolish, led astray, slaves to passions and pleasures, passing our days in malice and envy, hated by men and hating one another. But when the goodness and loving kindness of God our Savior appeared, he saved us, not because of deeds done by us in righteousness, but in virtue of his own mercy, by the washing of regeneration and renewal in the Holy Spirit, which he poured out upon us richly through Jesus Christ our Savior, that we might be justified by his grace and become heirs in hope of eternal life.

I desire you to insist on these things, so that those who have believed in God may be careful to apply themselves to good deeds. But avoid stupid controversies, dissensions, and quarrels over the law, for they are futile. As for a man who is factious, after admonishing him once or twice, have nothing more to do with him, knowing that such a person is perverted and sinful; he is self-condemned.

When I send Artemas or Tychicus to you, do your best to come to me at Nicopolis, for I have decided to spend the winter there. Speed Zenas the lawyer and Apollos on their way; see that they lack nothing. And let our people learn to help cases of urgent need, and not to be unfruitful.

All who are with me send greetings to you. Greet those who love us in the faith. Grace be with you all.

PHILEMON

Philemon was a Christian of Colossae in Phrygia, whose slave Onesimus had run away. Somehow the fugitive had come to meet Paul, who sent him back to his master with this brief personal note, the shortest of the Pauline Letters. Paul asks Philemon, for the sake of friendship, to forgive Onesimus, who is now a fellow Christian. As a runaway slave, Onesimus could be severely punished, and Paul's plea shows how Christian ways were changing the old harsh customs, though it was many generations before slavery was ended.

Paul, a prisoner for Christ Jesus, and Timothy our brother, to Philemon our beloved fellow worker and Apphia our sister and Archippus our fellow soldier, and the church in your house: Grace to you and peace from God our Father and the Lord Jesus Christ.

I thank my God always when I remember you in my prayers, because I hear of your love and of the faith which you have toward the Lord Jesus and all the saints, and I pray that the sharing of your faith may promote the knowledge of all the good that is ours in Christ. For I have derived much joy and comfort from your love, my brother, because the hearts of the saints have been refreshed through you.

Accordingly, though I am bold enough in Christ to command you to do what is required, yet for love's sake I prefer to appeal to you—I, Paul, an ambassador and now a prisoner also for Christ Jesus—I appeal to you for my child, Onesimus, whose father I have become in my imprisonment. (Formerly he was useless to you, but now he is indeed useful to you and to me.) I am sending him back to you, sending my very heart. I would have been glad to keep him with me, in order that he might serve me on your behalf during my imprisonment for the gospel; but I preferred to do nothing without your consent in order that your goodness might not be by compulsion but of your own free will.

Perhaps this is why he was parted from you for a while, that you might have him back for ever, no longer as a slave but more than a slave, as a beloved brother, especially to me but how much more to you, both in the flesh and in the Lord. So if you consider me your partner, receive him as you would receive me. If he has wronged you at all, or owes you anything, charge that to my account. I, Paul, write this with my own hand, I will repay it—to say nothing of your owing me even your own self. Yes, brother, I want some benefit from you in the Lord. Refresh my heart in Christ.

Confident of your obedience, I write to you, knowing that you will do even more than I say. At the same time, prepare a guest room for me, for I am hoping through your prayers to be granted to you.

Epaphras, my fellow prisoner in Christ Jesus, sends greetings to you, and so do Mark, Aristarchus, Demas, and Luke, my fellow workers.

The grace of the Lord Jesus Christ be with your spirit.

HEBREWS

This anonymous treatise, the longest sustained argument of any book in the Bible, was written to Jewish Christians who were on the point of returning to Judaism, perhaps because of persecution. In order to win them back to the Christian faith, the author emphasizes three points: the superiority of Jesus Christ over Old Testament figures (the prophets, the angels, and Moses himself); the superiority of Christ's priesthood over the priesthood of Aaron; and the superiority of Christ's sacrifice of himself over the Levitical sacrifices. Into his argument the author weaves sections of earnest exhortation, urging his readers to be steadfast, to persevere, and to have greater faith. Though the letter is traditionally ascribed to the apostle Paul, features of style and vocabulary show that it was written by some other leader in the early church. It is probably to be dated before the fall of Jerusalem in A.D. 70.

IN MANY AND various ways God spoke of old to our fathers by the prophets; but in these last days he has spoken to us by a Son, whom he appointed the heir of all things, through whom also he created the world. He reflects the glory of God and bears the very stamp of his nature, upholding the universe by his word of power. When he had made purification for sins, he sat down at the right hand of the Majesty on high, having become as much superior to angels as the name he has obtained is more excellent than theirs. For to what angel did God ever say, "Thou art my Son, today I have begotten thee"? To what angel has he ever said, "Sit at my right hand, till I make thy enemies a stool for thy feet"?

Therefore we must pay the closer attention to what we have heard, lest we drift away from it. For how shall we escape if we neglect such a great salvation? It was declared at first by the Lord, and it was attested to us by those who heard him, while God also bore witness by signs and wonders and various miracles and by gifts of the Holy Spirit.

For it was not to angels that God subjected the world to come, of which we are speaking. It has been testified somewhere, "What is man that thou art mindful of him, or the son of man, that thou carest for him? Thou didst make him for a little while lower than the angels, thou hast crowned him with glory and honor, putting everything in subjection under his feet." Now in putting everything in subjection to him, he left nothing outside his control. As it is, we do not yet see everything in subjection to him. But we see Jesus, who for a little while was made lower than the angels, crowned with glory and honor because of the suffering of death, so that by the grace of God he might taste death for every one.

It was fitting that he, for whom and by whom all things exist, should make the pioneer of their salvation perfect through suffering. For he who sanctifies and those who are sanctified have all one origin. That is why he is not ashamed to call them brethren, saying, "I will proclaim thy name to my brethren." And again, "Here am I, and the children God has given me." Since therefore the children share in flesh and blood, he himself likewise partook of the same nature, that through death he might destroy him who has the power of death, that is, the devil, and deliver all those who through fear of death were subject to lifelong bondage. He had to be made like his brethren in every respect, so that he might become a merciful and faithful high priest in the service of God, to make expiation for the sins of the people. Because he himself has suffered and been tempted, he is able to help those who are tempted.

Therefore, holy brethren, consider Jesus, the apostle and high priest of our confession. He was faithful to him who appointed him, just as Moses also was faithful in God's house as a servant, to testify to the things that were to be spoken later. But Christ was faithful over God's house as a son. And we are his house if we hold fast our confidence and pride in our hope.

Take care, brethren, lest there be in any of you an evil, unbelieving heart, leading you to fall away from the living God. But exhort one another every day, that none of you may be hardened by the deceitfulness of sin. For we share in Christ, if only we hold our first confidence firm to the end. The word of God is living and active, sharper than any two-edged sword, piercing to the division of soul and spirit, of joints and marrow, and discerning the thoughts and intentions of the heart. And before him no creature is hidden, but all are open and laid bare to the eyes of him with whom we have to do.

Since, then, we have a great high priest who has passed through the heavens, Jesus, the Son of God, let us hold fast our confession. For we have not a high priest who is unable to sympathize with our weaknesses, but one who in every respect has been tempted as we are, yet without sin. Let us, then, with confidence draw near to the throne of grace, that we may receive mercy and find grace to help in time of need.

For every high priest chosen from among men is appointed to act on behalf of men in relation to God, to offer gifts and sacrifices for sins. He can deal gently with the ignorant and wayward, since he himself is beset with weakness. Because of this he is bound to offer sacrifice for his own sins as well as for those of the people. And one does not take the honor upon himself, but he is called by God, just as Aaron was. So also Christ did not exalt himself to be made a high priest, but was appointed by him who said to him, "Thou art my Son, today I have begotten thee."

In the days of his flesh, Jesus offered up prayers and supplications, with loud cries and tears, to him who was able to save him from death, and he was heard for his godly fear. Although he was a Son, he learned obedience through what he suffered; and being made perfect he became the source of eternal salvation to all who obey him, being designated by God a high priest after the order of Melchizedek.

When God made a promise to Abraham, since he had no one greater by whom to swear, he swore by himself, saying, "Surely I will bless you and multiply you." And thus Abraham, having patiently endured, obtained the promise. Men indeed swear by a greater than themselves, and in all their disputes an oath is final for confirmation. So when God desired to show more convincingly to the heirs of the promise the unchangeable character of his purpose, he interposed with an oath, so that through two unchangeable things, in which it is impossible that God should prove false, we who have fled for refuge might have strong encouragement to seize the hope set before us. We have this as a sure and steadfast anchor of the soul, a hope that enters into the inner shrine behind the curtain, where Jesus has gone as a forerunner on our behalf, having become a high priest for ever, after the order of Melchizedek.

For this Melchizedek, king of Salem, priest of the Most High God, met Abraham returning from the slaughter of the kings and blessed him; and to him Abraham apportioned a tenth part of everything. He is first, by translation of his name, king of righteousness, and then he is also king of Salem, that is, king of peace. He is without father or mother or genealogy, and has neither beginning of days nor end of life, but resembling the Son of God he continues a priest for ever.

See how great he is! Abraham the patriarch gave him a tithe of the spoils. And those descendants of Levi who receive the priestly office have a commandment in the law to take tithes from the people, that is, from their brethren, though these also are descended from Abraham. But this man who has not their genealogy received tithes from Abraham and blessed him who had the promises. It is beyond dispute that the inferior is blessed by the superior. Here tithes are received by mortal men; there, by one of whom it is testified that he lives. One might even say that Levi himself, who receives tithes, paid tithes through Abraham, for he was still in the loins of his ancestor when Melchizedek met him.

Now if perfection had been attainable through the Levitical priesthood (for under it the people received the law), what further need would there have been for another priest to arise after the order of Melchizedek, rather

than one named after the order of Aaron? For when there is a change
in the priesthood, there is necessarily a change in the law as well. The one
of whom these things are spoken belonged to another tribe, from which
no one has ever served at the altar. For it is evident that our Lord was descended from Judah, and in connection with that tribe Moses said nothing
about priests.

This becomes even more evident when another priest arises in the likeness
of Melchizedek, who has become a priest, not according to a legal requirement concerning bodily descent but by the power of an indestructible life.
For it is witnessed of him, "Thou art a priest for ever, after the order of
Melchizedek."

On the one hand, a former commandment is set aside because of its weakness and uselessness (for the law made nothing perfect); on the other hand, a
better hope is introduced, through which we draw near to God.

And it was not without an oath. Those who formerly became priests took
their office without an oath, but this one was addressed with an oath, "The
Lord has sworn and will not change his mind, 'Thou art a priest for ever.'"
This makes Jesus the surety of a better covenant.

The former priests were many in number, because they were prevented by
death from continuing in office; but he holds his priesthood permanently,
because he continues for ever. Consequently he is able for all time to save
those who draw near to God through him, since he always lives to make
intercession for them.

It was fitting that we should have such a high priest, holy, blameless, unstained, separated from sinners, exalted above the heavens. He has no need to
offer sacrifices daily, first for his own sins and then for those of the people; he
did this once for all when he offered up himself. Indeed, the law appoints men
in their weakness as high priests, but the word of the oath, which came later
than the law, appoints a Son who has been made perfect for ever.

Now the point in what we are saying is this: we have such a high priest, one
who is seated at the right hand of the throne of the Majesty in heaven, a
minister in the sanctuary and the true tent which is set up not by man but by
the Lord. If he were on earth, he would not be a priest at all, since there are
priests who offer gifts according to the law. They serve a copy and shadow of
the heavenly sanctuary. But as it is, Christ has obtained a ministry which is as
much more excellent than the old as the covenant he mediates is better, since
it is enacted on better promises. For if that first covenant had been faultless,
there would have been no occasion for a second.

Now even the first covenant had regulations for worship and an earthly
sanctuary. For a tent was prepared, the outer one, in which were the lampstand and the table and the bread of the Presence; it is called the Holy Place.
Behind the second curtain stood a tent called the Holy of Holies, having the
golden altar of incense and the ark of the covenant covered on all sides with
gold, which contained a golden urn holding the manna, and Aaron's rod that

budded, and the tables of the covenant; above it were the cherubim of glory overshadowing the mercy seat.

These preparations having been made, the priests go continually into the outer tent, performing their ritual duties; but into the second only the high priest goes, and he but once a year, and not without taking blood, which he offers for himself and for the errors of the people. By this the Holy Spirit indicates that the way into the sanctuary is not yet opened as long as the outer tent is still standing (which is symbolic for the present age). According to this arrangement, gifts and sacrifices are offered which cannot perfect the conscience of the worshiper, but deal only with food and drink and various ablutions, regulations for the body imposed until the time of reformation.

But when Christ appeared as a high priest, then through the greater and more perfect tent (not made with hands, that is, not of this creation) he entered once for all into the Holy Place, taking not the blood of goats and calves but his own blood, thus securing an eternal redemption. For if the sprinkling of defiled persons with the blood of goats and bulls and with the ashes of a heifer sanctifies for the purification of the flesh, how much more shall the blood of Christ, who through the eternal Spirit offered himself without blemish to God, purify your conscience from dead works to serve the living God.

Therefore he is the mediator of a new covenant, so that those who are called may receive the promised eternal inheritance, since a death has occurred which redeems them from the transgressions under the first covenant. He has appeared once for all at the end of the age to put away sin by the sacrifice of himself. And just as it is appointed for men to die once, and after that comes judgment, so Christ, having been offered once to bear the sins of many, will appear a second time, not to deal with sin but to save those who are eagerly waiting for him. We have been sanctified through the offering of the body of Jesus Christ once for all.

Therefore, brethren, since we have confidence to enter the sanctuary by the blood of Jesus, by the new and living way which he opened for us through the curtain, that is, through his flesh, let us draw near in full assurance of faith, with our hearts sprinkled clean from an evil conscience and our bodies washed with pure water. Let us hold fast the confession of our hope without wavering, for he who promised is faithful; and let us consider how to stir up one another to love and good works, not neglecting to meet together, as is the habit of some, but encouraging one another, and all the more as you see the Day drawing near.

For if we sin deliberately after receiving the knowledge of the truth, there no longer remains a sacrifice for sins, but a fearful prospect of judgment, and a fury of fire which will consume the adversaries. A man who has violated the law of Moses dies without mercy at the testimony of two or three witnesses. How much worse punishment do you think will be deserved by the man who has spurned the Son of God, and profaned the blood of the covenant by which he was sanctified, and outraged the Spirit of grace? For we know him who said, "Vengeance is mine, I will repay." And again, "The Lord will judge his people." It is a fearful thing to fall into the hands of the living God.

But recall the former days when, after you were enlightened, you endured a hard struggle with sufferings, sometimes being publicly exposed to abuse and affliction, and sometimes being partners with those so treated. For you had compassion on the prisoners, and you joyfully accepted the plundering of your property, since you knew that you yourselves had a better possession and an abiding one. Therefore do not throw away your confidence, which has a great reward. For you have need of endurance, so that you may do the will of God and receive what is promised.

Now faith is the assurance of things hoped for, the conviction of things not seen. For by it the men of old received divine approval. By faith we understand that the world was created by the word of God, so that what is seen was made out of things which do not appear.

By faith Abel offered to God a more acceptable sacrifice than Cain; he died, but through his faith he is still speaking. By faith Enoch was taken up so that he should not see death; now before he was taken he was attested as having pleased God. And without faith it is impossible to please him. For whoever would draw near to God must believe that he exists and that he rewards those who seek him.

By faith Noah, being warned by God concerning events as yet unseen, took heed and constructed an ark for the saving of his household. By faith Abraham obeyed when he was called to go out to a place which he was to receive as an inheritance; and he went out, not knowing where he was to go. By faith Sarah herself received power to conceive, even when she was past the age. Therefore from one man, and him as good as dead, were born descendants as many as the stars of heaven and as the innumerable grains of sand by the seashore.

These all died in faith, not having received what was promised, but having seen it and greeted it from afar, and having acknowledged that they were strangers and exiles on the earth. They desire a better country, that is, a heavenly one. Therefore God is not ashamed to be called their God, for he has prepared for them a city.

By faith Moses left Egypt, not being afraid of the anger of the king; for he endured as seeing him who is invisible. By faith he kept the Passover and sprinkled the blood, so that the Destroyer of the first-born might not touch them. By faith the people crossed the Red Sea as if on dry land; but the Egyptians, when they attempted to do the same, were drowned. By faith the walls of Jericho fell down after they had been encircled for seven days. By faith Rahab the harlot did not perish with those who were disobedient, because she had given friendly welcome to the spies.

And what more shall I say? For time would fail me to tell of Gideon, Barak, Samson, Jephthah, of David and Samuel and the prophets—who through faith conquered kingdoms, enforced justice, received promises, stopped the mouths of lions, quenched raging fire, escaped the edge of the sword, won strength out of weakness, became mighty in war, put foreign armies to flight. Women received their dead by resurrection. Some were tortured, refusing to accept release, that they might rise again to a better life. Others suffered mocking and scourging, and even chains and imprisonment. They were stoned, they were sawn in two, they were killed with the sword; they went about in skins of sheep and goats, destitute, afflicted, ill-treated, wandering over deserts and mountains, and in dens and caves of the earth.

And all these, though well attested by their faith, did not receive what was promised, since God had foreseen something better for us, that apart from us they should not be made perfect.

Therefore, since we are surrounded by so great a cloud of witnesses, let us also lay aside every weight, and sin which clings so closely, and let us run with perseverance the race that is set before us, looking to Jesus the pioneer and perfecter of our faith, who for the joy that was set before him endured the cross, despising the shame, and is seated at the right hand of the throne of God.

Consider him who endured from sinners such hostility against himself, so that you may not grow weary or fainthearted. In your struggle against sin you have not yet resisted to the point of shedding your blood. And have you forgotten the exhortation which addresses you as sons?—"My son, do not regard lightly the discipline of the Lord, nor lose courage when you are punished by him. For the Lord disciplines him whom he loves, and chastises every son whom he receives."

God is treating you as sons; for what son is there whom his father does not discipline? If you are left without discipline, in which all have participated, then you are illegitimate children and not sons. Besides this, we have had earthly fathers to discipline us and we respected them. Shall we not much more be subject to the Father of spirits and live? For they disciplined us for a short time at their pleasure, but he disciplines us for our good, that we may share his holiness. For the moment all discipline seems painful rather than pleasant; later it yields the peaceful fruit of righteousness to those who have been trained by it.

Therefore lift your drooping hands and strengthen your weak knees, and make straight paths for your feet, so that what is lame may not be put out of joint but rather be healed. Strive for peace with all men, and for the holiness without which no one will see the Lord. See to it that no one fail to obtain the grace of God; that no "root of bitterness" spring up and cause trouble, and by it the many become defiled; that no one be immoral or irreligious like Esau, who sold his birthright for a single meal. You know that afterward, when he desired to inherit the blessing, he was rejected, for he found no chance to repent, though he sought it with tears.

You have not come to what may be touched, a blazing fire, and darkness, and gloom, and a tempest, and the sound of a trumpet, and a voice whose words made the hearers entreat that no further messages be spoken to them. You have come to Mount Zion and to the city of the living God, the heavenly Jerusalem, and to innumerable angels in festal gathering, and to the assembly of the first-born who are enrolled in heaven, and to a judge who is God of all, and to the spirits of just men made perfect, and to Jesus, the mediator of a new covenant, and to the sprinkled blood that speaks more graciously than the blood of Abel.

See that you do not refuse him who is speaking. For if they did not escape when they refused him who warned them on earth, much less shall we escape if we reject him who warns from heaven. His voice then shook the earth; but now he has promised, "Yet once more I will shake not only the earth but also the heaven." This phrase, "Yet once more," indicates the removal of what is shaken, as of what has been made, in order that what cannot be shaken may remain. Therefore let us be grateful for receiving a kingdom that cannot be shaken, and thus let us offer to God acceptable worship, with reverence and awe; for our God is a consuming fire.

Let brotherly love continue. Do not neglect to show hospitality to strangers, for thereby some have entertained angels unawares. Remember those who are in prison, as though in prison with them; and those who are ill-treated, since you also are in the body. Let marriage be held in honor among all, and let the marriage bed be undefiled; for God will judge the immoral and adulterous. Keep your life free from love of money, and be content with what you have; for he has said, "I will never fail you nor forsake you."

Remember your leaders, those who spoke to you the word of God; consider the outcome of their life, and imitate their faith. Jesus Christ is the same yesterday and today and for ever. Do not be led away by diverse and strange teachings; for it is well that the heart be strengthened by grace. Here we have no lasting city, but we seek the city which is to come. Through him, then, let us continually offer up a sacrifice of praise to God, that is, the fruit of lips that acknowledge his name. Do not neglect to do good and to share what you have, for such sacrifices are pleasing to God.

Now may the God of peace who brought again from the dead our Lord Jesus, the great shepherd of the sheep, by the blood of the eternal covenant, equip you with everything good, that you may do his will, working in you that which is pleasing in his sight, through Jesus Christ; to whom be glory for ever and ever. Amen.

LETTER OF
JAMES

Forceful in style, the Letter of James is more like a sermon than a letter. Its content, which is concerned with Christian conduct, is not very orderly, supplying many diverse admonitions, some more than once. Except for the opening greeting *"to the twelve tribes in the Dispersion"*—meaning all God's faithful scattered abroad—none of the usual parts of an ancient letter is present. Tradition ascribes the letter to James, the Lord's brother, writing about A.D. 45, but modern opinion is uncertain, and differs widely on both origin and date.

————

JAMES, A SERVANT of God and of the Lord Jesus Christ, to the twelve tribes in the Dispersion: Greeting.

Count it all joy, my brethren, when you meet various trials, for you know that the testing of your faith produces steadfastness. And let steadfastness have its full effect, that you may be perfect and complete, lacking in nothing.

If any of you lacks wisdom, let him ask God, and it will be given him. But let him ask in faith, with no doubting, for he who doubts is like a wave of the sea that is driven and tossed by the wind. Do not suppose that a double-minded man will receive anything from the Lord.

Blessed is the man who endures trial, for he will receive the crown of life which God has promised to those who love him. Let no one say when he is tempted, "I am tempted by God"; for God cannot be tempted with evil and he himself tempts no one; but each person is tempted when he is enticed by his own desire. Then desire when it has conceived gives birth to sin; and sin when it is full-grown brings forth death.

Do not be deceived, my beloved brethren. Every good endowment and every perfect gift is from above, coming down from the Father of lights, with whom there is no variation or shadow due to change. Of his own will he brought us forth by the word of truth, that we should be a kind of first fruits of his creatures.

Know this, my beloved brethren. Let every man be quick to hear, slow to speak, slow to anger, for the anger of man does not work the righteousness of God. But be doers of the word, and not hearers only, deceiving yourselves. For if any one is a hearer of the word and not a doer, he is like a man who observes his natural face in a mirror, and goes away and at once forgets what he was like. But he who looks into the perfect law, and perseveres, being a doer that acts, he shall be blessed.

If any one thinks he is religious, and does not bridle his tongue but deceives his heart, this man's religion is vain. Religion that is pure and undefiled before God and the Father is this: to visit orphans and widows in their affliction, and to keep oneself unstained from the world.

My brethren, show no partiality. If a man with gold rings and in fine clothing comes into your assembly, and a poor man in shabby clothing also comes in, and to the one who wears the fine clothing you say, "Have a seat here, please," while you say to the poor man, "Stand there," or, "Sit at my feet," have you not made distinctions among yourselves, and become judges with evil thoughts? Has not God chosen those who are poor in the world to be rich in faith and heirs of the kingdom which he has promised to those who love him?

If you really fulfil the royal law, "You shall love your neighbor as yourself," you do well. But if you show partiality, you commit sin, and are convicted by the law as transgressors. For whoever keeps the whole law but fails in one point has become guilty of all of it. Speak and act as those who are to be judged under the law of liberty. For judgment is without mercy to one who has shown no mercy; yet mercy triumphs over judgment.

What does it profit, my brethren, if a man says he has faith but has not works? Can his faith save him? If a brother or sister is ill-clad and in lack of daily food, and one of you says to them, "Go in peace, be warmed and filled," without giving them the things needed for the body, what does it profit? So faith by itself, if it has no works, is dead.

But some one will say, "You have faith and I have works." Show me your faith apart from your works, and I by my works will show you my faith. Do you want to be shown, you shallow man, that faith apart from works is barren? Was not Abraham our father justified by works, when he offered his son Isaac upon the altar? You see that faith was active along with his works, and faith was completed by works. You see that a man is justified by works and not by faith alone. As the body apart from the spirit is dead, so faith apart from works is dead.

Look at the ships; though they are so great and are driven by strong winds, they are guided by a very small rudder. So the tongue is a little member and boasts of great things. How great a forest is set ablaze by a small fire! And the tongue is a fire. The tongue is an unrighteous world among our members, setting on fire the cycle of nature, and set on fire by hell. For every kind of beast can be tamed and has been tamed by humankind, but no human being can tame the tongue—a restless evil, full of deadly poison. With it we bless the Lord and Father, and with it we curse men, who are made in the likeness of God. From the same mouth come blessing and cursing. My brethren, this ought not to be so.

Who is wise and understanding among you? By his good life let him show his works in the meekness of wisdom. But if you have bitter jealousy and selfish ambition in your hearts, do not boast and be false to the truth. This wisdom is not such as comes down from above, but is earthly, unspiritual, devilish. For where jealousy and selfish ambition exist, there will be disorder and every vile practice. But the wisdom from above is first pure, then peaceable, gentle, open to reason, full of mercy and good fruits, without uncertainty or insincerity.

What causes wars, and what causes fightings among you? Is it not your passions that are at war in your members? You desire and do not have; so you kill. And you covet and cannot obtain; so you fight and wage war. You do not have, because you do not ask. You ask and do not receive, because you ask wrongly, to spend it on your passions. Unfaithful creatures! Do you not know that friendship with the world is enmity with God? Therefore whoever wishes to be a friend of the world makes himself an enemy of God. Resist the devil and he will flee from you. Draw near to God and he will draw near to you. Humble yourselves before the Lord and he will exalt you.

Do not speak evil against one another, brethren. He that speaks evil against a brother or judges his brother, speaks evil against the law and judges the law. There is one lawgiver and judge, he who is able to save and to destroy. But who are you that you judge your neighbor?

Come now, you who say, "Tomorrow we will go into town and trade and get gain"; whereas you do not know about tomorrow. You are a mist that appears for a little time and then vanishes. Instead you ought to say, "If the Lord wills, we shall live and we shall do this or that." As it is, you boast in your arrogance. All such boasting is evil. Whoever knows what is right to do and fails to do it, for him it is sin.

Come now, you rich, weep and howl for the miseries that are coming upon you. Your riches have rotted and your garments are moth-eaten. Your gold and silver have rusted, and their rust will be evidence against you and will eat your flesh like fire. Behold, the wages of the laborers who mowed your fields, which you kept back by fraud, cry out; and the cries of the harvesters have reached the ears of the Lord of hosts.

Be patient, therefore, brethren, until the coming of the Lord. Behold, the farmer waits for the precious fruit of the earth, being patient over it until it receives the early and the late rain. You also be patient. Establish your hearts, for the coming of the Lord is at hand. Do not grumble, brethren, against one another, that you may not be judged; behold, the Judge is standing at the doors. But above all, my brethren, do not swear, either by heaven or by earth or with any other oath, but let your yes be yes and your no be no, that you may not fall under condemnation.

Is any one among you suffering? Let him pray. Is any cheerful? Let him sing praise. Is any among you sick? Let him call for the elders of the church, and let them pray over him, anointing him with oil in the name of the Lord; and the prayer of faith will save the sick man, and the Lord will raise him up; and if he has committed sins, he will be forgiven. Therefore confess your sins to one another, and pray for one another, that you may be healed. The prayer of a righteous man has great power in its effects.

My brethren, if any one among you wanders from the truth and some one brings him back, let him know that whoever brings back a sinner from the error of his way will save his soul from death and will cover a multitude of sins.

FIRST LETTER OF
PETER

Written to the Christians of five Roman provinces in Asia Minor (modern Turkey), this letter offers encouragement in difficult times. Some of the Christians in these provinces, threatened with renewed serious persecution, had already suffered in various ways for their faith. The author begins by reminding them of the central place occupied by Christ's redeeming death and resurrection in the Christian plan of salvation. He then passes to Christian duties: unity with each other and with God, and the obligations to be observed by various classes of believers, with repeated reference to the example of Christ. According to tradition, the apostle Peter wrote the letter from Rome, perhaps after the outbreak of persecution by the emperor Nero in A.D. 64. But this is questioned by some modern scholars, who prefer to date the letter nearer A.D. 100, with authorship unknown. In any case, it was accepted as canonical in the earliest times.

PETER, AN APOSTLE of Jesus Christ, to the exiles of the Dispersion in Pontus, Galatia, Cappadocia, Asia, and Bithynia, chosen and destined by God the Father and sanctified by the Spirit for obedience to Jesus Christ and for sprinkling with his blood: May grace and peace be multiplied to you.

Blessed be the God and Father of our Lord Jesus Christ! By his great mercy we have been born anew to a living hope through the resurrection of Jesus Christ from the dead, and to an inheritance which is imperishable, undefiled, and unfading, kept in heaven for you, who by God's power are guarded through faith for a salvation ready to be revealed in the last time. In this you rejoice, though now for a little while you may have to suffer various trials, so that the genuineness of your faith, more precious than gold which though perishable is tested by fire, may redound to praise and glory and honor at the revelation of Jesus Christ. Without having seen him, you love him; though you do not now see him, you believe in him and rejoice with unutterable and exalted joy.

The prophets who prophesied of the grace that was to be yours searched and inquired about this salvation; they inquired what person or time was indicated by the Spirit of Christ within them when predicting the sufferings of Christ and the subsequent glory. It was revealed to them that they were serving not themselves but you, in the things which have now been announced to you, things into which angels long to look.

Gird up your minds, be sober, set your hope fully upon the grace that is coming to you at the revelation of Jesus Christ. As he who called you is holy, be holy yourselves, since it is written, "You shall be holy, for I am holy." And if you invoke as Father him who judges each one impartially according to his deeds, conduct yourselves with fear throughout the time of your exile. You know that you were ransomed from the futile ways inherited from your fathers, not with perishable things such as silver or gold, but with the precious blood of Christ, like that of a lamb without blemish or spot. He was destined before the foundation of the world but was made manifest at the end of the times for your sake.

Having purified your souls, love one another earnestly from the heart. You have been born anew, not of perishable seed but of imperishable, through the living and abiding word of God; for "All flesh is like grass and all its glory like the flower of grass. The grass withers, and the flower falls, but the word of the Lord abides for ever." That word is the good news which was preached to you. So put away all malice and all guile and insincerity and envy and all slander. Like newborn babes, long for the pure spiritual milk, that by it you may grow up to salvation; for you have tasted the kindness of the Lord.

You are a chosen race, a royal priesthood, a holy nation, God's own people, that you may declare the wonderful deeds of him who called you out of darkness into his marvelous light. Once you were no people but now you are God's people; once you had not received mercy but now you have received mercy.

Beloved, I beseech you as aliens and exiles to abstain from the passions of the flesh that wage war against your soul. Maintain good conduct among the Gentiles, so that in case they speak against you as wrongdoers, they may see your good deeds and glorify God on the day of visitation.

Be subject for the Lord's sake to every human institution, whether it be to the emperor as supreme, or to governors as sent by him to punish those who do wrong and to praise those who do right. For it is God's will that by doing right you should put to silence the ignorance of foolish men. Live as free men, yet without using your freedom as a pretext for evil; but live as servants of God. Honor all men. Love the brotherhood. Fear God. Honor the emperor.

Servants, be submissive to your masters with all respect, not only to the kind and gentle but also to the overbearing. For one is approved if, mindful of God, he endures pain while suffering unjustly. For what credit is it, if when you do wrong and are beaten for it you take it patiently? But if when you do right and suffer for it you take it patiently, you have God's approval. For to this you have been called, because Christ also suffered for you, leaving you an example, that you should follow in his steps. He committed no sin; no guile was found on his lips. When he was reviled, he did not revile in return; when he suffered, he did not threaten; but he trusted to him who judges justly. He himself bore our sins in his body on the tree, that we might die to sin and live to righteousness. By his wounds you have been healed. For you were straying like sheep, but have now returned to the Shepherd and Guardian of your souls.

Likewise you wives, be submissive to your husbands, so that some, though they do not obey the word, may be won without a word by the behavior of their wives, when they see your reverent and chaste behavior. Let not yours be the outward adorning with braiding of hair, decoration of gold, and wearing of fine clothing, but let it be the hidden person of the heart with the imperishable jewel of a gentle and quiet spirit, which in God's sight is very precious.

Likewise you husbands, live considerately with your wives, bestowing honor on the woman as the weaker sex, since you are joint heirs of the grace of life, in order that your prayers may not be hindered.

Finally, all of you, have unity of spirit, sympathy, love of the brethren, a tender heart, and a humble mind. Do not return evil for evil or reviling for reviling; but on the contrary bless, that you may obtain a blessing.

Now who is there to harm you if you are zealous for what is right? But even if you do suffer for righteousness' sake, you will be blessed. Have no fear of them, nor be troubled, but in your hearts reverence Christ as Lord. Always be prepared to make a defense to any one who calls you to account for the hope that is in you, yet do it with gentleness and reverence; and keep your conscience clear, so that when you are abused, those who revile your good behavior in Christ may be put to shame. For it is better to suffer for doing right, if that should be God's will, than for doing wrong.

Since therefore Christ suffered in the flesh, arm yourselves with the same thought, for whoever has suffered in the flesh has ceased from sin, so as to live for the rest of the time in the flesh no longer by human passions but by the will of God. Let the time that is past suffice for doing what the Gentiles like to do, living in licentiousness, passions, drunkenness, revels, carousing, and lawless idolatry. They are surprised that you do not now join them in the same wild profligacy, and they abuse you; but they will give account to him who is ready to judge the living and the dead. For this is why the gospel was preached even to the dead, that though judged in the flesh like men, they might live in the spirit like God.

The end of all things is at hand; therefore keep sane and sober for your prayers. Above all, hold unfailing your love for one another, since love covers a multitude of sins. Practice hospitality ungrudgingly to one another. As each has received a gift, employ it for one another, as good stewards of God's varied grace: whoever speaks, as one who utters oracles of God; whoever renders service, as one who renders it by the strength which God supplies; in order that in everything God may be glorified through Jesus Christ. To him belong glory and dominion for ever and ever. Amen.

Beloved, do not be surprised at the fiery ordeal which comes upon you to prove you, as though something strange were happening to you. But rejoice in so far as you share Christ's sufferings, that you may also rejoice and be glad when his glory is revealed. If you are reproached for the name of Christ, you are blessed, because the spirit of glory and of God rests upon you. But let none of you suffer as a murderer, or a thief, or a wrongdoer, or a mischief-maker; yet if one suffers as a Christian, let him not be ashamed, but under that name let him glorify God. For the time has come for judgment to begin with the household of God; and if it begins with us, what will be the end of those who do not obey the gospel of God?

So I exhort the elders among you, as a fellow elder and a witness of the sufferings of Christ as well as a partaker in the glory that is to be revealed. Tend the flock of God that is your charge, not by constraint but willingly, not for shameful gain but eagerly, not as domineering over those in your charge but being examples to the flock. And when the chief Shepherd is manifested you will obtain the unfading crown of glory. Likewise you that are younger be subject to the elders. Clothe yourselves, all of you, with humility toward one another, for "God opposes the proud, but gives grace to the humble."

Humble yourselves therefore under the mighty hand of God, that in due time he may exalt you. Cast all your anxieties on him, for he cares about you. Be sober, be watchful. Your adversary the devil prowls around like a roaring lion, seeking some one to devour. Resist him, firm in your faith, knowing that the same experience of suffering is required of your brotherhood throughout the world. And after you have suffered a little while, the God of all grace, who has called you to his eternal glory in Christ, will himself restore, establish, and strengthen you. To him be the dominion for ever and ever. Amen.

By Silvanus, a faithful brother as I regard him, I have written briefly to you, exhorting and declaring that this is the true grace of God; stand fast in it. She who is at Babylon, who is likewise chosen, sends you greetings; and so does my son Mark. Greet one another with the kiss of love. Peace to all of you that are in Christ.

SECOND LETTER OF

PETER

Markedly different in content and manner from 1 Peter, this brief letter is
addressed to all Christians. It begins with an exhortation to maintain holiness
of character, followed by a warning (based on the Letter of Jude) against
heresy, which leads to immorality. It concludes with a reminder of the Second Coming of Christ, a hope that some individuals in that time had begun to
ridicule. Because the author refers to the letters of Paul as "scripture," a term
apparently not applied to them until long after Paul's death, most modern
scholars think that this letter was drawn up in Peter's name sometime between A.D. 100 and 150.

SIMEON PETER, a servant and apostle of Jesus Christ, to those who have obtained a faith of equal standing with ours in the righteousness of our God and
Savior Jesus Christ: May grace and peace be multiplied to you in the knowledge of God and of Jesus our Lord.

His divine power has granted to us all things that pertain to life and godliness, through the knowledge of him who called us to his own glory and excellence, by which he has granted to us his precious and very great promises,
that through these you may escape from the corruption that is in the world
because of passion, and become partakers of the divine nature. For this very
reason make every effort to supplement your faith with virtue, and virtue
with knowledge, and knowledge with self-control, and self-control with
steadfastness, and steadfastness with godliness, and godliness with brotherly
affection, and brotherly affection with love. For if these things are yours and
abound, they keep you from being ineffective or unfruitful in the knowledge
of our Lord Jesus Christ.

I think it right, as long as I am in this body, to arouse you by way of reminder, since I know that the putting off of my body will be soon, as our Lord
Jesus Christ showed me. And I will see to it that after my departure you may
be able at any time to recall these things.

For we did not follow cleverly devised myths when we made known to you the power and coming of our Lord Jesus Christ, but we were eyewitnesses of his majesty. For when he received honor and glory from God the Father and the voice was borne to him by the Majestic Glory, "This is my beloved Son, with whom I am well pleased," we heard this voice borne from heaven, for we were with him on the holy mountain. And we have the prophetic word made more sure. You will do well to pay attention to this as to a lamp shining in a dark place, until the day dawns and the morning star rises in your hearts. First of all you must understand this, that no prophecy of scripture is a matter of one's own interpretation, because no prophecy ever came by the impulse of man, but men moved by the Holy Spirit spoke from God.

But false prophets also arose among the people, just as there will be false teachers among you, who will secretly bring in destructive heresies, even denying the Master who bought them, bringing upon themselves swift destruction. For if God did not spare the angels when they sinned, but cast them into hell and committed them to pits of nether gloom until the judgment; if he did not spare the ancient world, but preserved Noah, a herald of righteousness, with seven others; if by turning the cities of Sodom and Gomorrah to ashes he condemned them to extinction; and if he rescued righteous Lot, then the Lord knows how to rescue the godly from trial, and to keep the unrighteous under punishment until the day of judgment, and especially those who indulge in the lust of defiling passion and despise authority.

Bold and wilful, they are not afraid to revile the glorious ones, whereas angels, though greater in might and power, do not pronounce a reviling judgment upon them before the Lord. But these, like irrational animals, creatures of instinct, born to be caught and killed, reviling in matters of which they are ignorant, will be destroyed in the same destruction with them, suffering wrong for their wrongdoing. They count it pleasure to revel in the daytime. They are blots and blemishes, reveling in their dissipation, carousing with you. They have eyes full of adultery, insatiable for sin. They entice unsteady souls. They have hearts trained in greed. Accursed children! They have followed the way of Balaam, who loved gain from wrongdoing, but was rebuked; a dumb ass spoke with human voice and restrained the prophet's madness.

These are waterless springs and mists driven by a storm; for them the nether gloom of darkness has been reserved. For they entice men who have barely escaped from those who live in error. They promise freedom, but they themselves are slaves of corruption; for whatever overcomes a man, to that he is enslaved. If, after men have escaped the defilements of the world through Jesus Christ, they are again entangled, the last state has become worse than the first. It has happened to them according to the true proverb: The dog turns back to his own vomit, and the sow is washed only to wallow in the mire.

This is now the second letter that I have written to you, beloved, and in both of them I have aroused your sincere mind by way of reminder; that you should remember the predictions of the holy prophets and the commandment of the Lord and Savior through your apostles. First of all you must understand this, that scoffers will come in the last days, following their own passions and saying, "Where is the promise of his coming? For ever since the fathers fell asleep, all things have continued as they were from the beginning of creation." They deliberately ignore this fact, that by the word of God heavens existed long ago, and an earth formed out of water and by means of water, through which the world that then existed was deluged with water and perished. But by the same word the heavens and earth that now exist have been stored up for fire, being kept until the day of judgment and destruction of ungodly men.

But do not ignore this one fact, beloved, that with the Lord one day is as a thousand years, and a thousand years as one day. The Lord is not slow about his promise as some count slowness, but is forbearing toward you, not wishing that any should perish, but that all should reach repentance. But the day of the Lord will come like a thief, and then the heavens will pass away with a loud noise, and the elements will be dissolved with fire, and the earth and the works that are upon it will be burned up.

Since all these things are thus to be dissolved, what sort of persons ought you to be in lives of holiness and godliness, waiting for and hastening the coming of the day of God, because of which the heavens will be kindled and dissolved, and the elements will melt with fire! But according to his promise we wait for new heavens and a new earth in which righteousness dwells.

Therefore, beloved, since you wait for these, be zealous to be found by him without spot or blemish, and at peace. And count the forbearance of our Lord as salvation. So also our beloved brother Paul wrote to you according to the wisdom given him, speaking of this as he does in all his letters. There are some things in them hard to understand, which the ignorant and unstable twist to their own destruction, as they do the other scriptures. You therefore, beloved, knowing this beforehand, beware lest you be carried away with the error of lawless men and lose your own stability. But grow in the grace and knowledge of our Lord and Savior Jesus Christ. To him be the glory both now and to the day of eternity. Amen.

FIRST LETTER OF

JOHN

The three letters of John give us a fascinating glimpse into the life of the Christian church in Asia Minor toward the close of the first century. Tradition ascribes all three to John the Apostle, author of the fourth Gospel. The writer, however, identifies himself only as "the Elder" (letters 2 and 3), though in the first letter he stresses that he knew Jesus in the flesh. Whoever he was, he obviously held a position of spiritual authority in the early church. Woven into the first letter are theology and ethics, doctrine and behavior, making it resemble a sermon or theological treatise. It was written to deepen the spiritual life of its readers and to correct false doctrines on the Person of Christ. The conception of God as light and life, prominent in the fourth Gospel, recurs here. Special emphasis is laid on the love of God, manifested in his Son, who was sent into the world as the remedy for sin and to give eternal life to all believers. The mark of Christians is love for God and for one another, and victory over sin.

———

THAT WHICH WAS from the beginning, which we have heard, which we have seen with our eyes and touched with our hands, concerning the word of life made manifest—this we proclaim to you so that you may have fellowship with us. Our fellowship is with the Father and with his Son Jesus Christ, and we are writing this that our joy may be complete.

This is the message we have heard from him, that God is light and in him is no darkness at all. If we say we have fellowship with him while we walk in darkness, we lie. But if we walk in the light, we have fellowship with one another, and the blood of Jesus his Son cleanses us from all sin. If we say we have no sin, we deceive ourselves. If we confess our sins, he will cleanse us from all unrighteousness.

My little children, I am writing this to you so that you may not sin; but if any one does sin, we have an advocate with the Father, Jesus Christ the righteous. He is the expiation for our sins, and for the sins of the whole world. We may be sure that we know him if we keep his commandments. He who says "I know him" but disobeys his commandments is a liar, but whoever keeps his word, in him love for God is perfected. He who says he abides in him ought to walk in the same way in which he walked.

Beloved, I am writing you no new commandment, but an old commandment which you had from the beginning, the word which you have heard. Yet I am writing you a new commandment, which is true in him and in you, because the darkness is passing away and the true light is already shining. He who says he is in the light and hates his brother is in the darkness still. He who loves his brother abides in the light, and there is no cause for stumbling.

I am writing to you, little children, because your sins are forgiven for Jesus' sake. I am writing to you, fathers, because you know him who is from the beginning. I write to you, young men, because you are strong, and the word of God abides in you, and you have overcome the evil one.

Do not love the world or the things in the world. If any one loves the world, love for the Father is not in him. For all that is in the world, the lust of the flesh and the lust of the eyes and the pride of life, is not of the Father but is of the world. And the world passes away, and the lust of it; but he who does the will of God abides for ever.

Children, it is the last hour; and as you have heard that antichrist is coming, so now many antichrists have come; therefore we know that it is the last hour. They went out from us, but they were not of us; they went out that it might be plain that they all are not of us. But you have been anointed by the Holy One, and you all know. I write to you, not because you do not know the truth, but because you know it, and know that no lie is of the truth. Who is the liar but he who denies that Jesus is the Christ? This is the antichrist, he who denies the Father and the Son. No one who denies the Son has the Father. He who confesses the Son has the Father also. If what you heard from the beginning abides in you, then you will abide in the Son and in the Father. And this is what he has promised us, eternal life.

I write this to you about those who would deceive you; but the anointing which you received from him abides in you, and you have no need that any one should teach you. As his anointing teaches you about everything, and is true, abide in him, so that when he appears we may not shrink from him in shame. You may be sure that every one who does right is born of him.

See what love the Father has given us, that we should be called children of God; and so we are. The reason why the world does not know us is that it did not know him. Beloved, we are God's children now; it does not yet appear what we shall be, but we know that when he appears we shall be like him, for we shall see him as he is. And every one who thus hopes in him purifies himself as he is pure.

Every one who commits sin is guilty of lawlessness. You know that he appeared to take away sins, and in him there is no sin. No one who abides in him sins; no one who sins has either seen him or known him. He who commits sin is of the devil; for the devil has sinned from the beginning. The reason the Son of God appeared was to destroy the works of the devil. No one born of God commits sin; by this it may be seen who are the children of God, and who are the children of the devil.

This is the message you have heard from the beginning, that we should love one another, and not be like Cain, who was of the evil one and murdered his brother. And why did he murder him? Because his own deeds were evil and his brother's righteous. Do not wonder, brethren, that the world hates you. We know that we have passed out of death into life, because we love the brethren. He who does not love abides in death. Any one who hates his brother is a murderer, and you know that no murderer has eternal life abiding in him. By this we know love, that he laid down his life for us; and we ought to lay down our lives for the brethren. But if any one has the world's goods and sees his brother in need, yet closes his heart against him, how does God's love abide in him? Little children, let us not love in word or speech but in deed and in truth.

By this we shall know that we are of the truth, and reassure our hearts before him whenever our hearts condemn us; for God is greater than our hearts, and he knows everything. Beloved, if our hearts do not condemn us, we have confidence before God; and we receive from him whatever we ask, because we keep his commandments. And this is his commandment, that we should believe in the name of his Son Jesus Christ and love one another. We know that he abides in us, by the Spirit which he has given us.

Beloved, do not believe every spirit, but test the spirits to see whether they are of God; for many false prophets have gone out into the world. Every spirit which confesses that Jesus Christ has come in the flesh is of God, and every spirit which does not confess Jesus is not of God. This is the spirit of antichrist, of which you heard that it was coming, and now it is in the world already. Little children, we are of God. Whoever knows God listens to us, and he who is not of God does not listen to us. By this we know the spirit of truth and the spirit of error.

Beloved, let us love one another; for love is of God, and he who loves is born of God. He who does not love does not know God; for God is love. In this the love of God was made manifest among us, that God sent his only Son into the world, so that we might live through him. In this is love, not that we loved God, but that he loved us and sent his Son to be the expiation for our sins. Beloved, if God so loved us, we also ought to love one another. No man has ever seen God; if we love one another, God abides in us and his love is perfected in us.

By this we know that we abide in him and he in us, because he has given us of his own Spirit. And we have seen and testify that the Father has sent his Son as the Savior of the world. Whoever confesses that Jesus is the Son of God, God abides in him, and he in God. God is love, and he who abides in love abides in God, and God abides in him. We may have confidence for the day of judgment, because as he is, so are we in this world. There is no fear in love, but perfect love casts out fear. For fear has to do with punishment, and he who fears is not perfected in love. We love, because he first loved us. If any one says, "I love God," and hates his brother, he is a liar; for he who does not love his brother whom he has seen, cannot love God whom he has not seen.

Every one who believes that Jesus is the Christ is a child of God, and every one who loves the parent loves the child. By this we know that we love the children of God, when we obey God's commandments. For this is the love of God, that we keep his commandments. Whatever is born of God overcomes the world; and this is the victory that overcomes the world, our faith.

This is he who came by water and blood, Jesus Christ, not with the water only but with the water and the blood. And the Spirit is the witness, because the Spirit is the truth. There are three witnesses, the Spirit, the water, and the blood; and these three agree. If we receive the testimony of men, the testimony of God is greater; for this is the testimony of God, that he has borne witness to his Son. He who believes in the Son of God has the testimony in himself. He who does not believe God has made him a liar, because he has not believed in the testimony that God has borne to his Son. And this is the testimony, that God gave us eternal life, and this life is in his Son. He who has the Son has life; he who has not the Son of God has not life.

I write this to you who believe in the name of the Son of God, that you may know that you have eternal life. And this is the confidence which we have in him, that if we ask anything according to his will he hears us. If we know that he hears us, we know that we have obtained the requests made of him. If any one sees his brother committing what is not a mortal sin, he will ask, and God will give him life for those whose sin is not mortal. There is sin which is mortal; I do not say that one is to pray for that. All wrongdoing is sin, but there is sin which is not mortal.

We know that we are of God, and the whole world is in the power of the evil one. And we know that the Son of God has come and has given us understanding to know him who is true; and we are in him who is true, in his Son Jesus Christ. This is the true God and eternal life. Little children, keep yourselves from idols.

SECOND LETTER OF

JOHN

The author, who calls himself "the Elder," repeats in briefer form the main teaching of 1 John, and adds a warning against showing hospitality to itinerant teachers of false doctrines. The addressees (*"the elect lady and her children"*) are usually understood to be a local church and its members. At the close of the letter the writer extends the greetings of the members of the "sister" church where he is now resident.

———

THE ELDER TO the elect lady and her children, whom I love in the truth, and not only I but also all who know the truth, because of the truth which abides in us and will be with us for ever: Grace, mercy, and peace will be with us, from God the Father and from Jesus Christ the Father's Son, in truth and love.

I rejoiced greatly to find some of your children following the truth, just as we have been commanded by the Father. And now I beg you, lady, not as though I were writing you a new commandment, but the one we have had from the beginning, that we love one another. And this is love, that we follow his commandments; this is the commandment, as you have heard from the beginning, that you follow love. For many deceivers have gone out into the world, men who will not acknowledge the coming of Jesus Christ in the flesh; such a one is the deceiver and the antichrist. Look to yourselves, that you may not lose what you have worked for, but may win a full reward. Any one who goes ahead and does not abide in the doctrine of Christ does not have God; he who abides in the doctrine has both the Father and the Son. If any one comes to you and does not bring this doctrine, do not receive him into the house or give him any greeting; for he who greets him shares his wicked work.

Though I have much to write to you, I would rather not use paper and ink, but I hope to come to see you and talk with you face to face, so that our joy may be complete.

The children of your elect sister greet you.

JOHN

In this personal letter the Elder expresses thanks to Gaius, an influential member of an unidentified church, for showing kindness and hospitality to Christian travelers. Mention is also made of a certain Diotrephes, who had opposed the Elder, and of someone named Demetrius, who is commended. The word "friends," at the letter's conventional close, refers to those members of the church who are loyal to the Elder and who oppose Diotrephes.

———

THE ELDER TO the beloved Gaius, whom I love in the truth.

Beloved, I pray that all may go well with you and that you may be in health; I know that it is well with your soul. For I greatly rejoiced when some of the brethren arrived and testified to the truth of your life, as indeed you do follow the truth. No greater joy can I have than this, to hear that my children follow the truth.

Beloved, it is a loyal thing you do when you render any service to the brethren, especially to strangers, who have testified to your love before the church. You will do well to send them on their journey as befits God's service. For they have set out for his sake and have accepted nothing from the heathen. So we ought to support such men, that we may be fellow workers in the truth.

I have written something to the church; but Diotrephes, who likes to put himself first, does not acknowledge my authority. So if I come, I will bring up what he is doing, prating against me with evil words. And not content with that, he refuses himself to welcome the brethren, and also stops those who want to welcome them and puts them out of the church.

Beloved, do not imitate evil but imitate good. He who does good is of God; he who does evil has not seen God. Demetrius has testimony from every one, and from the truth itself; I testify to him too, and you know my testimony is true.

I had much to write to you, but I would rather not write with pen and ink; I hope to see you soon, and we will talk together face to face.

Peace be to you. The friends greet you. Greet the friends, every one of them.

JUDE

The purpose of this forceful letter was to combat doctrines that were being spread by heretical teachers. Using examples drawn from the Old Testament, the writer graphically illustrates the dangers of such doctrines. The letter's date and destination cannot be determined with any precision; its author has usually been identified as one of the "brethren" of Jesus. Containing references to two Jewish apocryphal books (Enoch and the Assumption of Moses), the letter closes with a beautiful and moving benediction.

JUDE, A SERVANT of Jesus Christ and brother of James, to those who are called, beloved in God the Father and kept for Jesus Christ: May mercy, peace, and love be multiplied to you.

Beloved, being very eager to write to you of our common salvation, I found it necessary to write appealing to you to contend for the faith which was once for all delivered to the saints. For admission has been secretly gained by some who long ago were designated for this condemnation, ungodly persons who pervert the grace of our God into licentiousness and deny our only Master and Lord, Jesus Christ.

Now I desire to remind you, though you were once for all fully informed, that he who saved a people out of the land of Egypt, afterward destroyed those who did not believe. And the angels that did not keep their own position but left their proper dwelling have been kept by him in eternal chains in the nether gloom until the judgment of the great day; just as Sodom and Gomorrah and the surrounding cities, which likewise acted immorally and indulged in unnatural lust, serve as an example by undergoing a punishment of eternal fire.

Yet in like manner these men in their dreamings defile the flesh, reject authority, and revile the glorious ones. But when the archangel Michael, contending with the devil, disputed about the body of Moses, he did not presume to pronounce a reviling judgment upon him, but said, "The Lord rebuke you." But these men revile whatever they do not understand, and by those things that they know by instinct as irrational animals do, they are destroyed. Woe to them! For they walk in the way of Cain, and abandon themselves for the sake of gain to Balaam's error, and perish in Korah's rebellion. These are blemishes on your love feasts, as they boldly carouse together, looking after themselves; waterless clouds, carried along by winds; fruitless trees in late autumn, twice dead, uprooted; wild waves of the sea, casting up the foam of their own shame; wandering stars for whom the nether gloom of darkness has been reserved for ever.

It was of these also that Enoch in the seventh generation from Adam prophesied, saying, "Behold, the Lord came with his holy myriads, to execute judgment on all, and to convict all the ungodly of all their deeds of ungodliness which they have committed in such an ungodly way, and of all the harsh things which ungodly sinners have spoken against him." These are grumblers, malcontents, following their own passions, loudmouthed boasters, flattering people to gain advantage.

But you must remember, beloved, the predictions of the apostles of our Lord Jesus Christ; they said to you, "In the last time there will be scoffers, following their own ungodly passions." It is these who set up divisions, worldly people, devoid of the Spirit. But you, beloved, build yourselves up on your most holy faith; pray in the Holy Spirit; keep yourselves in the love of God; wait for the mercy of our Lord Jesus Christ unto eternal life. And convince some who doubt; save some, by snatching them out of the fire; on some have mercy with fear, hating even the garment spotted by the flesh.

Now to him who is able to keep you from falling and to present you without blemish before the presence of his glory with rejoicing, to the only God, our Savior through Jesus Christ our Lord, be glory, majesty, dominion, and authority, before all time and now and for ever. Amen.

THE
REVELATION
TO JOHN

Fifty miles offshore from Miletus in Asia Minor lies the rocky island of Patmos. Here a Christian prophet named John, who had been exiled for refusing to worship the image of the emperor Domitian (A.D. 81–96), experienced a series of remarkable visions. Some were beautiful, some horrible, but all of them proved to him the reality of his Christian faith, strengthening his belief that Christ and his church would ultimately triumph. When his harsh exile was over and he could obtain writing materials, John wrote the substance of his visions in a book in order to inspire hope, courage, and endurance among persecuted Christians. His book is arranged in elaborate patterns of sevens, and contains prophetic symbolism derived from Daniel and Zechariah. John's final visions of a new heaven and a new earth, predicted by Isaiah, describe the renewal of all creation, freed from imperfection and transformed by the glory of God.

THE REVELATION OF Jesus Christ, which God gave him to show to his servants what must soon take place; and he made it known by sending his angel to his servant John, who bore witness to the word of God and to the testimony of Jesus Christ, even to all that he saw. Blessed is he who reads aloud the words of the prophecy, and blessed are those who hear, and who keep what is written therein; for the time is near.

JOHN TO THE seven churches that are in Asia:
Grace to you and peace from him who is and who was and who is to come, and from the seven spirits before his throne, and from Jesus Christ the faithful witness, the first-born of the dead, and the ruler of kings on earth.

To him who loves us, and has freed us from our sins by his blood, and made us a kingdom, priests to his God and Father, to him be glory and dominion for ever. Behold, he is coming with the clouds, and every eye will see him, every one who pierced him; and all tribes of the earth will wail on account of him.

"I am the Alpha and the Omega," says the Lord God, who is and who was and who is to come, the Almighty.

I John, your brother, who share with you in Jesus the tribulation, was on the island called Patmos on account of the word of God and the testimony of Jesus. I was in the Spirit on the Lord's day, and I heard behind me a loud voice like a trumpet saying, "Write what you see in a book and send it to the seven churches."

Then I turned, and I saw seven golden lampstands, and in the midst one like a son of man, clothed with a long robe and with a golden girdle round his breast; his head and his hair were white as white wool; his eyes like a flame of fire, his feet like burnished bronze, and his voice like the sound of many waters; in his right hand he held seven stars, from his mouth issued a sharp two-edged sword, and his face was like the sun shining in full strength.

I fell at his feet as though dead, but he laid his right hand upon me, saying, "Fear not, I am the first and the last; I died, and behold, I am alive for ever-more, and I have the keys of Death and Hades. Now write what you see, what is and what is to take place hereafter. As for the mystery of the seven stars, they are the angels of the seven churches, and the lampstands are the seven churches.

"To the angel of the church in Ephesus write: 'The words of him who holds the seven stars in his right hand, who walks among the seven golden lamp-stands.

"'I know your works, and how you cannot bear evil men, but have tested those who call themselves apostles but are not, and found them to be false; I know you are enduring patiently for my name's sake. But I have this against you, that you have abandoned the love you had at first. Remember from what you have fallen, repent and do the works you did at first. If not, I will remove your lampstand from its place. To him who conquers I will grant to eat of the tree of life, in the paradise of God.'

"And to the angel of the church in Smyrna write: 'The words of the first and the last, who died and came to life.

"'I know your tribulation and your poverty (but you are rich) and the slander of those who say that they are Jews and are not, but are a synagogue of Satan. Behold, the devil is about to throw some of you into prison, that you may be tested, and for ten days you will have tribulation. Be faithful unto death, and I will give you the crown of life. He who conquers shall not be hurt by the second death.'

"And to the angel of the church in Pergamum write: 'The words of him who has the sharp two-edged sword.

"'I know you dwell where Satan's throne is; you did not deny my faith even in the days of Antipas my witness, who was killed among you. But I have a few things against you: you have some there who hold the teaching of Balaam, who taught Balak to put a stumbling block before the sons of Israel, that they might eat food sacrificed to idols and practice immorality. Repent then. If not, I will soon war against them with the sword of my mouth. To him who conquers I will give some of the hidden manna, and I will give him a white stone, with a new name written on the stone which no one knows except him who receives it.'

"And to the angel of the church in Thyatira write: 'The words of the Son of God, who has eyes like a flame of fire, and feet like burnished bronze.

"'I know your works, your faith and patient endurance, and that your latter works exceed the first. But the woman Jezebel, who calls herself a prophetess, is beguiling my servants to practice immorality and to eat food sacrificed to idols. I gave her time to repent, but she refuses. Behold, I will throw her and those with her into great tribulation, unless they repent; and I will strike her children dead. And all the churches shall know that I am he who searches mind and heart, and I will give to each of you as your works deserve. To the rest of you, who have not learned what some call the deep things of Satan, I say, hold fast what you have, until I come. He who keeps my works until the end, I will give power over the nations, even as I myself have received power from my Father; and I will give him the morning star.'

"And to the angel of the church in Sardis write: 'The words of him who has the seven spirits of God and the seven stars.

"'I know your works; you have the name of being alive, and you are dead. Awake, and strengthen what remains. Remember what you received, and repent. If you will not awake, I will come like a thief, and you will not know at what hour. Yet you have still a few in Sardis who have not soiled their garments; and they shall walk with me in white, for they are worthy. He who conquers shall be clad thus, and I will not blot his name out of the book of life; I will confess his name before my Father and before his angels.'

"And to the angel of the church in Philadelphia write: 'The words of the holy one, the true one, who has the key of David, who opens and no one shall shut, who shuts and no one opens.

"'I know your works. Behold, I have set before you an open door, which no one is able to shut; I know that you have but little power, and yet you have kept my word and have not denied my name. Those who say that they are Jews and are not, but lie—behold, I will make them come and bow down before your feet, and learn that I have loved you. Because you have kept my word, I will keep you from the hour of trial which is coming on the whole world. I am coming soon; hold fast what you have. He who conquers, I will make him a pillar in the temple of my God; I will write on him the name of my God, and of the city of my God, the new Jerusalem which comes down from my God out of heaven, and my own new name.'

"And to the angel of the church in Laodicea write: 'The words of the Amen, the faithful and true witness, the beginning of God's creation.

"'I know your works: you are neither cold nor hot. Because you are lukewarm, I will spew you out of my mouth. For you say, I am rich, I need nothing; not knowing that you are wretched, pitiable, poor, blind, and naked.

Therefore I counsel you to buy from me gold refined by fire, that you may be rich, and white garments to keep the shame of your nakedness from being seen, and salve to anoint your eyes, that you may see. Those whom I love, I reprove and chasten; so be zealous and repent. Behold, I stand at the door and knock; if any one hears my voice and opens the door, I will come in to him and eat with him, and he with me. He who conquers, I will grant him to sit with me on my throne, as I myself conquered and sat down with my Father on his throne.'"

AFTER THIS I looked, and lo, in heaven an open door! And the first voice, like a trumpet, said, "Come up hither, and I will show you what must take place after this." At once I was in the Spirit, and lo, a throne stood in heaven, with one seated on it who appeared like jasper and carnelian, and round the throne was a rainbow that looked like an emerald. Round the throne were twenty-four thrones, and seated on them twenty-four elders, clad in white garments, with golden crowns. From the throne issue flashes of lightning, and voices and peals of thunder, and before the throne burn seven torches of fire, which are the seven spirits of God; and before the throne there is as it were a sea of glass, like crystal. On each side of the throne are four living creatures, full of eyes in front and behind: the first living creature like a lion, the second like an ox, the third with the face of a man, and the fourth like a flying eagle. And the creatures, each with six wings, never cease to sing, "Holy, holy, holy, is the Lord God Almighty, who was and is and is to come!" And whenever the living creatures give glory and honor and thanks to him who is seated on the throne, who lives for ever and ever, the twenty-four elders fall down before him and worship, singing, "Worthy art thou, our Lord and God, to receive glory and honor and power, for thou didst create all things, and by thy will they existed and were created."

And I saw in the right hand of him seated on the throne a scroll sealed with seven seals; and I saw a strong angel proclaiming with a loud voice, "Who is worthy to open the scroll and break its seals?" No one in heaven or on earth or under the earth was able to open the scroll, and I wept much that no one was found. Then one of the elders said to me, "Weep not; lo, the Lion of the tribe of Judah, the Root of David, has conquered, so that he can open the scroll and its seven seals."

And I saw a Lamb standing, as though it had been slain, with seven horns and seven eyes, which are the seven spirits of God sent out into all the earth; and he took the scroll. Then the four living creatures and the twenty-four elders fell down before the Lamb, each holding a harp, and with golden bowls full of incense, which are the prayers of the saints; and they sang a new song, saying, "Worthy art thou to take the scroll and to open its seals, for thou wast slain and by thy blood didst ransom men for God from every tribe and tongue and people and nation, and hast made them a kingdom and priests to our God, and they shall reign on earth."

Then I heard around the throne the voice of many angels, numbering myriads of myriads and thousands of thousands, saying with a loud voice, "Worthy is the Lamb who was slain, to receive power and wealth and wisdom and might and honor and glory and blessing!" And I heard every creature in heaven, earth and sea saying, "To him who sits upon the throne and to the Lamb be blessing and honor and glory and might for ever and ever!" And the four living creatures said, "Amen!" and the elders fell down and worshiped.

When the Lamb opened one of the seven seals, I heard one of the four living creatures say, as with a voice of thunder, "Come!" And I saw a white horse, and its rider had a bow; and a crown was given to him, and he went out conquering and to conquer.

When he opened the second seal, I heard the second living creature say, "Come!" And out came another horse, bright red; its rider was permitted to take peace from the earth, so that men should slay one another; and he was given a great sword.

When he opened the third seal, I heard the third living creature say, "Come!" And behold, a black horse, and its rider had a balance in his hand; and I heard a voice in the midst of the four living creatures saying, "A quart of wheat for a denarius, and three quarts of barley for a denarius; but do not harm oil and wine!"

When he opened the fourth seal, I heard the voice of the fourth living creature say, "Come!" And I saw a pale horse, and its rider's name was Death, and Hades followed him; and they were given power over a fourth of the earth, to kill with sword and famine and pestilence and by wild beasts.

When he opened the fifth seal, I saw under the altar the souls of those who had been slain for the word of God and for the witness they had borne; they cried out, "O Sovereign Lord, holy and true, how long before thou wilt judge and avenge our blood on those who dwell upon the earth?" Then they were each given a white robe and told to rest a little longer, until the number of their fellow servants and their brethren should be complete, who were to be killed as they themselves had been.

When he opened the sixth seal, behold, there was a great earthquake; the sun became black as sackcloth, the full moon became like blood, and the stars of the sky fell to the earth as the fig tree sheds its winter fruit when shaken by a gale; the sky vanished like a scroll that is rolled up, and every mountain and island was removed from its place. Then the kings of the earth and the great men and the generals and the rich and the strong, and every one, slave and free, hid in the caves and among the rocks of the mountains, calling to the mountains and rocks, "Fall on us and hide us from the face of him seated on the throne, and from the wrath of the Lamb; for the great day of their wrath has come, and who can stand before it?"

After this I saw four angels standing at the four corners of the earth, holding back the four winds of the earth. Then I saw another angel ascend from the rising of the sun, with the seal of the living God, and he called to the four angels, saying, "Do not harm the earth or the sea or the trees, till we have sealed the servants of our God upon their foreheads." And I heard the number of the sealed, a hundred and forty-four thousand, out of every tribe of the sons of Israel, twelve thousand out of each.

After this, behold, a multitude which no man could number, from every nation, standing before the throne and before the Lamb, clothed in white robes, with palm branches in their hands, and crying out, "Salvation belongs to our God, who sits upon the throne, and to the Lamb!" And all the angels round the throne fell on their faces and worshiped God, saying, "Amen! Blessing and glory and wisdom and thanksgiving and honor and power and might be to our God for ever and ever! Amen."

Then one of the elders addressed me, saying, "Who are these, clothed in white robes, and whence have they come?" I said to him, "Sir, you know." And he said to me, "These are they who have come out of the great tribulation; they have washed their robes and made them white in the blood of the Lamb. Therefore are they before the throne of God, and serve him day and night within his temple; and he who sits upon the throne will shelter them with his presence. They shall hunger no more, neither thirst any more; the sun shall not strike them, nor any scorching heat. For the Lamb in the midst of the throne will be their shepherd, and he will guide them to springs of living water; and God will wipe away every tear from their eyes."

When the Lamb opened the seventh seal, there was silence in heaven for about half an hour. Then I saw the seven angels who stand before God, and seven trumpets were given to them. And another angel came and stood at the altar with a golden censer; and the smoke of the incense rose with the prayers of the saints. Then the angel took the censer and filled it with fire from the altar and threw it on the earth; and there were peals of thunder, voices, flashes of lightning, and an earthquake.

Now the seven angels made ready to blow the trumpets.

The first angel blew, and there followed hail and fire, mixed with blood, which fell on the earth; and a third of the earth was burned up, and a third of the trees, and all green grass.

The second angel blew, and something like a great mountain, burning with fire, was thrown into the sea; and a third of the sea became blood, a third of the living creatures in the sea died, and a third of the ships were destroyed.

The third angel blew, and a great star fell from heaven, blazing like a torch, and it fell on a third of the rivers and on the fountains of water. The name of the star is Wormwood. A third of the waters became wormwood, and many men died of the water, because it was made bitter.

The fourth angel blew, and a third of the sun was struck, and a third of the moon, and a third of the stars, so that a third of their light was darkened.

Then I heard an eagle crying as it flew in midheaven, "Woe, woe, woe to those who dwell on the earth, at the blasts of the other trumpets which the three angels are about to blow!"

And the fifth angel blew his trumpet, and I saw a star fallen from heaven to earth, and he was given the key of the shaft of the bottomless pit. He opened the shaft, and from it rose smoke like the smoke of a great furnace, and the sun and the air were darkened. Then from the smoke came locusts on the earth, and they were given power like the power of scorpions of the earth; they were told not to harm the grass of the earth or any green growth or any tree, but only those of mankind who have not the seal of God upon their foreheads; they were allowed to torture them for five months, but not to kill them, and their torture was like the torture of a scorpion, when it stings a man. And in those days men will long to die, and death will fly from them. In appearance the locusts were like horses arrayed for battle; on their heads were what looked like crowns of gold; their faces were like human faces, their hair like women's hair, and their teeth like lions' teeth; they had scales like iron breastplates, and the noise of their wings was like the noise of many chariots with horses rushing into battle. They have tails like scorpions, and stings. They have as king over them the angel of the bottomless pit; his name in Hebrew is Abaddon, and in Greek Apollyon.

The first woe has passed; behold, two woes are still to come.

Then the sixth angel blew his trumpet, and I heard a voice from the golden altar before God, saying to the sixth angel, "Release the four angels who are bound at the great river Euphrates." So the four angels were released, who had been held ready for the hour, the day, the month, and the year, to kill a third of mankind. The number of the troops of cavalry was twice ten thousand times ten thousand; I heard their number. And in my vision the riders wore breastplates the color of fire and of sapphire and of sulphur, and the heads of the horses were like lions' heads, and fire and smoke and sulphur issued from their mouths. A third of mankind was killed by the fire and smoke and sulphur. The horses' tails are like serpents, with heads, and by means of them they wound. The rest of mankind, who were not killed, did not repent of the works of their hands nor give up worshiping demons and idols; nor did they repent of their murders or their sorceries or their immorality or their thefts.

THEN I SAW another mighty angel coming down from heaven, wrapped in a cloud, with a rainbow over his head, his face like the sun, and his legs like pillars of fire. He had a little scroll open in his hand. And he set his right foot on the sea, and his left foot on the land, and called out like a lion roaring; when he called out, the seven thunders sounded. I was about to write, but I heard a voice from heaven saying, "Seal up what the seven thunders have said, and do not write it down." And the angel lifted up his right hand to heaven and swore by him who lives for ever and ever, who created heaven and earth and sea, that there should be no more delay, but that in the days of the trumpet call to be sounded by the seventh angel, the mystery of God, as he announced to his servants the prophets, should be fulfilled.

Then the voice which I had heard from heaven spoke to me again, saying, "Go, take the scroll." So I went to the angel and told him to give me the little scroll; and he said to me, "Take it and eat; it will be bitter to your stomach, but sweet as honey in your mouth." And I took the little scroll from the hand of the angel and ate it; it was sweet as honey in my mouth, but when I had eaten it my stomach was made bitter. And I was told, "You must again prophesy about many peoples and nations and tongues and kings."

Then I was given a measuring rod like a staff, and I was told: "Rise and measure the temple of God and the altar and those who worship there, but do not measure the court outside the temple; that is given over to the nations, and they will trample over the holy city for forty-two months. And I will grant my two witnesses power to prophesy for one thousand two hundred and sixty days." These are the two olive trees and the two lampstands which stand before the Lord of the earth. And if any one would harm them, fire pours from their mouth and consumes their foes. They have power to shut the sky, that no rain may fall during the days of their prophesying, and they have power over the waters to turn them into blood, and to smite the earth with every plague.

And when they have finished their testimony, the beast that ascends from the bottomless pit will conquer and kill them, and their dead bodies will lie in the street of the great city where their Lord was crucified. For three days and a half men from the peoples and nations gaze at their dead bodies and refuse to let them be placed in a tomb, and those who dwell on the earth will make merry, because these two prophets had been a torment to them. But after the three and a half days a breath of life from God entered them, and they stood up, and great fear fell on those who saw them. A loud voice from heaven said to them, "Come up hither!" And in the sight of their foes they went up to heaven in a cloud. At that hour there was a great earthquake, and a tenth of the city fell; seven thousand people were killed, and the rest were terrified and gave glory to the God of heaven.

The second woe has passed; behold, the third woe is soon to come.

Then the seventh angel blew his trumpet, and there were loud voices in heaven, saying, "The kingdom of the world has become the kingdom of our Lord and of his Christ, and he shall reign for ever and ever." And the twenty-four elders fell on their faces and worshiped God, saying, "We give thanks to thee, Lord God Almighty, who art and who wast, that thou hast taken thy great power and begun to reign. The nations raged, but thy wrath came, and the time for the dead to be judged, for rewarding thy servants, the prophets and saints, and those who fear thy name, both small and great, and for destroying the destroyers of the earth."

Then God's temple in heaven was opened, and the ark of his covenant was seen within; and there were flashes of lightning, voices, peals of thunder, an earthquake, and heavy hail.

A GREAT PORTENT APPEARED IN HEAVEN, a woman clothed with the sun, with the moon under her feet, and on her head a crown of twelve stars; she was with child and she cried out in her pangs of birth. And another portent appeared in heaven, a great red dragon, with seven heads and ten horns, and seven diadems upon his heads. His tail swept down a third of the stars of heaven, and cast them to the earth. And the dragon stood before the woman, that he might devour her child when she brought it forth. Then she brought forth a male child, one who is to rule all the nations with a rod of iron, but her child was caught up to God and to his throne, and the woman fled into the wilderness, where she has a place prepared by God, in which to be nourished for one thousand two hundred and sixty days.

Now war arose in heaven, Michael and his angels fighting against the dragon; and the dragon and his angels fought, but they were defeated and there was no longer any place for them in heaven. The great dragon, that ancient serpent, who is called the Devil and Satan, the deceiver of the whole world—he was thrown down to the earth, and his angels with him. I heard a loud voice in heaven, saying, "Now the salvation and the power and the kingdom of our God and the authority of his Christ have come, for the accuser of our brethren has been thrown down, who accuses them day and night before our God. They have conquered him by the blood of the Lamb and by the word of their testimony, for they loved not their lives even unto death. Rejoice then, O heaven and you that dwell therein! But woe to you, O earth and sea, for the devil has come down to you in great wrath, because he knows that his time is short!"

When the dragon saw that he had been thrown down to the earth, he pursued the woman who had borne the male child. But the woman was given the two wings of the great eagle, that she might fly into the wilderness, where she is to be nourished for a time, and times, and half a time. The serpent poured water like a river out of his mouth after the woman, to sweep her away with the flood. But the earth came to the help of the woman, and swallowed the river. Then the dragon was angry with the woman, and went off to make war on the rest of her offspring, on those who keep the commandments of God and bear testimony to Jesus.

And I saw a beast rising out of the sea, with ten horns and seven heads, with ten diadems upon its horns and a blasphemous name upon its heads. And the beast was like a leopard, its feet were like a bear's, and its mouth was like a lion's. To it the dragon gave his power and his throne and great authority. One of its heads seemed to have a mortal wound, but its mortal wound was healed, and the whole earth followed the beast with wonder. Men worshiped the dragon, for he had given his authority to the beast, and they worshiped the beast, saying, "Who is like the beast, and who can fight against it?"

And the beast was given a mouth uttering blasphemous words, and it was allowed to exercise authority for forty-two months, blaspheming God's name and his dwelling, that is, those who dwell in heaven. Also it was allowed to make war on the saints and to conquer them. And authority was given it over every tribe and nation, and all who dwell on earth will worship it, every one whose name has not been written before the foundation of the world in the book of life of the Lamb that was slain.

Then I saw another beast which rose out of the earth; it had two horns like a lamb and it spoke like a dragon. It exercises all the authority of the first beast in its presence, and makes the earth and its inhabitants worship the first beast, whose mortal wound was healed. It works great signs, even making fire come down from heaven to earth in the sight of men; and by the signs it deceives those who dwell on earth, bidding them make an image for the first beast; and it was allowed to give breath to the image, so that it should speak, and to cause those who would not worship the image to be slain. Also it causes all, both small and great, both rich and poor, both free and slave, to be marked on the right hand or the forehead, so that no one can buy or sell unless he has the mark, that is, the name of the beast or the number of its name. This calls for wisdom: let him who has understanding reckon the number of the beast, for it is a human number, its number is six hundred and sixty-six.

Then lo, on Mount Zion stood the Lamb, and with him a hundred and forty-four thousand who had his name and his Father's name written on their foreheads. And I heard a voice from heaven like the sound of many waters and like loud thunder; the voice I heard was like the sound of harpers, and they sing a new song before the throne. No one could learn that song except the hundred and forty-four thousand. It is these who are chaste; it is these who follow the Lamb wherever he goes; these have been redeemed from mankind as first fruits for God and the Lamb, and in their mouth no lie was found, for they are spotless.

Then I saw another angel flying in midheaven, with an eternal gospel to proclaim on earth to every nation; and he said with a loud voice, "Fear God and give him glory, for the hour of his judgment has come; and worship him who made heaven and earth, the sea and the fountains of water."

A second angel followed, saying, "Fallen, fallen is Babylon the great, she who made all nations drink the wine of her impure passion."

And a third followed, saying with a loud voice, "If any one worships the beast and its image, and receives a mark on his forehead or hand, he also shall drink the wine of God's wrath, and shall be tormented with fire and sulphur in the presence of the holy angels and of the Lamb. And the smoke of their torment goes up for ever and ever; and they have no rest, day or night."

I heard a voice from heaven saying, "Write this: Blessed are the dead who die in the Lord henceforth." "Blessed indeed," says the Spirit, "that they may rest from their labors, for their deeds follow them!"

Then lo, a white cloud, and seated on the cloud one like a son of man, with a golden crown on his head, and a sharp sickle in his hand. And another angel came out of the temple, calling to him upon the cloud, "Put in your sickle, and reap, for the hour to reap has come, for the harvest of the earth is fully ripe." So he swung his sickle on the earth, and the earth was reaped.

And another angel came out, and he too had a sharp sickle. Then another angel came out from the altar, the angel who has power over fire, and he called to him who had the sharp sickle, "Put in your sickle and gather the clusters of the vine of the earth, for its grapes are ripe." So the angel swung his sickle and gathered the vintage of the earth, and threw it into the great wine press of the wrath of God; and the wine press was trodden outside the city, and blood flowed from it, as high as a horse's bridle, for one thousand six hundred stadia.

THEN I SAW another portent in heaven, great and wonderful, seven angels with seven plagues, which are the last, for with them the wrath of God is ended.

And I saw what appeared to be a sea of glass mingled with fire, and those who had conquered the beast, standing beside the sea with harps of God in their hands. And they sing the song of Moses and the song of the Lamb, saying, "Great and wonderful are thy deeds, O Lord God the Almighty! Just and true are thy ways, O King of the ages! Who shall not fear and glorify thy name, O Lord? For thou alone art holy. All nations shall come and worship thee, for thy judgments have been revealed."

After this I looked, and the temple of the tent of witness in heaven was opened, and out came the seven angels with the seven plagues, robed in pure bright linen, and their breasts girded with golden girdles. And one of the four living creatures gave the angels seven golden bowls full of the wrath of God; and the temple was filled with smoke from the glory and power of God, and no one could enter the temple until the seven plagues were ended.

Then I heard a loud voice from the temple telling the seven angels, "Go and pour out on the earth the seven bowls of the wrath of God."

So the first angel poured his bowl on the earth, and foul and evil sores came upon the men who bore the mark of the beast and worshiped its image.

The second angel poured his bowl into the sea, and it became like the blood of a dead man, and every living thing died that was in the sea.

The third angel poured his bowl into the rivers and the fountains of water, and they became blood. And I heard the angel of water say, "Just art thou in these thy judgments, O Holy One. For men have shed the blood of saints and prophets, and thou hast given them blood to drink. It is their due!"

The fourth angel poured his bowl on the sun, and it was allowed to scorch men with fire and fierce heat, and they cursed the name of God who had power over these plagues, and they did not repent.

The fifth angel poured his bowl on the throne of the beast, and its kingdom was in darkness; men gnawed their tongues in anguish and cursed the God of heaven for their pain and sores, and did not repent of their deeds.

The sixth angel poured his bowl on the great river Euphrates, and its water was dried up, to prepare the way for the kings from the east. And I saw, issuing from the mouths of the dragon and the beast and the false prophet, three foul spirits like frogs; for they are demonic spirits, performing signs, who go abroad to the kings of the whole world, to assemble them for battle on the great day of God the Almighty. And they assembled them at the place which is called in Hebrew Armageddon.

The seventh angel poured his bowl into the air, and a loud voice came out of the temple, from the throne, saying, "It is done!" And there were flashes of lightning, voices, peals of thunder, and a great earthquake such as had never been since men were on the earth. The great city was split into three parts, and the cities of the nations fell, and God remembered great Babylon, to make her drain the cup of the fury of his wrath.

THEN ONE OF the angels said to me, "Come, I will show you the judgment of the great harlot who is seated upon many waters, with whom the kings of the earth have committed fornication." And he carried me away in the Spirit into a wilderness, and I saw a woman sitting on a scarlet beast which had seven heads and ten horns. The woman was arrayed in purple and scarlet, and bedecked with jewels, holding in her hand a golden cup full of abominations and the impurities of her fornication; and on her forehead was written a name of mystery: "Babylon the great, mother of harlots and of earth's abominations." And I saw the woman, drunk with the blood of the saints.

"I will tell you the mystery of the woman," the angel said, "and of the beast. The beast that you saw was, and is not, and is to ascend from the bottomless pit and go to perdition. The seven heads are seven mountains on which the woman is seated; they are also seven kings, five of whom have fallen. The ten horns are ten kings who have not yet received power, but they are to receive authority for one hour, together with the beast. They will make war on the Lamb, and the Lamb will conquer them, for he is Lord of lords and King of kings."

And he said to me, "The waters where the harlot is seated are peoples and nations. The ten horns and the beast will hate the harlot; they will make her desolate and naked. And the woman is the great city which has dominion over the kings of the earth."

After this I saw another angel coming down from heaven, and the earth was made bright with his splendor. And he called out with a mighty voice, "Fallen, fallen is Babylon the great! It has become a dwelling place of demons, a haunt of every foul spirit, and the merchants of the earth have grown rich with the wealth of her wantonness."

Then I heard another voice from heaven saying, "Come out of her, my people, lest you take part in her sins, for God has remembered her iniquities. Render to her as she herself has rendered, and repay her double for her deeds. So shall her plagues come in a single day, pestilence and mourning and famine, and she shall be burned with fire; for mighty is the Lord God who judges her."

And the kings of the earth will weep over her when they see the smoke of her burning, and they will say, "Alas! thou mighty city, Babylon! In one hour has thy judgment come."

And the merchants of the earth mourn for her, since no one buys their cargo any more. And all shipmasters and seafaring men stood far off and cried out, "What city was like the great city, where all who had ships at sea grew rich by her wealth? In one hour she has been laid waste. Rejoice over her, O heaven, O saints and apostles and prophets, for God has given judgment for you against her!"

After this I heard what seemed to be the loud voice of a great multitude in heaven, crying, "Hallelujah! Salvation and glory and power belong to our God, for his judgments are true and just; he has judged the great harlot, and he has avenged on her the blood of his servants. The smoke from her goes up for ever and ever." And the twenty-four elders and the four living creatures fell down and worshiped God, who is seated on the throne, saying, "Amen. Hallelujah!" Again I heard what seemed to be the voice of a great multitude, like the sound of many waters and of mighty thunderpeals, crying, "Hallelujah! For the Lord our God the Almighty reigns. Let us rejoice, for the marriage of the Lamb has come, and his Bride has made herself ready; it was granted her to be clothed with fine linen, bright and pure"—for the fine linen is the righteous deeds of the saints. And the angel said to me, "Write this: Blessed are those who are invited to the marriage supper of the Lamb."

Then I saw heaven opened, and behold, a white horse! He who sat upon it is called Faithful and True, and in righteousness he judges and makes war. His eyes are like a flame, and on his head are many diadems; and he has a name inscribed which no one knows but himself. He is clad in a robe dipped in blood, and the name by which he is called is The Word of God. And the armies of heaven, arrayed in fine linen, white and pure, followed him on white horses. From his mouth issues a sharp sword with which to smite the nations, and he will rule them with a rod of iron; he will tread the wine press of the wrath of God the Almighty. On his robe and on his thigh he has a name inscribed, King of kings and Lord of lords.

Then I saw an angel standing in the sun, and with a loud voice he called to all the birds that fly in midheaven, "Come, gather for the great supper of God, to eat the flesh of kings, of captains, of mighty men, the flesh of horses and their riders." And I saw the beast and the kings of the earth with their armies gathered to make war against him who sits upon the horse and against his army. And the beast was captured, and with it the false prophet who by signs had deceived those who had received the mark of the beast and worshiped its image. These two were thrown alive into the lake of fire that burns with sulphur. And the rest were slain by the sword of him who sits upon the horse, and all the birds were gorged with their flesh.

Then I saw an angel coming down from heaven, holding the key of the bottomless pit and a great chain. And he seized the dragon, that ancient serpent, the Devil and Satan, and bound him for a thousand years, and threw him into the pit, and shut it and sealed it over him, that he should deceive the nations no more, till the thousand years were ended. After that he must be loosed for a little while.

Then I saw thrones, and seated on them were those to whom judgment was committed. Also I saw the souls of those who had been beheaded for their testimony to Jesus and for the word of God. They came to life, and reigned with Christ a thousand years. The rest of the dead did not come to life until the thousand years were ended. This is the first resurrection. Blessed and holy is he who shares in the first resurrection! Over such the second death has no power, but they shall be priests of God and of Christ, and they shall reign with him a thousand years.

And when the thousand years are ended, Satan will be loosed from his prison and will come out to deceive the nations which are at the four corners of the earth, that is, Gog and Magog, to gather them for battle; their number is like the sand of the sea. And they marched up over the broad earth and surrounded the camp of the saints and the beloved city; but fire came down from heaven and consumed them, and the devil was thrown into the lake of fire and sulphur where the beast and the false prophet were, and they will be tormented day and night for ever.

Then I saw a great white throne and him who sat upon it; from his presence earth and sky fled away. And I saw the dead, great and small, standing before the throne, and books were opened. Also another book was opened, which is the book of life. And the dead were judged by what was written in the books, by what they had done. And the sea gave up the dead in it, Death and Hades gave up the dead in them, and all were judged by what they had done. Then Death and Hades were thrown into the lake of fire. This is the second death, the lake of fire; and if any one's name was not found written in the book of life, he was thrown into the lake of fire.

THEN I SAW a new heaven and a new earth; for the first heaven and the first earth had passed away, and the sea was no more. And I saw the holy city, new Jerusalem, coming down out of heaven from God, prepared as a bride adorned for her husband; and I heard a loud voice from the throne saying, "Behold, the dwelling of God is with men. They shall be his people; God will wipe away every tear from their eyes, and death shall be no more, neither shall there be mourning nor crying nor pain any more, for the former things have passed away."

And he who sat upon the throne said, "Behold, I make all things new. I am the Alpha and the Omega, the beginning and the end. To the thirsty I will give from the fountain of the water of life without payment. He who conquers shall have this heritage, and I will be his God and he shall be my son. But as for the cowardly, the faithless, the polluted, as for murderers, fornicators, sorcerers, idolaters, and all liars, their lot shall be in the lake that burns with fire and sulphur, which is the second death."

Then one of the seven angels who had the bowls full of the seven last plagues spoke to me, saying, "Come, I will show you the Bride, the wife of the Lamb." And in the Spirit he carried me away to a high mountain, and showed me the holy city Jerusalem coming down out of heaven from God, having the glory of God, its radiance like a most rare jewel. It had a great, high wall, with twelve gates, and at the gates twelve angels, and on the gates the names of the twelve tribes of Israel were inscribed. And the wall had twelve foundations, and on them the names of the twelve apostles of the Lamb. The city lies foursquare, twelve thousand stadia; its length and breadth and height are equal.

The wall was built of jasper, while the city was pure gold, clear as glass. The foundations of the wall were adorned with every jewel: jasper, sapphire, agate, emerald, onyx, carnelian, chrysolite, beryl, topaz, chrysoprase, jacinth, amethyst. The twelve gates were each made of a single pearl, and the street of the city was pure gold, transparent as glass. And I saw no temple in the city, for its temple is the Lord God the Almighty and the Lamb. And the city has no need of sun or moon to shine upon it, for the glory of God is its light, and its lamp is the Lamb. By its light shall the nations walk; and the kings of the earth shall bring their glory into it, and its gates shall never be shut by day—and there shall be no night there. But nothing unclean shall enter it, nor any one who practices abomination or falsehood, but only those who are written in the Lamb's book of life.

Then he showed me the river of the water of life, bright as crystal, flowing from the throne of God and of the Lamb through the middle of the street of the city; also, on either side of the river, the tree of life with its twelve kinds of fruit, yielding its fruit each month; and the leaves of the tree were for the healing of the nations. There shall no more be anything accursed, but the throne of God and of the Lamb shall be in it, and his servants shall worship him; they shall see his face, and his name shall be on their foreheads. And they shall reign for ever and ever.

AND HE SAID to me, "The Lord, the God of the spirits of the prophets, has sent his angel to show his servants what must soon take place. And behold, I am coming soon."

Blessed is he who keeps the words of the prophecy of this book.

I John am he who heard and saw these things. And when I heard and saw them, I fell down to worship at the feet of the angel who showed them to me; but he said to me, "You must not do that! I am a fellow servant with you and your brethren the prophets, and with those who keep the words of this book. Worship God." And he said to me, "Do not seal up the words of the prophecy of this book, for the time is near. Let the evildoer still do evil, and the filthy still be filthy, and the righteous still do right, and the holy still be holy."

Blessed are those who wash their robes, that they may have the right to the tree of life and that they may enter the city by the gates. Outside are the dogs and sorcerers and fornicators and murderers and idolaters, and every one who loves and practices falsehood.

"I Jesus have sent my angel to you with this testimony for the churches. I am the root and the offspring of David, the bright morning star."

The Spirit and the Bride say, "Come." And let him who hears say, "Come." And let him who is thirsty come, let him who desires take the water of life without price.

He who testifies to these things says, "Surely I am coming soon." Amen. Come, Lord Jesus!

The grace of the Lord Jesus be with all the saints. Amen.

INDEX

NUMBERS ⚬ GENESIS ⚬ JOSHU
DANIEL ⚬ LAMENTATIONS ⚬ Z
LUKE ⚬ ROMANS ⚬ REVELATIO
MATTHEW ⚬ TITUS ⚬ HOSEA ⚬ G
CORINTHIANS ⚬ JONAH ⚬ RUTH
MARK ⚬ THESSALONIANS ⚬ NE
SAMUEL ⚬ COLOSSIANS ⚬ JOHI
MICAH ⚬ HABAKKUK ⚬ PETER ⚬
ISAIAH ⚬ ZECHARIAH ⚬ JUDGE
EZRA ⚬ THESSALONIANS ⚬ HAG
ECCLESIASTES ⚬ CHRONICLE
PHILEMON ⚬ AMOS ⚬ DANIEL ⚬
RUTH ⚬ CORINTHIANS ⚬ JONAH
LAMENTATIONS ⚬ DANIEL ⚬ H
GENESIS ⚬ JOSHUA ⚬ LUKE ⚬ RO
CHRONICLES ⚬ ECCLESIASTE
HOSEA ⚬ GALATIANS ⚬ CORINT
HAGGAI ⚬ MARK ⚬ LEVITICUS ⚬
NEHEMIAH ⚬ EZEKIEL ⚬ ESTHEI
PHILIPPIANS ⚬ JAMES ⚬ MICAH
HABAKKUK ⚬ PETER ⚬ ISAIAH ⚬
GALATIANS ⚬ ACTS ⚬ JEREMIAH
HAGGAI ⚬ ECCLESIASTES ⚬ CH
ROMANS ⚬ REVELATION ⚬ PHIL
DANIEL ⚬ MALACHI ⚬ RUTH ⚬